BIG ROAD AT

BRITAIN

Contents

29th edition June 2019

© AA Media Limited 2019

Original edition printed 1991.

Cartography: All cartography in this atlas edited, designed and produced by the Mapping Services Department of AA Publishing (A05686).

This atlas contains Ordnance Survey data © Crown copyright and database right 2019.

Contains public sector information licensed under the Open Government Licence v3.0

Ireland mapping and Distances and journey times contains data available from openstreetmap.org © under the Open Database License found at opendatacommons.org

Publisher's Notes: Published by AA Publishing (a trading name of AA Media Limited, whose registered office is Fanum House, Basing View, Basingstoke, Hampshire RG21 4EA, UK. Registered number 06112600).

ISBN: 978 0 7495 8129 9 (spiral bound)
ISBN: 978 0 7495 8128 2 (paperback)

A CIP catalogue record for this book is available from The British Library.

The publishers would welcome information to correct any errors or omissions and to keep this atlas up to date. Please write to the Atlas Editor, AA Publishing, The Automobile Association, Fanum House, Basing View, Basingstoke, Hampshire RG21 4EA, UK.
E-mail: *roadatlasfeedback@theaa.com*

Acknowledgements: AA Publishing would like to thank the following for information used in the creation of this atlas:
Cadw, English Heritage, Forestry Commission, Historic Scotland, National Trust and National Trust for Scotland, RSPB, The Wildlife Trust, Scottish Natural Heritage, Natural England, The Countryside Council for Wales. Award winning beaches from 'Blue Flag' and 'Keep Scotland Beautiful' (summer 2018 data): for latest information visit *www.blueflag.org* and *www.keepscotlandbeautiful.org*. Road signs are © Crown Copyright 2019. Reproduced under the terms of the Open Government Licence.

Ireland mapping: Republic of Ireland census 2016 © Central Statistics Office and Northern Ireland census 2016 © NISRA (population data); Irish Public Sector Data (CC BY 4.0) (Gaeltacht); Logainm.ie (placenames); Roads Service and Transport Infrastructure Ireland

Printer: Elcograf S.p.A, Italy

Scale 1:190,000
or 3 miles to 1 inch

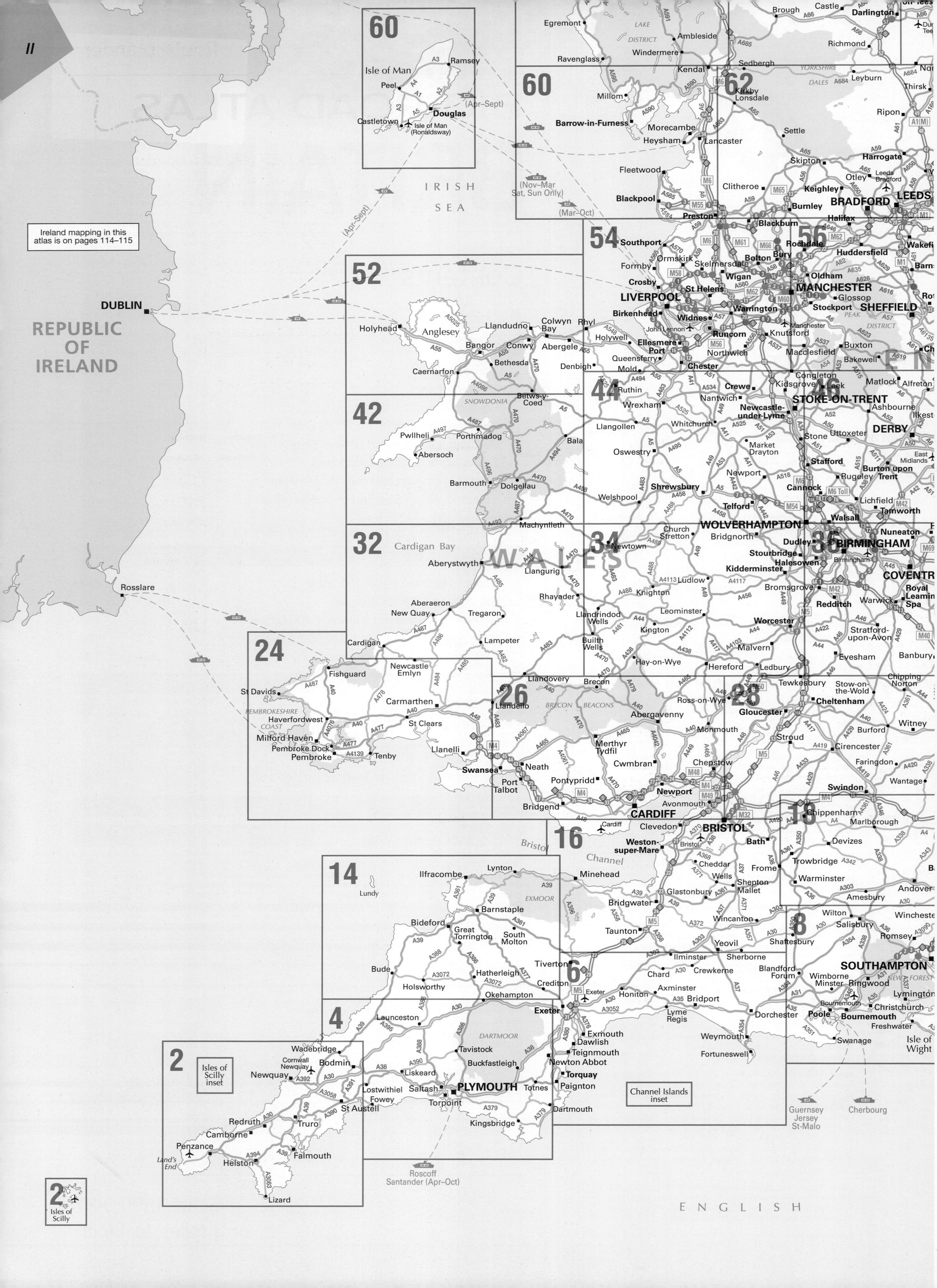

60

60

62

54

52

42

44

32

34

36

24

26

28

16

18

14

8

6

4

2

Ireland mapping in this atlas is on pages 114–115

IRISH SEA

REPUBLIC OF IRELAND

DUBLIN

Rosslare

Isle of Man

Ramsey

Peel

Douglas

Castletown • Isle of Man (Ronaldsway)

(Apr–Sept)

(Nov–Mar Sat, Sun Only)

(Mar–Oct)

Egremont

Ravenglass

Millom

Barrow-in-Furness

Ambleside

LAKE DISTRICT

Windermere

Kendal

Sedbergh

Morecambe

Heysham Lancaster

Fleetwood

Blackpool

Preston

Kirkby Lonsdale

YORKSHIRE DALES

Leyburn

Settle

Skipton

Clitheroe

Burnley

Blackburn

Harrogate

Keighley

Otley Leeds Bradford

BRADFORD

LEEDS

Southport

Ormskirk

Formby

Crosby

Skelmersdale

Bolton

Wigan

Bury

MANCHESTER

Rochdale

Oldham

Huddersfield

Wakefi

Barn

LIVERPOOL

St Helens

Birkenhead

Widnes

Warrington

Stockport

SHEFFIELD

John Lennon

Runcorn

Knutsford

Manchester

PEAK DISTRICT

Buxton

Ellesmere Port

Queensferry

Mold

Chester

Northwich

Macclesfield

Bakewell

Holyhead

Anglesey

Llandudno

Colwyn Bay

Rhyl

Conwy

Abergele

Holywell

Denbigh

Bangor

Bethesda

Caernarfon

Betws-y-Coed

SNOWDONIA

Ruthin

Wrexham

Crewe

Kidsgrove

Nantwich

STOKE-ON-TRENT

Newcastle-under-Lyme

Leek

Ashbourne

DERBY

Pwllheli

Abersoch

Porthmadog

Bala

Llangollen

Whitchurch

Market Drayton

Stone

Uttoxeter

Barmouth

Dolgellau

Welshpool

Oswestry

Newport

Stafford

Rugeley

Burton upon Trent

Machynlleth

Shrewsbury

Telford

Cannock

Lichfield

Tamworth

Cardigan Bay

WALES

Newtown

Church Stretton

Bridgnorth

WOLVERHAMPTON

Walsall

Nuneaton

Aberystwyth

Llangurig

Dudley

Stourbridge

BIRMINGHAM

COVENTRY

Llanidloes

Rhayader

Ludlow

Kidderminster

Halesowen

Birmingham

Aberaeron

New Quay

Tregaron

Llandrindod Wells

Knighton

Leominster

Bromsgrove

Redditch

Warwick

Royal Leamington Spa

Lampeter

Builth Wells

Kington

Malvern

Worcester

Stratford-upon-Avon

Banbury

Cardigan

Newcastle Emlyn

Llandovery

Brecon

Hay-on-Wye

Hereford

Ledbury

Evesham

Chipping Norton

St Davids

Fishguard

Carmarthen

Llandeilo

BRECON BEACONS

Ross-on-Wye

Tewkesbury

Stow-on-the-Wold

PEMBROKESHIRE COAST

Haverfordwest

St Clears

Abergavenny

Monmouth

Gloucester

Cheltenham

Burford

Witney

Milford Haven

Pembroke Dock

Pembroke

Tenby

Llanelli

Merthyr Tydfil

Cwmbran

Chepstow

Stroud

Cirencester

Faringdon

Wantage

Swansea

Neath

Pontypridd

Newport

Avonmouth

Swindon

Port Talbot

Bridgend

CARDIFF

Clevedon

BRISTOL

Chippenham

Marlborough

Cardiff

Weston-super-Mare

Bath

Devizes

Bristol Channel

Minehead

Cheddar

Wells

Frome

Trowbridge

Warminster

Amesbury

Andover

Ilfracombe

Lynton

EXMOOR

Bridgwater

Glastonbury

Shepton Mallet

Wilton

Salisbury

Winchester

Lundy

Barnstaple

Taunton

Wincanton

Shaftesbury

Romsey

SOUTHAMPTON

Bideford

Great Torrington

South Molton

Tiverton

Ilminster

Yeovil

Sherborne

Blandford Forum

Wimborne Minster

Ringwood

NEW FOREST

Lymington

Bude

Hatherleigh

Crediton

Chard

Crewkerne

Axminster

Bridport

Poole

Bournemouth

Christchurch

Freshwater

Holsworthy

Okehampton

Exeter

Honiton

Lyme Regis

Dorchester

Weymouth

Fortuneswell

Swanage

Isle of Wight

Launceston

DARTMOOR

Tavistock

Exmouth

Dawlish

Teignmouth

Newton Abbot

Torquay

Paignton

Channel Islands inset

Wadebridge

Bodmin

Liskeard

Buckfastleigh

Totnes

Guernsey Jersey St-Malo

Cherbourg

Isles of Scilly inset

Newquay

Cornwall Newquay

Lostwithiel Fowey

St Austell

Saltash

Torpoint

PLYMOUTH

Dartmouth

Kingsbridge

Redruth

Camborne

Truro

St Austell

Penzance

Land's End

Helston

Falmouth

Lizard

Roscoff Santander (Apr–Oct)

Isles of Scilly

ENGLISH

ENGLISH CHANNEL

Brough Castle

Darlington

Richmond

Thirsk

Ripon

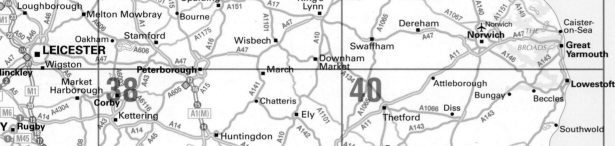

EMERGENCY DIVERSION ROUTES

In an emergency it may be necessary to close a section of motorway or other main road to traffic, so a temporary sign may advise drivers to follow a diversion route. To help drivers navigate the route, black symbols on yellow patches may be permanently displayed on existing direction signs, including motorway signs. Symbols may also be used on separate signs with yellow backgrounds.

For further information see *theaa.com/breakdown-cover/ advice/emergency-diversion-routes*

FERRY INFORMATION

Information on ferry routes and operators can be found on pages *XIV–XVI*.

Legend

Symbol	Description
	Motorway
	Toll motorway
	Primary route dual carriageway
	Primary route single carriageway
	Other A road
	Vehicle ferry
	Fast vehicle ferry or catamaran
	National Park
98	Atlas page number

0   10   20   30 miles
0 10 20 30   40 kilometres

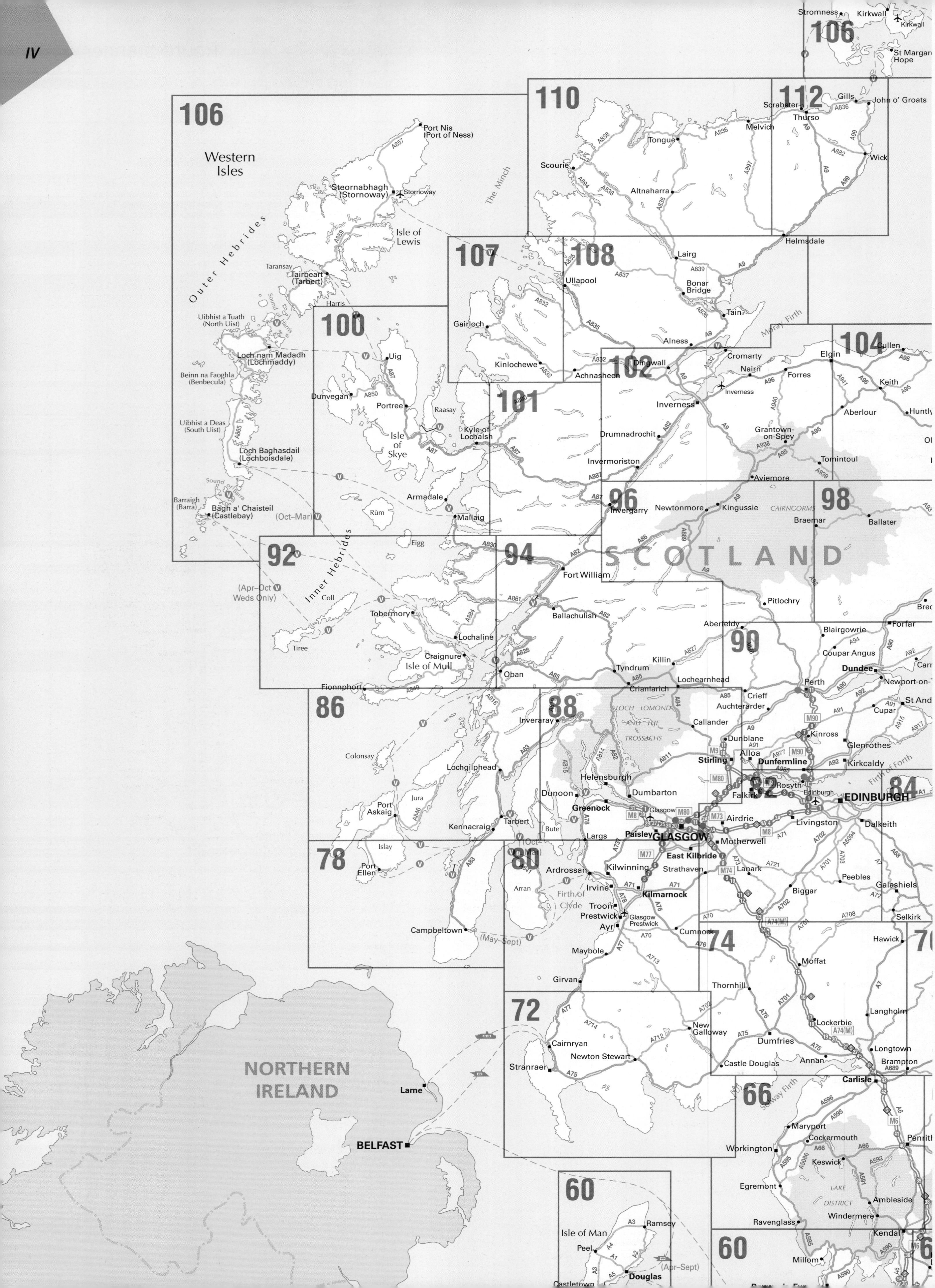
106
Western Isles
Outer Hebrides
Port Nis (Port of Ness)
Steornabhagh (Stornoway)
Stornoway
Isle of Lewis
The Minch
Taransay
Tairbeart (Tarbert)
Harris
Uibhist a Tuath (North Uist)
Loch nam Madadh (Lochmaddy)
Beinn na Faoghla (Benbecula)
Uibhist a Deas (South Uist)
Loch Baghasdail (Lochboisdale)
Sound of Barra
Barraigh (Barra)
Bàgh a' Chaisteil (Castlebay)
(Oct–Mar)
110
112
Stromness
Kirkwall
St Margaret's Hope
Gills
John o' Groats
Scrabster
Thurso
Melvich
Tongue
Scourie
Altnaharra
Wick
Helmsdale
107
108
Lairg
Ullapool
Bonar Bridge
Tain
Gairloch
Kinlochewe
Achnasheen
Alness
Moray Firth
Cromarty
100
Uig
Dunvegan
Portree
Raasay
Isle of Skye
Kyle of Lochalsh
101
102
Dingwall
Nairn
Forres
Elgin
Inverness
104
Cullen
Keith
Aberlour
Huntly
Drumnadrochit
Grantown-on-Spey
Invermoriston
Tomintoul
Aviemore
Armadale
Rùm
Mallaig
96
Invergarry
Newtonmore
Kingussie
CAIRNGORMS
98
Braemar
Ballater
Eigg
92
Inner Hebrides
(Apr–Oct Weds Only)
Coll
Tiree
94
Fort William
SCOTLAND
Pitlochry
Tobermory
Ballachulish
Lochaline
Craignure
Isle of Mull
Aberfeldy
90
Blairgowrie
Forfar
Coupar Angus
Dundee
Killin
Tyndrum
Oban
Fionnphort
Lochearnhead
Crianlarich
Perth
Newport-on-Tay
86
88
Inveraray
LOCH LOMOND AND THE TROSSACHS
Callander
Crieff
Auchterarder
Cupar
St Andrews
Colonsay
Dunblane
Kinross
Glenrothes
Stirling
Alloa
Dunfermline
Kirkcaldy
Firth of Forth
Lochgilphead
Helensburgh
Rosyth
Falkirk
82
84
Edinburgh
EDINBURGH
Jura
Port Askaig
Dunoon
Greenock
Dumbarton
Glasgow
Airdrie
Livingston
Dalkeith
Kennacraig
Tarbert
Bute
Largs
Paisley
GLASGOW
Motherwell
Islay
78
Port Ellen
80
Ardrossan
Kilwinning
East Kilbride
Strathaven
Lanark
Peebles
Galashiels
Arran
Irvine
Firth of Clyde
Kilmarnock
Biggar
Troon
Prestwick
Glasgow Prestwick
Ayr
Selkirk
Campbeltown
(May–Sept)
Cumnock
74
Hawick
Maybole
Moffat
Girvan
Thornhill
72
Langholm
Cairnryan
New Galloway
Lockerbie
Newton Stewart
Dumfries
Longtown
Brampton
Stranraer
Castle Douglas
Annan
NORTHERN IRELAND
Larne
Carlisle
66
Solway Firth
Maryport
Cockermouth
Penrith
BELFAST
Workington
Keswick
60
Isle of Man
Ramsey
Peel
Douglas
Castletown
(Apr–Sept)
Egremont
LAKE DISTRICT
Ambleside
Windermere
Ravenglass
Kendal
Millom

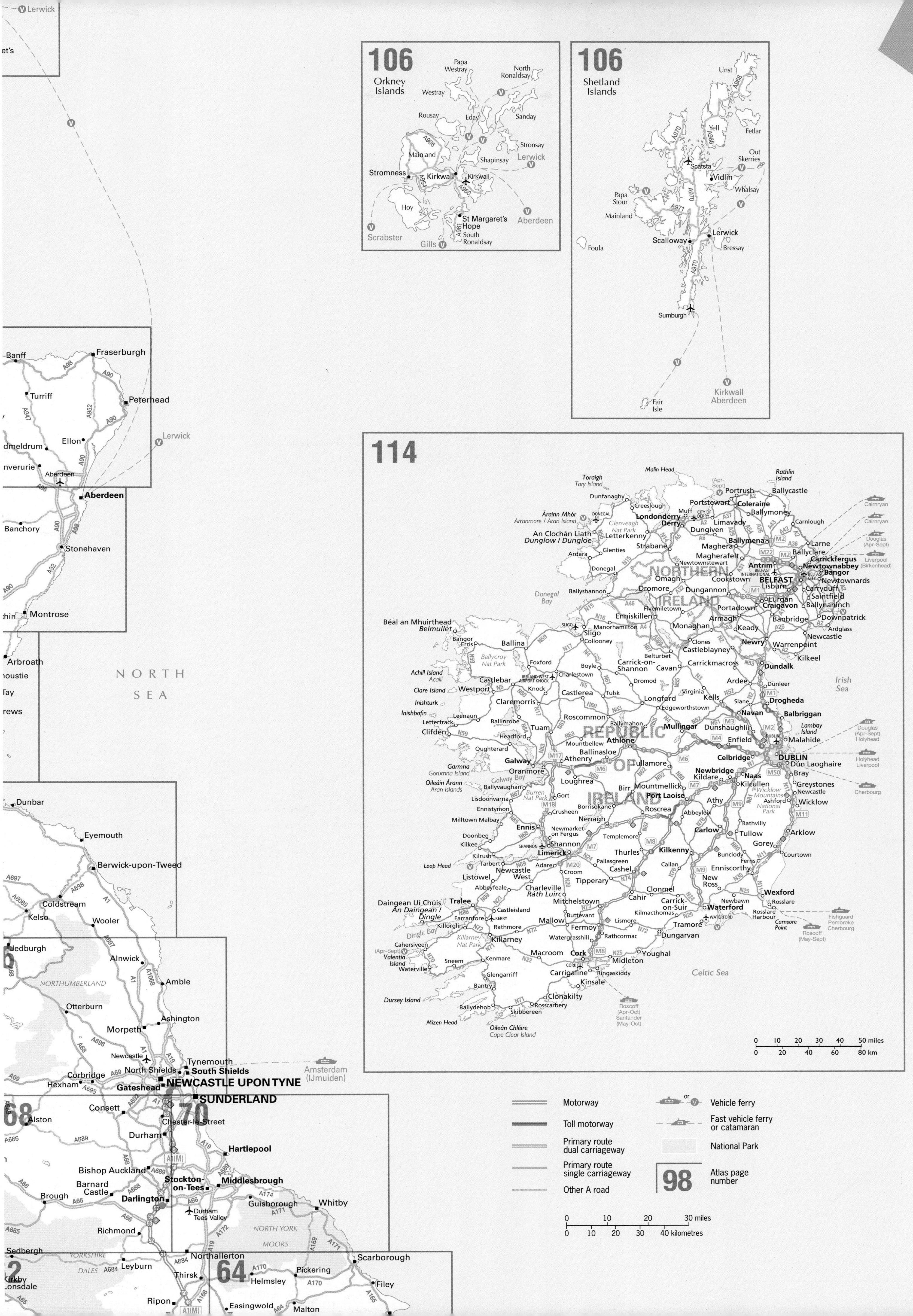

106 Orkney Islands

106 Shetland Islands

114

Motorway

Toll motorway

Primary route
dual carriageway

Primary route
single carriageway

Other A road

Vehicle ferry

Fast vehicle ferry
or catamaran

National Park

98 Atlas page
number

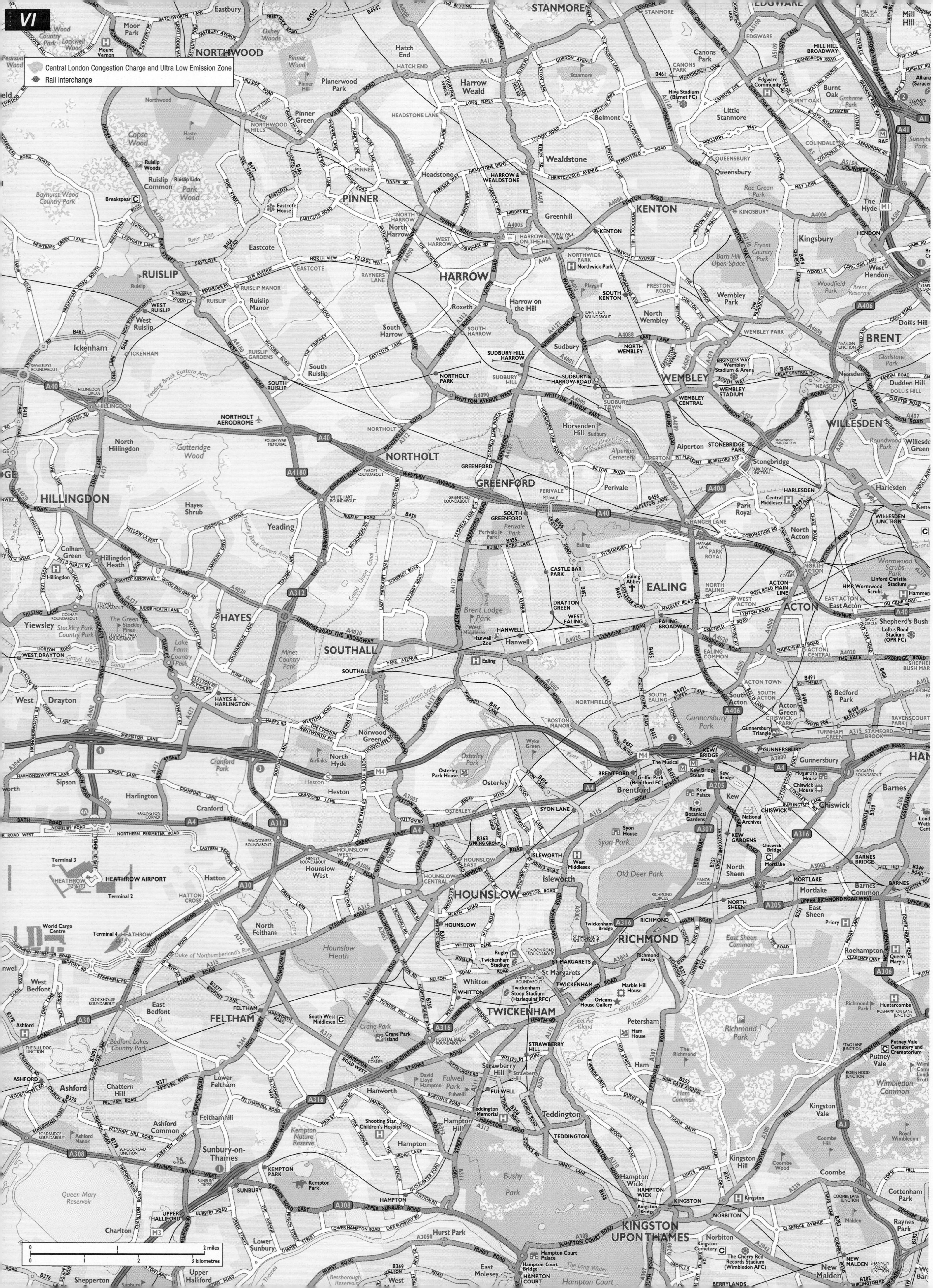
Central London Congestion Charge and Ultra Low Emission Zone
Rail interchange
STANMORE
EDGWARE
NORTHWOOD
PINNER
HARROW
KENTON
WEMBLEY
BRENT
RUISLIP
NORTHOLT
GREENFORD
WILLESDEN
HILLINGDON
HAYES
SOUTHALL
EALING
ACTON
HOUNSLOW
RICHMOND
FELTHAM
TWICKENHAM
KINGSTON UPON THAMES
HEATHROW AIRPORT
Terminal 2
Terminal 3
Terminal 4
Wealdstone
Harrow Weald
Hatch End
Eastcote
Ickenham
Uxbridge
Yiewsley
West Drayton
Harlington
Cranford
Heston
Isleworth
Brentford
Chiswick
Barnes
Mortlake
Kew
Hampton
Teddington
Sunbury-on-Thames
Ashford
Hanwell
Perivale
Alperton
Neasden
Hendon
Kingsbury
Queensbury
Park Royal
Richmond Park
Bushy Park
Hounslow Heath
Syon Park
Old Deer Park
Wimbledon Common
Kingston Hill
Coombe
New Malden
Norbiton
Petersham
Ham
Hampton Court
East Molesey
Shepperton
2 miles
3 kilometres

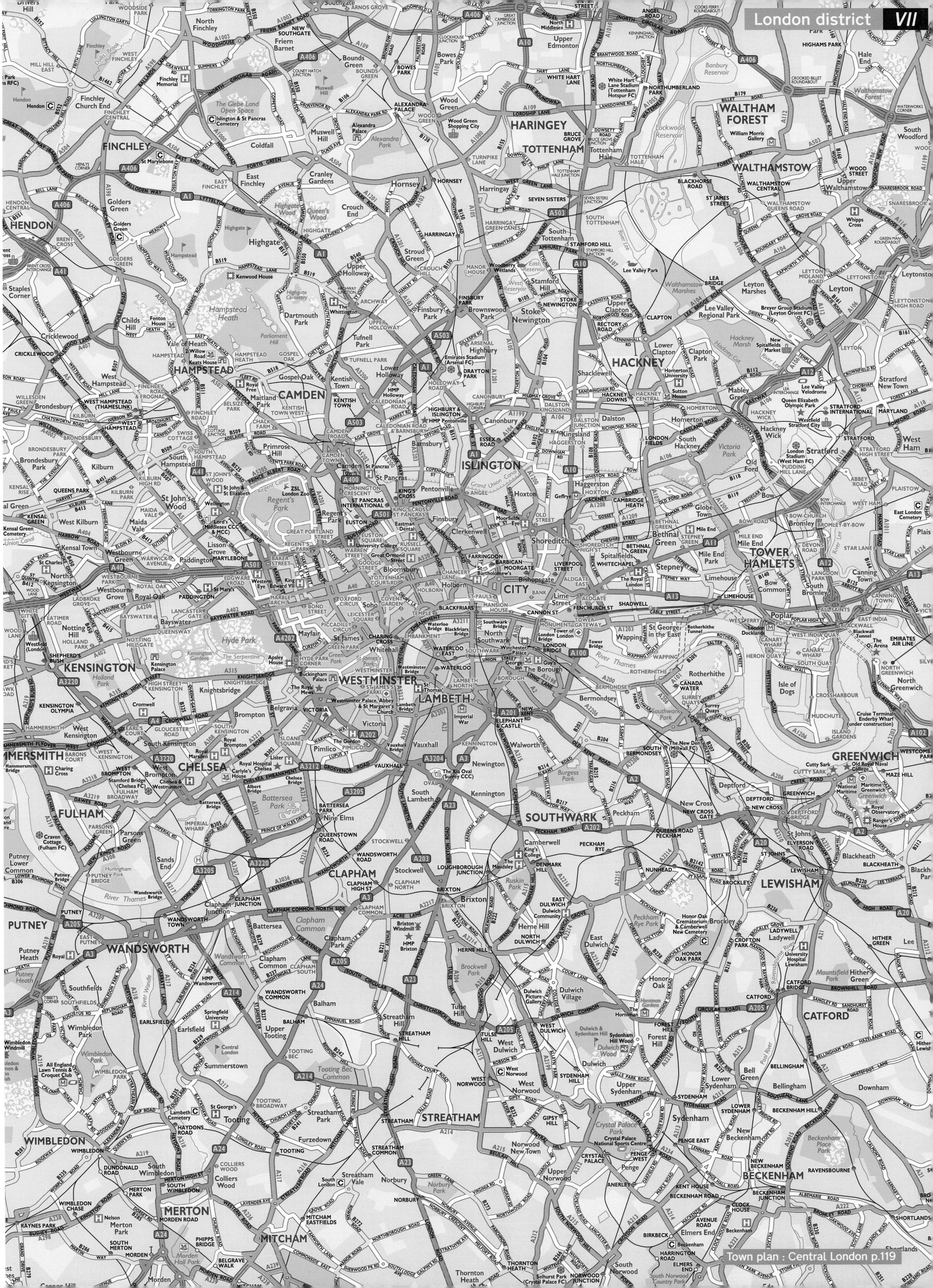
FINCHLEY
HENDON
HARINGEY
TOTTENHAM
WALTHAM FOREST
WALTHAMSTOW
HAMPSTEAD
CAMDEN
HACKNEY
ISLINGTON
CITY
TOWER HAMLETS
KENSINGTON
WESTMINSTER
LAMBETH
CHELSEA
HAMMERSMITH
FULHAM
SOUTHWARK
GREENWICH
LEWISHAM
CLAPHAM
PUTNEY
WANDSWORTH
CATFORD
STREATHAM
WIMBLEDON
MERTON
MITCHAM
BECKENHAM

Town plan : Central London p.119

Restricted junctions

Motorway and primary route junctions which have access or exit restrictions are shown on the map pages thus:

M1 London - Leeds

Junction	Northbound	Southbound
2	Access only from A1 *(northbound)*	Exit only to A1 *(southbound)*
4	Access only from A41 *(northbound)*	Exit only to A41 *(southbound)*
6A	Access only from M25 (no link from A405)	Exit only to M25 (no link from A405)
7	Access only from A414	Exit only to A414
17	Exit only to M45	Access only from M45
19	Exit only to M6 *(northbound)*	Exit only to A14 *(southbound)*
21A	Exit only, no access	Access only, no exit
24A	Access only, no exit	Access only from A50 *(eastbound)*
35A	Exit only, no access	Access only, no exit
43	Exit only to M621	Access only from M621
48	Exit only to A1(M) *(northbound)*	Access only from A1(M) *(southbound)*

M2 Rochester - Faversham

Junction	Westbound	Eastbound
1	No exit to A2 *(eastbound)*	No access from A2 *(westbound)*

M3 Sunbury - Southampton

Junction	Northeastbound	Southwestbound
8	Access only from A303, no exit	Exit only to A303, no access
10	Exit only, no access	Access only, no exit
14	Access from M27 only, no exit	No access to M27 *(westbound)*

M4 London - South Wales

Junction	Westbound	Eastbound
1	Access only from A4 *(westbound)*	Exit only to A4 *(eastbound)*
2	Access only from A4 *(westbound)*	Access only from A4 *(eastbound)*
21	Exit only to M48	Access only from M48
23	Access only from M48	Exit only to M48
25	Exit only, no access	Access only, no exit
25A	Exit only, no access	Access only, no exit
29	Exit only to A48(M)	Access only from A48(M)
38	Exit only, no access	No restriction
39	Access only, no exit	No access or exit
42	Exit only to A483	Access only from A483

M5 Birmingham - Exeter

Junction	Northeastbound	Southwestbound
10	Access only, no exit	Exit only, no access
11A	Access only from A417 *(westbound)*	Exit only to A417 *(eastbound)*
18A	Exit only to M49	Access only from M49
18	Exit only, no access	Access only, no exit

M6 Toll Motorway

Junction	Northwestbound	Southeastbound
T1	Access only, no exit	No access or exit
T2	No access or exit	Exit only, no access
T5	Access only, no exit	Exit only to A5148 *(northbound)*, no access
T7	Exit only, no access	Access only, no exit
T8	Exit only, no access	Access only, no exit

M6 Rugby - Carlisle

Junction	Northbound	Southbound
3A	Exit only to M6 Toll	Access only from M6 Toll
4	Exit only to M42 *(southbound)* & A446	Exit only to A446
4A	Access only from M42 *(southbound)*	Exit only to M42
5	Exit only, no access	Access only, no exit
10A	Exit only to M54	Access only from M54
11A	Access only from M6 Toll	Exit only to M6 Toll
with M56 (jct 20A)	No restriction	Access only from M56 *(eastbound)*
20	Exit only to M56 *(westbound)*	Access only from M56 *(eastbound)*
24	Access only, no exit	Exit only, no access
25	Exit only, no access	Access only, no exit
30	Access only from M61	Exit only to M61
31A	Exit only, no access	Access only, no exit
45	Exit only, no access	Access only, no exit

M8 Edinburgh - Bishopton

Junction	Westbound	Eastbound
6	Exit only, no access	Access only, no exit
6A	Access only, no exit	Exit only, no access
7	Access only, no exit	Exit only, no access
7A	Exit only, no access	Access only from A725 *(northbound)*, no exit
8	No access from M73 *(southbound)* or from A8 *(eastbound)* & A89	No exit to M73 *(northbound)* or to A8 *(westbound)* & A89
9	Access only, no exit	Exit only, no access
13	Access only from M80 *(southbound)*	Exit only to M80 *(northbound)*
14	Access only, no exit	Exit only, no access
16	Exit only to A804	Access only from A879
17	Exit only to A82	No restriction
18	Access only from A82 *(eastbound)*	Exit only to A814
19	No access from A814 *(westbound)*	Exit only to A814 *(westbound)*
20	Exit only, no access	Access only, no exit
21	Access only, no exit	Exit only to A8
22	Exit only to M77 *(southbound)*	Access only from M77 *(northbound)*
23	Exit only to B768	Access only from B768
25	No access or exit from or to A8	No access or exit from or to A8
25A	Exit only, no access	Access only, no exit
28	Exit only, no access	Access only, no exit
28A	Exit only to A737	Access only from A737
29A	Exit only to A8	Access only, no exit

M9 Edinburgh - Dunblane

Junction	Northwestbound	Southeastbound
2	Access only, no exit	Exit only, no access
3	Exit only, no access	Access only, no exit
6	Access only, no exit	Exit only to A905
8	Exit only to M876 *(southwestbound)*	Access only from M876 *(northeastbound)*

M11 London - Cambridge

Junction	Northbound	Southbound
4	Access only from A406 *(eastbound)*	Exit only to A406
5	Exit only, no access	Access only, no exit
8A	Exit only, no access	No direct access, use jct 8
9	Exit only to A11	Access only from A11
13	Exit only, no access	Access only, no exit
14	Exit only, no access	Access only, no exit

M20 Swanley - Folkestone

Junction	Northwestbound	Southeastbound
2	Staggered junction; follow signs - access only	Staggered junction; follow signs - exit only
3	Exit only to M26 *(westbound)*	Access only from M26 *(eastbound)*
5	Access only from A20	For access follow signs - exit only to A20
6	No restriction	For exit follow signs
11A	Access only, no exit	Exit only, no access

M23 Hooley - Crawley

Junction	Northbound	Southbound
7	Exit only to A23 *(northbound)*	Access only from A23 *(southbound)*
10A	Access only, no exit	Exit only, no access

M25 London Orbital Motorway

Junction	Clockwise	Anticlockwise
1B	No direct access, use slip road to jct 2 Exit only	Access only, no exit
5	No exit to M26 *(eastbound)*	No access from M26
19	Exit only, no access	Access only, no exit
21	Access only from M1 *(southbound)* Exit only to M1 *(northbound)*	Access only from M1 *(southbound)* Exit only to M1 *(northbound)*
31	No exit (use slip road via jct 30), access only	No access (use slip road via jct 30), exit only

M26 Sevenoaks - Wrotham

Junction	Westbound	Eastbound
with M25 (jct 5)	Exit only to clockwise M25 *(westbound)*	Access only from anticlockwise M25 *(eastbound)*
with M20 (jct 3)	Access only from M20 *(northwestbound)*	Exit only to M20 *(southeastbound)*

M27 Cadnam - Portsmouth

Junction	Westbound	Eastbound
4	Staggered junction; follow signs - access only from M3 *(southbound)*. Exit only to M3 *(northbound)*	Staggered junction; follow signs - access only from M3 *(southbound)*. Exit only to M3 *(northbound)*
10	Exit only, no access	Access only, no exit
12	Staggered junction; follow signs - exit only to M275 *(southbound)*	Staggered junction; follow signs - access only from M275 *(northbound)*

M40 London - Birmingham

Junction	Northwestbound	Southeastbound
3	Exit only, no access	Access only, no exit
7	Exit only, no access	Access only, no exit
8	Exit only to M40/A40	Access only from M40/A40
13	Exit only, no access	Access only, no exit
14	Access only, no exit	Exit only, no access
16	Access only, no exit	Exit only, no access

M42 Bromsgrove - Measham

Junction	Northeastbound	Southwestbound
1	Access only, no exit	Exit only, no access
7	Exit only to M6 *(northwestbound)*	Access only from M6 *(northwestbound)*
7A	Exit only to M6 *(southeastbound)*	No access or exit
8	Access only from M6 *(southeastbound)*	Exit only to M6 *(northwestbound)*

M45 Coventry - M1

Junction	Westbound	Eastbound
Dunchurch (unnumbered)	Access only from A45	Exit only, no access
with M1 (jct 17)	Access only from M1 *(northbound)*	Exit only to M1 *(southbound)*

M48 Chepstow

Junction	Westbound	Eastbound
21	Access only from M4 *(westbound)*	Exit only to M4 *(eastbound)*
23	No exit to M4 *(eastbound)*	No access from M4 *(westbound)*

M53 Mersey Tunnel - Chester

Junction	Northbound	Southbound
11	Access only from M56 *(westbound)* Exit only to M56 *(eastbound)*	Access only from M56 *(westbound)* Exit only to M56 *(eastbound)*

M54 Telford - Birmingham

Junction	Westbound	Eastbound
with M6 (jct 10A)	Access only from M6 *(northbound)*	Exit only to M6 *(southbound)*

M56 Chester - Manchester

Junction	Westbound	Eastbound
1	Access only from M60 *(westbound)*	Exit only to M60 *(eastbound)* & A34 *(northbound)*
2	Exit only, no access	Access only, no exit
3	Access only, no exit	Exit only, no access
4	Exit only, no access	Access only, no exit
7	Exit only, no access	No restriction
8	Access only, no exit	No access or exit
9	No exit to M6 *(southbound)*	No access from M6 *(northbound)*
15	Exit only to M53	Access only from M53
16	No access or exit	No restriction

M57 Liverpool Outer Ring Road

Junction	Northwestbound	Southeastbound
3	Access only, no exit	Exit only, no access
5	Access only from A580 *(westbound)*	Exit only, no access

M58 Liverpool - Wigan

Junction	Westbound	Eastbound
1	Exit only, no access	Access only, no exit

M60 Manchester Orbital

Junction	Clockwise	Anticlockwise
2	Access only, no exit	Exit only, no access
3	No access from M56	Access only from A34 *(northbound)*
4	Access only from A34 *(northbound)*. Exit only to M56	Access only from M56 *(eastbound)*. Exit only to A34 *(southbound)*
5	Access and exit only from and to A5103 *(northbound)*	Access and exit only from and to A5103 *(southbound)*
7	No direct access, use slip road to jct 8. Exit only to A56	Access only from A56. No exit, use jct 8
14	Access from A580 *(eastbound)*	Exit only to A580 *(westbound)*
16	Access only, no exit	Exit only, no access
20	Exit only, no access	Access only, no exit
22	No restriction	Exit only, no access
25	Exit only, no access	No restriction
26	No restriction	Exit only, no access
27	Access only, no exit	Exit only, no access

M61 Manchester - Preston

Junction	Northwestbound	Southeastbound
3	No access or exit	Exit only, no access
with M6 (jct 30)	Exit only to M6 *(northbound)*	Access only from M6 *(southbound)*

M62 Liverpool - Kingston upon Hull

Junction	Westbound	Eastbound
23	Access only, no exit	Exit only, no access
32A	No access to A1(M) *(southbound)*	No restriction

M65 Preston - Colne

Junction	Northeastbound	Southwestbound
9	Exit only, no access	Access only, no exit
11	Access only, no exit	Exit only, no access

M66 Bury

Junction	Northbound	Southbound
with A56	Exit only to A56 *(northbound)*	Access only from A56 *(southbound)*
1	Exit only, no access	Access only, no exit

M67 Hyde Bypass

Junction	Westbound	Eastbound
1	Access only, no exit	Exit only, no access
2	Exit only, no access	Access only, no exit
3	Exit only, no access	No restriction

M69 Coventry - Leicester

Junction	Northbound	Southbound
2	Access only, no exit	Exit only, no access

M73 East of Glasgow

Junction	Northbound	Southbound
1	No exit to A74 & A721	No exit to A74 & A721
2	No access from or exit to A89. No access from *(eastbound)*	No access from or exit to A89. No exit to M8 *(westbound)*

M74 and A74(M) Glasgow - Gretna

Junction	Northbound	Southbound
3	Exit only, no access	Access only, no exit
3A	Access only, no exit	Exit only, no access
4	No access from A74 & A721	Access only, no exit to A74 & A721
7	Access only, no exit	Exit only, no access
9	No access or exit	Exit only, no access
10	No restriction	Access only, no exit
11	Access only, no exit	Exit only, no access
12	Exit only, no access	Access only, no exit
18	Exit only, no access	Access only, no exit

M77 Glasgow - Kilmarnock

Junction	Northbound	Southbound
with M8 (jct 22)	No exit to M8 *(westbound)*	No access from M8 *(eastbound)*
4	Access only, no exit	Exit only, no access
6	Access only, no exit	Exit only, no access
7	Access only, no exit	No restriction
8	Exit only, no access	Exit only, no access

M80 Glasgow - Stirling

Junction	Northbound	Southbound
4A	Exit only, no access	Access only, no exit
6A	Access only, no exit	Exit only, no access
8	Exit only to M876 *(northeastbound)*	Access only from M876 *(southwestbound)*

M90 Edinburgh - Perth

Junction	Northbound	Southbound
1	No exit, access only	Exit only to A90 *(eastbound)*
2A	Exit only to A92 *(eastbound)*	Access only from A92 *(westbound)*
7	Access only, no exit	Exit only, no access
8	Exit only, no access	Access only, no exit
10	No access from A912. No exit to A912 *(southbound)*	No access from A912 *(northbound)* No exit to A912

M180 Doncaster - Grimsby

Junction	Westbound	Eastbound
1	Access only, no exit	Exit only, no access

M606 Bradford Spur

Junction	Northbound	Southbound
2	Exit only, no access	No restriction

M621 Leeds - M1

Junction	Clockwise	Anticlockwise
2A	Access only, no exit	Exit only, no access
4	No exit or access	No restriction
5	Access only, no exit	Exit only, no access
6	Exit only, no access	Access only, no exit
with M1 (jct 43)	Exit only to M1 *(southbound)*	Access only from M1 *(northbound)*

M876 Bonnybridge - Kincardine Bridge

Junction	Northeastbound	Southwestbound
with M80 (jct 5)	Access only from M80 *(northeastbound)*	Exit only to M80 *(southwestbound)*
with M9 (jct 8)	Exit only to M9 *(eastbound)*	Access only from M9 *(westbound)*

A1(M) South Mimms - Baldock

Junction	Northbound	Southbound
2	Exit only, no access	Access only, no exit
3	No restriction	Exit only, no access
5	Access only, no exit	No access or exit

A1(M) Pontefract - Bedale

Junction	Northbound	Southbound
41	No access to M62 *(eastbound)*	No restriction
43	Access only from M1 *(northbound)*	Exit only to M1 *(southbound)*

A1(M) Scotch Corner - Newcastle upon Tyne

Junction	Northbound	Southbound
57	Exit only to A66(M) *(eastbound)*	Access only from A66(M) *(westbound)*
65	No access Exit only to A194(M) & A1 *(northbound)*	No exit Access only from A194(M) & A1 *(southbound)*

A3(M) Horndean - Havant

Junction	Northbound	Southbound
1	Access only from A3	Exit only to A3
4	Exit only, no access	Access only, no exit

A38(M) Birmingham, Victoria Road (Park Circus)

Junction	Northbound	Southbound
with B4132	No exit	No access

A48(M) Cardiff Spur

Junction	Westbound	Eastbound
29	Access only from M4 *(westbound)*	Exit only to M4 *(eastbound)*
29A	Exit only to A48 *(westbound)*	Access only from A48 *(eastbound)*

A57(M) Manchester, Brook Street (A34)

Junction	Westbound	Eastbound
with A34	No exit	No access

A58(M) Leeds, Park Lane and Westgate

Junction	Northbound	Southbound
with A58	No restriction	No access

A64(M) Leeds, Clay Pit Lane (A58)

Junction	Westbound	Eastbound
with A58	No exit (to Clay Pit Lane)	No access (from Clay Pit Lane)

A66(M) Darlington Spur

Junction	Westbound	Eastbound
with A1(M) (jct 57)	Exit only to A1(M) *(southbound)*	Access only from A1(M) *(northbound)*

A74(M) Gretna - Abington

Junction	Northbound	Southbound
18	Exit only, no access	No exit

A194(M) Newcastle upon Tyne

Junction	Northbound	Southbound
with A1(M) (jct 65)	Access only from A1(M) *(northbound)*	Exit only to A1(M) *(southbound)*

A12 M25 - Ipswich

Junction	Northeastbound	Southwestbound
13	Access only, no exit	No restriction
14	Exit only, no access	Access only, no exit
20A	Exit only, no access	Access only, no exit
20B	Access only, no exit	Exit only, no access
21	No restriction	Access only, no exit
23	Exit only, no access	Access only, no exit
24	Access only, no exit	Exit only, no access
27	Exit only, no access	Access only, no exit
Dedham & Stratford St Mary (unnumbered)	Exit only	Access only

A14 M1 - Felixstowe

Junction	Westbound	Eastbound
with M1/M6 (jct19)	Exit only to M6 and M1 *(northbound)*	Access only from M6 and M1 *(southbound)*
4	Exit only, no access	Access only, no exit
31	Exit only to M11 *(for London)*	Access only, no exit
31A	Exit only to A14 *(northbound)*	Access only, no exit
34	Access only, no exit	Exit only, no access
36	Exit only to A11, access only from A1303	Access only from A11
38	Access only from A11	Exit only to A11
39	Exit only, no access	Access only, no exit
61	Access only, no exit	Exit only, no access

A55 Holyhead - Chester

Junction	Westbound	Eastbound
8A	Exit only, no access	Access only, no exit
23A	Access only, no exit	Exit only, no access
24A	Exit only, no access	No access or exit
27A	No restriction	No access or exit
33A	Exit only, no access	No access or exit
33B	Exit only, no access	Access only, no exit
36A	Exit only to A5104	Access only from A5104

Since Britain's first motorway (the Preston Bypass) opened in 1958, motorways have changed significantly. A vast increase in car journeys over the last 61 years has meant that motorways quickly filled to capacity. To combat this, the recent development of smart motorways uses technology to monitor and actively manage traffic flow and congestion.

How they work

Smart motorways utilise various active traffic management methods, monitored through a regional traffic control centre:

- Traffic flow is monitored using CCTV
- Speed limits are changed to smooth traffic flow and reduce stop-start driving
- Capacity of the motorway can be increased by either temporarily or permanently opening the hard shoulder to traffic
- Warning signs and messages alert drivers to hazards and traffic jams ahead
- Lanes can be closed in the case of an accident or emergency by displaying a red X sign

- Emergency refuge areas are located regularly along the motorway where there is no hard shoulder available

The map shows the main motorway network with the three different types of smart motorway in operation or planned to open over the next five years:

Controlled motorway
Variable speed limits without hard shoulder (the hard shoulder is used in emergencies only)

Hard shoulder running
Variable speed limits with part-time hard shoulder (the hard shoulder is open to traffic at busy times when signs permit)

All lane running
Variable speed limits with hard shoulder as permanent running lane (there is no hard shoulder); this is standard for all new motorway schemes since 2013

Standard motorway

Quick tips

- Never drive in a lane closed by a red X

- Keep to the speed limit shown on the gantries
- A solid white line indicates the hard shoulder – do not drive in it unless directed or in the case of an emergency
- A broken white line indicates a normal running lane
- Exit the smart motorway where possible if your vehicle is in difficulty. In an emergency, move onto the hard shoulder where there is one, or the nearest emergency refuge area
- Put on your hazard lights if you break down

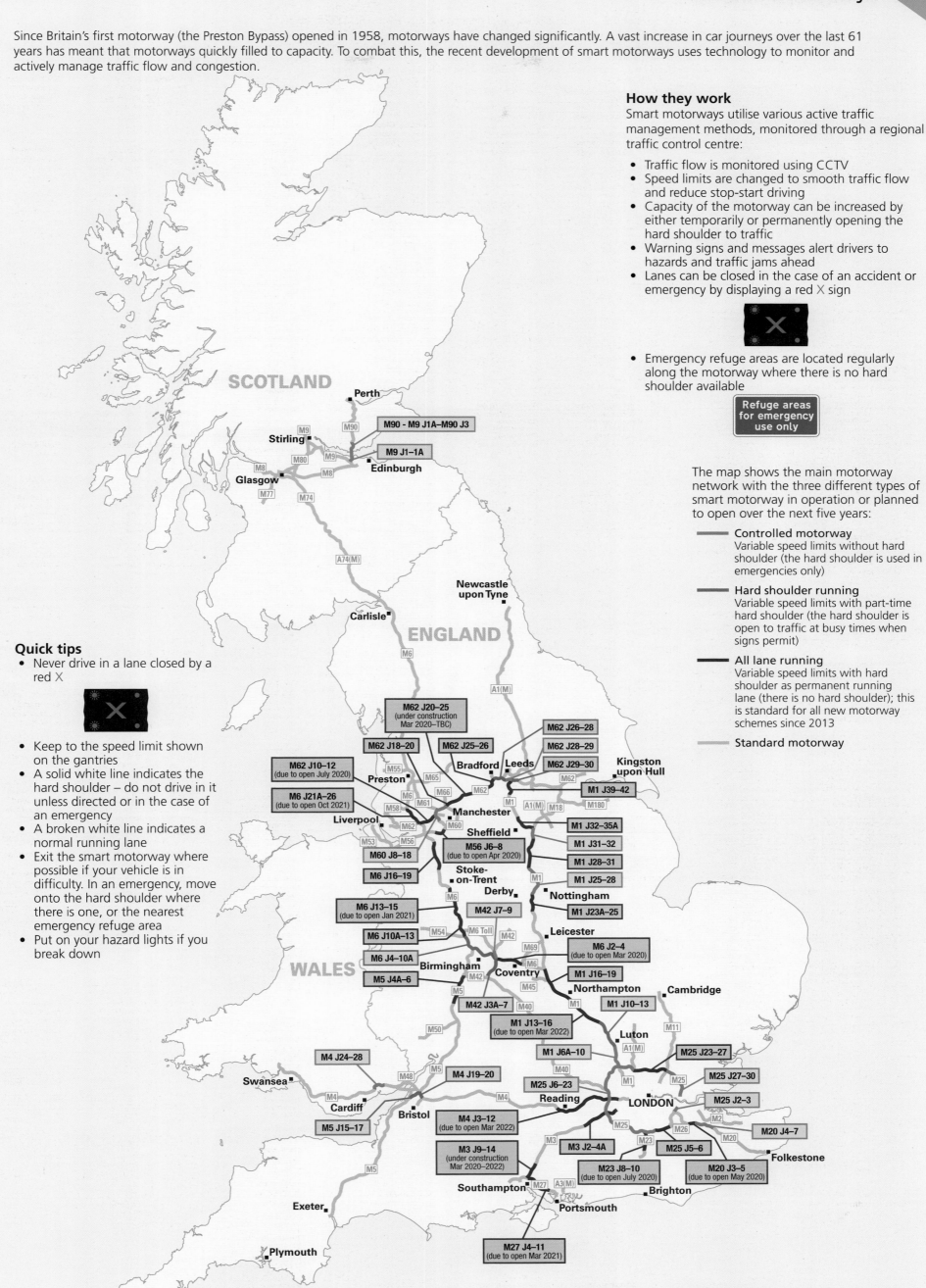

Smart motorways (*Intelligent Transport Systems* in Scotland) are the responsibility of Highways England, Transport Scotland and Transport for Wales

Caravan and camping sites in Britain

These pages list the top 300 AA-inspected Caravan and Camping (C & C) sites in the Pennant rating scheme. **Five Pennant Premier sites are shown in green,** Four Pennant sites are shown in blue.
Listings include addresses, telephone numbers and websites together with page and grid references to locate the sites in the atlas. The total number of touring pitches is also included for each site, together with the type of pitch available.
The following abbreviations are used: **C = Caravan CV = Campervan T = Tent**

To find out more about the AA's Pennant rating scheme and other rated caravan and camping sites not included on these pages please visit ***theAA.com***

ENGLAND

Alders Caravan Park
Home Farm, Alne, York
YO61 1RY
Tel: 01347 838722 64 C6
alderscaravanpark.co.uk
Total Pitches: 87 (C, CV & T)

Andrewshayes Holiday Park
Dalwood, Axminster
EX13 7DY
Tel: 01404 831225 6 H5
andrewshayes.co.uk
Total Pitches: 150 (C, CV & T)

Apple Tree Park C & C Site
A38, Claypits,
Stonehouse
GL10 3AL
Tel: 01452 742362 28 E6
appletreepark.co.uk
Total Pitches: 65 (C, CV & T)

Atlantic Bays Holiday Park
St Merryn, Padstow
PL28 8PY
Tel: 01841 520855 3 M2
atlanticbaysholidaypark.co.uk
Total Pitches: 70 (C, CV & T)

Ayr Holiday Park
St Ives, Cornwall
TR26 1EJ
Tel: 01736 795855 2 E8
ayrholidaypark.co.uk
Total Pitches: 40 (C, CV & T)

Back of Beyond Touring Park
234 Ringwood Road, St Leonards,
Dorset
BH24 2SB
Tel: 01202 876968 8 F8
backofbeyondtouringpark.co.uk
Total Pitches: 80 (C, CV & T)

Bagwell Farm Touring Park
Bethesda, Knights in the Bottom, Chickerell,
Weymouth
DT3 4EA
Tel: 01305 782575 7 R8
bagwellfarm.co.uk
Total Pitches: 320 (C, CV & T)

Bardsea Leisure Park
Priory Road, Ulverston
LA12 9QE
Tel: 01229 584712 61 P4
bardsealeisure.co.uk
Total Pitches: 83 (C & CV)

Barn Farm Campsite
Barn Farm, Birchover, Matlock
DE4 2BL
Tel: 01629 650245 46 H1
barnfarmcamping.com
Total Pitches: 62 (C, CV & T)

Bath Chew Valley Caravan Park
Ham Lane, Bishop Sutton
BS39 5TZ
Tel: 01275 332127 17 Q5
bathchewvalley.co.uk
Total Pitches: 45 (C, CV & T)

Bay View Holiday Park
Bolton le Sands, Carnforth
LA5 9TN
Tel: 01524 732854 61 T6
holgates.co.uk
Total Pitches: 100 (C, CV & T)

Beacon Cottage Farm Touring Park
Beacon Drive,
St Agnes
TR5 0NU
Tel: 01872 552347 2 J6
beaconcottagefarmholidays.co.uk
Total Pitches: 70 (C, CV & T)

Beaconsfield Farm Caravan Park
Battlefield,
Shrewsbury
SY4 4AA
Tel: 01939 210370 45 M10
beaconsfieldholidaypark.co.uk
Total Pitches: 60 (C & CV)

Beech Croft Farm
Beech Croft, Blackwell in the Peak,
Buxton
SK17 9TQ
Tel: 01298 85330 56 H12
beechcroftfarm.co.uk
Total Pitches: 30 (C, CV & T)

Bellingham C & C Club Site
Brown Rigg, Bellingham
NE48 2JY
Tel: 01434 220175 76 G9
campingandcaravanningclub.co.uk/bellingham
Total Pitches: 64 (C, CV & T)

Beverley Park C & C Park
Goodrington Road, Paignton
TQ4 7JE
Tel: 01803 661961 6 A13
beverley-holidays.co.uk
Total Pitches: 172 (C, CV & T)

Blue Rose Caravan Country Park
Star Carr Lane, Brandesburton
YO25 8RU
Tel: 01964 543366 65 Q10
bluerosepark.com
Total Pitches: 58 (C & CV)

Briarfields Motel & Touring Park
Gloucester Road, Cheltenham
GL51 0SX
Tel: 01242 235324 28 H3
briarfields.net
Total Pitches: 72 (C, CV & T)

Broadhembury C & C Park
Steeds Lane, Kingsnorth,
Ashford
TN26 1NQ
Tel: 01233 620859 12 K8
broadhembury.co.uk
Total Pitches: 110 (C, CV & T)

Budemeadows Touring Park
Widemouth Bay, Bude
EX23 0NA
Tel: 01288 361646 14 F12
budemeadows.com
Total Pitches: 145 (C, CV & T)

Burnham-on-Sea Holiday Village
Marine Drive,
Burnham-on-Sea
TA8 1LA
Tel: 01278 783391 16 K7
haven.com/burnhamonsea
Total Pitches: 781 (C, CV & T)

Burrowhayes Farm C & C Site & Riding Stables
West Luccombe, Porlock,
Minehead
TA24 8HT
Tel: 01643 862463 15 U3
burrowhayes.co.uk
Total Pitches: 120 (C, CV & T)

Burton Constable Holiday Park & Arboretum
Old Lodges, Sproatley, Hull
HU11 4LJ
Tel: 01964 562508 65 R12
burtonconstable.co.uk
Total Pitches: 105 (C, CV & T)

Caister-on-Sea Holiday Park
Ormesby Road, Caister-on-Sea,
Great Yarmouth
NR30 5NH
Tel: 01493 728931 51 T11
haven.com/caister
Total Pitches: 949 (C &CV)

Caistor Lakes Leisure Park
99a Brigg Road,
Caistor
LN7 6RX
Tel: 01472 859626 58 K6
caistorlakes.co.uk
Total Pitches: 36 (C &CV)

Cakes & Ale
Abbey Lane, Theberton, Leiston
IP16 4TE
Tel: 01728 831655 41 R8
cakesandale.co.uk
Total Pitches: 55 (C, CV & T)

Calloose C & C Park
Leedstown, Hayle
TR27 5ET
Tel: 01736 850431 2 F10
calloose.co.uk
Total Pitches: 109 (C, CV & T)

Camping Caradon Touring Park
Trelawne, Looe
PL13 2NA
Tel: 01503 272388 4 G10
campingcaradon.co.uk
Total Pitches: 75 (C, CV & T)

Capesthorne Hall
Congleton Road, Siddington,
Macclesfield
SK11 9JY
Tel: 01625 861221 55 T12
capesthorne.com
Total Pitches: 50 (C & CV)

Carlyon Bay C & C Park
Bethesda, Cypress Avenue,
Carlyon Bay
PL25 3RE
Tel: 01726 812735 3 R6
carlyonbay.net
Total Pitches: 180 (C, CV & T)

Carnon Downs C & C Park
Carnon Downs, Truro
TR3 6JJ
Tel: 01872 862283 3 L8
carnon-downs-caravanpark.co.uk
Total Pitches: 150 (C, CV & T)

Cartref C & C
Cartref, Ford Heath, Shrewsbury
SY5 9GD
Tel: 01743 821688 44 K11
cartrefcaravansite.co.uk
Total Pitches: 44 (C, CV & T)

Carvynick Country Club
Summercourt, Newquay
TR8 5AF
Tel: 01872 510716 3 M5
carvynick.co.uk
Total Pitches: 47 (C & CV)

Castlerigg Hall C & C Park
Castlerigg Hall, Keswick
CA12 4TE
Tel: 017687 74499 67 L8
castlerigg.co.uk
Total Pitches: 68 (C, CV & T)

Charris C & C Park
Candy's Lane, Corfe Mullen, Wimborne
BH21 3EF
Tel: 01202 885970 8 D9
charris.co.uk
Total Pitches: 45 (C, CV & T)

Cheddar Mendip Heights C & C Club Site
Townsend, Priddy, Wells
BA5 3BP
Tel: 01749 870241 17 P6
campingandcaravanningclub.co.uk/cheddar
Total Pitches: 90 (C, CV & T)

Chy Carne Holiday Park
Kuggar, Ruan Minor, Helston
TR12 7LX
Tel: 01326 290200 2 J13
chycarne.co.uk
Total Pitches: 30 (C, CV & T)

Clippesby Hall
Hall Lane, Clippesby,
Great Yarmouth
NR29 3BL
Tel: 01493 367800 51 R11
clippesbyhall.com
Total Pitches: 120 (C, CV & T)

Cofton Holidays
Starcross, Dawlish
EX6 8RP
Tel: 01626 890111 6 C8
coftonholidays.co.uk
Total Pitches: 450 (C, CV & T)

Concierge Camping
Ratham Estate, Ratham Lane,
West Ashling, Chichester
PO18 8DL
Tel: 01243 573118 10 C9
conciergecamping.co.uk
Total Pitches: 15 (C, CV & T)

Coombe Touring Park
Race Plain, Netherhampton, Salisbury
SP2 8PN
Tel: 01722 328451 8 F3
coombecaravanpark.co.uk
Total Pitches: 50 (C, CV & T)

Corfe Castle C & C Club Site
Bucknowle, Wareham
BH20 5PQ
Tel: 01929 480280 8 C12
campingandcaravanningclub.co.uk/corfecastle
Total Pitches: 80 (C, CV & T)

Cornish Farm Touring Park
Shoreditch, Taunton
TA3 7BS
Tel: 01823 327746 16 H12
cornishfarm.com
Total Pitches: 50 (C, CV & T)

Cosawes Park
Perranarworthal, Truro
TR3 7QS
Tel: 01872 863724 2 K9
cosawes.co.uk
Total Pitches: 59 (C, CV & T)

Cote Ghyll C & C Park
Osmotherley, Northallerton
DL6 3AH
Tel: 01609 883425 70 G13
coteghyll.com
Total Pitches: 77 (C, CV & T)

Country View Holiday Park
Sand Road, Sand Bay,
Weston-super-Mare
BS22 9UJ
Tel: 01934 627595 16 K4
cvhp.co.uk
Total Pitches: 190 (C, CV & T)

Crealy Adventure Park and Resort
Sidmouth Road, Clyst St Mary, Exeter
EX5 1DR
Tel: 01395 234888 6 D6
crealy.co.uk
Total Pitches: 120 (C, CV & T)

Crows Nest Caravan Park
Gristhorpe, Filey
YO14 9PS
Tel: 01723 582206 65 P3
crowsnestcaravanpark.com
Total Pitches: 49 (C, CV & T)

Deepdale Backpackers & Camping
Deepdale Farm,
Burnham Deepdale
PE31 8DD
Tel: 01485 210256 50 D5
deepdalebackpackers.co.uk
Total Pitches: 80 (CV & T)

Dolbeare Park C & C
St Ive Road, Landrake, Saltash
PL12 5AF
Tel: 01752 851332 4 K8
dolbeare.co.uk
Total Pitches: 60 (C, CV & T)

Dornafield
Dornafield Farm, Two Mile Oak,
Newton Abbot
TQ12 6DD
Tel: 01803 812732 5 U7
dornafield.com
Total Pitches: 135 (C, CV & T)

East Fleet Farm Touring Park
Chickerell, Weymouth
DT3 4DW
Tel: 01305 785768 7 R9
eastfleet.co.uk
Total Pitches: 400 (C, CV & T)

Eden Valley Holiday Park
Lanlivery, Nr Lostwithiel
PL30 5BU
Tel: 01208 872277 3 R5
edenvalleyholidaypark.co.uk
Total Pitches: 56 (C, CV & T)

Exe Valley Caravan Site
Mill House, Bridgetown, Dulverton
TA22 9JR
Tel: 01643 851432 16 B10
exevalleycamping.co.uk
Total Pitches: 48 (C, CV & T)

Eye Kettleby Lakes
Eye Kettleby, Melton Mowbray
LE14 2TN
Tel: 01664 565900 47 T10
eyekettlebylakes.com
Total Pitches: 130 (C, CV & T)

Fields End Water Caravan Park & Fishery
Benwick Road, Doddington,
March
PE15 0TY
Tel: 01354 740199 39 N2
fieldsendcaravans.co.uk
Total Pitches: 52 (C, CV & T)

Flower of May Holiday Park
Lebberston Cliff, Filey, Scarborough
YO11 3NU
Tel: 01723 584311 65 P3
flowerofmay.com
Total Pitches: 503 (C, CV & T)

Freshwater Beach Holiday Park
Burton Bradstock, Bridport
DT6 4PT
Tel: 01308 897317 7 N6
freshwaterbeach.co.uk
Total Pitches: 750 (C, CV & T)

Glenfield Caravan Park
Blackmoor Lane, Bardsey,
Leeds
LS17 9DZ
Tel: 01937 574657 63 S11
glenfieldcaravanpark.co.uk
Total Pitches: 31 (C, CV & T)

Globe Vale Holiday Park
Radnor, Redruth
TR16 4BH
Tel: 01209 891183 2 J8
globevale.co.uk
Total Pitches: 138 (C, CV & T)

Glororum Caravan Park
Glororum Farm, Bamburgh
NE69 7AW
Tel: 01670 860256 85 T12
northumbrianleisure.co.uk
Total Pitches: 213 (C & CV)

Golden Cap Holiday Park
Seatown, Chideock, Bridport
DT6 6JX
Tel: 01308 422139 7 M6
wdlh.co.uk
Total Pitches: 108 (C, CV & T)

Golden Coast Holiday Park
Station Road, Woolacombe
EX34 7HW
Tel: 01271 872302 15 L4
woolacombe.com
Total Pitches: 431 (C, CV & T)

Golden Sands Holiday Park
Quebec Road, Mablethorpe
LN12 1QJ
Tel: 01507 477871 59 S9
haven.com/goldensands
Total Pitches: 1672 (C, CV & T)

Golden Square C & C Park
Oswaldkirk, Helmsley
YO62 5YQ
Tel: 01439 788269 64 E4
goldensquarecaravanpark.com
Total Pitches: 129 (C, CV & T)

Goosewood Holiday Park
Sutton-on-the-Forest, York
YO61 1ET
Tel: 01347 810829 64 D7
flowerofmay.com
Total Pitches: 100 (C & CV)

Green Acres Caravan Park
High Knells, Houghton, Carlisle
CA6 4JW
Tel: 01228 675418 75 T13
caravanpark-cumbria.com
Total Pitches: 35 (C, CV & T)

Greenhill Farm C & C Park
Greenhill Farm, New Road,
Landford, Salisbury
SP5 2AZ
Tel: 01794 324117 8 K5
greenhillfarm.co.uk
Total Pitches: 160 (C, CV & T)

Greenhill Leisure Park
Greenhill Farm, Station Road,
Bletchingdon, Oxford
OX5 3BQ
Tel: 01869 351600 29 U4
greenhill-leisure-park.co.uk
Total Pitches: 92 (C, CV & T)

Grooby's Pit
Bridgefoot Farm, Steeping Road,
Thorpe St Peter
PE24 4QT
Tel: 07427 137463 49 Q1
fishskegness.co.uk
Total Pitches: 18 (C & CV)

Grouse Hill Caravan Park
Flask Bungalow Farm, Fylingdales,
Robin Hood's Bay
YO22 4QH
Tel: 01947 880543 71 R12
grousehill.co.uk
Total Pitches: 175 (C, CV & T)

Gunvenna Holiday Park
St Minver, Wadebridge
PL27 6QN
Tel: 01208 862405 4 B5
gunvenna.com
Total Pitches: 75 (C, CV & T)

Haggerston Castle Holiday Park
Beal, Berwick-upon-Tweed
TD15 2PA
Tel: 01289 381333 85 Q10
haven.com/haggerstoncastle
Total Pitches: 1340 (C & CV)

Harbury Fields
Harbury Fields Farm, Harbury,
Nr Leamington Spa
CV33 9JN
Tel: 01926 612457 37 L8
harburyfields.co.uk
Total Pitches: 59 (C & CV)

Harford Bridge Holiday Park
Peter Tavy, Tavistock
PL19 9LS
Tel: 01822 810349 5 N5
harfordbridge.co.uk
Total Pitches: 198 (C, CV & T)

Haw Wood Farm Caravan Park
Hinton, Saxmundham
IP17 3QT
Tel: 01502 359550 41 R6
hawwoodfarm.co.uk
Total Pitches: 60 (C, CV & T)

Heathfield Farm Camping
Heathfield Road, Freshwater, Isle of Wight
PO40 9SH
Tel: 01983 407822 9 L11
heathfieldcamping.co.uk
Total Pitches: 75 (C, CV & T)

Heathland Beach Caravan Park
London Road, Kessingland
NR33 7PJ
Tel: 01502 740337 41 T3
heathlandbeach.co.uk
Total Pitches: 63 (C, CV & T)

Hele Valley Holiday Park
Hele Bay, Ilfracombe
EX34 9RD
Tel: 01271 862460 15 M3
helevalley.co.uk
Total Pitches: 50 (C, CV & T)

Hendra Holiday Park
Newquay
TR8 4NY
Tel: 01637 875778 3 L4
hendra-holidays.com
Total Pitches: 548 (C, CV & T)

Hidden Valley Park
West Down, Braunton, Ilfracombe
EX34 8NU
Tel: 01271 813837 15 M4
hiddenvalleypark.com
Total Pitches: 100 (C, CV & T)

Highfield Farm Touring Park
Long Road, Comberton, Cambridge
CB23 7DG
Tel: 01223 262308 39 N9
highfieldfarmtouringpark.co.uk
Total Pitches: 120 (C, CV & T)

Highlands End Holiday Park
Eype, Bridport, Dorset
DT6 6AR
Tel: 01308 422139 7 N6
wdlh.co.uk
Total Pitches: 195 (C, CV & T)

Hill Cottage Farm C & C Park
Sandleheath Road, Alderholt, Fordingbridge
SP6 3EG
Tel: 01425 650513 8 G6
hillcottagefarmcampingandcaravanpark.co.uk
Total Pitches: 95 (C, CV & T)

Hill of Oaks & Blakeholme
Windermere
LA12 8NR
Tel: 015395 31578 61 R2
hillofoaks.co.uk
Total Pitches: 43 (C & CV)

Hillside Caravan Park
Canvas Farm, Moor Road, Knayton, Thirsk
YO7 4BR
Tel: 01845 537349 63 U2
hillsidecaravanpark.co.uk
Total Pitches: 50 (C & CV)

Holiday Resort Unity
Coast Road, Brean Sands, Brean
TA8 2RB
Tel: 01278 751235 16 J6
hru.co.uk
Total Pitches: 1114 (C, CV & T)

Hollins Farm C & C
Far Arnside, Carnforth
LA5 0SL
Tel: 01524 701767 61 S4
holgates.co.uk
Total Pitches: 12 (C, CV & T)

Hylton Caravan Park
Eden Street, Silloth
CA7 4AY
Tel: 016973 31707 66 H2
stanwix.com
Total Pitches: 90 (C, CV & T)

Island Lodge C & C Site
Stumpy Post Cross, Kingsbridge
TQ7 4BL
Tel: 01548 852956 5 S11
islandlodgesite.co.uk
Total Pitches: 30 (C, CV & T)

Isle of Avalon Touring Caravan Park
Godney Road, Glastonbury
BA6 9AF
Tel: 01458 833618 17 N9
avaloncaravanpark.co.uk
Total Pitches: 120 (C, CV & T)

Jasmine Caravan Park
Cross Lane, Snainton, Scarborough
YO13 9BE
Tel: 01723 859240 65 L3
jasminepark.co.uk
Total Pitches: 68 (C, CV & T)

Kenneggy Cove Holiday Park
Higher Kenneggy, Rosudgeon, Penzance
TR20 9AU
Tel: 01736 763453 2 F11
kenneggycove.co.uk
Total Pitches: 40 (C, CV & T)

Kennford International Caravan Park
Kennford, Exeter
EX6 7YN
Tel: 01392 833046 6 B7
kennfordinternational.co.uk
Total Pitches: 87 (C, CV & T)

King's Lynn C & C Park
New Road, North Runcton, King's Lynn
PE33 0RA
Tel: 01553 840004 49 T10
kl-cc.co.uk
Total Pitches: 150 (C, CV & T)

Kloofs Caravan Park
Sandhurst Lane, Bexhill
TN39 4RG
Tel: 01424 842839 12 D14
kloofs.com
Total Pitches: 125 (C, CV & T)

Kneps Farm Holiday Park
River Road, Stanah, Thornton-Cleveleys,
Blackpool
FY5 5LR
Tel: 01253 823632 61 R11
knepsfarm.co.uk
Total Pitches: 40 (C & CV)

Knight Stainforth Hall Caravan & Campsite
Stainforth, Settle
BD24 0DP
Tel: 01729 822200 62 G6
knightstainforth.co.uk
Total Pitches: 100 (C, CV & T)

Ladycross Plantation Caravan Park
Egton, Whitby
YO21 1UA
Tel: 01947 895502 71 P11
ladycrossplantation.co.uk
Total Pitches: 130 (C, CV & T)

Lady's Mile Holiday Park
Dawlish, Devon
EX7 0LX
Tel: 01626 863411 6 C9
ladysmile.co.uk
Total Pitches: 570 (C, CV & T)

Lakeland Leisure Park
Moor Lane, Flookburgh
LA11 7LT
Tel: 01539 558556 61 R5
haven.com/lakeland
Total Pitches: 977 (C, CV & T)

Lamb Cottage Caravan Park
Dalefords Lane, Whitegate, Northwich
CW8 2BN
Tel: 01606 882302 55 P13
lambcottage.co.uk
Total Pitches: 45 (C & CV)

Langstone Manor C & C Park
Moortown, Tavistock
PL19 9JZ
Tel: 01822 613371 5 N6
langstonemanor.co.uk
Total Pitches: 40 (C, CV & T)

Lanyon Holiday Park
Loscombe Lane, Four Lanes, Redruth
TR16 6LP
Tel: 01209 313474 2 H9
lanyonholidaypark.co.uk
Total Pitches: 25 (C, CV & T)

Lebberston Touring Park
Filey Road, Lebberston, Scarborough
YO11 3PE
Tel: 01723 585723 65 P3
lebberstontouring.co.uk
Total Pitches: 125 (C & CV)

Lickpenny Caravan Site
Lickpenny Lane, Tansley, Matlock
DE4 5GF
Tel: 01629 583040 46 K2
lickpennycaravanpark.co.uk
Total Pitches: 80 (C & CV)

Lime Tree Park
Dukes Drive, Buxton
SK17 9RP
Tel: 01298 22988 56 G12
limetreeparkbuxton.com
Total Pitches: 106 (C, CV & T)

Lincoln Farm Park Oxfordshire
High Street, Standlake
OX29 7RH
Tel: 01865 300239 29 S7
lincolnfarmpark.co.uk
Total Pitches: 90 (C, CV & T)

Little Lakeland Caravan Park
Wortwell, Harleston
IP20 0EL
Tel: 01986 788646 41 N4
littlelakelandcaravanparkandcamping.co.uk
Total Pitches: 58 (C, CV & T)

Littlesea Holiday Park
Lynch Lane, Weymouth
DT4 9DT
Tel: 01305 774414 7 S9
haven.com/littlesea
Total Pitches: 861 (C, CV & T)

Long Acres Touring Park
Station Road, Old Leake, Boston
PE22 9RF
Tel: 01205 871555 49 N3
long-acres.co.uk
Total Pitches: 40 (C, CV & T)

Longnor Wood Holiday Park
Newtown, Longnor, Nr Buxton
SK17 0NG
Tel: 01298 83648 56 G14
longnorwood.co.uk
Total Pitches: 47 (C, CV & T)

Lower Polladras Touring Park
Carleen, Breage, Helston
TR13 9NX
Tel: 01736 762220 2 G10
lower-polladras.co.uk
Total Pitches: 39 (C, CV & T)

Lowther Holiday Park
Eamont Bridge, Penrith
CA10 2JB
Tel: 01768 863631 67 R7
lowther-holidaypark.co.uk
Total Pitches: 180 (C, CV & T)

Manor Wood Country Caravan Park
Manor Wood, Coddington, Chester
CH3 9EN
Tel: 01829 782990 44 K3
cheshire-caravan-sites.co.uk
Total Pitches: 45 (C, CV & T)

Marton Mere Holiday Village
Mythop Road, Blackpool
FY4 4XN
Tel: 01253 767544 61 Q13
haven.com/martonmere
Total Pitches: 782 (C & CV)

Mayfield Park
Cheltenham Road, Cirencester
GL7 7BH
Tel: 01285 831301 28 K6
mayfieldpark.co.uk
Total Pitches: 105 (C, CV & T)

Meadowbank Holidays
Stour Way, Christchurch
BH23 2PQ
Tel: 01202 483597 8 G10
meadowbank-holidays.co.uk
Total Pitches: 41 (C & CV)

Middlewood Farm Holiday Park
Middlewood Lane, Fylingthorpe,
Robin Hood's Bay, Whitby
YO22 4UF
Tel: 01947 880414 71 R12
middlewoodfarm.com
Total Pitches: 100 (C, CV & T)

Minnows Touring Park
Holbrook Lane, Sampford Peverell
EX16 7EN
Tel: 01884 821770 16 D13
minnowstouringpark.co.uk
Total Pitches: 59 (C, CV & T)

Monkey Tree Holiday Park
Hendra Croft, Scotland Road, Newquay
TR8 5QR
Tel: 01872 572032 3 L6
monkeytreeholidaypark.co.uk
Total Pitches: 700 (C, CV & T)

Moon & Sixpence
Newbourn Road, Waldringfield,
Woodbridge
IP12 4PP
Tel: 01473 736650 41 N11
moonandsixpence.co.uk
Total Pitches: 50 (C & CV)

Moor Lodge Park
Blackmoor Lane, Bardsey, Leeds
LS17 9DZ
Tel: 01937 572424 63 T11
moorlodgecaravanpark.co.uk
Total Pitches: 12 (C & CV)

Moss Wood Caravan Park
Crimbles Lane, Cockerham
LA2 0ES
Tel: 01524 791041 61 T10
mosswood.co.uk
Total Pitches: 25 (C, CV & T)

Naburn Lock Caravan Park
Naburn
YO19 4RU
Tel: 01904 728697 64 E10
naburnlock.co.uk
Total Pitches: 100 (C, CV & T)

New Lodge Farm C & C Site
New Lodge Farm, Bulwick, Corby
NN17 3DU
Tel: 01780 450493 38 E1
newlodgefarm.com
Total Pitches: 72 (C, CV & T)

Newberry Valley Park
Woodlands, Combe Martin
EX34 0AT
Tel: 01271 882334 15 N3
newberryvalleypark.co.uk
Total Pitches: 110 (C, CV & T)

Newlands Holidays
Charmouth, Bridport
DT6 6RB
Tel: 01297 560259 7 L6
newlandsholidays.co.uk
Total Pitches: 240 (C, CV & T)

Newperran Holiday Park
Rejerrah, Newquay
TR8 5QJ
Tel: 01872 572407 2 K6
newperran.co.uk
Total Pitches: 357 (C, CV & T)

Ninham Country Holidays
Ninham, Shanklin, Isle of Wight
PO37 7PL
Tel: 01983 864243 9 R12
ninham-holidays.co.uk
Total Pitches: 135 (C, CV & T)

North Morte Farm C & C Park
North Morte Road, Mortehoe,
Woolacombe
EX34 7EG
Tel: 01271 870381 15 L3
northmortefarm.co.uk
Total Pitches: 180 (C, CV & T)

Northam Farm Caravan & Touring Park
Brean, Burnham-on-Sea
TA8 2SE
Tel: 01278 751244 16 K5
northamfarm.co.uk
Total Pitches: 350 (C, CV & T)

Oakdown Country Holiday Park
Gatedown Lane, Weston, Sidmouth
EX10 0PT
Tel: 01297 680387 6 G6
oakdown.co.uk
Total Pitches: 150 (C, CV & T)

Old Hall Caravan Park
Capernwray, Carnforth
LA6 1AD
Tel: 01524 733276 61 U5
oldhallcaravanpark.co.uk
Total Pitches: 38 (C & CV)

Ord House Country Park
East Ord, Berwick-upon-Tweed
TD15 2NS
Tel: 01289 305288 85 P8
ordhouse.co.uk
Total Pitches: 79 (C, CV & T)

Oxon Hall Touring Park
Welshpool Road, Shrewsbury
SY3 5FB
Tel: 01743 340868 45 L11
morris-leisure.co.uk
Total Pitches: 105 (C, CV & T)

Padstow Touring Park
Padstow
PL28 8LE
Tel: 01841 532061 3 N2
padstowtouringpark.co.uk
Total Pitches: 150 (C, CV & T)

Park Cliffe C & C Estate
Birks Road, Tower Wood, Windermere
LA23 3PG
Tel: 015395 31344 61 R1
parkcliffe.co.uk
Total Pitches: 60 (C, CV & T)

Parkers Farm Holiday Park
Higher Mead Farm, Ashburton, Devon
TQ13 7LJ
Tel: 01364 654869 5 T6
parkersfarmholidays.co.uk
Total Pitches: 100 (C, CV & T)

Park Foot C & C Park
Howtown Road, Pooley Bridge
CA10 2NA
Tel: 017684 86309 67 Q8
parkfootullswater.co.uk
Total Pitches: 454 (C, CV & T)

Parkland C & C Site
Sorley Green Cross, Kingsbridge
TQ7 4AF
Tel: 01548 852723 5 S11
parklandsite.co.uk
Total Pitches: 50 (C, CV & T)

Pebble Bank Caravan Park
Camp Road, Wyke Regis, Weymouth
DT4 9HF
Tel: 01305 774844 7 S9
pebblebank.co.uk
Total Pitches: 120 (C, CV & T)

Perran Sands Holiday Park
Perranporth, Truro
TR6 0AQ
Tel: 01872 573551 2 K5
haven.com/perransands
Total Pitches: 1012 (C, CV & T)

Petwood Caravan Park
Off Stixwould Road, Woodhall Spa
LN10 6QH
Tel: 01526 354799 59 L14
petwoodcaravanpark.com
Total Pitches: 98 (C, CV & T)

Polmanter Touring Park
Halsetown, St Ives
TR26 3LX
Tel: 01736 795640 2 E9
polmanter.co.uk
Total Pitches: 270 (C, CV & T)

Porthtowan Tourist Park
Mile Hill, Porthtowan, Truro
TR4 8TY
Tel: 01209 890256 2 H7
porthtowantouristpark.co.uk
Total Pitches: 80 (C, CV & T)

Primrose Valley Holiday Park
Filey
YO14 9RF
Tel: 01723 513771 65 Q4
haven.com/primrosevalley
Total Pitches: 1549 (C & CV)

Quantock Orchard Caravan Park
Flaxpool, Crowcombe, Taunton
TA4 4AW
Tel: 01984 618618 16 F9
quantock-orchard.co.uk
Total Pitches: 60 (C, CV & T)

Ranch Caravan Park
Station Road, Honeybourne, Evesham
WR11 7PR
Tel: 01386 830744 36 F12
ranch.co.uk
Total Pitches: 120 (C & CV)

Ripley Caravan Park
Knaresborough Road, Ripley, Harrogate
HG3 3AU
Tel: 01423 770050 63 R7
ripleycaravanpark.com
Total Pitches: 60 (C, CV & T)

River Dart Country Park
Holne Park, Ashburton
TQ13 7NP
Tel: 01364 652511 5 S7
riverdart.co.uk
Total Pitches: 170 (C, CV & T)

River Valley Holiday Park
London Apprentice, St Austell
PL26 7AP
Tel: 01726 73533 3 Q6
rivervalleyholidaypark.co.uk
Total Pitches: 45 (C, CV & T)

Riverside C & C Park
Marsh Lane, North Molton Road, South Molton
EX36 3HQ
Tel: 01769 579269 15 R7
exmoorriverside.co.uk
Total Pitches: 58 (C, CV & T)

Riverside Caravan Park
High Bentham, Lancaster
LA2 7FJ
Tel: 015242 61272 62 D6
riversidecaravanpark.co.uk
Total Pitches: 61 (C & CV)

Riverside Holiday Park
Southport New Road, Southport
PR9 8DF
Tel: 01704 228886 54 K3
riversideleisurecentre.co.uk
Total Pitches: 615 (C & CV)

Riverside Meadows Country Caravan Park
Ure Bank Top, Ripon
HG4 1JD
Tel: 01765 602964 63 S5
flowerofmay.com
Total Pitches: 80 (C, CV & T)

Robin Hood C & C Park
Green Dyke Lane, Slingsby
YO62 4AP
Tel: 01653 628391 64 G5
robinhoodcaravanpark.co.uk
Total Pitches: 32 (C, CV & T)

Rose Farm Touring & Camping Park
Stepshort, Belton, Nr Great Yarmouth
NR31 9JS
Tel: 01493 738292 51 S13
rosefarmtouringpark.co.uk
Total Pitches: 145 (C, CV & T)

Rosedale Abbey C & C Park
Rosedale Abbey, Pickering
YO18 8SA
Tel: 01751 417272 71 M13
rosedaleabbeycaravanpark.co.uk
Total Pitches: 100 (C, CV & T)

Ross Park
Park Hill Farm, Ipplepen, Newton Abbot
TQ12 5TT
Tel: 01803 812983 5 U7
rossparkcaravanpark.co.uk
Total Pitches: 110 (C, CV & T)

Rudding Holiday Park
Follifoot, Harrogate
HG3 1JH
Tel: 01423 870439 63 S9
ruddingholidaypark.co.uk
Total Pitches: 86 (C, CV & T)

Run Cottage Touring Park
Alderton Road, Hollesley, Woodbridge
IP12 3RQ
Tel: 01394 411309 41 Q12
runcottage.co.uk
Total Pitches: 45 (C, CV & T)

Rutland C & C
Park Lane, Greetham, Oakham
LE15 7FN
Tel: 01572 813520 48 D11
rutlandcaravanandcamping.co.uk
Total Pitches: 130 (C, CV & T)

St Helens Caravan Park
Wykeham, Scarborough
YO13 9QD
Tel: 01723 862771 65 M3
sthelenscaravanpark.co.uk
Total Pitches: 250 (C, CV & T)

St Ives Bay Holiday Park
73 Loggans Road, Upton Towans, Hayle
TR27 5BH
Tel: 01736 752274 2 F9
stivesbay.co.uk
Total Pitches: 507 (C, CV & T)

Salcombe Regis C & C Park
Salcombe Regis, Sidmouth
EX10 0JH
Tel: 01395 514303 6 G7
salcombe-regis.co.uk
Total Pitches: 110 (C, CV & T)

Sand le Mere Holiday Village
Southfield Lane, Tunstall
HU12 0JF
Tel: 01964 670403 65 U13
sand-le-mere.co.uk
Total Pitches: 89 (C & CV)

Sandy Balls Holiday Village
Sandy Balls Estate Ltd, Godshill, Fordingbridge
SP6 2JZ
Tel: 01442 508850 8 H6
awayresorts.co.uk
Total Pitches: 225 (C, CV & T)

Searles Leisure Resort
South Beach Road, Hunstanton
PE36 5BB
Tel: 01485 534211 49 U6
searles.co.uk
Total Pitches: 413 (C, CV & T)

Seaview Holiday Park
Preston, Weymouth
DT3 6DZ
Tel: 01305 832271 7 T8
haven.com/seaview
Total Pitches: 347 (C, CV & T)

Seaview International Holiday Park
Boswinger, Mevagissey
PL26 6LL
Tel: 01726 843425 3 P8
seaviewinternational.com
Total Pitches: 201 (C, CV & T)

Severn Gorge Park
Bridgnorth Road, Tweedale, Telford
TF7 4JB
Tel: 01952 684789 45 R12
severngorgepark.co.uk
Total Pitches: 12 (C & CV)

Shamba Holidays
East Moors Lane, St Leonards, Ringwood
BH24 2SB
Tel: 01202 873302 8 G8
shambaholidays.co.uk
Total Pitches: 150 (C, CV & T)

Shrubbery Touring Park
Rousdon, Lyme Regis
DT7 3XW
Tel: 01297 442227 6 J6
shrubberypark.co.uk
Total Pitches: 120 (C, CV & T)

Silverdale Caravan Park
Middlebarrow Plain, Cove Road, Silverdale, Nr Carnforth
LA5 0SH
Tel: 01524 701508 61 T4
holgates.co.uk
Total Pitches: 80 (C, CV & T)

Skelwith Fold Caravan Park
Ambleside, Cumbria
LA22 0HX
Tel: 015394 32277 67 N12
skelwith.com
Total Pitches: 150 (C & CV)

Skirlington Leisure Park
Driffield, Skipsea
YO25 8SY
Tel: 01262 468213 65 R9
skirlington.com
Total Pitches: 930 (C & CV)

Sleningford Watermill Caravan Camping Park
North Stainley, Ripon
HG4 3HQ
Tel: 01765 635201 63 R4
sleningfordwatermill.co.uk
Total Pitches: 135 (C, CV & T)

Somers Wood Caravan Park
Somers Road, Meriden
CV7 7PL
Tel: 01676 522978 36 H4
somerswood.co.uk
Total Pitches: 48 (C & CV)

South Lytchett Manor C & C Park
Dorchester Road, Lytchett Minster, Poole
BH16 6JB
Tel: 01202 622577 8 D10
southlytchettmanor.co.uk
Total Pitches: 150 (C, CV & T)

South Meadows Caravan Park
South Road, Belford
NE70 7DP
Tel: 01668 213326 85 S12
southmeadows.co.uk
Total Pitches: 83 (C, CV & T)

Stanmore Hall Touring Park
Stourbridge Road, Bridgnorth
WV15 6DT
Tel: 01746 761761 35 R2
morris-leisure.co.uk
Total Pitches: 129 (C, CV & T)

Stanwix Park Holiday Centre
Greenrow, Silloth
CA7 4HH
Tel: 016973 32666 66 H2
stanwix.com
Total Pitches: 337 (C, CV & T)

Stowford Farm Meadows
Berry Down, Combe Martin
EX34 0PW
Tel: 01271 882476 15 N4
stowford.co.uk
Total Pitches: 700 (C, CV & T)

Stroud Hill Park
Fen Road, Pidley, St Ives
PE28 3DE
Tel: 01487 741333 39 M5
stroudhillpark.co.uk
Total Pitches: 60 (C, CV & T)

Summer Valley Touring Park
Shortlanesend, Truro
TR4 9DW
Tel: 01872 277878 3 L7
summervalley.co.uk
Total Pitches: 60 (C, CV & T)

Sumners Ponds Fishery & Campsite
Chapel Road, Barns Green, Horsham
RH13 0PR
Tel: 01403 732539 10 J5
sumnersponds.co.uk
Total Pitches: 86 (C, CV & T)

Swiss Farm Touring & Camping
Marlow Road, Henley-on-Thames
RG9 2HY
Tel: 01491 573419 20 C6
swissfarmhenley.co.uk
Total Pitches: 140 (C, CV & T)

Tanner Farm Touring C & C Park
Tanner Farm, Goudhurst Road, Marden
TN12 9ND
Tel: 01622 832399 12 D7
tannerfarmpark.co.uk
Total Pitches: 120 (C, CV & T)

Tattershall Lakes Country Park
Sleaford Road, Tattershall
LN4 4LR
Tel: 01526 348800 48 K2
tattershall-lakes.com
Total Pitches: 186 (C, CV & T)

Tehidy Holiday Park
Harris Mill, Illogan, Portreath
TR16 4JQ
Tel: 01209 216489 2 H8
tehidy.co.uk
Total Pitches: 18 (C, CV & T)

Tencreek Holiday Park
Polperro Road, Looe
PL13 2JR
Tel: 01503 262447 4 G10
dolphinholidays.co.uk
Total Pitches: 355 (C, CV & T)

Teversal C & C Club Site
Silverhill Lane, Teversal
NG17 3JJ
Tel: 01623 551838 47 N1
campingandcaravanningclub.co.uk/teversal
Total Pitches: 126 (C, CV & T)

The Laurels Holiday Park
Padstow Road, Whitecross, Wadebridge
PL27 7JQ
Tel: 01208 813341 3 P2
thelaurelsholidaypark.co.uk
Total Pitches: 30 (C, CV & T)

The Old Brick Kilns
Little Barney Lane, Barney, Fakenham
NR21 0NL
Tel: 01328 878305 50 H7
old-brick-kilns.co.uk
Total Pitches: 65 (C, CV & T)

The Old Oaks Touring Park
Wick Farm, Wick, Glastonbury
BA6 8JS
Tel: 01458 831437 17 P9
theoldoaks.co.uk
Total Pitches: 98 (C, CV & T)

The Orchards Holiday Caravan Park
Main Road, Newbridge, Yarmouth, Isle of Wight
PO41 0TS
Tel: 01983 531331 9 N11
orchards-holiday-park.co.uk
Total Pitches: 160 (C, CV & T)

The Quiet Site
Ullswater, Watermillock
CA11 0LS
Tel: 07768 727016 67 P8
thequietsite.co.uk
Total Pitches: 100 (C, CV & T)

Thornwick Bay Holiday Village
North Marine Road, Flamborough
YO15 1AU
Tel: 01262 850569 65 S5
haven.com/parks/yorkshire/thornwick-bay
Total Pitches: 225 (C, CV & T)

Thorpe Park Holiday Centre
Cleethorpes
DN35 0PW
Tel: 01472 813395 59 P5
haven.com/thorpepark
Total Pitches: 1491 (C, CV & T)

Treago Farm Caravan Site
Crantock, Newquay
TR8 5QS
Tel: 01637 830277 2 K4
treagofarm.co.uk
Total Pitches: 90 (C, CV & T)

Tregoad Park
St Martin, Looe
PL13 1PB
Tel: 01503 262718 4 H9
tregoadpark.co.uk
Total Pitches: 200 (C, CV & T)

Treloy Touring Park
Newquay
TR8 4JN
Tel: 01637 872063 3 M4
treloy.co.uk
Total Pitches: 223 (C, CV & T)

Trencreek Holiday Park
Hillcrest, Higher Trencreek, Newquay
TR8 4NS
Tel: 01637 874210 3 L4
trencreekholidaypark.co.uk
Total Pitches: 194 (C, CV & T)

Trethem Mill Touring Park
St Just-in-Roseland, Nr St Mawes, Truro
TR2 5JF
Tel: 01872 580504 3 M9
trethem.com
Total Pitches: 84 (C, CV & T)

Trevalgan Touring Park
Trevalgan, St Ives
TR26 3BJ
Tel: 01736 791892 2 D9
trevalgantouringpark.co.uk
Total Pitches: 135 (C, CV & T)

Trevedra Farm C & C Site
Sennen, Penzance
TR19 7BE
Tel: 01736 871818 2 B11
trevedrafarm.co.uk
Total Pitches: 100 (C, CV & T)

Trevella Park
Crantock, Newquay
TR8 5EW
Tel: 01637 830308 3 L5
trevella.co.uk
Total Pitches: 165 (C, CV & T)

Trevornick
Holywell Bay, Newquay
TR8 5PW
Tel: 01637 830531 2 K5
trevornick.co.uk
Total Pitches: 688 (C, CV & T)

Truro C & C Park
Truro
TR4 8QN
Tel: 01872 560274 2 K7
trurocaravanandcampingpark.co.uk
Total Pitches: 51 (C, CV & T)

Tudor C & C
Shepherds Patch, Slimbridge, Gloucester
GL2 7BP
Tel: 01453 890483 28 D7
tudorcaravanpark.com
Total Pitches: 75 (C, CV & T)

Twitchen House Holiday Park
Mortehoe Station Road, Mortehoe, Woolacombe
EX34 7ES
Tel: 01271 872302 15 L4
woolacombe.com
Total Pitches: 569 (C, CV & T)

Two Mills Touring Park
Yarmouth Road, North Walsham
NR28 9NA
Tel: 01692 405829 51 N8
twomills.co.uk
Total Pitches: 81 (C, CV & T)

Ulwell Cottage Caravan Park
Ulwell Cottage, Ulwell, Swanage
BH19 3DG
Tel: 01929 422823 8 E12
ulwellcottagepark.co.uk
Total Pitches: 77 (C, CV & T)

Vale of Pickering Caravan Park
Carr House Farm, Allerston, Pickering
YO18 7PQ
Tel: 01723 859280 64 K3
valeofpickering.co.uk
Total Pitches: 120 (C, CV & T)

Wagtail Country Park
Cliff Lane, Marston, Grantham
NG32 2HU
Tel: 01400 251123 48 C5
wagtailcountrypark.co.uk
Total Pitches: 76 (C & CV)

Waldegraves Holiday Park
Mersea Island, Colchester
CO5 8SE
Tel: 01206 382898 23 P5
waldegraves.co.uk
Total Pitches: 30 (C, CV & T)

Warcombe Farm C & C Park
Station Road, Mortehoe, Woolacombe
EX34 7EJ
Tel: 01271 870690 15 L3
warcombefarm.co.uk
Total Pitches: 250 (C, CV & T)

Wareham Forest Tourist Park
North Trigon, Wareham
BH20 7NZ
Tel: 01929 551393 8 B10
warehamforest.co.uk
Total Pitches: 200 (C, CV & T)

Waren C & C Park
Waren Mill, Bamburgh
NE70 7EE
Tel: 01668 214366 85 T12
meadowhead.co.uk
Total Pitches: 150 (C, CV & T)

Warren Farm Holiday Centre
Brean Sands, Brean, Burnham-on-Sea
TA8 2RP
Tel: 01278 751227 16 J5
warrenfarm.co.uk
Total Pitches: 975 (C, CV & T)

Watergate Bay Touring Park
Watergate Bay, Tregurrian
TR8 4AD
Tel: 01637 860387 3 M3
watergatebaytouringpark.co.uk
Total Pitches: 171 (C, CV & T)

Waterrow Touring Park
Wiveliscombe, Taunton
TA4 2AZ
Tel: 01984 623464 16 E11
waterrowpark.co.uk
Total Pitches: 44 (C, CV & T)

Wayfarers C & C Park
Relubbus Lane, St Hilary, Penzance
TR20 9EF
Tel: 01736 763326 2 F10
wayfarerspark.co.uk
Total Pitches: 32 (C, CV & T)

Wells Touring Park
Haybridge, Wells
BA5 1AJ
Tel: 01749 676869 17 P7
wellstouringpark.co.uk
Total Pitches: 72 (C, CV & T)

Wheathill Touring Park
Wheathill, Bridgnorth
WV16 6QT
Tel: 01584 823456 35 P4
wheathillpark.co.uk
Total Pitches: 25 (C & CV)

Whitecliff Bay Holiday Park
Hillway Road, Bembridge, Whitecliff Bay
PO35 5PL
Tel: 01983 872671 9 S11
wight-holidays.com
Total Pitches: 653 (C, CV & T)

Whitefield Forest Touring Park
Brading Road, Ryde, Isle of Wight
PO33 1QL
Tel: 01983 617069 9 S11
whitefieldforest.co.uk
Total Pitches: 90 (C, CV & T)

Whitemead Caravan Park
East Burton Road, Wool
BH20 6HG
Tel: 01929 462241 8 A11
whitemeadcaravanpark.co.uk
Total Pitches: 105 (C, CV & T)

Widdicombe Farm Touring Park
Marldon, Paignton
TQ3 1ST
Tel: 01803 558325 5 V8
widdicombefarm.co.uk
Total Pitches: 180 (C, CV & T)

Wild Rose Park
Ormside, Appleby-in-Westmorland
CA16 6EJ
Tel: 017683 51077 68 E9
harrisonholidayhomes.co.uk
Total Pitches: 226 (C & CV)

Wilksworth Farm Caravan Park
Cranborne Road, Wimborne Minster
BH21 4HW
Tel: 01202 885467 8 E8
shorefield.co.uk/camping-touring-holidays/our-parks/wilksworth-caravan-park
Total Pitches: 85 (C, CV & T)

Willowbank Holiday Home & Touring Park
Coastal Road, Ainsdale, Southport
PR8 3ST
Tel: 01704 571566 54 H4
willowbankcp.co.uk
Total Pitches: 87 (C & CV)

Wolds View Touring Park
115 Brigg Road, Caistor
LN7 6RX
Tel: 01472 851099 58 K6
woldsviewtouringpark.co.uk
Total Pitches: 60 (C, CV & T)

Wood Farm C & C Park
Axminster Road, Charmouth
DT6 6BT
Tel: 01297 560697 7 L6
woodfarm.co.uk
Total Pitches: 175 (C, CV & T)

Wooda Farm Holiday Park
Poughill, Bude
EX23 9HJ
Tel: 01288 352069 14 F11
wooda.co.uk
Total Pitches: 200 (C, CV & T)

Woodclose Caravan Park
High Casterton, Kirkby Lonsdale
LA6 2SE
Tel: 015242 71597 62 C4
woodclosepark.com
Total Pitches: 22 (C, CV & T)

Woodhall Country Park
Stixwold Road, Woodhall Spa
LN10 6UJ
Tel: 01526 353710 59 L14
woodhallcountrypark.co.uk
Total Pitches: 115 (C, CV & T)

Woodland Springs Adult Touring Park
Venton, Drewsteignton
EX6 6PG
Tel: 01647 231695 5 R2
woodlandsprings.co.uk
Total Pitches: 81 (C, CV & T)

Woodlands Grove C & C Park
Blackawton, Dartmouth
TQ9 7DQ
Tel: 01803 712598 5 U10
woodlandsgrove.co.uk
Total Pitches: 350 (C, CV & T)

Woodovis Park
Gulworthy, Tavistock
PL19 8NY
Tel: 01822 832968 5 L6
woodovis.com
Total Pitches: 50 (C, CV & T)

Yeatheridge Farm Caravan Park
East Worlington, Crediton
EX17 4TN
Tel: 01884 860330 15 S10
yeatheridge.co.uk
Total Pitches: 122 (C, CV & T)

SCOTLAND

Auchenlarie Holiday Park
Gatehouse of Fleet
DG7 2EX
Tel: 01556 506200 73 N9
swalwellholidaygroup.co.uk
Total Pitches: 451 (C, CV & T)

Beecraigs C & C Site
Beecraigs Country Park, The Visitor Centre, Linlithgow
EH49 6PL
Tel: 01506 844516 82 K4
beecraigs.com
Total Pitches: 36 (C, CV & T)

Blair Castle Caravan Park
Blair Atholl, Pitlochry
PH18 5SR
Tel: 01796 481263 97 P10
blaircastlecaravanpark.co.uk
Total Pitches: 226 (C, CV & T)

Brighouse Bay Holiday Park
Brighouse Bay, Borgue, Kirkcudbright
DG6 4TS
Tel: 01557 870267 73 Q10
gillespie-leisure.co.uk
Total Pitches: 190 (C, CV & T)

Cairnsmill Holiday Park
Largo Road, St Andrews
KY16 8NN
Tel: 01334 473604 91 Q9
cairnsmill.co.uk
Total Pitches: 62 (C, CV & T)

Craig Tara Holiday Park
Ayr
KA7 4LB
Tel: 0800 975 7579 81 L9
haven.com/craigtara
Total Pitches: 1144 (C & CV)

Craigtoun Meadows Holiday Park
Mount Melville, St Andrews
KY16 8PQ
Tel: 01334 475959 91 Q8
craigtounmeadows.co.uk
Total Pitches: 56 (C, CV & T)

Faskally Caravan Park
Pitlochry
PH16 5LA
Tel: 01796 472007 97 Q12
faskally.co.uk
Total Pitches: 430 (C, CV & T)

Glen Nevis C & C Park
Glen Nevis, Fort William
PH33 6SX
Tel: 01397 702191 94 G4
glen-nevis.co.uk
Total Pitches: 380 (C, CV & T)

Hoddom Castle Caravan Park
Hoddom, Lockerbie
DG11 1AS
Tel: 01576 300251 75 N11
hoddomcastle.co.uk
Total Pitches: 200 (C, CV & T)

Huntly Castle Caravan Park
The Meadow, Huntly
AB54 4UJ
Tel: 01466 794999 104 G7
huntlycastle.co.uk
Total Pitches: 90 (C, CV & T)

Invercoe C & C Park
Ballachulish, Glencoe
PH49 4HP
Tel: 01855 811210 94 F7
invercoe.co.uk
Total Pitches: 66 (C, CV & T)

Linwater Caravan Park
West Clifton, East Calder
EH53 0HT
Tel: 0131 333 3326 83 M5
linwater.co.uk
Total Pitches: 64 (C, CV & T)

Loch Ken Holiday Park
Parton, Castle Douglas
DG7 3NE
Tel: 01644 470282 73 R5
lochkenholidaypark.co.uk
Total Pitches: 40 (C, CV & T)

Lomond Woods Holiday Park
Old Luss Road, Balloch, Loch Lomond
G83 8QP
Tel: 01389 755000 88 J9
woodleisure.co.uk
Total Pitches: 115 (C & CV)

Milton of Fonab Caravan Park
Bridge Road, Pitlochry
PH16 5NA
Tel: 01796 472882 97 Q12
fonab.co.uk
Total Pitches: 154 (C, CV & T)

River Tilt Caravan Park
Blair Atholl, Pitlochry
PH18 5TE
Tel: 01796 481467 97 P10
rivertiltpark.co.uk
Total Pitches: 30 (C, CV & T)

Sands of Luce Holiday Park
Sands of Luce, Sandhead, Stranraer
DG9 9JN
Tel: 01776 830456 72 E9
sandsofluceholidaypark.co.uk
Total Pitches: 80 (C, CV & T)

Seaward Caravan Park
Dhoon Bay, Kirkudbright
DG6 4TJ
Tel: 01557 870267 73 R10
gillespie-leisure.co.uk
Total Pitches: 25 (C, CV & T)

Seton Sands Holiday Village
Longniddry
EH32 0QF
Tel: 01875 813333 83 T3
haven.com/setonsands
Total Pitches: 640 (C & CV)

Silver Sands Holiday Park
Covesea, West Beach, Lossiemouth
IV31 6SP
Tel: 01343 813262 103 V1
silver-sands.co.uk
Total Pitches: 140 (C, CV & T)

Skye C & C Club Site
Loch Greshornish, Borve, Arnisort, Edinbane, Isle of Skye
IV51 9PS
Tel: 01470 582230 100 c4
campingandcaravanningclub.co.uk/skye
Total Pitches: 105 (C, CV & T)

Thurston Manor Leisure Park
Innerwick, Dunbar
EH42 1SA
Tel: 01368 840643 84 J4
thurstonmanor.co.uk
Total Pitches: 120 (C & CV)

Trossachs Holiday Park
Aberfoyle
FK8 3SA
Tel: 01877 382614 89 M6
trossachsholidays.co.uk
Total Pitches: 66 (C, CV & T)

Witches Craig C & C Park
Blairlogie, Stirling
FK9 5PX
Tel: 01786 474947 89 T6
witchescraig.co.uk
Total Pitches: 60 (C, CV & T)

WALES

Bron Derw Touring Caravan Park
Llanrwst
LL26 0YT
Tel: 01492 640494 53 N10
bronderw-wales.co.uk
Total Pitches: 48 (C & CV)

Bron-Y-Wendon Caravan Park
Wern Road, Llanddulas, Colwyn Bay
LL22 8HG
Tel: 01492 512903 53 R7
bronywendon.co.uk
Total Pitches: 130 (C & CV)

Bryn Gloch C & C Park
Betws Garmon, Caernarfon
LL54 7YY
Tel: 01286 650216 52 H11
campwales.co.uk
Total Pitches: 177 (C, CV & T)

Caerfai Bay Caravan & Tent Park
Caerfai Bay, St Davids, Haverfordwest
SA62 6QT
Tel: 01437 720274 24 C6
caerfaibay.co.uk
Total Pitches: 106 (C, CV & T)

Cenarth Falls Holiday Park
Cenarth, Newcastle Emlyn
SA38 9JS
Tel: 01239 710345 32 E12
cenarth-holipark.co.uk
Total Pitches: 30 (C, CV & T)

Daisy Bank Caravan Park
Snead, Montgomery
SY15 6EB
Tel: 01588 620471 34 H2
daisy-bank.co.uk
Total Pitches: 80 (C, CV & T)

Dinlle Caravan Park
Dinas Dinlle, Caernarfon
LL54 5TW
Tel: 01286 830324 52 F11
thornleyleisure.co.uk
Total Pitches: 175 (C, CV & T)

Eisteddfa
Eisteddfa Lodge, Pentrefelin, Criccieth
LL52 0PT
Tel: 01766 522696 42 K6
eisteddfapark.co.uk
Total Pitches: 100 (C, CV & T)

Fforest Fields C & C Park
Hundred House, Builth Wells
LD1 5RT
Tel: 01982 570406 34 D10
fforestfields.co.uk
Total Pitches: 120 (C, CV & T)

Fishguard Bay Resort
Garn Gelli, Fishguard
SA65 9ET
Tel: 01348 811415 24 G3
fishguardbay.com
Total Pitches: 102 (C, CV & T)

Greenacres Holiday Park
Black Rock Sands, Morfa Bychan, Porthmadog
LL49 9YF
Tel: 01766 512781 42 K6
haven.com/greenacres
Total Pitches: 945 (C & CV)

Hafan y Môr Holiday Park
Pwllheli
LL53 6HJ
Tel: 01758 612112 42 H6
haven.com/hafanymor
Total Pitches: 875 (C & CV)

Hendre Mynach Touring C & C Park
Llanaber Road, Barmouth
LL42 1YR
Tel: 01341 280262 43 M10
hendremynach.co.uk
Total Pitches: 240 (C, CV & T)

Home Farm Caravan Park
Marian-Glas, Isle of Anglesey
LL73 8PH
Tel: 01248 410614 52 G6
homefarm-anglesey.co.uk
Total Pitches: 102 (C, CV & T)

Islawrffordd Caravan Park
Tal-y-bont, Barmouth
LL43 2AQ
Tel: 01341 247269 43 L9
islawrffordd.co.uk
Total Pitches: 105 (C, CV & T)

Kiln Park Holiday Centre
Marsh Road, Tenby
SA70 8RB
Tel: 01834 844121 24 K10
haven.com/kilnpark
Total Pitches: 849 (C, CV & T)

Pencelli Castle C & C Park
Pencelli, Brecon
LD3 7LX
Tel: 01874 665451 26 K3
pencelli-castle.com
Total Pitches: 80 (C, CV & T)

Penisar Mynydd Caravan Park
Caerwys Road, Rhuallt, St Asaph
LL17 0TY
Tel: 01745 582227 54 C11
penisarmynydd.co.uk
Total Pitches: 71 (C, CV & T)

Plas Farm Caravan & Lodge Park
Betws-yn-Rhos, Abergele
LL22 8AU
Tel: 01492 680254 53 Q8
plasfarmcaravanpark.co.uk
Total Pitches: 54 (C & CV)

Plassey Holiday Park
The Plassey, Eyton, Wrexham
LL13 0SP
Tel: 01978 780277 44 H4
plassey.com
Total Pitches: 90 (C, CV & T)

Pont Kemys C & C Park
Chainbridge, Abergavenny
NP7 9DS
Tel: 01873 880688 27 Q6
pontkemys.com
Total Pitches: 65 (C, CV & T)

Presthaven Sands Holiday Park
Gronant, Prestatyn
LL19 9TT
Tel: 01745 856471 54 C10
haven.com/presthavensands
Total Pitches: 1102 (C & CV)

Red Kite Touring Park
Van Road, Llanidloes
SY18 6NG
Tel: 01686 412122 33 T3
redkitetouringpark.co.uk
Total Pitches: 66 (C & CV)

River View Touring Park
The Dingle, Llanedi, Pontarddulais
SA4 0FH
Tel: 01635 844876 25 U9
riverviewtouringpark.com
Total Pitches: 60 (C, CV & T)

Riverside Camping
Seiont Nurseries, Pont Rug, Caernarfon
LL55 2BB
Tel: 01286 678781 52 H10
riversidecamping.co.uk
Total Pitches: 73 (C, CV & T)

The Trotting Mare Caravan Park
Overton, Wrexham
LL13 0LE
Tel: 01978 711963 44 J6
thetrottingmare.co.uk
Total Pitches: 65 (C, CV & T)

Trawsdir Touring C & C Park
Llanaber, Barmouth
LL42 1RR
Tel: 01341 280999 43 L10
barmouthholidays.co.uk
Total Pitches: 70 (C, CV & T)

Trefalun Park
Devonshire Drive, St Florence, Tenby
SA70 8RD
Tel: 01646 651514 24 J10
trefalunpark.co.uk
Total Pitches: 90 (C, CV & T)

Tyddyn Isaf Caravan Park
Lligwy Bay, Dulas, Isle of Anglesey
LL70 9PQ
Tel: 01248 410203 52 G5
tyddynisaf.co.uk
Total Pitches: 80 (C, CV & T)

White Tower Caravan Park
Llandwrog, Caernarfon
LL54 5UH
Tel: 01286 830649 52 G11
whitetowerpark.co.uk
Total Pitches: 52 (C & CV)

CHANNEL ISLANDS

Daisy Cottage Campsite
Route de Vinchelez, St Ouen, Jersey
JE3 2DB
Tel: 01534 481700 7 b1
daisycottagecampsite.com
Total Pitches: 29 (C, CV & T)

Fauxquets Valley Campsite
Castel, Guernsey
GY5 7QL
Tel: 01481 255460 6 d3
fauxquets.co.uk
Total Pitches: 120 (C & T)

Rozel Camping Park
Summerville Farm, St Martin, Jersey
JE3 6AX
Tel: 01534 855200 7 f2
rozelcamping.com
Total Pitches: 100 (C, CV & T)

Traffic signs

Signs giving orders

Signs with red circles are mostly prohibitive.
Plates below signs qualify their message

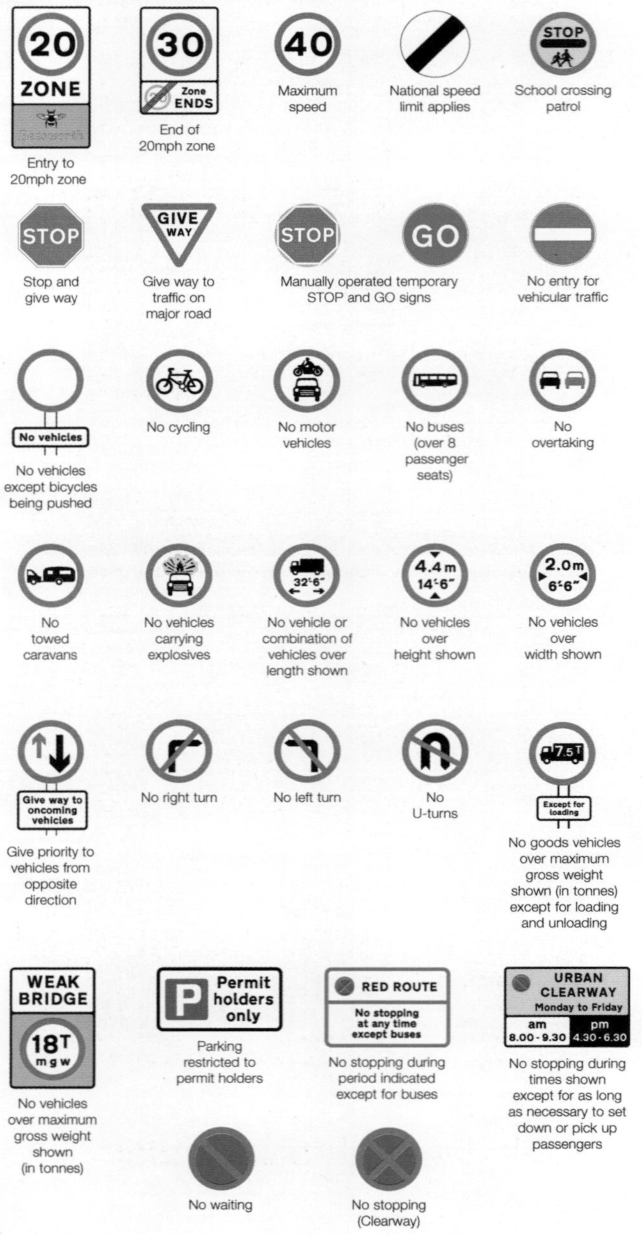

 Entry to 20mph zone

 End of 20mph zone

 Maximum speed

National speed limit applies

 School crossing patrol

Stop and give way

Give way to traffic on major road

Manually operated temporary STOP and GO signs

No entry for vehicular traffic

No vehicles except bicycles being pushed

No cycling

No motor vehicles

No buses (over 8 passenger seats)

No overtaking

No towed caravans

No vehicles carrying explosives

No vehicle or combination of vehicles over length shown

No vehicles over height shown

No vehicles over width shown

Give way to vehicles from opposite direction

No right turn

No left turn

No U-turns

No goods vehicles over maximum gross weight shown (in tonnes) except for loading and unloading

WEAK BRIDGE — No vehicles over maximum gross weight shown (in tonnes)

Permit holders only — Parking restricted to permit holders

RED ROUTE — No stopping at any time except buses

URBAN CLEARWAY Monday to Friday am 8.00-9.30 pm 4.30-6.30 — No stopping during times shown except for as long as necessary to set down or pick up passengers

No waiting

No stopping (Clearway)

Signs with blue circles but no red border mostly give positive instruction.

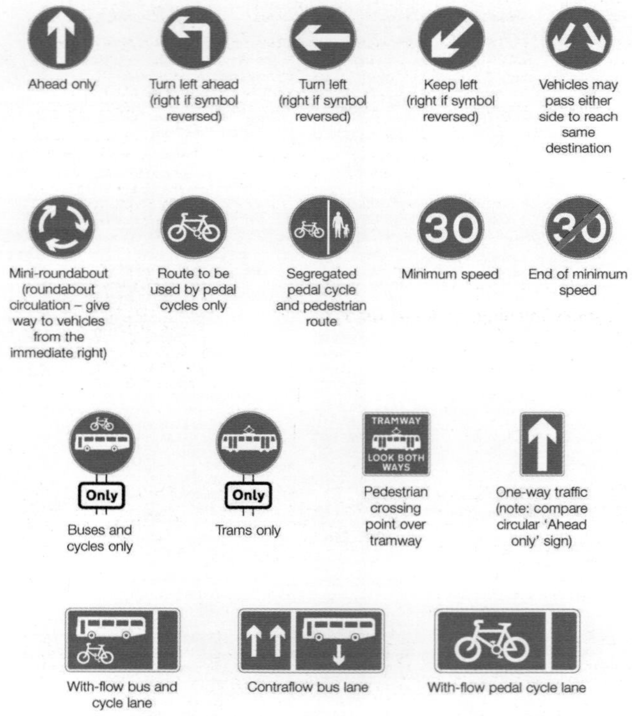

Ahead only

Turn left ahead (right if symbol reversed)

Turn left (right if symbol reversed)

Keep left (right if symbol reversed)

Vehicles may pass either side to reach same destination

Mini-roundabout (roundabout circulation – give way to vehicles from the immediate right)

Route to be used by pedal cycles only

Segregated pedal cycle and pedestrian route

Minimum speed

End of minimum speed

Buses and cycles only

Trams only

Pedestrian crossing point over tramway

One-way traffic (note: compare circular 'Ahead only' sign)

With-flow bus and cycle lane

Contraflow bus lane

With-flow pedal cycle lane

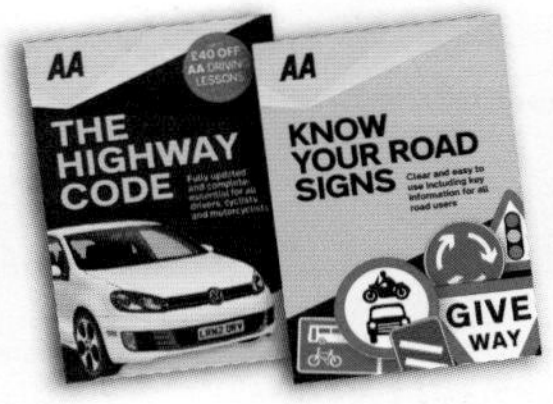

Note: The signs shown in this road atlas are those most commonly in use and are not all drawn to the same scale. In Scotland and Wales bilingual versions of some signs are used, showing both English and Gaelic or Welsh spellings. Some older designs of signs may still be seen on the roads. A comprehensive explanation of the signing system illustrating the vast majority of road signs can be found in the AA's handbook *Know Your Road Signs*. Where there is a reference to a rule number, this refers to *The Highway Code*.

Warning signs

Mostly triangular

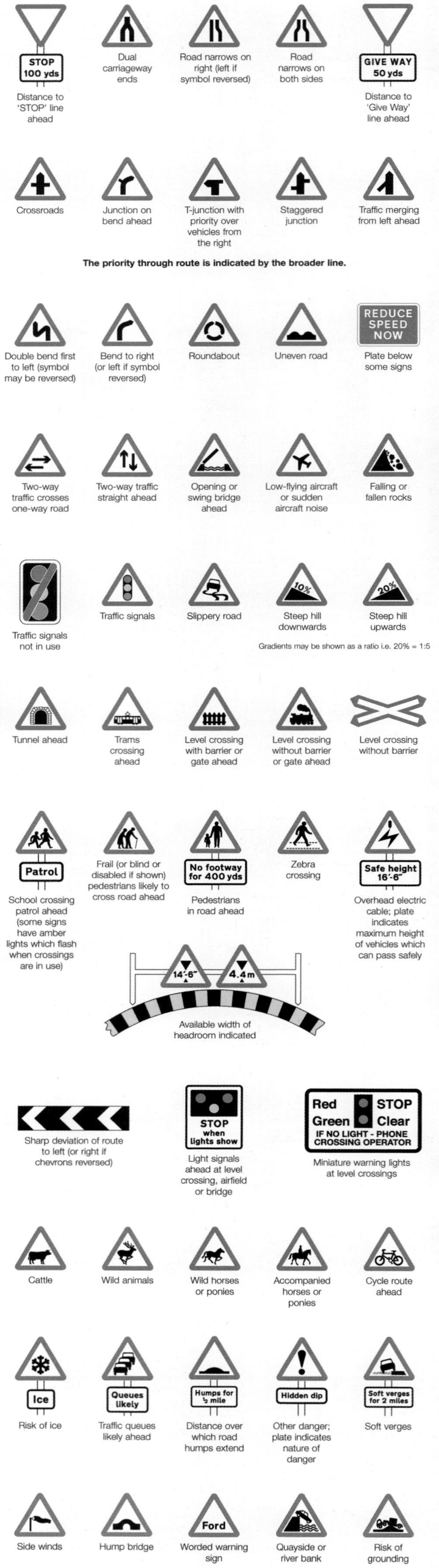

STOP 100 yds — Distance to 'STOP' line ahead

Dual carriageway ends

Road narrows on right (left if symbol reversed)

Road narrows on both sides

GIVE WAY 50 yds — Distance to 'Give Way' line ahead

Crossroads

Junction on bend ahead

T-junction with priority over vehicles from the right

Staggered junction

Traffic merging from left ahead

The priority through route is indicated by the broader line.

Double bend first to left (symbol may be reversed)

Bend to right (or left if symbol reversed)

Roundabout

Uneven road

REDUCE SPEED NOW — Plate below some signs

Two-way traffic crosses one-way road

Two-way traffic straight ahead

Opening or swing bridge ahead

Low-flying aircraft or sudden aircraft noise

Falling or fallen rocks

Traffic signals not in use

Traffic signals

Slippery road

Steep hill downwards

Steep hill upwards

Gradients may be shown as a ratio i.e. 20% = 1:5

Tunnel ahead

Trams crossing ahead

Level crossing with barrier or gate ahead

Level crossing without barrier or gate ahead

Level crossing without barrier

Patrol — School crossing patrol ahead (some signs have amber lights which flash when crossings are in use)

Frail (or blind or disabled if shown) pedestrians likely to cross road ahead

No footway for 400 yds — Pedestrians in road ahead

Zebra crossing

Safe height 16'-6" — Overhead electric cable; plate indicates maximum height of vehicles which can pass safely

14'-6" 4.4 m — Available width of headroom indicated

Sharp deviation of route to left (or right if chevrons reversed)

STOP when lights show — Light signals ahead at level crossing, airfield or bridge

Red STOP Green Clear IF NO LIGHT - PHONE CROSSING OPERATOR — Miniature warning lights at level crossings

Cattle

Wild animals

Wild horses or ponies

Accompanied horses or ponies

Cycle route ahead

Ice — Risk of ice

Queues likely — Traffic queues likely ahead

Humps for ½ mile — Distance over which road humps extend

Hidden dip — Other danger; plate indicates nature of danger

Soft verges for 2 miles — Soft verges

Side winds

Hump bridge

Ford — Worded warning sign

Quayside or river bank

Risk of grounding

Direction signs

Mostly retangular

Signs on motorways - blue backgrounds

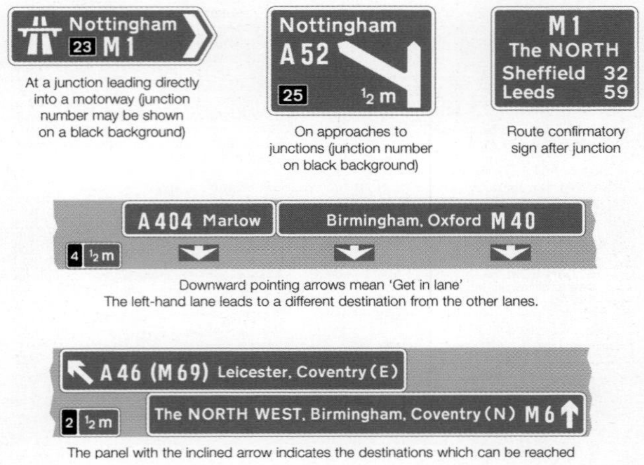

 Nottingham 23 M1 — At a junction leading directly into a motorway (junction number may be shown on a black background)

 Nottingham A 52 25 ½m — On approaches to junctions (junction number on black background)

 M1 The NORTH Sheffield 32 Leeds 59 — Route confirmatory sign after junction

 A 404 Marlow   Birmingham, Oxford M 40 — 4 ½m — Downward pointing arrows mean 'Get in lane' The left-hand lane leads to a different destination from the other lanes.

 A 46 (M 69) Leicester, Coventry (E) — The NORTH WEST, Birmingham, Coventry (N) M 6 — 2 ½m — The panel with the inclined arrow indicates the destinations which can be reached

Signs on primary routes - green backgrounds

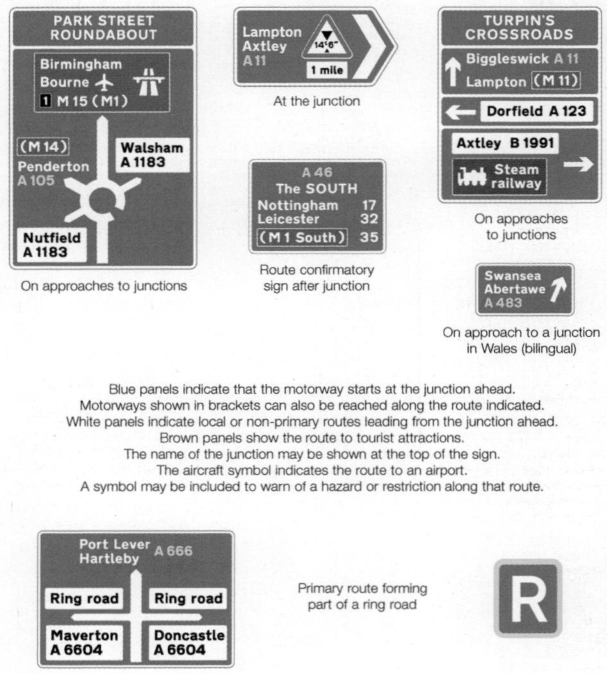

 PARK STREET ROUNDABOUT — Birmingham Bourne M 15 (M1) — Penderton A 105 — Nutfield A 1183 — Walsham A 1183 — On approaches to junctions

 Lampton Axtley A11 1 mile — At the junction

A 46 The SOUTH Nottingham 17 Leicester 32 (M1 South) 35 — Route confirmatory sign after junction

 TURPIN'S CROSSROADS — Biggleswick A 11 — Lampton (M 11) — Dorfield A 123 — Axtley B 1991 — Steam railway — On approaches to junctions

Swansea Abertawe A 483 — On approach to a junction in Wales (bilingual)

Blue panels indicate that the motorway starts at the junction ahead. Motorways shown in brackets can also be reached along the route indicated. White panels indicate local or non-primary routes leading from the junction ahead. Brown panels show the route to tourist attractions. The name of the junction may be shown at the top of the sign. The aircraft symbol indicates the route to an airport. A symbol may be included to warn of a hazard or restriction along that route.

Port Lever Hartleby A 666 — Ring road — Ring road — Maverton A 6604 — Doncastle A 6604 — Primary route forming part of a ring road

R

Signs on non-primary and local routes - black borders

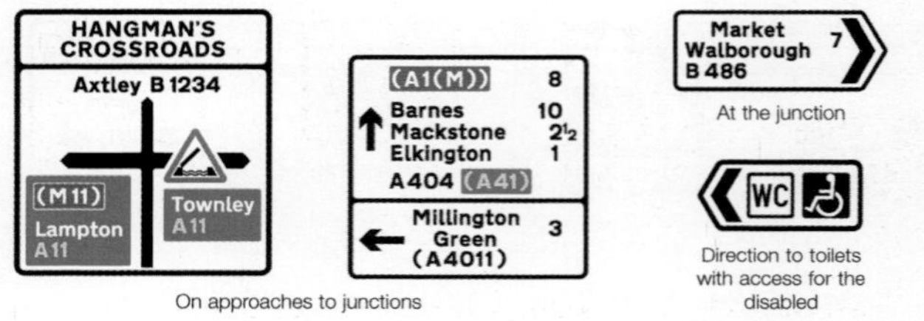

 HANGMAN'S CROSSROADS — Axtley B 1234 — (M 11) Lampton A 11 — Townley A 11 — On approaches to junctions

(A1(M)) 8 — Barnes 10 — Mackstone 2½ — Elkington — A 404 (A 41) — Millington Green (A 4011)

Market Walborough B 486 7 — At the junction

WC — Direction to toilets with access for the disabled

Green panels indicate that the primary route starts at the junction ahead. Route numbers on a blue background show the direction to a motorway. Route numbers on a green background show the direction to a primary route.

Signs on non-primary and local routes - black borders

 150 yds — Picnic site

Wrest Park — Ancient monument in the care of English Heritage

Saturday only — Direction to a car park

Zoo — Tourist attraction

300 yds — Direction to camping and caravan site

(A 33) (M 1) — Advisory route for lorries

4 — Route for pedal cycles forming part of a network

Marton 3 — Recommended route for pedal cycles to place shown

Public library Council offices — Route for pedestrians

Emergency diversion routes

 Symbols showing emergency diversion route for motorway and other main road traffic

Northtown — Diversion route

In an emergency it may be necessary to close a section of motorway or other main road to traffic, so a temporary sign may advise drivers to follow a diversion route. To help drivers navigate the route, black symbols on yellow patches may be permanently displayed on existing direction signs, including motorway signs. Symbols may also be used on separate signs with yellow backgrounds.

For further information visit:
theaa.com/breakdown-cover/advice/emergency-diversion-routes

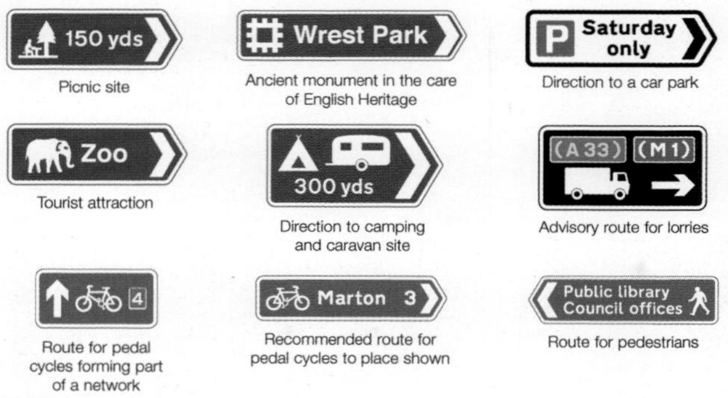

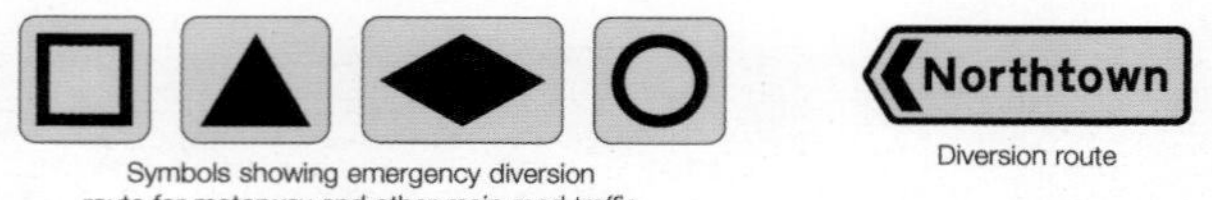

Road markings

Information signs

All retangular

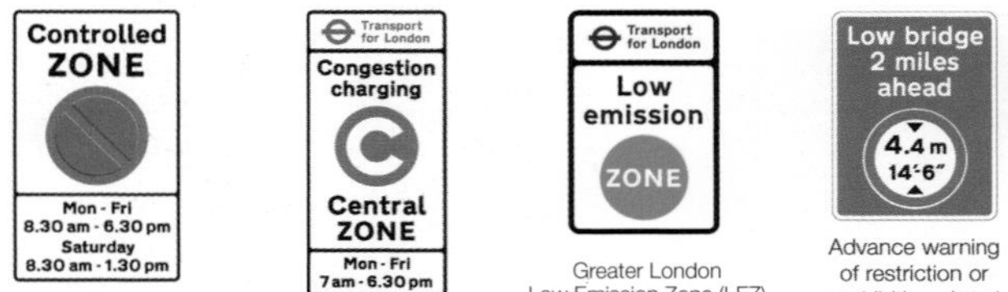

Entrance to controlled parking zone

Entrance to congestion charging zone

Greater London Low Emission Zone (LEZ)

Advance warning of restriction or prohibition ahead

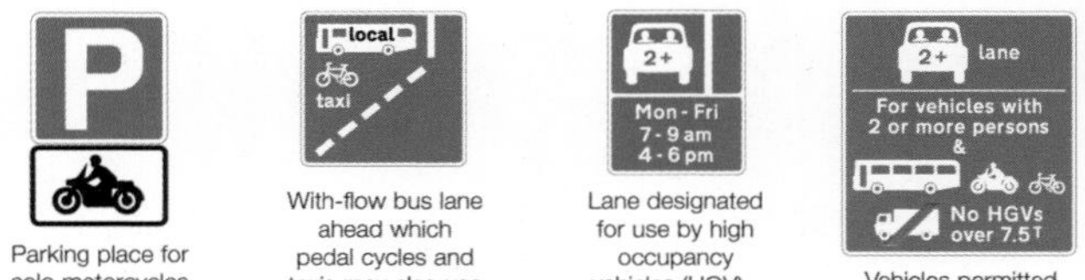

Parking place for solo motorcycles

With-flow bus lane ahead which pedal cycles and taxis may also use

Lane designated for use by high occupancy vehicles (HOV) – see rule 142

Vehicles permitted to use an HOV lane ahead

End of motorway

Start of motorway and point from which motorway regulations apply

Appropriate traffic lanes at junction ahead

Traffic on the main carriageway coming from right has priority over joining traffic

Additional traffic joining from left ahead. Traffic on main carriageway has priority over joining traffic from right hand lane of slip road

Traffic in right hand lane of slip road joining the main carriageway has prority over joining traffic from left hand lane

'Countdown' markers at exit from motorway (each bar represents 100 yards to the exit). Green-backed markers may be used on primary routes and white-backed markers with black bars on other routes. At approaches to concealed level crossings white-backed markers with red bars may be used. Although these will be erected at equal distances the bars do not represent 100 yard intervals.

Motorway service area sign showing the operator's name

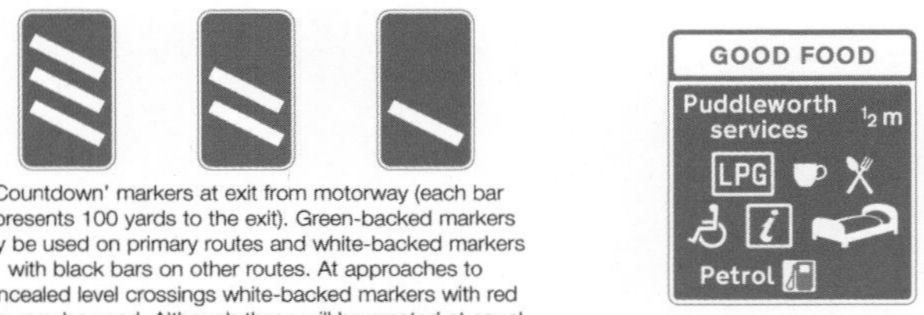

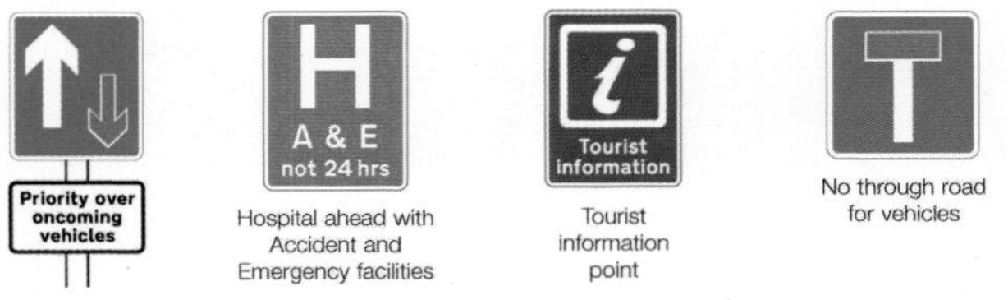

Traffic has priority over oncoming vehicles

Hospital ahead with Accident and Emergency facilities

Tourist information point

No through road for vehicles

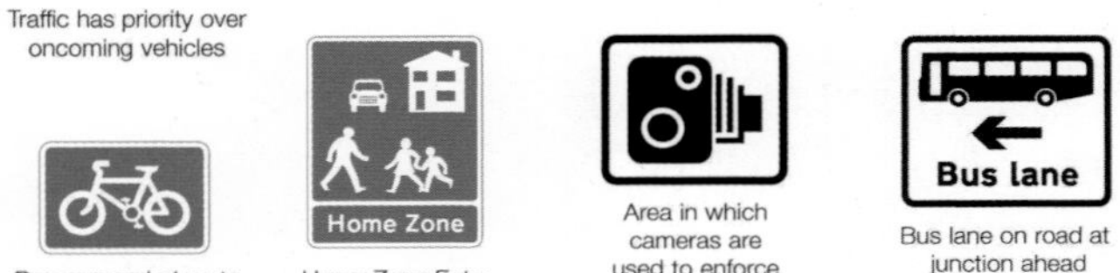

Recommended route for pedal cycles

Home Zone Entry

Area in which cameras are used to enforce traffic regulations

Bus lane on road at junction ahead

*Home Zone Entry – You are entering an area where people could be using the whole street for a range of activities. You should drive slowly and carefully and be prepared to stop to allow people time to move out of the way.

Roadworks signs

Road works

Loose chippings

Temporary hazard at roadworks

Temporary lane closure (the number and position of arrows and red bars may be varied according to lanes open and closed)

Slow-moving or stationary works vehicle blocking a traffic lane. Pass in the direction shown by the arrow.

Mandatory speed limit ahead

Roadworks 1 mile ahead

End of roadworks and any temporary restrictions including speed limits

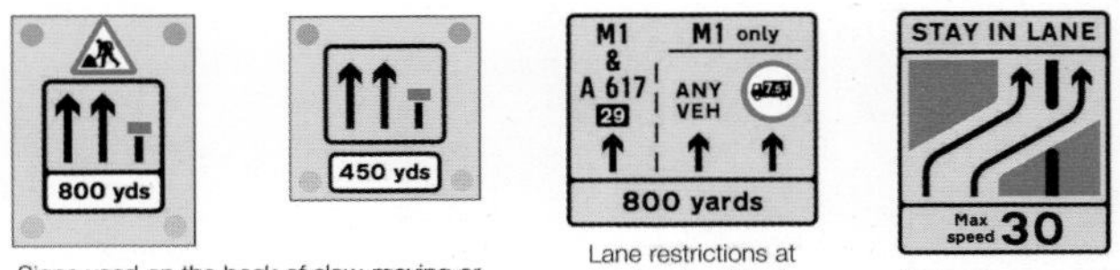

Signs used on the back of slow-moving or stationary vehicles warning of a lane closed ahead by a works vehicle. There are no cones on the road.

Lane restrictions at roadworks ahead

One lane crossover at contraflow roadworks

Across the carriageway

Stop line at signals or police control

Stop line at 'Stop' sign

Stop line for pedestrians at a level crossing

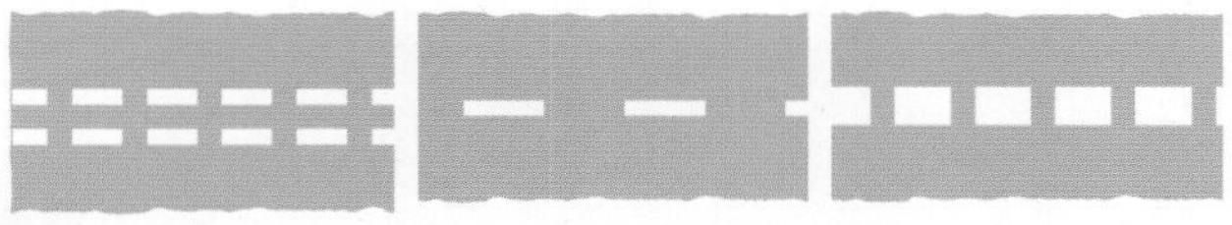

Give way to traffic on major road (can also be used at mini roundabouts)

Give way to traffic from the right at a roundabout

Give way to traffic from the right at a mini-roundabout

Along the carriageway

Edge line

Centre line See Rule 127

Hazard warning line See Rule 127

Double white lines See Rules 128 and 129

See Rule 130

Lane line See Rule 131

Along the edge of the carriageway

Waiting restrictions

Waiting restrictions indicated by yellow lines apply to the carriageway, pavement and verge. You may stop to load or unload (unless there are also loading restrictions as described below) or while passengers board or alight. Double yellow lines mean no waiting at any time, unless there are signs that specifically indicate seasonal restrictions. The times at which the restrictions apply for other road markings are shown on nearby plates or on entry signs to controlled parking zones. If no days are shown on the signs, the restrictions are in force every day including Sundays and Bank Holidays. White bay markings and upright signs (see below) indicate where parking is allowed.

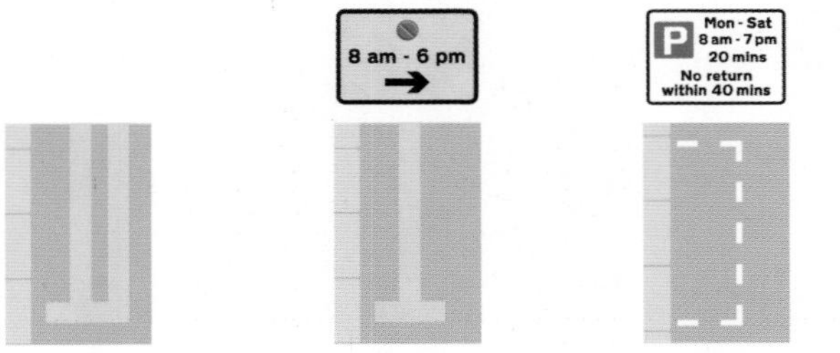

No waiting at any time

No waiting during times shown on sign

Waiting is limited to the duration specified during the days and times shown

Red Route stopping controls

Red lines are used on some roads instead of yellow lines. In London the double and single red lines used on Red Routes indicate that stopping to park, load/unload or to board and alight from a vehicle (except for a licensed taxi or if you hold a Blue Badge) is prohibited. The red lines apply to the carriageway, pavement and verge. The times that the red line prohibitions apply are shown on nearby signs, but the double red line ALWAYS means no stopping at any time. On Red Routes you may stop to park, load/unload in specially marked boxes and adjacent signs specify the times and purposes and duration allowed. A box MARKED IN RED indicates that it may only be available for the purpose specified for part of the day (e.g. between busy peak periods). A box MARKED IN WHITE means that it is available throughout the day.

RED AND SINGLE YELLOW LINES CAN ONLY GIVE A GUIDE TO THE RESTRICTIONS AND CONTROLS IN FORCE AND SIGNS, NEARBY OR AT A ZONE ENTRY, MUST BE CONSULTED.

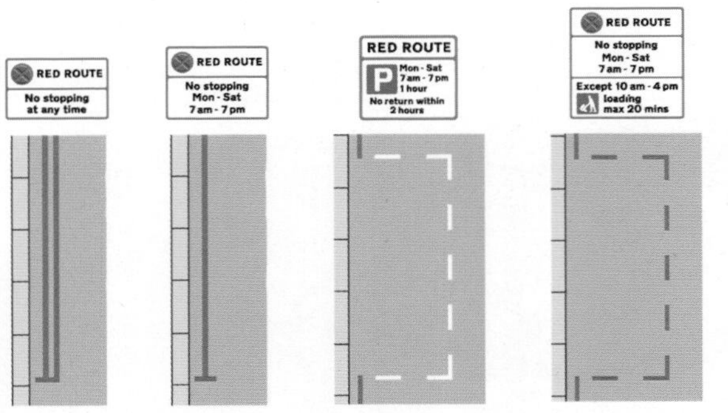

No stopping at any time

No stopping during times shown on sign

Parking is limited to the duration specified during the days and times shown

Only loading may take place at the times shown for up to a maximum duration of 20 mins

On the kerb or at the edge of the carriageway

Loading restrictions on roads other than Red Routes

Yellow marks on the kerb or at the edge of the carriageway indicate that loading or unloading is prohibited at the times shown on the nearby black and white plates. You may stop while passengers board or alight. If no days are indicated on the signs the restrictions are in force every day including Sundays and Bank Holidays.

ALWAYS CHECK THE TIMES SHOWN ON THE PLATES.

Lengths of road reserved for vehicles loading and unloading are indicated by a white 'bay' marking with the words 'Loading Only' and a sign with the white on blue 'trolley' symbol. This sign also shows whether loading and unloading is restricted to goods vehicles and the times at which the bay can be used. If no times or days are shown it may be used at any time. Vehicles may not park here if they are not loading or unloading.

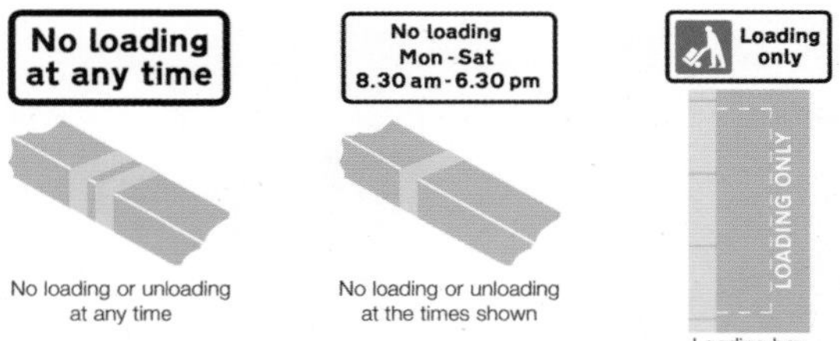

No loading or unloading at any time

No loading or unloading at the times shown

Loading bay

Other road markings

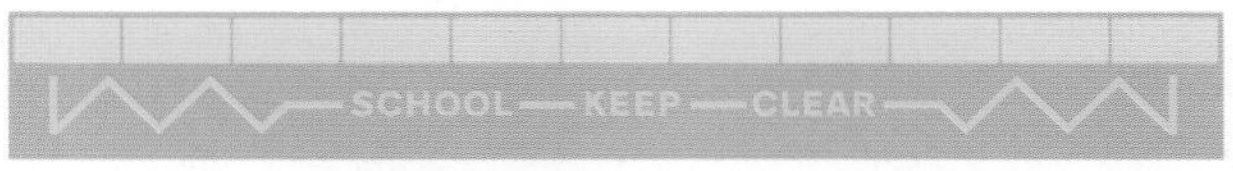

Keep entrance clear of stationary vehicles, even if picking up or setting down children

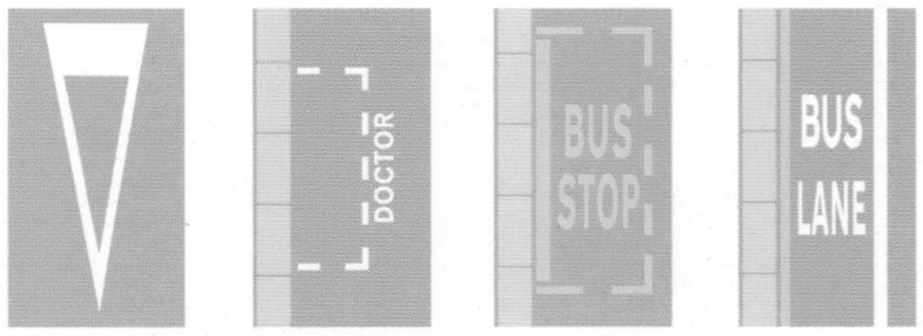

Warning of 'Give Way' just ahead

Parking space reserved for vehicles named

See Rule 243

See Rule 141

Box junction - See Rule 174

Do not block that part of the carriageway indicated

Indication of traffic lanes

Light signals controlling traffic

Traffic Light Signals

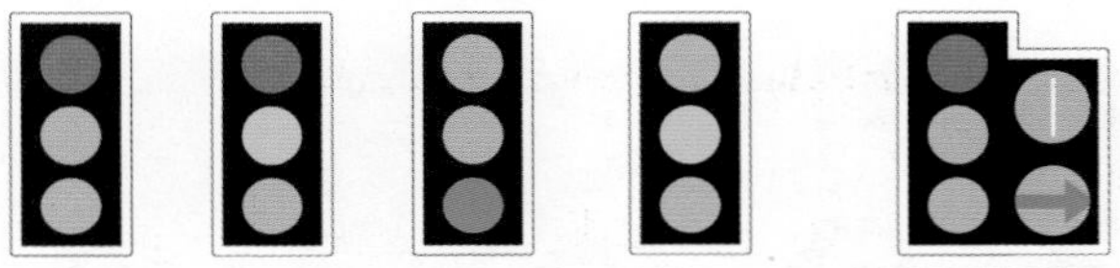

RED means 'Stop'. Wait behind the stop line on the carriageway

RED AND AMBER also means 'Stop'. Do not pass through or start until GREEN shows

GREEN means you may go on if the way is clear. Take special care if you intend to turn left or right and give way to pedestrians who are crossing

AMBER means 'Stop' at the stop line. You may go on only if the AMBER appears after you have crossed the stop line or are so close to it that to pull up might cause an accident

A GREEN ARROW may be provided in addition to the full green signal if movement in a certain direction is allowed before or after the full green phase. If the way is clear you may go but only in the direction shown by the arrow. You may do this whatever other lights may be showing. White light signals may be provided for trams

Flashing red lights

Alternately flashing red lights mean YOU MUST STOP

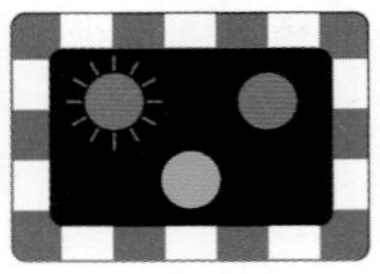

At level crossings, lifting bridges, airfields, fire stations, etc.

Motorway signals

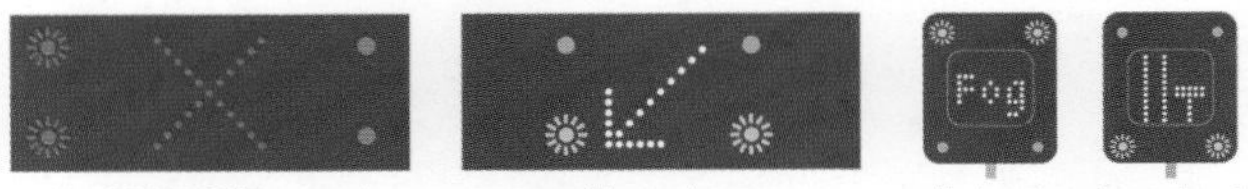

You MUST NOT proceed further in this lane

Change lane

Reduced visibility ahead

Lane ahead closed

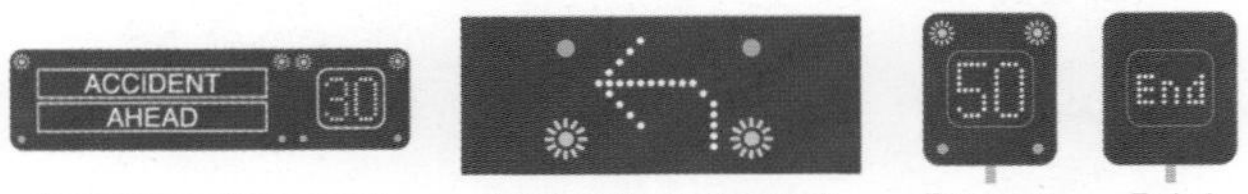

Temporary maximum speed advised and information message

Leave motorway at next exit

Temporary maximum speed advised

End of restriction

Lane control signals

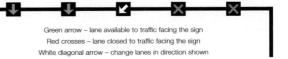

Green arrow – lane available to traffic facing the sign
Red crosses – lane closed to traffic facing the sign
White diagonal arrow – change lanes in direction shown

Channel hopping and the Isle of Wight

For business or pleasure, hopping on a ferry across to France, the Channel Islands or Isle of Wight has never been easier.

The vehicle ferry services listed in the table give you all the options, together with detailed port plans to help you navigate to and from the ferry terminals. Simply choose your preferred route, not forgetting the fast sailings (see 🚢). Bon voyage!

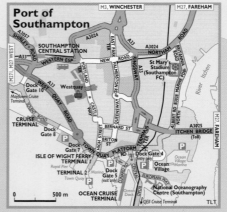

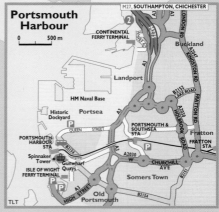

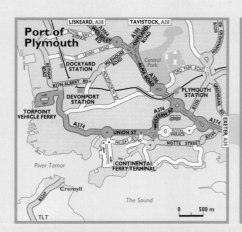

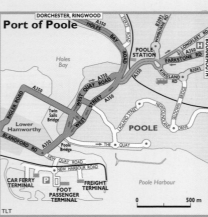

ENGLISH CHANNEL AND ISLE OF WIGHT FERRY CROSSINGS

From	To	Journey time	Operator website
Dover	Calais	1 hr 30 mins	dfdsseaways.co.uk
Dover	Calais	1 hr 30 mins	poferries.com
Dover	Dunkirk	2 hrs	dfdsseaways.co.uk
Folkestone	Calais (Coquelles)	35 mins	eurotunnel.com
Lymington	Yarmouth (IOW)	40 mins	wightlink.co.uk
Newhaven	Dieppe	4 hrs	dfdsseaways.co.uk
Plymouth	Roscoff	6–8 hrs	brittany-ferries.co.uk
Poole	Cherbourg	4 hrs 15 mins	brittany-ferries.co.uk
Poole	Guernsey	3 hrs 🚢	condorferries.co.uk
Poole	Jersey	4 hrs 30 mins 🚢	condorferries.co.uk
Poole	St-Malo	7–12 hrs (via Channel Is.) 🚢	condorferries.co.uk
Portsmouth	Caen (Ouistreham)	6–7 hrs	brittany-ferries.co.uk
Portsmouth	Cherbourg	3 hrs (May–Aug) 🚢	brittany-ferries.co.uk
Portsmouth	Fishbourne (IOW)	45 mins	wightlink.co.uk
Portsmouth	Guernsey	7 hrs	condorferries.co.uk
Portsmouth	Jersey	8–11 hrs	condorferries.co.uk
Portsmouth	Le Havre	5 hrs 30 mins	brittany-ferries.co.uk
Portsmouth	St-Malo	9–11 hrs	brittany-ferries.co.uk
Southampton	East Cowes (IOW)	1 hr	redfunnel.co.uk

The information listed is provided as a guide only, as services are liable to change at short notice. Services shown are for vehicle ferries only, operated by conventional ferry unless indicated as a fast ferry service (🚢). Please check sailings before planning your journey.

Travelling further afield? For ferry services to Northern Spain see *brittany-ferries.co.uk.*

ENGLISH

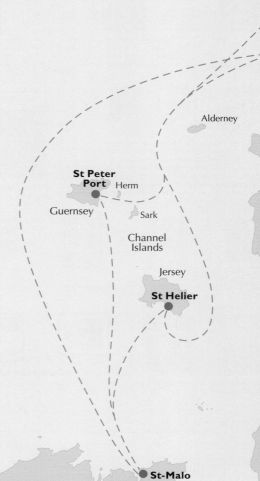

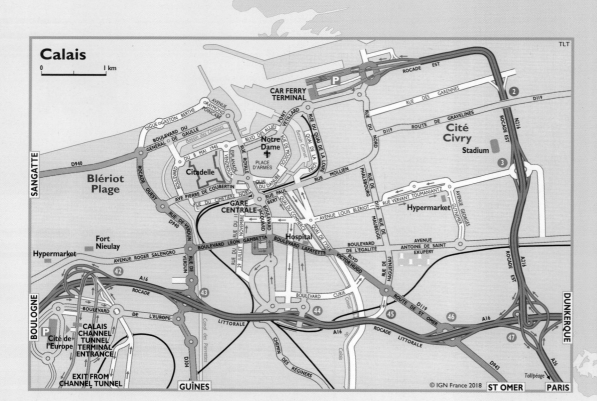

Newhaven Harbour

LEWES
RIVER OUSE
NORTH WAY
SOUTH WAY
DENTON ROAD
THE DROVE
A26
A259
BRIGHTON RD
BRIGHTON
NEWHAVEN
NEWHAVEN TOWN STATION
FERRY TERMINAL
RAILWAY ROAD
BEACH ROAD
Newhaven Harbour
NEWHAVEN HARBOUR STATION
EAST QUAY COMMERCIAL TERMINAL
EASTBOURNE
A259
FORT ROAD
GIBBON ROAD
Lifeboat Station
Newhaven Marina
Rec Ground
H&S
P
0   500 m
TLT

Port of Dover

LONDON
A256
A258
TOWNWALL ROAD
MAISON DIEU
DOVER
CANTERBURY, RAMSGATE
A256
Dover
FERRY TERMINAL
EASTERN DOCKS ROUNDABOUT
MARINE PARADE
TOWNWALL ST
A20
DOVER PRIORY STATION
B2011
FOLKESTONE ROAD
SNARGATE ST
Clarendon
Western Heights
LIMEKILN ST
WESTERN HEIGHTS
A20
Western Docks
Eastern Docks
Outer Harbour
Inner Harbour
CRUISE TERMINALS
LONDON, FOLKESTONE, CHANNEL TUNNEL
0   500 m
TLT

Folkestone Terminal

0   400 yards
0   500 metres

Ashley Wood
Peene
Newington
Cheriton
CREATE ROAD WEST
DANTON LANE
CHANNEL TUNNEL TERMINAL
Terminal Building
P
AA
Check-in
Police Station
Superstore
HIGH STREET
CHERITON
CHERITON INTERCHANGE
12
Cheriton
B2064
B2063
BIGGINS WOOD ROAD
FOLKESTONE
CHURCH ROAD
ASHFORD   ROAD
ASHFORD   ROAD
M20
M20
A20
A20
A20
11A
ASHFORD, MAIDSTONE, M25 & LONDON
DOVER, FOLKESTONE, CANTERBURY
TLT

Departures to France follow →
Arrivals from France follow ⇒

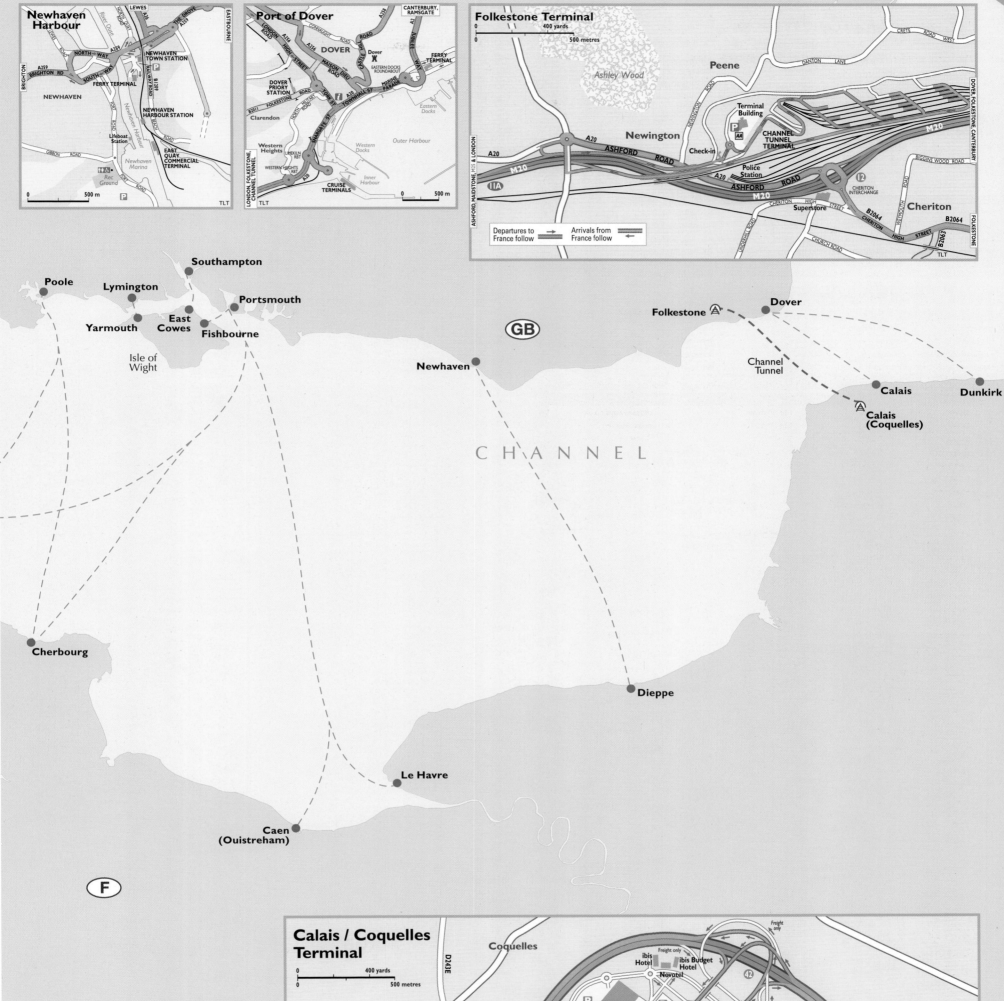

Poole
Lymington
Southampton
Yarmouth
East Cowes
Fishbourne
Portsmouth
Isle of Wight
Cherbourg

GB
Newhaven

Folkestone
Dover
Channel Tunnel
Calais
(Coquelles)
Calais
Dunkirk

CHANNEL

Dieppe
Le Havre
Caen
(Ouistreham)

F

Calais / Coquelles Terminal

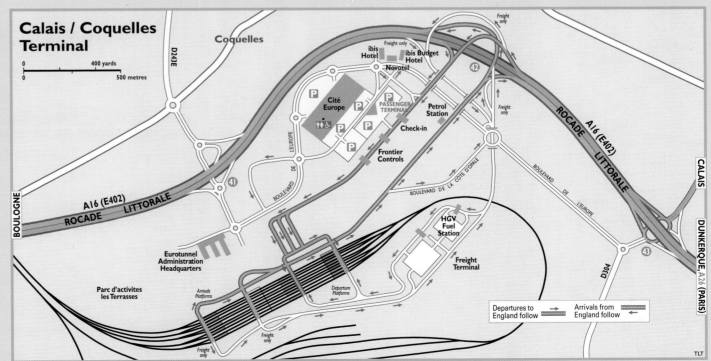

0   400 yards
0   500 metres

Coquelles
D243E
ibis Hotel
ibis Budget Hotel
Novotel
Cité Europe
P
P
P
PASSENGER TERMINAL
Petrol Station
Check-in
Frontier Controls
Eurotunnel Administration Headquarters
Parc d'activites les Terrasses
Arrivals Platforms
Departure Platforms
HGV Fuel Station
Freight Terminal
BOULOGNE
A16 (E402)
ROCADE   LITTORALE
ROCADE   LITTORALE
A16 (E402)
CALAIS
DUNKERQUE A26 (PARIS)
D304
BOULEVARD DE L'EUROPE
BOULEVARD DE LA CÔTE D'OPALE
BOULEVARD DE L'EUROPE
41
42
43
Freight only
Freight only
Freight only

Departures to England follow →
Arrivals from England follow ⇒

TLT

SCOTLAND FERRIES

From	To	Journey time	Operator website
Scottish Islands/west coast of Scotland			
Gourock	Dunoon	20 mins	western-ferries.co.uk
Glenelg	Skye	20 mins (Easter–Oct)	skyeferry.co.uk
Numerous and varied sailings from the west coast of Scotland to Scottish islands are provided by Caledonian MacBrayne. Please visit calmac.co.uk for all ferry information, including those of other operators.			
Orkney Islands			
Aberdeen	Kirkwall	6 hrs	northlinkferries.co.uk
Gills	St Margaret's Hope	1 hr	pentlandferries.co.uk
Scrabster	Stromness	1 hr 30 mins	northlinkferries.co.uk
Lerwick	Kirkwall	5 hrs 30 mins	northlinkferries.co.uk
Inter-island services are operated by Orkney Ferries. Please see orkneyferries.co.uk for details.			
Shetland Islands			
Aberdeen	Lerwick	12 hrs 30 mins	northlinkferries.co.uk
Kirkwall	Lerwick	7 hrs 45 mins	northlinkferries.co.uk
Inter-island services are operated by Shetland Island Council Ferries. Please see shetland.gov.uk/ferries for details.			

Please note that some smaller island services are day dependent and reservations are required for some routes. Book and confirm sailing schedules by contacting the operator.

NORTH SEA FERRY CROSSINGS

From	To	Journey time	Operator website
Harwich	Hook of Holland	7–8 hrs	stenaline.co.uk
Kingston upon Hull	Rotterdam (Europoort)	12 hrs	poferries.com
Kingston upon Hull	Zeebrugge	12 hrs	poferries.com
Newcastle upon Tyne	Amsterdam (IJmuiden)	15 hrs 30 mins	dfdsseaways.co.uk

Heysham Harbour

Liverpool Docks

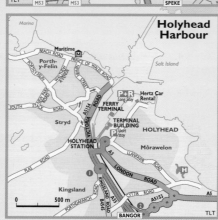

Holyhead Harbour

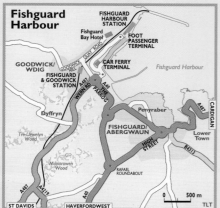

Fishguard Harbour

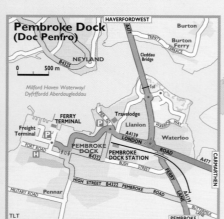

Pembroke Dock (Doc Penfro)

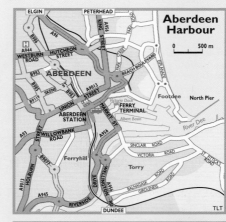

Aberdeen Harbour

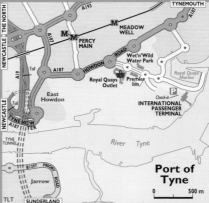

Port of Tyne

Port of Hull

Harwich International Port

IRISH SEA FERRY CROSSINGS

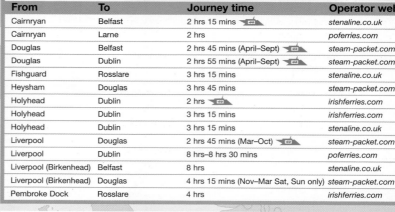

From	To	Journey time	Operator website
Cairnryan	Belfast	2 hrs 15 mins	stenaline.co.uk
Cairnryan	Larne	2 hrs	poferries.com
Douglas	Belfast	2 hrs 45 mins (April–Sept)	steam-packet.com
Douglas	Dublin	2 hrs 55 mins (April–Sept)	steam-packet.com
Fishguard	Rosslare	3 hrs 15 mins	stenaline.co.uk
Heysham	Douglas	3 hrs 45 mins	steam-packet.com
Holyhead	Dublin	2 hrs	irishferries.com
Holyhead	Dublin	3 hrs 15 mins	irishferries.com
Holyhead	Dublin	3 hrs 15 mins	stenaline.co.uk
Liverpool	Douglas	2 hrs 45 mins (Mar–Oct)	steam-packet.com
Liverpool	Dublin	8 hrs–8 hrs 30 mins	poferries.com
Liverpool (Birkenhead)	Belfast	8 hrs	stenaline.co.uk
Liverpool (Birkenhead)	Douglas	4 hrs 15 mins (Nov–Mar Sat, Sun only)	steam-packet.com
Pembroke Dock	Rosslare	4 hrs	irishferries.com

The information listed is provided as a guide only, as services are liable to change at short notice. Services shown are for vehicle ferries only, operated by conventional ferry unless indicated as a fast ferry service ( ). Please check sailings before planning your journey.

Motoring information

M4	Motorway with number	Primary route junction with and without number	Roundabout	Vehicle ferry	International freight terminal
Toll	Toll motorway with toll station	Restricted primary route junctions	Interchange/junction	Fast vehicle ferry or catamaran	24-hour Accident & Emergency hospital
6	Motorway junction with and without number	Primary route service area	Narrow primary/other A/B road with passing places (Scotland)	Railway line, in tunnel	Crematorium
5	Restricted motorway junctions	BATH	Primary route destination	Road under construction	Railway/tram station, level crossing	Park and Ride (at least 6 days per week)
Fleet S R	Motorway service area, rest area	A1123	Other A road single/dual carriageway	Road tunnel	Tourist railway	628 637 Lecht Summit	Height in metres, mountain pass
	Motorway and junction under construction	B2070	B road single/dual carriageway	Road toll, steep gradient (arrows point downhill)	City, town, village or other built-up area	Snow gates (on main routes)
A3	Primary route single/dual carriageway	Minor road more than 4 metres wide, less than 4 metres wide	Distance in miles between symbols	Airport (major/minor), heliport	National boundary, County or administrative boundary

Touring information To avoid disappointment, check opening times before visiting

	Scenic route	Industrial interest	RSPB site	Cave or cavern	National Trust site
	Tourist Information Centre	Aqueduct or viaduct	National Nature Reserve (England, Scotland, Wales)	Windmill, monument	National Trust for Scotland site
	Tourist Information Centre (seasonal)	Garden	Wildlife Trust reserve	Beach (award winning)	English Heritage site
	Visitor or heritage centre	Arboretum	Local nature reserve	Lighthouse	Historic Scotland site
	Picnic site	Vineyard	Forest drive	Golf course	Cadw (Welsh heritage) site
	Caravan site (AA inspected)	Brewery or distillery	National trail	Football stadium	Other place of interest
	Camping site (AA inspected)	Country park	Waterfall	County cricket ground	Boxed symbols indicate attractions within urban areas
	Caravan & camping site (AA inspected)	Agricultural showground	Viewpoint	Rugby Union national stadium	World Heritage Site (UNESCO)
	Abbey, cathedral or priory	Theme park	Hill-fort	International athletics stadium	National Park and National Scenic Area (Scotland)
	Ruined abbey, cathedral or priory	Farm or animal centre	Roman antiquity	Horse racing, show jumping	Forest Park
	Castle	Zoological or wildlife collection	Prehistoric monument	Motor-racing circuit	Sandy beach
	Historic house or building	Bird collection	Battle site with year	Air show venue	Heritage coast
	Museum or art gallery	Aquarium	Steam railway centre	Ski slope (natural, artificial)	Major shopping centre

Town plans

2	Motorway and junction	Railway station	Toilet, with facilities for the less able	Tourist Information Centre	Abbey, chapel, church
4	Primary road single/dual carriageway and numbered junction	Tramway	Building of interest	Visitor or heritage centre	Synagogue
37	A road single/dual carriageway and numbered junction	London Underground station	Ruined building	Post Office	Mosque
	B road single/dual carriageway	London Overground station	City wall	Public library	Golf course
	Local road single/dual carriageway	Rail interchange	Cliff lift	Shopping centre	Racecourse
	Other road single/dual carriageway, minor road	Docklands Light Railway (DLR) station	Escarpment	Shopmobility	Nature reserve
	One-way, gated/closed road	Light rapid transit system station	River/canal, lake	Theatre or performing arts centre	Aquarium
	Restricted access	Airport, heliport	Lock, weir	Cinema	World Heritage Site (UNESCO)
	Pedestrian area	Railair terminal	Park/sports ground/open space	Museum	English Heritage site
	Footpath	P+R Park and Ride (at least 6 days per week)	Cemetery	Castle	Historic Scotland site
	Road under construction	P P Car park, with electric charging point	Woodland	Castle mound	Cadw (Welsh heritage) site
	Road tunnel	Bus/coach station	Built-up area	Monument, statue	National Trust site
	Level crossing	H H 24-hour Accident & Emergency hospital, other hospital	Beach	Viewpoint	National Trust for Scotland site

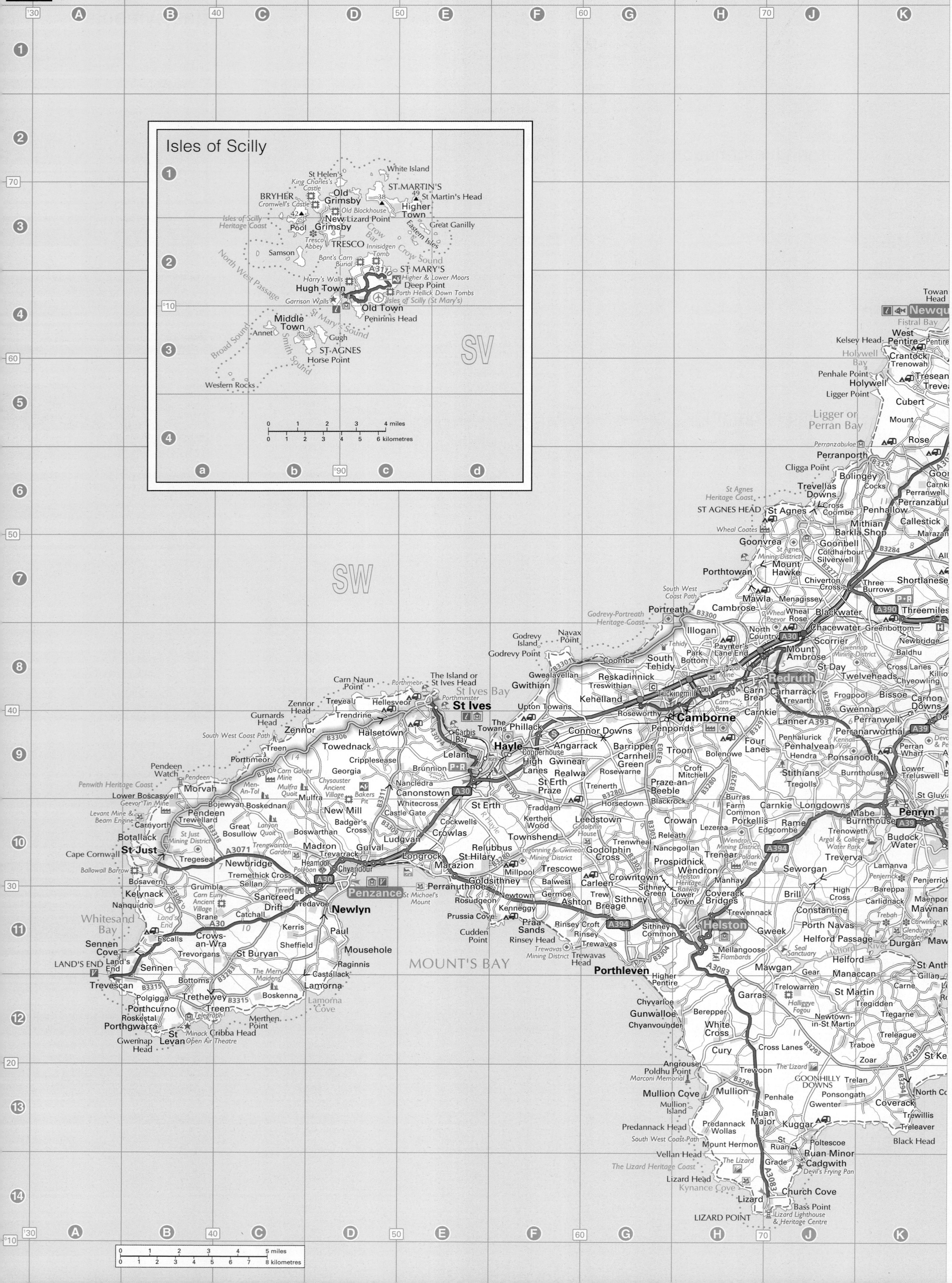

Isles of Scilly

St Helen's
White Island
King Charles's Castle
BRYHER
Old Grimsby
38
ST. MARTIN'S
St Martin's Head
Cromwell's Castle
Old Blockhouse
Higher Town
42
New Lizard Point
Isles of Scilly Heritage Coast
Grimsby
Pool
Tresco Abbey
TRESCO
Great Ganilly
Crow Bar
Eastern Isles
Innisidgen Tomb
Crow Sound
Samson
Bant's Carn Burial
ST. MARY'S
Higher & Lower Moors
North West Passage
Harry's Walls
Hugh Town
Deep Point
Porth Hellick Down Tombs
Garrison Walls
Old Town
Isles of Scilly (St Mary's)
Middle Town
Peninnis Head
Annet
Gugh
ST-AGNES
Broad Sound
Smith Sound
St Mary's Sound
Horse Point
Western Rocks

SV

0   1   2   3   4 miles
0 1 2 3 4 5 6 kilometres

SW

Newquay
Towan Head
Fistral Bay
Kelsey Head
West Pentire
Pentire
Holywell Bay
Crantock
Trenowah
Penhale Point
Holywell
Tresean
Treva
Ligger Point
Cubert
Ligger or Perran Bay
Mount
Rose
Perranzabuloe
Perranporth
Cligga Point
Bolingey
Cocks
Goon
Carnk
St Agnes Heritage Coast
Trevellas Downs
Perranwell
Perranzabul
ST AGNES HEAD
Cross
St Agnes
Penhallow
Coombe
Mithian
Callestick
Wheal Coates
Marazan
Goonvrea
St Agnes Mining District
Goonbell
Coldharbour
Silverwell
Porthtowan
Mount Hawke
Wheal Peevor
Chiverton Cross
Three Burrows
Shortlanese
Godrevy-Portreath Heritage-Coast
Portreath
B3300
Cambrose
Blackwater
Threemiles
South West Coast Path
Illogan
North Country
Scorrier
Greenbottom
Newbridge
Godrevy Island
Coombe
South Tehidy
Paynter's Lane End
Mount Ambrose
Baldhu
Godrevy Point
Tehidy
Park Bottom
St Day
Cross Lanes
Killio
Navax Point
Gwealavellan
Reskadinnick
Redruth
Twelveheads
Chyeowling
Carn Naun Point
Porthmeor
The Island or St Ives Head
St Ives Bay
Mine
Treswithian
Carn Brea
Carharrack
Trevarth
Frogpool
Carnon Downs
Zennor Head
Treyeal
Trendrine
Hellesveor
Porthminster
Gwithian
Trickingmill
Camborne
Carnkie
Gwennap
Perranwell
Gurnards Head
St Ives
Upton Towans
Roseworthy
Lanner
A393
Perranarworthal
Treen
Halsetown
The Towans
Phillack
Connor Downs
Penponds
Penhalurick
Perran Wharf
South West Coast Path
Zennor
Towednack
Carbis Bay
Hayle
Angarrack
Barripper
Troon
Bolenowe
Penhalvean
Lower
Treluswell
Penwith Heritage Coast
Cripplesease
High Lanes
Carnhell Green
Four Lanes
Hendra
Ponsanooth
Burnthouse
Pendeen Watch
Georgia
Brunnion
St Erth
Realwa
Rosewarne
Praze-an-Beeble
Stithians
Tregolls
St Gluvi
Pendeen
Morvah
Carn Galver Mine
Chysauster Ancient Village
Nancledra
St Erth Praze
Trenerth
Horsedown
Burras Farm Common
Carnkie
Longdowns
Levant Mine & Beam Engine
Lower Boscaswell
Men-An-Tol
Mulfra Quoit
Whitecross
Castle Gate
Kerthen Wood
Leedstown
B3280
Blackrock
Carnke
Rame
Mabe Burnthouse
Penryn
Geevor Tin Mine
Pendeen
Trewellard
Great Bosullow
Boskednan
New Mill
Cockwells
Crowlas
Townshend
Godolphin House
Crowan
Nancegollan
Godolphin Cross
Trenoweth
Argal & College Water Park
Budock Water
Botallack
Boswarthen
Badger's Cross
Ludgvan
Fraddam
Releath
Lezerea
Porkellis
Edgcombe
St Just Mining District
Madron
Trevarrack
Longrock
Relubbus
Reawnny & Gwinear Railway Heritage
Prospidnick
Wendron
Mining District
Trevarva
Cape Cornwall
Trengwainton Garden
Heamoor
Ponsanooth
Marazion
Crowntown
Wendron Heritage
Manhay
Sewor
St Just
Tregeseal
Newbridge
Tremethick Cross
Gulval
St Hilary
Trescowe
Godolphin Cross
Lower Town
Coverack Bridges
Lamanva
Ballowall Barrow
Bosavern
Grumbla
Carn Euny Ancient Village
Chyandour
Perranuthnoe
St Michael's Mount
Millpool
Balwest
Carleen
Trewennack
Penjerri
Kelynack
Sancreed
Drift
Tredavoe
Newlyn
Goldsithney
Rosudgeon
Newtown
Germoe
Ashton
Trew
Sithney
Gweek
Trewennack
Helston
Porth Navas
Nanquidno
Catchall
Rosemanowes
Prussia Cove
Kenneggy
Breage
Sithney Common
Constantine
Trebah
Whitesand Bay
Brane
Cudden Point
Rinsey Head
Trewavas
A394
Mellangoose
Flambards
Mawgan
Gear
Manaccan
Sennen Cove
Escalls
Crows-an-Wra
Kerris
Paul
Mousehole
Praa Sands
Rinsey
Trewavas Head
Seal Sanctuary
Helford Passage
Helford
St Anth
LAND'S END
Land's End
Sennen
Trevorgans
St Buryan
Sheffield
MOUNT'S BAY
Trewavas Mining District
Porthleven
Higher Pentire
Gunwalloe
Mawgan
Durgan
Maw
Trevescan
The Merry Maidens
Castallack
Raginnis
Lamorna
Chyvarloe
White Cross
Gweek
Helford
Polgigga
Trethewey
Treen
Boskenna
Lamorna Cove
Merthen Point
Garras
Trelowarren
St Martin
Carne
Porthcurno
Telegraph
Angrouse
Trewoon
The Lizard
Cury
Cross Lanes
Traboe
St Ke
Roskestal
Gwennap Head
Minack Open Air Theatre
Cribba Head
Poldhu Point
Marconi Memorial
Trevon
Penhale
Goonhilly Downs
Trelan
Halligye Fogou
Newton-in-St Martin
North Co
Porthgwarra
St Levan
Mullion Cove
Mullion
Ponsongath
Gwenter
Coverack
Mullion Island
Ruan Major
Kuggar
Treleague
Predannack Wollas
White Cross
Tregidden
Tregarne
Predannack Head
Ruan Minor
Poltescoe
Black Head
South West Coast-Path
Mount Hermon
St Ruan
Cadgwith
Treleaver
Vellan Head
Devil's Frying Pan
The Lizard Heritage Coast
Grade
Kynance Cove
Church Cove
Lizard Head
Lizard
Bass Point
LIZARD POINT
Lizard Lighthouse & Heritage Centre

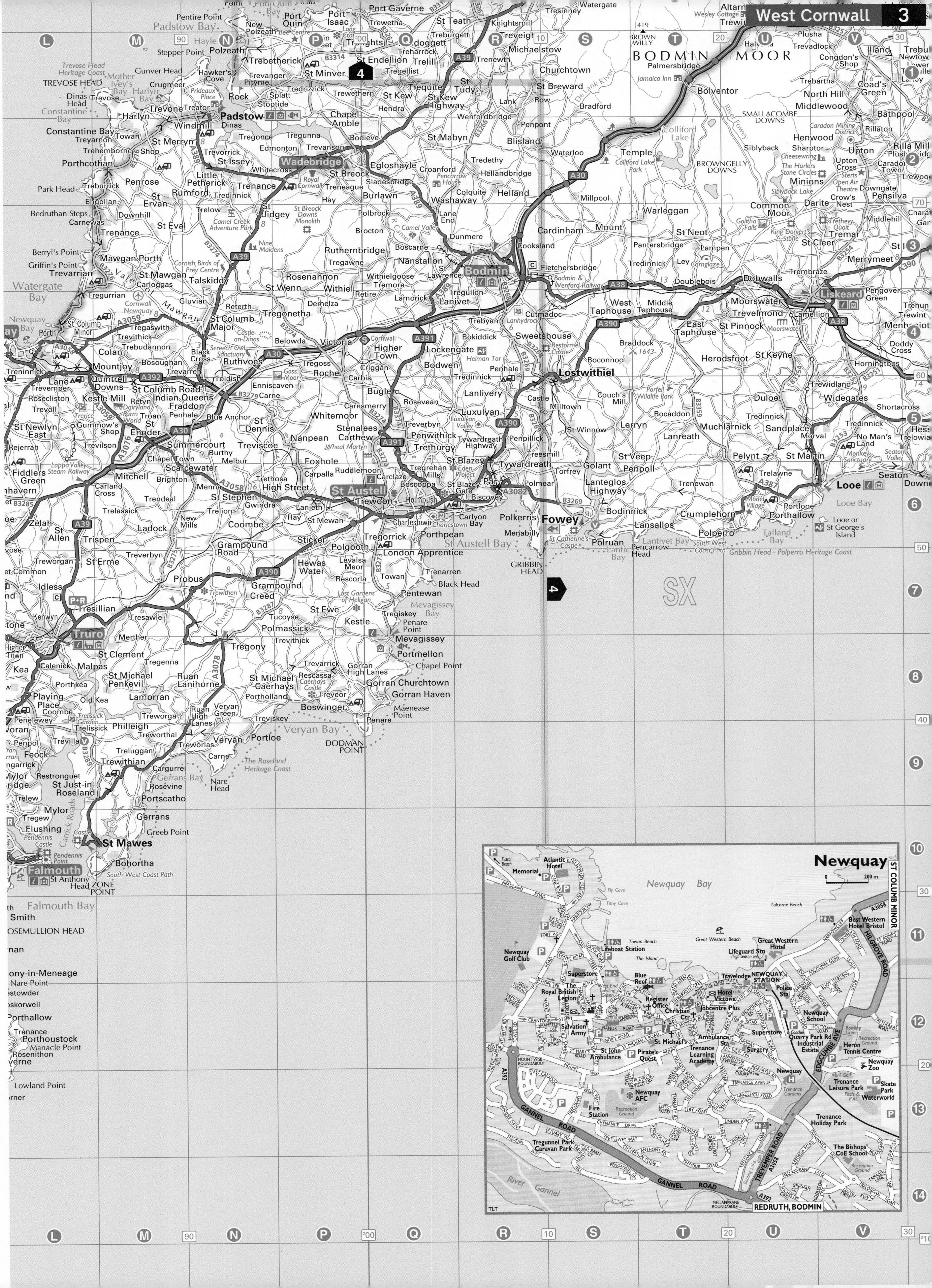

BODMIN MOOR
Padstow
Wadebridge
Bodmin
Lostwithiel
Liskeard
Looe
Fowey
St Austell
Truro
Falmouth
St Mawes
Mevagissey
Newquay
Newquay Bay
Padstow Bay
Watergate Bay
Veryan Bay
St Austell Bay
Falmouth Bay
Mevagissey Bay
Gerrans Bay
Lantivet Bay
Talland Bay
Looe Bay
GRIBBIN HEAD
DODMAN POINT
ZONE POINT
TREVOSE HEAD
ROSEMULLION HEAD
SX
Gribbin Head - Polperro Heritage Coast
The Roseland Heritage Coast
Trevose Head Heritage Coast
South West Coast Path
REDRUTH, BODMIN
ST COLUMB MINOR

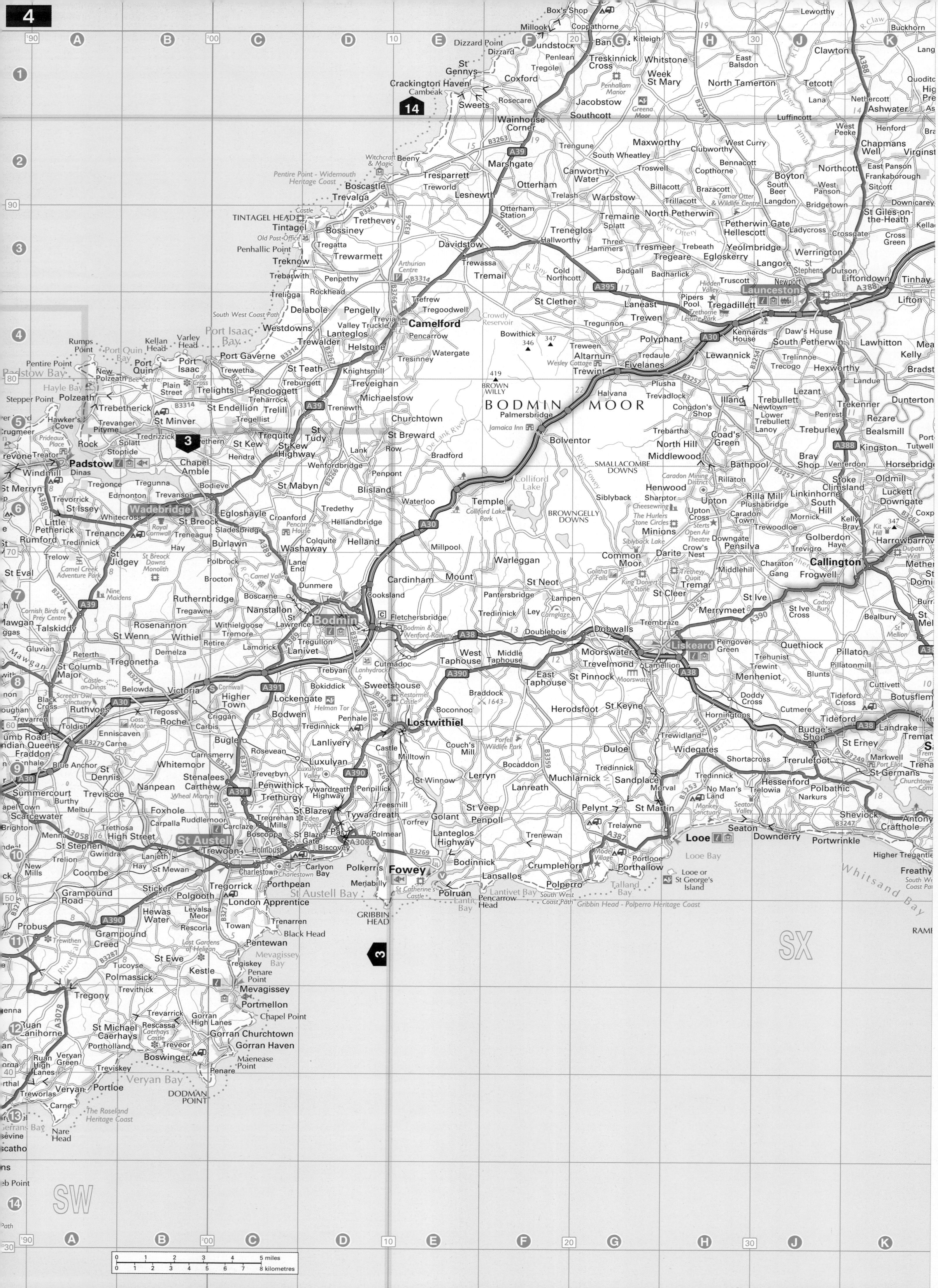

Box's Shop
Leworthy
Millook
Coppathorne
Buckhorn
Dizzard Point
Dizzard
Bangors
Kitleigh
Clawton
Penlean
Treskinnick Cross
Whitstone
East Balsdon
Tregole
St Gennys
Week St Mary
North Tamerton
Tetcott
Coxford
Crackington Haven
Cambeak
Penhallam Manor
Lana
Nethercott
Ashwater
Sweets
Rosecare
Jacobstow
Greena Moor
Southcott
Luffincott
Wainhouse Corner
Henford
West Peeke
Chapmans Well
Trengune
Maxworthy
West Curry
Clubworthy
South Wheatley
Virginstow
Witchcraft & Magic
Beeny
Marshgate
Bennacott
Canworthy Water
Troswell
Copthorne
Boyton
Northcott
East Panson
Frankaborough
Pentire Point - Widemouth Heritage Coast
Trespparrett
Treworld
Boscastle
Lesnewth
Otterham
Billacott
Brazacott
South Beer
West Panson
Sitcott
Trevalga
Trelash
Warbstow
Trillacott
Tamar Otter & Wildlife Centre
Langdon
Bridgetown
Downicarey
Trethevey
Otterham Station
Tremaine
North Petherwin
St Giles-on-the-Heath
TINTAGEL HEAD
Castle
Tintagel
Bossiney
Splatt
Petherwin Gate
Hellescott
Ladycross
Crossgate
Old Post Office
Treneglos
Hallworthy
Tregatta
Penhallic Point
Trewarmett
Davidstow
Three Hammers
Tresmeer
Trebeath
Tregeare
Egloskerry
Yeolmbridge
Werrington
Cross Green
Treknow
Trewassa
Arthurian Centre
Cold Northcott
Badgall
Badharlick
Langore
St Stephens
Dutson
Liftondown
Tinhay
Trebarwith
Tremail
Penpethy
Rockhead
Hidden Valley
Truscott
Newport
Launceston
Castle
Lifton
Treligga
Trefrew
St Clether
Laneast
Pipers Pool
Tregadillett
Delabole
Pengelly
Tregoodwell
Crowdy Reservoir
Trethorne Leisure Park
South West Coast Path
Valley Truckle
Trewen
Westdowns
Camelford
Tregunnon
Polyphant
Kennards House
Daw's House
Rumps Point
Kellan Head
Varley Head
Port Isaac Bay
Lanteglos
Bowithick
Pencarrow
Trewalder
346
347
South Petherwin
Lawhitton
Port Quin Bay
Helstone
Watergate
Treween
Lewannick
Kelly
Pentire Point
Port Quin
Port Isaac
Port Gaverne
Tresinney
Altarnun
Tredaule
Trelinnoe
Trecogo
Hexworthy
Bradstone
Padstow Bay
New Polzeath
Long Cross
Trewetha
St Teath
Knightsmill
Wesley Cottage
Trewint
Fivelanes
Landue
Hayle Bay
Plain Street
Trelights
Treburgett
Treveighan
419
BROWN WILLY
Plusha
Lezant
Stepper Point
Polzeath
Pendoggett
Treharrock
Halvana
Trevadlock
Illand
Trebullett
Dunterton
Trebetherick
St Endellion
Trelill
Trenewth
Michaelstow
BODMIN MOOR
Congdon's Shop
Newtown
Trekenner
Hawker's Cove
St Minver
Tregellist
Palmersbridge
Lower Trebullett
Penrest
Rezare
Trevanger
Pityme
Churchtown
Jamaica Inn
Trebartha
Lanoy
Treburley
Bealsmill
Prideaux Place
Splatt
Tredrizzick
Rock
St Kew
Trequite
St Tudy
St Breward
Bolventor
Coad's Green
North Hill
Kingston
Treator
Stoptide
Hendra
St Kew Highway
Lank
Row
Bradford
Middlewood
Tutwell
Trevone
Padstow
Chapel Amble
Wenfordbridge
Bray Shop
Windmill
Dinas
SMALLACOMBE DOWNS
Bathpool
Venterdon
Horsebridge
St Merryn
Tregonce
Tregunna
Trevanson
Bodieve
St Mabyn
Penpont
Colliford Lake
Caradon Mining District
Rillaton
Stoke Climsland
Oldmill
Edmonton
Blisland
Henwood
Luckett
Trevorrick
Wadebridge
Waterloo
Temple
Siblyback
Sharptor
Rilla Mill
Linkinhorne
Downgate
St Issey
Tredethy
Cheesewring
Plushabridge
South Hill
Little Petherick
Whitecross
St Breock
Egloshayle
Croanford
Colliford Lake Park
BROWNGELLY DOWNS
Upton
Upton Cross
The Hurlers Stone Circles
Caradon Town
Mornick
Kelly Bray
347
Coxpark
Royal Cornwall
Treneague
Sladesbridge
Pencarrow House
Hellandbridge
Sterts Open Air Theatre
Trewoodloe
Kit Hill
Trenance
Minions
Rumford
Tredinnick
Burlawn
Hay
Colquite
Helland
Millpool
Sibleyback Lake
Downgate
Golberdon
Harrowbarrow
Trelow
St Breock Downs Monolith
Washaway
Darite
Crow's Nest
Pensilva
Haye
St Jidgey
Polbrock
Common Moor
Trevigro
Dupath Well
St Eval
Camel Creek Adventure Park
Lane End
Warleggan
Charaton
Callington
Metherell
Brocton
Golitha Falls
Trethevy Quoit
Middlehill
Gang
Frogwell
Nine Maidens
Camel Valley
Dunmere
Cardinham
Mount
St Neot
Tremar
Cornish Birds of Prey Centre
Ruthernbridge
Boscarne
Cooksland
King Doniert's Stone
St Cleer
St Ive
Burraton
Tregawne
Nanstallon
Pantersbridge
Lampen
Cadson Bury
Mawgan
Bodmin
Fletchersbridge
Tredinnick
Ley
Carnglaze
Merrymeet
St Ive Cross
Bealbury
Talskiddy
Rosenannon
Withielgoose
St Lawrence
Bodmin & Wenford Railway
Trembraze
St Mellion
St Wenn
Withiel
Tremore
Tregullon
Doublebois
Dobwalls
Liskeard
Gluvian
Retire
Lamorick
Lanivet
Middle Taphouse
Moorswater
Pengover Green
Quethiock
Pillaton
Reterth
Demelza
West Taphouse
Trevelmond
Lamellion
Trehunist
Pillatonmill
St Columb Major
Tregonetha
Trebyan
Lanhydrock
Cutmadoc
East Taphouse
St Pinnock
Trewint
Menheniot
Blunts
Castle-an-Dinas
Belowda
Sweetshouse
Moorswater
Cuttivett
Black Cross
Screech Owl Sanctuary
Victoria
Higher Town
Bokiddick
Restormel Castle
Braddock
1643
Doddy Cross
Botusfleming
Ruthvoes
Tregoss
Lockengate
Helman Tor
Boconnoc
Herodsfoot
St Keyne
Tideford Cross
Goss Moor
Roche
Criggan
Bodwen
Penhale
Lostwithiel
Cutmere
Tideford
Toldish
Carbis
Tredinnick
Horningtops
Enniscaven
Carne
Bugle
Couch's Mill
Trewidland
Budge's Shop
Landrake
Indian Queens
Fraddon
Carnsmerry
Lanlivery
Castle
Porfell Wildlife Park
Duloe
Widegates
St Erney
Penhale
Blue Anchor
Rosevean
Milltown
Bocaddon
Shortacross
Trerulefoot
Markwell
Port Eliot
St Dennis
Whitemoor
Luxulyan
Luxulyan Valley
Tredinnick
Trehan
Stenalees
St Germans
Summercourt
Treviscoe
Nanpean
Carthew
Treverbyn
Penwithick
St Winnow
Lerryn
Muchlarnick
Sandplace
Tredinnick
Hessenford
Polbathic
Wheal Martyn
Tywardreath Highway
Penpillick
Lanreath
Morval
No Man's Land
Trelowia
Narkurs
Burthy
Melbur
Trethurgy
Treesmill
Foxhole
Rescorla
St Blazey
Tywardreath
Golant
St Veep
Pelynt
Trelawne
St Martin
Monkey Sanctuary
Seaton Valley
Sheviock
Antony
Scarcewater
Carpella
Ruddlemoor
Tregrehan Mills
Eden Project
Torfrey
Penpoll
Trenewan
Seaton
Crafthole
Brighton
Trethosa
Carclaze
St Blazey Gate
Par
Polmear
Lanteglos Highway
Looe
Downderry
Portwrinkle
Menna
High Street
St Austell
Boscoppa
Biscovey
A3082
Model Village
Portlooe
Looe Bay
Higher Tregantle
St Stephen
Gwindra
Lanjeth
Trewoon
Holmbush
Carlyon Bay
Polkerris
Fowey
Bodinnick
Crumplehorn
Porthallow
Looe or St George's Island
Freathy
Trelion
Hay
St Mewan
Charlestown
Menabilly
Lansallos
Polperro
Talland Bay
Whitsand Bay
South West Coast Path
New Mills
Coombe
Tregorrick
Porthpean
St Austell Bay
St Catherine's Castle
Polruan
Lantic Bay
Pencarrow Head
Lantivet Bay
Gribbin Head - Polperro Heritage Coast
Grampound Road
Sticker
Polgooth
London Apprentice
GRIBBIN HEAD
Hewas Water
Levalsa Meor
Trenarren
Probus
Trewithen
Grampound
Creed
Rescorla
Towan
Black Head
Lost Gardens of Heligan
Pentewan
Tucoyse
St Ewe
Mevagissey Bay
Tregiskey
Polmassick
Kestle
Penare Point
Tregony
Trevithick
Mevagissey
Portmellon
Chapel Point
Trevarrick
Gorran High Lanes
Ruan Lanihorne
St Michael Caerhays
Rescassa
Caerhays Castle
Gorran Churchtown
Portholland
Treveor
Gorran Haven
Veryan Green
Ruan High Lanes
Boswinger
Maenease Point
Treviskey
Penare
Veryan Bay
Treworlas
Veryan
Portloe
DODMAN POINT
Carne
The Roseland Heritage Coast
Gerrans Bay
Nare Head
Scatho
SW
SX
RAME
A30
A39
A38
A390
A391
A395
A388
A3058
A3078
A387
B3263
B3266
B3314
B3267
B3262
B3254
B3257
B3266
B3274
B3268
B3269
B3359
B3253
B3252
B3251
B3257
B3247
B3249
B3273
B3287
B3279
3
14
A B C D E F G H J K
1 2 3 4 5 6 7 8 9 10 11 12 13 14
90 00 10 20 30
0 1 2 3 4 5 miles
0 1 2 3 4 5 6 7 8 kilometres

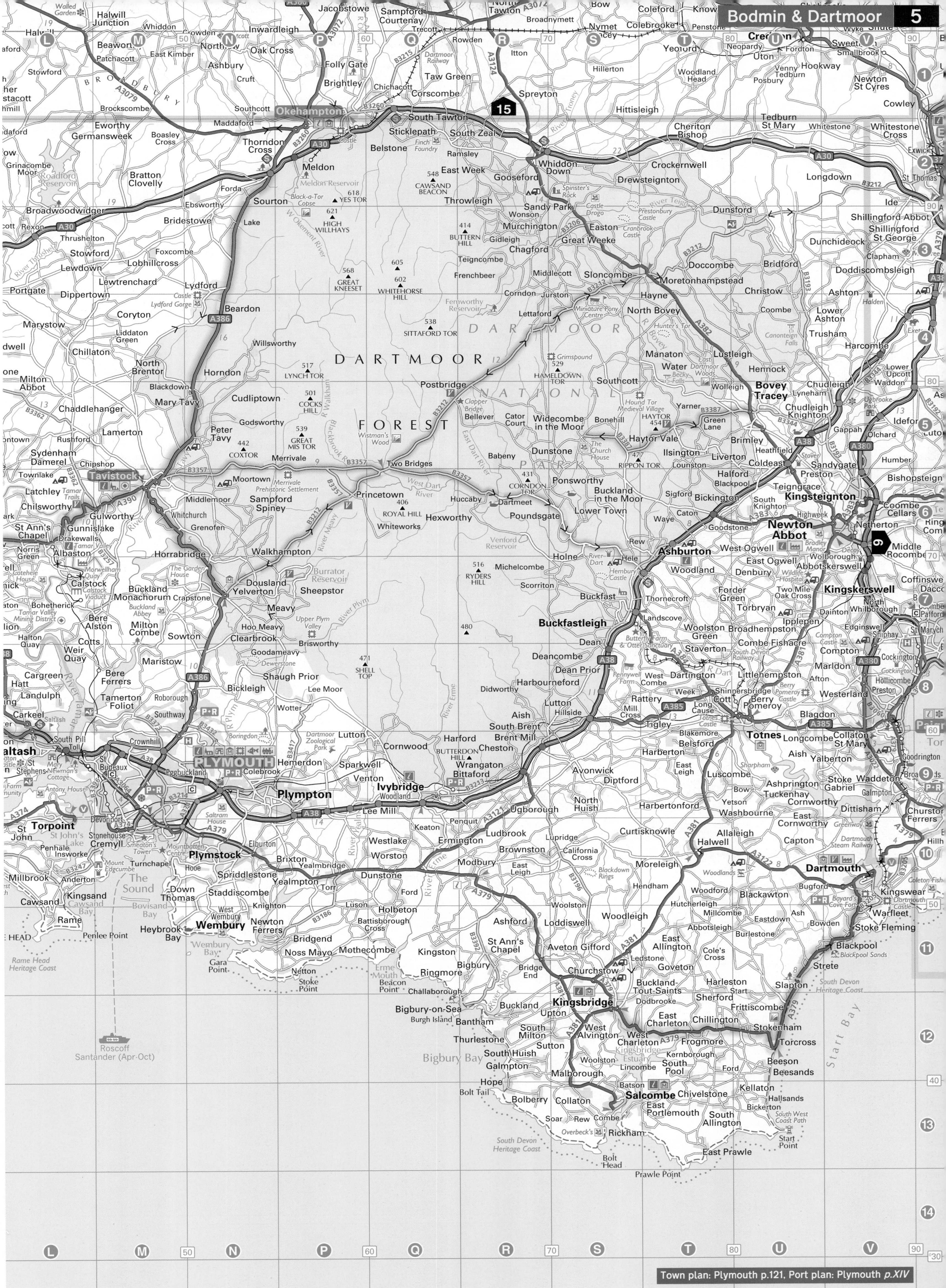
Walled Garden
Halwill Junction
Jacobstowe
Sampford Courtenay
North Tawton
Bow
Coleford
Knowle
Whiddon
Inwardleigh
Broadnymett
Nymet Tracey
Colebrooke
Penstone
Crediton
Beaworthy
Northlew
Oak Cross
Trecott
Rowden
Itton
Yeoford
Neopardy
Uton
Fordton
Sweetham
Smallbrook
Patchacott
East Kimber
Ashbury
Folly Gate
Dartmoor Railway
Hillerton
Woodland Head
Venny Tedburn
Hookway
Newton St Cyres
Stowford
Cruft
Brightley
Chichacott
Taw Green
Posbury
BROADBURY
Corscombe
Spreyton
Cowley
Brockscombe
Southcott
Okehampton
South Tawton
15
Hittisleigh
Tedburn St Mary
Whitestone
Whitestone Cross
Maddaford
Sticklepath
Cheriton Bishop
Eworthy
Germansweek
Boasley Cross
Thorndon Cross
Belstone
Finch Foundry
South Zeal
Exwick
Ramsley
Whiddon Down
Crockernwell
Grinacombe Moor
Roadford Reservoir
Meldon
Meldon Reservoir
East Week
Drewsteignton
Longdown
Bratton Clovelly
548 CAWSAND BEACON
Gooseford
St Thomas
Forda
Black-a-Tor Copse
618 YES TOR
Spinster's Rock
Sourton
621 HIGH WILLHAYS
Throwleigh
Castle Drogo
Ide
Ebsworthy
Sandy Park
Prestonbury Castle
Dunsford
Shillingford Abbot
Broadwoodwidger
Wonson
Easton
Shillingford St George
Rexon
Bridestowe
Lake
W Okement River
414 BUTTERN HILL
Murchington
Cranbrook Castle
Thrushelton
Gidleigh
Great Weeke
Dunchideock
Foxcombe
Chagford
Bridford
Clapham
Stowford
Lobhillcross
605
Teigncombe
Doccombe
Doddiscombsleigh
Lewdown
568 GREAT KNEESET
602 WHITEHORSE HILL
Frenchbeer
Middlecott
Sloncombe
Moretonhampstead
Lewtrenchard
Portgate
Lydford
Christow
Ashton
Dippertown
Lydford Gorge
Fernworthy Reservoir
Corndon
Jurston
Hayne
Halden
Beardon
Lettaford
Miniature Pony Centre
North Bovey
Coombe
Lower Ashton
Coryton
538 SITTAFORD TOR
DARTMOOR
Hunter's Tor
Canonteign Falls
Trusham
Marystow
Liddaton Green
Willsworthy
Harcombe
Chillaton
North Brentor
DARTMOOR
Grimspound
Manaton
Lustleigh
Lower Upcott
517 LYNCH TOR
529 HAMELDOWN TOR
Water
East Dartmoor Woods
Becky Falls
Hennock
Horndon
Southcott
Wolleigh
Milton Abbot
Blackdown
Postbridge
NATIONAL
Bovey Tracey
Chudleigh
Lyneham
Waddon
501 COCKS HILL
Clapper Bridge
Hound Tor Medieval Village
Chudleigh Knighton
Ugbrooke Park
Chaddlehanger
Mary Tavy
Cudliptown
Bellever
Cator Court
Widecombe in the Moor
Bonehill
454 HAYTOR
Yarner
Green Lane
Gappah
Idefor
Godsworthy
FOREST
Haytor Vale
Peter Tavy
539 GREAT MIS TOR
Wistman's Wood
Olchard
Lamerton
Rushford
442 COXTOR
Merrivale
The Church House
Brimley
Heathfield
Sydenham Damerel
Chipshop
Babeny
Dunstone
Ilsington
Liverton
Humber
477 RIPPON TOR
Lounston
Coldeast
Sandygate
Tavistock
Two Bridges
Preston
Townlake
Moortown
Merrivale Prehistoric Settlement
PARK
431 CORNDON TOR
Ponsworthy
Halford
Blackpool
Bishopsteign
Latchley
Tamar Trails
West Dart River
Buckland in the Moor
Teigngrace
Kingsteignton
Middlemoor
Sampford Spiney
Princetown
Huccaby
Dartmeet
Sigford
Bickington
Chilsworthy
406 ROYAL HILL
South Knighton
Coombe Cellars
Whitchurch
Hexworthy
Poundsgate
Lower Town
Gulworthy
Caton
Highweek
Gunnislake
Whiteworks
Waye
Goodstone
Newton Abbot
Netherton
St Ann's Chapel
Grenofen
Drakewalls
Venford Reservoir
Rew
Norris Green
Tamar Valley
Albaston
Horrabridge
Walkhampton
Holne
River Dart
Hele
Ashburton
West Ogwell
Bradley Manor
Decoy
Middle Rocombe
Cotehele House
Morwellham Quay
The Garden House
Burrator Reservoir
516 RYDERS HILL
Michelcombe
Hembury Castle
East Ogwell
Wolborough
Calstock
Calstock Viaduct
Dousland
Woodland
Denbury
Wildlife Hospital
Abbotskerswell
Coffinswell
Buckland Monachorum
Crapstone
Yelverton
Sheepstor
Scorriton
Forder Green
Two Mile Oak Cross
Kingskerswell
Bohetherick
Buckland Abbey
Meavy
Buckfast
Thornecroft
Torbryan
North Whilborough
Tamar Valley Mining District
Bere Alston
Milton Combe
Upper Plym Valley
480
Buckfastleigh
Landscove
Dainton
Ipplepen
Edginswell
Shiphay
Sowton
Hoo Meavy
Woolston Green
Broadhempston
Halton Quay
Cotts
Clearbrook
Briswörthy
Dean
Butterfly Farm & Otter Sanctuary
Combe Fishacre
Compton Castle
Weir Quay
Goodameavy
Dewerstone
Deancombe
Staverton
South Devon Railway
Compton
Cockington
Maristow
471 SHELL TOP
Dean Prior
Pennywell Farm
West Combe
Dartington
Littlehempston
Marldon
Afton
Hollicombe
Cargreen
Bere Ferrers
Shaugh Prior
Harbourneford
Week
Shinnersbridge
Berry Pomeroy Castle
Preston
Hatt
Bickleigh
Lee Moor
Didworthy
Rattery
Cott
Berry Pomeroy
Westerland
Landulph
Tamerton Foliot
Roborough
Lutton
Mill Cross
Long Cause
Blagdon
Carkeel
Saltash
Southway
Wotter
Aish
Hillside
Tigley
Totnes Castle
South Brent
Brent Mill
Blakemore
Totnes
Longcombe
Collaton St Mary
Saltash
South Pill
Crownhill
Boringdon
Dartmoor Zoological Park
Lutton
Harford
Cheston
Belsford
Harberton
Goodrington
St Budeaux
Newman's Cottage
PLYMOUTH
Hemerdon
Cornwood
Butterdon Hill
Aish
Yalberton
Eggbuckland
Colebrook
Sparkwell
Wrangaton
Bittaford
East Leigh
Sharpham
Antony House
Venton
Ivybridge
Avonwick
Diptford
Luscombe
Stoke Gabriel
Waddeton
Plympton
Woodland
Bow
Ashprington
Tuckenhay
Galmpton
Cornworthy
North Huish
Harbertonford
Yetson
Washbourne
Dittisham
Churston Ferrers
Torpoint
Devonport
Saltram House
Lee Mill
Keaton
Penquit
Ugborough
St John
St John's Lake
Stonehouse
Cremyll
Smeaton's Tower
Mountbatten Centre
Plymstock
Elburton
Ermington
Ludbrook
Lupridge
Curtisknowle
Allaleigh
East Cornworthy
Capton
Halwell
Greenway
Dartmouth Steam Railway
Penhale
Insworke
Brixton
Westlake
Brownston
California Cross
Mount Edgcumbe
Turnchapel
Hooe
Yealmbridge
Worston
Modbury
East Leigh
Blackdown Rings
Moreleigh
Woodlands
Dartmouth
Millbrook
Anderton
The Sound
Spriddlestone
Yealmpton
Torr
Dunstone
Coleton Fishacre
Kingsand
Cawsand
Cawsand Bay
Down Thomas
Staddiscombe
Ford
Hendham
Woodford
Bugford
Kingswear
Bayard's Cove Fort
Dartmouth Castle
Bovisand Bay
Knighton
Luson
Holbeton
Woolston
Blackawton
Hutcherleigh
Millcombe
Ash
Warfleet
Rame
West Wembury
Battisborough Cross
Ashford
Loddiswell
Woodleigh
Eastdown
Bowden
Heybrook Bay
Wembury
Newton Ferrers
Abbotsleigh
Burlestone
Stoke Fleming
Penlee Point
Bridgend
St Ann's Chapel
Aveton Gifford
East Allington
Cole's Cross
Blackpool
Blackpool Sands
Wembury Bay
Noss Mayo
Mothecombe
Kingston
Rame Head Heritage Coast
Gara Point
Bigbury
Ledstone
Goveton
Strete
Netton
Erme Mouth
Ringmore
Bridge End
Churchstow
Stoke Point
Beacon Point
Challaborough
Buckland-Tout-Saints
Harleston
Slapton
South Devon Heritage Coast
Dodbrooke
Start
Sherford
Kingsbridge
Frittiscombe
Bigbury-on-Sea
Burgh Island
Bantham
Buckland
Upton
East Charleton
Chillington
Thurlestone
South Milton
West Alvington
West Charleton
Stokenham
Frogmore
Roscoff Santander (Apr-Oct)
Bigbury Bay
South Huish
Sutton
Kingsbridge Estuary
Kernborough
Torcross
Galmpton
Woolston
Lincombe
South Pool
Beeson
Beesands
Start Bay
Malborough
Hope
Ford
Bolt Tail
Batson
Salcombe
Chivelstone
Kellaton
Bolberry
Collaton
East Portlemouth
Hallsands
Bickerton
South West Coast Path
Soar
Rew
Combe
South Allington
Overbeck's
Rickham
South Devon Heritage Coast
Start Point
East Prawle
Bolt Head
Prawle Point
A30
A3072
A386
A3079
A3124
B3215
B3260
B3212
A382
B3357
A390
A38
A380
A381
A385
A3121
A379
A374
A3122
B3193
B3344
B3387
B3362
B3213
B3196
B3392
B3186
B3205

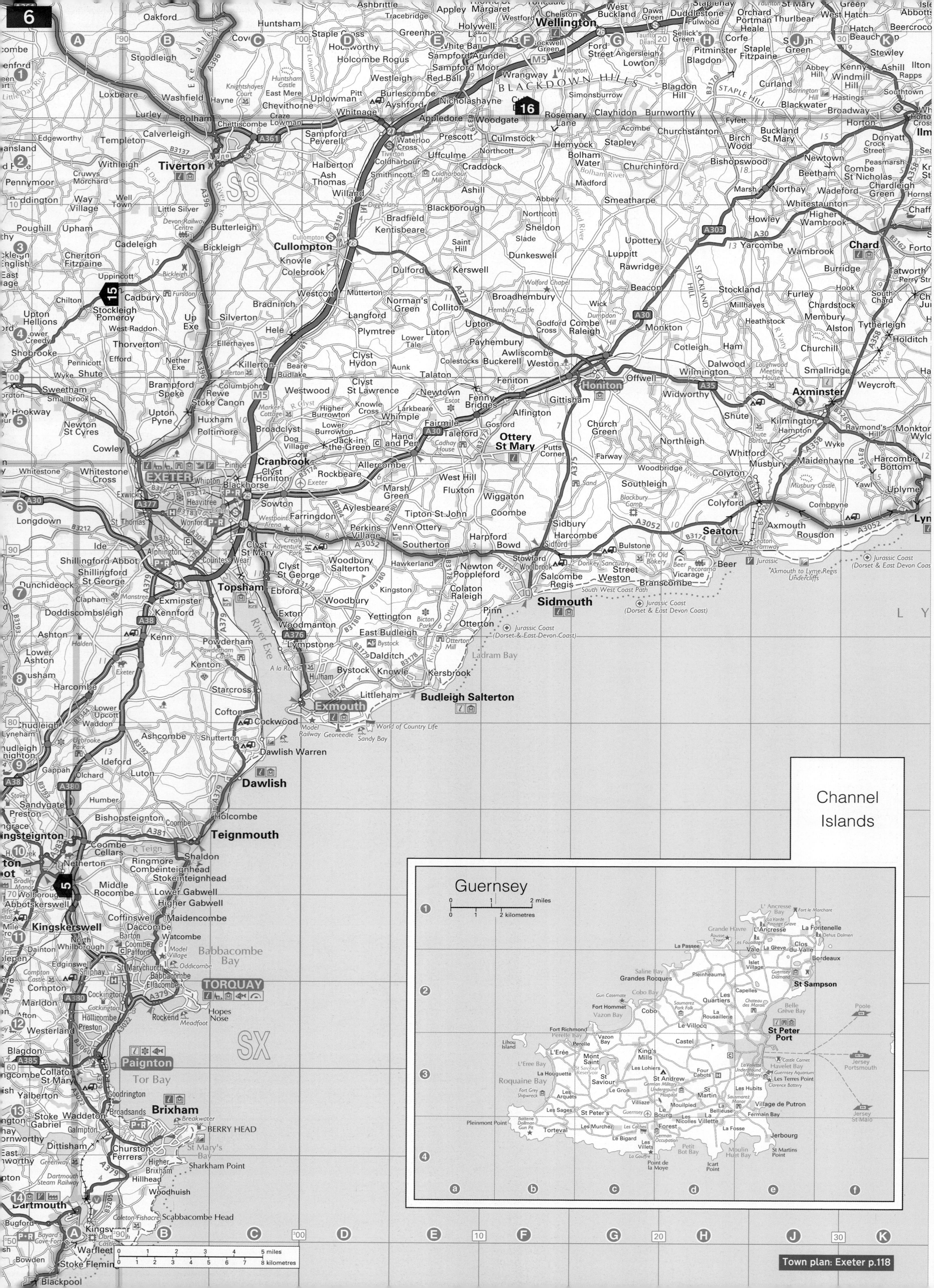
Oakford
Huntsham
Ashbrittle
Appley
Wellington
West Buckland
Duddlestone
Orchard Portman
Thurlbear
Stoodleigh
Staple Cross
Greenham
Holywell Lake
Hockworthy
Holcombe Rogus
White Ball
Sampford Arundel
Sampford Moor
Ford Street
Angersleigh
Lowton
Pitminster
Blagdon
Corfe
Staple Fitzpaine
Hatch Beauchamp
Stewley
Westleigh
Red Ball
Wrangway
BLACKDOWN HILLS
Blagdon Hill
Curland
Kenny
Ashill
Windmill Hill
Loxbeare
Washfield
Hayne
Knightshayes Court
Huntsham Castle
East Mere
Burlescombe
Uplowman
Pitt
Ayshford
Chevithorne
Nicholashayne
Simonsburrow
STAPLE HILL
Barrington Hill
Blackwater
Hastings
Broadway
Southtown
Lurley
Bolham
Chettiscombe
Craze Lowman
Whitnage
Appledore
Woodgate
Rosemary Lane
Clayhidon
Burnworthy
Fyfett
Buckland St Mary
Horton
Edgeworthy
Templeton
Calverleigh
A361
Sampford Peverell
Waterloo Cross
Prescott
Culmstock
Hemyock
Stapley
Churchstanton
Birch Wood
Donyatt
Tiverton
Withleigh
Cruwys Morchard
Halberton
Coldharbour
Uffculme
Northcott
Bolham Water
Churchinford
Bishopswood
Newtown
Beetham
Combe St Nicholas
Ash Thomas
Smithincott
Craddock
Chardleigh Green
Pennymoor
Way Village
Well Town
Willand
Ashill
Madford
Marsh
Northay
Wadeford
Whitestaunton
Little Silver
Devon Railway Centre
Butterleigh
Blackborough
Abbey
Smeatharpe
Howley
Higher Wambrook
Poughill
Upham
Cadeleigh
Bradfield
Kentisbeare
Northcott
Sheldon
Slade
Upottery
Yarcombe
Wambrook
Chard
Cheriton Fitzpaine
Bickleigh
Cullompton
Knowle
Colebrook
Saint Hill
Dunkeswell
Luppitt
Rawridge
Burridge
Tatworth
Uppincott
Dulford
Kerswell
Wolford Chapel
Beacon
Stockland
Hook
Cadbury
Fursdon
Westcott
Mutterton
Norman's Green
Colliton
Broadhembury
Hembury Castle
Wick
Dumpdon Hill
Millhayes
Furley
Chardstock
South Chard
Chilton
Stockleigh Pomeroy
Up Exe
Silverton
Bradninch
Langford
Upton
Godford Cross
Combe Raleigh
Monkton
Heathstock
Membury
Tytherleigh
Holditch
Upton Hellions
West Raddon
Hele
Plymtree
Luton
Lower Tale
Payhembury
Cotleigh
Ham
Alston
Churchill
Shobrooke
Thorverton
Ellerhayes
Clyst Hydon
Awliscombe
Buckerell
Colestocks
Weston
Dalwood
Wilmington
Loughwood Meeting House
Smallridge
Pennicott
Efford
Nether Exe
Killerton
Beare
Budlake
Aunk
Talaton
Feniton
Honiton
Offwell
Widworthy
Weycroft
Axminster
Shute
Sweetham
Smallbrook
Brampford Speke
Columbjohn
Rewe
Stoke Canon
Westwood
Clyst St Lawrence
Newtown
Escot
Fenny Bridges
Gittisham
Alfington
Shute Barton
Kilmington
Hampton
Raymond's Hill
Monkton Wyld
Hookway
Newton St Cyres
Upton Pyne
Huxham
Poltimore
Marker's Cottage
Higher Burrowton
Knowle Cross
Larkbeare
Whimple
Fairmile
Gosford
Church Green
Northleigh
Wyke
Harcombe Bottom
Cowley
Broadclyst
Dog Village
Lower Burrowton
Jack-in-the-Green
Hand and Pen
Taleford
Cadhay House
Ottery St Mary
Putts Corner
Farway
Whitford
Musbury
Maidenhayne
Uplyme
Whitestone
Whitestone Cross
EXETER
Pinhoe
Cranbrook
Clyst Honiton
Allercombe
Rockbeare
West Hill
Woodbridge
Colyton
Whipton
Blackhorse
Heavitree
Exwick
Exeter
Marsh Green
Fluxton
Southleigh
Mushbury Castle
Yawl
Longdown
St Thomas
Wonford
Sowton
Aylesbeare
Wiggaton
Blackbury Camp
Colyford
Combpyne
Farringdon
Westpoint Arena
Tipton St John
Coombe
Perkins Village
Venn Ottery
Sidbury
Harcombe
Seaton
Axmouth
Rousdon
Ide
Alphington
Countess Wear
Clyst St Mary
Crealy Adventure Park
Southerton
Harpford
Bowd
Sidford
Bulstone
Seaton Tramway
Jurassic Coast (Dorset & East Devon Coast)
Shillingford Abbot
Shillingford St George
Clyst St George
Woodbury Salterton
Hawkerland
Newton Poppleford
Stowford
Woolbrook
Donkey Sanctuary
The Old Bakery
Beer
Pecorama
Street
Weston
Branscombe
Vicarage
Axmouth to Lyme Regis Undercliffs
Dunchideock
Topsham
Exminster
Ebford
Woodbury
Kingston
Colaton Raleigh
Salcombe Regis
Sidmouth
South West Coast Path
Clapham
Doddiscombsleigh
Kennford
Exton
Yettington
Bicton Park
Pinn
Otterton
Ashton
Kenn
Woodmanton
East Budleigh
Powderham
Powderham Castle
River Exe
Lympstone
Bystock
Otterton Mill
Lower Ashton
Dalditch
Ladram Bay
Kenton
A la Ronde
Bystock
Knowle
Kersbrook
Harcombe
Hulham
Starcross
Littleham
Budleigh Salterton
Lower Upcott
Waddon
Cofton
Exmouth
Cockwood
Model Railway
Geoneedle
World of Country Life
Sandy Bay
Ashcombe
Shutterton
Dawlish Warren
Ideford
Luton
Dawlish
Olchard
Humber
Sandygate
Preston
Holcombe
Bishopsteignton
Teignmouth
Coombe Cellars
Shaldon
Ringmore
Netherton
Combeinteignhead
Stokeinteignhead
Middle Rocombe
Lower Gabwell
Higher Gabwell
Abbotskerswell
Coffinswell
Maidencombe
Kingskerswell
Daccombe
Barton
Watcombe
North Whilborough
Dainton
Babbacombe Bay
Model Village
Oddicombe
St Marychurch
Babbacombe
Ellacombe
TORQUAY
Compton Castle
Compton
Cockington
Marldon
Hopes Nose
Rockend
Meadfoot
Westerland
Preston
Hollicombe
SX
Blagdon
Paignton
Collaton St Mary
Tor Bay
Goodrington
Yalberton
Broadsands
Brixham
Breakwater
BERRY HEAD
Stoke Gabriel
Waddeton
Galmpton
Dittisham
Churston Ferrers
St Mary's Bay
Higher Brixham
Sharkham Point
Hillhead
Dartmouth Steam Railway
Woodhuish
Dartmouth
Coleton Fishacre
Scabbacombe Head
Bugford
Kingswear
Dartmouth Castle
Warfleet
Stoke Fleming
Bowden
Blackpool
0 1 2 3 4 5 miles
0 1 2 3 4 5 6 7 8 kilometres
Channel Islands
Guernsey
0 1 2 miles
0 1 2 kilometres
L'Ancresse Bay
Fort le Marchant
La Fontenelle
Grande Havre
L'Ancresse
Dehus Dolmen
La Passee
Vale
La Greve
Clos du Valle
Bordeaux
Saline Bay
Grandes Rocques
Pleinheaume
Islet Village
St Sampson
Cobo Bay
Capelles
Fort Hommet
Vazon Bay
Cobo
Les Quartiers
La Rousaillerie
Belle Greve Bay
Le Villocq
Fort Richmond
Perelle Bay
Perelle
Castel
St Peter Port
Lihou Island
L'Erée
King's Mills
Castle Cornet
Havelet Bay
Guernsey Aquarium
L'Eree Bay
Mont Saint
La Houguette
St Saviour
Les Lohiers
St Andrew
Four Cabots
Les Terres Point
Clarence Battery
Rocquaine Bay
Le Gron
German Military Underground Hospital
St Martin
Les Hubits
Les Arquets
Villiaze
Mouilpied
Bellieuse
Village de Putron
Fermain Bay
Les Sages
St Peter's
Le Bourg
Les Nicolles
Villette
Pleinmont Point
Torteval
Les Murchez
Forest
La Fosse
Jerbourg
Le Bigard
Les Villets
Petit Bot Bay
Moulin Huet Bay
St Martins Point
Point de la Moye
Icart Point
Poole
Jersey Portsmouth
Jersey St-Malo
Wellington
Honiton
Seaton
Sidmouth
Exmouth
Exeter

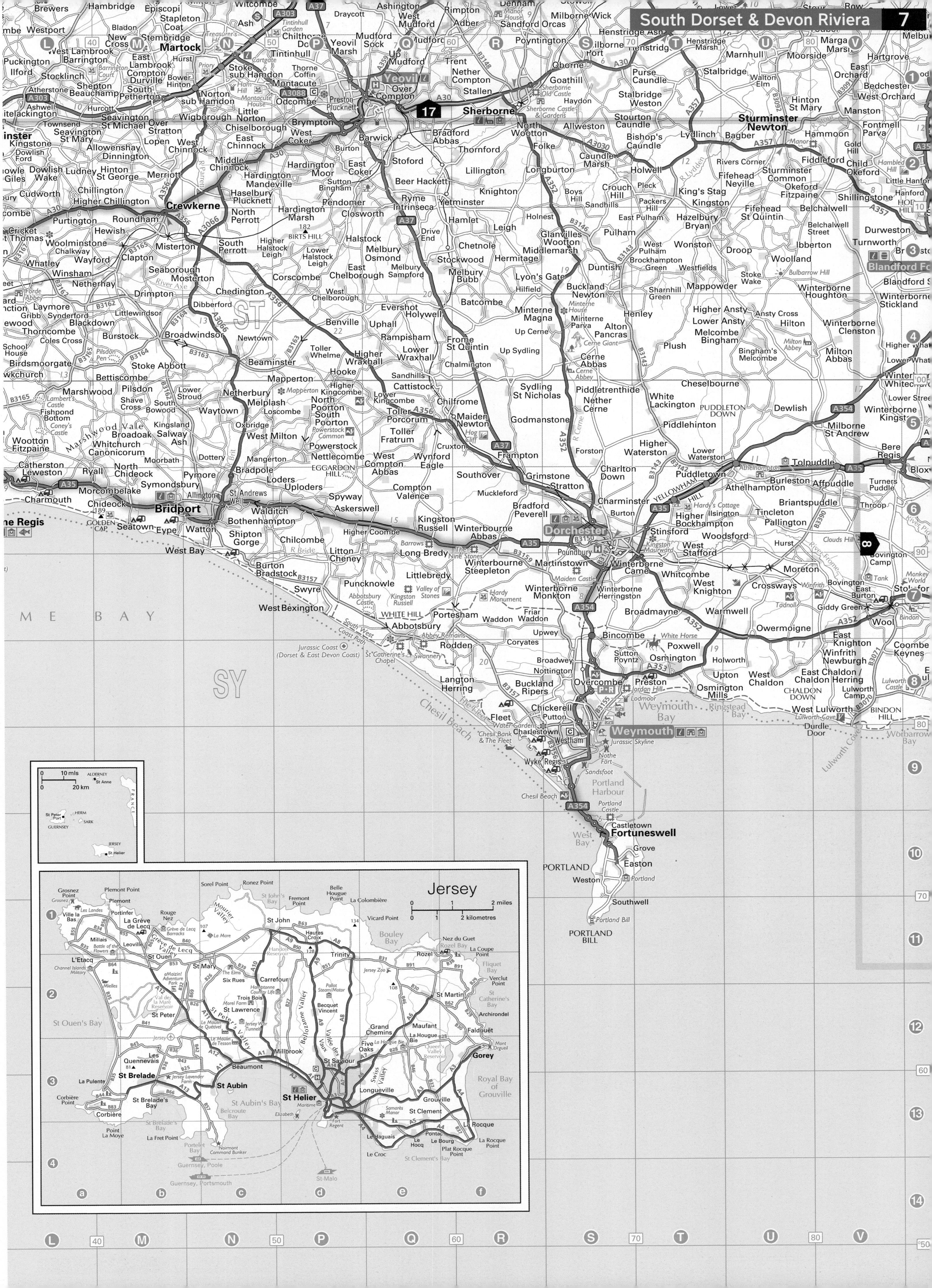

Yeovil
Sherborne
Martock
Crewkerne
Sturminster Newton
Bridport
Dorchester
Weymouth
Fortuneswell
Portland
Portland Bill
Chesil Beach
Lyme Bay
Abbotsbury
Beaminster
Maiden Newton
Cerne Abbas
Puddletown
Wool
Lulworth Cove
Jurassic Coast (Dorset & East Devon Coast)
Jersey
St Helier
St Aubin
St Brelade
Gorey
St Ouen's Bay
St Aubin's Bay
Royal Bay of Grouville
Alderney
Guernsey
Sark
Herm
St Peter Port
France

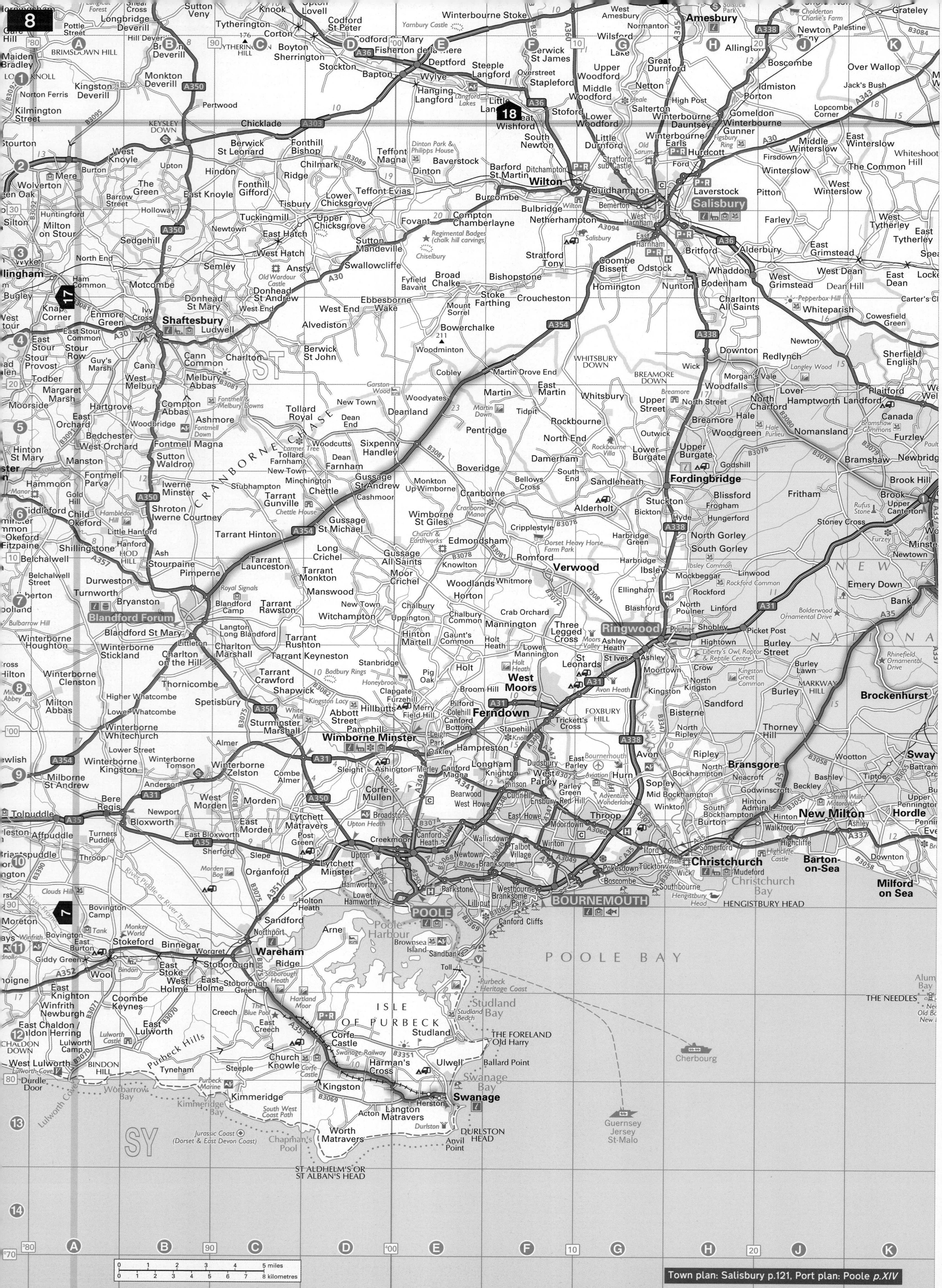
Amesbury
Wilton
Salisbury
Shaftesbury
Blandford Forum
Fordingbridge
Verwood
Ringwood
Ferndown
West Moors
Wimborne Minster
Wareham
POOLE
BOURNEMOUTH
Christchurch
New Milton
Barton-on-Sea
Milford on Sea
Swanage
Brockenhurst
CRANBORNE CHASE
ISLE OF PURBECK
POOLE BAY
Poole Harbour
Studland Bay
Swanage Bay
Christchurch Bay
HENGISTBURY HEAD
DURLSTON HEAD
ST ALDHELM'S OR ST ALBAN'S HEAD
THE FORELAND Old Harry
THE NEEDLES
Purbeck Hills
Cherbourg
Guernsey Jersey St-Malo
SY
ST
NEW FOREST NATIONAL PARK
A36
A30
A338
A354
A350
A31
A35
A303
A351
A348
A341
A343
A345
A360
A3094
A3049
A3060
A337
A352
A357
A347
0 1 2 3 4 5 miles
0 1 2 3 4 5 6 7 8 kilometres

Town plan: Salisbury p.121, Port plan: Poole p.XIV

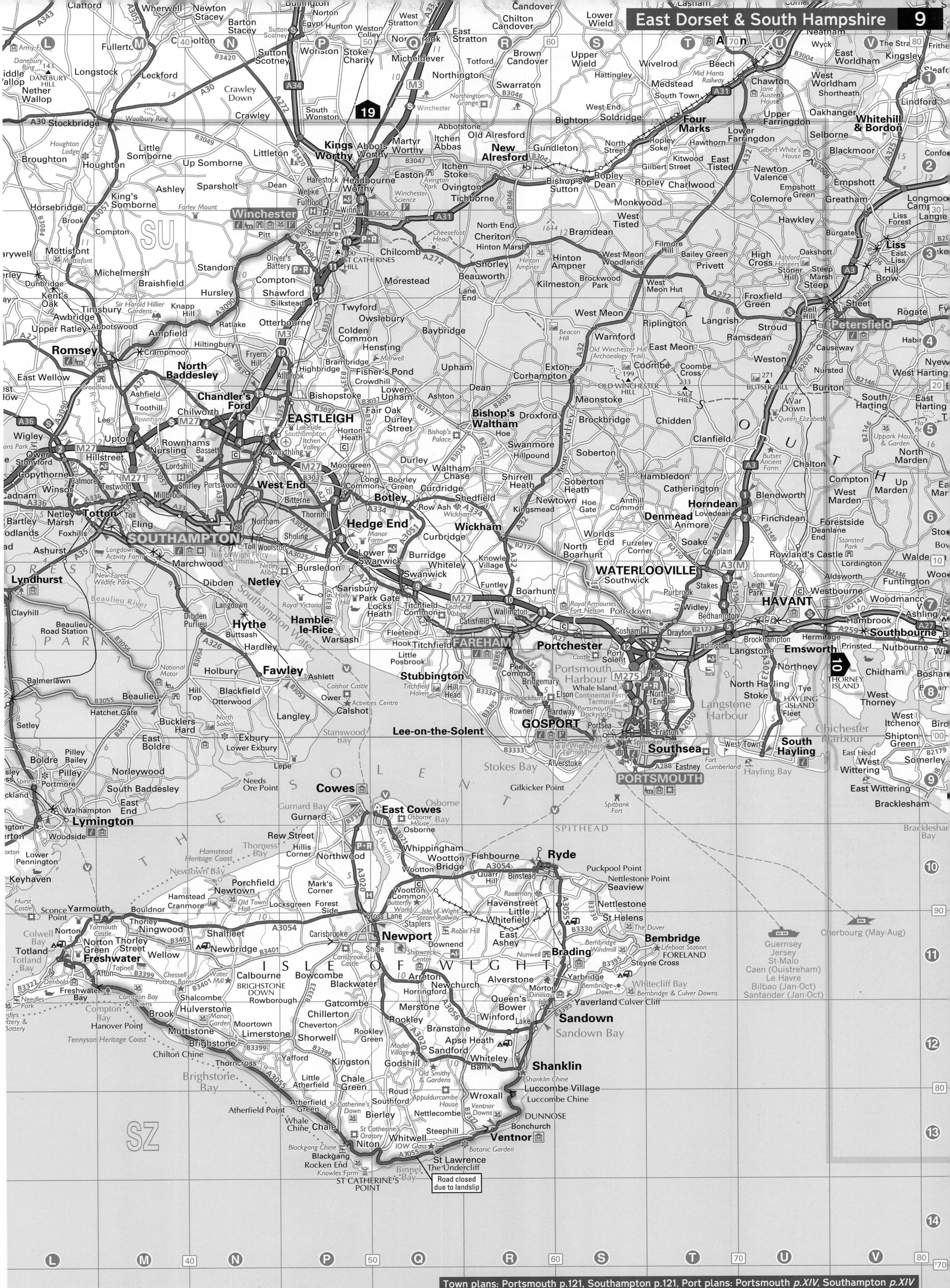
Winchester
Kings Worthy
New Alresford
Four Marks
Alton
Whitehill & Bordon
Liss
Petersfield
Romsey
North Baddesley
Chandler's Ford
EASTLEIGH
Bishop's Waltham
West End
Botley
Hedge End
Wickham
Denmead
Horndean
WATERLOOVILLE
HAVANT
Emsworth
Southbourne
SOUTHAMPTON
Totton
Lyndhurst
Netley
Hythe
Hamble-le-Rice
Fawley
FAREHAM
Portchester
Stubbington
Lee-on-the-Solent
GOSPORT
Southsea
PORTSMOUTH
South Hayling
Lymington
Cowes
East Cowes
Ryde
Yarmouth
Freshwater
Newport
Brading
Bembridge
Sandown
Shanklin
Ventnor
ISLE OF WIGHT
THE SOLENT
SOUTH DOWNS
Road closed due to landslip
Guernsey
Jersey
St-Malo
Caen (Ouistreham)
Le Havre
Bilbao (Jan-Oct)
Santander (Jan-Oct)
Cherbourg (May-Aug)
SU
SZ
19
10

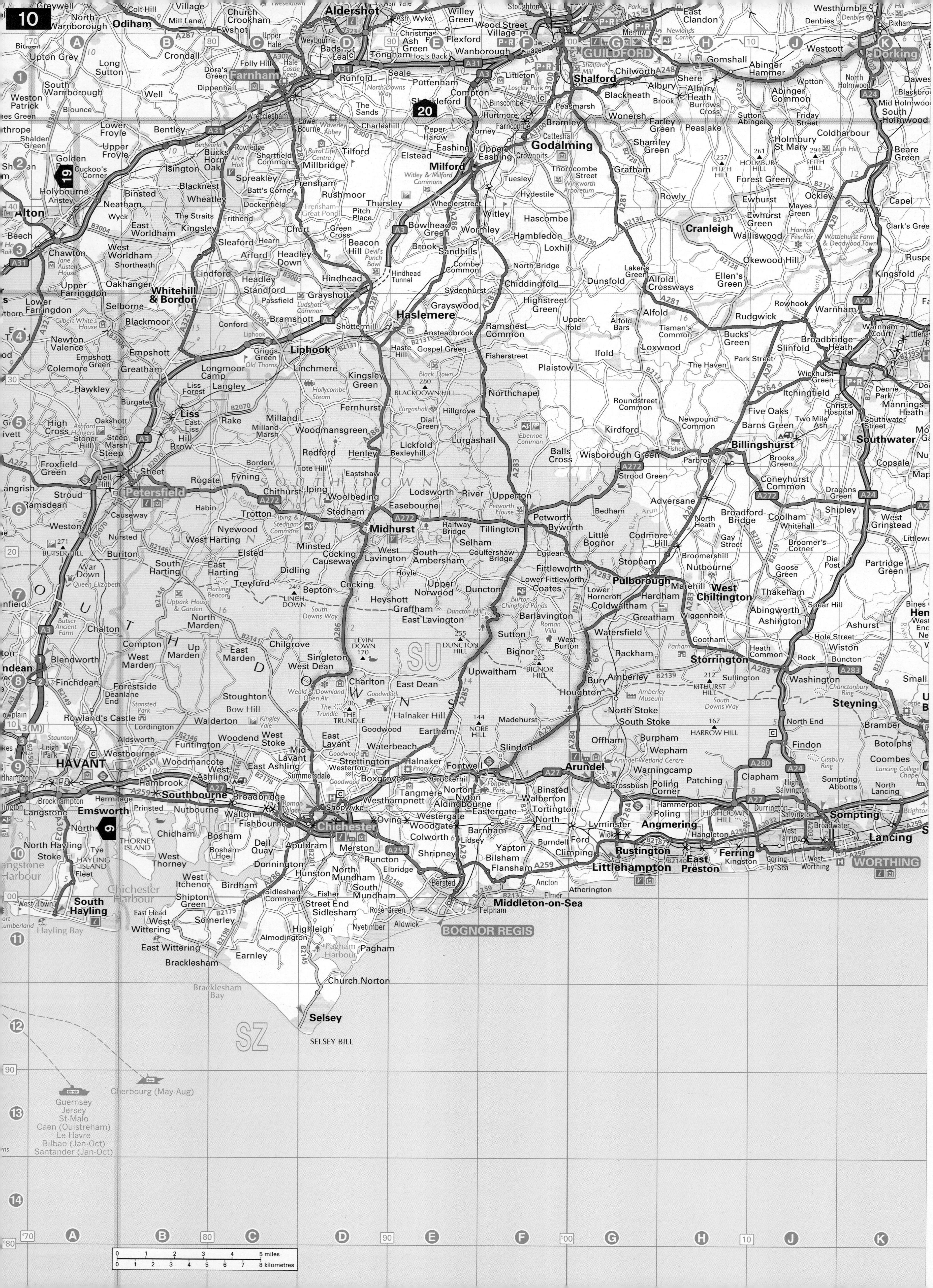

Odiham
North Warnborough
Greywell
Colt Hill
Mill Lane
Village
Church Crookham
Ewshot
Upper Hale
Aldershot
Ash Wyke
Willey Green
Wood Street Village
Stoughton
East Clandon
Westhumble
Denbies
Pixham
Upton Grey
Long Sutton
Crondall
Folly Hill
Hale
Weybourne
Badshot Lea
Christmas Ash Green
Flexford
Tongham
Hog's Back
Wanborough
GUILDFORD
Newlands Corner
Gomshall
Abinger Hammer
Westcott
Dorking
South Warnborough
Well
Dora's Green
Farnham
Dippenhall
Runfold
Seale
Puttenham
Compton
Littleton
Shalford
Chilworth
Shere
Albury
Wotton
North Holmwood
Dawes
Weston Patrick
Blounce
Wrecclesham
The Sands
Shackleford
Binscombe
Peasmarsh
Blackheath
Brook
Albury Heath
Burrows Cross
Abinger Common
Mid Holmwood
South Holmwood
Lower Froyle
Bentley
Lower Bourne
Charleshill
Waverley Abbey
Peper Harow
Hurtmore
Farncombe
Norney
Catteshall
Bramley
Wonersh
Farley Green
Peaslake
Sutton Abinger
Friday Street
Coldharbour
Upper Froyle
Birdworld
Bucks Horn Oak
Alice Holt
Rowledge
Shortfield Common
Rural Life Centre
Tilford
Eashing
Upper Eashing
Godalming
Crownpits
Shamley Green
Holmbury St Mary
Leith Hill
Beare Green
Golden Pot
Cuckoo's Corner
Isington
Millbridge
Elstead
Milford
Witley & Milford Commons
Thorncombe Street
Winkworth Arboretum
Grafham
Pitch Hill
Holmbury Hill
Leith Hill
Forest Green
Holybourne
Anstey
Binsted
Neatham
Blacknest
Spreakley
Batt's Corner
Frensham
Rushmoor
Tuesley
Hydestile
Rowly
Ewhurst
Mayes Green
Ockley
Capel
Alton
Wyck
East Worldham
Wheatley
The Straits
Kingsley
Dockenfield
Frithend
Frensham Great Pond
Thursley
Pitch Place
Wheelerstreet
Witley
Hascombe
Ewhurst Green
Cranleigh
Walliswood
Hannah Peschar
Wattlehurst Farm & Deadwood Town
Clark's Green
Beech
Chawton
Jane Austen's House
West Worldham
Shortheath
Sleaford
Hearn
Churt
Green Cross
Bowlhead Green
Wormley
Hambledon
Loxhill
Beacon Hill
Devil's Punch Bowl
Brook
Sandhills
Arford
Headley Down
Okewood Hill
Rusper
Lindford
Headley
Hindhead
Hindhead Tunnel
Combe Common
North Bridge
Lakers Green
Alfold Crossways
Ellen's Green
Kingsfold
Upper Farringdon
Oakhanger
Whitehill & Bordon
Standford
Passfield
Grayshott
Ludshott Common
Sydenhurst
Chiddingfold
Dunsfold
Lower Farringdon
Selborne
Bramshott
Grayswood
Haslemere
Highstreet Green
Rowhook
Warnham
Alfold
Rudgwick
Blackmoor
Gilbert White's House
Conford
Shottermill
Ramsnest Common
Upper Ifold
Alfold Bars
Tisman's Common
Bucks Green
Warnham Court
Littlehaven
Newton Valence
Empshott
Empshott Green
Liphook
Griggs Green
Old Thorns
Longmoor Camp
Anstead Brook
Haste Hill
Gospel Green
Fisherstreet
Ifold
Loxwood
Slinfold
Broadbridge Heath
Colemore
Greatham
Linchmere
Kingsley Green
Black Down
Plaistow
The Haven
Park Street
Wickhurst Green
Hawkley
Liss Forest
Langley
Hollycombe Steam
Blackdown Hill
Northchapel
Roundstreet Common
Itchingfield
Denne Park
Mannings Heath
Burgates
Liss
East Liss
Rake
Fernhurst
Lurgashall
Hillgrove
Newpound Common
Five Oaks
Christ's Hospital
Two Mile Ash
Southwater Street
High Cross
Ashford Hangers
Oakshott
Steep Marsh
Stoner Hill
Steep
Hill Brow
Milland
Milland Marsh
Woodmansgreen
Dial Green
Lickfold
Bexleyhill
Lurgashall
Ebernoe Common
Kirdford
Barns Green
Billingshurst
Southwater
Redford
Henley
Balls Cross
Wisborough Green
Fishers
Parbrook
Brooks Green
Copsale
Froxfield Green
Bell Hill
Sheet
Petersfield
Borden
Tote Hill
Eastshaw
Rogate
Fyning
SOUTH DOWNS NATIONAL PARK
Strood Green
Coneyhurst Common
Dragons Green
Langrish
Stroud
Ramsdean
Chithurst
Iping
Woolbeding
Lodsworth
River
Upperton
Petworth House
Adversane
Habin
Trotton
Iping & Stedham Commons
Stedham
Easebourne
Petworth
Bedham
Broadford Bridge
Coolham
Whitehall
Shipley
Causeway
Weston
Nyewood
West Harting
Midhurst
Halfway Bridge
Tillington
Byworth
Little Bognor
Codmore Hill
North Heath
Gay Street
Broomer's Corner
West Grinstead
Butser Hill
Nursted
Buriton
Elsted
Minsted
Selham
Egdean
Broomershill
Dial Post
War Down
Queen Elizabeth Country Park
South Harting
East Harting
Didling
Cocking Causeway
West Lavington
South Ambersham
Coultershaw Bridge
Fittleworth
Stopham
Nutbourne
Goose Green
Partridge Green
Treyford
Hoyle
Upper Norwood
Lower Fittleworth
Pulborough
West Chiltington
Harting Beacon
Bepton
Linch Down
Cocking
Heyshott
Duncton
Coates
Lower Horncroft
Marehill
Hardham
Thakeham
Spear Hill
Uppark House & Garden
North Marden
South Downs Way
Graffham
East Lavington
Burton & Chingford Ponds
Coldwaltham
Greatham
Wiggonholt
Abingworth
Ashington
Butser Ancient Farm
Chalton
Barlavington
Roman Villa
Watersfield
Ashurst
Compton
Up Marden
East Marden
Chilgrove
Levin Down
Duncton Hill
Sutton
West Burton
Bignor
Parham
Cootham
Hole Street
Wiston
Blendworth
West Marden
Singleton
West Dean
Bignor Hill
Rackham
Storrington
Heath Common
Rock
Buncton
Finchdean
Forestside
Deanlane End
Stoughton
Charlton
Weald & Downland Open Air Museum
Goodwood
East Dean
Upwaltham
Bury
Amberley
Kithurst Hill
Sullington
Washington
Chanctonbury Ring
Small
Rowland's Castle
Stansted Park
Bow Hill
Walderton
Kingley Vale
The Trundle
Halnaker Hill
Eartham
Nore Hill
Madehurst
Houghton
Amberley Museum
North Stoke
South Stoke
South Downs Way
Harrow Hill
Steyning
North End
Bramber
Lordington
Aldsworth
Funtington
Woodend
West Stoke
East Lavant
Mid Lavant
Goodwood
Waterbeach
Slindon
Offham
Burpham
Wepham
Findon
Botolphs
Staunton
Leigh Park
Westbourne
Woodmancote
East Ashling
West Ashling
Strettington
Westerton
Halnaker
Fontwell
Arundel
Arundel Wetland Centre
Warningcamp
Cissbury Ring
Coombes
Lancing College Chapel
HAVANT
Hambrook
Summersdale
Boxgrove
Crockerhill
Fontwell Park
Binsted
Walberton
Crossbush
Poling Corner
Patching
Clapham
Sompting Abbotts
North Lancing
Brockhampton
Langstone
Hermitage
Southbourne
Broadbridge
Emsworth
Prinsted
Nutbourne
Walton
Roman Palace
Fishbourne
Chichester
Shopwyke
Oving
Westhampnett
Tangmere
Norton
Nyton
Aldingbourne
Eastergate
Westergate
Woodgate
Tortington
North End
Lyminster
Hammerpot
Poling
Angmering
Highdown Hill
Durrington
Salvington
High Salvington
Sompting
Broadwater
Brighton
Lancing
North Hayling
Thorney Island
Chidham
Bosham
Bosham Hoe
Dell Quay
Apuldram
Merston
Colworth
Barnham
Lidsey
Yapton
Burndell
Ford
Wick
Climping
Rustington
Hangleton
Ferring
Kingston
East Preston
Goring-by-Sea
West Tarring
West Worthing
WORTHING
Stoke
Tye
Hayling Island
Fleet
Langstone Harbour
West Thorney
West Itchenor
Shipton Green
Birdham
Donnington
Runcton
Hunston
North Mundham
Elbridge
Shripney
Bilsham
Flansham
Bersted
Ancton
Elmer
Atherington
Littlehampton
South Hayling
West Town
Chichester Harbour
Sidlesham Common
Fisher
South Mundham
Street End
Sidlesham
Rose Green
Felpham
Middleton-on-Sea
Hayling Bay
East Head
West Wittering
Somerley
Highleigh
Nyetimber
Aldwick
BOGNOR REGIS
Almodington
Pagham Harbour
Pagham
East Wittering
Earnley
Bracklesham
Bracklesham Bay
Church Norton
Selsey
SELSEY BILL
SZ
SU
Cherbourg (May-Aug)
Guernsey
Jersey
St-Malo
Caen (Ouistreham)
Le Havre
Bilbao (Jan-Oct)
Santander (Jan-Oct)
A B C D E F G H J K
1 2 3 4 5 6 7 8 9 10 11 12 13 14
19
20
9
0 1 2 3 4 5 miles
0 1 2 3 4 5 6 7 8 kilometres

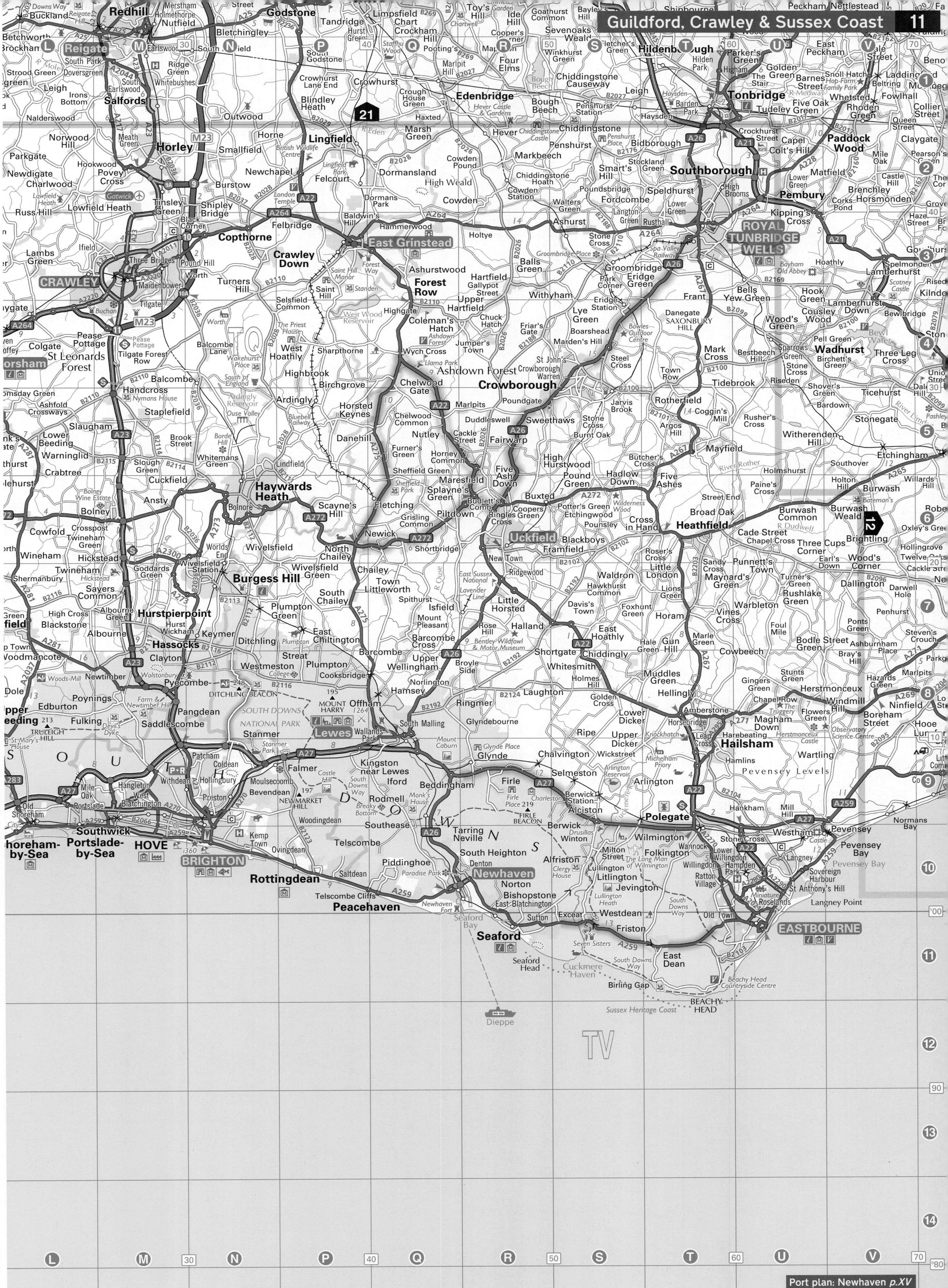

Redhill
Reigate
Godstone
Nutfield
Bletchingley
South Godstone
Limpsfield Chart
Tandridge
Crockham Hill
Sevenoaks Weald
Hildenborough
Tonbridge
Edenbridge
Salfords
Horley
Lingfield
Smallfield
Outwood
Chiddingstone
Penshurst
Bidborough
Southborough
Paddock Wood
Pembury
Dormansland
Felcourt
Newchapel
Burstow
Charlwood
Newdigate
Copthorne
Felbridge
East Grinstead
Crawley Down
CRAWLEY
Three Bridges
Pound Hill
Maidenbower
Tilgate
Turners Hill
ROYAL TUNBRIDGE WELLS
Groombridge
Eridge Green
Frant
Lamberhurst
Wadhurst
Forest Row
Hartfield
Ashurst
Langton Green
Rusthall
Withyham
Ashdown Forest
Crowborough
Rotherfield
Mayfield
Handcross
Balcombe
Staplefield
Cuckfield
Haywards Heath
Lindfield
Ardingly
West Hoathly
Sharpthorne
Horsted Keynes
Danehill
Nutley
Fairwarp
Maresfield
Uckfield
Framfield
Buxted
Heathfield
Burwash
Etchingham
Ticehurst
Bolney
Ansty
Wivelsfield
Burgess Hill
Hurstpierpoint
Hassocks
Keymer
Ditchling
Plumpton
Chailey
Newick
Fletching
Isfield
Barcombe
Ringmer
Halland
East Hoathly
Chiddingly
Hailsham
Herstmonceux
Pevensey
Lewes
Offham
Kingston near Lewes
Falmer
Patcham
Pyecombe
Clayton
Henfield
Poynings
Fulking
Southwick
Portslade-by-Sea
Shoreham-by-Sea
HOVE
BRIGHTON
Rottingdean
Peacehaven
Telscombe
Saltdean
Rodmell
Iford
Southease
Piddinghoe
Newhaven
Seaford
Bishopstone
South Heighton
Tarring Neville
Beddingham
Firle
Selmeston
Alciston
Berwick
Alfriston
Polegate
Wilmington
Folkington
Jevington
Friston
East Dean
Willingdon
EASTBOURNE
Beachy Head
Birling Gap
Cuckmere Haven
Seaford Head
Langney Point
Sovereign Harbour
Westham
Pevensey Bay
Dieppe
SOUTH DOWNS NATIONAL PARK
A22
A23
A26
A27
A259
A264
A275
M23
TQ
TV

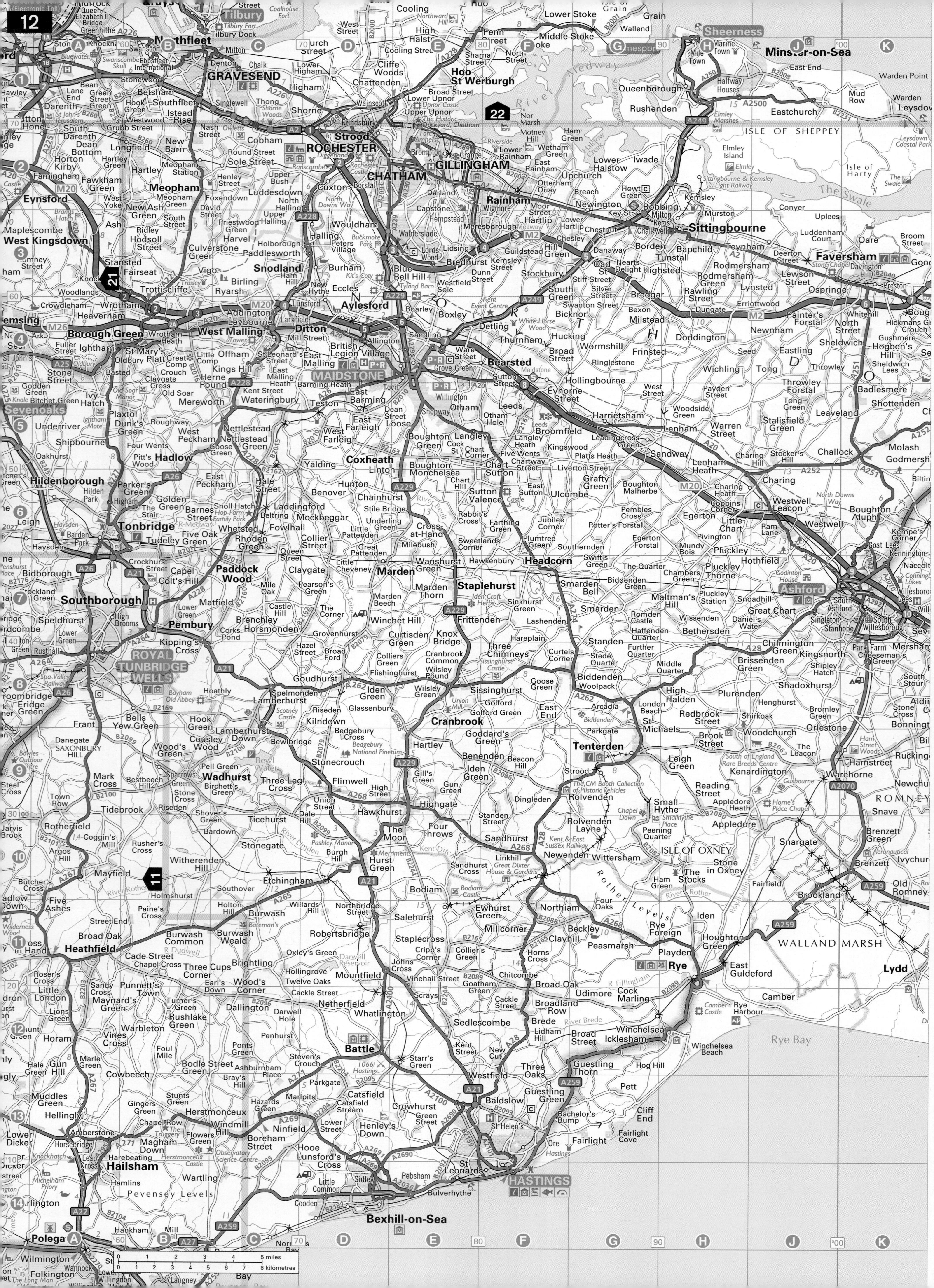

GRAVESEND
ROCHESTER
CHATHAM
GILLINGHAM
Sheerness
Minster-on-Sea
ISLE OF SHEPPEY
Sittingbourne
Faversham
Rainham
Hoo St Werburgh
Strood
Aylesford
Snodland
West Malling
Borough Green
MAIDSTONE
Bearsted
Sevenoaks
Tonbridge
Hildenborough
Southborough
ROYAL TUNBRIDGE WELLS
Pembury
Paddock Wood
Staplehurst
Headcorn
Marden
Coxheath
Ashford
Cranbrook
Tenterden
Hawkhurst
Wadhurst
Heathfield
Battle
Hailsham
Bexhill-on-Sea
HASTINGS
Rye
Lydd
ROMNEY
WALLAND MARSH
ISLE OF OXNEY
Rye Bay
Polegate
Pevensey Levels
5 miles
8 kilometres

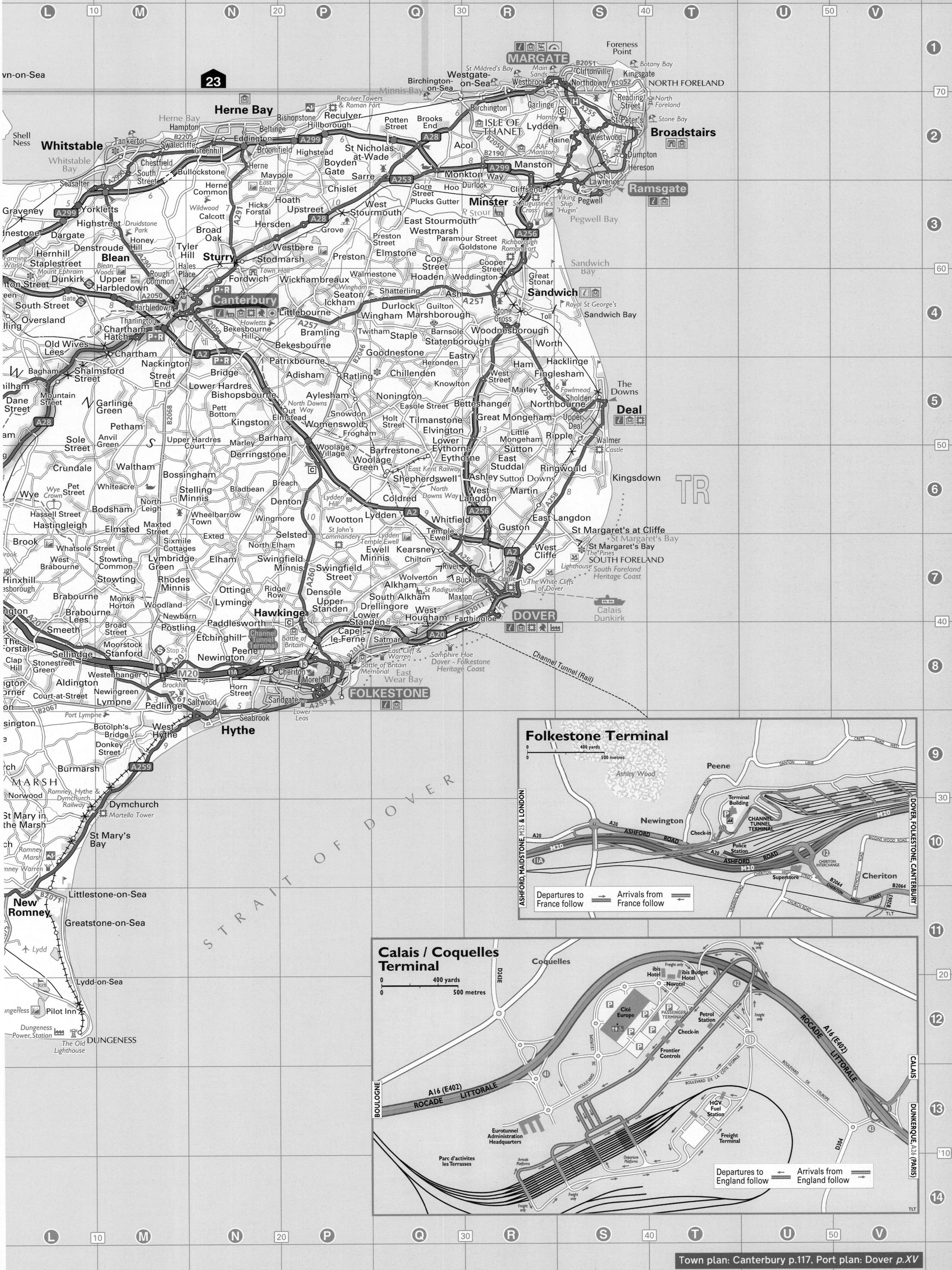

Folkestone Terminal

Departures to France follow →
Arrivals from France follow ←

Calais / Coquelles Terminal

Departures to England follow →
Arrivals from England follow ←

STRAIT OF DOVER

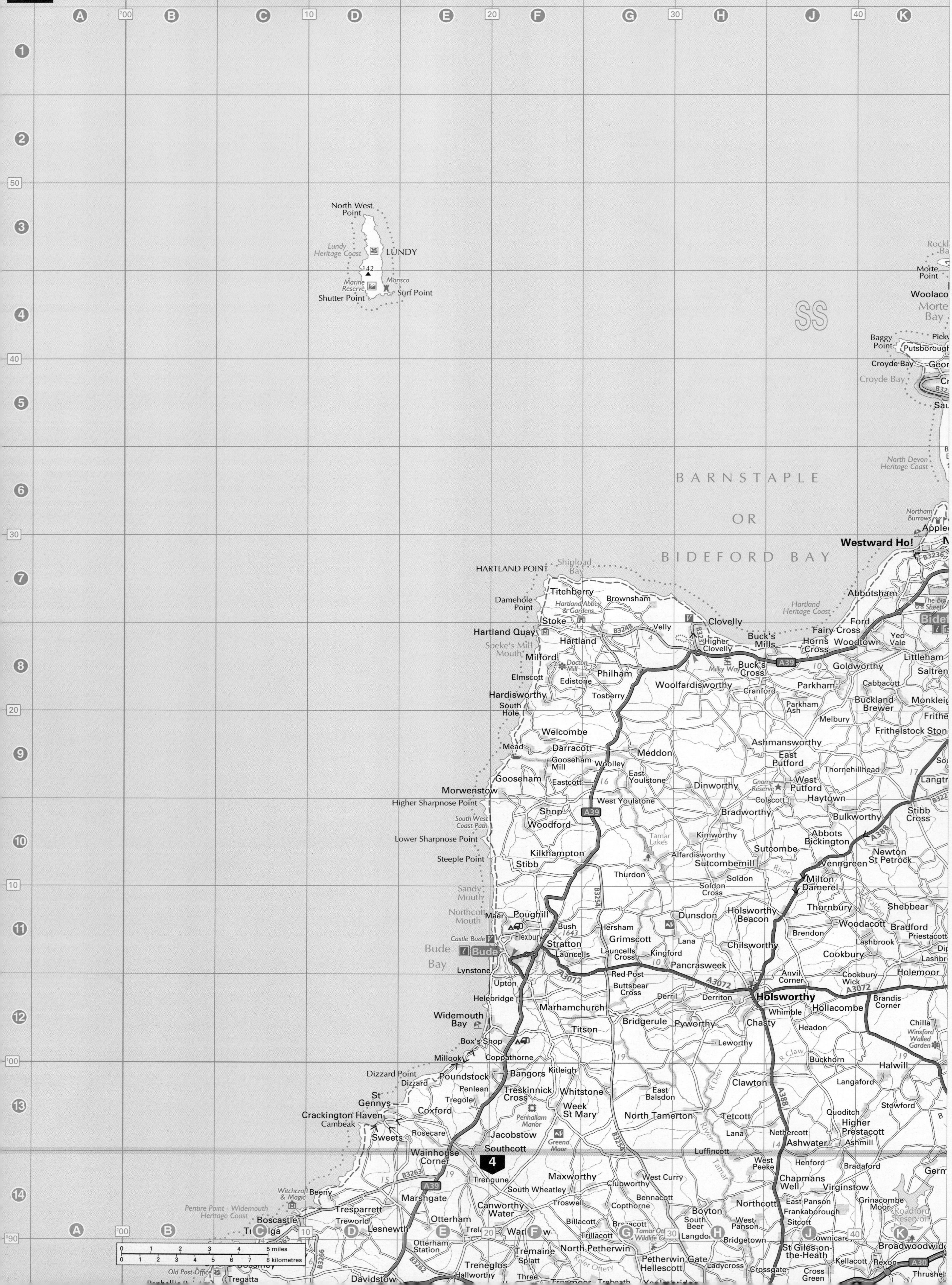
North West Point
Lundy Heritage Coast
LUNDY
Marine Reserve
Marisco
Shutter Point
Surf Point
SS
Morte Point
Morte Bay
Baggy Point
Putsborough
Croyde Bay
North Devon Heritage Coast
BARNSTAPLE
OR
BIDEFORD BAY
Westward Ho!
Northam Burrows
HARTLAND POINT
Shipload Bay
Titchberry
Brownsham
Damehole Point
Hartland Abbey & Gardens
Stoke
Hartland Quay
Hartland
Speke's Mill Mouth
Milford
Velly
Clovelly
Higher Clovelly
Buck's Mills
Hartland Heritage Coast
Abbotsham
Ford
Fairy Cross
Horns Cross
Woodtown
Yeo Vale
Littleham
Buck's Cross
Goldworthy
Milky Way
Elmscott
Edistone
Philham
Woolfardisworthy
Parkham
Cabbacott
Hardisworthy
Tosberry
Cranford
Buckland Brewer
South Hole
Parkham Ash
Melbury
Welcombe
Ashmansworthy
Frithelstock Stone
Mead
Darracott
Meddon
East Putford
Gooseham Mill
Woolley
Thornehillhead
Gooseham
Eastcott
East Youlstone
Dinworthy
Gnome Reserve
West Putford
Morwenstow
West Youlstone
Colscott
Haytown
Higher Sharpnose Point
Shop
Bradworthy
Bulkworthy
Stibb Cross
South West Coast Path
Woodford
Kimworthy
Abbots Bickington
Lower Sharpnose Point
Tamar Lakes
Sutcombe
Newton St Petrock
Kilkhampton
Alfardisworthy
Steeple Point
Stibb
Sutcombemill
Venngreen
Thurdon
Soldon
Milton Damerel
Soldon Cross
Sandy Mouth
Dunsdon
Holsworthy Beacon
Thornbury
Shebbear
Northcott Mouth
Maer
Poughill
Bush
Hersham
Woodacott
Bradford
Brendon
Flexbury
Grimscott
Castle Bude
Stratton
Lana
Chilsworthy
Lashbrook
Bude Bay
Bude
Launcells
Launcells Cross
Kingford
Cookbury
Lynstone
Pancrasweek
Red Post
Anvil Corner
Cookbury Wick
Holemoor
Upton
Buttsbear Cross
Holsworthy
Derril
Derriton
Brandis Corner
Helebridge
Marhamchurch
Whimble
Hollacombe
Widemouth Bay
Titson
Bridgerule
Pyworthy
Chasty
Chilla
Headon
Winsford Walled Garden
Box's Shop
Leworthy
Millook
Coppathorne
Buckhorn
Halwill
Dizzard Point
Dizzard
Poundstock
Bangors
Kitleigh
Clawton
Langaford
Penlean
Treskinnick Cross
Whitstone
East Balsdon
St Gennys
Tregole
Week St Mary
Stowford
Crackington Haven
Cambeak
Coxford
Penhallam Manor
North Tamerton
Tetcott
Quoditch
Higher Prestacott
Rosecare
Sweets
Jacobstow
Greena Moor
Lana
Nethercott
Ashwater
Ashmill
Wainhouse Corner
Southcott
Luffincott
West Peeke
Henford
Bradaford
Trengune
Maxworthy
West Curry
Chapmans Well
Virginstow
Clubworthy
Beeny
Marshgate
South Wheatley
Bennacott
Grinacombe Moor
Roadford Reservoir
Pentire Point - Widemouth Heritage Coast
Witchcraft & Magic
Tresparrett
Canworthy Water
Troswell
Copthorne
Northcott
East Panson
Frankaborough
Boscastle
Treworld
Otterham
Boyton
Sitcott
Lesnewth
Billacott
West Panson
South Beer
Tamar Otter Wildlife Centre
Langdon
Bridgetown
St Giles-on-the-Heath
Broadwoodwidger
Otterham Station
Trillacott
Tremaine
North Petherwin
Treneglos
Splatt
Petherwin Gate
Hellescott
Kellacott
Rexon
Hallworthy
River Ottery
Ladycross
Crossgate
Cross Green
Thrushel
Old Post Office
Tregatta
Davidstow
A39
A388
A3072
A30
B3248
B3237
B3236
B3254
B3263
B3266
B3262
0 1 2 3 4 5 miles
0 1 2 3 4 5 6 7 8 kilometres

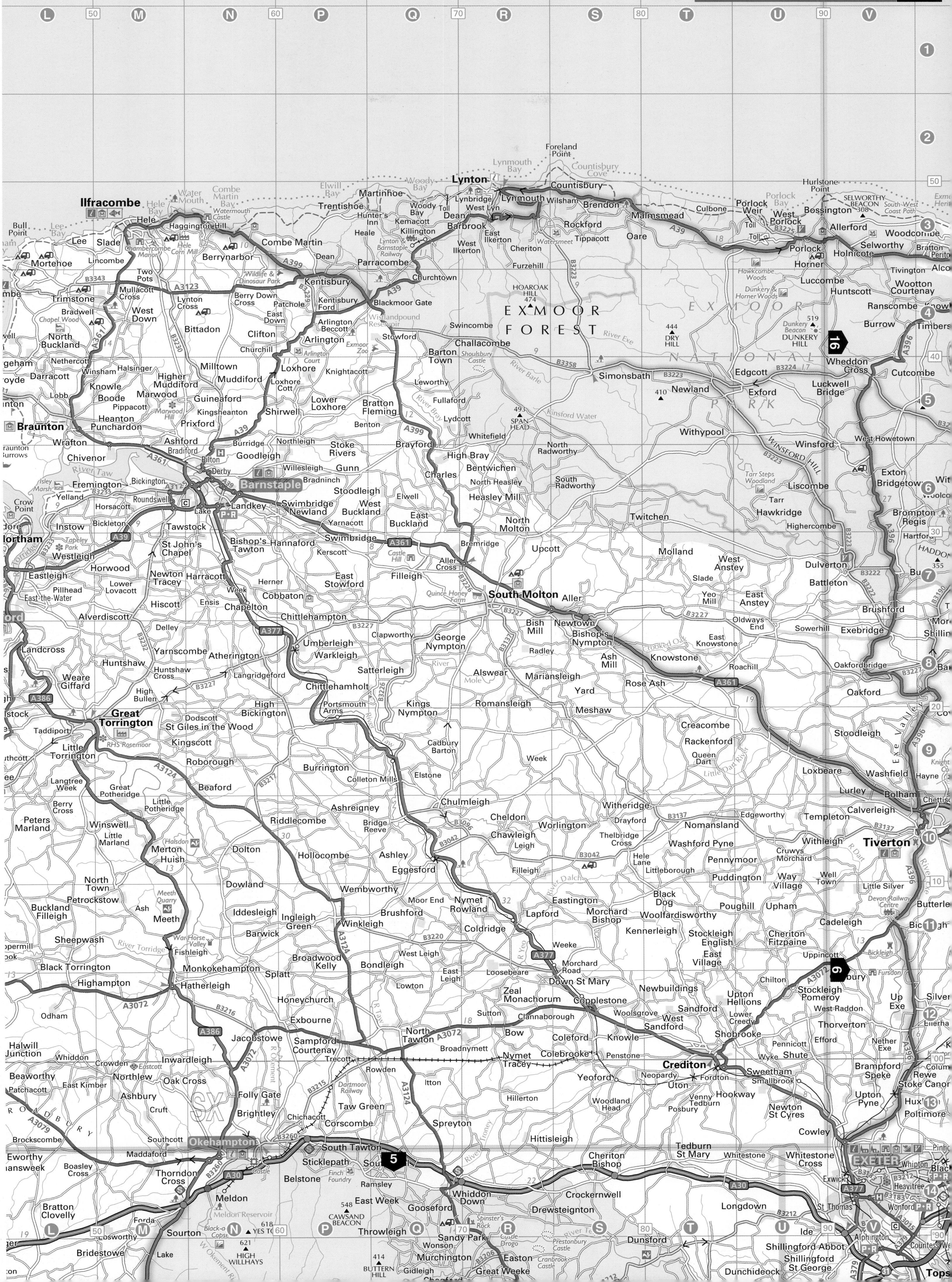

Foreland Point
Lynmouth Bay
Countisbury Cove
Lynton
Lynmouth
Countisbury
Wilsham
Brendon
Malmsmead
Culbone
Porlock Weir
Porlock Bay
West Porlock
Porlock
Hurlstone Point
Bossington
SELWORTHY BEACON 308
Allerford
Woodcombe
Selworthy
Holnicote
Horner
Luccombe
Tivington
Wootton Courtenay
Huntscott
Ranscombe
Burrow
Timbers
Wheddon Cross
Cutcombe
Luckwell Bridge
Dunkery Beacon
DUNKERY HILL
519
Hawkcombe Woods
Dunkery & Horner Woods
EXMOOR
NATIONAL PARK
EXMOOR FOREST
HOAROAK HILL 474
444 DRY HILL
Ilfracombe
Hele
Water Mouth
Combe Martin Bay
Watermouth Castle
Elwill Bay
Woody Bay
Martinhoe
Trentishoe
Hunter's Inn
Heale
Kemacott
Killington
Lynton & Barnstaple Railway
Lynbridge
West Lyn
Toll
Dean
Barbrook
East Ilkerton
West Ilkerton
Cheriton
Watersmeet
Rockford
Tippacott
Oare
Furzehill
Bull Point
Lee Bay
Lee
Slade
Haggington Hill
Chambercombe Manor
Hele Corn Mill
Combe Martin
Berrynarbor
Wildlife & Dinosaur Park
Mortehoe
Lincombe
Two Pots
Parracombe
Churchtown
Kentisbury
Kentisbury Ford
Blackmoor Gate
Trimstone
Mullacott Cross
Lynton Cross
Berry Down Cross
Patchole
East Down
Bradwell
Chapel Wood
West Down
Bittadon
North Buckland
Clifton
Arlington Beccott
Arlington
Arlington Court
Wistlandpound Reservoir
Stowford
Exmoor Zoo
Swincombe
Challacombe
Shoulsbury Castle
Barton Town
Churchill
Nethercott
Darracott
Croyde
Winsham
Halsinger
Milltown
Loxhore
Loxhore Cott
Knightacott
Simonsbath
Edgcott
Exford
Newland
410
Knowle
Higher Muddiford
Muddiford
Lobb
Boode
Marwood
Guineaford
Lower Loxhore
Bratton Fleming
Leworthy
Fullaford
Lydcott
Pippacott
Marwood Hill
Kingsheanton
Shirwell
Benton
Braunton
Heanton Punchardon
Prixford
Wrafton
Braunton Burrows
Ashford
Bradiford
Burridge
Northleigh
Stoke Rivers
Brayford
493 SPAN HEAD
Kinsford Water
Whitefield
North Radworthy
Withypool
Winsford
West Howetown
Winsford Hill
Chivenor
River Taw
Pilton
Derby
Goodleigh
Willesleigh
Gunn
High Bray
Bentwichen
North Heasley
South Radworthy
Isley Marsh
Fremington
Bickington
Barnstaple
Bradninch
Charles
Tarr Steps Woodland
Liscombe
Exton
Bridgetown
Yelland
Roundswell
Lake
Landkey
Swimbridge Newland
Stoodleigh
West Buckland
Elwell
Heasley Mill
Tarr
Hawkridge
Brompton Regis
Crow Point
Horsacott
East Buckland
North Molton
Twitchen
Highercombe
Hartford
Instow
Bickleton
Tawstock
Yarnacott
Swimbridge
Bremridge
Northam
Tapeley Park
St John's Chapel
Bishop's Tawton
Hannaford
Kerscott
Castle Hill
Upcott
Molland
West Anstey
Dulverton
Westleigh
Horwood
Aller Cross
Filleigh
Slade
Battleton
Eastleigh
Newton Tracey
Harracott
Lower Lovacott
Herner
East Stowford
South Molton
Aller
Yeo Mill
East Anstey
Brushford
Pillhead
East-the-Water
Hiscott
Ensis
Week
Cobbaton
Quince Honey Farm
Chapelton
Alverdiscott
Chittlehampton
Bish Mill
Newtown
Bishop's Nympton
Oldways End
Sowerhill
Exebridge
Delley
Clapworthy
George Nympton
East Knowstone
Crooked Oak
Landcross
Yarnscombe
Atherington
Umberleigh
Warkleigh
Radley
Ash Mill
Knowstone
Roachill
Oakfordbridge
Huntshaw
Huntshaw Cross
Langridgeford
Satterleigh
Alswear
River Mole
Mariansleigh
Rose Ash
Weare Giffard
High Bullen
Chittlehamholt
Yard
Oakford
Great Torrington
Dodscott
High Bickington
Portsmouth Arms
Kings Nympton
Romansleigh
Meshaw
Taddiport
St Giles in the Wood
Creacombe
Stoodleigh
Little Torrington
RHS Rosemoor
Kingscott
Cadbury Barton
Rackenford
Queen Dart
Little Dart River
Week
Roborough
Burrington
Elstone
Loxbeare
Washfield
Hayne
Langtree Week
Great Potheridge
Beaford
Colleton Mills
Lurley
Bolham
Berry Cross
Little Potheridge
Chulmleigh
Witheridge
Drayford
Edgeworthy
Templeton
Calverleigh
Peters Marland
Winswell
Little Marland
Ashreigney
Riddlecombe
Bridge Reeve
Cheldon
Chawleigh
Leigh
Worlington
Thelbridge Cross
Nomansland
Withleigh
Tiverton
Halsdon
Merton
Huish
Dolton
Hollocombe
Ashley
Eggesford
Filleigh
Hele Lane
Washford Pyne
Cruwys Morchard
Pennymoor
Littleborough
Puddington
Way Village
Well Town
North Town
Petrockstowe
Dowland
Wembworthy
Moor End
Nymet Rowland
Eastington
Black Dog
Little Silver
Devon Railway Centre
Buckland Filleigh
Ash
Meeth Quarry
Meeth
Iddesleigh
Ingleigh Green
Brushford
Lapford
Morchard Bishop
Woolfardisworthy
Poughill
Upham
Butterleigh
Barwick
Winkleigh
Coldridge
Kennerleigh
Stockleigh English
Cheriton Fitzpaine
Cadeleigh
Bickleigh
Sheepwash
War Horse Valley
River Torridge
Fishleigh
West Leigh
Weeke
East Village
Uppincott
Black Torrington
Monkokehampton
Broadwood Kelly
Bondleigh
Morchard Road
Highampton
Hatherleigh
Splatt
East Leigh
Lowton
Loosebeare
Down St Mary
Chilton
Stockleigh Pomeroy
Fursdon
Up Exe
Silverton
Odham
Honeychurch
Zeal Monachorum
Copplestone
Newbuildings
Upton Hellions
West Raddon
Exbourne
Sutton
Bow
Clannaborough
Woolsgrove
Sandford
West Sandford
Lower Creedy
Thorverton
Ellerhayes
Halwill Junction
Jacobstowe
Sampford Courtenay
North Tawton
Broadnymett
Coleford
Knowle
Shobrooke
Pennicott
Efford
Nether Exe
Whiddon
Crowden
Eastcott
Inwardleigh
River Okement
Trecott
Nymet Tracey
Colebrooke
Penstone
Crediton
Wyke
Shute
Brampford Speke
Beaworthy
Northlew
Oak Cross
Rowden
Itton
Yeoford
Neopardy
Fordton
Uton
Sweetham
Smallbrook
Rewe
Stoke Canon
Patchacott
East Kimber
Ashbury
Folly Gate
Dartmoor Railway
Hillerton
Woodland Head
Venny Tedburn
Posbury
Hookway
Upton Pyne
Huxham
Poltimore
Roadford
Cruft
Brightley
Taw Green
Newton St Cyres
Brockscombe
Southcott
Chichacott
Corscombe
Spreyton
Hittisleigh
Cowley
Okehampton
South Tawton
Tedburn St Mary
Whitestone
Whitestone Cross
Exeter
Pinhoe
Whipton
Eworthy
Hanswek
Maddaford
Boasley Cross
Sticklepath
Cheriton Bishop
Thorndon Cross
Belstone
Finch Foundry
Ramsley
Exwick
Heavitree
Blackhorse
Meldon
Meldon Reservoir
East Week
Whiddon Down
Crockernwell
Longdown
St Thomas
Wonford
Bratton Clovelly
548 CAWSAND BEACON
Gooseford
Drewsteignton
Ide
Alphington
Sourton
Black-a-Tor Copse
618 YES TOR
Throwleigh
Spinster's Rock
Castle Drogo
River Teign
Prestonbury Castle
Dunsford
Shillingford Abbot
Countess Wear
Ebsworthy
621 HIGH WILLHAYS
Wonson
Sandy Park
Bridestowe
Lake
W Okement River
414 BUTTERN HILL
Murchington
Gidleigh
Easton
Cranbrook Castle
Dunchideock
Shillingford St George
Great Weeke
Topsham
A39
A399
A361
A3123
A377
A386
A3124
A3072
A30
A396
A3079
B3343
B3230
B3229
B3358
B3223
B3224
B3225
B3227
B3226
B3217
B3137
B3042
B3216
B3220
B3215
B3260
B3212
B3222
B3221
B3213
B3183
SX
L
M
N
P
Q
R
S
T
U
V
50
60
70
80
90
1
2
3
4
5
6
7
8
9
10
11
12
13
14
16

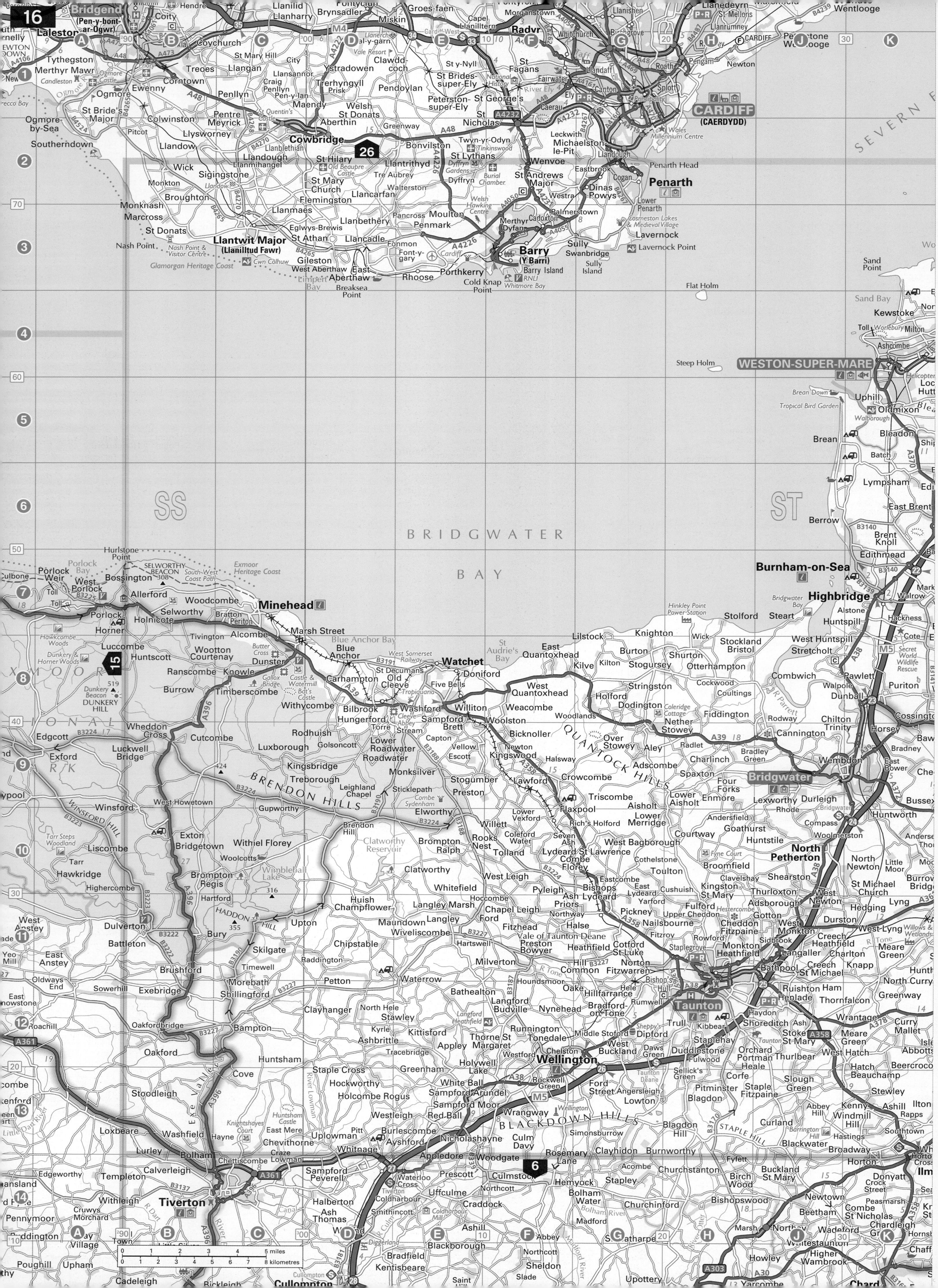
Bridgend
(Pen-y-bont-ar-Ogwr)
Laleston
Coity
Coychurch
Tythegston
Merthyr Mawr
Ewenny
Ogmore
Ogmore-by-Sea
Southerndown
St Bride's Major
Colwinston
Pentre Meyrick
Llysworney
Llandow
Wick
Sigingstone
Monknash
Marcross
St Donats
Nash Point
Llantwit Major
(Llanilltud Fawr)
Glamorgan Heritage Coast
Cowbridge
Llanblethian
St Hilary
Llandough
Flemingston
Llanmaes
Eglwys-Brewis
St Athan
Gileston
West Aberthaw
East Aberthaw
Breaksea Point
Rhoose
Porthkerry
Llancarfan
Llantrithyd
Bonvilston
St Nicholas
St Lythans
Dyffryn
Wenvoe
Barry
(Y Barri)
Barry Island
Cold Knap Point
Whitmore Bay
Sully
Swanbridge
Sully Island
Lavernock
Lavernock Point
Penarth
Penarth Head
Dinas Powys
Llandough
Michaelston-le-Pit
Leckwith
St Fagans
St Georges
Peterston-super-Ely
St Brides-super-Ely
Pendoylan
Welsh St Donats
Ystradowen
Llanharry
Miskin
Groes-faen
Radyr
Whitchurch
Llandaff
Canton
Fairwater
Ely
Caerau
Roath
Splott
CARDIFF
(CAERDYDD)
Wales Millennium Centre
Pengam
Newton
Llanrumney
Peterstone Wentlooge
Wentlooge
SEVERN
Flat Holm
Steep Holm
Sand Point
Sand Bay
Kewstoke
Milton
Ashcombe
WESTON-SUPER-MARE
Uphill
Oldmixon
Bleadon
Brean
Brean Down
Tropical Bird Garden
Lympsham
Berrow
East Brent
Brent Knoll
Edithmead
Burnham-on-Sea
Highbridge
Alstone
Huntspill
West Huntspill
Stretcholt
Pawlett
Puriton
Dunball
Stolford
Steart
Hinkley Point Power Station
Wick
Stockland Bristol
Combwich
Knighton
Lilstock
Burton
Shurton
Otterhampton
Stogursey
Kilve
Kilton
East Quantoxhead
West Quantoxhead
Holford
Dodington
Stringston
Nether Stowey
Over Stowey
Aley
Fiddington
Cannington
Bridgwater
Wembdon
Chilton Trinity
Horsey
Durleigh
North Petherton
Huntworth
Woolmerston
Enmore
Spaxton
Four Forks
Charlinch
Lexworthy
Goathurst
Huntstile
Courtway
Broomfield
Kingston St Mary
Thurloxton
West Newton
Creech Heathfield
Monkton Heathfield
Cheddon Fitzpaine
Bathpool
Creech St Michael
Taunton
Ruishton
Henlade
Thornfalcon
Ham
Stoke St Mary
Orchard Portman
Thurlbear
Staplehay
Trull
Dipford
Corfe
Pitminster
Blagdon
Staple Fitzpaine
Bishops Lydeard
Ash Priors
Lydeard St Lawrence
West Bagborough
Combe Florey
Halse
Cotford St Luke
Norton Fitzwarren
Hillfarrance
Bradford-on-Tone
Oake
Heathfield
Nynehead
Wellington
West Buckland
Rockwell Green
Sampford Arundel
Holywell Lake
Thorne St Margaret
Langford Budville
Runnington
Milverton
Wiveliscombe
Fitzhead
Chipstable
Waterrow
Petton
Clayhanger
Stawley
Kittisford
Ashbrittle
Appley
Greenham
Huntsham
Bampton
Morebath
Shillingford
Skilgate
Upton
Huish Champflower
Clatworthy
Clatworthy Reservoir
Brompton Ralph
Tolland
Elworthy
Monksilver
Stogumber
Preston
Sampford Brett
Williton
Doniford
Watchet
Washford
Old Cleeve
Carhampton
Blue Anchor
Blue Anchor Bay
Dunster
Minehead
Alcombe
Selworthy
Porlock
Porlock Weir
Porlock Bay
West Porlock
Bossington
Allerford
Hurlstone Point
Exmoor Heritage Coast
Luccombe
Wootton Courtenay
Timberscombe
Cutcombe
Luxborough
Wheddon Cross
Exford
Winsford
Dulverton
Brushford
Exebridge
Oakford
Tiverton
Bolham
Washfield
Cove
Stoodleigh
Loxbeare
Calverleigh
Templeton
Chettiscombe
Halberton
Sampford Peverell
Uplowman
Burlescombe
Holcombe Rogus
Hockworthy
Westleigh
Uffculme
Culmstock
Hemyock
Clayhidon
Churchinford
Churchstanton
Buckland St Mary
Bishopswood
Cullompton
Bradninch
Kentisbeare
Blackborough
Sheldon
BRIDGWATER BAY
BRENDON HILLS
QUANTOCK HILLS
BLACKDOWN HILLS
HADDON HILL
EXMOOR NATIONAL PARK
SS
ST

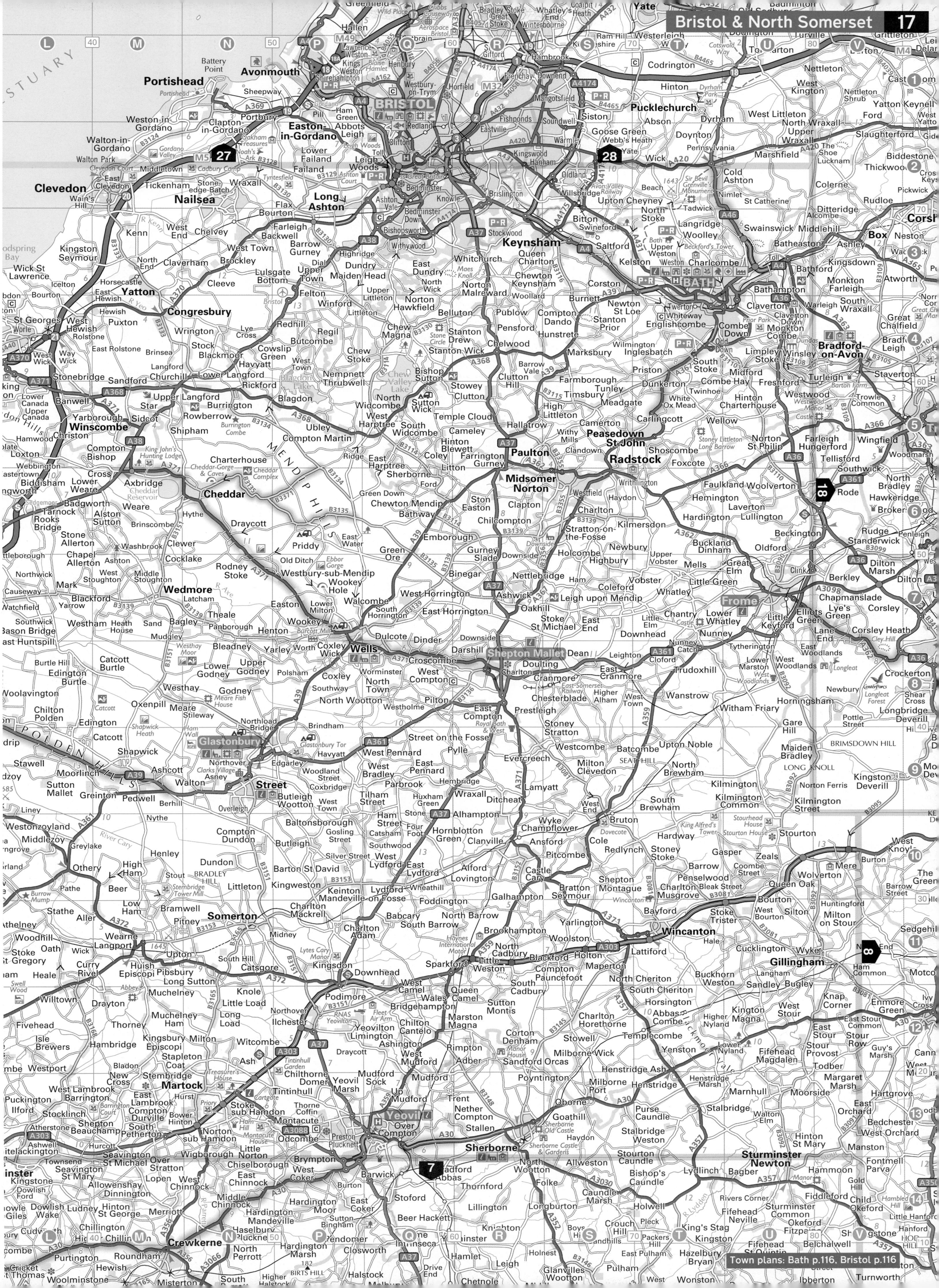
Portishead
Avonmouth
Clevedon
Nailsea
Long Ashton
BRISTOL
Keynsham
Pucklechurch
Yatton
Congresbury
Winscombe
Cheddar
Wedmore
MENDIP HILLS
Wells
Glastonbury
Street
Shepton Mallet
Midsomer Norton
Radstock
Paulton
Peasedown St John
BATH
Bradford-on-Avon
Frome
Somerton
Castle Cary
Wincanton
Gillingham
Yeovil
Sherborne
Martock
Crewkerne
Sturminster Newton
Ilchester
Langport
POLDEN HILLS

Town plans: Bath p.116, Bristol p.116

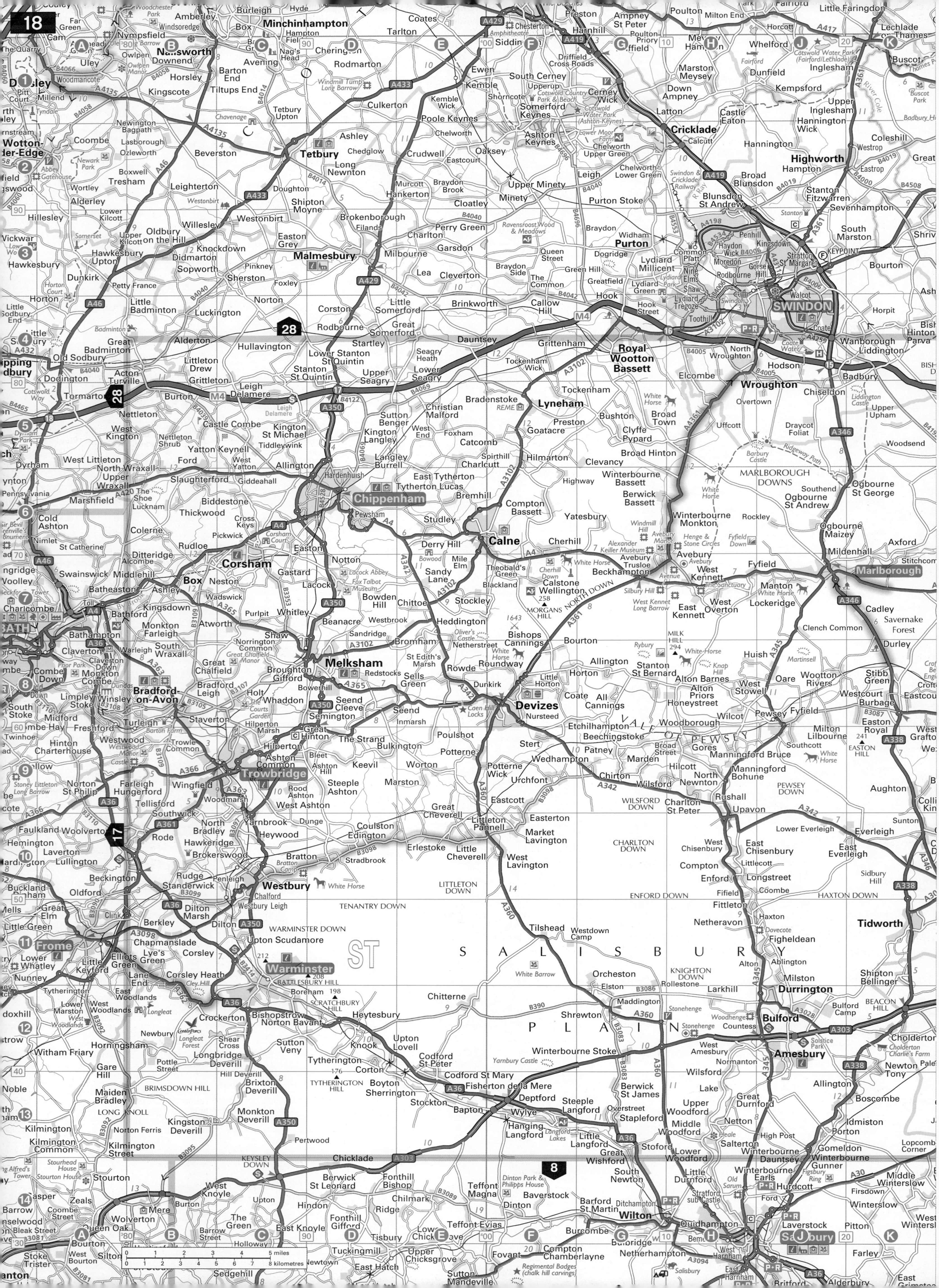
Minchinhampton
Nailsworth
Amberley
Burleigh
Box
Avening
Cherington
Rodmarton
Tarlton
Coates
Siddington
Preston
Ampney St Peter
Poulton
Fairford
Little Faringdon
Lechlade on Thames
Nympsfield
Uley
Owlpen
Dursley
Horsley
Barton End
Tiltups End
Kingscote
Ewen
Kemble
South Cerney
Cerney Wick
Somerford Keynes
Marston Meysey
Meysey Hampton
Whelford
Dunfield
Down Ampney
Kempsford
Inglesham
Buscot
Culkerton
Tetbury Upton
Tetbury
Ashley
Long Newton
Poole Keynes
Chelworth
Ashton Keynes
Oaksey
Crudwell
Eastcourt
Latton
Cricklade
Calcutt
Castle Eaton
Hannington
Hannington Wick
Highworth
Coleshill
Wotton-under-Edge
Coombe
Newington Bagpath
Lasborough
Ozleworth
Beverston
Boxwell
Tresham
Leighterton
Doughton
Shipton Moyne
Hankerton
Braydon Brook
Cloatley
Upper Minety
Minety
Leigh
Chelworth Lower Green
Purton Stoke
Broad Blunsdon
Blunsdon St Andrew
Hampton
Stanton Fitzwarren
Sevenhampton
Alderley
Hillesley
Lower Kilcott
Oldbury on the Hill
Willesley
Westonbirt
Brokenborough
Perry Green
Charlton
Braydon
Widham
Purton
South Marston
Hawkesbury
Hawkesbury Upton
Didmarton
Knockdown
Sopworth
Easton Grey
Malmesbury
Milbourne
Garsdon
Lea
Cleverton
Queen Street
Dogridge
Lydiard Millicent
Common Platt
Penhill
Haydon Wick
Kingsdown
Stratton St Margaret
Bourton
Dunkirk
Petty France
Sherston
Pinkney
Foxley
Braydon Side
The Common
Green Hill
Greatfield
Lydiard Green
Rodbourne
Gorse Hill
Horton
Little Badminton
Luckington
Norton
Corston
Little Somerford
Brinkworth
Callow Hill
Hook
Hook Street
Lydiard Tregoze
Toothill
SWINDON
Walcot
Coate
Horpit
Little Sodbury
Great Badminton
Alderton
Hullavington
Rodbourne
Great Somerford
Startley
Dauntsey
Grittenham
Royal Wootton Bassett
Wroughton
Wanborough
Liddington
Old Sodbury
Chipping Sodbury
Littleton Drew
Lower Stanton St Quintin
Stanton St Quintin
Seagry Heath
Upper Seagry
Lower Seagry
Tockenham Wick
Elcombe
Hodson
Badbury
Chiseldon
Acton Turville
Dodington
Tormarton
Burton
Grittleton
Leigh Delamere
Tockenham
Lyneham
Bradenstoke
Christian Malford
Sutton Benger
Nettleton
Castle Combe
West Kington
Nettleton Shrub
Kington St Michael
Kington Langley
Tiddleywink
West End
Foxham
Preston
Bushton
Broad Town
Goatacre
Clyffe Pypard
Upper Upham
Overtown
Uffcott
Draycot Foliat
Catcomb
Dyrham
West Littleton
North Wraxall
Yatton Keynell
West Yatton
Ford
Allington
Langley Burrell
Spirthill
Charlcutt
Hilmarton
Clevancy
Broad Hinton
Woodsend
Upper Wraxall
Slaughterford
Giddeahall
East Tytherton
Tytherton Lucas
Highway
Winterbourne Bassett
MARLBOROUGH DOWNS
Marshfield
The Shoe
Biddestone
Chippenham
Bremhill
Berwick Bassett
Southend
Ogbourne St George
Ogbourne St Andrew
Cold Ashton
Thickwood
Lucknam
Compton Bassett
Yatesbury
Winterbourne Monkton
Rockley
Pewsham
Colerne
Cross Keys
Pickwick
Studley
Ogbourne Maizey
St Catherine
Rudloe
Easton
Derry Hill
Calne
Cherhill
Avebury
Avebury Trusloe
Mildenhall
Axford
Ditteridge
Corsham
Notton
Bowood
Mile Elm
Fyfield
Marlborough
Swainswick
Middlehill
Box
Neston
Gastard
Lacock
Sandy Lane
Theobald's Green
Blackland
Calstone Wellington
Beckhampton
West Kennett
Manton
Cadley
Batheaston
Ashley
Wadswick
Bowden Hill
Chittoe
Stockley
East Kennett
West Overton
Lockeridge
Savernake Forest
Charlcombe
Bathford
Kingsdown
Purlpit
Whitley
Beanacre
Westbrook
Heddington
Bishops Cannings
Bourton
Clench Common
BATH
Bathampton
Monkton Farleigh
Atworth
Shaw
Sandridge
Bromham
Claverton
South Wraxall
Norrington Common
Melksham
St Edith's Marsh
Rowde
Roundway
Allington
Stanton St Bernard
Huish
Durley
Great Chalfield
Broughton Gifford
Redstocks
Sells Green
Dunkirk
Horton
Alton Barnes
Oare
Wootton Rivers
Stibb Green
Combe Down
Monkton Combe
Bradford-on-Avon
Bradford Leigh
Holt
Whaddon
Bowerhill
Seend Cleeve
Seend
Devizes
Nurstead
Coate
All Cannings
Alton Priors
Honeystreet
West Stowell
Westcourt
Burbage
Limpley Stoke
Winsley
South Stoke
Midford
Freshford
Turleigh
Staverton
Semington
Inmarsh
Poulshot
Etchilhampton
Beechingstoke
VALE OF PEWSEY
Woodborough
Wilcot
Pewsey
Fyfield
Easton Royal
Hinton Charterhouse
Westwood
Trowle Common
Hilperton Marsh
Great Hinton
The Strand
Bulkington
Potterne
Stert
Wedhampton
Patney
Broad Street
Marden
Gores
Manningford Bruce
Milton Lilbourne
Wingfield
Trowbridge
Hilperton
Ashton Common
Steeple Ashton
Keevil
Worton
Marston
Potterne Wick
Urchfont
Chirton
Wilsford
Hilcott
North Newton
Manningford Bohune
Norton St Philip
Farleigh Hungerford
Tellisford
Southwick
Rood Ashton
West Ashton
Eastcott
WILSFORD DOWN
Charlton St Peter
Rushall
Upavon
PEWSEY DOWN
Aughton
Faulkland
Woolverton
North Bradley
Rode
Hawkeridge
Yarnbrook
Heywood
Dunge
Great Cheverell
Littleton Pannell
Easterton
Market Lavington
CHARLTON DOWN
Lower Everleigh
Everleigh
Hemington
Laverton
Lullington
Brokerswood
Coulston
Edington
Erlestoke
Little Cheverell
West Lavington
West Chisenbury
East Chisenbury
East Everleigh
Beckington
Rudge
Standerwick
Penleigh
Bratton
Stradbrook
Westbury
Chalford
Westbury Leigh
LITTLETON DOWN
Compton
Enford
Littlecott
Longstreet
Coombe
ENFORD DOWN
Fifield
HAXTON DOWN
Sidbury Hill
Buckland Dinham
Oldford
Great Elm
Dilton Marsh
Berkley
Dilton
TENANTRY DOWN
Fittleton
Haxton
Netheravon
Tidworth
Frome
Chapmanslade
WARMINSTER DOWN
Upton Scudamore
Tilshead
Westdown Camp
Figheldean
Lower Whatley
Little Keyford
Elliots Green
Lye's Green
Corsley
Corsley Heath
Warminster
SALISBURY PLAIN
Orcheston
Elston
KNIGHTON DOWN
Rollestone
Larkhill
Ablington
Alton
Milston
Durrington
Shipton Bellinger
Nunney
Tytherington
East Woodlands
Lane End
BATTLESBURY HILL
Boreham
SCRATCHBURY HILL
Chitterne
Maddington
Stonehenge
Bulford
Bulford Camp
BEACON HILL
Lower Marston
West Woodlands
Longleat
Crockerton
Bishopstrow
Norton Bavant
Heytesbury
Shrewton
Woodhenge
Countess
Cholderton
Witham Friary
Newbury
Horningsham
Shear Cross
Sutton Veny
Upton Lovell
Knook
Tytherington
Codford St Peter
Winterbourne Stoke
West Amesbury
Amesbury
Normanton
Newton Tony
Gare Hill
Pottle Street
Longbridge Deverill
Hill Deverill
Brixton Deverill
Corton
Boyton
Sherrington
Codford St Mary
Fisherton de la Mere
Deptford
Wylye
Steeple Langford
Berwick St James
Wilsford
Lake
Great Durnford
Upper Woodford
Allington
Boscombe
Noble
Maiden Bradley
BRIMSDOWN HILL
LONG KNOLL
Monkton Deverill
Kingston Deverill
Stockton
Bapton
Hanging Langford
Overstreet
Stapleford
Middle Woodford
Netton
Idmiston
Porton
Kilmington
Norton Ferris
Kilmington Common
Kilmington Street
Pertwood
Little Langford
Great Wishford
Stoford
Lower Woodford
Salterton
High Post
Winterbourne Dauntsey
Gomeldon
Winterbourne Gunner
Lopcombe Corner
KEYSLEY DOWN
Chicklade
Stourhead House
Stourton
West Knoyle
Berwick St Leonard
Fonthill Bishop
Teffont Magna
Baverstock
Dinton
South Newton
Little Durnford
Stratford sub Castle
Old Sarum
Winterbourne Earls
Hurdcott
Middle Winterslow
Firsdown
Winterslow
Zeals
Mere
Burton
Hindon
Ridge
Chilmark
Teffont Evias
Barford St Martin
Ditchampton
Wilton
Quidhampton
Laverstock
Pitton
West Winterslow
Wolverton
Queen Oak
Barrow Street
The Green
Holloway
East Knoyle
Fonthill Gifford
Tisbury
Lower Chicksgrove
Burcombe
Bulbridge
Netherhampton
Bemerton
West Harnham
Salisbury
Farley
Bourton
West Bourton
Silton
Stoke Trister
Tuckingmill
Upper Chicksgrove
Fovant
Compton Chamberlayne
East Hatch
Sedgehill
Sutton Mandeville
East Harnham
Britford
Alderbury
East Grimstead
miles
kilometres

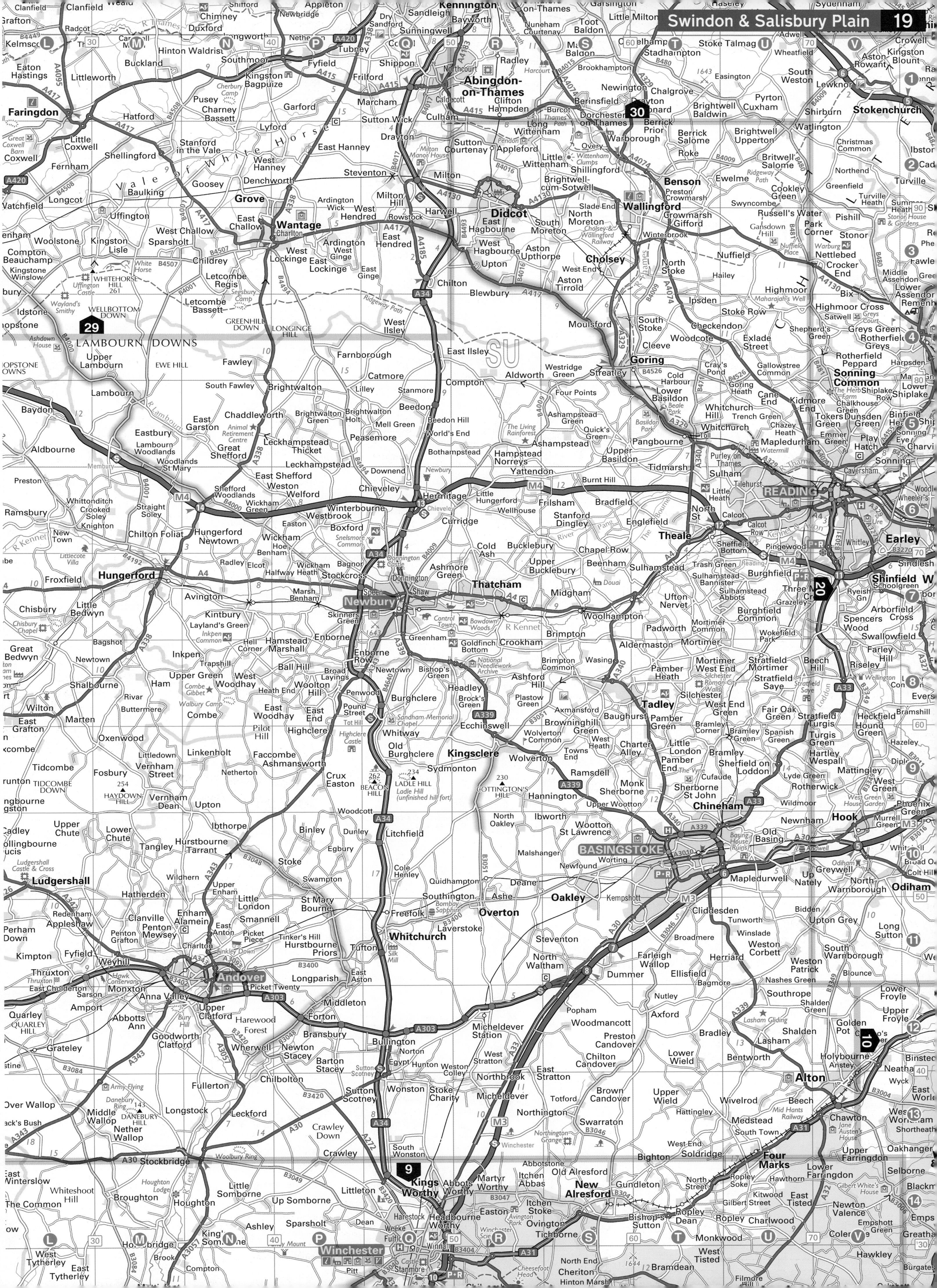
Faringdon
Abingdon-on-Thames
Wantage
Grove
Didcot
Wallingford
Benson
Cholsey
Goring
Streatley
Pangbourne
READING
Earley
Theale
Newbury
Hungerford
Thatcham
Kingsclere
Tadley
BASINGSTOKE
Oakley
Overton
Whitchurch
Andover
Alton
New Alresford
Kings Worthy
Winchester
Stockbridge
Ludgershall
Lambourn
LAMBOURN DOWNS
Vale of White Horse
Hook
Odiham
Stokenchurch
Chineham
Four Marks
Sonning Common
Shinfield
Upper Lambourn
Kintbury
Hermitage
Chieveley
Compton
Woolhampton
Burghclere
Wolverton
Sherborne St John
Micheldever
Sutton Scotney
Longparish
Harwell
Milton
Steventon
Upton
Blewbury
Aldworth
Bradfield
Mortimer
Upper Clatford
Anna Valley
Middle Wallop
Broughton
Houghton
Abbotts Ann
Wherwell
Chilbolton
Barton Stacey
Bullington
Dummer
Preston Candover
Ropley
Medstead
Chawton
Upper Froyle
Lower Froyle
Greatham
Empshott
Itchen Abbas
Ovington
Tichborne
Cheriton
Bramdean
Hinton Marsh
Twyford
Compton
Pitt
Dean
Sparsholt
Up Somborne
Little Somborne
Crawley
King's Somborne
West Tytherley
East Tytherley
The Common
Kimpton
Thruxton
Fyfield
Weyhill
Monxton
Amport
Quarley
Grateley
Over Wallop
Nether Wallop
Longstock
Leckford
Fullerton
Wonston
Stoke Charity
Northington
Swarraton
Brown Candover
Chilton Candover
Upper Wield
Lower Wield
Bentworth
Lasham
Shalden
Herriard
Ellisfield
Farleigh Wallop
Cliddesden
Upton Grey
Mapledurwell
Greywell
North Warnborough
South Warnborough
Long Sutton
Bentley
Holybourne
Binsted
Neatham
East Worldham
West Worldham
Selborne
Newton Valence
Colemore
Hawkley
West Tisted
East Tisted
Bishop's Sutton
Gundleton
Old Alresford
Abbotstone
Itchen Stoke
Bighton
Soldridge
Wield
Four Marks
Lower Farringdon
Upper Farringdon
M3
M4
A34
A303
A339
A343
A338
A4
A417
A420
A329
A30
A31
A33
A340
A4130
A415
20
29
30
9
10

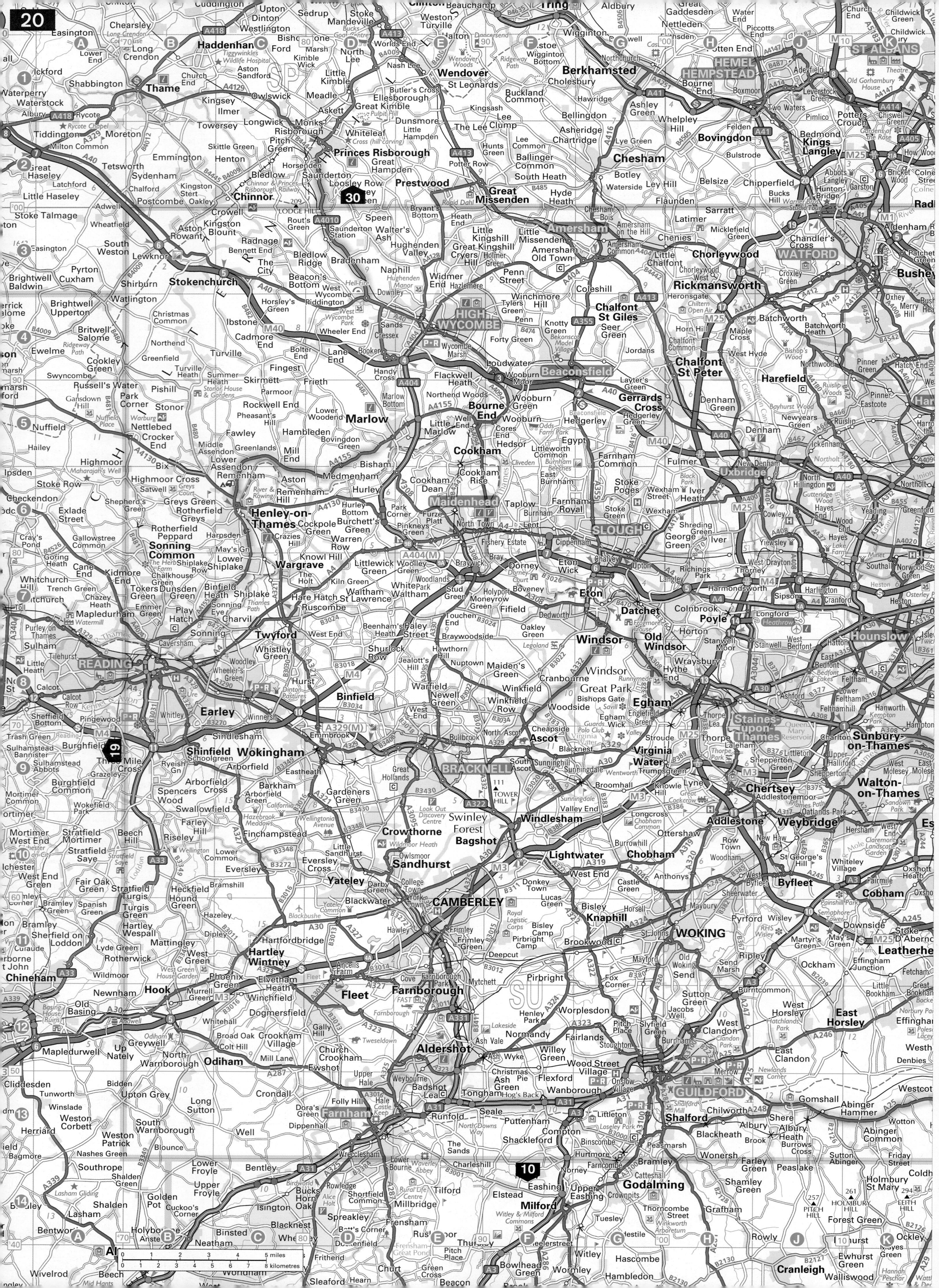
Haddenhan
Thame
Wendover
Berkhamsted
HEMEL HEMPSTEAD
ST ALBANS
Princes Risborough
Chinnor
Prestwood
Great Missenden
Chesham
Amersham
Bovingdon
Kings Langley
WATFORD
Chorleywood
Rickmansworth
Stokenchurch
HIGH WYCOMBE
Chalfont St Giles
Chalfont St Peter
Beaconsfield
Harefield
Marlow
Bourne End
Gerrards Cross
Cookham
Uxbridge
Maidenhead
Henley-on-Thames
SLOUGH
Sonning Common
Wargrave
Eton
Datchet
Twyford
Windsor
Old Windsor
READING
Binfield
Egham
Earley
Ascot
Staines-upon-Thames
Sunbury-on-Thames
Shinfield
Wokingham
Virginia Water
BRACKNELL
Chertsey
Walton-on-Thames
Windlesham
Addlestone
Weybridge
Crowthorne
Bagshot
Sandhurst
Lightwater
Chobham
Yateley
CAMBERLEY
Byfleet
Cobham
Knaphill
WOKING
Hartley Wintney
Chineham
Hook
Fleet
Farnborough
Aldershot
Odiham
GUILDFORD
Farnham
Shalford
Godalming
Milford
Cranleigh
Leatherhead
East Horsley
0 1 2 3 4 5 miles
0 1 2 3 4 5 6 7 8 kilometres

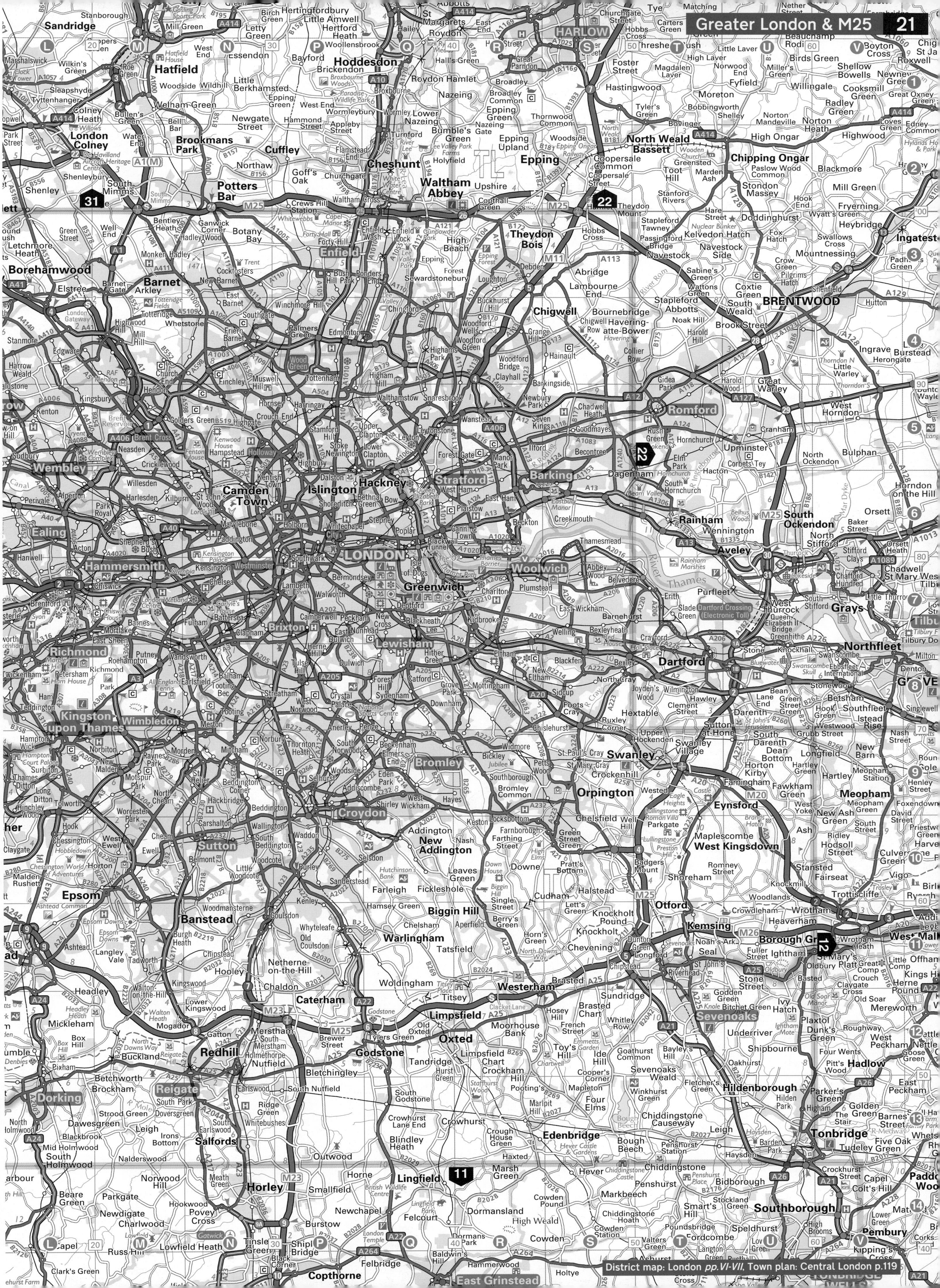

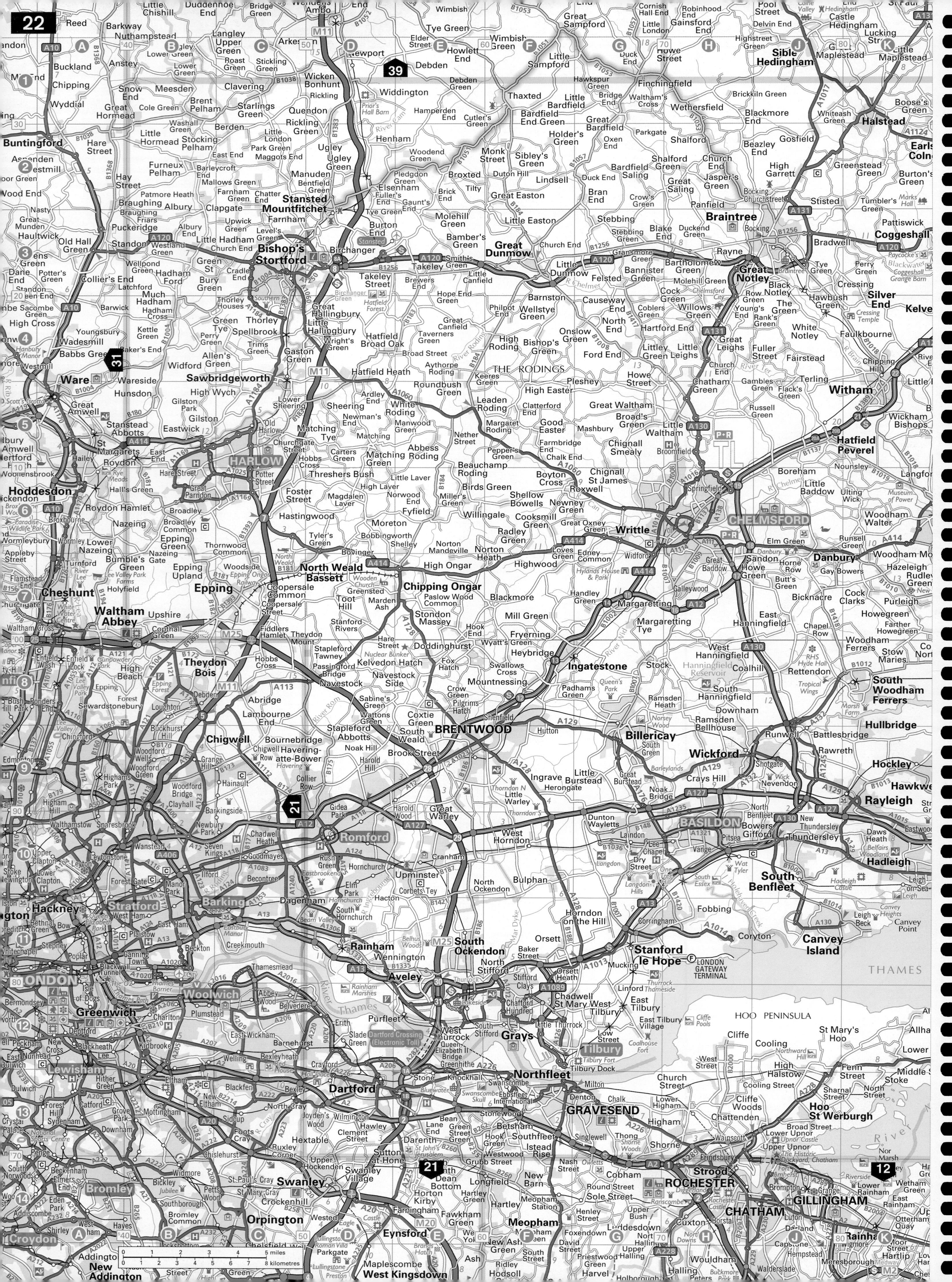
Bishop's Stortford
Stansted Mountfitchet
Great Dunmow
Braintree
Coggeshall
Halstead
Sible Hedingham
Thaxted
Saffron Walden
Buntingford
Ware
Sawbridgeworth
Harlow
Hoddesdon
Cheshunt
Waltham Abbey
Epping
North Weald Bassett
Chipping Ongar
Witham
Great Notley
Hatfield Peverel
Chelmsford
Writtle
Ingatestone
Brentwood
Billericay
Wickford
Basildon
Rayleigh
South Woodham Ferrers
Danbury
Chigwell
Theydon Bois
Romford
Upminster
Dagenham
Barking
Hackney
Stratford
London
Greenwich
Woolwich
Lewisham
Bromley
Croydon
Rainham
Aveley
South Ockendon
Grays
Tilbury
Stanford le Hope
Canvey Island
South Benfleet
Hadleigh
Dartford
Swanley
Orpington
Northfleet
Gravesend
Strood
Rochester
Chatham
Gillingham
Hoo St Werburgh
HOO PENINSULA
THAMES
THE RODINGS
Dartford Crossing (Electronic Toll)
LONDON GATEWAY TERMINAL
39
31
21
12

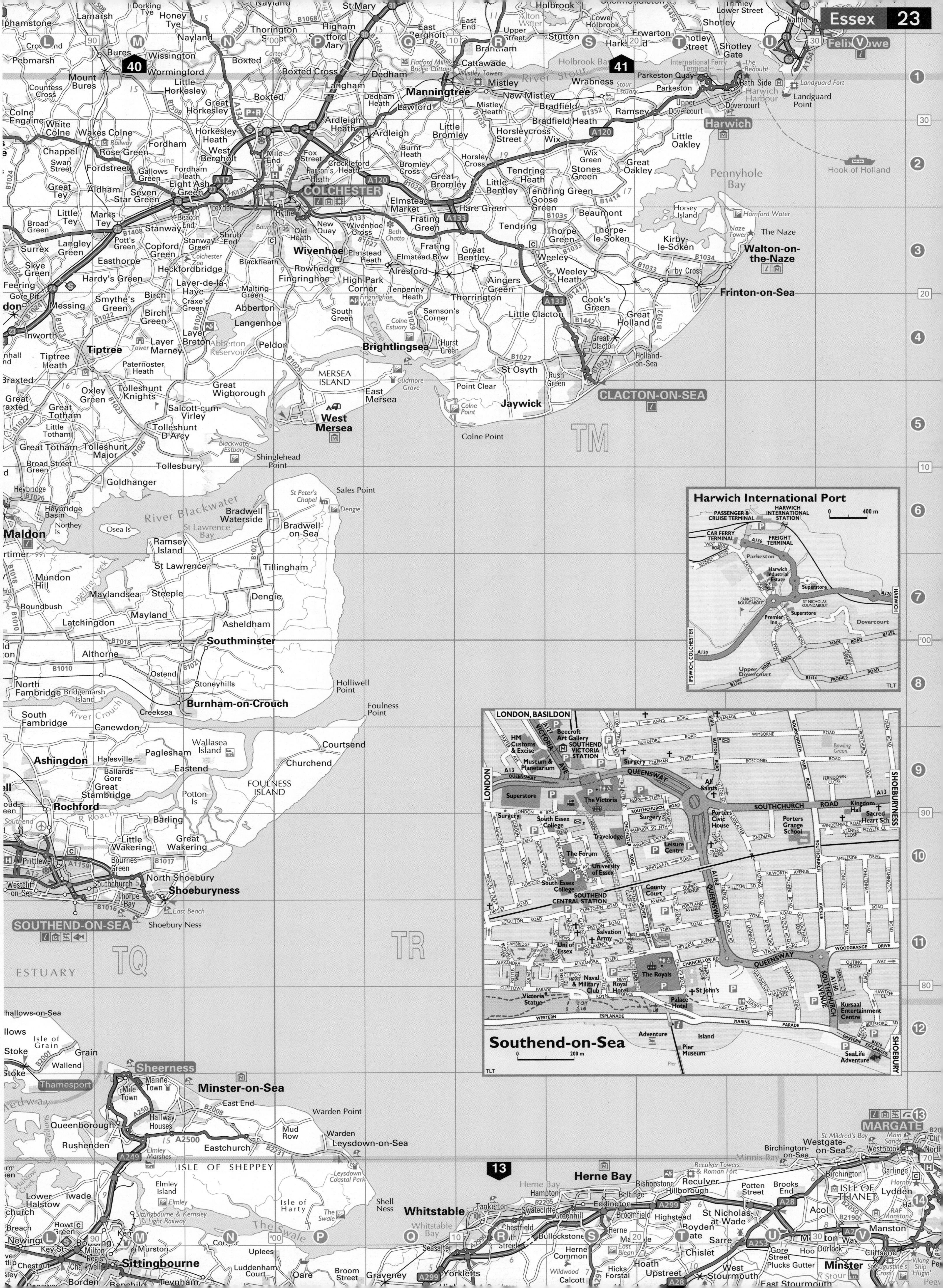
Colchester
Wivenhoe
Brightlingsea
West Mersea
Mersea Island
Tiptree
Manningtree
Mistley
Harwich
Dovercourt
Walton-on-the-Naze
Frinton-on-Sea
Clacton-on-Sea
Jaywick
St Osyth
Maldon
Burnham-on-Crouch
Southminster
Rochford
Shoeburyness
Southend-on-Sea
Sheerness
Minster-on-Sea
Sittingbourne
Whitstable
Herne Bay
Margate
Isle of Sheppey
Foulness Island
River Blackwater
River Stour
Hook of Holland
TM
TQ
TR
Harwich International Port
Southend-on-Sea
Estuary

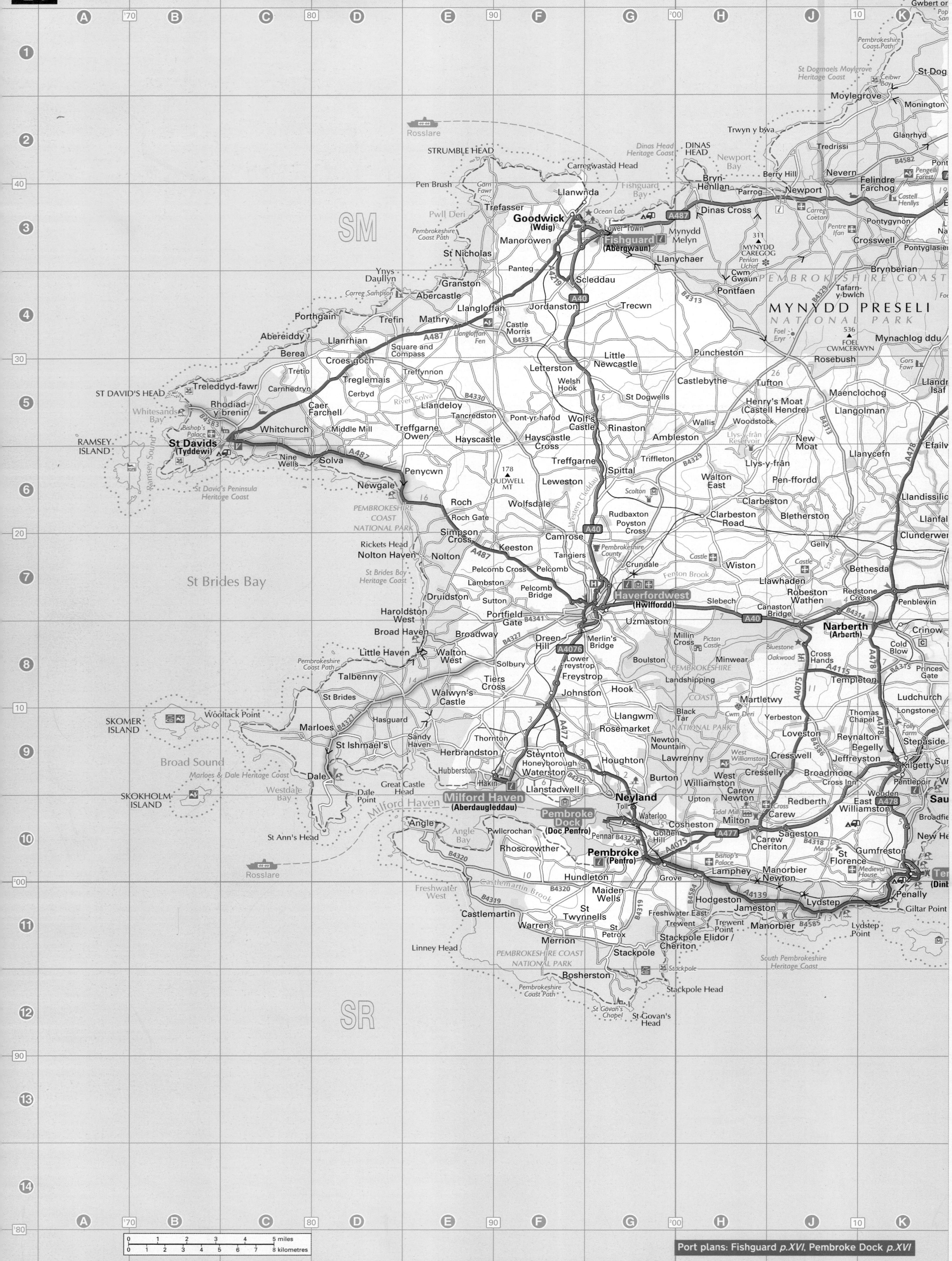
SM
SR
St Brides Bay
Broad Sound
Milford Haven
Rosslare
STRUMBLE HEAD
Carregwastad Head
Pen Brush
Llanwnda
Trefasser
Goodwick
(Wdig)
Fishguard
(Abergwaun)
Fishguard Bay
Dinas Head Heritage Coast
DINAS HEAD
Newport Bay
Trwyn y bwa
Bryn-Henllan
Dinas Cross
Newport
Berry Hill
Nevern
Felindre Farchog
Moylegrove
Monington
St Dogmaels Moylgrove Heritage Coast
Pembrokeshire Coast Path
Gwbert on Sea
Glanrhyd
Tredrissi
Pontygynon
Crosswell
Pontyglasier
Brynberian
Mynydd Melyn
Llanychaer
MYNYDD CAREGOG
Cwm Gwaun
Pontfaen
PEMBROKESHIRE COAST
MYNYDD PRESELI
NATIONAL PARK
Tafarn-y-bwlch
FOEL CWMCERWYN
Mynachlog ddu
Rosebush
Puncheston
Pwll Deri
St Nicholas
Manorowen
Panteg
Scleddau
Ynys Daullyn
Granston
Abercastle
Carreg Sampson
Porthgain
Trefin
Mathry
Llangloffan
Jordanston
Castle Morris
Trecwn
Abereiddy
Llanrhian
Berea
Square and Compass
Croes-goch
Tretio
Treglemais
Treffynnon
Letterston
Little Newcastle
Castlebythe
Tufton
Maenclochog
Llangolman
ST DAVID'S HEAD
Treleddyd-fawr
Carnhedryn
Cerbyd
Welsh Hook
St Dogwells
Henry's Moat (Castell Hendre)
Whitesands Bay
Rhodiad-y-brenin
Caer Farchell
Llandeloy
Tancredston
Pont-yr-hafod
Wolf's Castle
Rinaston
Ambleston
Wallis
Woodstock
Llys-y-frân Reservoir
New Moat
Llanycefn
RAMSEY ISLAND
Ramsey Sound
St Davids
(Tyddewi)
Whitchurch
Middle Mill
Treffgarne Owen
Hayscastle
Hayscastle Cross
Treffgarne
Spittal
Triffleton
Llys-y-frân
Nine Wells
Solva
Penycwn
DUDWELL MT
Leweston
Walton East
Pen-ffordd
Newgale
St David's Peninsula Heritage Coast
Scolton
Clarbeston
Bletherston
Roch
Wolfsdale
Rudbaxton
Poyston Cross
Clarbeston Road
Llandissilio
Roch Gate
PEMBROKESHIRE COAST NATIONAL PARK
Simpson Cross
Camrose
Clunderwen
Rickets Head
Nolton Haven
Nolton
Keeston
Tangiers
Crundale
Wiston
Gelly
Bethesda
St Brides Bay Heritage Coast
Pelcomb Cross
Pelcomb
Lambston
Fenton Brook
Llawhaden
Druidston
Sutton
Pelcomb Bridge
Haverfordwest
(Hwlffordd)
Slebech
Robeston Wathen
Redstone Cross
Penblewin
Haroldston West
Portfield Gate
Uzmaston
Canaston Bridge
Narberth
(Arberth)
Crinow
Broad Haven
Broadway
Dreen Hill
Merlin's Bridge
Millin Cross
Picton Castle
Bluestone
Oakwood
Cross Hands
Cold Blow
Little Haven
Walton West
Lower Freystrop
Boulston
Minwear
Princes Gate
Talbenny
Solbury
Freystrop
Landshipping
Templeton
Tiers Cross
Johnston
Hook
Ludchurch
St Brides
Walwyn's Castle
Martletwy
Longstone
SKOMER ISLAND
Wooltack Point
Llangwm
Black Tar
Cwm Deri
Yerbeston
Thomas Chapel
Marloes
Hasguard
Rosemarket
Loveston
Reynalton
Stepaside
Thornton
Newton Mountain
Begelly
St Ishmael's
Sandy Haven
Herbrandston
Steynton
Houghton
Lawrenny
Cresswell
Jeffreyston
Kilgetty
Marloes & Dale Heritage Coast
Dale
Hubberston
Honeyborough
Waterston
Burton
West Williamston
Cresselly
Broadmoor
Cross Inn
Pentlepoir
SKOKHOLM ISLAND
Westdale Bay
Great Castle Head
Hakin
Llanstadwell
Neyland
Carew Newton
Upton
Redberth
East Williamston
Wooden
Saundersfoot
Dale Point
Milford Haven
(Aberdaugleddau)
Pembroke Dock
(Doc Penfro)
Toll
Waterloo
Tidal Mill
Milton
Carew
Angle
Pwllcrochan
Cosheston
Pennar
Golden Hill
Sageston
Broadfield
New Hedges
St Ann's Head
Angle Bay
Rhoscrowther
Pembroke
(Penfro)
Carew Cheriton
Gumfreston
Bishop's Palace
St Florence
Lamphey
Manorbier Newton
Tenby
(Dinbych-y-pysgod)
Hundleton
Grove
Penally
Freshwater West
Castlemartin Brook
Maiden Wells
Hodgeston
Lydstep
Jameston
Giltar Point
Castlemartin
St Twynnells
Freshwater East
Trewent
Trewent Point
Manorbier
Warren
St Petrox
Stackpole Elidor / Cheriton
Lydstep Point
Linney Head
Merrion
Stackpole
South Pembrokeshire Heritage Coast
Bosherston
Stackpole Head
St Govan's Chapel
St Govan's Head
A40
A487
A4219
A4076
A477
A4075
A478
A4115
A4139
B4313
B4329
B4330
B4331
B4341
B4327
B4320
B4319
B4322
B4325
B4583
B4582
B4584
B4585
B4586
B4314
B4315
B4318
0 1 2 3 4 5 miles
0 1 2 3 4 5 6 7 8 kilometres

Port plans: Fishguard p.XVI, Pembroke Dock p.XVI

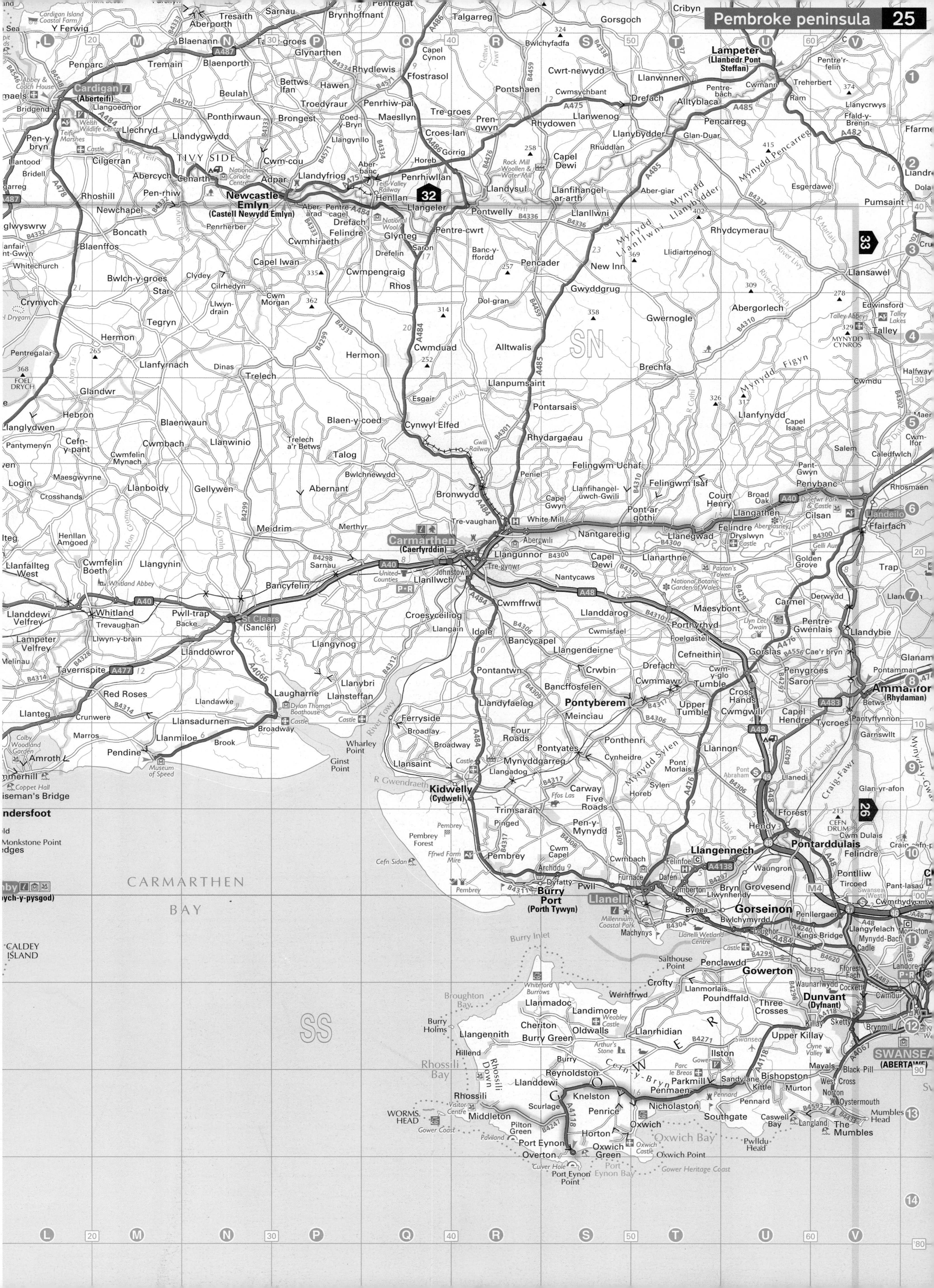
Cardigan (Aberteifi)
Newcastle Emlyn (Castell Newydd Emlyn)
Lampeter (Llanbedr Pont Steffan)
Aberporth
Tresaith
Sarnau
Brynhoffnant
Talgarreg
Gorsgoch
Cribyn
Y Ferwig
Blaenannerch
Glynarthen
Penparc
Tremain
Blaenporth
Rhydlewis
Capel Cynon
Ffostrasol
Bwlchyfadfa
Cwrt-newydd
Llanwnnen
Beulah
Bettws Ifan
Hawen
Pontshaen
Cwmsychbant
Drefach
Alltyblaca
Llangoedmor
Troedyraur
Penrhiw-pal
Tre-groes
Ponthirwaun
Brongest
Coed-y-Bryn
Maesllyn
Pren-gwyn
Rhydowen
Llanwenog
Llanybydder
Pencarreg
Llechryd
Llandygwydd
Cwm-cou
Croes-lan
Gorrig
Capel Dewi
Cilgerran
Abercych
Cenarth
Adpar
Llandyfriog
Henllan
Penrhiwllan
Llandysul
Llanfihangel-ar-arth
Pen-y-bryn
Rhoshill
Pen-rhiw
Newchapel
Llangeler
Pontwelly
Llanllwni
Rhydcymerau
Boncath
Penrherber
Drefach
Felindre
Cwmhiraeth
Glynteg
Pentre-cwrt
Blaenffos
Capel Iwan
Saron
Pencader
New Inn
Whitechurch
Clydey
Cilrhedyn
Cwmpengraig
Rhos
Bwlch-y-groes
Star
Crymych
Cwm Morgan
Llwyn-drain
Gwyddgrug
Tegryn
Dol-gran
Abergorlech
Gwernogle
Edwinsford
Talley
Hermon
Cwmduad
Alltwalis
SN
Pentregalar
Llanfyrnach
Dinas
Trelech
Brechfa
Glandwr
Llanpumsaint
Esgair
Pontarsais
Hebron
Blaenwaun
Blaen-y-coed
Cynwyl Elfed
Llanfynydd
Capel Isaac
Llanglydwen
Cefn-y-pant
Cwmbach
Llanwinio
Trelech a'r Betws
Talog
Rhydargaeau
Pantymenyn
Cwmfelin Mynach
Salem
Login
Maesgwynne
Llanboidy
Gellywen
Bwlchnewydd
Abernant
Felingwm Uchaf
Felingwm Isaf
Peniel
Llanfihangel-uwch-Gwili
Crosshands
Bronwydd
Capel Gwyn
Court Henry
Broad Oak
Penybanc
Rhosmaen
White Mill
Pont-ar-gothi
Llangathen
Cilsan
Llandeilo
Tre-vaughan
Henllan Amgoed
Meidrim
Merthyr
Carmarthen (Caerfyddin)
Abergwili
Nantgaredig
Llanegwad
Felindre
Dryslwyn
Ffairfach
Llangunnor
Capel Dewi
Llanarthne
Golden Grove
Sarnau
Johnstown
Tre-gynwr
Trap
Llanfallteg West
Cwmfelin Boeth
Llangynin
Llanllwch
Nantycaws
Bancyfelin
Llanddarog
Carmel
Derwydd
Whitland
Llanddewi Velfrey
Pwll-trap
Backe
St Clears (Sanclêr)
Trevaughan
Croesyceiliog
Cwmffrwd
Maesybont
Pentre-Gwenlais
Lampeter Velfrey
Llwyn-y-brain
Llangain
Idole
Cwmisfael
Porthyrhyd
Llandybie
Llanddowror
Llangynog
Bancycapel
Llangendeirne
Foelgastell
Cefneithin
Gorslas
Cae'r bryn
Glanamman
Tavernspite
Crwbin
Drefach
Cwm-y-glo
Penygroes
Saron
Pontamman
Red Roses
Llanybri
Llansteffan
Pontantwn
Bancffosfelen
Cwmmawr
Tumble
Ammanford (Rhydaman)
Llanteg
Crunwere
Llandawke
Laugharne
Pontyberem
Meinciau
Upper Tumble
Cross Hands
Cwmgwili
Capel Hendre
Tycroes
Betws
Pantyffynnon
Llansadurnen
Broadway
Ferryside
Llandyfaelog
Marros
Llanmiloe
Brook
Broadlay
Four Roads
Ponthenri
Llannon
Garnswllt
Pendine
Amroth
Wharley Point
Ginst Point
Llansaint
Pontyates
Mynyddgarreg
Cynheidre
Pont Morlais
Llangadog
Kidwelly (Cydweli)
Carway
Five Roads
Sylen
Horeb
Pont Abraham
Llanedi
Glan-yr-afon
Saundersfoot
Monkstone Point
Trimsaran
Pinged
Pembrey
Pembrey Forest
Pen-y-Mynydd
Cwm Capel
Cwmbach
Llangennech
Fforest
Hendy
Pontarddulais
Cwm Dulais
Felindre
Cefn Sidan
Burry Port (Porth Tywyn)
Pwll
Dyfatty
Furnace
Felinfoel
Dafen
Llanelli
Pemberton
Bryn
Llwynhendy
Waungron
Grovesend
Pontlliw
Tircoed
Pant-lasau
CARMARTHEN BAY
Bynea
Gorseinon
Penllergaer
Bwlchymyrdd
Llangyfelach
Morriston
Machynys
Loughor
Kings Bridge
Mynydd-Bach
CALDEY ISLAND
Burry Inlet
Salthouse Point
Penclawdd
Gowerton
Fforest Fach
Cadle
Landore
Crofty
Llanmorlais
Waunarlwydd
Cockett
Cwmdu
Broughton Bay
Whiteford Burrows
Wernffrwd
Poundffald
Dunvant (Dyfnant)
Llanmadoc
Landimore
Weobley Castle
Three Crosses
SS
Burry Holms
Cheriton
Llangennith
Burry Green
Oldwalls
Llanrhidian
Killay
Sketty
Brynmill
Upper Killay
Clyne Valley
Hillend
Arthur's Stone
Burry
Ilston
Swansea (Abertawe)
Rhossili Bay
Rhossili Down
Reynoldston
Parc le Breos
Cefn-y-Bryn
GOWER
Mayals
Black Pill
Sandylane
Bishopston
West Cross
Llanddewi
Parkmill
Penmaen
Kittle
Murton
Norton
Oystermouth
Rhossili
Knelston
Pennard
Scurlage
Nicholaston
WORMS HEAD
Middleton
Penrice
Southgate
Caswell Bay
Langland
Mumbles Head
The Mumbles
Pilton Green
Oxwich
Gower Coast
Paviland
Horton
Port Eynon
Oxwich Bay
Oxwich Green
Overton
Oxwich Castle
Oxwich Point
Pwlldu Head
Culver Hole
Port Eynon Point
Port Eynon Bay
Gower Heritage Coast
32
33
26

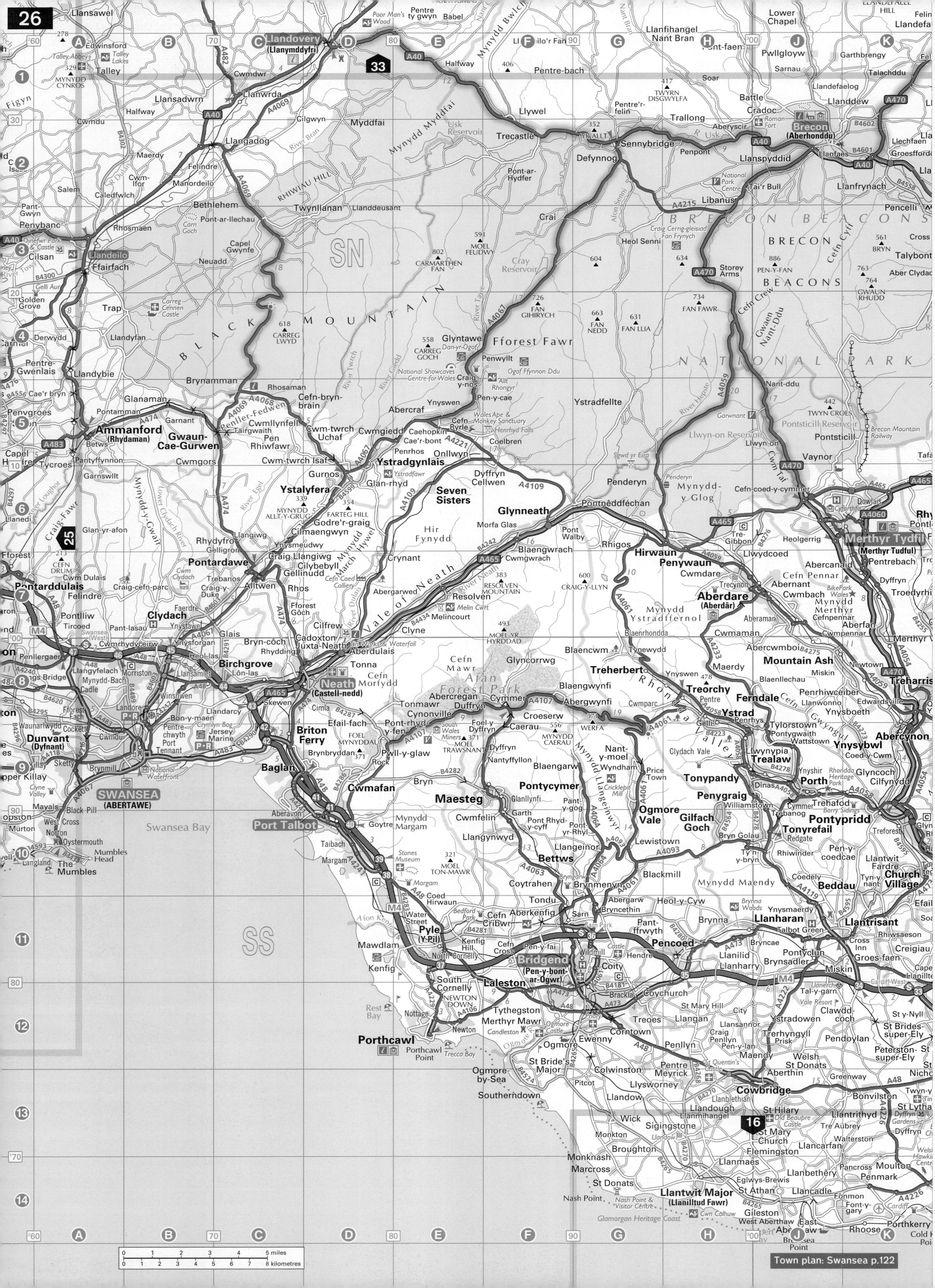
Llandovery (Llanymddyfri)
Talley
Llanwrda
Llangadog
Myddfai
Trecastle
Sennybridge
Defynnog
Brecon (Aberhonddu)
Llanspyddid
Libanus
Llanfrynach
BRECON BEACONS
NATIONAL PARK
BLACK MOUNTAIN
Fforest Fawr
Glyntawe
Llandeilo
Ffairfach
Llandybie
Ammanford (Rhydaman)
Gwaun-Cae-Gurwen
Brynamman
Ystradgynlais
Ystalyfera
Seven Sisters
Glynneath
Hirwaun
Penderyn
Merthyr Tydfil (Merthyr Tudful)
Aberdare (Aberdâr)
Mountain Ash
Treorchy
Ferndale
Tonypandy
Porth
Pontypridd
Pontardawe
Pontarddulais
Clydach
Birchgrove
Neath (Castell-nedd)
Vale of Neath
Resolven
Briton Ferry
Baglan
Cwmafan
Maesteg
Port Talbot
Swansea (Abertawe)
Swansea Bay
Dunvant (Dyfnant)
The Mumbles
Pyle (Y Pîl)
Bridgend (Pen-y-bont-ar-Ogwr)
Porthcawl
Pencoed
Llanharan
Llantrisant
Tonyrefail
Cowbridge
Llantwit Major (Llanilltud Fawr)
St Athan
Rhoose
Glamorgan Heritage Coast
SN
SS
Town plan: Swansea p.122

Town plan: Swansea p.122

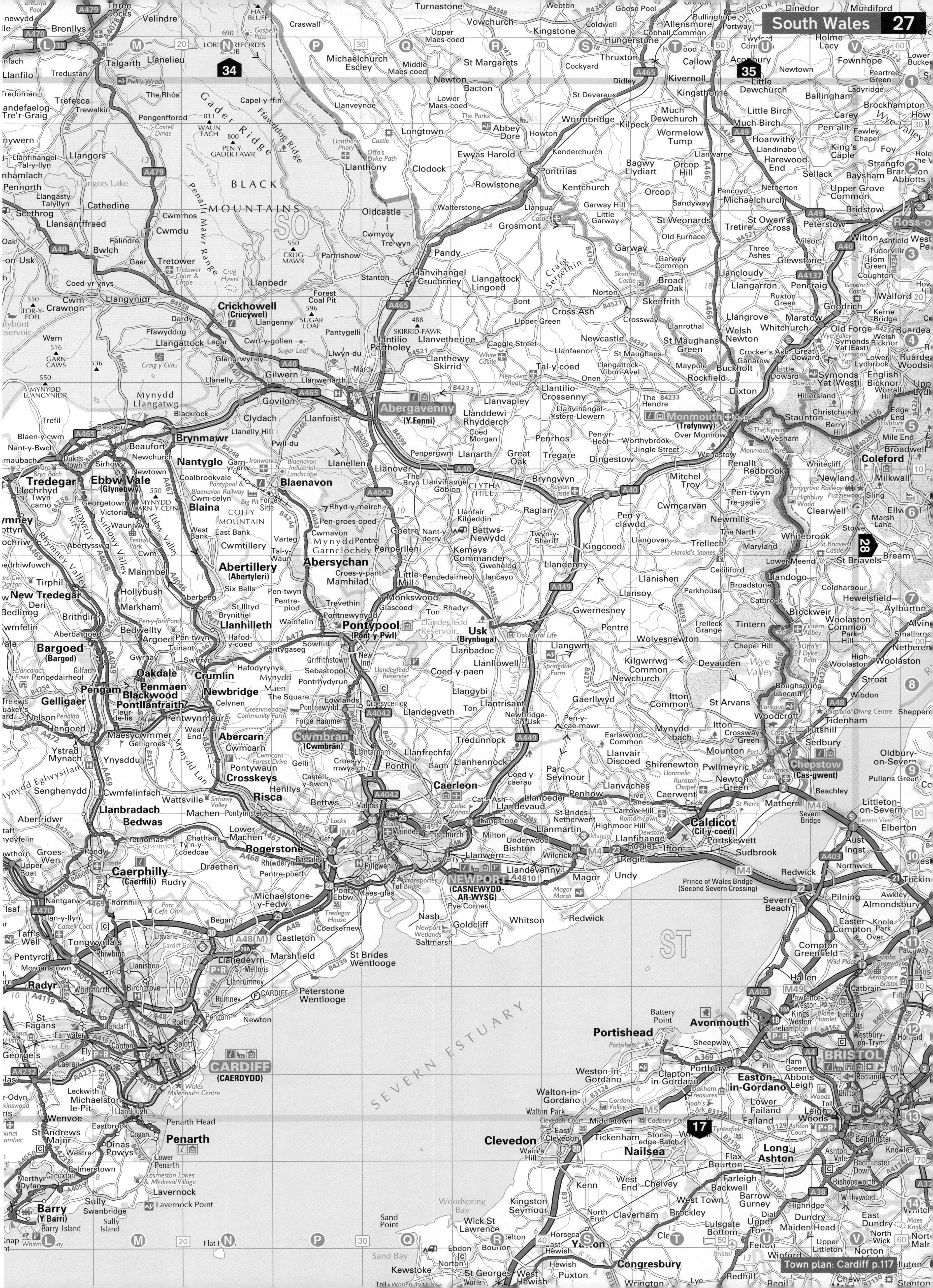
BLACK MOUNTAINS
SEVERN ESTUARY
Crickhowell (Crucywel)
Abergavenny (Y Fenni)
Monmouth (Trefynwy)
Brynmawr
Nantyglo
Tredegar
Ebbw Vale (Glynebwy)
Blaenavon
Blaina
Abertillery (Abertyleri)
Abersychan
Pontypool (Pont-y-Pwl)
Usk (Brynbuga)
Raglan
Llanhilleth
Bargoed (Bargod)
Oakdale
Crumlin
Newbridge
Gelligaer
Pengam
Penmaen
Blackwood
Pontllanfraith
Cwmbran (Cwmbrân)
Abercarn
Crosskeys
Risca
Caerleon
Caerphilly (Caerffili)
Rogerstone
NEWPORT (CASNEWYDD-AR-WYSG)
Caldicot (Cil-y-coed)
Chepstow (Cas-gwent)
CARDIFF (CAERDYDD)
Penarth
Barry (Y Barri)
Radyr
Portishead
Avonmouth
BRISTOL
Clevedon
Nailsea
Easton-in-Gordano
Long Ashton
Congresbury
Coleford
Ross-on-Wye
Talgarth
Grosmont
Skenfrith
Pandy
Pontrilas
Llanbradach
Bedwas
Tongwynlais
Magor
Undy
Portskewett
Tintern
St Briavels
Goodrich
Symonds Yat (West)
Lydney
Woolaston
Tidenham
Sedbury
Severn Beach
Pilning
Thornbury
Clifton
Redland
Bedminster
Yatton
Wrington
Sand Point
Kewstoke

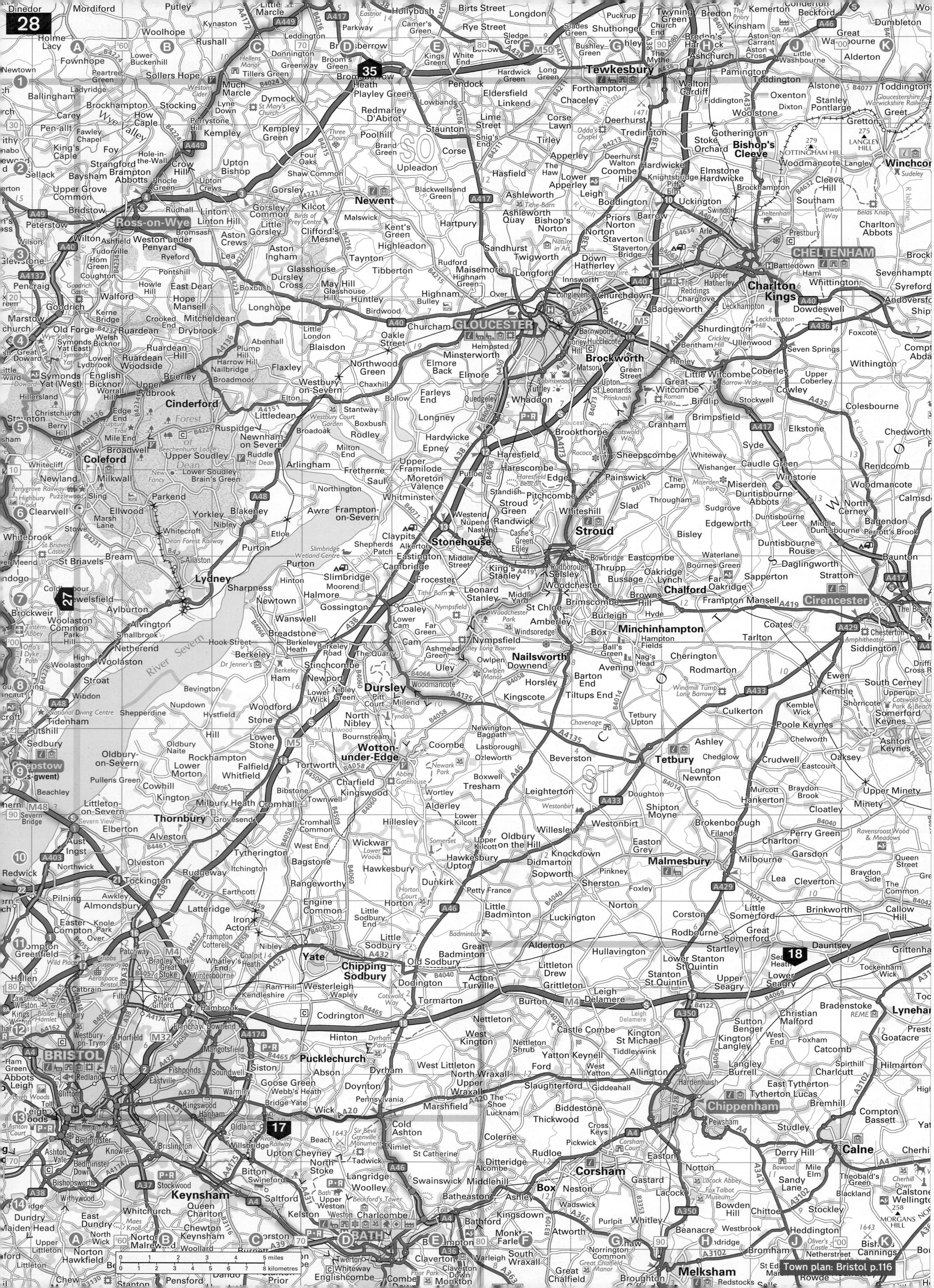
Ross-on-Wye
Newent
Tewkesbury
Bishop's Cleeve
Winchcombe
CHELTENHAM
Charlton Kings
GLOUCESTER
Brockworth
Cinderford
Coleford
Lydney
Chepstow
Stonehouse
Stroud
Chalford
Cirencester
Nailsworth
Minchinhampton
Dursley
Tetbury
Wotton-under-Edge
Thornbury
Malmesbury
Yate
Chipping Sodbury
BRISTOL
Pucklechurch
Chippenham
Calne
Corsham
Keynsham
BATH
Melksham
River Severn
M5
M4
M50
M48
M32
A38
A417
A419
A46
A40
A429
A433
A4
35
27
18
17
Town plan: Bristol p.116

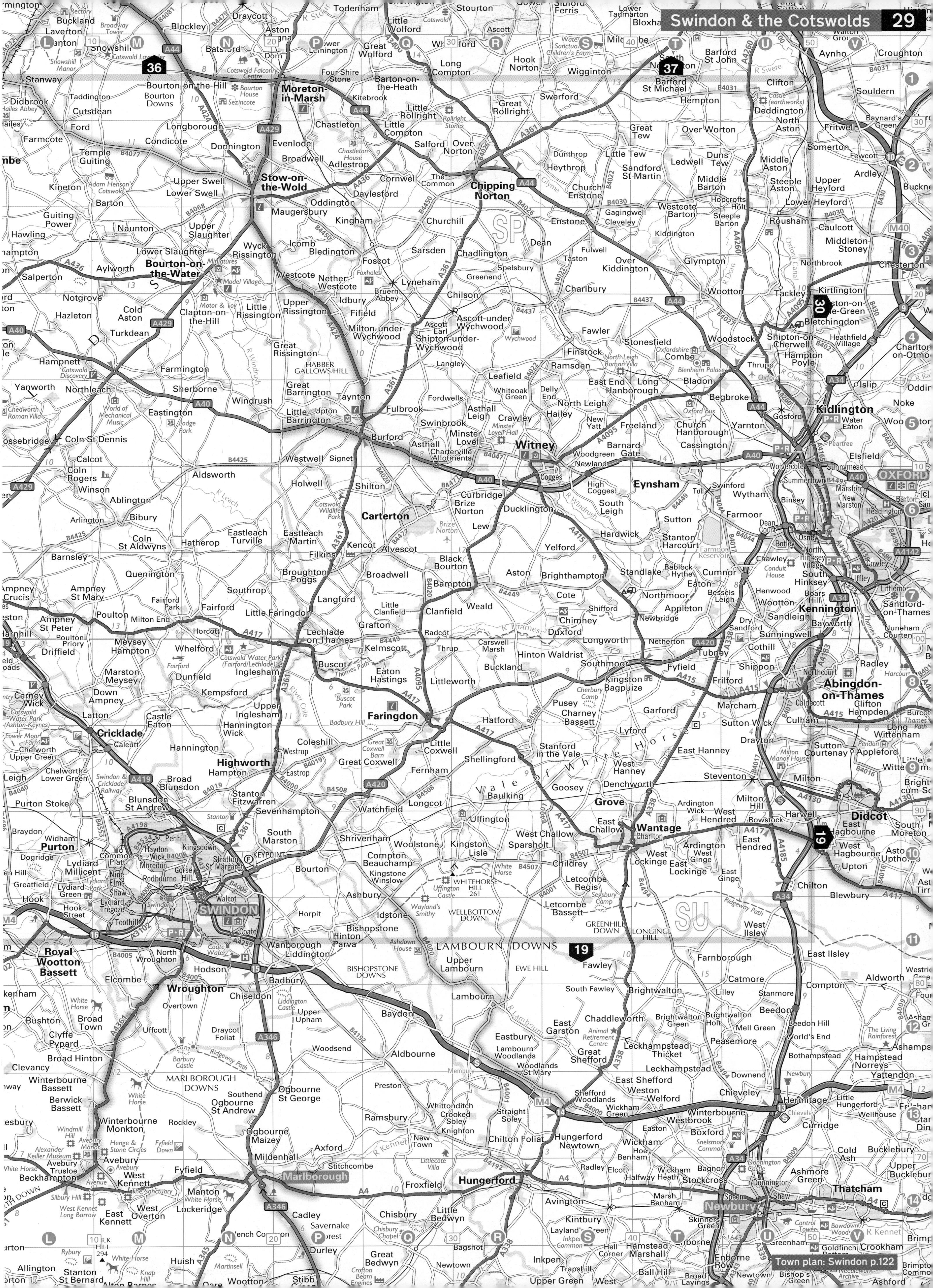

Moreton-in-Marsh
Stow-on-the-Wold
Bourton-on-the-Water
Chipping Norton
Witney
Burford
Carterton
Eynsham
Kidlington
OXFORD
Abingdon-on-Thames
Kennington
Faringdon
Highworth
Cricklade
Purton
Royal Wootton Bassett
SWINDON
Wroughton
Wantage
Grove
Didcot
Hungerford
Marlborough
Newbury
Thatcham
Lambourn
Chiseldon
Fairford
Lechlade on Thames
Northleach
Charlbury
Woodstock
Bicester
Vale of White Horse
LAMBOURN DOWNS
MARLBOROUGH DOWNS
36
37
30
19

Town plan: Swindon p.122

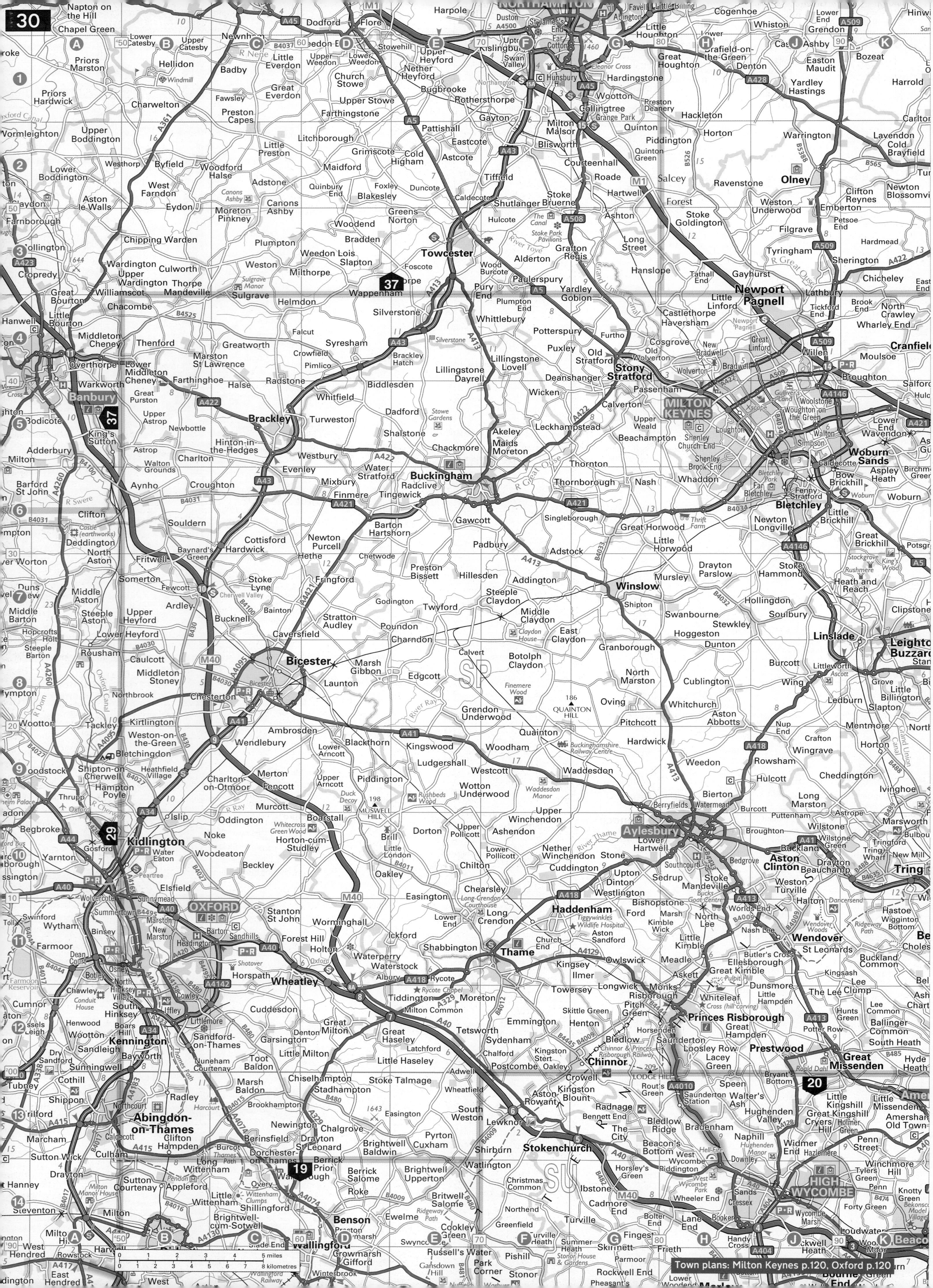
Northampton
Towcester
Brackley
Buckingham
Banbury
Bicester
Kidlington
Oxford
Abingdon-on-Thames
Wallingford
Thame
Wheatley
Aylesbury
Princes Risborough
Chinnor
Stokenchurch
High Wycombe
Great Missenden
Wendover
Tring
Leighton Buzzard
Linslade
Bletchley
Milton Keynes
Newport Pagnell
Olney
Stony Stratford
Woburn Sands
Winslow
Kennington
Benson
Watlington
Haddenham
Daventry
0 1 2 3 4 5 miles
0 1 2 3 4 5 6 7 8 kilometres
Town plans: Milton Keynes p.120, Oxford p.120

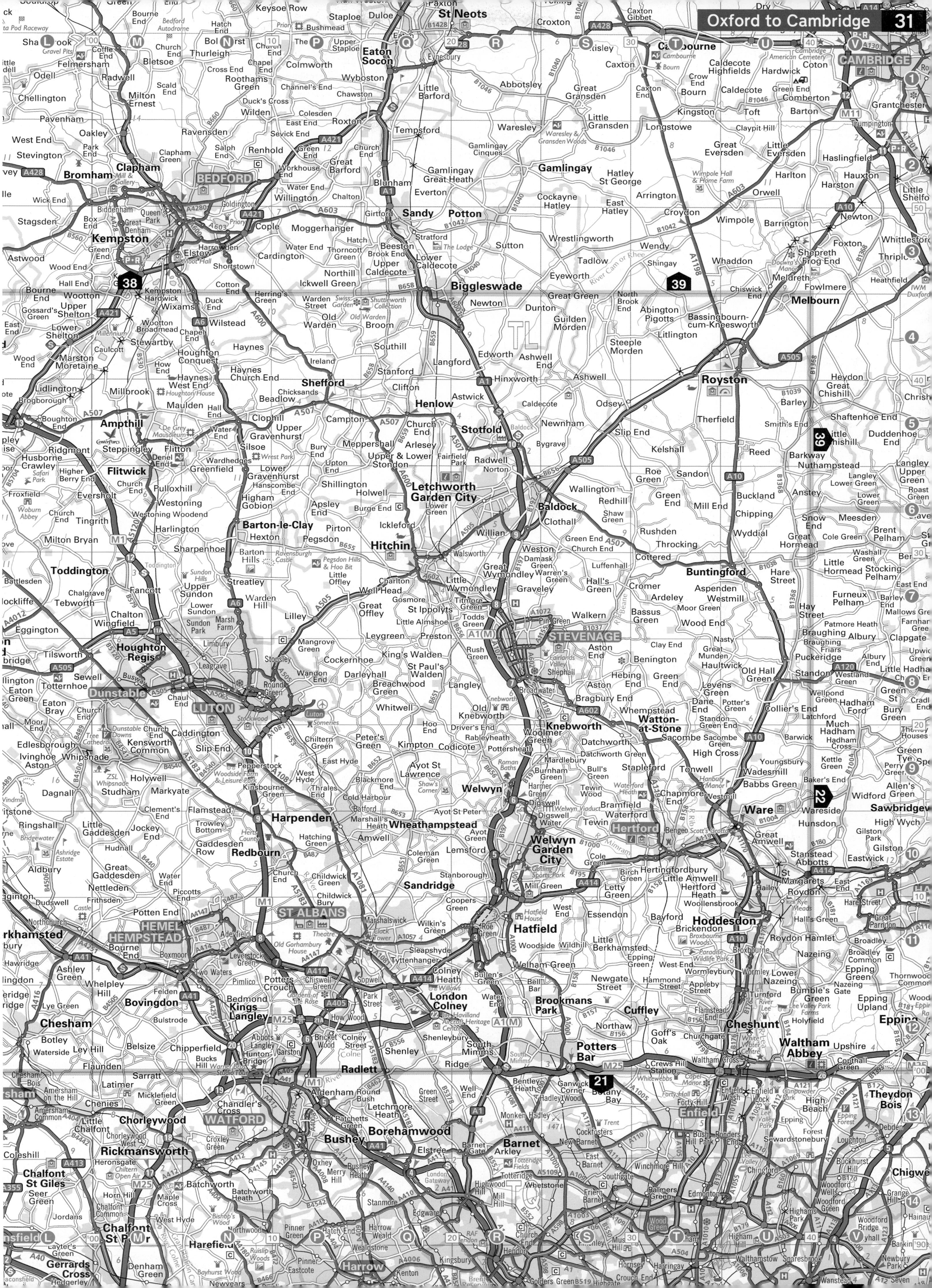
St Neots
Eaton Socon
CAMBRIDGE
Bedford
BEDFORD
Clapham
Bromham
Kempston
Sandy
Potton
Biggleswade
Gamlingay
Royston
Melbourn
Shefford
Henlow
Stotfold
Baldock
Letchworth Garden City
Hitchin
Ampthill
Flitwick
Toddington
Houghton Regis
Dunstable
LUTON
Harpenden
Stevenage
STEVENAGE
Knebworth
Welwyn
Welwyn Garden City
Hertford
Ware
Buntingford
Hoddesdon
Hatfield
ST ALBANS
HEMEL HEMPSTEAD
Berkhamsted
Chesham
Bovingdon
Kings Langley
London Colney
Potters Bar
Cheshunt
Waltham Abbey
Enfield
Barnet
Borehamwood
Bushey
WATFORD
Rickmansworth
Chorleywood
Chalfont St Giles
Chalfont St Peter
Harefield
Harrow
Theydon Bois
Epping
Radlett
Shenley
Brookmans Park
Cuffley
Sawbridgeworth
Tempsford
Blunham
Wilstead
Barton-le-Clay
Whipsnade
Redbourn
Sandridge
Wheathampstead
Abbots Langley
Chipperfield

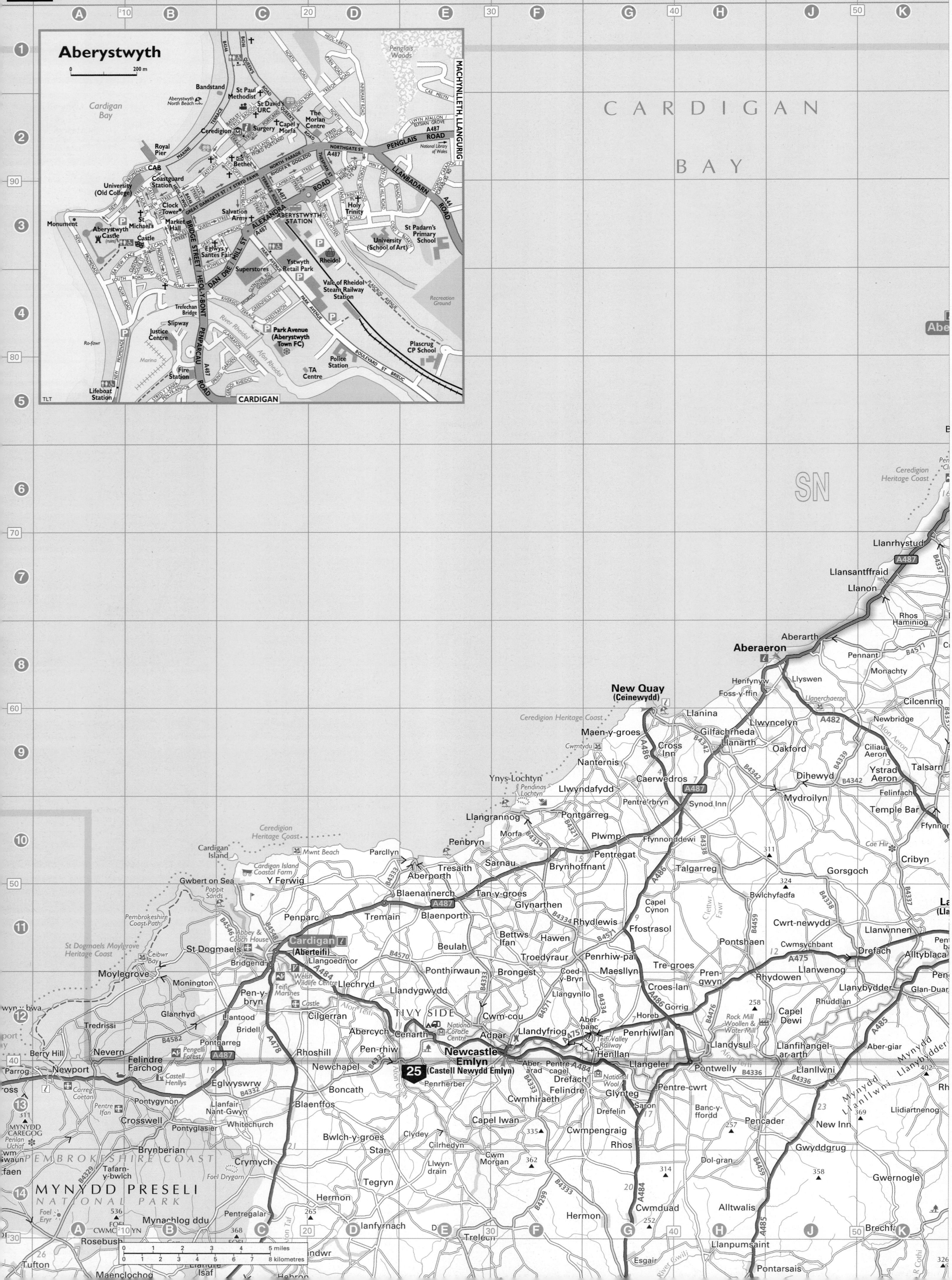

Aberystwyth

0   100   200 m

Cardigan Bay

C A R D I G A N

B A Y

SN

Ceredigion Heritage Coast

Llanrhystud

Llansantffraid

Llanon

Rhos Haminiog

Aberarth

Aberaeron

Pennant

Monachty

Cilcennin

Henfynyw

Foss-y-ffin

Llyswen

Newbridge

New Quay
(Ceinewydd)

Llanina

Llwyncelyn

Oakford

Ciliau
Aeron

Ceredigion Heritage Coast

Maen-y-groes

Gilfachrheda

Llanarth

Talsarn

Cwmtydu

Cross
Inn

Nanternis

Caerwedros

Dihewyd

Ystrad
Aeron

Ynys-Lochtyn

Pendinas
Lochtyn

Llwyndafydd

Mydroilyn

Felinfach

Llangrannog

Pontgarreg

Pentre'rbryn

Synod Inn

Temple Bar

Ffynnon

Penbryn

Morfa

Plwmp

Ffynnonddewi

Cae Hir

Parcllyn

Mwnt Beach

Tresaith

Aberporth

Sarnau

Brynhoffnant

Pentregat

Talgarreg

Gorsgoch

Cribyn

Cardigan
Island

Cardigan Island
Coastal Farm

Y Ferwig

Blaenannerch

Tan-y-groes

Glynarthen

Rhydlewis

Capel
Cynon

Bwlchyfadfa

Gwbert on Sea

Poppit
Sands

Penparc

Tremain

Blaenporth

Bettws
Ifan

Hawen

Ffostrasol

Cwrt-newydd

Llanwnnen

Ceredigion
Heritage Coast

Pembrokeshire
Coast Path

Abbey &
Coach House

Beulah

Troedyraur

Penrhiw-pal

Pontshaen

Cwmsychbant

Drefach

St Dogmaels Moylegrove
Heritage Coast

Ceibwr
Bay

St-Dogmaels

Bridgend

Llangoedmor

Ponthirwaun

Brongest

Coed-
y-Bryn

Maesllyn

Tre-groes

Prengwyn

Rhydowen

Llanwenog

Glan-Duar

Moylegrove

Monington

Glanrhyd

Pen-y-
bryn

Llechryd

Llandygwydd

Llangynllo

Croes-lan

Rhuddlan

Capel
Dewi

La
(Lla

Welsh
Wildlife Centre

Teifi
Marshes

Castle

Cardigan
(Aberteifi)

Cilgerran

NVY SIDE

Cwm-cou

Aber-
banc

Gorrig

Horeb

Rock Mill
Woollen &
Water Mill

Llandysul

Llanfihangel
ar-arth

Aber-giar

wyn y bwa

Tredissi

Nevern

Berry Hill

Pengelli
Forest

Pontgarreg

Abercych

Cenarth

National
Coracle Centre

Adpar

Llandyfriog

Penrhiwllan

Teifi Valley
Railway

Henllan

Llangeler

Pontwelly

Llanllwni

Pen-rhiw

Newcastle
Emlyn
(Castell Newydd Emlyn)

Aber-
arad

Pentre
cagel

Drefach

National
Wool

Glynteg

Pentre-cwrt

Felindre
Farchog

Castell
Henllys

Eglwyswrw

Newport

Boncath

Penrherber

Felindre

Saron

Banc-y-
ffordd

Pencader

New Inn

MYNYDD
CAREGOG

Pontygynon

Pentre
Ifan

Lanfair-
Nant-Gwyn

Blaenffos

Capel Iwan

Cwmhiraeth

Drefelin

Gwyddgrug

Crosswell

Pontyglasier

Whitechurch

Newchapel

Clydey

Cilrhedyn

Rhos

Dol-gran

Gwernogle

Brynberian

Crymych

Star

Cwm
Morgan

Cwmpengraig

Foel Drygarn

Bwlch-y-groes

PEMBROKESHIRE COAST

Tafarn-
y-bwlch

Llwyn-
drain

Tegryn

Hermon

Alltwalis

MYNYDD PRESELI

NATIONAL PARK

Foel
Eryr

Mynachlog
ddu

Pentregalar

Hermon

Cwmduad

Brechf

Rosebush

Tufton

Maenclochog

lanfyrnach

Treleen

Esgair

Llanpumsaint

Pontarsais

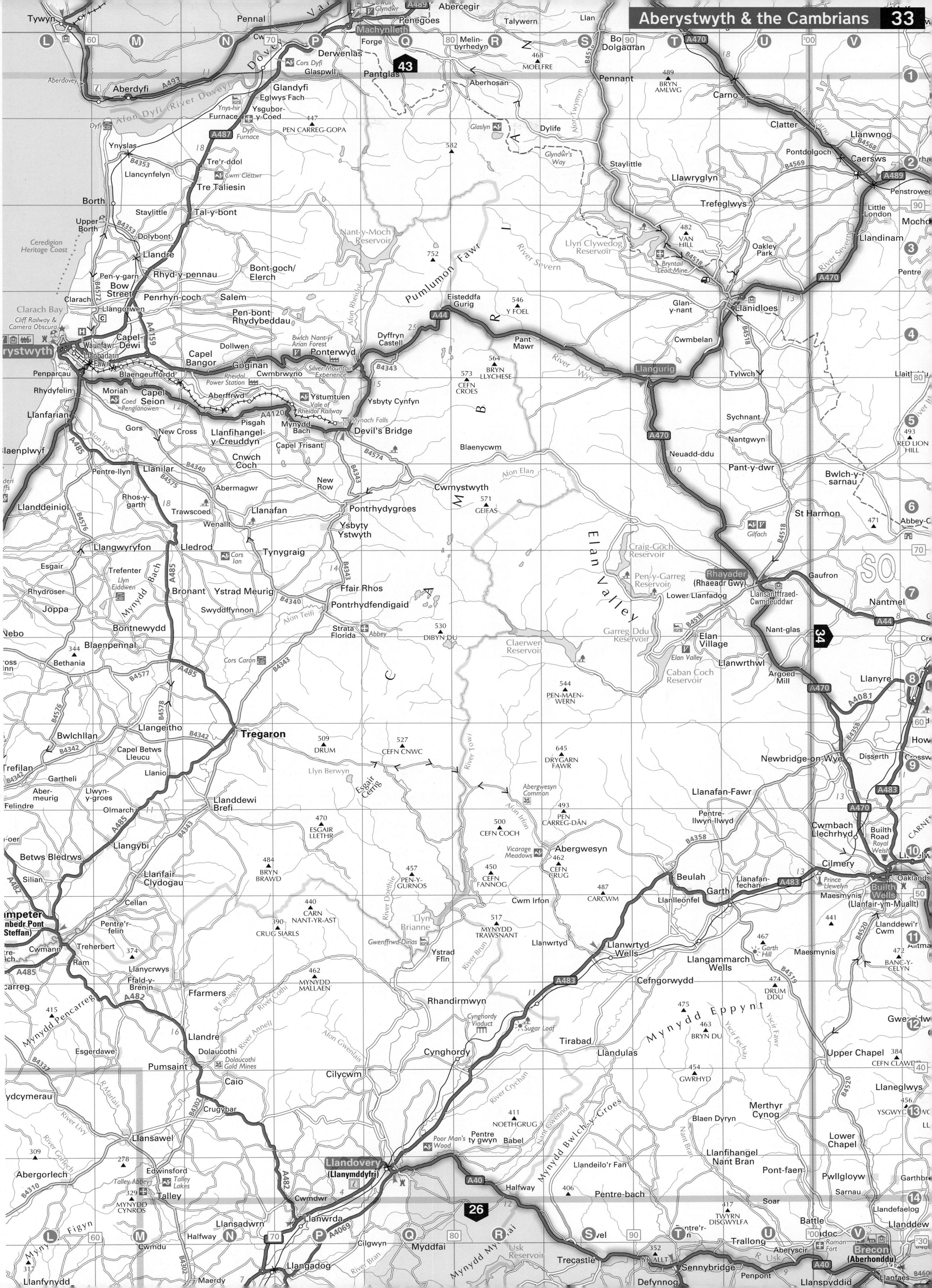
Tywyn
Pennal
Penegoes
Abercegir
Talywern
Llan
Machynlleth
Forge
Melin-byrhedyn
Bont Dolgadfan
Derwenlas
Glaspwll
Pantglas
43
MOELFRE
Pennant
BRYN AMLWG
Carno
Aberdovey
Aberdyfi
Glandyfi
Eglwys Fach
Ynys-hir
Furnace
Ysgubor-y-Coed
Dyfi Furnace
PEN CARREG-GOPA
Aberhosan
Cors Dyfi
Dovey
Afon Dyfi (River Dovey)
Glaslyn
Dylife
Clatter
Llanwnog
Ynyslas
Tre'r-ddol
Cwm Clettwr
Llancynfelyn
Tre Taliesin
Glyndŵr's Way
Staylittle
Llawryglyn
Pontdolgoch
Caersws
Penstrowed
Borth
Upper Borth
Tal-y-bont
Staylittle
Dolybont
Llandre
Trefeglwys
Little London
Mochdre
Ceredigion Heritage Coast
Nant-y-Moch Reservoir
Llyn Clywedog Reservoir
VAN HILL
Bryntail Lead Mine
Oakley Park
Llandinam
Pen-y-garn
Bow Street
Rhyd-y-pennau
Bont-goch/ Elerch
Pumlumon Fawr
River Severn
Pentre
Clarach Bay
Clarach
Cliff Railway & Camera Obscura
Penrhyn-coch
Salem
Llangorwen
Pen-bont Rhydybeddau
Eisteddfa Gurig
Y FOEL
Glan-y-nant
Llanidloes
Aberystwyth
Waunfawr
Capel-Dewi
Llanbadarn Fawr
Dollwen
Bwlch Nant-yr Arian Forest
Dyffryn Castell
Pant Mawr
Cwmbelan
Capel Bangor
Goginan
Ponterwyd
Penparcau
Blaengeufforrdd
Cwmbrwyno
Rheidol Power Station
Silver Mountain Experience
BRYN LLYCHESE
CEFN CROES
Llangurig
Tylwch
Llaithddu
Rhydyfelin
Moriah
Capel Seion
Coed Penglanowen
Aberffrwd
Ystumtuen
Vale of Rheidol Railway
Ysbyty Cynfyn
River Wye
Llanfarian
Gors
New Cross
Llanfihangel-y-Creuddyn
Pisgah
Mynydd Bach
Mynach Falls
Devil's Bridge
Capel Trisant
Blaenycwm
Sychnant
Nantgwyn
RED LION HILL
Blaenplwyf
Afon Ystwyth
Cnwch Coch
Pentre-llyn
Llanilar
Neuadd-ddu
Pant-y-dwr
Bwlch-y-sarnau
Abermagwr
New Row
Cwmystwyth
Afon Elan
Rhos-y-garth
GEIFAS
Llanddeiniol
Trawscoed
Wenallt
Llanafan
Pontrhydygroes
Ysbyty Ystwyth
St Harmon
Gilfach
Abbey-Cwmhir
Llangwyryfon
Lledrod
Cors Ian
Tynygraig
Elan Valley
Craig-Goch Reservoir
Esgair
Trefenter
Llyn Eiddwen
Mynydd Bach
Pen-y-Garreg Reservoir
Rhayader (Rhaeadr Gwy)
Gaufron
Rhydroser
Bronant
Ystrad Meurig
Ffair Rhos
Lower Llanfadog
Llansantffraed-Cwmdeuddwr
Nantmel
Joppa
Swyddffynnon
Pontrhydfendigaid
Afon Teifi
Nebo
Bontnewydd
Strata Florida
Abbey
DIBYN DU
Garreg-Ddu Reservoir
Elan Village
Nant-glas
34
Blaenpennal
Bethania
Cors Caron
Claerwen Reservoir
Elan Valley
Caban Coch Reservoir
Llanwrthwl
Argoed Mill
Llanyre
PEN-MAEN-WERN
Bwlchllan
Llangeitho
Tregaron
DRUM
CEFN CNWC
DRYGARN FAWR
Capel Betws Lleucu
Llanio
Newbridge-on-Wye
Disserth
Trefilan
Gartheli
Llyn Berwyn
Esgair Cerrig
River Towi
Abergwesyn Common
Aber-meurig
Llwyn-y-groes
Felindre
Olmarch
Llanddewi Brefi
ESGAIR LLETHR
CEFN COCH
PEN CARREG-DÂN
Llanafan-Fawr
Pentre-llwyn-llwyd
Cwmbach Llechrhyd
Builth Road
Afon Irfon
Vicarage Meadows
Abergwesyn
CEFN CRUG
Llangybi
Betws Bledrws
BRYN BRAWD
PEN-Y-GURNOS
CEFN FANNOG
Beulah
Llanafan-fechan
Cilmery
Silian
Llanfair Clydogau
River Doethie
CARCWM
Garth
Prince Llewelyn
Maesmynis
Builth Wells (Llanfair-ym-Muallt)
Oaklands
Cellan
CARN NANT-YR-AST
Llyn Brianne
Cwm Irfon
Llanlleonfel
Lampeter (Llanbedr Pont Steffan)
Pentre'r-felin
CRUG SIARLS
MYNYDD TRAWSNANT
Llanwrtyd
Llanwrtyd Wells
Garth Hill
Llanddewi'r Cwm
Treherbert
Cwmann
Gwenffrwd-Dinas
Ystrad Ffin
River Brun
Llangammarch Wells
Maesmynis
BANC-Y-CELYN
Ram
Llanycrwys
Ffald-y-Brenin
MYNYDD MALLAEN
Cefngorwydd
DRUM DDU
Ffarmers
Rhandirmwyn
Mynydd Eppynt
Mynydd Pencarreg
Cynghordy Viaduct
Sugar Loaf
BRYN DU
Llandre
River Annell
Afon Gwenlais
Tirabad
Llandulas
Gwenddwr
Esgerdawe
Dolaucothi
Dolaucothi Gold Mines
Cynghordy
Upper Chapel
CEFN CLAWDD
Pumsaint
Caio
Cilycwm
GWRHYD
Llaneglwys
Llanycrwys
Crugybar
River Crychan
NOETHGRUG
Merthyr Cynog
YSGWYDD
Llansawel
Poor Man's Wood
Pentre ty gwyn
Babel
Mynydd Bwlch-y-Groes
Blaen Dyryn
Lower Chapel
River Gorlech
Edwinsford
Llandovery (Llanymddyfri)
Llandeilo'r Fan
Llanfihangel Nant Bran
Pont-faen
Pwllgloyw
Abergorlech
Talley Abbey
Talley Lakes
Halfway
Pentre-bach
MYNYDD CYNROS
Talley
Cwmdwr
26
Sarnau
Soar
Llanwrda
TWYRN DISGWYLFA
Battle
Llandefaelog
Figyn
Llansadwrn
Halfway
Cilgwyn
Myddfai
Usk Reservoir
Trallong
Aberyscir
Roman Fort
Brecon (Aberhonddu)
Cwmdu
Llangadog
River Bran
Mynydd Myddfai
Trecastle
Sennybridge
Defynnog
Penpont
Llanspyddid
Llanfaes
Llanfynydd
Maerdy
A487
A44
A470
A483
A485
A482
A40
A4120
A4159
A4069
A4081
A489
A493
B4343
B4340
B4342
B4578
B4576
B4577
B4353
B4572
B4574
B4575
B4518
B4358
B4519
B4520
B4337
B4310
B4302
B4569
B4568

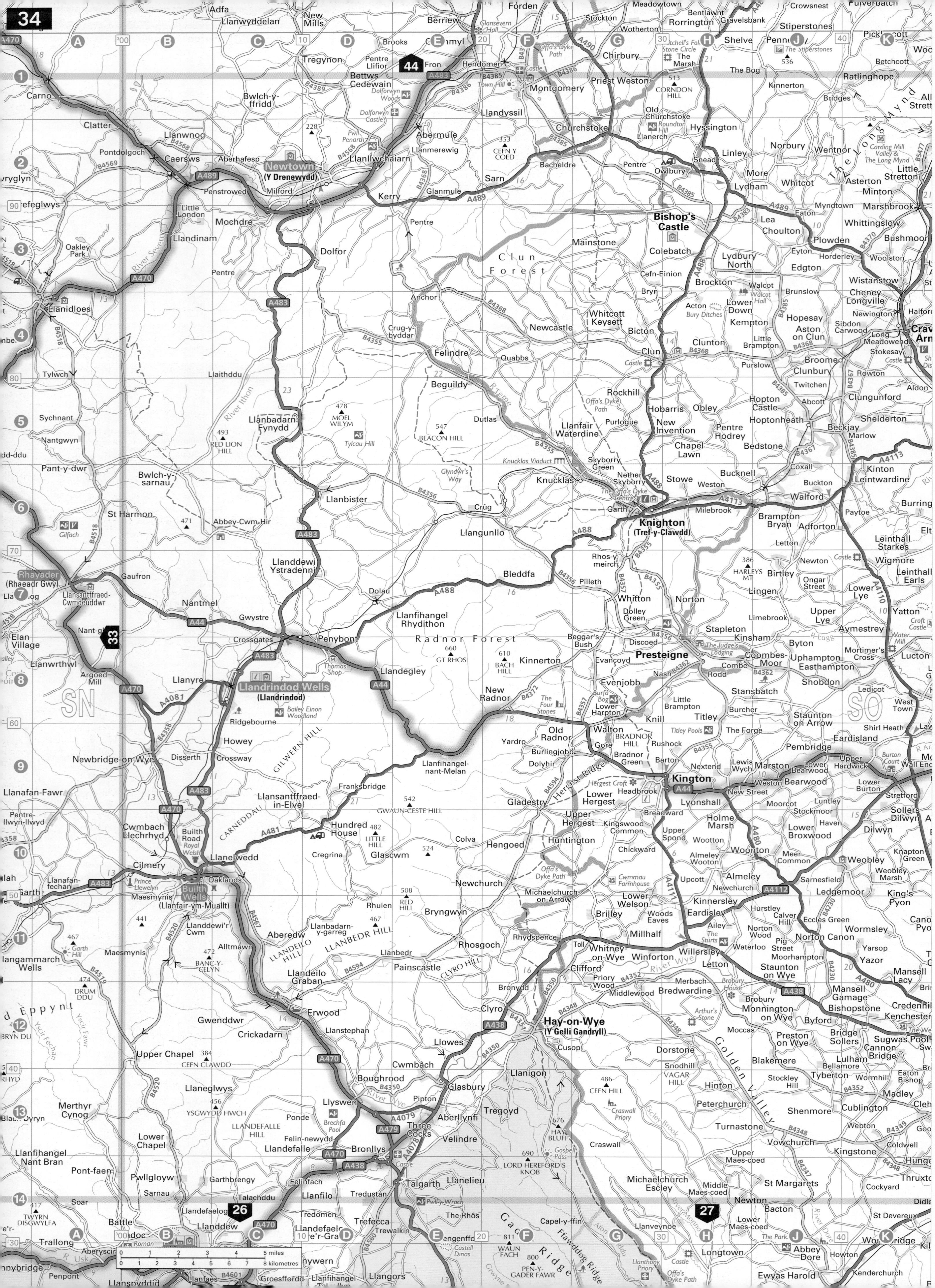

Adfa
Llanwyddelan
New Mills
Berriew
Forden
Stockton
Meadowtown
Bentlawnt
Rorrington
Gravelsbank
Crowsnest
Stiperstones
Wotherton
Tregynon
Brooks
Fron
Hendomen
Chirbury
Shelve
Pennerley
The Stiperstones
Carno
Bettws Cedewain
Montgomery
Priest Weston
Corndon Hill
The Bog
Ratlinghope
Bwlch-y-ffridd
Llandyssil
Old Churchstoke
Kinnerton
Clatter
Abermule
Churchstoke
Hyssington
Llanwnog
Pontdolgoch
Caersws
Aberhafesp
Newtown
(Y Drenewydd)
Llanllwchaiarn
Llanmerewig
Cefn y Coed
Bacheldre
Pentre
Snead
Linley
Norbury
Wentnor
The Long Mynd
Penstrowed
Milford
Kerry
Glanmule
Sarn
Owlbury
More
Lydham
Whitcot
Asterton
Little Stretton
Minton
Little London
Mochdre
Bishop's Castle
Lea
Eaton
Myndtown
Marshbrook
Oakley Park
Llandinam
Pentre
Chouiton
Plowden
Whittingslow
Bushmoor
River Severn
Dolfor
Mainstone
Colebatch
Lydbury North
Eyton
Horderley
Edgton
Woolston
Clun Forest
Cefn-Einion
Llanidloes
Brockton
Walcot
Brunslow
Wistanstow
Bryn
Acton
Lower Down
Cheney Longville
Anchor
Whitcott Keysett
Bury Ditches
Kempton
Hopesay
Newington
Crug-y-byddar
Newcastle
Bicton
Clunton
Little Brampton
Aston on Clun
Sibdon Carwood
Craven Arms
Felindre
Quabbs
Clun
Purslow
Broome
Stokesay Castle
Long Meadowend
Tylwch
Llaithddu
Clunbury
Twitchen
Rowton
Beguildy
Rockhill
Hopton Castle
Abcott
Clungunford
Aldon
Sychnant
Llanbadarn Fynydd
Moel Wilym
Dutlas
Hobarris
Obley
Shelderton
Nantgwyn
Red Lion Hill
Tylcau Hill
Beacon Hill
Purlogue
Llanfair Waterdine
New Invention
Hoptonheath
Pentre Hodrey
Beckjay
Marlow
Chapel Lawn
Bedstone
Pant-y-dwr
Knucklas Viaduct
Skyborry Green
Coxall
Kinton
Bwlch-y-sarnau
Glyndŵr's Way
Knucklas
Nether Skyborry
Stowe
Bucknell
Weston
Buckton
Leintwardine
Llanbister
Walford
St Harmon
Crûg
Knighton
(Tref-y-Clawdd)
Milebrook
Brampton Bryan
Adforton
Paytoe
Burrington
Abbey-Cwm-Hir
Llangunllo
Garth
Gilfach
Leinthall Starkes
Letton
Rhayader
(Rhaeadr Gwy)
Gaufron
Llanddewi Ystradenni
Rhos-y-meirch
Harleys Mt
Birtley
Newton
Wigmore
Llansantffraed-Cwmdeuddwr
Bleddfa
Pilleth
Ongar Street
Leinthall Earls
Lingen
Lower Lye
Elan Village
Dolau
Nantmel
Whitton
Norton
Upper Lye
Yatton
Gwystre
Llanfihangel Rhydithon
Dolley Green
Limebrook
Stapleton
Aymestrey
Croft Castle
Crossgates
Penybont
Radnor Forest
Beggar's Bush
Discoed
Kinsham
Byton
Llanwrthwl
Gt Rhos
Bach Hill
Kinnerton
Evancoyd
Presteigne
The Judge's Lodging
Combe
Coombes-Moor
Uphampton
Mortimer's Cross
Lucton
Llandegley
Easthampton
Argoed Mill
Llanyre
Llandrindod Wells
(Llandrindod)
Thomas Shop
Nash
Rodd
Shobdon
New Radnor
Evenjobb
Stansbatch
Ledicot
The Four Stones
Burfa Bog
Lower Harpton
Little Brampton
Burcher
Ridgebourne
Bailey Einon Woodland
Knill
Titley
Staunton on Arrow
West Town
Howey
Walton
Old Radnor
Yardro
Bradnor Hill
Titley Pools
The Forge
Shirl Heath
Disserth
Crossway
Gilwern Hill
Gore
Burlingjobb
Rushock
Pembridge
Eardisland
Newbridge-on-Wye
Llanfihangel-nant-Melan
Dolyhir
Bradnor Green
Barton
Nextend
Lewis Wych
Marston
Lower Bearwood
Upper Hardwick
Burton Court
Kington
Weston
Bearwood
Hergest Ridge
Hergest Croft
Headbrook
New Street
Lower Burton
Stretford
Llanafan-Fawr
Franksbridge
Llansantffraed-in-Elvel
Gwaun-Ceste Hill
Gladestry
Lower Hergest
Lyonshall
Moorcot
Luntley
Stockmoor
Sollers Dilwyn
Pentre-llwyn-llwyd
Cwmbach Llechrhyd
Builth Road
Royal Welsh
Carneddau
Hundred House
Little Hill
Upper Hergest
Kingswood Common
Breadward
Holme Marsh
Haven
Lower Broxwood
Dilwyn
Colva
Hengoed
Huntington
Upper Spond
Wootton
Chickward
Llanelwedd
Cregrina
Glascwm
Almeley Wooton
Woonton
Meer Common
Weobley
Knapton Green
Cilmery
Oaklands
Offa's Dyke Path
Cwmmau Farmhouse
Upcott
Almeley
Sarnesfield
Weobley Marsh
Llanafan-fechan
Prince Llewelyn
Builth Wells
(Llanfair-ym-Muallt)
Maesmynis
Newchurch
Michaelchurch-on-Arrow
Lower Welson
Newchurch
Ledgemoor
King's Pyon
Rhulen
Red Hill
Bryngwyn
Kinnersley
Brilley
Woods Eaves
Eardisley
Hurstley
Calver Hill
Eccles Green
Llanddewi'r Cwm
Aberedw
Llanbadarn-y-garreg
Llanbedr Hill
Llandeilo Hill
Millhalf
Ailey
The Sturts
Norton Wood
Wormsley
Norton Canon
Rhydspence
Rhosgoch
Alltmawr
Garth Hill
Banc-y-Celyn
Toll
Whitney-on-Wye
Winforton
Willersley
Pig Street
Waterloo
Moorhampton
Yarsop
Yazor
Llangammarch Wells
Maesmynis
Llanbedr
Painscastle
Clyro Hill
Clifford
Letton
River Wye
Staunton on Wye
Mansell Lacy
Llandeilo Graban
Priory Wood
Merbach
Bredwardine
Middlewood
Brobury House
Brobury
Mansell Gamage
Bishopstone
Credenhill
Drum Ddu
Bronydd
Monnington on Wye
Byford
Kenchester
Eppynt
Erwood
Clyro
Hay-on-Wye
(Y Gelli Gandryll)
Arthur's Stone
Gwenddwr
Llanstephan
Moccas
Preston on Wye
Bridge Sollers
Sugwas Pool
Crickadarn
Llowes
Cusop
Dorstone
Cannon Bridge
Upper Chapel
Cefn Clawdd
Blakemere
Lulham
Bellamore
Snodhill
Vagar Hill
Tyberton
Eaton Bishop
Cwmbach
Llanigon
Cefn Hill
Hinton
Stockley Hill
Wormhill
Madley
Boughrood
Glasbury
Golden Valley
Llaneglwys
Llyswen
River Wye
Pipton
Peterchurch
Cublington
Merthyr Cynog
Ysgwydd Hwch
Ponde
Aberllynfi
Tregoyd
Craswall Priory
Shenmore
Three Cocks
Hay Bluff
Escley Brook
Turnastone
Webton
Llandefalle Hill
Brechfa Pool
Felin-newydd
Velindre
Vowchurch
Lower Chapel
Llandefalle
Bronllys
Gospel Pass
Craswall
Kingstone
Coldwell
Llanfihangel Nant Bran
Pont-faen
Lord Hereford's Knob
Upper Maes-coed
Hungerstone
Thruxton
Pwllgloyw
Garthbrengy
Felinfach
Talgarth
Llanelieu
Michaelchurch Escley
Middle Maes-coed
St Margarets
Cockyard
Sarnau
Talachddu
Llanfilo
Tredustan
Pwll-y-Wrach
Soar
Newton
Didley
Twyn Disgwylfa
Battle
Llandefaelog
Llanddew
Tredomen
Trefecca
The Rhôs
Gadair Ridge
Capel-y-ffin
Llanveynoe
Lower Maes-coed
Bacton
St Devereux
Trallong
Trewalkin
Waun Fach
Pen-y-Gader Fawr
Flwddog Ridge
Llanthony Priory
The Park
Abbey Dore
Aberyscir
Castell Dinas
Longtown
Offa's Dyke Path
Howton
Kenderchurch
Penpont
Llanspyddid
Llanfaes
Groesffordd
Llanfihangel
Llangors
Ewyas Harold
SN
SO
A470
A483
A489
A44
A488
A481
A4081
A4113
A480
A4111
A4112
A438
A479
A4079
A4110
B4518
B4568
B4569
B4385
B4386
B4389
B4355
B4356
B4357
B4362
B4368
B4372
B4594
B4520
B4519
B4567
B4358
B4350
B4352
B4348
B4347
B4349
B4230
B4360
B4361
B4367
B4370
B4385
0 1 2 3 4 5 miles
0 1 2 3 4 5 6 7 8 kilometres
44
33
26
27

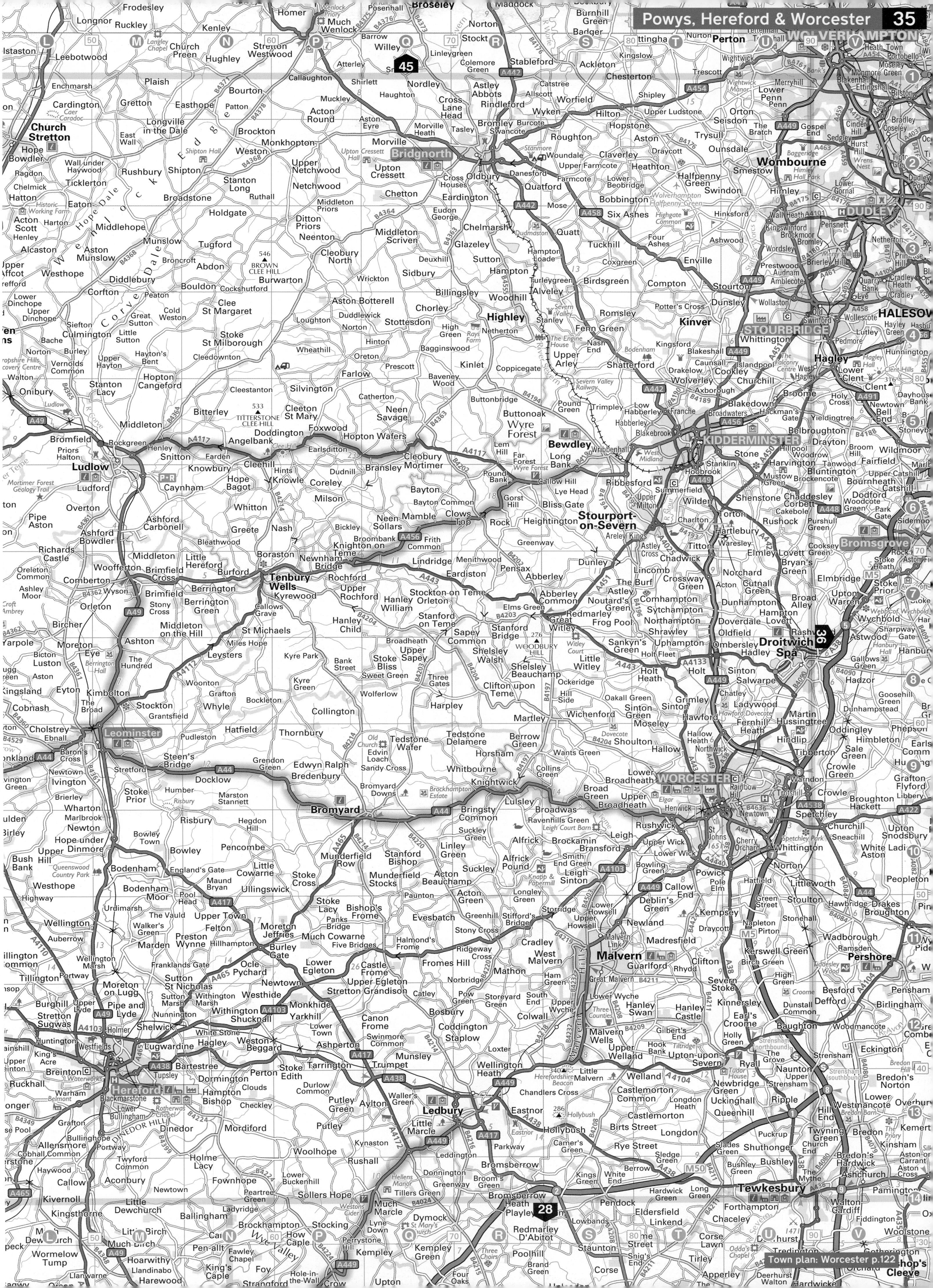
Much Wenlock
Bridgnorth
Church Stretton
Wombourne
Dudley
Highley
Kinver
Stourbridge
Hagley
Halesowen
Bewdley
Kidderminster
Ludlow
Cleobury Mortimer
Stourport-on-Severn
Tenbury Wells
Bromsgrove
Droitwich Spa
Leominster
Bromyard
Worcester
Malvern
Pershore
Hereford
Ledbury
Tewkesbury
Upton-upon-Severn
Wyre Forest
Titterstone Clee Hill
Brown Clee Hill
Woodbury Hill
Herefordshire Beacon
Wenlock Edge
Corve Dale
Hope Dale
Wolverley
Blakedown
Ombersley
Great Witley
Martley
Kingsland
Wellington
Moreton on Lugg
Withington
Stoke Lacy
Much Cowarne
Colwall
Eastnor
Kempsey
Powick
Severn Stoke
Ripple

Town plan: Worcester p.122

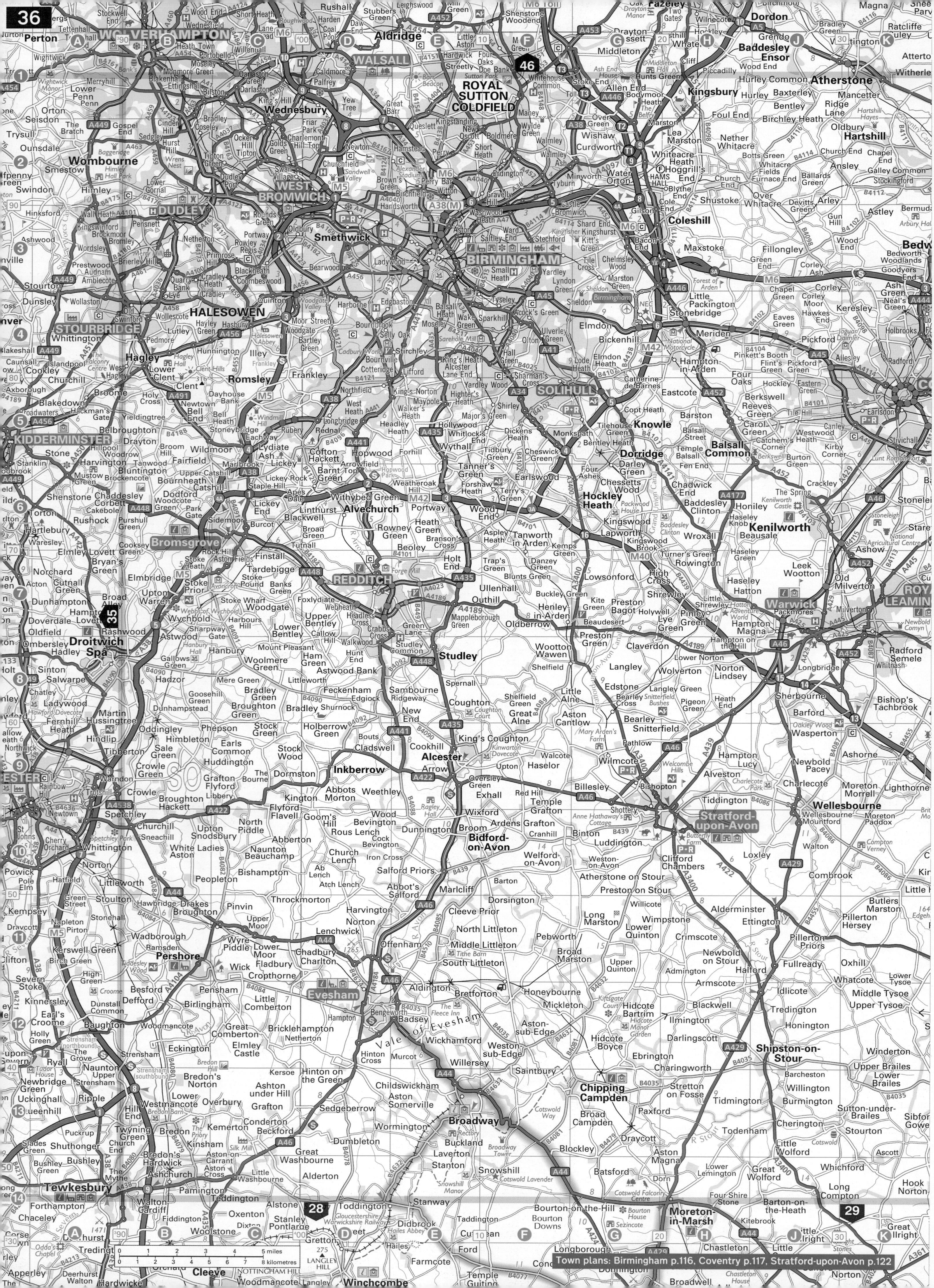

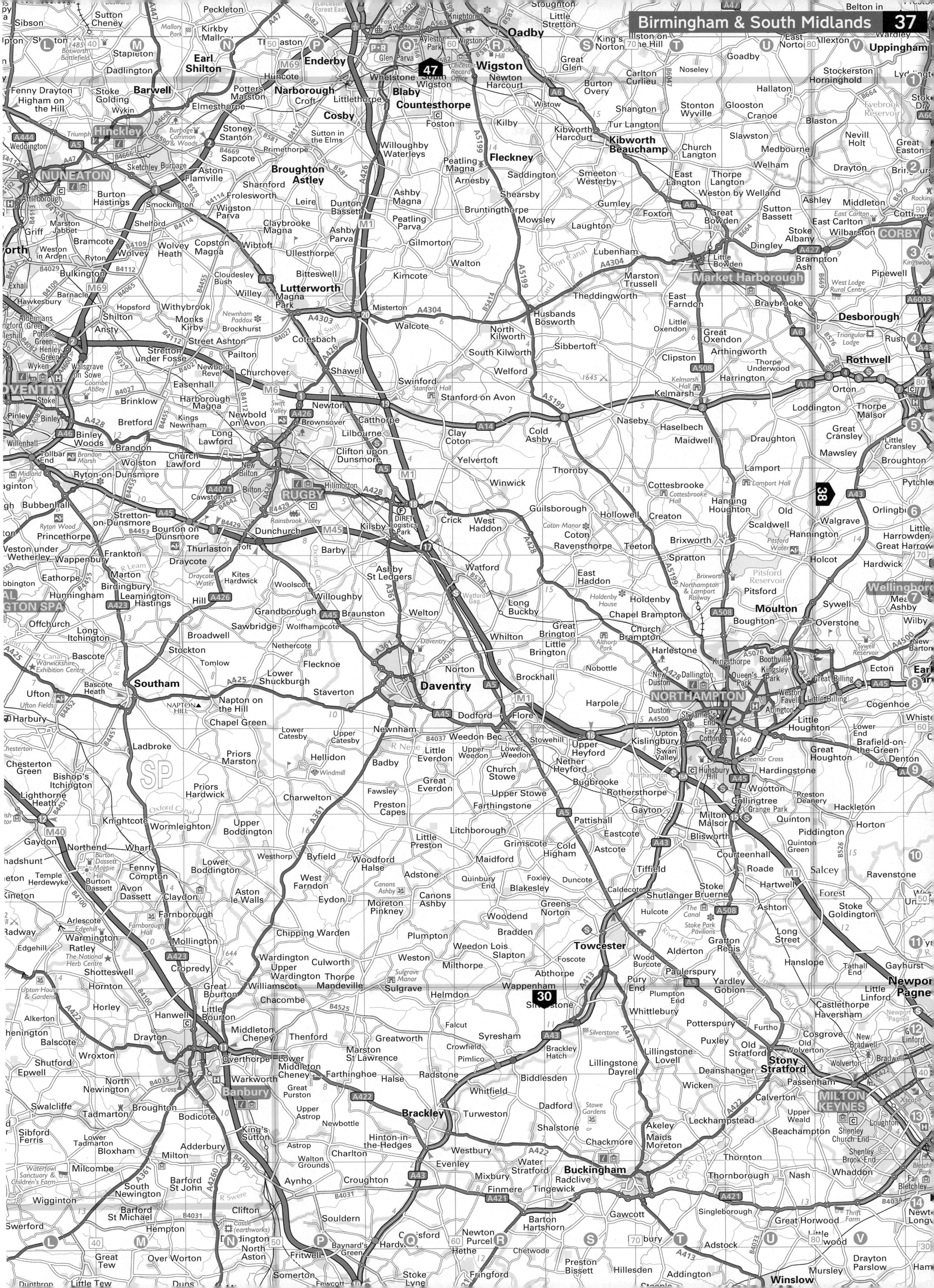

Sibson
Sutton Cheney
Peckleton
Kirkby Mallory
Stoughton
Little Stretton
Oadby
Belton in Rutland
Stapleton
Earl Shilton
Enderby
Aylestone
Wigston
King's Norton
Great Glen
Goadby
Uppingham
Dadlington
Huncote
Whetstone
South Wigston
Blaby
Newton Harcourt
Burton Overy
Carlton Curlieu
Noseley
Stockerston
Horninghold
Fenny Drayton
Higham on the Hill
Stoke Golding
Barwell
Potters Marston
Narborough
Croft
Littlethorpe
Countesthorpe
Foston
Wistow
Kilby
Shangton
Stonton Wyville
Glooston
Cranoe
Hallaton
Blaston
Elmesthorpe
Wykin
Cosby
Stoney Stanton
Sutton in the Elms
Willoughby Waterleys
Kibworth Harcourt
Kibworth Beauchamp
Tur Langton
Church Langton
Slawston
Medbourne
Nevill Holt
Great Easton
Hinckley
Sapcote
Primethorpe
Peatling Magna
Fleckney
Saddington
Smeeton Westerby
Welham
Drayton
Nuneaton
Aston Flamville
Broughton Astley
Sharnford
Frolesworth
Arnesby
East Langton
Thorpe Langton
Weston by Welland
Ashby Magna
Shearsby
Burton Hastings
Smockington
Leire
Dunton Bassett
Bruntingthorpe
Gumley
Sutton Bassett
Ashley
Middleton
Cottingham
Wigston Parva
Claybrooke Magna
Peatling Parva
Mowsley
Laughton
Foxton
Great Bowden
East Carlton
Marston Jabbet
Griff
Shelford
Bramcote
Wolvey
Wolvey Heath
Copston Magna
Wibtoft
Ashby Parva
Ullesthorpe
Gilmorton
Lubenham
Dingley
Stoke Albany
Wilbarston
Corby
Weston in Arden
Ryton
Bulkington
Bitteswell
Walton
Kimcote
Little Bowden
Brampton Ash
Market Harborough
Pipewell
Exhall
Barnacle
Cloudesley Bush
Willey
Lutterworth
Marston Trussell
Theddingworth
East Farndon
Braybrooke
Hawkesbury
Hopsford
Withybrook
Shilton
Monks Kirby
Ansty
Magna Park
Misterton
Walcote
Husbands Bosworth
Little Oxendon
Great Oxendon
Desborough
Street Ashton
Cotesbach
North Kilworth
South Kilworth
Sibbertoft
Arthingworth
Rush
Stretton under Fosse
Pailton
Newbold Revel
Churchover
Shawell
Swinford
Stanford Hall
Welford
Clipston
Thorpe Underwood
Harrington
Rothwell
Wyken
Walsgrave on Sowe
Coombe Abbey
Coventry
Easenhall
Harborough Magna
Brinklow
Newton
Stanford on Avon
Kelmarsh
Orton
Loddington
Thorpe Malsor
Stoke
Binley
Pinley
Binley Woods
Bretford
Kings Newnham
Newbold on Avon
Brownsover
Catthorpe
Lilbourne
Clay Coton
Cold Ashby
Naseby
Haselbech
Maidwell
Draughton
Great Cransley
Little Cransley
Willenhall
Tollbar End
Brandon
Long Lawford
Church Lawford
Wolston
Ryton-on-Dunsmore
New Bilton
Bilton
Clifton upon Dunsmore
Yelvertoft
Mawsley
Broughton
Baginton
Bubbenhall
Cawston
Rugby
Hillmorton
Winwick
Thornby
Lamport
Cottesbrooke
Pytchley
Stretton-on-Dunsmore
Bourton on Dunsmore
Princethorpe
Dunchurch
Crick
West Haddon
Guilsborough
Hollowell
Creaton
Hanging Houghton
Old
Walgrave
Orlingbury
Kilsby
DIRFT Logistics Park
Coton Manor
Coton
Ravensthorpe
Teeton
Brixworth
Scaldwell
Hannington
Little Harrowden
Great Harrowden
Weston under Wetherley
Wappenbury
Frankton
Thurlaston
Toft
Barby
Spratton
Pitsford Water
Holcot
Hardwick
Eathorpe
Marton
Birdingbury
Kites Hardwick
Ashby St Ledgers
Watford
East Haddon
Pitsford Reservoir
Pitsford
Hunningham
Leamington Hastings
Hill
Woolscott
Willoughby
Watford Gap
Long Buckby
Holdenby
Moulton
Sywell
Wellingborough
Mears Ashby
Leamington Spa
Offchurch
Grandborough
Sawbridge
Wolfhampcote
Braunston
Welton
Chapel Brampton
Church Brampton
Boughton
Overstone
Wilby
Long Itchington
Broadwell
Nethercote
Great Brington
Little Brington
Whilton
Harlestone
Kingsthorpe
Boothville
Kingsley
Bascote
Stockton
Tomlow
Flecknoe
Daventry
Norton
Nobottle
New Duston
Dallington
Queen's Park
Great Billing
Ecton
Earls Barton
Bascote Heath
Southam
Lower Shuckburgh
Brockhall
Duston
Northampton
Weston Favell
Little Billing
Abington
Cogenhoe
Ufton
Napton on the Hill
Napton Hill
Staverton
Harpole
Flore
Dodford
St James's End
Far Cotton
Little Houghton
Harbury
Chapel Green
Newnham
Weedon Bec
Stowehill
Upper Heyford
Kislingbury
Swan Valley
Lower End
Brafield-on-the-Green
Denton
Lower Catesby
Upper Catesby
Little Everdon
Upper Weedon
Lower Weedon
Nether Heyford
Hunsbury Hill
Eleanor Cross
Great Houghton
Ladbroke
Chesterton
Chesterton Green
Priors Marston
Hellidon
Badby
Church Stowe
Bugbrooke
Hardingstone
Bishop's Itchington
Great Everdon
Rothersthorpe
Wootton
Preston Deanery
Fawsley
Upper Stowe
Collingtree
Grange Park
Lighthorne Heath
Priors Hardwick
Charwelton
Preston Capes
Farthingstone
Gayton
Milton Malsor
Hackleton
Knightcote
Wormleighton
Upper Boddington
Pattishall
Eastcote
Quinton
Horton
Gaydon
Northend
Wharf
Little Preston
Litchborough
Grimscote
Cold Higham
Astcote
Blisworth
Piddington
Quinton Green
Lower Boddington
Westhorp
Byfield
Woodford Halse
Maidford
Tiffield
Courteenhall
Hadshunt
Temple Herdewyke
Burton Dassett
Fenny Compton
Adstone
Quinbury End
Foxley
Duncote
Roade
Salcey Forest
Ravenstone
Kineton
Avon Dassett
Claydon
Aston le Walls
West Farndon
Canons Ashby
Blakesley
Caldecote
Stoke Bruerne
Shutlanger
Hartwell
Eydon
Moreton Pinkney
Greens Norton
Hulcote
Ashton
Stoke Goldington
Arlescote
Farnborough
Woodend
The Canal
Stoke Park Pavilions
Long Street
Radway
Edgehill
Warmington
Chipping Warden
Plumpton
Bradden
Towcester
Grafton Regis
Ratley
Mollington
Wardington
Culworth
Weedon Lois
Slapton
Wood Burcote
Alderton
Hanslope
The National Herb Centre
Shotteswell
Cropredy
Upper Wardington
Weston
Milthorpe
Abthorpe
Foscote
Tathall End
Gayhurst
Hornton
Great Bourton
Williamscot
Thorpe Mandeville
Sulgrave Manor
Sulgrave
Wappenham
Pury End
Paulerspury
Plumpton End
Yardley Gobion
Little Linford
Newport Pagnell
Upton House & Gardens
Horley
Little Bourton
Chacombe
Helmdon
Silverstone
Whittlebury
Castlethorpe
Haversham
Alkerton
Hanwell
Middleton Cheney
Falcut
Syresham
Potterspury
Furtho
Shenington
Balscote
Drayton
Thenford
Greatworth
Crowfield
Pimlico
Brackley Hatch
Lillingstone Lovell
Puxley
Old Stratford
Cosgrove
Old Wolverton
New Bradwell
Bradwell
Shutford
Wroxton
Overthorpe
Marston St Lawrence
Lower Middleton Cheney
Farthinghoe
Radstone
Lillingstone Dayrell
Stony Stratford
Wolverton
Epwell
Banbury
Warkworth
Great Purston
Halse
Whitfield
Biddlesden
Deanshanger
Passenham
North Newington
Swalcliffe
Broughton
Tadmarton
Bodicote
Upper Astrop
Newbottle
Brackley
Turweston
Dadford
Stowe Gardens
Wicken
Calverton
Milton Keynes
Upper Weald
Shenley Church End
Shenley Brook End
Loughton
Sibford Ferris
Lower Tadmarton
Bloxham
King's Sutton
Adderbury
Hinton-in-the-Hedges
Astrop
Shalstone
Leckhampstead
Akeley
Maids Moreton
Chackmore
Beachampton
Milton
Milcombe
Walton Grounds
Charlton
Westbury
Evenley
Water Stratford
Buckingham
Thornton
Whaddon
Waterfowl Sanctuary & Children's Farm
South Newington
Barford St John
Aynho
Croughton
Mixbury
Finmere
Tingewick
Radclive
Thornborough
Nash
Bletchley
Wigginton
Barford St Michael
Souldern
Gawcott
Singleborough
Great Horwood
Thrift Farm
Newton Longville
Swerford
Hempton
Deddington
North Aston
Fritwell
Baynard's Green
Hardwick
Cottisford
Newton Purcell
Hethe
Chetwode
Barton Hartshorn
Tingewick
Preston Bissett
Adstock
Little Horwood
Swanbourne
Drayton Parslow
Great Tew
Over Worton
Somerton
Stoke Lyne
Fringford
Hillesden
Addington
Mursley
Winslow
Little Tew
Dunthrop
Duns Tew
Fewcott

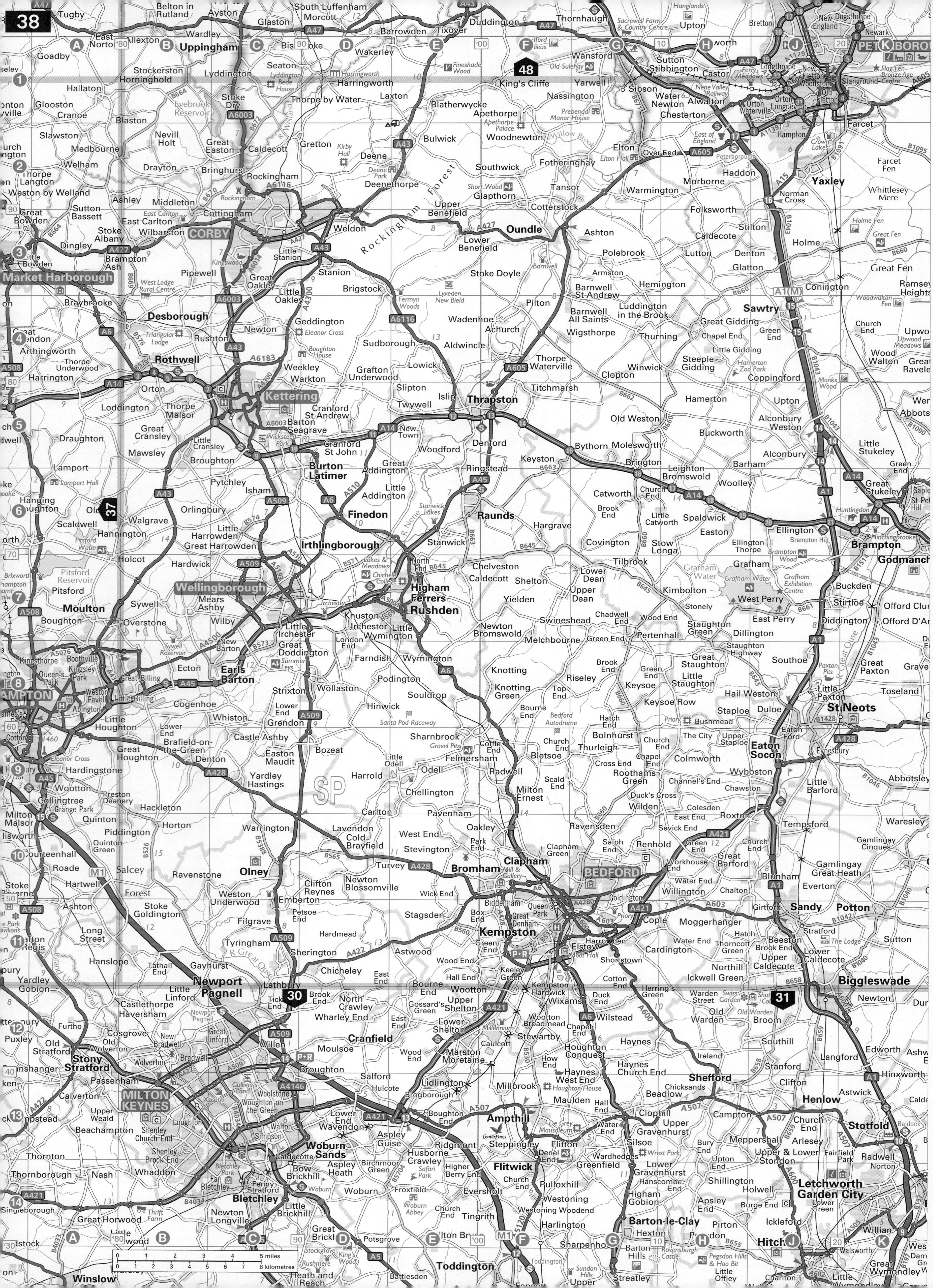

Tugby
Belton in Rutland
Ayston
Glaston
South Luffenham
Morcott
Duddington
Thornhaugh
Upton
Bretton
Wardley
Uppingham
Barrowden
Tixover
Wansford
Sutton
Stibbington
Castor
Peterborough
Goadby
Stockerston
Horninghold
Lyddington
Seaton
Harringworth
Wakerley
King's Cliffe
Yarwell
Nassington
Sibson
Water Newton
Alwalton
Chesterton
Orton Waterville
Orton Longueville
Hampton
Farcet
Hallaton
Glooston
Cranoe
Blaston
Stoke Dry
Eyebrook Reservoir
Thorpe by Water
Laxton
Blatherwycke
Apethorpe
Woodnewton
Slawston
Medbourne
Nevill Holt
Great Easton
Caldecott
Gretton
Kirby Hall
Bulwick
Deene
Fotheringhay
Elton
Over End
Haddon
Yaxley
Welham
Drayton
Bringhurst
Rockingham
Deenethorpe
Southwick
Tansor
Morborne
Norman Cross
Farcet Fen
Whittlesey Mere
Thorpe Langton
Weston by Welland
Ashley
Middleton
Cottingham
Upper Benefield
Glapthorn
Cotterstock
Warmington
Folksworth
Stilton
Great Bowden
Sutton Bassett
Stoke Albany
East Carlton
Wilbarston
CORBY
Weldon
Rockingham Forest
Lower Benefield
Oundle
Ashton
Caldecote
Holme
Dingley
Brampton Ash
Little Bowden
Little Stanion
Stanion
Polebrook
Lutton
Denton
Glatton
Great Fen
Market Harborough
Pipewell
Great Oakley
Little Oakley
Brigstock
Stoke Doyle
Armston
Barnwell
Hemington
Conington
Ramsey Heights
Braybrooke
Desborough
Rushton
Geddington
Lyveden New Bield
Pilton
Barnwell St Andrew
Barnwell All Saints
Luddington in the Brook
Sawtry
Wadenhoe
Achurch
Aldwincle
Wigsthorpe
Thurning
Great Gidding
Chapel End
Green End
Little Gidding
Church End
Upwood
Arthingworth
Thorpe Underwood
Rothwell
Newton
Sudborough
Thorpe Waterville
Winwick
Steeple Gidding
Coppingford
Wood Walton
Great Raveley
Harrington
Orton
Kettering
Weekley
Warkton
Grafton Underwood
Lowick
Slipton
Twywell
Islip
Thrapston
Titchmarsh
Clopton
Hamerton
Upton
Wennington
Abbots Ripton
Loddington
Thorpe Malsor
Cranford St Andrew
Barton Seagrave
Cranford St John
Old Weston
Alconbury Weston
Alconbury
Buckworth
Little Stukeley
Great Stukeley
Draughton
Great Cransley
Little Cransley
Mawsley
Broughton
Burton Latimer
Woodford
Denford
Keyston
Bythorn
Molesworth
Brington
Leighton Bromswold
Barham
Woolley
Lamport
Hanging Houghton
Pytchley
Isham
Great Addington
Little Addington
Ringstead
Raunds
Catworth
Brook End
Little Catworth
Spaldwick
Easton
Ellington
Ellington Thorpe
Brampton
Huntingdon
Godmanchester
Old
Orlingbury
Walgrave
Scaldwell
Hannington
Finedon
Stanwick
Hargrave
Covington
Stow Longa
Tilbrook
Grafham
Grafham Water
Buckden
Holcot
Little Harrowden
Great Harrowden
Irthlingborough
Chelveston
Caldecott
Shelton
Lower Dean
Upper Dean
Kimbolton
West Perry
East Perry
Stirtloe
Offord Cluny
Offord D'Arcy
Diddington
Brixworth
Pitsford Reservoir
Pitsford
Hardwick
Wellingborough
Mears Ashby
Sywell
Higham Ferrers
Rushden
Yielden
Swineshead
Chadwell End
Wood End
Pertenhall
Stonely
Staughton Green
Dillington
Moulton
Boughton
Overstone
Wilby
Little Irchester
Irchester
Knuston
Little Wymington
Newton Bromswold
Melchbourne
Green End
Great Staughton
Staughton Highway
Southoe
Great Paxton
Kingsthorpe
Boothville
Kingsley Park
Ecton
Earls Barton
Great Doddington
London End
Farndish
Wymington
Knotting
Knotting Green
Riseley
Keysoe
Little Staughton
Hail Weston
Little Paxton
St Neots
Toseland
Great Billing
Little Billing
Weston Favell
Abington
Cogenhoe
Strixton
Wollaston
Podington
Souldrop
Top End
Bourne End
Keysoe Row
Staploe
Duloe
Little Houghton
Whiston
Lower End
Grendon
Hinwick
Santa Pod Raceway
Bedford Autodrome
Hatch End
Bolnhurst
Upper Staploe
Eaton Ford
Eaton Socon
Eynesbury
Brafield-on-the-Green
Great Houghton
Castle Ashby
Denton
Easton Maudit
Bozeat
Sharnbrook
Felmersham
Bletsoe
Thurleigh
Church End
Colmworth
Cross End
Ravensden
Hardingstone
Wootton
Collingtree
Yardley Hastings
Little Odell
Odell
Harrold
Radwell
Milton Ernest
Roothams Green
Channel's End
Wyboston
Chawston
Little Barford
Abbotsley
Preston Deanery
Hackleton
Horton
Chellington
Carlton
Pavenham
Oakley
Duck's Cross
Wilden
Colesden
Roxton
Tempsford
Waresley
Milton Malsor
Quinton
Piddington
Warrington
Lavendon
Cold Brayfield
West End
Stevington
Park End
Clapham
Salph End
Renhold
Great Barford
Gamlingay
Courteenhall
Roade
Salcey
Ravenstone
Olney
Turvey
Bromham
BEDFORD
Willington
Blunham
Gamlingay Great Heath
Stoke Bruerne
Hartwell
Forest
Weston Underwood
Clifton Reynes
Newton Blossomville
Emberton
Wick End
Biddenham
Queen's Park
Goldington
Cople
Moggerhanger
Girtford
Sandy
Potton
Everton
Ashton
Stoke Goldington
Petsoe End
Stagsden
Box End
Kempston
Great Denham
Elstow
Harrowden
Shortstown
Cardington
Water End
Thorncote Green
Beeston
Upper Caldecote
Lower Caldecote
Sutton
Long Street
Filgrave
Tyringham
Hardmead
Astwood
Sherington
Hanslope
Tathall End
Gayhurst
Chicheley
East End
Wood End
Hall End
Keeley Green
Kempston Hardwick
Cotton End
Ickwell Green
Northill
Biggleswade
Yardley Gobion
Little Linford
Newport Pagnell
Lathbury
Tickford End
Brook End
North Crawley
Bourne End
Wootton
Upper Shelton
Lower Shelton
Wixams
Duck End
Wilstead
Herring's Green
Warden Street
Old Warden
Broom
Newton
Castlethorpe
Haversham
Wharley End
Cranfield
Gossard's Green
Stewartby
Broadmead
Chapel End
Haynes
Southill
Puxley
Old Stratford
Furtho
Cosgrove
Old Wolverton
New Bradwell
Great Linford
Willen
Moulsoe
Marston Moretaine
Caulcott
Houghton Conquest
Ireland
Langford
Edworth
Stony Stratford
Bradwell
Wolverton
Broughton
Wood End
How End
Haynes West End
Haynes Church End
Shefford
Stanford
Hinxworth
Passenham
Calverton
Salford
Hulcote
Lidlington
Millbrook
Chicksands
Clifton
Astwick
MILTON KEYNES
Woolstone
Woughton on the Green
Brogborough
Maulden
Hall End
Beadlow
Henlow
Upper Weald
Loughton
Lower End
Wavendon
Boughton End
Ampthill
Clophill
Campton
Church End
Stotfold
Beachampton
Shenley Church End
Walton
Simpson
Aspley Guise
Ridgmont
Steppingley
Water End
Upper Gravenhurst
Silsoe
Meppershall
Arlesey
Thornton
Shenley Brook End
Woburn Sands
Husborne Crawley
Flitton
Wardhedges
Bury End
Upper & Lower Stondon
Fairfield Park
Radwell
Norton
Thornborough
Nash
Whaddon
Caldecotte
Bow Brickhill
Aspley Heath
Birchmoor Green
Higher Berry End
Flitwick
Denel End
Greenfield
Lower Gravenhurst
Hanscombe End
Upton End
Shillington
Holwell
Letchworth Garden City
Fenny Stratford
Far Bletchley
Bletchley
Woburn
Froxfield
Eversholt
Church End
Pulloxhill
Higham Gobion
Apsley End
Burge End
Lower Green
Singleborough
Great Horwood
Newton Longville
Little Brickhill
Woburn Abbey
Church End
Tingrith
Westoning
Westoning Woodend
Barton-le-Clay
Ickleford
Little Horwood
Great Brickhill
Potsgrove
Harlington
Hexton
Pirton
Hitchin
William
Walsworth
Istock
Stockgrove
Rushmere
Sharpenhoe
Barton Hills
Pegsdon Hills & Hoo Bit
Great Wymondley
Little Wymondley
Winslow
Heath and Reach
Battlesden
Toddington
Sundon Hills
Upper
Streatley
Charlton
Little Offley
30
31
37
48
SP

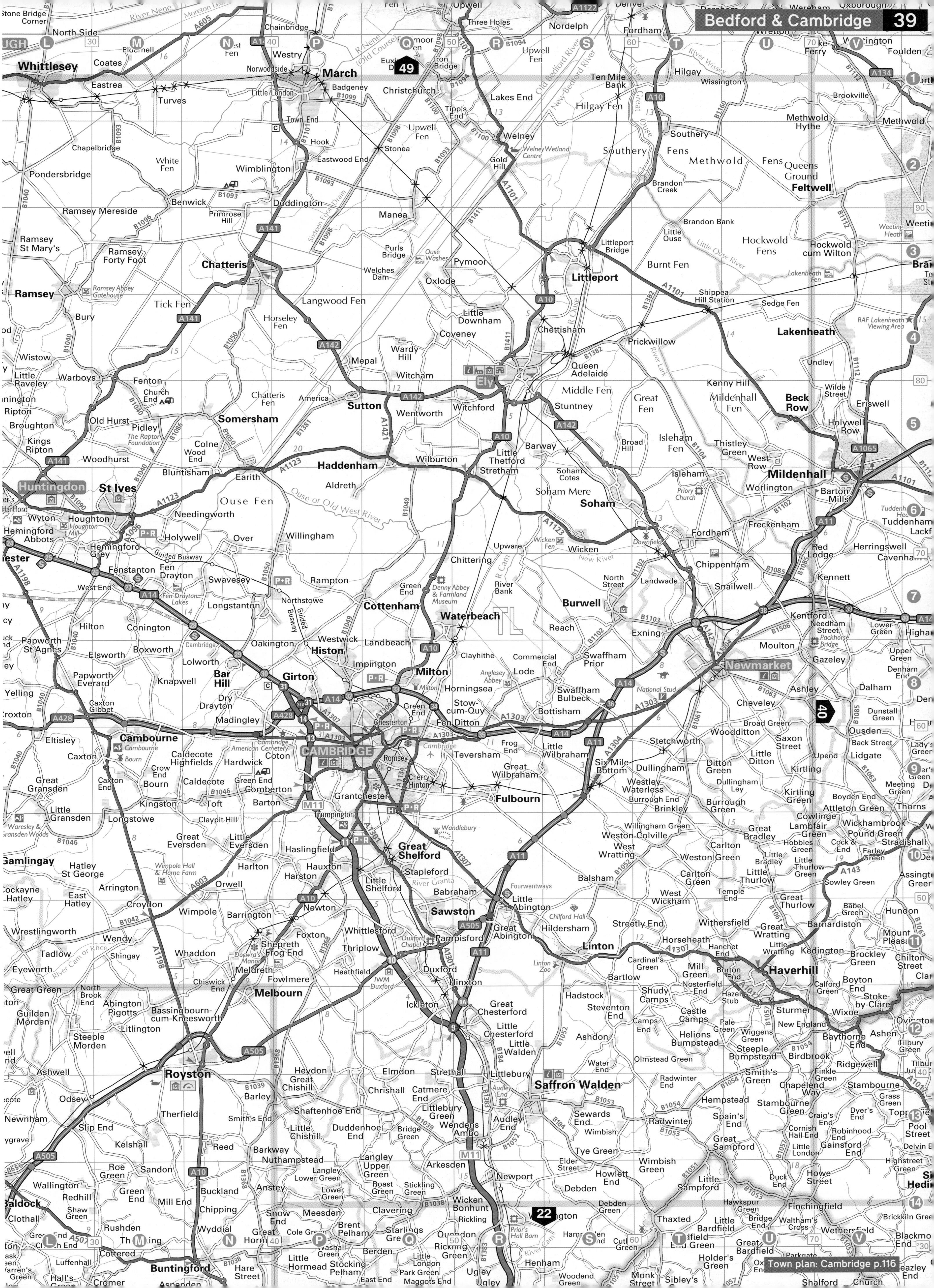
Whittlesey
March
Chatteris
Ramsey
Littleport
Ely
Sutton
Somersham
Haddenham
St Ives
Huntingdon
Mildenhall
Soham
Burwell
Newmarket
Cottenham
Waterbeach
Histon
Girton
Milton
CAMBRIDGE
Cambourne
Great Shelford
Fulbourn
Sawston
Linton
Haverhill
Melbourn
Royston
Saffron Walden
Buntingford
Baldock
Lakenheath
Feltwell
Beck Row
Gamlingay
Town plan: Cambridge p.116

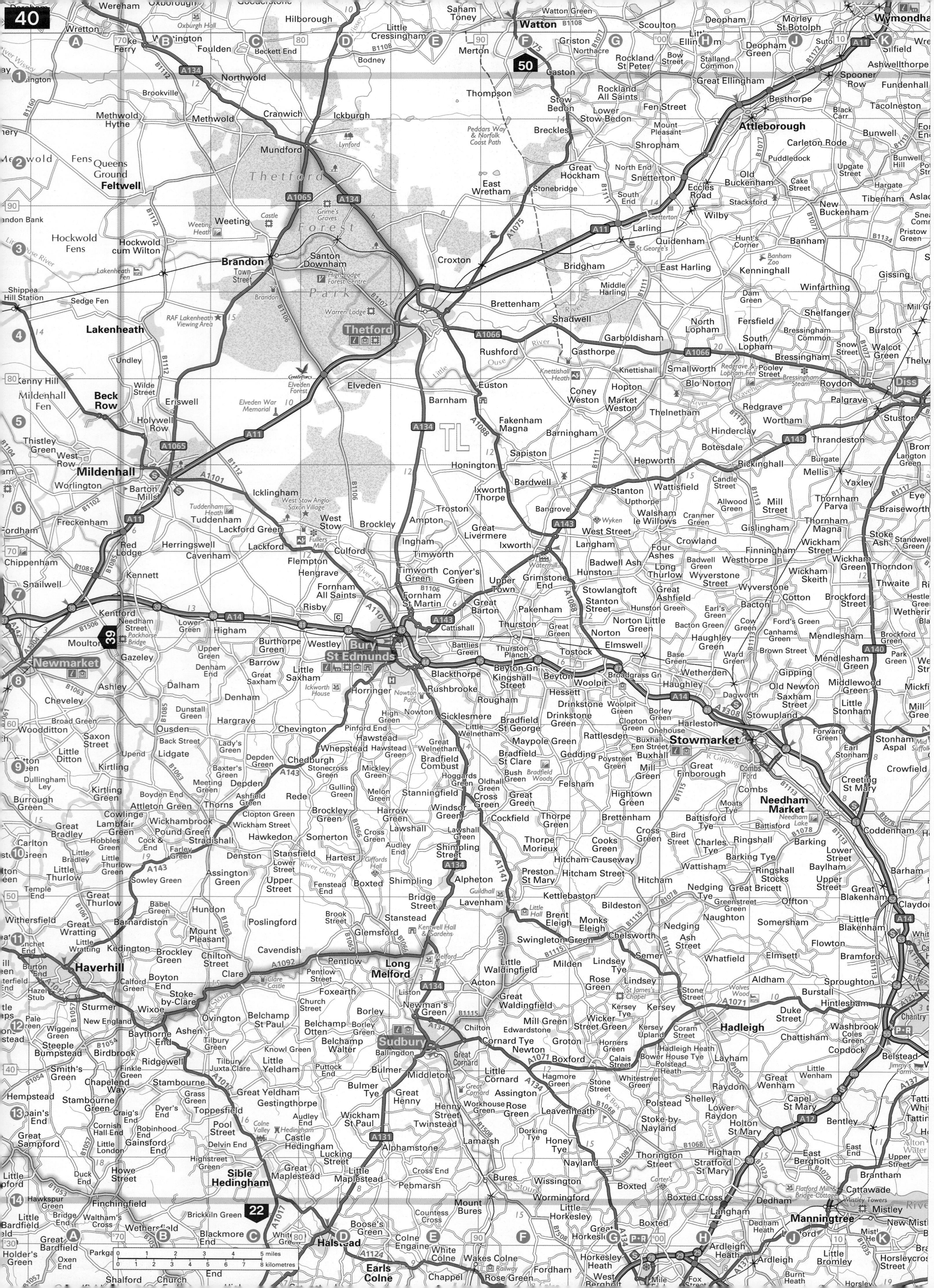

Wereham
Oxborough
Hilborough
Saham Toney
Watton
Watton Green
Scoulton
Deopham
Morley St Botolph
Wymondham
Wretton
Stoke Ferry
Wretton
Foulden
Beckett End
Little Cressingham
Bodney
Merton
Griston
Northacre
Rockland St Peter
Bow Street
Little Ellingham
Stalland Common
Deopham Green
Suton
Silfield
Ashwellthorpe
Oxburgh Hall
50
Northwold
Caston
Great Ellingham
Spooner Row
Fundenhall
Brookville
Thompson
Rockland All Saints
Stow Bedon
Fen Street
Lower Stow Bedon
Besthorpe
Tacolneston
Methwold Hythe
Methwold
Cranwich
Ickburgh
Attleborough
Black Carr
Breckles
Mount Pleasant
Lynford
Peddars Way & Norfolk Coast Path
Shropham
Carleton Rode
Bunwell
Mundford
Great Hockham
North End
Snetterton
Old Buckenham
Puddledock
Upgate Street
Bunwell Hill
Fens
Queens Ground
Feltwell
Thetford
East Wretham
Stonebridge
South End
Eccles Road
Cake Street
Hargate
Tibenham
Aslacton
Grime's Graves
Stacksford
New Buckenham
Hockwold Fens
Hockwold cum Wilton
Weeting
Weeting Heath
Castle
Forest
Larling
Wilby
Pristow Green
Quidenham
Hunt's Corner
Banham
Banham Zoo
Brandon
Town Street
Santon Downham
Croxton
St George's
Bridgham
East Harling
Kenninghall
Gissing
Lakenheath Fen
High Lodge Forest Centre
Shippea Hill Station
Sedge Fen
Brandon
Park
Middle Harling
Winfarthing
Warren Lodge
Brettenham
Dam Green
Mill Green
RAF Lakenheath Viewing Area
Shadwell
Shelfanger
Lakenheath
Thetford
North Lopham
Fersfield
Burston
Garboldisham
South Lopham
Bressingham Common
Walcot Green
Undley
Rushford
River Ouse
Gasthorpe
Snow Street
Bressingham
Knettishall Heath
Knettishall
Smallworth
Redgrave & Lopham Fen
Pooley Street
Bressingham Steam
Roydon
Diss
Kenny Hill
Mildenhall Fen
Beck Row
Wilde Street
Eriswell
Center Parcs Elveden Forest
Elveden
Euston
Barnham
Coney Weston
Hopton
Market Weston
Blo Norton
Palgrave
Thelnetham
Redgrave
Wortham
Stuston
Elveden War Memorial
Holywell Row
Fakenham Magna
Barningham
Hinderclay
Botesdale
Thrandeston
Thistley Green
West Row
Mildenhall
Worlington
Barton Mills
Sapiston
Honington
Hepworth
Rickinghall
Burgate
Mellis
Yaxley
Icklingham
West Stow Anglo-Saxon Village
Bardwell
Ixworth Thorpe
Stanton
Wattisfield
Candle Street
Upthorpe
Allwood Green
Mill Street
Thornham Parva
Eye
Braiseworth
Tuddenham Heath
Tuddenham
Freckenham
Troston
West Stow
Brockley
Ampton
Great Livermere
Bangrove
Walsham le Willows
Cranmer Green
Wyken
West Street
Gislingham
Thornham Magna
Stoke Ash
Lackford Green
Lackford
Herringswell
Cavenham
Red Lodge
Fullers Mill
Culford
Ingham
Timworth
Ixworth
Langham
Four Ashes
Crowland
Finningham
Wickham Street
Fordham
Chippenham
Kennett
Flempton
Hengrave
Timworth Green
Conyer's Green
Upper Town
Grimstone End
Badwell Ash
Hunston
Long Thurlow
Badwell Green
Wyverstone Street
Westhorpe
Wickham Skeith
Wickham Green
Thorndon
Snailwell
Fornham All Saints
Fornham St Martin
Great Barton
Stowlangtoft
Stanton Street
Great Ashfield
Wyverstone
Cotton
Brockford Street
Thwaite
Kentford
Needham Street
Packhorse Bridge
Lower Green
Higham
Risby
Pakenham
Hunston Green
Earl's Green
Bacton
Wetheringsett
Newmarket
Moulton
Gazeley
Upper Green
Burthorpe Green
Westley
Bury St Edmunds
Cattishall
Thurston
Great Green
Norton
Norton Little Green
Bacton Green
Cow Green
Ford's Green
Canhams Green
Mendlesham
Brockford Green
Battlies Green
Thurston Planch
Tostock
Elmswell
Haughley Green
Ward Green
Brown Street
Park Green
Denham End
Barrow
Great Saxham
Little Saxham
Ickworth House
Horringer
Nowton Park
Beyton Green
Kingshall Street
Beyton
Woolpit
Broadgrass Green
Base Green
Wetherden
Haughley
Gipping
Old Newton
Mendlesham Green
Middlewood Green
Mickfield
Cheveley
Ashley
Dalham
Denham
Dunstall Green
Blackthorpe
Rushbrooke
Rougham
Hessett
Drinkstone
Drinkstone Green
Woolpit Green
Borley Green
Dagworth
Saxham Street
Little Stonham
Broad Green
Woodditton
Saxon Street
Ousden
Hargrave
Chevington
High Green
Nowton
Sicklesmere
Little Welnetham
Bradfield St George
Clopton Green
Onehouse
Harleston
Stowupland
Forward Green
Stonham Aspal
Earl Stonham
Little Ditton
Back Street
Lady's Green
Upend
Lidgate
Pinford End
Hawstead
Hawstead Green
Great Welnetham
Maypole Green
Rattlesden
Buxhall Fen Street
Stowmarket
Buxhall
Gedding
Poystreet Green
Bradfield Combust
Bradfield St Clare
Bradfield Woods
Chedburgh
Depden Green
Baxter's Green
Kirtling
Dullingham Ley
Stonecross Green
Whepstead
Mickley Green
Hoggards Green
Oldhall Green
Bush Green
Mill Green
Great Finborough
Combs Ford
Crowfield
Creeting St Mary
Depden
Meeting Green
Gulling Green
Cross Green
Felsham
Combs
Kirtling Green
Burrough Green
Boyden End
Ashfield Green
Rede
Melon Green
Stanningfield
Great Green
Hightown Green
Needham Market
Cowlinge
Attleton Green
Thorns
Brockley Green
Harrow Green
Windsor Green
Cockfield
Thorpe Green
Brettenham
Moats Tye
Battisford Tye
Battisford
Needham Lake
Coddenham
Great Bradley
Lambfair Green
Wickhambrook
Clopton Green
Wickham Street
Lawshall
Lawshall Green
Cross Green
Bird Street
Charles Tye
Ringshall
Barking
Hobbles Green
Pound Green
Cock & End
Stradishall
Hawkedon
Somerton
Audley End
Shimpling Street
Thorpe Morieux
Cooks Green
Barking Tye
Lower Street
Carlton Green
Little Bradley
Farley Green
Denston
Stansfield
Hartest
Gifford Hall
Hitcham Causeway
Ringshall Stocks
Baylham
Barham
Little Thurlow Green
Little Thurlow
Lower Street
River Glem
Preston St Mary
Hitcham Street
Wattisham
Upper Street
Sowley Green
Assington Green
Upper Street
Fenstead End
Boxted
Shimpling
Alpheton
Hitcham
Nedging Tye
Great Bricett
Great Blakenham
Temple End
Great Thurlow
Guildhall
Kettlebaston
Greenstreet Green
Offton
Claydon
Babel Green
Hundon
Brook Street
Bridge Street
Lavenham
Little Hall
Bildeston
Naughton
Somersham
Little Blakenham
Withersfield
Great Wratting
Barnardiston
Poslingford
Stanstead
Kentwell Hall & Gardens
Brent Eleigh
Monks Eleigh
Nedging
Flowton
Little Wratting
Mount Pleasant
Glemsford
Swingleton Green
Chelsworth
Ash Street
Kedington
Cavendish
Semer
Whatfield
Elmsett
Bramford
Brockley Green
Chilton Street
Pentlow
Long Melford
Melford Hall
Little Waldingfield
Milden
Lindsey Tye
Haverhill
Boyton End
Clare
Pentlow Street
Clare Castle
Foxearth
Acton
Rose Green
Lindsey
Aldham
Sproughton
Calford Green
Stoke-by-Clare
Liston
St James's Chapel
Stone Street
Burstall
Hazel Stub
Sturmer
Wixoe
Church Street
Great Waldingfield
Kersey Tye
Kersey
Wolves Wood
Duke Street
Hintlesham
Chantry
New England
Ovington
Belchamp St Paul
Belchamp Otten
Borley
Borley Green
Newman's Green
Chilton
Mill Green
Edwardstone
Wicker Street Green
Kersey Upland
Coram Street
Hadleigh
Chattisham
Washbrook
Wiggens Green
Baythorne End
Ashen
Tilbury Green
Belchamp Walter
Sudbury
Ballingdon
Cornard Tye
Newton
Groton
Horners Green
Hadleigh Heath
Copdock
Steeple Bumpstead
Birdbrook
Ridgewell
Knowl Green
Tilbury Juxta Clare
Little Yeldham
Puttock End
Great Cornard
Boxford
Calais Street
Bower House Tye
Polstead Heath
Layham
Belstead
Smith's Green
Finkle Green
Stambourne
Bulmer
Middleton
Little Cornard
Hagmore Green
Whitestreet Green
Wenham
Chapelend Way
Great Yeldham
Bulmer Tye
Great Henny
Great Cornard
Assington
Stone Street
Raydon
Great Wenham
Hempstead
Stambourne Green
Grass Green
Gestingthorpe
Henny Street
Workhouse Green
Rose Green
Leavenheath
Polstead
Shelley
Capel St Mary
Tattingstone
Toppesfield
Dyer's End
Craig's End
Audley End
Wickham St Paul
Twinstead
Stoke-by-Nayland
Lower Raydon
Holton St Mary
Bentley
Cornish Hall End
Robinhood End
Pool Street
Colne Valley
Hedingham Castle
Castle Hedingham
Dorking Tye
Honey Tye
Great Sampford
Little London
Gainsford End
Delvin End
Alphamstone
Lamarsh
Thorington Street
Higham
Stratford St Mary
East End
East Bergholt
Alton Water
Highstreet Green
Lucking Street
Nayland
Upper Street
Howe Street
Duck End
Sible Hedingham
Great Maplestead
Little Maplestead
Cross End
Pebmarsh
Bures
Wissington
Boxted
Carter's
Brantham
Flatford Mill & Bridge Cottage
Cattawade
Hawkspur Green
Finchingfield
Mount Bures
Wormingford
Boxted Cross
Dedham
Mistley Towers
Mistley
Manningtree
Little Bardfield
Bridge Green
Waltham's Cross
Brickkiln Green
22
Countess Cross
Little Horkesley
Langham
New Mistley
Great Bardfield
Wethersfield
Blackmore End
White Green
Boose's Green
Colne Engaine
Great Horkesley
Dedham Heath
Lawford
Mistley Heath
Holder's Green
Parkgate
Oxen End
Halstead
White Colne
Wakes Colne
Colne Valley Railway
Horkesley Heath
Ardleigh Heath
Ardleigh
Little Bromley
Horsleycross Street
Earls Colne
Shalford
Church End
Chappel
Rose Green
Fordham
West Bergholt
Mile End
Fox Street
Burnt Heath
0 1 2 3 4 5 miles
0 1 2 3 4 5 6 7 8 kilometres

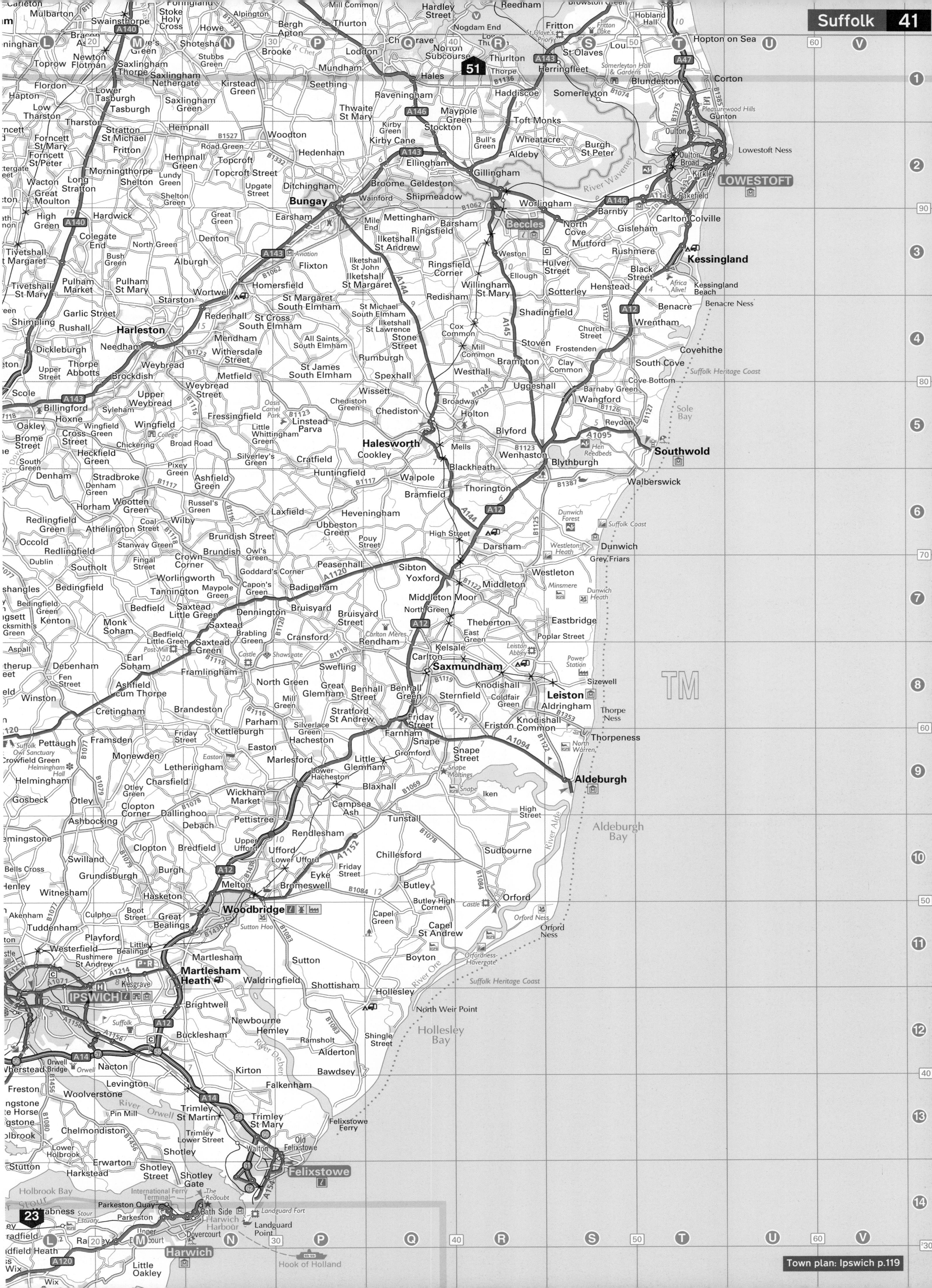
LOWESTOFT
Lowestoft Ness
Beccles
Bungay
Kessingland
Halesworth
Southwold
Walberswick
Dunwich
Saxmundham
Leiston
Aldeburgh
Aldeburgh Bay
Woodbridge
Martlesham Heath
IPSWICH
Felixstowe
Harwich
Hook of Holland
Harleston
Framlingham
Orford
Orford Ness
Hollesley Bay
Suffolk Heritage Coast
Sole Bay
TM
Haddiscoe
Somerleyton
Blundeston
Corton
Hopton on Sea
Gillingham
Ditchingham
Earsham
Wrentham
Covehithe
Benacre Ness
Wangford
Reydon
Blythburgh
Wenhaston
Yoxford
Kelsale
Snape
Thorpeness
Sizewell
Wickham Market
Melton
Shotley Gate
Landguard Point
River Orwell
River Deben
River Ore
River Alde
Hen Reedbeds
Minsmere
Dunwich Heath
Sutton Hoo
Holbrook Bay
Parkeston Quay
A12
A14
A143
A144
A145
A146
A1094
A1095
A1120
A1152
51
23

Town plan: Ipswich p.119

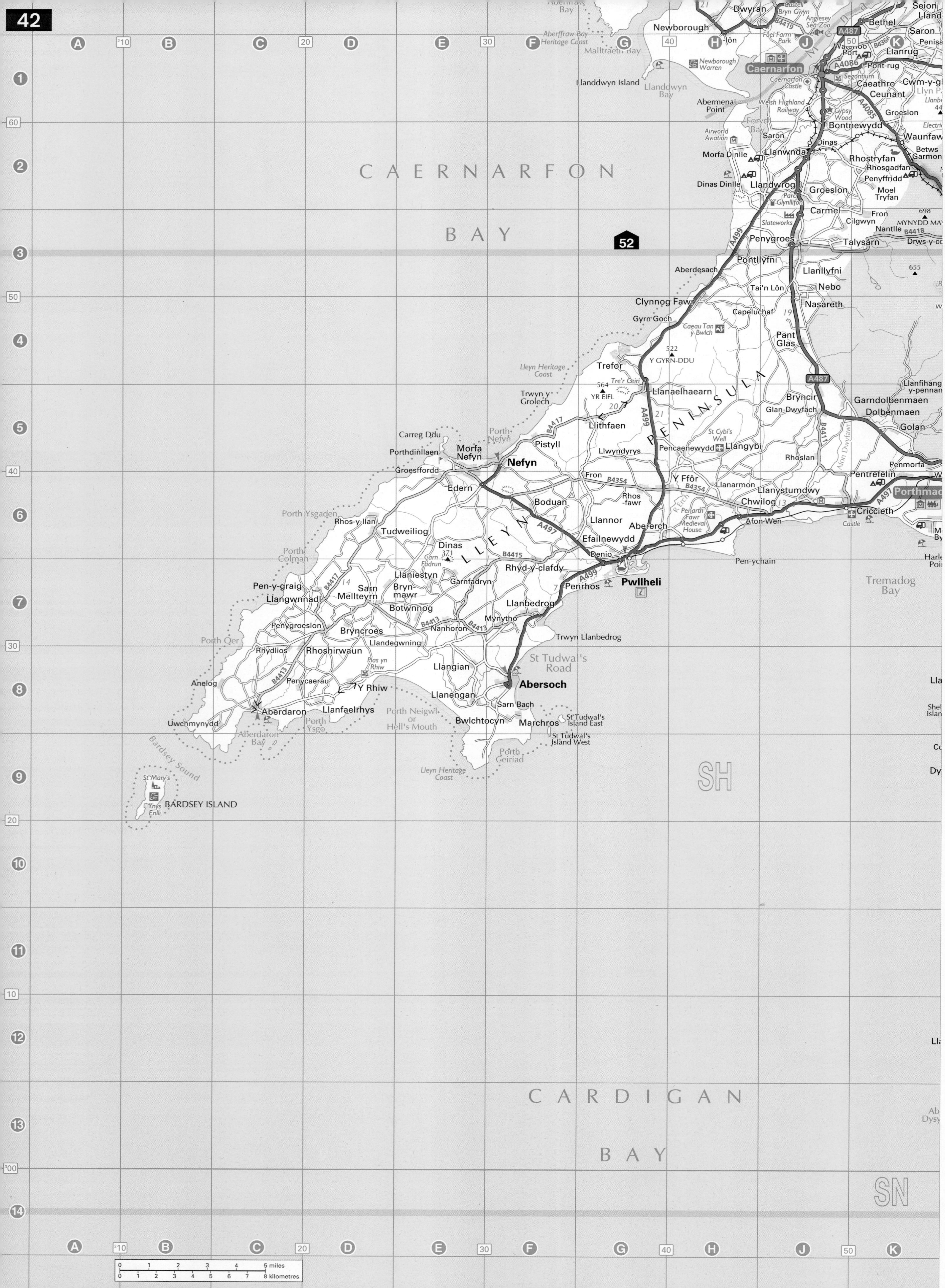
CAERNARFON
BAY
CARDIGAN
BAY
52
Newborough
Dwyran
Malltraeth Bay
Aberffraw Bay Heritage Coast
Llanddwyn Island
Llanddwyn Bay
Newborough Warren
Abermenai Point
Caernarfon
Caernarfon Castle
Bethel
Saron
Llanrug
Pont-rug
Caeathro
Ceunant
Cwm-y-glo
Bontnewydd
Waunfawr
Groeslon
Foryd Bay
Airworld Aviation
Saron
Dinas
Morfa Dinlle
Llanwnda
Rhostryfan
Rhosgadfan
Penyffridd
Dinas Dinlle
Llandwrog
Groeslon
Moel Tryfan
Carmel
Cilgwyn
Nantlle
Slateworks
Penygroes
Talysarn
Pontllyfni
Llanllyfni
Aberdesach
Tai'n Lôn
Nebo
Clynnog Fawr
Nasareth
Capeluchaf
Gyrn Goch
Caeau Tan y Bwlch
Pant Glas
Y GYRN-DDU
Trefor
Lleyn Heritage Coast
Tre'r Ceiri
YR EIFL
Llanaelhaearn
Trwyn y Grolech
PENINSULA
Bryncir
Glan-Dwyfach
Garndolbenmaen
Dolbenmaen
Golan
Llithfaen
Carreg Ddu
Porth Nefyn
Pistyll
St Cybi's Well
Pencaenewydd
Llangybi
Porthdinllaen
Morfa Nefyn
Nefyn
Llwyndyrys
Rhoslan
Penmorfa
Groesffordd
Fron
Y Ffôr
Llanarmon
Pentrefelin
Llanystumdwy
Edern
Rhos-fawr
Chwilog
Porthmadog
Boduan
Penarth Fawr Medieval House
Criccieth
Criccieth Castle
Porth Ysgaden
Rhos-y-llan
Llannor
Abererch
Afon-Wen
Tudweiliog
LLEYN
Efailnewydd
Porth Colmon
Dinas
Carn Fadrun
Denio
Pen-ychain
Rhyd-y-clafdy
Pwllheli
Tremadog Bay
Llaniestyn
Pen-y-graig
Sarn Mellteyrn
Bryn-mawr
Garnfadryn
Penrhos
Llangwnnadl
Botwnnog
Llanbedrog
Penygroeslon
Mynytho
Bryncroes
Nanhoron
Porth Oer
Trwyn Llanbedrog
Rhydlios
Rhoshirwaun
Llandegwning
St Tudwal's Road
Plas yn Rhiw
Llangian
Anelog
Penycaerau
Y Rhiw
Abersoch
Llanengan
Sarn Bach
Aberdaron
Llanfaelrhys
Porth Neigwl or Hell's Mouth
Uwchmynydd
Porth Ysgo
Bwlchtocyn
Marchros
St Tudwal's Island East
St Tudwal's Island West
Aberdaron Bay
Bardsey Sound
Porth Ceiriad
Lleyn Heritage Coast
St Mary's
Ynys Enlli
BARDSEY ISLAND
SH
SN
A
B
C
D
E
F
G
H
J
K
10
20
30
40
50
60
1
2
3
4
5
6
7
8
9
10
11
12
13
14
0 1 2 3 4 5 miles
0 1 2 3 4 5 6 7 8 kilometres

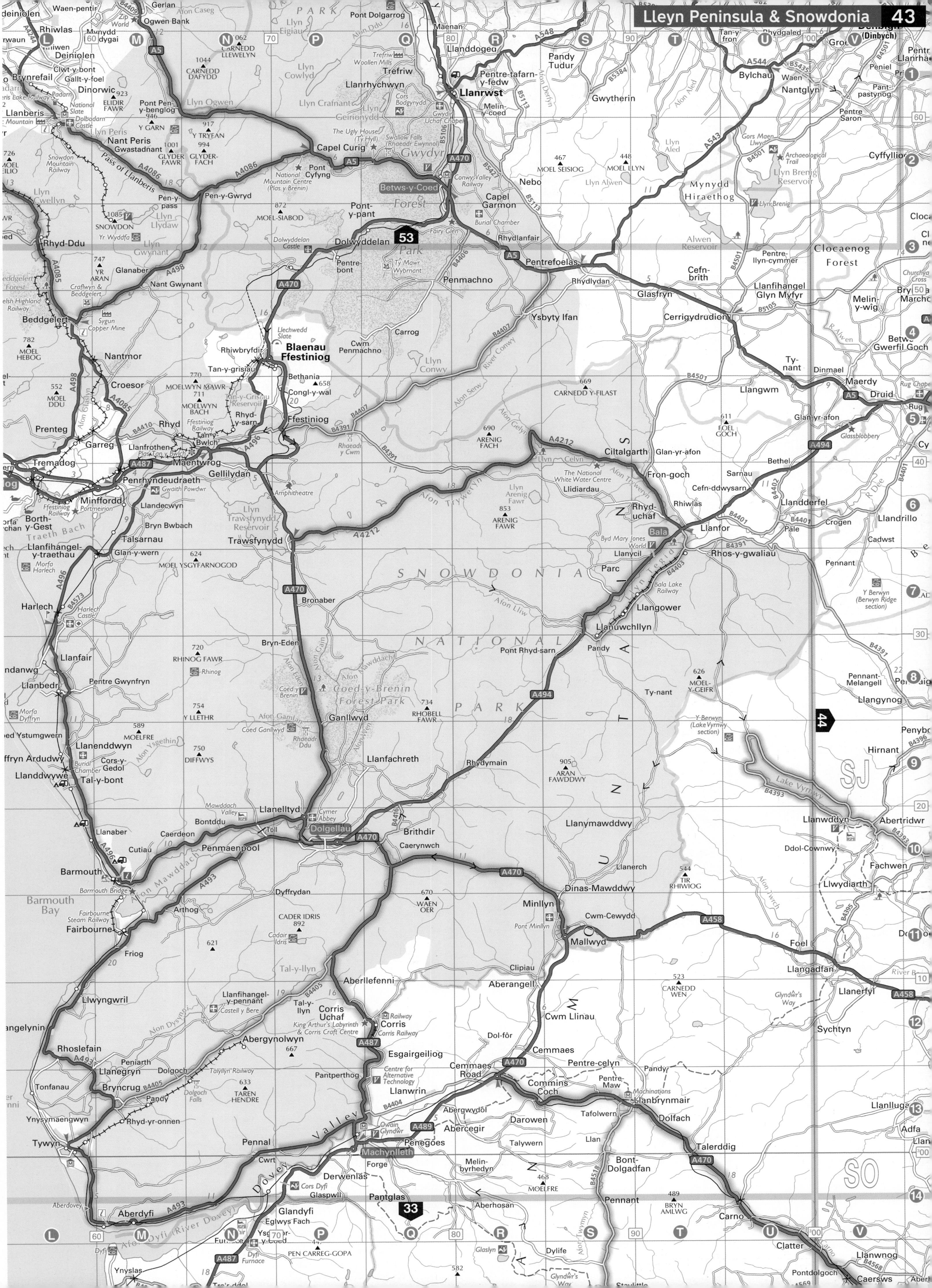

Llanberis
Nant Peris
Capel Curig
Betws-y-Coed
Llanrwst
Trefriw
Pentrefoelas
Dolwyddelan
Blaenau Ffestiniog
Ffestiniog
Beddgelert
Nantmor
Croesor
Rhyd-Ddu
Maentwrog
Penrhyndeudraeth
Minffordd
Tremadog
Porthmadog
Talsarnau
Harlech
Trawsfynydd
Llanfair
Llanbedr
Tal-y-bont
Barmouth
Fairbourne
Dolgellau
Penmaenpool
Llanelltyd
Bala
Llanfor
Cerrigydrudion
Druid
Llandderfel
Llanuwchllyn
Dinas-Mawddwy
Mallwyd
Corris
Abergynolwyn
Tywyn
Aberdyfi
Machynlleth
Llanbrynmair
Carno
Llanwddyn
Cyffylliog
Nebo
Ysbyty Ifan
SNOWDONIA
NATIONAL
PARK
53
44
33

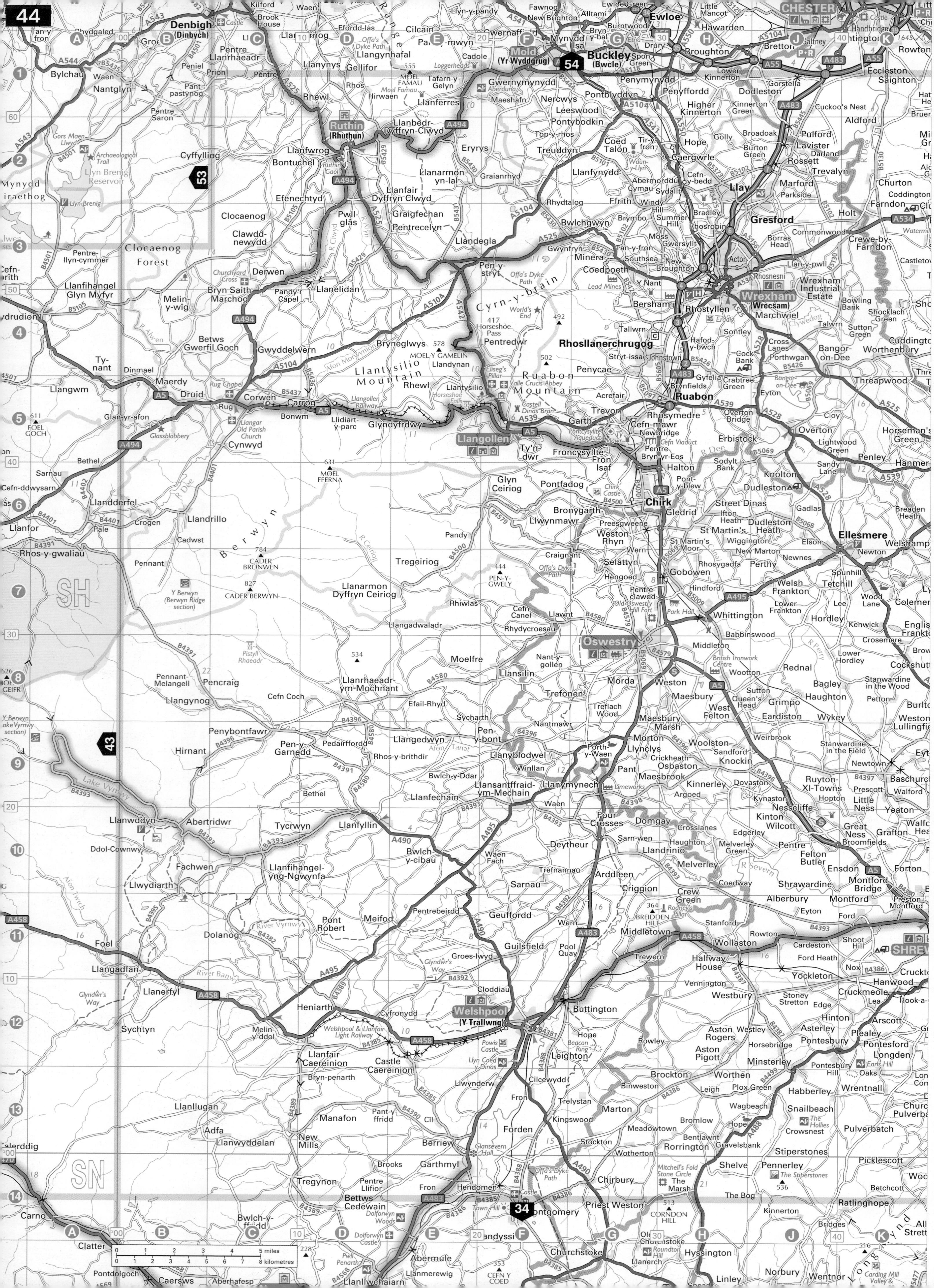
Denbigh (Dinbych)
Mold (Yr Wyddgrug)
Buckley (Bwcle)
Ewloe
Hawarden
CHESTER
Ruthin (Rhuthun)
Wrexham (Wrecsam)
Gresford
Llay
Ruabon
Llangollen
Chirk
Ellesmere
Oswestry
Whittington
Welshpool (Y Trallwng)
Llanfyllin
Corwen
Llandrillo
Cyrn-y-brain
Ruabon Mountain
Llantysilio Mountain
Clocaenog Forest
Berwyn
Llanrhaeadr-ym-Mochnant
Llangynog
Llanwddyn
Lake Vyrnwy
Llanfair Caereinion
Llangadfan
Montgomery
Churchstoke
Chirbury
Minsterley
Pontesbury
Westbury
Four Crosses
Llanymynech
Maesbrook
Knockin
Ruyton-XI-Towns
Nesscliffe
Wollaston
Middletown
Forden
Berriew
Garthmyl
Cyfronydd
Meifod
Guilsfield
Trefonen
Weston Rhyn
St Martin's
Overton
Bangor-on-Dee
Holt
Farndon
Rhosllanerchrugog
Coedpoeth
Caergwrle
Hope
Penyffordd
Llanarmon Dyffryn Ceiriog
Glyn Ceiriog
Tregeiriog
Cynwyd
Gwyddelwern
Bryneglwys
Llandegla
Llanbedr-Dyffryn-Clwyd
Cyffylliog
Carno
Sychtyn
Llanerfyl
Foel
Dolanog
Pont Robert
Manafon
Tregynon
Bettws Cedewain
Abermule
Priest Weston
Hyssington
Ratlinghope
Snailbeach
Stiperstones
Pulverbatch
Hanwood
Cruckmeole
Yockleton
Halfway House
Shrawardine
Montford Bridge
Baschurch
Welsh Frankton
Hordley
Cockshutt
Dudleston Heath
Penley
Hanmer
SH
SN
43
53
54
34

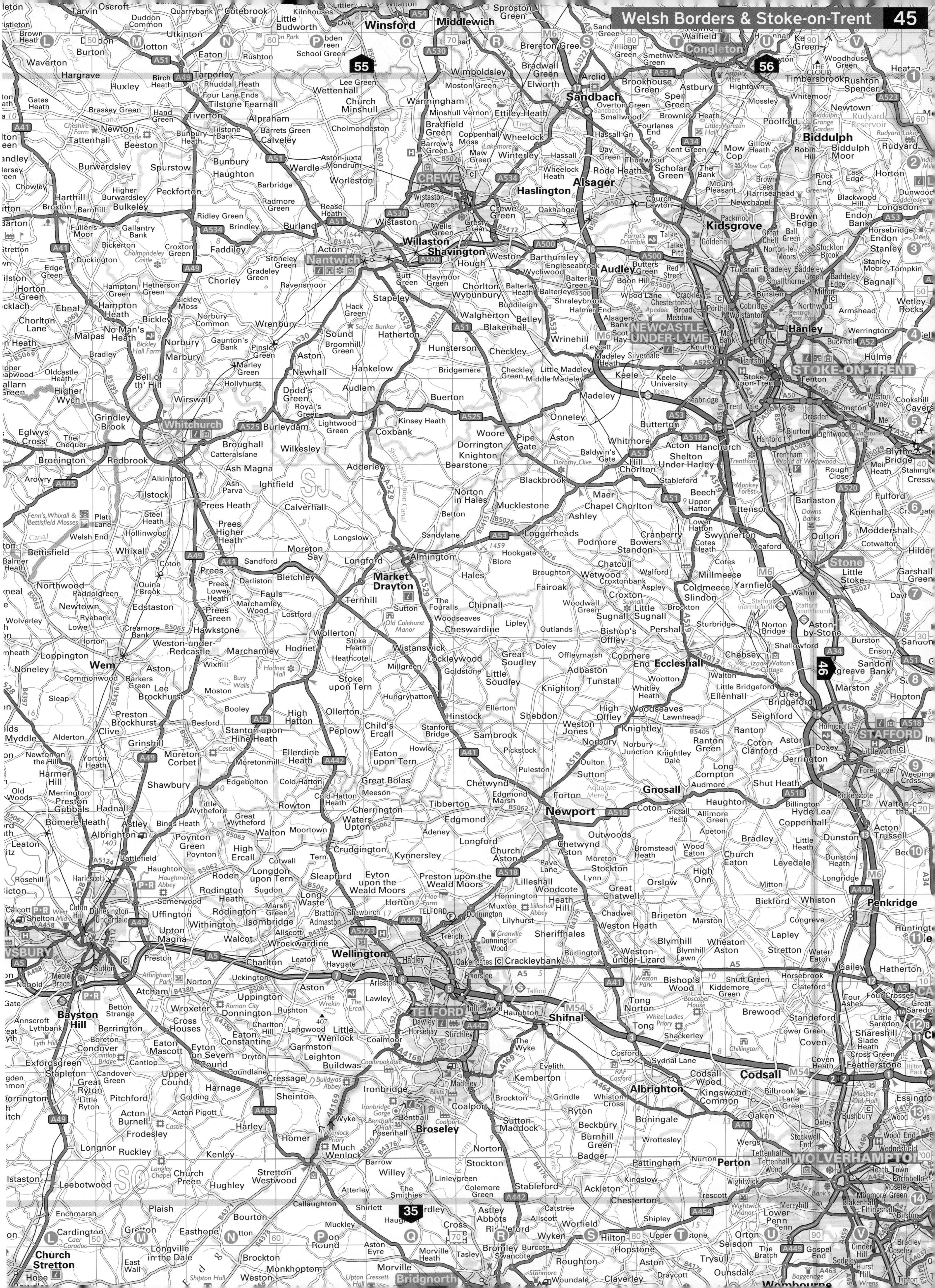

Winsford
Middlewich
Congleton
Sandbach
Crewe
Alsager
Biddulph
Kidsgrove
Nantwich
Willaston
Shavington
Audley
Hanley
Newcastle-under-Lyme
Stoke-on-Trent
Whitchurch
Market Drayton
Stone
Eccleshall
Wem
Hodnet
Stafford
Newport
Gnosall
Penkridge
Wellington
Telford
Shifnal
Codsall
Albrighton
Wolverhampton
Bayston Hill
Broseley
Much Wenlock
Church Stretton
Bridgnorth
SJ
SO
55
56
46
35

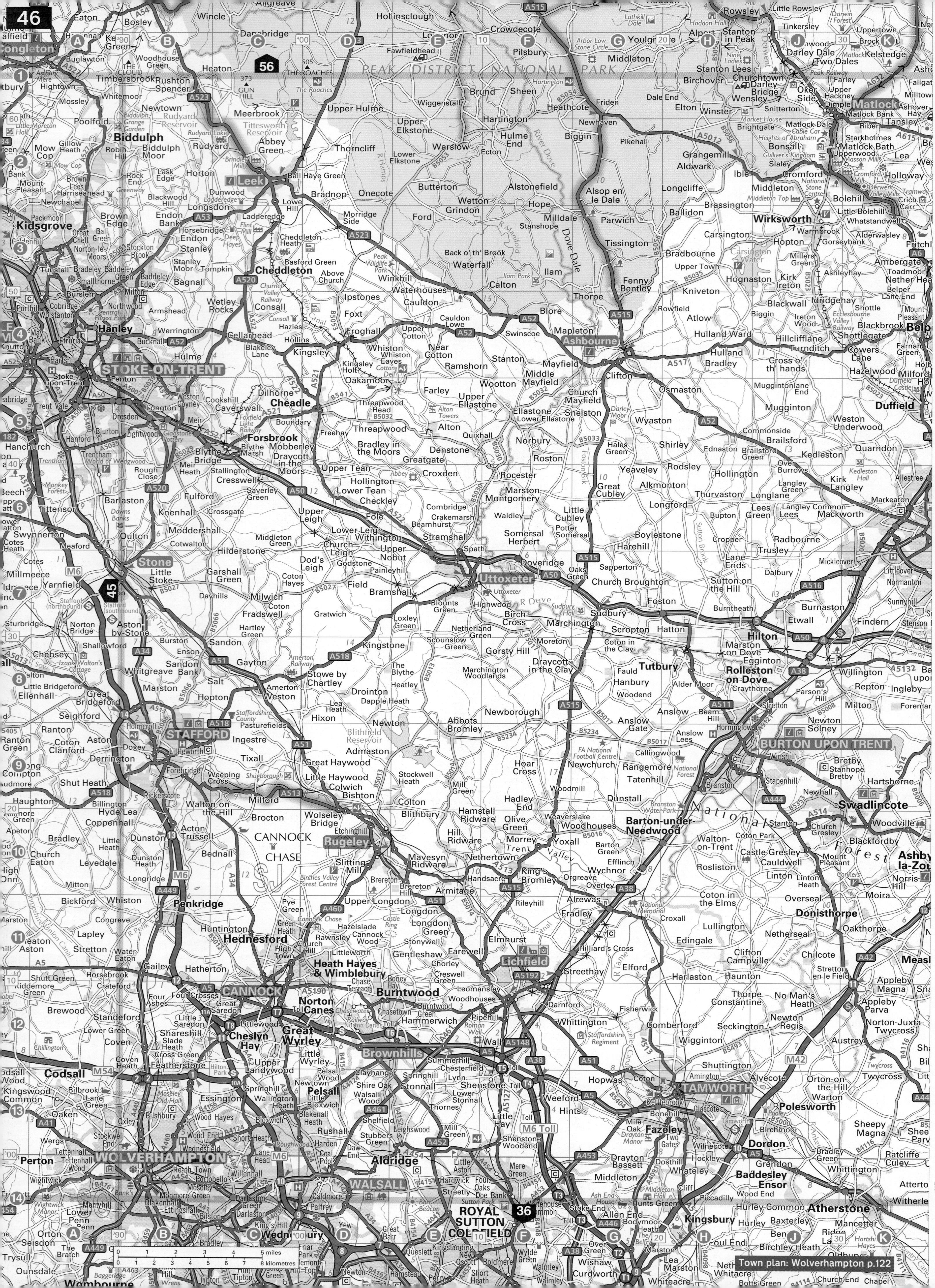
Congleton
Biddulph
Kidsgrove
Leek
Hanley
STOKE-ON-TRENT
Cheadle
Cheddleton
Stone
Uttoxeter
Ashbourne
Matlock
Wirksworth
Duffield
Hilton
Tutbury
Rolleston on Dove
BURTON UPON TRENT
Swadlincote
STAFFORD
Rugeley
CANNOCK
Lichfield
Burntwood
Brownhills
Cheslyn Hay
Great Wyrley
Codsall
WOLVERHAMPTON
WALSALL
Aldridge
ROYAL SUTTON COLDFIELD
TAMWORTH
Fazeley
Dordon
Polesworth
Atherstone
Kingsbury
Barton-under-Needwood
Donisthorpe
PEAK DISTRICT NATIONAL PARK
CANNOCK CHASE
National Forest
56
45
36

Town plan: Wolverhampton p.122

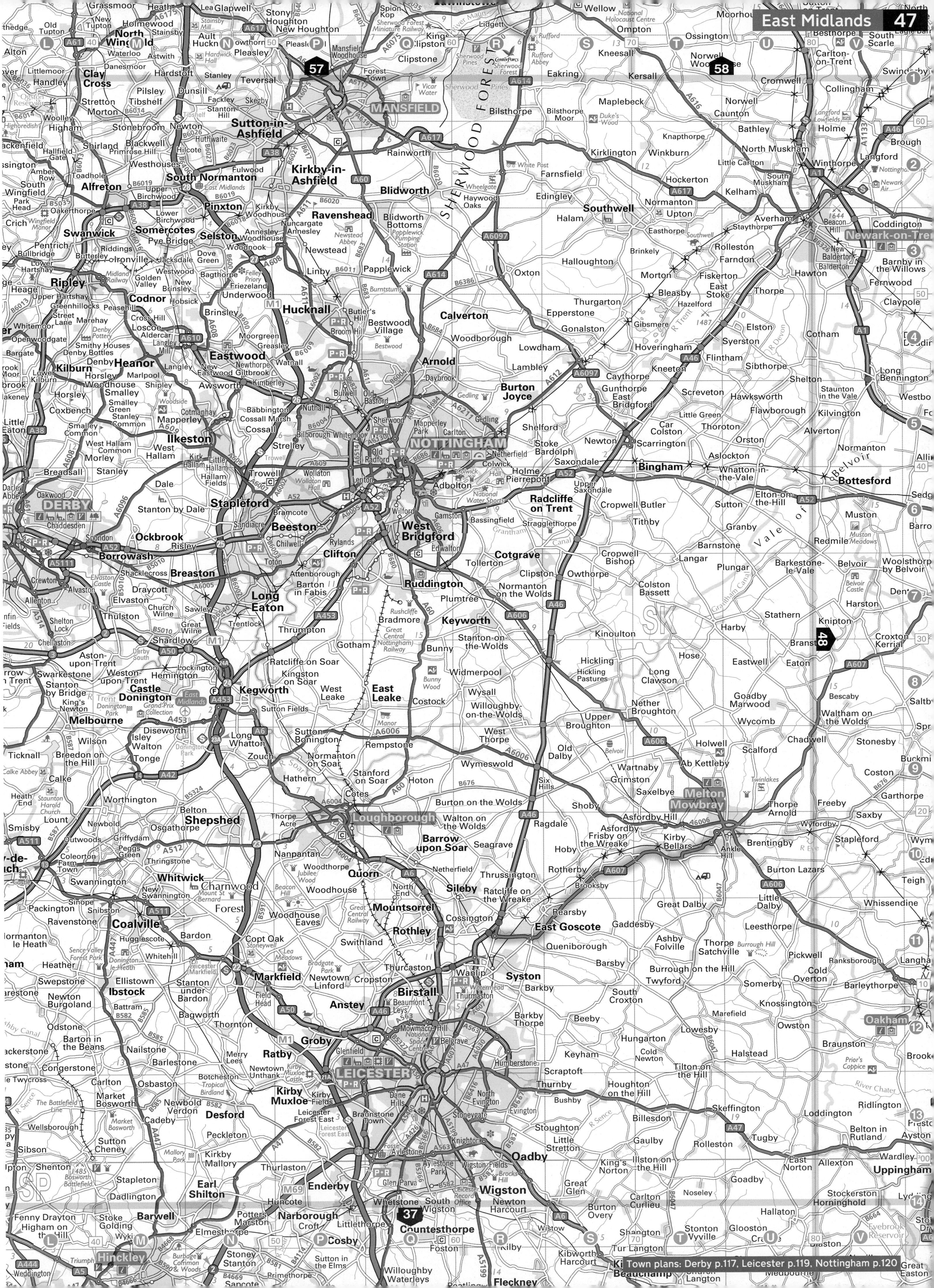

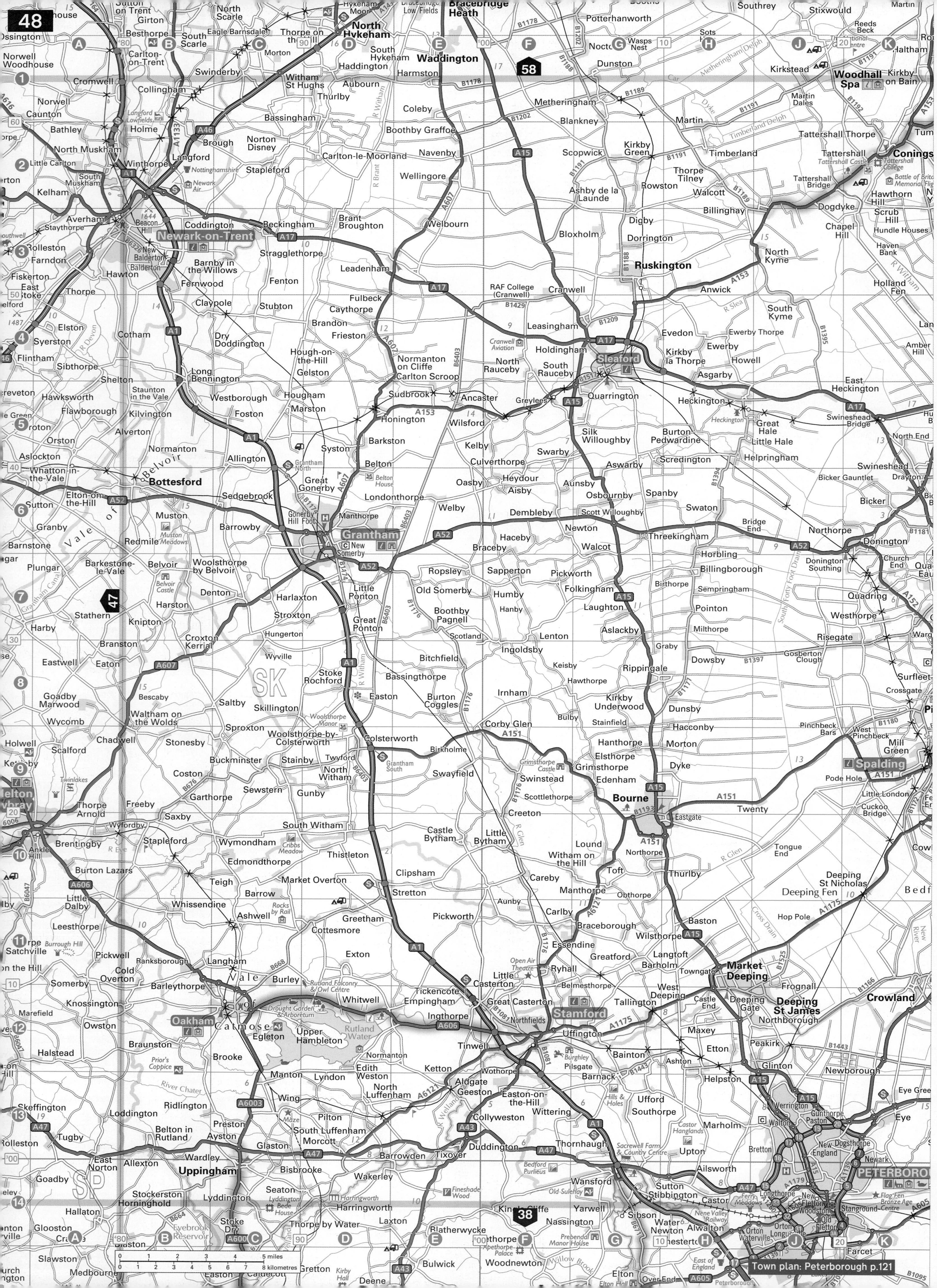
North Hykeham
Bracebridge Heath
Waddington
South Hykeham
Haddington
Harmston
Potterhanworth
Southrey
Stixwould
Woodhall Spa
Kirkby on Bain
Kirkstead
Dunston
Nocton
Wasps Nest
Metheringham
Martin
Martin Dales
Blankney
Timberland
Kirkby Green
Scopwick
Tattershall Thorpe
Tattershall
Tattershall Castle
Tattershall Bridge
Conings
Thorpe Tilney
Rowston
Walcott
Billinghay
Ashby de la Launde
Digby
Dorrington
Bloxholm
Ruskington
North Kyme
South Kyme
Anwick
Dogdyke
Chapel Hill
Hawthorn Hill
Scrub Hill
Haven Bank
Holland Fen
Hundle Houses
Cranwell
RAF College (Cranwell)
Leasingham
Holdingham
Sleaford
Quarrington
Evedon
Ewerby
Ewerby Thorpe
Kirkby la Thorpe
Howell
Asgarby
East Heckington
Heckington
Great Hale
Little Hale
Swineshead Bridge
North End
Helpringham
Swineshead
Bicker Gauntlet
Bicker
Drayton
Donington
Donington Southing
Northorpe
Quadring
Westhorpe
Risegate
Gosberton Clough
Surfleet
Crossgate
Pinchbeck Bars
West Pinchbeck
Mill Green
Spalding
Pode Hole
Little London
Cuckoo Bridge
Twenty
Tongue End
Deeping St Nicholas
Deeping Fen
Hop Pole
Crowland
Frognall
Deeping St James
Northborough
Deeping Gate
Market Deeping
Towngate
Peakirk
Glinton
Newborough
Eye Green
Eye
Werrington
Gunthorpe
Paston
Walton
Dogsthorpe
New England
Newark
PETERBOROUGH
Longthorpe
Woodston
Fletton
Stanground
Flag Fen Bronze Age Centre
Orton Longueville
Orton Waterville
Farcet
Town plan: Peterborough p.121
Castor
Ailsworth
Upton
Marholm
Bretton
Helpston
Etton
Maxey
Ashton
Bainton
Barnack
Pilsgate
Ufford
Southorpe
Wittering
Thornhaugh
Wansford
Sutton
Stibbington
Sibson
Water Newton
Alwalton
Chesterton
Yarwell
Nassington
Kings Cliffe
Apethorpe
Woodnewton
Elton
Bulwick
Blatherwycke
Laxton
Harringworth
Wakerley
Duddington
Collyweston
Easton-on-the-Hill
Stamford
Uffington
Tallington
West Deeping
Castle End
Greatford
Barholm
Langtoft
Baston
Wilsthorpe
Braceborough
Belmesthorpe
Ryhall
Essendine
Carlby
Careby
Aunby
Little Bytham
Castle Bytham
Witham on the Hill
Toft
Manthorpe
Obthorpe
Thurlby
Northorpe
Lound
Bourne
Eastgate
Dyke
Edenham
Grimsthorpe
Grimsthorpe Castle
Elsthorpe
Hanthorpe
Morton
Hacconby
Dunsby
Stainfield
Kirkby Underwood
Rippingale
Dowsby
Aslackby
Laughton
Pointon
Milthorpe
Sempringham
Birthorpe
Billingborough
Horbling
Threekingham
Bridge End
Folkingham
Pickworth
Walcot
Newton
Scott Willoughby
Spanby
Swaton
Osbournby
Aunsby
Aswarby
Scredington
Silk Willoughby
Burton Pedwardine
Swarby
Heydour
Aisby
Culverthorpe
Kelby
Oasby
Welby
Dembleby
Haceby
Braceby
Sapperton
Humby
Hanby
Ropsley
Old Somerby
Boothby Pagnell
Lenton
Ingoldsby
Keisby
Hawthorpe
Bulby
Irnham
Corby Glen
Birkholme
Swayfield
Swinstead
Scottlethorpe
Creeton
Bitchfield
Bassingthorpe
Burton Coggles
Easton
Stoke Rochford
Great Ponton
Little Ponton
Colsterworth
Woolsthorpe-by-Colsterworth
Woolsthorpe Manor
North Witham
South Witham
Twyford
Stainby
Gunby
Sewstern
Buckminster
Coston
Garthorpe
Saxby
Wymondham
Edmondthorpe
Thistleton
Market Overton
Clipsham
Stretton
Pickworth
Greetham
Cottesmore
Exton
Barrow
Ashwell
Whissendine
Teigh
Langham
Burley
Whitwell
Empingham
Tickencote
Great Casterton
Little Casterton
Ingthorpe
Tinwell
Ketton
Aldgate
Geeston
Wothorpe
Edith Weston
Normanton
North Luffenham
South Luffenham
Pilton
Morcott
Barrowden
Tixover
Wing
Lyndon
Manton
Upper Hambleton
Rutland Water
Egleton
Oakham
Vale of Catmose
Barleythorpe
Cold Overton
Knossington
Owston
Braunston
Brooke
Ridlington
Preston
Ayston
Uppingham
Glaston
Bisbrooke
Seaton
Lyddington
Stoke Dry
Caldecott
Thorpe by Water
Gretton
Horninghold
Stockerston
Hallaton
Allexton
Wardley
East Norton
Belton in Rutland
Loddington
Tugby
Skeffington
Rolleston
Goadby
Glooston
Slawston
Medbourne
Halstead
Marefield
Somerby
Pickwell
Ranksborough
Leesthorpe
Little Dalby
Burton Lazars
Melton Mowbray
Brentingby
Wyfordby
Stapleford
Freeby
Thorpe Arnold
Scalford
Chadwell
Wycomb
Goadby Marwood
Eastwell
Eaton
Branston
Waltham on the Wolds
Saltby
Skillington
Sproxton
Stonesby
Harby
Stathern
Knipton
Croxton Kerrial
Denton
Harston
Harlaxton
Stroxton
Hungerton
Wyville
Barkestone-le-Vale
Plungar
Belvoir
Belvoir Castle
Woolsthorpe by Belvoir
Redmile
Barrowby
Muston
Grantham
Sedgebrook
Bottesford
Elton-on-the-Hill
Granby
Barnstone
Whatton-in-the-Vale
Aslockton
Orston
Normanton
Allington
Great Gonerby
Gonerby Hill Foot
Manthorpe
Londonthorpe
Belton
Belton House
Syston
Barkston
Honington
Sudbrook
Ancaster
Wilsford
Carlton Scroop
Normanton on Cliffe
North Rauceby
South Rauceby
Greylees
Marston
Hougham
Foston
Westborough
Long Bennington
Staunton in the Vale
Kilvington
Alverton
Flawborough
Hawksworth
Shelton
Sibthorpe
Flintham
Syerston
Elston
Cotham
Dry Doddington
Claypole
Stubton
Fenton
Hough-on-the-Hill
Gelston
Brandon
Frieston
Caythorpe
Fulbeck
Leadenham
Stragglethorpe
Beckingham
Brant Broughton
Welbourn
Wellingore
Navenby
Carlton-le-Moorland
Boothby Graffoe
Coleby
Bassingham
Thurlby
Aubourn
Witham St Hughs
Norton Disney
Stapleford
Brough
Collingham
Swinderby
Morton
Thorpe on the Hill
Eagle Barnsdale
North Scarle
South Scarle
Besthorpe
Girton
Sutton on Trent
Carlton-on-Trent
Norwell Woodhouse
Cromwell
Norwell
Caunton
Bathley
Holme
North Muskham
South Muskham
Little Carlton
Winthorpe
Langford
Kelham
Averham
Staythorpe
Newark-on-Trent
Coddington
Barnby in the Willows
Fernwood
Balderton
New Balderton
Hawton
Farndon
Rolleston
Fiskerton
East Stoke
Thorpe
Nottinghamshire
Newark Air
Beacon Hill
Cranwell Aviation
Rutland Falconry & Owl Centre
Drought Garden & Arboretum
Rocks by Rail
Cribbs Meadow
Burghley House
Hills & Holes
Sacrewell Farm & Country Centre
Castor Hanglands
Bedford Purlieus
Fineshade Wood
Old Sulehay
Prebendal Manor House
Nene Valley Railway
Ferry Meadows
Lyddington Bede House
Prior's Coppice
Eyebrook Reservoir
Burrough Hill
Twinlakes
Open Air Theatre
Muston Meadows
Vale of Belvoir
Grantham Canal
South Forty Foot Drain
R Witham
R Glen
R Welland
River Chater
Car Dyke
SK
SP
47
58
38
A1
A15
A17
A52
A153
A151
A607
A606
A6003
A47
A43
A46
A1133
A6121
A1175
A16
A152
A605
A1179
B1176
B6403
B1081
B1443
B1166
B1191
B1188
B1189
B1202
B1178
B1209
B1429
B1394
B1397
B1177
B1180
B1181
B1395
B1525
B1443
B1095
B676
B668
B664
0 1 2 3 4 5 miles
0 1 2 3 4 5 6 7 8 kilometres

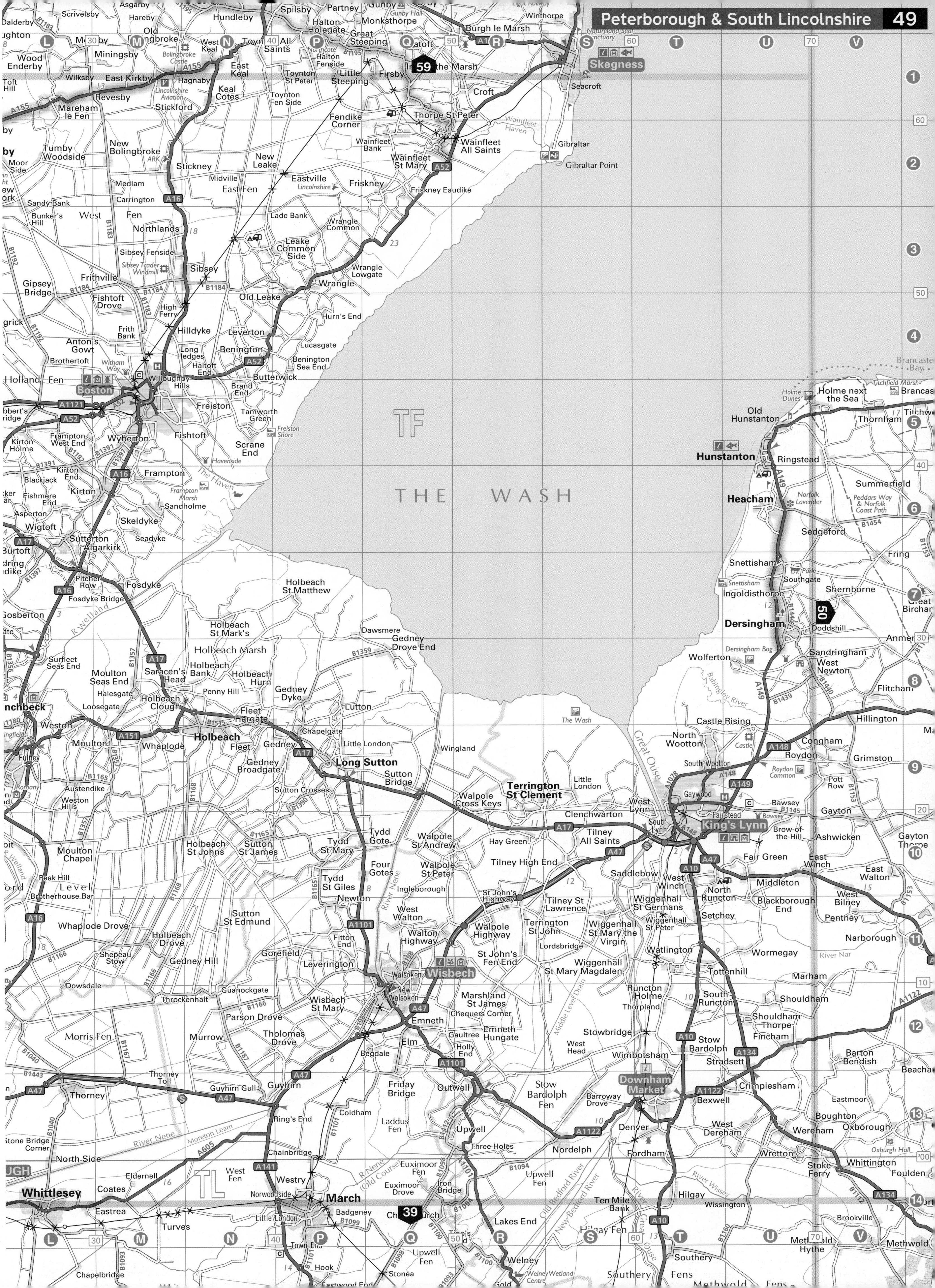

Asgarby
Scrivelsby
Hareby
Hundleby
Spilsby
Partney
Gunby
Gunby Hall
Winthorpe
Burgh le Marsh
Dalderby
Old Bolingbroke
West Keal
Toynton All Saints
Halton Holegate
Great Steeping
Monksthorpe
Skegness
Wood Enderby
Miningsby
Bolingbroke Castle
East Keal
Halton Fenside
Little Steeping
Firsby
Ingoldmells
Wilksby
East Kirkby
Hagnaby
Toynton St Peter
Croft
Seacroft
Toft Hill
Revesby
Keal Cotes
Toynton Fen Side
Lincolnshire Aviation
Mareham le Fen
Stickford
Fendike Corner
Thorpe St Peter
Wainfleet Haven
Tumby Woodside
New Bolingbroke
Wainfleet Bank
Wainfleet All Saints
Gibraltar
Wainfleet St Mary
Gibraltar Point
Moor Side
Stickney
New Leake
Eastville
Midville
East Fen
Friskney
Friskney Eaudike
Medlam
Carrington
Sandy Bank
Bunker's Hill
West Fen
Northlands
Lade Bank
Wrangle Common
Leake Common Side
Sibsey Fenside
Sibsey Trader Windmill
Sibsey
Wrangle Lowgate
Wrangle
Frithville
Gipsey Bridge
Fishtoft Drove
High Ferry
Old Leake
Hurn's End
Hilldyke
Leverton
Frith Bank
Anton's Gowt
Long Hedges
Benington
Lucasgate
Brothertoft
Benington Sea End
Holland Fen
Boston
Haltoft End
Butterwick
Willoughby Hills
Brand End
Freiston
Tamworth Green
Freiston Shore
Wyberton
Fishtoft
Scrane End
Frampton West End
Kirton Holme
Kirton End
Frampton
Haven
Blackjack
Kirton
Fishmere End
Frampton Marsh
Sandholme
Asperton
Skeldyke
Wigtoft
Seadyke
Sutterton
Algarkirk
Surfleet
Pitcher Row
Fosdyke
Fosdyke Bridge
Gosberton
Holbeach St Matthew
TF
THE WASH
Old Hunstanton
Holme next the Sea
Brancaster Bay
Titchwell
Thornham
Hunstanton
Ringstead
Heacham
Summerfield
Norfolk Lavender
Peddars Way & Norfolk Coast Path
Sedgeford
Fring
Snettisham
Southgate
Ingoldisthorpe
Shernborne
Dersingham
Dersingham Bog
Doddshill
Anmer
Great Bircham
Wolferton
Sandringham
West Newton
Babingley River
Flitcham
Castle Rising
Hillington
North Wootton
Congham
Roydon
Grimston
South Wootton
Roydon Common
Pott Row
Gaywood
Bawsey
Gayton
King's Lynn
Brow-of-the-Hill
Ashwicken
Gayton Thorpe
Fair Green
East Winch
East Walton
Middleton
West Bilney
Pentney
Narborough
River Nar
Wormegay
Tottenhill
Marham
Shouldham
Shouldham Thorpe
Fincham
Barton Bendish
Beachamwell
Crimplesham
Eastmoor
Boughton
Wereham
Oxborough
Oxburgh Hall
Wretton
Stoke Ferry
Whittington
Foulden
Wissington
Brookville
Methwold
Methwold Hythe
Holbeach St Mark's
Holbeach Marsh
Dawsmere
Gedney Drove End
Surfleet Seas End
Moulton Seas End
Saracen's Head
Holbeach Bank
Holbeach Hurn
Halesgate
Penny Hill
Gedney Dyke
Holbeach Clough
Loosegate
Spalding
Pinchbeck
Fleet Hargate
Lutton
Weston
Moulton
Whaplode
Holbeach
Fleet
Gedney
Chapelgate
Little London
Long Sutton
Gedney Broadgate
Sutton Bridge
Sutton Crosses
Wingland
The Wash
Great Ouse
Terrington St Clement
Little London
Walpole Cross Keys
Clenchwarton
West Lynn
South Lynn
Tilney All Saints
Austendike
Weston Hills
Moulton Chapel
Holbeach St Johns
Sutton St James
Tydd St Mary
Tydd Gote
Walpole St Andrew
Hay Green
Tilney High End
Walpole St Peter
Four Gotes
Tydd St Giles
Saddlebow
West Winch
North Runcton
Peak Hill
Ingleborough
St John's Highway
Tilney St Lawrence
Wiggenhall St Germans
Brotherhouse Bar
Newton
River Nene
West Walton
Terrington St John
Wiggenhall St Mary the Virgin
Wiggenhall St Peter
Setchey
Blackborough End
Sutton St Edmund
Whaplode Drove
Walton Highway
Walpole Highway
Holbeach Drove
Fitton End
Lordsbridge
Watlington
Shepeau Stow
Gorefield
Leverington
St John's Fen End
Wiggenhall St Mary Magdalen
Gedney Hill
Wisbech
Walsoken
New Walsoken
Runcton Holme
South Runcton
Dowsdale
Guanockgate
Marshland St James
Thorpland
Throckenholt
Wisbech St Mary
Chequers Corner
Parson Drove
Emneth
Emneth Hungate
Stowbridge
Morris Fen
Murrow
Tholomas Drove
Gaultree
Holly End
Elm
Middle Level Main Drain
West Head
Stow Bardolph
Begdale
Wimbotsham
Stradsett
Thorney Toll
Downham Market
Guyhirn Gull
Guyhirn
Friday Bridge
Outwell
Stow Bardolph Fen
Barroway Drove
Thorney
Bexwell
Ring's End
Coldham
Laddus Fen
Upwell
Denver
West Dereham
Stone Bridge Corner
River Nene
Moreton Leam
Chainbridge
Three Holes
Nordelph
Fordham
North Side
Eldernell
West Fen
Westry
Euximoor Fen
Iron Bridge
Upwell Fen
Old Bedford River
New Bedford River
River Wissey
Whittlesey
Coates
TL
Norwoodside
March
Euximoor Drove
Ten Mile Bank
Hilgay
Eastrea
Turves
Little London
Badgeney
Christchurch
Lakes End
Hilgay Fen
Town End
Upwell Fen
Welney
Welney Wetland Centre
Southery
Southery Fens
Hook
Chapelbridge
Stonea
Eastwood End
59
39
50

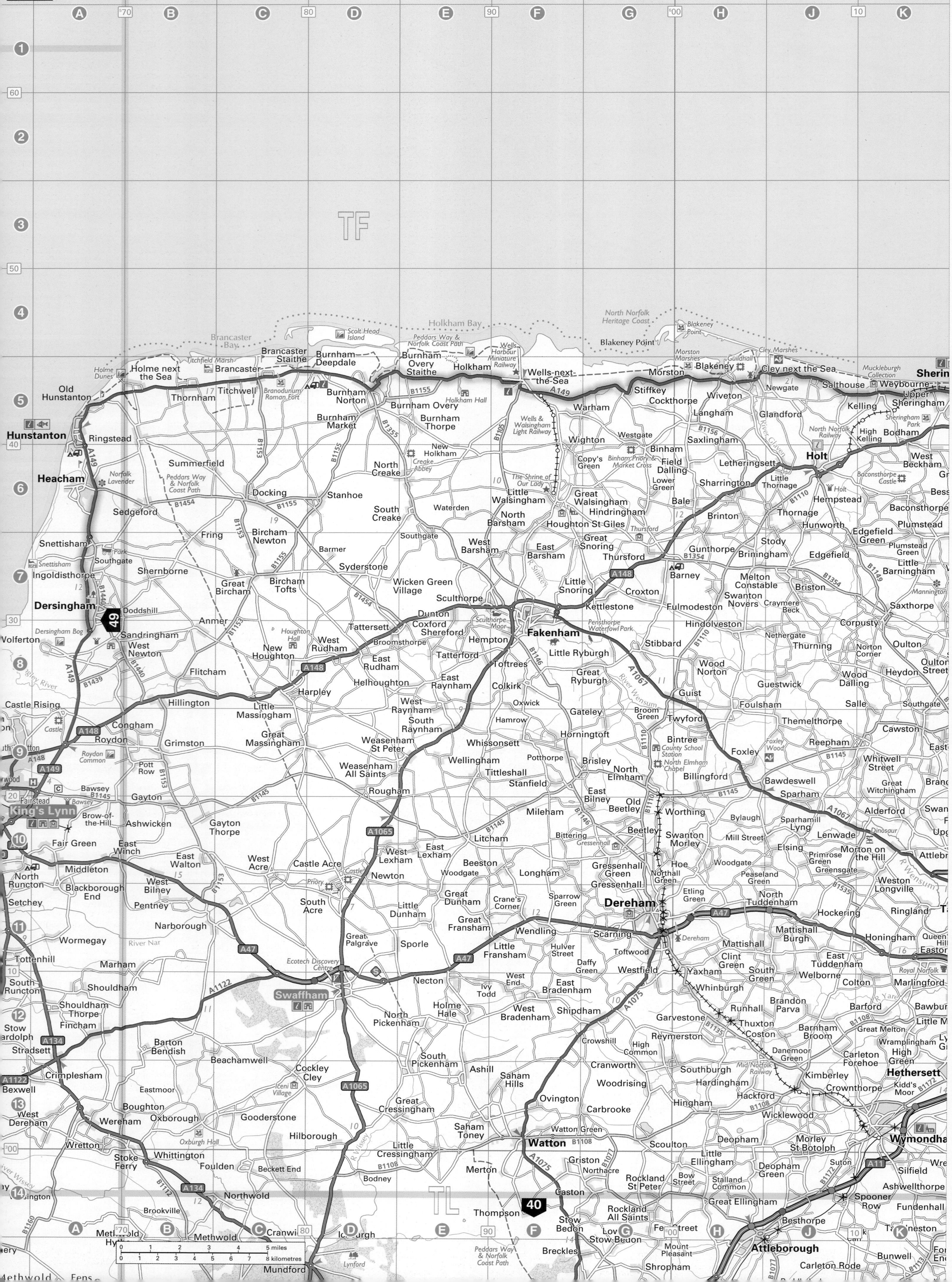

TF

TL

Holkham Bay

Peddars Way &
Norfolk Coast Path

North Norfolk
Heritage Coast

Brancaster
Bay

Blakeney Point

Holme
Dunes

Old
Hunstanton

Holme next
the Sea

Titchfield Marsh

Brancaster

Brancaster
Staithe

Burnham
Deepdale

Burnham
Overy
Staithe

Holkham

Wells
Harbour
Miniature
Railway

Wells-next-
the-Sea

Morston

Blakeney

Cley next the Sea

Muckleburgh
Collection

Sherin

Thornham

Titchwell

Branodunum
Roman Fort

Burnham
Norton

Burnham Overy

Holkham Hall

A149

Stiffkey

Cockthorpe

Warham

Salthouse

Weybourne

Upper
Sheringham

Hunstanton

Ringstead

Burnham
Market

Burnham
Thorpe

Wells &
Walsingham
Light Railway

Wighton

Westgate

Langham

Newgate

Glandford

Kelling

High
Kelling

West
Beckham

Heacham

Norfolk
Lavender

Summerfield

B1153

New
Holkham

Creake
Abbey

The Shrine of
Our Lady

Copy's
Green

Binham
Priory Market Cross

Binham

Field
Dalling

Saxlingham

North Norfolk
Railway

Holt

Bodham

Bess

Peddars Way
& Norfolk
Coast Path

Docking

Stanhoe

North
Creake

Waterden

Little
Walsingham

Great
Walsingham

Hindringham

Lower
Green

Bale

Sharrington

Little
Thornage

Thornage

Hempstead

Baconsthorpe

Sedgeford

B1454

Houghton St Giles

Brinton

Hunworth

Edgefield
Green

Plumstead

Snettisham

Fring

Bircham
Newton

Barmer

Southgate

West Barsham

East
Barsham

Great
Snoring

Thursford

Gunthorpe

Stody

Briningham

Edgefield

Plumstead
Green

Little
Barningham

Ingoldisthorpe

Southgate

Shernborne

Great
Bircham

Bircham
Tofts

Syderstone

Wicken Green
Village

Sculthorpe

Little
Snoring

A148

Barney

Croxton

Melton
Constable

Swanton
Novers

Craymere
Beck

Briston

Saxthorpe

Mannington

Dersingham

Doddshill

Anmer

New
Houghton

Tattersett

Broomsthorpe

Dunton
Coxford
Shereford

Hempton

Sculthorpe
Moor

Fakenham

Penthorpe
Waterfowl Park

Kettlestone

Fulmodeston

Hindolveston

Thurning

Norton
Corner

Oulton

Oulton
Street

Heydon

Volferton

Dersingham Bog

Sandringham

West
Newton

Houghton
Hall

Flitcham

West Rudham

East
Rudham

Tatterford

Toftrees

Little Ryburgh

Great
Ryburgh

Stibbard

B1110

Wood
Norton

Guestwick

Wood
Dalling

Salle

Southgate

Castle Rising

A148

Hillington

Harpley

Little
Massingham

Helhoughton

West
Raynham

East
Raynham

Colkirk

Oxwick

Gateley

Hamrow

Broom
Green

Twyford

Bintree

Foxley

Foxley
Wood

Reepham

Cawston

East

Congham

Roydon

Grimston

Great
Massingham

South
Raynham

Weasenham
St Peter

Whissonsett

Wellingham

Potthorpe

Brisley

North
Elmham

County School
Station

North Elmham
Chapel

Billingford

Bawdeswell

Themelthorpe

Whitwell
Street

Great

Roydon
Common

Pott
Row

Gayton

Gayton
Thorpe

Weasenham
All Saints

Tittleshall

Stanfield

East
Bilney

Old
Beetley

Worthing

Bylaugh

Sparham

A1067

Alderford

Swan

Upp

King's Lynn

Brow-of-
the-Hill

Ashwicken

Bawsey

B1145

Rougham

Mileham

Beetley

Swanton
Morley

Mill Street

Sparhamhill

Lyng

Elsing

Lenwade

Morton on
the Hill

Weston
Longville

R Wensum

Attle

Fair Green

East
Winch

West
Acre

Castle Acre

Newton

West
Lexham

East
Lexham

Beeston

Woodgate

Longham

Litcham

Bittering

Gressenhall

Northall
Green

Hoe

Woodgate

Peaseland
Green

Greengate

Hockering

Ringland

T

North
Runcton

Middleton

East
Walton

Priory

Castle

Castle Acre
Priory

South
Acre

Little
Dunham

Great
Dunham

Great
Fransham

Crane's
Corner

Sparrow
Green

Gressenhall
Green

Gressenhall

Dereham

A47

North
Tuddenham

Mattishall
Burgh

Honingham

Queen's
Hill

Easton

Blackborough
End

West
Bilney

Narborough

River Nar

A47

Great
Palgrave

Sporle

Little
Dunham

Great
Fransham

Wendling

Scarning

Dereham

Mattishall

Clint Green

South
Green

Welborne

Colton

Marlingford

Setchey

Pentney

Wormegay

Ecotech Discovery
Centre

Necton

Little
Fransham

Hulver
Street

Daffy
Green

Toftwood

Westfield

Yaxham

Whinburgh

Brandon
Parva

Barford

Bawbur

Great Melton

Little M

Tottenhill

Marham

Shouldham

A1122

Swaffham

North
Pickenham

Holme
Hale

West End

Ivy
Todd

East
Bradenham

West
Bradenham

Shipdham

A1075

Garveston

Runhall

Thuxton

Coston

Barnham
Broom

Wramplingham

High
Green

Lith

South
Runcton

Shouldham
Thorpe

Fincham

Barton
Bendish

Beachamwell

Cockley
Cley

Iceni
Village

South
Pickenham

Ashill

Saham
Hills

Crowshill

High
Common

Cranworth

Reymerston

Danemead
Green

Carleton
Forehoe

Kimberley

Crownthorpe

Kidd's
Moor

Hethersett

Stow
Bardolph

Stradsett

A134

Stow

Fincham

Eastmoor

Oxborough

Gooderstone

Hilborough

Great
Cressingham

Saham
Toney

Ovington

Carbrooke

Hingham

Woodrising

Southburgh

Hardingham

Hackford

Wicklewood

Deopham

Morley
St Botolph

Suton

A11

Silfield

Wymondha

Crimplesham

Bexwell

A1122

West
Dereham

Wretton

Whittington

Foulden

Beckett End

Bodney

Little
Cressingham

B1108

Merton

Watton

Griston

Northacre

Watton Green

Scoulton

Little
Ellingham

Deopham
Green

Great
Ellingham

Besthorpe

Spooner
Row

Ashwellthorpe

Wre

ington

Stoke
Ferry

A134

B1112

Northwold

Brookville

Whittington

Lynford

Mundford

Thompson

40

Stow
Bedon

Lov
Stow Bedon

Fe
street

Rockland
St Peter

Rockland
All Saints

Stalland
Common

Bow
Street

Mount
Pleasant

Great Ellingham

Carleton Rode

Attleborough

Fundenhall

Bunwell

For

Methwold
Hythe

Methwold

Cranwi

Iс
urgh

Breckles

Sho

Peddars Way &
Norfolk Coast Path

0   1   2   3   4   5 miles
0 1 2 3 4 5 6 7   8 kilometres

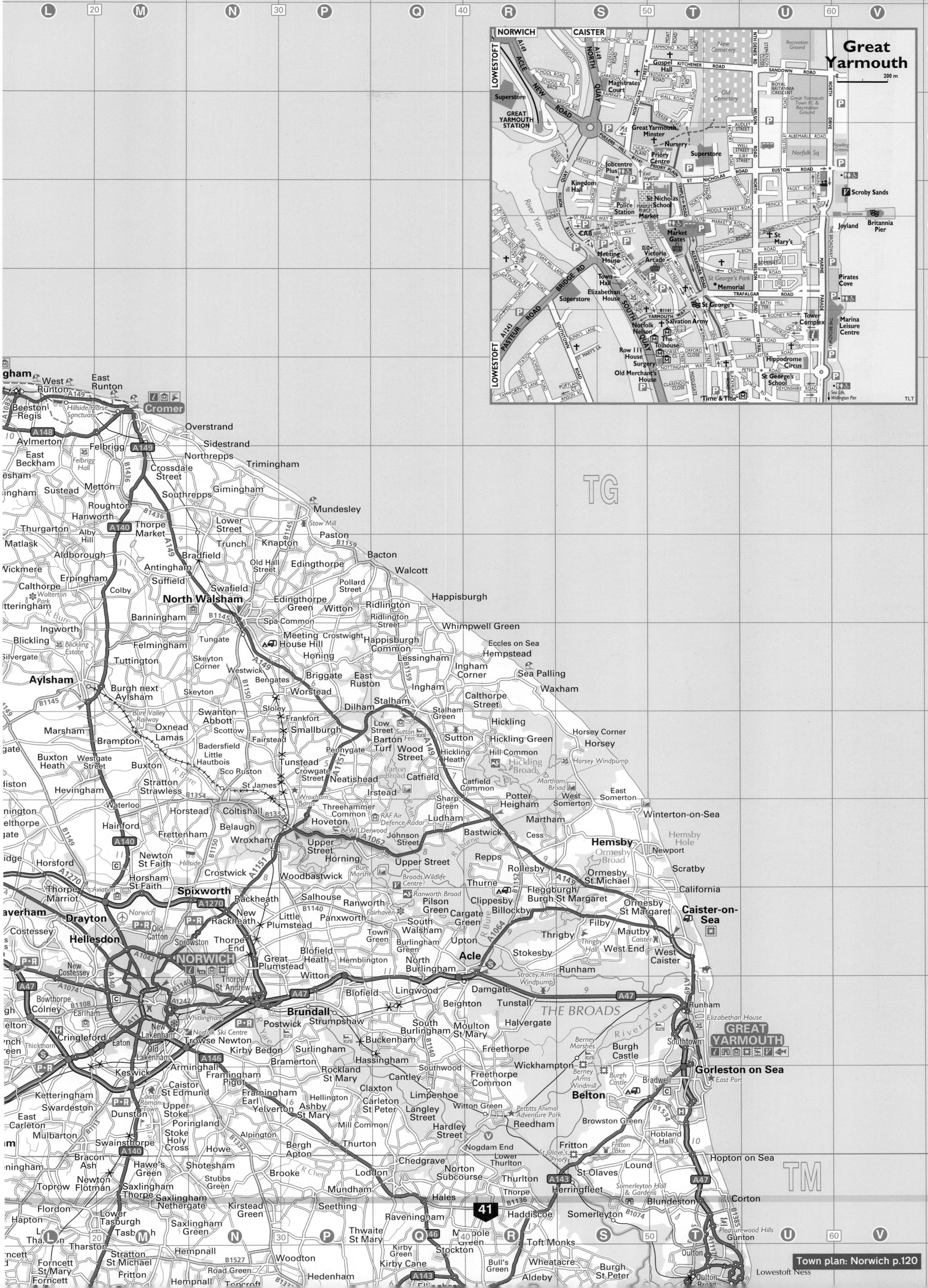
Great Yarmouth
200 m
Cromer
Overstrand
Sidestrand
Northrepps
Trimingham
Mundesley
Paston
Bacton
Walcott
Happisburgh
Whimpwell Green
Eccles on Sea
Sea Palling
Waxham
Horsey Corner
Horsey
Winterton-on-Sea
Hemsby
Newport
Scratby
California
Caister-on-Sea
North Walsham
Aylsham
Coltishall
Wroxham
Hoveton
Horning
Ludham
Potter Heigham
Martham
Stalham
Hickling
Acle
Drayton
Hellesdon
NORWICH
Spixworth
Brundall
Blofield
Reedham
Belton
Gorleston on Sea
GREAT YARMOUTH
Hopton on Sea
Corton
Lowestoft Ness
Haddiscoe
Loddon
Framingham Earl
Poringland
THE BROADS
TG
TM
41

Town plan: Norwich p.120

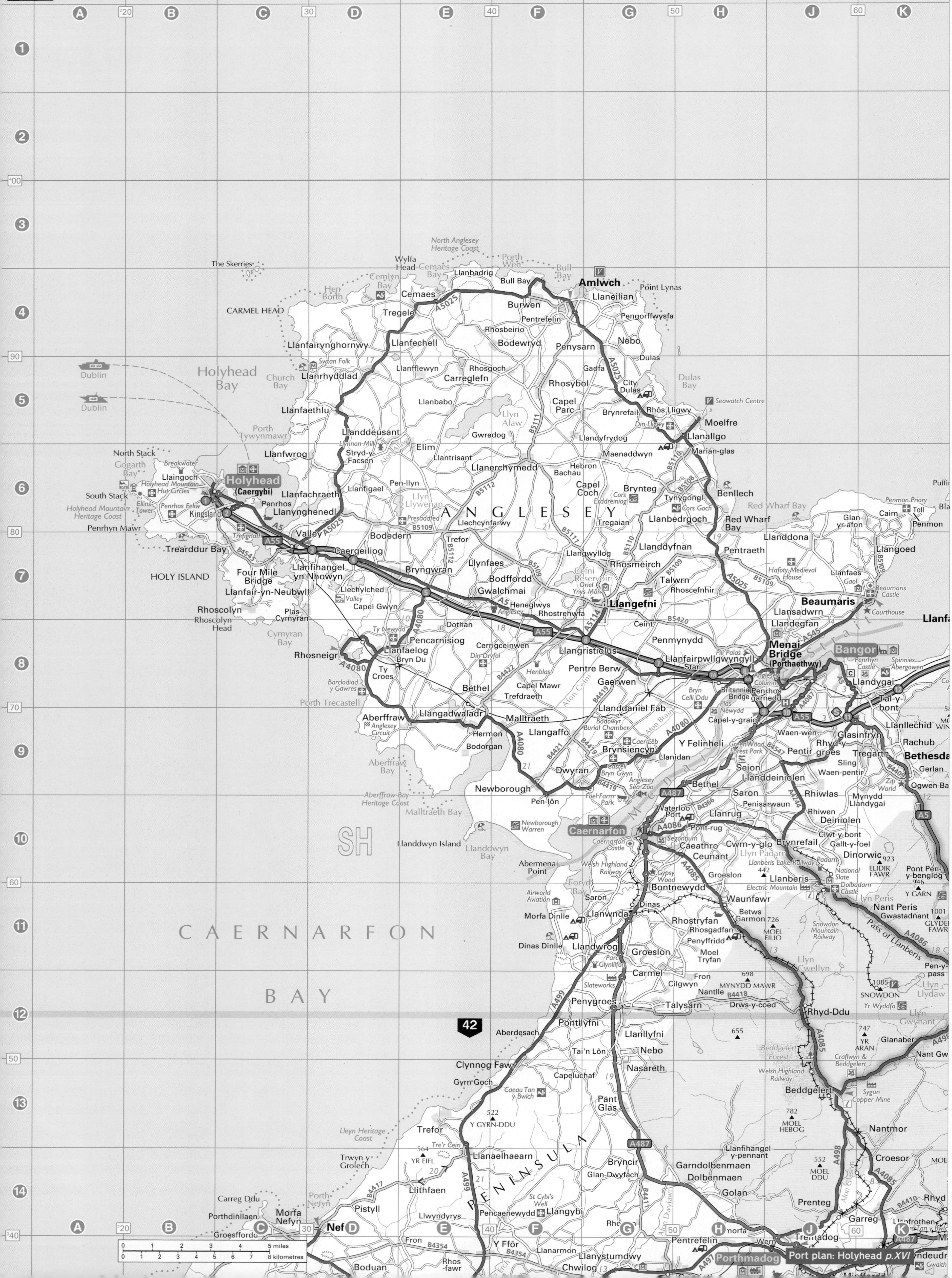

CAERNARFON
BAY
Holyhead Bay
ANGLESEY
HOLY ISLAND
CARMEL HEAD
The Skerries
North Anglesey Heritage Coast
Wylfa Head
Cemlyn Bay
Cemaes
Llanbadrig
Porth Wen
Bull Bay
Amlwch
Point Lynas
Llaneilian
Pengorffwysfa
Burwen
Pentrefelin
Rhosbeirio
Tregele
Hen Borth
Llanfechell
Bodewryd
Penysarn
Nebo
Dulas
Llanfairynghornwy
Swtan Folk
Llanrhyddlad
Church Bay
Llanfflewyn
Rhosgoch
Carreglefn
Gadfa
Rhosybol
City Dulas
Dulas Bay
Seawatch Centre
Llanfaethlu
Llanbabo
Llyn Alaw
Capel Parc
Brynrefail
Rhôs Lligwy
Din Lligwy
Moelfre
Dublin
Porth Tywynmawr
Llanddeusant
Llynnon Mill
Gwredog
Llandyfrydog
Llanallgo
Marian-glas
North Stack
Gogarth Bay
Breakwater
Llanfwrog
Stryd-y-Facsen
Elim
Llantrisant
Maenaddwyn
Llaingoch
Holyhead Mountain Hut Circles
Holyhead (Caergybi)
Llanerchymedd
Hebron
Bachau
South Stack
Ellins Tower
Holyhead Mountain Heritage Coast
Penrhos Feliw
Llanfachraeth
Llanfigael
Pen-llyn
Llyn Llywenan
Capel Coch
Cors Erddreiniog
Brynteg
Tynygongl
Cors Goch
Benllech
Penmon Priory
Puffin
Kingsland
Penrhos
Llanynghenedl
Presaddfed
Llechcynfarwy
Tregaian
Llanbedrgoch
Red Wharf Bay
Caim
Toll
Penmon
Glan-yr-afon
Penrhyn Mawr
Trefignath
Valley
Bodedern
Trefor
Llanddyfnan
Pentraeth
Llanddona
Llangoed
Trearddur Bay
Caergeiliog
Llangwyllog
Rhosmeirch
Cefni Reservoir
Talwrn
Hafoty Medieval House
Llanfaes
Four Mile Bridge
Llanfihangel yn Nhowyn
Bryngwran
Llynfaes
Bodffordd
Oriel Ynys Môn
Rhoscefnhir
Beaumaris
Beaumaris Castle
Gaol
Llanfair-yn-Neubwll
Llechylched
Gwalchmai
Llangefni
Courthouse
Rhoscolyn
Rhoscolyn Head
Plas Cymyran
Capel Gwyn
Heneglwys
Anglesey Showground
Rhostrehwfa
Llansadwrn
Dothan
Ceint
Llandegfan
Cymyran Bay
Ty Newydd
Pencarnisiog
Cerrigceinwen
Llangristiolus
Penmynydd
Menai Bridge (Porthaethwy)
Pili Palas
Bangor
Rhosneigr
Llanfaelog
Bryn Du
Din Dryfol
Llanfairpwllgwyngyll
Star
Penrhyn Castle
Spinnies Aberogwen
Barclodiad y Gawres
Ty Croes
Henblas
Pentre Berw
Anglesey Column
Llandygai
Bethel
Capel Mawr
Gaerwen
Britannia Bridge
Penrhos garnedd
Porth Trecastell
Trefdraeth
Bryn Celli Ddu
Plas Newydd
Tal-y-bont
Aberffraw
Anglesey Circuit
Llangadwaladr
Malltraeth
Llanddaniel Fab
Capel-y-graig
Llanllechid
Bodowyr Burial Chamber
Waen-wen
Glasinfryn
Hermon
Llangaffo
Caer Leb
Y Felinheli
Rhyd-y-groes
Rachub
Bodorgan
Brynsiencyn
Llanidan
Pentir
Tregarth
Bethesda
Aberffraw Bay
Greenwood Forest Park
Sling
Gerlan
Dwyran
Castell Bryn Gwyn
Seion
Waen-pentir
Llanddeiniolen
Ogwen Bank
Newborough
Anglesey Sea Zoo
Bethel
Rhiwlas
Mynydd Llandygai
Zip World
Aberffraw Bay Heritage Coast
Pen-lôn
Foel Farm Park
Saron
Penisarwaun
Malltraeth Bay
Waterloo Port
Llanrug
Rhiwen
Deiniolen
Newborough Warren
Caernarfon
Pont-rug
Clwt-y-bont
SH
Llanddwyn Island
Llanddwyn Bay
Segontium
Caeathro
Cwm-y-glo
Brynrefail
Gallt-y-foel
Caernarfon Castle
Llyn Padarn
Dinorwic
Ceunant
Llanberis Lake Railway
Padarn
923
ELIDIR FAWR
Abermenai Point
Welsh Highland Railway
Gypsy Wood
442
Llanberis
Groeslon
National Slate
Pont Pen-y-benglog
Foryd Bay
Bontnewydd
Electric Mountain
Dolbadarn Castle
946
Y GARN
Llyn Peris
Airworld Aviation
Saron
Waunfawr
Nant Peris
Dinas
1001
Gwastadnant
GLYDER FAWR
Morfa Dinlle
Llanwnda
Rhostryfan
Betws Garmon
726
MOEL EILIO
Snowdon Mountain Railway
Pass of Llanberis
Rhosgadfan
Penyffridd
Dinas Dinlle
Llandwrog
Groeslon
Moel Tryfan
Llyn Cwellyn
Parc Glynllifon
Carmel
Pen-y-pass
698
MYNYDD MAWR
Fron
1085
SNOWDON
Slateworks
Cilgwyn
Nantlle
Llyn Llydaw
Yr Wyddfa
Penygroes
Talysarn
Drws-y-coed
Rhyd-Ddu
Llyn Gwynant
42
Aberdesach
Pontllyfni
655
747
YR ARAN
Glanaber
Llanllyfni
Beddgelert Forest
Nant Gw
Tai'n Lôn
Nebo
Craflwyn & Beddgelert
Clynnog Fawr
Nasareth
Welsh Highland Railway
Capeluchaf
Beddgelert
Gyrn Goch
Sygun Copper Mine
Caeau Tan y Bwlch
Pant Glas
522
Y GYRN-DDU
782
MOEL HEBOG
Lleyn Heritage Coast
Nantmor
Trefor
Tre'r Ceiri
564
YR EIFL
Llanaelhaearn
Bryncir
Garndolbenmaen
Llanfihangel-y-pennant
Croesor
Trwyn y Gorlech
Glan-Dwyfach
Dolbenmaen
552
MOEL DDU
LLEYN PENINSULA
Llithfaen
Golan
Carreg Ddu
Porth Nefyn
Pistyll
St Cybi's Well
Llangybi
Prenteg
Rhyd
Porthdinllaen
Morfa Nefyn
Nefyn
Llwyndyrys
Pencaenewydd
Garreg
Llanfrothen
Groesffordd
Fron
Y Ffôr
Pentrefelin
Tremadog
Boduan
Rhos-fawr
Llanarmon
Llanystumdwy
Chwilog
Porthmadog
Afon Dwyfawr
Afon Glaslyn
Menai Strait
Afon Cefni
Afon Braint
A5
A55
A5025
A4080
A5114
A4086
A4087
A487
A499
A498
A4085
A4244
A545
B5109
B5110
B5111
B5112
B5108
B4545
B4422
B4419
B4421
B4420
B4366
B4547
B4409
B4418
B4417
B4354
B4411
B4410
0 1 2 3 4 5 miles
0 1 2 3 4 5 6 7 8 kilometres

Port plan: Holyhead p.XVI

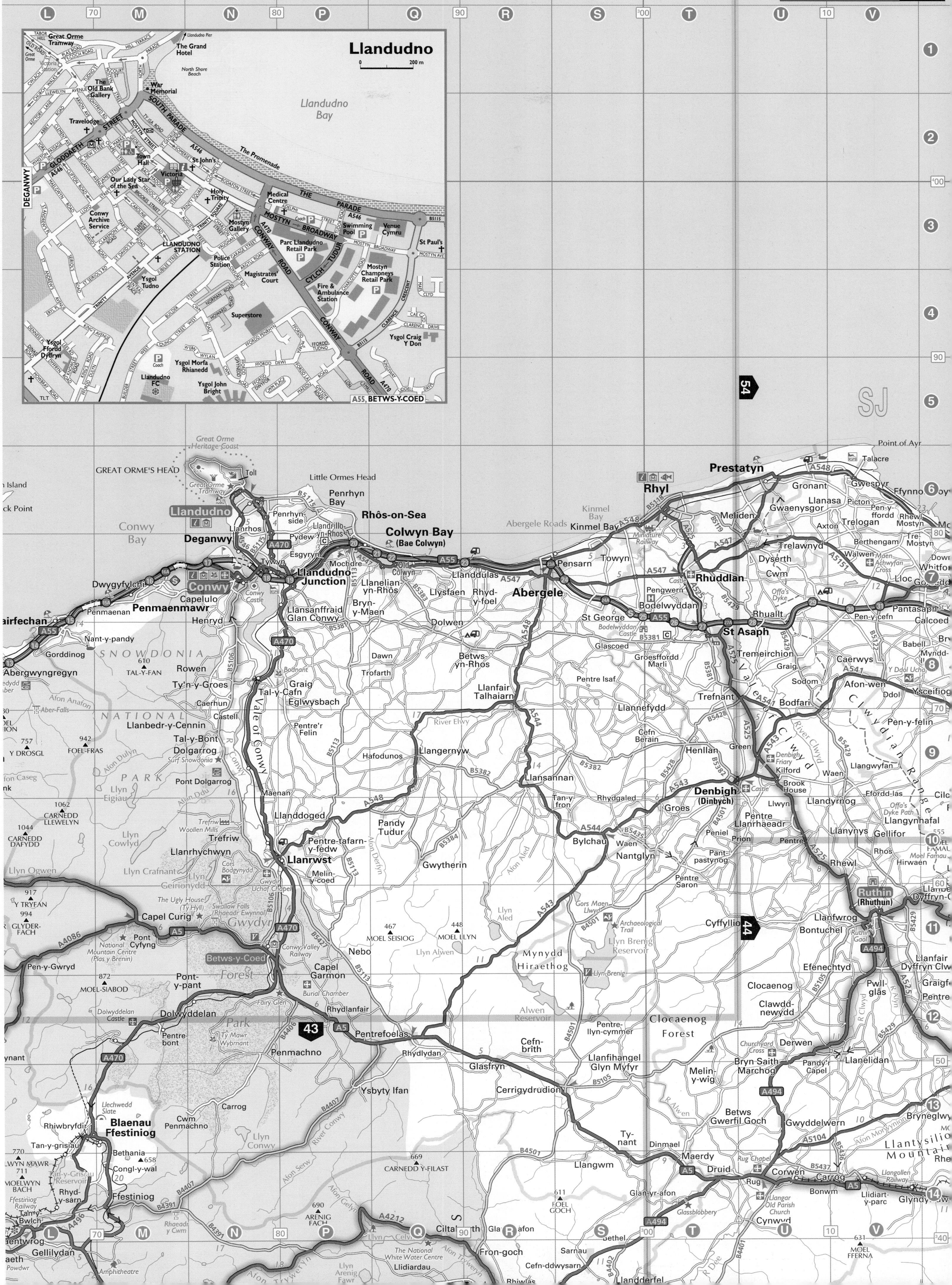

Llandudno

0 200 m

Great Orme Tramway
Llandudno Pier
The Grand Hotel
North Shore Beach
The Old Bank Gallery
War Memorial
Travelodge
The Promenade
Llandudno Bay
Town Hall
Our Lady Star of the Sea
St John's
Holy Trinity
Victoria
Conwy Archive Service
LLANDUDNO STATION
Medical Centre
Swimming Pool
Venue Cymru
THE PARADE
St Paul's
Mostyn Gallery
Parc Llandudno Retail Park
Police Station
Magistrates' Court
Mostyn Champneys Retail Park
Fire & Ambulance Station
Ysgol Tudno
Superstore
Ysgol Craig Y Don
Ysgol Ffordd Dyffryn
Coach
Ysgol Morfa Rhianedd
Llandudno FC
Ysgol John Bright
A55, BETWS-Y-COED

SJ

54

Great Orme Heritage Coast
GREAT ORME'S HEAD
Great Orme Tramway
Toll
Point of Ayr
Talacre
Prestatyn
Rhyl
Gwespyr
Ffynno
Gronant
Llanasa
Picton
Meliden
Gwaenysgor
Pen-y-ffordd
Rhewl
Mostyn
Axton
Trelogan
Tre Mostyn
Walwen
Whitfo
Down

Little Ormes Head
Penrhyn Bay
Rhôs-on-Sea
Kinmel Bay
Abergele Roads
Kinmel Bay
Llandudno
Conwy Bay
Deganwy
Penrhynside
Llandrillo yn-Rhos
Pydew yn-Rhos
Colwyn Bay (Bae Colwyn)
Towyn
Pensarn
Rhuddlan
Dyserth
Cwm
Trelawnyd
Berthengam
Aethwyan Cross
Lloc
Llanrhos
Esgyrryn
Mochdre
Old Colwyn
Llanddulas
A547
Pengwern
Bodelwyddan
Rhuallt
Pen-y-cefn
Calcoed
Babell
Dwygyfylchi
Conwy
Conwy Castle
Llandudno Junction
Llanelian yn-Rhôs
Bryn-y-Maen
Dolwen
St George
Bodelwyddan Castle
St Asaph
Tremeirchion
Caerwys
Mynedd
Capelulo
Penmaenmawr
Llansanffraid Glan Conwy
Betws-yn-Rhos
Glascoed
Groesffordd Marli
Graig
Sodom
Y Dol Uch
Fairfechan
Penmaen
Henryd
Dawn
Llanfair Talhaiarn
Pentre Isaf
Trefnant
Bodfari
Afon-wen
Ysceifio
Gorddinog
Nant-y-pandy
Rowen
Ty'n-y-Groes
Trofarth
Llannefydd
Ddol
Pen-y-felin
Abergwyngregyn
SNOWDONIA
TAL-Y-FAN
Graig
Eglwysbach
Tal-y-Cafn
Caerhun
Castell
Pentre'r Felin
River Elwy
Llangernyw
Cefn Berain
Henllan
Green
Llangwyfan
FOEL-FRAS
Bodnant
Hafodunos
A544
Llansannan
Tan-y-fron
Rhydgaled
Denbigh (Dinbych)
Kilford
Brook House
Llandyrnog
Y DROSGL
NATIONAL
Llanbedr-y-Cennin
Tal-y-Bont
Dolgarrog
Surf Snowdonia
Maenan
Llanddoged
Bylchau
Waen
Nantglyn
Groes
Peniel
Prion
Pentre Saron
Llanrhaeadr
Llanynys
Gellifor
Rhos
Pentre
CARNEDD LLEWELYN
Llyn Eigiau
Trefriw
Woollen Mills
PARK
A548
Pandy Tudur
Gwytherin
Llyn Aled
Pentre Llanrhaeadr
Llangynhafal
CARNEDD DAFYDD
Llyn Cowlyd
Trefriw
Llanrhychwyn
Pentre-tafarn-y-fedw
Melin-y-coed
FAMAU
Rhewl
Llyn Ogwen
Y TRYFAN
Llyn Crafnant
Llanrwst
Gwytherin
MOEL SEISIOG
MOEL LLYN
Gors Maen Llwyd
Archaeological Trail
Cyffylliog
Ruthin (Rhuthun)
Llanfwrog
GLYDER-FACH
Llyn Geirionydd
Cors Bodgynydd
Uchaf Chapel
Nebo
Llyn Alwen
Mynydd Hiraethog
Llyn Brenig Reservoir
44
Bontuchel
Capel Curig
The Ugly House (Ty Hyll)
Swallow Falls (Rhaeadr Ewynnol)
Llyn Brenig
Efenechtyd
Pont Cyfyng
National Mountain Centre (Plas y Brenin)
Betws-y-Coed
Conwy Valley Railway
Capel Garmon
Llyn Brenig
Clocaenog
Clawdd-newydd
Pwll-glâs
Pen-y-Gwryd
MOEL-SIABOD
Gwydyr Forest
Burial Chamber
Clocaenog Forest
Derwen
Llanelidan
Fairy Glen
Rhydlanfair
Alwen Reservoir
Dolwyddelan
Dolwyddelan Castle
43
A5
Pentrefoelas
Bryn Saith Marchog
Pandy'r Capel
Pentre-bont
Ty Mawr Wybrnant
Rhydlydan
Cefn-brith
Llanfihangel Glyn Myfyr
Melin-y-wig
Penmachno
Glasfryn
Churchyard Cross
Derwen
Llechwedd Slate
Cwm Penmachno
Carrog
Cerrigydrudion
Betws Gwerfil Goch
Gwyddelwern
Llantysilio Mountain
Blaenau Ffestiniog
Rhiwbryfdir
Llyn Conwy
River Conwy
Ysbyty Ifan
Ty-nant
Brynegl
Bethania
Congl-y-wal
Maerdy
Druid
Rug Chapel
Corwen
Llangollen Railway
Ffestiniog Railway
Rhyd-y-sarn
Llangwm
Glan-yr-afon
Rug
Bonwm
Glyndy
Ffestiniog
CARNEDD Y-FILAST
FOEL GOCH
Llidiart-y-parc
MOELWYN MAWR
Tan-y-grisiau Reservoir
ARENIG FACH
Bethel
Cynwyd
MOEL FFERNA
MOELWYN BACH
Rhaeadr y Cwm
The National White Water Centre
Cefn-ddwysarn
Llidiardau
Llanddefel
Gelililydan
Gentryn
Powdwr
Fron-goch
Sarnau
Llyn Arenig Fawr
Rhiwlas

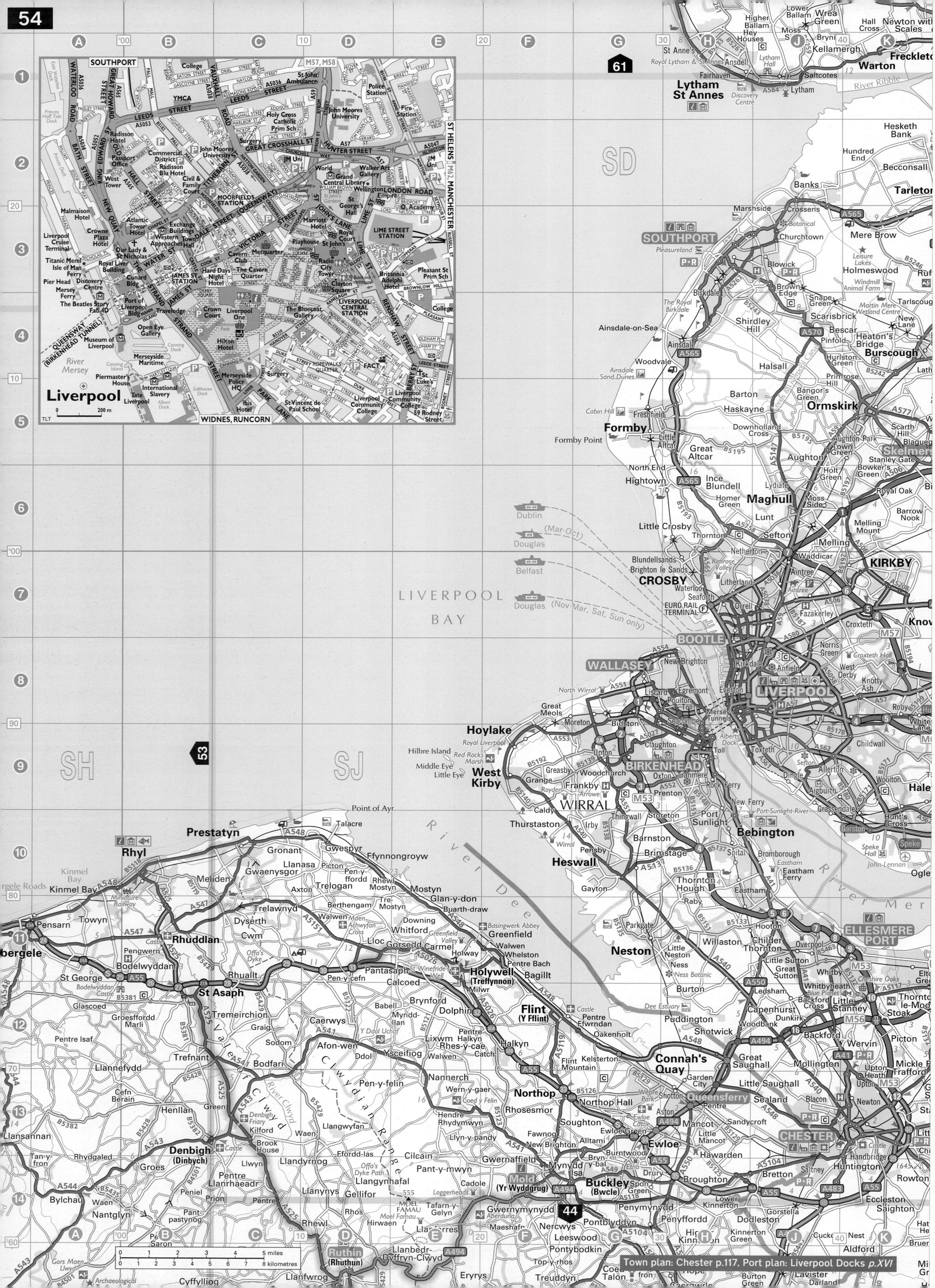

Liverpool
SOUTHPORT
WIDNES, RUNCORN
M57, M58
ST HELENS M62 MANCHESTER
John Moores University
Liverpool Cruise Terminal
Royal Liver Building
Cunard Bldg
Port of Liverpool Bldg
Museum of Liverpool
Merseyside Maritime
International Slavery
Tate Liverpool
LIME STREET STATION
LIVERPOOL CENTRAL STATION
MOORFIELDS STATION
JAMES ST STATION
World Museum
Central Library
Walker Art Gallery
St George's Hall
Empire
Liverpool One
Metquarter
Cavern Club
The Beatles Story
Radio City Tower
Liverpool Community College
QUEENSWAY (BIRKENHEAD TUNNEL)
River Mersey
200 m
Lytham St Annes
Lytham
Warton
Freckleton
Ansdell
Saltcoates
River Ribble
Hesketh Bank
Becconsall
Tarleton
Banks
SOUTHPORT
Churchtown
Birkdale
Ainsdale
Ainsdale-on-Sea
Woodvale
Formby
Formby Point
Freshfield
Hightown
Ince Blundell
Halsall
Barton
Haskayne
Downholland Cross
Ormskirk
Aughton
Maghull
Lydiate
Lunt
Sefton
Melling
KIRKBY
Little Crosby
Thornton
CROSBY
Litherland
Waterloo
Seaforth
Netherton
Aintree
Fazakerley
BOOTLE
Kirkdale
Anfield
Everton
LIVERPOOL
WALLASEY
New Brighton
Egremont
Liscard
Seacombe
Mersey Tunnels
Dublin
Douglas
Belfast
(Mar-Oct)
(Nov-Mar, Sat, Sun only)
LIVERPOOL BAY
SD
SH
SJ
Hoylake
West Kirby
Hilbre Island
Middle Eye
Little Eye
Moreton
Great Meols
Bidston
Claughton
Upton
BIRKENHEAD
Oxton
Tranmere
Rock Ferry
Greasby
Frankby
Woodchurch
Prenton
Grange
Caldy
WIRRAL
Thurstaston
Irby
Thingwall
Storeton
Port Sunlight
Bebington
Barnston
Pensby
Heswall
Brimstage
Spital
Bromborough
Eastham
Gayton
Thornton Hough
Raby
Parkgate
Neston
Little Neston
Ness
Willaston
Burton
Childer Thornton
Hooton
ELLESMERE PORT
Little Sutton
Great Sutton
Ledsham
Capenhurst
Puddington
Shotwick
Woodbank
Backford
Mollington
Great Saughall
Little Saughall
Saughall
Sealand
Blacon
CHESTER
Hoole
Upton
Newton
Huntington
Handbridge
Saltney
Bretton
Broughton
Hawarden
Mancot
Queensferry
Sandycroft
Connah's Quay
Shotton
Garden City
Aston
Ewloe
Buckley (Bwcle)
Penyffordd
Dodleston
Kinnerton
Mold (Yr Wyddgrug)
Gwernaffield
Mynydd Isa
Northop
Northop Hall
Sychdyn
Soughton
Rhosesmor
Halkyn
Flint (Y Fflint)
Oakenholt
Bagillt
Holywell (Treffynnon)
Greenfield
Mostyn
Point of Ayr
Talacre
Gronant
Gwespyr
Ffynnongroyw
Llanasa
Trelogan
Prestatyn
Rhyl
Meliden
Gwaenysgor
Dyserth
Cwm
Trelawnyd
Rhuddlan
Bodelwyddan
St Asaph
Kinmel Bay
Towyn
Pensarn
Abergele
St George
Tremeirchion
Caerwys
Afon-wen
Ysceifiog
Nannerch
Pen-y-felin
Denbigh (Dinbych)
Henllan
Trefnant
Llannefydd
Bodfari
Llandyrnog
Llangwyfan
Llangynhafal
Gellifor
Llanynys
Rhewl
Ruthin (Rhuthun)
Llanbedr-Dyffryn-Clwyd
Cilcain
Pant-y-mwyn
Moel Famau
Clwydian Range
Vale of Clwyd
River Dee
River Mersey
Speke
Garston
Allerton
Aigburth
Dingle
Toxteth
Wavertree
Childwall
Woolton
Knotty Ash
West Derby
Norris Green
Croxteth
Halewood
Ellesmere Port
Whitby
Overpool
Stanney
Picton
Mickle Trafford
Rowton
Eccleston
Saighton
Aldford
Burscough
Scarisbrick
Bescar
Pinfold
Holmeswood
Mere Brow
Crossens
Marshside
Shirdley Hill
Bickerstaffe
Skelmersdale
Lathom
Town plan: Chester p.117, Port plan: Liverpool Docks p.XVI
44
53
61
miles
kilometres

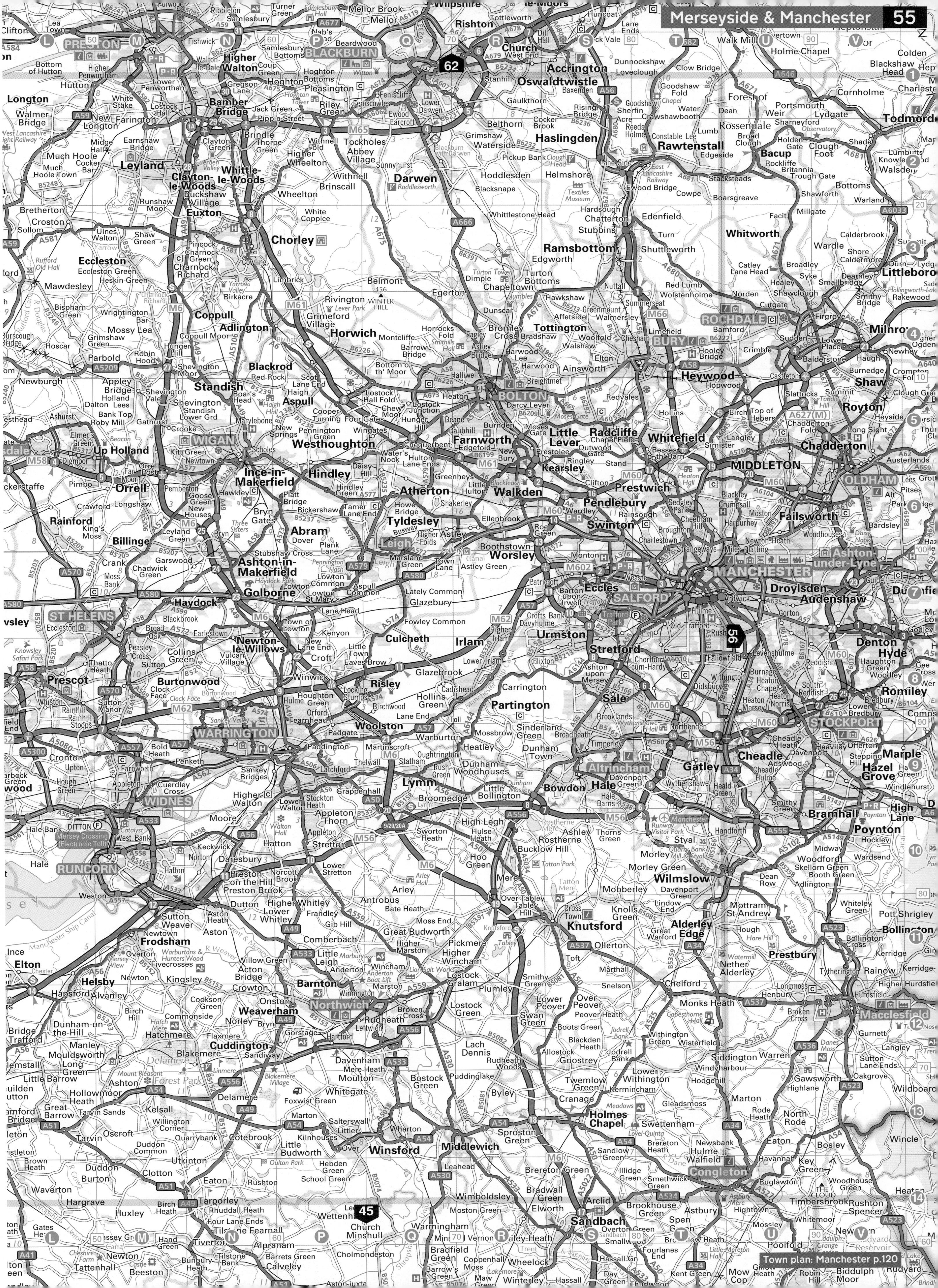
PRESTON
BLACKBURN
Accrington
Oswaldtwistle
Haslingden
Rawtenstall
Bacup
Todmorden
Leyland
Chorley
Darwen
Ramsbottom
Whitworth
Littleborough
ROCHDALE
BURY
Heywood
Milnrow
Shaw
Royton
BOLTON
Horwich
Standish
WIGAN
Westhoughton
Farnworth
Little Lever
Radcliffe
Whitefield
MIDDLETON
Chadderton
OLDHAM
Up Holland
Orrell
Ince-in-Makerfield
Hindley
Atherton
Walkden
Prestwich
Pendlebury
Failsworth
Swinton
Tyldesley
Leigh
Worsley
Ashton-in-Makerfield
Golborne
Haydock
ST HELENS
Eccles
SALFORD
MANCHESTER
Ashton-under-Lyne
Droylsden
Audenshaw
Newton-le-Willows
Prescot
Urmston
Stretford
Irlam
Denton
Hyde
Romiley
Sale
Partington
Culcheth
Risley
WARRINGTON
Woolston
STOCKPORT
Cheadle
Gatley
Altrincham
Hale
Bowdon
Lymm
Marple
Hazel Grove
Bramhall
Poynton
High Lane
WIDNES
RUNCORN
Wilmslow
Alderley Edge
Knutsford
Frodsham
Helsby
Weaverham
Northwich
Bollington
Prestbury
Macclesfield
Holmes Chapel
Middlewich
Winsford
Congleton
Sandbach
Tarporley
Biddulph

Town plan: Manchester p.120

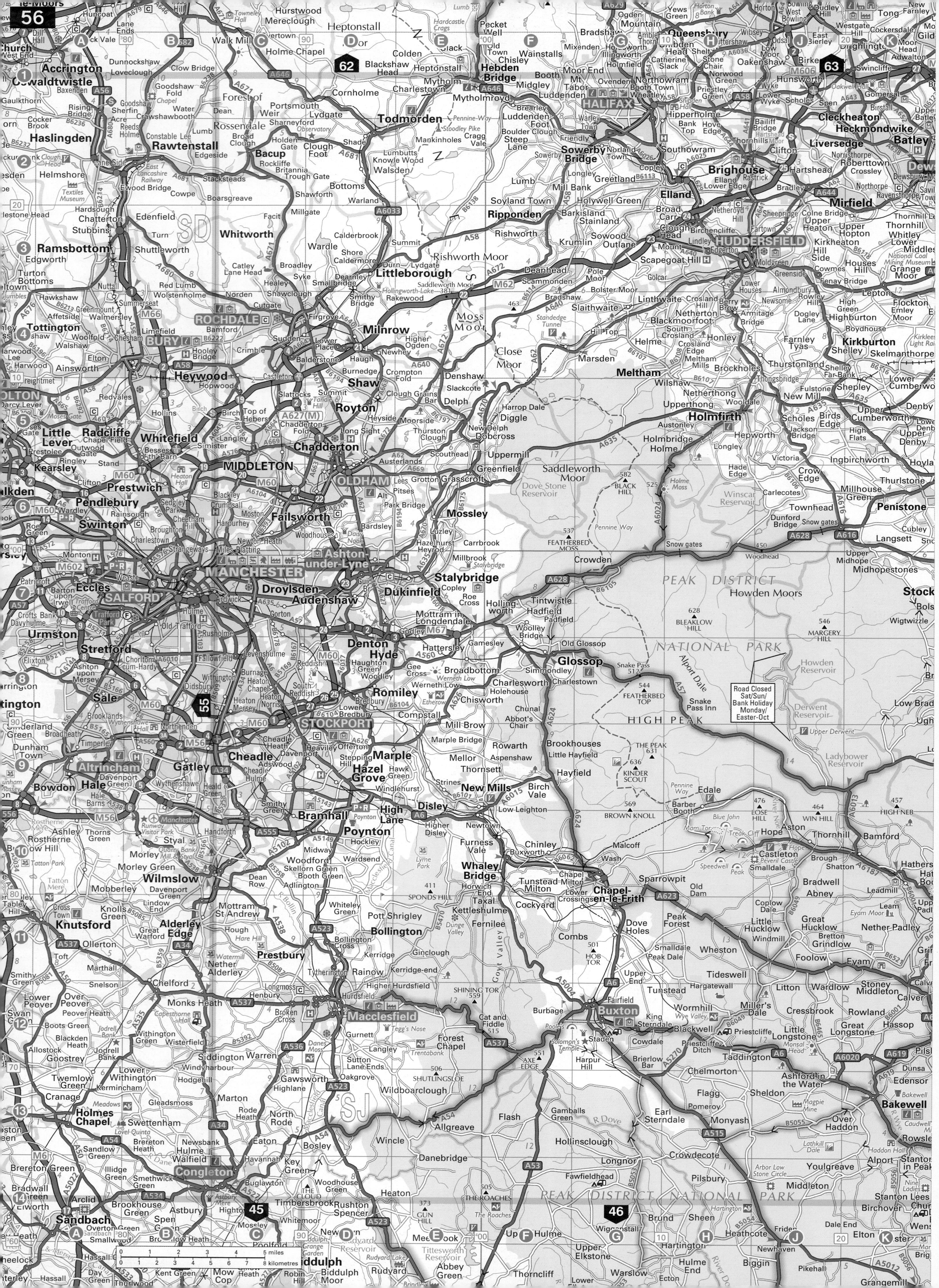
Accrington
Oswaldtwistle
Haslingden
Rawtenstall
Bacup
Todmorden
Hebden Bridge
Heptonstall
Queensbury
Halifax
Sowerby Bridge
Brighouse
Elland
Cleckheaton
Heckmondwike
Liversedge
Batley
Mirfield
Huddersfield
Ripponden
Ramsbottom
Whitworth
Littleborough
Rochdale
Milnrow
Bury
Tottington
Heywood
Shaw
Royton
Radcliffe
Whitefield
Middleton
Chadderton
Oldham
Prestwich
Pendlebury
Swinton
Failsworth
Eccles
Salford
Manchester
Ashton-under-Lyne
Droylsden
Audenshaw
Stalybridge
Dukinfield
Mossley
Urmston
Stretford
Sale
Denton
Hyde
Romiley
Glossop
Stockport
Cheadle
Gatley
Altrincham
Hale
Bowdon
Marple
Hazel Grove
Bramhall
Poynton
Disley
New Mills
High Lane
Whaley Bridge
Chapel-en-le-Frith
Wilmslow
Knutsford
Alderley Edge
Prestbury
Bollington
Macclesfield
Buxton
Bakewell
Holmes Chapel
Congleton
Sandbach
Biddulph
Holmfirth
Meltham
Marsden
Slaithwaite
Penistone
Kirkburton
Saddleworth Moor
Peak District National Park
High Peak
Kinder Scout
Edale
Hope
Castleton
Tideswell
Monyash
Hartington
SD
SJ
62
63
55
45
46
M60
M62
M66
M56
M6
M67
A6
A628
A57
A523
A54
A34
A537
A53
A515
A623
A635
A616
Road Closed Sat/Sun/ Bank Holiday Monday/ Easter-Oct
5 miles
8 kilometres

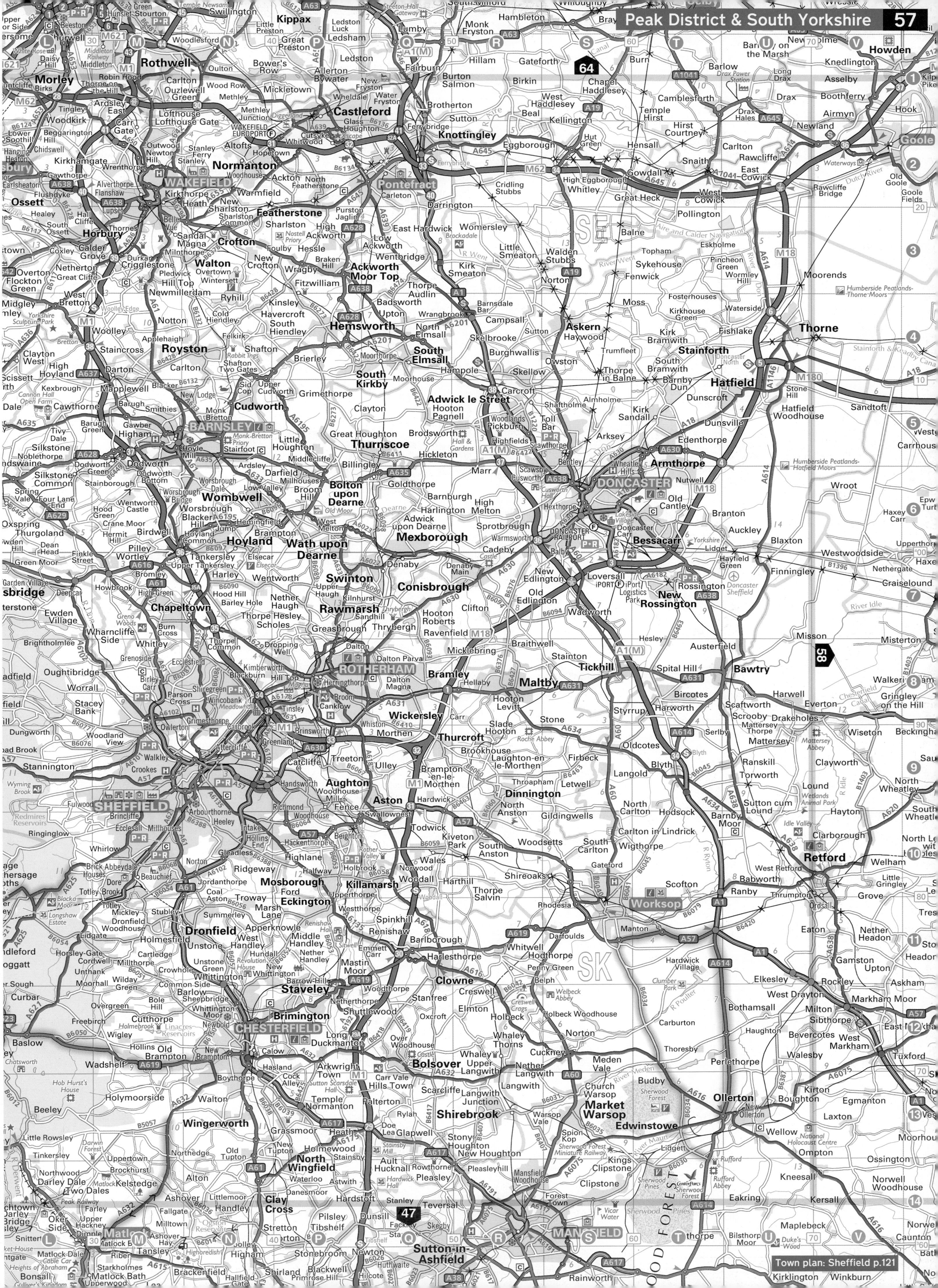
Rothwell
Morley
Castleford
Knottingley
Normanton
Pontefract
Wakefield
Ossett
Horbury
Featherstone
Hemsworth
South Elmsall
South Kirkby
Royston
Cudworth
Barnsley
Askern
Thorne
Stainforth
Hatfield
Adwick le Street
Thurnscoe
Bolton upon Dearne
Wombwell
Hoyland
Wath upon Dearne
Mexborough
Conisbrough
Armthorpe
Doncaster
Bessacarr
New Rossington
Swinton
Rawmarsh
Chapeltown
Rotherham
Maltby
Tickhill
Bawtry
Bramley
Wickersley
Thurcroft
Sheffield
Aughton
Aston
Dinnington
Retford
Worksop
Mosborough
Killamarsh
Eckington
Dronfield
Staveley
Clowne
Brimington
Chesterfield
Bolsover
Shirebrook
Market Warsop
Edwinstowe
Ollerton
North Wingfield
Clay Cross
Mansfield
Sutton-in-Ashfield
Howden
Goole

Town plan: Sheffield p.121

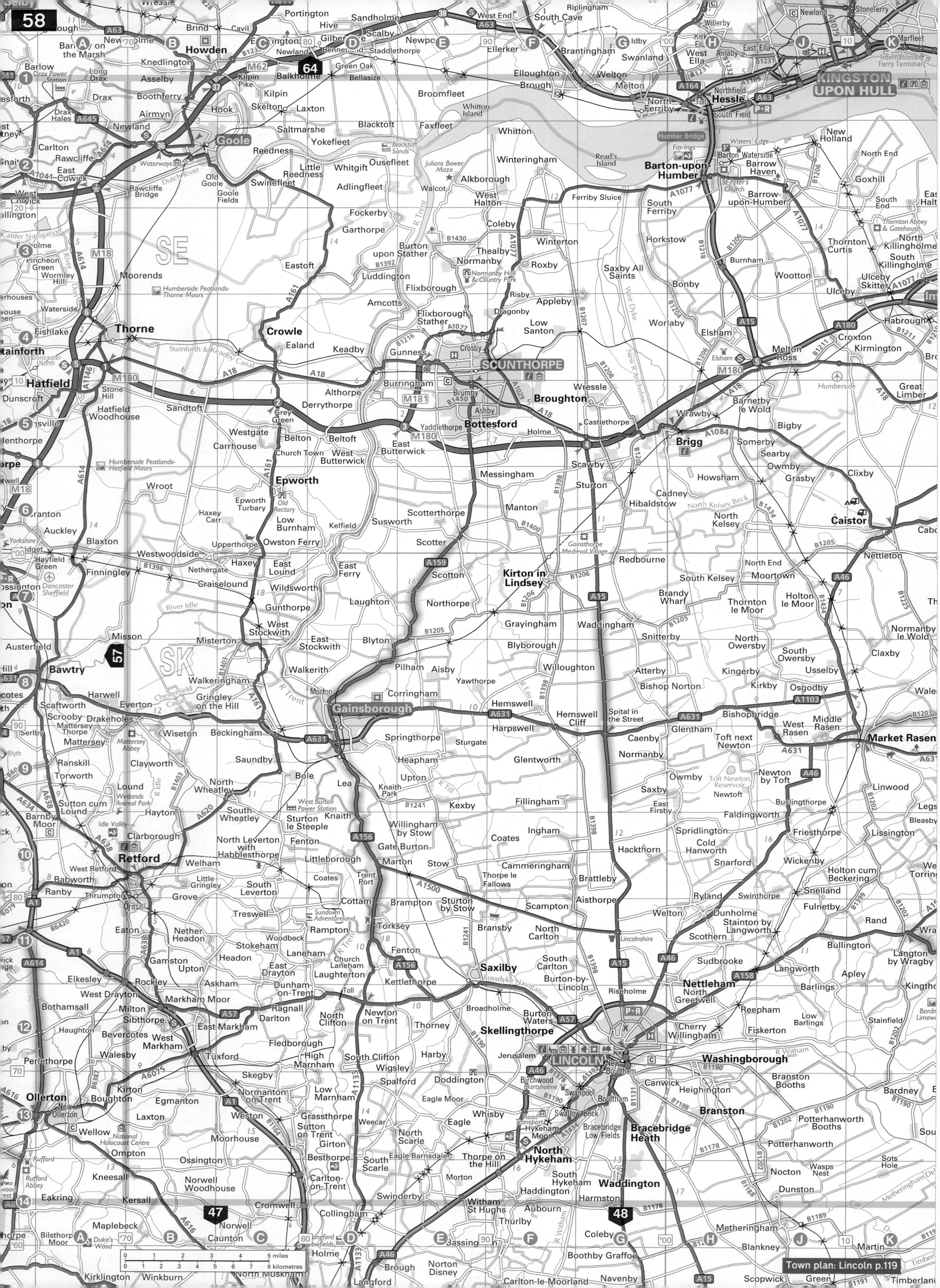
Portington
Sandholme
Hive
Gilberdyke
Scalby
Newport
West End
South Cave
Riplingham
Newland
Willerby
Stoneferry
Marfleet
Howden
Brind
Cavil
Barlby on the Marsh
Newsholme
Knedlington
Asselby
Barlow
Drax Power Station
Long Drax
Drax
Boothferry
Airmyn
Hook
Kilpin Pike
Kilpin
Skelton
Laxton
Balkholme
Bennetland
Staddlethorpe
Green Oak
Bellasize
Ellerker
Brantingham
Idby
Swanland
Kirk Ella
West Ella
Anlaby
East Ella
International Ferry Terminal
KINGSTON UPON HULL
Elloughton
Brough
Welton
Melton
North Ferriby
Hessle
South Field
Broomfleet
Whitton Island
Faxfleet
Whitton
Blacktoft
Blacktoft Sands
Saltmarshe
Yokefleet
Newland
Drax Hales
Carlton
Rawcliffe
East Cowick
West Cowick
Goole
Waterways
Old Goole
Goole Fields
Rawcliffe Bridge
Dutch River
Reedness
Little Reedness
Whitgift
Ousefleet
Swinefleet
Adlingfleet
Julians Bower Maze
Walcot
Alkborough
Winteringham
Read's Island
Humber Bridge
Far Ings
Waters' Edge
Barton Waterside
Barton-upon-Humber
Barrow Haven
St Peter's Church
Barrow-upon-Humber
New Holland
North End
Goxhill
East Halton
South End
Thornton Abbey & Gatehouse
Thornton Curtis
North Killingholme
South Killingholme
West Halton
Ferriby Sluice
South Ferriby
Horkstow
Coleby
Winterton
Fockerby
Garthorpe
Burton upon Stather
Thealby
Normanby
Normanby Hall & Country Park
Roxby
Saxby All Saints
Burnham
Wootton
Bonby
Ulceby
Ulceby Skitter
Habrough
Worlaby
Elsham
Croxton
Kirmington
Melton Ross
Humberside
Great Limber
SE
Calder Navigation
Pincheon Green
Wormley Hill
Moorends
Humberside Peatlands-Thorne Moors
Eastoft
Luddington
Flixborough
Amcotts
Flixborough Stather
Risby
Appleby
Dragonby
Low Santon
Weir Dyke
New R. Ancholme
Waterside
Thorne
Fishlake
Stainforth
Stainforth & Keadby Canal
Crowle
Ealand
Keadby
Gunness
Crosby
SCUNTHORPE
Burringham
Brumby
Ashby
Bottesford
Yaddlethorpe
Holme
Broughton
Wressle
Castlethorpe
Wrawby
Barnetby le Wold
Brigg
Bigby
Somerby
Searby
Owmby
Grasby
Clixby
Caistor
Cabourne
Hatfield
Dunscroft
Stone Hill
Hatfield Woodhouse
Sandtoft
Althorpe
Derrythorpe
Grey Green
Belton
Beltoft
Westgate
Carrhouse
Church Town
West Butterwick
East Butterwick
Humberside Peatlands-Hatfield Moors
Epworth
Wroot
Epworth Turbary
Old Rectory
Haxey Carr
Low Burnham
Kelfield
Susworth
Scotterthorpe
Messingham
Scawby
Sturton
Manton
Hibaldstow
Cadney
Howsham
North Kelsey Beck
North Kelsey
Auckley
Blaxton
Upperthorpe
Owston Ferry
Scotter
Gainsthorpe Medieval Village
Redbourne
Nettleton
Hayfield Green
Finningley
Westwoodside
Nethergate
Haxey
Craiselound
East Lound
East Ferry
Scotton
Kirton in Lindsey
North End
Moortown
South Kelsey
Doncaster Sheffield
River Idle
Wildsworth
Gunthorpe
Laughton
Northorpe
Brandy Wharf
Thornton le Moor
Holton le Moor
Misson
Austerfield
West Stockwith
East Stockwith
Misterton
Blyton
Grayingham
Waddingham
Snitterby
North Owersby
South Owersby
Normanby le Wold
Claxby
Bawtry
SK
Walkerith
Pilham
Aisby
Blyborough
Willoughton
Yawthorpe
Atterby
Kingerby
Usselby
Walkeringham
Chesterfield Canal
Gringley on the Hill
Morton
Corringham
Bishop Norton
Kirkby
Osgodby
Harwell
Everton
Scaftworth
Scrooby
Drakeholes
Mattersey Thorpe
Mattersey
Mattersey Abbey
Serlby
Wiseton
Beckingham
Gainsborough
Hemswell
Harpswell
Hemswell Cliff
Spital in the Street
Glentham
Bishopbridge
West Rasen
Middle Rasen
Market Rasen
Springthorpe
Sturgate
Caenby
Toft next Newton
Normanby
Heapham
Glentworth
Ranskill
Torworth
Clayworth
Saundby
Bole
Lea
Upton
Knaith Park
Owmby
Saxby
Toft Newton Reservoir
Newtoft
Newton by Toft
Linwood
Lound
Lound Wetlands Animal Park
North Wheatley
Sutton cum Lound
Hayton
South Wheatley
West Burton Power Station
Knaith
Sturton le Steeple
Kexby
Fillingham
East Firsby
Faldingworth
Buslingthorpe
Barnby Moor
Idle Valley
Clarborough
Retford
North Leverton with Habblesthorpe
Fenton
Willingham by Stow
Gate Burton
Ingham
Coates
Spridlington
Cold Hanworth
Hackthorn
Friesthorpe
Lissington
Legsby
Welham
West Retford
Babworth
Little Gringley
Littleborough
Marton
Stow
Cammeringham
Snarford
Wickenby
Holton cum Beckering
Ranby
Thrumpton
Ordsall
Grove
South Leverton
Coates
Trent Port
Thorpe le Fallows
Brattleby
Aisthorpe
Ryland
Swinthorpe
Snelland
Fulnetby
Rand
Treswell
Cottam
Brampton
Sturton by Stow
Scampton
Welton
Dunholme
Stainton by Langworth
Sundown Adventureland
Torksey
Eaton
Nether Headon
Rampton
Bransby
North Carlton
Scothern
Bullington
Woodbeck
Stokeham
Laneham
Church Laneham
Fenton
Lincolnshire
Headon
Gamston
Upton
East Drayton
Laughterton
Saxilby
Fossdyke Navigation
South Carlton
Burton-by-Lincoln
Sudbrooke
Langworth
Langton by Wragby
Apley
Barlings
Elkesley
Rockley
West Drayton
Askham
Dunham-on-Trent
Kettlethorpe
Riseholme
Nettleham
North Greetwell
Markham Moor
Ragnall
Darlton
Bothamsall
Milton
Sibthorpe
East Markham
North Clifton
Newton on Trent
Broadholme
Burton Waters
Reepham
Low Barlings
Stainfield
Haughton
Bevercotes
West Markham
Thorney
Skellingthorpe
Cherry Willingham
Fiskerton
Walesby
Tuxford
Fledborough
Harby
Jerusalem
LINCOLN
Washingborough
R. Witham
Perlethorpe
High Marnham
South Clifton
Wigsley
Spalford
Doddington
Birchwood
Hartsholme
New Boultham
Canwick
Heighington
Branston Booths
Bardney
Skegby
Normanton on Trent
Kirton
Boughton
Egmanton
Low Marnham
Eagle Moor
Swanpool
Boultham
Branston
Potterhanworth Booths
Ollerton
New Ollerton
Laxton
Weston
Grassthorpe
Whisby
Swallow Beck
Bracebridge Low Fields
Bracebridge Heath
Wellow
National Holocaust Centre
Moorhouse
Sutton on Trent
Weecar
Eagle
Road Transport
Hykeham Moor
North Scarle
Girton
Ompton
Rufford
Rufford Abbey
Ossington
Besthorpe
Eagle Barnsdale
Thorpe on the Hill
North Hykeham
Potterhanworth
Sots Hole
Kneesall
Norwell Woodhouse
South Scarle
Carlton-on-Trent
Morton
South Hykeham
Waddington
Nocton
Wasps Nest
Dunston
Metheringham Delph
Eakring
Kersall
Cromwell
Swinderby
Haddington
Harmston
Witham St Hughs
Thurlby
Aubourn
Maplebeck
Norwell
Collingham
Bilsthorpe Moor
Duke's Wood
Caunton
Langford Lowfields
Holme
Bassingham
Coleby
Metheringham
Blankney
Martin
Boothby Graffoe
R. Witham
Kirklington
Winkburn
North Muskham
Brough
Norton Disney
Langford
Carlton-le-Moorland
Navenby
Scopwick
Timberland
Town plan: Lincoln p.119
5 miles
8 kilometres

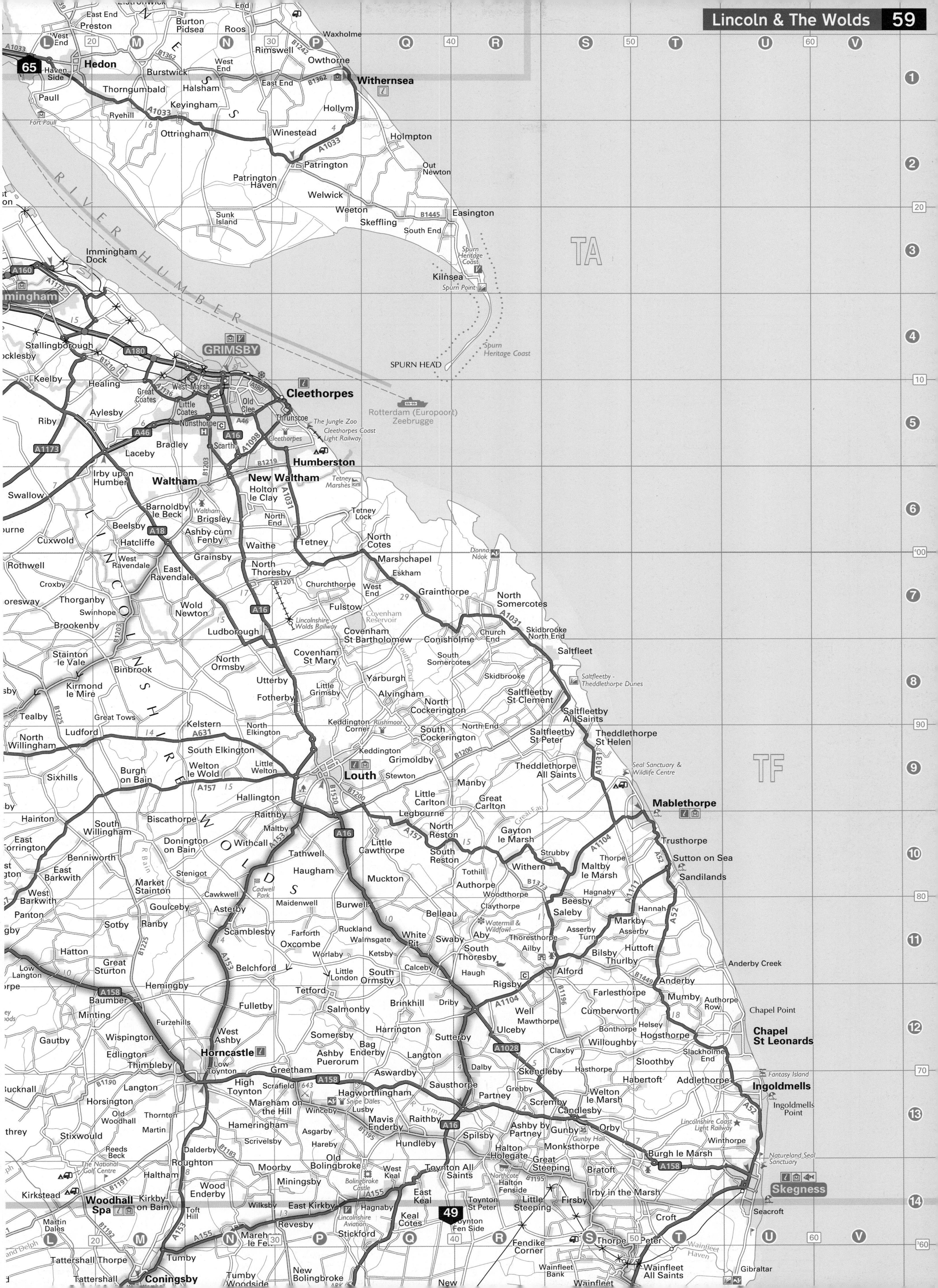

49

East End
Preston
Burton Pidsea
Roos
Waxholme
West End
Hedon
Haven Side
Paull
Fort Paull
Thorngumbald
Burstwick
Halsham
Rimswell
Owthorne
Withernsea
West End
East End
Hollym
Keyingham
Ryehill
Ottringham
Winestead
Holmpton
Patrington
Patrington Haven
Welwick
Out Newton
RIVER HUMBER
Sunk Island
Weeton
Skeffling
Easington
South End
Immingham Dock
Kilnsea
Spurn Point
Spurn Heritage Coast
TA
Stallingborough
Keelby
Immingham
GRIMSBY
Healing
Great Coates
West Marsh
Riby
Aylesby
Little Coates
Nunsthorpe
Old Clee
Cleethorpes
SPURN HEAD
Spurn Heritage Coast
Rotterdam (Europoort) Zeebrugge
Laceby
Bradley
Scartho
Thrunscoe
The Jungle Zoo
Cleethorpes Coast Light Railway
Irby upon Humber
Waltham
New Waltham
Humberston
Swallow
Barnoldby le Beck
Brigsley
Holton le Clay
New Waltham
Tetney Marshes
Beelsby
Ashby cum Fenby
North End
Tetney Lock
Cuxwold
Hatcliffe
Waithe
Tetney
North Cotes
Rothwell
West Ravendale
Grainsby
North Thoresby
Marshchapel
Eskham
Donna Nook
Croxby
East Ravendale
Churchthorpe
West End
Grainthorpe
Thoresway
Swinhope
Wold Newton
Fulstow
Covenham Reservoir
North Somercotes
Brookenby
Thorganby
Ludborough
Lincolnshire Wolds Railway
A1031
Stainton le Vale
Covenham St Bartholomew
Conisholme
Skidbrooke North End
Saltfleet
Binbrook
North Ormsby
Covenham St Mary
South Somercotes
Church End
Kirmond le Mire
Utterby
Little Grimsby
Yarburgh
Skidbrooke
Saltfleetby - Theddlethorpe Dunes
Tealby
Fotherby
Alvingham
North Cockerington
Saltfleetby St Clement
Ludford
Great Tows
Kelstern
North Elkington
Keddington Corner
Rushmoor
South Cockerington
North End
Saltfleetby All Saints
North Willingham
Sixhills
South Elkington
Little Welton
Keddington
Grimoldby
Saltfleetby St Peter
Theddlethorpe St Helen
TF
Burgh on Bain
Welton le Wold
Louth
Stewton
Manby
Theddlethorpe All Saints
Seal Sanctuary & Wildlife Centre
Hainton
Biscathorpe
Raithby
Little Carlton
Great Carlton
Mablethorpe
Haltham
South Willingham
Maltby
Hallington
Legbourne
North Reston
Gayton le Marsh
Trusthorpe
East Barkwith
Benniworth
Donington on Bain
Withcall
Tathwell
South Reston
Withern
Strubby
Thorpe
Maltby le Marsh
Sutton on Sea
Sandilands
West Barkwith
Panton
Stenigot
Haugham
Muckton
Authorpe
Woodthorpe
Beesby
Hagnaby
Hannah
Market Stainton
Cawkwell
Cadwell Park
Maidenwell
Burwell
Claythorpe
Saleby
Markby
Asserby
Huttoft
Great Sturton
Goulceby
Asterby
Ranby
Scamblesby
Farforth
Oxcombe
Ruckland
Walmsgate
White Pit
Swaby
Aby
Thoresthorpe
Ailby
Bilsby
Thurlby
Anderby
Hatton
Sotby
Belchford
Worlaby
Ketsby
South Thoresby
Watermill & Wildfowl
Alford
Anderby Creek
Low Langton
Hemingby
Tetford
Little London
South Ormsby
Calceby
Haugh
Rigsby
Farlesthorpe
Mumby
Authorpe Row
Baumber
Minting
Fulletby
Salmonby
Brinkhill
Driby
Well
Mawthorpe
Ulceby
Bonthorpe
Cumberworth
Helsey
Hogsthorpe
Chapel Point
Wispington
Furzehills
West Ashby
Somersby
Bag Enderby
Sutterby
Mavis Enderby
Langton
Willoughby
Sloothby
Slackholme End
Chapel St Leonards
Gautby
Edlington
Thimbleby
Horncastle
Low Toynton
Greetham
Ashby Puerorum
Harrington
Aswardby
Skendleby
Claxby
Hasthorpe
Habertoft
Addlethorpe
Fantasy Island
Ingoldmells
Bucknall
Langton
Horsington
Old Woodhall
Thornton
Martin
High Toynton
Scrafield
Mareham on the Hill
Hameringham
Winceby
Lusby
Asgarby
Hareby
Snipe Dales
Hagworthingham
Raithby
Mavis Enderby
Sausthorpe
Partney
Screlby
Welton le Marsh
Candlesby
Orby
Winthorpe
Lincolnshire Coast Light Railway
Ingoldmells Point
Stixwould
Old Bolingbroke
Dalby
Grebby
Gunby
Gunby Hall
Burgh le Marsh
Natureland Seal Sanctuary
Woodhall Spa
Kirkby on Bain
Roughton
Haltham
Moorby
Miningsby
Wood Enderby
Bolingbroke Castle
Mareham le Fen
West Keal
Hundleby
Spilsby
Ashby by Partney
Monksthorpe
Great Steeping
Halton Holegate
Bratoft
Skegness
Martin Dales
Reeds Beck
Kirkstead
The National Golf Centre
Dalderby
Scrivelsby
Revesby
Lincolnshire Aviation
Keal Cotes
East Keal
Toynton All Saints
Toynton St Peter
Toynton Fen Side
Northcote
Fendike Corner
Little Steeping
Irby in the Marsh
Firsby
Croft
Seacroft
Tattershall Thorpe
Tumby
Tumby Woodside
New Bolingbroke
Stickford
Toft Hill
Hagnaby
East Kirkby
Wilksby
Stickney
Thorpe St Peter
Wainfleet All Saints
Wainfleet Bank
Wainfleet Haven
Gibraltar
Coningsby
Tattershall
New Bolingbroke

L M N P Q R S T U V

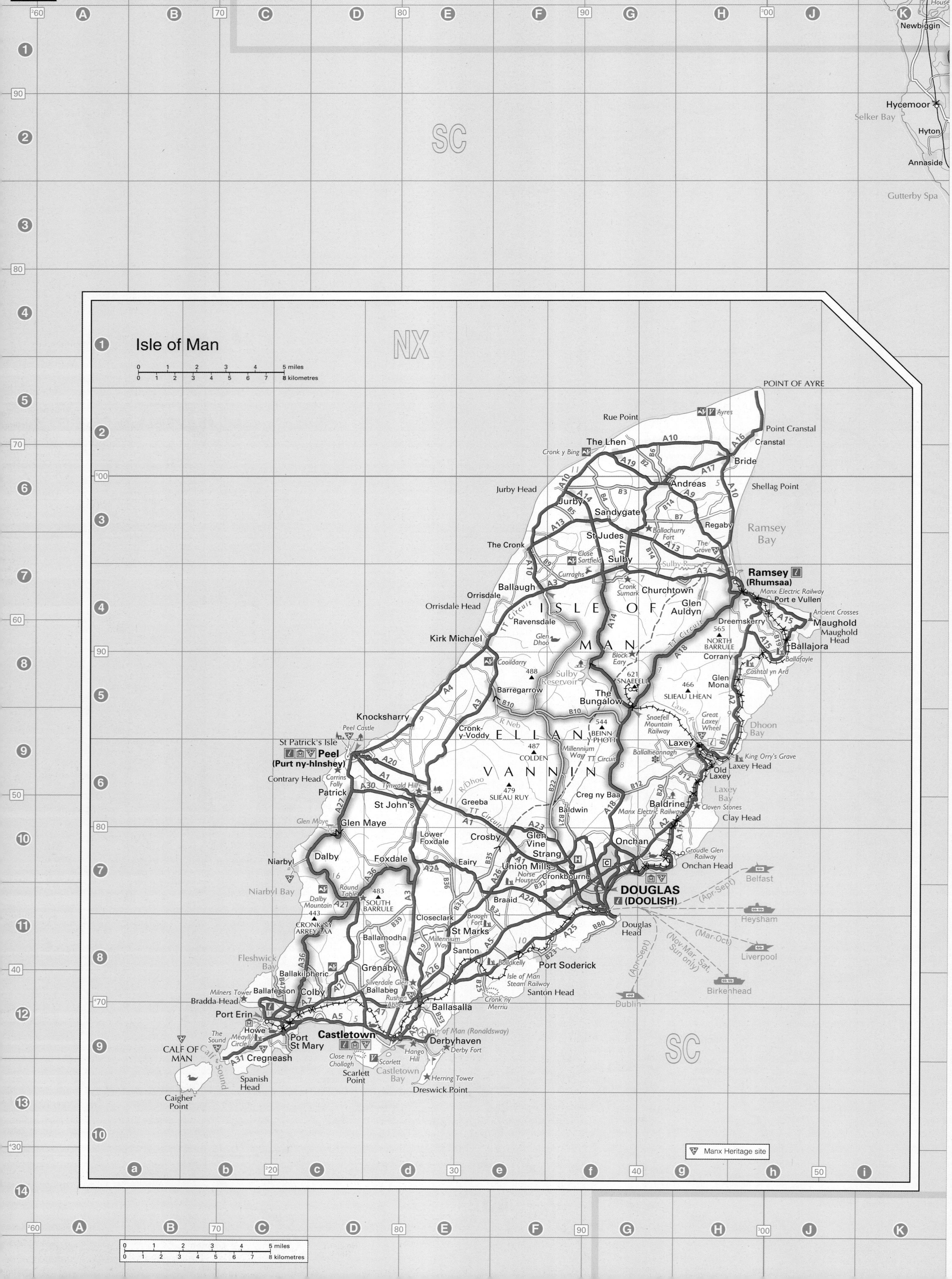

Isle of Man

0 1 2 3 4 5 miles
0 1 2 3 4 5 6 7 8 kilometres

NX

POINT OF AYRE

Rue Point
Ayres
Point Cranstal
The Lhen
Cranstal
Cronk y Bing
A10
A16
Bride
A19
B9
A17
Jurby Head
A10
A14
Andreas
Shellag Point
Jurby
A9
A10
B5
B3
Sandygate
B7
Regaby
Ramsey
Bay
St Judes
Ballachurry
Fort
A13
The
Grove
The Cronk
B9
Close
Sartfield
Sulby
B14
Sulby R.
Ramsey
(Rhumsaa)
A3
Curraghs
Ballaugh
A10
Cronk
Sumark
Churchtown
Manx Electric Railway
Port e Vullen
Orrisdale
A14
Glen
Auldyn
A2
Ancient Crosses
Orrisdale Head
TT Circuit
Ravensdale
Dreemskerry
A15
Maughold
565
A18
Maughold
Head
Kirk Michael
Glen
Dhoo
NORTH
BARRULE
Corrany
Ballajora
Cooildarry
Block
Eary
A13
621
466
Ballafayle
488
Sulby
Reservoir
SNAEFELL
Glen
Mona
Cashtal yn Ard
Barregarrow
B10
The
Bungalow
SLIEAU LHEAN
Knocksharry
R.Neb
B10
Snaefell
Mountain
Railway
Laxey R.
Great
Laxey
Wheel
Dhoon
Bay
Peel Castle
Cronk-
y-Voddy
544
BEINN
Y PHOTT
Ballaheannagh
Laxey
St Patrick's Isle
487
COLDEN
Millennium
Way
TT Circuit
King Orry's Grave
Peel
(Purt ny-hInshey)
A20
Old
Laxey
Contrary Head
Corrins
Folly
A1
Greeba
B12
Laxey
Bay
Patrick
A30
Tynwald Hill
SLIEAU RUY
Creg ny Baa
B20
Cloven Stones
R.Dhoo
479
B22
Clay Head
St John's
Baldwin
B21
Manx Electric Railway
Glen Maye
Glen Maye
TT Circuit
A1
Baldrine
479
A23
A18
Lower
Foxdale
Crosby
Glen
Vine
A2
Niarbyl
Dalby
Foxdale
Eairy
Strang
Onchan
16
A24
Union Mills
H
Norse
Houses
Cronkbourne
C
Onchan Head
Niarbyl Bay
Round
Table
B35
B32
Groudle Glen
Railway
483
A27
A26
B36
Braaid
DOUGLAS
(DOOLISH)
Belfast
Dalby
Mountain
SOUTH
BARRULE
A24
(Apr-Sept)
443
B33
Douglas
Head
Heysham
(Mar-Oct)
CRONK NY
ARREY LAA
Closeclark
Millennium
Way
St Marks
Santon
A5
10
(Nov-Mar Sat.
Sun only)
Liverpool
Fleshwick
Bay
B41
Ballamodha
B39
Brough
Fort
A25
B80
Grenaby
Silverdale Glen
Ballakelly
Port Soderick
(Apr-Sept)
Birkenhead
Ballakilpheric
A7
Ballabeg
Rushen
Abbey
Isle of Man
Steam Railway
Santon Head
Milners Tower
Ballafesson
Colby
A26
Cronk ny
Merriu
Dublin
Bradda Head
A31
Port Erin
A5
Ballasalla
Isle of Man (Ronaldsway)
SC
Howe
Meayll
Circle
Port
St Mary
Castletown
Derby Fort
CALF OF
MAN
The
Sound
A31
Cregneash
Close ny
Chollagh
Derbyhaven
Hango Hill
Spanish
Head
Scarlett
Point
Scarlett
Point
Castletown
Bay
Herring Tower
Caigher
Point
Dreswick Point
SC

Manx Heritage site

0 1 2 3 4 5 miles
0 1 2 3 4 5 6 7 8 kilometres

Ravenglass
Newbiggin
Hycemoor
Selker Bay
Hyton
Annaside
Gutterby Spa

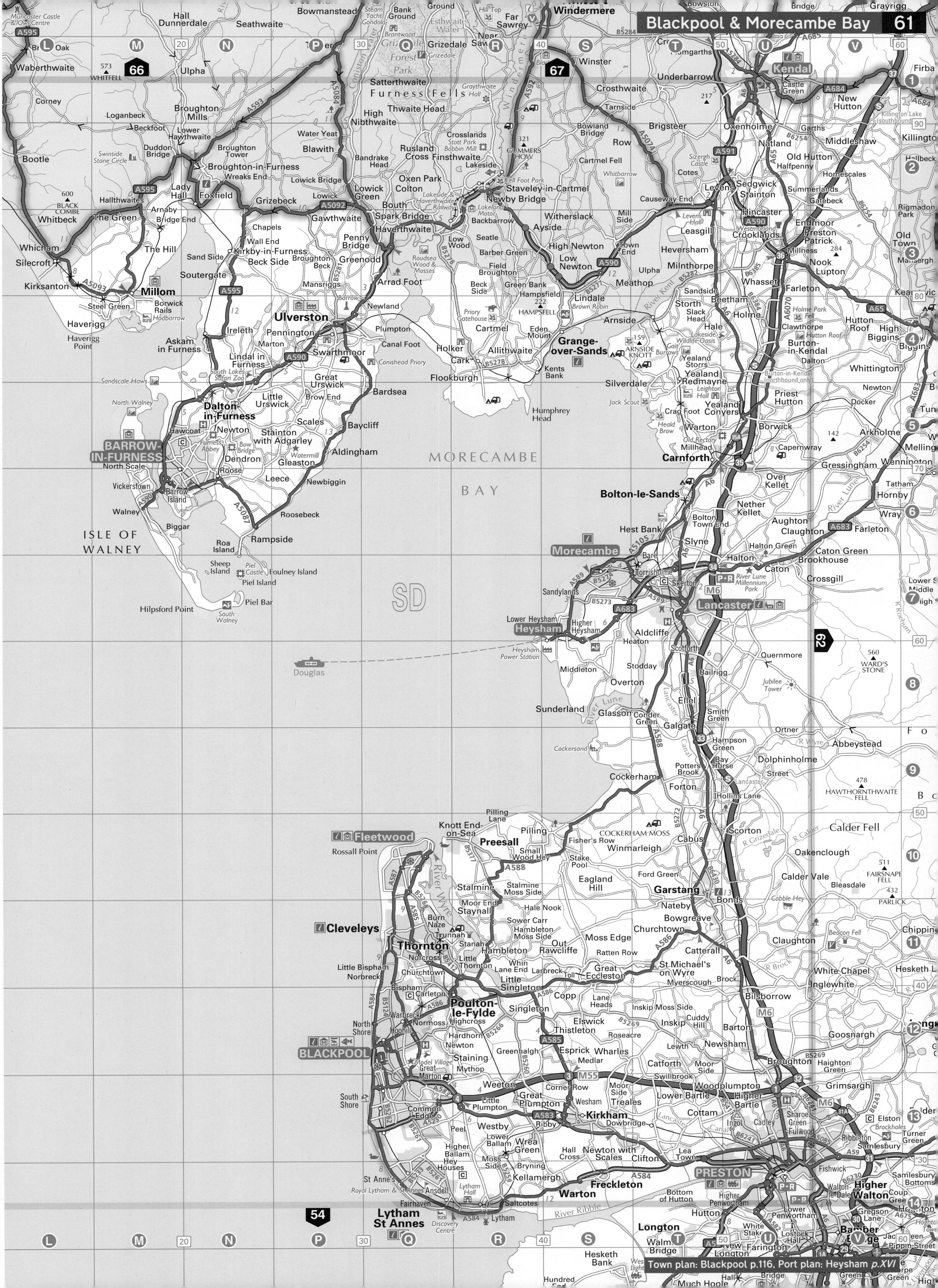
Windermere
Kendal
Ulverston
Millom
Barrow-in-Furness
Dalton-in-Furness
Grange-over-Sands
Carnforth
Bolton-le-Sands
Morecambe
Lancaster
Heysham
Morecambe Bay
Isle of Walney
SD
Douglas
Fleetwood
Cleveleys
Thornton
Poulton-le-Fylde
Blackpool
Garstang
Kirkham
Preston
Lytham St Annes
Freckleton
Warton
Longton
Preesall
Knott End-on-Sea
Cockerham
Silverdale
Arnside
Milnthorpe
Cartmel
Flookburgh
Newby Bridge
Broughton-in-Furness
Coniston Water
Grizedale Forest Park
Calder Fell
Abbeystead
Dolphinholme
Grayrigg
Killington
Kirkby-in-Furness
Askam in Furness
Haverigg
Bootle
Corney
Seathwaite
Ulpha
M6
M55
A6
A590
A595
A583
A584
A585
A586
A587
A588
A589
A683
A5105
A5087
A5093
A5092
A5074
A591
A592
A593
A65
A6070
A59
A5085

Town plan: Blackpool p.116, Port plan: Heysham p.XVI

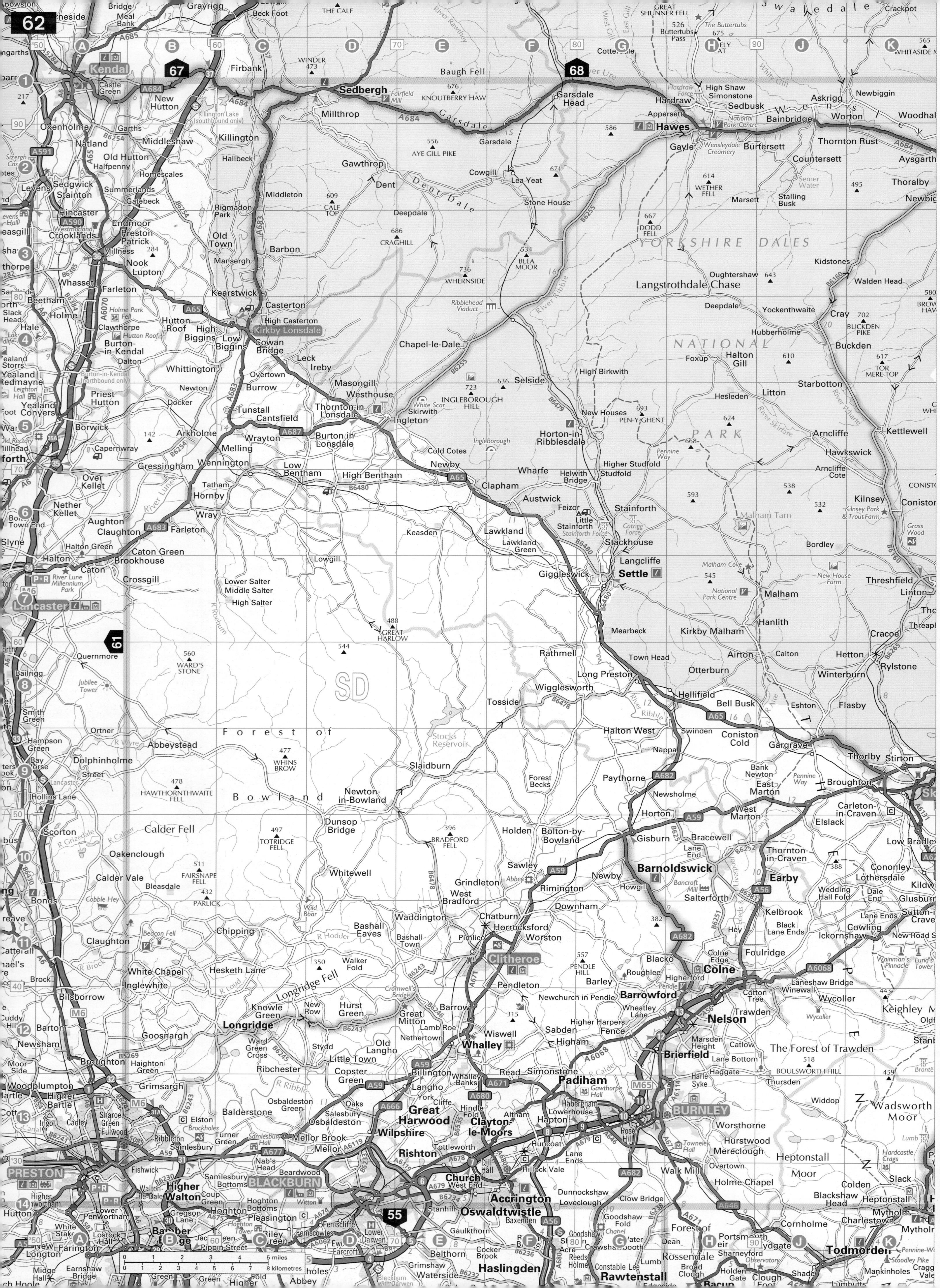
Kendal
Sedbergh
Firbank
Baugh Fell
Garsdale Head
Hawes
Hardraw
Askrigg
Bainbridge
Swaledale
Great Shunner Fell
The Buttertubs
Oxenholme
Natland
Killington
Garsdale
Gawthrop
Dent
Dent Dale
Cowgill
Lea Yeat
Gayle
Burtersett
Countersett
Thoralby
Aysgarth
Middleshaw
Old Hutton
Sedgwick
Levens
Stainton
Hincaster
Endmoor
Preston Patrick
Crooklands
Milnthorpe
Middleton
Calf Top
Deepdale
Craghill
Stone House
Blea Moor
Whernside
Dodd Fell
Yorkshire Dales
National Park
Langstrothdale Chase
Kidstones
Oughtershaw
Walden Head
Barbon
Nook
Lupton
Farleton
Kearstwick
Casterton
High Casterton
Kirkby Lonsdale
Cowan Bridge
Beetham
Holme
Hale
Hutton Roof
High Biggins
Low Biggins
Burton-in-Kendal
Dalton
Whittington
Leck
Ireby
Chapel-le-Dale
Ribblehead Viaduct
Yockenthwaite
Deepdale
Cray
Hubberholme
Buckden
Foxup
Halton Gill
High Birkwith
Selside
Ingleborough Hill
Pen-y-ghent
New Houses
Litton
Starbotton
Hesleden
Arncliffe
Kettlewell
Hawkswick
Yealand Conyers
Yealand Redmayne
Priest Hutton
Borwick
Capernwray
Newton
Docker
Burrow
Overtown
Masongill
Westhouse
Thornton in Lonsdale
Ingleton
Tunstall
Cantsfield
Burton in Lonsdale
Horton-in-Ribblesdale
Helwith Bridge
Higher Studfold
Studfold
Wharfe
Clapham
Austwick
Newby
Cold Cotes
Arkholme
Wrayton
Melling
Wennington
Gressingham
Low Bentham
High Bentham
Over Kellet
Hornby
Tatham
Wray
Nether Kellet
Aughton
Claughton
Farleton
Bolton-le-Sands
Keasden
Lawkland
Lawkland Green
Feizor
Little Stainforth
Stainforth
Stackhouse
Langcliffe
Settle
Giggleswick
Malham Tarn
Malham Cove
Malham
Kirkby Malham
Hanlith
Kilnsey
Conistone
Grass Wood
Bordley
Threshfield
Linton
Cracoe
Halton Green
Caton Green
Brookhouse
Halton
Caton
Crossgill
Lowgill
Lancaster
Lower Salter
Middle Salter
High Salter
Great Harlow
Mearbeck
Airton
Calton
Hetton
Rylstone
Rathmell
Long Preston
Otterburn
Winterburn
Quernmore
Ward's Stone
Jubilee Tower
SD
Wigglesworth
Hellifield
Bell Busk
Eshton
Flasby
Tosside
Forest of Bowland
Halton West
Swinden
Coniston Cold
Gargrave
Thorlby
Stirton
Ortner
Abbeystead
Hampson Green
Dolphinholme
Whins Brow
Slaidburn
Stocks Reservoir
Nappa
Forest Becks
Paythorne
Bank Newton
East Marton
Broughton
Hawthornthwaite Fell
Newton-in-Bowland
Newsholme
Horton
West Marton
Carleton-in-Craven
Elslack
Scorton
Calder Fell
Dunsop Bridge
Totridge Fell
Bradford Fell
Holden
Bolton-by-Bowland
Gisburn
Bracewell
Lane End
Thornton-in-Craven
Low Bradley
Oakenclough
Sawley
Barnoldswick
Earby
Cononley
Lothersdale
Calder Vale
Fairsnape Fell
Parlick
Whitewell
Grindleton
Rimington
Newby
Howgill
Salterforth
Wedding Hall Fold
Kildwick
Bonds
Bleasdale
West Bradford
Downham
Kelbrook
Black Lane Ends
Sutton-in-Craven
Cowling
Ickornshaw
Chipping
Waddington
Chatburn
Horrocksford
Worston
Pimlico
Bashall Eaves
Bashall Town
Claughton
Clitheroe
Pendle Hill
Blacko
Roughlee
Higherford
Colne
Foulridge
Hey
Colne Edge
Walker Fold
Hesketh Lane
White Chapel
Inglewhite
Longridge Fell
Pendleton
Barley
Barrowford
Laneshaw Bridge
Winewall
Cotton Tree
Wycoller
Keighley Moor
Bilsborrow
Knowle Green
New Row
Hurst Green
Great Mitton
Barrow
Newchurch in Pendle
Wheatley Lane
Nelson
Trawden
Barton
Longridge
Goosnargh
Lamb Roe
Nethertown
Wiswell
Sabden
Higher Harpers
Fence
Higham
Brierfield
Marsden Height
Catlow
Lane Bottom
The Forest of Trawden
Boulsworth Hill
Newsham
Ward Green Cross
Stydd
Old Langho
Little Town
Whalley
Broughton
Haighton Green
Ribchester
Copster Green
Billington
Whalley Banks
Read
Simonstone
Padiham
Gawthorpe Hall
Haggate
Harle Syke
Thursden
Woodplumpton
Higher Bartle
Bartle
Grimsargh
Langho
York
Cliffe
Hindle Fold
Altham
Habergham
Lowerhouse
Burnley
Widdop
Wadsworth Moor
Cadley
Sharoe Green
Fulwood
Elston
Balderstone
Osbaldeston Green
Osbaldeston
Salesbury
Great Harwood
Clayton-le-Moors
Hapton
Worsthorne
Hurstwood
Mereclough
Ribbleton
Samlesbury
Turner Green
Mellor Brook
Mellor
Wilpshire
Rishton
Tottleworth
Huncoat
Lane Ends
Towneley Hall
Heptonstall Moor
Preston
Fishwick
Nab's Head
Beardwood
Blackburn
Dill Hall
Hillock Vale
Walk Mill
Overtown
Holme Chapel
Colden
Slack
Higher Walton
Walton-le-Dale
Samlesbury Bottoms
Church
West End
Accrington
Oswaldtwistle
Dunnockshaw
Loveclough
Clow Bridge
Blackshaw Head
Heptonstall
Hoghton Bottoms
Hoghton
Pleasington
Gregson Lane
Penwortham
Lower Penwortham
Lostock Hall
Bamber Bridge
Riley Green
Feniscowles
Feniscliffe
Lower Darwen
Stanhill
Baxenden
Goodshaw Fold
Forest of Rossendale
Portsmouth
Cornholme
Charlestown
Mytholm
Longton
Farington
Pippin Street
Earcroft
Belthorn
Gaulkthorn
Cocker Brook
Haslingden
Crawshawbooth
Acre
Reedsholme
Dean
Rossendale
Sharneyford
Todmorden
Midge Hall
Earnshaw Bridge
Abbey
Grimshaw
Waterside
Rawtenstall
Constable Lee
Lumb
Broad Clough
Bacup
Holden Gate
Clough Foot
Shade
Lumbutts
Mankinholes
Cragg Vale
0 1 2 3 4 5 miles
0 1 2 3 4 5 6 7 8 kilometres

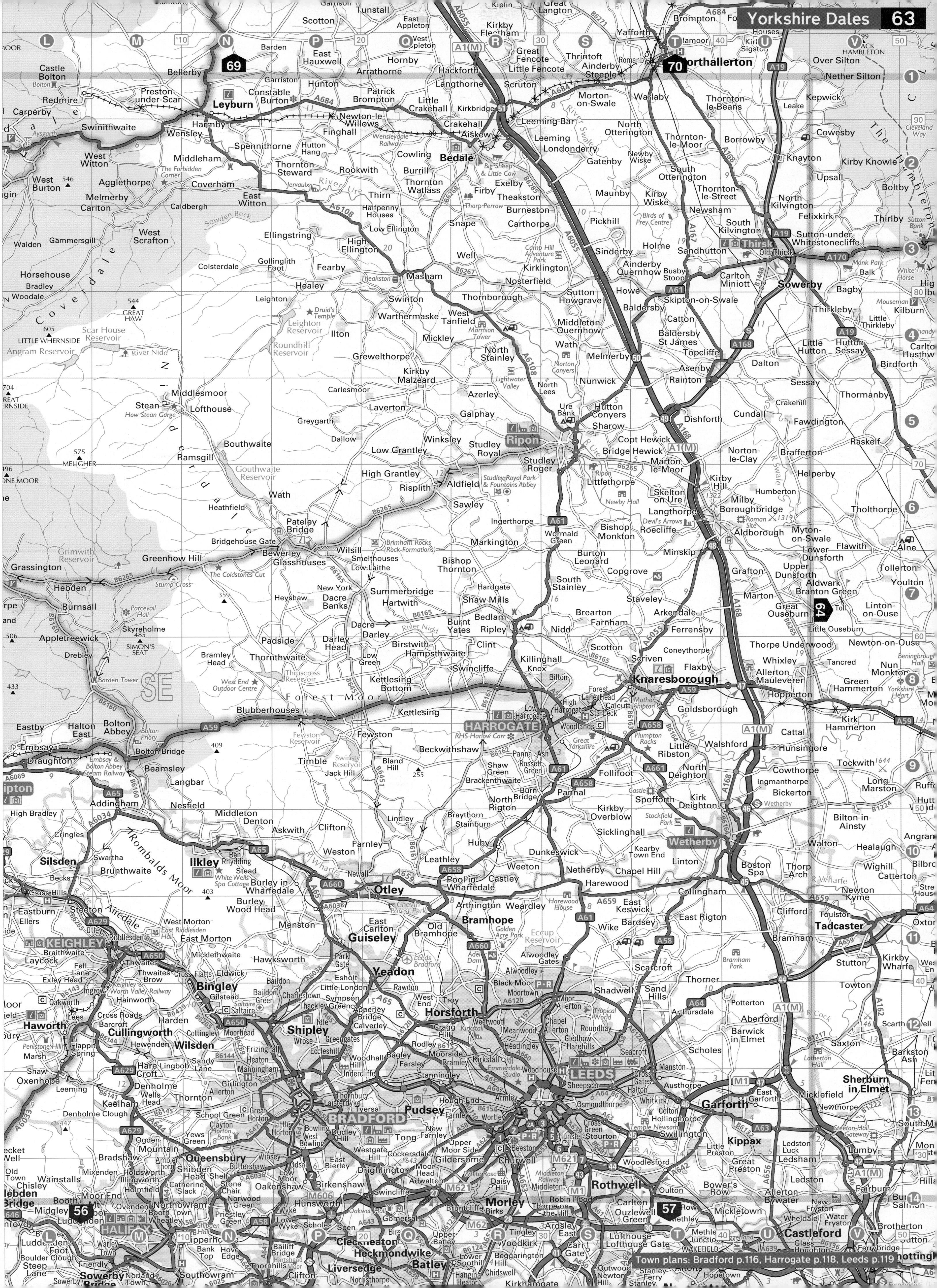
69
70
64
56
57
Leyburn
Northallerton
Bedale
Thirsk
Sowerby
Masham
Ripon
Knaresborough
HARROGATE
Wetherby
Tadcaster
Ilkley
Otley
Guiseley
Yeadon
Bingley
KEIGHLEY
Haworth
Shipley
Horsforth
LEEDS
BRADFORD
Pudsey
Queensbury
HALIFAX
Morley
Rothwell
Garforth
Castleford
Batley
Heckmondwike
Cleckheaton
Liversedge
Tunstall
Scotton
Great Langton
Kiplin
Brompton
Yafforth
East Appleton
West Appleton
Kirkby Fleetham
Barden
East Hauxwell
Hornby
Great Fencote
Little Fencote
Thrintoft
Ainderby Steeple
Romanby
Castle Bolton
Bellerby
Garriston
Hunton
Arrathorne
Hackforth
Scruton
Morton-on-Swale
Warlaby
Thornton-le-Beans
Over Silton
Nether Silton
Redmire
Preston-under-Scar
Constable Burton
Patrick Brompton
Little Crakehall
Langthorne
Kirkbridge
Carperby
Harmby
Newton-le-Willows
Finghall
Crakehall
Aiskew
Leeming Bar
Leeming
North Otterington
Thornton-le-Moor
Borrowby
Kepwick
Cowesby
Swinithwaite
Wensley
Spennithorne
Hutton Hang
Cowling
Londonderry
Gatenby
Newby Wiske
South Otterington
Knayton
Kirby Knowle
West Witton
Middleham
Thornton Steward
Rookwith
Burrill
Exelby
Thornton-le-Street
Upsall
Boltby
West Burton
Agglethorpe
Coverham
Thornton Watlass
Firby
Theakston
Maunby
Kirby Wiske
North Kilvington
Melmerby
Carlton
East Witton
Thirn
Burneston
Newsham
South Kilvington
Felixkirk
Thirlby
Caldbergh
Halfpenny Houses
Snape
Carthorpe
Pickhill
Sutton-under-Whitestonecliffe
Walden
Gammersgill
West Scrafton
Low Ellington
Ellingstring
High Ellington
Holme
Sandhutton
Sinderby
Well
Kirklington
Ainderby Quernhow
Busby Stoop
Carlton Miniott
Horsforth
Colsterdale
Gollinglith Foot
Fearby
Nosterfield
Balk
Bagby
Bradley
Woodale
Healey
Thornborough
Sutton Howgrave
Howe
Baldersby
Skipton-on-Swale
Thirkleby
Kilburn
Leighton
Swinton
Warthermaske
West Tanfield
Middleton Quernhow
Catton
Little Thirkleby
Great Haw
Leighton Reservoir
Ilton
Mickley
Baldersby St James
Little Hutton
Hutton Sessay
Scar House Reservoir
Little Whernside
Angram Reservoir
Roundhill Reservoir
Grewelthorpe
North Stainley
Wath
Melmerby
Topcliffe
Dalton
Birdforth
Kirkby Malzeard
Asenby
Rainton
Sessay
Carlesmoor
Nunwick
North Lees
Middlesmoor
Stean
Lofthouse
Laverton
Azerley
Ure Bank
Hutton Conyers
Sharow
Dishforth
Cundall
Crakehill
Thormanby
Greygarth
Galphay
Fawdington
Dallow
Winksley
Copt Hewick
Raskelf
Bouthwaite
Low Grantley
Studley Royal
Bridge Hewick
Norton-le-Clay
Brafferton
Ramsgill
Studley Roger
Marton-le-Moor
Meugher
Gouthwaite Reservoir
High Grantley
Littlethorpe
Kirby Hill
Helperby
Risplith
Aldfield
Skelton on Ure
Humberton
Wath
Sawley
Milby
Boroughbridge
Tholthorpe
Heathfield
Langthorpe
Pateley Bridge
Ingerthorpe
Bishop Monkton
Roecliffe
Aldborough
Myton-on-Swale
Wormald Green
Markington
Minskip
Flawith
Alne
Bridgehouse Gate
Wilsill
Greenhow Hill
Beverley
Glasshouses
Smelthouses
Low Laithe
Bishop Thornton
Burton Leonard
Copgrove
Grafton
Lower Dunsforth
Upper Dunsforth
Tollerton
Youlton
Grassington
Aldwark
Hebden
Stump Cross
The Coldstones Cut
Hardgate
South Stainley
Staveley
Marton
Brantton Green
Linton-on-Ouse
New York
Summerbridge
Dacre Banks
Hartwith
Shaw Mills
Brearton
Arkendale
Great Ouseburn
Burnsall
Heyshaw
Farnham
Little Ouseburn
Bedlam
Dacre
Burnt Yates
Ripley
Nidd
Ferrensby
Skyreholme
Darley
Appletreewick
Padside
Darley Head
Birstwith
Clint
Scotton
Coneythorpe
Thorpe Underwood
Newton-on-Ouse
Simon's Seat
Drebley
Hampsthwaite
Killinghall
Scriven
Whixley
Tancred
Bramley Head
Thornthwaite
Low Green
Knox
Flaxby
Allerton Mauleverer
Nun Monkton
Swincliffe
Bilton
Kettlesing Bottom
Green Hammerton
Barden Tower
Thruscross Reservoir
West End Outdoor Centre
Forest Moor
Forest Lane Head
Hopperton
Blubberhouses
Kettlesing
Low Harrogate
High Harrogate
Starbeck
Calcutt
Goldsborough
Kirk Hammerton
Eastby
Halton East
Bolton Abbey
Woodlands
Embsay
Fewston
Fewston Reservoir
Beckwithshaw
Plumpton Rocks
Little Ribston
Walshford
Cattal
Hunsingore
Draughton
Bolton Bridge
Swinsty Reservoir
Timble
Bland Hill
Pannal Ash
Rossett Green
Shaw Green
Brackenthwaite
North Deighton
Cowthorpe
Tockwith
Beamsley
Jack Hill
Follifoot
Ingmanthorpe
Long Marston
Langbar
Pannal
Spofforth
Kirk Deighton
Bickerton
Skipton
Addingham
Nesfield
Burn Bridge
North Rigton
Kirkby Overblow
High Bradley
Middleton
Denton
Askwith
Clifton
Lindley
Braythorn
Stainburn
Sicklinghall
Bilton-in-Ainsty
Cringles
Farnley
Huby
Kearby Town End
Linton
Walton
Healaugh
Silsden
Swartha
Ben Rhydding
Weston
Leathley
Dunkeswick
Boston Spa
Thorp Arch
Wighill
Catterton
Brunthwaite
Stead
Rombalds Moor
Burley in Wharfedale
Newall
Pool in Wharfedale
Castley
Weeton
Netherby
Chapel Hill
Becks
Harewood
Collingham
Newton Kyme
Cross Hills
Burley Wood Head
Arthington
Weardley
East Keswick
Clifford
Toulston
Eastburn
Steeton
Airedale
Chevin Forest Park
Bramhope
Bardsey
East Rigton
Ellers
West Morton
East Carlton
Old Bramhope
Wike
Bramham
Menston
East Morton
Riddlesden
Golden Acre Park
Eccup Reservoir
Braithwaite
Micklethwaite
Hawksworth
Park Gate
Adel Dam
Alwoodley Gates
Scarcroft
Bramham Park
Stutton
Kirkby Wharfe
Laycock
Fell Lane
Thwaites
Thwaites Brow
Cross Flatts
Eldwick
Esholt
Rawdon
Alwoodley
Black Moor
Moortown
Shadwell
Sand Hills
Thorner
Towton
Exley Head
Ingrow
Worth Valley Railway
Gilstead
Baildon
Baildon Green
Little London
Sympson Green
Charlestown
Saltaire
Thackley
West End
Troy
Moor Allerton
Tropical World
Potterton
Oakworth
Lees
Cross Roads
Harden
Hainworth
Apperley Bridge
Idle
Calverley
Chapel Allerton
Roundhay
Arthursdale
Aberford
Barwick in Elmet
Scarth
Barcroft
Cullingworth
Cottingley
Moorhead
Wrose
Greengates
Cragg Hill
Weetwood
Meanwood
Gledhow
Harehills
Scholes
Saxton
Flappit Spring
Penistone Hill
Marsh
Wilsden
Hewenden
Sandy Lane
Eccleshill
Frizinghall
Woodhall Hill
Bagley
Rodley
Farsley
Moorside
Bramley
Kirkstall
Headingley
Woodhouse
Seacroft
Manston
Barkston Ash
Shaw
Oxenhope
Hare Croft
Lingbob
Heaton
Manningham
Undercliffe
Stanningley
Cross Gates
Halton
Austhorpe
Sherburn in Elmet
Leeming
Denholme
Denholme Clough
Allerton
Girlington
Thornbury
Laisterdyke
Tyersal
Hough End
Armley
Wortley
Sheepscar
Osmondthorpe
Whitkirk
Colton
Hollingthorpe
East Garforth
Micklefield
Newthorpe
South Milford
Keelham
Wells Head
Thornton
School Green
Clayton
Clayton Heights
Great Horton
Little Horton
West Bowling
Dudley Hill
Tong
New Farnley
Farnley
Beeston
Hunslet
Stourton
Cross Green
Temple Newsam
Swillington
Kippax
Ledston
Ledston Luck
Ledsham
Lumby
Ogden
Mountain
Yews Green
Wibsey
Low Moor
Buttershaw
Westgate Hill
East Bierley
Cockersdale
Drighlington
Gildersome
Upper Moor Side
Churwell
Middleton Railway
Middleton
Woodlesford
Little Preston
Great Preston
Fairburn
Old Town
Chisley
Wainstalls
Bradshaw
Mixenden
Holdsworth
Illingworth
Holmfield
Shibden Head
Shelf
Catherine Slack
Stone Chair
Oakenshaw
Birkenshaw
Moor Head
Adwalton
White Rose
Daisy Hill
Oulton
Bower's Row
Allerton Bywater
Ledston
Booth
Mount Tabor
Moor End
Ovenden
Northowram
Norwood Green
Swincliffe
Robin Hood
Carlton
Ouzlewell Green
Mickletown
New Fryston
Water Fryston
Midgley
Luddenden
Boothtown
Wheatley
Priestley Green
Hunsworth
Wyke
Gomersal
Bruntcliffe
Birks
Thorpe on the Hill
Methley
Methley Junction
Wheldale
Brotherton
Ferrybridge
Luddenden Foot
Warley
Shibden Hall
Lower Wyke
Scholes
Spen
Birstall
Upper Batley
Tingley
Ardsley East
Lofthouse
Lofthouse Gate
Glass Houghton
Boulder Clough
Steep Lane
Friendly
Sowerby Bridge
Bank Top
Hove Edge
Bailiff Bridge
Hartshead Moor
Hipperholme
Norwood Green
Soothill
Woodkirk
Carr Gate
Outwood
Stanley
Stanley Ferry
Hanging Heaton
Chidswell
Kirkhamgate
Bunn
Hopetown
Southowram
Norland Town
Norristhorpe
Thornhills
Clifton
Bagby
Leake
Tollerton
Middleton
Coverdale
Nidderdale
Sowden Beck
River Ure
River Nidd
River Wharfe
River Swale
The Hambleton Hills
Forest Moor
Fountains Abbey
Studley Royal Park
Newby Hall
Lightwater Valley
Norton Conyers
Marmion Tower
Druid's Temple
Jervaulx Abbey
The Forbidden Corner
Thorp Perrow
Big Sheep & Little Cow
Camp Hill Adventure Park
Birds of Prey Centre
Devil's Arrows
Roman Site
Mother Shipton's Cave
Great Yorkshire Showground
RHS Harlow Carr
Stockfield Park
Castle
Harewood House
Leeds Bradford Airport
Kirkstall Abbey
Emmerdale Studio
Middleton Railway
Embsay & Bolton Abbey Steam Railway
Bolton Priory
Parcevall Hall
Grimwith Reservoir
Brimham Rocks (Rock Formations)
How Stean Gorge
Wensleydale Railway
Theakston
White Wells Spa Cottage
Lotherton Hall
Steeton Hall Gateway
Yorkshire Heart
Beningbrough Hall
Monk Park
White Horse
Mouseman
Cleveland Way
Sutton Bank
Aysgarth
Bolton
East Riddlesden Hall
SE

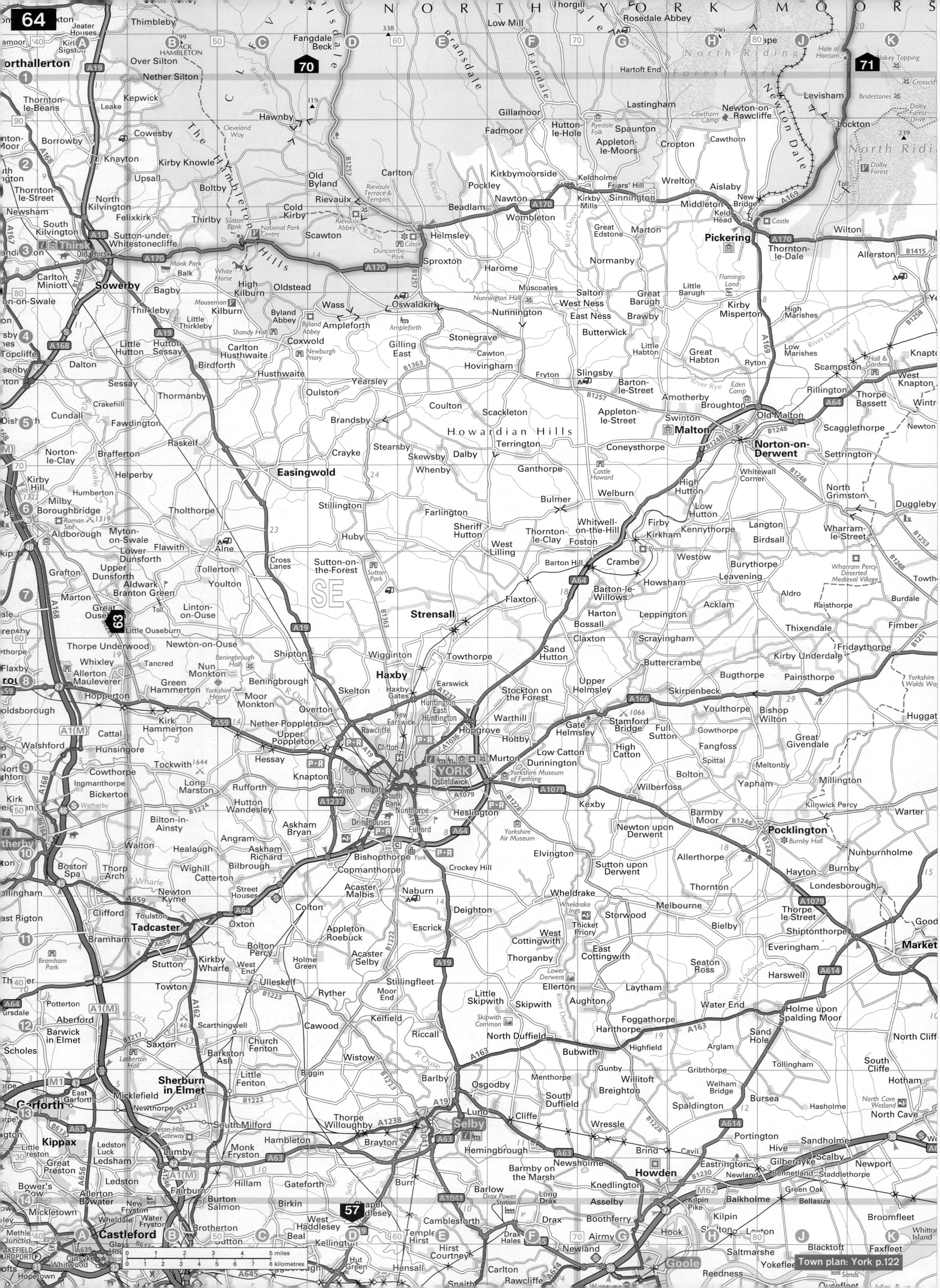
NORTH YORK MOORS
North Riding Forest Park
Northallerton
Thirsk
Sowerby
Thimbleby
Over Silton
Nether Silton
Kepwick
Cowesby
Borrowby
Knayton
Kirby Knowle
Upsall
Boltby
Thornton-le-Beans
Thornton-le-Street
North Kilvington
South Kilvington
Newsham
Felixkirk
Thirlby
Sutton-under-Whitestonecliffe
Carlton Miniott
Bagby
Thirkleby
Little Thirkleby
Kilburn
High Kilburn
Oldstead
Byland Abbey
Coxwold
Carlton Husthwaite
Husthwaite
Birdforth
Dalton
Sessay
Thormanby
Cundall
Fawdington
Raskelf
Brafferton
Norton-le-Clay
Helperby
Kirby Hill
Milby
Boroughbridge
Aldborough
Humberton
Tholthorpe
Myton-on-Swale
Flawith
Alne
Easingwold
Lower Dunsforth
Upper Dunsforth
Aldwark
Tollerton
Youlton
Branton Green
Grafton
Marton
Great Ouseburn
Little Ouseburn
Linton-on-Ouse
Newton-on-Ouse
Thorpe Underwood
Whixley
Allerton Mauleverer
Hopperton
Tancred
Nun Monkton
Green Hammerton
Kirk Hammerton
Beningbrough
Moor Monkton
Cattal
Hunsingore
Walshford
Tockwith
Cowthorpe
Ingmanthorpe
Bickerton
Long Marston
Hutton Wandesley
Rufforth
Bilton-in-Ainsty
Wetherby
Walton
Healaugh
Angram
Askham Bryan
Askham Richard
Boston Spa
Thorp Arch
Wighill
Bilbrough
Catterton
Clifford
Newton Kyme
Tadcaster
Toulston
Street Houses
Oxton
Bramham
Stutton
Kirkby Wharfe
Towton
Potterton
Aberford
Barwick in Elmet
Scholes
Saxton
Barkston Ash
Scarthingwell
Church Fenton
Little Fenton
Sherburn in Elmet
Micklefield
Garforth
Kippax
Ledsham
Ledston
Great Preston
Allerton Bywater
Castleford
Fairburn
Burton Salmon
Brotherton
Monk Fryston
Hillam
South Milford
Hambleton
Gateforth
Birkin
Thorpe Willoughby
Brayton
Selby
Barlby
Osgodby
Riccall
Kelfield
Cawood
Wistow
Biggin
Ryther
Ulleskelf
Stillingfleet
Moor End
Acaster Selby
Appleton Roebuck
Acaster Malbis
Colton
Bolton Percy
Escrick
Deighton
Naburn
Bishopthorpe
Copmanthorpe
Crockey Hill
Fulford
Heslington
Dringhouses
Acomb
Holgate
Knapton
Hessay
Nether Poppleton
Upper Poppleton
Rawcliffe
Clifton
York
Osbaldwick
Murton
Dunnington
Holtby
Hopgrove
Huntington
New Earswick
Earswick
Haxby
Wigginton
Skelton
Overton
Shipton
Towthorpe
Strensall
Flaxton
Stockton on the Forest
Warthill
Gate Helmsley
Upper Helmsley
Sand Hutton
Claxton
Harton
Bossall
Stamford Bridge
Full Sutton
High Catton
Low Catton
Kexby
Wilberfoss
Elvington
Sutton upon Derwent
Newton upon Derwent
Wheldrake
Thicket Priory
Storwood
Melbourne
Cottingwith
Thorganby
Ellerton
Aughton
Skipwith
Little Skipwith
North Duffield
Bubwith
Foggathorpe
Harlthorpe
Highfield
Menthorpe
South Duffield
Breighton
Willitoft
Gunby
Spaldington
Wressle
Cliffe
Lund
Hemingbrough
Barmby on the Marsh
Newsholme
Howden
Knedlington
Asselby
Barlow
Drax
Long Drax
Camblesforth
Carlton
Airmy
Hook
Goole
Kilpin
Saltmarshe
Laxton
Blacktoft
Faxfleet
Yokefleet
Reedness
Balkholme
Bellasize
Broomfleet
Newport
Gilberdyke
Eastrington
Portington
Cavil
Brind
Hive
Sandholme
Scalby
Bursea
Hasholme
Welham Bridge
Gribthorpe
Holme upon Spalding Moor
Sand Hole
Arglam
Water End
Laytham
Seaton Ross
Harswell
Everingham
Bielby
Thornton
Allerthorpe
Pocklington
Barmby Moor
Yapham
Meltonby
Millington
Kilnwick Percy
Warter
Nunburnholme
Hayton
Burnby
Londesborough
Thorpe le Street
Shiptonthorpe
Market Weighton
North Cliffe
South Cliffe
Tollingham
Hotham
North Cave
Huggate
Great Givendale
Bishop Wilton
Youlthorpe
Bolton
Fangfoss
Spittal
Gowthorpe
Skirpenbeck
Bugthorpe
Buttercrambe
Scrayingham
Leppington
Painsthorpe
Kirby Underdale
Thixendale
Fridaythorpe
Fimber
Acklam
Leavening
Burythorpe
Westow
Howsham
Crambe
Barton Hill
Barton-le-Willows
Foston
Thornton-le-Clay
Whitwell-on-the-Hill
Kirkham
Firby
Langton
Kennythorpe
Birdsall
Welburn
Bulmer
Castle Howard
Ganthorpe
Terrington
Howardian Hills
Coneysthorpe
Malton
Old Malton
Norton-on-Derwent
Settrington
Scagglethorpe
North Grimston
Duggleby
Wharram-le-Street
Wharram Percy Deserted Medieval Village
Burdale
Raisthorpe
Aldro
Rillington
Thorpe Bassett
Scampston
West Knapton
Knapton
Wintringham
Low Marishes
High Marishes
Great Habton
Little Habton
Ryton
Amotherby
Broughton
Swinton
Appleton-le-Street
Barton-le-Street
Slingsby
Fryton
Hovingham
Cawton
Scackleton
Coulton
Dalby
Skewsby
Whenby
Stearsby
Brandsby
Crayke
Yearsley
Oulston
Stillington
Farlington
Sheriff Hutton
West Lilling
Huby
Sutton-on-the-Forest
Cross Lanes
Gilling East
Stonegrave
Ampleforth
Wass
Oswaldkirk
Nunnington
Harome
Sproxton
Helmsley
Duncombe Park
Rievaulx
Scawton
Cold Kirby
Old Byland
Hawnby
Carlton
Beadlam
Pockley
Nawton
Wombleton
Kirkbymoorside
Keldholme
Kirkby Mills
Great Edstone
Marton
Normanby
Salton
West Ness
East Ness
Butterwick
Great Barugh
Little Barugh
Brawby
Kirby Misperton
Pickering
Thornton-le-Dale
Allerston
Wilton
Keld Head
Middleton
Aislaby
Wrelton
Sinnington
Cropton
Appleton-le-Moors
Spaunton
Lastingham
Hutton-le-Hole
Fadmoor
Gillamoor
Low Mill
Farndale
Bransdale
Fangdale Beck
Rosedale Abbey
Hartoft End
Newton-on-Rawcliffe
Newton Dale
Levisham
Lockton
Cawthorn
Dalby Forest
Flamingo Land
Eden Camp
Town plan: York p.122
5 miles
8 kilometres

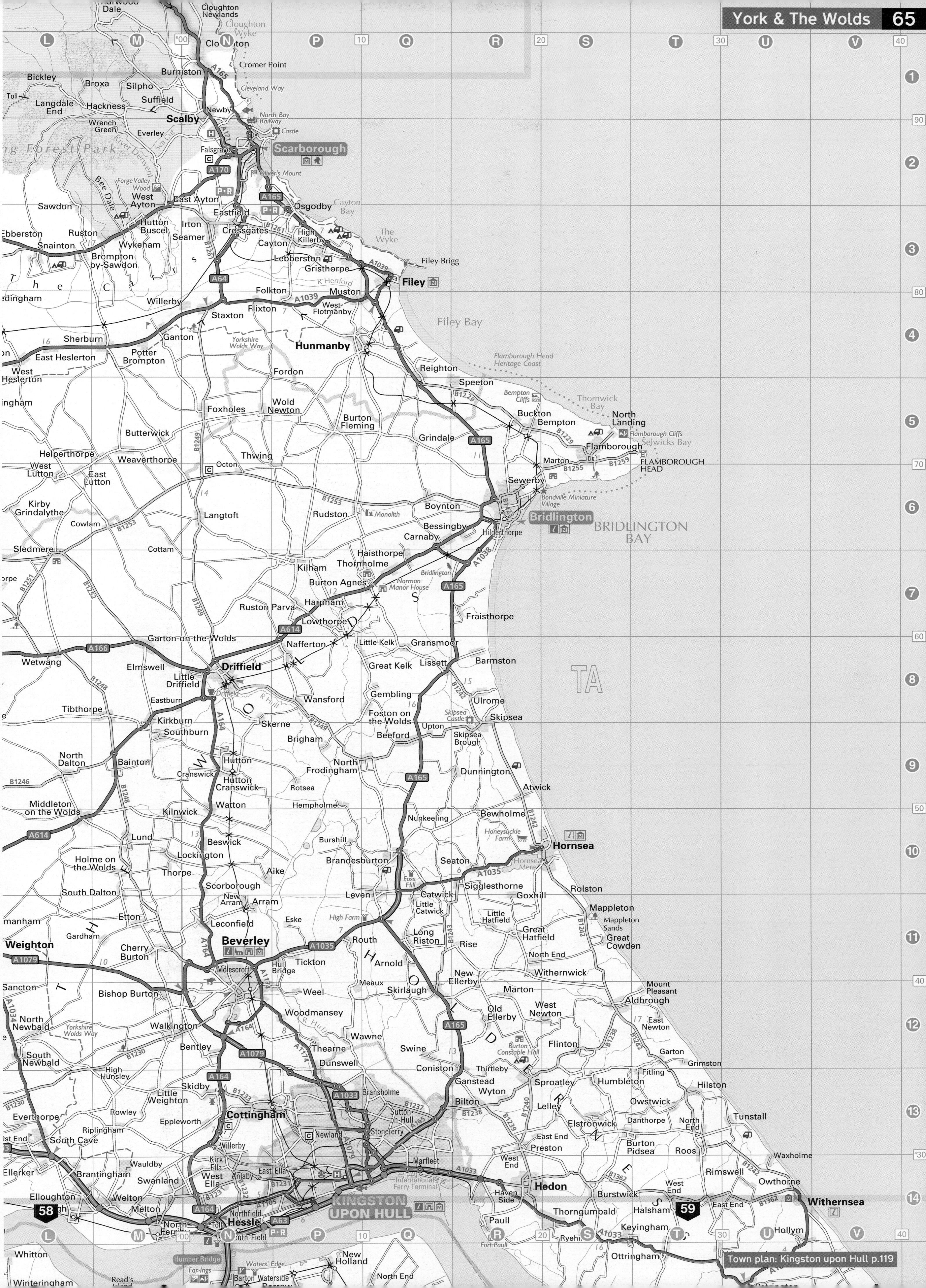
Cloughton Newlands
Cloughton Wyke
Cloughton
Cromer Point
Cleveland Way
Burniston
Bickley
Broxa
Silpho
Suffield
Langdale End
Hackness
Newby
North Bay Railway
Castle
Scalby
Wrench Green
Everley
Forest Park
River Derwent
Sea Cut
Falsgrave
Scarborough
A170
A171
A165
Oliver's Mount
Forge Valley Wood
Bee Dale
West Ayton
East Ayton
Sawdon
Eastfield
Osgodby
Cayton Bay
Hutton Buscel
Irton
Crossgates
B1261
High Killerby
Ebberston
Ruston
Seamer
Cayton
The Wyke
Snainton
Wykeham
Brompton-by-Sawdon
Lebberston
Gristhorpe
Filey Brigg
A1039
R Hertford
A64
Folkton
Muston
Filey
Willerby
Flixton
West Flotmanby
Staxton
Filey Bay
Sherburn
Ganton
Yorkshire Wolds Way
Hunmanby
East Heslerton
Potter Brompton
West Heslerton
Fordon
Reighton
Flamborough Head Heritage Coast
Speeton
Bempton Cliffs
Thornwick Bay
B1229
Foxholes
Wold Newton
Buckton
Bempton
North Landing
Burton Fleming
Butterwick
Grindale
Flamborough Cliffs
Selwicks Bay
Flamborough
Helperthorpe
Thwing
Weaverthorpe
B1249
Octon
Marton
B1255
B1259
FLAMBOROUGH HEAD
West Lutton
East Lutton
Sewerby
Bondville Miniature Village
B1253
Kirby Grindalythe
Langtoft
Rudston
Monolith
Boynton
Cowlam
Bridlington
BRIDLINGTON BAY
Bessingby
Hilderthorpe
Carnaby
Sledmere
Cottam
Haisthorpe
Thornholme
A1038
Kilham
Burton Agnes
Bridlington
Norman Manor House
B1251
B1252
Harpham
A165
Ruston Parva
Fraisthorpe
Lowthorpe
A614
Garton-on-the-Wolds
A166
Nafferton
Little Kelk
Gransmoor
Wetwang
Barmston
Elmswell
Driffield
Great Kelk
Lissett
Little Driffield
TA
B1248
Eastburn
Gembling
B1242
Ulrome
Wansford
Tibthorpe
Foston on the Wolds
Skipsea Castle
Skipsea
Kirkburn
Skerne
Upton
Southburn
A164
Beeford
Skipsea Brough
Brigham
North Dalton
Bainton
Hutton
North Frodingham
Dunnington
B1246
Cranswick
Hutton Cranswick
Atwick
Rotsea
Middleton on the Wolds
Kilnwick
Hempholme
Watton
Nunkeeling
Bewholme
A614
Honeysuckle Farm
Lund
Beswick
Burshill
Hornsea
Holme on the Wolds
Lockington
Brandesburton
Seaton
Hornsea Mere
Thorpe
Aike
A1035
Scorborough
Foss Hill
Sigglesthorne
Rolston
South Dalton
New Arram
Arram
Leven
Catwick
Goxhill
Little Catwick
Mappleton
Etton
Leconfield
Eske
High Farm
Little Hatfield
Mappleton Sands
Great Hatfield
Gardham
Long Riston
Great Cowden
Weighton
Beverley
Routh
Rise
A1079
Cherry Burton
North End
Tickton
Arnold
Molescroft
Hull Bridge
Withernwick
Sancton
Bishop Burton
Meaux
New Ellerby
Weel
Skirlaugh
Marton
Mount Pleasant
Aldbrough
West Newton
Old Ellerby
Woodmansey
North Newbald
Walkington
Wawne
East Newton
Flinton
Burton Constable Hall
B1238
South Newbald
Bentley
Thearne
Swine
Garton
Grimston
B1230
Dunswell
Coniston
Thirtleby
Fitling
High Hunsley
A1033
Ganstead
Humbleton
Sproatley
Hilston
Skidby
Bransholme
Wyton
Little Weighton
Bilton
Owstwick
B1233
B1237
Lelley
Tunstall
Everthorpe
Rowley
Cottingham
Sutton-on-Hull
B1240
Elstronwick
North End
Danthorpe
Riplingham
Newland
Stoneferry
B1239
East End
South Cave
Willerby
East End
Preston
Burton Pidsea
Roos
Waxholme
Ellerker
Brantingham
Wauldby
Kirk Ella
Marfleet
West End
Rimswell
Swanland
East Ella
International Ferry Terminal
B1362
Owthorne
West Ella
Anlaby
Hedon
Ellougton
Welton
B1231
Haven Side
Burstwick
West End
Withernsea
East End
KINGSTON UPON HULL
Thorngumbald
Halsham
Melton
Northfield
A63
Paull
Keyingham
North Ferriby
Hessle
South Field
Hollym
Fort Paull
Ryehill
Whitton
Humber Bridge
Ottringham
New Holland
Far Ings
Waters' Edge
Barton Waterside
Winteringham
North End

58
59
Town plan: Kingston upon Hull p.119

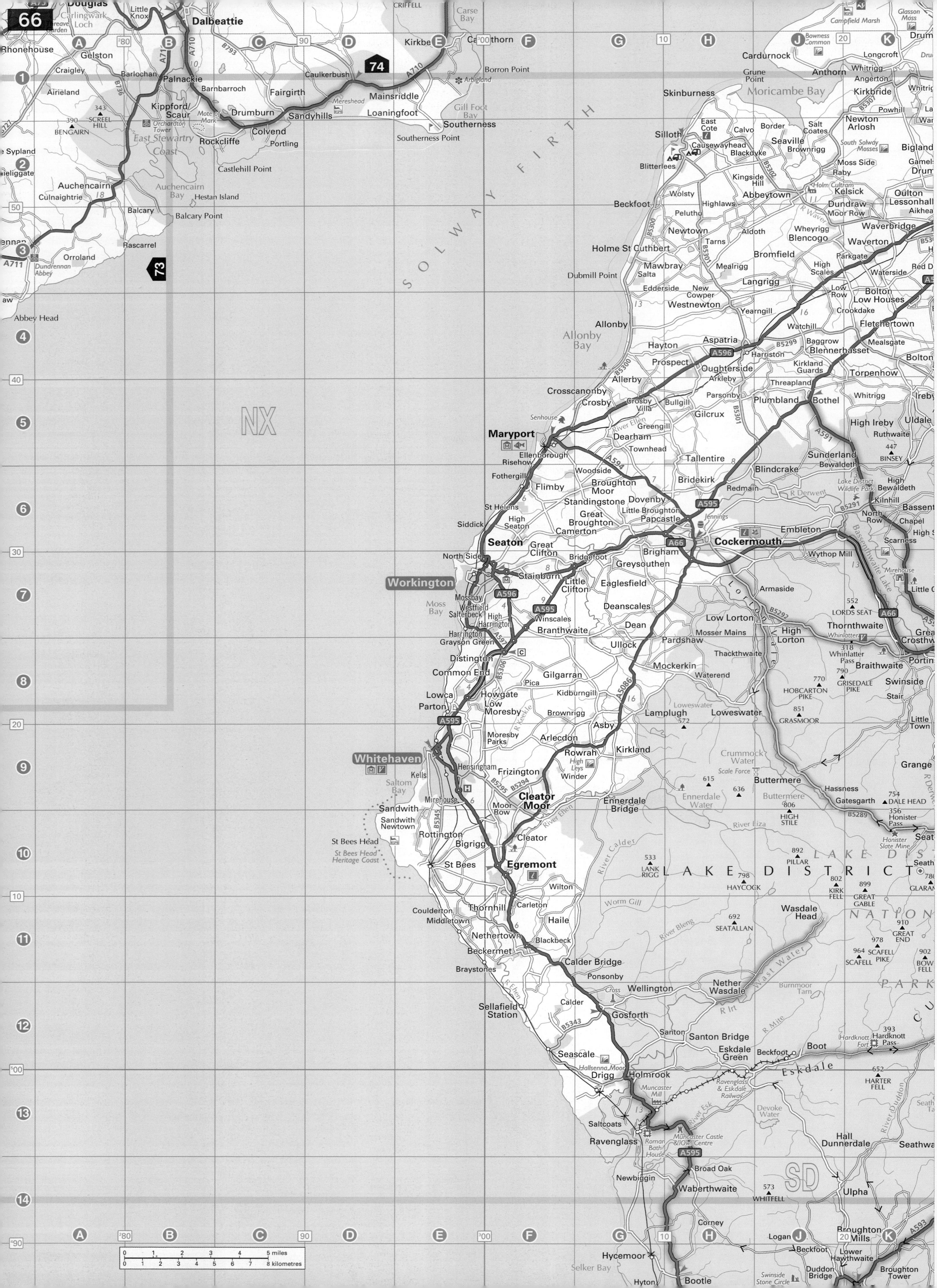
Douglas
Little Knox
Dalbeattie
CRIFFELL
Carse Bay
Glasson Moss
Campfield Marsh
Carlingwark Loch
Rhonehouse
Gelston
Kirkbean
Carsethorn
Bowness Common
Drumburgh
Craigley
Barlochan
Palnackie
Caulkerbush
74
Borron Point
Cardurnock
Longcroft
Airieland
Barnbarroch
Fairgirth
Arbigland
Grune Point
Anthorn
Whitrigg
Angerton
Kirkbride
Mainsriddle
Moricambe Bay
Skinburness
343 SCREEL HILL
Kippford/Scaur
Mote of Mark
Drumburn
Colvend
Sandyhills
Mereshead
Loaningfoot
Gill Foot Bay
Southerness
Powhill
Newton Arlosh
390 BENGAIRN
Orchardton Tower
East Stewartry Coast
Rockcliffe
Portling
Southerness Point
Silloth
East Cote
Calvo
Border
Salt Coates
Sypland
Auchencairn
Castlehill Point
Auchencairn Bay
Hestan Island
Causewayhead
Blackdyke
Seaville
Brownrigg
South Solway Mosses
Bigland
Blitterlees
Kingside Hill
Moss Side
Raby
Holm Cultram
Abbeytown
Kelsick
Culnaightrie
Balcary
Balcary Point
Wolsty
Highlaws
Pelutho
Beckfoot
Dundraw
Moor Row
Oulton
Lessonhall
Aikhead
Rascarrel
Orroland
Dundrennan Abbey
Newtown
Tarns
Aldoth
Wheyrigg
Blencogo
Waverbridge
Waverton
73
Holme St Cuthbert
Mawbray
Salta
Mealrigg
Bromfield
Parkgate
High Scales
Waterside
SOLWAY FIRTH
Dubmill Point
Edderside
New Cowper
Langrigg
Low Row
Bolton Low Houses
Westnewton
Yearngill
Crookdake
Abbey Head
Allonby
Allonby Bay
Watchill
Fletchertown
Hayton
Aspatria
Baggrow
Blennerhasset
Mealsgate
Bolton
Harriston
Prospect
Oughterside
Kirkland Guards
Torpenhow
Allerby
Arkleby
Threapland
Crosscanonby
Crosby
Parsonby
Plumbland
Bothel
Whitrigg
Ireby
NX
Senhouse
Crosby Villa
Bullgill
Gilcrux
High Ireby
Uldale
River Ellen
Greengill
Ruthwaite
Maryport
Dearham
Townhead
447 BINSEY
Ellenborough
Risehow
Tallentire
Sunderland
Bewaldeth
Woodside
Fothergill
Flimby
Broughton Moor
Bridekirk
Blindcrake
Lake District Wildlife Park
High Bewaldeth
Redmain
Standingstone
Dovenby
R Derwent
Kilnhill
St Helens
Little Broughton
Papcastle
Great Broughton
Jennings
Bassenthwaite
North Row
Chapel
High Seaton
Camerton
Siddick
Embleton
Scarness
Seaton
Great Clifton
Brigham
Cockermouth
Wythop Mill
North Side
Bridgefoot
Greysouthen
Workington
Stainburn
Little Clifton
Eaglesfield
Mirehouse
Little Crosthwaite
Armaside
Moss Bay
Mossbay
Westfield
Salterbeck
High Harrington
Winscales
Deanscales
552 LORDS SEAT
Lorton
Harrington
Branthwaite
Dean
Low Lorton
Thornthwaite
Grayson Green
Mosser Mains
Pardshaw
High Lorton
Whinlatter
Crosthwaite
Ullock
Thackthwaite
318 Whinlatter Pass
Braithwaite
Portinscale
Distington
Mockerkin
Common End
Waterend
770 HOBCARTON PIKE
790 GRISEDALE PIKE
Swinside
Stair
Pica
Gilgarran
Lowca
Howgate
Kidburngill
Parton
Low Moresby
Loweswater
Lamplugh
Loweswater
851 GRASMOOR
Little Town
Brownrigg
572
Asby
Moresby Parks
Arlecdon
Whitehaven
Rowrah
Kirkland
Crummock Water
High Leys
Grange
Hensingham
Frizington
Winder
Scale Force
Kells
Saltom Bay
615
Buttermere
Cleator Moor
636
Buttermere
Hassness
Sandwith
Mirehouse
Ennerdale Water
Ennerdale Bridge
Gatesgarth
754 DALE HEAD
806 HIGH STILE
356 Honister Pass
Sandwith Newtown
Moor Row
River Ehen
River Liza
Honister Slate Mine
Rottington
Cleator
St Bees Head
St Bees Head Heritage Coast
Bigrigg
River Calder
892 PILLAR
St Bees
Egremont
533 LANK RIGG
LAKE DISTRICT
798 HAYCOCK
802 KIRK FELL
899 GREAT GABLE
Wilton
Worm Gill
Coulderton
Thornhill
Carleton
Wasdale Head
Middletown
Haile
692 SEATALLAN
NATIONAL PARK
910 GREAT END
Nethertown
River Bleng
Blackbeck
978 SCAFELL PIKE
964 SCAFELL
902 BOW FELL
Beckermet
Calder Bridge
Braystones
Ponsonby
Wast Water
Cross
Wellington
Nether Wasdale
Burnmoor Tarn
Sellafield Station
Calder
R Irt
Gosforth
R Mite
393 Hardknott Pass
Hardknott Fort
Santon
Santon Bridge
Eskdale Green
Beckfoot
Boot
Seascale
Hallsenna Moor
Holmrook
Eskdale
Drigg
Muncaster Mill
Ravenglass & Eskdale Railway
652 HARTER FELL
River Esk
Devoke Water
Saltcoats
Muncaster Castle & Owl Centre
Ravenglass
Roman Bath House
Hall Dunnerdale
Seathwaite
River Duddon
SD
Broad Oak
Newbiggin
Waberthwaite
573 WHITFELL
Ulpha
Corney
Logan
Broughton Mills
Beckfoot
Lower Hawthwaite
Hycemoor
Duddon Bridge
Broughton Tower
Selker Bay
Hyton
Bootle
Swinside Stone Circle
A711
A710
A596
A595
A594
A591
A597
A66
A5086
A593
B793
B736
B5300
B5302
B5301
B5299
B5291
B5292
B5289
B5306
B5295
B5294
B5345
B5343
A B C D E F G H J K
1 2 3 4 5 6 7 8 9 10 11 12 13 14
0 1 2 3 4 5 miles
0 1 2 3 4 5 6 7 8 kilometres

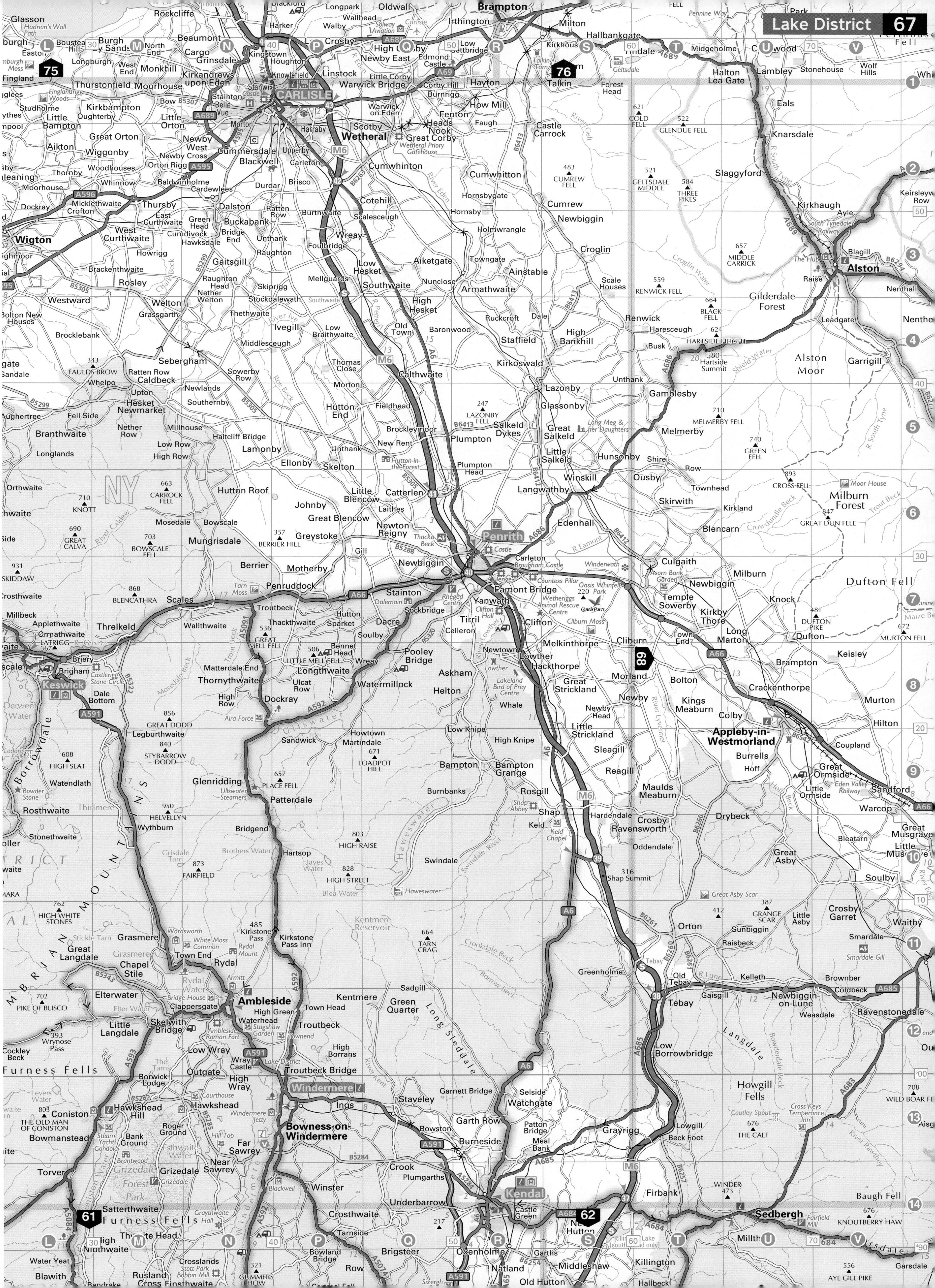

CARLISLE
Brampton
Wetheral
Wigton
Penrith
Alston
Keswick
Appleby-in-Westmorland
Ambleside
Windermere
Bowness-on-Windermere
Kendal
Sedbergh
Hawkshead
Coniston
Shap
Tebay
Orton
Kirkoswald
Lazonby
Langwathby
Dalston
Rockcliffe
Glasson
Burgh by Sands
Thursby
Sebergham
Caldbeck
Hesket Newmarket
Greystoke
Pooley Bridge
Glenridding
Patterdale
Grasmere
Rydal
Troutbeck
Staveley
Burneside
Kirkby Thore
Temple Sowerby
Long Marton
Dufton
Brough Castle
Eamont Bridge
Lowther
Askham
Bampton
Haweswater
Ullswater
Thirlmere
Kentmere Reservoir
Kentmere
Longsleddale
Howgill Fells
Alston Moor
Dufton Fell
Milburn Forest
Gilderdale Forest
Grizedale Forest Park
Furness Fells
Cumbrian Mountains
Helvellyn 950
Skiddaw 931
Blencathra 868
Great Dodd 856
Fairfield 873
High Street 828
High Raise 803
Place Fell 657
Great Calva 690
Knott 710
Carrock Fell 663
Bowscale Fell 703
Cross Fell 893
Hartside Height 624
Black Fell 664
Melmerby Fell 710
Green Fell 740
Great Dun Fell 847
Murton Fell 672
Dufton Pike 481
Great Mell Fell 536
Little Mell Fell 506
Loadpot Hill 671
Kirkstone Pass 485
Tarn Crag 664
The Old Man of Coniston 803
Wrynose Pass 393
Pike of Blisco 702
The Calf 676
Wild Boar Fell 708
Baugh Fell
Knoutberry Haw 676
Aye Gill Pike 556
Shap Summit 316
Grange Scar 387
Glendue Fell 522
Cold Fell 621
Cumrew Fell 483
Geltsdale Middle 521
Three Pikes 584
Middle Carrick 657
Renwick Fell 559
Lazonby Fell 247
M6
A6
A66
A69
A591
A592
A593
A595
A596
A683
A684
A685
A686
A689

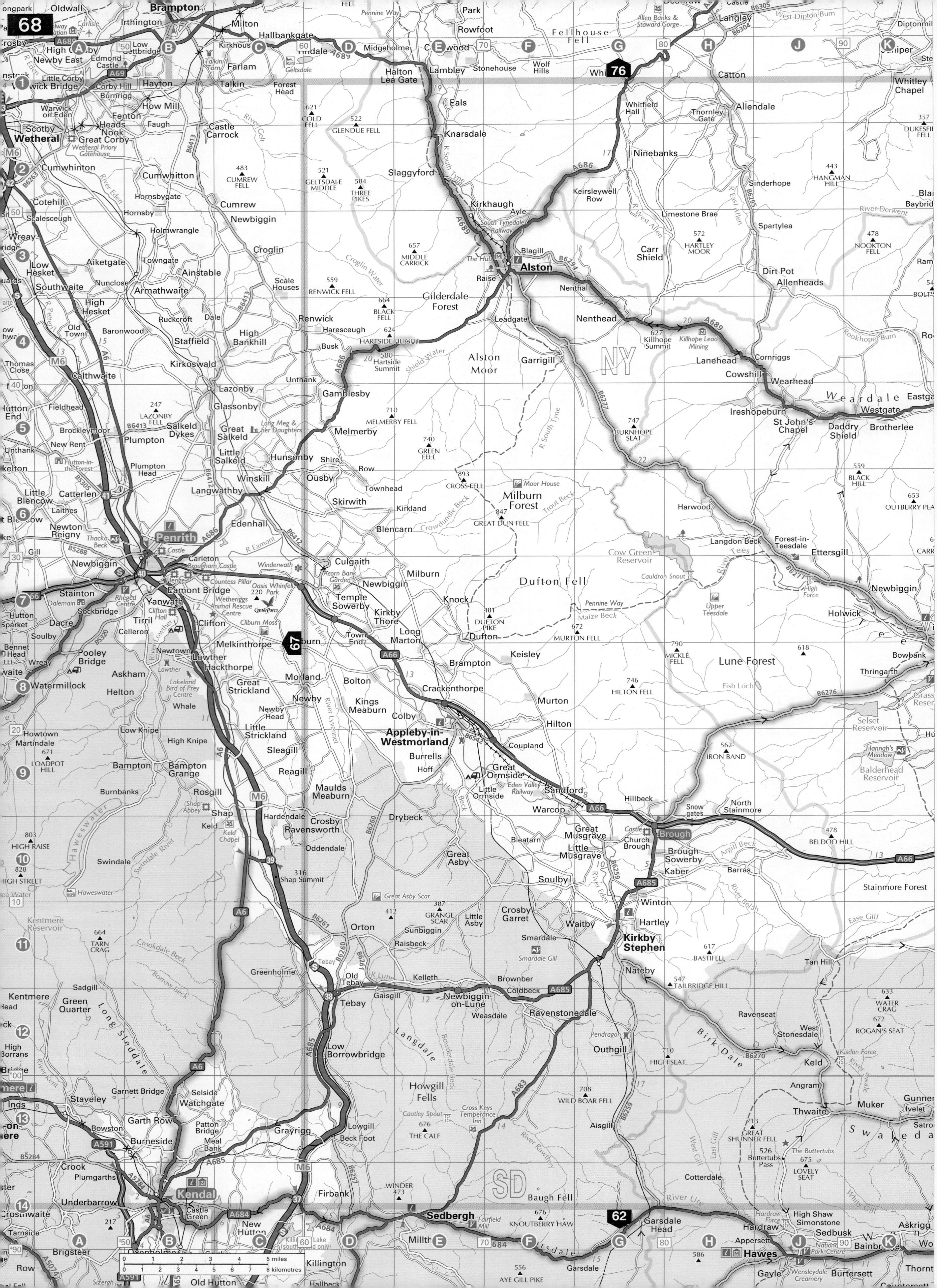

Brampton
Irthington
Milton
Hallbankgate
Midgeholme
Park
Rowfoot
Fellhouse Fell
Allen Banks & Staward Gorge
Langley
Diptonmill
Crosby
Newby East
Low Row
Edmond Castle
Kirkhouse
Talkin Tarn
Farlam
Halton Lea Gate
Lambley
Stonehouse
Wolf Hills
Whitfield
Catton
Whitley Chapel
Little Corby
Warwick Bridge
Corby Hill
Hayton
Talkin
Forest Head
Burnrigg
How Mill
Warwick-on-Eden
Fenton
Heads Nook
Faugh
Eals
Whitfield Hall
Thornley Gate
Allendale
Scotby
Wetheral
Great Corby
Wetheral Priory Gatehouse
Castle Carrock
621 COLD FELL
522 GLENDUE FELL
Knarsdale
357 DUKESFIELD FELL
Cumwhinton
Cumwhitton
483 CUMREW FELL
521 GELTSDALE MIDDLE
584 THREE PIKES
Slaggyford
Ninebanks
Keirsleywell Row
Sinderhope
443 HANGMAN HILL
Cotehill
Hornsbygate
Cumrew
Newbiggin
Kirkhaugh
Ayle
South Tynedale Railway
Limestone Brae
Spartylea
Baybridge
Scalesceugh
Hornsby
Holmwrangle
Wreay
Low Hesket
Aiketgate
Towngate
Croglin
657 MIDDLE CARRICK
The Hub
Blagill
Alston
Carr Shield
572 HARTLEY MOOR
478 NOOKTON FELL
Ainstable
Southwaite
Nunclose
Armathwaite
Scale Houses
559 RENWICK FELL
Raise
Nenthall
Dirt Pot
Allenheads
High Hesket
664 BLACK FELL
Gilderdale Forest
Ruckcroft
Dale
Renwick
Leadgate
Nenthead
Old Town
Baronwood
High Bankhill
Staffield
Haresceugh
624 HARTSIDE HEIGHT
627 Killhope Summit
Killhope Lead Mining
Busk
580 Hartside Summit
Alston Moor
Garrigill
NY
Lanehead
Cornriggs
Cowshill
Wearhead
Thomas Close
Calthwaite
Kirkoswald
Unthank
Lazonby
Gamblesby
Hutton End
Fieldhead
247 LAZONBY FELL
Glassonby
710 MELMERBY FELL
Weardale
Eastgate
Westgate
Ireshopeburn
St John's Chapel
Daddry Shield
Brotherlee
Brockleymoor
Salkeld Dykes
Great Salkeld
Long Meg & her Daughters
Melmerby
747 BURNHOPE SEAT
New Rent
Plumpton
Little Salkeld
740 GREEN FELL
Hunsonby
Shire
Row
Hutton-in-the-Forest
Plumpton Head
Ousby
893 CROSS FELL
Moor House
Milburn Forest
559 BLACK HILL
Little Blencow
Catterlen
Langwathby
Winskill
Townhead
Skirwith
Kirkland
653 OUTBERRY PLAIN
Laithes
Newton Reigny
Penrith
Edenhall
Blencarn
847 GREAT DUN FELL
Harwood
Thacka Beck
Castle
Carleton
Brougham Castle
Winderwath
Culgaith
Cow Green Reservoir
Langdon Beck
Forest-in-Teesdale
Ettersgill
Newbiggin
Acorn Bank Garden
Milburn
Dufton Fell
Cauldron Snout
High Force
Countess Pillar
Oasis Whinfell 220 Park
Temple Sowerby
Stainton
Dalemain
Rheged Centre
Eamont Bridge
Yanwath
Wetheriggs Animal Rescue Centre
Knock
Pennine Way
Maize Beck
Upper Teesdale
Holwick
Hutton
Sockbridge
Tirril
Clifton Hall
Kirkby Thore
481 DUFTON PIKE
Dacre
Celleron
Clifton
Cliburn Moss
Long Marton
672 MURTON FELL
Soulby
Pooley Bridge
Newtown
Melkinthorpe
Town End
Dufton
790 MICKLE FELL
Lune Forest
618
Bowbank
Watermillock
Askham
Lowther
Hackthorpe
Lakeland Bird of Prey Centre
Great Strickland
Morland
Bolton
Brampton
Keisley
Helton
Whale
Newby
Newby Head
Kings Meaburn
Crackenthorpe
746 HILTON FELL
Fish Loch
Thringarth
Howtown
Martindale
Low Knipe
Little Strickland
Colby
Appleby-in-Westmorland
Murton
Hilton
Selset Reservoir
671 LOADPOT HILL
High Knipe
Sleagill
Burrells
Coupland
562 IRON BAND
Hannah's Meadow
Balderhead Reservoir
Bampton
Bampton Grange
Reagill
Hoff
Great Ormside
Little Ormside
Eden Valley Railway
Sandford
Burnbanks
Rosgill
Maulds Meaburn
Hillbeck
Snow gates
North Stainmore
Shap Abbey
Shap
Hardendale
Crosby Ravensworth
Drybeck
Warcop
Brough
Castle
Church Brough
Brough Sowerby
478 BELDOO HILL
803 HIGH RAISE
Keld
Keld Chapel
Oddendale
Bleatarn
Great Musgrave
Little Musgrave
Kaber
Barras
Haweswater
Swindale
828 HIGH STREET
316 Shap Summit
Great Asby
Soulby
Winton
Stainmore Forest
Great Asby Scar
387 GRANGE SCAR
412
Little Asby
Crosby Garret
Hartley
Waitby
Kentmere Reservoir
664 TARN CRAG
Orton
Sunbiggin
Raisbeck
Smardale
Smardale Gill
Kirkby Stephen
617 BASTIFELL
Tan Hill
Tebay
Greenholme
Old Tebay
Kelleth
Brownber
Coldbeck
Nateby
547 TAILBRIDGE HILL
633 WATER CRAG
Kentmere
Sadgill
Green Quarter
Gaisgill
Newbiggin-on-Lune
Weasdale
Ravenstonedale
Ravenseat
West Stonesdale
672 ROGAN'S SEAT
Long Sleddale
Langdale
Bowderdale Beck
Pendragon
Outhgill
Birk Dale
710 HIGH SEAT
Keld
Kisdon Force
High Borrans
Low Borrowbridge
Angram
Garnett Bridge
Selside
Watchgate
Howgill Fells
708 WILD BOAR FELL
Muker
Gunnerside
Ivelet
Staveley
Thwaite
Garth Row
Patton Bridge
Meal Bank
Lowgill
Beck Foot
Cautley Spout
Cross Keys Temperance Inn
676 THE CALF
713 GREAT SHUNNER FELL
Swaledale
Bowston
Burneside
Grayrigg
Aisgill
526 Buttertubs Pass
The Buttertubs
675 LOVELY SEAT
Crook
Plumgarths
SD
Cotterdale
Winder 473
Underbarrow
Kendal
Firbank
Baugh Fell
Castle Green
Sedbergh
Fairfield Mill
676 KNOUTBERRY HAW
Garsdale Head
Hardraw Force
High Shaw
Simonstone
Hardraw
Sedbusk
Askrigg
Crosthwaite
Tarnside
New Hutton
Killington Lake
Millthrop
Garsdale
Appersett
Hawes
Bainbridge
National Park Centre
Brigsteer
Oxenholme
Killington
586
556 AYE GILL PIKE
Gayle
Burtersett
Wensleydale Creamery
Thornton
Old Hutton
Sizergh
Row
0 1 2 3 4 5 miles
0 1 2 3 4 5 6 7 8 kilometres
76
67
62

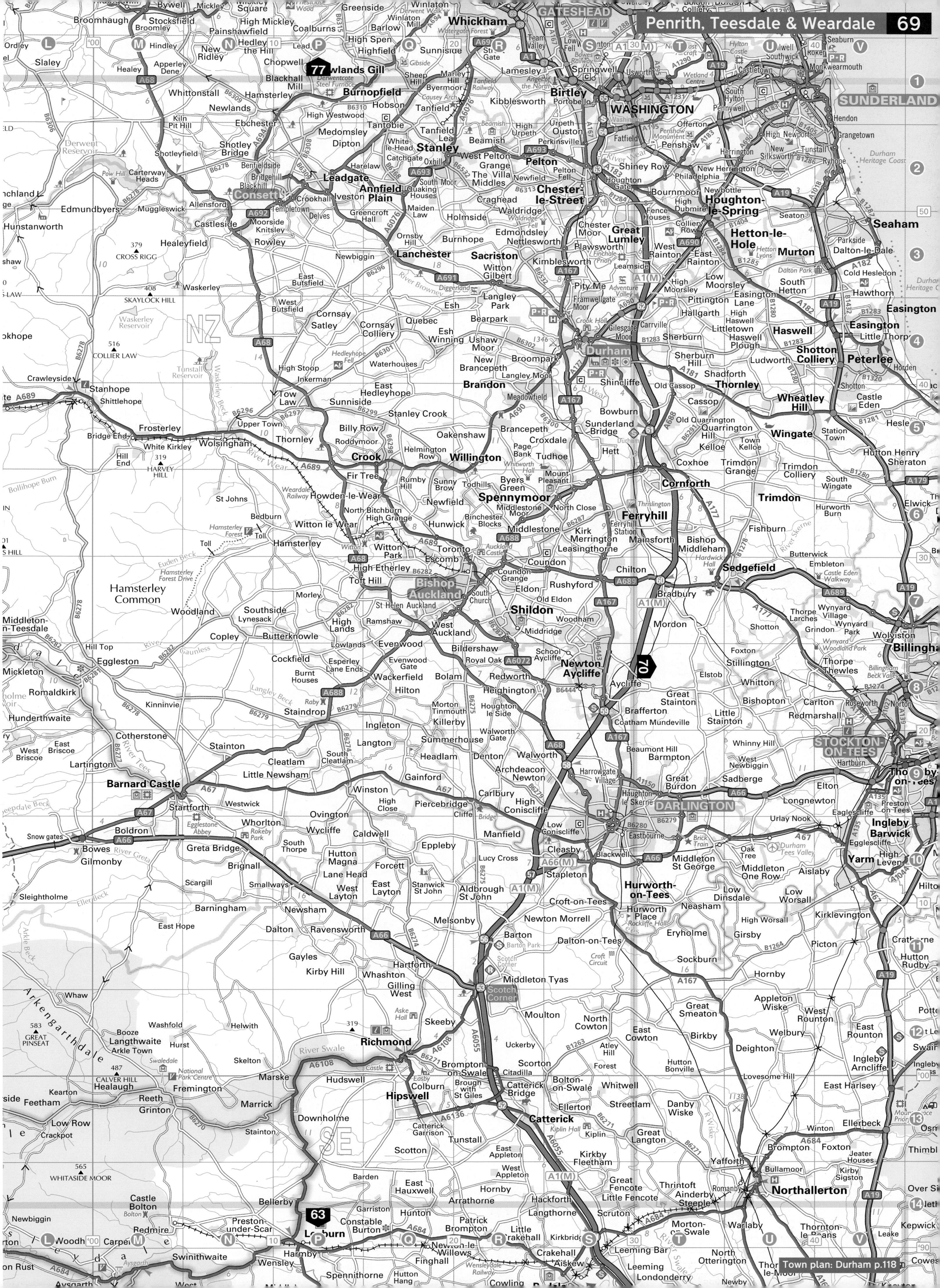
GATESHEAD
Whickham
Birtley
WASHINGTON
SUNDERLAND
77
Rowlands Gill
Burnopfield
Stanley
Pelton
Chester-le-Street
Consett
Leadgate
Annfield Plain
Lanchester
Sacriston
Great Lumley
Houghton-le-Spring
Hetton-le-Hole
Seaham
Murton
Easington
Peterlee
Shotton Colliery
Haswell
Durham
Brandon
Thornley
Wheatley Hill
Wingate
Trimdon
Crook
Willington
Spennymoor
Ferryhill
Cornforth
Sedgefield
Bishop Auckland
Shildon
Newton Aycliffe
70
Stanhope
Frosterley
Wolsingham
Hamsterley
Hamsterley Common
Middleton-in-Teesdale
Eggleston
Romaldkirk
Cotherstone
Barnard Castle
Staindrop
Gainford
Piercebridge
DARLINGTON
STOCKTON-ON-TEES
Billingham
Yarm
Ingleby Barwick
Hurworth-on-Tees
Middleton St George
Scotch Corner
Richmond
Catterick
Hipswell
Northallerton
Brompton
Bedale
Leyburn
63
Derwent Reservoir
Waskerley Reservoir
Tunstall Reservoir
River Wear
River Tees
River Swale
Arkengarthdale
Swaledale
Wensleydale
A1(M)
A19
A66
A67
A68
A167
A689
A688
A684
A6108
Town plan: Durham p.118

Town plan: Durham p.118

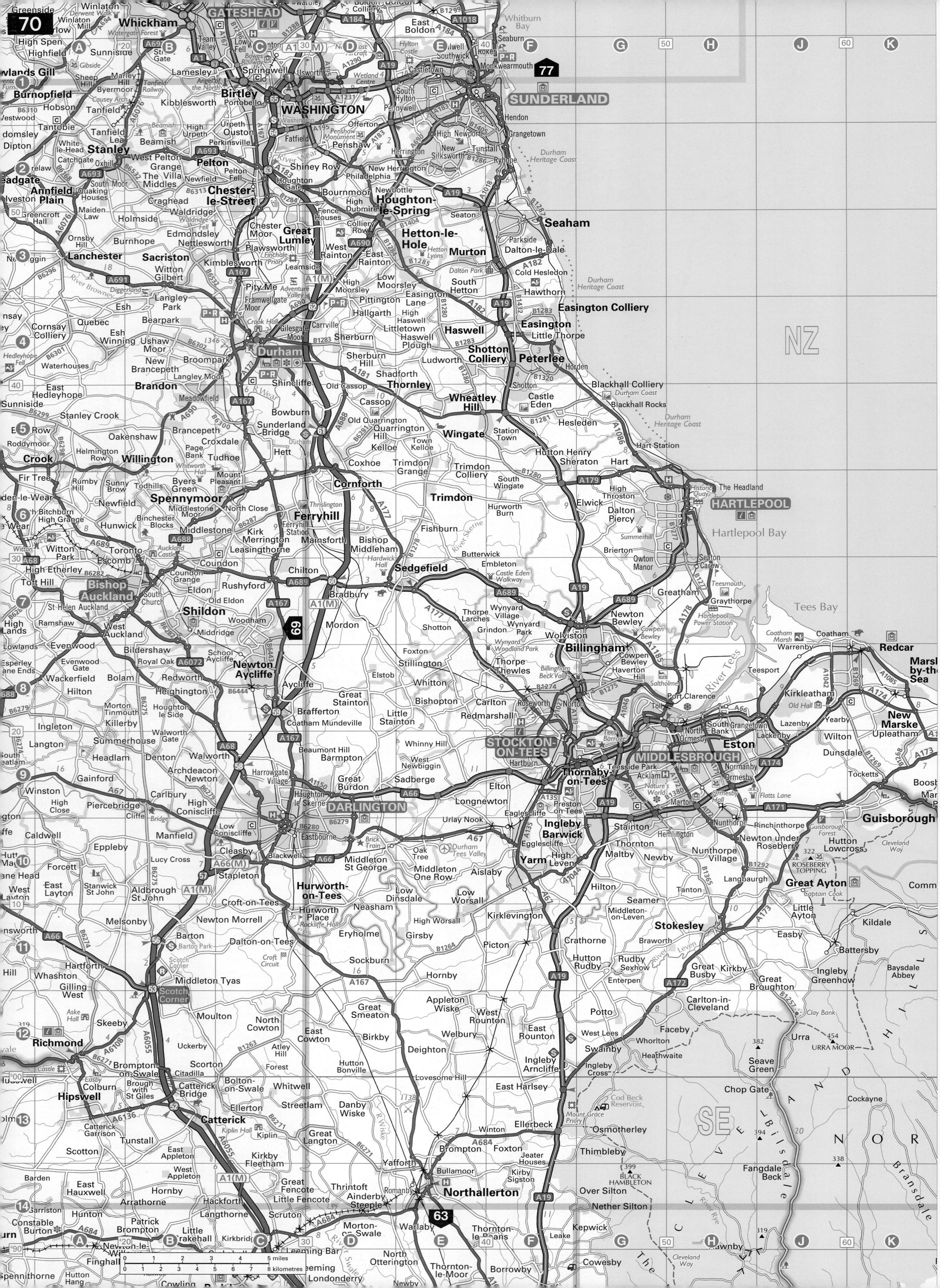
70
77
69
63
GATESHEAD
Whickham
Sunniside
Lamesley
Birtley
Springwell
Usworth
WASHINGTON
East Boldon
Whitburn Bay
Seaburn
Roker
Monkwearmouth
SUNDERLAND
Hendon
Grangetown
Ryhope
Tunstall
Silksworth
Penshaw
Fatfield
Burnopfield
Tanfield
Stanley
Pelton
Chester-le-Street
Annfield Plain
Beamish
Shiney Row
Philadelphia
Houghton-le-Spring
Seaton
Seaham
Durham Heritage Coast
Dalton-le-Dale
Murton
Hetton-le-Hole
Great Lumley
West Rainton
Lanchester
Sacriston
Witton Gilbert
Pity Me
Easington Colliery
Easington
Haswell
Shotton Colliery
Peterlee
Horden
Blackhall Colliery
Blackhall Rocks
Durham
Brandon
Esh Winning
Ushaw Moor
New Brancepeth
Shincliffe
Sherburn
Thornley
Wheatley Hill
Castle Eden
Hesleden
Wingate
Station Town
Bowburn
Sunderland Bridge
Quarrington Hill
Kelloe
Coxhoe
Trimdon Grange
Trimdon Colliery
Hart Station
Hutton Henry
Sheraton
Hart
Crook
Willington
Brancepeth
Tudhoe
Spennymoor
Cornforth
Ferryhill
Trimdon
Elwick
High Throston
The Headland
HARTLEPOOL
Hartlepool Bay
Dalton Piercy
Fishburn
Bishop Middleham
Mainsforth
Kirk Merrington
Middlestone
Leasingthorne
Coundon
Bishop Auckland
Escomb
Toronto
Witton Park
Shildon
Eldon
Chilton
Sedgefield
Bradbury
Butterwick
Embleton
Brierton
Owton Manor
Seaton Carew
Greatham
Graythorpe
Tees Bay
Coatham
Redcar
Marske-by-the-Sea
Newton Bewley
Wolviston
Billingham
Wynyard
Thorpe Thewles
Grindon
Mordon
Shotton
Foxton
Stillington
Newton Aycliffe
Aycliffe
Evenwood
West Auckland
Redworth
Heighington
Bolam
Hilton
Ingleton
Brafferton
Great Stainton
Little Stainton
Whitton
Bishopton
Carlton
Redmarshall
Roseworth
Norton
Cowpen Bewley
Haverton Hill
Port Clarence
Teesport
Kirkleatham
New Marske
Yearby
Lazenby
Wilton
Upleatham
STOCKTON-ON-TEES
Hartburn
Thornaby-on-Tees
MIDDLESBROUGH
Eston
Normanby
Ormesby
South Bank
Grangetown
Dunsdale
Tocketts
Whinny Hill
West Newbiggin
Sadberge
Elton
Longnewton
Great Burdon
Barmpton
Walworth
Gainford
Winston
Summerhouse
Headlam
Denton
Archdeacon Newton
Carlbury
Piercebridge
High Coniscliffe
DARLINGTON
Haughton le Skerne
Eastbourne
Low Coniscliffe
Manfield
Cleasby
Blackwell
Stapleton
Middleton St George
Middleton One Row
Durham Tees Valley
Urlay Nook
Eaglescliffe
Preston on Tees
Ingleby Barwick
Yarm
High Leven
Aislaby
Egglescliffe
Stainton
Thornton
Maltby
Hemlington
Marton
Nunthorpe
Nunthorpe Village
Pinchinthorpe
Guisborough
Newton under Roseberry
Hutton Lowcross
Roseberry Topping
Great Ayton
Newby
Langbaugh
Hilton
Seamer
Tanton
Middleton-on-Leven
Stokesley
Little Ayton
Kildale
Easby
Battersby
Hurworth-on-Tees
Hurworth Place
Neasham
Low Dinsdale
Low Worsall
High Worsall
Kirklevington
Croft-on-Tees
Newton Morrell
Barton
Dalton-on-Tees
Eryholme
Girsby
Picton
Crathorne
Braworth
Hutton Rudby
Rudby
Sexhow
Great Busby
Kirkby
Enterpen
Great Broughton
Ingleby Greenhow
Baysdale Abbey
Sockburn
Hornby
Melsonby
Middleton Tyas
Scotch Corner
Gilling West
Whashton
Skeeby
Moulton
North Cowton
East Cowton
Great Smeaton
Birkby
Appleton Wiske
West Rounton
East Rounton
Welbury
Deighton
Potto
Carlton-in-Cleveland
Faceby
Whorlton
Swainby
Ingleby Arncliffe
Urra
Urra Moor
Seave Green
Richmond
Brompton-on-Swale
Colburn
Catterick Bridge
Catterick
Hipswell
Bolton-on-Swale
Scorton
Uckerby
Whitwell
Streetlam
Danby Wiske
Lovesome Hill
East Harlsey
Chop Gate
Cockayne
Osmotherley
Ellerbeck
Winton
Brompton
Thimbleby
Tunstall
Scotton
Kiplin
Great Langton
Kirkby Fleetham
Yafforth
Bullamoor
Northallerton
Romanby
Thrintoft
Ainderby Steeple
Great Fencote
Little Fencote
Hornby
Arrathorne
Hackforth
Langthorne
Scruton
Morton-on-Swale
Warlaby
Thornton-le-Beans
Leake
Kepwick
Nether Silton
Over Silton
Black Hambleton
Fangdale Beck
Hawnby
Cowesby
Borrowby
North Otterington
Thornton-le-Moor
Leeming Bar
Patrick Brompton
Constable Burton
Hunton
Finghall
Cleveland Way
Bilsdale
Bransdale
NZ
SE
0 1 2 3 4 5 miles
0 1 2 3 4 5 6 7 8 kilometres

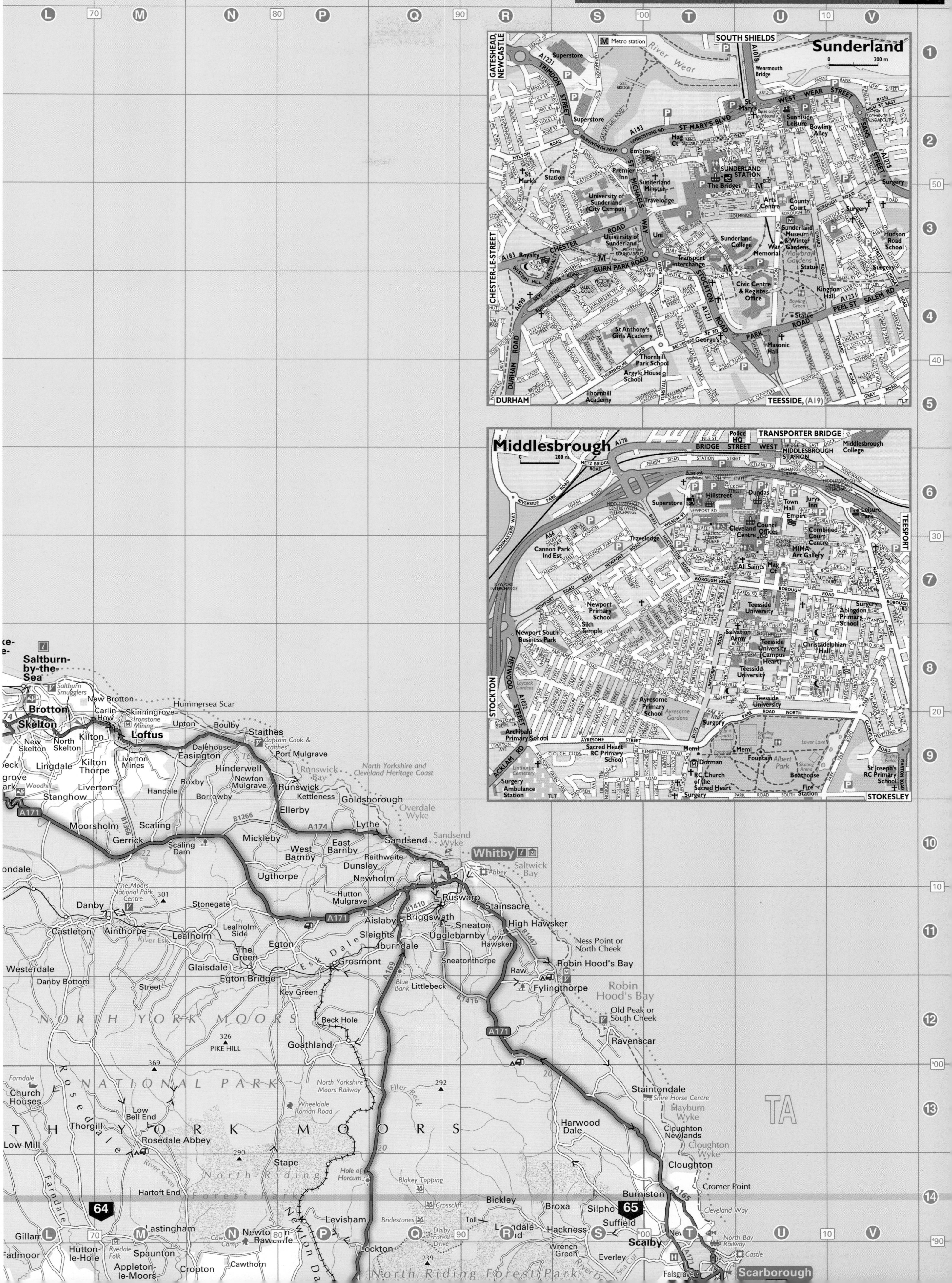

Sunderland

SOUTH SHIELDS

GATESHEAD, NEWCASTLE

Metro station

River Wear

Wearmouth Bridge

WEST WEAR STREET

Superstore

TRIMDON STREET

Superstore

Sunniside Leisure

Bowling Alley

St Mary's

A183

St Michael's Way

Premier Inn

Empire

St Mary's Blvd

Mag Ct

Fire Station

Sunderland Minster

Travelodge

SUNDERLAND STATION

The Bridges

Arts Centre

County Court

Surgery

St Mark's

University of Sunderland (City Campus)

University of Sunderland

Sunderland College

War Memorial

Sunderland Museum & Winter Gardens

Hudson Road School

CHESTER-LE-STREET

CHESTER ROAD

BURN PARK ROAD

STOCKTON ROAD

Transport Interchange

Park Lane

Mowbray Gardens

Statue

Surgery

Civic Centre & Register Office

Kingdom Hall

PEEL ST

SALEM RD

St Anthony's Girls' Academy

George's

Masonic Hall

PARK

ROAD

Bowling Green

Statue

Thornhill Park School

Argyle House School

Thornhill Academy

DURHAM

TEESSIDE, (A19)

Middlesbrough

Police HQ

TRANSPORTER BRIDGE

A178

BRIDGE STREET WEST

MIDDLESBROUGH STATION

Middlesbrough College

METZ BRIDGE ROAD

MARSH ROAD

STATION STREET

TEESPORT

RIVERSIDE PARK ROAD

Superstore

Hillstreet

Dundas

Town Hall

Jury's Inn

Empire

Leisure Park

Cannon Park Ind Est

Travelodge

Cleveland Centre

Council Offices

Combined Court Centre

MIMA Art Gallery

STOCKTON STREET

Newport South Business Park

All Saints

Mag Ct

Teesside University

Surgery

Abingdon Primary School

Newport Primary School

Sikh Temple

Salvation Army

Teesside University (Campus Heart)

Christadelphian Hall

ACKLAM ROAD

Ayresome Primary School

Teesside University

Ayresome Gardens

Surgery

Archibald Primary School

Sacred Heart RC Primary School

Meml

Meml

Albert Park

Lower Lake

Surgery Ambulance Station

Linthorpe Cemetery

Dorman

RC Church of the Sacred Heart

Fountain

Boathouse

Fire Station

St Joseph's RC Primary School

STOKESLEY

Saltburn-by-the-Sea

Saltburn Smugglers

New Brotton

Hummersea Scar

Brotton

Skelton

Carlin How

Skinningrove

Ironstone Mining

Upton

Boulby

Staithes

Captain Cook & Staithes

North Yorkshire and Cleveland Heritage Coast

New Skelton

North Skelton

Kilton

Loftus

Dalehouse

Easington

Port Mulgrave

Runswick Bay

Lingdale

Kilton Thorpe

Liverton Mines

Hinderwell

Roxby

Runswick

Kettleness

A171

Stanghow

Liverton

Handale

Newton Mulgrave

Borrowby

Goldsborough

Moorsholm

Scaling

Mickleby

Ellerby

A174

Lythe

Overdale Wyke

Gerrick

Scaling Dam

West Barnby

East Barnby

Sandsend

Sandsend Wyke

B1266

Dunsley

Raithwaite

Whitby

Saltwick Bay

Ugthorpe

Newholm

Abbey

Danby

The Moors National Centre

Stonegate

Hutton Mulgrave

Ruswarp

Stainsacre

Castleton

Ainthorpe

Lealholm

Lealholm Side

Aislaby

Briggswath

Sneaton

High Hawsker

B1467

NORTH YORK MOORS

Westerdale

The Green

Egton

Sleights

Iburndale

Ugglebarnby

Low Hawsker

Ness Point or North Cheek

Danby Bottom

Glaisdale

Grosmont

Sneatonthorpe

Robin Hood's Bay

Street

Egton Bridge

Key Green

Blue Bank

Littlebeck

Raw

Fylingthorpe

Robin Hood's Bay

Beck Hole

B1416

Old Peak or South Cheek

PIKE HILL

Goathland

A171

Ravenscar

NATIONAL PARK

North Yorkshire Moors Railway

Eller Beck

Staintondale

Shire Horse Centre

Hayburn Wyke

TA

Church Houses

Farndale

Low Bell End

Wheeldale Roman Road

Harwood Dale

Cloughton Newlands

Cloughton Wyke

Thorgill

YORK MOORS

Rosedale Abbey

Cloughton

Low Mill

River Seven

Stape

North Riding

Hole of Horcum

Blakey Topping

Cromer Point

Burniston

Cleveland Way

Gillan

Hartoft End

Forest Park

Levisham

Bridestones

Crosscliff

Toll

Bickley

Broxa

Silpho

Suffield

Cloughton

North Bay Railway

Hutton-le-Hole

Lastingham

Newton-on-Rawcliffe

Dalby Forest Drive

Lockton

Lowdale

Hackness

Scalby

Scarborough

Fadmoor

Spaunton

Appleton-le-Moors

Cropton

Cawthorn

North Riding Forest Park

Everley

Wrench Green

Falsgrave

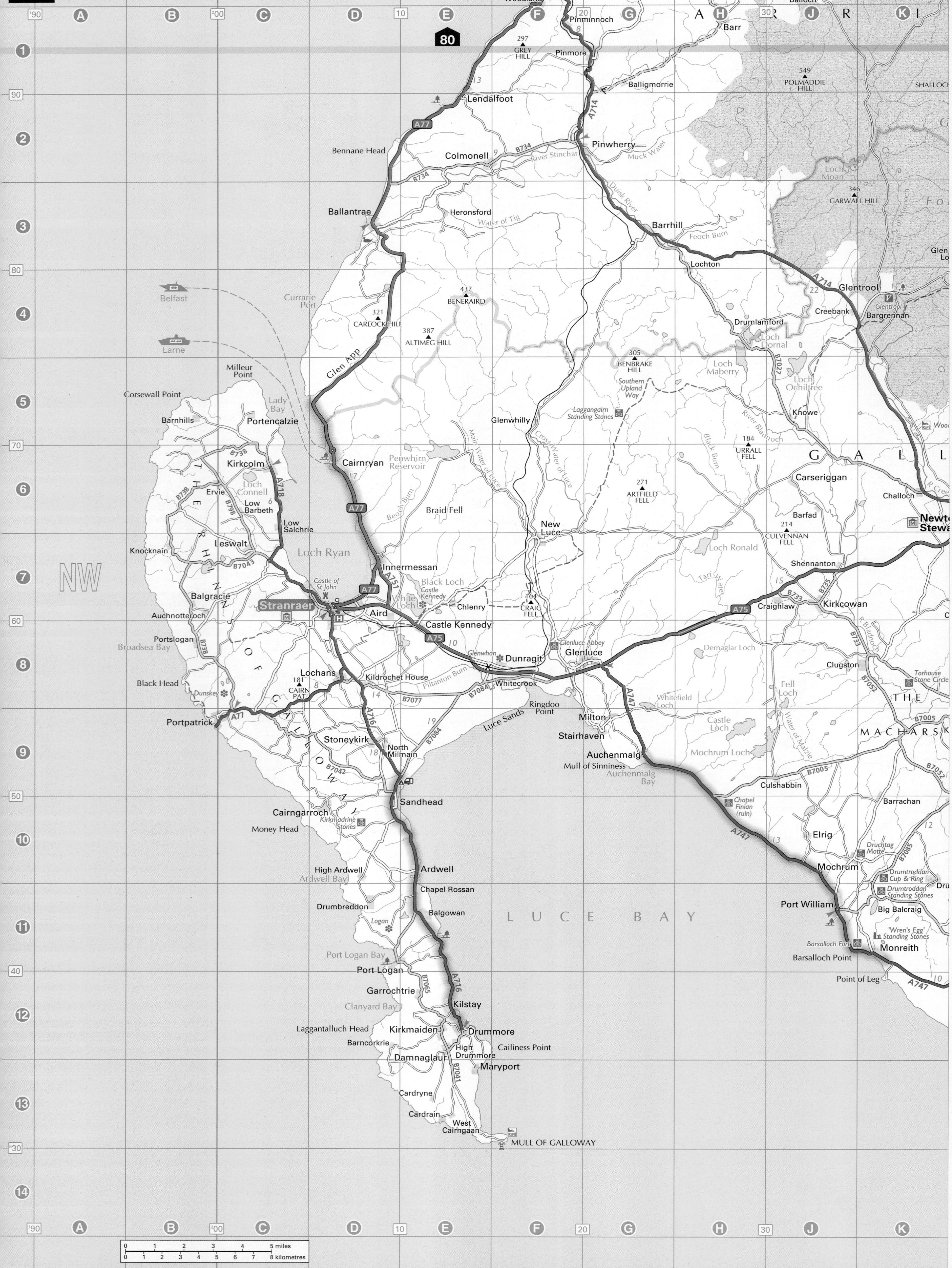
80
NW
Woodland
Pinmminnoch
Pinmore
Dalquhairn
Knockeen
Balloch
Barr
River Stinchar
297 GREY HILL
549 POLMADDIE HILL
SHALLOCH
Balligmorrie
Lendalfoot
A77
A714
Pinwherry
Muck Water
Bennane Head
Colmonell
B734
River Stinchar
Loch Moan
346 GARWALL HILL
Ballantrae
Heronsford
Water of Tig
Dusk River
Barrhill
Feoch Burn
Lochton
Glentrool
Creebank
Bargrennan
Belfast
Larne
Currarie Port
437 BENERAIRD
321 CARLOCK HILL
387 ALTIMEG HILL
Drumlamford
Loch Dornal
305 BENBRAKE HILL
Loch Maberry
B7027
Loch Ochiltree
Southern Upland Way
Glen App
Milleur Point
Corsewall Point
Lady Bay
Barnhills
Portencalzie
Laggangairn Standing Stones
Glenwhilly
Knowe
River Bladnoch
184 URRALL FELL
G A L L
Main Water of Luce
Cross Water of Luce
Black Burn
Kirkcolm
B738
A718
Cairnryan
Penwhirn Reservoir
271 ARTFIELD FELL
Carseriggan
Challoch
Ervie
Loch Connell
Low Barbeth
B798
B738
Braid Fell
Beoch Burn
Barfad
214 CULVENNAN FELL
Newton Stewart
Low Salchrie
New Luce
Leswalt
Loch Ryan
Loch Ronald
Shennanton
Knocknain
B7043
Innermessan
A751
Tarf Water
B733
B735
Castle of St John
Black Loch
Balgracie
Castle Kennedy
A77
Craiglaw
Kirkcowan
Stranraer
White Loch
Chlenry
184 CRAIG FELL
A75
Auchnotteroch
Aird
Castle Kennedy
Portslogan
Broadsea Bay
B738
Glenwhan
Dunragit
Glenluce Abbey
Glenluce
Dernaglar Loch
Clugston
Torhouse Stone Circle
Lochans
Kildrochet House
Piltanton Burn
Black Head
181 CAIRN PAT
Dunskey
B7084
Whitecrook
A747
Whitefield Loch
Fell Loch
B7052
THE
B7077
Ringdoo Point
Portpatrick
Luce Sands
Milton
Castle Loch
B7005
MACHARS
Stoneykirk
North Milmain
Stairhaven
Auchenmalg
Mochrum Loch
Water of Malzie
Mull of Sinniness
Auchenmalg Bay
B7042
Culshabbin
B7005
Sandhead
Chapel Finian (ruin)
Barrachan
Cairngarroch
Kirkmadrine Stones
Money Head
Elrig
A747
Druchtag Motte
B7085
Ardwell
High Ardwell
Ardwell Bay
Mochrum
Drumtroddan Cup & Ring
Drumtroddan Standing Stones
Chapel Rossan
Port William
Drumbreddon
Big Balcraig
Balgowan
L U C E B A Y
Logan
'Wren's Egg' Standing Stones
Barsalloch Fort
Monreith
Port Logan Bay
Barsalloch Point
Port Logan
Point of Leg
B7065
A716
A747
Garrochtrie
Clanyard Bay
Kilstay
Laggantalluch Head
Kirkmaiden
Drummore
Barncorkrie
Cailiness Point
High Drummore
Damnaglaur
Maryport
B7041
Cardryne
Cardrain
West Cairngaan
MULL OF GALLOWAY
A B C D E F G H J K
1 2 3 4 5 6 7 8 9 10 11 12 13 14
0 1 2 3 4 5 miles
0 1 2 3 4 5 6 7 8 kilometres

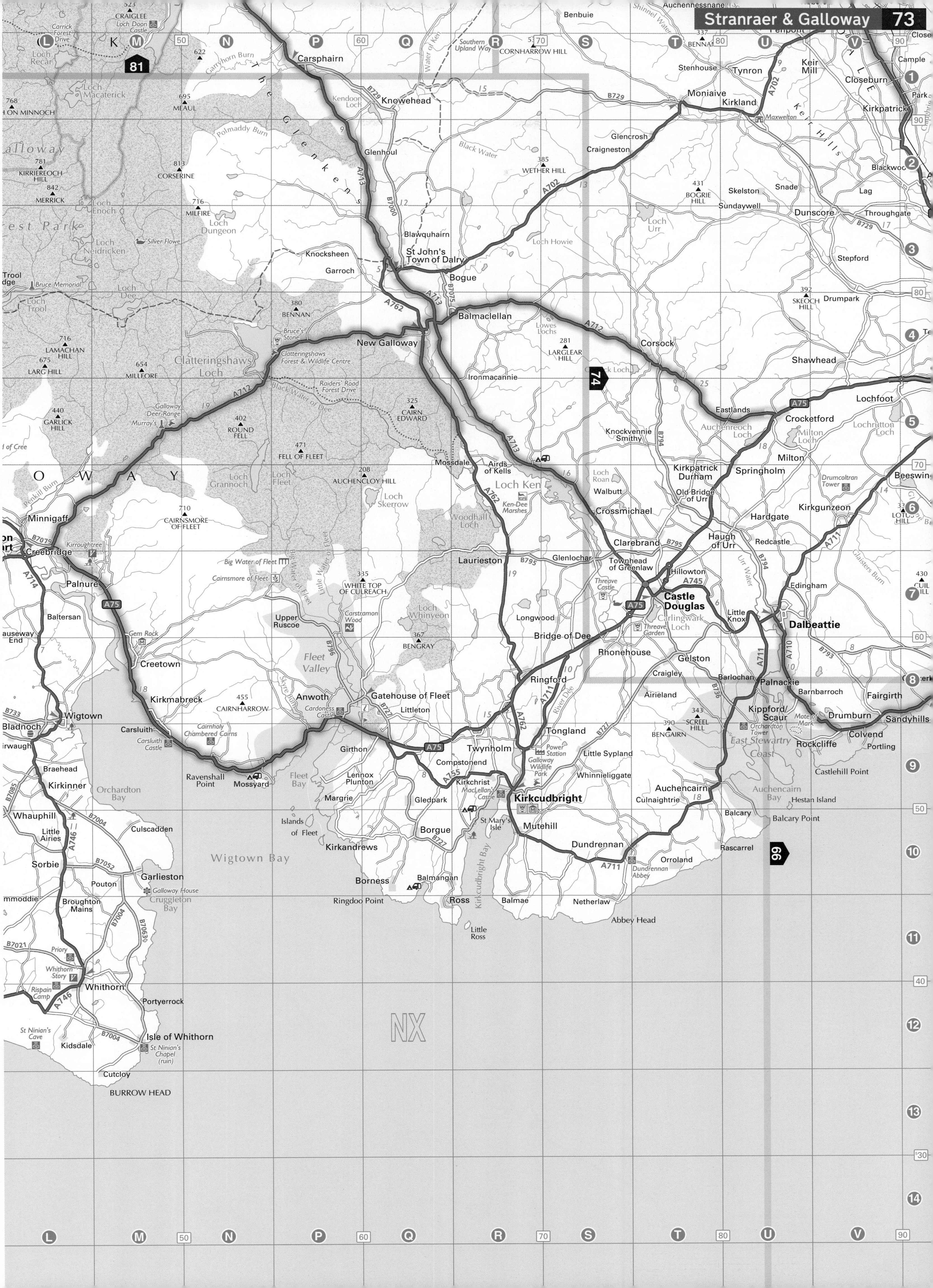
Carsphairn
Knowehead
Glenhoul
Blawquhairn
St John's Town of Dalry
Bogue
Knocksheen
Garroch
Balmaclellan
New Galloway
Ironmacannie
Mossdale
Airds of Kells
Loch Ken
Laurieston
Crossmichael
Clarebrand
Glenlochar
Townhead of Greenlaw
Castle Douglas
Rhonehouse
Gelston
Bridge of Dee
Ringford
Tongland
Twynholm
Kirkcudbright
Mutehill
Dundrennan
Auchencairn
Palnackie
Dalbeattie
Kippford/ Scaur
Rockcliffe
Colvend
Sandyhills
Moniaive
Tynron
Kirkland
Closeburn
Kirkpatrick
Dunscore
Corsock
Shawhead
Crocketford
Lochfoot
Springholm
Milton
Kirkpatrick Durham
Haugh of Urr
Hardgate
Kirkgunzeon
Minnigaff
Creebridge
Palnure
Creetown
Kirkmabreck
Gatehouse of Fleet
Anworth
Wigtown
Bladnoch
Kirkinner
Whauphill
Sorbie
Garlieston
Whithorn
Isle of Whithorn
Burrow Head
Wigtown Bay
Clatteringshaws Loch
Cairnsmore of Fleet
Fleet Valley
Borgue
Kirkandrews
Ross
Abbey Head
NX

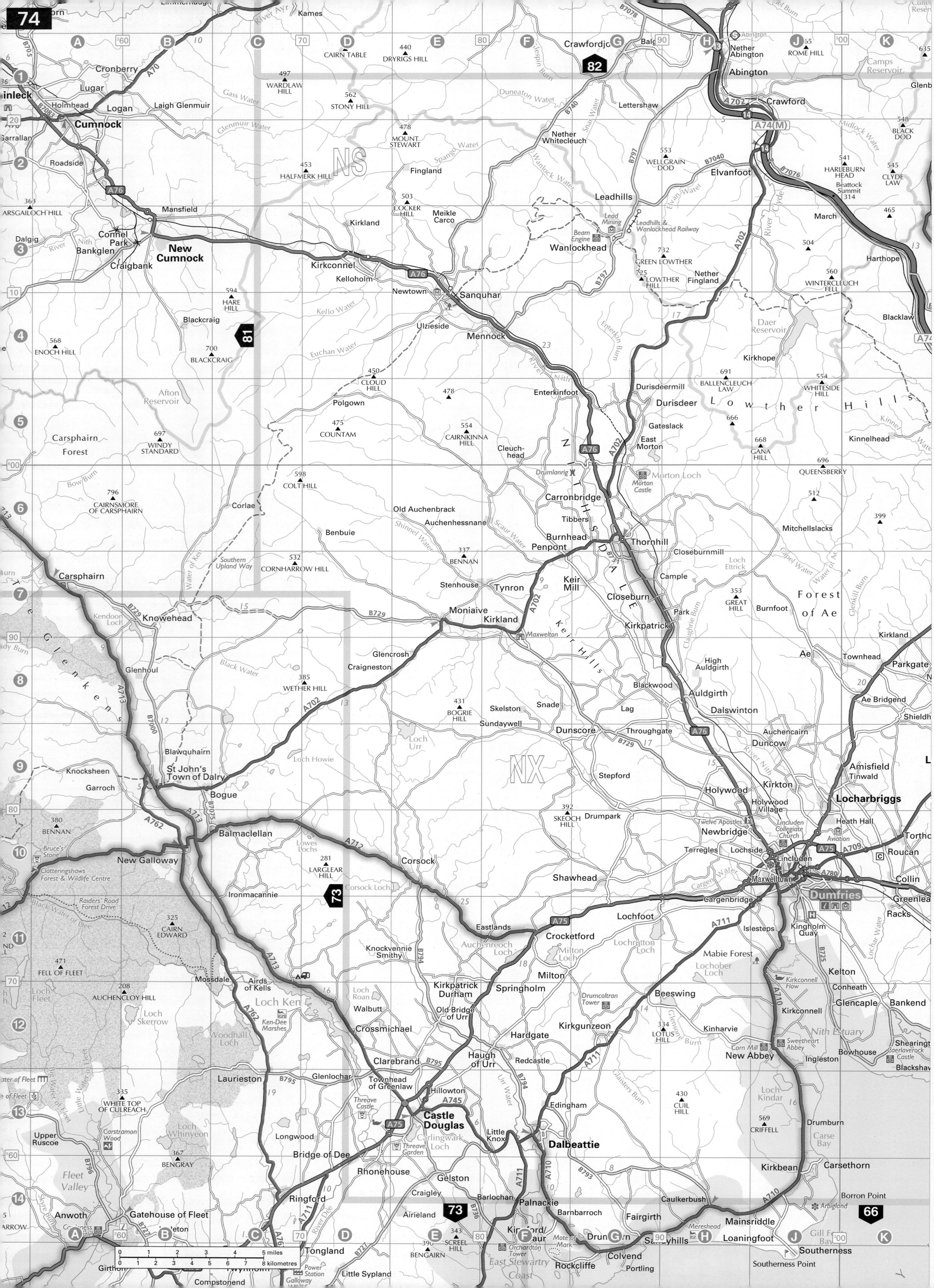

Kames
Crawfordjohn
Abington
Nether Abington
ROME HILL
Camps Reservoir
CAIRN TABLE
DRYRIGS HILL
WARDLAW HILL
STONY HILL
Cronberry
Lugar
Holmhead
Logan
Laigh Glenmuir
Cumnock
Crawford
Lettershaw
Duneaton Water
A74(M)
MOUNT STEWART
Nether Whitecleuch
WELLGRAIN DOD
Elvanfoot
BLACK DOD
Roadside
HALFMERK HILL
Fingland
Leadhills
HARLEBURN HEAD
CLYDE LAW
Beattock Summit
COCKER HILL
Meikle Carco
Kirkland
Lead Mining
Leadhills & Wanlockhead Railway
March
ARSGAILOCH HILL
Mansfield
Dalgig
Connel Park
Bankglen
New Cumnock
Craigbank
Kirkconnel
Kelloholm
Beam Engine
Wanlockhead
GREEN LOWTHER
LOWTHER HILL
Nether Fingland
WINTERCLEUCH FELL
Harthope
Newtown
Sanquhar
HARE HILL
Kello Water
Blackcraig
Ulzieside
Mennock
Daer Reservoir
Blacklaw
ENOCH HILL
BLACKCRAIG
Euchan Water
Kirkhope
CLOUD HILL
Afton Reservoir
Polgown
Enterkinfoot
Durisdeermill
Durisdeer
BALLENCLEUCH LAW
WHITESIDE HILL
Lowther Hills
COUNTAM
CAIRNKINNA HILL
Gateslack
East Morton
GANA HILL
Kinnelhead
Carsphairn Forest
WINDY STANDARD
Cleuchhead
Drumlanrig
Morton Loch
Morton Castle
QUEENSBERRY
COLT HILL
CAIRNSMORE OF CARSPHAIRN
Corlae
Carronbridge
Old Auchenbrack
Auchenhessnane
Tibbers
NITHSDALE
Mitchellslacks
Benbuie
Burnhead
Penpont
Thornhill
Closeburnmill
BENNAN
CORNHARROW HILL
Southern Upland Way
Carsphairn
Stenhouse
Tynron
Keir Mill
Cample
Forest of Ae
GREAT HILL
Burnfoot
Closeburn
Park
Kendoon Loch
Knowehead
Moniaive
Kirkland
Maxwelton
Keir Hills
Kirkpatrick
Glenkens
Glencrosh
Craigneston
Ae
Townhead
Parkgate
Glenhoul
Black Water
High Auldgirth
WETHER HILL
Blackwood
Auldgirth
Ae Bridgend
BOGRIE HILL
Skelston
Snade
Lag
Dalswinton
Sundaywell
Dunscore
Throughgate
Auchencairn
Loch Urr
Duncow
Blawquhairn
Loch Howie
Amisfield
Tinwald
Knocksheen
St John's Town of Dalry
Stepford
Holywood
Kirkton
Garroch
Bogue
Holywood Village
Locharbriggs
BENNAN
SKEOCH HILL
Drumpark
Balmaclellan
Twelve Apostles
Newbridge
Lincluden Collegiate Church
Heath Hall
Aviation
Bruce's Stone
New Galloway
Lowes Lochs
LARGLEAR HILL
Corsock
Terregles
Lochside
Lincluden
Roucan
Clatteringshaws Forest & Wildlife Centre
Shawhead
Maxwelltown
Collin
Raiders' Road Forest Drive
Ironmacannie
Corsock Loch
Dumfries
Cargenbridge
CAIRN EDWARD
Eastlands
Lochfoot
Crocketford
Islesteps
Kingholm Quay
Auchenreoch Loch
Milton Loch
Lochrutton Loch
Knockvennie Smithy
Mabie Forest
FELL OF FLEET
Lochaber Loch
Kelton
Mossdale
Airds of Kells
Milton
Kirkpatrick Durham
Springholm
Beeswing
Kirkconnell Flow
Conheath
AUCHENCLOY HILL
Loch Fleet
Loch Roan
Drumcoltran Tower
Glencaple
Bankend
Loch Ken
Walbutt
Old Bridge of Urr
Kirkconnell
Loch Skerrow
Ken-Dee Marshes
Crossmichael
Kirkgunzeon
LOTUS HILL
Kinharvie
Nith Estuary
Woodhall Loch
Hardgate
Corn Mill
Sweetheart Abbey
New Abbey
Shearington
Bowhouse
Caerlaverock Castle
Ingleston
Blackshaw
Clarebrand
Haugh of Urr
Redcastle
Laurieston
Glenlochar
Townhead of Greenlaw
Hillowton
Edingham
CUIL HILL
Loch Kindar
WHITE TOP OF CULREACH
Threave Castle
Castle Douglas
CRIFFELL
Drumburn
Carstramon Wood
Loch Whinyeon
Upper Ruscoe
Longwood
Carlingwark Loch
Threave Garden
Little Knox
Dalbeattie
Carse Bay
BENGRAY
Bridge of Dee
Fleet Valley
Rhonehouse
Gelston
Kirkbean
Carsethorn
Craigley
Barlochan
Palnackie
Caulkerbush
Borron Point
Ringford
Arbigland
Anwoth
Gatehouse of Fleet
Airieland
Barnbarroch
Fairgirth
Mainsriddle
Meikle
Kippford/Scaur
Mote of Mark
Drum
Sandyhills
Mereshead
Loaningfoot
Southerness
Tongland
SCREEL HILL
Orchardton Tower
BENGAIRN
Rough Island
Colvend
Portling
Southerness Point
East Stewartry Coast
Rockcliffe
Girthon
Compstonend
Power Station
Little Sypland
Galloway
NS
NX
73
81
82
66
0 1 2 3 4 5 miles
0 1 2 3 4 5 6 7 8 kilometres

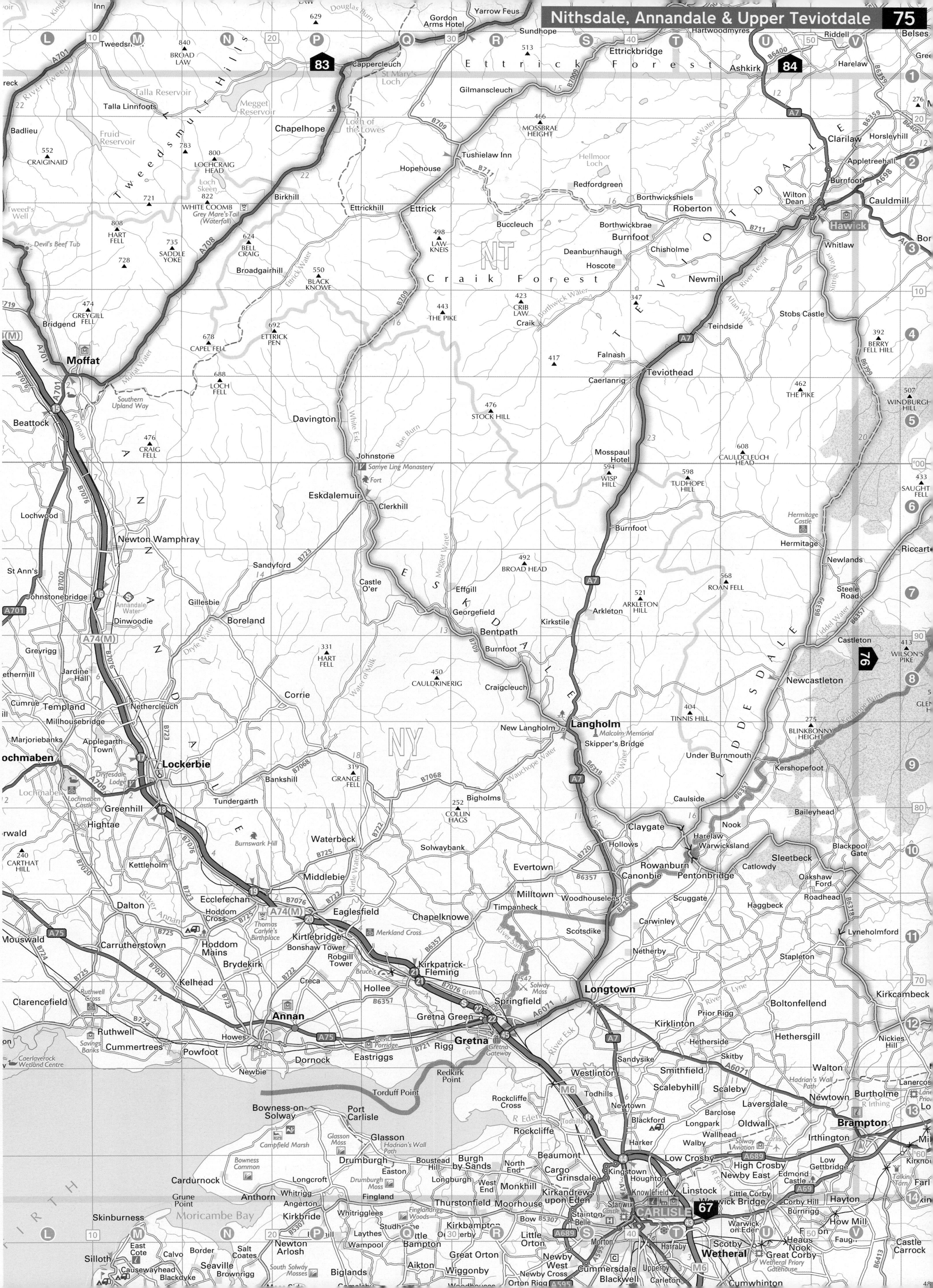
83
84
76
67
NT
NY
Ettrick Forest
Tweedsmuir Hills
Craik Forest
Teviotdale
Annandale
Eskdale
Liddesdale
Moffat
Lockerbie
Langholm
Annan
Gretna
Longtown
Hawick
Carlisle
Brampton
Lochmaben
Beattock
Johnstone
Eskdalemuir
Clerkhill
Samye Ling Monastery
Fort
Davington
Tushielaw Inn
Hopehouse
Ettrick
Ettrickhill
Buccleuch
Birkhill
Chapelhope
Cappercleuch
Gordon Arms Hotel
Yarrow Feus
Sundhope
Ettrickbridge
Ashkirk
Gilmanscleuch
Talla Reservoir
Talla Linnfoots
Megget Reservoir
Fruid Reservoir
St Mary's Loch
Loch of the Lowes
Badlieu
552 CRAIGINAID
840 BROAD LAW
800 LOCHCRAIG HEAD
783
822 WHITE COOMB
Grey Mare's Tail (Waterfall)
Loch Skeen
721
Tweed's Well
Devil's Beef Tub
808 HART FELL
735 SADDLE YOKE
728
624 BELL CRAIG
Broadgairhill
550 BLACK KNOWE
498 LAW KNEIS
466 MOSSBRAE HEIGHT
Hellmoor Loch
Redfordgreen
Borthwickshiels
Roberton
Borthwickbrae
Burnfoot
Chisholme
Deanburnhaugh
Hoscote
Newmill
443 THE PIKE
423 CRIB LAW
Craik
347
474 GREYGILL FELL
Bridgend
678 CAPEL FELL
692 ETTRICK PEN
688 LOCH FELL
Southern Upland Way
Teviothead
Caerlanrig
Falnash
417
476 STOCK HILL
Mosspaul Hotel
594 WISP HILL
598 TUDHOPE HILL
608 CAULDCLEUCH HEAD
462 THE PIKE
392 BERRY FELL HILL
Teindside
Stobs Castle
Clarilaw
Horsleyhill
Appletreehall
Wilton Dean
Cauldmill
Whitlaw
Harelaw
Riddell
Hartwoodmyres
Belses
507 WINDBURGH HILL
433 SAUGHTREE FELL
Hermitage Castle
Hermitage
Newlands
Riccarton
Steele Road
Castleton
413 WILSON'S PIKE
Newcastleton
476 CRAIG FELL
Lochwood
Newton Wamphray
St Ann's
Johnstonebridge
Annandale Water
Dinwoodie
Gillesbie
Boreland
Sandyford
Castle O'er
Effgill
Georgefield
Bentpath
Burnfoot
Kirkstile
Arkleton
521 ARKLETON HILL
492 BROAD HEAD
568 ROAN FELL
Greyrigg
Jardine Hall
331 HART FELL
450 CAULDKINERIG
Craigcleuch
Corrie
Templand
Nethercleuch
Millhousebridge
Marjoriebanks
Applegarth Town
New Langholm
Malcolm Memorial
Skipper's Bridge
404 TINNIS HILL
275 BLINKBONNY HEIGHT
Under Burnmouth
Kershopefoot
Bankshill
319 GRANGE FELL
Dryfesdale Lodge
Lochmaben Castle
Greenhill
Hightae
Tundergarth
252 COLLIN HAGS
Bigholms
Caulside
Baileyhead
Waterbeck
Burnswark Hill
Solwaybank
Claygate
Hollows
Harelaw
Warwicksland
Nook
Blackpool Gate
240 CARTHAT HILL
Kettleholm
Middlebie
Evertown
Rowanburn
Canonbie
Pentonbridge
Sleetbeck
Catlowdy
Oakshaw Ford
Roadhead
Dalton
Ecclefechan
Hoddom Cross
Thomas Carlyle's Birthplace
Eaglesfield
Chapelknowe
Milltown
Timpanheck
Woodhouselees
Scuggate
Haggbeck
Mouswald
Carrutherstown
Hoddom Mains
Kirtlebridge
Merkland Cross
Bonshaw Tower
Robgill Tower
Scotsdike
Carwinley
Lyneholmford
Netherby
Stapleton
Brydekirk
Kirkpatrick-Fleming
Bruce's Cave
Kelhead
Creca
Hollee
542 Solway Moss
Springfield
Gretna Green
Clarencefield
Ruthwell Cross
Ruthwell
Savings Banks
Cummertrees
Powfoot
Howes
Dornock
Eastriggs
Devil's Porridge
Rigg
Gretna Gateway
Kirkcambeck
Boltonfellend
Prior Rigg
Kirklinton
Hethersgill
Netherside
Nickies Hill
Caerlaverock Wetland Centre
Newbie
Redkirk Point
Torduff Point
Westlinton
Sandysike
Smithfield
Skitby
Walton
Todhills
Scalebyhill
Scaleby
Newtown
Burtholme
Lanercost
Hadrian's Wall Path
Bowness-on-Solway
Port Carlisle
Rockcliffe Cross
Rockcliffe
Blackford
Barclose
Laversdale
Longpark
Oldwall
Irthington
Glasson Moss
Glasson
Hadrian's Wall Path
Campfield Marsh
Bowness Common
Drumburgh
Boustead Hill
Burgh by Sands
Eastern
North End
West End
Longburgh
Beaumont
Cargo
Grinsdale
Kingstown
Harker
Walby
Wallhead
Low Crosby
High Crosby
Newby East
Edmond Castle
Low Gettbridge
Houghton
Linstock
Little Corby
Warwick Bridge
Corby Hill
Hayton
Talkin Tarn
Cardurnock
Longcroft
Drumburgh Moss
Whitrigg
Anthorn
Fingland
Grune Point
Angerton
Moricambe Bay
Kirkbride
Whitrigglees
Finglandrigg Woods
Thurstonfield
Moorhouse
Kirkandrews upon Eden
Stanwix
Stainton
Belle
Knowlefield
Burnrigg
How Mill
Skinburness
Laythes
Kirkbampton
Bow
Warwick-on-Eden
Heads Nook
Great Corby
Wetheral Priory Gatehouse
Wetheral
Scotby
Harraby
Castle Carrock
Silloth
East Cote
Calvo
Border
Salt Coates
Newton Arlosh
Wampool
Bampton
Great Orton
Little Orton
Newby West
Newby Cross
Cummersdale
Upperby
Carleton
Causewayhead
Blackdyke
Seaville
Brownrigg
South Solway Mosses
Biglands
Aikton
Wiggonby
Orton Rigg
Blackwell
Cumwhinton
Faugh
Firth
River Tweed
River Annan
River Esk
River Teviot
Ettrick Water
Moffat Water
White Esk
Rae Burn
Megget Water
Dryfe Water
Water of Milk
Kirtle Water
Wauchope Water
Tarras Water
Liddel Water
Borthwick Water
Allan Water
Slitrig Water
Ale Water
Kershope Burn
River Sark
River Lyne
R Eden
River Irthing
A7
A74(M)
A701
A708
A709
A75
A6071
A698
A689
A69
A595
A596
M6
B709
B711
B723
B7068
B7076
B7020
B724
B725
B6357
B6318
B6399
B6355
B6359
B6400
B6405
B721
B722
B7009
B6357
B6413
B5307
B5299

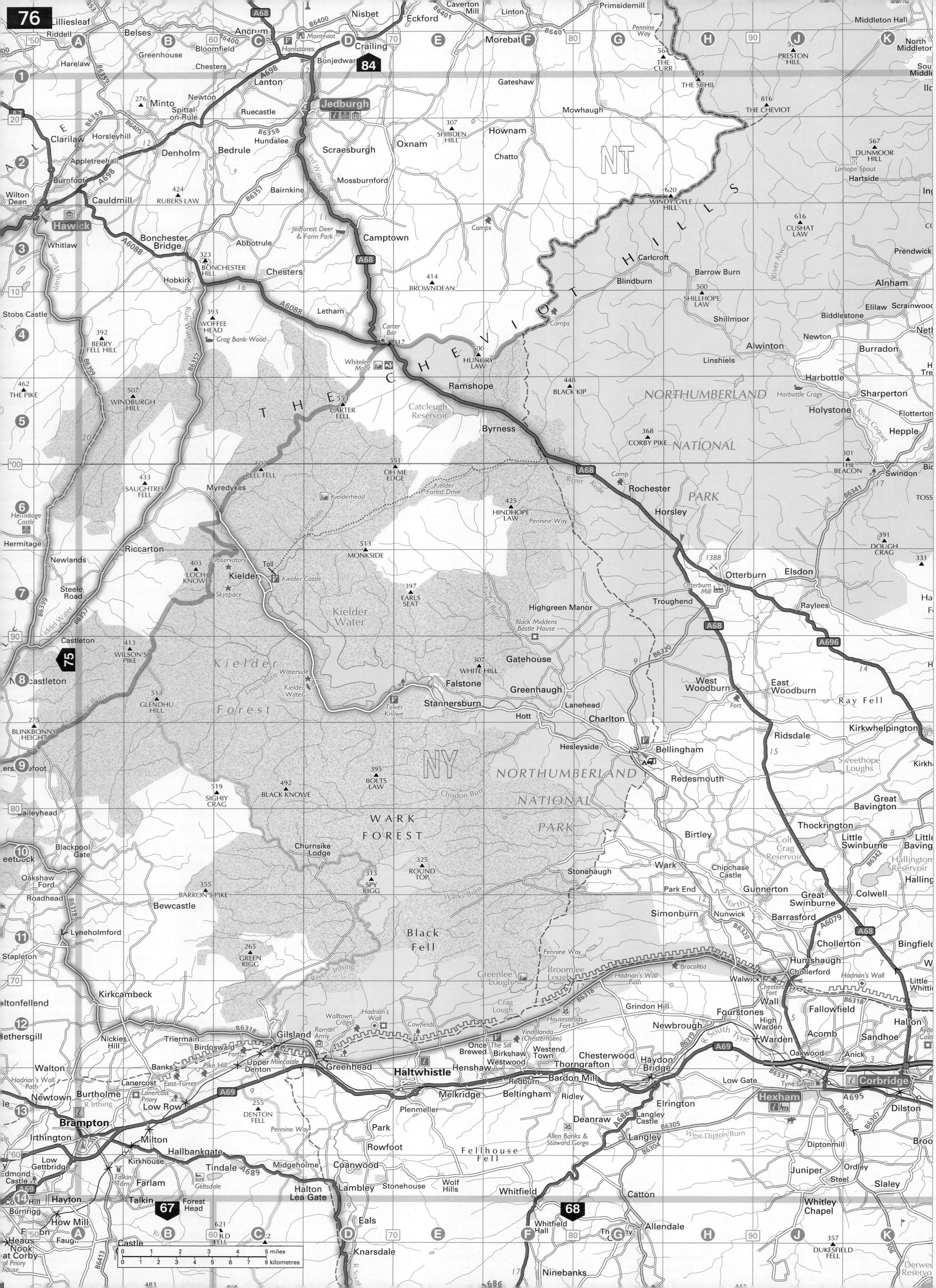

Lilliesleaf
Riddell
Belses
Ancrum
Nisbet
Eckford
Caverton Mill
Linton
Primsidemill
Middleton Hall
Bloomfield
Greenhouse
Harestanes
Monteviot
Crailing
Bonjedward
84
Morebattle
Pennine Way
THE CURR
PRESTON HILL
North Middleton
Harelaw
Chesters
Lanton
Gateshaw
THE SCHIL
Minto
Newton
Spittal-on-Rule
Ruecastle
Jedburgh
Mowhaugh
THE CHEVIOT
Clarilaw
Horsleyhill
Hundalee
SHIBDEN HILL
Hownam
DUNMOOR HILL
Denholm
Bedrule
Scraesburgh
Oxnam
Chatto
NT
Appletreehall
Burnfoot
Wilton Dean
Caudmill
Hawick
RUBERS LAW
Bairnkine
Mossburnford
WINDY GYLE HILL
Linhope Spout
Hartside
CUSHAT LAW
Whitlaw
Bonchester Bridge
Abbotrule
Jedforest Deer & Farm Park
Camptown
Camps
Prendwick
BONCHESTER HILL
Chesters
Hobkirk
BROWNDEAN
Carlcroft
Blindburn
Barrow Burn
SHILLHOPE LAW
Alnham
Stobs Castle
WOFFEE HEAD
Letham
Carter Bar
Shillmoor
Eilaw
Biddlestone
Crag Bank Wood
BERRY FELL HILL
HUNGRY LAW
Whitelee Moor
Alwinton
Newton
Burradon
Linshiels
Harbottle
THE CHEVIOT HILLS
THE PIKE
WINDBURGH HILL
CARTER FELL
Ramshope
BLACK KIP
NORTHUMBERLAND NATIONAL PARK
Harbottle Crags
Sharperton
Holystone
Catcleugh Reservoir
Byrness
CORBY PIKE
River Coquet
Hepple
PEEL FELL
OH ME EDGE
THE BEACON
Swindon
SAUGHTREE FELL
Myredykes
Kielderhead
Kielder Forest Drive
River Rede
Rochester
Hermitage Castle
HINDHOPE LAW
Horsley
Pennine Way
Hermitage
Riccarton
MONKSIDE
DOUGH CRAG
Newlands
LOCH KNOWE
Observatory
Kielder
Toll
Kielder Castle
Skyspace
Otterburn
Elsdon
Steele Road
EARLS SEAT
Otterburn Mill
Troughend
Kielder Water
Highgreen Manor
Raylees
Black Middens Bastle House
Castleton
WILSON'S PIKE
75
Kielder Forest
WHITE HILL
Gatehouse
Newcastleton
Waterside
Kielder Water
Falstone
Greenhaugh
West Woodburn
East Woodburn
Ray Fell
GLENDHU HILL
Tower Knowe
Stannersburn
Hott
Lanehead
Charlton
Kirkwhelpington
Ridsdale
BLINKBONNY HEIGHT
Hesleyside
Bellingham
Sweethope Loughs
NY
BOLTS LAW
BLACK KNOWE
SIGHTY CRAG
Redesmouth
Chirdon Burn
Great Bavington
Baileyhead
WARK FOREST
Thockrington
Little Swinburne
Birtley
Colt Crag Reservoir
Hallington Reservoir
Blackpool Gate
Churnsike Lodge
ROUND TOP
Wark
Chipchase Castle
Stonehaugh
Oakshaw Ford
SPY RIGG
BARRON'S PIKE
Park End
Gunnerton
Colwell
Roadhead
Bewcastle
Wark Burn
Great Swinburne
Simonburn
Nunwick
Barrasford
Lyneholmford
Black Fell
Chollerton
Bingfield
Stapleton
GREEN RIGG
River Irthing
Pennine Way
Humshaugh
Greenlee Lough
Broomlee Lough
Brocolitia
Walwick
Chollerford
Hadrian's Wall Path
Chesters Roman Fort
Little Whittington
Kirkcambeck
Crag Lough
Grindon Hill
Wall
Fallowfield
Fourstones
Walltown Crags
Hadrian's Wall
Cawfields
Housesteads Fort
Newbrough
High Warden
Halton
Nickies Hill
Triermain
Gilsland
Roman Army Museum
Vindolanda (Chesterholm)
Warden
Acomb
Sandhoe
Birdoswald Fort
Once Brewed
The Sill
Birkshaw
Westwood
Westend Town
Chesterwood
Haydon Bridge
Oakwood
Anick
Walton
Banks
Pike Hill
Upper Denton
Milecastle
Greenhead
Haltwhistle
Henshaw
Thorngrafton
Hadrian's Wall Path
Lanercost
Lanercost Priory
East Turret
Redburn
Bardon Mill
Low Gate
Tyne Green
Corbridge
Newtown
Burtholme
River Irthing
Low Row
Melkridge
Beltingham
Ridley
Elrington
Hexham
Dilston
DENTON FELL
Plenmeller
Brampton
Deanraw
Langley Castle
Irthington
Milton
Pennine Way
Park
Allen Banks & Staward Gorge
Langley
West Dipton Burn
Rowfoot
Fellhouse Fell
Diptonmill
Hallbankgate
Tindale
Midgeholme
Coanwood
Low Gettbridge
Kirkhouse
Talkin Tarn
Geltsdale
Juniper
Ordley
Edmond Castle
Farlam
Lambley
Stonehouse
Wolf Hills
Steel
Slaley
Halton Lea Gate
Whitfield
Catton
Hayton
Talkin
67
Forest Head
68
Whitley Chapel
Burnrigg
How Mill
Eals
Whitfield Hall
Allendale
OLD FELL
DUKESFIELD FELL
Faugh
Heads Nook
Castle
Knarsdale
Warwick
at Corby
Corby Priory House
Ninebanks
Derwent Reservoir
5 miles
8 kilometres

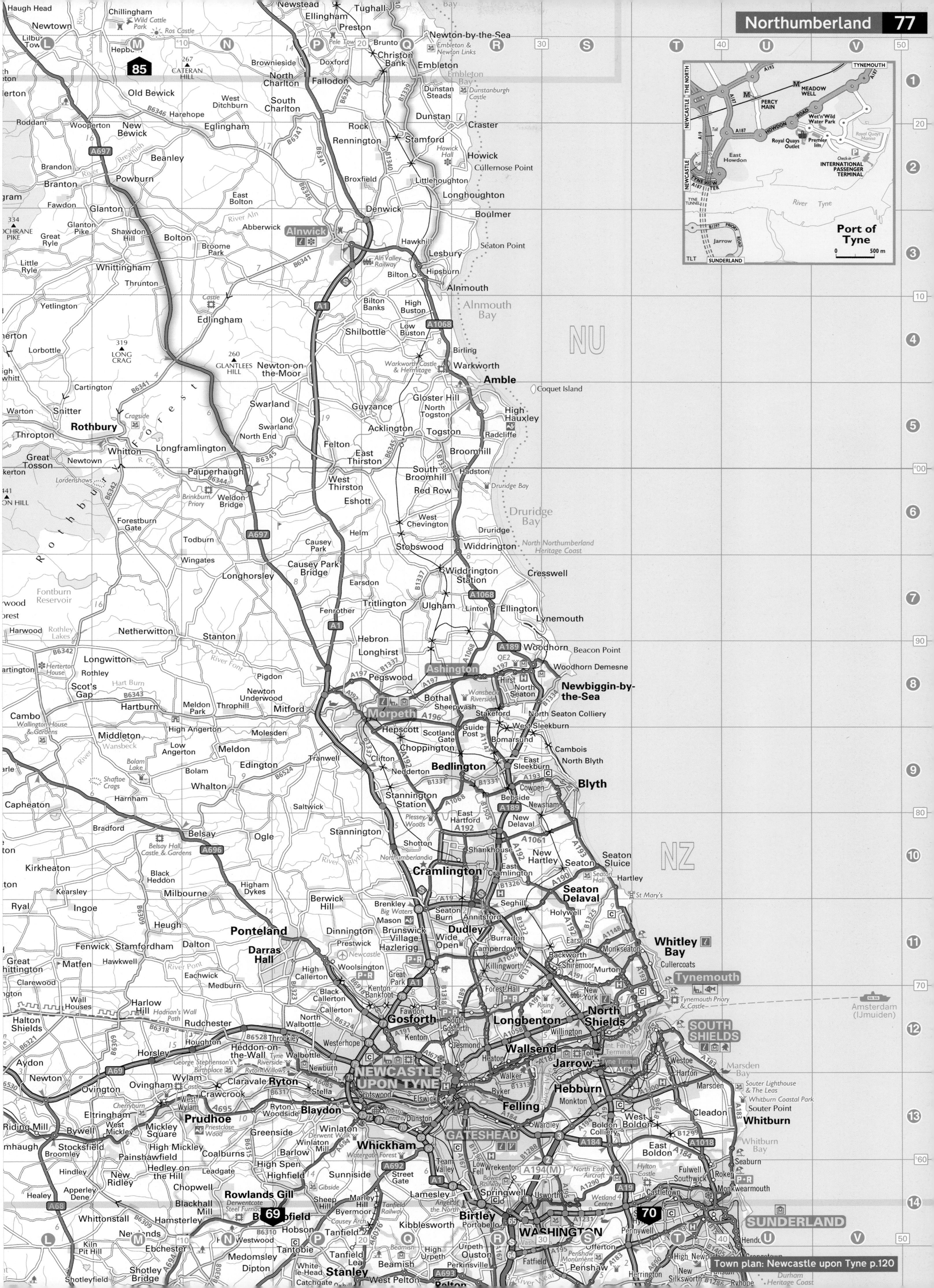

Port of Tyne

NU

NZ

Town plan: Newcastle upon Tyne p.120

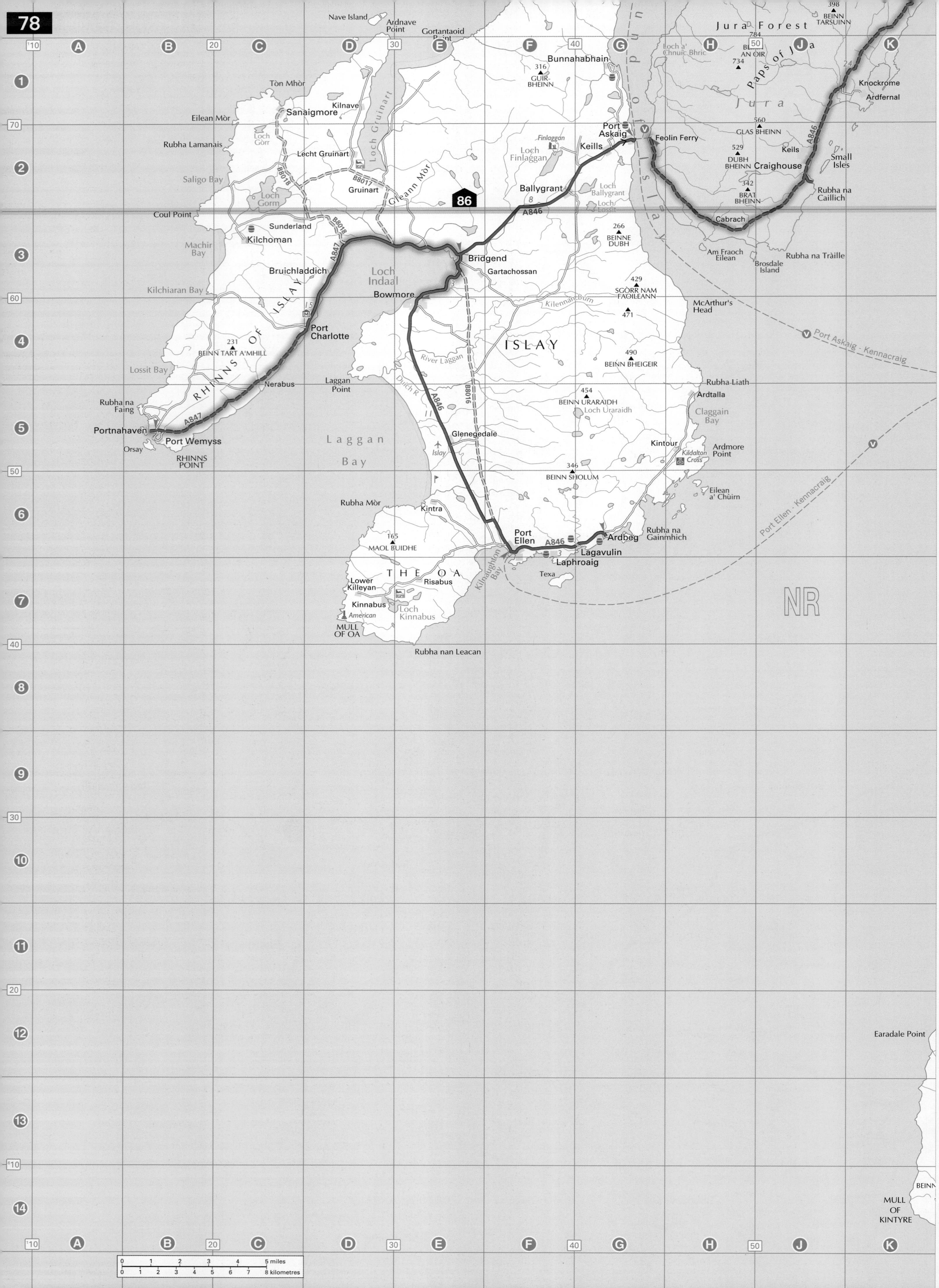
Nave Island
Ardnave Point
Gortantaoid Point
Jura Forest
398 BEINN TARSUINN
784 BEINN AN OIR
734
Paps of Jura
Loch a' Chnuic Bhric
Bunnahabhain
316 GUIR-BHEINN
Tòn Mhòr
Kilnave
Sanaigmore
Eilean Mòr
Loch Gorm
Rubha Lamanais
Lecht Gruinart
Loch Gruinart
Saligo Bay
B8018
B8017
Gruinart
Gleann Mòr
Loch Finlaggan
Finlaggan
Keills
Port Askaig
Feolin Ferry
Jura
560 GLAS BHEINN
529 DUBH BHEINN
Craighouse
Keills
Small Isles
342 BRAT BHEINN
Rubha na Caillich
Knockrome
Ardfernal
A846
Ballygrant
Loch Ballygrant
Loch Lossit
86
Coul Point
Sunderland
Kilchoman
Machir Bay
A846
266 BEINNE DUBH
Cabrach
Am Fraoch Eilean
Brosdale Island
Rubha na Tràille
Sound of Islay
Bridgend
Gartachossan
Loch Indaal
Bruichladdich
Kilchiaran Bay
A847
Bowmore
429 SGÒRR NAM FAOILEANN
471
Kilennan Burn
McArthur's Head
Port Charlotte
RHINNS OF ISLAY
231 BEINN TART A'MHILL
ISLAY
490 BEINN BHEIGEIR
Port Askaig - Kennacraig
Lossit Bay
River Laggan
Nerabus
Laggan Point
Duich R.
B8016
A846
Rubha Liath
Ardtalla
454 BEINN URARAIDH
Loch Uraraidh
Rubha na Faing
Claggain Bay
Portnahaven
A847
Port Wemyss
Orsay
RHINNS POINT
Laggan Bay
Glenegedale
Islay
Kintour
Kildalton Cross
Ardmore Point
346 BEINN SHOLUM
Eilean a' Chùirn
Rubha Mòr
Kintra
Port Ellen - Kennacraig
165 MAOL BUIDHE
Port Ellen
A846
Ardbeg
Rubha na Gainmhich
Lagavulin
Laphroaig
Texa
Kilnaughton Bay
THE OA
Lower Killeyan
Risabus
Kinnabus
Loch Kinnabus
American
MULL OF OA
Rubha nan Leacan
NR
Earadale Point
BEINN
MULL OF KINTYRE
A B C D E F G H J K
1 2 3 4 5 6 7 8 9 10 11 12 13 14
10 20 30 40 50
70 60 50 40 30 20 10
0 1 2 3 4 5 miles
0 1 2 3 4 5 6 7 8 kilometres

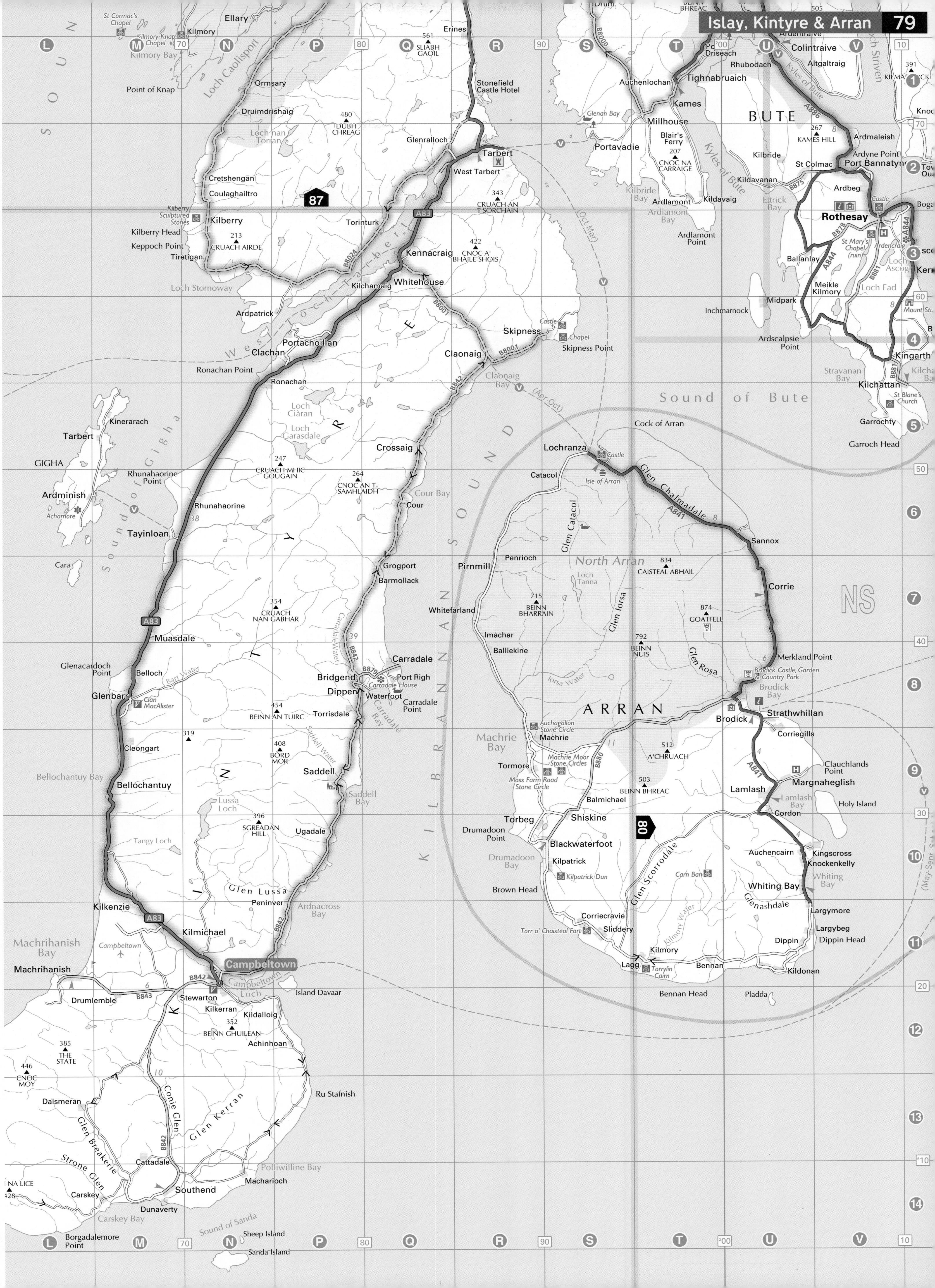

St Cormac's Chapel
Ellary
Kilmory
Kilmory Knap Chapel
Kilmory Bay
Loch Caolisport
Erines
561 SLIABH GAOIL
Ormsary
Point of Knap
Stonefield Castle Hotel
Druimdrishaig
480 DUBH CHREAG
Loch nan Torran
Glenralloch
Tarbert
West Tarbert
Cretshengan
Coulaghailtro
87
343 CRUACH AN T SORCHAIN
Kilberry Sculptured Stones
Kilberry
Kilberry Head
Keppoch Point
Tiretigan
213 CRUACH AIRDE
Torinturk
A83
422 CNOC A' BHAILE-SHOIS
Kennacraig
West Loch Tarbert
B8024
Loch Stornoway
Kilchamaig
Whitehouse
B8001
Ardpatrick
Skipness
Castle
Chapel
Skipness Point
Portachoillan
Clachan
Claonaig
Ronachan Point
Ronachan
Claonaig Bay
(Apr-Oct)
(Oct-Mar)
Loch Ciaran
Loch Garasdale
Kinerarach
Tarbert
GIGHA
Sound of Gigha
Rhunahaorine Point
247 CRUACH MHIC GOUGAIN
264 CNOC AN T-SAMHLAIDH
Crossaig
Ardminish
Achamore
Rhunahaorine
Cour Bay
Cour
Tayinloan
Cara
KINTYRE
Grogport
Barmollack
354 CRUACH NAN GABHAR
Muasdale
Carradale Water
B842
Carradale
B879
Port Righ
Carradale House
Glenacardoch Point
Belloch
Barr Water
Bridgend
Dippen
Waterfoot
Carradale Point
Carradale Bay
Glenbarr
Clan MacAlister
454 BEINN AN TUIRC
Torrisdale
319
Cleongart
408 BORD MOR
Saddell Water
Bellochantuy Bay
Bellochantuy
Saddell
Saddell Bay
Lussa Loch
396 SGREADAN HILL
Ugadale
Tangy Loch
Glen Lussa
Peninver
Ardnacross Bay
Kilkenzie
Kilmichael
Machrihanish Bay
Campbeltown
Machrihanish
B842
B843
Campbeltown Loch
Island Davaar
Drumlemble
Stewarton
Kilkerran
Kildalloig
352 BEINN GHUILEAN
Achinhoan
385 THE STATE
446 CNOC MOY
Conie Glen
Glen Kerran
Ru Stafnish
Dalsmeran
Glen Breakerie
Strone Glen
Cattadale
Polliwilline Bay
Southend
Macharioch
Carskey
Dunaverty
Carskey Bay
Sound of Sanda
Sheep Island
Sanda Island
Borgadalemore Point
Drum
B8000
Colintraive
Pol Driseach
Rhubodach
Altgaltraig
Auchenlochan
Tighnabruaich
Kyles of Bute
Loch Striven
Kames
Glenan Bay
Millhouse
BUTE
A886
Blair's Ferry
207 CNOC NA CARRAIGE
267 KAMES HILL
Ardmaleish
Portavadie
Kilbride
Ardyne Point
St Colmac
Port Bannatyne
Kildavanan
Kilbride Bay
Ardlamont
Kildavaig
Ettrick Bay
Ardbeg
Ardlamont Bay
Rothesay
Castle
Ardlamont Point
B878
St Mary's Chapel (ruin)
Ardencraig
Ballanlay
A844
B881
Loch Ascog
Meikle Kilmory
Loch Fad
Midpark
Inchmarnock
Ardscalpsie Point
Kingarth
Stravanan Bay
Kilchattan
St Blane's Church
Sound of Bute
Garrochty
Garroch Head
Cock of Arran
Lochranza
Castle
Catacol
Isle of Arran
Glen Chalmadale
A841
Glen Catacol
KILBRANNAN SOUND
Sannox
Penrioch
Pirnmill
North Arran
834 CAISTEAL ABHAIL
Loch Tanna
Corrie
NS
715 BEINN BHARRAIN
Glen Iorsa
874 GOATFELL
Whitefarland
Imachar
Balliekine
792 BEINN NUIS
Glen Rosa
Merkland Point
Brodick Castle, Garden & Country Park
Brodick Bay
Iorsa Water
ARRAN
Strathwhillan
Brodick
Auchagallon Stone Circle
Machrie
Machrie Bay
Corriegills
512 A'CHRUACH
Machrie Moor Stone Circles
Tormore
B880
Clauchlands Point
Moss Farm Road Stone Circle
503 BEINN BHREAC
Margnaheglish
Lamlash
Lamlash Bay
Balmichael
Holy Island
Torbeg
Shiskine
80
Cordon
Drumadoon Point
Blackwaterfoot
Auchencairn
Kingscross
Knockenkelly
Kilpatrick
Drumadoon Bay
Glen Scorrodale
Carn Ban
Kilpatrick Dun
Whiting Bay
Brown Head
Glenashdale
Largymore
Corriecravie
Kilmory Water
Torr a' Chaisteal Fort
Sliddery
Largybeg
Dippin
Dippin Head
Kilmory
Lagg
Torrylin Cairn
Bennan
Kildonan
Bennan Head
Pladda
(May-Sept)

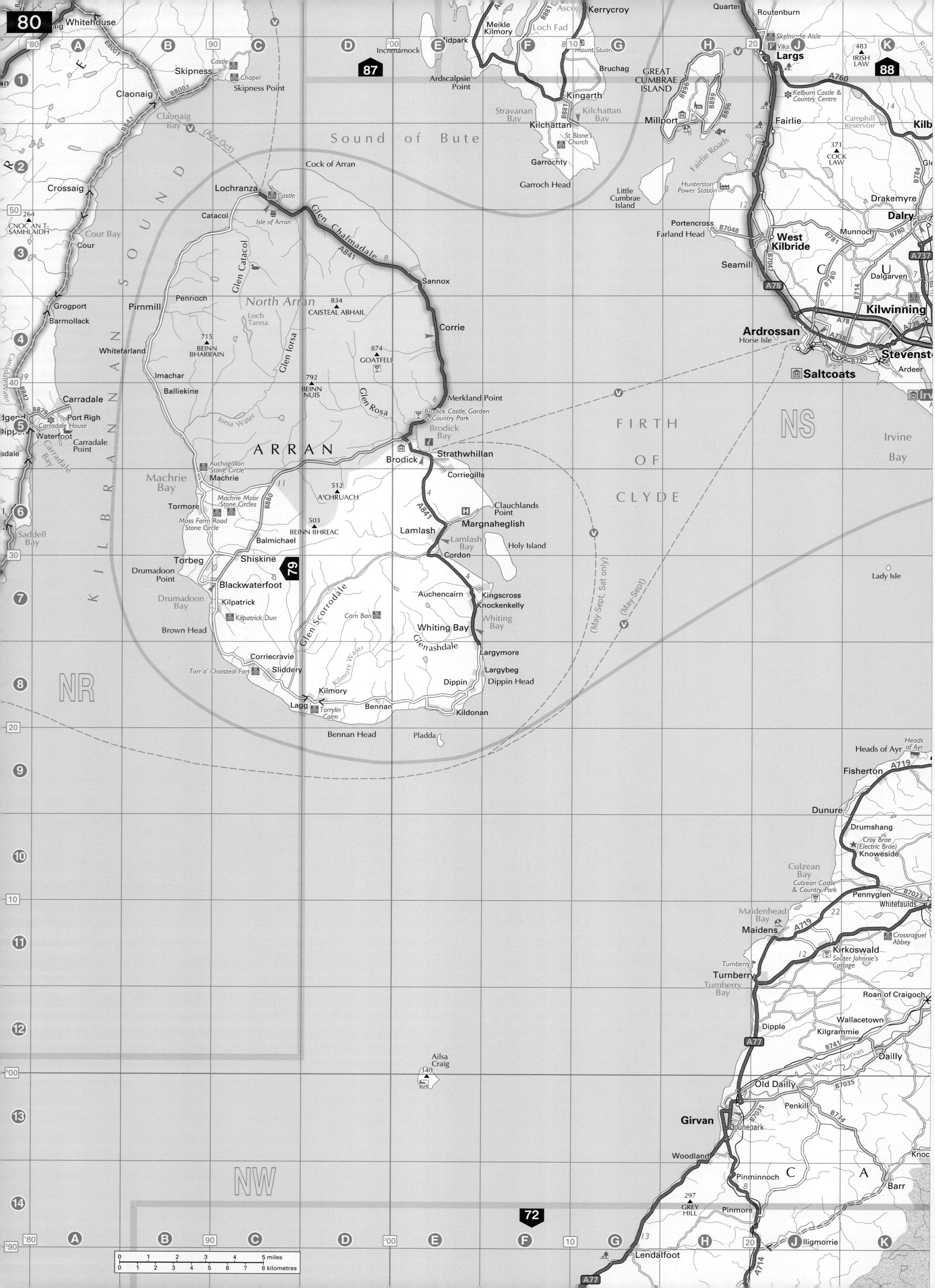
Whitehouse
Skipness
Castle
Chapel
Skipness Point
Claonaig
Claonaig Bay
(Apr-Oct)
Crossaig
CNOC AN T-SAMHLAIDH
Cour Bay
Cour
Grogport
Barmollack
Whitefarland
Pirnmill
Carradale
Port Righ
Carradale House
Waterfoot
Carradale Point
Carradale Bay
Saddell Bay
K I L B R A N N A N   S O U N D
Sound of Bute
Inchmarnock
Ardscalpsie Point
Meikle Kilmory
Loch Fad
Kerrycroy
Mount Stuart
Bruchag
Kingarth
Stravanan Bay
Kilchattan
Kilchattan Bay
St Blane's Church
Garrochty
Garroch Head
GREAT CUMBRAE ISLAND
Millport
Little Cumbrae Island
Fairlie Roads
Hunterston Power Station
Portencross
Farland Head
Seamill
West Kilbride
Quarter
Routenburn
Skelmorlie Aisle
Vikingar!
Largs
IRISH LAW
Kelburn Castle & Country Centre
Fairlie
Camphill Reservoir
COCK LAW
Drakemyre
Dalry
Munnoch
Dalgarven
Kilwinning
Ardrossan
Horse Isle
Saltcoats
Stevenston
Ardeer
Cock of Arran
Lochranza
Castle
Isle of Arran
Catacol
Glen Catacol
Glen Chalmadale
Sannox
North Arran
CAISTEAL ABHAIL
Loch Tanna
Penrioch
BEINN BHARRAIN
Glen Iorsa
Corrie
GOATFELL
Imachar
Balliekine
BEINN NUIS
Glen Rosa
Merkland Point
Iorsa Water
Brodick Castle, Garden & Country Park
Brodick Bay
A R R A N
Brodick
Strathwhillan
Corriegills
Auchagallon Stone Circle
Machrie Bay
Machrie
A'CHRUACH
Machrie Moor Stone Circles
Tormore
Moss Farm Road Stone Circle
BEINN BHREAC
Clauchlands Point
Margnaheglish
Lamlash
Lamlash Bay
Holy Island
Cordon
Balmichael
Torbeg
Shiskine
Drumadoon Point
Blackwaterfoot
Drumadoon Bay
Kilpatrick
Kilpatrick Dun
Brown Head
Glen Scorrodale
Auchencairn
Kingscross
Knockenkelly
Carn Ban
Whiting Bay
Glenashdale
Largymore
Largybeg
Dippin Head
Dippin
Corriecravie
Sliddery
Torr a' Chaisteal Fort
Kilmory Water
Kilmory
Lagg
Torrylin Cairn
Bennan
Kildonan
Bennan Head
Pladda
F I R T H   O F   C L Y D E
(May-Sept, Sat only)
(May-Sept)
Irvine Bay
Lady Isle
NS
NR
NW
Heads of Ayr
Fisherton
Dunure
Drumshang
Cray Brae (Electric Brae)
Knoweside
Culzean Bay
Culzean Castle & Country Park
Pennyglen
Whitefaulds
Maidenhead Bay
Maidens
Crossraguel Abbey
Kirkoswald
Souter Johnnie's Cottage
Turnberry
Turnberry Bay
Roan of Craigoch
Dipple
Wallacetown
Kilgrammie
Water of Girvan
Dailly
Ailsa Craig
Old Dailly
Penkill
Girvan
Dounepark
Woodland
Pinminnoch
Barr
GREY HILL
Pinmore
Lendalfoot
Illigmorrie
87
88
79
72
0 1 2 3 4 5 miles
0 1 2 3 4 5 6 7 8 kilometres

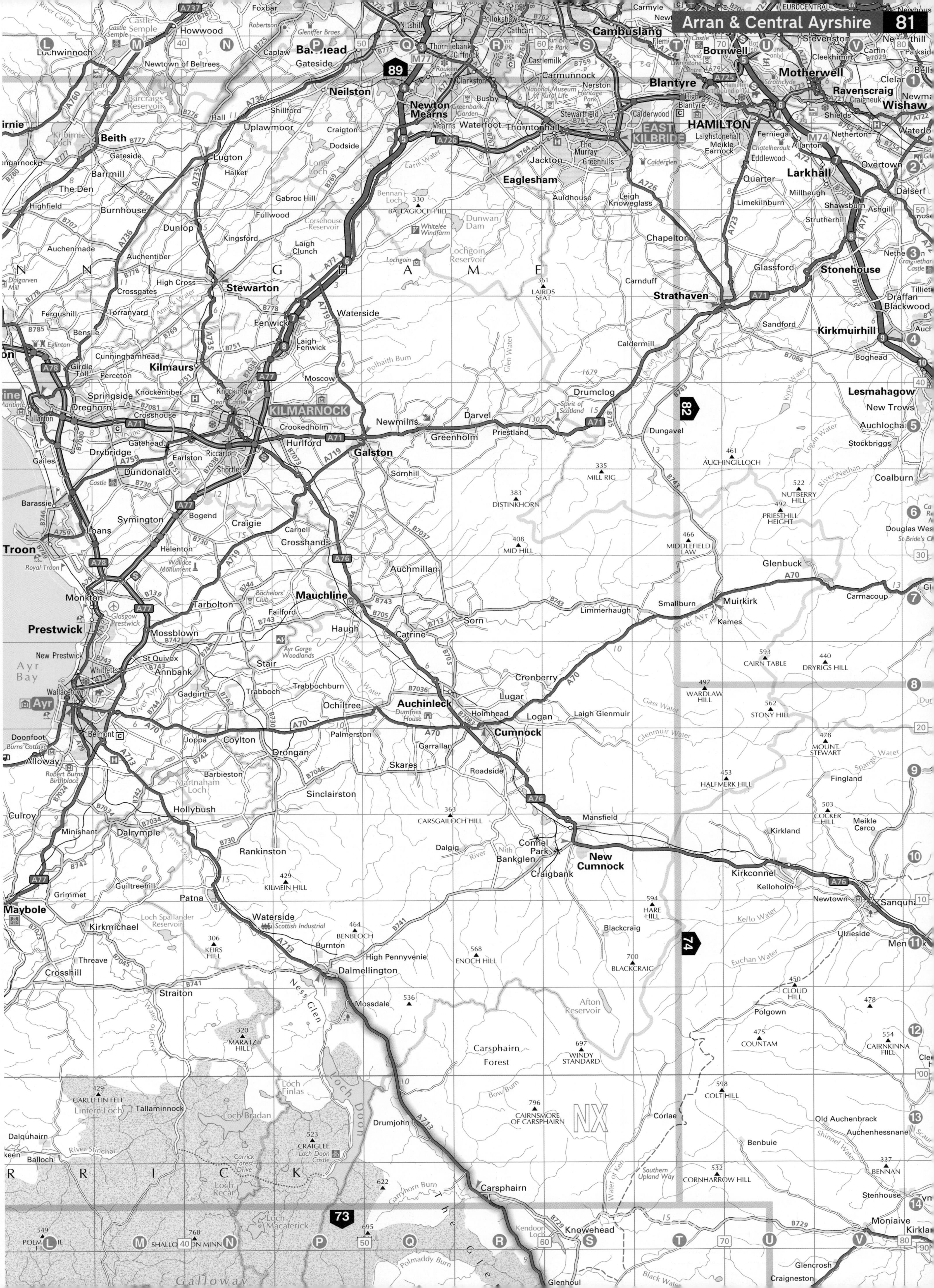

Lochwinnoch
Howwood
Castle Semple
Barrhead
Gateside
Neilston
Newton Mearns
Busby
Clarkston
Giffnock
Thornliebank
Cathcart
Castlemilk
Carmunnock
Cambuslang
Bothwell
Blantyre
Motherwell
Ravenscraig
Wishaw
Hamilton
East Kilbride
Eaglesham
Jackton
Auldhouse
Larkhall
Stonehouse
Strathaven
Chapelton
Glassford
Sandford
Kirkmuirhill
Lesmahagow
New Trows
Auchlochan
Coalburn
Beith
Barrmill
Burnhouse
Dunlop
Lugton
Uplawmoor
Shillford
Stewarton
Fenwick
Kilmaurs
Kilmarnock
Crosshouse
Springside
Dreghorn
Irvine
Drybridge
Dundonald
Riccarton
Hurlford
Galston
Newmilns
Darvel
Greenholm
Priestland
Drumclog
Symington
Troon
Loans
Craigie
Crosshands
Mauchline
Tarbolton
Monkton
Prestwick
Mossblown
Annbank
Stair
Catrine
Sorn
Muirkirk
Glenbuck
Ayr
Ayr Bay
Alloway
Coylton
Drongan
Ochiltree
Auchinleck
Cumnock
Lugar
Cronberry
Logan
Dalrymple
Hollybush
Patna
Maybole
Kirkmichael
Crosshill
Straiton
Waterside
Dalmellington
New Cumnock
Kirkconnel
Sanquhar
Carsphairn
Loch Doon
Carsphairn Forest
Afton Reservoir
Moniaive
Knowehead
NX

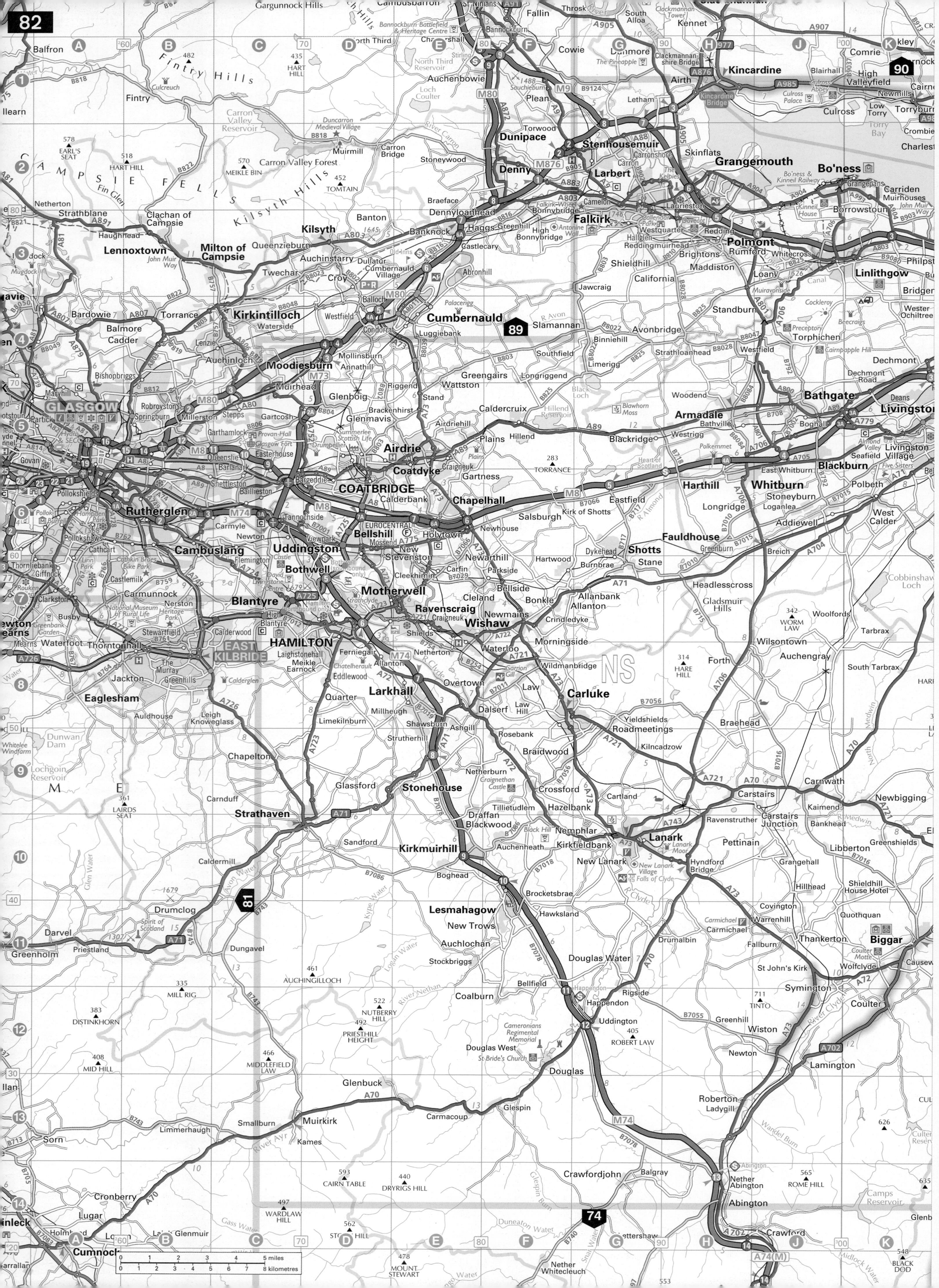
Gargunnock Hills
Balfron
Fintry Hills
Fintry
Culcreuch
Killearn
Carron Valley Reservoir
Duncarron Medieval Village
Carron Valley Forest
578 EARL'S SEAT
518 HART HILL
570 MEIKLE BIN
452 TOMTAIN
482
435 HART HILL
Campsie Fells
Fin Glen
Kilsyth Hills
Netherton
Strathblane
Clachan of Campsie
Haughhead
Lennoxtown
Milton of Campsie
Queenzieburn
Kilsyth
Banton
Mugdock
Bardowie
Torrance
Balmore
Cadder
Kirkintilloch
Waterside
Lenzie
Auchinloch
Bishopbriggs
Moodiesburn
Annathill
Mollinsburn
Muirhead
Robroyston
Springburn
Millerston
Stepps
Gartcosh
Glenboig
Glenmavis
GLASGOW
Partick
Govan
Garthamlock
Provan Hall
Queenslie
Barlanark
Easterhouse
Shettleston
Baillieston
Pollokshields
Rutherglen
Carmyle
Cambuslang
Cathcart
Pollokshaws
Thornliebank
Giffnock
Linn Park
Castlemilk
Carmunnock
Clarkston
Busby
Nerston
National Museum of Rural Life
Stewartfield
Mearns
Waterfoot
Thorntonhall
EAST KILBRIDE
The Murray
Greenhills
Jackton
Eaglesham
Auldhouse
Calderglen
Leigh Knoweglass
Dunwan Dam
Whitelee Windfarm
Lochgoin Reservoir
Chapelton
361 LAIRDS SEAT
Carnduff
Strathaven
Caldermill
1679
Drumclog
Spirit of Scotland
Darvel
Priestland
Greenholm
Dungavel
335 MILL RIG
383 DISTINKHORN
408 MID HILL
466 MIDDLEFIELD LAW
461 AUCHINGILLOCH
522 NUTBERRY HILL
492 PRIESTHILL HEIGHT
Glenbuck
Muirkirk
Smallburn
Limmerhaugh
Kames
Sorn
Cronberry
Lugar
Holmhead
Logan
Glenmuir
Cumnock
593 CAIRN TABLE
440 DRYRIGS HILL
497 WARDLAW HILL
562
478 MOUNT STEWART
Carmacoup
Glespin
Douglas
Douglas West
St Bride's Church
Cameronians Regimental Memorial
Coalburn
Bellfield
Stockbriggs
Auchlochan
New Trows
Lesmahagow
Douglas Water
Happendon
Uddington
405 ROBERT LAW
Rigside
Crawfordjohn
Balgray
Abington
Nether Abington
Crawford
Roberton
Ladygill
Lamington
Wiston
Newton
Greenhill
711 TINTO
Symington
Coulter
Biggar
Wolfclyde
Thankerton
Quothquan
Covington
Carmichael
Warrenhill
Fallburn
St John's Kirk
565 ROME HILL
626
548 BLACK DOD
Camps Reservoir
Campsie
Cumbernauld
Condorrat
Luggiebank
Westfield
Palacerigg
Abronhill
Croy
Twechar
Auchinstarry
Dullatur
Cumbernauld Village
Castlecary
Banknock
Haggs
Dennyloanhead
Braeface
Denny
Dunipace
Torwood
Stoneywood
Carron Bridge
Muirmill
Stenhousemuir
Larbert
Carron
Carronshore
Falkirk
Camelon
Falkirk Wheel
Bonnybridge
High Bonnybridge
Greenhill
Antonine Wall
Westquarter
Redding
Reddingmuirhead
Hallglen
Brightons
Polmont
Rumford
Whitecross
Shieldhill
California
Maddiston
Loany
Linlithgow
Grangemouth
Skinflats
Bo'ness
Bo'ness & Kinneil Railway
Kinneil House
Borrowstoun
Grangepans
Carriden
Muirhouses
Airth
Letham
Plean
Bannockburn
Bannockburn Battlefield & Heritage Centre
St Ninians
Chartershall
Fallin
Throsk
Cowie
Dunmore
The Pineapple
South Alloa
Kennet
Clackmannan
Clackmannanshire Bridge
Kincardine
Kincardine Bridge
Blairhall
High Valleyfield
Culross
Culross Palace
Low Torry
Torry Bay
Torryburn
Newmills
Comrie
North Third Reservoir
North Third
Auchenbowie
Loch Coulter
Jawcraig
Slamannan
Avonbridge
Binniehill
Standburn
Limerigg
Southfield
Greengairs
Longriggend
Wattston
Riggend
Stand
Brackenhirst
Airdriehill
Caldercruix
Hillend Reservoir
Black Loch
Blawhorn Moss
Plains
Hillend
Airdrie
Coatdyke
Craigneuk
Gartness
COATBRIDGE
Calderbank
Chapelhall
Drumpellier
Summerlee Scottish Life
Bargeddie
Tannochside
Viewpark
Uddingston
Bothwell
Bellshill
Holytown
Mossend
New Stevenston
Newarthill
Carfin
Cleekhimin
Motherwell
Ravenscraig
Craigneuk
Wishaw
Shields
Cleland
Newmains
Bellside
Parkside
Bonkle
Hartwood
Salsburgh
Kirk of Shotts
Eastfield
Newhouse
283 TORRANCE
Blackridge
Westrigg
Armadale
Bathville
Polkemmet
Harthill
Whitburn
East Whitburn
Blackburn
Longridge
Stoneyburn
Loganlea
Addiewell
Fauldhouse
Greenburn
Breich
West Calder
Polbeth
Seafield
Livingston Village
Livingston
Bathgate
Boghall
Deans
Dechmont
Dechmont Road
Torphichen
Westfield
Woodend
Preceptory
Cockleroy
Beecraigs
Cairnpapple Hill
Wester Ochiltree
Dykehead
Shotts
Stane
Burnbrae
Headlesscross
Allanbank
Allanton
Crindledyke
Gladsmuir Hills
342 WORM LAW
Woolfords
Cobbinshaw Loch
Tarbrax
Wilsontown
Auchengray
South Tarbrax
Forth
314 HARE HILL
Morningside
Wildmanbridge
Waterloo
Overtown
Garrion Bridge
Law
Carluke
Dalserf
Yieldshields
Roadmeetings
Kilncadzow
Braehead
Rosebank
Braidwood
Ashgill
Shawsburn
Larkhall
Millheugh
Netherton
Allanton
Ferniegair
Chatelherault
Eddlewood
Quarter
Limekilnburn
Strutherhill
HAMILTON
Laighstonehall
Meikle Earnock
Blantyre
Calderwood
High Blantyre
Flemington
Newton
Stonehouse
Glassford
Sandford
Kirkmuirhill
Boghead
Nethrburn
Craignethan Castle
Crossford
Tillietudlem
Hazelbank
Draffan
Blackwood
Auchenheath
Black Hill
Nemphlar
Kirkfieldbank
Cartland
Lanark
Lanark Moor
New Lanark
New Lanark Village
Falls of Clyde
Hyndford Bridge
Brocketsbrae
Hawksland
Drumalbin
Ravenstruther
Carstairs
Carstairs Junction
Pettinain
Grangehall
Libberton
Greenshields
Hillhead
Shieldhill House Hotel
Carnwath
Kaimend
Bankhead
Newbigging
NS
Auchenheath

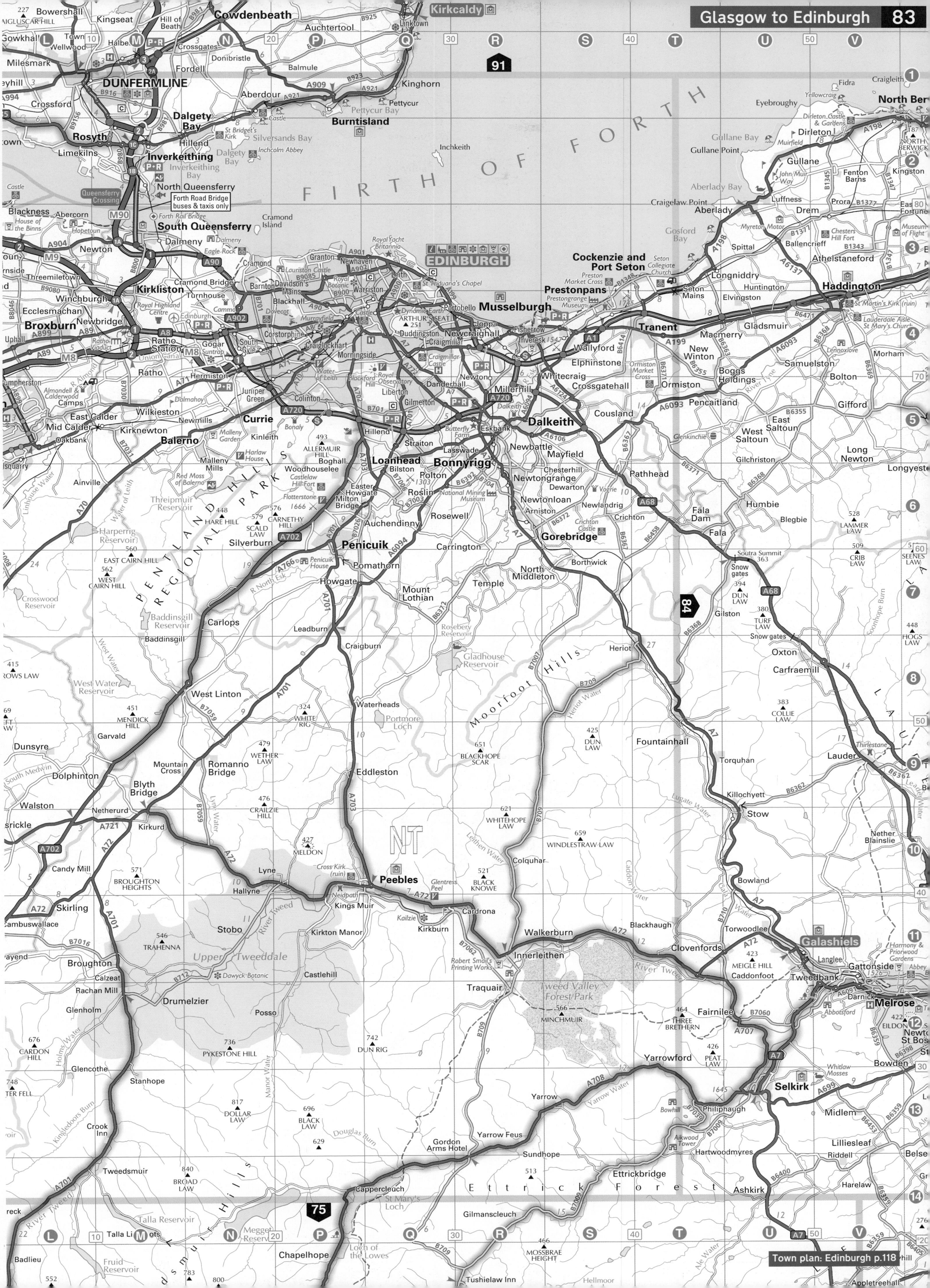
Kirkcaldy
Cowdenbeath
Auchtertool
Kingseat
Bowershall
Hill of Beath
Halbeath
Crossgates
Donibristle
Balmule
Linktown
Wellwood
Milesmark
DUNFERMLINE
Fordell
Aberdour
Kinghorn
Pettycur
Pettycur Bay
Burntisland
Crossford
Dalgety Bay
Castle
St Bridget's Kirk
Silversands Bay
Inchcolm Abbey
Rosyth
Limekilns
Hillend
Inverkeithing
Dalgety Bay
Inverkeithing Bay
Inchkeith
FIRTH OF FORTH
North Queensferry
Queensferry Crossing
Forth Road Bridge buses & taxis only
Forth Rail Bridge
Blackness
Abercorn
House of the Binns
Hopetoun
South Queensferry
Cramond Island
Dalmeny
Newton
Eagle Rock
Royal Yacht Britannia
EDINBURGH
Granton
Newhaven
Leith
Cramond
Lauriston Castle
Cramond Bridge
Barnton
Davidson's Mains
Royal Botanic
Warriston
St Triduana's Chapel
Threemiletown
Kirkliston
Winchburgh
Turnhouse
Blackhall
Portobello
Musselburgh
Ecclesmachan
Royal Highland Centre
Edinburgh
Dovecot
Murrayfield
Castle
Dynamic Earth
ARTHUR'S SEAT 251
Joppa
Broxburn
Newbridge
Uphall
Corstorphine
Duddingston
Newcraighall
Craigmillar
Craigmillar Castle
Fisherrow
Inveresk
Ratho Viaduct
Ratho Station
Gogar
Suntrap
South Gyle
Craiglockhart
Morningside
Union Canal
Ratho
Hermiston
Water of Leith
Blackford Hill
Royal Observatory
Liberton
Danderhall
Newton
Whitecraig
Millerhill
Juniper Green
Colinton
Gilmerton
Almondell & Calderwood Camps
Dalmahoy
Wilkieston
Currie
Newmills
Bonaly
East Calder
Mid Calder
Oakbank
Kirknewton
Balerno
Malleny Garden
Kinleith
Hillend
Butterfly Farm
Eskbank
Dalkeith
Straiton
Lasswade
Harlaw House
493 ALLERMUIR HILL
Boghall
Loanhead
Bilston
Bonnyrigg
Newbattle
Mayfield
Malleny Mills
Ainville
Red Moss of Balerno
Woodhouselee
Castlelaw Hill Fort
Easter Howgate
Milton Bridge
Polton
Roslin
1303
National Mining Museum
Newtongrange
Dewarton
Chesterhill
Vogrie
Newtonloan
Arniston
Newlandrig
Crichton
Crichton Castle
Gorebridge
Threipmuir Reservoir
Flotterstone
1666
448 HARE HILL
579 SCALD LAW
576 CARNETHY HILL
PENTLAND HILLS REGIONAL PARK
Harperrig Reservoir
Silverburn
Auchendinny
Rosewell
Penicuik
Carrington
560 EAST CAIRN HILL
562 WEST CAIRN HILL
Penicuik House
Pomathorn
Howgate
R North Esk
North Middleton
Borthwick
Temple
Mount Lothian
Crosswood Reservoir
Baddinsgill Reservoir
Baddinsgill
Carlops
Leadburn
Rosebery Reservoir
Craigburn
Gladhouse Reservoir
Heriot
Moorfoot Hills
415 ROWS LAW
West Water Reservoir
West Linton
451 MENDICK HILL
Garvald
324 WHITE RIG
Waterheads
Portmore Loch
425 DUN LAW
Fountainhall
651 BLACKHOPE SCAR
Dunsyre
479 WETHER LAW
Mountain Cross
Romanno Bridge
Dolphinton
Eddleston
Blyth Bridge
Walston
Netherurd
Kirkurd
476 CRAILZIE HILL
621 WHITEHOPE LAW
659 WINDLESTRAW LAW
NT
427 MELDON
Colquhar
Candy Mill
571 BROUGHTON HEIGHTS
Lyne
Hallyne
Cross Kirk (ruin)
Peebles
Glentress Peel
521 BLACK KNOWE
Neidpath
Kings Muir
Cardrona
Skirling
Cambuswallace
Kailzie
Kirkburn
Stobo
Kirkton Manor
Walkerburn
546 TRAHENNA
Upper Tweeddale
Innerleithen
Robert Smail's Printing Works
Broughton
Calzeat
Dawyck Botanic
Castlehill
Traquair
Rachan Mill
Drumelzier
Tweed Valley Forest Park
566 MINCHMUIR
Glenholm
Posso
676 CARDON HILL
736 PYKESTONE HILL
742 DUN RIG
Glencothe
Stanhope
748 TER FELL
817 DOLLAR LAW
696 BLACK LAW
629
Crook Inn
Gordon Arms Hotel
Yarrow Feus
Yarrow
Sundhope
Tweedsmuir
840 BROAD LAW
513
Ettrick Forest
Cappercleuch
St Mary's Loch
Talla Reservoir
Talla Linfoots
Megget Reservoir
Gilmanscleuch
Chapelhope
Loch of the Lowes
466 MOSSBRAE HEIGHT
Badlieu
Fruid Reservoir
552
783
800
Tushielaw Inn
Hellmoor
Fidra
Craigleith
Yellowcraig
Eyebrowghy
North Berwick
Dirleton Castle & Gardens
Dirleton
Gullane Bay
Muirfield
Gullane Point
Gullane
John Muir Way
Fenton Barns
Kingston
Aberlady Bay
Craigelaw Point
Aberlady
Luffness
Drem
Prora
East Fortune
Gosford Bay
Myreton Motor
Chesters Hill Fort
Museum of Flight
Ballencrieff
Spittal
Athelstaneford
Cockenzie and Port Seton
Seton Collegiate Church
Longniddry
Preston Market Cross
Prestonpans
Prestongrange Museum
1745
Seton Mains
Huntington
Haddington
Elvingston
St Martin's Kirk (ruin)
Lauderdale Aisle St Mary's Church
Tranent
Gladsmuir
Macmerry
Wallyford
New Winton
Elphinstone
Lennoxlove
Morham
Samuelston
Ormiston Market Cross
Ormiston
Boggs Holdings
Crossgatehall
Bolton
River Tyne
Cousland
Pencaitland
Gifford
Glenkinchie
East Saltoun
West Saltoun
Long Newton
Gilchriston
Longyester
Pathhead
Humbie
Blegbie
Fala Dam
Fala
528 LAMMER LAW
Soutra Summit 363
509 CRIB LAW
SEENES LAW
Snow gates
394 DUN LAW
Gilston
380 TURF LAW
Snow gates
448 HOGS LAW
Oxton
Carfraemill
383 COLLIE LAW
Torquhan
Thirlestane
Lauder
Killochyett
Lugate Water
Stow
Nether Blainslie
Bowland
Gala Water
Caddon Water
Blackhaugh
Torwoodlee
Galashiels
Clovenfords
423 MEIGLE HILL
Caddonfoot
Langlee
Harmony & Priorwood Gardens
Gattonside
Abbey
Tweedbank
1526
Darnick
Melrose
Abbotsford
Fairnilee
464 THREE BRETHREN
422 EILDON
Newtown St Boswells
426 PEAT LAW
Yarrowford
Whitlaw Mosses
Bowden
Selkirk
1645
Philiphaugh
Bowhill
Midlem
Aikwood Tower
Hartwoodmyres
Lilliesleaf
Riddell
Ettrickbridge
Ashkirk
Harelaw
Appletreehall
91
84
75

Town plan: Edinburgh p.118

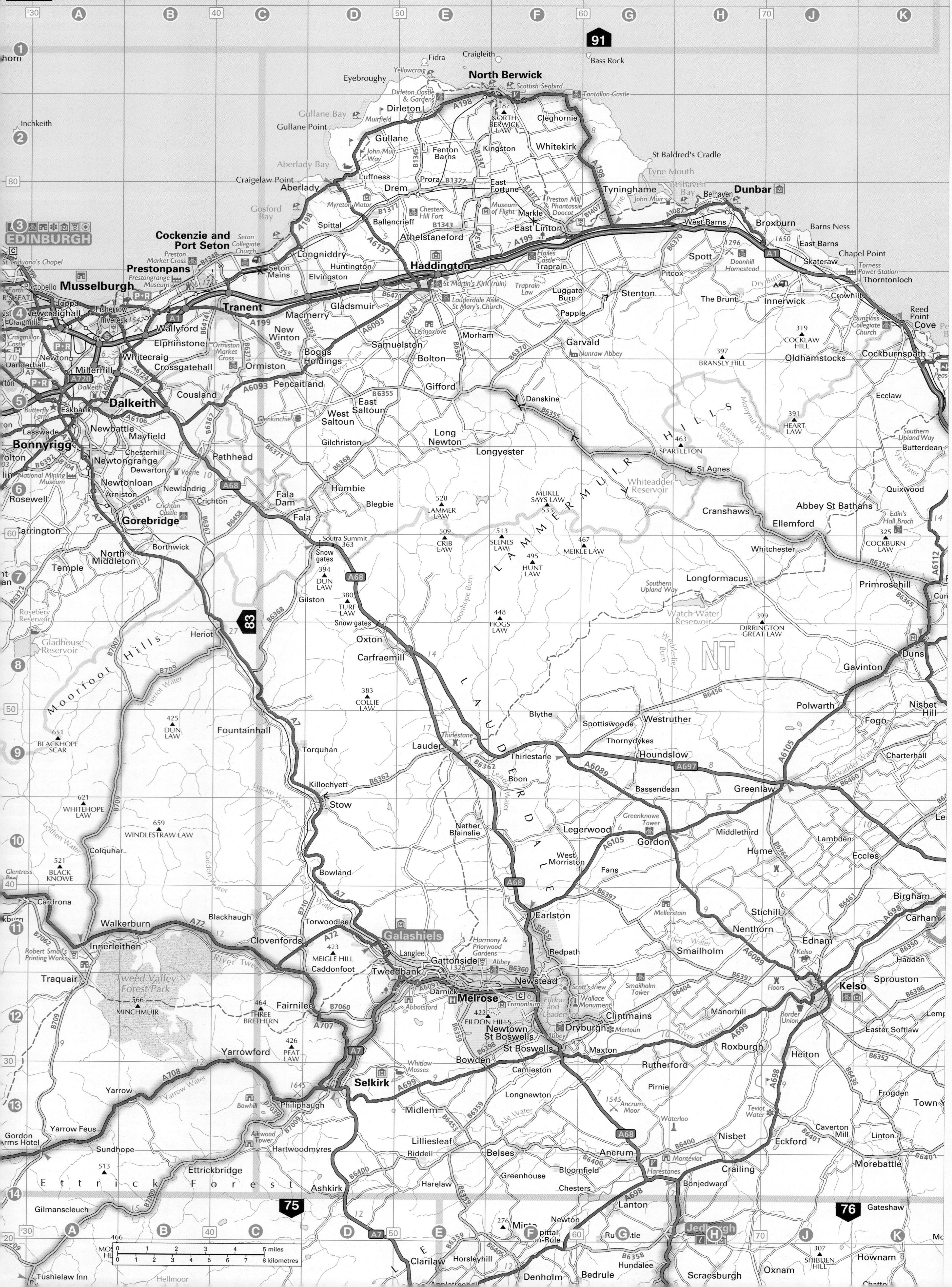
91
Fidra
Craigleith
Bass Rock
Eyebroughy
Yellowcraig
North Berwick
Scottish Seabird
Dirleton Castle & Gardens
Tantallon Castle
Dirleton
Muirfield
Gullane Bay
Gullane Point
187 NORTH BERWICK LAW
Cleghornie
Inchkeith
Gullane
John Muir Way
Fenton Barns
Kingston
Whitekirk
St Baldred's Cradle
Aberlady Bay
Tyne Mouth
Belhaven Bay
Craigelaw Point
Aberlady
Luffness
Drem
Prora
East Fortune
Tyninghame
Belhaven
Dunbar
Gosford Bay
Myreton Motor
Museum of Flight
Preston Mill & Phantassie Doocot
Markle
Chesters Hill Fort
Ballencrieff
East Linton
West Barns
Broxburn
Barns Ness
Spittal
Athelstaneford
EDINBURGH
Cockenzie and Port Seton
Seton Collegiate Church
Longniddry
Hailes Castle
Traprain
Spott
Doonhill Homestead
East Barns
Chapel Point
Preston Market Cross
Prestongrange Museum
Prestonpans
Seton Mains
Huntington
Haddington
Skateraw
Torness Power Station
Thorntonloch
St Triduana's Chapel
Portobello
Musselburgh
Elvingston
St Martin's Kirk (ruin)
Traprain Law
Luggate Burn
Pitcox
Dry Burn
Stenton
The Brunt
Innerwick
Crowhill
Joppa
Fisherrow
Newcraighall
Inveresk
Craigmillar
Tranent
Macmerry
Gladsmuir
Lauderdale Aisle St Mary's Church
Pappple
Reed Point
Cove
Dunglass Collegiate Church
Wallyford
Elphinstone
Ormiston Market Cross
New Winton
Samuelston
Lennoxlove
Morham
Garvald
319 COCKLAW HILL
Craigmillar Castle
Newton
Danderhall
Whitecraig
Crossgatehill
Ormiston
Boggs Holdings
Bolton
Nunraw Abbey
397 BRANSLY HILL
Oldhamstocks
Cockburnspath
Millerhill
Dalkeith
Cousland
Pencaitland
Gifford
Danskine
Ecclaw
Eskbank
Butterfly Farm
Glenkinchie
East Saltoun
West Saltoun
Lasswade
Newbattle
Mayfield
Long Newton
Bonnyrigg
Gilchriston
Longyester
391 HEART LAW
Southern Upland Way
Butterdean
463 SPARTLETON
St Agnes
Chesterhill
Newtongrange
Pathhead
Polton
Dewarton
Vogrie
National Mining Museum
Newtonloan
Newlandrig
Humbie
Whiteadder Reservoir
Quixwood
Rosewell
Arniston
Crichton
Crichton Castle
Fala Dam
Blegbie
528 LAMMER LAW
MEIKLE SAYS LAW 533
Cranshaws
Abbey St Bathans
Gorebridge
Fala
Ellemford
Edin's Hall Broch
Carrington
Soutra Summit 363
509 CRIB LAW
513 SEENES LAW
467 MEIKLE LAW
325 COCKBURN LAW
Borthwick
Snow gates
495 HUNT LAW
Whitchester
North Middleton
Temple
394 DUN LAW
LAMMERMUIR HILLS
Longformacus
Primrosehill
Gilston
380 TURF LAW
Southern Upland Way
Rosebery Reservoir
448 HOGS LAW
Watch Water Reservoir
399 DIRRINGTON GREAT LAW
Snow gates
Heriot
83
Oxton
Gladhouse Reservoir
Moorfoot Hills
Carfraemill
NT
Duns
Gavinton
Heriot Water
383 COLLIE LAW
Nisbet Hill
Polwarth
Fogo
425 DUN LAW
Fountainhall
Blythe
Westruther
Spottiswoode
651 BLACKHOPE SCAR
Thornydykes
Lauder
Thirlestane
Torquhan
Houndslow
Charterhall
LAUDERDALE
Boon
Bassendean
Greenlaw
Killochyett
Stow
621 WHITEHOPE LAW
Lugate Water
Leader Water
Greenknowe Tower
659 WINDLESTRAW LAW
Nether Blainslie
Legerwood
Gordon
Middlethird
Lambden
Leithen Water
Colquhar
West Morriston
Hume
Eccles
521 BLACK KNOWE
Bowland
Fans
Glentress Peel
Cardrona
Caddon Water
Mellerstain
Birgham
Stichill
Carham
Walkerburn
Blackhaugh
Torwoodlee
Galashiels
Nenthorn
Ednam
Innerleithen
Clovenfords
Harmony & Priorwood Gardens
Redpath
Smailholm
Robert Smail's Printing Works
423 MEIGLE HILL
Langlee
Gattonside
Abbey
Kelso
Hadden
Traquair
Caddonfoot
Tweedbank
Newstead
Scott's View
Smailholm Tower
Floors
Sprouston
Tweed Valley Forest Park
Darnick
Melrose
Trimontium
Eildon and Leaderfoot
Wallace Monument
Clintmains
Manorhill
Border Union
566 MINCHMUIR
464 THREE BRETHREN
Fairnilee
Abbotsford
422 EILDON HILLS
Newtown St Boswells
Dryburgh
Dryburgh Abbey
Mertoun
Easter Softlaw
Yarrowford
426 PEAT LAW
St Boswells
Maxton
Roxburgh
Bowden
Heiton
Camieston
Rutherford
Whitlaw Mosses
Selkirk
Yarrow
Philiphaugh
Pirnie
Bowhill
Longnewton
1545 Ancrum Moor
Frogden
Midlem
Teviot Water
Town Yetholm
Yarrow Feus
Waterloo
Caverton Mill
Gordon Arms Hotel
Aikwood Tower
Hartwoodmyres
Lilliesleaf
Nisbet
Eckford
Linton
Sundhope
Riddell
Belses
Ancrum
Monteviot
Harestanes
Crailing
Morebattle
513
Ettrickbridge
Bloomfield
Ettrick Forest
Ashkirk
Harelaw
Greenhouse
Chesters
Bonjedward
Gilmanscleuch
75
Lanton
76
Gateshaw
276 Minto
Newton
Denholm
Spittal-on-Rule
Rulecastle
Jedburgh
307 SHIBDEN HILL
Hownam
Clarilaw
Horsleyhill
Hundalee
Oxnam
Scraesburgh
Bedrule
Tushielaw Inn
Hellmoor
0 1 2 3 4 5 miles
0 1 2 3 4 5 6 7 8 kilometres

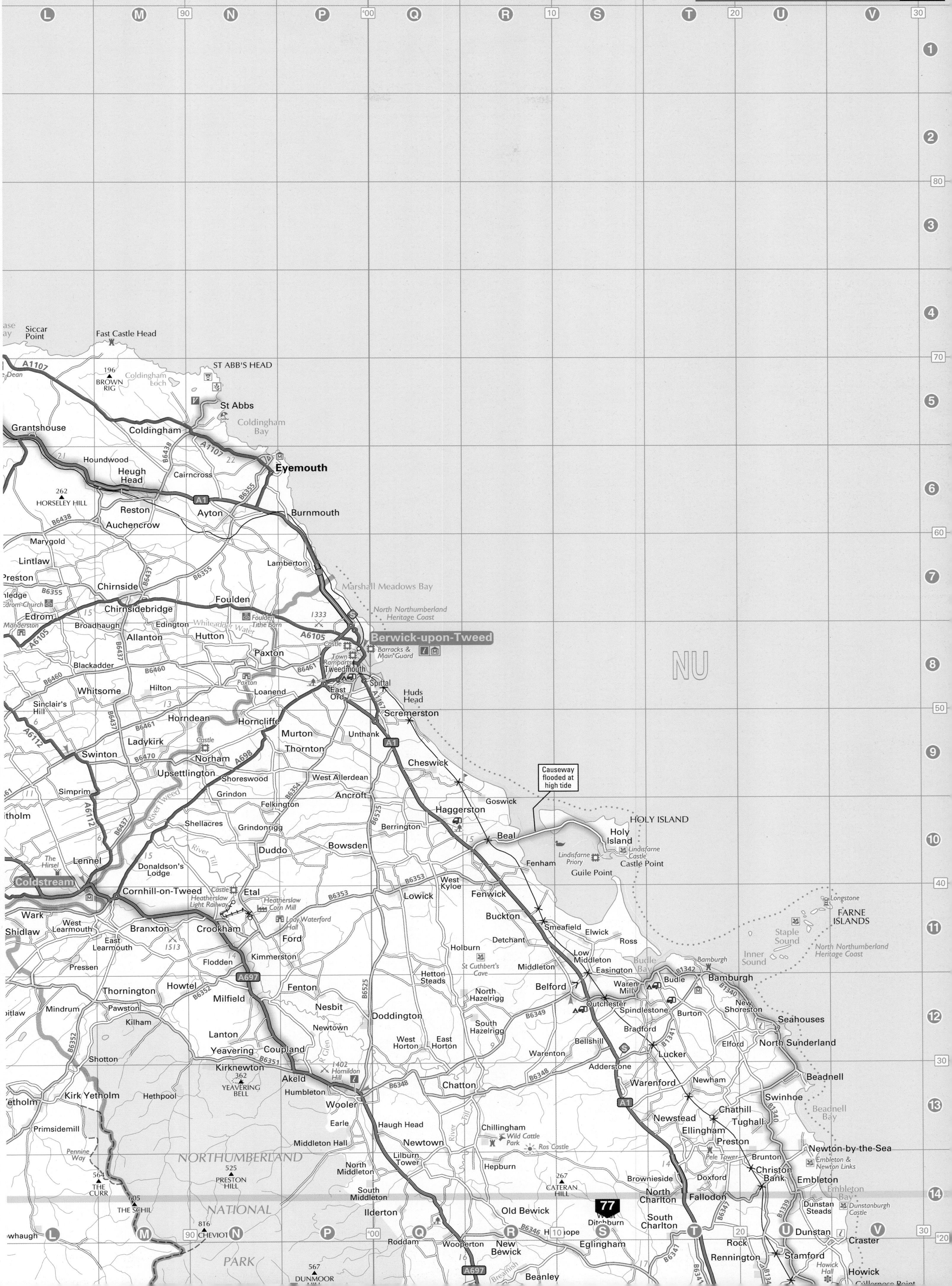

Siccar Point
Fast Castle Head
A1107
196 BROWN RIG
Coldingham Loch
ST ABB'S HEAD
St Abbs
Coldingham Bay
Grantshouse
Coldingham
Houndwood
Heugh Head
Cairncross
Eyemouth
262 HORSELEY HILL
Reston
Ayton
Burnmouth
Auchencrow
Marygold
Lintlaw
Lamberton
Preston
Chirnside
Marshall Meadows Bay
Foulden
Edrom Church
Edrom
Chirnsidebridge
North Northumberland Heritage Coast
Manderston
Broadhaugh
Edington
Whiteadder Water
Foulden Tithe Barn
Allanton
Hutton
A6105
Berwick-upon-Tweed
Castle
Barracks & Main Guard
Paxton
Town Ramparts
Blackadder
Tweedmouth
Whitsome
Hilton
Paxton
Loanend
Spittal
Huds Head
East Ord
Sinclair's Hill
Scremerston
Horndean
Horncliffe
Unthank
Ladykirk
Murton
Thornton
Swinton
Norham
Cheswick
Upsettlington
Shoreswood
West Allerdean
Causeway flooded at high tide
Simprim
Grindon
Ancroft
Goswick
HOLY ISLAND
Felkington
Haggerston
Shellacres
Grindonrigg
Berrington
Beal
Holy Island
River Tweed
River Till
Lindisfarne Castle
Duddo
Bowsden
Lindisfarne Priory
Castle Point
The Hirsel
Lennel
Donaldson's Lodge
Fenham
Guile Point
Coldstream
Cornhill-on-Tweed
Castle
Etal
West Kyloe
Fenwick
Heatherslaw Light Railway
Heatherslaw Corn Mill
Lowick
Longstone
Wark
West Learmouth
Lady Waterford Hall
Buckton
FARNE ISLANDS
Shidlaw
Branxton
Crookham
Smeafield
Elwick
Ross
East Learmouth
Ford
Staple Sound
Detchant
Holburn
Pressen
Kimmerston
Inner Sound
North Northumberland Heritage Coast
Flodden
St Cuthbert's Cave
Middleton
Low Middleton
Budle Bay
Bamburgh
Easington
Thornington
Howtel
Fenton
Hetton Steads
Budle
Waren Mill
Belford
North Hazelrigg
Milfield
Outchester
New Shoreston
Mindrum
Pawston
Nesbit
Spindlestone
Burton
Kilham
Doddington
South Hazelrigg
Seahouses
Newtown
Bradford
Lanton
West Horton
East Horton
Bellshill
Elford
North Sunderland
Yeavering
Coupland
Lucker
Warenton
Shotton
Kirknewton
1402 Homildon Hill
Adderstone
362 YEAVERING BELL
Akeld
Beadnell
Kirk Yetholm
Hethpool
Humbleton
Chatton
Warenford
Newham
Yetholm
Wooler
Swinhoe
Chathill
Newstead
Beadnell Bay
Earle
Haugh Head
Tughall
Primsidemill
Ellingham
Chillingham Wild Cattle Park
Ros Castle
Middleton Hall
Newtown
Preston
Newton-by-the-Sea
Pennine Way
NORTHUMBERLAND
Lilburn Tower
Pele Tower
Brunton
Embleton & Newton Links
Hepburn
Christon Bank
525 PRESTON HILL
North Middleton
Doxford
Embleton
564 THE CURR
Brownieside
267 CATERAN HILL
Embleton Bay
South Middleton
North Charlton
Falloden
605 THE SCHIL
NATIONAL
77
Dunstan Steads
Dunstanburgh Castle
Ilderton
Old Bewick
West Ditchburn
South Charlton
816 CHEVIOT
Dunstan
Craster
Roddam
Wooperton
New Bewick
Eglingham
Rock
PARK
Rennington
Stamford
567 DUNMOOR HILL
Beanley
Howick Hall
Howick
Cullernose Point
NU

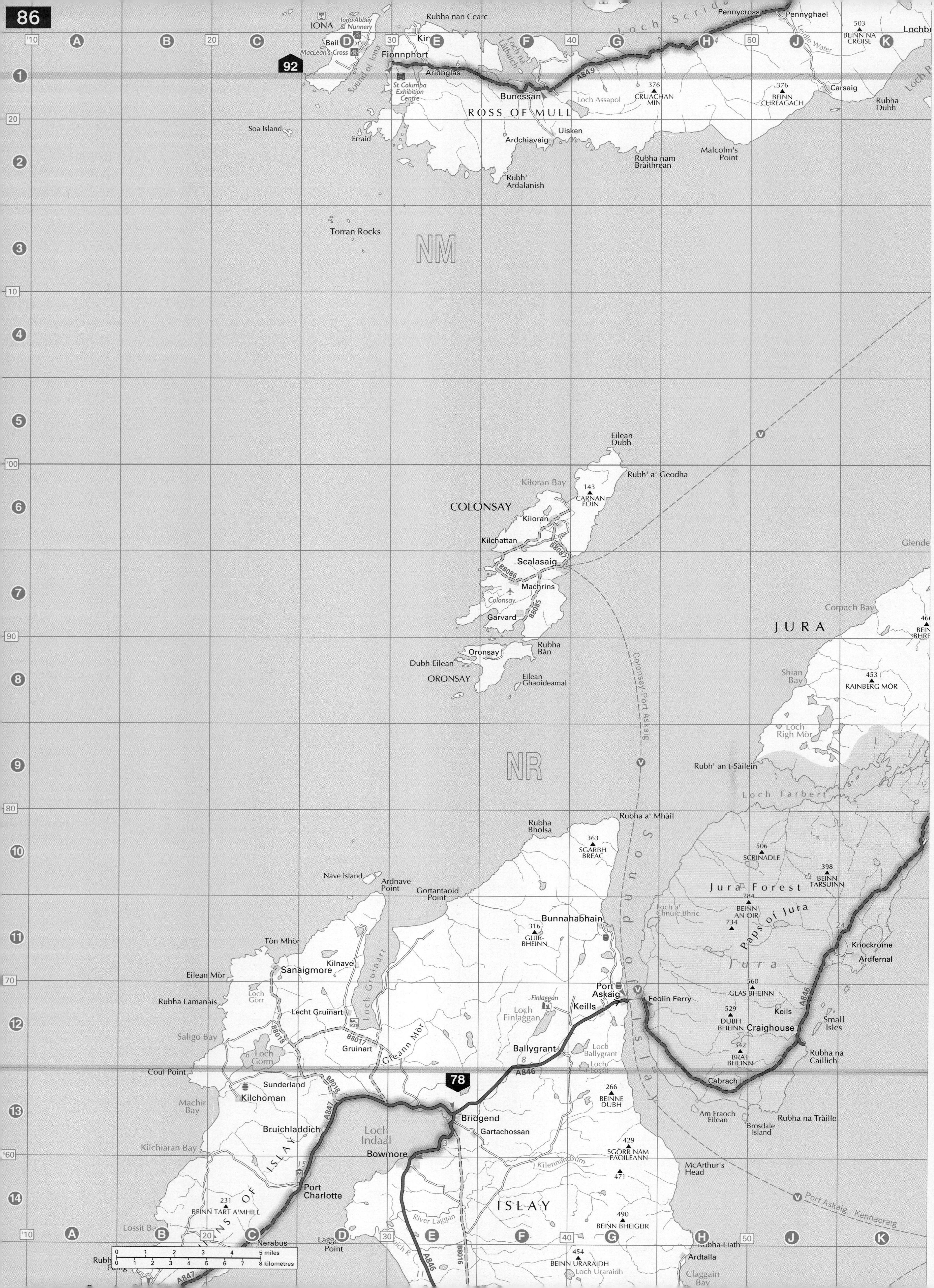
IONA
Iona Abbey & Nunnery
Baile Mòr
MacLean's Cross
Sound of Iona
Rubha nan Cearc
Fionnphort
Aridhglas
St Columba Exhibition Centre
Loch na Làthaich
Bunessan
A849
Loch Scridain
Pennycross
Pennyghael
Leidle Water
503 BEINN NA CROISE
Lochbuie
Loch Assapol
376 CRUACHAN MIN
376 BEINN CHREAGACH
Carsaig
Rubha Dubh
ROSS OF MULL
Soa Island
Erraid
Uisken
Ardchiavaig
Malcolm's Point
Rubha nam Bràithrean
Rubh' Ardalanish
Torran Rocks
NM
92
Eilean Dubh
Rubh' a' Geodha
Kiloran Bay
143 CARNAN EOIN
COLONSAY
Kiloran
Kilchattan
B8087
Scalasaig
B8086
Machrins
Colonsay
Garvard
B8085
Glendebadel
Corpach Bay
JURA
Rubha Bàn
Oronsay
Dubh Eilean
ORONSAY
Eilean Ghaoideamal
Colonsay-Port Askaig
Shian Bay
453 RAINBERG MÒR
Loch Righ Mòr
Rubh' an t-Sàilein
NR
Loch Tarbert
Rubha a' Mhàil
Rubha Bholsa
363 SGARBH BREAC
Sound of Islay
506 SCRINADLE
398 BEINN TARSUINN
Nave Island
Ardnave Point
Gortantaoid Point
Jura Forest
784 BEINN AN OIR
Loch a' Chnuic Bhric
734
Paps of Jura
Bunnahabhain
316 GUIR-BHEINN
Tòn Mhòr
Knockrome
Ardfernal
Kilnave
Eilean Mòr
Sanaigmore
Loch Gruinart
Jura
560 GLAS BHEINN
Port Askaig
Feolin Ferry
Loch Gòrr
Rubha Lamanais
Lecht Gruinart
Finlaggan
Loch Finlaggan
Keills
529 DUBH BHEINN
Keils
Craighouse
A846
Small Isles
Saligo Bay
B8018
B8017
Gruinart
Gleann Mòr
Ballygrant
Loch Ballygrant
342 BRAT BHEINN
Rubha na Caillich
Loch Gorm
Coul Point
78
A846
Loch Lossit
Sunderland
Kilchoman
Machir Bay
Cabrach
266 BEINNE DUBH
Bridgend
A847
Bruichladdich
Loch Indaal
Gartachossan
Am Fraoch Eilean
Brosdale Island
Rubha na Tràille
Kilchiaran Bay
Bowmore
429 SGÒRR NAM FAOILEANN
Kilennan Burn
McArthur's Head
471
Port Charlotte
RHINNS OF ISLAY
231 BEINN TART A'MHILL
ISLAY
Port Askaig - Kennacraig
490 BEINN BHEIGEIR
River Laggan
Lossit Bay
Nerabus
Laggan Point
B8016
Rubha Liath
Ardtalla
454 BEINN URARAIDH
Loch Uraraidh
Claggain Bay
0 1 2 3 4 5 miles
0 1 2 3 4 5 6 7 8 kilometres

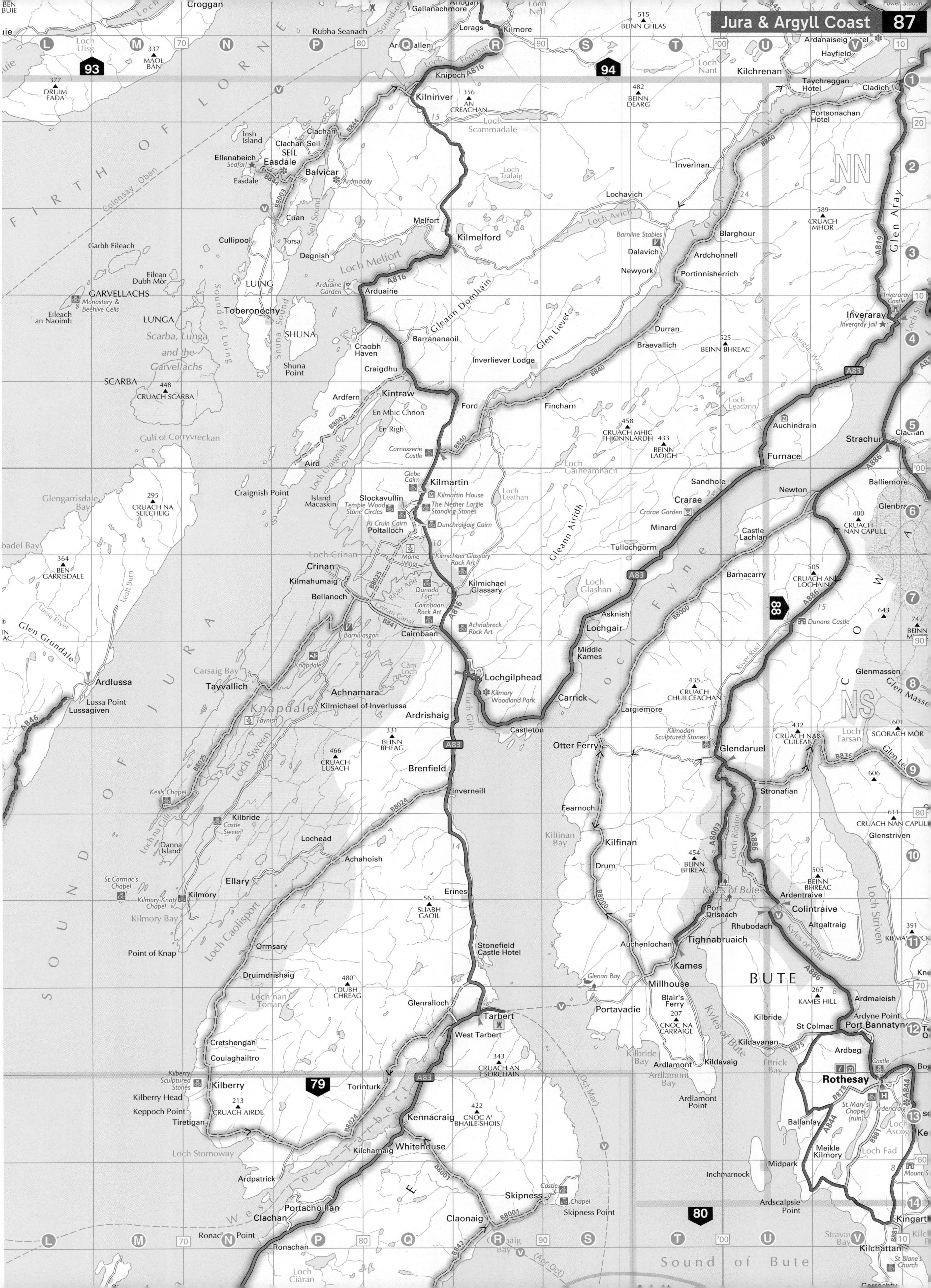

FIRTH OF LORNE
SOUND OF JURA
Loch Fyne
BUTE
Sound of Bute
Kilninver
Knipoch
Loch Feochan
Kilmore
Lerags
Gallanachmore
Croggan
Kilchrenan
Taychreggan Hotel
Cladich
Portsonachan Hotel
Inverinan
Lochavich
Loch Avich
Barnline Stables
Dalavich
Newyork
Blarghour
Ardchonnell
Portinnisherrich
Loch Awe
Glen Aray
Inveraray
Inveraray Castle
Inveraray Jail
Durran
Braevallich
Douglas Water
Clachan
Clachan-Seil
SEIL
Insh Island
Ellenabeich
Easdale
Balvicar
Ardmaddy
Cuan
Torsa
Degnish
Cullipool
LUING
Toberonochy
SHUNA
Shuna Point
Garbh Eileach
Eilean Dubh Mòr
GARVELLACHS
Monastery & Beehive Cells
Eileach an Naoimh
LUNGA
Scarba, Lunga and the Garvellachs
SCARBA
CRUACH SCARBA
Gulf of Corryvreckan
Melfort
Kilmelford
Loch Melfort
Arduaine Garden
Arduaine
Gleann Domhain
Barrananaoil
Inverliever Lodge
Glen Liever
Craobh Haven
Craigdhu
Kintraw
Ardfern
En Mhic Chrion
En Righ
Ford
Fincharn
Carnasserie Castle
Kilmartin
Kilmartin House
Glebe Cairn
The Nether Largie Standing Stones
Temple Wood Stone Circles
Slockavullin
Ri Cruin Cairn
Poltalloch
Dunchraigaig Cairn
Loch Crinan
Moine Mhor
Crinan
Kilmahumaig
Bellanoch
Dunadd Fort
Cairnbaan Rock Art
Crinan Canal
Cairnbaan
Kilmichael Glassary
Achnabreck Rock Art
Lochgilphead
Kilmory Woodland Park
Loch Gilp
Ardrishaig
Castleton
Carrick
Lochgair
Middle Kames
Asknish
Minard
Tullochgorm
Crarae
Crarae Garden
Sandhole
Furnace
Auchindrain
Strachur
Newton
Castle Lachlan
Barnacarry
Dunans Castle
Glenbranter
Glenmassen
Glendaruel
Kilmodan Sculptured Stones
Otter Ferry
Stronafian
Kilfinan
Drum
Fearnoch
Largiemore
Kyles of Bute
Port Driseach
Colintraive
Ardentraive
Rhubodach
Altgaltraig
Tighnabruaich
Auchenlochan
Kames
Millhouse
Blair's Ferry
Glenan Bay
Portavadie
Kilbride Bay
Ardlamont
Ardlamont Point
Kildavaig
Kildavanan
Ettrick Bay
St Colmac
Port Bannatyne
Ardmaleish
Ardyne Point
Kilbride
Ardbeg
Rothesay
Ballanlay
Meikle Kilmory
Loch Fad
Loch Ascog
St Mary's Chapel (ruin)
Midpark
Inchmarnock
Ardscalpsie Point
Kingarth
Kilchattan
St Blane's Church
Loch Striven
Craignish Point
Loch Craignish
Aird
Island Macaskin
Barnluasgan
Knapdale
Carsaig Bay
Tayvallich
Achnamara
Kilmichael of Inverlussa
Taynish
Loch Sween
Keills Chapel
Kilbride
Castle Sween
Danna Island
Loch na Cille
St Cormac's Chapel
Kilmory Knap Chapel
Kilmory
Kilmory Bay
Point of Knap
Loch Caolisport
Ellary
Achahoish
Lochead
Ormsary
Brenfield
Inverneill
Erines
Stonefield Castle Hotel
Druimdrishaig
Glenralloch
Tarbert
West Tarbert
Cretshengan
Coulaghailtro
Kilberry Sculptured Stones
Kilberry
Kilberry Head
Keppoch Point
Tiretigan
Torinturk
Kennacraig
Whitehouse
Kilchamaig
Loch Stornoway
Ardpatrick
Portachoillan
Clachan
Ronachan
Ronachan Point
Claonaig
Skipness
Skipness Castle
Skipness Point
West Loch Tarbert
Glengarrisdale Bay
CRUACH NA SEILCHEIG
BEN GARRISDALE
Glen Grundale
Lussa River
Ardlussa
Lussa Point
Lussagiven
JURA

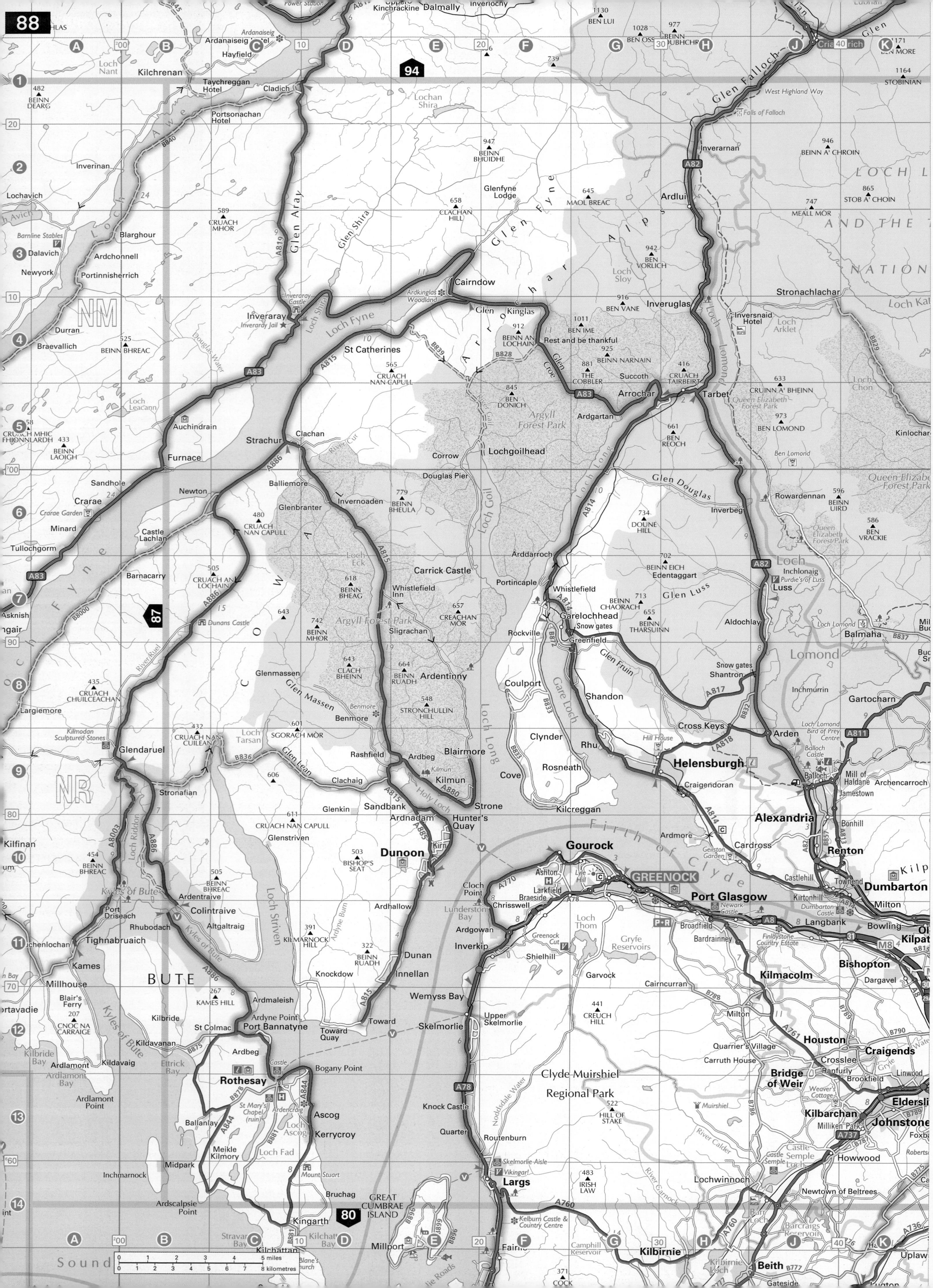

Kinchrackine
Dalmally
Inverlochy
BEN LUI
BEN OSS
BEINN DUBHCHRAIG
Ardanaiseig
Hayfield
Loch Nant
Kilchrenan
Taychreggan Hotel
Cladich
94
Lochan Shira
BEINN DEARG
Portsonachan Hotel
Glen Falloch
West Highland Way
Falls of Falloch
BEN MORE
STOBINIAN
Inverinan
BEINN BHUIDHE
Inverarnan
A82
BEINN A' CHROIN
Lochavich
CRUACH MHOR
Glenfyne Lodge
CLACHAN HILL
MAOL BREAC
Ardlui
MEALL MOR
STOB A' CHOIN
Barnline Stables
Dalavich
Blarghour
Ardchonnell
Portinnisherrich
Newyork
Glen Aray
Glen Shira
Glen Fyne
Arrochar Alps
BEN VORLICH
Loch Sloy
Cairndow
Ardkinglas Woodland
Inveraray Castle
Inveraray
Inveraray Jail
Loch Fyne
Glen Kinglas
BEN VANE
Inveruglas
Stronachlachar
Inversnaid Hotel
Loch Arklet
Loch Katrine
NM
Durran
Braevallich
BEINN BHREAC
St Catherines
B839
B828
BEINN AN LOCHAIN
BEN IME
Rest and be thankful
BEINN NARNAIN
THE COBBLER
Succoth
CRUACH TAIRBEIRT
Tarbet
Loch Lomond
CRUACH NAN CAPULL
A83
Arrochar
CRUINN A' BHEINN
Loch Chon
Queen Elizabeth Forest Park
BEN LOMOND
Loch Leacann
Auchindrain
BEN DONICH
Argyll Forest Park
Ardgartan
BEN REOCH
Kinlochard
Strachur
Clachan
Furnace
Lochgoilhead
Corrow
Ben Lomond
Douglas Pier
Glen Douglas
Rowardennan
BEINN UIRD
Sandhole
Balliemore
Newton
Crarae
Crarae Garden
Invernoaden
BEINN BHEULA
Inverbeg
Glenbranter
CRUACH NAN CAPULL
DOUNE HILL
BEN VRACKIE
Minard
Castle Lachlan
Loch Goil
Loch Long
Tullochgorm
Arddarroch
Carrick Castle
Loch Eck
A83
Barnacarry
CRUACH AN LOCHAIN
BEINN EICH
Edentaggart
Inchlonaig
Purdie's of Luss
Luss
BEINN BHEAG
Portincaple
Whistlefield Inn
Whistlefield
Glen Luss
87
Dunans Castle
CREACHAN MOR
BEINN CHAORACH
BEINN THARSUINN
Garelochhead
Snow gates
Aldochlay
Loch Lomond
Balmaha
BEINN MHOR
Argyll Forest Park
Sligrachan
Rockville
Greenfield
B837
Lomond
Glen Fruin
Snow gates
Shantron
Glenmassen
CLACH BHEINN
BEINN RUADH
Ardentinny
Coulport
Inchmurrin
Gartocharn
CRUACH CHUILCEACHAN
Glen Massen
Benmore
Shandon
A817
Largiemore
STRONCHULLIN HILL
Gare Loch
Kilmodan Sculptured Stones
CRUACH NAN CUILEAN
Loch Tarsan
SGORACH MOR
Clynder
Cross Keys
Arden
Loch Lomond Bird of Prey Centre
A811
Glendaruel
B836
Glen Lean
Rashfield
Blairmore
Rhu
Hill House
A818
Balloch Castle
Balloch
Mill of Haldane
Archencarroch
Jamestown
Ardbeg
Kilmun
Rosneath
Helensburgh
Craigendoran
NR
Stronafian
Clachaig
Cove
A880
Holy Loch
Glenkin
Sandbank
Strone
Kilcreggan
Alexandria
Ardnadam
Hunter's Quay
Firth of Clyde
Ardmore
Bonhill
CRUACH NAN CAPULL
Glenstriven
A8003
Loch Riddon
A886
Kirn
Gourock
Cardross
Renton
Kilfinan
BEINN BHREAC
BISHOP'S SEAT
Dunoon
Ashton
Lyle Hill
GREENOCK
Geilston Garden
Castlehill
Kilpatrick
BEINN BHREAC
Kyles of Bute
Ardentraive
Cloch Point
Larkfield
Braeside
Port Glasgow
Newark Castle
Townend
Dumbarton
Port Driseach
Colintraive
Chrisswell
Kirtonhill
Milton
Dumbarton Castle
Rhubodach
Altgaltraig
Loch Striven
Ardhallow
Lunderston Bay
Loch Thom
Broadfield
Langbank
Bowling
Tighnabruaich
Kames
KILMARNOCK HILL
Ardyne Burn
Ardgowan
Greenock Cut
Gryfe Reservoirs
Bardrainney
Finlaystone Country Estate
M8
Kilpatrick
Inverkip
Shielhill
BEINN RUADH
Dunan
Kilmacolm
Bishopton
BUTE
Knockdow
Innellan
Garvock
Dargavel
Millhouse
Blair's Ferry
CNOC NA CARRAIGE
KAMES HILL
Ardmaleish
Wemyss Bay
Cairncurran
Kilbride
Ardyne Point
Port Bannatyne
St Colmac
Toward
Toward Quay
Upper Skelmorlie
Skelmorlie
CREUCH HILL
Milton
Kildavanan
Houston
Quarrier's Village
Craigends
Kilbride Bay
Ardlamont Bay
Ardlamont
Kildavaig
Ettrick Bay
Ardbeg
Castle
Bogany Point
Carruth House
Crosslee
Ranfurly
Bridge of Weir
Brookfield
Linwood
Rothesay
A844
A78
Clyde Muirshiel Regional Park
Noddsdale Water
Weaver's Cottage
Elderslie
Ardlamont Point
B878
St Mary's Chapel (ruin)
Ascog
Knock Castle
HILL OF STAKE
Muirshiel
Kilbarchan
Johnstone
Milliken Park
Ballanlay
Loch Ascog
Kerrycroy
Quarter
Routenburn
A737
Foxbar
River Calder
Castle Semple
Howwood
Meikle Kilmory
Loch Fad
B881
Inchmarnock
Midpark
Mount Stuart
Skelmorlie Aisle
Vikingar!
Largs
IRISH LAW
River Garnock
Lochwinnoch
Bruchag
Ardscalpsie Point
GREAT CUMBRAE ISLAND
80
Newtown of Beltrees
Kingarth
A760
Kelburn Castle & Country Centre
Strayar Bay
Kilchattan Bay
Millport
Fairlie
Camphill Reservoir
Kilbirnie
Kilbirnie Loch
Barcraigs Reservoir
Beith
Uplawmoor
Sound
Kilchattan
Blane's Church
COCK
Gateside
B777
5 miles
5 kilometres

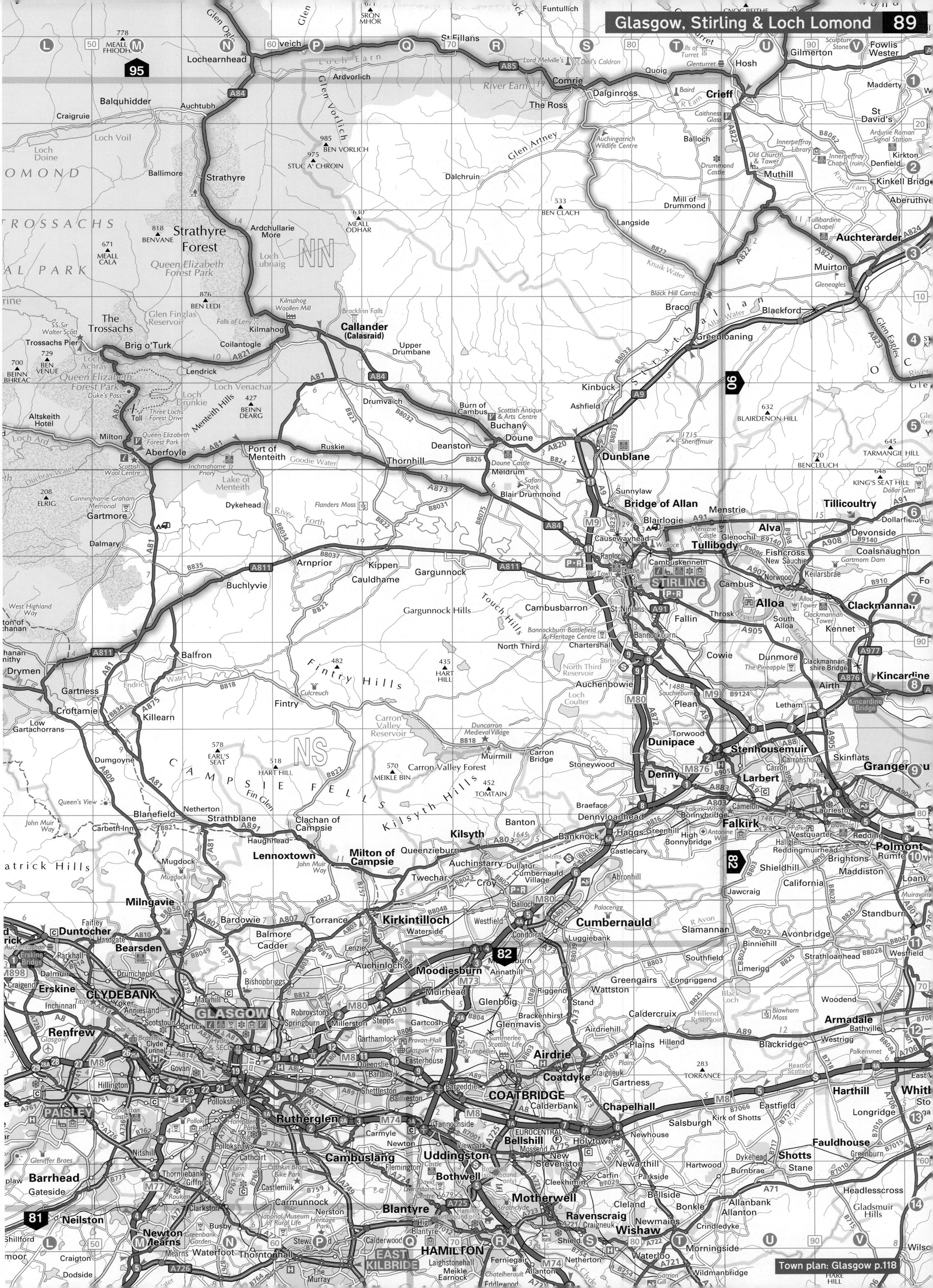
Lochearnhead
St Fillans
Comrie
Crieff
Gilmerton
Loch Earn
Balquhidder
Strathyre
Strathyre Forest
Queen Elizabeth Forest Park
TROSSACHS
BEN VORLICH
STUC A' CHROIN
BEN LEDI
BEN CLACH
Muthill
Auchterarder
Braco
Blackford
Gleneagles
Callander (Calasraid)
The Trossachs
Brig o'Turk
Kilmahog
Aberfoyle
Port of Menteith
Lake of Menteith
Menteith Hills
Thornhill
Deanston
Doune
Dunblane
Bridge of Allan
Tillicoultry
Alva
Tullibody
STIRLING
Cambuskenneth
Alloa
Clackmannan
Kincardine
Fallin
Bannockburn
Gartmore
Arnprior
Kippen
Gargunnock
Buchlyvie
Cambusbarron
Drymen
Balfron
Killearn
Fintry
Fintry Hills
Touch Hills
Gargunnock Hills
CAMPSIE FELLS
Kilsyth Hills
Carron Valley Reservoir
Carron Valley Forest
Denny
Dunipace
Larbert
Stenhousemuir
Falkirk
Grangemouth
Polmont
Kilsyth
Lennoxtown
Milton of Campsie
Strathblane
Blanefield
Milngavie
Bearsden
Kirkintilloch
Cumbernauld
Moodiesburn
CLYDEBANK
GLASGOW
Renfrew
Erskine
PAISLEY
Barrhead
Rutherglen
Cambuslang
Airdrie
COATBRIDGE
Chapelhall
Bellshill
Uddingston
Bothwell
Motherwell
Wishaw
Blantyre
HAMILTON
EAST KILBRIDE
Newton Mearns
Neilston
Shotts
Harthill
Armadale
Fauldhouse
Whitburn
NN
NS

Town plan: Glasgow p.118

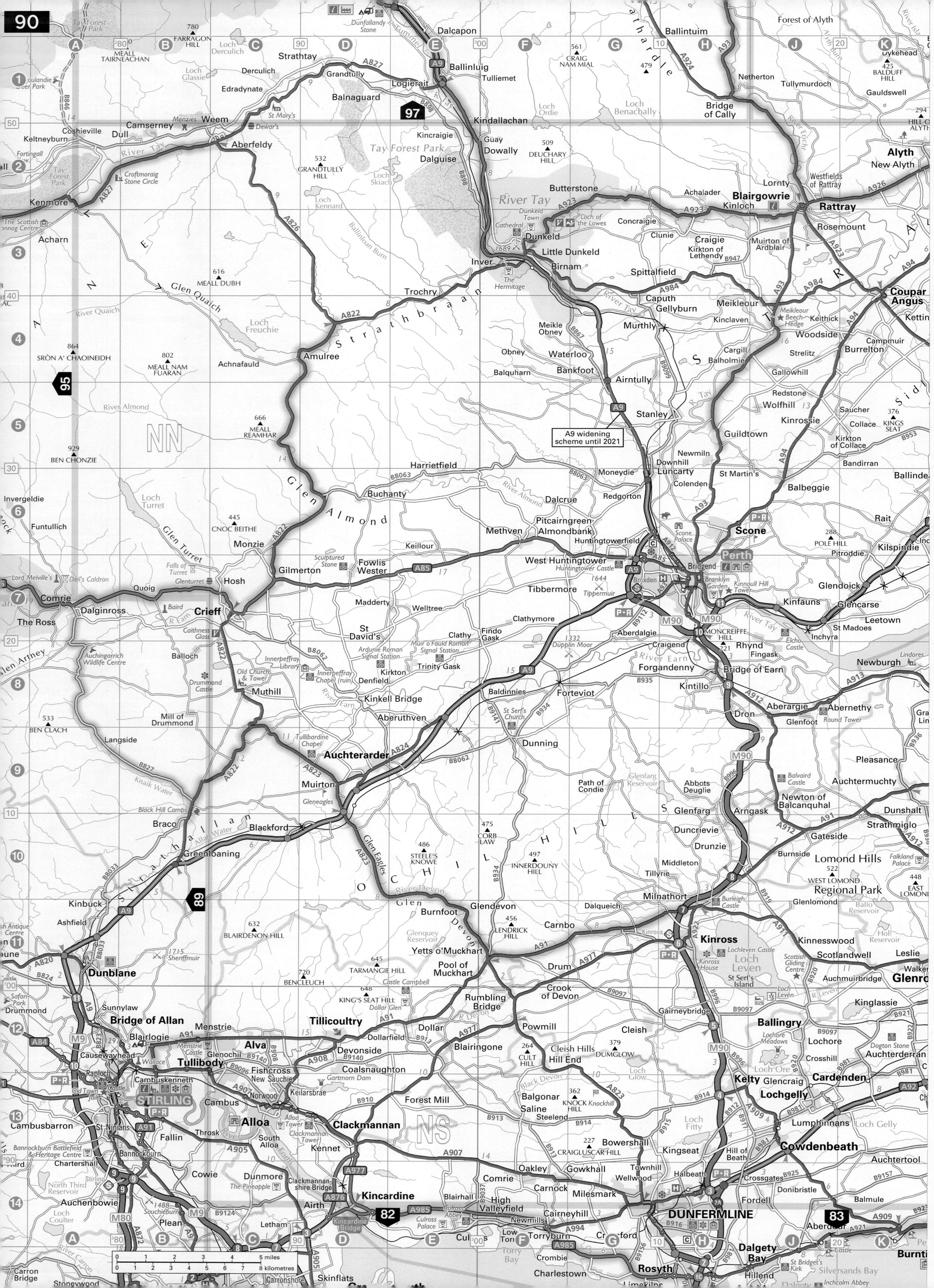
Dalcapon
Ballintuim
Forest of Alyth
Strathtay
Ballinluig
Tulliemet
Grandtully
Logierait
Derculich
Edradynate
Balnaguard
Dykehead
Netherton
Tullymurdoch
Gauldswell
Bridge of Cally
Camserney
Weem
Dull
Coshieville
Keltneyburn
Kindallachan
Kincraigie
Aberfeldy
Guay
Dowally
Tay Forest Park
Dalguise
Alyth
New Alyth
Kenmore
Butterstone
Blairgowrie
Kinloch
Rattray
River Tay
Dunkeld
Little Dunkeld
Birnam
Inver
Concraigie
Clunie
Craigie
Kirkton of Lethendy
Muirton of Ardblair
Rosemount
Acharn
Spittalfield
Trochry
Caputh
Gellyburn
Meikleour
Kinclaven
Coupar Angus
Glen Quaich
Strathbraan
Murthly
Woodside
Burrelton
Amulree
Achnafauld
Obney
Waterloo
Bankfoot
Balquharn
Cargill
Balholmie
Strelitz
Airntully
Gallowhill
Wolfhill
Stanley
Kinrossie
Guildtown
Saucher
Collace
A9 widening scheme until 2021
Newmiln
Downhill
Luncarty
Colenden
Harrietfield
Moneydie
St Martin's
Balbeggie
Bandirran
Ballindean
Buchanty
Dalcrue
Redgorton
Glen Almond
Invergeldie
Funtullich
Monzie
Methven
Pitcairngreen
Almondbank
Scone
Rait
Huntingtowerfield
Keillour
Fowlis Wester
West Huntingtower
Perth
Bridgend
Kilspindie
Pitroddie
Gilmerton
Hosh
Comrie
Quoig
Tibbermore
Glendoick
Kinfauns
Glencarse
Dalginross
The Ross
Crieff
Madderty
Welltree
Clathymore
Leetown
St Madoes
St David's
Clathy
Findo Gask
Aberdalgie
Moncreiffe Hill
Inchyra
Balloch
Craigend
Rhynd
Fingask
Forgandenny
Newburgh
Muthill
Kirkton
Trinity Gask
Denfield
Bridge of Earn
Kinkell Bridge
Baldinnies
Forteviot
Kintillo
Aberargie
Abernethy
Aberuthven
Dron
Glenfoot
Mill of Drummond
Dunning
Langside
Auchterarder
Pleasance
Muirton
Path of Condie
Abbots Deuglie
Auchtermuchty
Newton of Balcanquhal
Glenfarg
Arngask
Dunshalt
Braco
Blackford
Duncrievie
Strathmiglo
Gateside
Greenloaning
Drunzie
Middleton
Lomond Hills
Regional Park
Tillyrie
Kinbuck
Burnfoot
Glendevon
Milnathort
Glenlomond
Ashfield
Carnbo
Kinross
Kinnesswood
Yetts o'Muckhart
Scotlandwell
Leslie
Dunblane
Pool of Muckhart
Drum
Loch Leven
Auchmuirbridge
Glenrothes
Rumbling Bridge
Crook of Devon
Kinglassie
Sunnylaw
Drummond
Bridge of Allan
Menstrie
Tillicoultry
Dollar
Powmill
Gairneybridge
Cleish
Ballingry
Blairlogie
Alva
Dollarfield
Blairingone
Lochore
Causewayhead
Tullibody
Devonside
Cleish Hills
Hill End
Crosshill
Auchterderran
Coalsnaughton
Cambuskenneth
Fishcross
New Sauchie
Kelty
Glencraig
Cardenden
Stirling
Cambus
Keilarsbrae
Forest Mill
Balgonar
Saline
Steelend
Lochgelly
Cambusbarron
Alloa
Clackmannan
Lumphinnans
Fallin
Throsk
South Alloa
Kennet
Bowershall
Kingseat
Cowdenbeath
Bannockburn
Chartershall
Cowie
Dunmore
Oakley
Gowkhall
Townhill
Auchtertool
Comrie
Wellwood
Halbeath
Crossgates
Donibristle
Kincardine
Airth
Carnock
Milesmark
Auchenbowie
High Valleyfield
Fordell
Balmule
Plean
Letham
Newmills
Cairneyhill
Dunfermline
Aberdour
Torryburn
Crombie
Charlestown
Rosyth
Dalgety Bay
Carron Bridge
Stoneywood
Skinflats
Burntisland
NN
NS
5 miles
8 kilometres

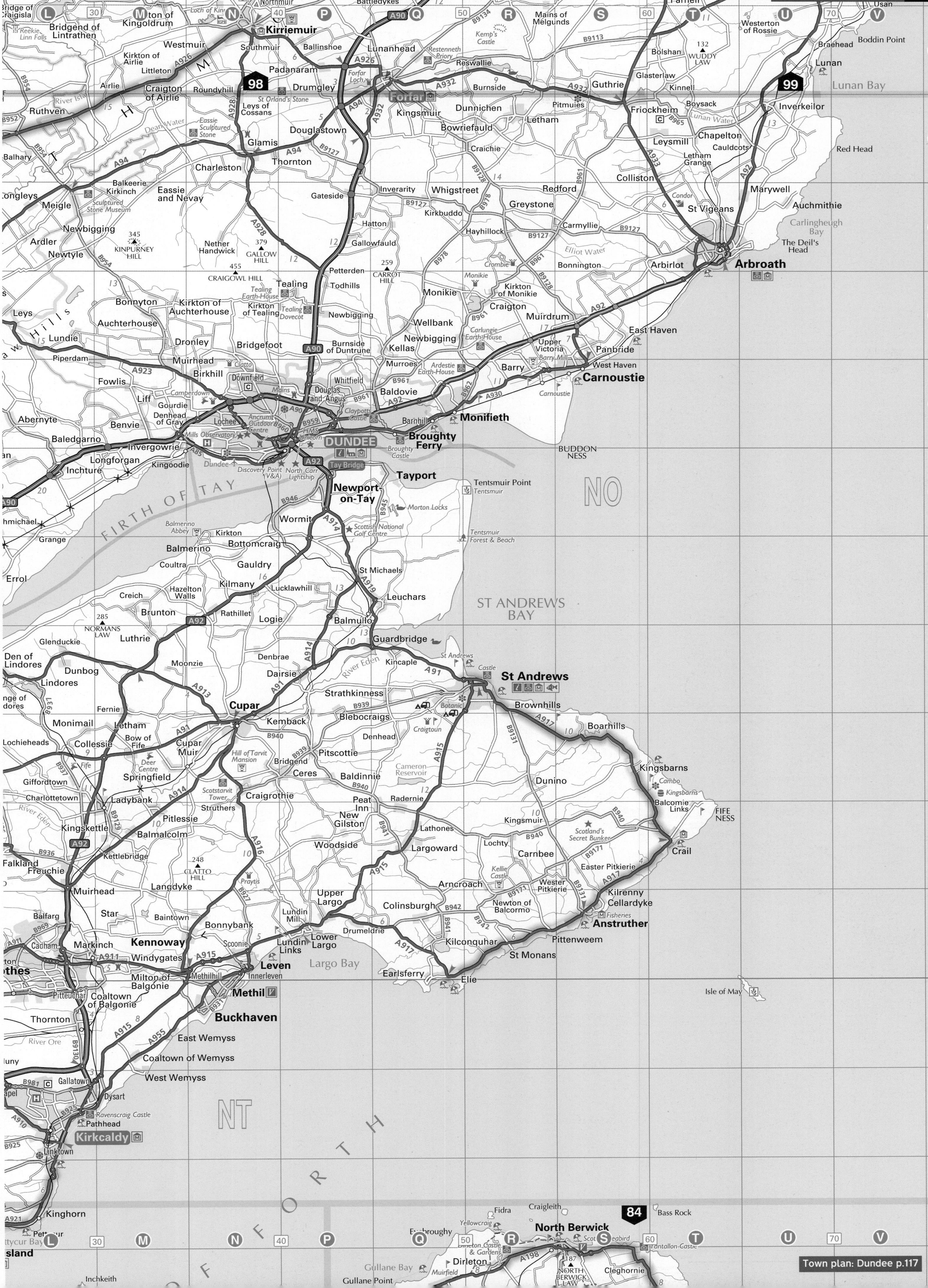
Kirriemuir
Forfar
Brechin
Arbroath
Carnoustie
Monifieth
Broughty Ferry
DUNDEE
Tay Bridge
Newport-on-Tay
Tayport
Wormit
FIRTH OF TAY
Leuchars
Guardbridge
St Andrews
ST ANDREWS BAY
Cupar
Crail
FIFE NESS
Anstruther
Pittenweem
St Monans
Elie
Earlsferry
Largo Bay
Leven
Methil
Buckhaven
East Wemyss
West Wemyss
Kirkcaldy
Kinghorn
Glenrothes
Falkland
Kingskettle
Ladybank
Newburgh
Lindores
Auchtermuchty
Errol
Inchture
Longforgan
Invergowrie
Meigle
Newtyle
Glamis
Letham
Friockheim
Inverkeilor
Lunan Bay
Auchmithie
Red Head
Isle of May
North Berwick
Bass Rock
Dirleton
Gullane Bay
Gullane Point
FIRTH OF FORTH
NO
NT
A90
A92
A91
A914
A915
A917
A919
A921
A955
A94
A932
A933
A926
A928
A923
A930

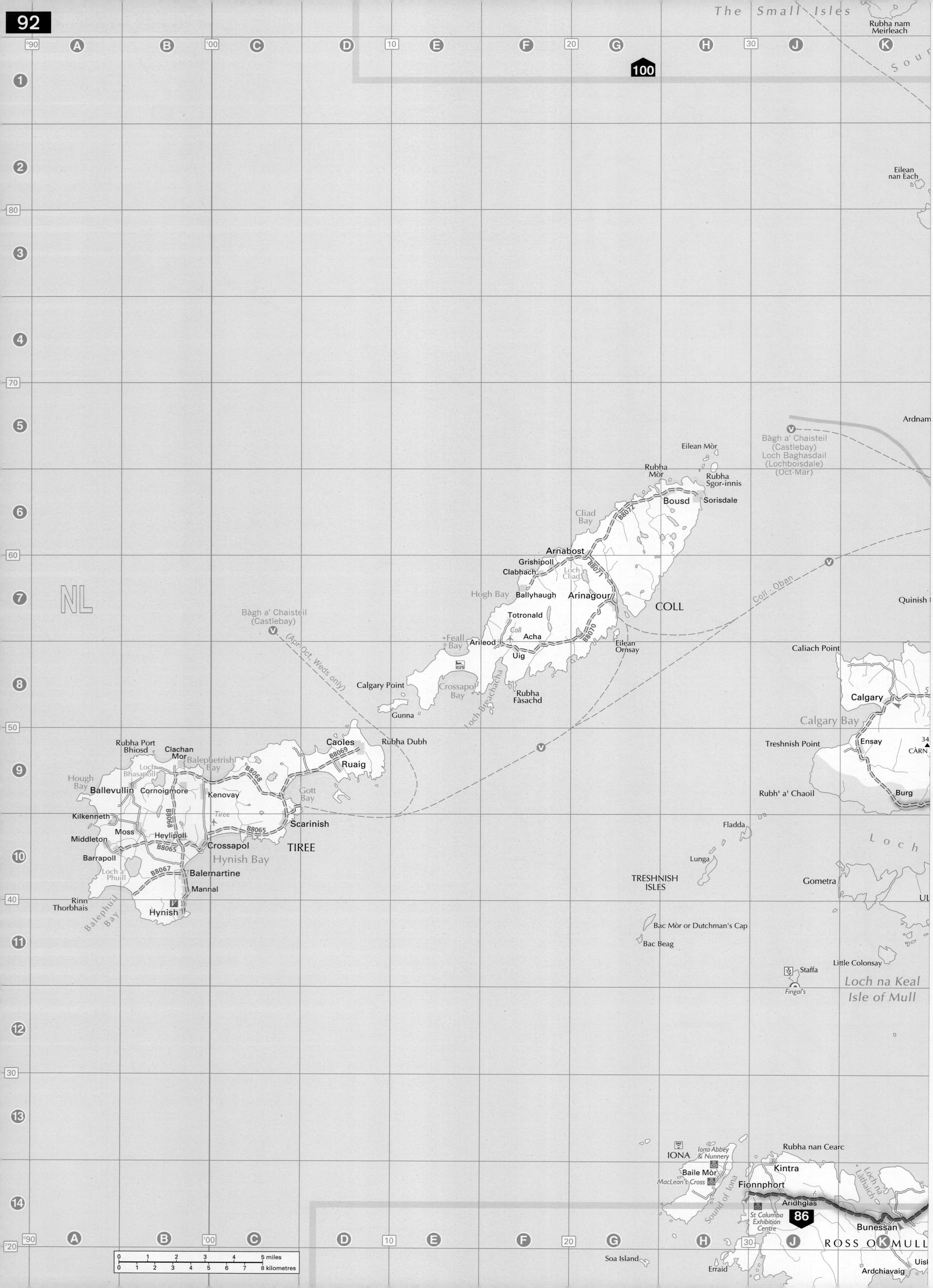

100

86

NL

COLL

TIREE

Rubha nam
Meirleach

Eilean
nan Each

Ardnam

Bàgh a' Chaisteil
(Castlebay)
Loch Baghasdail
(Lochboisdale)
(Oct-Mar)

Eilean Mòr

Rubha
Mòr

Rubha
Sgor-innis

Bousd   Sorisdale

Cliad
Bay

Arnabost

Grishipoll
Clabhach

Loch
Cliad

Hogh Bay   Ballyhaugh   Arinagour

Totronald

Coll
Acha

Arileod

Uig

Coll - Oban

Eilean
Ornsay

Quinish

Caliach Point

Calgary

Calgary Bay

Treshnish Point

Ensay

CÀRN

Rubh' a' Chaoil

Burg

Bàgh a' Chaisteil
(Castlebay)

(Apr-Oct, Weds only)

Feall
Bay

Calgary Point

Crossapol
Bay

Gunna

Loch Breachacha

Rubha
Fàsachd

Rubha Dubh

Caoles

Ruaig

B8069

Fladda

Lunga

Loch

Rubha Port
Bhiosd

Clachan
Mor

Balephetrish
Bay

Loch
Bhasapoll

B8068

Gott
Bay

Tiree

Scarinish

Treshnish Point

Hough
Bay

Ballevullin   Cornoigmore

Kenovay

Kilkenneth

B8068

Moss

Heylipoll

B8065

Middleton

Barrapoll

Crossapol

Hynish Bay

TIREE

B8067

Balemartine

Mannal

Rinn
Thorbhais

Loch a
Phuill

Balephuil Bay

Hynish

TRESHNISH
ISLES

Gometra

UL

Bac Mòr or Dutchman's Cap

Bac Beag

Little Colonsay

Staffa

Fingal's

Loch na Keal

Isle of Mull

IONA

Iona Abbey
& Nunnery

Rubha nan Cearc

Baile Mòr

Kintra

MacLean's Cross

Fionnphort

Sound of Iona

Aridhglas

St Columba
Exhibition
Centre

Bunessan

ROSS OF MULL

Soa Island

Erraid

Ardchiavaig

Uisk

0   1   2   3   4   5 miles
0   1   2   3   4   5   6   7   8 kilometres

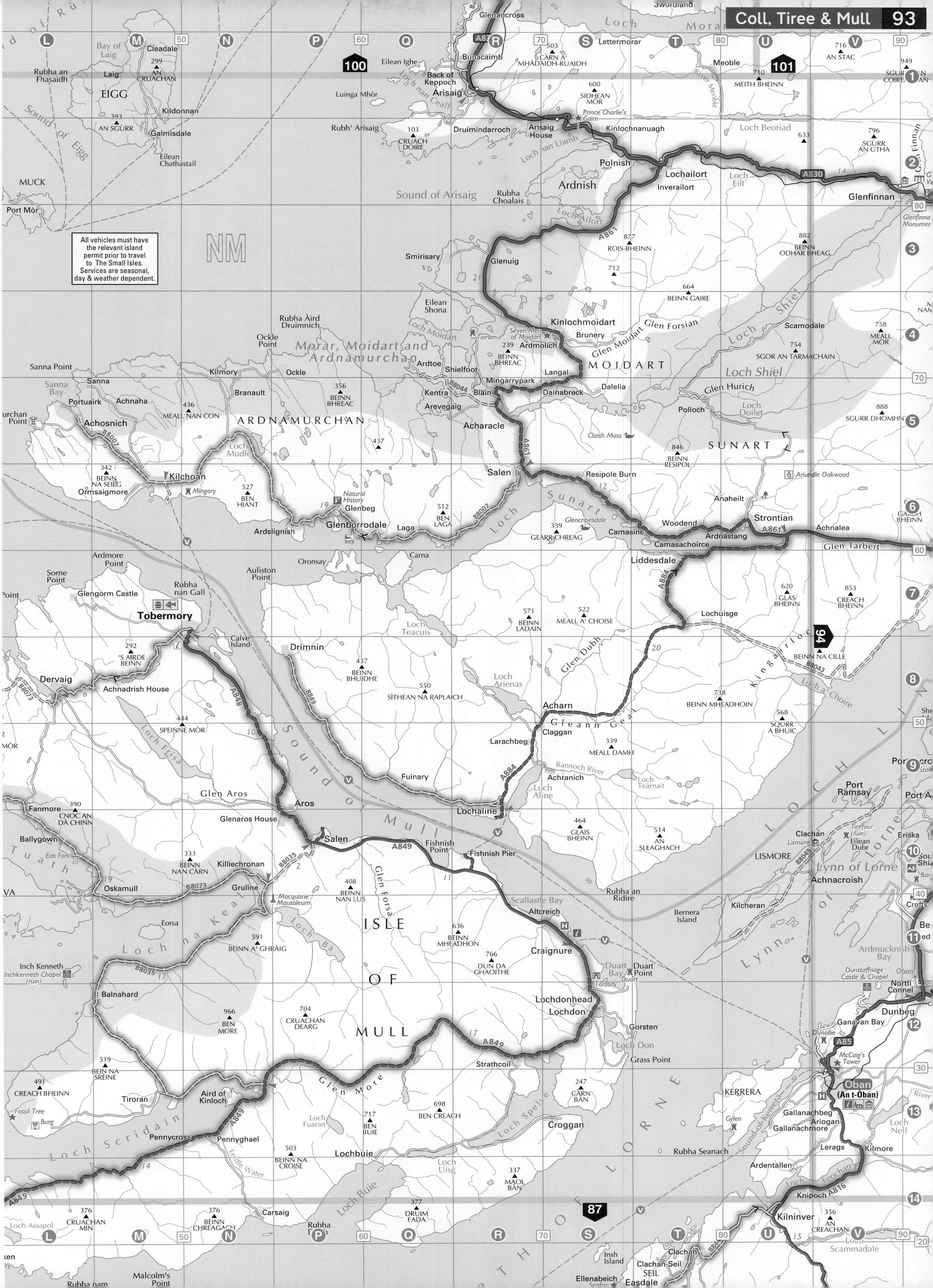

All vehicles must have the relevant island permit prior to travel to The Small Isles. Services are seasonal, day & weather dependent.
NM
EIGG
Cleadale
Laig
Bay of Laig
Rubha an Fhasaidh
299 AN CRUACHAN
Kildonnan
393 AN SGURR
Galmisdale
Eilean Chathastail
Sound of Eigg
MUCK
Port Mòr
100
101
Glenancross
Bunacaimb
Eilean Ighe
Back of Keppoch
Arisaig
Luinga Mhòr
Loch nan Ceall
Rubh' Arisaig
103 CRUACH DOIRE
Druimindarroch
Arisaig House
Loch nan Uamh
Sound of Arisaig
Rubha Choalais
503 CÀRN A' MHADAIDH-RUAIDH
Lettermorar
600 SIDHEAN MÒR
Prince Charlie's Cairn
Kinlochnanuagh
Polnish
Lochailort
Inveraillort
Ardnish
Loch Ailort
Meoble
River Meoble
710 MEITH BHEINN
716 AN STAC
949 SGURR COIRE
Loch Beoriad
633
796 SGÙRR AN UTHA
Loch Eilt
A830
Glenfinnan
Glenfinnan Monument
A861
877 ROIS-BHEINN
712
882 BEINN ODHAR BHEAG
Smirisary
Glenuig
Eilean Shona
664 BEINN GAIRE
Kinlochmoidart
Glen Forsian
Brunery
Glen Moidart
Seven Men of Moidart
Ardmolich
Loch Shiel
Scamodale
758 MEALL MÒR
754 SGOR AN TARMACHAIN
Rubha Àird Druimnich
Ockle Point
Loch Moidart
Tioram
239 BEINN BHREAC
Morar, Moidart and Ardnamurchan
MOIDART
Sanna Point
Sanna
Sanna Bay
Kilmory
Ockle
Ardtoe
Shielfoot
Langal
Mingarrypark
Dalelia
Glen Hurich
Portuairk
Achnaha
Branault
356 BEINN BHREAC
B8044
Kentra
Blain
Dalnabreck
Polloch
Loch Doilet
888 SGURR DHOMHNUILL
Achosnich
436 MEALL NAN CON
ARDNAMURCHAN
Arevegaig
Acharacle
Claish Moss
SUNART
B8007
Loch Mudle
437
846 BEINN RESIPOL
342 BEINN NA SEILG
Kilchoan
Mingary
527 BEN HIANT
Ormsaigmore
Natural History
Glenbeg
Salen
Resipole Burn
Ariundle Oakwood
Anaheilt
512 BEN LAGA
Laga
Glenborrodale
Ardslignish
Loch Sunart
Glencripesdale
339 GEARR CHREAG
Camasine
Woodend
Strontian
Ardnastang
Camasachoirce
Achnalea
Glen Tarbert
Ardmore Point
Sorne Point
Oronsay
Carna
Auliston Point
Liddesdale
A884
Glengorm Castle
Rubha nan Gall
Tobermory
620 GLAS BHEINN
853 CREACH BHEINN
571 BEINN LADAIN
522 MEALL A' CHOISE
Lochuisge
Loch Teacuis
Calve Island
Drimnin
292 'S AIRDE BHEINN
94
Glen Dubh
Kingairloch
BEINN NA CILLE
B8043
Dervaig
Achnadrish House
437 BEINN BHUIDHE
550 SÌTHEAN NA RAPLAICH
Loch Arienas
Acharn
738 BEINN MHEADHOIN
Loch a' Choire
B8073
A848
B849
Gleann Geal
568 SGURR A BHUIC
444 SPEINNE MÒR
Loch Frisa
Sound of Mull
Claggan
Larachbeg
339 MEALL DAMH
Rannoch River
Achranich
Loch Tearnait
Loch Aline
Funiary
Glen Aros
Aros
Lochaline
Port Ramsay
390 CNOC AN DÀ CHINN
Fanmore
Glenaros House
464 GLAIS BHEINN
514 AN SLEAGHACH
Ballygown
Salen
A849
Fishnish Point
Fishnish Pier
Clachan
Lismore
Tirefour (ruin)
Eilean Dubh
Eriska
Eas Fors
333 BEINN NAN CÀRN
Killiechronan
B8035
LISMORE
Lynn of Lorne
Achnacroish
B8045
Oskamull
Gruline
408 BEINN NAN LUS
Glen Forsa
Macquarie Mausoleum
Scallastle Bay
Rubha an Ridire
Altcreich
Kilcheran
Bernera Island
Loch na Keal
Eorsa
ISLE OF MULL
591 BEINN A' GHRÀIG
Loch Bà
636 BEINN MHEADHON
Craignure
Ardmucknish Bay
Inch Kenneth
Inchkenneth Chapel (ruin)
766 DÙN DA GHAOITHE
Duart Bay
Duart Point
Torosay
Duart
Dunstaffnage Castle & Chapel
North Connel
Balnahard
Lochdonhead
Lochdon
966 BEN MORE
704 CRUACHAN DEARG
Gorsten
Dunbeg
Ganavan Bay
Dunollie
A85
McCaig's Tower
Loch Don
Grass Point
Strathcoil
519 BEINN NA SREINE
Glen More
Oban (An t-Oban)
491 CREACH BHEINN
Tiroran
Aird of Kinloch
247 CARN BAN
KERRERA
Fossil Tree
Burg
698 BEN CREACH
Loch Spelve
Gallanachbeg
Gallanachmore
Ariogan
Loch Nell
Loch Scridain
Pennycross
Pennyghael
717 BEN BUIE
Loch Fuaran
Croggan
Gylen
Sound of Kerrera
Rubha Seanach
Lerags
Kilmore
Leidle Water
503 BEINN NA CROISE
Lochbuie
Loch Uisg
337 MAOL BAN
Ardentallen
Loch Feochan
Loch Buie
Firth of Lorne
Knipoch
A816
87
Loch Assapol
376 CRUACHAN MIN
376 BEINN CHREAGACH
Carsaig
Rubha
377 DRUIM FADA
Kilninver
356 AN CREACHAN
Loch Scammadale
Clachan
Clachan-Seil
SEIL
Insh Island
Ellenabeich
Easdale
Malcolm's Point

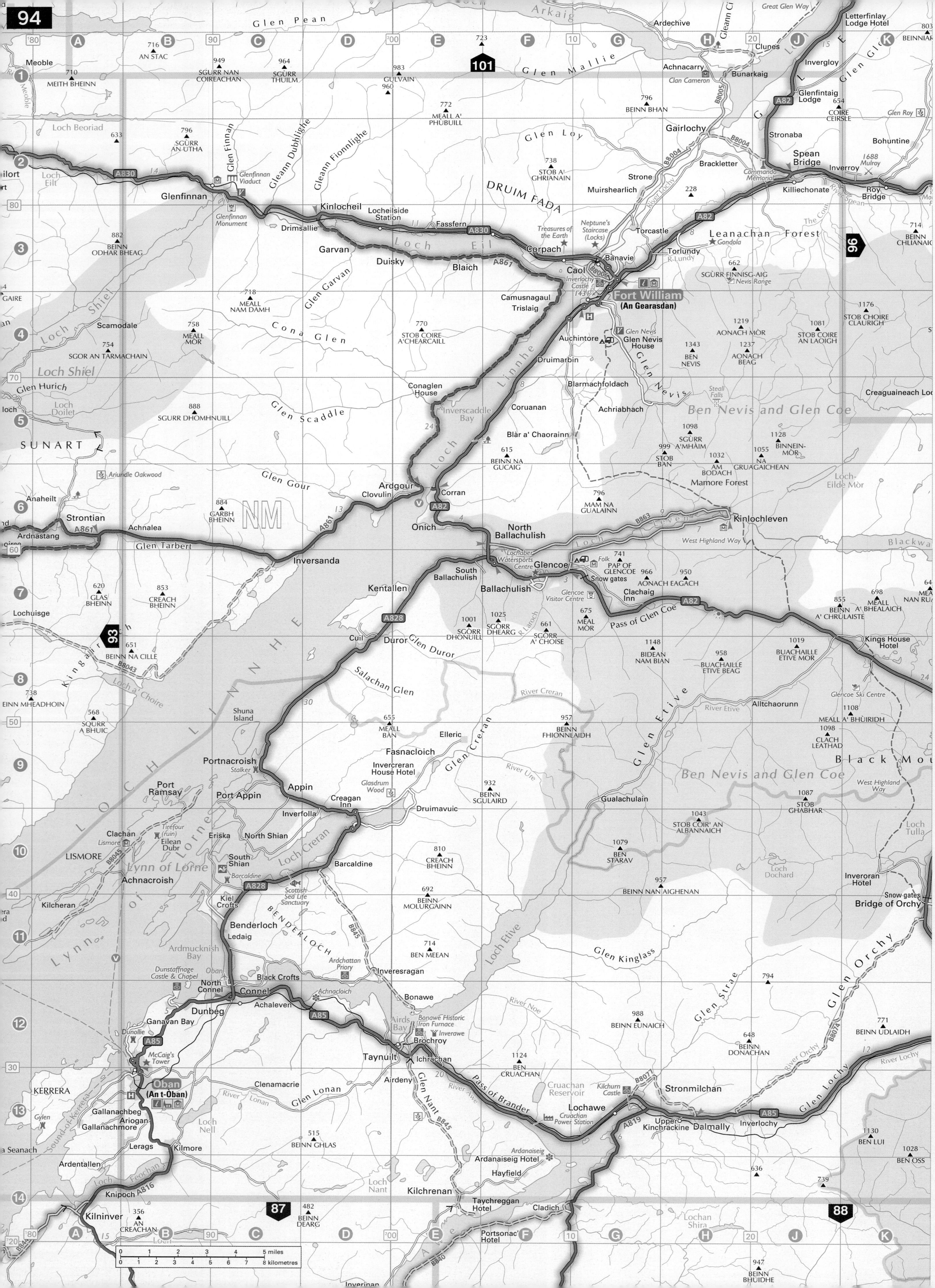

Glen Pean
Arkaig
Great Glen Way
Ardechive
Letterfinlay Lodge Hotel
Meoble
716 AN STAC
949 SGURR NAN COIREACHAN
964 SGURR THUILM
983 GULVAIN
960
723
101
Glen Mallie
Achnacarry
Clan Cameron
Clunes
Bunarkaig
Invergloy
Glen Gloy
803 BEINNIAR
710 MEITH BHEINN
772 MEALL A' PHUBUILL
796 BEINN BHAN
Glenfintaig Lodge
654 COIRE CEIRSLE
Glen Roy
Loch Beoriad
633
796 SGURR AN UTHA
Glen Finnan
Gleann Dubhlighe
Gleann Fionnlighe
Glen Loy
Gairlochy
Stronaba
Bohuntine
B8005
B8004
A82
Spean Bridge
Inverroy
1688 Mulroy
Brackletter
Commando Memorial
A830
Loch Eilt
Glenfinnan Viaduct
Glenfinnan
Glenfinnan Monument
738 STOB A' GHRIANAIN
DRUIM FADA
Strone
Muirshearlich
228
Killiechonate
Roy Bridge
River Spean
Kinlocheil
Locheilside Station
Drimsallie
Fassfern
Loch Eil
A830
Treasures of the Earth
Neptune's Staircase (Locks)
Torcastle
Leanachan Forest
Gondola
882 BEINN ODHAR BHEAG
Garvan
Duisky
Blaich
A861
Corpach
Banavie
Torlundy
R. Lundy
Caol
B8006
Inverlochy Castle
662 SGÙRR FINNISG-AIG
Nevis Range
714 BEINN CHLIANAIG
96
Loch Shiel
718 MEALL NAM DAMH
Glen Garvan
Camusnagaul
Trislaig
Fort William
(An Gearasdan)
GAIRE
1176 STOB CHOIRE CLAURIGH
Scamodale
758 MEALL MÒR
Cona Glen
770 STOB COIRE A'CHEARCAILL
Auchintore
Glen Nevis
Glen Nevis House
1219 AONACH MÒR
1081 STOB COIRE AN LAOIGH
754 SGOR AN TARMACHAIN
1343 BEN NEVIS
1237 AONACH BEAG
Druimarbin
Loch Linnhe
Glen Hurich
Loch Doilet
Conaglen House
Blarmachfoldach
Glen Nevis
Steall Falls
Creaguaineach Lodge
888 SGURR DHOMHNUILL
Glen Scaddle
Inverscaddle Bay
Coruanan
Achriabhach
Ben Nevis and Glen Coe
SUNART
Blàr a' Chaorainn
615 BEINN NA GUCAIG
1098 SGÙRR A'MHÀIM
999 STOB BAN
1032 AM BODACH
1128 BINNEIN MÒR
1055 NA GRUAGAICHEAN
Mamore Forest
Loch Eilde Mòr
Ariundle Oakwood
Glen Gour
Ardgour
Clovullin
Corran
Anaheilt
884 GARBH BHEINN
NM
796 MAM NA GUALAINN
Strontian
A82
A861
Onich
North Ballachulish
B863
Kinlochleven
Ardnastang
A861
Achnalea
Glen Tarbert
Lochaber Watersports Centre
West Highland Way
Blackwater
Inversanda
South Ballachulish
Glencoe
741 PAP OF GLENCOE
966
950 AONACH EAGACH
Folk
Snow gates
620 GLAS BHEINN
853 CREACH BHEINN
Kentallen
Ballachulish
Glencoe Visitor Centre
Clachaig Inn
A82
Pass of Glen Coe
855 BEINN A' CHRULAISTE
698 MEALL A' BHEALAICH
Lochuisge
A828
1001 SGORR DHONUILL
1025 SGORR DHEARG
661 SGORR A' CHOISE
675 MEAL MÒR
93
Cuil
Duror
Glen Duror
1148 BIDEAN NAM BIAN
958 BUACHAILLE ETIVE BEAG
1019 BUACHAILLE ETIVE MOR
Kings House Hotel
651 BEINN NA CILLE
B8043
Kingairloch
Loch a' Choire
Salachan Glen
River Creran
738 EINN MHEADHOIN
568 SGURR A BHUIC
Shuna Island
655 MEALL BÀN
957 BEINN FHIONNLAIDH
Glen Etive
River Etive
Alltchaorunn
Glencoe Ski Centre
1108 MEALL A' BHÙIRIDH
1098 CLACH LEATHAD
Elleric
Glen Creran
Fasnacloich
Portnacroish
Stalker
Invercreran House Hotel
River Ure
Black Mount
Ben Nevis and Glen Coe
West Highland Way
LOCH LINNHE
Port Ramsay
Port Appin
Appin
Glasdrum Wood
932 BEINN SGULAIRD
Creagan Inn
Inverfolla
Druimavuic
Gualachulain
1087 STOB GHABHAR
1043 STOB COIR' AN ALBANNAICH
Clachan
Lismore
Tirefour (ruin)
Eilean Dubh
Eriska
North Shian
Loch Creran
810 CREACH BHEINN
1079 BEN STARAV
Loch Tulla
LISMORE
B8045
Lynn of Lorne
Achnacroish
South Shian
Barcaldine
Barcaldine
Loch Dochard
957 BEINN NAN AIGHENAN
Inveroran Hotel
A828
Scottish Sea Life Sanctuary
692 BEINN MOLURGAINN
Snow gates
Bridge of Orchy
Kilcheran
Kiel Crofts
BENDERLOCH
Benderloch
Ledaig
B845
Lynn of Lorne
714 BEN MEEAN
Loch Etive
Glen Kinglass
Glen Orchy
Ardmucknish Bay
Dunstaffnage Castle & Chapel
Ardchattan Priory
Inveresragan
Black Crofts
North Connel
Connel
794
Achnacloich
Bonawe
River Noe
Glen Strae
Dunbeg
Achaleven
A85
988 BEINN EUNAICH
Ganavan Bay
Airds Bay
Bonawe Historic Iron Furnace
Inverawe
Brochroy
648 BEINN DONACHAN
771 BEINN UDLAIDH
B8074
Dunollie
A85
McCaig's Tower
Taynuilt
Ichrachan
1124 BEN CRUACHAN
River Orchy
River Lochy
KERRERA
Oban
(An t-Oban)
Clenamacrie
Glen Lonan
Airdeny
River Awe
Pass of Brander
Cruachan Reservoir
Kilchurn Castle
B8077
Stronmilchan
Glen Lochy
Gylen
Gallanachbeg
Ariogan
Gallanachmore
Sound of Kerrera
Loch Nell
Glen Nant
B845
Lochawe
Cruachan Power Station
A819
Upper Kinchrackine
Dalmally
A85
Inverlochy
1130 BEN LUI
Seanach
Lerags
Kilmore
515 BEINN GHLAS
Ardanaiseig
Ardanaiseig Hotel
Ardentallen
Loch Feochan
A816
Hayfield
636
1028 BEN OSS
Knipoch
Loch Nant
Kilchrenan
739
87
482 BEINN DEARG
Taychreggan Hotel
Cladich
88
Kilninver
356 AN CREACHAN
Portsonachan Hotel
Lochan Shira
B844
Loch Awe
B840
0 1 2 3 4 5 miles
0 1 2 3 4 5 6 7 8 kilometres
947 BEINN BHUIDHE
Inverinan

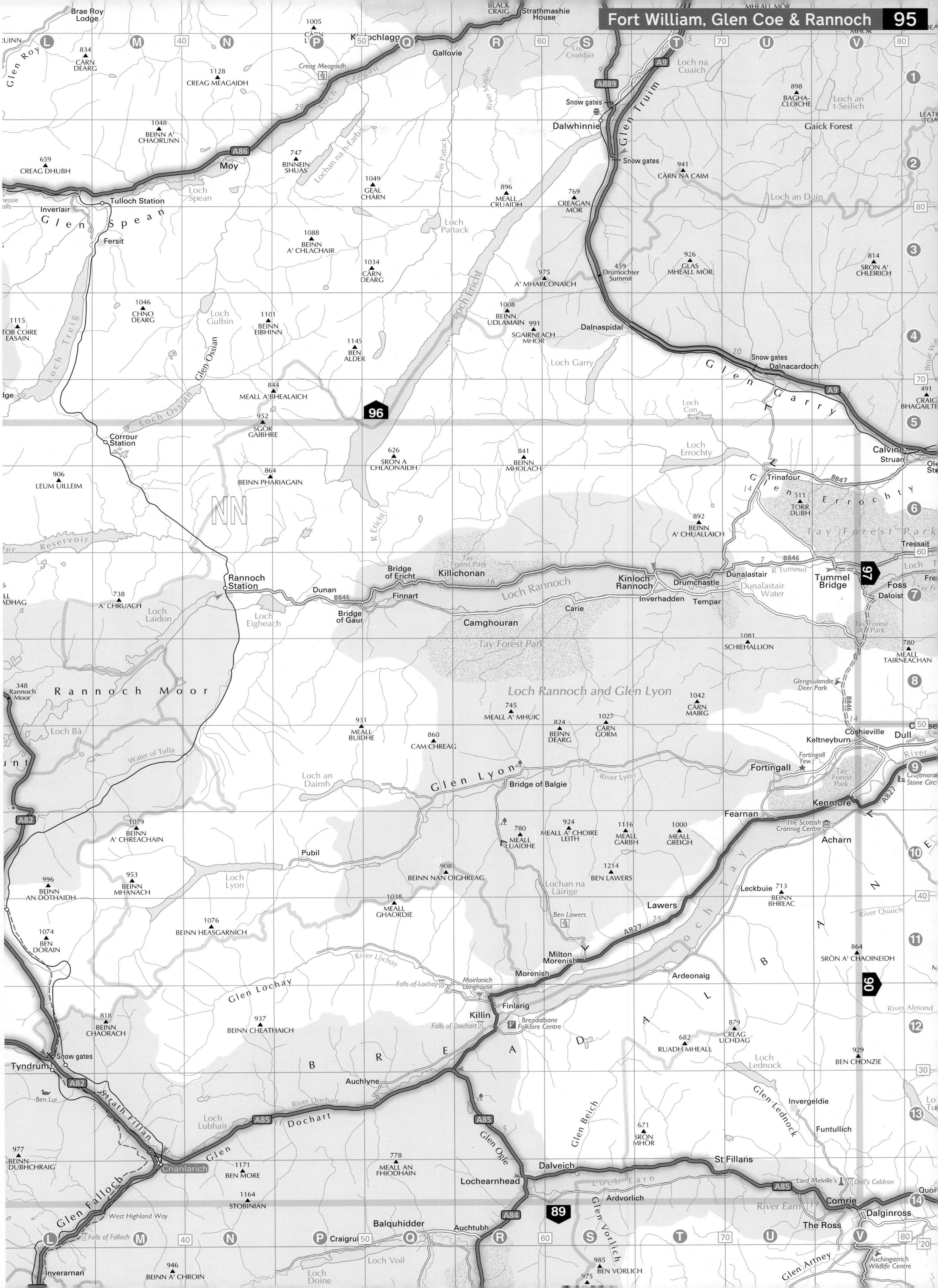
Brae Roy Lodge
Glen Roy
834 CARN DEARG
1128 CREAG MEAGAIDH
1005
Creag Meagaidh
Loch Laggan
Kinlochlaggan
Gallovie
Strathmashie House
BLACK CRAIG
Loch Coaldair
Loch na Cuaich
A9
A889
Snow gates
Dalwhinnie
Glen Truim
898 BAGHA-CLOICHE
Loch an t-Seilich
Gaick Forest
1048 BEINN A' CHAORUNN
A86
747 BINNEIN SHUAS
Lochan na h-Earba
River Pattack
River Maghie
659 CREAG DHUBH
Moy
Loch Spean
1049 GEAL CHÀRN
896 MEALL CRUAIDH
769 CREAGAN MÒR
941 CÀRN NA CAIM
Loch an Duin
Inverlair
Tulloch Station
Glen Spean
Fersit
Loch Pattack
1088 BEINN A' CHLACHAIR
1034 CÀRN DEARG
975 A' MHARCONAICH
459 Drumochter Summit
926 GLAS MHEALL MÒR
814 SRON A' CHLEIRICH
1115 STOB COIRE EASAIN
Loch Treig
1046 CHNO DEARG
Loch Gulbin
1101 BEINN EIBHINN
Glen Ossian
1145 BEN ALDER
Loch Ericht
1008 BEINN UDLAMAIN
991 SGAIRNEACH MHOR
Dalnaspidal
Loch Garry
Snow gates
Dalnacardoch
Glen Garry
A9
491 CRAIG BHAGAILTE
844 MEALL A'BHEALAICH
96
952 SGÒR GAIBHRE
Loch Ossian
Corrour Station
Loch Con
Loch Errochty
Calvine
Struan
626 SRON A CHLAONAIDH
841 BEINN MHOLACH
906 LEUM UILLEIM
864 BEINN PHARIAGAIN
NN
Trinafour
B847
511 TORR DUBH
Glen Errochty
892 BEINN A' CHUALLAICH
Tay Forest Park
R Ericht
Reservoir
Tay Forest Park
Killichonan
Bridge of Ericht
Rannoch Station
Dunan
B846
Finnart
Loch Rannoch
Kinloch Rannoch
Drumchastle
Dunalastair
R Tummel
Tummel Bridge
97
Foss
Daloist
Tressait
738 A' CHRUACH
Loch Laidon
Loch Eigheach
Bridge of Gaur
Camghouran
Carie
Inverhadden
Tempar
Dunalastair Water
Tay Forest Park
1081 SCHIEHALLION
780 MEALL TAIRNEACHAN
348 Rannoch Moor
Rannoch Moor
Loch Rannoch and Glen Lyon
Glengoulandie Deer Park
1042 CÀRN MAIRG
745 MEALL A' MHUIC
931 MEALL BUIDHE
860 CAM CHREAG
824 BEINN DEARG
1027 CÀRN GORM
Coshieville
Dull
Keltneyburn
Loch Bà
Water of Tulla
Glen Lyon
Bridge of Balgie
River Lyon
Fortingall
Fortingall Yew
Tay Forest Park
Croftmoraig Stone Circle
Loch an Daimh
Fearnan
Kenmore
A827
A82
1079 BEINN A' CHREACHAIN
780 MEALL LUAIDHE
924 MEALL A' CHOIRE LEITH
1116 MEALL GARBH
1000 MEALL GREIGH
The Scottish Crannog Centre
Acharn
Pubil
Loch Lyon
908 BEINN NAN OIGHREAG
1214 BEN LAWERS
996 BEINN AN DOTHAIDH
953 BEINN MHANACH
1038 MEALL GHAORDIE
Lochan na Lairige
Leckbuie
713 BEINN BHREAC
Lawers
Ben Lawers
River Quaich
1074 BEN DORAIN
1076 BEINN HEASGARNICH
River Lochay
A827
Loch Tay
Milton Morenish
Morenish
864 SRÒN A' CHAOINEIDH
Ardeonaig
Glen Lochay
Falls-of-Lochay
Moirlanich Longhouse
90
Finlarig
River Almond
818 BEINN CHAORACH
937 BEINN CHEATHAICH
Killin
Falls of Dochart
Breadalbane Folklore Centre
879 CREAG UCHDAG
682 RUADH MHEALL
929 BEN CHONZIE
Tyndrum
Snow gates
BREADALBANE
Loch Lednock
A82
Auchlyne
Ben Lui
Strath Fillan
River Dochart
Loch Lubhair
A85
Glen Dochart
A85
Glen Ogle
Glen Beich
Glen Lednock
Invergeldie
Funtullich
977 BEINN DUBHCHRAIG
671 SRÒN MHOR
Crianlarich
1171 BEN MORE
778 MEALL AN FHIODHAIN
Dalveich
St Fillans
Lochearnhead
Loch Earn
Lord Melville's
Deil's Caldron
1164 STOBINIAN
Ardvorlich
A85
River Earn
Comrie
Glen Falloch
West Highland Way
A84
89
Balquhidder
Auchtubh
Glen Vorlich
Dalginross
The Ross
Falls of Falloch
Craigruie
Loch Voil
Glen Artney
Auchingarrich Wildlife Centre
Inverarnan
946 BEINN A' CHROIN
Loch Doine
985 BEN VORLICH
975

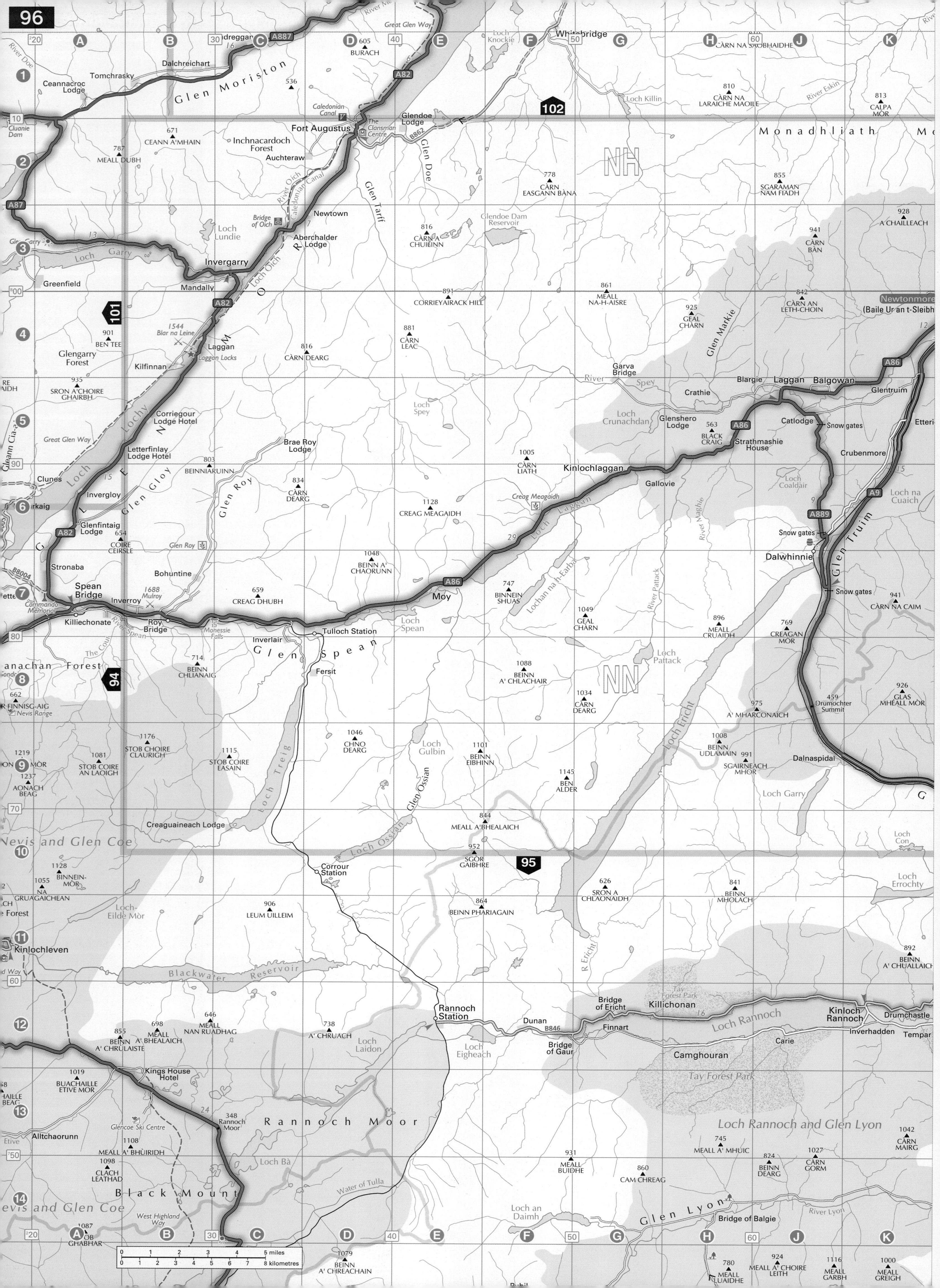

Glen Moriston
Dalchreichart
Tomchrasky
Ceannacroc Lodge
605 BURACH
536
Great Glen Way
Fort Augustus
Caledonian Canal
The Clansman Centre
Glendoe Lodge
Whitebridge
Loch Knockie
Loch Killin
810 CÀRN NA SAOBHAIDHE
810 CÀRN NA LARAICHE MAOILE
River Eskin
813 CALPA MÒR
102
Monadhliath
671 CEANN A' MHAIN
787 MEALL DUBH
Inchnacardoch Forest
Auchteraw
Cluanie Dam
River Oich
Caledonian Canal
Glen Doe
Glen Tarff
NH
778 CÀRN EASGANN BÀNA
855 SGARAMAN NAM FIADH
Bridge of Oich
Newtown
Loch Lundie
Aberchalder Lodge
816 CÀRN A' CHUILINN
Glendoe Dam Reservoir
928 A CHAILLEACH
941 CÀRN BÀN
Loch Garry
Invergarry
Greenfield
Mandally
Loch Oich
891 CORRIEYAIRACK HILL
861 MEALL NA-H-AISRE
925 GEAL CHÀRN
842 CÀRN AN LEITH-CHOIN
Newtonmore
(Baile Ùr an t-Slèibh)
101
901 BEN TEE
1544 Blar na Leine
Laggan
Laggan Locks
816 CÀRN DEARG
881 CÀRN LEAC
Glen Markie
Glengarry Forest
Kilfinnan
Garva Bridge
River Spey
Blargie
Laggan
Balgowan
Glentruim
Crathie
935 SRON A' CHOIRE GHAIRBH
Corriegour Lodge Hotel
Loch Spey
Loch Crunachdan
Glenshero Lodge
563 BLACK CRAIG
Catlodge
Snow gates
Strathmashie House
Crubenmore
Great Glen Way
Loch Lochy
Letterfinlay Lodge Hotel
Brae Roy Lodge
803 BEINNIARUINN
1005 CÀRN LIATH
Kinlochlaggan
Gallovie
Loch Coaldair
Clunes
Glen Gloy
Glen Roy
834 CÀRN DEARG
Invergloy
1128 CREAG MEAGAIDH
Creag Meagaidh
Loch Laggan
Loch na Cuaich
Glenfintaig Lodge
654 COIRE CEIRSLE
Glen Roy
River Maighe
Snow gates
Glen Truim
Dalwhinnie
Stronaba
1048 BEINN A' CHAORUNN
Lochan na h-Earba
747 BINNEIN SHUAS
River Pattack
Snow gates
941 CÀRN NA CAIM
Spean Bridge
Bohuntine
Inverroy
1688 Mulroy
659 CREAG DHUBH
Moy
Commando Memorial
Killiechonate
Roy Bridge
Monessie Falls
River Spean
Tulloch Station
Loch Spean
1049 GEAL CHÀRN
896 MEALL CRUAIDH
769 CREAGAN MÒR
Inverlair
Glen Spean
Fersit
714 BEINN CHLIANAIG
1088 BEINN A' CHLACHAIR
Loch Pattack
NN
94
662
Nevis Range
1034 CÀRN DEARG
926 GLAS MHEALL MÒR
975 A' MHARCONAICH
459 Drumochter Summit
1176 STOB CHOIRE CLAURIGH
1046 CHNO DEARG
Loch Gulbin
1101 BEINN EIBHINN
Loch Ericht
1008 BEINN UDLAMAIN
991 SGAIRNEACH MHOR
Dalnaspidal
1219
1081 STOB COIRE AN LAOIGH
1237 AONACH BEAG
1115 STOB COIRE EASAIN
Loch Treig
Glen Ossian
1145 BEN ALDER
Loch Garry
Creaguaineach Lodge
844 MEALL A' BHEALAICH
Loch Ossian
Loch Con
Nevis and Glen Coe
952 SGOR GAIBHRE
95
1128 BINNEIN MÒR
1055 NA GRUAGAICHEAN
Corrour Station
626 SRON A CHLAONAIDH
841 BEINN MHOLACH
Loch Errochty
Loch Eilde Mòr
906 LEUM UILLEIM
864 BEINN PHARIAGAIN
R Ericht
Kinlochleven
892 BEINN A' CHUALLAICH
Blackwater Reservoir
Tay Forest Park
Rannoch Station
646 MEALL NAN RUADHAG
738 A' CHRUACH
Loch Laidon
Dunan
Bridge of Ericht
Killichonan
Loch Rannoch
Kinloch Rannoch
Drumchastle
855 BEINN A' CHRULAISTE
698 MEALL A' BHEALAICH
Loch Eigheach
Finnart
Bridge of Gaur
Inverhadden
Carie
Tempar
Camghouran
Kings House Hotel
1019 BUACHAILLE ETIVE MOR
Tay Forest Park
348 Rannoch Moor
Rannoch Moor
Glencoe Ski Centre
Loch Rannoch and Glen Lyon
1042 CÀRN MAIRG
Alltchaorunn
1108 MEALL A' BHÙIRIDH
745 MEALL A' MHUIC
931 MEALL BUIDHE
1098 CLACH LEATHAD
Loch Bà
860 CAM CHREAG
824 BEINN DEARG
1027 CÀRN GORM
Black Mount
Water of Tulla
Glen Lyon
Nevis and Glen Coe
West Highland Way
Loch an Daimh
Bridge of Balgie
River Lyon
1087
1079 BEINN A' CHREACHAIN
780 MEALL LUAIDHE
924 MEALL A' CHOIRE LEITH
1116 MEALL GARBH
1000 MEALL GREIGH
A82
A87
A86
A9
A889
B862
B8004
B846
0 1 2 3 4 5 miles
0 1 2 3 4 5 6 7 8 kilometres

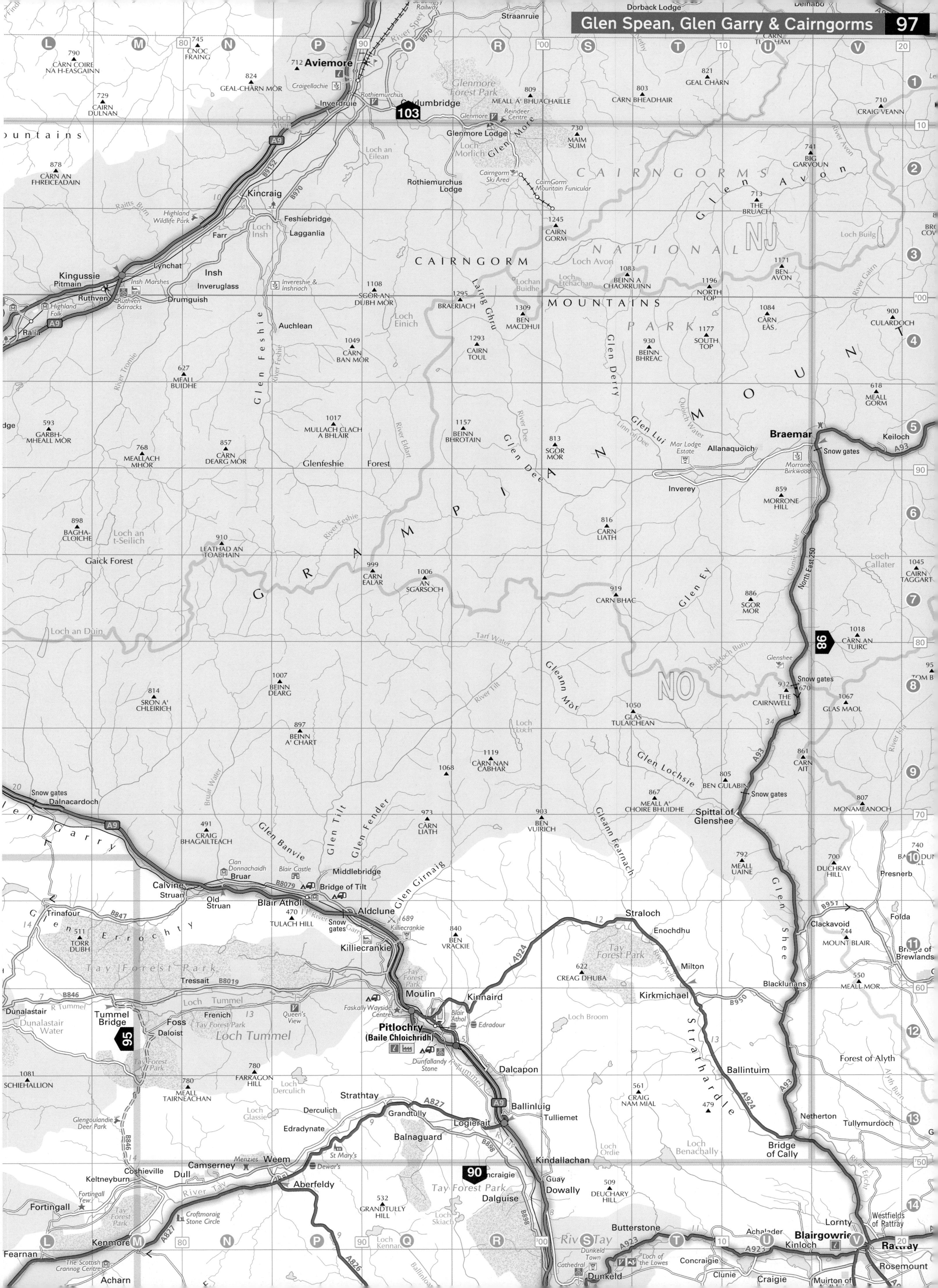

Aviemore
Coylumbridge
Inverdruie
Rothiemurchus
Glenmore Lodge
Glenmore Forest Park
Cairngorm Ski Area
CairnGorm Mountain Funicular
Rothiemurchus Lodge
Kincraig
Highland Wildlife Park
Feshiebridge
Lagganlia
Farr
Kingussie
Pitmain
Lynchat
Insh
Inveruglass
Ruthven
Ruthven Barracks
Drumguish
Highland Folk
Ralia
Auchlean
Glen Feshie
Glenfeshie Forest
CAIRNGORM MOUNTAINS
CAIRNGORMS NATIONAL PARK
GRAMPIAN MOUNTAINS
Glen Avon
1245 CAIRN GORM
1309 BEN MACDHUI
1295 BRAERIACH
1293 CAIRN TOUL
1083 BEINN A CHAORRUINN
1196 NORTH TOP
1171 BEN AVON
1177 SOUTH TOP
930 BEINN BHREAC
1108 SGOR AN DUBH MOR
1049 CARN BAN MOR
1017 MULLACH CLACH A BHLAIR
1157 BEINN BHROTAIN
813 SGOR MOR
Braemar
Keiloch
Inverey
Allanaquoich
Mar Lodge Estate
Morrone Birkwood
859 MORRONE HILL
816 CARN LIATH
919 CARN BHAC
886 SGOR MOR
1018 CARN AN TUIRC
1045 CAIRN TAGGART
Loch Callater
Glen Ey
Glen Dee
Glen Lui
Glen Derry
Lairig Ghru
Glenshee
932 THE CAIRNWELL
1067 GLAS MAOL
1050 GLAS TULAICHEAN
861 CARN AIT
805 BEN GULABIN
867 MEALL A' CHOIRE BHUIDHE
807 MONAMEANOCH
Spittal of Glenshee
Glen Lochsie
Gleann Mòr
Gleann Fearnach
Glen Shee
1119 CARN NAN CABHAR
1068
973 CARN LIATH
903 BEN VUIRICH
1007 BEINN DEARG
897 BEINN A' CHART
999 CARN EALAR
1006 AN SGARSOCH
910 LEATHAD AN TOABHAIN
898 BAGHA-CLOICHE
Gaick Forest
Loch an t-Seilich
Loch an Dùin
814 SRON A' CHLEIRICH
627 MEALL BUIDHE
593 GARBH-MHEALL MOR
768 MEALLACH MHOR
857 CARN DEARG MOR
790 CÀRN COIRE NA H-EASGAINN
745 CNOC FRAING
824 GEAL-CHÀRN MÒR
729 CAIRN DULNAN
878 CÀRN AN FHREICEADAIN
809 MEALL A' BHUACHAILLE
803 CARN BHEADHAIR
821 GEAL CHÀRN
710 CRAIG VEANN
730 MAIM SUIM
741 BIG GARVOUN
713 THE BRUACH
1084 CARN EAS
900 CULARDOCH
618 MEALL GORM
Dalnacardoch
Glen Garry
491 CRAIG BHAGAILTEACH
Glen Banvie
Glen Tilt
Glen Fender
Glen Girnaig
Calvine
Struan
Old Struan
Bruar
Clan Donnachaidh
Blair Castle
Blair Atholl
Bridge of Tilt
Middlebridge
Aldclune
470 TULACH HILL
689
840 BEN VRACKIE
Killiecrankie
Trinafour
Glen Errochty
511 TORR DUBH
Tay Forest Park
Tressait
Straloch
Enochdhu
Milton
622 CREAG DHUBA
Kirkmichael
Strathardle
Moulin
Kinnaird
Edradour
Pitlochry (Baile Chloichridh)
Dunfallandy Stone
Faskally Wayside Centre
Queen's View
Dunalastair
Dunalastair Water
Tummel Bridge
Foss
Daloist
Frenich
Loch Tummel
1081 SCHIEHALLION
780 MEALL TAIRNEACHAN
780 FARRAGON HILL
Loch Broom
Dalcapon
Ballintuim
561 CRAIG NAM MIAL
479
Ballinluig
Tulliemet
Strathtay
Derculich
Grandtully
Logierait
Edradynate
Balnaguard
Kindallachan
Glengoulandie Deer Park
Camserney
Weem
Coshieville
Dull
Keltneyburn
Fortingall
Aberfeldy
St Mary's
Dewar's
Guay
Dowally
Dalguise
509 DEUCHARY HILL
532 GRANDTULLY HILL
Croftmoraig Stone Circle
Kenmore
Fearnan
The Scottish Crannog Centre
Acharn
Butterstone
Dunkeld
Loch of the Lowes
Concraigie
Clunie
Craigie
Blairgowrie
Kinloch
Rattray
Rosemount
Lornty
Westfields of Rattray
Achalader
Bridge of Cally
Netherton
Tullymurdoch
Forest of Alyth
Blacklunans
550 MEALL MOR
744 MOUNT BLAIR
Clackavoid
Folda
Bridge of Brewlands
700 DUCHRAY HILL
Presnerb
792 MEALL UAINE
Snow gates
A9
A93
A924
A827
B8079
B847
B846
B8019
B950
B951
B898
B970
B9152
A923
North East 250
103
98
95
90
NJ
NO

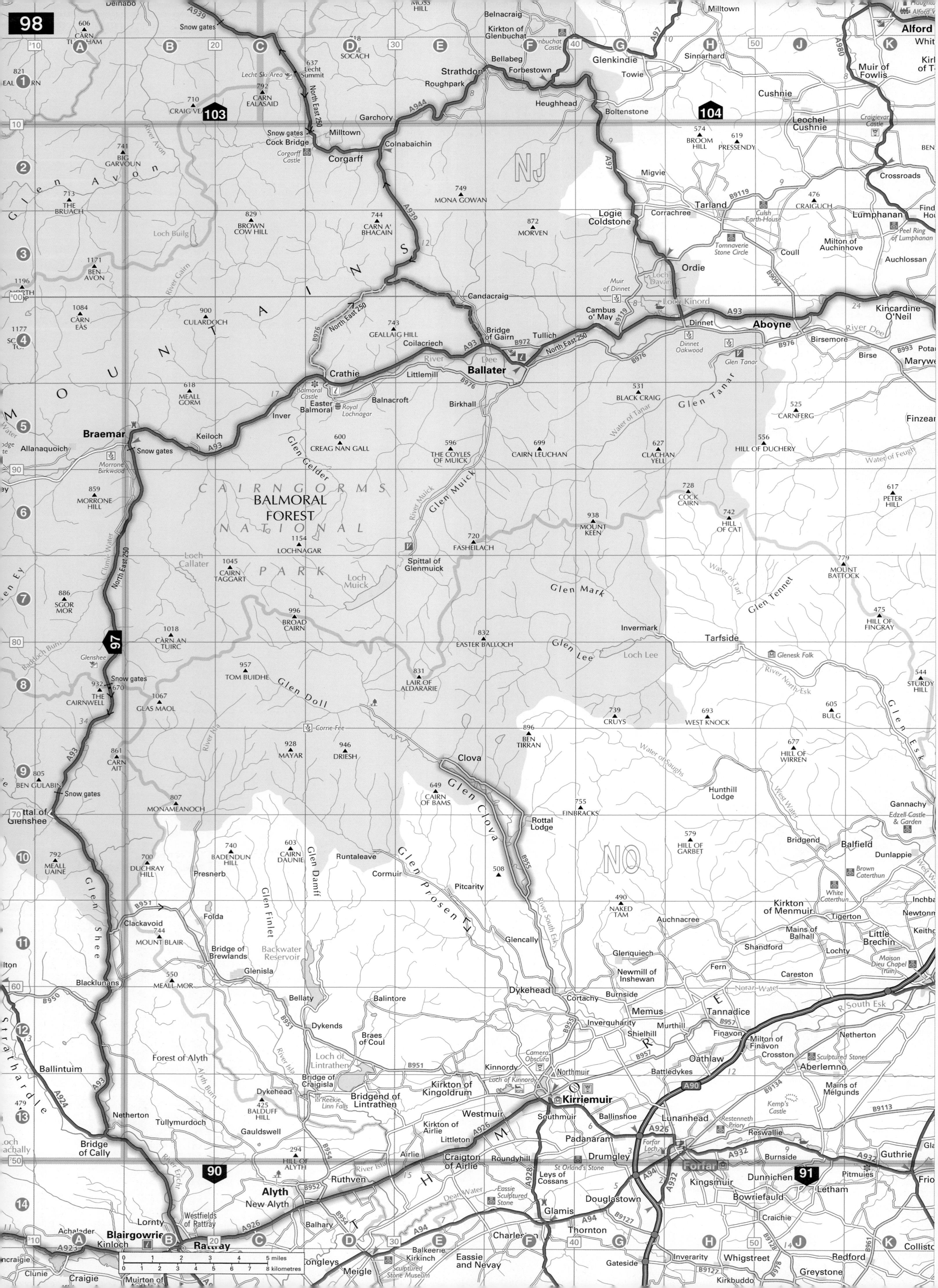

Snow gates
Lecht Ski Area
Lecht Summit
North East 250
CARN EALASAID
CRAIG VEAN
103
Corgarff Castle
Cock Bridge
Milltown
Corgarff
Colnabaichin
Garchory
Strathdon
Roughpark
Bellabeg
Forbestown
Kirkton of Glenbuchat
Belnacraig
Glenkindie
Towie
Heughhead
Boltenstone
Milltown
Sinnarhard
Alford
Muir of Fowlis
Cushnie
Leochel-Cushnie
Craigievar Castle
104
BROOM HILL
PRESSENDY
Migvie
Crossroads
Tarland
Corrachree
Culsh Earth-House
CRAIGUCH
Lumphanan
Peel Ring of Lumphanan
Milton of Auchinhove
Coull
Auchlossan
Tomnaverie Stone Circle
Logie Coldstone
MONA GOWAN
MORVEN
CARN A' BHACAIN
BROWN COW HILL
BIG GARVOUN
THE BRUACH
Loch Builg
BEN AVON
Glen Avon
River Avon
River Gairn
NJ
MOUNTAINS
Ordie
Loch Davan
Muir of Dinnet
Loch Kinord
Candacraig
Cambus o' May
Dinnet
Aboyne
Kincardine O'Neil
Dinnet Oakwood
Birsemore
Birse
River Dee
Glen Tanar
Potarch
Marywell
CULARDOCH
CARN EAS
GEALLAIG HILL
Coilacriech
Bridge of Gairn
Tullich
Crathie
Balmoral Castle
Easter Balmoral
Royal Lochnagar
Littlemill
Ballater
Balnacroft
Birkhall
BLACK CRAIG
CARNFERG
Finzean
MEALL GORM
Inver
Keiloch
Braemar
Allanaquoich
Snow gates
Morrone Birkwood
CREAG NAN GALL
THE COYLES OF MUICK
CAIRN LEUCHAN
CLACHAN YELL
HILL OF DUCHERY
Water of Tanar
Water of Feugh
MORRONE HILL
Glen Gelder
CAIRNGORMS NATIONAL PARK
BALMORAL FOREST
Glen Muick
River Muick
COCK CAIRN
PETER HILL
MOUNT KEEN
HILL OF CAT
FASHEILACH
LOCHNAGAR
Loch Callater
CAIRN TAGGART
Spittal of Glenmuick
Loch Muick
Clunie Water
SGOR MOR
MOUNT BATTOCK
Water of Tarf
Glen Tennet
Glen Mark
97
BROAD CAIRN
CARN AN TUIRC
EASTER BALLOCH
Invermark
Tarfside
HILL OF FINGRAY
Glenshee
Glen Lee
Loch Lee
Glenesk Folk
River North Esk
STURDY HILL
THE CAIRNWELL
GLAS MAOL
TOM BUIDHE
LAIR OF ALDARARIE
Glen Doll
CRUYS
WEST KNOCK
BULG
Corrie Fee
MAYAR
DRIESH
BEN TIRRAN
Clova
HILL OF WIRREN
Glen Esk
CARN AIT
River Isla
Water of Saughs
BEN GULABIN
Snow gates
Spittal of Glenshee
MONAMEANOCH
CAIRN OF BAMS
Glen Clova
FINBRACKS
Hunthill Lodge
West Water
Gannachy
Edzell Castle & Garden
Rottal Lodge
Bridgend
Balfield
Dunlappie
HILL OF GARBET
MEALL UAINE
DUCHRAY HILL
BADENDUN HILL
CAIRN DAUNIE
Glen Damff
Runtaleave
Glen Prosen
Cormuir
NO
Brown Caterthun
White Caterthun
Presnerb
Pitcarity
Glen Shee
Glen Finlet
NAKED TAM
Kirkton of Menmuir
Inchbare
Newtonmill
Folda
Clackavoid
MOUNT BLAIR
Bridge of Brewlands
Backwater Reservoir
Glencally
Auchnacree
Mains of Balhall
Tigerton
Little Brechin
Keithock
Shandford
Lochty
Glenisla
Glenquiech
Newmill of Inshewan
Fern
Careston
Maison Dieu Chapel (ruin)
Blacklunans
MEALL MOR
Dykehead
Cortachy
Burnside
Noran Water
Bellaty
Balintore
Memus
Tannadice
River South Esk
Strathardle
Dykends
Inverquharity
Murthill
Shielhill
Finavon
Milton of Finavon
Netherton
Braes of Coul
Loch of Lintrathen
Forest of Alyth
Kinnordy
Camera Obscura
Northmuir
Oathlaw
Crosston
Sculptured Stones
Aberlemno
Ballintuim
Battledykes
Loch of Kinnordy
Bridge of Craigisla
Reekie Linn Falls
Bridgend of Lintrathen
Kirkton of Kingoldrum
Kirriemuir
Mains of Melgunds
Dykehead
BALDUFF HILL
Kemp's Castle
Netherton
Tullymurdoch
Westmuir
Southmuir
Ballinshoe
Lunanhead
Restenneth Priory
Gauldswell
Kirkton of Airlie
Littleton
Padanaram
Reswallie
Bridge of Cally
HILL OF ALYTH
Airlie
Craigton of Airlie
Roundyhill
Drumgley
Forfar Loch
Forfar
Burnside
Guthrie
90
River Isla
Leys of Cossans
St Orland's Stone
Kingsmuir
Dunnichen
91
Pitmuies
Letham
Alyth
New Alyth
Ruthven
Dean Water
Eassie Sculptured Stone
Glamis
Douglastown
Bowriefauld
Lornty
Westfields of Rattray
Achalader
Blairgowrie
Kinloch
Rattray
Balhary
Charleston
Thornton
Craichie
Balkeerie
Kirkinch
Eassie and Nevay
Inverarity
Whigstreet
Redford
Colliston
Craigie
Clunie
Longleys
Meigle
Sculptured Stone Museum
Gateside
Kirkbuddo
Greystone
Muirton of Ardblair
0 1 2 3 4 5 miles
0 1 2 3 4 5 6 7 8 kilometres

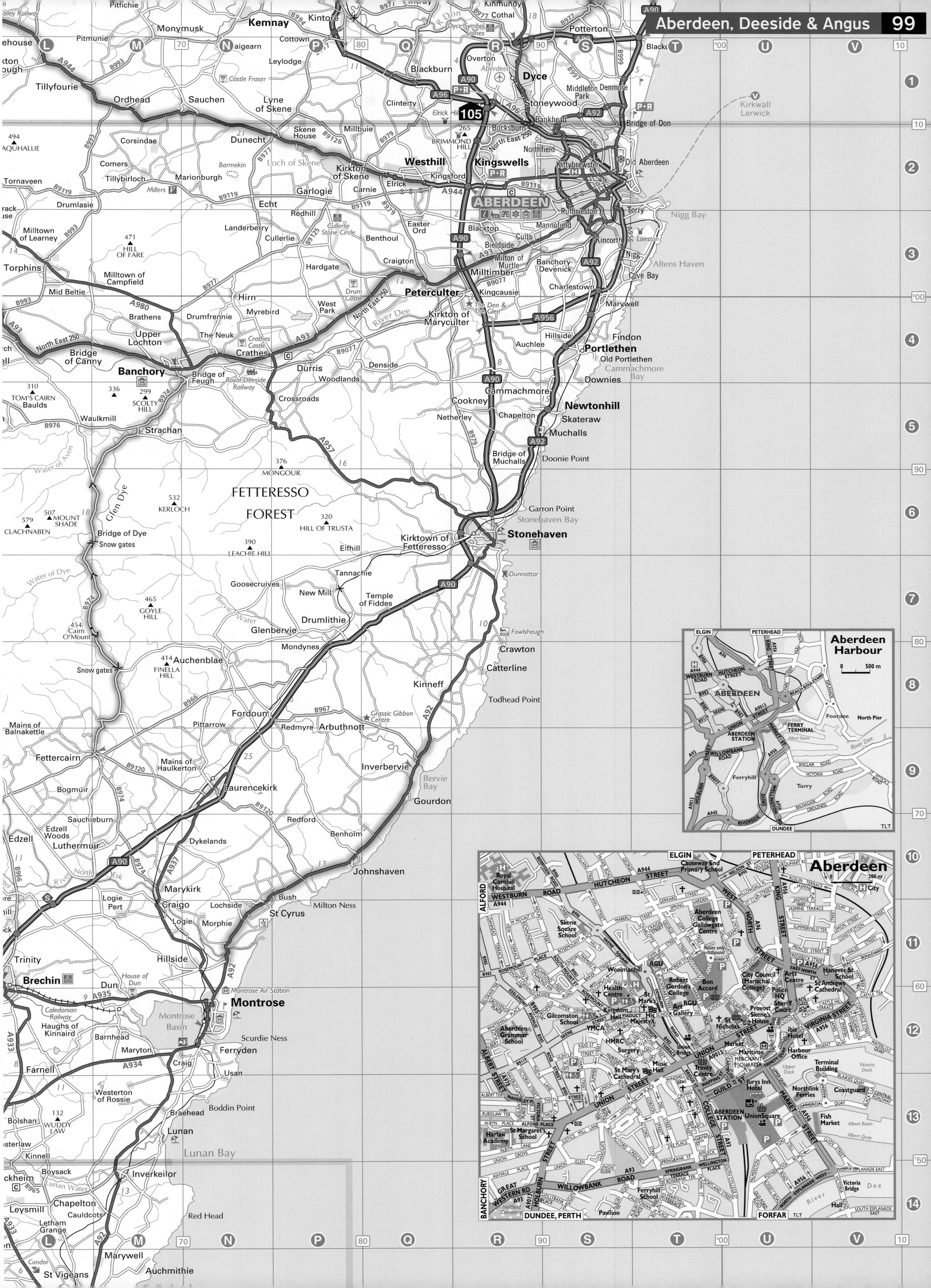
Kemnay
Kintore
Monymusk
Pitmunie
Nairgarn
Cottown
Leylodge
Blackburn
Overton
Dyce
Potterton
Tillyfourie
Ordhead
Sauchen
Lyne of Skene
Clinterty
Middleton Park
Denmore
Stoneywood
Bankhead
Bridge of Don
Kirkwall
Lerwick
Dunecht
Skene House
Millbuie
Bucksburn
Brimmond Hill
Corsindae
Westhill
Kingswells
Northfield
Kittybrewster
Old Aberdeen
Comers
Tillybirloch
Marionburgh
Kirkton of Skene
Kingsford
Tornaveen
Garlogie
Carnie
Elrick
ABERDEEN
Drumlasie
Echt
Redhill
Ruthrieston
Torry
Nigg Bay
Milltown of Learney
Landerberry
Cullerlie
Easter Ord
Mannofield
Hill of Fare
Benthoul
Blacktop
Bieldside
Cults
Kincorth
Torphins
Hardgate
Craigton
Milltimber
Milton of Murtle
Banchory-Devenick
Nigg
Altens Haven
Cove Bay
Milltown of Campfield
Mid Beltie
Hirn
Peterculter
Kingcausie
Charlestown
Drum Castle
West Park
The Den & The Glen
Marywell
Brathens
Drumfrennie
Myrebird
River Dee
Kirkton of Maryculter
Upper Lochton
The Neuk
Crathes Castle
Crathes
Bridge of Canny
Banchory
Bridge of Feugh
Royal Deeside Railway
Durris
Denside
Woodlands
Auchlee
Hillside
Findon
Portlethen
Old Portlethen
Cammachmore Bay
Downies
Tom's Cairn
Baulds
Scolty Hill
Crossroads
Cammachmore
Cookney
Newtonhill
Skateraw
Chapelton
Netherley
Muchalls
Waulkmill
Strachan
Water of Aven
Bridge of Muchalls
Doonie Point
Mongour
Glen Dye
FETTERESSO FOREST
Kerloch
Mount Shade
Clachnaben
Hill of Trusta
Garron Point
Stonehaven Bay
Bridge of Dye
Snow gates
Kirktown of Fetteresso
Stonehaven
Leachie Hill
Elfhill
Water of Dye
Dunnottar
Tannachie
Goosecruives
New Mill
Temple of Fiddes
Goyle Hill
Bervie Water
Drumlithie
Cairn O'Mount
Glenbervie
Fowlsheugh
Mondynes
Crawton
Auchenblae
Finella Hill
Catterline
Kinneff
Todhead Point
Fordoun
Grassic Gibbon Centre
Mains of Balnakettle
Pittarrow
Redmyre
Arbuthnott
Fettercairn
Mains of Haulkerton
Inverbervie
Bervie Bay
Bogmuir
Laurencekirk
Gourdon
Sauchieburn
Edzell Woods
Edzell
Luthermuir
Redford
Benholm
Dykelands
River North Esk
Johnshaven
Marykirk
Logie Pert
Craigo
Lochside
Logie
Morphie
Bush
Milton Ness
St Cyrus
Trinity
Hillside
House of Dun
Brechin
Dun
Caledonian Railway
Montrose Air Station
Montrose
Montrose Basin
Haughs of Kinnaird
Barnhead
Scurdie Ness
Maryton
Ferryden
Farnell
Craig
Usan
Westerton of Rossie
Boddin Point
Braehead
Bolshan
Wuddy Law
Lunan
Lunan Bay
Kinnell
Boysack
Inverkeilor
Lunan Water
Chapelton
Leysmill
Cauldcots
Red Head
Letham Grange
Marywell
Condor
St Vigeans
Auchmithie
Aberdeen Harbour
Elgin
Peterhead
Westburn Road
Hutcheon Street
Aberdeen Station
Ferry Terminal
Willowbank Road
Footdee
North Pier
River Dee
Ferryhill
Torry
Riverside
Dundee
Aberdeen
Royal Cornhill Hospital
Causeway End Primary School
Skene Square School
Aberdeen College Gallowgate Centre
Woolmanhill
RGU
Robert Gordon's College
City Council (Marischal College)
Police HQ
Sheriff Court
Hanover St School
St Andrew's Cathedral
Health Centre
St Mark's
Bon Accord
Art Gallery
His Majesty's
Provost Skene's House
Gilcomston School
YMCA
St Nicholas
ibis Hotel
Aberdeen Grammar School
HMRC
Surgery
Music Hall
Union Bridge
Trinity Centre
Maritime Museum
Merchant Quarter
Harbour Office
Terminal Building
St Mary's Cathedral
Jurys Inn Hotel
Northlink Ferries
Coastguard
Fish Market
Aberdeen Station
Union Square
Harlaw Academy
St Margaret's School
Ferryhill School
Pavilion
Victoria Bridge
Banchory
Dundee, Perth
Forfar

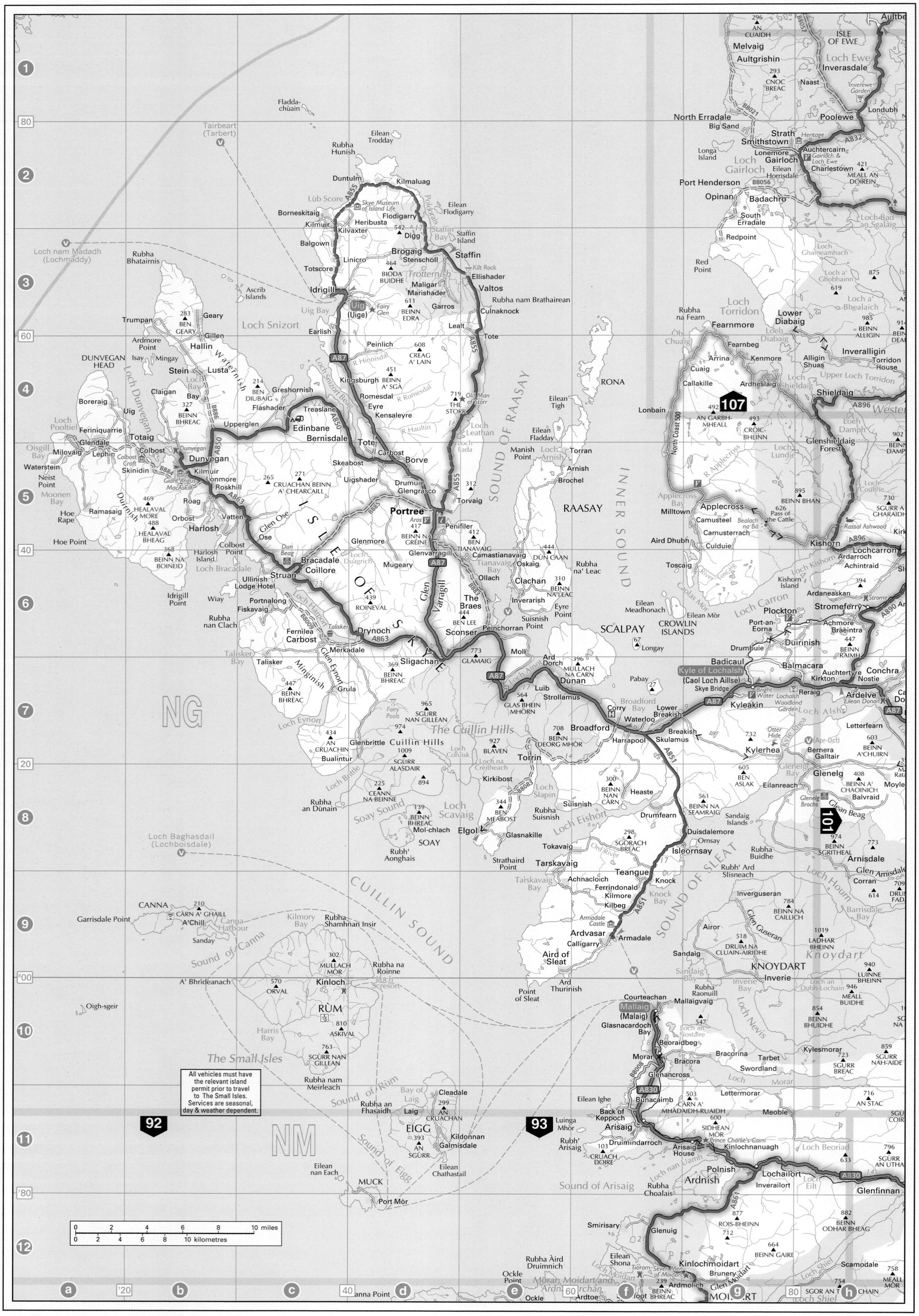

All vehicles must have the relevant island permit prior to travel to The Small Isles. Services are seasonal, day & weather dependent.

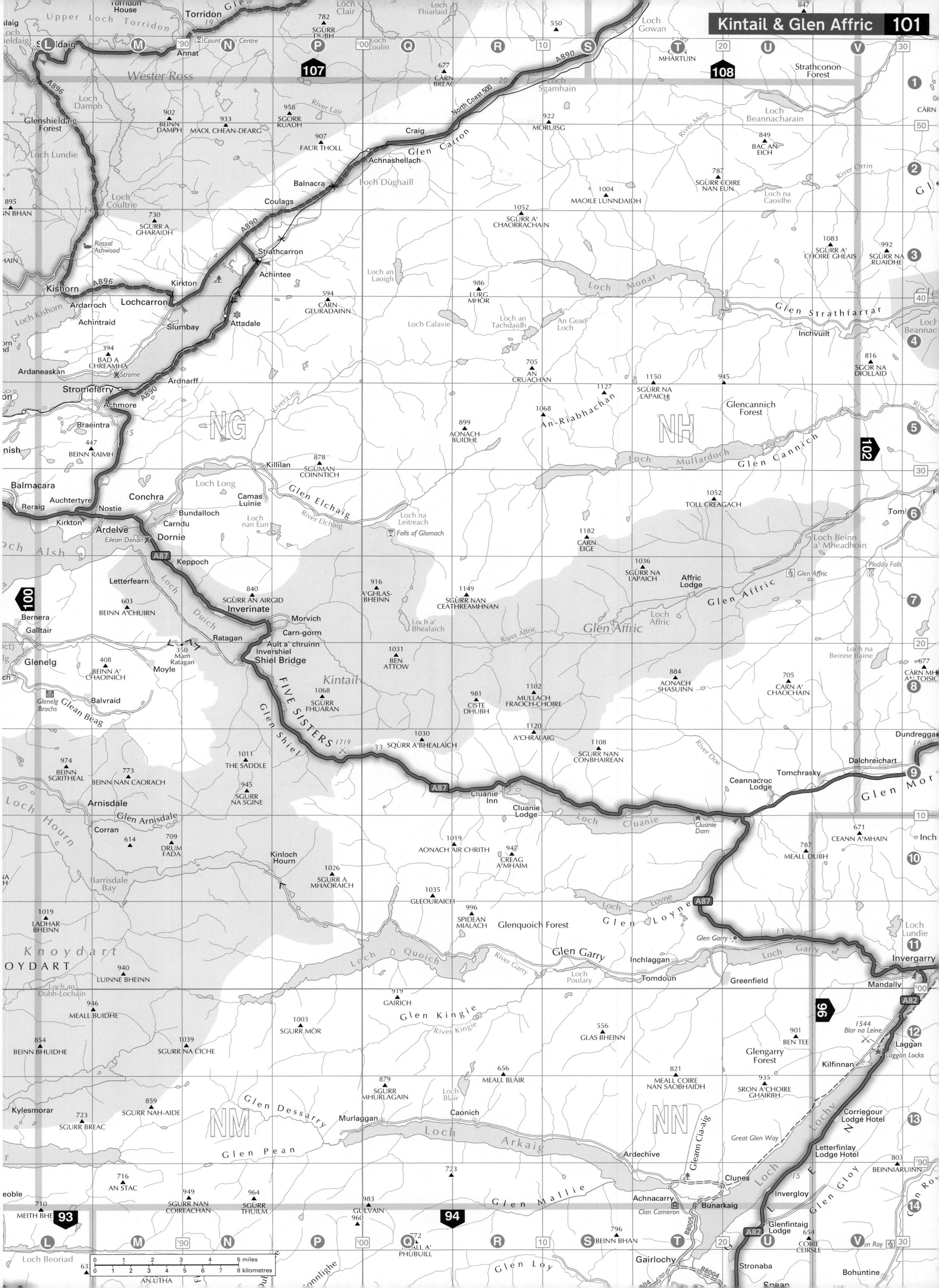
Torridon
Upper Loch Torridon
Shieldaig
Annat
Wester Ross
Loch Damph
Glenshieldaig Forest
Loch Lundie
Loch Coultrie
Rassal Ashwood
Kishorn
Ardarroch
Achintraid
Lochcarron
Kirkton
Slumbay
Attadale
Strathcarron
Achintee
Coulags
Balnacra
Loch Dùghaill
Achnashellach
Craig
Glen Carron
North Coast 500
Loch Sgamhain
Loch Beannacharain
Loch Gowan
Strathconon Forest
River Meig
River Orrin
Loch na Caoidhe
Loch Monar
Glen Strathfarrar
Inchvuilt
Loch an Laoigh
Loch Calavie
Loch an Tachdaidh
An Gead Loch
Ardaneaskan
Stromeferry
Achmore
Ardnarff
Strome
Braeintra
Balmacara
Reraig
Auchtertyre
Nostie
Conchra
Kirkton
Ardelve
Eilean Donan
Dornie
Carndu
Bundalloch
Loch Long
Camas Luinie
Killilan
Loch nan Eun
Glen Elchaig
River Elchaig
River Ling
Loch na Leitreach
Falls of Glomach
An-Riabhachan
Loch Mullardoch
Glen Cannich
Glencannich Forest
Keppoch
Letterfearn
Loch Duich
Inverinate
Morvich
Carn-gorm
Ault a' chruinn
Inversheil
Shiel Bridge
Ratagan
Bernera
Galltair
Glenelg
Moyle
Mam Ratagan
Balvraid
Glenelg Brochs
Glean Beag
Kintail
Five Sisters
Glen Shiel
Loch a' Bhealaich
River Affric
Glen Affric
Affric Lodge
Loch Affric
Loch Beinn a' Mheadhoin
Plodda Falls
Loch na Beinne Baine
Tomich
Dundreggan
Dalchreichart
Tomchrasky
Glen Moriston
Ceannacroc Lodge
River Doe
Cluanie Inn
Cluanie Lodge
Loch Cluanie
Cluanie Dam
Arnisdale
Glen Arnisdale
Corran
Loch Hourn
Kinloch Hourn
Barrisdale Bay
Knoydart
Glenquoich Forest
Loch Loyne
Glen Loyne
Glen Garry
Loch Garry
Inchlaggan
Tomdoun
Greenfield
Invergarry
Mandally
Loch Lundie
Loch Quoich
River Garry
Loch Poulary
Loch an Dubh-Lochain
Glen Kingie
River Kingie
Glengarry Forest
Laggan
Laggan Locks
Kilfinnan
Blar na Leine
Kylesmorar
Glen Dessarry
Murlaggan
Caonich
Loch Blair
Loch Arkaig
Glen Pean
Glen Mallie
Ardechive
Achnacarry
Clan Cameron
Bunarkaig
Clunes
Gleann Cia-aig
Great Glen Way
Loch Lochy
Corriegour Lodge Hotel
Letterfinlay Lodge Hotel
Glen Gloy
Invergloy
Glenfintaig Lodge
Spean
Stronaba
Gairlochy
Glen Loy
Loch Beoriad
Bohuntine
A896
A890
A87
A82
B8005
B8004
NG
NH
NM
NN
100
102
107
108
93
94
96
1544
1052 Sgùrr a' Chaorrachain
1004 Maoile Lunndaidh
787 Sgùrr Coire nan Eun
849 Bac an Eich
1083 Sgùrr a' Choire Ghlais
992 Sgùrr na Ruaidhe
986 Lurg Mhòr
594 Càrn Geuradainn
730 Sgùrr a' Gharaidh
902 Beinn Damph
933 Maol Chean-dearg
958 Sgorr Ruadh
907 Fuar Tholl
677 Càrn Breac
922 Moruisg
782 Sgùrr Dubh
394 Bad a' Chreamha
447 Beinn Raimh
705 An Cruachan
1150 Sgùrr na Lapaich
1127
1068
899 Aonach Buidhe
878 Sguman Coinntich
816 Sgor na Diollaid
1052 Toll Creagach
1182 Càrn Eige
1036 Sgùrr na Lapaich
916 A' Ghlas-bheinn
1149 Sgùrr nan Ceathreamhnan
840 Sgùrr an Airgid
603 Beinn a' Chuirn
408 Beinn a' Chaoinich
350 Mam Ratagan
1031 Ben Attow
1068 Sgùrr Fhuaran
981 Ciste Dhubh
1102 Mullach Fraoch-choire
884 Aonach Shasuinn
705 Càrn a' Chaochain
677 Càrn an Tòisich
1120 A'Chralaig
1108 Sgùrr nan Conbhairean
1030 Sgùrr a'Bhealaich
1011 The Saddle
974 Beinn Sgritheall
773 Beinn nan Caorach
945 Sgùrr na Sgine
614
709 Druim Fada
1019 Aonach air Chrith
947 Creag a'Mhaim
671 Ceann a'Mhaim
787 Meall Dubh
1026 Sgùrr a Mhaoraich
1035 Gleouraich
996 Spidean Mialach
1019 Ladhar Bheinn
940 Luinne Bheinn
946 Meall Buidhe
919 Gairich
1003 Sgùrr Mòr
556 Glas Bheinn
901 Ben Tee
854 Beinn Bhuidhe
1039 Sgùrr na Ciche
879 Sgùrr Mhurlagain
656 Meall Blair
821 Meall Coire nan Saobhaidh
935 Sron a'Choire Ghairbh
859 Sgùrr nah-Aide
723 Sgùrr Breac
723
716 An Stac
949 Sgùrr nan Coireachan
964 Sgùrr Thuilm
983 Gulvain
960
796 Beinn Bhan
803 Beinn Iaruinn
654 Coire Ceirsle
710 Meith Bheinn
772 Meall a' Phubuill
An Utha
0 1 2 3 4 5 miles
0 1 2 3 4 5 6 7 8 kilometres

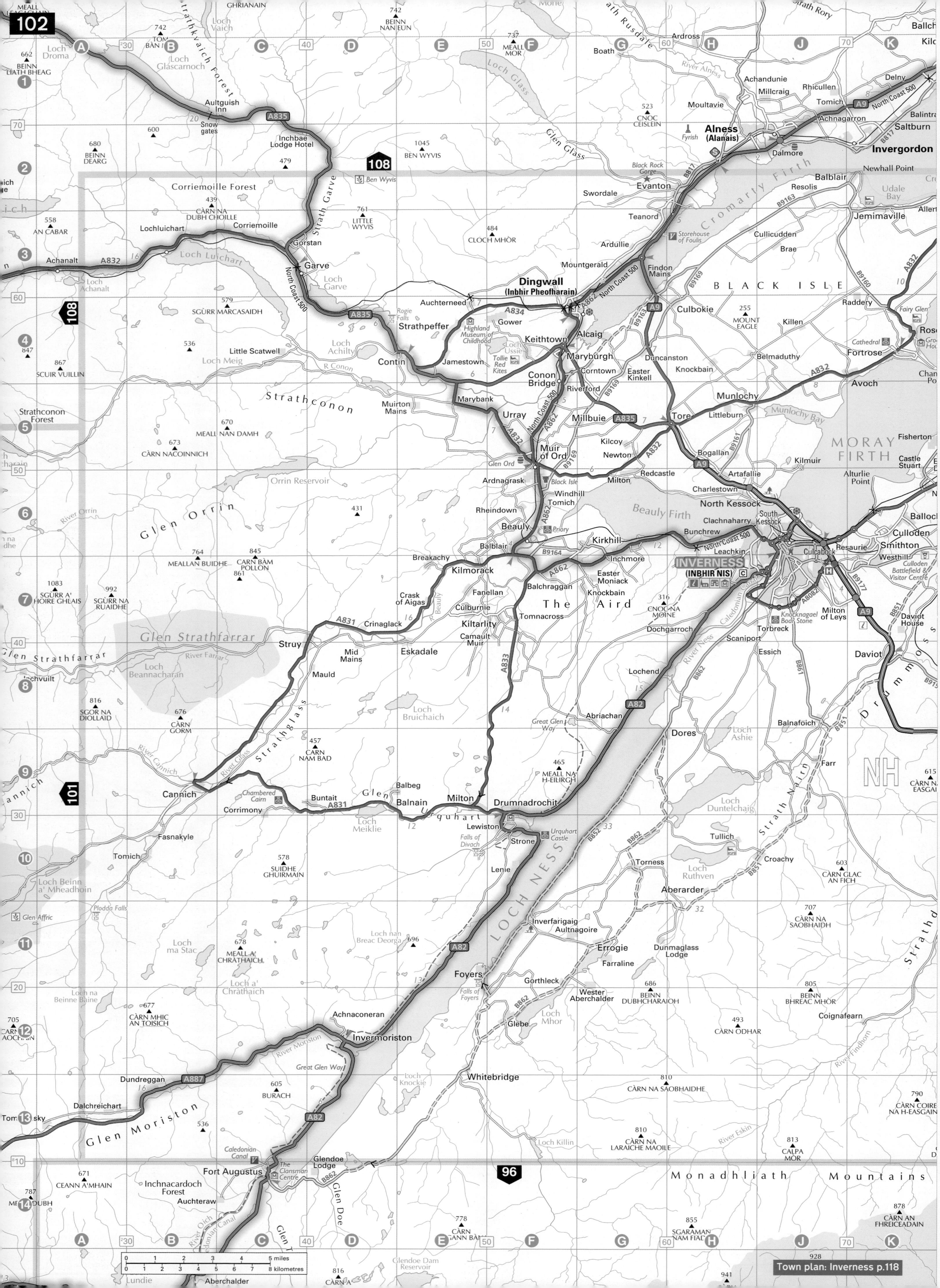
Loch Vaich
Loch Droma
Loch Glascarnoch
Strathvaich Forest
Ben Wyvis
BEN WYVIS
Loch Glass
Glen Glass
Achandunie
Millcraig
Rhicullen
Delny
Moultavie
Tomich
Achnagarron
Alness (Alanais)
Saltburn
Invergordon
Dalmore
North Coast 500
Newhall Point
Balblair
Resolis
Udale Bay
Jemimaville
Black Rock Gorge
Evanton
Swordale
Cromarty Firth
Teanord
Storehouse of Foulis
Ardullie
Cullicudden
Brae
Findon Mains
Mountgerald
Dingwall (Inbhir Pheofharain)
BLACK ISLE
Raddery
Fairy Glen
Auchterneed
Culbokie
MOUNT EAGLE
Killen
Aultguish Inn
Snow gates
Inchbae Lodge Hotel
Corriemoille Forest
CÀRN NA DUBH CHOILLE
Corriemoille
LITTLE WYVIS
Strath Garve
Lochluichart
AN CABAR
Gorstan
CLOCH MHÒR
Achanalt
Loch Luichart
Garve
Loch Garve
Loch Achanalt
SGÙRR MARCASAIDH
Rogie Falls
Strathpeffer
Highland Museum of Childhood
Gower
Keithtown
Alcaig
Maryburgh
Loch Ussie
Tollie Red Kites
Jamestown
Contin
Loch Achilty
Little Scatwell
Loch Meig
R Conon
SCUIR VUILLIN
Conon Bridge
Corntown
Easter Kinkell
Duncanston
Knockbain
Belmaduthy
Fortrose
Cathedral
Rosemarkie
Avoch
Munlochy
Munlochy Bay
Littleburn
Strathconon Forest
Strathconon
Muirton Mains
Marybank
Urray
Riverford
Millbuie
Tore
MEALL NAN DAMH
CÀRN NACOINNICH
Muir of Ord
Glen Ord
Kilcoy
Newton
Bogallan
Kilmuir
MORAY FIRTH
Fisherton
Castle Stuart
Alturlie Point
Orrin Reservoir
Ardnagrask
Black Isle
Milton
Redcastle
Artafallie
Charlestown
North Kessock
Glen Orrin
River Orrin
Windhill
Tomich
Rheindown
Beauly Firth
South Kessock
Clachnaharry
Beauly
Priory
Bunchrew
Kirkhill
Leachkin
Balloch
Culloden
Smithton
Culcabock
Resaurie
Westhill
Culloden Battlefield & Visitor Centre
INVERNESS (INBHIR NIS)
Balblair
MEALLAN BUIDHE
CÀRN BÀN POLLON
Breakachy
Kilmorack
Inchmore
Easter Moniack
Balchraggan
Knockbain
The Aird
SGÙRR A' CHOIRE GHLAIS
SGÙRR NA RUAIDHE
Crask of Aigas
Fanellan
Culburnie
Tomnacross
CNOC NA MOINE
Knocknagael Boar Stone
Milton of Leys
Daviot House
Glen Strathfarrar
A831
Crinaglack
Kiltarlity
Dochgarroch
Torbreck
Caledonian Canal
Struy
Camault Muir
Scaniport
Mid Mains
Eskadale
Essich
Daviot
Loch Beannacharan
River Farrar
Inchvuilt
Mauld
Lochend
River Ness
SGOR NA DIOLLAID
CÀRN GORM
Loch Bruiachaich
Abriachan
Great Glen Way
Dores
Loch Ashie
Balnafoich
Drummossie
Strathglass
CARN NAM BAD
MEALL NA H-EILIRGH
Farr
NH
CÀRN NA EASGAIN
River Cannich
River Glass
Cannich
Chambered Cairn
Buntait
Balbeg
Glen Urquhart
Balnain
Milton
Drumnadrochit
Corrimony
Loch Meiklie
Lewiston
Loch Duntelchaig
Strath Nairn
Fasnakyle
Falls of Divach
Strone
Urquhart Castle
Tullich
Tomich
SUIDHE GHUIRMAIN
Lenie
LOCH NESS
Torness
Croachy
Loch Ruthven
CÀRN GLAC AN FICH
Loch Beinn a' Mheadhoin
Aberarder
Plodda Falls
Glen Affric
CÀRN NA SAOBHAIDH
Inverfarigaig
Aultnagoire
Loch nan Breac Deorga
Loch ma Stac
MEALL A' CHRATHAICH
Errogie
Dunmaglass Lodge
Farraline
Foyers
Falls of Foyers
Loch a' Chràthaich
Gorthleck
Wester Aberchalder
BEINN DUBHCHARAIDH
BEINN BHREAC MHÒR
Loch na Beinne Baine
CÀRN MHIC AN TOISICH
Achnaconeran
Glebe
Loch Mhor
Coignafearn
CÀRN ODHAR
Invermoriston
River Moriston
Great Glen Way
River Findhorn
Loch Knockie
Whitebridge
Dundreggan
BURACH
CÀRN NA SAOBHAIDHE
Dalchreichart
CÀRN COIRE NA H-EASGAIN
Glen Moriston
Loch Killin
CÀRN NA LARAICHE MAOILE
River Eskin
CALPA MÒR
Caledonian Canal
Glendoe Lodge
Fort Augustus
The Clansman Centre
CEANN A' MHAIN
Inchnacardoch Forest
Auchteraw
Monadhliath Mountains
Glen Doe
River Oich
CÀRN AN FHREICEADAIN
SGARAMAN NAM FIAD
Glendoe Dam Reservoir
Lundie
Aberchalder
5 miles
8 kilometres

Town plan: Inverness p.118

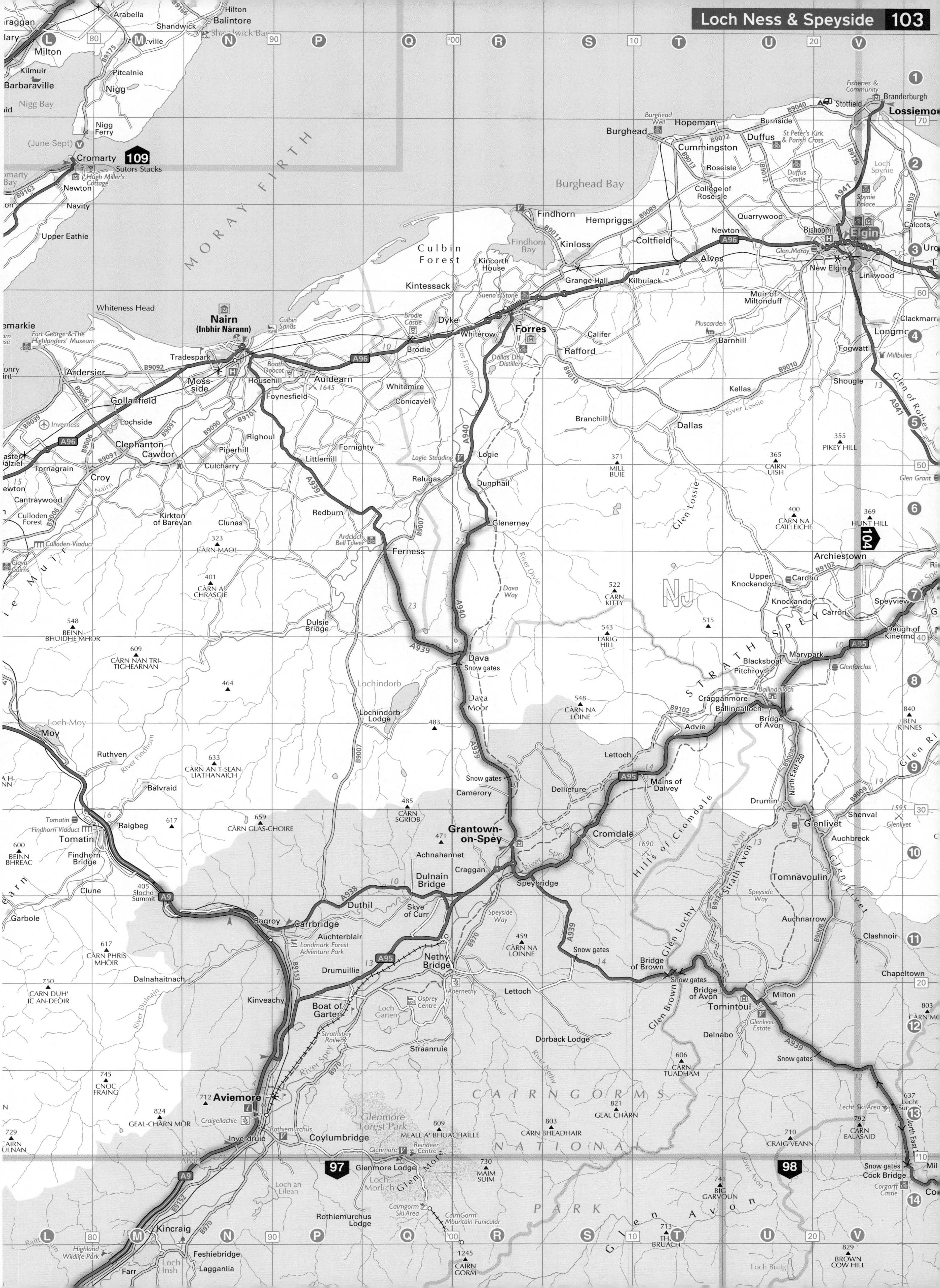
Arabella
Hilton
Balintore
Shandwick
Shandwick Bay
Milton
Kilmuir
Barbaraville
Pitcalnie
Nigg
Nigg Bay
Nigg Ferry
(June-Sept)
Cromarty
109
Sutors Stacks
Hugh Miller's Cottage
Newton
Navity
Upper Eathie
MORAY FIRTH
Burghead Bay
Burghead
Burghead Well
Hopeman
Cummingston
Duffus
St Peter's Kirk & Parish Cross
Duffus Castle
Roseisle
College of Roseisle
Fisheries & Community
Branderburgh
Stotfield
Lossiemouth
Loch Spynie
Spynie Palace
Quarrywood
Findhorn
Hempriggs
Findhorn Bay
Kinloss
Coltfield
Newton
Bishopmill
Elgin
Calcots
Glen Moray
New Elgin
Linkwood
Alves
Kilbuiack
Grange Hall
Culbin Forest
Kincorth House
Kintessack
Sueno's Stone
Muir of Miltonduff
Whiteness Head
Nairn (Inbhir Nàrann)
Culbin Sands
Brodie Castle
Dyke
Whiterow
Forres
Califer
Pluscarden
Barnhill
Clackmarras
Longmorn
Fort George & The Highlanders' Museum
Tradespark
Boath Doocot
Brodie
Dallas Dhu Distillery
Rafford
Fogwatt
Millbuies
Ardersier
Moss-side
Househill
Auldearn
1645
Whitemire
Conicavel
Kellas
Shougle
Glen of Rothes
Gollanfield
Foynesfield
River Findhorn
River Lossie
Lochside
Inverness
Branchill
Dallas
Clephanton
Cawdor
Righoul
Piperhill
Culcharry
Fornighty
Littlemill
Logie Steading
Logie
Dunphail
Relugas
371 MILL BUIE
365 CAIRN UISH
355 PIKEY HILL
Glen Grant
Tornagrain
Croy
River Nairn
Cantraywood
Culloden Forest
Kirkton of Barevan
Clunas
Redburn
Glenerney
Glen Lossie
400 CARN NA CAILLEICHE
369 HUNT HILL
104
Culloden Viaduct
323 CARN MAOL
Ardclach Bell Tower
Ferness
River Divie
Archiestown
Clava Cairns
401 CARN A' CHRASGIE
Dava Way
522 CARN KITTY
NJ
Upper Knockando
Cardhu
Knockando
Speyview
Carron
548 BEINN BHUIDHE MHOR
Dulsie Bridge
543 LARIG HILL
515
Daugh of Kinermony
609 CARN NAN TRI-TIGHEARNAN
Dava
Snow gates
STRATH SPEY
Marypark
Blacksboat
Pitchroy
Glenfarclas
464
Lochindorb
Dava Moor
548 CARN NA LOINE
Cragganmore
Ballindalloch
Bridge of Avon
840 BEN RINNES
Loch Moy
Moy
Lochindorb Lodge
483
Advie
Ruthven
River Findhorn
633 CARN AN T-SEAN-LIATHANAICH
Lettoch
Glen Rinnes
Snow gates
Mains of Dalvey
Balvraid
Camerory
Dellefure
North East 250
Drumin
Shenval
Glenlivet
Tomatin
Findhorn Viaduct
Raigbeg
617
659 CARN GLAS-CHOIRE
485 CARN SGRIOB
Grantown-on-Spey
471
Cromdale
Auchbreck
600 BEINN BHREAC
Findhorn Bridge
Achnahannet
Craggan
Hills of Cromdale
1690
Strath Avon
River Avon
Tomnavoulin
Glen Livet
405 Slochd Summit
Clune
Dulnain Bridge
Speybridge
River Spey
Speyside Way
Duthil
Skye of Curr
Auchnarrow
Garbole
Bogroy
Carrbridge
Auchterblair
Landmark Forest Adventure Park
Speyside Way
459 CARN NA LOINNE
Snow gates
Glen Lochy
Clashnoir
617 CARN PHRIS MHÒIR
Drumuillie
Nethy Bridge
Abernethy
Lettoch
Bridge of Brown
Snow gates
Chapeltown
750 CARN DUH' IC AN-DEÒIR
Dalnahaitnach
Kinveachy
River Dulnain
Boat of Garten
Loch Garten
Osprey Centre
Bridge of Avon
Tomintoul
Milton
Glen Brown
Glenlivet Estate
803
Strathspey Railway
Dorback Lodge
Delnabo
River Spey
Straanruie
River Nethy
606 CARN TUADHAM
Snow gates
745 CNOC FRAING
CAIRNGORMS
637 Lecht Summit
Lecht Ski Area
712 Aviemore
824 GEAL-CHÀRN MÒR
Craigellachie
Rothiemurchus
Glenmore Forest Park
809 MEALL A' BHUACHAILLE
803 CARN BHEADHAIR
821 GEAL CHÀRN
792 CARN EALASAID
710 CRAIG VEANN
729 CAIRN ULNAN
Inverdruie
Coylumbridge
Glenmore
Reindeer Centre
NATIONAL
Loch Alvie
97
Glenmore Lodge
730 MAIM SUIM
98
Snow gates
Cock Bridge
Corgarff Castle
Loch an Eilean
Loch Morlich
Glen More
741 BIG GARVOUN
River Avon
Glen Avon
Cairngorm Ski Area
CairnGorm Mountain Funicular
PARK
Rothiemurchus Lodge
Kincraig
713 THE BRUACH
Highland Wildlife Park
Feshiebridge
Loch Insh
Farr
Lagganlia
1245 CAIRN GORM
829 BROWN COW HILL
Loch Builg
A9
A95
A96
A938
A939
A940
A941
B9006
B9007
B9008
B9009
B9010
B9012
B9013
B9040
B9089
B9090
B9091
B9092
B9101
B9102
B9103
B9135
B9152
B9153
B9163
B9175
B970
L M N P Q R S T U V
80 90 00 10 20
60 50 40 30 20 10
1 2 3 4 5 6 7 8 9 10 11 12 13 14

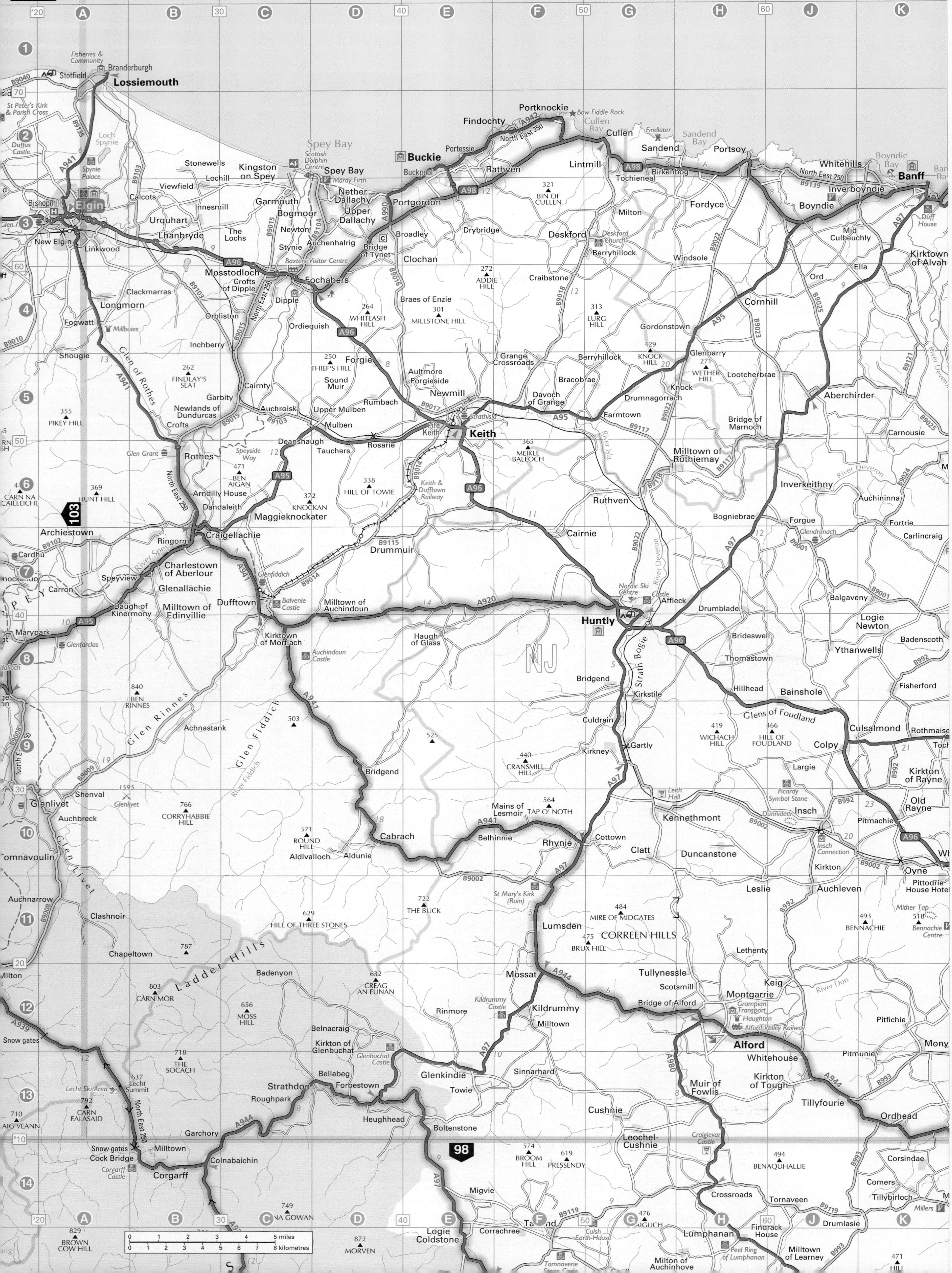

Lossiemouth
Branderburgh
Stotfield
Fisheries & Community
St Peter's Kirk & Parish Cross
Duffus Castle
Loch Spynie
Spynie Palace
Elgin
Bishopmill
New Elgin
Linkwood
Stonewells
Lochill
Kingston on Spey
Spey Bay
Scottish Dolphin Centre
Moray Firth
Viewfield
Calcots
Innesmill
Urquhart
Lhanbryde
Garmouth
Bogmoor
The Lochs
Newton
Stynie
Auchenhalrig
Nether Dallachy
Upper Dallachy
Bridge of Tynet
Baxters Visitor Centre
Mosstodloch
Crofts of Dipple
Dipple
Fochabers
Clackmarras
Longmorn
Fogwatt
Millbuies
Orbliston
Ordiequish
Inchberry
Shougle
Glen of Rothes
262 FINDLAY'S SEAT
Garbity
Cairnty
Newlands of Dundurcas
Crofts
Auchroisk
355 PIKEY HILL
Glen Grant
Rothes
Speyside Way
471 BEN AIGAN
Arndilly House
Dandaleith
369 HUNT HILL
CARN NA CAILLEICHE
Archiestown
Ringorm
Craigellachie
Cardhu
Charlestown of Aberlour
Speyview
Carron
Glenallachie
Dufftown
Glenfiddich
Balvenie Castle
Daugh of Kinermony
Milltown of Edinvillie
Marypark
Glenfarclas
Kirktown of Mortlach
Auchindoun Castle
Milltown of Auchindoun
840 BEN RINNES
Glen Rinnes
Achnastank
Glen Fiddich
River Fiddich
503
Glenlivet
Shenval
Auchbreck
766 CORRYHABBIE HILL
571 ROUND HILL
Aldivalloch
Aldunie
Cabrach
Bridgend
Tomnavoulin
Glen Livet
Auchnarrow
Clashnoir
629 HILL OF THREE STONES
Chapeltown
787
Ladder Hills
Badenyon
803 CÀRN MÒR
656 MOSS HILL
632 CREAG AN EUNAN
Snow gates
718 THE SOCACH
637 Lecht Summit
Lecht Ski Area
792 CARN EALASAID
710 AIG VEANN
Strathdon
Roughpark
Bellabeg
Forbestown
Glenbuchat Castle
Kirkton of Glenbuchat
Belnacraig
Heughhead
Garchory
Snow gates
Cock Bridge
Milltown
Corgarff Castle
Corgarff
Colnabaichin
749 NA GOWAN
829 BROWN COW HILL
872 MORVEN
Buckie
Portessie
Bucknool
Findochty
Portknockie
Bow Fiddle Rock
Cullen Bay
Cullen
Findlater
Sandend Bay
Sandend
Portsoy
Rathven
Portgordon
Lintmill
Tochieneal
Birkenbog
321 BIN OF CULLEN
Milton
Fordyce
Whitehills
Boyndie Bay
Banff
Inverboyndie
Boyndie
Duff House
Mid Culbeuchly
Kirktown of Alvah
Broadley
Clochan
Drybridge
Deskford
Deskford Church
Berryhillock
Windsole
Ella
Ord
272 ADDIE HILL
Craibstone
Braes of Enzie
264 WHITEASH HILL
301 MILLSTONE HILL
313 LURG HILL
Gordonstown
Cornhill
250 THIEF'S HILL
Forgie
Sound Muir
Upper Mulben
Mulben
Rumbach
Aultmore
Forgieside
Newmill
Grange Crossroads
Berryhillock
429 KNOCK HILL
Glenbarry
271 WETHER HILL
Lootcherbrae
Bracobrae
Davoch of Grange
Knock
Drumnagorrach
Farmtown
Aberchirder
Bridge of Marnoch
Carnousie
Strathisla
Fife Keith
Keith
Rosarie
Deanshaugh
Tauchers
365 MEIKLE BALLOCH
Milltown of Rothiemay
River Isla
River Deveron
338 HILL OF TOWIE
Keith & Dufftown Railway
372 KNOCKAN
Maggieknockater
Ruthven
Inverkeithny
Auchininna
Bogniebrae
Forgue
Glendronach
Fortrie
Carlincraig
Drummuir
Cairnie
Nordic Ski Centre
Castle
Affleck
Huntly
Drumblade
Balgaveny
Logie Newton
Haugh of Glass
NJ
Brideswell
Thomastown
Ythanwells
Badenscoth
Bridgend
Strath Bogie
Kirkstile
Hillhead
Bainshole
Fisherford
Glens of Foudland
Culdrain
419 WICHACH HILL
466 HILL OF FOUDLAND
Culsalmond
Rothmaise
Colpy
525
440 CRANSMILL HILL
Kirkney
Gartly
Largie
Kirkton of Rayne
Leith Hall
Picardy Symbol Stone
Insch
Old Rayne
Dunnideer
Pitmachie
Mains of Lesmoir
564 TAP O' NOTH
Belhinnie
Rhynie
Cottown
Kennethmont
Clatt
Duncanstone
Insch Connection
Kirkton
Oyne
Pittodrie House Hotel
St Mary's Kirk (Ruin)
722 THE BUCK
Leslie
Auchleven
484 MIRE OF MIDGATES
Lumsden
475 BRUX HILL
CORREEN HILLS
493 BENNACHIE
518 Mither Tap
Bennachie Centre
Lethenty
Mossat
Tullynessle
Scotsmill
Keig
River Don
Kildrummy Castle
Kildrummy
Milltown
Rinmore
Bridge of Alford
Montgarrie
Grampian Transport
Haughton
Alford Valley Railway
Alford
Whitehouse
Pitfichie
Pitmunie
Mony
Sinnarhard
Glenkindie
Towie
Muir of Fowlis
Kirkton of Tough
Tillyfourie
Cushnie
Ordhead
Boltenstone
Leochel-Cushnie
Craigievar Castle
574 BROOM HILL
619 PRESSENDY
494 BENAQUHALLIE
Corsindae
Migvie
Crossroads
Tornaveen
Comers
Tillybirloch
Millers
Logie Coldstone
Corrachree
Tarland
Cush Earth-House
476 AIGUCH
Lumphanan
Peel Ring of Lumphanan
Findrack House
Drumlasie
Milton of Auchinhove
Milltown of Learney
471 HILL
North East 250
103
98
A98 A96 A95 A941 A920 A97 A944 A980 A939 A990 A942
B9040 B9135 B9103 B9015 B9104 B9016 B9018 B9022 B9139 B9025 B9023 B9121 B9017 B9117 B9014 B9115 B9116 B9024 B9001 B9002 B992 B9102 B9009 B9008 B9010 B993 B9119
0 1 2 3 4 5 miles
0 1 2 3 4 5 6 7 8 kilometres

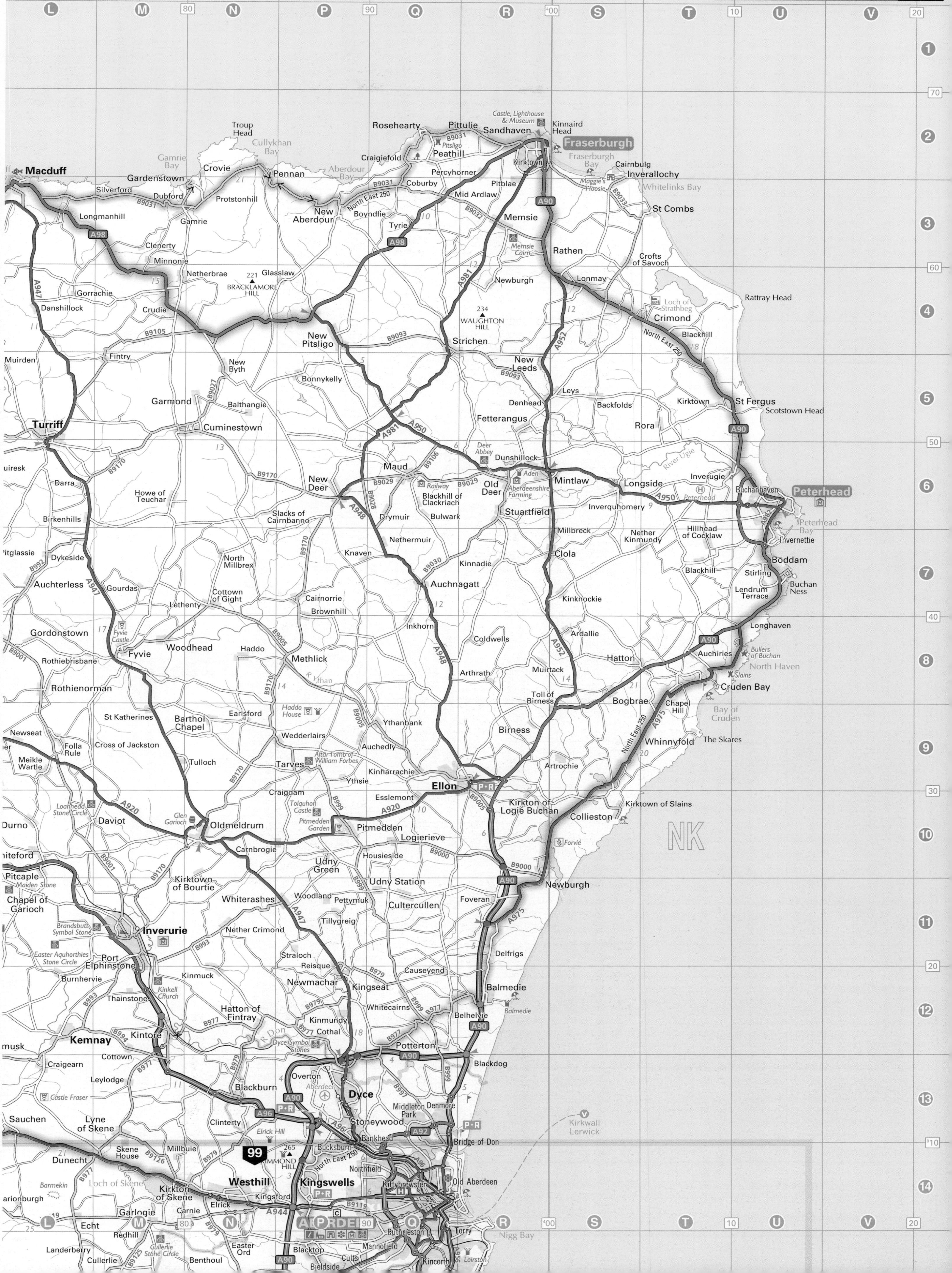
Fraserburgh
Peterhead
Macduff
Turriff
Inverurie
Ellon
Westhill
Kingswells
Dyce
Rosehearty
Pittulie
Sandhaven
Kinnaird Head
Castle, Lighthouse & Museum
Troup Head
Cullykhan Bay
Gamrie Bay
Crovie
Pennan
Aberdour Bay
Craigiefold
Peathill
Pitsligo
Kirktown
Fraserburgh Bay
Cairnbulg
Inverallochy
Maggie's Hoosie
Whitelinks Bay
Gardenstown
Silverford
Dubford
Protstonhill
New Aberdour
Coburby
Percyhorner
Mid Ardlaw
Pitblae
Boyndlie
Tyrie
Memsie
Memsie Cairn
Rathen
St Combs
Crofts of Savoch
Longmanhill
Gamrie
Clenerty
Minnonie
Netherbrae
Glasslaw
Bracklamore Hill
Gorrachie
Danshillock
Crudie
New Pitsligo
Newburgh
Lonmay
Loch of Strathbeg
Rattray Head
Crimond
Blackhill
Waughton Hill
Strichen
New Leeds
Muirden
Fintry
New Byth
Bonnykelly
Garmond
Balthangie
Cuminestown
Leys
Denhead
Backfolds
Kirktown
St Fergus
Scotstown Head
Fetterangus
Rora
Deer Abbey
Dunshillock
Aden
Aberdeenshire Farming
Mintlaw
Longside
Inverugie
River Ugie
Buchanhaven
Darra
Howe of Teuchar
Maud
Railway
New Deer
Blackhill of Clackriach
Old Deer
Stuartfield
Inverquhomery
Birkenhills
Slacks of Cairnbanno
Drymuir
Bulwark
Millbreck
Nether Kinmundy
Hillhead of Cocklaw
Peterhead Bay
Invernettie
Dykeside
Nethermuir
Knaven
Clola
Boddam
North Millbrex
Kinnadie
Blackhill
Stirling
Auchterless
Gourdas
Cottown of Gight
Auchnagatt
Buchan Ness
Lendrum Terrace
Lethenty
Cairnorrie
Brownhill
Kinknockie
Longhaven
Gordonstown
Fyvie Castle
Inkhorn
Ardallie
Coldwells
Fyvie
Woodhead
Haddo
Methlick
Hatton
Auchiries
Bullers of Buchan
North Haven
Rothiebrisbane
Arthrath
Muirtack
Slains
Cruden Bay
Rothienorman
Toll of Birness
Bogbrae
Chapel Hill
Bay of Cruden
St Katherines
Barthol Chapel
Earlsford
Haddo House
Ythanbank
Newseat
Folla Rule
Cross of Jackston
Wedderlairs
Auchedly
Birness
Whinnyfold
The Skares
Meikle Wartle
Tulloch
Altar Tomb of William Forbes
Tarves
Kinharrachie
Ythsie
Artrochie
Craigdam
Loanhead Stone Circle
Daviot
Glen Garioch
Oldmeldrum
Tolquhon Castle
Pitmedden Garden
Pitmedden
Esslemont
Kirkton of Logie Buchan
Kirktown of Slains
Collieston
Durno
Logierieve
Forvie
NK
Carnbrogie
Housieside
Pitcaple
Maiden Stone
Chapel of Garioch
Kirktown of Bourtie
Udny Green
Udny Station
Newburgh
Whiterashes
Woodland
Pettymuk
Culterculien
Foveran
Tillygreig
Brandsbutt Symbol Stone
Nether Crimond
Easter Aquhorthies Stone Circle
Port Elphinstone
Straloch
Reisque
Delfrigs
Causeyend
Burnhervie
Kinmuck
Newmachar
Kingseat
Balmedie
Kinkell Church
Thainstone
Hatton of Fintray
Whitecairns
Belhelvie
Kinmundy
Cothal
Kemnay
Kintore
Dyce Symbol Stones
Potterton
Cottown
Craigearn
Blackdog
Leylodge
Overton
Aberdeen
Blackburn
Castle Fraser
Middleton Park
Denmore
Sauchen
Lyne of Skene
Clinterty
Stoneywood
Kirkwall Lerwick
Elrick Hill
Bankhead
Bridge of Don
Dunecht
Skene House
Millbuie
Bucksburn
Brimmond Hill
Northfield
Barmekin
Loch of Skene
Kirkton of Skene
Kittybrewster
Old Aberdeen
Kingsford
Garlogie
Elrick
Carnie
Echt
Redhill
Aberdeen
Ruthrieston
Torry
Nigg Bay
Landerberry
Cullerlie
Gullerne Stone Circle
Benthoul
Easter Ord
Blacktop
Mannofield
Cults
Bieldside
Kincorth
Loirston
A90
A98
A947
A981
A950
A952
A948
A920
A975
A96
A92
A944
B9031
B9032
B9033
B9093
B9105
B9027
B9170
B9106
B9029
B9028
B9030
B9005
B9000
B999
B992
B9001
B993
B979
B977
B9126
B9119
B9125
B9077
B9997
North East 250
99
L M N P Q R S T U V
80 90 00 10 20
1 2 3 4 5 6 7 8 9 10 11 12 13 14
70 60 50 40 30 20 10

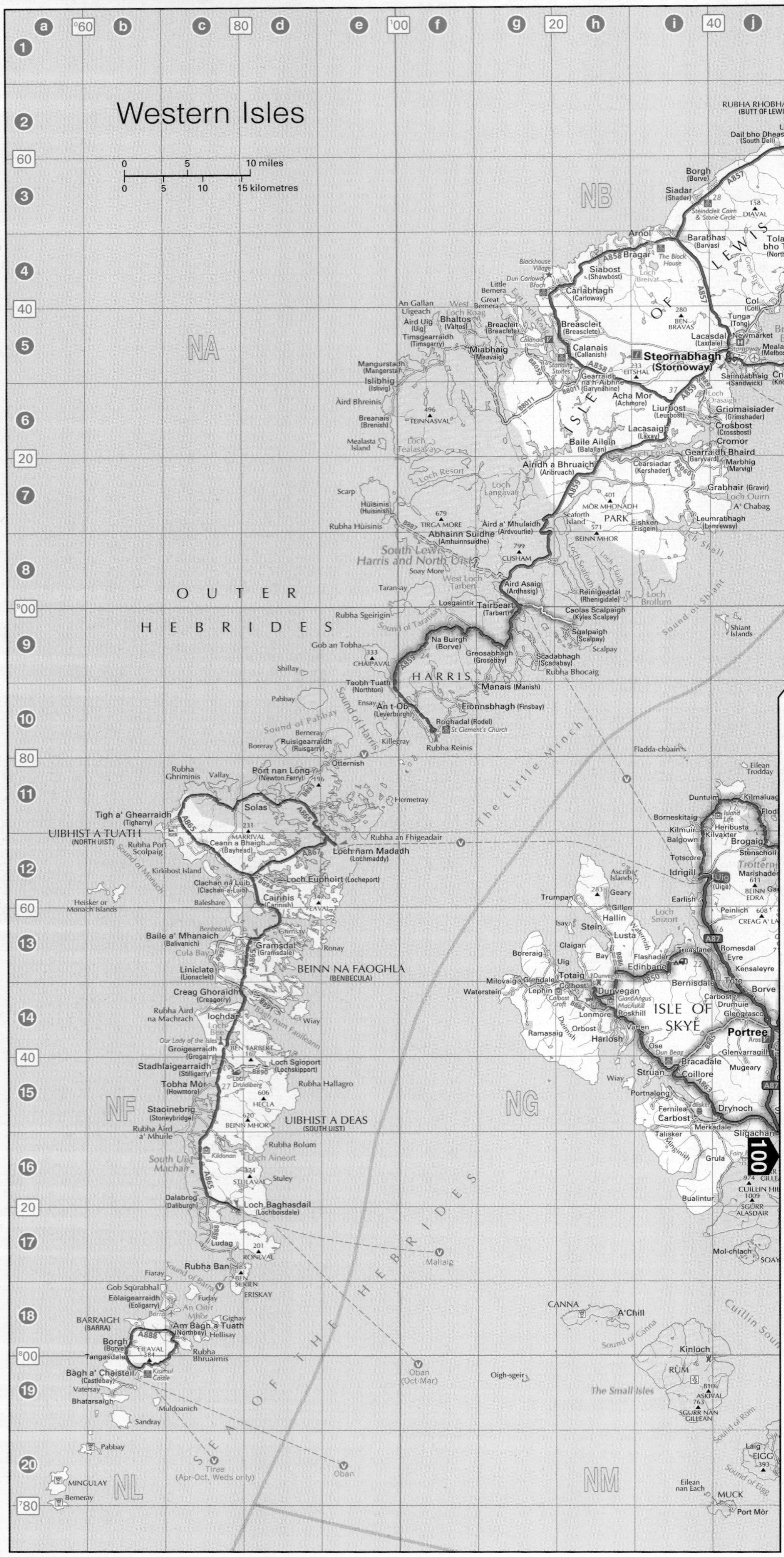

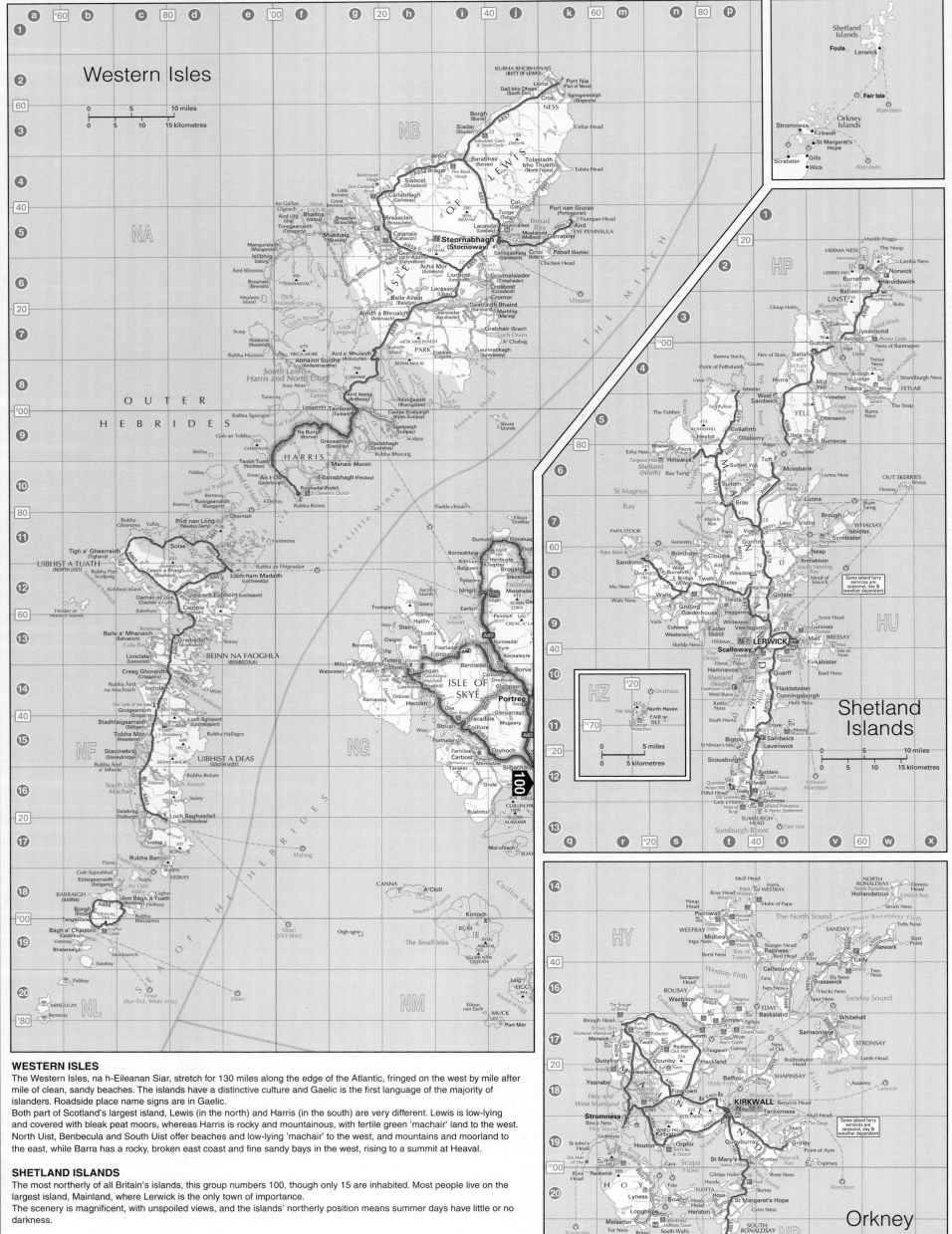

WESTERN ISLES

The Western Isles, na h-Eileanan Siar, stretch for 130 miles along the edge of the Atlantic, fringed on the west by mile after mile of clean, sandy beaches. The islands have a distinctive culture and Gaelic is the first language of the majority of islanders. Roadside place name signs are in Gaelic.

Both part of Scotland's largest island, Lewis (in the north) and Harris (in the south) are very different. Lewis is low-lying and covered with bleak peat moors, whereas Harris is rocky and mountainous, with fertile green 'machair' land to the west. North Uist, Benbecula and South Uist offer beaches and low-lying 'machair' to the west, and mountains and moorland to the east, while Barra has a rocky, broken east coast and fine sandy bays in the west, rising to a summit at Heaval.

SHETLAND ISLANDS

The most northerly of all Britain's islands, this group numbers 100, though only 15 are inhabited. Most people live on the largest island, Mainland, where Lerwick is the only town of importance.

The scenery is magnificent, with unspoiled views, and the islands' northerly position means summer days have little or no darkness.

ORKNEY ISLANDS

Lying approximately 10 miles north of the Scottish mainland, Orkney comprises 70 islands, 18 of which are inhabited, Mainland being the largest.

Apart from Hoy, Orkney is generally green and flat, with few trees. The islands abound with prehistoric antiquities and rare birds. The climate is one of even temperatures and 'twilight' summer nights, but with violent winds at times.

For information on ferry services see page XVI.

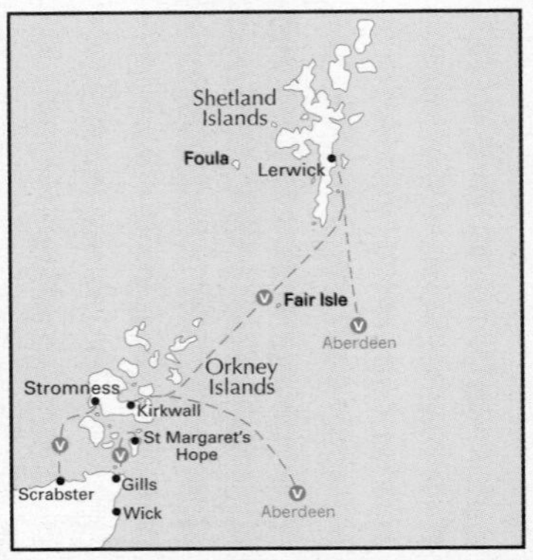

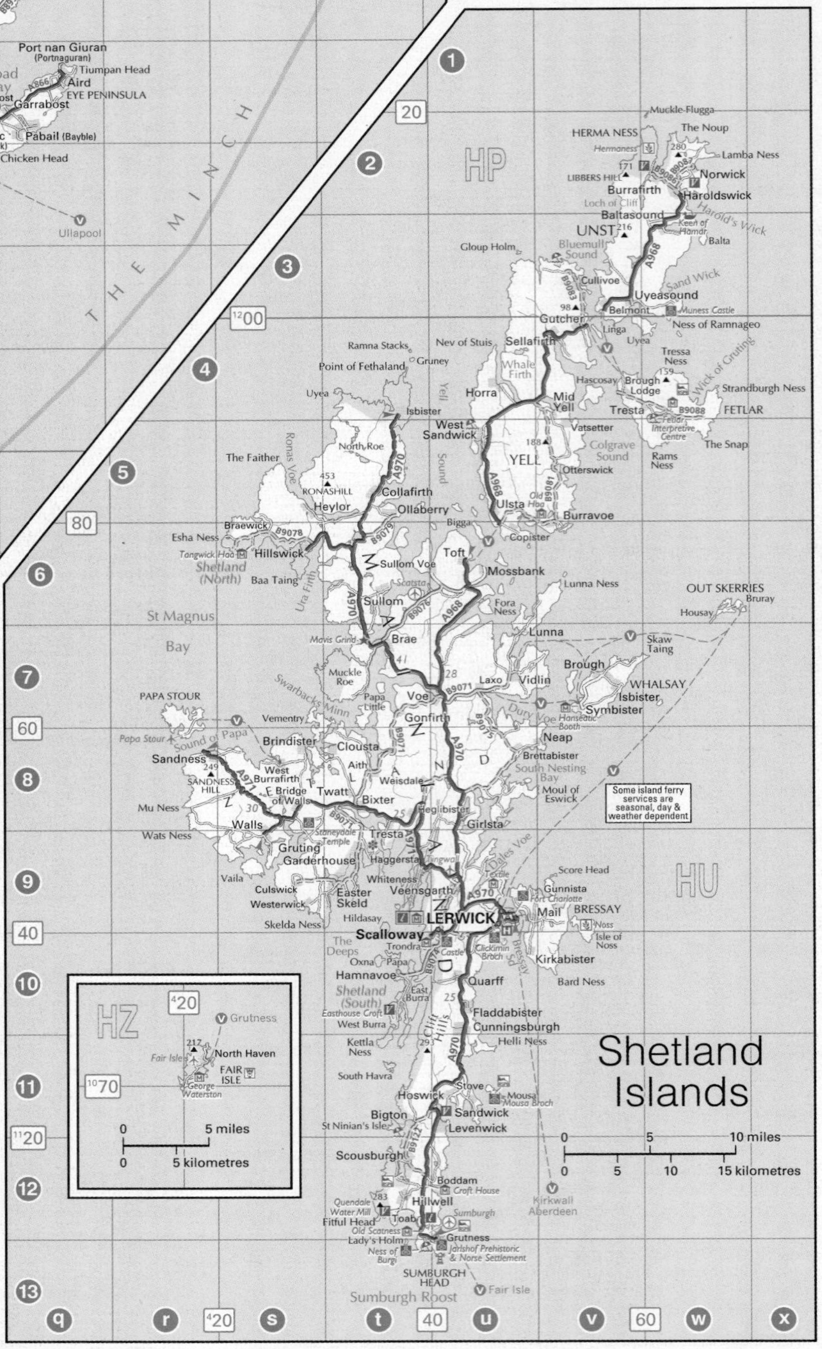

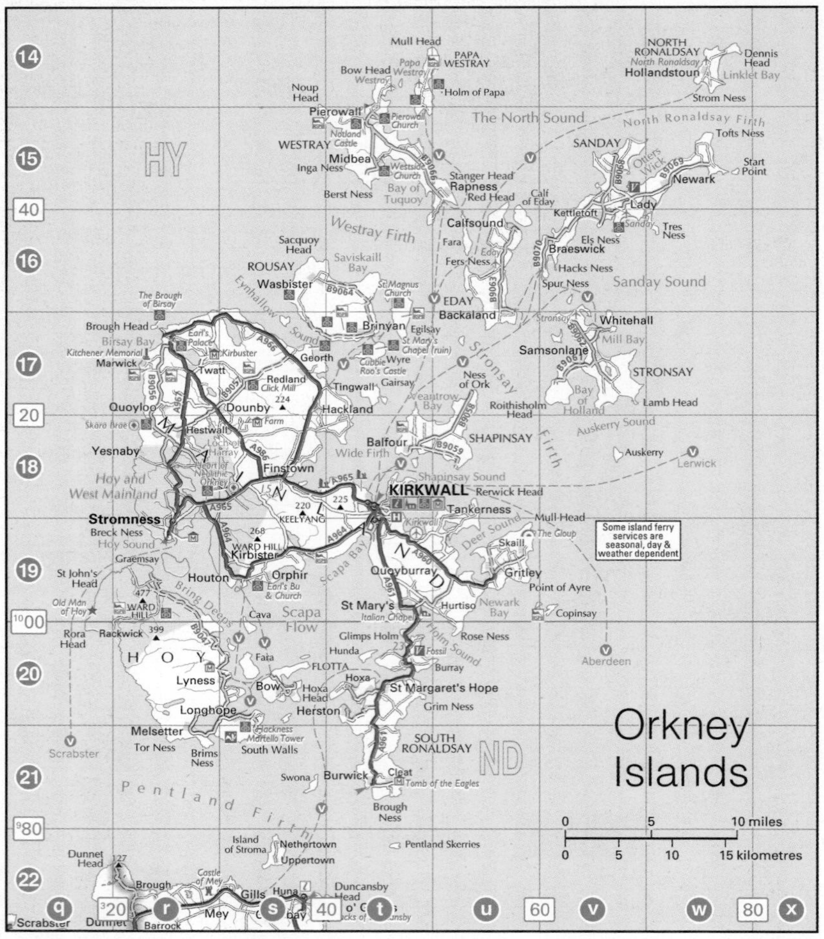

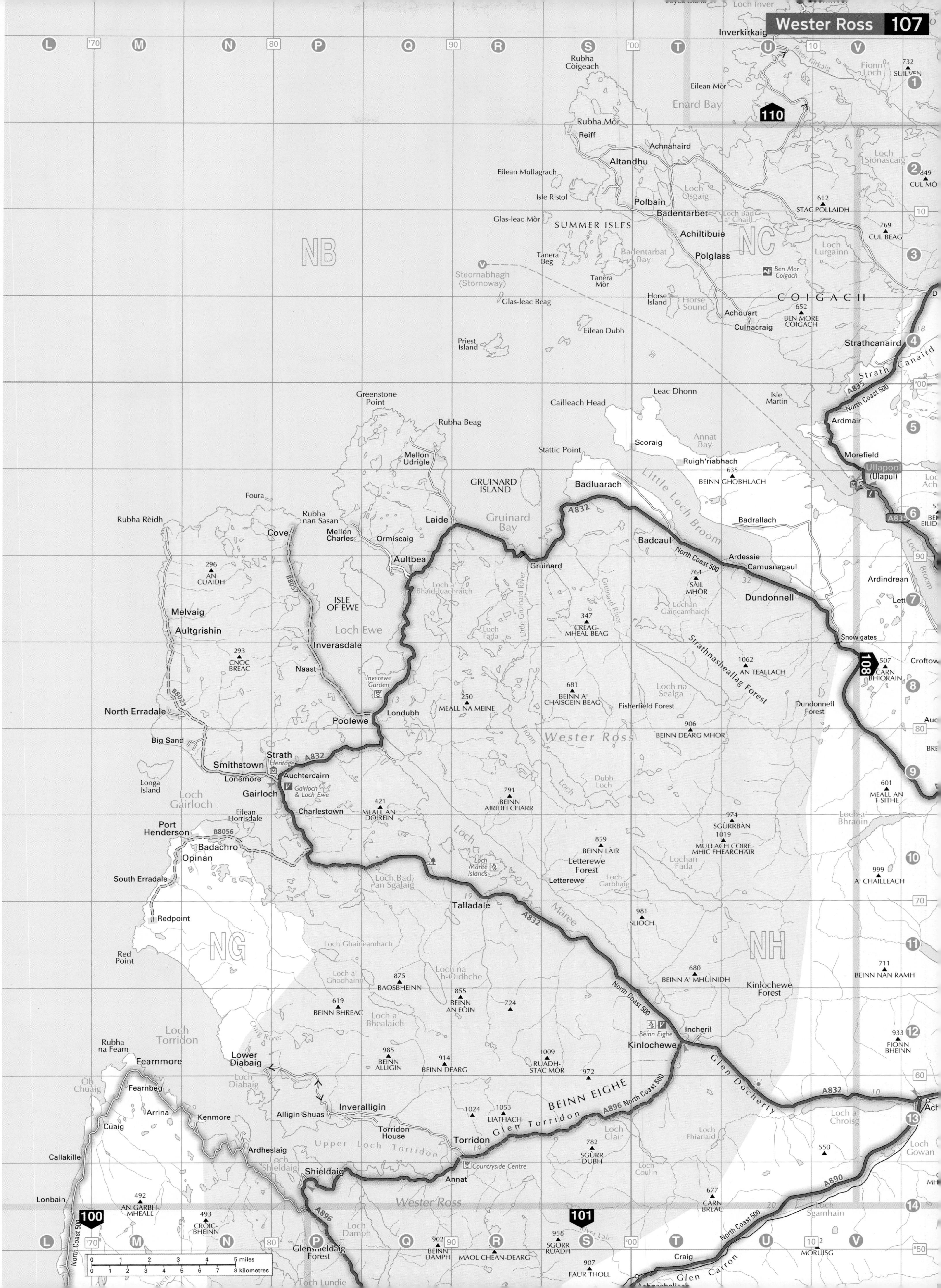
Loch Inver
Inverkirkaig
River Kirkaig
Fionn Loch
732 SUILVEN
Rubha Còigeach
Eilean Mòr
Enard Bay
110
Rubha Mòr
Reiff
Achnahaird
Altandhu
Loch Sionascaig
849 CUL MÒR
Eilean Mullagrach
Isle Ristol
Loch Osgaig
Polbain
612 STAC POLLAIDH
Badentarbet
Loch Bad a' Ghaill
Glas-leac Mòr
SUMMER ISLES
Achiltibuie
769 CUL BEAG
NB
NC
Tanera Beg
Badentarbat Bay
Polglass
Loch Lurgainn
Steornabhagh (Stornoway)
Tanera Mòr
Ben Mor Coigach
Horse Island
Horse Sound
COIGACH
Glas-leac Beag
Achduart
652 BEN MORE COIGACH
Eilean Dubh
Culnacraig
Strathcanaird
Priest Island
Strath Canaird
A835
North Coast 500
Leac Dhonn
Isle Martin
Greenstone Point
Cailleach Head
Ardmair
Rubha Beag
Scoraig
Annat Bay
Stattic Point
Mellon Udrigle
Morefield
Rugh'riabhach
Ullapool (Ulapul)
635 BEINN GHOBHLACH
GRUINARD ISLAND
Badluarach
Little Loch Broom
Foura
A832
Badrallach
Rubha Rèidh
Rubha nan Sasan
Laide
Gruinard Bay
Cove
Mellon Charles
Ormiscaig
Badcaul
Aultbea
Gruinard
Ardessie
Camusnagaul
296 AN CUAIDH
B8057
Loch a' Bhaid-luachraich
764 SAIL MHÒR
Ardindrean
ISLE OF EWE
Little Gruinard River
Gruinard River
Dundonnell
Melvaig
Lochan Gaineamhaich
Loch Ewe
347 CREAG-MHEAL BEAG
Aultgrishin
Loch Fada
Inverasdale
Strathnasheallag Forest
Snow gates
293 CNOC BREAC
Naast
1062 AN TEALLACH
108
507 CARN BHIORAIN
Croftown
Inverewe Garden
681 BEINN A' CHAISGEIN BEAG
Loch na Sealga
B8021
250 MEALL NA MEINE
Fisherfield Forest
Dundonnell Forest
North Erradale
Londubh
Poolewe
906 BEINN DEARG MHOR
Fionn Loch
Wester Ross
Big Sand
Strath Heritage
Smithstown
A832
Auchtercairn
Dubh Loch
601 MEALL AN T-SITHE
Longa Island
Lonemore
Gairloch & Loch Ewe
Loch Gairloch
Gairloch
791 BEINN AIRIDH CHARR
Eilean Horrisdale
Charlestown
421 MEALL AN DOIREIN
974 SGÙRRBÀN
Loch a' Bhraoin
Port Henderson
B8056
1019 MULLACH COIRE MHIC FHEARCHAIR
Badachro
859 BEINN LÀIR
Opinan
Loch Maree
Loch Maree Islands
Letterewe Forest
Lochan Fada
10
999 A' CHAILLEACH
South Erradale
Loch Bad an Sgalaig
Letterewe
Loch Garbhaig
Talladale
981 SLIOCH
Redpoint
NG
NH
Loch Ghaineamhach
11
Red Point
Loch a' Ghodhainn
Loch na h-Oidhche
680 BEINN A' MHÙINIDH
711 BEINN NAN RAMH
875 BAOSBHEINN
Kinlochewe Forest
855 BEINN AN EOIN
619 BEINN BHREAC
724
Loch a' Bhealaich
Loch Torridon
Craig River
Beinn Eighe
Incheril
933 FIONN BHEINN
Rubha na Fearn
Kinlochewe
Fearnmore
Lower Diabaig
985 BEINN ALLIGIN
914 BEINN DEARG
1009 RUADH-STAC MÒR
Ob Chuaig
Loch Diabaig
972
Glen Docherty
Fearnbeg
A832
BEINN EIGHE
Inveralligin
Arrina
Alligin Shuas
1024
1053 LIATHACH
Glen Torridon
A896
Loch a' Chroisg
Kenmore
Cuaig
Torridon House
Torridon
Loch Clair
Loch Fhiarlaid
Upper Loch Torridon
782 SGÙRR DUBH
550
Loch Gowan
Callakille
Ardheslaig
Loch Shieldaig
Countryside Centre
Loch Coulin
Shieldaig
Annat
A890
677 CARN BREAC
Lonbain
492 AN GARBH-MHEALL
Wester Ross
101
Loch Sgamhain
100
493 CROIC-BHEINN
Loch Damph
River Lair
Glenshieldaig Forest
902 BEINN DAMPH
MAOL CHEAN-DEARG
958 SGORR RUADH
MORUISG
Craig
Glen Carron
907 FAUR THOLL
Loch Lundie
5 miles
8 kilometres

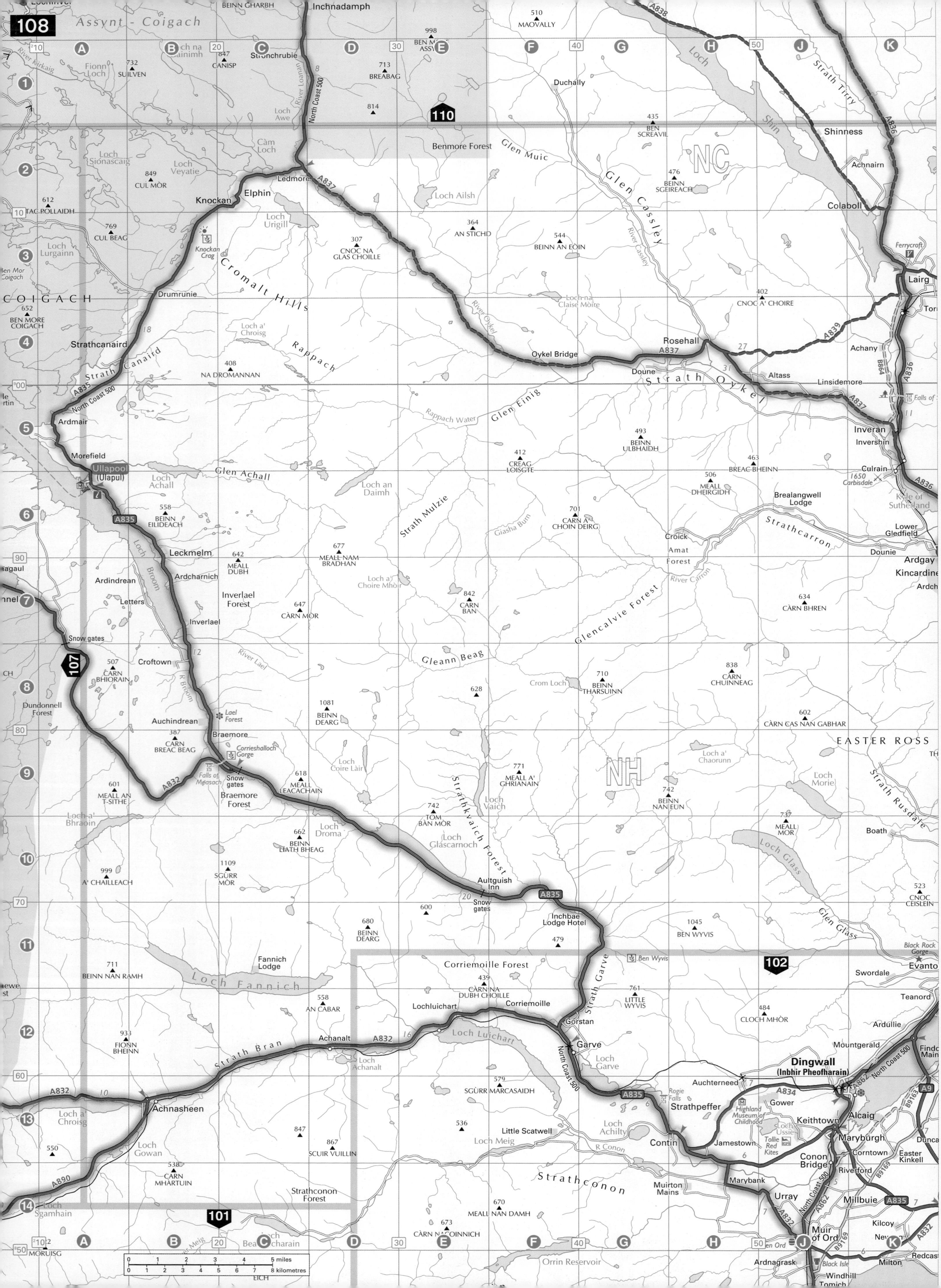
Assynt - Coigach
Inchnadamph
BEINN GHARBH
River Kirkaig
Fionn Loch
732 SUILVEN
847 CANISP
Stronchrubie
998 BEN MORE ASSYNT
713 BREABAG
510 MAOVALLY
Duchally
814
110
Loch Awe
River Loanan
North Coast 500
Benmore Forest
Glen Muic
435 BEN SCREAVIL
NC
476 BEINN SGEIREACH
Glen Cassley
River Cassley
Loch Shin
Strath Tirry
Shinness
Achnairn
Colaboll
A838
A836
Càm Loch
Loch Sionascaig
Loch Veyatie
849 CUL MÒR
612 STAC POLLAIDH
Ledmore
A837
Knockan
Elphin
Loch Urigill
Loch Ailsh
364 AN STICHD
544 BEINN AN EOIN
307 CNOC NA GLAS CHOILLE
769 CUL BEAG
Loch Lurgainn
Knockan Crag
Cromalt Hills
Ben Mor Coigach
COIGACH
652 BEN MORE COIGACH
Drumrunie
Loch a' Chroisg
Rappach
Loch na Claise Mòire
River Oykel
Ferrycroft
Lairg
402 CNOC A' CHOIRE
A839
Strathcanaird
Strath Canaird
408 NA DROMANNAN
Oykel Bridge
Rosehall
Achany
Doune
Strath Oykel
Altass
Linsidemore
B864
Falls of Shin
A835
Ardmair
Rappach Water
Glen Einig
Inveran
Invershin
493 BEINN ULBHAIDH
Morefield
Ullapool (Ulapul)
Loch Achall
Glen Achall
Loch an Daimh
412 CREAG LOISGTE
463 BREAC-BHEINN
Culrain
1650 Carbisdale
506 MEALL DHEIRGIDH
Brealangwell Lodge
Kyle of Sutherland
558 BEINN EILIDEACH
701 CARN A' CHOIN DEIRG
Strath Mulzie
Giasha Burn
Croick
Amat Forest
Strathcarron
Lower Gledfield
Loch Broom
Leckmelm
642 MEALL DUBH
677 MEALL NAM BRADHAN
Dounie
Ardgay
Kincardine
Ardindrean
Ardcharnich
Letters
Inverlael Forest
Loch a' Choire Mhòir
River Carron
647 CÀRN MÒR
842 CARN BAN
Glencalvie Forest
634 CÀRN BHREN
Inverlael
Snow gates
107
507 CARN BHIORAIN
Croftown
River Lael
Gleann Beag
Crom Loch
710 BEINN THARSUINN
838 CARN CHUINNEAG
Dundonnell Forest
Lael Forest
628
1081 BEINN DEARG
Auchindrean
602 CÀRN CAS NAN GABHAR
387 CARN BREAC BEAG
Braemore
Corrieshalloch Gorge
EASTER ROSS
Loch a' Chaorunn
Loch Coire Làir
NH
771 MEALL A' GHRIANAIN
Loch Morie
Strath Rusdale
A832
Falls of Measach
Snow gates
601 MEALL AN T-SITHE
618 MEALL LEACACHAIN
Braemore Forest
Strathvaich Forest
Loch Vaich
742 BEINN NAN EUN
Loch a' Bhraoin
742 TOM BÀN MÒR
737 MEALL MÒR
Boath
Loch Droma
662 BEINN LIATH BHEAG
Loch Glascarnoch
Loch Glass
1109 SGÙRR MÒR
999 A' CHAILLEACH
Aultguish Inn
523 CNOC CEISLEIN
Snow gates
600
Inchbae Lodge Hotel
680 BEINN DEARG
1045 BEN WYVIS
Glen Glass
479
Black Rock Gorge
Ben Wyvis
102
Fannich Lodge
Corriemoille Forest
711 BEINN NAN RAMH
Loch Fannich
439 CÀRN NA DUBH CHOILLE
Strath Garve
761 LITTLE WYVIS
Swordale
Evanton
558 AN CABAR
Lochluichart
Corriemoille
484 CLOCH MHÒR
Teanord
Gorstan
Ardullie
933 FIONN BHEINN
Achanalt
Loch Luichart
Mountgerald
Strath Bran
Garve
Loch Garve
Loch Achanalt
Dingwall (Inbhir Pheofharain)
579 SGÙRR MARCASAIDH
Auchterneed
A834
A862
A9
B9163
Rogie Falls
Strathpeffer
Gower
Highland Museum of Childhood
Loch a' Chroisg
Achnasheen
Keithtown
Alcaig
536
Little Scatwell
Loch Achilty
Loch Ussie
847
Loch Meig
Contin
Jamestown
Maryburgh
Tollie Red Kites
Loch Gowan
867 SCUIR VUILLIN
R Conon
Conon Bridge
Corntown
Easter Kinkell
550
538 CARN MHARTUIN
Riverford
B9169
A890
Strathconon
Muirton Mains
Marybank
Urray
Millbuie
Strathconon Forest
Loch Sgamhain
670 MEALL NAN DAMH
101
Kilcoy
673 CÀRN NA COINNICH
Muir of Ord
Beauly
1012 MORUISG
Loch Beannacharain
River Meig
Orrin Reservoir
Ardnagrask
Black Isle
Milton
Redcastle
Windhill
Tomich
EICH
5 miles
8 kilometres

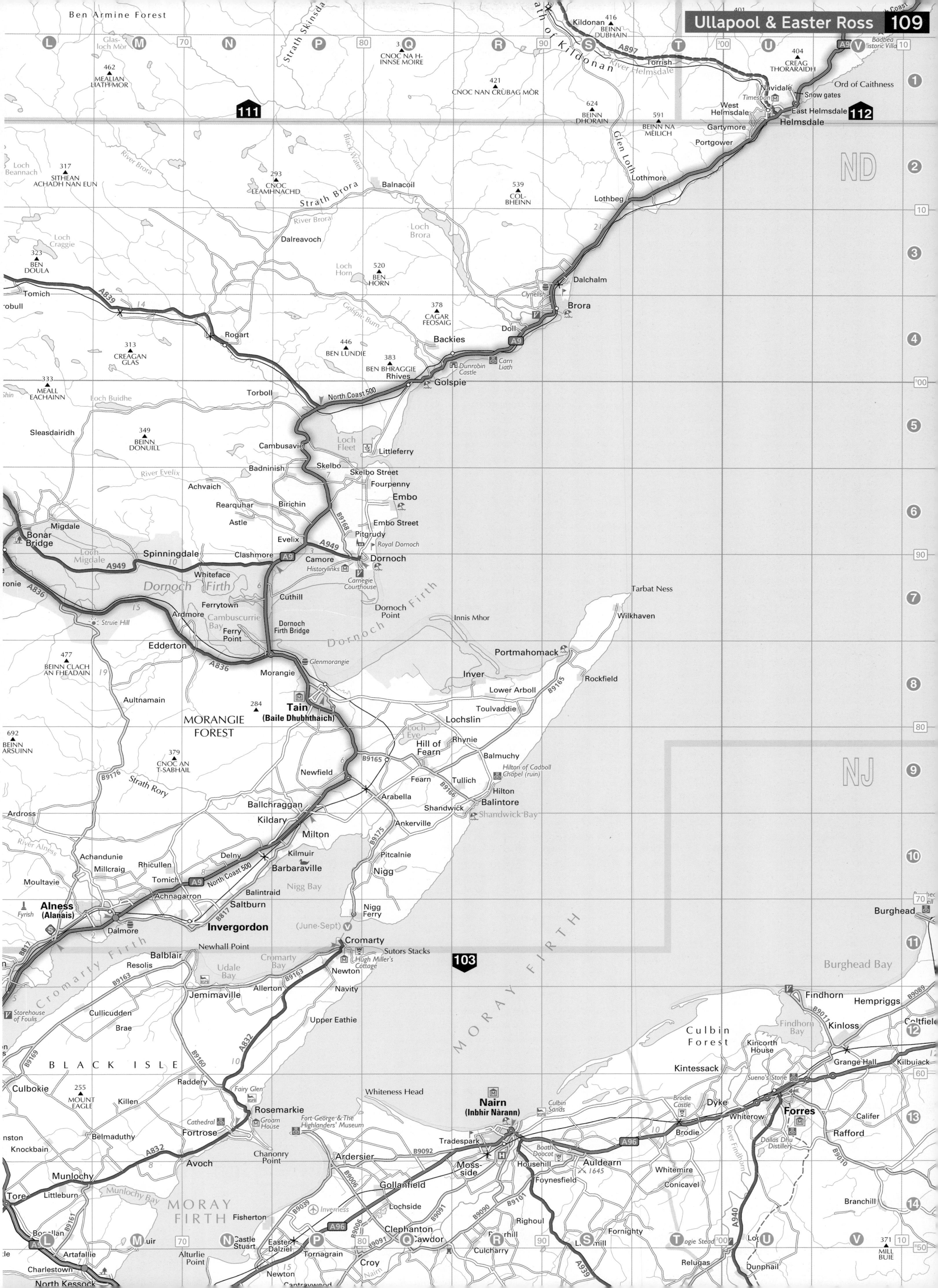
Ben Armine Forest
Kildonan
416 BEINN DUBHAIN
Strath of Kildonan
River Helmsdale
Torrish
404 CREAG THORARAIDH
Badbea Historic Village
Ord of Caithness
Navidale
Snow gates
Timespan
West Helmsdale
East Helmsdale
Helmsdale
Gartymore
Portgower
462 MEALLAN LIATH MÒR
CNOC NA H-INNSE MOIRE
421 CNOC NAN CRÙBAG MÒR
624 BEINN DHORAIN
591 BEINN NA MEILICH
111
112
ND
Glen Loth
Lothmore
Lothbeg
Loch Beannach
317 SITHEAN ACHADH NAN EUN
River Brora
293 CNOC LEAMHNACHD
Strath Brora
Balnacoil
539 COL-BHEINN
Loch Brora
Dalreavoch
Loch Craggie
323 BEN DOULA
Loch Horn
520 BEN HORN
Dalchalm
Clynelish
Brora
Tomich
A830
Golspie Burn
378 CAGAR FEOSAIG
Rogart
313 CREAGAN GLAS
446 BEN LUNDIE
Backies
Doll
A9
383 BEN BHRAGGIE
Rhives
Dunrobin Castle
Carn Liath
Golspie
333 MEALL EACHAINN
Loch Buidhe
Torboll
North Coast 500
Sleasdairidh
349 BEINN DONUILL
Cambusavie
Loch Fleet
Littleferry
Badninish
Skelbo
Skelbo Street
River Evelix
Achvaich
Fourpenny
Embo
Rearquhar
Birichin
Embo Street
Astle
B9168
Migdale
Bonar Bridge
Pitgrudy
Royal Dornoch
Evelix
A949
Loch Migdale
Spinningdale
Clashmore
Camore
Dornoch
Historylinks
Carnegie Courthouse
Whiteface
Dornoch Firth
A836
Cuthill
Tarbat Ness
Ferrytown
Dornoch Point
Wilkhaven
Ardmore
Cambuscurrie Bay
Dornoch Firth Bridge
Innis Mhor
Struie Hill
Ferry Point
Edderton
Portmahomack
Glenmorangie
477 BEINN CLACH AN FHEADAIN
Morangie
Inver
Rockfield
Lower Arbol
B9165
Aultnamain
284
Tain (Baile Dhubhthaich)
Toulvaddie
MORANGIE FOREST
Lochslin
Loch Eye
692 BEINN ARSUINN
379 CNOC AN T-SABHAIL
Hill of Fearn
Rhynie
Balmuchy
NJ
B9176
Strath Rory
Newfield
Hilton of Cadboll Chapel (ruin)
Fearn
Tullich
Hilton
Arabella
Balintore
Ardross
Ballchraggan
Shandwick
Shandwick Bay
Kildary
Ankerville
Milton
River Alness
B9175
Achandunie
Delny
Kilmuir
Pitcalnie
Millcraig
Rhicullen
Barbaraville
Nigg
Moultavie
Tomich
Nigg Bay
Achnagarron
Balintraid
Alness (Alanais)
Saltburn
Nigg Ferry
Fyrish
B817
Invergordon
(June-Sept)
Burghead
Dalmore
Cromarty
Newhall Point
Sutors Stacks
103
Balblair
Cromarty Bay
Hugh Miller's Cottage
Cromarty Firth
Resolis
Udale Bay
Newton
B9163
Allerton
Navity
Burghead Bay
Jemimaville
MORAY FIRTH
Findhorn
Hempriggs
Storehouse of Foulis
Cullicudden
Upper Eathie
Findhorn Bay
Kinloss
Brae
Culbin Forest
Kincorth House
A832
Kintessack
Grange Hall
Kilbuiack
B9169
BLACK ISLE
B9160
Sueno's Stone
Culbokie
255 MOUNT EAGLE
Raddery
Whiteness Head
Nairn (Inbhir Nàrann)
Killen
Fairy Glen
Culbin Sands
Dyke
Forres
Rosemarkie
Brodie Castle
Whiterow
Califer
Cathedral
Groam House
Fort George & The Highlanders' Museum
Brodie
River Findhorn
Dallas Dhu Distillery
Rafford
Fortrose
Belmaduthy
Tradespark
A96
Knockbain
Chanonry Point
Ardersier
B9092
Boath Doocot
Auldearn
1645
Avoch
Moss-side
Househill
Whitemire
B9010
Munlochy
Foynesfield
Gollanfield
Conicavel
Tore
Littleburn
Munlochy Bay
MORAY FIRTH
B9006
Lochside
Branchill
B9161
Fisherton
Inverness
B9039
B9091
B9090
B9101
Righoul
A940
Castle Stuart
Easter Dalziel
Clephanton
Fornighty
Cawdor
Tornagrain
Culcharry
Logie Steading
371 MILL BUIE
Artafallie
Alturlie Point
Croy
Relugas
Charlestown
Newton
Dunphail
North Kessock
A939
Nairn

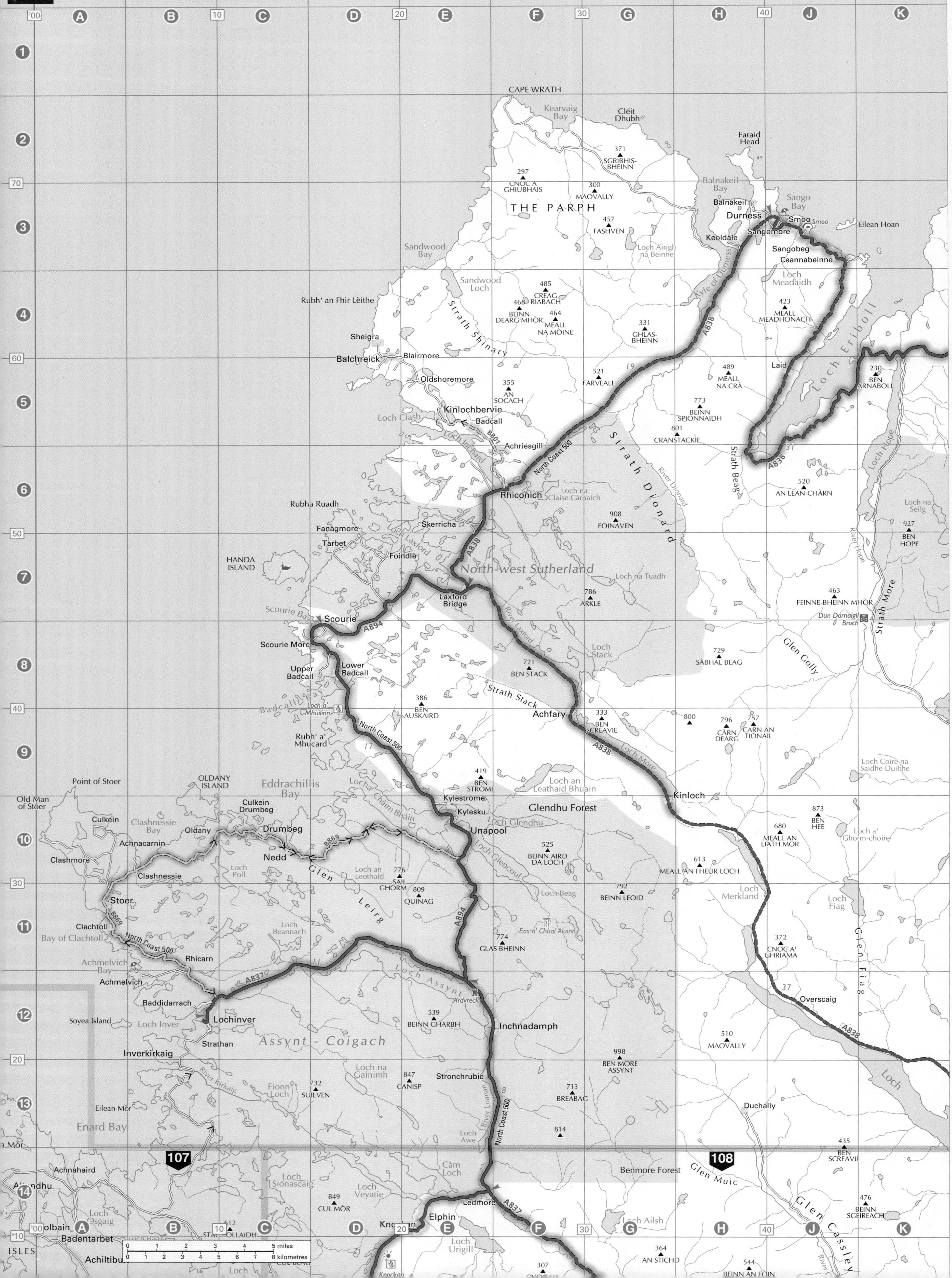

CAPE WRATH
Kearvaig Bay
Cléit Dhubh
Faraid Head
371 SGRIBHIS-BHEINN
297 CNOC A' GHIUBHAIS
300 MAOVALLY
THE PARPH
457 FASHVEN
Balnakeil Bay
Balnakeil
Durness
Sango Bay
Smoo
Eilean Hoan
Sangomore
Keoldale
Sangobeg
Ceannabeinne
Loch Airigh na Beinne
Sandwood Bay
Sandwood Loch
Loch Meadaidh
Kyle of Durness
485 CREAG RIABACH
468 BEINN DEARG MHÒR
464 MEALL NA MÒINE
423 MEALL MEADHONACH
Rubh' an Fhir Lèithe
Strath Shinary
331 GHLAS-BHEINN
Loch Eriboll
Sheigra
Balchreick
Blairmore
Oldshoremore
355 AN SOCACH
521 FARVEALL
489 MEALL NA CRÀ
Laid
230 BEN ARNABOLL
Kinlochbervie
Loch Clash
Badcall
Loch Inchard
Achriesgill
773 BEINN SPIONNAIDH
801 CRANSTACKIE
Strath Dionard
River Dionard
Strath Beag
Loch Hope
North Coast 500
A838
B801
520 AN LEAN-CHÀRN
Rhiconich
Loch na Claise Càrnaich
Rubha Ruadh
908 FOINAVEN
Loch na Seilg
927 BEN HOPE
Fanagmore
Skerricha
Tarbet
Loch Laxford
Foindle
HANDA ISLAND
River Hope
North-west Sutherland
Loch na Tuadh
Laxford Bridge
786 ARKLE
463 FEINNE-BHEINN MHÒR
Dun Dornaigil Broch
Strath More
Scourie Bay
Scourie
A894
River Laxford
Scourie More
Loch Stack
729 SÀBHAL BEAG
Glen Golly
Lower Badcall
Upper Badcall
721 BEN STACK
Badcall Bay
Loch a' Mhuilinn
386 BEN AUSKAIRD
Strath Stack
Achfary
333 BEN SCREAVIE
800
796 CÀRN DEARG
757 CARN AN TIONAIL
Rubh' a' Mhucard
Loch More
Loch Coire na Saidhe Duibhe
Point of Stoer
OLDANY ISLAND
Eddrachillis Bay
419 BEN STROME
Loch an Leathaid Bhuain
Kinloch
Old Man of Stoer
Culkein Drumbeg
Kylestrome
Kylesku
Glendhu Forest
Loch Glendhu
Loch a' Chàirn Bhain
Culkein
Clashnessie Bay
Oldany
Drumbeg
Unapool
873 BEN HEE
680 MEALL AN LIATH MOR
Loch a' Ghorm-choire
Achnacarnin
B869
Nedd
Clashmore
Loch Glencoul
525 BEINN AIRD DA LOCH
613 MEALL AN FHEUR LOCH
Clashnessie
Loch Poll
Glen Leirg
Loch an Leothaid
776 SAIL GHORM
809 QUINAG
Loch Beag
792 BEINN LEOID
Loch Merkland
Loch Fiag
Stoer
Clachtoll
Bay of Clachtoll
Loch Beannach
Eas a' Chùal Aluinn
774 GLAS BHEINN
372 CNOC A' GHRIAMA
Glen Fiag
Rhicarn
Achmelvich Bay
Achmelvich
A837
Loch Assynt
Ardvreck
Overscaig
Baddidarrach
Lochinver
539 BEINN GHARBH
Inchnadamph
Soyea Island
Loch Inver
Strathan
Assynt - Coigach
510 MAOVALLY
Inverkirkaig
998 BEN MORE ASSYNT
River Kirkaig
Loch na Gainimh
847 CANISP
Stronchrubie
Fionn Loch
732 SUILVEN
713 BREABAG
River Loanan
Eilean Mòr
Duchally
Enard Bay
814
Loch Awe
435 BEN SCREAVIL
107
108
Achnahaird
Càm Loch
Benmore Forest
Glen Muic
Loch Sionascaig
Loch Veyatie
849 CUL MÒR
Ledmore
476 BEINN SGEIREACH
Glen Cassley
Loch Osgaig
Elphin
Loch Ailsh
Badentarbet
612 STAC POLLAIDH
Loch Urigill
364 AN STICHD
Achiltibuie
307
544 BEINN AN FÒIN
0 1 2 3 4 5 miles
0 1 2 3 4 5 6 7 8 kilometres

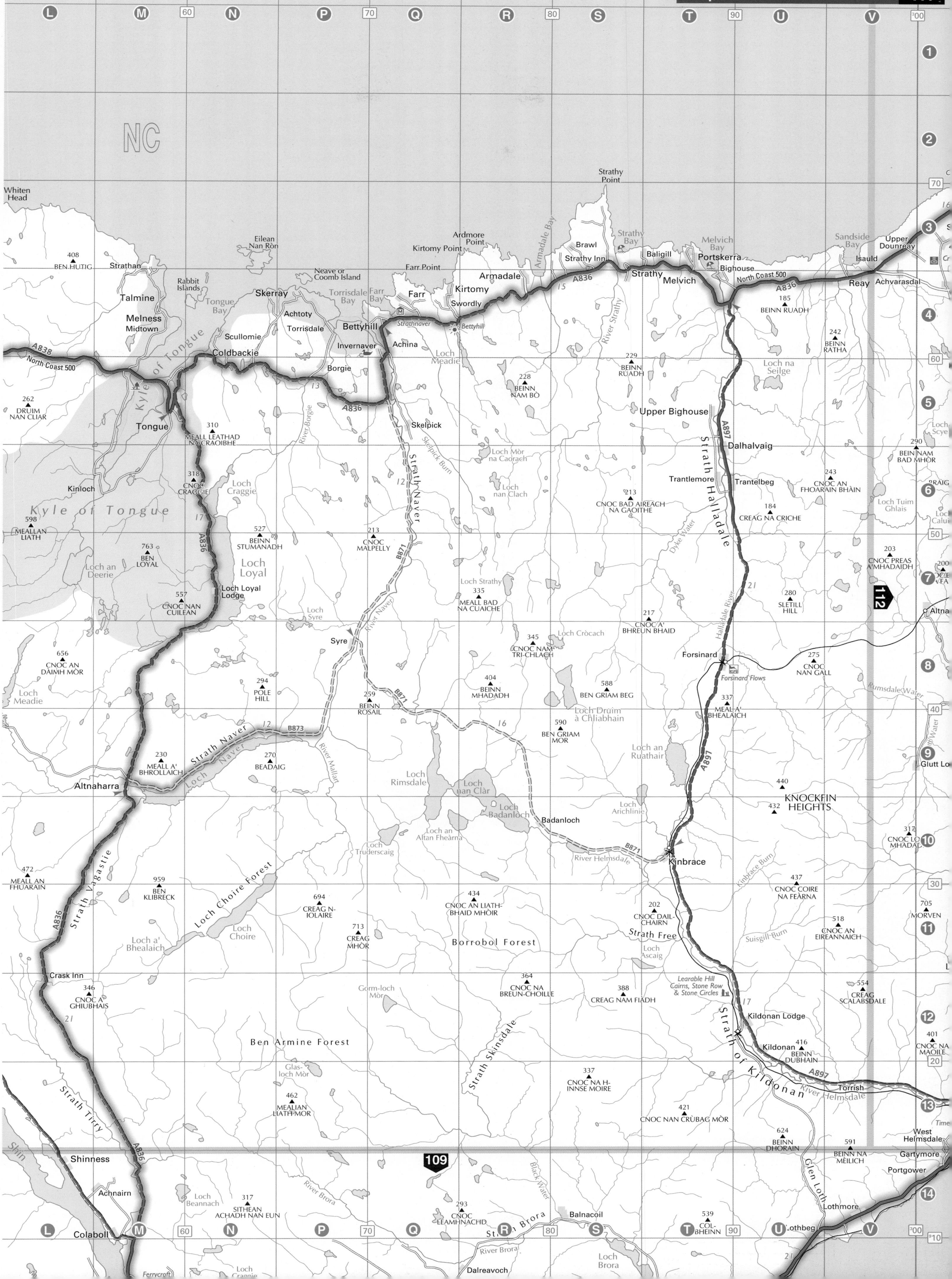

NC

L M 60 N P 70 Q R 80 S T 90 U V 00

Whiten Head

408 ▲ BEN HUTIG
Strathan
Talmine
Melness
Midtown

A838
North Coast 500

262 ▲ DRUIM NAN CLIAR

Kinloch

Kyle of Tongue

598 ▲ MEALLAN LIATH

Loch an Deerie

763 ▲ BEN LOYAL

Eilean Nan Ròn
Rabbit Islands
Tongue Bay

Skerray
Achtoty
Scullomie
Torrisdale
Coldbackie
Borgie

Tongue

310 ▲ MEALL LEATHAD NA CRAOIBHE

318 ▲ CNOC CRAGGIE

Loch Craggie

527 ▲ BEINN STUMANADH

Loch Loyal

557 ▲ CNOC NAN CUILEAN

Loch Loyal Lodge

656 ▲ CNOC AN DÀIMH MÒR

Loch Meadie

Neave or Coomb Island
Torrisdale Bay
Farr Bay
Farr Point

Farr
Bettyhill
Invernaver
Achina
A836

Strathnaver
Bettyhill
Achina

Loch Meadie

Skelpick

Skelpick Burn

Strath Naver

294 ▲ POLE HILL

259 ▲ BEINN ROSAIL

213 ▲ CNOC MALPELLY

Loch Syre

River Naver

Syre

Loch Mòr na Caorach

Loch nan Clach

335 ▲ MEALL BAD NA CUAICHE

Loch Strathy

345 ▲ CNOC NAM TRI-CHLACH

404 ▲ BEINN MHADADH

Ardmore Point
Kirtomy Point
Farr Point

Armadale
Kirtomy
Swordly

228 ▲ BEINN NAM BÒ

229 ▲ BEINN RUADH

213 ▲ CNOC BAD AIREACH NA GAOITHE

Loch Cròcach

588 ▲ BEN GRIAM BEG

590 ▲ BEN GRIAM MÒR

Loch Druim à Chliabhain

Strathy Point

Brawl
Strathy Inn
Strathy

Baligill
Bighouse
Strathy
Melvich

A836

Upper Bighouse

Trantlemore
Trantelbeg

Dalhalvaig

185 ▲ BEINN RUADH

242 ▲ BEINN RATHA

243 ▲ CNOC AN FHOARAIN BHÀIN

184 ▲ CREAG NA CRICHE

217 ▲ CNOC A' BHREUN BHAID

Loch an Ruathair

Melvich Bay
Portskerra

North Coast 500

Sandside Bay

Upper Dounreay
Isauld
Reay
Achvarasdal

290 ▲ BEINN NAM BAD MHÒR

RAIG

Loch Scye

Loch Calui

Loch Tuim Ghlais

203 ▲ CNOC PREAS A'MHADAIDH

200 ▲ VA

Altna

280 ▲ SLETILL HILL

112

275 ▲ CNOC NAN GALL

Rumsdale Water

337 ▲ MEALL A' BHEALAICH

Loch na Seilge

Strath Halladale

Strath Free

A897

Forsinard
Forsinard Flows

Halladale River

440

432

KNOCKFIN HEIGHTS

312 ▲ CNOC LO MHADAL

Glutt Lo

472 ▲ MEALL AN FHUARAIN

Strath Vagastie

Altnaharra

230 ▲ MEALL A' BHROLLAICH

270 ▲ BEADAIG

Strath Naver

Loch Naver

River Mallart

Loch Rimsdale

Loch nan Clàr

Loch an Altan Fheàrna

Loch Badanloch

Loch Truderscaig

Badanloch

B871

River Helmsdale

Kinbrace

Loch Arichlinie

Kinbrace Burn

437 ▲ CNOC COIRE NA FEÀRNA

705 ▲ MORVEN

518 ▲ CNOC AN EIREANNAICH

959 ▲ BEN KLIBRECK

Loch Choire Forest

694 ▲ CREAG N-IOLAIRE

713 ▲ CREAG MHÒR

Loch a' Bhealaich

Loch Choire

434 ▲ CNOC AN LIATH-BHAID MHÒIR

Borrobol Forest

202 ▲ CNOC DAIL-CHAIRN

Loch Ascaig

Strath Free

Suisgill Burn

Crask Inn

346 ▲ CNOC A' GHIUBHAIS

A836

Ben Armine Forest

Gorm-loch Mòr

364 ▲ CNOC NA BREUN-CHOILLE

388 ▲ CREAG NAM FIADH

Learable Hill Cairns, Stone Row & Stone Circles

554 ▲ CREAG SCALABSDALE

Strath Skinsdale

337 ▲ CNOC NA H-INNSE MOIRE

421 ▲ CNOC NAN CRÙBAG MÒR

Kildonan Lodge

Kildonan

416 ▲ BEINN DUBHAIN

Strath of Kildonan

401 ▲ CNOC NA MAOILE

Torrish

River Helmsdale

462 ▲ MEALIAN LIATH MÒR

Glas-loch Mòr

Strath Tirry

Shinness

Achnairn

Loch Beannach

317 ▲ SITHEAN ACHADH NAN EUN

Loch Brora

River Brora

293 ▲ CNOC LEAMHNACHD

Strath Brora

Balnacoil

624 ▲ BEINN DHORAIN

591 ▲ BEINN NA MÈILICH

West Helmsdale

Gartymore
Portgower

539 ▲ COL-BHEINN

Glen Loth

Lothmore
Lothbeg

Shin

Colaboll

Ferrycroft

Loch Crannie

Dalreavoch

109

L M 60 N P 70 Q R 80 S T 90 U V 00

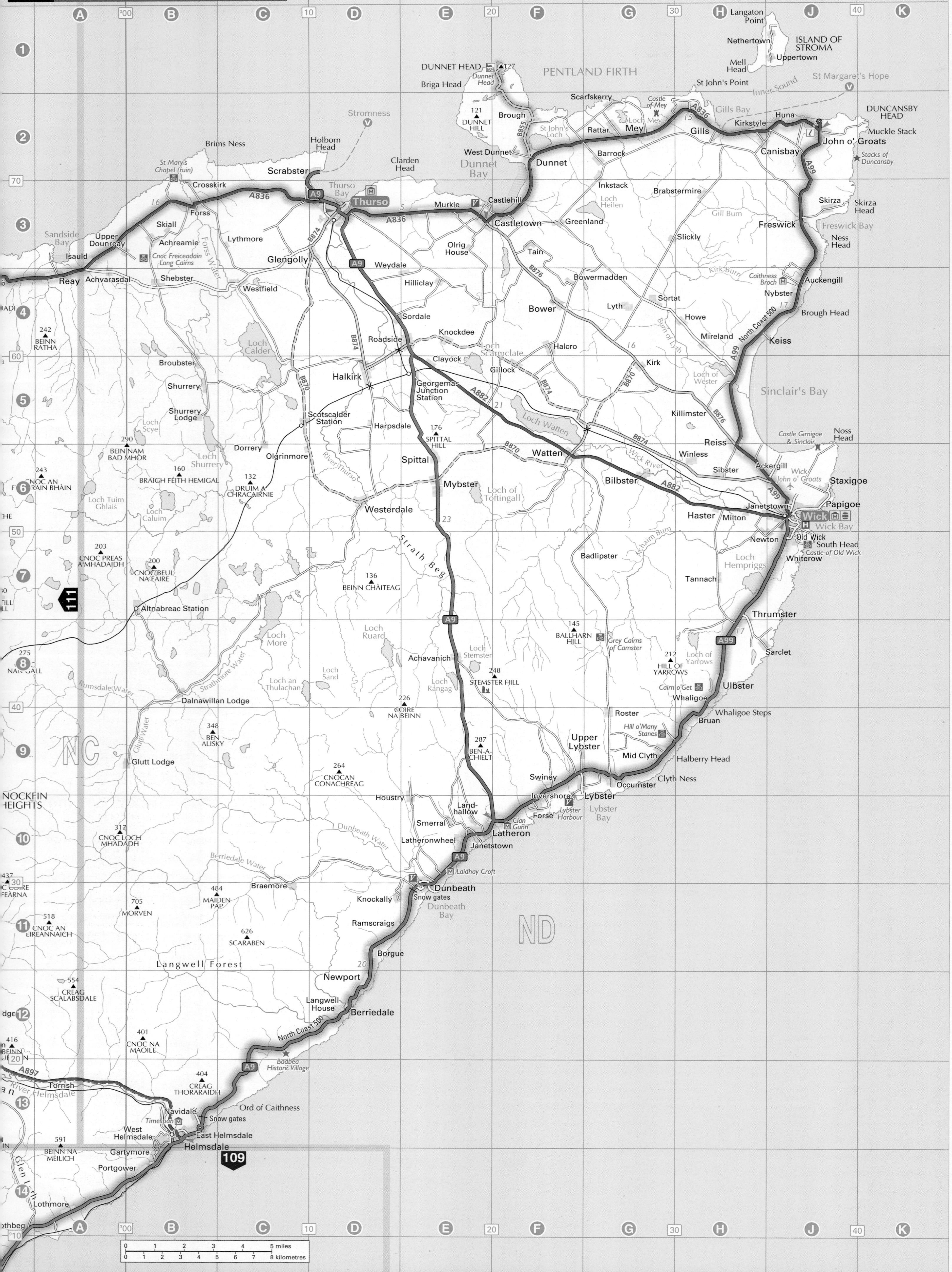
Langaton Point
ISLAND OF STROMA
Nethertown
Uppertown
Mell Head
DUNNET HEAD
127
Dunnet Head
PENTLAND FIRTH
Briga Head
St John's Point
St Margaret's Hope
Inner Sound
Scarfskerry
Castle of Mey
DUNCANSBY HEAD
121 DUNNET HILL
Brough
St John's Loch
Loch Mey
A836
Gills Bay
Huna
Stromness
Rattar
Mey
Gills
Kirkstyle
Muckle Stack
John o' Groats
Brims Ness
Holborn Head
Clarden Head
West Dunnet
Dunnet Bay
Dunnet
Barrock
Canisbay
Stacks of Duncansby
St Mary's Chapel (ruin)
Scrabster
A99
Crosskirk
Thurso Bay
Thurso
Inkstack
Brabstermire
Loch Heilen
A836
A9
Murkle
Castlehill
Skirza
Skirza Head
Forss
Skiall
Castletown
Greenland
Gill Burn
Freswick
Freswick Bay
Sandside Bay
Upper Dounreay
Achreamie
Lythmore
Forss Water
B874
Olrig House
Tain
Slickly
Ness Head
Isauld
Cnoc Freiceadain Long Cairns
Glengolly
Weydale
B876
Kirk Burn
Caithness Broch
Auckengill
Reay
Achvarasdal
Shebster
Westfield
Hilliclay
Bowermadden
Nybster
Sortat
Lyth
Bower
Howe
Brough Head
242 BEINN RATHA
Sordale
Knockdee
Burn of Lyth
Mireland
North Coast 500
Loch Calder
B874
Roadside
Loch Scarmclate
Halcro
Keiss
Broubster
Clayock
Gillock
Kirk
Halkirk
B870
Georgemas Junction Station
B874
B870
Loch of Wester
Shurrery
Sinclair's Bay
A882
Shurrery Lodge
Scotscalder Station
Loch Watten
Killimster
Loch Scye
Harpsdale
176 SPITTAL HILL
B876
Castle Girnigoe & Sinclair
Noss Head
290 BEIN NAM BAD MHOR
Dorrery
Spittal
B870
Watten
B874
Reiss
Olgrinmore
Loch Shurrery
Winless
River Thurso
Wick River
Ackergill
243 CNOC AN RAIN BHAIN
160 BRAIGH FEITH HEMIGAL
132 DRUIM A' CHRACAIRNIE
Mybster
Bilbster
Sibster
Wick John o' Groats
Staxigoe
Loch of Toftingall
A882
A99
Loch Tuim Ghlais
Westerdale
Janetstown
Papigoe
Loch Caluim
23
Haster
Milton
Wick
Wick Bay
Strath Beg
Achairn Burn
Newton
Old Wick
South Head
Castle of Old Wick
203 CNOC PREAS A' MHADAIDH
200 CNOC BEUL NA FAIRE
Badlipster
Whiterow
Loch Hempriggs
136 BEINN CHAITEAG
Tannach
111
Altnabreac Station
A9
Thrumster
Loch Ruard
145 BALLHARN HILL
Grey Cairns of Camster
A99
Loch More
Loch Stemster
Sarclet
275 NAN GALL
Achavanich
212 HILL OF YARROWS
Loch of Yarrows
Loch Sand
248 STEMSTER HILL
Loch an Thulachan
Loch Rangag
Cairn o'Get
Ulbster
Strathmore Water
Rumsdale Water
Whaligoe
226 COIRE NA BEINN
Dalnawillan Lodge
Roster
Whaligoe Steps
Bruan
348 BEN ALISKY
Hill o'Many Stanes
Glutt Water
Upper Lybster
287 BEN-A-CHIELT
NC
Mid Clyth
Halberry Head
Glutt Lodge
264 CNOCAN CONACHREAG
Swiney
Clyth Ness
Occumster
Invershore
Lybster
NOCKFIN HEIGHTS
Houstry
Landhallow
Forse
Lybster Harbour
Lybster Bay
Clan Gunn
Smerral
Latheron
312 CNOC LOCH MHADADH
Dunbeath Water
Latheronwheel
Janetstown
A9
Berriedale Water
Laidhay Croft
Braemore
Dunbeath
484 MAIDEN PAP
Snow gates
705 MORVEN
Knockally
Dunbeath Bay
518 CNOC AN EIREANNAICH
Ramscraigs
ND
626 SCARABEN
Borgue
Langwell Forest
Newport
554 CREAG SCALABSDALE
Langwell House
Berriedale
401 CNOC NA MAOILE
North Coast 500
416
Badbea Historic Village
A897
A9
Torrish
404 CREAG THORARAIDH
River Helmsdale
Ord of Caithness
Navidale
Snow gates
Timespan
West Helmsdale
East Helmsdale
591 BEINN NA MEILICH
Helmsdale
109
Gartymore
Portgower
Glen Loth
Lothmore
0 1 2 3 4 5 miles
0 1 2 3 4 5 6 7 8 kilometres

ENGLAND

- **Acorn Bank Garden** CA10 1SP Cumb 68 D7
- **Aldborough Roman Site** YO51 9ES N York 63 U6
- **Alfriston Clergy House** BN26 5TL E Susx 11 S10
- **Alton Towers** ST10 4DB Staffs 46 E5
- **Anglesey Abbey** CB25 9EJ Cambs 39 R8
- **Anne Hathaway's Cottage** CV37 9HH Warwks 36 G10
- **Antony House** PL11 2QA Cnwll 5 L9
- **Appuldurcombe House** PO38 3EW IoW 9 Q13
- **Apsley House** W1J 7NT Gt Lon 21 N7
- **Arlington Court** EX31 4LP Devon 15 P4
- **Ascott** LU7 0PS Bucks 30 J8
- **Ashby-de-la-Zouch Castle** LE65 1BR Leics 47 L10
- **Athelhampton House & Gardens** DT2 7LG Dorset 7 U6
- **Attingham Park** SY4 4TP Shrops 45 M11
- **Audley End House & Gardens** CB11 4JF Essex 39 R13
- **Avebury Manor & Garden** SN8 1RF Wilts 18 G6
- **Baconsthorpe Castle** NR25 6LN Norfk 50 K6
- **Baddesley Clinton Hall** B93 0DQ Warwks 36 H6
- **Bamburgh Castle** NE69 7DF Nthumb 85 T11
- **Barnard Castle** DL12 8PR Dur 69 M9
- **Barrington Court** TA19 0NQ Somset 17 L13
- **Basildon Park** RG8 9NR W Berk 19 T5
- **Bateman's** TN19 7DS E Susx 12 C11
- **Battle of Britain Memorial Flight Visitor Centre** LN4 4SY Lincs 48 K2
- **Beamish Museum** DH9 0RG Dur 69 R2
- **Beatrix Potter Gallery** LA22 0NS Cumb 67 N13
- **Beaulieu** SO42 7ZN Hants 9 M8
- **Belton House** NG32 2LS Lincs 48 D6
- **Belvoir Castle** NG32 1PE Leics 48 B7
- **Bembridge Windmill** PO35 5SQ IoW 9 S11
- **Beningbrough Hall & Gardens** YO30 1DD N York 64 C8
- **Benthall Hall** TF12 5RX Shrops 45 Q13
- **Berkeley Castle** GL13 9PJ Gloucs 28 C8
- **Berrington Hall** HR6 0DW Herefs 35 M8
- **Berry Pomeroy Castle** TQ9 6LJ Devon 5 U8
- **Beth Chatto Gardens** CO7 7DB Essex 23 Q3
- **Biddulph Grange Garden** ST8 7SD Staffs 45 U2
- **Bishop's Waltham Palace** SO32 1DH Hants 9 Q5
- **Blackpool Zoo** FY3 8PP Bpool 61 Q12
- **Blenheim Palace** OX20 1PX Oxon 29 T4
- **Blickling Estate** NR11 6NF Norfk 51 L8
- **Blue John Cavern** S33 8WA Derbys 56 H10
- **Bodiam Castle** TN32 5UA E Susx 12 E10
- **Bolsover Castle** S44 6PR Derbys 57 Q12
- **Boscobel House** ST19 9AR Staffs 45 T12
- **Bovington Tank Museum** BH20 6JG Dorset 8 A11
- **Bowes Castle** DL12 9LD Dur 69 L10
- **Bradford Industrial Museum** BD2 3HP W Yorks 63 P13
- **Bradley Manor** TQ12 6BN Devon 5 U6
- **Bramber Castle** BN44 3WW W Susx 10 K8
- **Brinkburn Priory** NE65 8AR Nthumb 77 N6
- **Bristol Zoo Gardens** BS8 3HA Bristl 27 V13
- **Brockhampton Estate** WR6 5TB Herefs 35 Q9
- **Brough Castle** CA17 4EJ Cumb 68 G10
- **Buckfast Abbey** TQ11 0EE Devon 5 S7
- **Buckingham Palace** SW1A 1AA Gt Lon 21 N7
- **Buckland Abbey** PL20 6EY Devon 5 M7
- **Buscot Park** SN7 8BU Oxon 29 P8
- **Byland Abbey** YO61 4BD N York 64 C4
- **Cadbury World** B30 1JR Birm 36 D4
- **Calke Abbey** DE73 7LE Derbys 47 L9
- **Canons Ashby House** NN11 3SD Nhants 37 Q10
- **Canterbury Cathedral** CT1 2EH Kent 13 N4
- **Carisbrooke Castle** PO30 1XY IoW 9 P11
- **Carlyle's House** SW3 5HL Gt Lon 21 N7
- **Castle Drogo** EX6 6PB Devon 5 S2
- **Castle Howard** YO60 7DA N York 64 G5
- **Castle Rising Castle** PE31 6AH Norfk 49 U9
- **Charlecote Park** CV35 9ER Warwks 36 J9
- **Chartwell** TN16 1PS Kent 21 S12
- **Chastleton House** GL56 0SU Oxon 29 P2
- **Chatsworth** DE45 1PP Derbys 57 L12
- **Chedworth Roman Villa** GL54 3LJ Gloucs 29 L5
- **Chessington World of Adventures** KT9 2NE Gt Lon 21 L10
- **Chester Cathedral** CH1 2HU Ches W 54 K13
- **Chester Zoo** CH2 1EU Ches W 54 K12
- **Chesters Roman Fort & Museum** NE46 4EU Nthumb 76 J11
- **Chiswick House & Gardens** W4 2RP Gt Lon 21 M7
- **Chysauster Ancient Village** TR20 8XA Cnwll 2 D10
- **Claremont Landscape Garden** KT10 9JG Surrey 20 K10
- **Claydon House** MK18 2EY Bucks 30 F7
- **Cleeve Abbey** TA23 0PS Somset 16 D8
- **Clevedon Court** BS21 6QU N Som 17 M2
- **Cliveden** SL6 0JA Bucks 20 F5
- **Clouds Hill** BH20 7NQ Dorset 7 V6
- **Clumber Park** S80 3AZ Notts 57 T12
- **Colchester Zoo** CO3 0SL Essex 23 N3
- **Coleridge Cottage** TA5 1NQ Somset 16 G9
- **Coleton Fishacre** TQ6 0EQ Devon 6 B14
- **Compton Castle** TQ3 1TA Devon 5 V8
- **Conisbrough Castle** DN12 3BU Donc 57 R7
- **Corbridge Roman Town** NE45 5NT Nthumb 76 K13
- **Corfe Castle** BH20 5EZ Dorset 8 D12
- **Corsham Court** SN13 0BZ Wilts 18 C6
- **Cotehele** PL12 6TA Cnwll 5 L7
- **Coughton Court** B49 5JA Warwks 36 E8
- **Courts Garden** BA14 6RR Wilts 18 C8
- **Cragside** NE65 7PX Nthumb 77 M5
- **Crealy Adventure Park** EX5 1DR Devon 6 D6
- **Crich Tramway Village** DE4 5DP Derbys 46 K2
- **Croft Castle** HR6 9PW Herefs 34 K7
- **Croome Park** WR8 9JS Worcs 35 U12
- **Deddington Castle** OX15 0TE Oxon 29 U1
- **Didcot Railway Centre** OX11 7NJ Oxon 19 R2
- **Dover Castle** CT16 1HU Kent 13 R7
- **Drayton Manor Theme Park** B78 3SA Staffs 46 G13
- **Dudmaston Estate** WV15 6QN Shrops 35 R3
- **Dunham Massey** WA14 4SJ Traffd 55 R9
- **Dunstanburgh Castle** NE66 3TT Nthumb 77 R1
- **Dunster Castle** TA24 6SL Somset 16 C8
- **Durham Cathedral** DH1 3EH Dur 69 S4
- **Dyrham Park** SN14 8HY S Glos 28 D12
- **East Riddlesden Hall** BD20 5EL Brad 63 M11
- **Eden Project** PL24 2SG Cnwll 3 R6
- **Eltham Palace & Gardens** SE9 5QE Gt Lon 21 R8
- **Emmetts Garden** TN14 6BA Kent 21 S12
- **Exmoor Zoo** EX31 4SG Devon 15 Q4
- **Farleigh Hungerford Castle** BA2 7RS Somset 18 B9
- **Farnborough Hall** OX17 1DU Warwks 37 M11
- **Felbrigg Hall** NR11 8PR Norfk 51 L6
- **Fenton House & Garden** NW3 6SP Gt Lon 21 N5
- **Finch Foundry** EX20 2NW Devon 5 Q2
- **Finchale Priory** DH1 5SH Dur 69 S3
- **Fishbourne Roman Palace** PO19 3QR W Susx 10 C10
- **Flamingo Land** YO17 6UX N York 64 H4
- **Forde Abbey** TA20 4LU Somset 7 L3
- **Fountains Abbey & Studley Royal** HG4 3DY N York 63 R6
- **Gawthorpe Hall** BB12 8UA Lancs 62 G13
- **Gisborough Priory** TS14 6HG R & Cl 70 K9
- **Glendurgan Garden** TR11 5JZ Cnwll 2 K11
- **Goodrich Castle** HR9 6HY Herefs 28 A4
- **Great Chalfield Manor & Garden** SN12 8NH Wilts 18 C8
- **Great Coxwell Barn** SN7 7LZ Oxon 29 Q9
- **Greenway** TQ5 0ES Devon 5 V10
- **Haddon Hall** DE45 1LA Derbys 56 K13
- **Hailes Abbey** GL54 5PB Gloucs 29 L1
- **Ham House & Garden** TW10 7RS Gt Lon 21 L8
- **Hampton Court Palace** KT8 9AU Gt Lon 21 L9
- **Hanbury Hall** WR9 7EA Worcs 36 B8
- **Hardwick Hall** S44 5QJ Derbys 57 Q14
- **Hardy's Cottage** DT2 8QJ Dorset 7 T6
- **Hare Hill** SK10 4PY Ches E 56 C11
- **Hatchlands Park** GU4 7RT Surrey 20 J12
- **Heale Gardens** SP4 6NU Wilts 18 H13
- **Helmsley Castle** YO62 5AB N York 64 E3
- **Hereford Cathedral** HR1 2NG Herefs 35 M13
- **Hergest Croft Gardens** HR5 3EG Herefs 34 G9
- **Hever Castle & Gardens** TN8 7NG Kent 21 S13
- **Hidcote Manor Garden** GL55 6LR Gloucs 36 G12
- **Hill Top** LA22 0LF Cumb 67 N13
- **Hinton Ampner** SO24 0LA Hants 9 R3
- **Holkham Hall** NR23 1AB Norfk 50 E5
- **Housesteads Roman Fort** NE47 6NN Nthumb 76 F12
- **Howletts Wild Animal Park** CT4 5EL Kent 13 N4
- **Hughenden Manor** HP14 4LA Bucks 20 E3
- **Hurst Castle** SO41 0TP Hants 9 L11
- **Hylands House & Park** CM2 8WQ Essex 22 G7
- **Ickworth** IP29 5QE Suffk 40 D8
- **Ightham Mote** TN15 0NT Kent 21 U12
- **Ironbridge Gorge Museums** TF8 7DQ Wrekin 45 Q13
- **Kedleston Hall** DE22 5JH Derbys 46 K5
- **Kenilworth Castle & Elizabethan Garden** CV8 1NE Warwks 36 J6
- **Kenwood House** NW3 7JR Gt Lon 21 N5
- **Killerton** EX5 3LE Devon 6 C4
- **King John's Hunting Lodge** BS26 2AP Somset 17 M6
- **Kingston Lacy** BH21 4EA Dorset 8 D8
- **Kirby Hall** NN17 3EN Nhants 38 D2
- **Knightshayes Court** EX16 7RQ Devon 16 C13
- **Knole House** TN13 1HU Kent 21 T12
- **Knowsley Safari Park** L34 4AN Knows 55 L8
- **Lacock Abbey** SN15 2LG Wilts 18 D7
- **Lamb House** TN31 7ES E Susx 12 H11
- **Lanhydrock House** PL30 5AD Cnwll 3 R4
- **Launceston Castle** PL15 7DR Cnwll 4 J4
- **Leeds Castle** ME17 1PB Kent 12 F5
- **Legoland** SL4 4AY W&M 20 F8
- **Lindisfarne Castle** TD15 2SH Nthumb 85 S10
- **Lindisfarne Priory** TD15 2RX Nthumb 85 S10
- **Little Moreton Hall** CW12 4SD Ches E 45 T2
- **Liverpool Cathedral** L1 7AZ Lpool 54 J9
- **London Zoo ZSL** NW1 4RY Gt Lon 21 N6
- **Longleat** BA12 7NW Wilts 18 B12
- **Loseley Park** GU3 1HS Surrey 20 G13
- **Ludgershall Castle** SP11 9QR Wilts 19 L10
- **Lydford Castle** EX20 4BH Devon 5 N4
- **Lyme Park, House & Garden** SK12 2NX Ches E 56 E10
- **Lytes Cary Manor** TA11 7HU Somset 17 P11
- **Lyveden New Bield** PE8 5AT Nhant 38 E3
- **Maiden Castle** DT2 9PP Dorset 7 S7
- **Mapledurham Estate** RG4 7TR Oxon 19 U5
- **Marble Hill House** TW1 2NL Gt Lon 21 L8
- **Marwell Zoo** SO21 1JH Hants 9 Q4
- **Melford Hall** CO10 9AA Suffk 40 E11
- **Merseyside Maritime Museum** L3 4AQ Lpool 54 H9
- **Minster Lovell Hall** OX29 0RR Oxon 29 R5
- **Mompesson House** SP1 2EL Wilts 8 G3
- **Monk Bretton Priory** S71 5QD Barns 57 N5
- **Montacute House** TA15 6XP Somset 17 N13
- **Morwellham Quay** PL19 8JL Devon 5 L7
- **Moseley Old Hall** WV10 7HY Staffs 46 B13
- **Mottisfont** SO51 0LP Hants 9 L3
- **Mottistone Manor Garden** PO30 4ED IoW 9 N12
- **Mount Grace Priory** DL6 3JG N York 70 F13
- **National Maritime Museum** SE10 9NF Gt Lon 21 Q7
- **National Motorcycle Museum** B92 0ED Solhll 36 H4
- **National Portrait Gallery** WC2H 0HE Gt Lon 21 N6
- **National Railway Museum** YO26 4XJ York 64 D9
- **National Space Centre** LE4 5NS C Leic 47 Q12
- **Natural History Museum** SW7 5BD Gt Lon 21 N7
- **Needles Old Battery** PO39 0JH IoW 9 L12
- **Nene Valley Railway** PE8 6LR Cambs 38 H1
- **Netley Abbey** SO31 5FB Hants 9 P7
- **Newark Air Museum** NG24 2NY Notts 48 B2
- **Newtown Old Town Hall** PO30 4PA IoW 9 N10
- **North Leigh Roman Villa** OX29 6QB Oxon 29 S4
- **Norwich Cathedral** NR1 4DH Norfk 51 M12
- **Nostell Priory** WF4 1QE Wakefd 57 P3
- **Nunnington Hall** YO62 5UY N York 64 F4
- **Nymans House** RH17 6EB W Susx 11 M5
- **Old Royal Naval College** SE10 9NN Gt Lon 21 Q7
- **Old Sarum** SP1 3SD Wilts 8 G2
- **Old Wardour Castle** SP3 6RR Wilts 8 C3
- **Oliver Cromwell's House** CB7 4HF Cambs 39 R4
- **Orford Castle** IP12 2ND Suffk 41 R10
- **Ormesby Hall** TS3 0SR R & Cl 70 H9
- **Osborne House** PO32 6JX IoW 9 Q9
- **Osterley Park & House** TW7 4RB Gt Lon 20 K7
- **Overbeck's** TQ8 8LW Devon 5 S13
- **Oxburgh Hall** PE33 9PS Norfk 50 B13
- **Packwood House** B94 6AT Warwks 36 G6
- **Paignton Zoo** TQ4 7EU Torbay 6 A13
- **Paycocke's House & Garden** CO6 1NS Essex 22 K3
- **Peckover House & Garden** PE13 1JR Cambs 49 Q12
- **Pendennis Castle** TR11 4LP Cnwll 3 L10
- **Petworth House & Park** GU28 0AE W Susx 10 F6
- **Pevensey Castle** BN24 5LE E Susx 11 U10
- **Peveril Castle** S33 8WQ Derbys 56 J10
- **Polesden Lacey** RH5 6BD Surrey 20 K12
- **Portland Castle** DT5 1AZ Dorset 7 S10
- **Portsmouth Historic Dockyard** PO1 3LJ C Port 9 S8
- **Powderham Castle** EX6 8JQ Devon 6 C8
- **Prior Park Landscape Garden** BA2 5AH BaNES 17 U4
- **Prudhoe Castle** NE42 6NA Nthumb 77 M13
- **Quarry Bank Mill & Styal** SK9 4LA Ches E 55 T10
- **Quebec House** TN16 1TD Kent 21 R12
- **Ramsey Abbey Gatehouse** PE17 1DH Cambs 39 L3
- **Reculver Towers & Roman Fort** CT6 6SU Kent 13 P2
- **Red House** DA6 8JF Gt Lon 21 S7
- **Restormel Castle** PL22 0EE Cnwll 4 E8
- **Richborough Roman Fort** CT13 9JW Kent 13 R3
- **Richmond Castle** DL10 4QW N York 69 Q12
- **Roche Abbey** S66 8NW Rothm 57 R9
- **Rochester Castle** ME1 1SW Medway 12 D2
- **Rockbourne Roman Villa** SP6 3PG Hants 8 G5
- **Roman Baths & Pump Room** BA1 1LZ BaNES 17 U4
- **Royal Botanic Gardens, Kew** TW9 3AB Gt Lon 21 L7
- **Royal Observatory Greenwich** SE10 8XJ Gt Lon 21 Q7
- **Rufford Old Hall** L40 1SG Lancs 55 L3
- **Runnymede** SL4 2JJ W & M 20 G8
- **Rushton Triangular Lodge** NN14 1RP Nhants 38 B4
- **Rycote Chapel** OX9 2PA Oxon 30 E12
- **St Leonard's Tower** ME19 6PE Kent 12 C4
- **St Michael's Mount** TR17 0HT Cnwll 2 E11
- **St Paul's Cathedral** EC4M 8AD Gt Lon 21 P6
- **Salisbury Cathedral** SP1 2EJ Wilts 8 G3
- **Saltram** PL7 1UH C Plym 5 N9
- **Sandham Memorial Chapel** RG20 9JT Hants 19 Q8
- **Sandringham House & Grounds** PE35 6EH Norfk 49 U8
- **Saxtead Green Post Mill** IP13 9QQ Suffk 41 N8
- **Scarborough Castle** YO11 1HY N York 65 P2
- **Science Museum** SW7 2DD Gt Lon 21 N7
- **Scotney Castle** TN3 8JN Kent 12 C8
- **Shaw's Corner** AL6 9BX Herts 31 Q9
- **Sheffield Park & Garden** TN22 3QX E Susx 11 Q6
- **Sherborne Old Castle** DT9 3SA Dorset 17 R13
- **Sissinghurst Castle Garden** TN17 2AB Kent 12 F8
- **Sizergh Castle & Garden** LA8 8AE Cumb 61 T2
- **Smallhythe Place** TN30 7NG Kent 12 G10
- **Snowshill Manor & Garden** WR12 7JU Gloucs 36 E14
- **Souter Lighthouse** SR6 7NH S Tyne 77 U13
- **Speke Hall, Garden & Estate** L24 1XD Lpool 54 K10
- **Spinnaker Tower, Emirates** PO1 3TT C Port 9 S9
- **Stokesay Castle** SY7 9AH Shrops 34 K4
- **Stonehenge** SP4 7DE Wilts 18 H12
- **Stourhead** BA12 6QD Wilts 17 U10
- **Stowe Gardens** MK18 5EQ Bucks 30 E5
- **Sudbury Hall** DE6 5HT Derbys 46 G7
- **Sulgrave Manor** OX17 2SD Nhants 37 Q11
- **Sunnycroft** TF1 2DR Wrekin 45 Q11
- **Sutton Hoo** IP12 3DJ Suffk 41 N11
- **Sutton House** E9 6JQ Gt Lon 21 Q5
- **Tate Britain** SW1P 4RG Gt Lon 21 N7
- **Tate Liverpool** L3 4BB Lpool 54 H9
- **Tate Modern** SE1 9TG Gt Lon 21 P6
- **Tattershall Castle** LN4 4LR Lincs 48 K2
- **Tatton Park** WA16 6QN Ches E 55 R10
- **The British Library** NW1 2DB Gt Lon 21 N6
- **The British Museum** WC1B 3DG Gt Lon 21 N6
- **The Lost Gardens of Heligan** PL26 6EN Cnwll 3 P7
- **The Lowry** M50 3AZ Salfd 55 T7
- **The National Gallery** WC2N 5DN Gt Lon 21 N6
- **The Vyne** RG24 9HL Hants 19 T9
- **The Weir Garden** HR4 7QF Herefs 34 K12
- **Thornton Abbey & Gatehouse** DN39 6TU N Linc 58 K3
- **Thorpe Park** KT16 8PN Surrey 20 H9
- **Tilbury Fort** RM18 7NR Thurr 22 G12
- **Tintagel Castle** PL34 0HE Cnwll 4 C3
- **Tintinhull Garden** BA22 8PZ Somset 17 P13
- **Totnes Castle** TQ9 5NU Devon 5 U8
- **Tower of London** EC3N 4AB Gt Lon 21 P6
- **Townend** LA23 1LB Cumb 67 P12
- **Treasurer's House** YO1 7JL York 64 E9
- **Trelissick Garden** TR3 6QL Cnwll 3 L9
- **Trengwainton Garden** TR20 8RZ Cnwll 2 C10
- **Trerice** TR8 4PG Cnwll 3 L5
- **Twycross Zoo** CV9 3PX Leics 46 K12
- **Upnor Castle** ME2 4XG Medway 22 J13
- **Uppark House & Garden** GU31 5QR W Susx 10 B7
- **Upton House & Garden** OX15 6HT Warwks 37 L11
- **Victoria & Albert Museum** SW7 2RL Gt Lon 21 N7
- **Waddesdon Manor** HP18 0JH Bucks 30 F9
- **Wakehurst Place** RH17 6TN W Susx 11 N4
- **Wall Roman Site** WS14 0AW Staffs 46 E12
- **Wallington** NE61 4AR Nthumb 77 L9
- **Walmer Castle & Gardens** CT14 7LJ Kent 13 S6
- **Warkworth Castle & Hermitage** NE65 0UJ Nthumb 77 Q4
- **Warner Bros. Studio Tour London** WD25 7LS Herts 31 N12
- **Warwick Castle** CV34 4QU Warwks 36 J8
- **Washington Old Hall** NE38 7LE Sundld 70 D1
- **Waterperry Gardens** OX33 1LG Oxon 30 D11
- **Weeting Castle** IP27 0RQ Norfk 40 C3
- **Wenlock Priory** TF13 6HS Shrops 45 P13
- **West Midland Safari & Leisure Park** DY12 1LF Worcs 35 T5
- **West Wycombe Park** HP14 3AJ Bucks 20 D4
- **Westbury Court Garden** GL14 1PD Gloucs 28 D5
- **Westminster Abbey** SW1P 3PA Gt Lon 21 N7
- **Westonbirt Arboretum** GL8 8QS Gloucs 28 G9
- **Westwood Manor** BA15 2AF Wilts 18 B9
- **Whipsnade Zoo ZSL** LU6 2LF Beds C 31 M9
- **Whitby Abbey** YO22 4JT N York 71 R10
- **Wicksteed Park** NN15 6NJ Nhants 38 C5
- **Wightwick Manor & Gardens** WV6 8EE Staffs 45 U14
- **Wimpole Estate** SG8 0BW Cambs 39 M10
- **Winchester Cathedral** SO23 9LS Hants 9 P3
- **Winchester City Mill** SO23 0EJ Hants 9 P3
- **Windsor Castle** SL4 1NJ W & M 20 G7
- **Winkworth Arboretum** GU8 4AD Surrey 10 F2
- **Wisley RHS Garden** GU23 6QB Surrey 20 J11
- **Woburn Safari Park** MK17 9QN Beds C 31 L6
- **Wookey Hole Caves** BA5 1BA Somset 17 P7
- **Woolsthorpe Manor** NG33 5PD Lincs 48 D9
- **Wordsworth House** CA13 9RX Cumb 66 H6
- **Wrest Park** MK45 4HR Beds C 31 N5
- **Wroxeter Roman City** SY5 6PR Shrops 45 N12
- **WWT Arundel Wetland Centre** BN18 9PB W Susx 10 G9
- **WWT Slimbridge Wetland Centre** GL2 7BT Gloucs 28 D6
- **Yarmouth Castle** PO41 0PB IoW 9 M11
- **York Minster** YO1 7HH York 64 E9

SCOTLAND

- **Aberdour Castle** KY3 0SL Fife 83 N1
- **Alloa Tower** FK10 1PP Clacks 90 C13
- **Arbroath Abbey** DD11 1EG Angus 91 T3
- **Arduaine Garden** PA34 4XQ Ag & B 87 P3
- **Bachelors' Club** KA5 5RB S Ayrs 81 N7
- **Balmoral Castle Grounds** AB35 5TB Abers 98 D5
- **Balvenie Castle** AB55 4DH Moray 104 C7
- **Bannockburn Battlefield & Heritage Centre** FK7 0LJ Stirlg 89 S7
- **Blackness Castle** EH49 7NH Falk 83 L2
- **Blair Castle** PH18 5TL P & K 97 P10
- **Bothwell Castle** G71 8BL S Lans 82 C7
- **Branklyn Garden** PH2 7BB P & K 90 H7
- **Brodick Castle, Garden & Country Park** KA27 8HY N Ayrs 80 E5
- **Brodie Castle** IV36 2TE Moray 103 Q4
- **Broughton House & Garden** DG6 4JX D & G 73 R9
- **Burleigh Castle** KY13 9GG P & K 90 H11
- **Caerlaverock Castle** DG1 4RU D & G 74 K12
- **Cardoness Castle** DG7 2EH D & G 73 P8
- **Castle Campbell & Garden** FK14 7PP Clacks 90 E12
- **Castle Fraser, Garden & Estate** AB51 7LD Abers 105 L13
- **Castle Kennedy & Gardens** DG9 8BX D & G 72 E7
- **Castle Menzies** PH15 2JD P & K 90 B2
- **Corgarff Castle** AB36 8YP Abers 98 D2
- **Craigievar Castle** AB33 8JF Abers 98 K2
- **Craigmillar Castle** EH16 4SY C Edin 83 Q4
- **Crarae Garden** PA32 8YA Ag & B 87 T6
- **Crathes Castle & Garden** AB31 5QJ Abers 99 N4
- **Crichton Castle** EH37 5XA Mdloth 83 S6
- **Crossraguel Abbey** KA19 8HQ S Ayrs 80 K11
- **Culloden Battlefield** IV2 5EU Highld 102 K6
- **Culross Palace** KY12 8JH Fife 82 J1
- **Culzean Castle & Country Park** KA19 8LE S Ayrs 80 J10
- **Dallas Dhu Distillery** IV36 2RR Moray 103 R4
- **David Livingstone Centre** G72 9BY S Lans 82 C7
- **Dirleton Castle & Garden** EH39 5ER E Loth 84 E2
- **Doune Castle** FK16 6EA Stirlg 89 R5
- **Drum Castle, Garden & Estate** AB31 5EY Abers 99 P3
- **Dryburgh Abbey** TD6 0RQ Border 84 F12
- **Duff House** AB45 3SX Abers 104 K3
- **Dumbarton Castle** G82 1JJ W Duns 88 J11
- **Dundrennan Abbey** DG6 4QH D & G 73 S10
- **Dunnottar Castle** AB39 2TL Abers 99 R7
- **Dunstaffnage Castle & Chapel** PA37 1PZ Ag & B 94 B12
- **Edinburgh Castle** EH1 2NG C Edin 83 Q4
- **Edinburgh Zoo RZSS** EH12 6TS C Edin 83 P4
- **Edzell Castle & Garden** DD9 7UE Angus 98 K10
- **Eilean Donan Castle** IV40 8DX Highld 101 M6
- **Elgin Cathedral** IV30 1HU Moray 103 V3
- **Falkland Palace & Garden** KY15 7BU Fife 91 L10
- **Fort George** IV2 7TE Highld 103 L4
- **Fyvie Castle** AB53 8JS Abers 105 M8
- **Georgian House** EH2 4DR C Edin 83 P4
- **Gladstone's Land** EH1 2NT C Edin 83 Q4
- **Glamis Castle** DD8 1RJ Angus 91 N2
- **Glasgow Botanic Gardens** G12 0UE C Glas 89 N12
- **Glasgow Cathedral** G4 0QZ C Glas 89 P12
- **Glasgow Science Centre** G51 1EA C Glas 89 N12
- **Glen Grant Distillery** AB38 7BS Moray 104 B6
- **Glenluce Abbey** DG8 0AF D & G 72 F8
- **Greenbank Garden** G76 8RB E Rens 81 R1
- **Haddo House** AB41 7EQ Abers 105 P9
- **Harmony Garden** TD6 9LJ Border 84 E12
- **Hermitage Castle** TD9 0LU Border 75 U6
- **Highland Wildlife Park RZSS** PH21 1NL Highld 97 N3
- **Hill House** G84 9AJ Ag & B 88 G9
- **Hill of Tarvit Mansion & Garden** KY15 5PB Fife 91 N9
- **Holmwood** G44 3YG C Glas 89 N14
- **House of Dun** DD10 9LQ Angus 99 M12
- **House of the Binns** EH49 7NA W Loth 83 L3
- **Huntingtower Castle** PH1 3JL P & K 90 G7
- **Huntly Castle** AB54 4SH Abers 104 G7
- **Hutchesons' Hall** G1 1EJ C Glas 89 N12
- **Inchmahome Priory** FK8 3RA Stirlg 89 N5
- **Inveresk Lodge Garden** EH21 7TE E Loth 83 R4
- **Inverewe Garden & Estate** IV22 2LG Highld 107 Q8
- **Inverlochy Castle** PH33 6SN Highld 94 G3
- **Kellie Castle & Garden** KY10 2RF Fife 91 R10
- **Kildrummy Castle** AB33 8RA Abers 104 F12
- **Killiecrankie** PH16 5LG P & K 97 Q11
- **Leith Hall Garden & Estate** AB54 4NQ Abers 104 G10
- **Linlithgow Palace** EH49 7AL W Loth 82 K3
- **Lochleven Castle** KY13 8UF P & K 90 H11
- **Logan Botanic Garden** DG9 9ND D & G 72 D11
- **Malleny Garden** EH14 7AF C Edin 83 N5
- **Melrose Abbey** TD6 9LG Border 84 E12
- **National Museum of Scotland** EH1 1JF C Edin 83 Q4
- **Newark Castle** PA14 5NH Inver 88 H11
- **Palace of Holyroodhouse** EH8 8DX C Edin 83 Q4
- **Pitmedden Garden** AB41 7PD Abers 105 P10
- **Preston Mill & Phantassie Doocot** EH40 3DS E Loth 84 F3
- **Priorwood Garden** TD6 9PX Border 84 E12
- **Robert Smail's Printing Works** EH44 6HA Border 83 R11
- **Rothesay Castle** PA20 0DA Ag & B 88 C13
- **Royal Botanic Garden Edinburgh** EH3 5LR C Edin 83 P3
- **Royal Yacht Britannia** EH6 6JJ C Edin 83 Q3
- **St Andrews Aquarium** KY16 9AS Fife 91 R8
- **Scone Palace** PH2 6BD P & K 90 H6
- **Smailholm Tower** TD5 7PG Border 84 G12
- **Souter Johnnie's Cottage** KA19 8HY S Ayrs 80 J11
- **Stirling Castle** FK8 1EJ Stirlg 89 S7
- **Sweetheart Abbey** DG2 8BU D & G 74 J12
- **Tantallon Castle** EH39 5PN E Loth 84 F1
- **Tenement House** G3 6QN C Glas 89 N12
- **The Burrell Collection** G43 1AT C Glas 89 N13
- **The Falkirk Wheel** FK1 4RS Falk 82 G2
- **The Hunterian Museum** G12 8QQ C Glas 89 N12
- **Threave Castle** DG7 1TJ D & G 74 D13
- **Threave Garden** DG7 1RX D & G 74 E13
- **Tolquhon Castle** AB41 7LP Abers 105 P10
- **Traquair House** EH44 6PW Border 83 R11
- **Urquhart Castle** IV63 6XJ Highld 102 F10
- **Weaver's Cottage** PA10 2JG Rens 88 K13
- **Whithorn Priory & Museum** DG8 8PY D & G 73 L11

WALES

- **Aberconwy House** LL32 8AY Conwy 53 N7
- **Aberdulais Tin Works & Waterfall** SA10 8EU Neath 26 D8
- **Beaumaris Castle** LL58 8AP IoA 52 K7
- **Big Pit: National Coal Museum** NP4 9XP Torfn 27 N6
- **Bodnant Garden** LL28 5RE Conwy 53 P8
- **Caerleon Roman Fortress & Baths** NP18 1AE Newpt 27 Q9
- **Caernarfon Castle** LL55 2AY Gwynd 52 G10
- **Caldicot Castle & Country Park** NP26 4HU Mons 27 T10
- **Cardiff Castle** CF10 3RB Cardif 27 M12
- **Castell Coch** CF15 7JS Cardif 27 L11
- **Chirk Castle** LL14 5AF Wrexhm 44 G6
- **Colby Woodland Garden** SA67 8PP Pembks 25 L9
- **Conwy Castle** LL32 8AY Conwy 53 N7
- **Criccieth Castle** LL52 0DP Gwynd 42 K6
- **Dinefwr Park & Castle** SA19 6RT Carmth 25 V6
- **Dolaucothi Gold Mines** SA19 8US Carmth 33 N12
- **Erddig** LL13 0YT Wrexhm 44 H4
- **Ffestiniog Railway** LL49 9NF Gwynd 43 N5
- **Harlech Castle** LL46 2YH Gwynd 43 L7
- **Llanerchaeron** SA48 8DG Cerdgn 32 J8
- **National Showcaves Centre for Wales** SA9 1GJ Powys 26 E4
- **Penrhyn Castle** LL57 4HT Gwynd 52 K8
- **Plas Newydd** LL61 6DQ IoA 52 H9
- **Plas yn Rhiw** LL53 8AB Gwynd 42 D8
- **Portmeirion** LL48 6ER Gwynd 43 L6
- **Powis Castle & Garden** SY21 8RF Powys 44 F12
- **Raglan Castle** NP15 2BT Mons 27 S6
- **Sygun Copper Mine** LL55 4NE Gwynd 43 M4
- **Tintern Abbey** NP16 6SE Mons 27 U7
- **Tudor Merchant's House** SA70 7BX Pembks 24 K10
- **Tŷ Mawr Wybrnant** LL25 0HJ Conwy 43 Q3
- **Valle Crucis Abbey** LL20 8DD Denbgs 44 F5

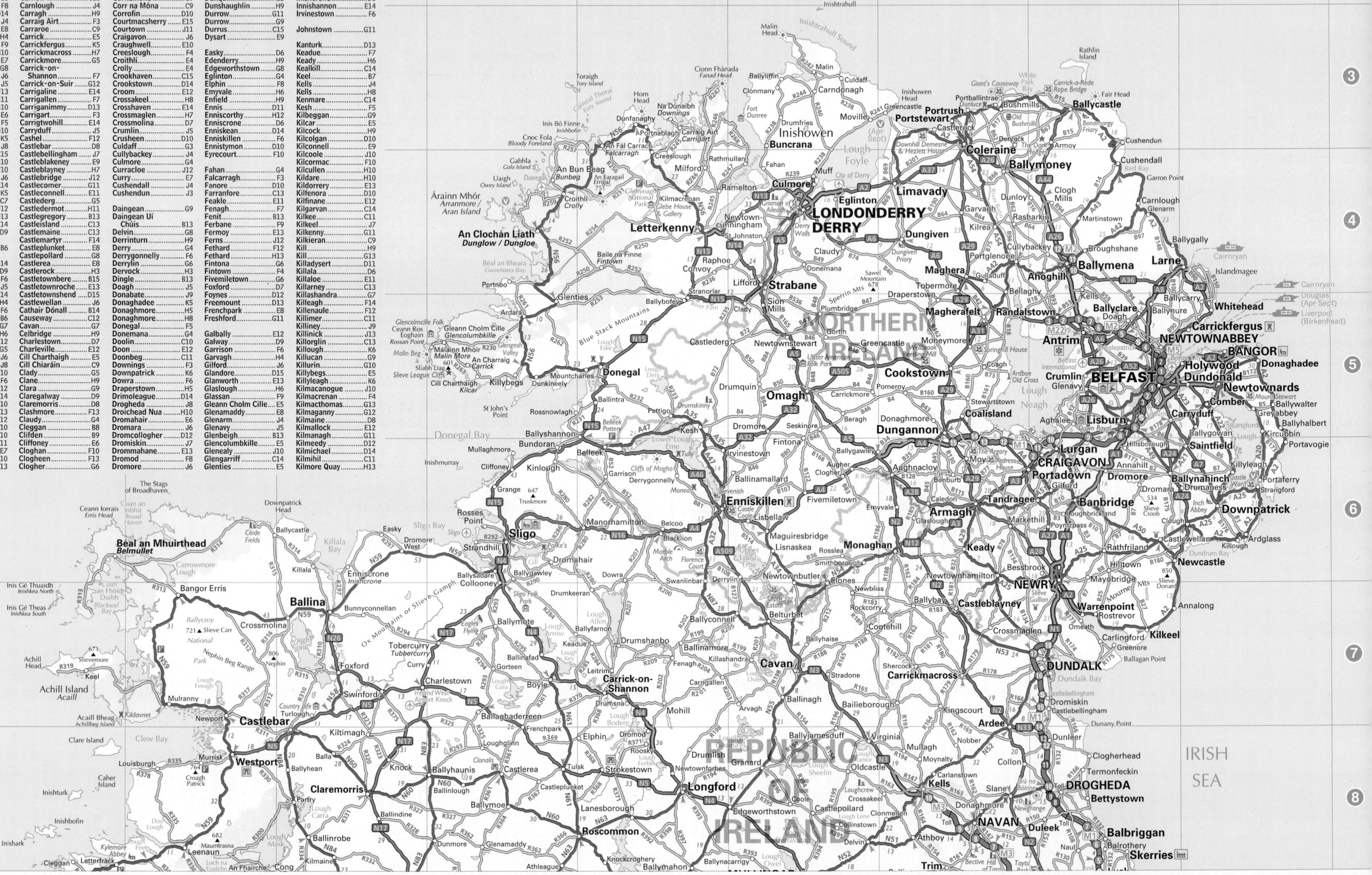

A
B
C
D
E
F
G
H
J
K
1
2
3
4
5
6
7
8
NORTHERN IRELAND
REPUBLIC OF IRELAND
IRISH SEA
BELFAST
LONDONDERRY
DERRY
NEWTOWNABBEY
BANGOR
Carrickfergus
Newtownards
Lisburn
Lurgan
CRAIGAVON
Portadown
Armagh
NEWRY
DUNDALK
DROGHEDA
NAVAN
Coleraine
Ballymoney
Ballymena
Larne
Antrim
Limavady
Strabane
Omagh
Cookstown
Dungannon
Enniskillen
Monaghan
Cavan
Letterkenny
Buncrana
Donegal
Sligo
Ballina
Castlebar
Westport
Claremorris
Carrick-on-Shannon
Longford
Roscommon
Kells
Downpatrick
Banbridge
Newcastle
Kilkeel
Ardee
Balbriggan
Skerries
Donegal Bay
Sligo Bay
Clew Bay
Dundalk Bay
Achill Island
Rathlin Island
Malin Head
Inishtrahull
Lough Neagh
Lough Foyle
Inishowen

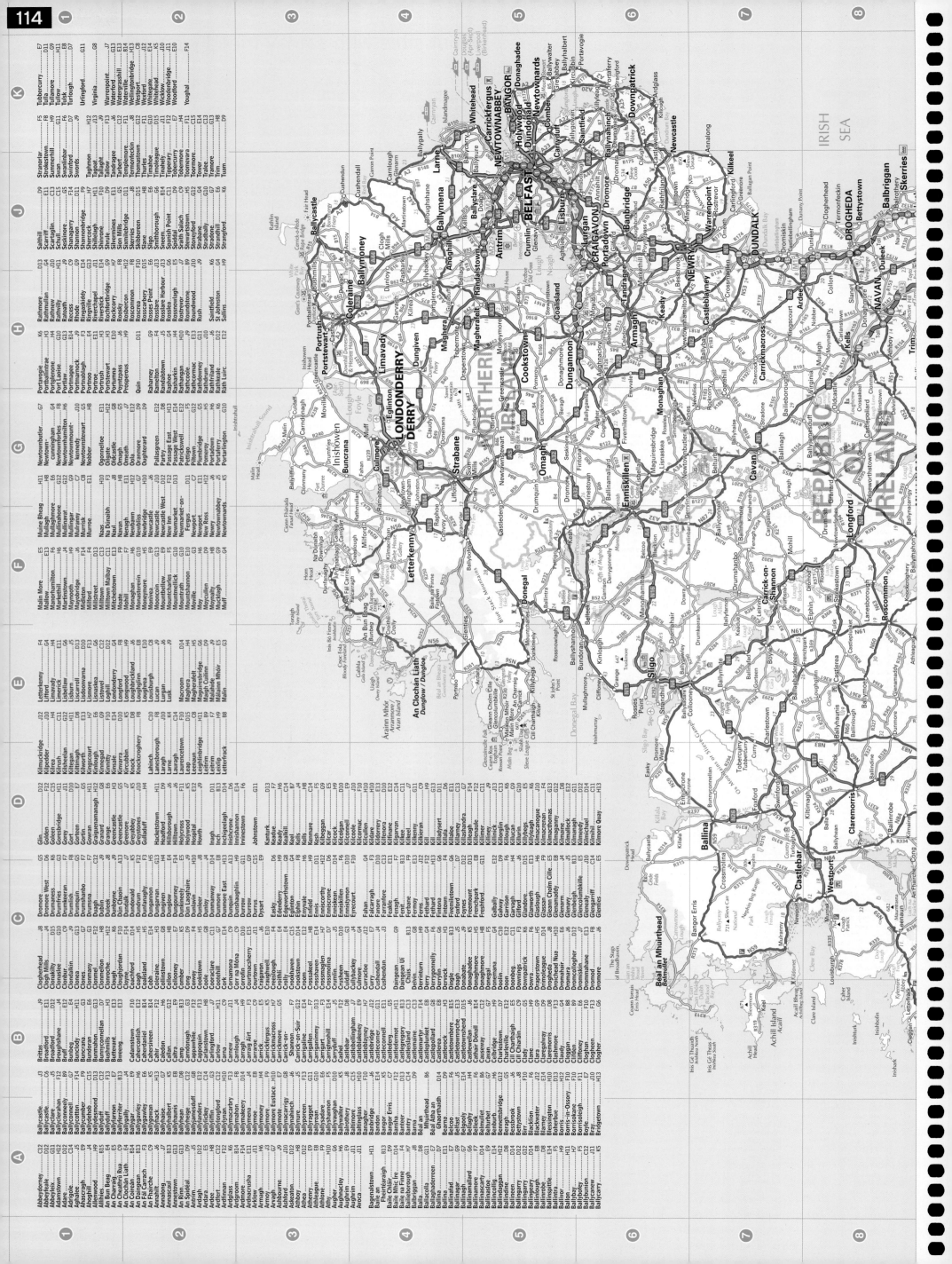

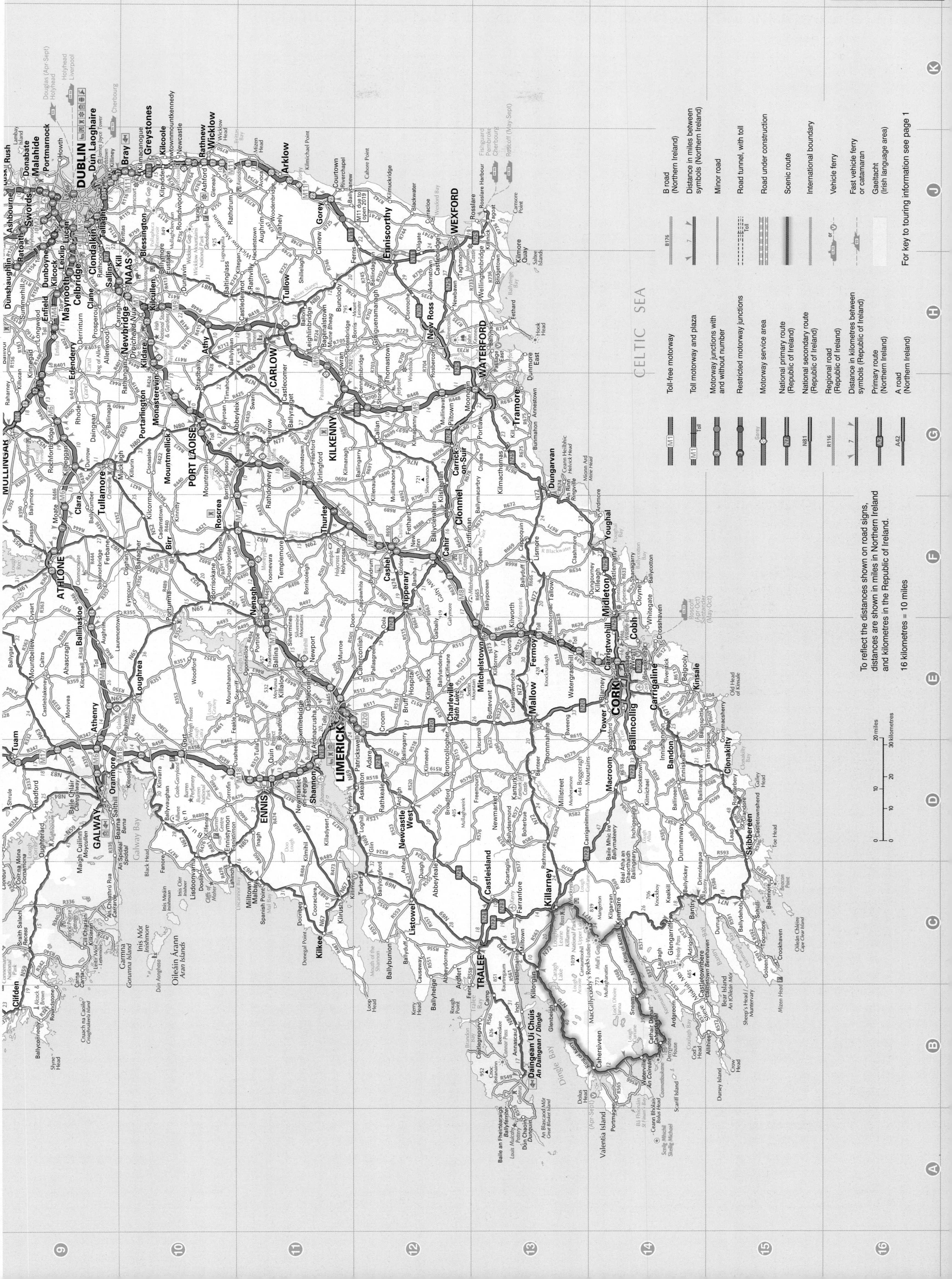
CELTIC SEA
DUBLIN
Dún Laoghaire
GALWAY
LIMERICK
CORK
WATERFORD
WEXFORD
KILKENNY
ATHLONE
Toll-free motorway
Toll motorway and plaza
Motorway junctions with and without number
Restricted motorway junctions
Motorway service area
National primary route (Republic of Ireland)
National secondary route (Republic of Ireland)
Regional road (Republic of Ireland)
Distance in kilometres between symbols (Republic of Ireland)
Primary route (Northern Ireland)
A road (Northern Ireland)
B road (Northern Ireland)
Distance in miles between symbols (Northern Ireland)
Minor road
Road tunnel, with toll
Road under construction
Scenic route
International boundary
Vehicle ferry
Fast vehicle ferry or catamaran
Gaeltacht (Irish language area)
For key to touring information see page 1
To reflect the distances shown on road signs, distances are shown in miles in Northern Ireland and kilometres in the Republic of Ireland.
16 kilometres = 10 miles
0 10 20 miles
0 10 20 30 kilometres

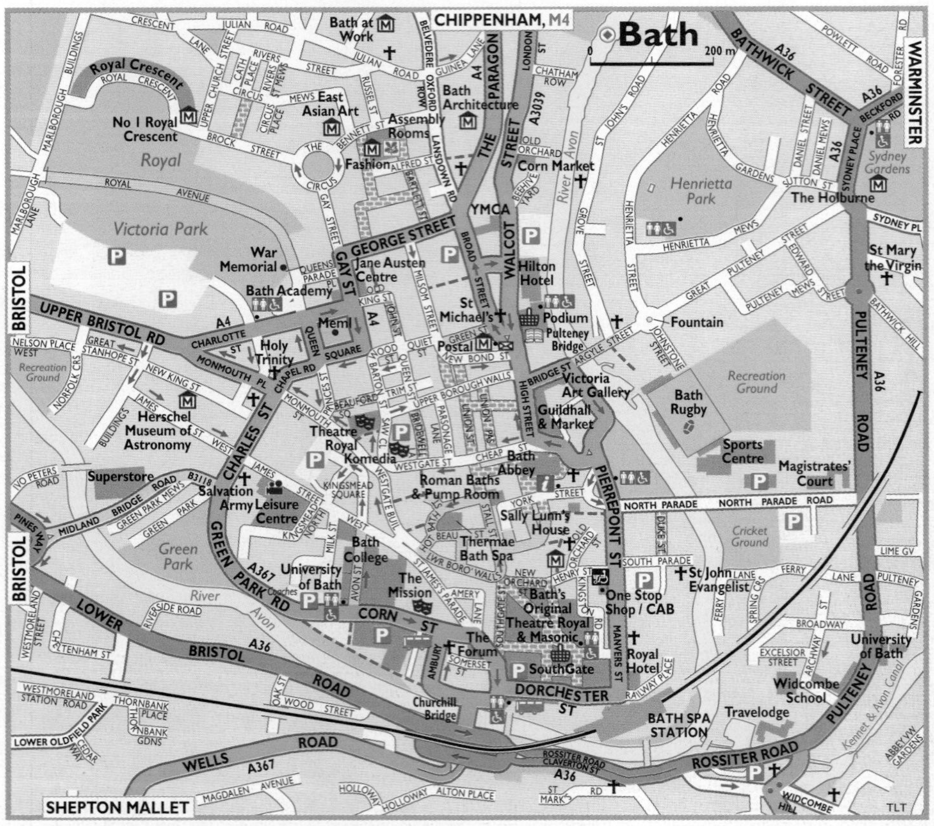
Bath
200 m
CHIPPENHAM, M4
WARMINSTER
BRISTOL
SHEPTON MALLET
Royal Crescent
No 1 Royal Crescent
Victoria Park
Assembly Rooms
Fashion
Bath Architecture
Corn Market
The Holburne
Henrietta Park
YMCA
Hilton Hotel
Podium
Pulteney Bridge
Fountain
Victoria Art Gallery
Guildhall & Market
Bath Rugby
Recreation Ground
Sports Centre
Magistrates' Court
Holy Trinity
Herschel Museum of Astronomy
Theatre Royal
Komedia
Bath Abbey
Roman Baths & Pump Room
Sally Lunn's House
Thermae Bath Spa
Superstore
Salvation Army
Leisure Centre
Green Park
Bath College
University of Bath
The Mission
Theatre Royal & Masonic
One Stop Shop / CAB
St John Evangelist
Royal Hotel
The Forum
SouthGate
BATH SPA STATION
Travelodge
Widcombe School
University of Bath
Churchill Bridge
TLT

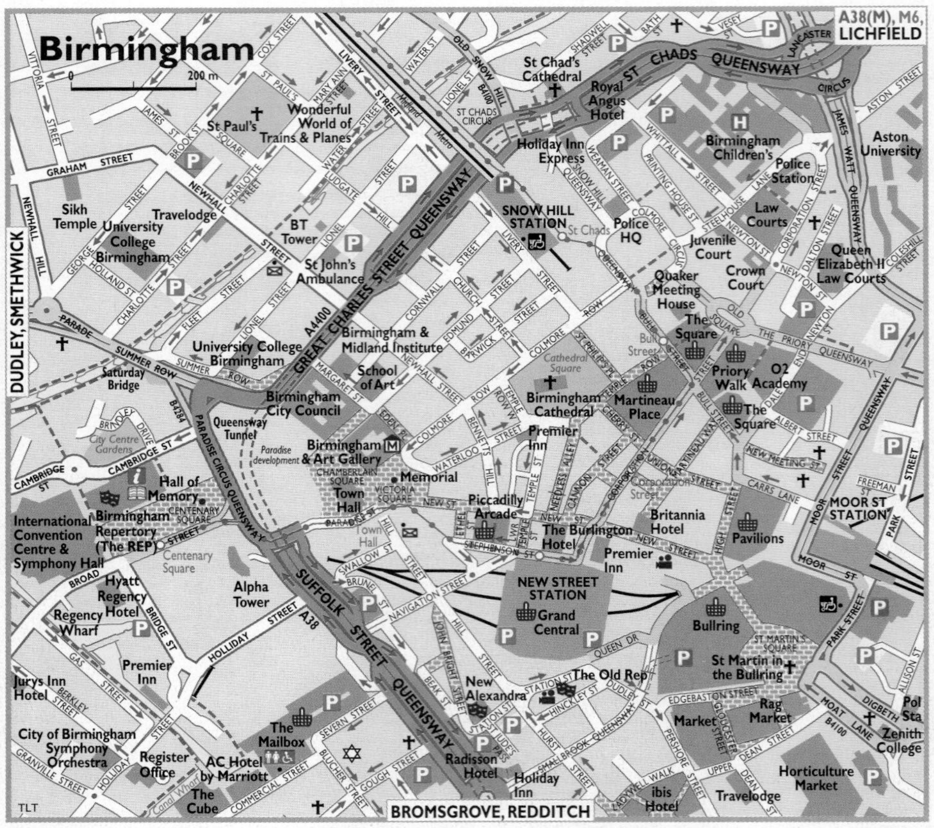
Birmingham
200 m
A38(M), M6, LICHFIELD
DUDLEY, SMETHWICK
BROMSGROVE, REDDITCH
St Chad's Cathedral
Royal Angus Hotel
Birmingham Children's
Aston University
Police Station
Law Courts
Police HQ
Crown Court
Queen Elizabeth II Law Courts
Wonderful World of Trains & Planes
St Paul's
Holiday Inn Express
SNOW HILL STATION
Sikh Temple
Travelodge
University College Birmingham
BT Tower
St John's Ambulance
Birmingham & Midland Institute
School of Art
University College Birmingham
Birmingham City Council
Birmingham Cathedral
Martineau Place
Priory Walk
O2 Academy
The Square
Birmingham Museum & Art Gallery
Memorial
Town Hall
Hall of Memory
International Convention Centre & Symphony Hall
Birmingham Repertory (The REP)
Piccadilly Arcade
The Burlington Hotel
Britannia Hotel
Premier Inn
Pavilions
MOOR ST STATION
Alpha Tower
NEW STREET STATION
Grand Central
Bullring
St Martin in the Bullring
Hyatt Regency Hotel
Regency Wharf
Premier Inn
Jurys Inn Hotel
New Alexandra
The Old Rep
Market
Rag Market
Zenith College
City of Birmingham Symphony Orchestra
Register Office
AC Hotel by Marriott
The Mailbox
The Cube
Radisson Hotel
Holiday Inn
Ibis Hotel
Travelodge
Horticulture Market
TLT

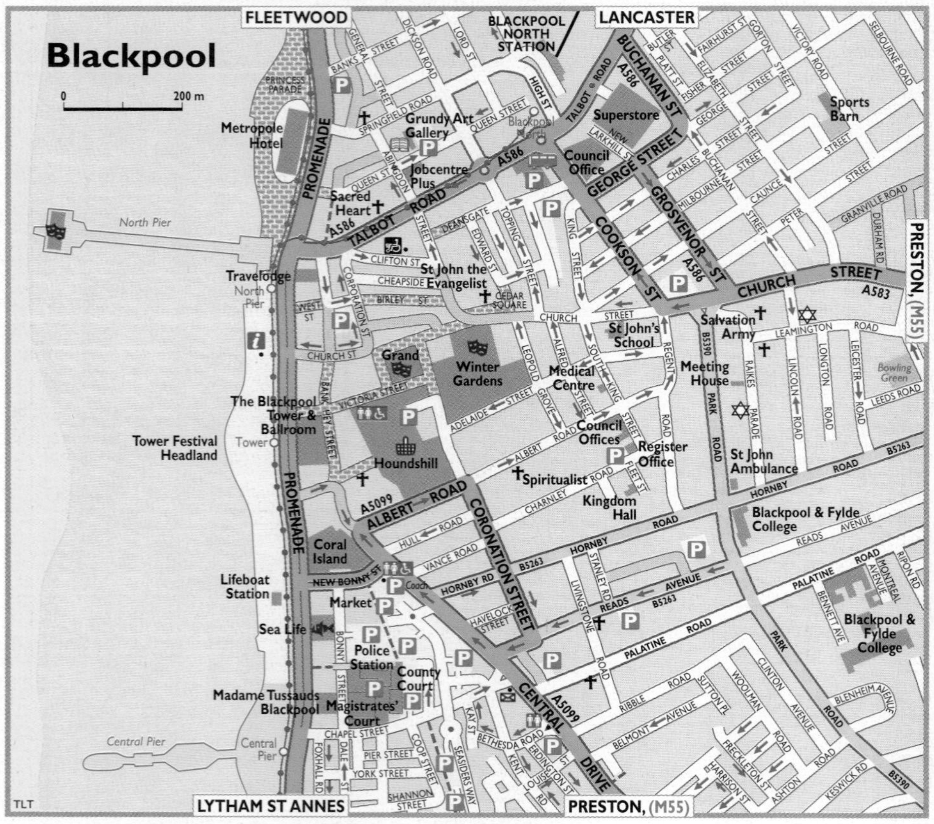
Blackpool
200 m
FLEETWOOD
BLACKPOOL NORTH STATION
LANCASTER
PRESTON, (M55)
LYTHAM ST ANNES
Sports Barn
Metropole Hotel
Grundy Art Gallery
Superstore
Council Office
Jobcentre Plus
Sacred Heart
North Pier
St John the Evangelist
Travelodge
Salvation Army
St John's School
Grand
Winter Gardens
Medical Centre
Meeting House
The Blackpool Tower & Ballroom
Tower Festival Headland
Houndshill
Council Offices
Register Office
St John Ambulance
Spiritualist
Kingdom Hall
Blackpool & Fylde College
Coral Island
Lifeboat Station
Market
Sea Life
Police Station
County Court
Madame Tussauds Blackpool
Magistrates' Court
Blackpool & Fylde College
Central Pier
TLT

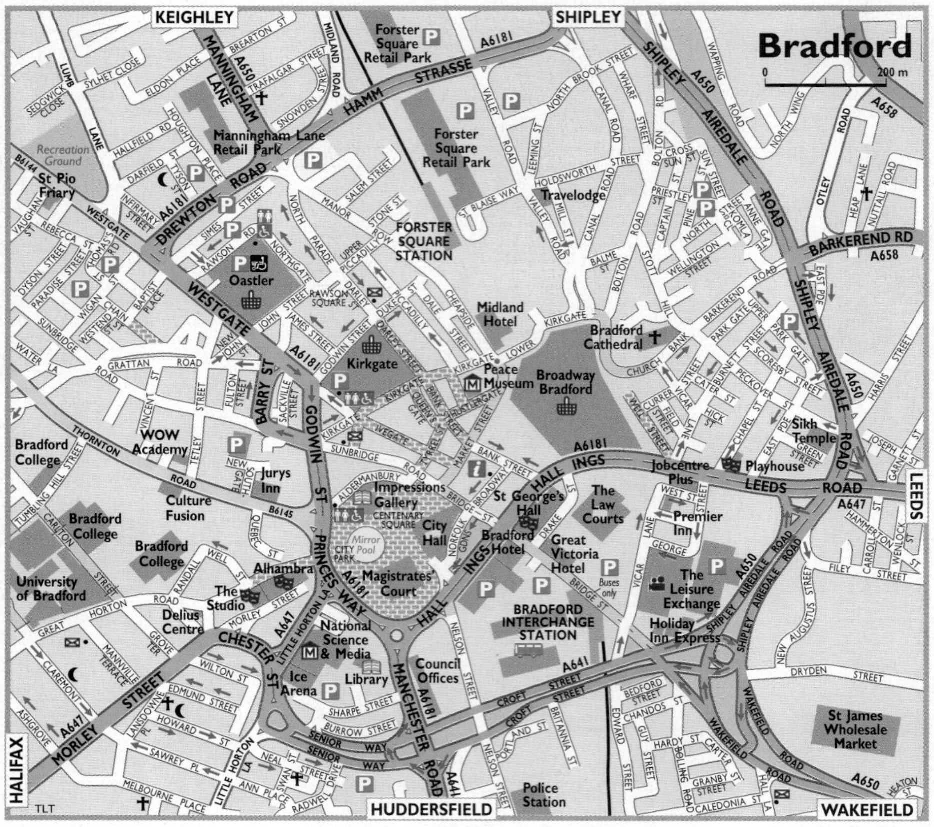
Bradford
200 m
KEIGHLEY
SHIPLEY
LEEDS
HALIFAX
HUDDERSFIELD
WAKEFIELD
Forster Square Retail Park
Manningham Lane Retail Park
Forster Square Retail Park
St Pio Friary
Travelodge
FORSTER SQUARE STATION
Oastler
Midland Hotel
Bradford Cathedral
Kirkgate
Peace Museum
Broadway Bradford
Bradford College
WOW Academy
Jurys Inn
Impressions Gallery
City Hall
St George's Hall
The Law Courts
Jobcentre Plus
Premier Inn
Sikh Temple
Playhouse
Culture Fusion
Bradford College
Bradford College
University of Bradford
Bradford Hotel
Great Victoria Hotel
The Leisure Exchange
Holiday Inn Express
Alhambra
Magistrates' Court
BRADFORD INTERCHANGE STATION
The Studio
Delius Centre
National Science & Media
Council Offices
Ice Arena
Library
St James Wholesale Market
Police Station
TLT

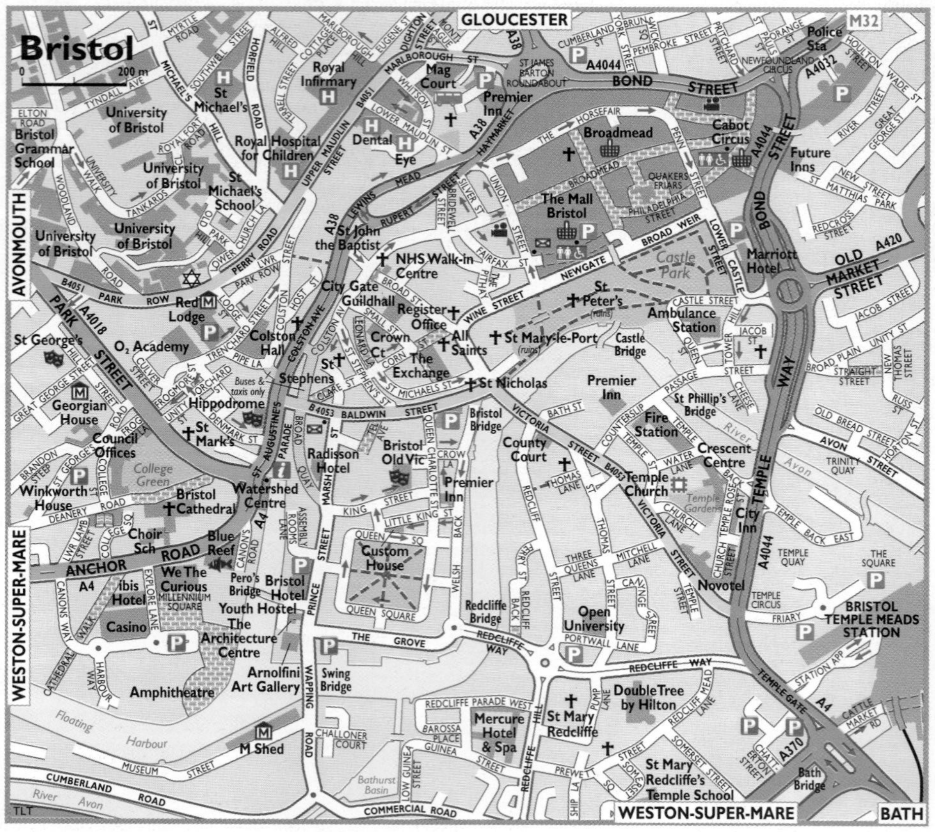
Bristol
200 m
GLOUCESTER
M32
AVONMOUTH
WESTON-SUPER-MARE
WESTON-SUPER-MARE
BATH
Royal Infirmary
Police Sta
Mag Court
Premier Inn
University of Bristol
St Michael's
Bristol Grammar School
Royal Hospital for Children
Dental
Eye
Broadmead
Cabot Circus
Future Inns
University of Bristol
St Michael's School
University of Bristol
The Mall Bristol
St John the Baptist
NHS Walk-in Centre
Marriott Hotel
Castle Park
City Gate Guildhall
Red Lodge
Register Office
St Peter's
Ambulance Station
St Mary-le-Port
St George's
O2 Academy
Colston Hall
Crown Court
All Saints
The Exchange
St Nicholas
St Stephens
Georgian House
Hippodrome
St Mark's
Council Offices
Bristol Bridge
Bristol Old Vic
Premier Inn
St Phillip's Bridge
Fire Station
County Court
Crescent Centre
Temple Church
Radisson Hotel
Premier Inn
Winkworth House
Bristol Cathedral
Watershed Centre
Choir Sch
Blue Reef
Ibis Hotel
We The Curious
Bristol Hotel
Youth Hostel
Custom House
Casino
The Architecture Centre
Novotel
Open University
BRISTOL TEMPLE MEADS STATION
Redcliffe Bridge
Amphitheatre
Arnolfini Art Gallery
Swing Bridge
Mercure Hotel & Spa
St Mary Redcliffe
Double Tree by Hilton
St Mary Redcliffe's Temple School
M Shed
Bath Bridge
Floating Harbour
TLT

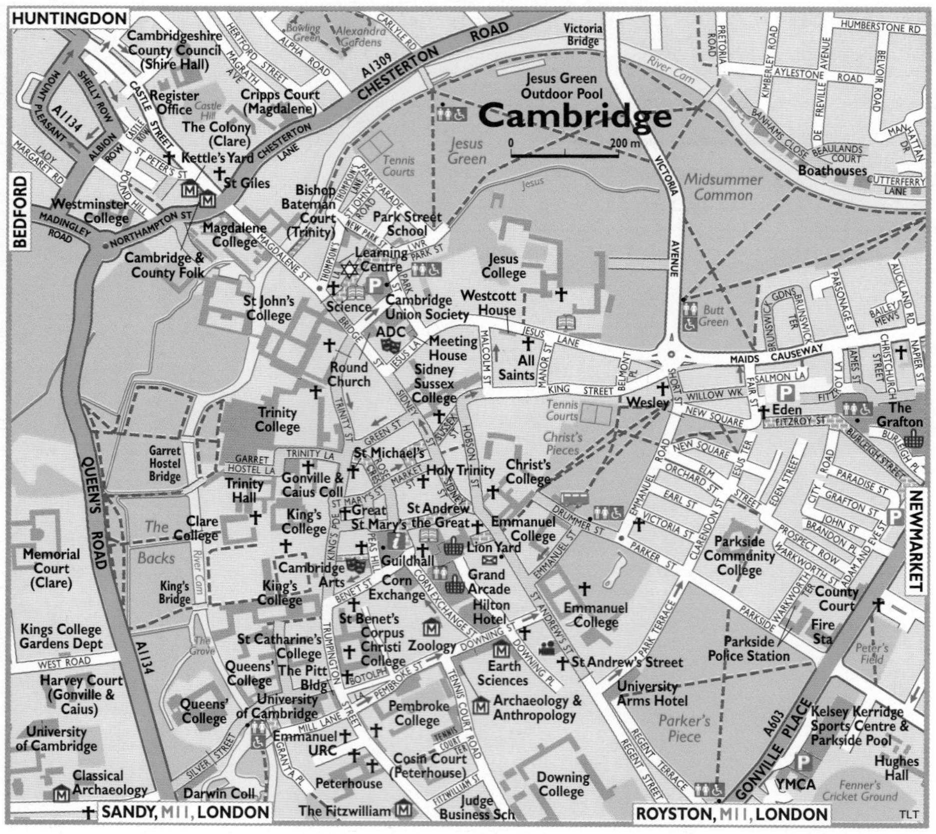
Cambridge
200 m
HUNTINGDON
BEDFORD
NEWMARKET
SANDY, M11, LONDON
ROYSTON, M11, LONDON
Victoria Bridge
Cambridgeshire County Council (Shire Hall)
Jesus Green Outdoor Pool
Register Office
Cripps Court (Magdalene)
The Colony (Clare)
Kettle's Yard
St Giles
Jesus Green
Boathouses
Midsummer Common
Westminster College
Bishop Bateman Court (Trinity)
Park Street School
Magdalene College
Cambridge & County Folk
Jesus College
Westcott House
St John's College
Cambridge Union Society
Meeting House
All Saints
Sidney Sussex College
Round Church
Trinity College
Wesley
Eden
The Grafton
Garret Hostel Bridge
Trinity Hall
St Michael's
Holy Trinity
Christ's College
Gonville & Caius Coll
King's College
St Andrew the Great
Emmanuel College
Lion Yard
Guildhall
Grand Arcade
Hilton Hotel
Parkside Community College
Clare College
Memorial Court (Clare)
King's Bridge
Cambridge Arts
Corn Exchange
Emmanuel College
Kings College Gardens Dept
St Catharine's College
Corpus Christi College
Zoology
Earth Sciences
St Andrew's Street
Parkside Police Station
Fire Sta
Harvey Court (Gonville & Caius)
Queens' College
The Pitt Bldg
University of Cambridge
Queens' College
Archaeology & Anthropology
University Arms Hotel
Parker's Piece
Kelsey Kerridge Sports Centre & Parkside Pool
University of Cambridge
Emmanuel URC
Pembroke College
Cosin Court (Peterhouse)
Hughes Hall
Classical Archaeology
Darwin Coll
Peterhouse
Downing College
YMCA
The Fitzwilliam
Judge Business Sch
TLT

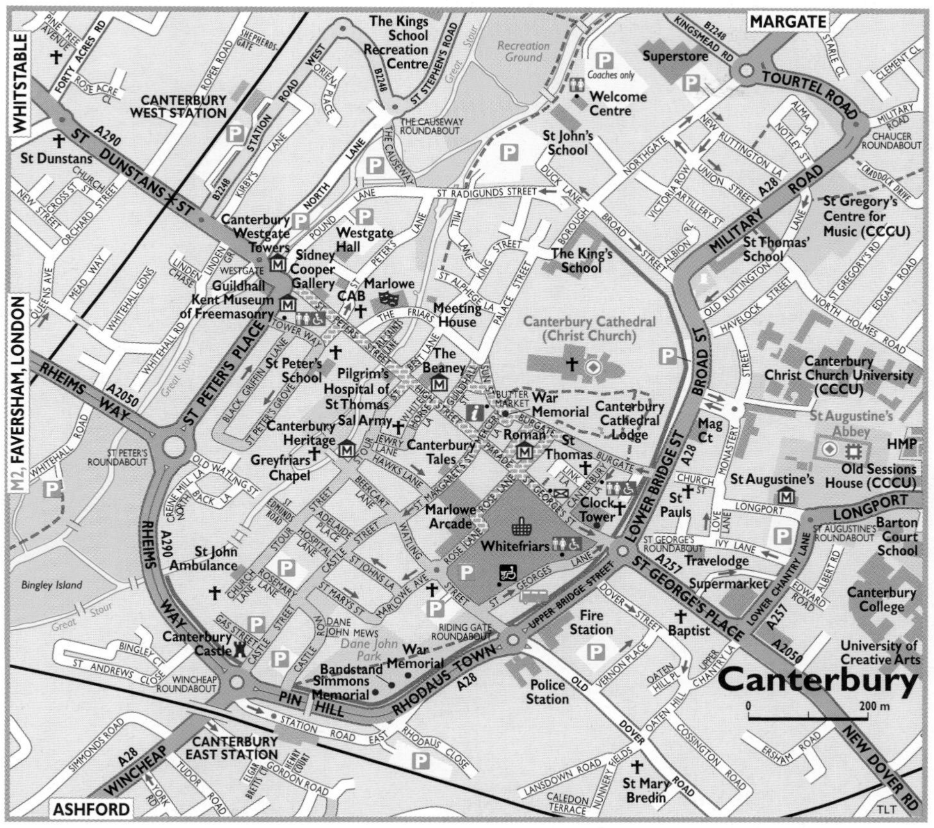

Canterbury

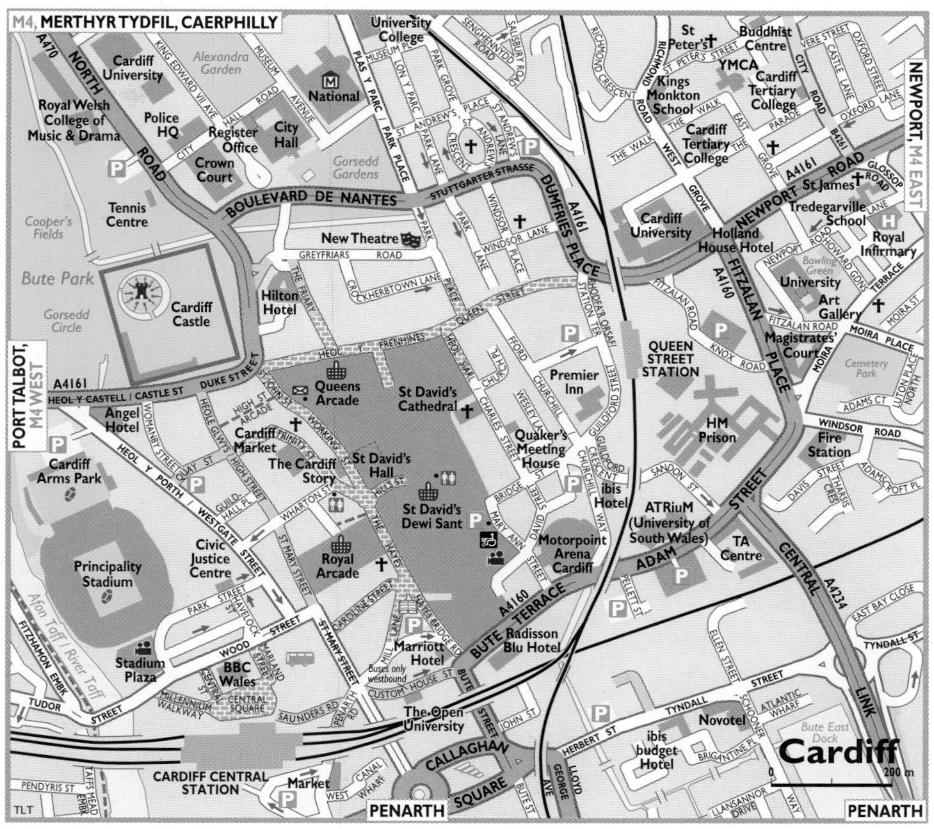

Cardiff

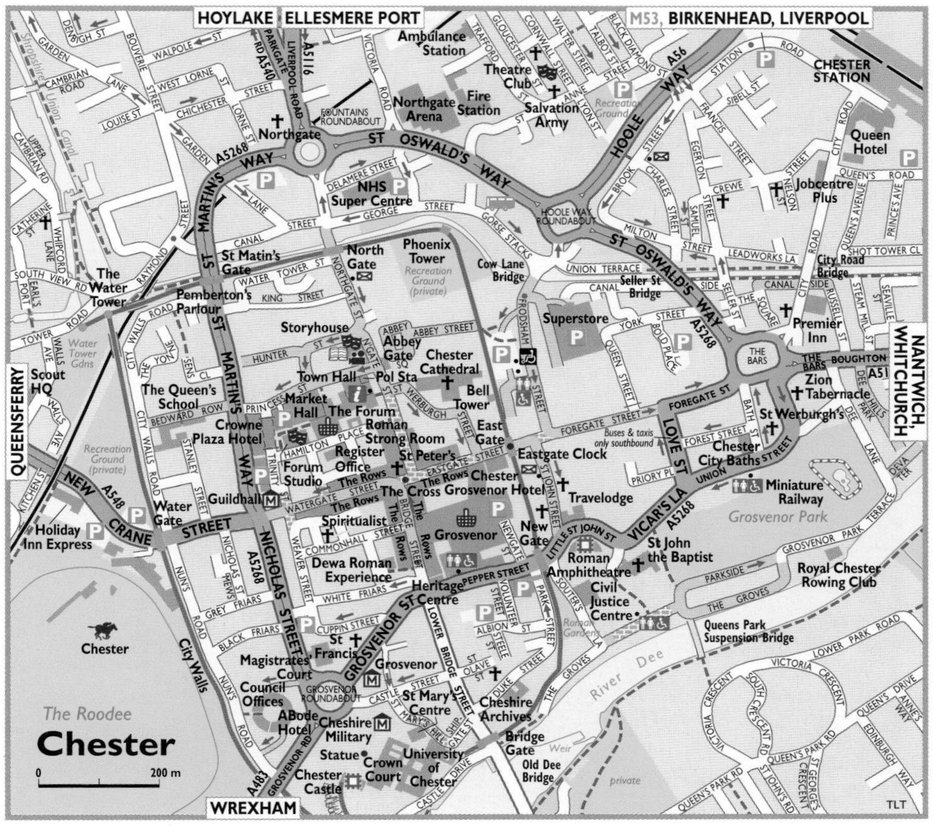

Chester

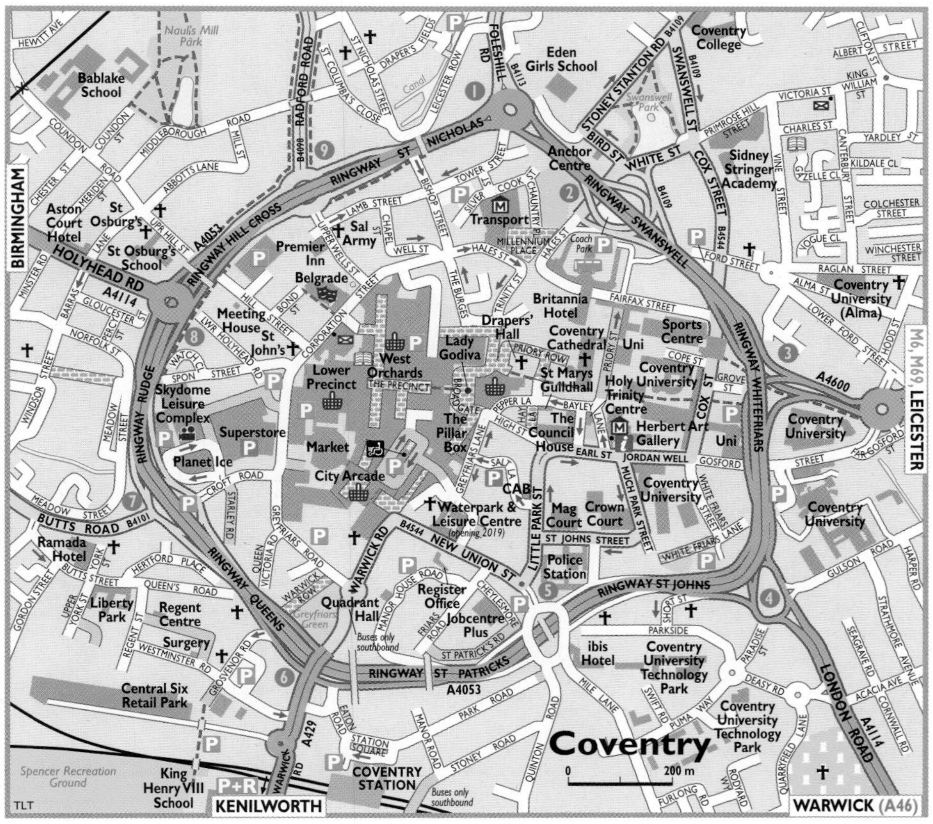

Coventry

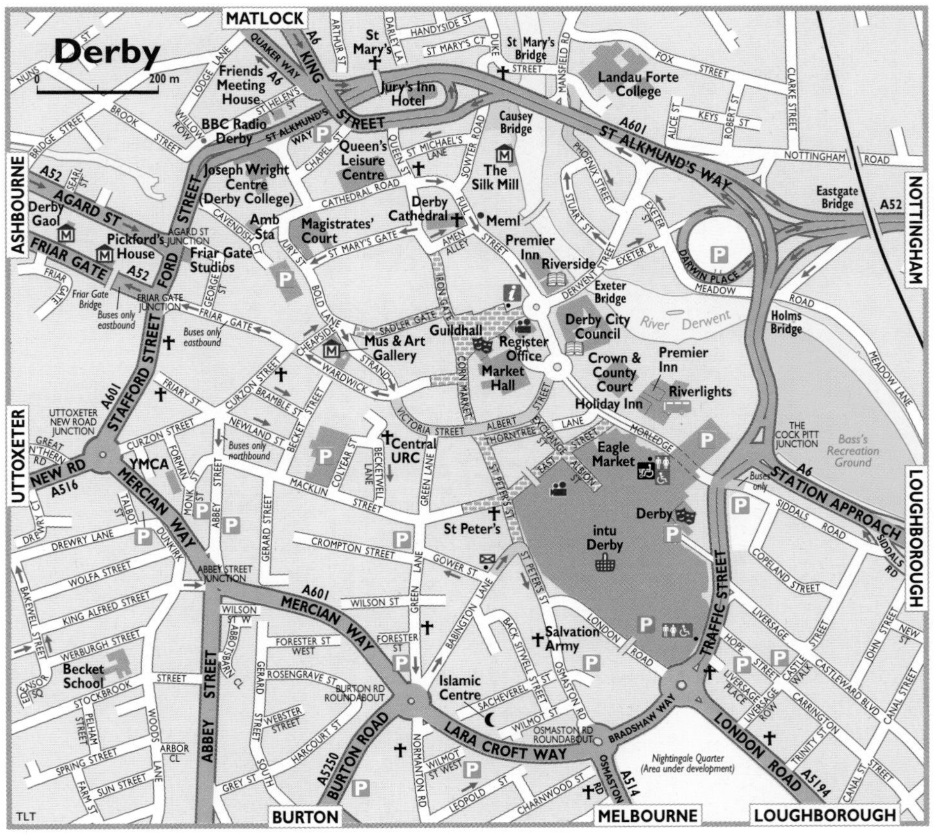

Derby

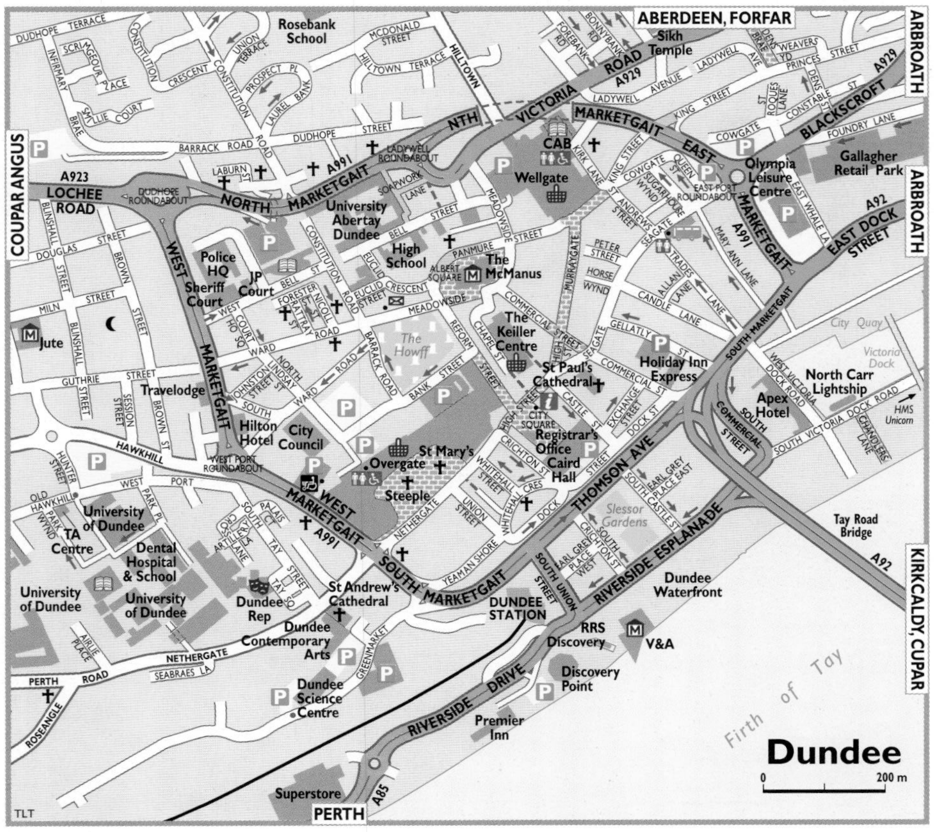

Dundee

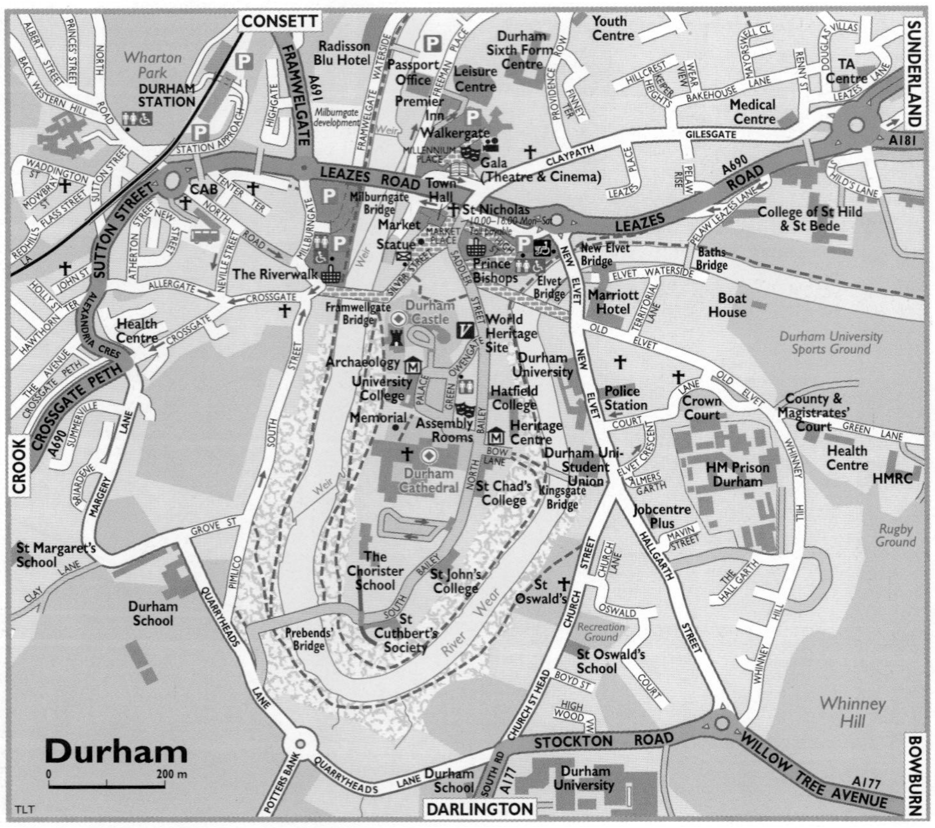

Durham

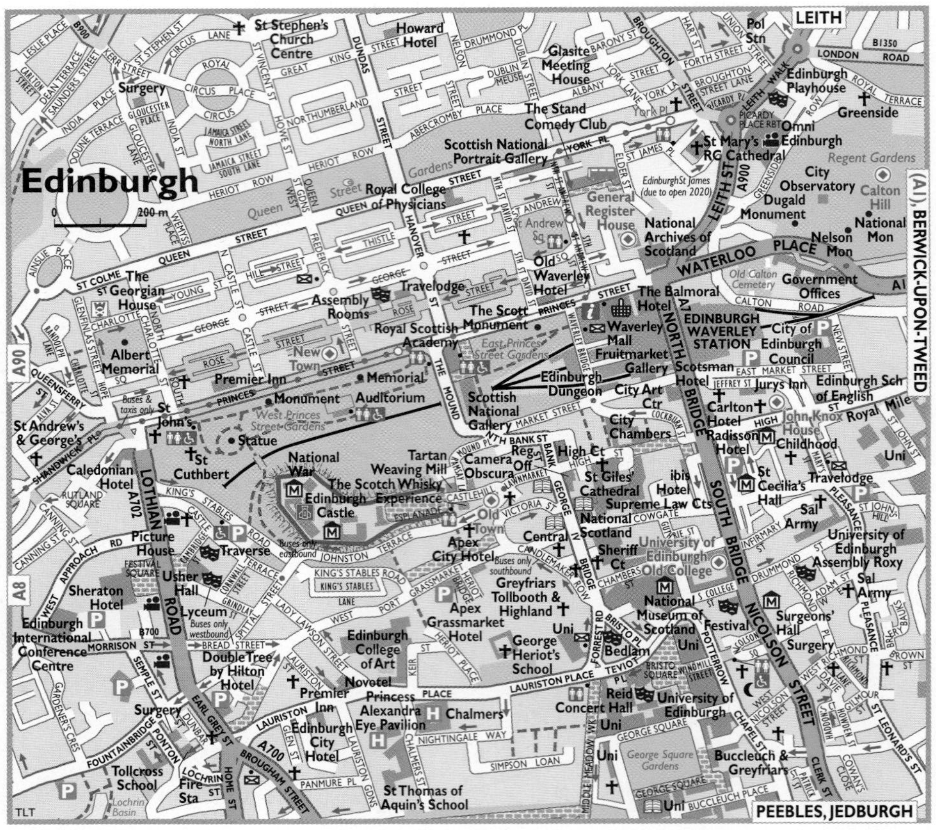

Edinburgh

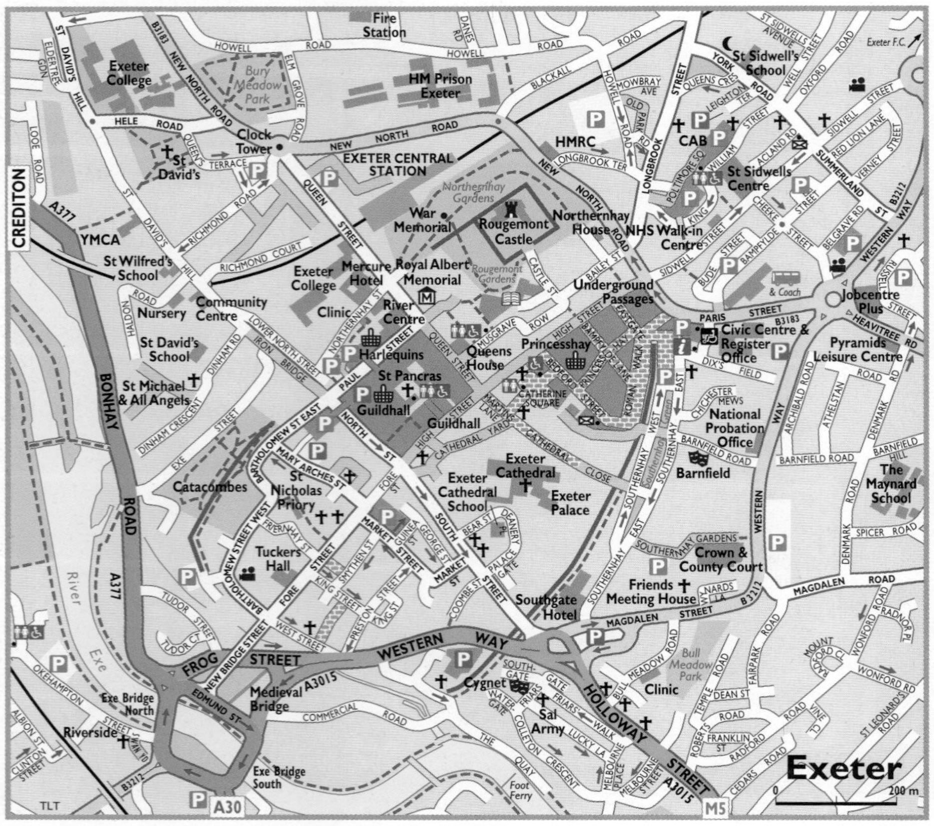

Exeter

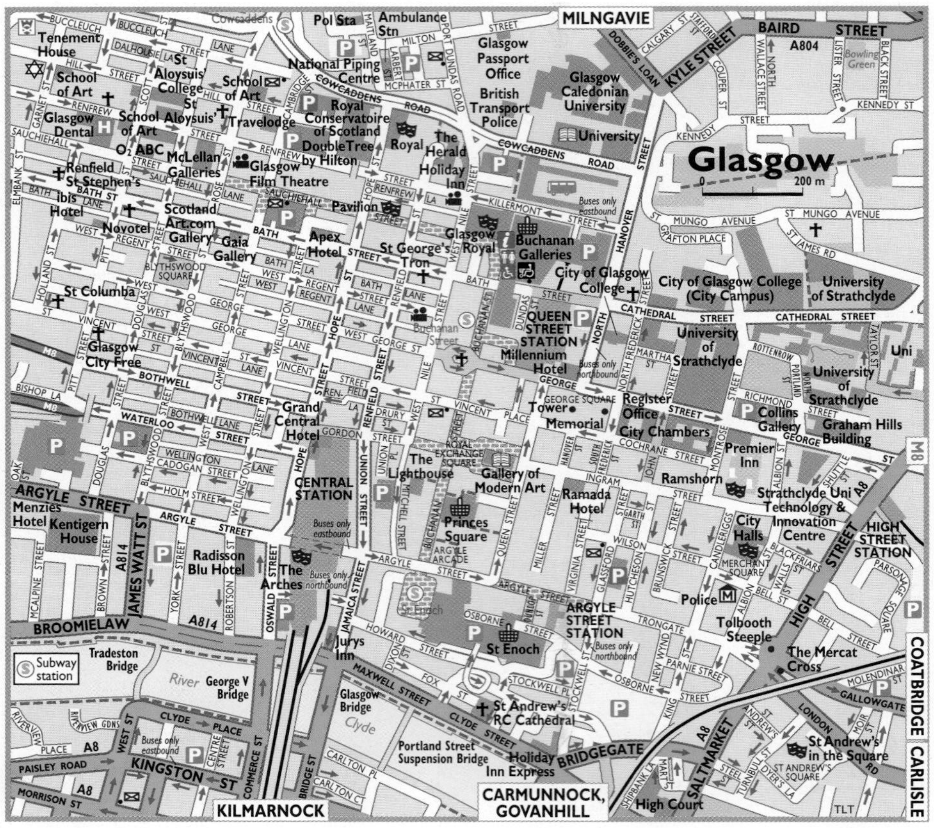

Glasgow

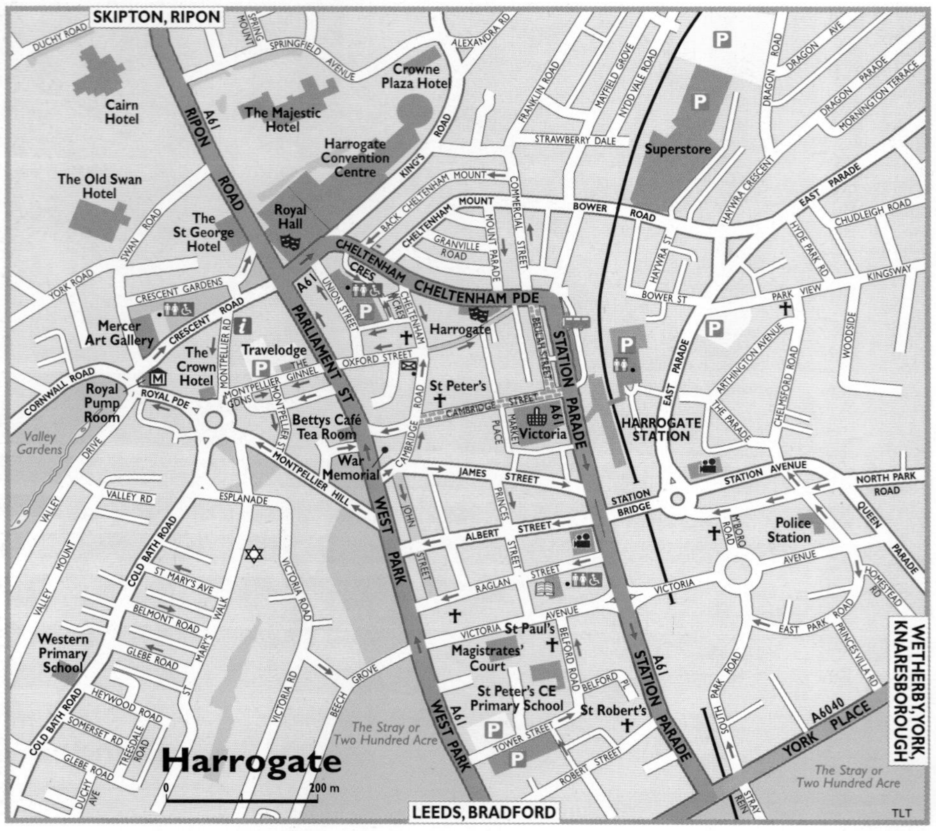

Harrogate

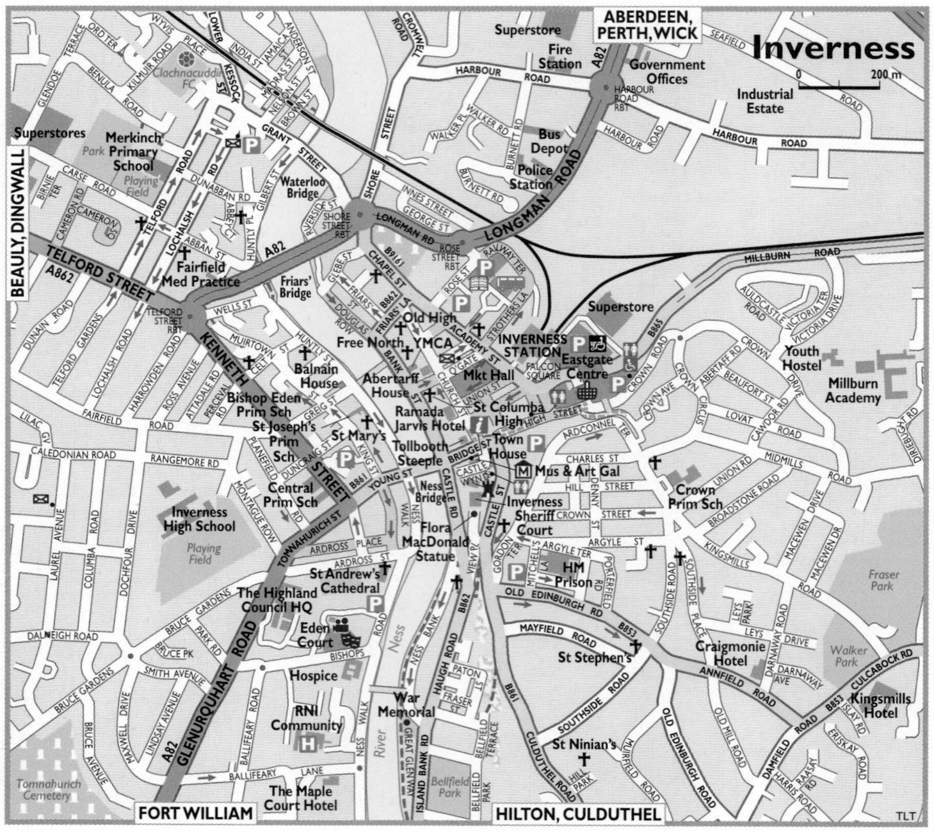

Inverness

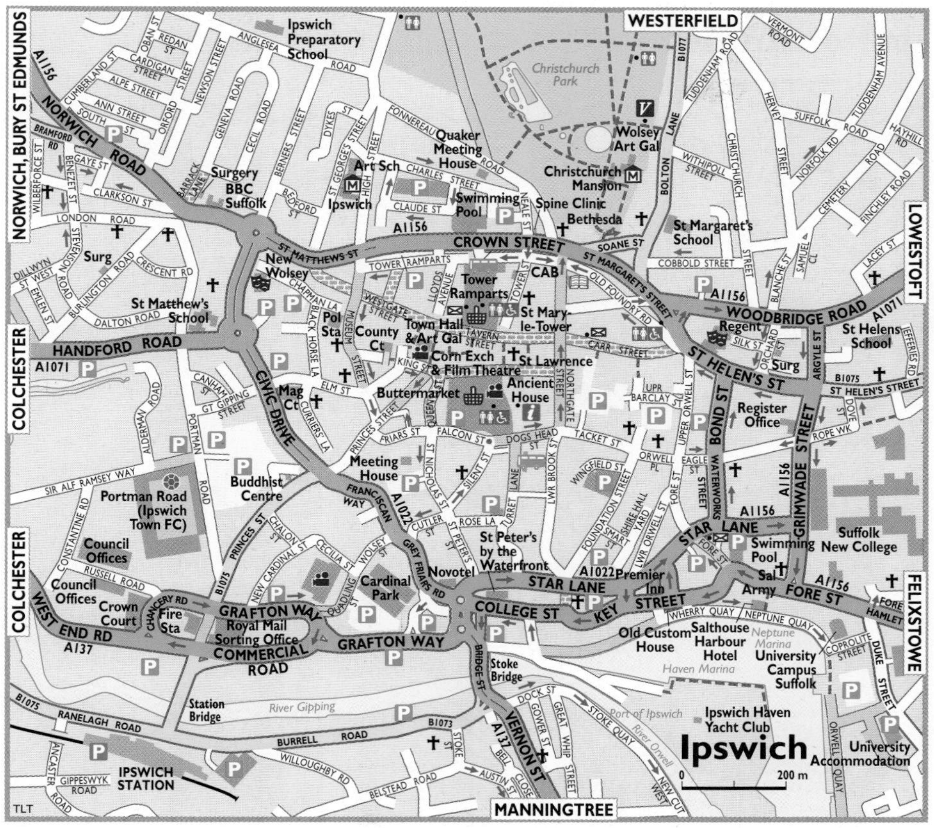

Ipswich

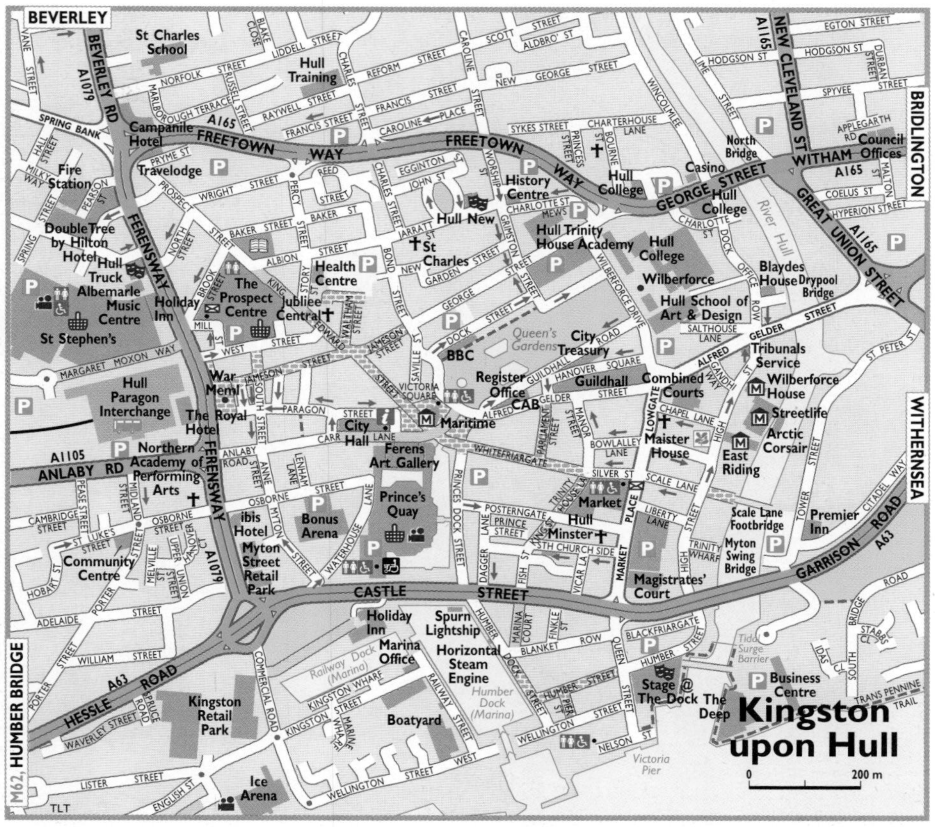

Kingston upon Hull

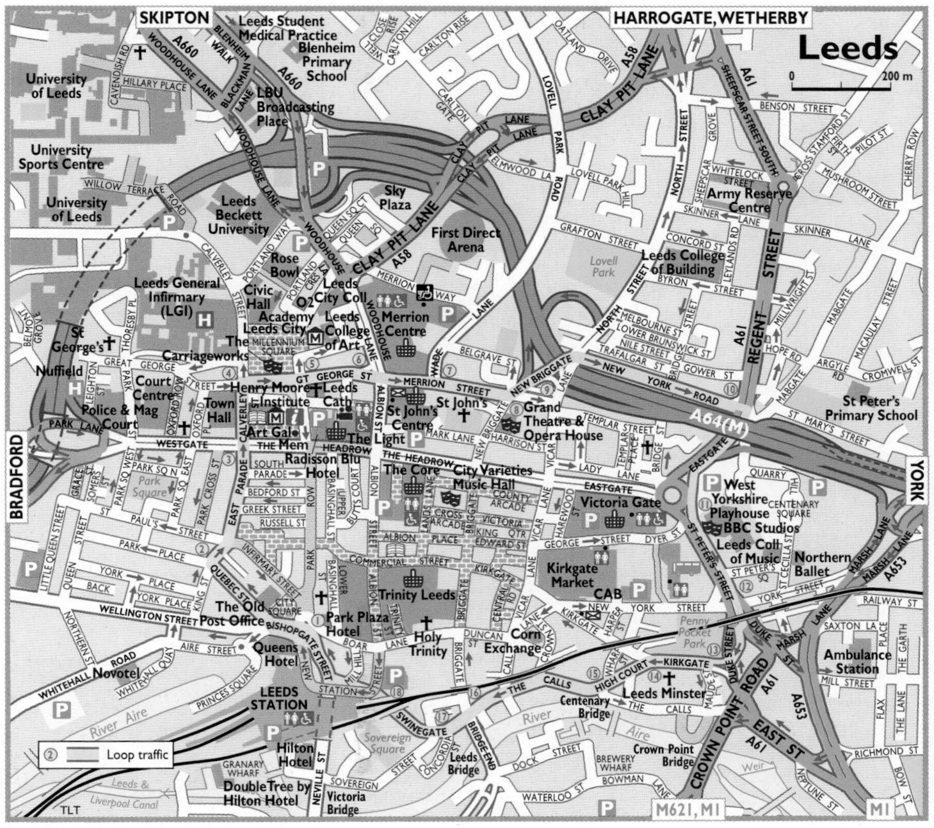

Leeds

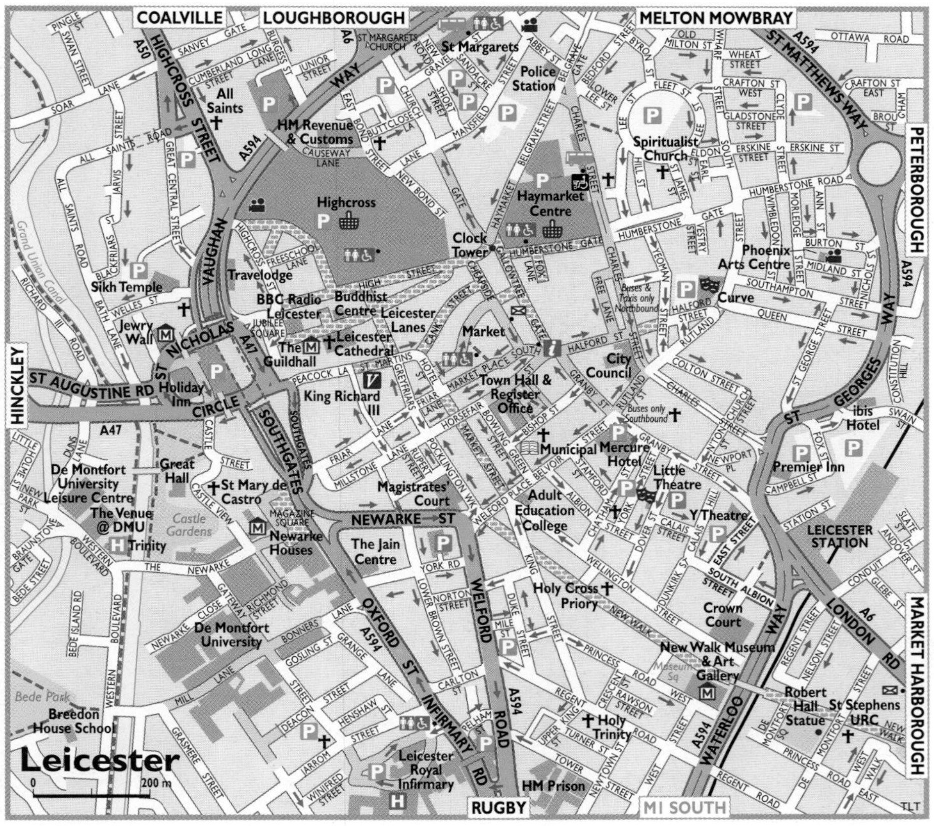

Leicester

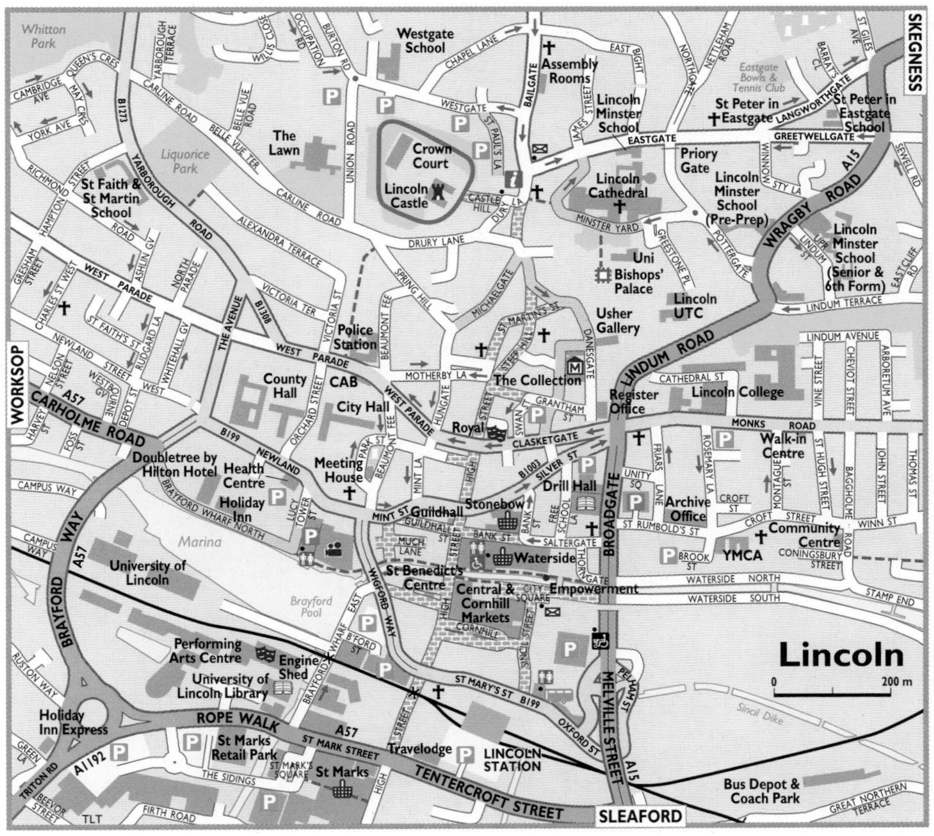

Lincoln

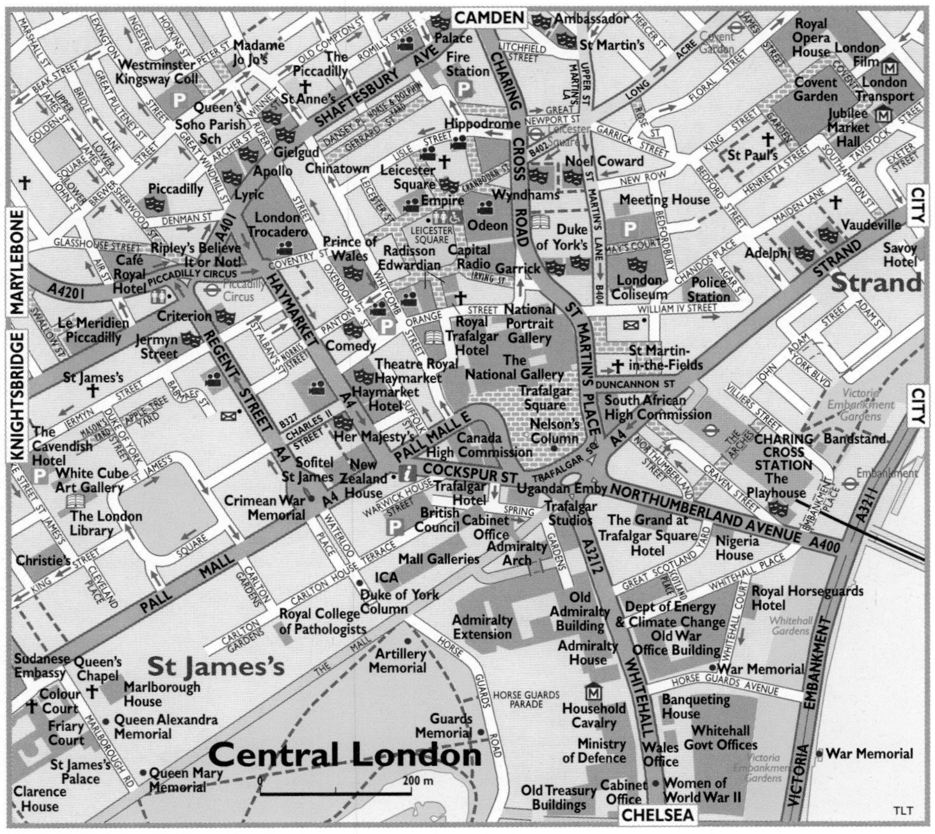

Central London

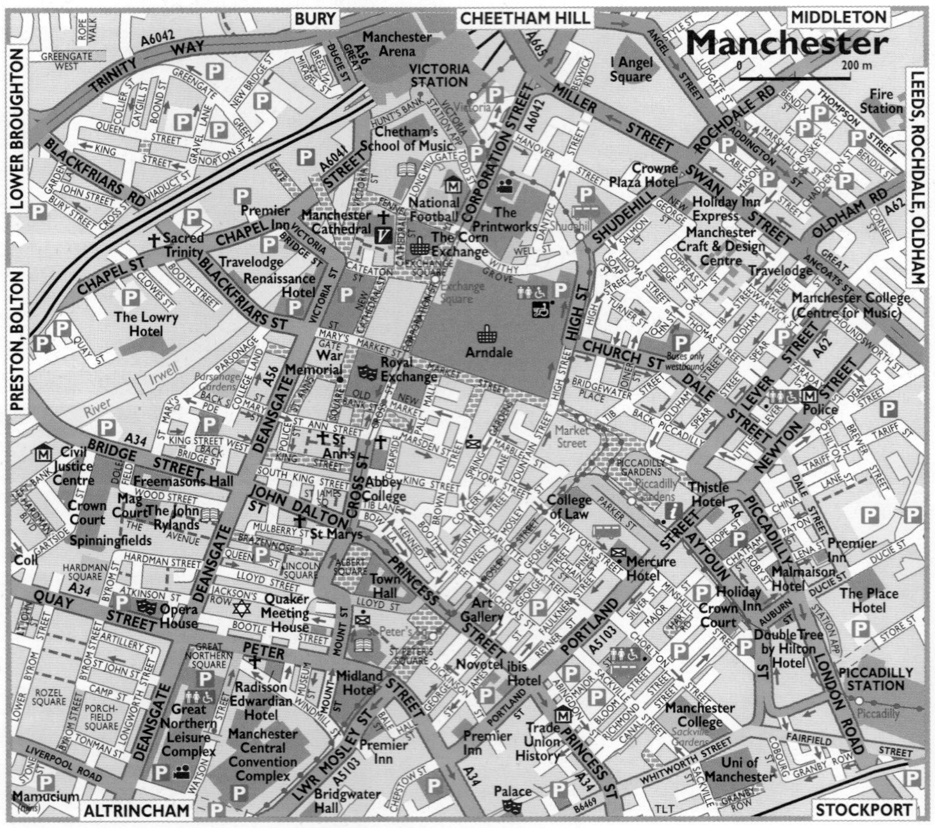
Manchester
0 200 m
BURY
CHEETHAM HILL
MIDDLETON
LEEDS, ROCHDALE, OLDHAM
LOWER BROUGHTON
PRESTON, BOLTON
ALTRINCHAM
STOCKPORT
Manchester Arena
VICTORIA STATION
I Angel Square
Fire Station
Chetham's School of Music
Crowne Plaza Hotel
Holiday Inn Express
Manchester Craft & Design Centre
National Football Museum
The Printworks
The Corn Exchange
Manchester Cathedral
Premier Inn
Sacred Trinity
Travelodge
Renaissance Hotel
The Lowry Hotel
Arndale
Manchester College (Centre for Music)
War Memorial
Royal Exchange
Police
Civil Justice Centre
Freemasons Hall
Abbey College
Mag Court
Crown Court
The John Rylands
Spinningfields
St Mary's
St Ann's
College of Law
Thistle Hotel
Mercure Hotel
Malmaison Hotel
Holiday Inn
Crown Court
The Place Hotel
Double Tree by Hilton Hotel
PICCADILLY STATION
PICCADILLY GARDENS
Opera House
Quaker Meeting House
Town Hall
Art Gallery
Novotel
ibis Hotel
Midland Hotel
Radisson Edwardian Hotel
Great Northern Leisure Complex
Manchester Central Convention Complex
Premier Inn
Trade Union History
Manchester College
Uni of Manchester
Palace
Bridgewater Hall
Mamucium
DEANSGATE
PORTLAND
PRINCESS ST
LWR MOSLEY ST
QUAY ST
BRIDGE ST
JOHN DALTON ST
CROSS ST
MARKET ST
CHURCH ST
OLDHAM RD
ROCHDALE RD
SWAN ST
MILLER STREET
CHAPEL ST
BLACKFRIARS RD
TRINITY WAY
PETER ST
LONDON ROAD
PICCADILLY
A34
A56
A6
A665
A62
A6041
A6042
TLT

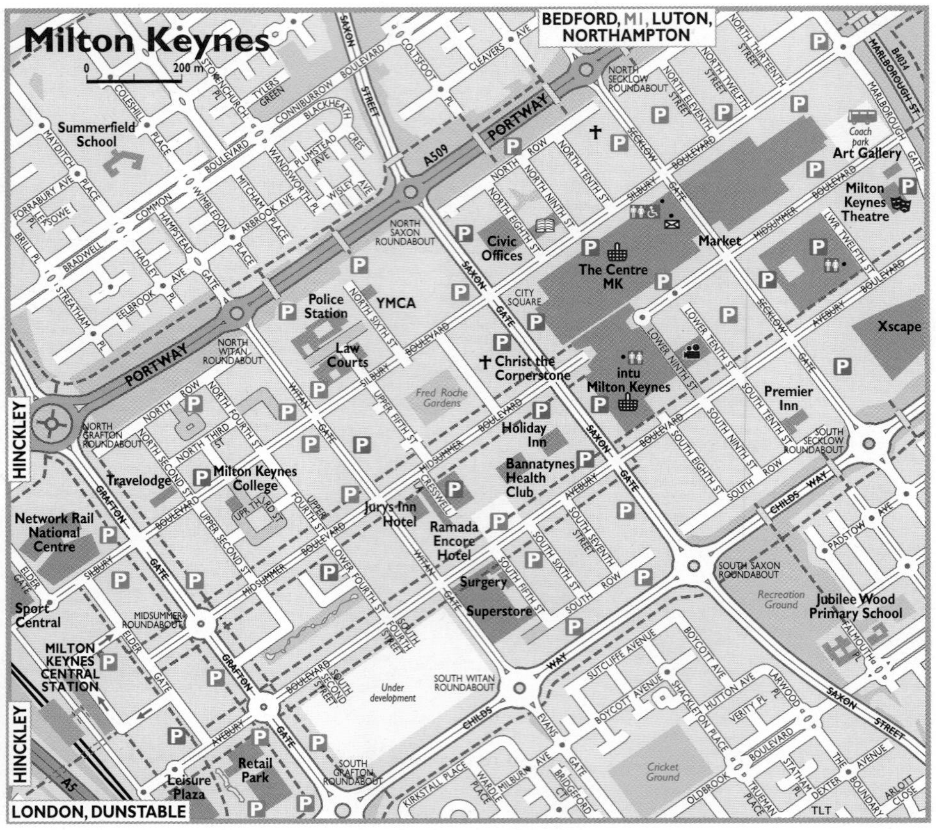
Milton Keynes
0 200 m
BEDFORD, M1, LUTON, NORTHAMPTON
HINCKLEY
LONDON, DUNSTABLE
Summerfield School
PORTWAY
A509
NORTH SAXON ROUNDABOUT
NORTH WITAN ROUNDABOUT
NORTH GRAFTON ROUNDABOUT
NORTH SECKLOW ROUNDABOUT
SOUTH SECKLOW ROUNDABOUT
SOUTH SAXON ROUNDABOUT
SOUTH WITAN ROUNDABOUT
SOUTH GRAFTON ROUNDABOUT
MIDSUMMER ROUNDABOUT
Art Gallery
Milton Keynes Theatre
Civic Offices
The Centre MK
Market
Xscape
Police Station
YMCA
Law Courts
Christ the Cornerstone
intu Milton Keynes
Premier Inn
Fred Roche Gardens
Holiday Inn
Bannatynes Health Club
Travelodge
Milton Keynes College
Network Rail National Centre
Jurys Inn Hotel
Ramada Encore Hotel
Surgery
Superstore
Sport Central
MILTON KEYNES CENTRAL STATION
Under development
Retail Park
Leisure Plaza
Recreation Ground
Jubilee Wood Primary School
Cricket Ground
A5
TLT

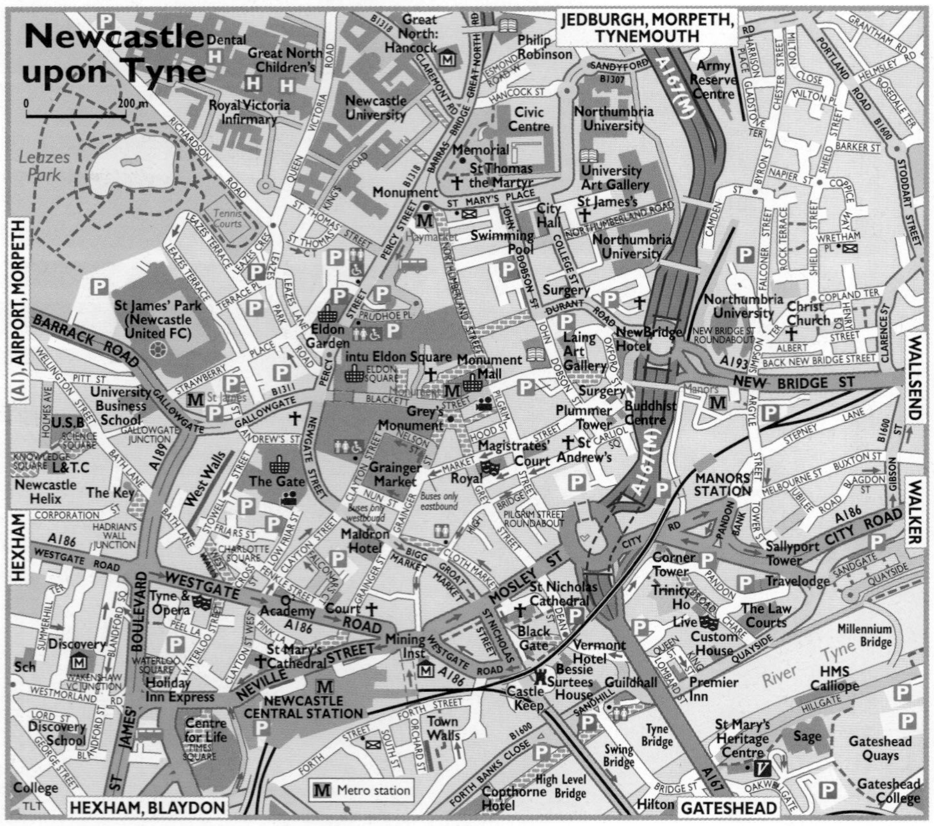
Newcastle upon Tyne
0 200 m
JEDBURGH, MORPETH, TYNEMOUTH
(A1), AIRPORT, MORPETH
HEXHAM
HEXHAM, BLAYDON
GATESHEAD
WALLSEND
WALKER
Dental
Great North: Hancock
Great North Children's
Royal Victoria Infirmary
Philip Robinson
Army Reserve Centre
Newcastle University
Civic Centre
Northumbria University
Leazes Park
Memorial
St Thomas the Martyr
University Art Gallery
St James's
Monument
City Hall
Swimming Pool
Northumbria University
St James' Park (Newcastle United FC)
Eldon Garden
intu Eldon Square
Monument Mall
Surgery
Laing Art Gallery
NewBridge Hotel
Northumbria University
Christ Church
Plummer Tower
Buddhist Centre
University Business School
Grey's Monument
Grainger Market
Magistrates Court
St Andrew's
Royal
U.S.B
L&T.C
Newcastle Helix
The Key
West Walls
The Gate
MANORS STATION
Malcolm Hotel
Sallyport Tower
Travelodge
Tyne & Opera
Academy
Court
St Nicholas Cathedral
Corner Tower
Trinity Ho
Live
The Law Courts
Millennium Bridge
Discovery
Mining Inst
St Mary's Cathedral
NEWCASTLE CENTRAL STATION
Black Gate
Vermont Hotel
Bessie Surtees House
Castle Keep
Guildhall
Custom House
HMS Calliope
Holiday Inn Express
Centre for Life
Town Walls
Premier Inn
Tyne Bridge
Swing Bridge
High Level Bridge
St Mary's Heritage Centre
Sage
Gateshead Quays
Gateshead College
Copthorne Hotel
Hilton
College
Discovery School
Metro station
River Tyne
BARRACK ROAD
WESTGATE ROAD
NEW BRIDGE ST
CITY ROAD
NEVILLE STREET
A167(M)
A186
A193
TLT

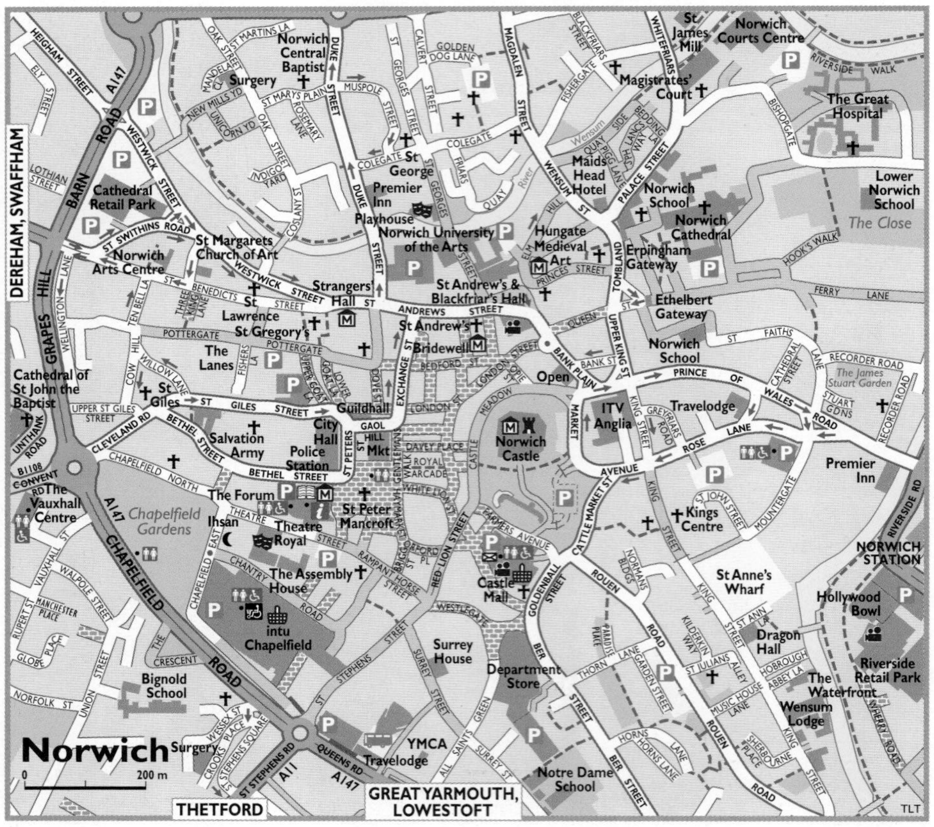
Norwich
0 200 m
DEREHAM, SWAFFHAM
THETFORD
GREAT YARMOUTH, LOWESTOFT
Norwich Central Baptist
St James Mill
Norwich Courts Centre
Surgery
Magistrates' Court
The Great Hospital
Cathedral Retail Park
St George
Premier Inn
Maids Head Hotel
Norwich School
Norwich Cathedral
Lower Norwich School
The Close
St Margarets Church of Art
Norwich Arts Centre
Playhouse
Norwich University of the Arts
Hungate Medieval Art
Erpingham Gateway
Strangers' Hall
St Andrew's & Blackfriar's Hall
Lawrence
St Gregory's
St Andrew's
Bridewell
Ethelbert Gateway
The Lanes
Norwich School
Cathedral of St John the Baptist
St Giles
Guildhall
ITV Anglia
Travelodge
Salvation Army
City Hall
Police Station
Mkt
Norwich Castle
Premier Inn
The Vauxhall Centre
The Forum
St Peter Mancroft
Kings Centre
Chapelfield Gardens
Theatre Royal
The Assembly House
Castle Mall
St Anne's Wharf
NORWICH STATION
intu Chapelfield
Hollywood Bowl
Dragon Hall
Riverside Retail Park
Surrey House
Department Store
The Waterfront
Wensum Lodge
Bignold School
YMCA
Travelodge
Surgery
Notre Dame School
GRAPES HILL
CHAPELFIELD ROAD
PRINCE OF WALES ROAD
A147
A11
A1242
TLT

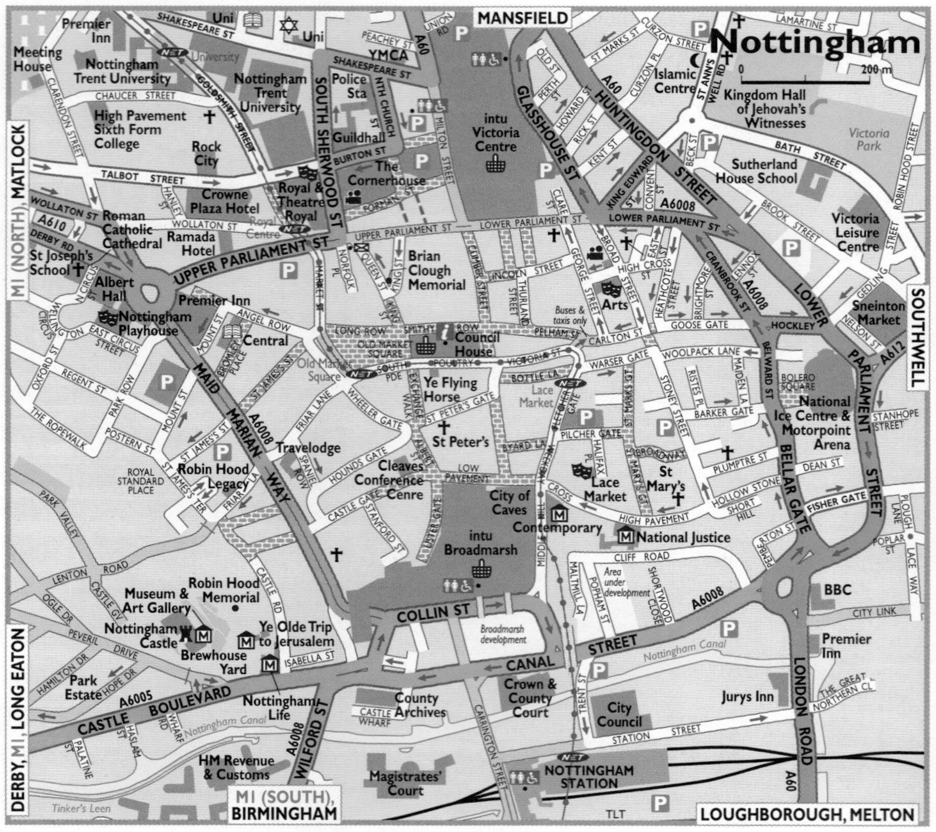
Nottingham
0 200 m
MANSFIELD
M1 (NORTH), MATLOCK
DERBY, M1, LONG EATON
M1 (SOUTH), BIRMINGHAM
LOUGHBOROUGH, MELTON
SOUTHWELL
Premier Inn
Uni
YMCA
Meeting House
Nottingham Trent University
Nottingham Trent University
Police Sta
intu Victoria Centre
Islamic Centre
Kingdom Hall of Jehovah's Witnesses
Victoria Park
High Pavement Sixth Form College
Rock City
Guildhall
The Cornerhouse
Sutherland House School
Crowne Plaza Hotel
Royal Theatre
Royal Concert Hall
Roman Catholic Cathedral
Ramada Hotel
Victoria Leisure Centre
St Joseph's School
Albert Hall
Brian Clough Memorial
Nottingham Playhouse
Premier Inn
Central
Council House
Arts
Sneinton Market
Ye Flying Horse
Travelodge
St Peter's
National Ice Centre & Motorpoint Arena
Robin Hood Legacy
Cleaves Conference Centre
City of Caves
Contemporary
Lace Market
St Mary's
National Justice
intu Broadmarsh
Area under development
Broadmarsh development
BBC
Museum & Art Gallery
Robin Hood Memorial
Nottingham Castle
Ye Olde Trip to Jerusalem
Brewhouse Yard
Premier Inn
Park Estate
Nottingham Life
County Archives
Crown & County Court
City Council
Jurys Inn
HM Revenue & Customs
Magistrates' Court
NOTTINGHAM STATION
Nottingham Canal
UPPER PARLIAMENT ST
MAID MARIAN WAY
COLLIN ST
CANAL STREET
CASTLE BOULEVARD
WILFORD ST
LONDON ROAD
HUNTINGDON STREET
GLASSHOUSE ST
BELLAR GATE
A60
A610
A6008
A6005
A612
TLT

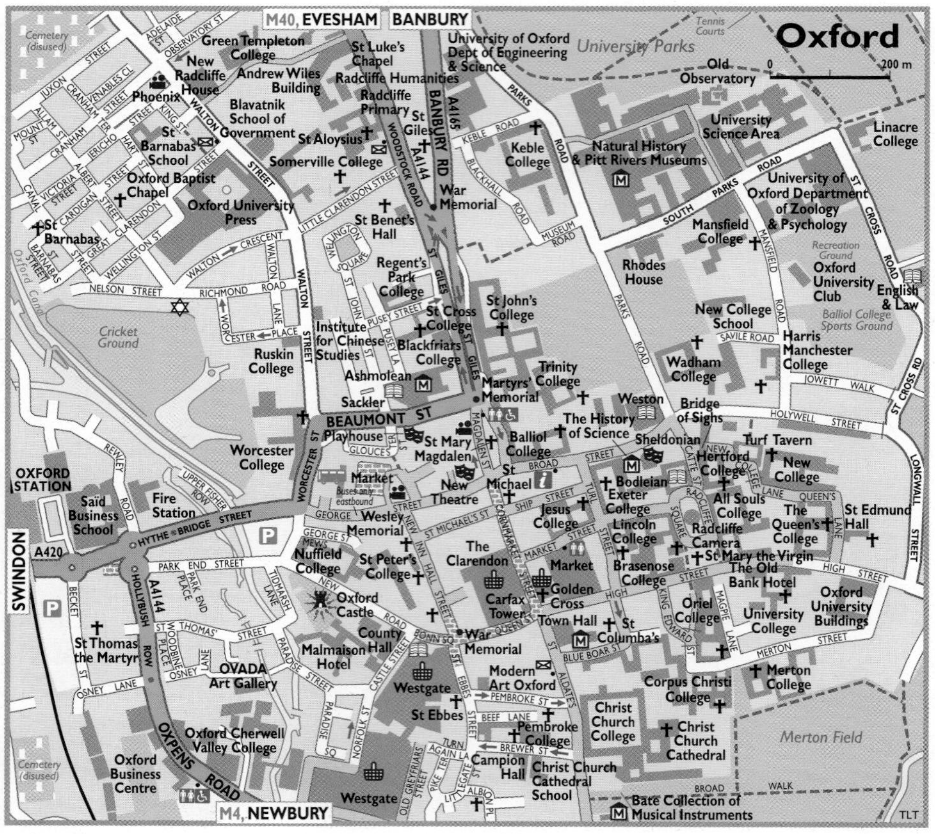
Oxford
0 200 m
M40, EVESHAM
BANBURY
SWINDON
M4, NEWBURY
Green Templeton College
St Luke's Chapel
Radcliffe Humanities
University of Oxford Dept of Engineering & Science
University Parks
Old Observatory
New Radcliffe House
Phoenix
Andrew Wiles Building
Radcliffe Primary
Blavatnik School of Government
St Aloysius
St Giles
Keble College
University Science Area
Natural History & Pitt Rivers Museums
Linacre College
St Barnabas School
Somerville College
Oxford Baptist Chapel
War Memorial
University of Oxford Department of Zoology & Psychology
St Barnabas
Oxford University Press
St Benet's Hall
Mansfield College
Rhodes House
Regent's Park College
Oxford University Club
English & Law
Cricket Ground
Institute for Chinese Studies
St Cross College
St John's College
Blackfriars College
New College School
Balliol College Sports Ground
Harris Manchester College
Ruskin College
Ashmolean
Trinity College
Wadham College
Martyrs' Memorial
Sackler
St Mary Magdalen
The History of Science
Weston
Bridge of Sighs
Playhouse
Balliol College
Sheldonian
Turf Tavern
Worcester College
Hertford College
New College
OXFORD STATION
Said Business School
Fire Station
Market
New Theatre
St Michael
Bodleian
Exeter College
All Souls College
St Edmund Hall
Jesus College
Lincoln College
Radcliffe Camera
The Queen's College
Wesley Memorial
St Mary the Virgin
Nuffield College
St Peter's College
The Clarendon
Brasenose College
The Old Bank Hotel
Oxford Castle
Golden Cross
Oriel College
University College
Oxford University Buildings
Carfax Tower
Town Hall
St Columba's
Malmaison Hotel
County Hall
War Memorial
St Thomas the Martyr
OVADA Art Gallery
Westgate
St Ebbes
Modern Art Oxford
Corpus Christi College
Merton College
Christ Church College
Pembroke College
Christ Church Cathedral
Merton Field
Oxford Fire Valley College
Campion Hall
Christ Church Cathedral School
Oxford Business Centre
Westgate
Bate Collection of Musical Instruments
Cemetery (disused)
Recreation Ground
BEAUMONT ST
HIGH STREET
HYTHE BRIDGE STREET
PARK END STREET
OXPENS ROAD
BANBURY RD
A420
A4144
A4165
TLT

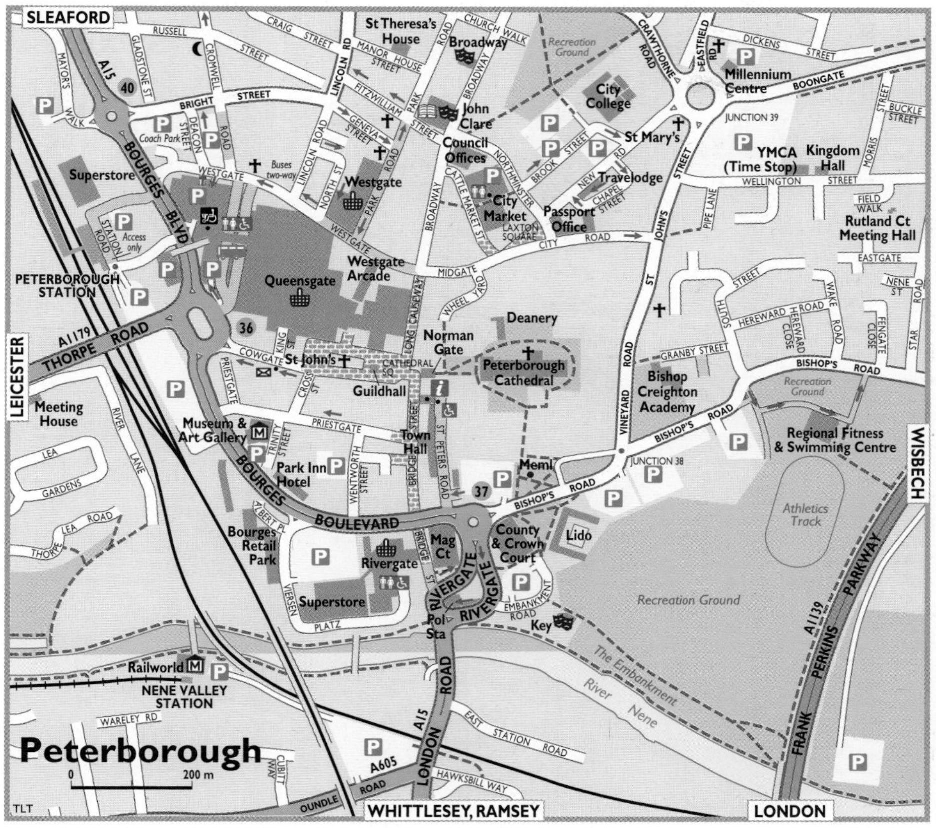

Peterborough

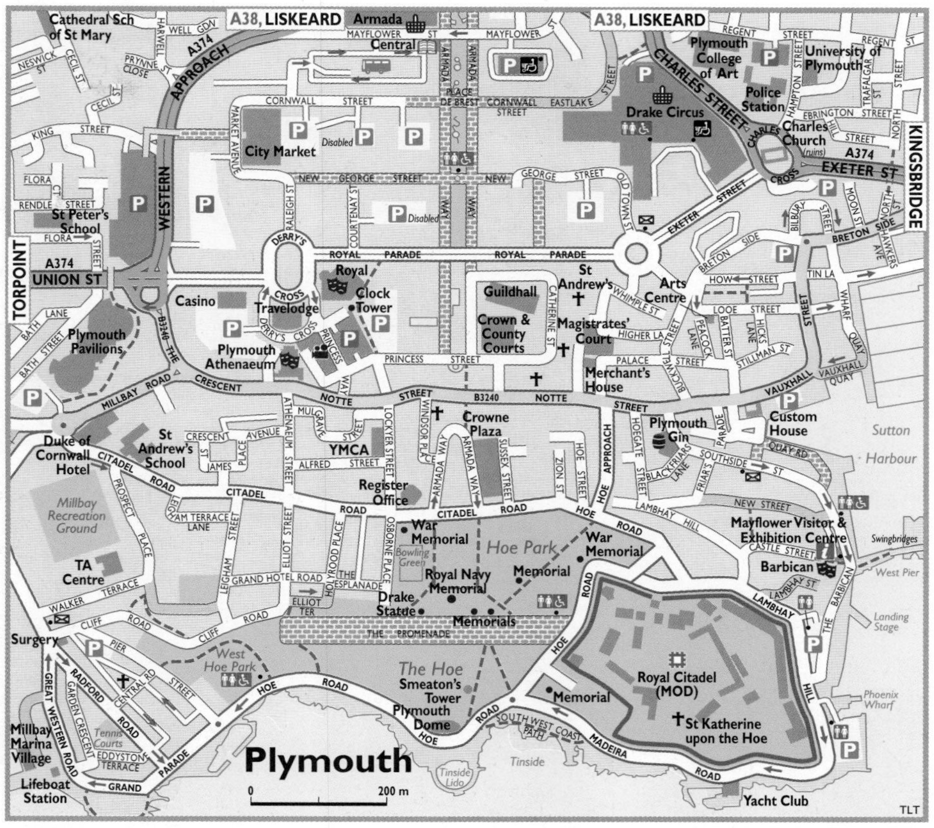

Plymouth

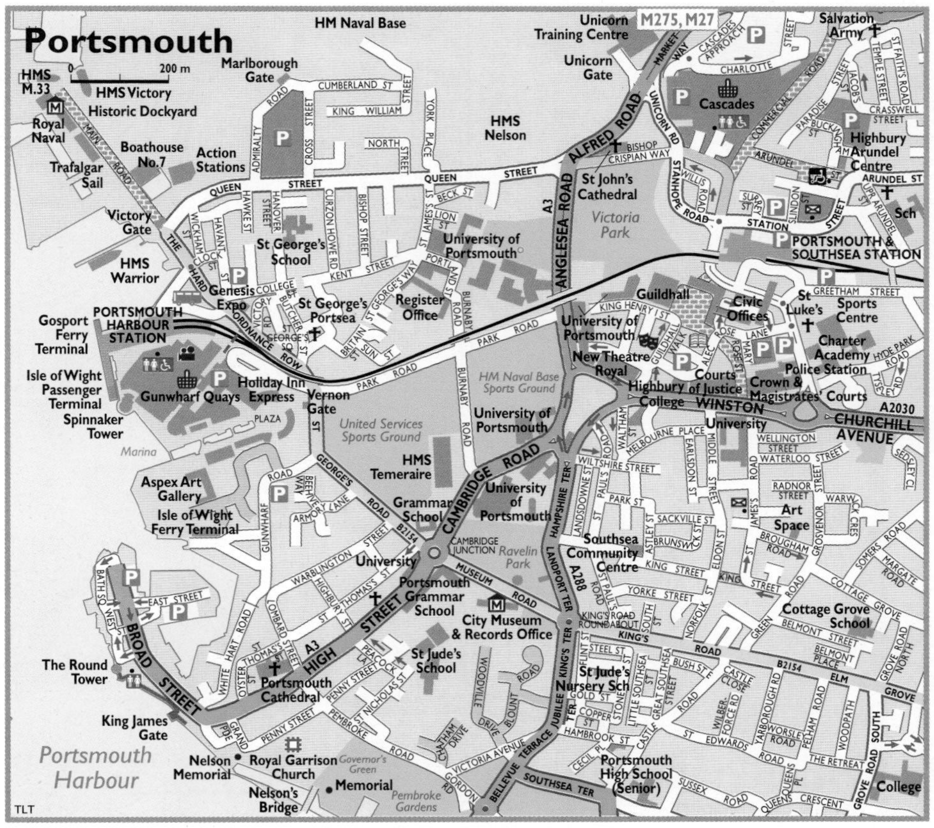

Portsmouth

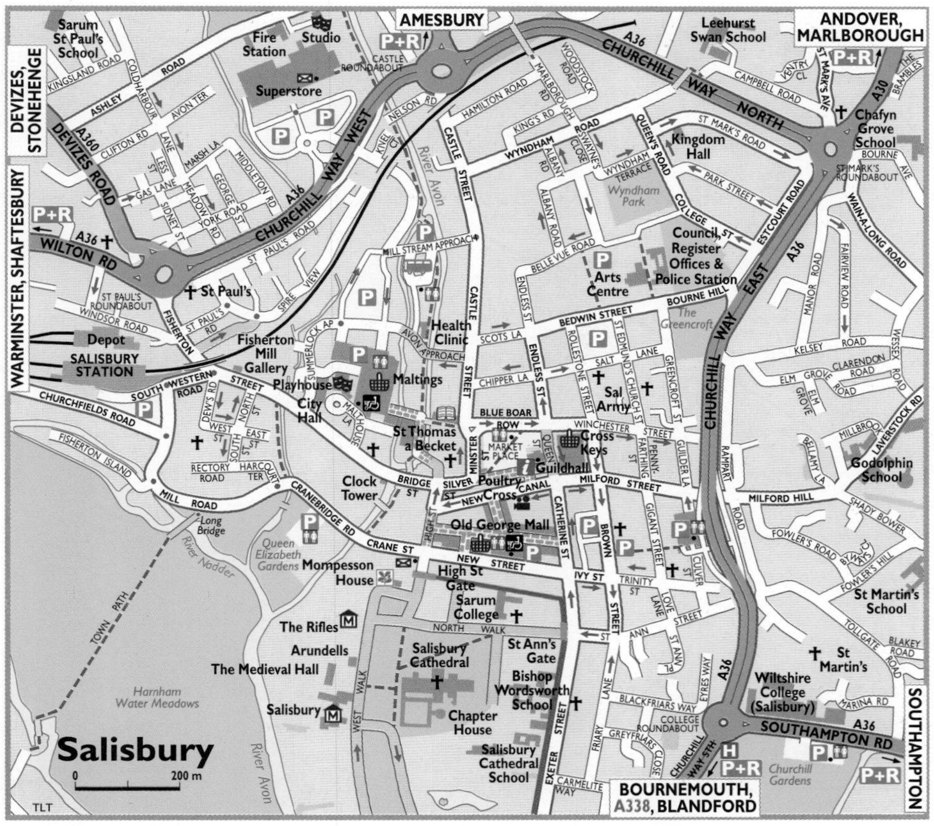

Salisbury

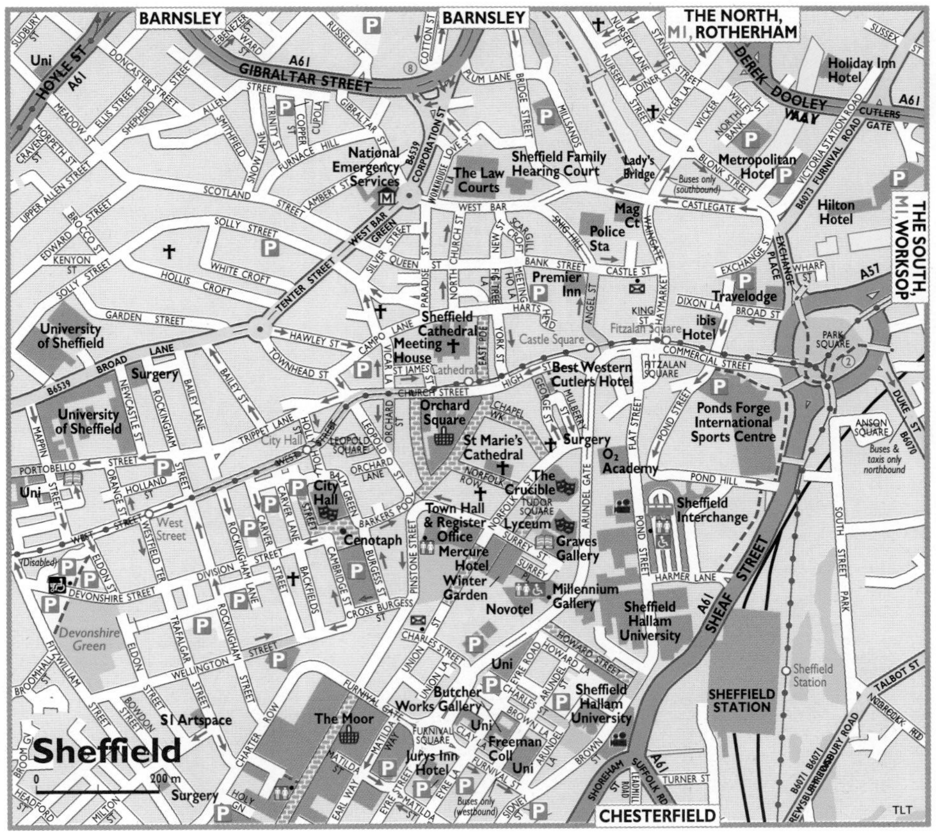

Sheffield

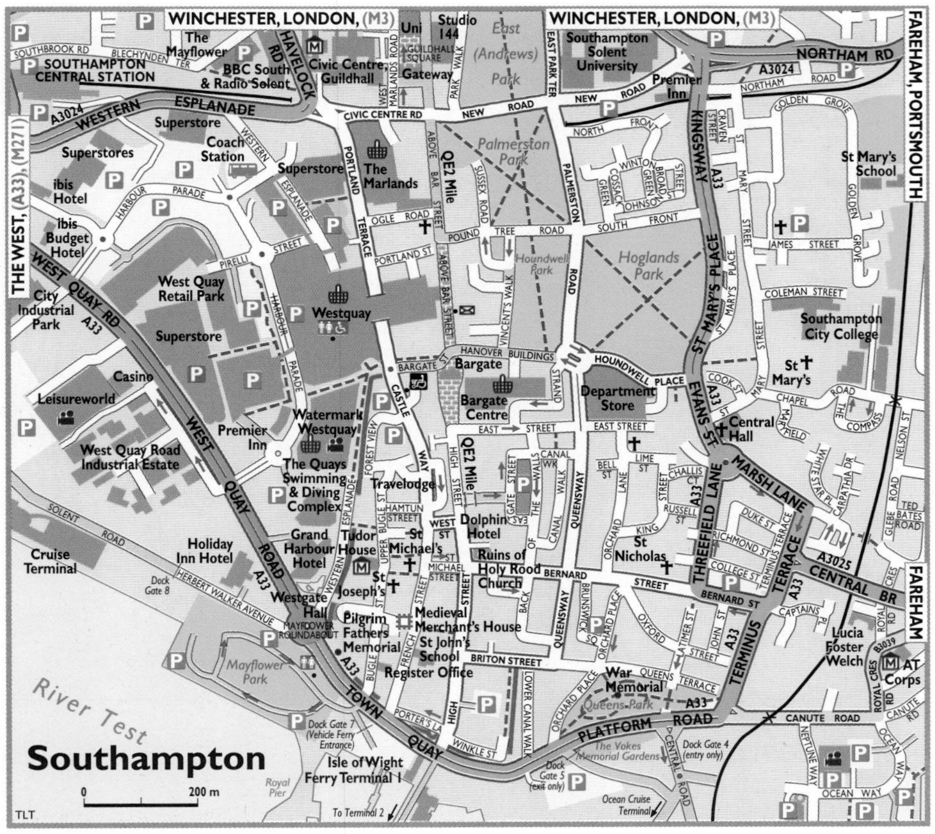

Southampton

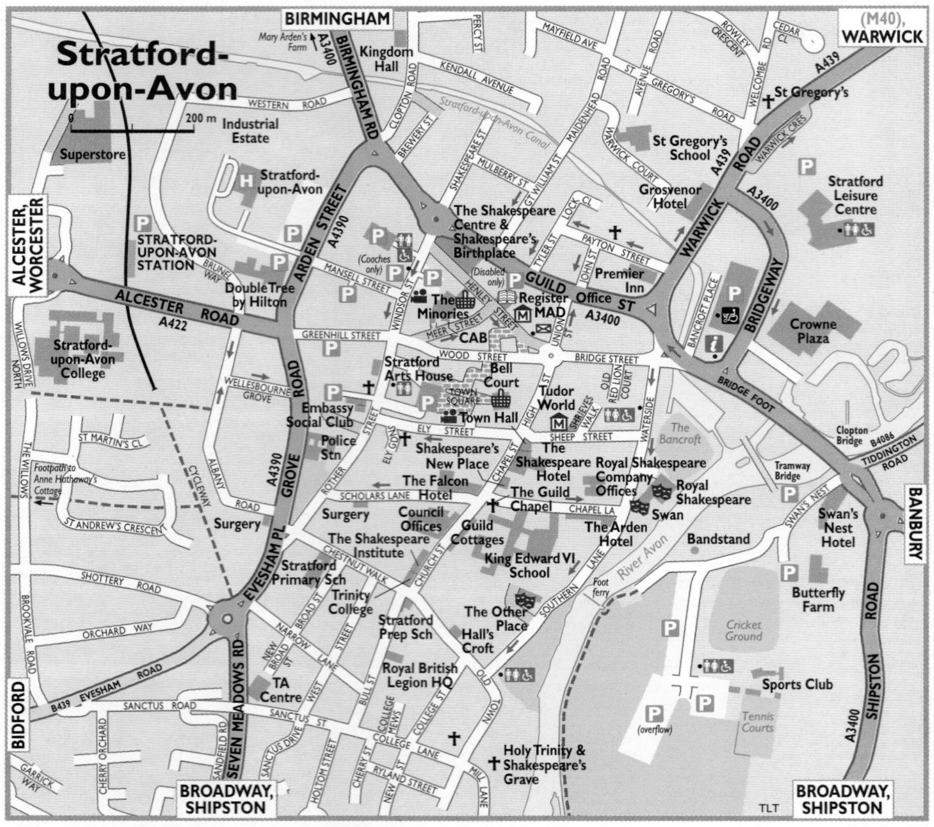
Stratford-upon-Avon
200 m
BIRMINGHAM
(M40), WARWICK
ALCESTER, WORCESTER
BANBURY
BIDFORD
BROADWAY, SHIPSTON
BROADWAY, SHIPSTON
Kingdom Hall
Industrial Estate
Superstore
Stratford-upon-Avon
STRATFORD-UPON-AVON STATION
DoubleTree by Hilton
Stratford-upon-Avon College
St Gregory's
St Gregory's School
Grosvenor Hotel
Stratford Leisure Centre
The Shakespeare Centre & Shakespeare's Birthplace
Premier Inn
Crowne Plaza
The Minories
Register Office
MAD
CAB
Stratford Arts House
Bell Court
Tudor World
Embassy Social Club
Town Hall
Police Stn
Shakespeare's New Place
The Shakespeare Hotel
Royal Shakespeare Company Offices
Royal Shakespeare
Swan
The Falcon Hotel
The Guild Chapel
Council Offices
Guild Cottages
The Arden Hotel
Swan's Nest Hotel
Surgery
Surgery
The Shakespeare Institute
King Edward VI School
Bandstand
Butterfly Farm
Stratford Primary Sch
Trinity College
Stratford Prep Sch
The Other Place
Hall's Croft
Cricket Ground
Royal British Legion HQ
TA Centre
Sports Club
Tennis Courts
Holy Trinity & Shakespeare's Grave
River Avon
ALCESTER ROAD
EVESHAM PL
SEVEN MEADOWS RD
ARDEN STREET
BIRMINGHAM RD
GROVE
GUILD ST
WARWICK ROAD
BRIDGEWAY
BRIDGE FOOT
SHIPSTON ROAD
TLT

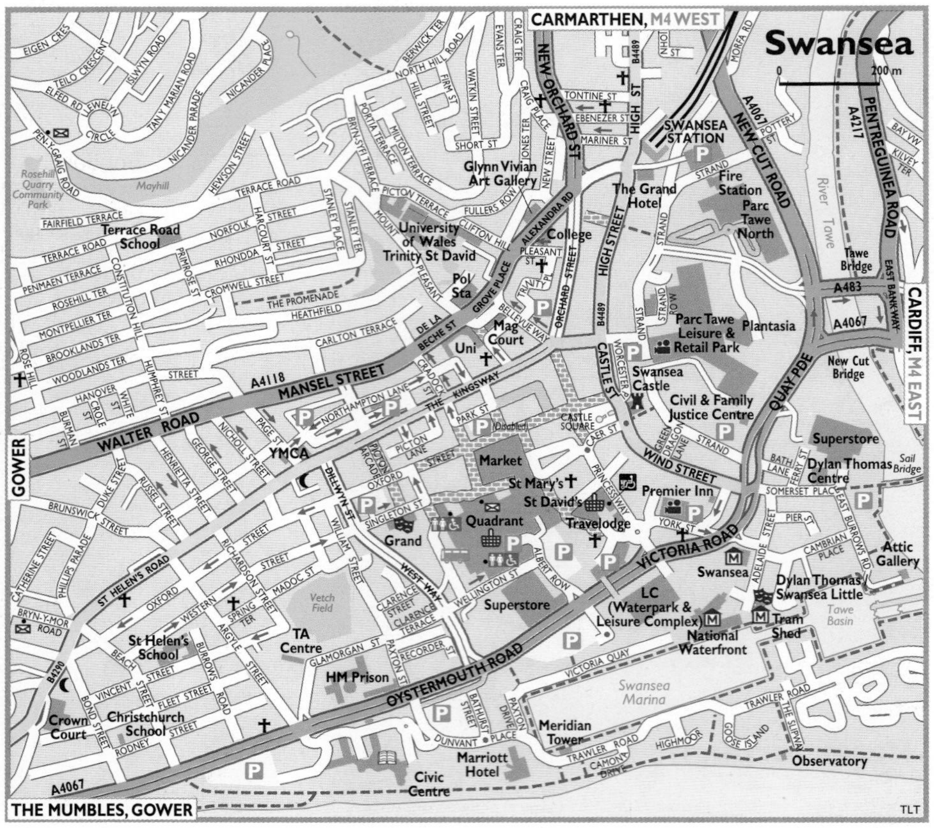
Swansea
200 m
CARMARTHEN, M4 WEST
CARDIFF, M4 EAST
GOWER
THE MUMBLES, GOWER
SWANSEA STATION
Glynn Vivian Art Gallery
The Grand Hotel
Fire Station
Parc Tawe North
Terrace Road School
University of Wales Trinity St David
College
Tawe Bridge
Pol Sta
Mag Court
Uni
Parc Tawe Leisure & Retail Park
Plantasia
Swansea Castle
Civil & Family Justice Centre
New Cut Bridge
YMCA
Market
St Mary's
St David's
Premier Inn
Superstore
Dylan Thomas
Sail Bridge
Grand
Quadrant
Travelodge
Attic Gallery
Swansea
Dylan Thomas Swansea Little Centre
Superstore
LC (Waterpark & Leisure Complex)
National Waterfront
Team Shed
St Helen's School
TA Centre
HM Prison
Crown Court
Christchurch School
Meridian Tower
Marriott Hotel
Civic Centre
Observatory
Swansea Marina
WALTER ROAD
MANSEL STREET
VICTORIA ROAD
OYSTERMOUTH ROAD
QUAY PDE
NEW CUT ROAD
TLT

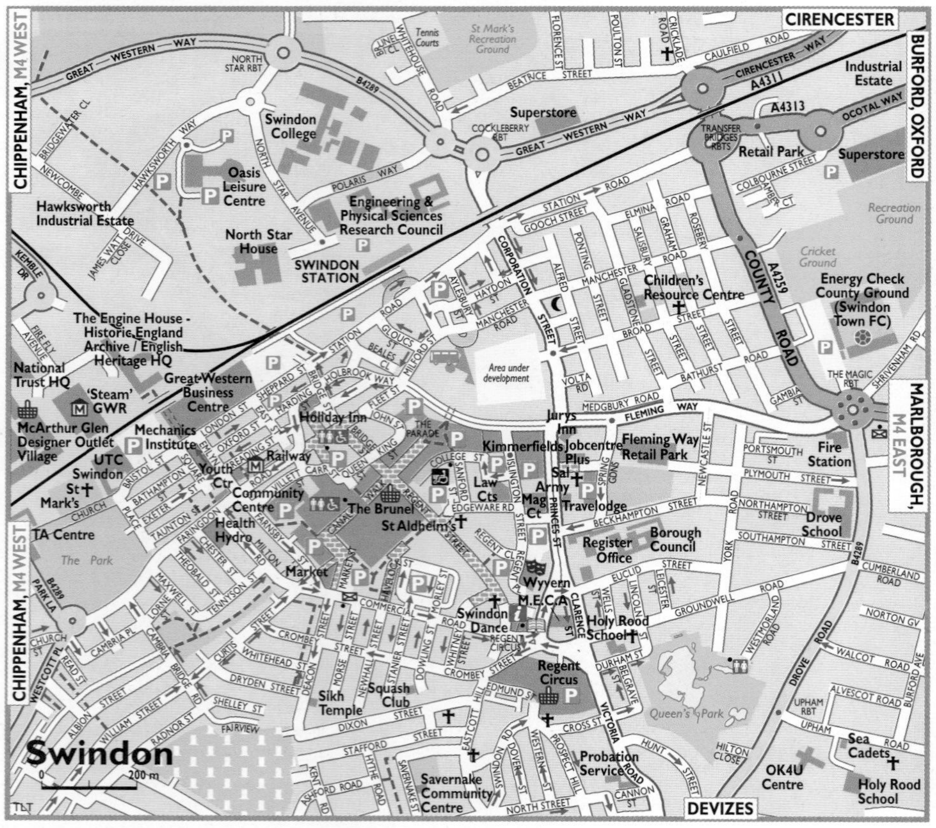
Swindon
200 m
CIRENCESTER
BURFORD, OXFORD
CHIPPENHAM, M4 WEST
MARLBOROUGH, M4 EAST
DEVIZES
Industrial Estate
Superstore
Retail Park
Superstore
Swindon College
Oasis Leisure Centre
Hawksworth Industrial Estate
North Star House
Engineering & Physical Sciences Research Council
SWINDON STATION
Children's Resource Centre
Energy Check County Ground (Swindon Town FC)
The Engine House - Historic England Archive / English Heritage HQ
National Trust HQ
'Steam' GWR
Great Western Business Centre
McArthur Glen Designer Outlet Village
Mechanics Institute
Holiday Inn
Railway
Jarys Inn
Kimmerfields
Jobcentre Plus
Fleming Way Retail Park
Fire Station
UTC Swindon
St Mark's
Youth Ctr
Community Centre
The Brunel
St Aldhelm's
Law Cts
Salv Army
Travelodge
Drove School
TA Centre
Health Hydro
Register Office
Borough Council
Market
Wyvern
M.E.C.A
Swindon Dance
Holy Rood School
Regent Circus
Queen's Park
Sikh Temple
Squash Club
Sea Cadets
Probation Service
OK4U Centre
Holy Rood School
Savernake Community Centre
COUNTY ROAD
TLT

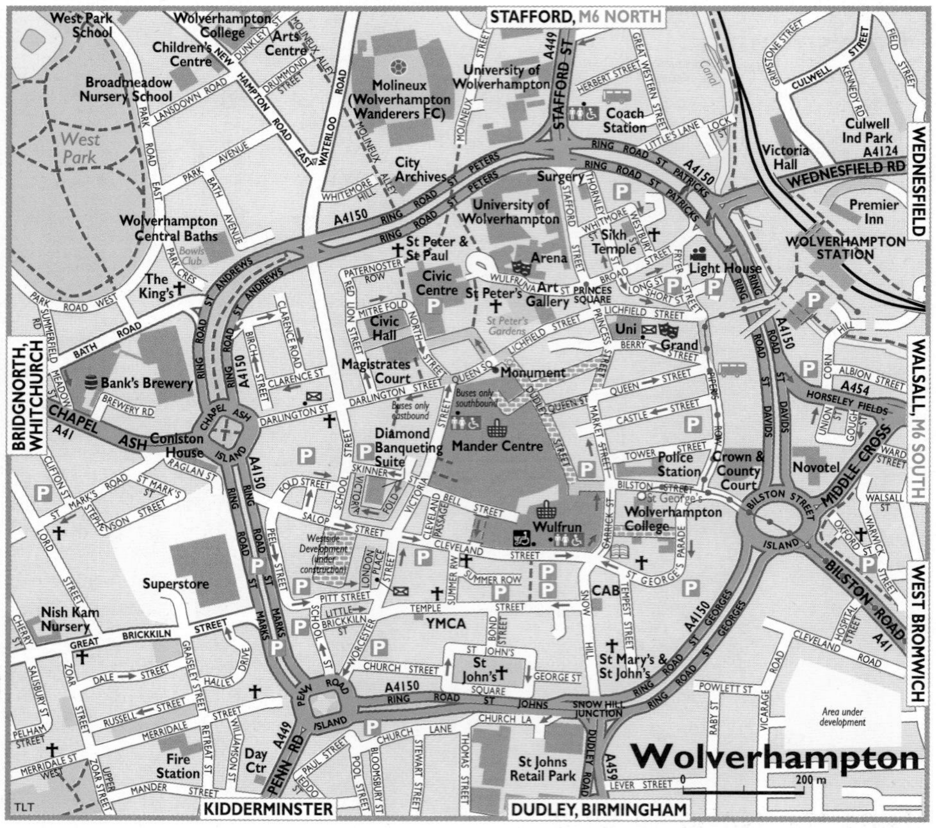
Wolverhampton
200 m
STAFFORD, M6 NORTH
WEDNESFIELD
WALSALL, M6 SOUTH
WEST BROMWICH
BRIDGNORTH, WHITCHURCH
KIDDERMINSTER
DUDLEY, BIRMINGHAM
West Park School
Wolverhampton College
Children's Centre
Arts Centre
Molineux (Wolverhampton Wanderers FC)
University of Wolverhampton
Broadmeadow Nursery School
West Park
Coach Station
Culwell Ind Park
Victoria Hall
City Archives
Surgery
University of Wolverhampton
Premier Inn
WOLVERHAMPTON STATION
Wolverhampton Central Baths
Sikh Temple
St Peter & St Paul
Arena
Light House
The King's
Civic Centre
St Peter's
Art Gallery
Civic Hall
Uni
Grand
Bank's Brewery
Magistrates Court
Monument
Coniston House
Diamond Banqueting Suite
Mander Centre
Police Station
Crown & County Court
Novotel
Wolverhampton College
Wulfrun
Superstore
CAB
YMCA
Nish Kam Nursery
St John's
St Mary's & St John's
Fire Station
Day Ctr
St Johns Retail Park
Area under development
RING ROAD
TLT

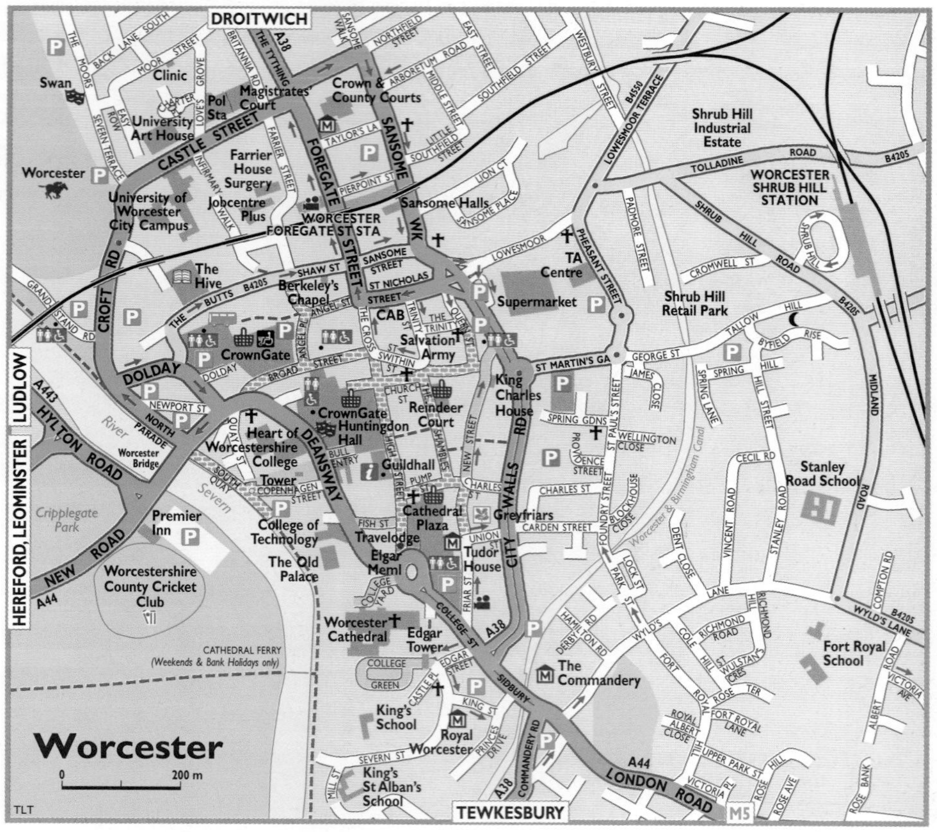
Worcester
200 m
DROITWICH
LUDLOW
HEREFORD, LEOMINSTER
TEWKESBURY
M5
Swan
Clinic
Pol Sta
Magistrates Court
Crown & County Courts
University Art House
Worcester
Farrier House
Surgery
Jobcentre Plus
University of Worcester City Campus
Sansome Halls
WORCESTER FOREGATE ST STA
Shrub Hill Industrial Estate
WORCESTER SHRUB HILL STATION
The Hive
Berkeley's Chapel
TA Centre
Supermarket
Shrub Hill Retail Park
CAB
CrownGate
Salvation Army
King Charles House
CrownGate Huntingdon Hall
Reindeer Court
Heart of Worcestershire College
Worcester Bridge
Guildhall
Tower
Cathedral Plaza
Greyfriars
Stanley Road School
Cripplegate Park
Premier Inn
College of Technology
Travelodge
Elgar Meml
Tudor House
The Old Palace
Worcestershire County Cricket Club
Worcester Cathedral
Edgar Tower
The Commandery
Fort Royal School
CATHEDRAL FERRY (Weekends & Bank Holidays only)
King's School
Royal Worcester
King's St Alban's School
CASTLE STREET
FOREGATE STREET
SANSOME WK
DEANSWAY
CITY WALLS RD
NEW ROAD
HYLTON ROAD
LONDON ROAD
TLT

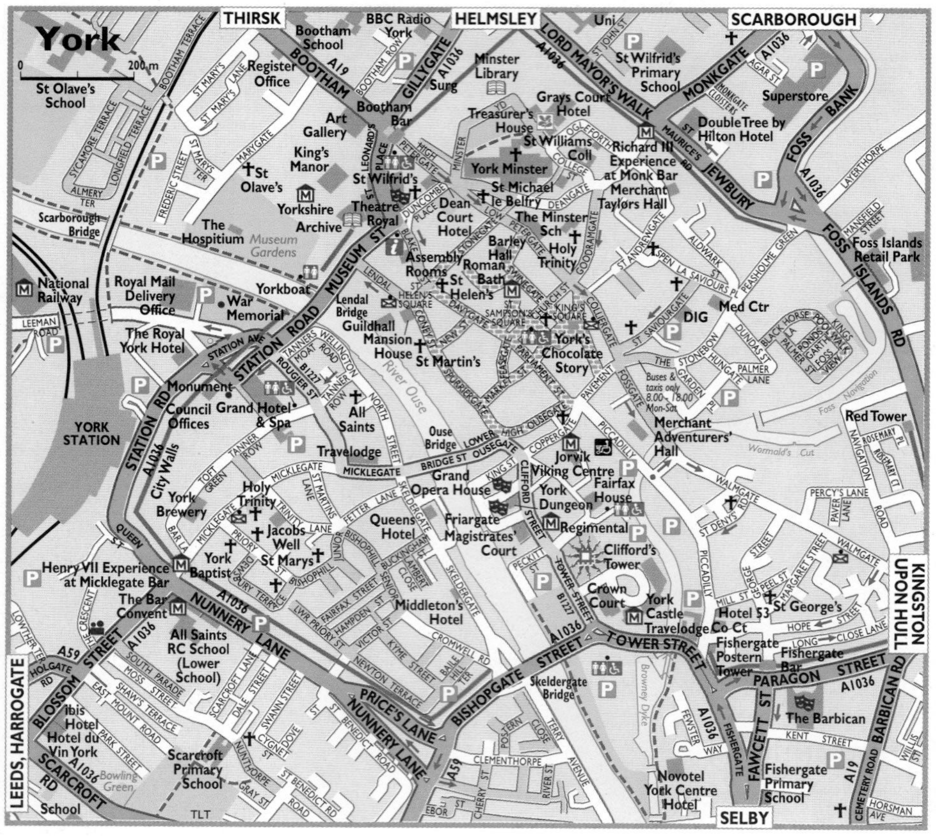
York
200 m
THIRSK
HELMSLEY
SCARBOROUGH
KINGSTON UPON HULL
LEEDS, HARROGATE
SELBY
Bootham School
BBC Radio York
Uni
St Wilfrid's Primary School
Register Office
Minster Library
St Olave's School
Superstore
Grays Court Hotel
Treasurer's House
St Williams Coll
Richard III Experience at Monk Bar
DoubleTree by Hilton Hotel
Art Gallery
King's Manor
St Olave's
York Minster
Merchant Taylors Hall
Yorkshire Museum
Dean Court Hotel
The Minster Sch
Foss Islands Retail Park
The Hospitium
Museum Gardens
Assembly Rooms
Holy Trinity
National Railway
Royal Mail Delivery Office
Yorkboat
War Memorial
Guildhall
Mansion House
St Martin's
York's Chocolate Story
Med Ctr
DIG
The Royal York Hotel
Grand Hotel & Spa
Red Tower
YORK STATION
Council Offices
All Saints
Travelodge
Merchant Adventurers' Hall
Jorvik Viking Centre
Fairfax House
York Dungeon
Grand Opera House
York Brewery
Holy Trinity
Jacobs Well
St Mary's
Queens Hotel
Friargate Magistrates' Court
Regimental Museum
Clifford's Tower
Henry VII Experience at Micklegate Bar
The Bar Convent
York Baptist
Crown Court
York Castle
Travelodge
St George's
Hotel 53
All Saints RC School (Lower School)
Middleton's Hotel
Skeldergate Bridge
Fishergate Postern Tower
Fishergate
The Barbican
Ibis Hotel
Hotel du Vin York
Scarcroft Primary School
Fishergate Primary School
Novotel York Centre Hotel
School
BOOTHAM
GILLYGATE
LORD MAYOR'S WALK
MONKGATE
FOSS BANK
FOSS ISLANDS RD
STATION ROAD
MUSEUM ST
TOWER STREET
PARAGON STREET
NUNNERY LANE
PRICE'S LANE
BISHOPGATE STREET
BLOSSOM STREET
TLT

This index lists places appearing in the main map section of the atlas in alphabetical order. The reference following each name gives the atlas page number and grid reference of the square in which the place appears. The map shows counties, unitary authorities and administrative areas, together with a list of the abbreviated name forms used in the index. The top 100 places of tourist interest are indexed in red, World Heritage sites in green, motorway service areas in blue, airports in blue *italic* and National Parks in green *italic*.

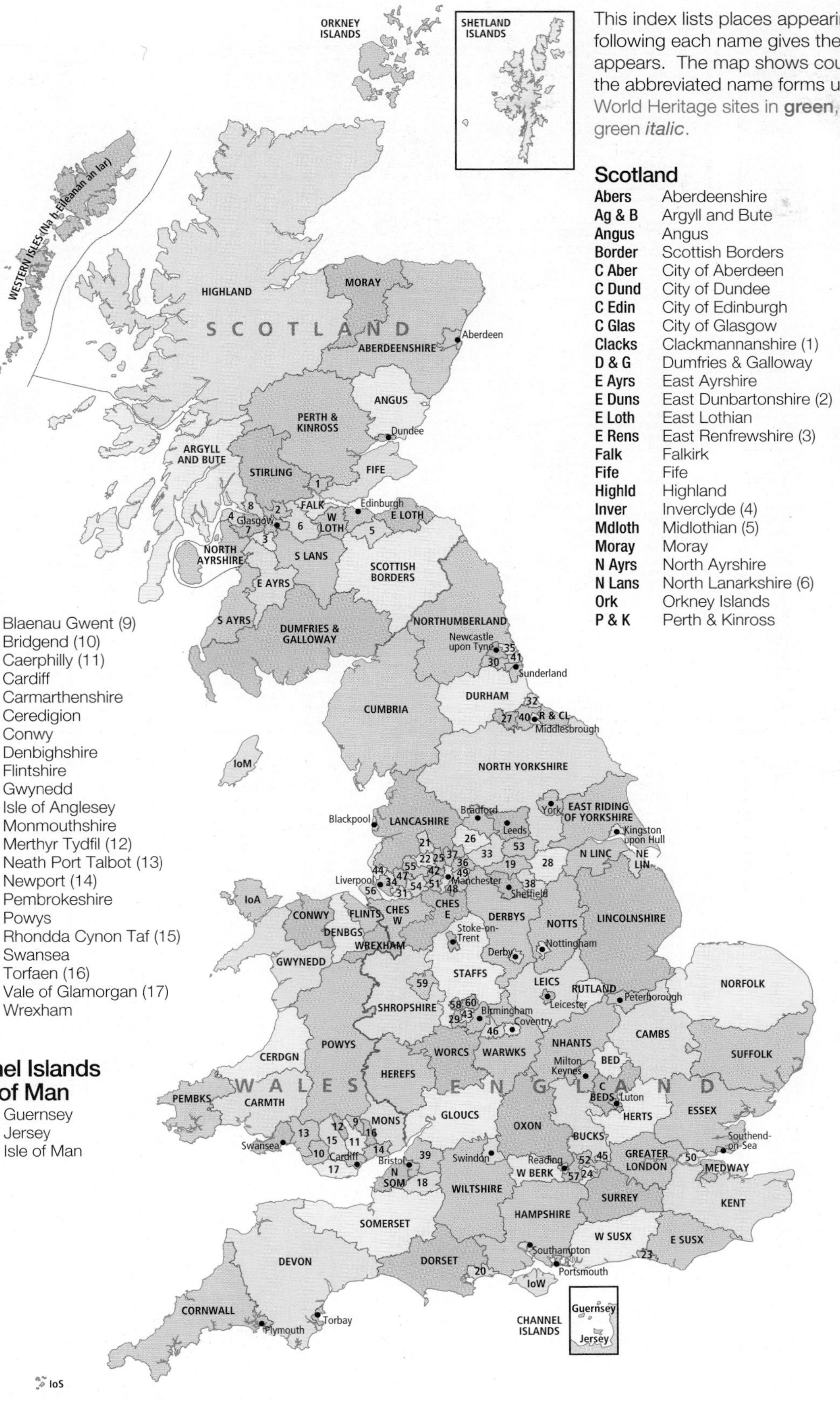

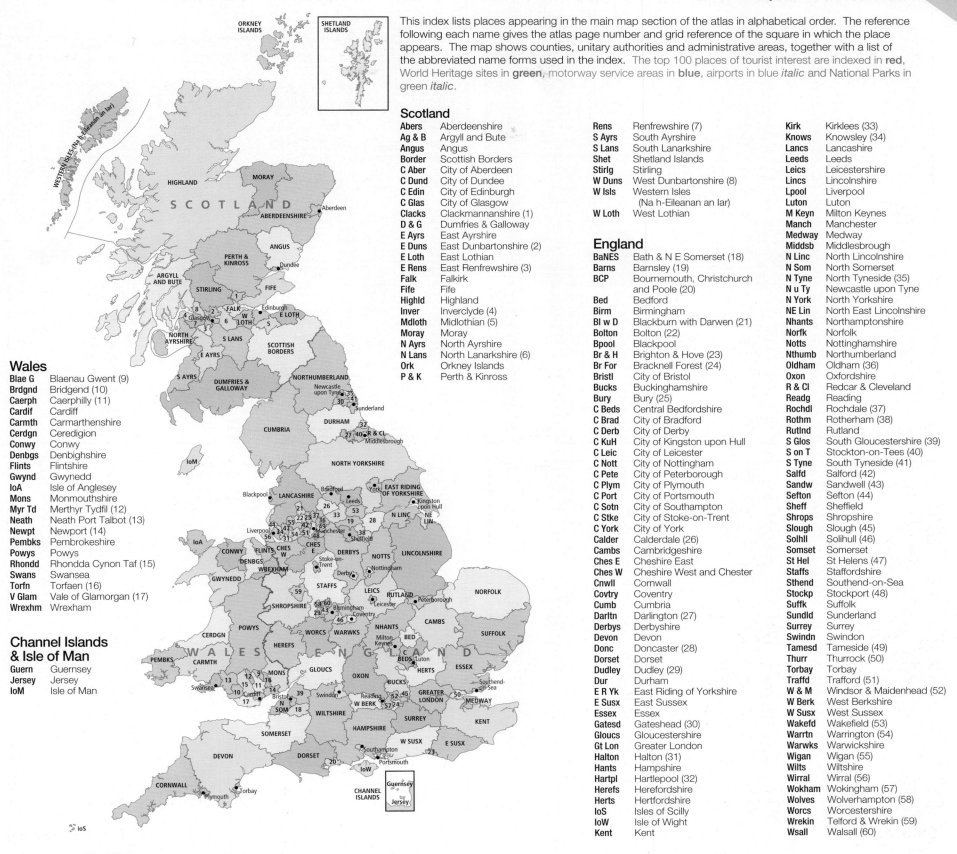

ORKNEY ISLANDS

SHETLAND ISLANDS

WESTERN ISLES (Na h-Eileanan an Iar)

HIGHLAND

MORAY

SCOTLAND

ABERDEENSHIRE

Aberdeen

ANGUS

PERTH & KINROSS

Dundee

ARGYLL AND BUTE

STIRLING

FIFE

FALK

W LOTH

Edinburgh

E LOTH

Glasgow

NORTH AYRSHIRE

S LANS

SCOTTISH BORDERS

E AYRS

S AYRS

DUMFRIES & GALLOWAY

NORTHUMBERLAND

Newcastle upon Tyne

Sunderland

IoM

CUMBRIA

DURHAM

R & CL

Middlesbrough

NORTH YORKSHIRE

Blackpool

LANCASHIRE

Bradford

Leeds

EAST RIDING OF YORKSHIRE

Kingston upon Hull

N LINC

NE LIN

Liverpool

Manchester

Sheffield

CHES E

CHES W

DERBYS

NOTTS

LINCOLNSHIRE

Stoke-on-Trent

Derby

Nottingham

CONWY

FLINTS

DENBGS

GWYNEDD

WREXHM

STAFFS

LEICS

RUTLAND

NORFOLK

SHROPSHIRE

Birmingham

WARWKS

Coventry

WORCS

NHANTS

CAMBS

SUFFOLK

Peterborough

Milton Keynes

BED

HEREFS

W A L E S

CERDGN

POWYS

E N G L A N D

BEDS

HERTS

ESSEX

PEMBKS

CARMTH

GLOUCS

OXON

BUCKS

GREATER LONDON

Southend-on-Sea

Swansea

MONS

Cardiff

Bristol

39

Swindon

Reading

W BERK

MEDWAY

KENT

N SOM

18

WILTSHIRE

SURREY

W SUSX

E SUSX

SOMERSET

HAMPSHIRE

DEVON

DORSET

IoW

Southampton

Portsmouth

CORNWALL

Plymouth

Torbay

IoS

CHANNEL ISLANDS

Guernsey

Jersey

Wales
Blae G	Blaenau Gwent (9)
Brdgnd	Bridgend (10)
Caerph	Caerphilly (11)
Cardif	Cardiff
Carmth	Carmarthenshire
Cerdgn	Ceredigion
Conwy	Conwy
Denbgs	Denbighshire
Flints	Flintshire
Gwynd	Gwynedd
IoA	Isle of Anglesey
Mons	Monmouthshire
Myr Td	Merthyr Tydfil (12)
Neath	Neath Port Talbot (13)
Newpt	Newport (14)
Pembks	Pembrokeshire
Powys	Powys
Rhondd	Rhondda Cynon Taf (15)
Swans	Swansea
Torfn	Torfaen (16)
V Glam	Vale of Glamorgan (17)
Wrexhm	Wrexham

Channel Islands & Isle of Man
Guern	Guernsey
Jersey	Jersey
IoM	Isle of Man

Scotland
Abers	Aberdeenshire
Ag & B	Argyll and Bute
Angus	Angus
Border	Scottish Borders
C Aber	City of Aberdeen
C Dund	City of Dundee
C Edin	City of Edinburgh
C Glas	City of Glasgow
Clacks	Clackmannanshire (1)
D & G	Dumfries & Galloway
E Ayrs	East Ayrshire
E Duns	East Dunbartonshire (2)
E Loth	East Lothian
E Rens	East Renfrewshire (3)
Falk	Falkirk
Fife	Fife
Highld	Highland
Inver	Inverclyde (4)
Mdloth	Midlothian (5)
Moray	Moray
N Ayrs	North Ayrshire
N Lans	North Lanarkshire (6)
Ork	Orkney Islands
P & K	Perth & Kinross
Rens	Renfrewshire (7)
S Ayrs	South Ayrshire
S Lans	South Lanarkshire
Shet	Shetland Islands
Stirlg	Stirling
W Duns	West Dunbartonshire (8)
W Isls	Western Isles (Na h-Eileanan an Iar)
W Loth	West Lothian

England
BaNES	Bath & N E Somerset (18)
Barns	Barnsley (19)
BCP	Bournemouth, Christchurch and Poole (20)
Bed	Bedford
Birm	Birmingham
Bl w D	Blackburn with Darwen (21)
Bolton	Bolton (22)
Bpool	Blackpool
Br & H	Brighton & Hove (23)
Br For	Bracknell Forest (24)
Bristl	City of Bristol
Bucks	Buckinghamshire
Bury	Bury (25)
C Beds	Central Bedfordshire
C Brad	City of Bradford
C Derb	City of Derby
C KuH	City of Kingston upon Hull
C Leic	City of Leicester
C Nott	City of Nottingham
C Pete	City of Peterborough
C Plym	City of Plymouth
C Port	City of Portsmouth
C Sotn	City of Southampton
C Stke	City of Stoke-on-Trent
C York	City of York
Calder	Calderdale (26)
Cambs	Cambridgeshire
Ches E	Cheshire East
Ches W	Cheshire West and Chester
Cnwll	Cornwall
Covtry	Coventry
Cumb	Cumbria
Darltn	Darlington (27)
Derbys	Derbyshire
Devon	Devon
Donc	Doncaster (28)
Dorset	Dorset
Dudley	Dudley (29)
Dur	Durham
E R Yk	East Riding of Yorkshire
E Susx	East Sussex
Essex	Essex
Gatesd	Gateshead (30)
Gloucs	Gloucestershire
Gt Lon	Greater London
Halton	Halton (31)
Hants	Hampshire
Hartpl	Hartlepool (32)
Herefs	Herefordshire
Herts	Hertfordshire
IoS	Isles of Scilly
IoW	Isle of Wight
Kent	Kent
Kirk	Kirklees (33)
Knows	Knowsley (34)
Lancs	Lancashire
Leeds	Leeds
Leics	Leicestershire
Lincs	Lincolnshire
Lpool	Liverpool
Luton	Luton
M Keyn	Milton Keynes
Manch	Manchester
Medway	Medway
Middsb	Middlesbrough
N Linc	North Lincolnshire
N Som	North Somerset
N Tyne	North Tyneside (35)
N u Ty	Newcastle upon Tyne
N York	North Yorkshire
NE Lin	North East Lincolnshire
Nhants	Northamptonshire
Norfk	Norfolk
Notts	Nottinghamshire
Nthumb	Northumberland
Oldham	Oldham (36)
Oxon	Oxfordshire
R & Cl	Redcar & Cleveland
Readg	Reading
Rochdl	Rochdale (37)
Rothm	Rotherham (38)
Rutlnd	Rutland
S Glos	South Gloucestershire (39)
S on T	Stockton-on-Tees (40)
S Tyne	South Tyneside (41)
Salfd	Salford (42)
Sandw	Sandwell (43)
Sefton	Sefton (44)
Sheff	Sheffield
Shrops	Shropshire
Slough	Slough (45)
Solhll	Solihull (46)
Somset	Somerset
St Hel	St Helens (47)
Staffs	Staffordshire
Sthend	Southend-on-Sea
Stockp	Stockport (48)
Suffk	Suffolk
Sundld	Sunderland
Surrey	Surrey
Swindn	Swindon
Tamesd	Tameside (49)
Thurr	Thurrock (50)
Torbay	Torbay
Traffd	Trafford (51)
W & M	Windsor & Maidenhead (52)
W Berk	West Berkshire
W Susx	West Sussex
Wakefd	Wakefield (53)
Warrtn	Warrington (54)
Warwks	Warwickshire
Wigan	Wigan (55)
Wilts	Wiltshire
Wirral	Wirral (56)
Wokham	Wokingham (57)
Wolves	Wolverhampton (58)
Worcs	Worcestershire
Wrekin	Telford & Wrekin (59)
Wsall	Walsall (60)

Using the National Grid

With an Ordnance Survey National Grid reference you can pinpoint anywhere in the country in this atlas. The blue grid lines which divide the main-map pages into 5km squares for ease of indexing also match the National Grid. A National Grid reference gives two letters and some figures. An example is how to find the summit of mount Snowdon using its 4-figure grid reference of **SH6154**.

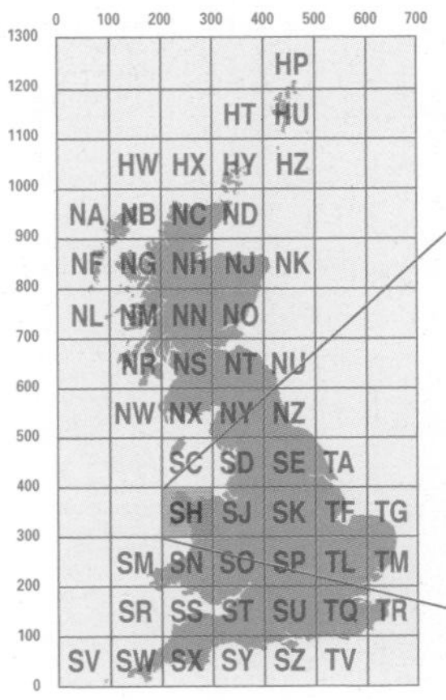

The letters **SH** indicate the 100km square of the National Grid in which Snowdon is located.

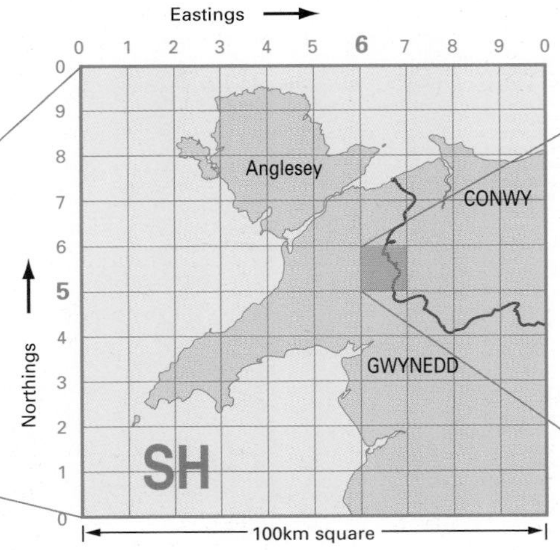

In a 4-figure grid reference the first two figures (eastings) are read along the map from left to right, the second two (northings) up the map. The figures **6** and **5**, the first and third figures of the Snowdon reference, indicate the 10km square within the **SH** square, lying above (north) and right (east) of the intersection of the vertical (easting) line **6** and horizontal (northing) line **5**.

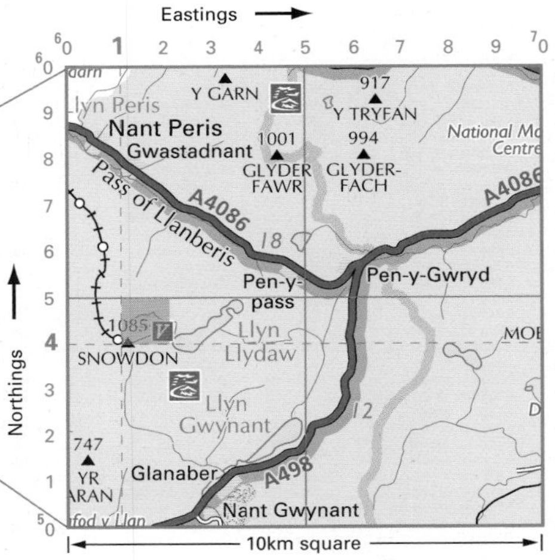

The summit is finally pinpointed by figures **1** and **4** which locate a 1km square within the 10km square. At road atlas scales these grid lines are normally estimated by eye.

Column 1

Bolton Nthumb 77 N3
Bolton Abbey N York 63 M9
Bolton Bridge N York 63 M9
Bolton-by-Bowland Lancs 62 H10
Boltonfellend Cumb 75 U12
Boltongate Cumb 66 K4
Bolton Low Houses Cumb 66 K4
Bolton New Houses Cumb 66 K4
Bolton-on-Swale N York 69 S13
Bolton Percy N York 64 C11
Bolton Town End Lancs 61 T6
Bolton upon Dearne Barns 57 P6
Bolventor Cnwll 4 F5
Bomarsund Nthumb 77 R9
Bomere Heath Shrops 45 L10
Bonar Bridge Highld 109 L6
Bonawe Ag & B 94 E12
Bonby N Linc 58 H3
Boncath Pembks 25 M3
Bonchester Bridge Border 76 B3
Bonchurch IoW 9 R13
Bondleigh Devon 15 Q12
Bonds Lancs 61 T11
Bonehill Devon 5 S5
Bonehill Staffs 46 G13
Boness Falk 82 H2
Boney Hay Staffs 46 D11
Bonhill W Duns 88 J10
Boningale Shrops 45 T13
Bonjedward Border 84 H14
Bonkle N Lans 82 F7
Bonnington Angus 91 S4
Bonnington Kent 13 L8
Bonnybank Fife 91 N11
Bonnybridge Falk 89 T10
Bonnykelly Abers 105 P5
Bonnyrigg Mdloth 83 R5
Bonnyton Angus 91 M4
Bonsall Derbys 56 K1
Bonshaw Tower D & G 75 P11
Bont Mons 27 R4
Bontddu Gwynd 43 N10
Bont-Dolgadfan Powys 43 S13
Bont-goch Cerdgn 33 N3
Bonthorpe Lincs 59 S12
Bontnewydd Gwynd 52 G11
Bontnewydd Cerdgn 33 M7
Bontuchel Denbgs 44 C2
Bonvilston V Glam 26 K13
Bonwm Denbgs 44 D5
Bon-y-maen Swans 26 B8
Boode Devon 15 M5
Booker Bucks 20 D4
Booley Shrops 45 N8
Boon Border 84 F9
Boorley Green Hants 9 Q6
Boosbeck R & Cl 71 L9
Boose's Green Essex 22 K1
Boot Cumb 66 J12
Booth Calder 56 G1
Boothby Graffoe Lincs 48 E2
Boothby Pagnell Lincs 48 E7
Boothferry E R Yk 58 B1
Booth Green Ches E 56 D10
Boothstown Salfd 55 R6
Booth Town Calder 56 G1
Boothville Nhants 37 U8
Bootle Cumb 61 L2
Bootle Sefton 54 H7
Boots Green Ches W 55 S12
Boot Street Suffk 41 M11
Booze N York 69 M12
Boraston Shrops 35 P7
Bordeaux Guern 6 e2
Borden Kent 12 G3
Borden W Susx 10 C6
Border Cumb 66 J2
Bordley N York 62 H7
Bordon Hants 10 B3
Boreham Essex 22 H6
Boreham Wilts 18 C12
Boreham Street E Susx 11 V8
Borehamwood Herts 21 L3
Boreland D & G 75 N7
Boreraig Highld 100 a4
Borgh W Isls 106 b18
Borgh W Isls 106 j9
Borgie Highld 111 P5
Borgue D & G 73 Q10
Borgue Highld 112 D11
Borley Essex 40 D12
Borley Green Essex 40 D12
Borley Green Suffk 40 G8
Borneskitaig Highld 100 c2
Borness D & G 73 Q10
Boroughbridge N York 63 T6
Borough Green Kent 12 B4
Borras Head Wrexhm 44 J3
Borrowash Derbys 47 M7
Borrowby N York 63 T13
Borrowby N York 71 N9
Borrowdale Cumb 66 K10
Borrowstoun Falk 82 H2
Borstal Medway 12 D2
Borth Cerdgn 33 M2
Borthwick Mdloth 83 S6
Borthwickbrae Border 75 T4
Borthwickshiels Border 75 T3
Borth-y-Gest Gwynd 42 K6
Borve Highld 100 d5
Borve W Isls 106 i6
Borve W Isls 106 b13
Borve W Isls 106 i9
Borwick Lancs 61 U5
Borwick Lodge Cumb 67 M7
Borwick Rails Cumb 61 M4
Bosavern Cnwll 2 B10
Bosbury Herefs 35 Q12
Boscarne Cnwll 4 D7
Boscastle Cnwll 4 D2
Boscombe BCP 8 G10
Boscombe Wilts 18 J13
Boscoppa Cnwll 3 Q5
Bosham W Susx 10 C10
Bosham Hoe W Susx 10 C10
Bosherston Pembks 24 G12
Boskednan Cnwll 2 C10
Boskenna Cnwll 2 C11
Bosley Ches E 56 D13
Bosoughan Cnwll 3 M4
Bossall N York 64 G7
Bossiney Cnwll 4 D3
Bossingham Kent 13 M6
Bossington Somset 15 U3
Bostock Green Ches W 55 Q13
Boston Lincs 49 M5
Boston Spa Leeds 63 U10
Boswarthan Cnwll 2 C10
Boswinger Cnwll 3 P8
Botallack Cnwll 2 B10
Botany Bay Gt Lon 21 N3
Botcheston Leics 47 N13
Botesdale Suffk 40 H5
Bothal Nthumb 77 Q8
Bothampstead W Berk 19 R5
Bothamsall Notts 57 U12
Bothel Cumb 66 J5
Bothenhampton Dorset 7 N6
Bothwell S Lans 82 C7
Bothwell Services S Lans 82 D7
Botley Bucks 31 L3
Botley Hants 9 Q6
Botley Oxon 29 U6
Botolph Claydon Bucks 30 F8
Botolphs W Susx 10 K9
Botolph's Bridge Kent 13 M9
Bottesford Leics 48 B6
Bottesford N Linc 58 E5
Bottisham Cambs 39 R8
Bottomcraig Fife 91 N7
Bothwell Services S Lans 82 D7
Botley Bucks 31 L3
Bottom o'th' Moor Bolton 55 R4
Bottom of Hutton Lancs 61 L1
Bottoms Calder 56 D2
Bottoms Cnwll 2 B12
Botts Green Warwks 36 H2
Botusfleming Cnwll 5 L8
Botwnnog Gwynd 42 E7
Bough Beech Kent 21 S13
Boughrood Powys 34 D13
Boughspring Gloucs 27 V8
Boughton Nhants 37 U7
Boughton Norfk 49 V13
Boughton Notts 57 U13
Boughton End C Beds 31 L5
Boughton Green Kent 12 E5
Boughton Monchelsea Kent 12 E5
Boughton Street Kent 13 L4
Boughton Aluph Kent 13 L6
Boughton Lees Kent 13 L6
Boughton Malherbe Kent 12 G6
Boulder Clough Calder 56 F2
Bouldnor IoW 9 M11
Bouldon Shrops 35 M3
Boulmer Nthumb 77 R2
Boulston Pembks 24 G8
Boultham Lincs 58 G13
Boundary Staffs 46 C5
Boundary Leics 47 L11
Bourn Cambs 39 M9
Bourne Lincs 48 G9
Bournbrook Birm 36 D4
Bourne End Bucks 20 E5
Bourne End C Beds 31 L4
Bourne End Herts 31 M11
Bourne End Bed 38 F8

Column 2

Bourne End Bucks 20 E5
Bourne End C Beds 31 L4
Bourne End Herts 31 M11
Bournemouth BCP 8 F10
Bournemouth Airport BCP 8 G9
Bournes Green Gloucs 28 H7
Bournes Green Sthend 23 M10
Bournheath Worcs 36 B6
Bournmoor Dur 70 D2
Bournstream Gloucs 28 D9
Bournville Birm 36 D4
Bourton Dorset 17 U10
Bourton N Som 17 L4
Bourton Oxon 29 P10
Bourton Shrops 35 N1
Bourton on Dunsmore Warwks 37 M6
Bourton-on-the-Hill Gloucs 29 N1
Bourton-on-the-Water Gloucs 29 N3
Bousd Ag & B 92 G7
Boustead Hill Cumb 75 Q14
Bouth Cumb 61 Q2
Bouthwaite N York 63 N5
Bouts Worcs 36 D9
Boveney Bucks 20 F7
Boveridge Dorset 8 F6
Boverton V Glam 16 C3
Bovey Tracey Devon 5 U5
Bovingdon Herts 31 M12
Bovingdon Green Bucks 20 D5
Bovinger Essex 22 C6
Bovington Dorset 8 A11
Bovington Camp Dorset 8 A11
Bow Cumb 67 N11
Bow Devon 15 S11
Bow Devon 5 U9
Bow Gt Lon 21 R6
Bow Ork 106 s20
Bow Brickhill M Keyn 30 K6
Bowbridge Gloucs 28 G6
Bowburn Dur 70 D5
Bowcombe IoW 9 P11
Bowd Devon 6 F6
Bowden Border 84 F12
Bowden Devon 5 U11
Bowden Hill Wilts 18 D7
Bowdon Traffd 55 R9
Bower Highld 112 F4
Bower Hinton Somset 7 N13
Bower House Tye Suffk 40 G12
Bowermadden Highld 112 F4
Bowers Staffs 45 T7
Bowers Gifford Essex 22 J10
Bowershall Fife 90 G13
Bower's Row Leeds 57 N1
Bowes Dur 69 L10
Bowgreave Lancs 61 T11
Bowhouse D & G 74 K2
Bowithick Cnwll 4 F4
Bowker's Green Lancs 54 K6
Bowland Border 84 D11
Bowland Bridge Cumb 61 R2
Bowley Herefs 35 M10
Bowley Town Herefs 35 M10
Bowlhead Green Surrey 10 E3
Bowling Brad 63 P13
Bowling W Duns 88 K11
Bowling Bank Wrexhm 44 J4
Bowling Green Worcs 35 T10
Bowmanstead Cumb 67 M13
Bowmore Ag & B 78 F4
Bowness-on-Solway Cumb 75 P13
Bowness-on-Windermere Cumb 67 P13
Bow of Fife Fife 91 M9
Bowriefauld Angus 91 R2
Bowscale Cumb 67 N6
Bowsden Nthumb 85 P10
Bowston Cumb 67 Q13
Bow Street Cerdgn 33 M3
Bowthorpe Norfk 51 L12
Box Gloucs 28 G7
Box Wilts 18 B7
Boxbush Gloucs 28 C3
Boxbush Gloucs 28 D5
Box End Bed 38 F11
Boxford Suffk 40 G12
Boxford W Berk 19 P6
Boxgrove W Susx 10 E9
Box Hill Surrey 21 L12
Boxley Kent 12 E4
Boxmoor Herts 31 M11
Box's Shop Cnwll 14 F12
Boxted Essex 23 P1
Boxted Suffk 40 D10
Boxted Cross Essex 23 P1
Boxwell Gloucs 28 F9
Boxworth Cambs 39 M8
Boyden End Suffk 40 B9
Boyden Gate Kent 13 P2
Boylestone Derbys 46 G6
Boyndie Abers 104 J3
Boyndlie Abers 105 Q3
Boynton E R Yk 65 Q7
Boysack Angus 91 T2
Boys Hill Dorset 7 S2
Boythorpe Derbys 57 N13
Boyton Cnwll 4 J2
Boyton Suffk 41 Q12
Boyton Wilts 18 E13
Boyton Cross Essex 22 F6
Boyton End Suffk 40 B12
Bozeat Nhants 38 D9
Braaid IoM 60 f7
Brabling Green Suffk 41 N8
Brabourne Kent 13 L7
Brabourne Lees Kent 13 L7
Brabstermire Highld 112 H3
Bracadale Highld 100 c6
Braceborough Lincs 48 G11
Bracebridge Heath Lincs 58 G13
Bracebridge Low Fields Lincs 58 G13
Braceby Lincs 48 G6
Bracewell Lancs 62 H10
Brackenfield Derbys 47 L2
Brackenhirst N Lans 82 D5
Brackenthwaite Cumb 67 L3
Brackenthwaite N York 63 R9
Brackla Brdgnd 26 G12
Bracklesham W Susx 10 C11
Brackletter Highld 96 C3
Brackley Nhants 30 C5
Brackley Hatch Nhants 30 D5
Bracknell Br For 20 E9
Braco P & K 89 R4
Bracobrae Moray 104 G5
Bracon Ash Norfk 51 L14
Bracora Highld 100 g10
Bracorina Highld 100 g10
Bradaford Devon 14 K2
Bradbourne Derbys 46 H3
Bradbury Dur 70 D7
Bradda IoM 60 b8
Bradden Nhants 37 R11
Braddock Cnwll 4 F8
Bradeley C Stke 45 U3
Bradenham Bucks 20 D3
Bradenstoke Wilts 18 F5
Bradfield Devon 6 F3
Bradfield Essex 23 R1
Bradfield Norfk 51 N7
Bradfield Sheff 57 L7
Bradfield W Berk 19 T6
Bradfield Combust Suffk 40 E9
Bradfield Green Ches E 45 Q2
Bradfield Heath Essex 23 R2
Bradfield St Clare Suffk 40 F9
Bradfield St George Suffk 40 F9
Bradford Cnwll 4 E5
Bradford Derbys 56 K14
Bradford Devon 14 K11
Bradford Nthumb 77 R7
Bradford Nthumb 85 T11
Bradford C Brad 63 P13
Bradford Abbas Dorset 7 R2
Bradford Leigh Wilts 18 B8
Bradford-on-Avon Wilts 18 B8
Bradford-on-Tone Somset 16 G12
Bradford Peverell Dorset 7 S5
Bradiford Devon 15 N6
Brading IoW 9 S11
Bradley Derbys 46 H4
Bradley Hants 19 T12
Bradley N E Lin 59 M5
Bradley NE Lin 59 M5
Bradley Staffs 45 U10
Bradley Wolves 46 B14
Bradley Worcs 36 C8
Bradley Green Ches W 45 N4
Bradley Green Somset 16 H9
Bradley Green Warwks 46 J13
Bradley Green Worcs 36 C8
Bradley in the Moors Staffs 46 E5
Bradley Stoke S Glos 28 B11
Bradmore Notts 47 Q7

Column 3

Bradney Somset 16 K9
Bradninch Devon 6 C4
Bradnop Staffs 46 D2
Bradnor Green Herefs 34 G9
Bradpole Dorset 7 N6
Bradshaw Bolton 55 R4
Bradshaw Calder 63 L2
Bradshaw Kirk 56 G4
Bradstone Devon 5 K4
Bradwall Green Ches E 55 S14
Bradwell Derbys 56 J10
Bradwell Essex 22 K3
Bradwell M Keyn 30 J5
Bradwell Norfk 51 T13
Bradwell-on-Sea Essex 23 P6
Bradwell Waterside Essex 23 N6
Bradworthy Devon 14 H9
Brae Shet 106 t7
Braeface Falk 89 S9
Braehead Angus 91 M9
Braehead D & G 73 M9
Braehead S Lans 82 H8
Braeintra Highld 101 M5
Braemar Abers 98 C5
Braemore Highld 108 B9
Braemore Highld 112 C11
Brae Roy Lodge Highld 96 C5
Braeside Inver 88 F11
Braes of Coul Angus 98 D12
Braes of Enzie Moray 104 D4
Braeswick Shet 106 v16
Braevallich Ag & B 87 T1
Brafferton Darltn 69 S8
Brafferton N York 63 U5
Brafield-on-the-Green Nhants 38 B9
Bragar W Isls 106 h4
Bragbury End Herts 31 S9
Braidwood S Lans 82 F9
Brailsford Derbys 46 H5
Brailsford Green Derbys 46 H5
Brain's Green Gloucs 28 C6
Braintree Essex 22 H2
Braiseworth Suffk 40 K6
Braishfield Hants 9 M3
Braithwaite C Brad 63 L11
Braithwaite Cumb 66 K8
Braithwaite Donc 57 S4
Braithwell Donc 57 R8
Braken Hill Wakefd 57 P3
Bramber W Susx 10 K8
Brambridge Hants 9 P4
Bramcote Notts 47 N6
Bramcote Warwks 37 M3
Bramdean Hants 9 S3
Bramerton Norfk 51 N13
Bramfield Herts 31 S9
Bramfield Suffk 41 Q6
Bramford Suffk 40 K11
Bramhall Stockp 56 C10
Bramham Leeds 63 U11
Bramhope Leeds 63 R11
Bramley Hants 19 U9
Bramley Leeds 63 R13
Bramley Rothm 57 P8
Bramley Surrey 10 G2
Bramley Corner Hants 19 T9
Bramley Green Hants 19 U9
Bramley Head N York 63 N9
Bramling Kent 13 P4
Brampford Speke Devon 6 B5
Brampton Cambs 38 K6
Brampton Cumb 76 A13
Brampton Cumb 68 E8
Brampton Lincs 58 E11
Brampton Norfk 51 M9
Brampton Rothm 57 P6
Brampton Suffk 41 R4
Brampton Abbotts Herefs 28 B2
Brampton Ash Nhants 37 U3
Brampton Bryan Herefs 34 J6
Brampton-en-le-Morthen Rothm 57 Q9
Bramshall Staffs 46 E7
Bramshaw Hants 8 K5
Bramshill Hants 20 B10
Bramshott Hants 10 C4
Bramwell Somset 17 M11
Branault Highld 93 N5
Brancaster Norfk 50 C5
Brancaster Staithe Norfk 50 C5
Brancepeth Dur 69 S5
Branchill Moray 103 S5
Brand End Lincs 49 M4
Branderburgh Moray 104 A1
Brandesburton E R Yk 65 Q10
Brandeston Suffk 41 M8
Brand Green Gloucs 28 D2
Brandiston Norfk 50 K9
Brandon Dur 69 S5
Brandon Lincs 48 D4
Brandon Nthumb 77 L2
Brandon Suffk 40 B3
Brandon Warwks 37 M5
Brandon Bank Norfk 39 T3
Brandon Creek Norfk 39 T2
Brandon Parva Norfk 50 J12
Brandsby N York 64 D5
Brandy Wharf Lincs 58 H7
Brane Cnwll 2 C11
Bran End Essex 22 G2
Branksome BCP 8 E10
Branksome Park BCP 8 E10
Bransbury Hants 19 P12
Bransby Lincs 58 E11
Branscombe Devon 6 G7
Bransford Worcs 35 S10
Bransgore Hants 8 H9
Bransholme C KuH 65 Q13
Branson's Cross Worcs 36 F6
Branston Leics 48 B8
Branston Lincs 58 H13
Branston Staffs 46 H9
Branston Booths Lincs 58 H13
Branstone IoW 9 R12
Brant Broughton Lincs 48 D3
Brantham Suffk 23 R1
Branthwaite Cumb 66 G7
Branthwaite Cumb 67 L4
Brantingham E R Yk 65 L14
Branton Donc 57 T6
Branton Nthumb 77 L2
Branton Green N York 63 U7
Branxton Nthumb 85 N11
Brassey Green Ches W 45 M1
Brassington Derbys 46 H2
Brasted Kent 21 S11
Brasted Chart Kent 21 S12
Brathens Abers 99 M4
Bratoft Lincs 59 S14
Brattleby Lincs 58 F10
Bratton Somset 16 B7
Bratton Wilts 18 D10
Bratton Wrekin 45 P10
Bratton Clovelly Devon 5 M2
Bratton Fleming Devon 15 P5
Bratton Seymour Somset 17 S11
Braughing Herts 31 U7
Braughing Friars Herts 22 B3
Braunston Nhants 37 P7
Braunston Rutlnd 48 B12
Braunstone Leics 47 Q13
Braunton Devon 15 L5
Brawby N York 64 G4
Brawl Highld 111 S4
Braworth N York 70 H11
Bray W & M 20 F7
Braybrooke Nhants 37 U4
Brayford Devon 15 Q6
Bray Shop Cnwll 4 J6
Braystones Cumb 66 F11
Braythorn N York 63 Q10
Brayton N York 64 D13
Braywick W & M 20 D7
Braywoodside W & M 20 D7
Brazacott Cnwll 4 J2
Breach Kent 12 H3
Breachwood Green Herts 31 Q8
Breacleit W Isls 106 g6
Breaden Heath Shrops 44 K6
Breadsall Derbys 47 L5
Breadstone Gloucs 28 D7
Breage Cnwll 2 G11
Breakachy Highld 102 E6
Breakish Highld 100 f7
Brealeagnach Lodge Highld 108 J8
Bream Gloucs 28 B6
Breamore Hants 8 H5
Breanais W Isls 106 e6
Brean Somset 16 J6
Brearley Calder 56 F1
Brearton N York 63 S7
Breascleit W Isls 106 h5

Column 4

Breascleit W Isls 106 h5
Breaston Derbys 47 N7
Brechfa Carmth 25 T4
Brechin Angus 99 L11
Breckles Norfk 40 F1
Brecon Powys 26 J2
Brecon Beacons National Park 26 J3
Bredbury Stockp 56 D8
Brede E Susx 12 F12
Bredenbury Herefs 35 P9
Bredfield Suffk 41 N10
Bredgar Kent 12 G3
Bredhurst Kent 12 E3
Bredon Worcs 36 B13
Bredon's Hardwick Worcs 36 B13
Bredon's Norton Worcs 36 B13
Bredwardine Herefs 34 H12
Breedon on the Hill Leics 47 M9
Breich W Loth 82 H6
Breightmet Bolton 55 R5
Breighton E R Yk 64 G13
Breinton Herefs 35 L13
Breinton Common Herefs 35 L13
Bremhill Wilts 18 E6
Bremridge Devon 15 Q7
Brenchley Kent 12 C7
Brendon Devon 14 J11
Brendon Devon 15 S3
Brendon Hill Somset 16 D10
Brenfield Ag & B 87 Q9
Brenish W Isls 106 e6
Brenkley N u Ty 77 Q11
Brent Cross Gt Lon 21 M5
Brent Eleigh Suffk 40 F11
Brentford Gt Lon 21 L7
Brentingby Leics 47 U11
Brent Knoll Somset 16 K6
Brent Mill Devon 5 R9
Brent Pelham Herts 22 C1
Brentwood Essex 22 E9
Brenzett Kent 12 K10
Brenzett Green Kent 12 K10
Brereton Staffs 46 D10
Brereton Green Ches E 55 S14
Brereton Heath Ches E 55 T14
Brereton Hill Staffs 46 D10
Bressay Shet 106 v9
Bressingham Norfk 40 J4
Bressingham Common Norfk 40 J4
Bretby Derbys 46 J9
Bretford Warwks 37 M5
Bretforton Worcs 36 E12
Bretherton Lancs 55 L2
Brettabister Shet 106 u8
Brettenham Norfk 40 F3
Brettenham Suffk 40 G10
Bretton C Pete 48 J13
Bretton Derbys 56 K11
Bretton Flints 54 J1
Brewers End Essex 22 D4
Brewer Street Surrey 21 P12
Brewood Staffs 45 U11
Briantspuddle Dorset 7 V6
Brick End Essex 22 E2
Brickendon Herts 31 T11
Bricket Wood Herts 31 P11
Brick Houses Sheff 57 M10
Brickkiln Green Essex 22 H1
Bricklehampton Worcs 36 C12
Bride IoM 60 g2
Bridekirk Cumb 66 H5
Bridell Pembks 32 C12
Bridestowe Devon 5 N3
Brideswell Abers 104 H8
Bridford Devon 5 U3
Bridge Cnwll 2 H9
Bridge Kent 13 N5
Bridge End Cumb 67 N3
Bridge End Devon 5 R11
Bridge End Dur 69 N5
Bridge End Essex 22 F1
Bridge End Lincs 48 G5
Bridgefoot Angus 91 M5
Bridgefoot Cumb 66 G7
Bridge Green Essex 39 Q14
Bridgehampton Somset 17 Q12
Bridge Hewick N York 63 S5
Bridgehill Dur 69 N2
Bridgemary Hants 9 R8
Bridgemere Ches E 45 R4
Bridgend Abers 104 J7
Bridgend Ag & B 79 P9
Bridgend Ag & B 87 T6
Bridgend Angus 98 J10
Bridgend Brdgnd 26 G11
Bridgend Cerdgn 32 F10
Bridgend Cumb 67 P9
Bridgend D & G 75 M3
Bridgend Devon 5 N10
Bridgend Fife 91 L9
Bridgend Moray 104 D8
Bridgend P & K 90 G6
Bridgend W Loth 82 K4
Bridgend of Lintrathen Angus 98 D13
Bridge of Alford Abers 104 H12
Bridge of Allan Stirlg 89 S6
Bridge of Avon Moray 103 U9
Bridge of Avon Moray 103 U8
Bridge of Balgie P & K 95 R9
Bridge of Brewlands Angus 98 B11
Bridge of Brown Highld 103 T11
Bridge of Cally P & K 90 H1
Bridge of Canny Abers 99 M4
Bridge of Craigisla Angus 98 D13
Bridge of Dee D & G 74 D14
Bridge of Don C Aber 99 S2
Bridge of Dye Abers 99 N6
Bridge of Earn P & K 90 H7
Bridge of Ericht P & K 95 R6
Bridge of Feugh Abers 99 N4
Bridge of Gairn Abers 98 F4
Bridge of Gaur P & K 95 R6
Bridge of Marnoch Abers 104 H5
Bridge of Muchalls Abers 99 R5
Bridge of Orchy Ag & B 94 K11
Bridge of Tilt P & K 97 P10
Bridge of Tynet Moray 104 D3
Bridge of Walls Shet 106 s8
Bridge of Weir Rens 88 J13
Bridge Reeve Devon 15 Q10
Bridgerule Devon 14 G12
Bridges Shrops 34 J1
Bridge Sollers Herefs 34 K12
Bridge Street Suffk 40 E11
Bridgetown Cnwll 4 H3
Bridgetown Somset 16 B9
Bridge Trafford Ches W 55 L12
Bridge Yate S Glos 28 C13
Bridgham Norfk 40 G3
Bridgnorth Shrops 35 R2
Bridgwater Somset 16 K9
Bridgwater Services Somset 16 K10
Bridlington E R Yk 65 R6
Bridport Dorset 7 N6
Bridstow Herefs 28 A3
Brierfield Lancs 62 G12
Brierley Barns 57 P4
Brierley Gloucs 28 B4
Brierley Herefs 35 L9
Brierley Hill Dudley 36 B3
Brierton Hartpl 70 G7
Briery Cumb 67 L8
Brigg N Linc 58 H5
Briggate Norfk 51 P8
Briggswath N York 71 R11
Brigham Cumb 66 G6
Brigham E R Yk 65 P9
Brighouse Calder 56 H1
Brighstone IoW 9 N12
Brightgate Derbys 46 J2
Brightholmlee Sheff 57 L7
Brightley Devon 15 P13
Brightling E Susx 12 C11
Brightlingsea Essex 23 Q4
Brighton Cnwll 3 N6
Brighton Br & H 11 N9
Brighton City Airport W Susx 10 K9
Brighton le Sands Sefton 54 H7
Brightons Falk 82 H3
Brightwalton W Berk 19 P5
Brightwalton Green W Berk 19 P5
Brightwalton Holt W Berk 19 P5
Brightwell Suffk 41 N12
Brightwell Baldwin Oxon 30 D13
Brightwell-cum-Sotwell Oxon 19 S2
Brightwell Upperton Oxon 19 S2
Brigmerston Wilts 18 J11
Brignall Dur 69 N10
Brig o'Turk Stirlg 89 M4
Brigsley N Linc 59 M6
Brigsteer Cumb 61 T2
Brigstock Nhants 38 D3
Brill Bucks 30 E10
Brill Cnwll 2 J11
Brilley Herefs 34 G11

Column 5

Brimfield Herefs 35 M7
Brimfield Cross Herefs 35 M7
Brimington Derbys 57 P12
Brimley Devon 5 U5
Brimpsfield Gloucs 28 H5
Brimpton W Berk 19 S8
Brimscombe Gloucs 28 G7
Brimstage Wirral 54 H10
Brincliffe Sheff 57 M10
Brind E R Yk 64 G13
Brindham Somset 17 P9
Brindister Shet 106 t9
Brindle Lancs 55 P1
Brineton Staffs 45 T11
Bringhurst Leics 38 B2
Bringsty Common Herefs 35 R9
Brington Cambs 38 G5
Briningham Norfk 50 H7
Brinkhill Lincs 59 Q12
Brinkley Cambs 39 T10
Brinklow Warwks 37 M5
Brinkworth Wilts 18 H4
Brinscall Lancs 55 P2
Brinscombe Somset 17 M6
Brinsea N Som 17 M4
Brinsley Notts 47 N4
Brinsworth Rothm 57 P8
Brinton Norfk 50 H6
Brisco Cumb 67 P2
Brisley Norfk 50 G9
Brislington Bristl 28 B13
Brissenden Green Kent 12 J8
Bristol Brist 28 A12
Bristol Airport N Som 17 N3
Bristol Zoo Gardens Bristl 27 V13
Briston Norfk 50 J7
Brisworthy Devon 5 P7
Britannia Lancs 56 C2
Britford Wilts 8 G3
Brithdir Caerph 27 L7
Brithdir Gwynd 43 Q10
British Legion Village Kent 12 D4
Briton Ferry Neath 26 D9
Britwell Salome Oxon 19 U2
Brixham Torbay 6 B13
Brixton Devon 5 P10
Brixton Gt Lon 21 P7
Brixton Deverill Wilts 18 C13
Brixworth Nhants 37 U6
Brize Norton Oxon 29 Q6
Brize Norton Airport Oxon 29 Q6
Broad Alley Worcs 35 U7
Broad Blunsdon Swindn 29 M9
Broadbottom Tamesd 56 E8
Broadbridge W Susx 10 C9
Broadbridge Heath W Susx 10 J4
Broad Campden Gloucs 36 F13
Broad Carr Calder 56 G3
Broad Chalke Wilts 8 E3
Broad Clough Lancs 56 C2
Broadfield Lancs 55 N1
Broadford Highld 100 f7
Broadford Bridge W Susx 10 H6
Broadgairhill Border 75 P4
Broadgrass Green Suffk 40 G8
Broad Green Cambs 39 U9
Broad Green Essex 22 K3
Broad Green Worcs 35 S10
Broad Green Worcs 36 C6
Broad Green W Susx 10 H5
Broad Haven Pembks 24 E8
Broadhaugh Border 85 R9
Broadheath Traffd 55 R9
Broad Heath Worcs 35 Q7
Broadhembury Devon 6 F4
Broadhempston Devon 5 U7
Broad Hill Cambs 39 T5
Broad Hinton Wilts 18 H5
Broadland Row E Susx 12 F12
Broadlay Carmth 25 Q8
Broad Laying Hants 19 P8
Broadley Lancs 56 C3
Broadley Moray 104 D3
Broadley Common Essex 22 B6
Broad Marston Worcs 36 F11
Broadmayne Dorset 7 T6
Broadmere Hants 19 T11
Broadmoor Pembks 24 J9
Broadnymett Devon 15 R12
Broad Oak Carmth 25 U6
Broad Oak Cumb 66 J13
Broad Oak E Susx 11 U6
Broad Oak E Susx 12 C11
Broad Oak E Susx 12 F12
Broad Oak Hants 9 S5
Broad Oak Herefs 27 T3
Broad Oak Kent 13 N3
Broad Oak St Hel 55 M7
Broadoak Dorset 7 M6
Broad Road Suffk 41 N6
Broadsands Torbay 6 A13
Broad's Green Essex 22 G5
Broadstairs Kent 13 S2
Broadstone BCP 8 E9
Broadstone Shrops 35 M3
Broad Street E Susx 12 G11
Broad Street Essex 22 D6
Broad Street Kent 12 E4
Broad Street Kent 13 L9
Broad Street Medway 12 J2
Broad Street Green Essex 23 L5
Broad Town Wilts 18 G5
Broadwas Worcs 35 S9
Broadwater Herts 31 R8
Broadwaters Worcs 35 U5
Broadway Carmth 25 P8
Broadway Carmth 25 L5
Broadway Pembks 24 E8
Broadway Somset 16 K13
Broadway Suffk 41 Q6
Broadway Worcs 36 E13
Broadwell Gloucs 28 A4
Broadwell Gloucs 29 P2
Broadwell Oxon 29 Q7
Broadwell Warwks 37 N7
Broadwey Dorset 7 S8
Broadwindsor Dorset 7 M4
Broadwood Kelly Devon 15 P11
Broadwoodwidger Devon 4 K3
Brobury Herefs 34 H12
Brochel Highld 100 e5
Brochroy Ag & B 94 E12
Brock Lancs 61 T11
Brockamin Worcs 35 S10
Brockbridge Hants 9 S5
Brockdish Norfk 41 M4
Brockencote Worcs 35 U6
Brockenhurst Hants 8 K8
Brocketsbrae S Lans 82 F11
Brockford Green Suffk 40 K7
Brockford Street Suffk 40 K7
Brockhall Nhants 37 R8
Brockham Surrey 21 L13
Brockhampton Gloucs 28 H2
Brockhampton Gloucs 28 K4
Brockhampton Hants 9 U8
Brockhampton Herefs 27 T1
Brockhampton Green Dorset 7 T3
Brockholes Kirk 56 J4
Brockhurst Derbys 57 M14
Brockhurst Warwks 37 M5
Brocklebank Cumb 67 L3
Brocklesby Lincs 58 K4
Brockley N Som 17 N3
Brockley Suffk 40 D7
Brockley Green Suffk 40 C10
Brockley Green Suffk 40 D10
Brockleymoor Cumb 67 Q5
Brockmoor Dudley 35 U3
Brockscombe Devon 15 L13
Brock's Green Hants 19 Q8
Brockton Shrops 34 J2
Brockton Shrops 35 N1
Brockton Shrops 35 P3
Brockton Shrops 45 R12
Brockton Staffs 45 T7
Brockweir Gloucs 27 U7
Brockwood Park Hants 9 S4
Brockworth Gloucs 28 G4
Brocton Cnwll 4 G6
Brocton Staffs 46 C10
Brodick N Ayrs 80 E5
Brodie Moray 103 R4
Brodsworth Donc 57 R5
Brogaig Highld 100 d3
Brogborough C Beds 31 L5
Brokenborough Wilts 28 H10
Broken Cross Ches E 55 T12
Broken Cross Ches W 55 Q12

Column 6

Brokerswood Wilts 18 B10
Bromborough Wirral 54 J10
Brome Suffk 40 K5
Brome Street Suffk 41 L5
Bromeswell Suffk 41 P10
Bromfield Cumb 66 J3
Bromfield Shrops 35 L5
Bromford Birm 36 F2
Bromham Bed 38 F10
Bromham Wilts 18 E7
Bromley Barns 57 M7
Bromley Dudley 36 B3
Bromley Gt Lon 21 R9
Bromley Shrops 35 R1
Bromley Common Gt Lon 21 R9
Bromley Cross Bolton 55 R4
Bromley Cross Essex 23 R2
Bromley Green Kent 12 K8
Bromlow Shrops 44 H13
Brompton Medway 12 E2
Brompton N York 70 H13
Brompton-by-Sawdon N York 65 L3
Brompton-on-Swale N York 69 R13
Brompton Ralph Somset 16 E10
Brompton Regis Somset 16 C10
Bromsash Herefs 28 C3
Bromsberrow Gloucs 28 E1
Bromsberrow Heath Gloucs 28 E1
Bromsgrove Worcs 36 C6
Bromstead Heath Staffs 45 S10
Bromyard Herefs 35 Q9
Bromyard Downs Herefs 35 Q9
Bronaber Gwynd 43 P7
Broncroft Shrops 35 M3
Brongest Cerdgn 32 G11
Bronington Wrexhm 45 L6
Bronllys Powys 34 E13
Bronwydd Carmth 25 R5
Bronydd Powys 34 F12
Bronygarth Shrops 44 G6
Brook Carmth 25 N8
Brook Hants 8 K6
Brook Hants 9 L3
Brook IoW 9 M12
Brook Kent 13 L6
Brook Surrey 10 F2
Brook Surrey 20 G13
Brooke Norfk 41 P1
Brooke Rutlnd 48 C12
Brookenby Lincs 59 L7
Brook End Bed 38 G7
Brook End M Keyn 38 D11
Brook End Cambs 38 J6
Brookfield Rens 88 K13
Brookhampton Somset 17 R11
Brookhouse Lancs 61 U7
Brookhouse Rothm 57 R9
Brookhouse Green Ches E 55 T14
Brookland Kent 12 K10
Brooklands Traffd 55 S8
Brookmans Park Herts 31 S11
Brooks Powys 34 D1
Brooksby Leics 47 S11
Brooks End Kent 13 Q2
Brooks Green W Susx 10 J5
Brook Street Essex 22 E9
Brook Street Kent 12 K9
Brook Street Suffk 40 E11
Brook Street W Susx 11 N5
Brookthorpe Gloucs 28 F5
Brookville Norfk 50 B14
Brookwood Surrey 20 G11
Broom C Beds 31 Q4
Broom Rothm 57 P8
Broom Warwks 36 E10
Broom Hill Barns 57 N5
Broome Norfk 41 Q2
Broome Shrops 34 K5
Broome Worcs 36 B5
Broomedge Warrtn 55 R9
Broome Park Nthumb 77 N3
Broomer's Corner W Susx 10 J6
Broomershill W Susx 10 H6
Broomfield Essex 22 H5
Broomfield Kent 12 K4
Broomfield Kent 13 N3
Broomfield Somset 16 H10
Broomfields Shrops 44 K10
Broomfleet E R Yk 58 E1
Broom Green Norfk 50 G8
Broomhall W & M 20 G9
Broomhaugh Nthumb 77 L13
Broom Hill Dorset 8 F8
Broomhill Nthumb 77 Q5
Broomhill Cumb 67 L1
Broom Hill Worcs 36 B5
Broomley Nthumb 77 L13
Broompark Dur 69 S4
Brooms Green Gloucs 35 S14
Broomsthorpe Norfk 50 E8
Brora Highld 109 T3
Brotherlee Dur 69 L5
Brotherhouse Bar Lincs 49 L10
Brothertoft Lincs 49 L4
Brotherton N York 57 P1
Brotton R & Cl 71 L9
Broubster Highld 112 B4
Brough Cumb 68 G10
Brough Derbys 56 J10
Brough E R Yk 58 G1
Brough Highld 112 G2
Brough Notts 48 B2
Brough Shet 106 u6
Brough Shet 106 v4
Broughall Shrops 45 N4
Brough Lodge Shet 106 v4
Brough Sowerby Cumb 68 G10
Broughton Border 83 M11
Broughton Bucks 30 J10
Broughton Cambs 39 L5
Broughton Flints 54 H14
Broughton Hants 9 L2
Broughton Lancs 55 M1
Broughton M Keyn 30 J5
Broughton N Linc 58 G5
Broughton N York 62 J9
Broughton N York 64 H4
Broughton Nhants 38 B5
Broughton Oxon 37 M13
Broughton Salfd 55 T7
Broughton Staffs 45 T7
Broughton V Glam 26 G12
Broughton Astley Leics 37 P2
Broughton Beck Cumb 61 P3
Broughton Gifford Wilts 18 C8
Broughton Green Worcs 36 C8
Broughton Hackett Worcs 36 C10
Broughton-in-Furness Cumb 61 N2
Broughton Mains D & G 73 M10
Broughton Mills Cumb 61 M1
Broughton Moor Cumb 66 G5
Broughton Poggs Oxon 29 P7
Broughton Tower Cumb 61 N2
Broughtown Ork 106 v15
Broughty Ferry C Dund 91 P5
Brough with St Giles N York 69 R13
Brow End Cumb 61 N5
Browland Shet 106 s8
Brown Candover Hants 19 S13
Brown Edge Lancs 54 J4
Brown Edge Staffs 46 B3
Brown Heath Ches W 54 K13
Brownheath Shrops 45 L8
Brownhill Abers 105 N6
Brownhills Fife 91 R8
Brownhills Wsall 46 E13
Brownieside Nthumb 85 T14
Browninghill Green Hants 19 S9
Brown Lees Staffs 45 U2
Brownlow Heath Ches E 55 T14
Brownrigg Cumb 66 F8
Brownrigg Cumb 66 K4
Brown's Green Birm 36 D2
Brownsham Devon 14 F7
Brownshill Gloucs 28 G7
Brownston Devon 5 Q10
Brownstone Devon 5 T11
Browston Green Norfk 51 S13
Broxa N York 65 L1
Broxbourne Herts 31 U11
Broxburn E Loth 84 F3
Broxburn W Loth 82 K4
Broxfield Nthumb 77 R2
Broxted Essex 22 E2
Broxton Ches W 44 K3
Broxwood Herefs 34 J10
Broyle Side E Susx 11 Q8
Bruan Highld 112 H9
Bruar P & K 97 M10
Brucefield Highld 109 Q8
Bruchag Ag & B 88 C14
Bruera Ches W 54 K13

Column 7

Bruern Abbey Oxon 29 Q3
Bruichladdich Ag & B 78 D3
Bruisyard Suffk 41 P7
Bruisyard Street Suffk 41 P7
Brund Staffs 46 F1
Brundall Norfk 51 P12
Brundish Suffk 41 N7
Brundish Street Suffk 41 N6
Brunery Highld 93 S4
Brunnion Cnwll 2 F9
Brunshaw Lancs 62 H13
Brunswick Village N u Ty 77 Q11
Bruntcliffe Leeds 57 L1
Bruntingthorpe Leics 37 R3
Brunton Fife 91 M7
Brunton Nthumb 85 U14
Brunton Wilts 18 K9
Brushford Devon 15 R11
Brushford Somset 16 B11
Bruton Somset 17 S10
Bryan's Green Worcs 35 U7
Bryanston Dorset 8 B8
Bryant's Bottom Bucks 20 D3
Brydekirk D & G 75 N11
Brymbo Wrexhm 44 G3
Brympton Somset 17 P13
Bryn Carmth 26 A8
Bryn Ches W 55 N6
Bryn Neath 26 D9
Bryn Shrops 34 G4
Bryn Wigan 55 N6
Brynamman Carmth 26 C6
Brynberian Pembks 24 K2
Brynbryddan Neath 26 D9
Bryncethin Brdgnd 26 G11
Bryncir Gwynd 42 H4
Bryn-côch Neath 26 C8
Bryncroes Gwynd 42 D7
Bryncrug Gwynd 43 M12
Bryn Du IoA 52 D8
Bryn-Eden Gwynd 43 P8
Bryneglwys Denbgs 44 E4
Brynfields Wrexhm 44 H5
Brynford Flints 54 E12
Bryn Gates Wigan 55 N6
Bryn Golau Rhondd 26 J10
Bryngwran IoA 52 D7
Bryngwyn Mons 27 R6
Bryngwyn Powys 34 E11
Bryn-Henllan Pembks 24 H3
Brynhoffnant Cerdgn 32 F10
Bryning Lancs 61 S13
Brynithel Blae G 27 N6
Brynmawr Blae G 27 M5
Bryn-mawr Gwynd 42 D7
Brynmenyn Brdgnd 26 G10
Brynmill Swans 26 A9
Brynna Rhondd 26 H11
Bryn-penarth Powys 44 D13
Brynrefail Gwynd 52 J10
Brynrefail IoA 52 G5
Brynsadler Rhondd 26 K11
Bryn Saith Marchog Denbgs 44 C3
Brynsiencyn IoA 52 G9
Brynteg IoA 52 G6
Bryn-y-bal Flints 54 F14
Bryn-y-Maen Conwy 53 P7
Bryn-yr-Eos Wrexhm 44 G5
Buailntur Highld 100 c7
Buarth-draw Flints 54 E11
Bubbenhall Warwks 37 L6
Bubwith E R Yk 64 G12
Buccleuch Border 75 R3
Buchanan Smithy Stirlg 89 L6
Buchanhaven Abers 105 U6
Buchanty P & K 90 D6
Buchany Stirlg 89 R5
Buchlyvie Stirlg 89 M6
Buckabank Cumb 67 N3
Buckden Cambs 38 J7
Buckden N York 62 J4
Buckenham Norfk 51 Q13
Buckerell Devon 6 F4
Buckfast Devon 5 S8
Buckfastleigh Devon 5 S8
Buckhaven Fife 91 M12
Buckholm Border 84 D12
Buckholt Mons 27 U5
Buckhorn Weston Dorset 17 U12
Buckhurst Hill Essex 21 R4
Buckie Moray 104 E2
Buckingham Bucks 30 F6
Buckland Bucks 30 K10
Buckland Devon 5 R11
Buckland Gloucs 36 E13
Buckland Hants 9 L9
Buckland Herts 31 U6
Buckland Kent 13 R7
Buckland Oxon 29 R8
Buckland Surrey 21 M13
Buckland Brewer Devon 14 K8
Buckland Common Bucks 31 L11
Buckland Dinham Somset 17 U6
Buckland Filleigh Devon 15 L11
Buckland in the Moor Devon 5 S6
Buckland Monachorum Devon 5 M7
Buckland Newton Dorset 7 S3
Buckland Ripers Dorset 7 S8
Buckland St Mary Somset 16 H13
Buckland-Tout-Saints Devon 5 S11
Bucklebury W Berk 19 T6
Bucklers Hard Hants 9 N9
Bucklesham Suffk 41 M12
Buckley Flints 54 G14
Buckley Green Warwks 36 F7
Bucklow Hill Ches E 55 R10
Buckminster Leics 48 C9
Bucknall C Stke 46 B4
Bucknall Lincs 59 L13
Bucknell Oxon 30 B7
Bucknell Shrops 34 J6
Buckpool Moray 104 E2
Bucksburn C Aber 99 R2
Buck's Cross Devon 14 H8
Buckshaw Village Lancs 55 N2
Bucks Hill Herts 31 N12
Bucks Horn Oak Hants 10 C2
Buck's Mills Devon 14 H8
Buckton E R Yk 65 R5
Buckton Herefs 34 J6
Buckton Nthumb 85 R11
Buckworth Cambs 38 H5
Budby Notts 57 T13
Buddileigh Staffs 45 S3
Buddon Angus 91 R5
Budc Cnwll 14 F12
Budge's Shop Cnwll 4 J9
Budlake Devon 6 C4
Budle Nthumb 85 S11
Budleigh Salterton Devon 6 E8
Budlett's Common E Susx 11 R6
Budock Water Cnwll 2 K10
Buerton Ches E 45 Q5
Bugbrooke Nhants 37 S9
Bugford Devon 5 T7
Buglawton Ches E 56 C14
Bugle Cnwll 3 Q5
Bugthorpe E R Yk 64 G8
Buildwas Shrops 45 P13
Builth Road Powys 34 C10
Builth Wells Powys 34 C10
Bulbourne Herts 31 L10
Bulbridge Wilts 8 F2
Bulby Lincs 48 G9
Bulcote Notts 47 R5
Buldoo Highld 112 A3
Bulford Wilts 18 H12
Bulford Camp Wilts 18 J12
Bulkeley Ches E 45 M3
Bulkington Warwks 37 L3
Bulkington Wilts 18 D9
Bulkworthy Devon 14 J9
Bullamoor N York 70 D14
Bull Bay IoA 52 G3
Bullbrook Br For 20 E9
Bullen's Green Herts 31 R11
Bulley Gloucs 28 E4
Bullgill Cumb 66 G4
Bullingham Herefs 35 M13
Bullinghope Herefs 35 M13
Bullington Hants 19 Q12
Bullington Lincs 58 J11
Bull's Green Herts 31 S9
Bull's Green Norfk 41 R2
Bullwood Ag & B 88 E10
Bulmer Essex 40 E12
Bulmer N York 64 F6
Bulmer Tye Essex 40 E13
Bulphan Thurr 22 F10
Bulstone Devon 6 F7
Bulstrode Herts 31 M12
Bulverhythe E Susx 12 E14
Bulwark Abers 105 Q5
Bulwell C Nott 47 P4
Bulwick Nhants 48 D14
Bumble's Green Essex 22 B6
Bunacaimb Highld 100 f11
Bunarkaig Highld 101 T14

Column 8

Bunbury Ches E 45 N2
Bunbury Heath Ches E 45 N2
Bunchrew Highld 102 J6
Buncton W Susx 10 J7
Bundalloch Highld 101 M6
Bunessan Ag & B 92 K13
Bungay Suffk 41 Q3
Bunker's Hill Lincs 49 L3
Bunnahabhain Ag & B 86 G13
Bunny Notts 47 Q8
Buntait Highld 102 D9
Buntingford Herts 31 U7
Bunwell Norfk 40 K2
Bunwell Hill Norfk 40 K2
Burbage Derbys 56 F12
Burbage Leics 37 M2
Burbage Wilts 18 K8
Burchett's Green W & M 20 D6
Burcombe Wilts 8 F2
Burcot Oxon 19 S2
Burcote Shrops 35 R1
Burcott Bucks 30 H8
Burdale N York 64 K6
Bures Essex 40 F14
Burford Oxon 29 P5
Burford Shrops 35 N7
Burg Ag & B 92 K9
Burgates Hants 10 B5
Burge End Herts 31 Q6
Burgess Hill W Susx 11 M6
Burgh Suffk 41 M10
Burgh by Sands Cumb 75 R14
Burghclere Hants 19 Q8
Burghead Moray 103 T2
Burghfield W Berk 19 U7
Burghfield Common W Berk 19 U7
Burgh Heath Surrey 21 M11
Burgh Hill E Susx 12 D10
Burghill Herefs 35 L12
Burgh Island Devon 5 R11
Burgh le Marsh Lincs 59 T13
Burgh next Aylsham Norfk 51 M8
Burgh on Bain Lincs 59 M9
Burgh St Margaret Norfk 51 R11
Burgh St Peter Norfk 41 S2
Burghwallis Donc 57 R4
Burham Kent 12 D3
Buriton Hants 9 U5
Burland Ches E 45 P3
Burlawn Cnwll 3 P2
Burleigh Gloucs 28 G7
Burlescombe Devon 16 E13
Burleston Dorset 7 U5
Burlestone Devon 5 U11
Burley Hants 8 J8
Burley Rutlnd 48 C11
Burley Shrops 35 L4
Burleydam Ches E 45 P4
Burley Gate Herefs 35 N11
Burley in Wharfedale C Brad 63 P10
Burley Lawn Hants 8 J8
Burley Street Hants 8 J8
Burley Wood Head C Brad 63 P11
Burlingham Green Norfk 51 Q11
Burlington Shrops 45 S11
Burlton Shrops 45 L8
Burmarsh Kent 13 M9
Burmington Warwks 36 J13
Burn N York 57 T1
Burnage Manch 56 C8
Burnaston Derbys 46 J7
Burnbanks Cumb 67 R9
Burnbrae N Lans 82 F7
Burn Bridge N York 63 R9
Burnby E R Yk 64 K10
Burndell W Susx 10 F9
Burnden Bolton 55 R5
Burnedge Rochdl 56 D4
Burneside Cumb 67 R13
Burneston N York 63 S3
Burnett BaNES 17 S3
Burnfoot Border 75 S4
Burnfoot Border 75 T2
Burnfoot D & G 74 K7
Burnfoot D & G 75 R8
Burnfoot P & K 90 C10
Burngreave Sheff 57 N9
Burnham Bucks 20 F6
Burnham N Linc 58 H4
Burnham Deepdale Norfk 50 D5
Burnham Green Herts 31 S9
Burnham Market Norfk 50 D5
Burnham Norton Norfk 50 D5
Burnham-on-Crouch Essex 23 M8
Burnham-on-Sea Somset 16 K7
Burnham Overy Norfk 50 D5
Burnham Overy Staithe Norfk 50 D5
Burnham Thorpe Norfk 50 E5
Burnhaven Abers 105 U6
Burnhead D & G 74 G5
Burnhervie Abers 105 L12
Burnhill Green Staffs 45 S13
Burnhope Dur 69 R3
Burnhouse N Ayrs 81 M2
Burniston N York 65 N1
Burnley Lancs 62 G13
Burnmouth Border 85 M7
Burn Naze Lancs 61 R11
Burn of Cambus Stirlg 89 R5
Burnopfield Dur 69 R2
Burnrigg Cumb 67 Q1
Burnsall N York 63 L7
Burnside Angus 98 H12
Burnside Fife 90 J10
Burnside Moray 103 U2
Burnside W Loth 83 L3
Burnside of Duntrune Angus 91 P5
Burntcommon Surrey 20 H12
Burntheath Derbys 46 J7
Burnt Heath Essex 23 Q2
Burnt Hill W Berk 19 S6
Burnt Houses Dur 69 Q8
Burntisland Fife 83 M1
Burnt Oak E Susx 11 S5
Burnton E Ayrs 81 N11
Burntwood Staffs 46 E12
Burntwood Green Staffs 46 E12
Burnt Yates N York 63 R7
Burnworthy Somset 16 G13
Burpham Surrey 20 H12
Burpham W Susx 10 G9
Burradon N Tyne 77 Q11
Burradon Nthumb 76 K4
Burrafirth Shet 106 w2
Burras Cnwll 2 H10
Burraton Cnwll 5 L8
Burravoe Shet 106 v6
Burrells Cumb 68 E9
Burrelton P & K 90 K4
Burridge Devon 6 K5
Burridge Hants 9 Q6
Burrill N York 63 Q2
Burringham N Linc 58 D5
Burrington Devon 15 P9
Burrington Herefs 34 K6
Burrington N Som 17 N5
Burrough End Cambs 39 U9
Burrough Green Cambs 39 U9
Burrough on the Hill Leics 47 U11
Burrow Somset 16 C8
Burrow Somset 16 K12
Burrow Bridge Somset 16 K11
Burrowhill Surrey 20 G10
Burrows Cross Surrey 20 J13
Burry Swans 25 S11
Burry Port Carmth 25 S10
Burscough Lancs 54 K4
Burscough Bridge Lancs 54 K4
Bursea E R Yk 64 J13
Bursledon Hants 9 P7
Burslem C Stke 45 U4
Burstall Suffk 40 J12
Burstock Dorset 7 M4
Burston Norfk 40 K3
Burston Staffs 46 B7
Burstow Surrey 11 N2
Burstwick E R Yk 65 U14
Burtersett N York 62 J2
Burtholme Cumb 76 A13
Burthorpe Suffk 40 C8
Burthwaite Cumb 67 N3
Burtle Somset 17 L8
Burtoft Lincs 49 L6
Burton BCP 8 H9
Burton Ches W 54 G13
Burton Ches W 55 N14
Burton Pembks 24 G9
Burton Somset 16 F8
Burton Wilts 18 B5
Burton Wilts 17 U9
Burton Agnes E R Yk 65 Q7
Burton Bradstock Dorset 7 N7
Burton-by-Lincoln Lincs 58 F12
Burton Coggles Lincs 48 E8
Burton Dassett Warwks 37 L10
Burton End Essex 22 D3
Burton End Suffk 40 B12
Burton Fleming E R Yk 65 P5
Burton Green Warwks 36 J5
Burton Green Wrexhm 44 H2
Burton Hastings Warwks 37 L3
Burton-in-Kendal Cumb 61 U4
Burton in Lonsdale N York 62 C5
Burton Joyce Notts 47 R5
Burton Latimer Nhants 38 D5
Burton Lazars Leics 47 U11
Burton Leonard N York 63 S7
Burton on the Wolds Leics 47 R10
Burton Overy Leics 37 S1
Burton Pedwardine Lincs 48 H5
Burton Pidsea E R Yk 65 U13
Burton Salmon N York 57 P1
Burton's Green Essex 22 K2
Burton upon Stather N Linc 58 E3
Burton upon Trent Staffs 46 H9
Burton Waters Lincs 58 F12
Burtonwood Warrtn 55 N8
Burtonwood Services Warrtn 55 N8
Burwardsley Ches W 45 M2
Burwarton Shrops 35 P4
Burwash E Susx 12 C11
Burwash Common E Susx 11 U5
Burwash Weald E Susx 11 U5
Burwell Cambs 39 S7
Burwell Lincs 59 Q11
Burwen IoA 52 F3
Burwick Ork 106 t21
Bury Bury 55 S4
Bury Cambs 39 L4
Bury Somset 16 C11
Bury W Susx 10 G8
Burybank Staffs 45 U7
Bury End Bed 38 G11
Bury Green Herts 22 C3
Bury St Edmunds Suffk 40 E7
Burythorpe N York 64 H6
Busby E Rens 81 R1
Buscot Oxon 29 P8
Bush Abers 99 N9
Bush Cnwll 14 F12
Bushbury Wolves 46 B13
Bushby Leics 47 R13
Bush Green Norfk 41 L3
Bush Green Suffk 40 G10
Bushey Herts 31 N12
Bushey Heath Herts 21 L3
Bush Hill Park Gt Lon 21 P4
Bushley Worcs 35 U14
Bushley Green Worcs 35 U14
Bushmead Bed 38 H8
Bushmoor Shrops 34 K4
Bushton Wilts 18 G5
Bushy Common Norfk 50 G11
Busk Cumb 68 C4
Buslingthorpe Lincs 58 H9
Bussage Gloucs 28 G7
Bussex Somset 16 K9
Busta Shet 106 t7
Butcher's Cross E Susx 11 S6
Butcher's Pasture Essex 22 F3
Butchers Row Devon 15 L6
Butcombe N Som 17 P4
Bute Town Caerph 27 L6
Butleigh Somset 17 P10
Butleigh Wootton Somset 17 P9
Butlers Marston Warwks 36 K11
Butley Suffk 41 Q11
Butley High Corner Suffk 41 R12
Butterambe N York 64 F8
Buttercrambe N York 64 G8
Butterdean Border 84 K6
Butterknowle Dur 69 Q8
Butterleigh Devon 6 C3
Buttermere Cumb 66 J10
Buttermere Wilts 19 M8
Butters Green Staffs 45 T3
Buttershaw C Brad 63 N14
Butterstone P & K 90 F2
Butterton Staffs 45 T4
Butterton Staffs 46 E2
Butterwick Dur 70 E7
Butterwick Lincs 49 N4
Butterwick N York 64 H5
Butterwick N York 65 M4
Buttington Powys 44 F12
Buttonbridge Shrops 35 R5
Buttonoak Shrops 35 R5
Buttsash Hants 9 N8
Buttsbear Cross Cnwll 14 G12
Butt's Green Essex 22 H7
Buttsole Kent 13 Q5
Buxhall Suffk 40 H9
Buxted E Susx 11 R6
Buxton Derbys 56 F12
Buxton Norfk 51 M9
Buxton Heath Norfk 51 L9
Bwlch Powys 27 M3
Bwlchgwyn Wrexhm 44 G3
Bwlch-Llan Cerdgn 33 L9
Bwlchnewydd Carmth 25 P6
Bwlchtocyn Gwynd 42 F8
Bwlch-y-cibau Powys 44 E10
Bwlch-y-Ddar Powys 44 E9
Bwlch-y-ffridd Powys 34 C2
Bwlchyfadfa Cerdgn 32 H11
Bwlch-y-groes Pembks 25 M3
Bwlchymyrdd Swans 25 U11
Bwlch-y-sarnau Powys 34 C6
Byermoor Gatesd 77 P14
Byers Green Dur 69 S5
Byfield Nhants 37 P9
Byfleet Surrey 20 J10
Byford Herefs 34 J12
Bygrave Herts 31 S5
Byker N u Ty 77 R13
Bylane End Cnwll 4 G9
Bylchau Conwy 53 R10
Byley Ches W 55 S13
Bynea Carmth 25 U11
Byrness Nthumb 76 F4
Bystock Devon 6 E7
Bythorn Cambs 38 G5
Byton Herefs 34 J8
Bywell Nthumb 77 L13
Byworth W Susx 10 F6

Hackbridge Gt Lon 21 N9
Hackenthorpe Sheff 57 P10
Hackford Norfk 50 J13
Hackforth N York 69 R14
Hack Green Ches E 45 P4
Hackland Ork 106 s17
Hackleton Nhants 38 B9
Hacklinge Kent 13 R5
Hackman's Gate Worcs 35 U5
Hackness N York 65 M1
Hackness Somset 16 K7
Hackney Gt Lon 21 P6
Hackthorn Lincs 58 G10
Hackthorpe Cumb 67 R8
Hacton Gt Lon 22 E10
Hadden Border 84 K11
Haddenham Bucks 30 F11
Haddenham Cambs 39 Q5
Haddington E Loth 84 E4
Haddington Lincs 58 F14
Haddiscoe Norfk 41 R1
Haddo Abers 105 N8
Haddon Cambs 38 H2
Hade Edge Kirk 56 H6
Hadfield Derbys 56 F7
Hadham Cross Herts 22 B4
Hadham Ford Herts 22 B3
Hadleigh Essex 22 K10
Hadleigh Suffk 40 H12
Hadleigh Heath Suffk 40 G12
Hadley Worcs 35 U8
Hadley Wrekin 45 Q11
Hadley End Staffs 46 F9
Hadley Wood Gt Lon 21 N3
Hadlow Kent 12 B5
Hadlow Down E Susx 11 S6
Hadnall Shrops 45 M9
Hadrian's Wall 76 K12
Hadstock Essex 39 S12
Hadston Nthumb 77 R5
Hadzor Worcs 36 B8
Haffenden Quarter Kent 12 G7
Hafodunos Conwy 53 Q9
Hafod-y-bwch Wrexhm 44 H4
Hafod-y-coed Blae G 27 N7
Hafodyrynys Caerph 27 N8
Haggate Lancs 62 H12
Haggbeck Cumb 75 U11
Haggersta Shet 106 t9
Haggerston Nthumb 85 Q10
Haggington Hill Devon 15 N3
Haggs Falk 89 S10
Hagley Herefs 35 N12
Hagley Worcs 36 B4
Hagmore Green Suffk 40 G13
Hagnaby Lincs 59 P14
Hagnaby Lincs 59 S11
Hagworthingham Lincs 59 P13
Haigh Wigan 55 P5
Haighton Green Lancs 62 B13
Haile Cumb 66 F11
Hailes Gloucs 28 K1
Hailey Herts 31 U10
Hailey Oxon 19 T3
Hailey Oxon 29 S5
Hailsham E Susx 11 T9
Hail Weston Cambs 38 J8
Hainault Gt Lon 21 S4
Haine Kent 13 S2
Hainford Norfk 51 M10
Hainton Lincs 59 L10
Hainworth C Brad 63 M12
Haisthorpe E R Yk 65 Q7
Hakin Pembks 24 E9
Halam Notts 47 S3
Halbeath Fife 90 H14
Halberton Devon 6 D2
Halcro Highld 112 F4
Hale Cumb 61 U4
Hale Halton 55 L10
Hale Hants 8 H5
Hale Somset 17 T11
Hale Surrey 20 D13
Hale Traffd 55 S9
Hale Bank Halton 55 L10
Hale Barns Traffd 55 S9
Hale Green E Susx 11 T8
Hale Nook Lancs 61 R11
Hales Norfk 41 Q1
Hales Staffs 45 R7
Halesgate Lincs 49 M8
Hales Green Derbys 46 G5
Halesowen Dudley 36 C4
Hales Place Kent 13 M4
Hale Street Kent 12 C6
Halesville Essex 23 M9
Halesworth Suffk 41 Q5
Halewood Knows 55 L9
Halford Devon 5 U6
Halford Shrops 34 K4
Halford Warwks 36 J11
Halfpenny Cumb 61 U2
Halfpenny Green Staffs 35 T2
Halfpenny Houses N York 63 Q3
Halfway Carmth 26 A1
Halfway Carmth 33 R14
Halfway Sheff 57 P10
Halfway W Berk 19 P7
Halfway Bridge W Susx 10 E6
Halfway House Shrops 44 H11
Halfway Houses Kent 23 M13
Halifax Calder 56 G1
Halket E Ayrs 81 N2
Halkirk Highld 112 D5
Halkyn Flints 54 F12
Hall E Rens 81 N2
Hallam Fields Derbys 47 N6
Halland E Susx 11 R7
Hallaton Leics 37 U1
Hallatrow BaNES 17 R5
Hallbankgate Cumb 76 B14
Hallbeck Cumb 62 C2
Hall Cliffe Wakefd 57 L3
Hall Cross Lancs 61 S13
Hall Dunnerdale Cumb 66 K13
Hallen S Glos 27 U11
Hall End Bed 38 F11
Hall End C Beds 31 N5
Hallfield Gate Derbys 47 L2
Hallgarth Dur 70 D4
Hallglen Falk 82 G3
Hall Green Birm 36 F4
Hallin Highld 100 b4
Halling Medway 12 D3
Hallington Lincs 59 P9
Hallington Nthumb 76 K10
Halliwell Bolton 55 Q4
Halloughton Notts 47 S3
Hallow Worcs 35 T9
Hallow Heath Worcs 35 T9
Hallsands Devon 5 U13
Hall's Green Essex 22 B6
Hall's Green Herts 31 S7
Hallthwaites Cumb 61 M2
Hallworthy Cnwll 4 F3
Hallyne Border 83 N10
Halmer End Staffs 45 S4
Halmond's Frome Herefs 35 Q11
Halmore Gloucs 28 D7
Halnaker W Susx 10 E9
Halsall Lancs 54 J4
Halse Nhants 30 C4
Halse Somset 16 F11
Halsetown Cnwll 2 E9
Halsham E R Yk 59 N1
Halsinger Devon 15 M5
Halstead Essex 40 D14
Halstead Kent 21 S10
Halstead Leics 47 U12
Halstock Dorset 7 P3
Halsway Somset 16 F9
Haltcliff Bridge Cumb 67 N5
Haltham Lincs 59 M14
Haltoft End Lincs 49 N4
Halton Bucks 30 J11
Halton Halton 55 M10
Halton Lancs 61 U7
Halton Leeds 63 T13
Halton Nthumb 76 K12
Halton Wrexhm 44 H6
Halton East N York 63 L9
Halton Fenside Lincs 59 R14
Halton Gill N York 62 H4
Halton Green Lancs 61 U6
Halton Holegate Lincs 59 R13
Halton Lea Gate Nthumb 76 C14
Halton Quay Cnwll 5 L8
Halton Shields Nthumb 77 L12
Halton West N York 62 G9
Haltwhistle Nthumb 76 E13
Halvana Cnwll 4 G5
Halvergate Norfk 51 R12
Halwell Devon 5 T10
Halwill Devon 14 K13
Halwill Junction Devon 14 K12
Ham Devon 6 H4
Ham Gloucs 28 C8
Ham Gloucs 28 J3
Ham Gt Lon 21 L8
Ham Kent 13 R5
Ham Somset 16 J11
Ham Somset 17 T6
Ham Wilts 19 M8
Hambleden Bucks 20 C5
Hambledon Hants 9 S6
Hambledon Surrey 10 F3
Hamble-le-Rice Hants 9 P7
Hambleton Lancs 61 R11
Hambleton N York 64 D13
Hambleton Moss Side Lancs 61 R11
Hambridge Somset 17 L12
Hambrook S Glos 28 B12
Hambrook W Susx 10 B9
Ham Common Dorset 17 V11
Hameringham Lincs 59 P13
Hamerton Cambs 38 H5
Ham Green Herefs 35 S12
Ham Green Kent 12 F2
Ham Green Kent 12 G10
Ham Green N Som 27 U12
Ham Green Worcs 36 D8
Ham Hill Kent 12 C3
Hamilton S Lans 82 D7
Hamilton Services S Lans 82 D7
Hamlet Dorset 7 Q3
Hamlins E Susx 11 T9
Hammerpot W Susx 10 H9
Hammersmith Gt Lon 21 M7
Hammerwich Staffs 46 E12
Hammerwood E Susx 11 Q3
Hammond Street Herts 31 T12
Hammoon Dorset 7 V2
Hamnavoe Shet 106 t10
Hampden Park E Susx 11 U10
Hamperden End Essex 22 E1
Hampnett Gloucs 29 L4
Hampole Donc 57 R4
Hampreston Dorset 8 F9
Hampsfield Cumb 61 S3
Hampson Green Lancs 61 T9
Hampstead Gt Lon 21 N5
Hampstead Norreys W Berk 19 R5
Hampsthwaite N York 63 R8
Hampton C Pete 38 J2
Hampton Devon 6 J5
Hampton Gt Lon 20 K9
Hampton Kent 13 N2
Hampton Shrops 35 R3
Hampton Swindn 29 N9
Hampton Worcs 36 D12
Hampton Bishop Herefs 35 N13
Hampton Court Palace Gt Lon 21 L9
Hampton Fields Gloucs 28 G8
Hampton Green Ches W 45 M4
Hampton Heath Ches W 45 M4
Hampton-in-Arden Solhll 36 H4
Hampton Loade Shrops 35 R3
Hampton Lovett Worcs 35 U7
Hampton Lucy Warwks 36 J9
Hampton Magna Warwks 36 J7
Hampton on the Hill Warwks 36 J8
Hampton Poyle Oxon 30 B9
Hampton Wick Gt Lon 21 L9
Hamptworth Wilts 8 J5
Hamrow Norfk 50 F9
Hamsey E Susx 11 Q8
Hamsey Green Surrey 21 Q11
Hamstall Ridware Staffs 46 F10
Hamstead Birm 36 E2
Hamstead IoW 9 N10
Hamstead Marshall W Berk 19 P7
Hamsterley Dur 69 P6
Hamsterley Dur 69 P2
Hamstreet Kent 12 K9
Ham Street Somset 17 Q10
Hamwood N Som 17 L5
Hamworthy BCP 8 D10
Hanbury Staffs 46 G8
Hanbury Worcs 36 C8
Hanby Lincs 48 F7
Hanchet End Suffk 39 T11
Hanchurch Staffs 45 T5
Handa Island Highld 110 C7
Handale R & Cl 71 M9
Hand and Pen Devon 6 D5
Handbridge Ches W 54 K13
Handcross W Susx 11 M5
Handforth Ches E 56 C10
Hand Green Ches W 45 M1
Handley Ches W 45 L2
Handley Derbys 47 L1
Handley Green Essex 22 G7
Handsacre Staffs 46 E10
Handsworth Birm 36 D3
Handsworth Sheff 57 P9
Handy Cross Bucks 20 E4
Hanford C Stke 45 U5
Hanford Dorset 8 A6
Hanging Heaton Kirk 57 L2
Hanging Houghton Nhants 37 U6
Hanging Langford Wilts 18 F13
Hangleton Br & H 11 M9
Hangleton W Susx 10 H10
Hanham S Glos 17 S2
Hankelow Ches E 45 Q4
Hankerton Wilts 28 J9
Hankham E Susx 11 U9
Hanley C Stke 45 U4
Hanley Castle Worcs 35 T12
Hanley Child Worcs 35 Q7
Hanley Swan Worcs 35 T12
Hanley William Worcs 35 Q7
Hanlith N York 62 J7
Hanmer Wrexhm 45 L6
Hannaford Devon 15 P7
Hannah Lincs 59 S11
Hannington Hants 19 R9
Hannington Nhants 38 B6
Hannington Swindn 29 N9
Hannington Wick Swindn 29 N8
Hanscombe End C Beds 31 P6
Hanslope M Keyn 38 B11
Hanthorpe Lincs 48 G9
Hanwell Gt Lon 21 L7
Hanwell Oxon 37 M12
Hanwood Shrops 44 K12
Hanworth Gt Lon 20 K8
Hanworth Norfk 51 L6
Happendon S Lans 82 G12
Happendon Services S Lans 82 G12
Happisburgh Norfk 51 Q7
Happisburgh Common Norfk 51 Q8
Hapsford Ches W 55 L12
Hapton Lancs 62 F13
Hapton Norfk 41 L1
Harberton Devon 5 T9
Harbertonford Devon 5 T9
Harbledown Kent 13 M4
Harborne Birm 36 D4
Harborough Magna Warwks 37 N5
Harbottle Nthumb 76 J5
Harbourneford Devon 5 S8
Harbours Hill Worcs 36 C7
Harbridge Hants 8 G6
Harbridge Green Hants 8 G6
Harburn W Loth 83 L6
Harbury Warwks 37 L9
Harby Leics 47 T7
Harby Notts 58 E12
Harcombe Devon 6 A8
Harcombe Devon 6 H6
Harcombe Bottom Devon 6 K5
Harden C Brad 63 M12
Harden Wsall 46 D13
Hardendale Cumb 67 S10
Hardenhuish Wilts 18 D6
Hardgate Abers 99 P3
Hardgate D & G 74 F12
Hardgate N York 63 R7
Hardgate W Duns 89 M11
Hardham W Susx 10 G7
Hardingham Norfk 50 H13
Hardingstone Nhants 37 U9
Hardington Somset 17 T6
Hardington Mandeville Somset 7 P2
Hardington Marsh Somset 7 P3
Hardington Moor Somset 7 P2
Hardisworthy Devon 14 F8
Hardley Hants 9 N8
Hardley Street Norfk 51 Q13
Hardmead M Keyn 38 D11
Hardraw N York 62 H1
Hardsough Lancs 55 S2
Hardstoft Derbys 57 P14
Hardway Hants 9 S8
Hardway Somset 17 T10
Hardwick Bucks 30 H9
Hardwick Cambs 39 N9
Hardwick Nhants 38 B7
Hardwick Norfk 41 M3
Hardwick Oxon 29 S6
Hardwick Oxon 30 C7
Hardwick Rothm 57 Q9
Hardwick Wsall 46 E14
Hardwicke Gloucs 28 E5
Hardwicke Gloucs 28 H3
Hardwick Hall Derbys 57 Q14
Hardwick Village Notts 57 T11
Hardy's Green Essex 23 M3
Harebeating E Susx 11 T8
Hareby Lincs 59 P13
Hare Croft C Brad 63 M12
Harefield Gt Lon 20 J4
Hare Green Essex 23 R2
Hare Hatch Wokham 20 D7
Harehill Derbys 46 G6
Harehills Leeds 63 S13
Harehope Nthumb 77 M1
Harelaw Border 75 V2
Harelaw D & G 75 T10
Harelaw Dur 69 Q2
Hareplain Kent 12 F8
Haresceugh Cumb 68 D4
Harescombe Gloucs 28 F5
Haresfield Gloucs 28 F5
Harestock Hants 9 P2
Hare Street Essex 22 B6
Hare Street Essex 22 D7
Hare Street Herts 31 U7
Harewood Leeds 63 S10
Harewood End Herefs 27 U2
Harford Devon 5 Q9
Hargate Norfk 40 K2
Hargatewall Derbys 56 H11
Hargrave Ches W 45 L1
Hargrave Nhants 38 F6
Hargrave Suffk 40 C9
Harker Cumb 75 S13
Harkstead Suffk 41 L13
Harlaston Staffs 46 H11
Harlaxton Lincs 48 C7
Harlech Gwynd 43 L7
Harlech Castle Gwynd 43 L7
Harlescott Shrops 45 L10
Harlesden Gt Lon 21 M6
Harlesthorpe Derbys 57 Q11
Harleston Devon 5 T11
Harleston Norfk 41 N4
Harleston Suffk 40 H8
Harlestone Nhants 37 T8
Harle Syke Lancs 62 H12
Harley Rothm 57 N7
Harley Shrops 45 N13
Harlington C Beds 31 M6
Harlington Donc 57 Q6
Harlington Gt Lon 20 J7
Harlosh Highld 100 b5
Harlow Essex 22 B5
Harlow Carr RHS N York 63 R9
Harlow Hill Nthumb 77 M12
Harlthorpe E R Yk 64 G12
Harlton Cambs 39 N10
Harlyn Cnwll 3 M1
Harman's Cross Dorset 8 D12
Harmby N York 63 N2
Harmer Green Herts 31 S9
Harmer Hill Shrops 45 L9
Harmondsworth Gt Lon 20 J7
Harmston Lincs 48 E1
Harnage Shrops 45 N13
Harnham Nthumb 77 M9
Harnhill Gloucs 29 L7
Harold Hill Gt Lon 22 D9
Haroldston West Pembks 24 E7
Haroldswick Shet 106 w2
Harold Wood Gt Lon 22 E9
Harome N York 64 E3
Harpenden Herts 31 P10
Harpford Devon 6 E6
Harpham E R Yk 65 P7
Harpley Norfk 50 C8
Harpley Worcs 35 Q8
Harpole Nhants 37 S8
Harpsdale Highld 112 D5
Harpsden Oxon 20 C6
Harpswell Lincs 58 F9
Harpurhey Manch 55 T6
Harpur Hill Derbys 56 G12
Harraby Cumb 67 P2
Harracott Devon 15 N7
Harrapool Highld 100 f7
Harrietfield P & K 90 E6
Harrietsham Kent 12 G5
Harringay Gt Lon 21 P5
Harrington Cumb 66 E7
Harrington Lincs 59 Q12
Harrington Nhants 37 U4
Harringworth Nhants 38 D1
Harris W Isls 106 f9
Harriseahead Staffs 45 U2
Harriston Cumb 66 J4
Harrogate N York 63 S8
Harrold Bed 38 D9
Harrop Dale Oldham 56 F5
Harrow Gt Lon 21 L5
Harrowbarrow Cnwll 5 L7
Harrowden Bed 38 G11
Harrowgate Village Darltn 69 S9
Harrow Green Suffk 40 E10
Harrow Hill Gloucs 28 C4
Harrow on the Hill Gt Lon 21 L5
Harrow Weald Gt Lon 21 L4
Harston Cambs 39 P10
Harston Leics 48 B7
Harswell E R Yk 64 J11
Hart Hartpl 70 G5
Hartburn Nthumb 77 M8
Hartburn S on T 70 F9
Hartest Suffk 40 D10
Hartfield E Susx 11 R3
Hartford Cambs 39 L6
Hartford Ches W 55 P12
Hartford Somset 16 C11
Hartfordbridge Hants 20 C11
Hartford End Essex 22 G4
Hartforth N York 69 Q11
Hartgrove Dorset 8 A5
Harthill Ches W 45 M2
Harthill N Lans 82 H6
Harthill Rothm 57 Q10
Harthope D & G 75 M3
Hartington Derbys 46 F1
Hartington Nthumb 77 L8
Hartland Devon 14 G8
Hartland Quay Devon 14 F8
Hartlebury Worcs 35 T6
Hartlepool Hartpl 70 H6
Hartley Cumb 68 G11
Hartley Kent 12 E9
Hartley Kent 12 B2
Hartley Nthumb 77 S10
Hartley Green Kent 12 B2
Hartley Green Staffs 46 C8
Hartley Wespall Hants 19 U9
Hartley Wintney Hants 20 C11
Hartlip Kent 12 F3
Hartoft End N York 71 M14
Harton N York 64 G7
Harton S Tyne 77 T12
Harton Shrops 35 L3
Hartpury Gloucs 28 E2
Hartshead Kirk 56 J2
Hartshead Moor Services Calder 56 J2
Hartshill C Stke 45 U4
Hartshill Warwks 36 K2
Hartshorne Derbys 46 K9
Hartside Nthumb 85 N14
Hartsop Cumb 67 P10
Hart Station Hartpl 70 G5
Hartswell Somset 16 E11
Hartwell Nhants 37 U10
Hartwith N York 63 Q7
Hartwood N Lans 82 F7
Hartwoodmyres Border 84 C14
Harvel Kent 12 C3
Harvington Worcs 36 E11
Harvington Worcs 35 U6
Harwell Notts 57 U8
Harwell Oxon 29 U10
Harwich Essex 23 U1
Harwood Bolton 55 R4
Harwood Dur 68 H6
Harwood Nthumb 76 K7
Harwood Dale N York 71 S13
Harwood Lee Bolton 55 R4
Harworth Notts 57 U8
Hasbury Dudley 36 C4
Hascombe Surrey 10 G3
Haselbech Nhants 37 T5
Haselbury Plucknett Somset 7 N2
Haseley Warwks 36 H7
Haseley Green Warwks 36 H7
Haseley Knob Warwks 36 H6
Haselor Warwks 36 F9
Hasfield Gloucs 28 F2
Hasguard Pembks 24 E9
Haskayne Lancs 54 J5
Hasketon Suffk 41 M10
Hasland Derbys 57 N13
Haslemere Surrey 10 E4
Haslingden Lancs 55 S1
Haslingfield Cambs 39 P10
Haslington Ches E 45 R2
Hassall Ches E 45 S2
Hassall Green Ches E 45 S2
Hassell Street Kent 13 L6
Hassingham Norfk 51 Q12
Hassness Cumb 66 J9
Hassocks W Susx 11 N7
Hassop Derbys 56 K12
Haste Hill Surrey 10 E4
Haster Highld 112 H6
Hasthorpe Lincs 59 S13
Hastingleigh Kent 13 L6
Hastings E Susx 12 F14
Hastings Somset 16 K13
Hastingwood Essex 22 C6
Hastoe Herts 30 K11
Haswell Dur 70 E4
Haswell Plough Dur 70 E4
Hatch C Beds 38 J11
Hatch Beauchamp Somset 16 K12
Hatch End Bed 38 G8
Hatch End Gt Lon 20 K4
Hatchet Gate Hants 9 M8
Hatching Green Herts 31 P10
Hatchmere Ches W 55 N12
Hatcliffe NE Lin 59 M6
Hatfield Donc 57 U5
Hatfield Herefs 35 N9
Hatfield Herts 31 R11
Hatfield Worcs 35 U10
Hatfield Broad Oak Essex 22 D4
Hatfield Heath Essex 22 D4
Hatfield Peverel Essex 22 J5
Hatfield Woodhouse Donc 57 U5
Hatford Oxon 29 R8
Hatherden Hants 19 M10
Hatherleigh Devon 15 M12
Hathern Leics 47 P9
Hatherop Gloucs 29 N6
Hathersage Derbys 56 K10
Hathersage Booths Derbys 56 K10
Hatherton Ches E 45 Q4
Hatherton Staffs 46 C11
Hatley St George Cambs 39 L10
Hatt Cnwll 5 L8
Hattersley Tamesd 56 E8
Hattingley Hants 19 T13
Hatton Abers 105 T8
Hatton Angus 91 Q3
Hatton Derbys 46 H7
Hatton Gt Lon 20 J7
Hatton Lincs 59 L11
Hatton Shrops 35 L2
Hatton Warrtn 55 N10
Hatton Warwks 36 H7
Hatton Heath Ches W 45 L1
Hatton of Fintray Abers 105 N12
Haugh E Ayrs 81 P7
Haugh Lincs 59 R11
Haugh Rochdl 56 D4
Haugham Lincs 59 P10
Haughhead E Duns 89 P10
Haugh Head Nthumb 85 Q13
Haughley Suffk 40 H8
Haughley Green Suffk 40 H8
Haugh of Glass Moray 104 E8
Haugh of Urr D & G 74 F12
Haugh of Kinnaird Angus 99 L12
Haughton Ches E 45 N2
Haughton Notts 57 U12
Haughton Powys 44 H10
Haughton Shrops 35 Q1
Haughton Shrops 44 J8
Haughton Shrops 45 N11
Haughton Shrops 45 P13
Haughton Staffs 45 U9
Haughton Green Tamesd 56 D8
Haughton le Skerne Darltn 70 D9
Haultwick Herts 31 T8
Haunton Staffs 46 H11
Hautes Croix Jersey 7 d1
Hauxton Cambs 39 P10
Havannah Ches E 56 C14
Havant Hants 9 U7
Haven Herefs 34 K10
Haven Bank Lincs 48 K3
Haven Side E R Yk 65 R14
Havenstreet IoW 9 R10
Havercroft Wakefd 57 N4
Haverfordwest Pembks 24 G7
Haverhill Suffk 39 U11
Haverigg Cumb 61 M4
Havering-atte-Bower Gt Lon 22 D9
Haversham M Keyn 30 H4
Haverthwaite Cumb 61 Q3
Haverton Hill S on T 70 G8
Havyatt N Som 17 N4
Havyatt Somset 17 P9
Hawarden Flints 54 H13
Hawbridge Worcs 36 B11
Hawbush Green Essex 22 J3
Hawcoat Cumb 61 N5
Hawen Cerdgn 32 F11
Hawes N York 62 H2
Hawe's Green Norfk 51 M14
Hawford Worcs 35 T8
Hawick Border 75 V3
Hawkchurch Devon 6 K4
Hawkedon Suffk 40 C10
Hawkenbury Kent 12 F7
Hawkeridge Wilts 18 C10
Hawkerland Devon 6 E7
Hawker's Cove Cnwll 3 N1
Hawkesbury S Glos 28 E10
Hawkesbury Warwks 37 L4
Hawkesbury Upton S Glos 28 E10
Hawkes End Covtry 36 J4
Hawk Green Stockp 56 E9
Hawkhill Nthumb 77 Q3
Hawkhurst Kent 12 E9
Hawkhurst Common E Susx 11 S7
Hawkinge Kent 13 P7
Hawkley Hants 9 U3
Hawkridge Somset 15 U7
Hawksdale Cumb 67 N3
Hawkshaw Bury 55 S3
Hawkshead Cumb 67 N13
Hawkshead Hill Cumb 67 M13
Hawksland S Lans 82 F11
Hawkspur Green Essex 22 G1
Hawkstone Shrops 45 N7
Hawkswick N York 62 K5
Hawksworth Leeds 63 P11
Hawksworth Notts 47 U5
Hawkwell Essex 23 L9
Hawkwell Nthumb 77 M11
Hawley Hants 20 E11
Hawley Kent 22 D13
Hawling Gloucs 29 L3
Hawnby N York 64 C1
Haworth C Brad 63 L12
Hawridge Bucks 30 K11
Hawstead Suffk 40 E9
Hawstead Green Suffk 40 E9
Hawthorn Dur 70 F3
Hawthorn Hants 9 T2
Hawthorn Rhondd 26 K10
Hawthorn Hill Br For 20 E8
Hawthorn Hill Lincs 48 K2
Hawthorpe Lincs 48 F8
Hawton Notts 47 U3
Haxby C York 64 E8
Haxby Gates C York 64 E8
Haxey N Linc 58 C7
Haxey Carr N Linc 58 C6
Haxted Surrey 11 Q2
Haxton Wilts 18 H11
Hay Cnwll 3 P2
Hay Cnwll 3 Q3
Haydock St Hel 55 N7
Haydon BaNES 17 S6
Haydon Dorset 17 S13
Haydon Somset 16 K12
Haydon Bridge Nthumb 76 H13
Haydon Wick Swindn 29 M10
Haye Cnwll 4 K6
Hayes Gt Lon 20 J6
Hayes Gt Lon 21 R9
Hayes End Gt Lon 20 J6
Hayfield Ag & B 94 F13
Hayfield Derbys 56 F9
Hayfield Green Donc 57 U7
Haygate Wrekin 45 P11
Hay Green Norfk 49 R10
Hayhillock Angus 91 R3
Hayle Cnwll 2 F9
Hayle Port Cnwll 2 F9
Hayley Green Dudley 36 B4
Hayling Island Hants 9 U8
Haymoor Green Ches E 45 Q3
Hayne Devon 5 U3
Hayne Devon 16 C13
Haynes C Beds 31 N4
Haynes Church End C Beds 31 N4
Haynes West End C Beds 31 N4
Hay-on-Wye Powys 34 F12
Hayscastle Pembks 24 E5
Hayscastle Cross Pembks 24 F5
Haysden Kent 21 U13
Hay Street Herts 31 U7
Hayton Cumb 66 H4
Hayton Cumb 67 R1
Hayton E R Yk 64 J10
Hayton Notts 58 B10
Hayton's Bent Shrops 35 M4
Haytor Vale Devon 5 T5
Haytown Devon 14 J10
Haywards Heath W Susx 11 N6
Haywood Donc 57 S4
Haywood Herefs 27 T1
Haywood Oaks Notts 47 R2
Hazards Green E Susx 12 C13
Hazelbank S Lans 82 F9
Hazelbury Bryan Dorset 7 T3
Hazeleigh Essex 22 K7
Hazeley Hants 20 B11
Hazelford Notts 47 T4
Hazel Grove Stockp 56 D9
Hazelhurst Tamesd 56 E6
Hazelslade Staffs 46 D11
Hazel Street Kent 12 C8
Hazel Stub Suffk 39 U12
Hazelton Walls Fife 91 M7
Hazelwood Derbys 46 K4
Hazlemere Bucks 20 E3
Hazlerigg N u Ty 77 Q11
Hazles Staffs 46 D4
Hazleton Gloucs 29 L4
Heacham Norfk 49 U6
Headbourne Worthy Hants 9 P2
Headbrook Herefs 34 G9
Headcorn Kent 12 F7
Headingley Leeds 63 R12
Headington Oxon 30 B11
Headlam Dur 69 Q9
Headlesscross N Lans 82 H7
Headless Cross Worcs 36 D7
Headley Hants 10 C3
Headley Hants 19 R8
Headley Surrey 21 M12
Headley Down Hants 10 C3
Headley Heath Worcs 36 E5
Headon Devon 14 J12
Headon Notts 58 B11
Heads Nook Cumb 67 Q1
Heage Derbys 47 L3
Healaugh N York 64 C10
Healaugh N York 69 M13
Heald Green Stockp 55 T9
Heale Devon 15 P3
Heale Somset 16 H12
Heale Somset 17 L11
Healey N York 63 P3
Healey Nthumb 77 L14
Healey Rochdl 56 C3
Healey Wakefd 57 L3
Healeyfield Dur 69 N3
Healing NE Lin 59 M4
Heamoor Cnwll 2 D10
Heanor Derbys 47 M4
Heanton Punchardon Devon 15 M5
Heapham Lincs 58 E9
Hearn Hants 10 C3
Heart of Scotland Services N Lans 82 H6
Hearts Delight Kent 12 G3
Heasley Mill Devon 15 R6
Heaste Highld 100 f8
Heath Derbys 57 P13
Heath Wakefd 57 N2
Heath and Reach C Beds 30 K7
Heath Common W Susx 10 J7
Heathcote Derbys 46 F1
Heathcote Shrops 45 Q8
Heath End Bucks 20 E3
Heath End Hants 19 Q8
Heath End Leics 47 L9
Heath End Warwks 36 H8
Heather Leics 47 L11
Heathfield Cambs 39 Q11
Heathfield Devon 5 U5
Heathfield E Susx 11 T6
Heathfield N York 63 N6
Heathfield Somset 16 G11
Heathfield Village Oxon 30 B9
Heath Green Worcs 36 E6
Heath Hall D & G 74 J10
Heath Hayes & Wimblebury Staffs 46 D11
Heath Hill Shrops 45 S11
Heath House Somset 17 M7
Heathrow Airport Gt Lon 20 J7
Heathstock Devon 6 H3
Heathton Shrops 35 T2
Heath Town Wolves 46 B14
Heathwaite N York 70 G12
Heatley Staffs 46 E8
Heatley Warrtn 55 R9
Heaton Bolton 55 Q5
Heaton C Brad 63 N12
Heaton Lancs 61 S7
Heaton N u Ty 77 R12
Heaton Staffs 56 E14
Heaton Chapel Stockp 56 C8
Heaton Mersey Stockp 56 C8
Heaton Norris Stockp 56 C8
Heaton's Bridge Lancs 54 K4
Heaverham Kent 21 U11
Heaviley Stockp 56 D9
Heavitree Devon 6 B6
Hebburn S Tyne 77 S13
Hebden N York 63 L7
Hebden Bridge Calder 56 E1
Hebden Green Ches W 55 P13
Hebing End Herts 31 T8
Hebron Carmth 25 L5
Hebron IoA 52 G6
Hebron Nthumb 77 P8
Heckfield Hants 20 B10
Heckfield Green Suffk 41 L5
Heckfordbridge Essex 23 M3
Heckington Lincs 48 H5
Heckmondwike Kirk 56 K2
Heddington Wilts 18 E7
Heddon-on-the-Wall Nthumb 77 N12
Hedenham Norfk 41 P2
Hedge End Hants 9 P6
Hedgerley Bucks 20 G5
Hedgerley Green Bucks 20 G5
Hedging Somset 16 K11
Hedley on the Hill Nthumb 77 M14
Hednesford Staffs 46 C10
Hedon E R Yk 65 R14
Hedsor Bucks 20 F5
Heeley Sheff 57 N10
Hegdon Hill Herefs 35 N10
Heglibister Shet 106 t8
Heighington Darltn 69 R8
Heighington Lincs 58 H13
Heightington Worcs 35 S6
Heiton Border 84 J12
Hele Devon 5 Q2
Hele Devon 6 C4
Hele Devon 15 M3
Hele Somset 16 G12
Helebridge Cnwll 14 F12
Hele Lane Devon 15 S11
Helensburgh Ag & B 88 G9
Helenton S Ayrs 81 M6
Helford Cnwll 2 K11
Helford Passage Cnwll 2 K11
Helhoughton Norfk 50 E8
Helions Bumpstead Essex 39 U12
Hellaby Rothm 57 R8
Helland Cnwll 3 R2
Hellandbridge Cnwll 3 R2
Hell Corner W Berk 19 N8
Hellescott Cnwll 4 H3
Hellesdon Norfk 51 M11
Hellesveor Cnwll 2 E8
Hellidon Nhants 37 P9
Hellifield N York 62 H8
Hellingly E Susx 11 T8
Hellington Norfk 51 P13
Helm Nthumb 77 P6
Helmdon Nhants 30 C4
Helme Kirk 56 G4
Helmingham Suffk 41 L9
Helmington Row Dur 69 Q5
Helmsdale Highld 112 B13
Helmshore Lancs 55 S2
Helmsley N York 64 E3
Helperby N York 63 U6
Helperthorpe N York 65 L5
Helpringham Lincs 48 H5
Helpston C Pete 48 H12
Helsby Ches W 55 L11
Helsey Lincs 59 T12
Helston Cnwll 2 H11
Helstone Cnwll 4 D4
Helton Cumb 67 R8
Helwith N York 69 N12
Helwith Bridge N York 62 G6
Hemblington Norfk 51 P11
Hembridge Somset 17 Q9
Hemel Hempstead Herts 31 N11
Hemerdon Devon 5 P9
Hemingbrough N York 64 F13
Hemingby Lincs 59 M12
Hemingfield Barns 57 N6
Hemingford Abbots Cambs 39 L6
Hemingford Grey Cambs 39 L6
Hemingstone Suffk 40 K10
Hemington Leics 47 N8
Hemington Nhants 38 G3
Hemington Somset 17 T6
Hemley Suffk 41 N12
Hemlington Middsb 70 H10
Hempholme E R Yk 65 P10
Hempnall Norfk 41 M2
Hempnall Green Norfk 41 M2
Hemprigs Moray 103 T3
Hempstead Essex 39 T13
Hempstead Medway 12 E3
Hempstead Norfk 50 K6
Hempstead Norfk 51 R8
Hempsted Gloucs 28 F4
Hempton Norfk 50 F8
Hempton Oxon 29 T1
Hemsby Norfk 51 S10
Hemswell Lincs 58 F8
Hemswell Cliff Lincs 58 F9
Hemsworth Wakefd 57 P4
Hemyock Devon 6 F2
Henbury Bristl 27 V12
Henbury Ches E 56 C12
Hendham Devon 5 S10
Hendomen Powys 34 F1
Hendon Gt Lon 21 M5
Hendon Sundld 70 F1
Hendra Cnwll 2 J9
Hendra Cnwll 3 Q1
Hendre Brdgnd 26 G11
Hendre Flints 54 E13
Hendy Carmth 25 U10
Heneglwys IoA 52 F7
Henfield W Susx 11 L7
Henford Devon 4 K2
Henfynyw Cerdgn 32 J8
Henghurst Kent 12 J8
Hengoed Caerph 27 M9
Hengoed Powys 34 F10
Hengoed Shrops 44 G7
Hengrave Suffk 40 D7
Henham Essex 22 D2
Henhurst Powys 44 D12
Henlade Somset 16 J12
Henley Dorset 7 S4
Henley Gloucs 28 H4
Henley Shrops 35 L3
Henley Shrops 35 N5
Henley Somset 17 M10
Henley Suffk 41 L10
Henley W Susx 10 D5
Henley Green Covtry 37 L4
Henley-in-Arden Warwks 36 G7
Henley-on-Thames Oxon 20 C6
Henley Park Surrey 20 F12
Henley's Down E Susx 12 D13
Henley Street Kent 12 C2
Henllan Cerdgn 32 G12
Henllan Denbgs 53 T9
Henllan Amgoed Carmth 25 L7
Henllys Torfn 27 P9
Henlow C Beds 31 Q5
Hennock Devon 5 U4
Henny Street Essex 40 E13
Henryd Conwy 53 N8
Henry's Moat (Castell Hendre) Pembks 24 H5
Hensall N York 57 S2
Henshaw Nthumb 76 F13
Hensingham Cumb 66 E9
Henstead Suffk 41 S3
Hensting Hants 9 P4
Henstridge Somset 17 T13
Henstridge Ash Somset 17 T12
Henstridge Marsh Somset 17 T12
Henton Oxon 30 G12
Henton Somset 17 N7
Henwick Worcs 35 T9
Henwood Cnwll 4 H6
Henwood Oxon 29 U7
Heolgerrig Myr Td 26 J6
Heol-las Swans 26 B8
Heol Senni Powys 26 G3
Heol-y-Cyw Brdgnd 26 G11
Hepburn Nthumb 85 R14
Hepple Nthumb 76 K5
Hepscott Nthumb 77 Q9
Heptonstall Calder 62 K14
Hepworth Kirk 56 J5
Hepworth Suffk 40 G6
Herbrandston Pembks 24 E9
Hereford Herefs 35 M13
Hereson Kent 13 S2
Heribusta Highld 100 c2
Heriot Border 83 T8
Hermiston C Edin 83 N4
Hermitage Border 75 V6
Hermitage Dorset 7 R3
Hermitage W Berk 19 R6
Hermitage W Susx 10 B9
Hermit Hill Barns 57 M6
Hermon Carmth 25 Q4
Hermon IoA 52 E9
Hermon Pembks 25 M4
Herne Kent 13 N2
Herne Bay Kent 13 N2
Herne Common Kent 13 N2
Herne Hill Gt Lon 21 P8
Herne Pound Kent 12 C5
Herner Devon 15 N7
Hernhill Kent 13 L3
Herodsfoot Cnwll 4 G8
Heronden Kent 13 Q5
Herongate Essex 22 F9
Heronsford S Ayrs 72 E3
Heronsgate Herts 20 H4
Herriard Hants 19 U11
Herringfleet Suffk 41 S1
Herring's Green Bed 31 N4
Herringswell Suffk 40 B6
Herringthorpe Rothm 57 P8
Herrington Sundld 70 D2
Hersden Kent 13 P3
Hersham Cnwll 14 G11
Hersham Surrey 20 K10
Herstmonceux E Susx 11 U8
Herston Dorset 8 E13
Herston Ork 106 t20
Hertford Herts 31 T10
Hertford Heath Herts 31 U10
Hertingfordbury Herts 31 T10
Hesketh Bank Lancs 54 K2
Hesketh Lane Lancs 62 C11
Hesket Newmarket Cumb 67 M5
Heskin Green Lancs 55 M3
Hesleden Dur 70 F5
Hesleden N York 62 H5
Hesley Donc 57 U8
Hesleyside Nthumb 76 G9
Heslington C York 64 E9
Hessay C York 64 C9
Hessenford Cnwll 4 J9
Hessett Suffk 40 F8
Hessle E R Yk 58 H1
Hessle Wakefd 57 P3
Hest Bank Lancs 61 T6
Hestley Green Suffk 40 K7
Heston Gt Lon 20 K7
Heston Services Gt Lon 20 K7
Hestwall Ork 106 r18
Heswall Wirral 54 G10
Hethe Oxon 30 C7
Hethersett Norfk 51 L13
Hethersgill Cumb 75 U12
Hetherside Cumb 75 T12
Hetherson Green Ches W 45 M3
Hethpool Nthumb 85 N13
Hett Dur 69 S5
Hetton N York 62 K8
Hetton-le-Hole Sundld 70 E3
Hetton Steads Nthumb 85 Q11
Heugh Nthumb 77 M11
Heughhead Abers 104 D13
Heugh Head Border 85 M6
Heveningham Suffk 41 P6
Hever Kent 21 S13
Heversham Cumb 61 T3
Hevingham Norfk 51 L9
Hewas Water Cnwll 3 P7
Hewelsfield Gloucs 27 V7
Hewenden C Brad 63 M12
Hewish N Som 17 M4
Hewish Somset 7 M3
Hewood Dorset 7 L4
Hexham Nthumb 76 J13
Hextable Kent 22 D13
Hexthorpe Donc 57 S6
Hexton Herts 31 P6
Hexworthy Cnwll 4 K4
Hexworthy Devon 5 R6
Hey Lancs 62 H11
Heybridge Essex 22 F9
Heybridge Essex 22 L6
Heybridge Basin Essex 22 L6
Heybrook Bay Devon 5 M11
Heydon Cambs 39 P12
Heydon Norfk 50 K8
Heydour Lincs 48 F6
Hey Houses Lancs 54 H1
Heylipoll Ag & B 92 B10
Heylor Shet 106 s5
Heyrod Tamesd 56 E7
Heysham Lancs 61 S7
Heyshaw N York 63 P7
Heyshott W Susx 10 D7
Heyside Oldham 56 D5
Heytesbury Wilts 18 D12
Heythrop Oxon 29 S2
Heywood Rochdl 56 C4
Heywood Wilts 18 C10
Hibaldstow N Linc 58 G6
Hickleton Donc 57 Q5
Hickling Norfk 51 R9
Hickling Notts 47 S8
Hickling Green Norfk 51 R9
Hickling Heath Norfk 51 R9
Hickling Pastures Notts 47 S8
Hickmans Green Kent 13 L4
Hicks Forstal Kent 13 N3
Hickstead W Susx 11 M6
Hidcote Bartrim Gloucs 36 G12
Hidcote Boyce Gloucs 36 G12
High Ackworth Wakefd 57 P3
Higham Barns 57 M5
Higham Derbys 47 L2
Higham Kent 12 B6
Higham Kent 22 H13
Higham Lancs 62 G12
Higham Suffk 40 B7
Higham Suffk 40 H13
Higham Dykes Nthumb 77 N10
Higham Ferrers Nhants 38 E7
Higham Gobion C Beds 31 P6
Higham Hill Gt Lon 21 Q4
Higham on the Hill Leics 37 L1
Highampton Devon 15 L12
Highams Park Gt Lon 21 Q4
High Angerton Nthumb 77 M8
High Ardwell D & G 72 D10
High Auldgirth D & G 74 H8
High Bankhill Cumb 67 S4
High Beach Essex 21 Q3
High Bentham N York 62 D6
High Bewaldeth Cumb 66 K6
High Bickington Devon 15 P8
High Biggins Cumb 62 C4
High Birkwith N York 62 G4
High Blantyre S Lans 82 C7
High Bonnybridge Falk 82 G3
High Borrans Cumb 67 P12
High Bradley N York 63 L10
High Bray Devon 15 Q6
Highbridge Hants 9 P4
Highbridge Somset 16 K7
Highbrook W Susx 11 P4
High Brooms Kent 11 T2
High Bullen Devon 15 M8
Highburton Kirk 56 J4
Highbury Gt Lon 21 P5
Highbury Somset 17 S7
High Buston Nthumb 77 Q4
High Callerton Nthumb 77 P11
High Casterton Cumb 62 C4
High Catton E R Yk 64 G9
Highclere Hants 19 P8
Highcliffe BCP 8 J10
High Close Dur 69 Q9
High Cogges Oxon 29 S6
High Common Norfk 50 G12
High Coniscliffe Darltn 69 R9
High Crosby Cumb 75 U14
High Cross Cnwll 2 J11
High Cross E Ayrs 81 N3
High Cross Hants 9 U3
High Cross Herts 31 U9
Highcross Lancs 61 Q12
High Cross W Susx 11 L7
High Cross Warwks 36 H7
High Drummore D & G 72 E12
High Dubmire Sundld 70 D3
High Easter Essex 22 F5
High Eggborough N York 57 S2
High Ellington N York 63 P3
Higher Alham Somset 17 S8
Higher Ansty Dorset 7 U4
Higher Ballam Lancs 61 R13
Higher Bartle Lancs 61 U13
Higher Berry End C Beds 31 L6
Higher Bockhampton Dorset 7 T6
Higher Brixham Torbay 6 B14
Higher Burrowton Devon 6 D5
Higher Burwardsley Ches W 45 M2
High Ercall Wrekin 45 N10
Higher Chillington Somset 7 L2
Higher Clovelly Devon 14 H8
Highercombe Somset 16 B10
Higher Coombe Dorset 7 P6
Higher Disley Ches E 56 E10
Higher Folds Wigan 55 Q6
Higherford Lancs 62 H11
Higher Gabwell Devon 6 B11
Higher Halstock Leigh Dorset 7 P3
Higher Harpers Lancs 62 G12
Higher Heysham Lancs 61 S7
Higher Hurdsfield Ches E 56 D12
Higher Irlam Salfd 55 R8
Higher Kingcombe Dorset 7 P5
Higher Kinnerton Flints 44 H1
Higher Marston Ches W 55 Q11
Higher Muddiford Devon 15 N5
Higher Nyland Dorset 17 T12
Higher Ogden Rochdl 56 E4
Higher Pentire Cnwll 2 H11
Higher Penwortham Lancs 61 U14
Higher Prestacott Devon 14 J13
Higher Studfold N York 62 G5
Higher Town Cnwll 3 Q4
Higher Town Cnwll 3 Q4
Higher Town IoS 2 c1
Higher Tregantle Cnwll 5 L10
Higher Walton Lancs 55 N1
Higher Walton Warrtn 55 N9
Higher Wambrook Somset 6 J3
Higher Waterston Dorset 7 T5
Higher Whatcombe Dorset 8 A8
Higher Wheelton Lancs 55 P2
Higher Whitley Ches W 55 P10
Higher Wincham Ches W 55 Q11
Higher Wraxhall Dorset 7 Q4
Higher Wych Ches W 45 L5
High Etherley Dur 69 Q7
High Ferry Lincs 49 N4
Highfield E R Yk 64 G12
Highfield Gatesd 77 N14
Highfield N Ayrs 81 L2
Highfields Donc 57 R5
High Flats Kirk 56 K5
High Garrett Essex 22 J2
Highgate E Susx 11 Q4
Highgate Gt Lon 21 N5
Highgate Kent 12 E9
High Grange Dur 69 Q6
High Grantley N York 63 Q6
High Green Cumb 67 P12
High Green Kirk 56 K4
High Green Norfk 41 L2
High Green Norfk 50 K12
High Green Sheff 57 M7
High Green Shrops 35 R4
High Green Suffk 40 E8
High Green Worcs 35 U11
Highgreen Manor Nthumb 76 H6
High Halden Kent 12 G8
High Halstow Medway 22 J12
High Ham Somset 17 M10
High Harrington Cumb 66 F8
High Harrogate N York 63 S8
High Haswell Dur 70 E4
High Hatton Shrops 45 P9
High Hauxley Nthumb 77 R5
High Hawsker N York 71 R11
High Hesket Cumb 67 Q4
High Hoyland Barns 57 L5
High Hunsley E R Yk 65 M12
High Hurstwood E Susx 11 R5
High Hutton N York 64 H6
High Ireby Cumb 66 K5
High Kelling Norfk 50 K5
High Kilburn N York 64 C4
High Killerby N York 65 P3
High Knipe Cumb 67 R9
High Lands Dur 69 P7
Highlane Ches E 56 C13
Highlane Derbys 57 P10
High Lane Stockp 56 E9
High Lanes Cnwll 2 F9
High Laver Essex 22 D6
Highlaws Cumb 66 H3
Highleadon Gloucs 28 E3
High Legh Ches E 55 R10
Highleigh W Susx 10 C11
High Leven S on T 70 G10
Highley Shrops 35 R4
High Littleton BaNES 17 R5
High Lorton Cumb 66 J7
High Marishes N York 64 J4
High Marnham Notts 58 D12
High Melton Donc 57 R6
High Mickley Nthumb 77 M13
Highmoor Cumb 67 L3
Highmoor Oxon 20 B6
Highmoor Cross Oxon 20 B6
Highmoor Hill Mons 27 T10
High Moorsley Sundld 70 D3
Highnam Gloucs 28 E4
Highnam Green Gloucs 28 E4
High Newport Sundld 70 E2
High Newton Cumb 61 S3
High Nibthwaite Cumb 61 P2
High Offley Staffs 45 S8
High Ongar Essex 22 E7
High Onn Staffs 45 T10
High Park Corner Essex 23 P4
High Pennyvenie E Ayrs 81 P12
High Post Wilts 18 H13
Highridge N Som 17 Q3
High Roding Essex 22 F4
High Row Cumb 67 M5
High Row Cumb 67 N8
High Salter Lancs 62 C7
High Salvington W Susx 10 J9
High Scales Cumb 66 J3
High Seaton Cumb 66 F6
High Shaw N York 62 H1
High Side Cumb 66 K6
High Spen Gatesd 77 N14
Highstead Kent 13 P2
Highsted Kent 12 H3
High Stoop Dur 69 P4
High Street Cnwll 3 P6
High Street Kent 12 D9
High Street Suffk 40 E11
High Street Suffk 41 R6
High Street Suffk 41 R9
Highstreet Green Essex 40 C14
Highstreet Green Surrey 10 F4
Hightae D & G 75 L10
Highter's Heath Birm 36 E5
High Throston Hartpl 70 G6
Hightown Ches E 45 U1
Hightown Hants 8 H8
Hightown Sefton 54 H6
High Town Staffs 46 C11
Hightown Green Suffk 40 G9
High Toynton Lincs 59 N13
High Trewhitt Nthumb 77 L4
High Urpeth Dur 69 R2
High Valleyfield Fife 82 K1
High Warden Nthumb 76 J12
Highway Herefs 35 L11
Highway Wilts 18 F6
Highweek Devon 5 U6
High Westwood Dur 69 P1
Highwood Essex 22 F7
Highwood Staffs 46 E7
Highwood Hill Gt Lon 21 M4
High Woolaston Gloucs 28 A8
High Worsall N York 70 E11
Highworth Swindn 29 P9
High Wray Cumb 67 N13
High Wych Herts 22 C5
High Wycombe Bucks 20 E4
Hilborough Norfk 50 D13
Hilcote Derbys 47 N2
Hilcott Wilts 18 H9
Hildenborough Kent 21 U13
Hilden Park Kent 21 U13
Hildersham Cambs 39 R11
Hilderstone Staffs 46 C7
Hilderthorpe E R Yk 65 R6
Hilfield Dorset 7 R3
Hilgay Norfk 49 T14
Hill S Glos 28 B8
Hill Warwks 37 N7
Hillam N York 64 C14
Hillbeck Cumb 68 G9
Hillborough Kent 13 P2
Hill Brow Hants 10 B5
Hillbutts Dorset 8 D8
Hill Chorlton Staffs 45 S6
Hillclifflane Derbys 46 J4
Hill Common Norfk 51 R9
Hill Common Somset 16 F11
Hill Deverill Wilts 18 C12
Hilldyke Lincs 49 M4
Hill End Dur 69 M5
Hill End Fife 83 M2
Hill End Fife 90 F12
Hill End Gloucs 35 U13
Hillend Mdloth 83 Q5
Hillend N Lans 82 F5
Hillend Swans 25 R12
Hillersland Gloucs 27 V5
Hillerton Devon 15 R13
Hillesden Bucks 30 E7
Hillesley Gloucs 28 E10
Hillfarrance Somset 16 G12
Hill Green Kent 12 F3
Hillgrove W Susx 10 E5
Hillhampton Herefs 35 N11
Hillhead Abers 104 H8
Hillhead Devon 6 B14
Hill Head Hants 9 Q8
Hillhead S Lans 82 J10
Hillhead of Cocklaw Abers 105 T7
Hilliard's Cross Staffs 46 G11
Hilliclay Highld 112 E3
Hillingdon Gt Lon 20 J6
Hillington C Glas 89 M13
Hillington Norfk 50 B8
Hillis Corner IoW 9 P10
Hillmorton Warwks 37 P6
Hillock Vale Lancs 62 F14
Hill of Beath Fife 90 J13
Hill of Fearn Highld 109 Q9
Hillowton D & G 74 E13
Hillpool Worcs 35 U5
Hillpound Hants 9 R6
Hill Ridware Staffs 46 E10
Hillside Abers 99 S4
Hillside Angus 99 N11
Hillside Devon 5 S8
Hill Side Kirk 56 J3
Hill Side Worcs 35 S8
Hills Town Derbys 57 Q13
Hillstreet Hants 9 L5
Hillswick Shet 106 s6
Hill Top Dur 69 L8
Hill Top Hants 9 N8
Hill Top Kirk 56 H4
Hill Top Rothm 57 N8
Hill Top Sandw 36 C2
Hill Top Wakefd 57 M3
Hillwell Shet 106 t12
Hilmarton Wilts 18 F5
Hilperton Wilts 18 C9
Hilperton Marsh Wilts 18 C9
Hilsea C Port 9 T8
Hilston E R Yk 65 T13
Hiltingbury Hants 9 N4
Hilton Border 85 M8
Hilton Cambs 39 L7
Hilton Cumb 68 F8
Hilton Derbys 46 H7
Hilton Dorset 7 U4
Hilton Dur 69 Q8
Hilton Highld 109 R9
Hilton S on T 70 G10
Hilton Shrops 35 S1
Hilton Park Services Staffs 46 C13
Himbleton Worcs 36 B9
Himley Staffs 35 U2
Hincaster Cumb 61 U3
Hinchley Wood Surrey 21 L9
Hinckley Leics 37 M2
Hinderclay Suffk 40 H6
Hinderwell N York 71 N9
Hindford Shrops 44 H7
Hindhead Surrey 10 D3
Hindhead Tunnel Surrey 10 D3
Hindle Fold Lancs 62 E13
Hindley Nthumb 77 L14
Hindley Wigan 55 P6
Hindley Green Wigan 55 P6
Hindlip Worcs 35 U9
Hindolveston Norfk 50 H8
Hindon Wilts 8 C2
Hindringham Norfk 50 G6
Hingham Norfk 50 H13
Hinksford Staffs 35 U3
Hinstock Shrops 45 Q8
Hintlesham Suffk 40 J12
Hinton Gloucs 28 C7
Hinton Hants 8 J9
Hinton Herefs 34 H13
Hinton S Glos 28 D12
Hinton Shrops 44 K12
Hinton Shrops 35 Q4
Hinton Admiral Hants 8 J9
Hinton Ampner Hants 9 S3
Hinton Blewett BaNES 17 Q5
Hinton Charterhouse BaNES 17 U5
Hinton Green Worcs 36 D12
Hinton-in-the-Hedges Nhants 30 C5
Hinton Marsh Hants 9 R3
Hinton Martell Dorset 8 E7
Hinton on the Green Worcs 36 D12
Hinton Parva Swindn 29 P11
Hinton St George Somset 7 M2
Hinton St Mary Dorset 17 U13
Hinton Waldrist Oxon 29 S8
Hints Shrops 35 P6
Hints Staffs 46 G13
Hinwick Bed 38 D8
Hinxhill Kent 13 K7
Hinxton Cambs 39 Q11
Hinxworth Herts 31 R4
Hipperholme Calder 56 H1
Hipsburn Nthumb 77 Q3
Hipswell N York 69 Q13
Hirn Abers 99 N3
Hirnant Powys 44 B9
Hirst Nthumb 77 R8
Hirst Courtney N York 57 T2
Hirwaen Denbgs 44 D1
Hirwaun Rhondd 26 H6
Hiscott Devon 15 M7
Histon Cambs 39 P8
Hitcham Suffk 40 G10
Hitcham Causeway Suffk 40 G10
Hitcham Street Suffk 40 G10
Hitchin Herts 31 Q7

Hither Green – Kimmerston 133

Hither Green Gt Lon 21 Q8
Hittisleigh Devon 15 R13
Hive E R Yk 64 J13
Hixon Staffs 46 D8
Hoaden Kent 13 Q4
Hoar Cross Staffs 46 F9
Hoarwithy Herefs 27 U2
Hoath Kent 13 P3
Hoathly Kent 12 C8
Hobarris Shrops 34 H5
Hobbles Green Suffk 40 B10
Hobbs Cross Essex 21 S3
Hobbs Cross Essex 22 C5
Hobkirk Border 76 B3
Hobland Hall Norfk 51 T13
Hobsick Notts 47 N4
Hobson Dur 69 Q1
Hoby Leics 47 S10
Hoccombe Somset 16 F11
Hockering Norfk 50 J11
Hockerton Notts 47 T2
Hockley Ches E 56 D10
Hockley Covtry 36 J5
Hockley Essex 22 K9
Hockley Staffs 46 H13
Hockley Heath Solhll 36 G6
Hockliffe C Beds 31 L7
Hockwold cum Wilton Norfk 40 B3
Hockworthy Devon 16 D13
Hoddesdon Herts 31 U11
Hoddlesden Bl w D 55 R2
Hoddom Cross D & G 75 N11
Hoddom Mains D & G 75 N11
Hodgehill Ches E 55 T13
Hodgeston Pembks 24 H11
Hodnet Shrops 45 P8
Hodsock Notts 57 T9
Hodsoll Street Kent 12 B3
Hodson Swindn 18 J4
Hodthorpe Derbys 57 R11
Hoe Hants 9 R5
Hoe Norfk 50 G10
Hoe Benham W Berk 19 P7
Hoe Gate Hants 9 S6
Hoff Cumb 68 E9
Hogben's Hill Kent 12 K4
Hoggards Green Suffk 40 E9
Hoggeston Bucks 30 H8
Hoggrill's End Warwks 36 H2
Hog Hill E Susx 12 G12
Hoghton Lancs 55 P1
Hoghton Bottoms Lancs 55 P1
Hognaston Derbys 46 H3
Hogsthorpe Lincs 59 T12
Holbeach Lincs 49 N9
Holbeach Bank Lincs 49 N8
Holbeach Clough Lincs 49 N8
Holbeach Drove Lincs 49 M11
Holbeach Hurn Lincs 49 N8
Holbeach St Johns Lincs 49 N10
Holbeach St Mark's Lincs 49 N7
Holbeach St Matthew Lincs 49 P7
Holbeck Notts 57 R12
Holbeck Woodhouse Notts 57 R12
Holberrow Green Worcs 36 D9
Holbeton Devon 5 Q10
Holborn Gt Lon 21 P6
Holborough Kent 12 D3
Holbrook Derbys 47 L5
Holbrook Sheff 57 P10
Holbrook Suffk 41 L13
Holbrook Moor Derbys 47 L4
Holbrooks Covtry 36 K4
Holburn Nthumb 85 Q11
Holbury Hants 9 N8
Holcombe Devon 6 C10
Holcombe Somset 17 S7
Holcombe Rogus Devon 16 E13
Holcot Nhants 37 U7
Holden Lancs 62 F10
Holdenby Nhants 37 S7
Holden Gate Calder 56 C2
Holder's Green Essex 22 F2
Holdgate Shrops 35 N3
Holdingham Lincs 48 G4
Holditch Dorset 6 K4
Holdsworth Calder 63 M14
Holehouse Derbys 56 F8
Hole-in-the-Wall Herefs 28 B2
Holemoor Devon 14 K11
Hole Street W Susx 10 J8
Holford Somset 16 G8
Holgate C York 64 D9
Holker Cumb 61 R4
Holkham Norfk 50 E5
Hollacombe Devon 14 J12
Holland Fen Lincs 48 K4
Holland Lees Lancs 55 M5
Holland-on-Sea Essex 23 S4
Hollandstoun Ork 106 w14
Hollee D & G 75 Q12
Hollesley Suffk 41 Q12
Hollicombe Torbay 6 A12
Hollingbourne Kent 12 F4
Hollingbury Br & H 11 N9
Hollingdon Bucks 30 J7
Hollingrove E Susx 12 C11
Hollingthorpe Leeds 63 T13
Hollington Derbys 46 H6
Hollington Staffs 46 E6
Hollingworth Tamesd 56 F7
Hollins Bury 55 T5
Hollins Derbys 57 M12
Hollins Staffs 46 C4
Hollinsclough Staffs 56 G13
Hollins End Sheff 57 N10
Hollins Green Warrtn 55 Q8
Hollins Lane Lancs 61 T9
Hollinswood Wrekin 45 R12
Hollinwood Shrops 45 M6
Hollocombe Devon 15 P10
Holloway Derbys 46 K2
Holloway Gt Lon 21 P5
Holloway Wilts 8 B2
Hollowell Nhants 37 S6
Hollowmoor Heath Ches W 55 L13
Hollows D & G 75 S10
Hollybush Caerph 27 M7
Hollybush E Ayrs 81 M9
Hollybush Herefs 35 S13
Holly End Norfk 49 Q12
Holly Green Worcs 35 U12
Hollyhurst Ches E 45 N5
Hollym E R Yk 59 P1
Hollywood Worcs 36 E5
Holmbridge Kirk 56 H5
Holmbury St Mary Surrey 10 J2
Holmbush Cnwll 3 Q6
Holmcroft Staffs 46 B9
Holme Cambs 38 J3
Holme Cumb 61 U4
Holme Kirk 56 H5
Holme N Linc 58 F5
Holme N York 63 T3
Holme Notts 48 B2
Holme Chapel Lancs 62 H14
Holme Green N York 64 D11
Holme Hale Norfk 50 E12
Holme Lacy Herefs 35 N13
Holme Marsh Herefs 34 H10
Holme next the Sea Norfk 50 B5
Holme on the Wolds E R Yk 65 M10
Holme Pierrepont Notts 47 R6
Holmer Herefs 35 M12
Holmer Green Bucks 20 F3
Holme St Cuthbert Cumb 66 H3
Holmes Chapel Ches E 55 S13
Holmesfield Derbys 57 M11
Holmes Hill E Susx 11 S8
Holmeswood Lancs 54 K3
Holmethorpe Surrey 21 N12
Holme upon Spalding Moor E R Yk 64 J12
Holmewood Derbys 57 P13
Holmfield Calder 63 M14
Holmfirth Kirk 56 H5
Holmhead E Ayrs 81 R8
Holmpton E R Yk 59 Q2
Holmrook Cumb 66 G13
Holmshurst E Susx 12 B10
Holmside Dur 69 R3
Holmwrangle Cumb 67 R3
Holne Devon 5 S7
Holnest Dorset 7 S3
Holnicote Somset 16 B7
Holsworthy Devon 14 H12
Holsworthy Beacon Devon 14 J11
Holt Dorset 8 E8
Holt Norfk 50 J6
Holt Wilts 18 C8
Holt Worcs 35 T8
Holt Wrexhm 44 K3
Holtby C York 64 F9
Holt End Worcs 36 E7
Holt Fleet Worcs 35 T8
Holt Green Lancs 54 J5
Holt Heath Dorset 8 F8
Holt Heath Worcs 35 T8
Holton Oxon 30 D11
Holton Somset 17 S11
Holton Suffk 41 R5
Holton cum Beckering Lincs 58 K10
Holton Heath Dorset 8 C10
Holton Hill E Susx 12 C10
Holton le Clay Lincs 59 N6
Holton le Moor Lincs 58 J7
Holton St Mary Suffk 40 J13
Holt Street Kent 13 Q5
Holtye E Susx 11 R3
Holway Flints 54 E11
Holwell Dorset 7 S2
Holwell Herts 31 Q6
Holwell Leics 47 T9
Holwell Oxon 29 P6
Holwick Dur 68 K7
Holworth Dorset 7 U8
Holybourne Hants 10 A2
Holy Cross Worcs 36 B5
Holyfield Essex 31 U12
Holyhead IoA 52 B6
Holy Island IoA 52 C6
Holy Island Nthumb 85 S10
Holy Island Nthumb 85 S10
Holymoorside Derbys 57 M13
Holyport W & M 20 E7
Holystone Nthumb 76 K5
Holytown N Lans 82 E6
Holywell C Beds 31 M9
Holywell Cambs 39 M6
Holywell Cnwll 2 K5
Holywell Dorset 7 Q4
Holywell Flints 54 E11
Holywell Nthumb 77 S11
Holywell Warwks 36 H7
Holywell Green Calder 56 G3
Holywell Lake Somset 16 F12
Holywell Row Suffk 40 B5
Holywood D & G 74 H9
Holywood Village D & G 74 J10
Homer Shrops 45 P13
Homer Green Sefton 54 H6
Homersfield Suffk 41 N3
Homescales Cumb 62 B2
Hom Green Herefs 28 A3
Homington Wilts 8 G3
Honeyborough Pembks 24 F9
Honeybourne Worcs 36 F12
Honeychurch Devon 15 P12
Honey Hill Kent 13 M3
Honeystreet Wilts 18 H8
Honey Tye Suffk 40 G13
Honiley Warwks 36 H6
Honing Norfk 51 P8
Honingham Norfk 50 K11
Honington Lincs 48 D5
Honington Suffk 40 F6
Honington Warwks 36 J12
Honiton Devon 6 G4
Honley Kirk 56 H4
Honnington Wrekin 45 R10
Hoo Kent 13 Q3
Hoobrook Worcs 35 T6
Hood Green Barns 57 M6
Hood Hill Rothm 57 N7
Hooe C Plym 5 N10
Hooe E Susx 12 C13
Hoo End Herts 31 Q8
Hoo Green Ches E 55 R10
Hoohill Bpool 61 Q12
Hook Cambs 39 P2
Hook Devon 6 K3
Hook E R Yk 58 C1
Hook Gt Lon 21 L10
Hook Hants 9 Q7
Hook Hants 20 B12
Hook Pembks 24 G8
Hook Wilts 29 L11
Hook-a-Gate Shrops 45 L12
Hook Bank Worcs 35 T12
Hooke Dorset 7 P4
Hook End Essex 22 E7
Hookgate Staffs 45 R6
Hook Green Kent 12 C8
Hook Green Kent 22 F13
Hook Norton Oxon 37 L14
Hook Street Gloucs 28 C8
Hook Street Wilts 29 L11
Hookway Devon 15 U13
Hookwood Surrey 11 M2
Hooley Surrey 21 N11
Hooley Bridge Rochdl 56 C4
Hoo Meavy Devon 5 N7
Hoo St Werburgh Medway 22 J13
Hooton Ches W 54 J11
Hooton Levitt Rothm 57 R8
Hooton Pagnell Donc 57 Q5
Hooton Roberts Rothm 57 Q7
Hopcrofts Holt Oxon 29 U2
Hope Derbys 56 J10
Hope Devon 5 R12
Hope Flints 44 H2
Hope Powys 44 G12
Hope Shrops 44 H13
Hope Staffs 46 F3
Hope Bagot Shrops 35 N6
Hope Bowdler Shrops 35 L2
Hope End Green Essex 22 E3
Hopehouse Border 75 Q2
Hopeman Moray 103 T2
Hope Mansell Herefs 28 B4
Hopesay Shrops 34 J4
Hopetown Wakefd 57 N2
Hope under Dinmore Herefs 35 M10
Hopgrove C York 64 E9
Hopperton N York 63 U8
Hop Pole Lincs 48 J11
Hopsford Warwks 37 M4
Hopstone Shrops 35 S2
Hopton Derbys 46 J3
Hopton Shrops 44 J9
Hopton Staffs 46 B8
Hopton Suffk 40 G5
Hopton Cangeford Shrops 35 M4
Hopton Castle Shrops 34 J5
Hoptonheath Shrops 34 J5
Hopton on Sea Norfk 51 T14
Hopton Wafers Shrops 35 P5
Hopwas Staffs 46 G13
Hopwood Rochdl 56 C5
Hopwood Worcs 36 D5
Hopwood Park Services Worcs 36 D6
Horam E Susx 11 T7
Horbling Lincs 48 H6
Horbury Wakefd 57 L3
Horcott Gloucs 29 N7
Horden Dur 70 F4
Horderley Shrops 34 K3
Hordle Hants 8 K9
Hordley Shrops 44 J7
Horeb Carmth 25 S9
Horeb Cerdgn 32 G12
Horfield Bristl 28 A12
Horham Suffk 41 M6
Horkesley Heath Essex 23 N2
Horkstow N Linc 58 G3
Horley Oxon 37 M12
Horley Surrey 11 M2
Hornblotton Green Somset 17 Q10
Hornby Lancs 62 B6
Hornby N York 69 R14
Hornby N York 70 E11
Horncastle Lincs 59 N13
Hornchurch Gt Lon 22 D10
Horncliffe Nthumb 85 N9
Horndean Border 85 N9
Horndean Hants 9 U6
Horndon Devon 5 N4
Horndon on the Hill Thurr 22 G11
Horne Surrey 11 N2
Horner Somset 16 B7
Horne Row Essex 22 J7
Horners Green Suffk 40 G12
Horney Common E Susx 11 R5
Horn Hill Bucks 20 H4
Horning Norfk 51 P10
Horninghold Leics 38 B1
Horninglow Staffs 46 H8
Horningsea Cambs 39 Q8
Horningsham Wilts 18 B12
Horningtoft Norfk 50 F9
Horningtops Cnwll 4 H8
Hornsbury Somset 6 K2
Hornsby Cumb 67 R2
Hornsbygate Cumb 67 R2
Horns Cross Devon 14 J8
Horns Cross E Susx 12 F11
Hornsea E R Yk 65 R10
Hornsey Gt Lon 21 P5
Horn's Green Gt Lon 21 S11
Horn Street Kent 13 N8
Hornton Oxon 37 L11
Horpit Swindn 29 P11
Horra Shet 106 u4
Horrabridge Devon 5 N7
Horringer Suffk 40 D8
Horringford IoW 9 Q11
Horrocks Fold Bolton 55 R4
Horrocksford Lancs 62 F11
Horsacott Devon 15 M6
Horsebridge Devon 5 L5
Horsebridge E Susx 11 T8
Horsebridge Hants 9 L2
Horsebridge Shrops 44 J12
Horsebridge Staffs 46 C3
Horsebrook Staffs 45 U11
Horsecastle N Som 17 M3
Horsedown Cnwll 2 G10
Horsehay Wrekin 45 Q12
Horseheath Cambs 39 T11
Horsehouse N York 63 L3
Horsell Surrey 20 G11
Horseman's Green Wrexhm 44 K5
Horsenden Bucks 30 G12
Horsey Norfk 51 S9
Horsey Somset 16 K9
Horsey Corner Norfk 51 S9
Horsford Norfk 51 L10
Horsforth Leeds 63 Q12
Horsham W Susx 10 K4
Horsham Worcs 35 R9
Horsham St Faith Norfk 51 M10
Horsington Lincs 59 L13
Horsington Somset 17 T12
Horsley Derbys 47 L5
Horsley Gloucs 28 F8
Horsley Nthumb 76 G6
Horsley Nthumb 77 M12
Horsley Cross Essex 23 R2
Horsleycross Street Essex 23 R2
Horsley-Gate Derbys 57 M11
Horsleyhill Border 76 A2
Horsley's Green Bucks 20 C4
Horsley Woodhouse Derbys 47 L5
Horsmonden Kent 12 D7
Horspath Oxon 30 C11
Horstead Norfk 51 N10
Horsted Keynes W Susx 11 P5
Horton Bucks 30 K9
Horton Dorset 8 E7
Horton Lancs 62 H9
Horton Nhants 38 B10
Horton S Glos 28 E11
Horton Shrops 45 L8
Horton Somset 6 K2
Horton Staffs 46 B2
Horton Surrey 21 L10
Horton Swans 25 S13
Horton W & M 20 H7
Horton Wilts 18 F8
Horton Wrekin 45 Q11
Horton Cross Somset 16 K13
Horton-cum-Studley Oxon 30 C10
Horton Green Ches W 45 L4
Horton Heath Hants 9 P5
Horton-in-Ribblesdale N York 62 G5
Horton Kirby Kent 21 U9
Horwich Bolton 55 P4
Horwich End Derbys 56 F10
Horwood Devon 15 M7
Hoscar Lancs 55 L4
Hoscote Border 75 S3
Hose Leics 47 T8
Hosey Hill Kent 21 S12
Hosh P & K 90 C7
Hoswick Shet 106 u11
Hotham E R Yk 64 K13
Hothfield Kent 12 J7
Hoton Leics 47 Q9
Hott Nthumb 76 F8
Hough Ches E 45 R3
Hough Ches E 56 C11
Hougham Lincs 48 C5
Hough End Leeds 63 Q13
Hough Green Halton 55 L9
Hough-on-the-Hill Lincs 48 D4
Houghton Cambs 39 L6
Houghton Cumb 75 T14
Houghton Hants 9 L2
Houghton Nthumb 77 N12
Houghton Pembks 24 G9
Houghton W Susx 10 G8
Houghton Conquest C Beds 31 M4
Houghton Gate Dur 70 D2
Houghton Green E Susx 12 H11
Houghton Green Warrtn 55 P8
Houghton le Side Darltn 69 R8
Houghton-le-Spring Sundld 70 D3
Houghton on the Hill Leics 47 S13
Houghton Regis C Beds 31 M8
Houghton St Giles Norfk 50 F6
Hound Green Hants 20 B11
Houndslow Border 84 G9
Houndsmoor Somset 16 F11
Houndwood Border 85 L6
Hounslow Gt Lon 20 K7
Househill Highld 103 N4
Houses Hill Kirk 56 J3
Housieside Abers 105 P10
Houston Rens 88 K12
Houstry Highld 112 E10
Houton Ork 106 s19
Hove Br & H 11 M10
Hove Edge Calder 56 H2
Hoveringham Notts 47 S4
Hoveton Norfk 51 P10
Hovingham N York 64 F4
Howbrook Barns 57 M7
How Caple Herefs 28 B1
Howden E R Yk 64 G14
Howden-le-Wear Dur 69 Q6
Howe Highld 112 H4
Howe IoM 60 b9
Howe N York 63 T3
Howe Norfk 51 N14
Howe Bridge Wigan 55 Q6
Howe Green Essex 22 H7
Howegreen Essex 22 K7
Howell Lincs 48 H4
How End C Beds 31 M4
Howe of Teuchar Abers 105 M6
Howes D & G 75 N12
Howe Street Essex 22 G5
Howe Street Essex 39 U14
Howey Powys 34 C9
Howgate Cumb 66 E8
Howgate Mdloth 83 P7
Howgill Lancs 62 G10
Howick Nthumb 77 R2
Howle Wrekin 45 Q9
Howle Hill Herefs 28 B3
Howlett End Essex 39 S14
Howley Somset 6 J3
How Mill Cumb 67 R1
Howmore W Isls 106 c15
Hownam Border 76 F2
Howrigg Cumb 67 M3
Howsham N Linc 58 H6
Howsham N York 64 G7
Howtel Nthumb 85 M12
Howt Green Kent 12 G2
Howton Herefs 27 S2
Howtown Cumb 67 P9
How Wood Herts 31 P12
Howwood Rens 88 J13
Hoxa Ork 106 t20
Hoxne Suffk 41 L5
Hoy Ork 106 r20
Hoylake Wirral 54 F9
Hoyland Barns 57 N6
Hoyland Common Barns 57 N6
Hoylandswaine Barns 57 L6
Hoyle W Susx 10 E7
Hoyle Mill Barns 57 N5
Hubberholme N York 62 J4
Hubberston Pembks 24 E9
Hubbert's Bridge Lincs 49 L5
Huby N York 63 R10
Huby N York 64 D6
Huccaby Devon 5 R6
Hucclecote Gloucs 28 G4
Hucking Kent 12 F4
Hucknall Notts 47 P4
Huddersfield Kirk 56 H3
Huddington Worcs 36 B9
Hudnall Herts 31 M10
Hudswell N York 69 P12
Huggate E R Yk 64 K8
Hugglescote Leics 47 M11
Hughenden Valley Bucks 20 E3
Hughley Shrops 45 N14
Hugh Town IoS 2 c2
Huish Devon 15 M10
Huish Wilts 18 H8
Huish Champflower Somset 16 E11
Huish Episcopi Somset 17 M11
Hùisinis W Isls 106 e7
Huisinish W Isls 106 e7
Hulcote C Beds 30 K5
Hulcote Nhants 37 T11
Hulcott Bucks 30 J9
Hulham Devon 6 D8
Hulland Derbys 46 H4
Hulland Ward Derbys 46 J4
Hullavington Wilts 18 C4
Hull Bridge E R Yk 65 P11
Hullbridge Essex 22 K8
Hull, Kingston upon C KuH 65 P14
Hulme Manch 55 T7
Hulme Staffs 46 B4
Hulme Warrtn 55 P8
Hulme End Staffs 46 F2
Hulme Walfield Ches E 55 T13
Hulse Heath Ches E 55 R10
Hulton Lane Ends Bolton 55 Q5
Hulverstone IoW 9 M12
Hulver Street Norfk 50 F11
Hulver Street Suffk 41 S3
Humber Devon 6 A9
Humber Herefs 35 M9
Humber Bridge N Linc 58 H2
Humberside Airport N Linc 58 J4
Humberston NE Lin 59 P5
Humberstone C Leic 47 R12
Humberton N York 63 U6
Humbie E Loth 84 D6
Humbleton E R Yk 65 S13
Humbleton Nthumb 85 P13
Humby Lincs 48 F7
Hume Border 84 J10
Humshaugh Nthumb 76 J11
Huna Highld 112 J2
Huncoat Lancs 62 F13
Huncote Leics 47 P14
Hundalee Border 76 C2
Hundall Derbys 57 N11
Hunderthwaite Dur 69 L8
Hundleby Lincs 59 Q13
Hundle Houses Lincs 48 K3
Hundleton Pembks 24 G10
Hundon Suffk 40 B11
Hundred End Lancs 54 K2
Hundred House Powys 34 D10
Hungarton Leics 47 S12
Hungerford Hants 8 H6
Hungerford Somset 16 D8
Hungerford W Berk 19 M7
Hungerford Newtown W Berk 19 N6
Hunger Hill Bolton 55 Q5
Hunger Hill Lancs 55 M4
Hungerstone Herefs 34 K13
Hungerton Lincs 48 C8
Hungryhatton Shrops 45 Q8
Hunmanby N York 65 P4
Hunningham Warwks 37 L7
Hunnington Worcs 36 C4
Hunsbury Hill Nhants 37 T9
Hunsdon Herts 22 B5
Hunsingore N York 63 U9
Hunslet Leeds 63 S13
Hunsonby Cumb 67 S5
Hunstanton Norfk 49 U5
Hunstanworth Dur 68 K3
Hunsterson Ches E 45 Q4
Hunston Suffk 40 G7
Hunston W Susx 10 D10
Hunston Green Suffk 40 G7
Hunstrete BaNES 17 R4
Hunsworth Kirk 56 J1
Hunt End Worcs 36 D8
Hunter's Inn Devon 15 Q3
Hunter's Quay Ag & B 88 E10
Huntham Somset 16 K11
Hunthill Lodge Angus 98 H9
Huntingdon Cambs 38 K6
Huntingfield Suffk 41 P6
Huntingford Dorset 17 V11
Huntington C York 64 E8
Huntington Ches W 54 K14
Huntington E Loth 84 D4
Huntington Herefs 34 G10
Huntington Herefs 35 L12
Huntington Staffs 46 C11
Huntingtowerfield P & K 90 G6
Huntley Gloucs 28 D4
Huntly Abers 104 G8
Hunton Hants 19 Q12
Hunton Kent 12 D6
Hunton N York 63 P1
Hunton Bridge Herts 31 N12
Hunt's Corner Norfk 40 J3
Huntscott Somset 16 B8
Hunt's Cross Lpool 54 K9
Hunts Green Bucks 30 J12
Hunts Green Warwks 36 G1
Huntsham Devon 16 D12
Huntshaw Devon 15 M8
Huntshaw Cross Devon 15 M8
Huntspill Somset 16 K7
Huntstile Somset 16 J10
Huntworth Somset 16 K10
Hunwick Dur 69 Q6
Hunworth Norfk 50 J6
Hurcott Somset 17 L13
Hurdcott Wilts 8 H2
Hurdsfield Ches E 56 D12
Hurley W & M 20 D6
Hurley Warwks 36 H1
Hurley Bottom W & M 20 D6
Hurley Common Warwks 36 H1
Hurlford E Ayrs 81 P5
Hurlston Green Lancs 54 J4
Hurn BCP 8 G9
Hurn's End Lincs 49 P4
Hursley Hants 9 N3
Hurst Dorset 7 U6
Hurst N York 69 M12
Hurst Somset 17 N13
Hurst Wokham 20 C8
Hurstbourne Priors Hants 19 P11
Hurstbourne Tarrant Hants 19 N10
Hurst Green E Susx 12 D10
Hurst Green Essex 23 Q4
Hurst Green Lancs 62 D12
Hurst Green Surrey 21 R12
Hurst Hill Dudley 36 B2
Hurstley Herefs 34 J11
Hurstpierpoint W Susx 11 M7
Hurst Wickham W Susx 11 M7
Hurstwood Lancs 62 H13
Hurtiso Ork 106 u19
Hurtmore Surrey 20 F13
Hurworth Burn Dur 70 F6
Hurworth-on-Tees Darltn 70 D11
Hurworth Place Darltn 69 S11
Hury Dur 69 L9
Husbands Bosworth Leics 37 R4
Husborne Crawley C Beds 31 L5
Husthwaite N York 64 C5
Hutcherleigh Devon 5 T10
Hut Green N York 57 S2
Huthwaite Notts 47 N2
Huttoft Lincs 59 T11
Hutton Border 85 N8
Hutton Cumb 67 P7
Hutton E R Yk 65 N9
Hutton Essex 22 F8
Hutton Lancs 55 L1
Hutton N Som 17 L5
Hutton Bonville N York 70 D12
Hutton Buscel N York 65 M3
Hutton Conyers N York 63 S5
Hutton Cranswick E R Yk 65 N9
Hutton End Cumb 67 Q5
Hutton Hang N York 63 P2
Hutton Henry Dur 70 F5
Hutton-le-Hole N York 64 G1
Hutton Lowcross R & Cl 70 J10
Hutton Magna Dur 69 P10
Hutton Mulgrave N York 71 P11
Hutton Roof Cumb 62 B4
Hutton Roof Cumb 67 N6
Hutton Rudby N York 70 G11
Hutton Sessay N York 64 B4
Hutton Wandesley N York 64 C9
Huxham Devon 6 B5
Huxham Green Somset 17 Q9
Huxley Ches W 45 M1
Huyton Knows 54 K8
Hycemoor Cumb 60 K2
Hyde Gloucs 28 G7
Hyde Hants 8 H6
Hyde Tamesd 56 D8
Hyde Heath Bucks 30 K12
Hyde Lea Staffs 46 B10
Hydestile Surrey 10 F2
Hykeham Moor Lincs 58 F13
Hylands House & Park Essex 22 G7
Hyndford Bridge S Lans 82 H10
Hynish Ag & B 92 B11
Hyssington Powys 34 H2
Hystfield Gloucs 28 C8
Hythe Essex 23 P2
Hythe Hants 9 N7
Hythe Kent 13 N9
Hythe Somset 17 M6
Hythe End W & M 20 H8
Hyton Cumb 60 K2

I

Ibberton Dorset 7 U3
Ible Derbys 46 H2
Ibsley Hants 8 H7
Ibstock Leics 47 M12
Ibstone Bucks 20 C4
Ibthorpe Hants 19 N10
Iburndale N York 71 Q11
Ibworth Hants 19 S10
Icelton N Som 17 L3
Ichrachan Ag & B 94 E12
Ickburgh Norfk 40 D1
Ickenham Gt Lon 20 J5
Ickford Bucks 30 D11
Ickham Kent 13 P4
Ickleford Herts 31 Q6
Icklesham E Susx 12 G12
Ickleton Cambs 39 Q12
Icklingham Suffk 40 C6
Ickornshaw N York 62 K11
Ickwell Green C Beds 38 J11
Icomb Gloucs 29 P3
Idbury Oxon 29 P4
Iddesleigh Devon 15 N11
Ide Devon 6 A6
Ideford Devon 6 A9
Ide Hill Kent 21 S12
Iden E Susx 12 H11
Iden Green Kent 12 D8
Iden Green Kent 12 F9
Idle C Brad 63 P12
Idless Cnwll 3 L7
Idlicote Warwks 36 J12
Idmiston Wilts 18 J13
Idole Carmth 25 R7
Idridgehay Derbys 46 J4
Idrigill Highld 100 c3
Idstone Oxon 29 Q11
Iffley Oxon 30 B12
Ifield W Susx 11 M3
Ifold W Susx 10 G4
Iford BCP 8 G10
Iford E Susx 11 Q9
Ifton Mons 27 T10
Ifton Heath Shrops 44 H6
Ightfield Shrops 45 N6
Ightham Kent 21 U11
Iken Suffk 41 R9
Ilam Staffs 46 F3
Ilchester Somset 17 P12
Ilderton Nthumb 77 L1
Ilford Gt Lon 21 R5
Ilford Somset 17 L13
Ilfracombe Devon 15 M3
Ilkeston Derbys 47 N5
Ilketshall St Andrew Suffk 41 Q3
Ilketshall St John Suffk 41 Q3
Ilketshall St Lawrence Suffk 41 Q4
Ilketshall St Margaret Suffk 41 P3
Ilkley C Brad 63 N10
Illand Cnwll 4 H5
Illey Dudley 36 C4
Illidge Green Ches E 55 S14
Illingworth Calder 63 M14
Illogan Cnwll 2 H8
Illston on the Hill Leics 47 T14
Ilmer Bucks 30 G11
Ilmington Warwks 36 H12
Ilminster Somset 7 L2
Ilsington Devon 5 T5
Ilsington Dorset 7 U6
Ilston Swans 25 U12
Ilton N York 63 P4
Ilton Somset 17 L13
Imachar N Ayrs 79 R7
Immingham NE Lin 59 L4
Immingham Dock NE Lin 59 L3
Impington Cambs 39 P8
Ince Ches W 55 L11
Ince Blundell Sefton 54 H6
Ince-in-Makerfield Wigan 55 N6
Inchbae Lodge Hotel Highld 108 G11
Inchbare Angus 99 L10
Inchberry Moray 104 C4
Incheril Highld 107 T12
Inchinnan Rens 89 L12
Inchlaggan Highld 101 T11
Inchmichael P & K 90 K6
Inchmore Highld 102 G6
Inchnadamph Highld 110 F12
Inchture P & K 91 L6
Inchvuilt Highld 101 U4
Inchyra P & K 90 J7
Indian Queens Cnwll 3 N5
Ingatestone Essex 22 F8
Ingbirchworth Barns 56 K5
Ingerthorpe N York 63 R6
Ingestre Staffs 46 C9
Ingham Lincs 58 F10
Ingham Norfk 51 Q8
Ingham Suffk 40 E6
Ingham Corner Norfk 51 Q8
Ingleborough Norfk 49 Q10
Ingleby Derbys 46 K8
Ingleby Arncliffe N York 70 F12
Ingleby Barwick S on T 70 F10
Ingleby Cross N York 70 G12
Ingleby Greenhow N York 70 J11
Ingleigh Green Devon 15 P11
Inglesbatch BaNES 17 T4
Inglesham Swindn 29 P8
Ingleston D & G 74 J12
Ingleton Dur 69 Q8
Ingleton N York 62 D5
Inglewhite Lancs 61 U12
Ingmanthorpe N York 63 U9
Ingoe Nthumb 77 L11
Ingol Lancs 61 U13
Ingoldisthorpe Norfk 49 U7
Ingoldmells Lincs 59 U13
Ingoldsby Lincs 48 F8
Ingram Nthumb 77 L2
Ingrave Essex 22 F9
Ingrow C Brad 63 M12
Ings Cumb 67 P13
Ingst S Glos 28 A10
Ingthorpe Rutlnd 48 E12
Ingworth Norfk 51 L8
Inkberrow Worcs 36 D9
Inkerman Dur 69 P5
Inkhorn Abers 105 Q8
Inkpen W Berk 19 N8
Inkstack Highld 112 G2
Inmarsh Wilts 18 D8
Innellan Ag & B 88 E11
Innerleithen Border 83 R11
Innerleven Fife 91 N11
Innermessan D & G 72 D7
Innerwick E Loth 84 J4
Innesmill Moray 104 B3
Innsworth Gloucs 28 G3
Insch Abers 104 J10
Insh Highld 97 N3
Inskip Lancs 61 T12
Inskip Moss Side Lancs 61 T12
Instow Devon 15 L6
Insworke Cnwll 5 L10
Intake Sheff 57 N10
Inver Abers 98 C5
Inver Highld 109 R8
Inver P & K 90 F3
Inverailort Highld 93 T2
Inveralligin Highld 107 P13
Inverallochy Abers 105 S2
Inveran Highld 108 K5
Inveraray Ag & B 88 C4
Inverarish Highld 100 e6
Inverarity Angus 91 Q3
Inverarnan Stirlg 88 H2
Inverasdale Highld 107 P8
Inverbeg Ag & B 88 H6
Inverbervie Abers 99 Q9
Inverboyndie Abers 104 K3
Invercreran House Hotel Ag & B 94 E9
Inverdruie Highld 103 N13
Inveresk E Loth 83 R4
Inveresragan Ag & B 94 D11
Inverey Abers 97 T6
Inverfarigaig Highld 102 F11
Inverfolla Ag & B 94 D10
Invergarry Highld 96 C3
Invergeldie P & K 95 U13
Invergloy Highld 101 U14
Invergordon Highld 109 N11
Invergowrie P & K 91 M5
Inverguseran Highld 100 g9
Inverhadden P & K 95 T7
Inverie Highld 100 g9
Inverinan Ag & B 87 T2
Inverinate Highld 101 N7
Inverkeilor Angus 91 U2
Inverkeithing Fife 83 M2
Inverkeithny Abers 104 J6
Inverkip Inver 88 F11
Inverkirkaig Highld 110 B13
Inverlael Highld 108 B7
Inverlair Highld 96 C8
Inverliever Lodge Ag & B 87 R4
Inverlochy Ag & B 94 H13
Invermark Angus 98 G7
Invermoriston Highld 102 D12
Invernaver Highld 111 Q4
Inverneill Ag & B 87 Q9
Inverness Highld 102 J6
Inverness Airport Highld 103 L5
Invernettie Abers 105 U7
Invernoaden Ag & B 88 D6
Inveroran Hotel Ag & B 94 K10
Inverquharity Angus 98 G12
Inverquhomery Abers 105 S6
Inverroy Highld 96 B7
Inversanda Highld 94 C7
Invershiel Highld 101 N8
Invershin Highld 108 K5
Invershore Highld 112 F9
Inversnaid Hotel Stirlg 88 H4
Inverugie Abers 105 T6
Inveruglas Ag & B 88 H4
Inveruglass Highld 97 N3
Inverurie Abers 105 M11
Inwardleigh Devon 15 N13
Inworth Essex 23 L4
Iochdar W Isls 106 c14
Iona Ag & B 92 H13
Iping W Susx 10 D6
iPort Logistics Park Donc 57 T7
Ipplepen Devon 5 U7
Ipsden Oxon 19 T3
Ipstones Staffs 46 D4
Ipswich Suffk 41 L12
Irby Wirral 54 G10
Irby in the Marsh Lincs 59 S14
Irby upon Humber NE Lin 59 L6
Irchester Nhants 38 D7
Ireby Cumb 66 K5
Ireby Lancs 62 D4
Ireland C Beds 31 P4
Ireleth Cumb 61 N4
Ireshopeburn Dur 68 J5
Ireton Wood Derbys 46 J4
Irlam Salfd 55 R8
Irnham Lincs 48 F8
Iron Acton S Glos 28 C11
Iron Bridge Cambs 49 Q14
Ironbridge Wrekin 45 Q13
Ironbridge Gorge Wrekin 45 Q13
Iron Cross Warwks 36 E10
Ironmacannie D & G 73 R4
Irons Bottom Surrey 21 M13
Ironville Derbys 47 M3
Irstead Norfk 51 Q9
Irthington Cumb 75 U13
Irthlingborough Nhants 38 D6
Irton N York 65 N3
Irvine N Ayrs 81 L5
Isauld Highld 112 A3
Isbister Shet 106 t4
Isbister Shet 106 v7
Isfield E Susx 11 Q7
Isham Nhants 38 C6
Isington Hants 10 B2
Islandpool Worcs 35 U4
Islay Ag & B 86 F10
Islay Airport Ag & B 78 E5
Isle Abbotts Somset 17 L12
Isle Brewers Somset 17 L12
Isleham Cambs 39 T6
Isle of Dogs Gt Lon 21 Q7
Isle of Grain Medway 23 L12
Isle of Lewis W Isls 106 i5
Isle of Man IoM 60 f5
Isle of Man Ronaldsway Airport IoM 60 d9
Isle of Mull Ag & B 93 Q11
Isle of Purbeck Dorset 8 E12
Isle of Sheppey Kent 12 J2
Isle of Skye Highld 100 d6
Isle of Thanet Kent 13 R2
Isle of Walney Cumb 61 M6
Isle of Whithorn D & G 73 M12
Isle of Wight IoW 9 Q11
Isleornsay Highld 100 g8
Isles of Scilly IoS 2 c2
Isles of Scilly St Mary's Airport IoS 2 c2
Islesteps D & G 74 J11
Islet Village Guern 6 e2
Isleworth Gt Lon 21 L7
Isley Walton Leics 47 M9
Islibhig W Isls 106 f6
Islington Gt Lon 21 P6
Islip Nhants 38 E5
Islip Oxon 30 B10
Islivig W Isls 106 f6
Isombridge Wrekin 45 P11
Istead Rise Kent 22 F13
Itchen Abbas Hants 9 Q2
Itchen Stoke Hants 9 R2
Itchingfield W Susx 10 J5
Itchington S Glos 28 C10
Itteringham Norfk 50 K7
Itton Devon 15 Q13
Itton Mons 27 T8
Itton Common Mons 27 T8
Ivegill Cumb 67 P4
Ivelet N York 68 K13
Iver Bucks 20 H6
Iver Heath Bucks 20 H6
Iveston Dur 69 P2
Ivinghoe Bucks 30 K9
Ivinghoe Aston Bucks 31 L9
Ivington Herefs 35 L9
Ivington Green Herefs 35 L9
Ivybridge Devon 5 Q9
Ivychurch Kent 12 K10
Ivy Cross Dorset 8 B4
Ivy Hatch Kent 21 U12
Ivy Todd Norfk 50 E12
Iwade Kent 12 H2
Iwerne Courtney Dorset 8 B6
Iwerne Minster Dorset 8 B6
Ixworth Suffk 40 F6
Ixworth Thorpe Suffk 40 F6

J

Jack Green Lancs 55 N1
Jack Hill N York 63 P9
Jack-in-the-Green Devon 6 D5
Jack's Bush Hants 19 L13
Jacksdale Notts 47 M3
Jackson Bridge Kirk 56 J5
Jackton S Lans 81 R2
Jacobstow Cnwll 14 E13
Jacobstowe Devon 15 N12
Jacobs Well Surrey 20 G12
Jameston Pembks 24 J11
Jamestown Highld 102 E4
Jamestown W Duns 88 J9
Janetstown Highld 112 E10
Janetstown Highld 112 J6
Jardine Hall D & G 75 M8
Jarrow S Tyne 77 S13
Jarvis Brook E Susx 11 S5
Jasper's Green Essex 22 H2
Jawcraig Falk 89 T10
Jaywick Essex 23 S5
Jealott's Hill Br For 20 E8
Jeater Houses N York 70 F14
Jedburgh Border 76 C1
Jeffreyston Pembks 24 J9
Jemimaville Highld 102 K2
Jerbourg Guern 6 e4
Jersey Jersey 7 d2
Jersey Airport Jersey 7 b2
Jersey Marine Neath 26 C9
Jerusalem Lincs 58 F12
Jesmond N u Ty 77 R12
Jevington E Susx 11 T10
Jingle Street Mons 27 T5
Jockey End Herts 31 M10
Jodrell Bank Ches E 55 S12
Johnby Cumb 67 P6
John Lennon Airport Lpool 54 K10
John o' Groats Highld 112 J2
Johns Cross E Susx 12 D11
Johnshaven Abers 99 P10
Johnson Street Norfk 51 Q10
Johnston Pembks 24 F8
Johnstone D & G 75 P5
Johnstone Rens 88 K13
Johnstonebridge D & G 75 M7
Johnstown Carmth 25 Q7
Johnstown Wrexhm 44 H4
Joppa C Edin 83 R4
Joppa Cerdgn 33 L7
Joppa S Ayrs 81 N9
Jordans Bucks 20 G4
Jordanston Pembks 24 F4
Jordanthorpe Sheff 57 N10
Joyden's Wood Kent 22 D13
Jubilee Corner Kent 12 F6
Jump Barns 57 N6
Jumper's Town E Susx 11 R4
Juniper Nthumb 76 J14
Juniper Green C Edin 83 N5
Jura Ag & B 86 J9
Jurassic Coast Devon 6 K7
Jurby IoM 60 f3
Jurston Devon 5 R4

K

Kaber Cumb 68 G10
Kaimend S Lans 82 J9
Kames Ag & B 87 T11
Kames E Ayrs 82 C13
Kea Cnwll 3 L8
Keadby N Linc 58 D4
Keal Cotes Lincs 49 N1
Kearby Town End N York 63 S10
Kearsley Bolton 55 S6
Kearsley Nthumb 77 L10
Kearsney Kent 13 Q7
Kearstwick Cumb 62 C4
Kearton N York 69 L13
Keasden N York 62 E6
Keaton Devon 5 Q10
Keckwick Halton 55 N10
Keddington Lincs 59 P9
Keddington Corner Lincs 59 Q9
Kedington Suffk 40 B11
Kedleston Derbys 46 K5
Keelby Lincs 59 L4
Keele Staffs 45 T4
Keele Services Staffs 45 T5
Keele University Staffs 45 T4
Keeley Green Bed 38 F11
Keelham C Brad 63 M13
Keeres Green Essex 22 E5
Keeston Pembks 24 F7
Keevil Wilts 18 D9
Kegworth Leics 47 N8
Kehelland Cnwll 2 G8
Keig Abers 104 J12
Keighley C Brad 63 M11
Keilarsbrae Clacks 90 C13
Keillour P & K 90 E6
Keiloch Abers 98 B5
Keils Ag & B 86 J12
Keinton Mandeville Somset 17 P10
Keir Mill D & G 74 G7
Keirsleywell Row Nthumb 68 G2
Keisby Lincs 48 F8
Keisley Cumb 68 F8
Keiss Highld 112 H4
Keith Moray 104 E5
Keithick P & K 90 K4
Keithock Angus 99 L11
Keithtown Highld 102 F4
Kelbrook Lancs 62 J11
Kelby Lincs 48 F5
Keld Cumb 67 S10
Keld N York 68 J12
Keld Head N York 64 H3
Keldholme N York 64 G2
Kelfield N Linc 58 D6
Kelfield N York 64 D12
Kelham Notts 47 U2
Kelhead D & G 75 M12
Kellacott Devon 5 L3
Kellamergh Lancs 61 S14
Kellas Angus 91 Q4
Kellas Moray 103 U5
Kellaton Devon 5 U13
Kelleth Cumb 68 E11
Kelling Norfk 50 J5
Kellington N York 57 S2
Kelloe Dur 70 D5
Kelloholm D & G 74 D3
Kells Cumb 66 E9
Kelly Devon 4 K4
Kelly Bray Cnwll 4 K6
Kelmarsh Nhants 37 T5
Kelmscott Oxon 29 P8
Kelsale Suffk 41 Q7
Kelsall Ches W 55 M13
Kelshall Herts 31 T5
Kelsick Cumb 66 J2
Kelso Border 84 J12
Kelstedge Derbys 57 M14
Kelstern Lincs 59 M9
Kelsterton Flints 54 G12
Kelston BaNES 17 T3
Keltneyburn P & K 95 V9
Kelton D & G 74 J11
Kelty Fife 90 H13
Kelvedon Essex 23 L4
Kelvedon Hatch Essex 22 E8
Kelynack Cnwll 2 B11
Kemacott Devon 15 Q3
Kemback Fife 91 P9
Kemberton Shrops 45 R13
Kemble Gloucs 28 J8
Kemble Wick Gloucs 28 J8
Kemerton Worcs 36 C13
Kemeys Commander Mons 27 Q7
Kemnay Abers 105 L12
Kempe's Corner Kent 12 K6
Kempley Gloucs 28 C2
Kempley Green Gloucs 28 C2
Kempsey Worcs 35 T11
Kempsford Gloucs 29 N8
Kemps Green Warwks 36 F6
Kempshott Hants 19 T10
Kempston Bed 38 F11
Kempston Hardwick Bed 31 M4
Kempton Shrops 34 J4
Kemp Town Br & H 11 N10
Kemsing Kent 21 U11
Kemsley Kent 12 H2
Kemsley Street Kent 12 F3
Kenardington Kent 12 J9
Kenchester Herefs 34 K12
Kencot Oxon 29 Q7
Kendal Cumb 67 R14
Kenderchurch Herefs 27 S2
Kendleshire S Glos 28 C12
Kenfig Brdgnd 26 E11
Kenfig Hill Brdgnd 26 E11
Kenilworth Warwks 36 J6
Kenley Gt Lon 21 P10
Kenley Shrops 45 N13
Kenmore Highld 107 N13
Kenmore P & K 95 V9
Kenn Devon 6 B7
Kenn N Som 17 M3
Kennacraig Ag & B 79 Q3
Kennall Vale Cnwll 2 J9
Kennards House Cnwll 4 H4
Kenneggy Cnwll 2 F11
Kennerleigh Devon 15 T11
Kennet Clacks 90 D13
Kennethmont Abers 104 G10
Kennett Cambs 39 U7
Kennford Devon 6 B7
Kenninghall Norfk 40 H3
Kennington Kent 12 K6
Kennington Oxon 30 B12
Kennoway Fife 91 N11
Kenny Somset 16 K13
Kenny Hill Suffk 39 U5
Kennythorpe N York 64 H6
Kenovay Ag & B 92 B9
Kensaleyre Highld 100 d4
Kensington Gt Lon 21 N7
Kensington Palace Gt Lon 21 N6
Kensworth Common C Beds 31 M9
Kentallen Highld 94 E7
Kentchurch Herefs 27 S2
Kentford Suffk 40 B7
Kent Green Ches E 45 T2
Kentisbeare Devon 6 E3
Kentisbury Devon 15 P4
Kentisbury Ford Devon 15 P4
Kentish Town Gt Lon 21 N6
Kentmere Cumb 67 Q12
Kenton Devon 6 C8
Kenton Gt Lon 21 L5
Kenton N u Ty 77 Q12
Kenton Suffk 41 L7
Kenton Bankfoot N u Ty 77 Q12
Kentra Highld 93 R5
Kents Bank Cumb 61 R4
Kent's Green Gloucs 28 D3
Kent's Oak Hants 9 L4
Kent Street E Susx 12 E12
Kent Street Kent 12 C5
Kenwick Shrops 44 K7
Kenwyn Cnwll 3 L7
Kenyon Warrtn 55 P7
Keoldale Highld 110 H3
Keppoch Highld 101 M7
Kepwick N York 64 B1
Keresley Covtry 36 K4
Kermincham Ches E 55 T13
Kernborough Devon 5 T12
Kerne Bridge Herefs 28 A4
Kerrera Ag & B 93 U13
Kerridge Ches E 56 D11
Kerridge-end Ches E 56 D11
Kerris Cnwll 2 C11
Kerry Powys 34 D2
Kerrycroy Ag & B 88 D13
Kersall Notts 47 T1
Kersbrook Devon 6 E8
Kerscott Devon 15 P7
Kersey Suffk 40 H12
Kersey Tye Suffk 40 G12
Kersey Upland Suffk 40 G12
Kershader W Isls 106 i7
Kershopefoot Cumb 75 U9
Kersoe Worcs 36 C12
Kerswell Devon 6 E3
Kerswell Green Worcs 35 U11
Kerthen Wood Cnwll 2 F10
Kesgrave Suffk 41 M11
Kessingland Suffk 41 T3
Kessingland Beach Suffk 41 T3
Kestle Cnwll 3 P7
Kestle Mill Cnwll 3 L5
Keston Gt Lon 21 R10
Keswick Cumb 67 L8
Keswick Norfk 51 M13
Ketsby Lincs 59 Q11
Kettering Nhants 38 C5
Ketteringham Norfk 51 L13
Kettins P & K 90 K4
Kettlebaston Suffk 40 G10
Kettlebridge Fife 91 M10
Kettlebrook Staffs 46 H13
Kettleburgh Suffk 41 N8
Kettle Green Herts 22 B4
Kettleholm D & G 75 M10
Kettleness N York 71 P9
Kettleshulme Ches E 56 E11
Kettlesing N York 63 Q8
Kettlesing Bottom N York 63 Q8
Kettlestone Norfk 50 G7
Kettlethorpe Lincs 58 D11
Kettletoft Ork 106 v16
Kettlewell N York 62 K5
Ketton Rutlnd 48 E13
Kew Gt Lon 21 L7
Kew Royal Botanic Gardens Gt Lon 21 L7
Kewstoke N Som 16 K4
Kexbrough Barns 57 M5
Kexby C York 64 G9
Kexby Lincs 58 E9
Key Green Ches E 56 C14
Key Green N York 71 P12
Keyham Leics 47 S12
Keyhaven Hants 9 L10
Keyingham E R Yk 59 M1
Keymer W Susx 11 N7
Keynsham BaNES 17 S3
Keysoe Bed 38 G8
Keysoe Row Bed 38 G8
Keyston Cambs 38 F5
Key Street Kent 12 G3
Keyworth Notts 47 R7
Kibbear Somset 16 H12
Kibblesworth Gatesd 69 R1
Kibworth Beauchamp Leics 37 S2
Kibworth Harcourt Leics 37 S2
Kidbrooke Gt Lon 21 R7
Kidburngill Cumb 66 G8
Kiddemore Green Staffs 45 U12
Kidderminster Worcs 35 T5
Kiddington Oxon 29 T3
Kidd's Moor Norfk 50 K13
Kidlington Oxon 29 U5
Kidmore End Oxon 19 U5
Kidsdale D & G 73 L12
Kidsgrove Staffs 45 T3
Kidstones N York 62 K3
Kidwelly Carmth 25 R9
Kiel Crofts Ag & B 94 C11
Kielder Nthumb 76 C7
Kielder Forest 76 C8
Kiells Ag & B 86 G12
Kilbarchan Rens 88 K13
Kilbeg Highld 100 f9
Kilberry Ag & B 79 N3
Kilbirnie N Ayrs 81 L2
Kilbride Ag & B 87 N10
Kilbride Ag & B 88 B12
Kilbuiack Moray 103 S3
Kilburn Derbys 47 L4
Kilburn Gt Lon 21 M6
Kilburn N York 64 C4
Kilby Leics 37 R1
Kilchamaig Ag & B 79 Q3
Kilchattan Ag & B 80 G2
Kilchattan Ag & B 86 F6
Kilcheran Ag & B 93 U11
Kilchoan Highld 93 M6
Kilchoman Ag & B 78 C3
Kilchrenan Ag & B 94 E14
Kilconquhar Fife 91 Q11
Kilcot Gloucs 28 C2
Kilcoy Highld 102 G5
Kilcreggan Ag & B 88 F9
Kildale N York 70 K11
Kildalloig Ag & B 79 P12
Kildary Highld 109 P10
Kildavaig Ag & B 87 T12
Kildavanan Ag & B 88 B12
Kildonan Highld 111 U12
Kildonan N Ayrs 80 E8
Kildonan Lodge Highld 111 U12
Kildonnan Highld 93 M1
Kildrochet House D & G 72 D8
Kildrummy Abers 104 F12
Kildwick N York 63 L10
Kilfinan Ag & B 87 S10
Kilfinnan Highld 96 B4
Kilford Denbgs 54 C13
Kilgetty Pembks 24 K9
Kilgrammie S Ayrs 80 K12
Kilgwrrwg Common Mons 27 T8
Kilham E R Yk 65 P7
Kilham Nthumb 85 M12
Kilkenneth Ag & B 92 A10
Kilkenzie Ag & B 79 M11
Kilkerran Ag & B 79 N12
Kilkhampton Cnwll 14 G10
Killamarsh Derbys 57 Q10
Killay Swans 25 V12
Killearn Stirlg 89 M8
Killen Highld 102 J4
Killerby Darltn 69 Q9
Killerton Devon 6 C4
Killichonan P & K 95 Q7
Killiechonate Highld 94 J2
Killiechronan Ag & B 93 N10
Killiecrankie P & K 97 Q11
Killilan Highld 101 N5
Killimster Highld 112 H5
Killin Stirlg 95 R12
Killinghall N York 63 R8
Killington Cumb 62 C2
Killington Devon 15 Q3
Killington Lake Services Cumb 62 B1
Killingworth N Tyne 77 R11
Killiow Cnwll 3 L8
Killochyett Border 84 D9
Kilmacolm Inver 88 J11
Kilmahog Stirlg 89 P4
Kilmahumaig Ag & B 87 P7
Kilmaluag Highld 100 d2
Kilmany Fife 91 N7
Kilmarnock E Ayrs 81 N5
Kilmartin Ag & B 87 Q6
Kilmaurs E Ayrs 81 N4
Kilmelford Ag & B 87 R3
Kilmersdon Somset 17 S6
Kilmeston Hants 9 R3
Kilmichael Ag & B 79 M11
Kilmichael Glassary Ag & B 87 R7
Kilmichael of Inverlussa Ag & B 87 P8
Kilmington Devon 6 J5
Kilmington Wilts 17 U9
Kilmington Common Wilts 17 U9
Kilmington Street Wilts 17 U9
Kilmorack Highld 102 E7
Kilmore Ag & B 94 B13
Kilmore Highld 100 f9
Kilmory Ag & B 87 N11
Kilmory Highld 93 N5
Kilmory N Ayrs 80 D8
Kilmuir Highld 100 b5
Kilmuir Highld 100 c2
Kilmuir Highld 102 J6
Kilmuir Highld 109 P10
Kilmun Ag & B 88 E9
Kilnave Ag & B 86 D11
Kilncadzow S Lans 82 G9
Kilndown Kent 12 D8
Kiln Green Wokham 20 D7
Kilnhill Cumb 66 K6
Kilnhouses Ches W 55 P13
Kilnhurst Rothm 57 Q7
Kilninver Ag & B 87 Q1
Kiln Pit Hill Nthumb 69 M1
Kilnsea E R Yk 59 R3
Kilnsey N York 62 K6
Kilnwick E R Yk 65 M10
Kilnwick Percy E R Yk 64 J10
Kiloran Ag & B 86 F6
Kilpatrick N Ayrs 79 S10
Kilpeck Herefs 27 S1
Kilpin E R Yk 58 C1
Kilpin Pike E R Yk 58 C1
Kilrenny Fife 91 S11
Kilsby Nhants 37 Q6
Kilspindie P & K 90 K6
Kilstay D & G 72 E12
Kilsyth N Lans 89 R10
Kiltarlity Highld 102 F7
Kilton R & Cl 71 M9
Kilton Somset 16 G8
Kilton Thorpe R & Cl 71 L9
Kilvaxter Highld 100 c3
Kilve Somset 16 F8
Kilvington Notts 48 B5
Kilwinning N Ayrs 81 L4
Kimberley Norfk 50 J13
Kimberley Notts 47 N5
Kimberworth Rothm 57 P8
Kimblesworth Dur 69 S3
Kimble Wick Bucks 30 H11
Kimbolton Cambs 38 H7
Kimbolton Herefs 35 M8
Kimcote Leics 37 Q3
Kimmeridge Dorset 8 C13
Kimmerston Nthumb 85 P11

134 Kimpton – Little Knox

Kimpton Hants 19 L11
Kimpton Herts 31 Q9
Kimworthy Devon 14 H10
Kinbrace Highld 111 T10
Kinbuck Stirlg 89 S4
Kincaple Fife 91 Q8
Kincardine Fife 90 D14
Kincardine Highld 109 L7
Kincardine Bridge Fife 82 H1
Kincardine O'Neil Abers 98 K4
Kinclaven P & K 90 J4
Kincorth C Aber 99 S3
Kincorth House Moray 103 R3
Kincraig Highld 97 N2
Kincraigie P & K 90 E2
Kindallachan P & K 90 E2
Kinerarach Ag & B 79 M5
Kineton Gloucs 29 L2
Kineton Warwks 36 K10
Kinfauns P & K 90 J7
Kingarth Ag & B 80 F1
Kingcausie Abers 99 R4
Kingcoed Mons 27 S6
Kingerby Lincs 58 J8
Kingford Devon 14 G11
Kingham Oxon 29 Q3
Kingholm Quay D & G 74 J11
Kinghorn Fife 83 Q1
Kinglassie Fife 90 K12
Kingoodie P & K 91 M6
King's Acre Herefs 35 L12
Kingsand Cnwll 5 L10
Kingsash Bucks 30 J11
Kingsbarns Fife 91 S9
Kingsbridge Devon 5 S12
Kingsbridge Somset 16 C9
Kings Bridge Swans 25 U11
King's Bromley Staffs 46 F10
Kingsburgh Highld 100 c4
Kingsbury Gt Lon 21 L5
Kingsbury Warwks 36 H1
Kingsbury Episcopi Somset 17 M12
King's Caple Herefs 27 V2
Kingsclere Hants 19 R9
King's Cliffe Nhants 38 F1
Kings Clipstone Notts 57 T14
Kingscote Gloucs 28 F8
Kingscott Devon 15 M9
King's Coughton Warwks 36 E9
Kingscross N Ayrs 80 E7
Kingsdon Somset 17 P11
Kingsdown Kent 13 S6
Kingsdown Swindn 29 N10
Kingsdown Wilts 18 B7
Kingseat Abers 105 Q12
Kingseat Fife 90 H13
Kingsey Bucks 30 F11
Kingsfold W Susx 10 K3
Kingsford C Aber 99 R2
Kingsford E Ayrs 81 N3
Kingsford Worcs 35 T4
Kingsgate Kent 13 S1
Kings Green Gloucs 35 S14
Kingshall Street Suffk 40 F8
Kingsheanton Devon 15 N5
King's Heath Birm 36 E4
Kings Hill Kent 12 C4
King's Hill Wsall 36 C1
Kings House Hotel Highld 94 K8
Kingshurst Solhll 36 G3
Kingside Hill Cumb 66 J2
Kingskerswell Devon 6 A11
Kingskettle Fife 91 M10
Kingsland Dorset 7 N5
Kingsland Herefs 34 K8
Kingsland IoA 52 C6
Kings Langley Herts 31 N12
Kingsley Ches W 55 N12
Kingsley Hants 10 B3
Kingsley Staffs 46 D4
Kingsley Green W Susx 10 D4
Kingsley Holt Staffs 46 D4
Kingsley Park Nhants 37 U8
Kingslow Shrops 45 S14
King's Lynn Norfk 49 T9
Kings Meaburn Cumb 68 D8
Kingsmead Hants 9 R6
King's Mills Guern 6 c3
King's Moss St Hel 55 M6
Kingsmuir Angus 91 Q2
Kings Muir Border 83 Q11
Kingsmuir Fife 91 R10
Kings Newnham Warwks 37 N5
King's Newton Derbys 47 L8
Kingsnorth Kent 12 K8
King's Norton Birm 36 E5
King's Norton Leics 47 S13
Kings Nympton Devon 15 Q9
King's Pyon Herefs 34 K10
Kings Ripton Cambs 39 L5
King's Somborne Hants 9 M2
King's Stag Dorset 7 T2
King's Stanley Gloucs 28 F7
King's Sutton Nhants 37 N13
Kingstanding Birm 36 E2
Kingsteignton Devon 5 V6
King Sterndale Derbys 56 G12
Kingsthorne Herefs 27 T1
Kingsthorpe Nhants 37 U8
Kingston Cambs 39 M9
Kingston Cnwll 4 K5
Kingston Devon 5 Q11
Kingston Devon 6 E7
Kingston Dorset 7 U3
Kingston Dorset 8 D13
Kingston E Loth 84 E2
Kingston Hants 8 G8
Kingston IoW 9 P12
Kingston Kent 13 N5
Kingston W Susx 10 H10
Kingston Bagpuize Oxon 29 T8
Kingston Blount Oxon 20 B3
Kingston Deverill Wilts 18 B13
Kingstone Herefs 34 K13
Kingstone Somset 7 L2
Kingstone Staffs 46 E8
Kingstone Winslow Oxon 29 Q10
Kingston Lacy House & Gardens Dorset 8 D8
Kingston Lisle Oxon 29 R10
Kingston near Lewes E Susx 11 P9
Kingston on Soar Notts 47 P8
Kingston on Spey Moray 104 C2
Kingston Russell Dorset 7 Q6
Kingston St Mary Somset 16 H11
Kingston Seymour N Som 17 M3
Kingston Stert Oxon 30 F12
Kingston upon Hull C KuH 65 P14
Kingston upon Thames Gt Lon 21 L9
Kingstown Cumb 75 S14
King's Walden Herts 31 Q8
Kingswear Devon 5 V10
Kingswells C Aber 99 R2
Kings Weston Bristl 27 U12
Kingswinford Dudley 35 U3
Kingswood Bucks 30 E9
Kingswood Gloucs 28 D9
Kingswood Kent 12 F5
Kingswood Powys 44 F13
Kingswood S Glos 28 B13
Kingswood Somset 16 F9
Kingswood Surrey 21 M11
Kingswood Warwks 36 G6
Kingswood Brook Warwks 36 G6
Kingswood Common Herefs 34 G10
Kingswood Common Staffs 45 T13
Kings Worthy Hants 9 P2
Kingthorpe Lincs 58 K11
Kington Herefs 34 G9
Kington S Glos 28 B9
Kington Worcs 36 C9
Kington Langley Wilts 18 D5
Kington Magna Dorset 17 U12
Kington St Michael Wilts 18 D5
Kingussie Highld 97 M3
Kingweston Somset 17 P10
Kinharrachie Abers 105 Q9
Kinharvie D & G 74 H12
Kinkell Bridge P & K 90 D8
Kinknockie Abers 105 S7
Kinleith C Edin 83 N5
Kinlet Shrops 35 R4
Kinloch Highld 100 d10
Kinloch Highld 110 G10
Kinloch Highld 111 M6
Kinloch P & K 90 H3
Kinlochard Stirlg 89 L5
Kinlochbervie Highld 110 E5
Kinlocheil Highld 94 D3
Kinlochewe Highld 107 T12
Kinloch Hourn Highld 101 P10
Kinlochlaggan Highld 96 G6
Kinlochleven Highld 94 H6
Kinlochmoidart Highld 93 S4
Kinlochnanuagh Highld 93 S2
Kinloch Rannoch P & K 95 T7
Kinloss Moray 103 S3
Kinmel Bay Conwy 53 S6
Kinmuck Abers 105 N12
Kinmundy Abers 105 P12
Kinnabus Ag & B 78 D7
Kinnadie Abers 105 R7
Kinnaird P & K 97 R12
Kinneff Abers 99 Q8
Kinnelhead D & G 74 K5
Kinnell Angus 99 L13
Kinnerley Shrops 44 H9
Kinnersley Herefs 34 H11
Kinnersley Worcs 35 U12
Kinnerton Powys 34 F8
Kinnerton Shrops 34 J1
Kinnerton Green Flints 44 H1
Kinnesswood P & K 90 J11
Kinninvie Dur 69 N8
Kinnordy Angus 98 F12
Kinoulton Notts 47 S7
Kinross P & K 90 H11
Kinrossie P & K 90 J5
Kinross Services P & K 90 H11
Kinsbourne Green Herts 31 P9
Kinsey Heath Ches E 45 Q5
Kinsham Herefs 34 J7
Kinsham Worcs 36 B13
Kinsley Wakefd 57 P4
Kinson BCP 8 F9
Kintail Highld 101 P8
Kintbury W Berk 19 N7
Kintessack Moray 103 R3
Kintillo P & K 90 H8
Kinton Herefs 34 K6
Kinton Shrops 44 J10
Kintore Abers 105 M12
Kintour Ag & B 78 H5
Kintra Ag & B 78 E6
Kintra Ag & B 92 J13
Kintraw Ag & B 87 Q5
Kintyre Ag & B 79 N8
Kinveachy Highld 103 P12
Kinver Staffs 35 T4
Kiplin N York 69 S13
Kippax Leeds 63 U13
Kippen Stirlg 89 P7
Kippford D & G 66 B2
Kipping's Cross Kent 12 B7
Kirbister Ork 106 s19
Kirby Bedon Norfk 51 N12
Kirby Bellars Leics 47 T10
Kirby Cane Norfk 41 Q2
Kirby Corner Covtry 36 J5
Kirby Cross Essex 23 T3
Kirby Fields Leics 47 P13
Kirby Green Norfk 41 Q2
Kirby Grindalythe N York 65 L6
Kirby Hill N York 63 T6
Kirby Hill N York 69 P11
Kirby Knowle N York 64 B2
Kirby-le-Soken Essex 23 T3
Kirby Misperton N York 64 H4
Kirby Muxloe Leics 47 P13
Kirby Sigston N York 70 F14
Kirby Underdale E R Yk 64 J8
Kirby Wiske N York 63 T3
Kirdford W Susx 10 G5
Kirk Highld 112 G5
Kirkabister Shet 106 u10
Kirkandrews D & G 73 Q10
Kirkandrews upon Eden Cumb 75 S14
Kirkbampton Cumb 67 M1
Kirkbean D & G 74 J14
Kirk Bramwith Donc 57 T4
Kirkbride Cumb 66 K1
Kirkbridge N York 63 R1
Kirkbuddo Angus 91 R3
Kirkburn Border 83 Q11
Kirkburn E R Yk 65 M8
Kirkburton Kirk 56 J4
Kirkby Knows 54 K7
Kirkby Lincs 58 J8
Kirkby N York 70 H11
Kirkby Fleetham N York 69 S14
Kirkby Green Lincs 48 G2
Kirkby-in-Ashfield Notts 47 P2
Kirkby-in-Furness Cumb 61 N3
Kirkby la Thorpe Lincs 48 G4
Kirkby Lonsdale Cumb 62 C4
Kirkby Malham N York 62 H7
Kirkby Mallory Leics 47 N13
Kirkby Malzeard N York 63 Q5
Kirkby Mills N York 64 G2
Kirkbymoorside N York 64 F2
Kirkby on Bain Lincs 48 K1
Kirkby Overblow N York 63 S10
Kirkby Stephen Cumb 68 G11
Kirkby Thore Cumb 68 D7
Kirkby Underwood Lincs 48 G8
Kirkby Wharf N York 64 C11
Kirkby Woodhouse Notts 47 N3
Kirkcaldy Fife 91 L13
Kirkcambeck Cumb 76 A12
Kirkchrist D & G 73 R9
Kirkcolm D & G 72 C6
Kirkconnel D & G 74 D3
Kirkconnell D & G 74 J12
Kirkcowan D & G 72 J7
Kirkcudbright D & G 73 R9
Kirkdale Lpool 54 H8
Kirk Deighton N York 63 T9
Kirk Ella E R Yk 65 N14
Kirkfieldbank S Lans 82 G10
Kirkgunzeon D & G 74 G12
Kirk Hallam Derbys 47 N5
Kirkham Lancs 61 S13
Kirkham N York 64 G6
Kirkhamgate Wakefd 57 L2
Kirk Hammerton N York 64 B8
Kirkharle Nthumb 77 L9
Kirkhaugh Nthumb 68 E3
Kirkheaton Kirk 56 J3
Kirkheaton Nthumb 77 L10
Kirkhill Highld 102 G6
Kirkhope S Lans 74 J4
Kirkhouse Cumb 76 B14
Kirkhouse Green Donc 57 T4
Kirkibost Highld 100 e8
Kirkinch P & K 91 M3
Kirkinner D & G 73 L9
Kirkintilloch E Duns 89 Q11
Kirk Ireton Derbys 46 J3
Kirkland Cumb 66 G9
Kirkland Cumb 68 D6
Kirkland D & G 74 D3
Kirkland D & G 74 F7
Kirkland D & G 74 K8
Kirkland Guards Cumb 66 J4
Kirk Langley Derbys 46 J6
Kirkleatham R & Cl 70 J8
Kirklevington S on T 70 F11
Kirkley Suffk 41 T2
Kirklington N York 63 S3
Kirklington Notts 47 S2
Kirklinton Cumb 75 T12
Kirkliston C Edin 83 M4
Kirkmabreck D & G 73 M8
Kirkmaiden D & G 72 E12
Kirk Merrington Dur 69 S6
Kirk Michael IoM 60 e4
Kirkmichael P & K 97 T12
Kirkmichael S Ayrs 81 L11
Kirkmuirhill S Lans 82 E10
Kirknewton Nthumb 85 N12
Kirknewton W Loth 83 M5
Kirkney Abers 104 G9
Kirk of Shotts N Lans 82 F6
Kirkoswald Cumb 67 S4
Kirkoswald S Ayrs 80 J11
Kirkpatrick D & G 74 H7
Kirkpatrick Durham D & G 74 E11
Kirkpatrick-Fleming D & G 75 Q11
Kirk Sandall Donc 57 T5
Kirksanton Cumb 61 L3
Kirk Smeaton N York 57 R3
Kirkstall Leeds 63 R12
Kirkstead Lincs 48 J1
Kirkstile Abers 104 G8
Kirkstile D & G 75 S7
Kirkstone Pass Inn Cumb 67 P11
Kirkstyle Highld 112 H2
Kirkthorpe Wakefd 57 N2
Kirkton Abers 104 J10
Kirkton D & G 74 J9
Kirkton Fife 91 N6
Kirkton Highld 101 L6
Kirkton Highld 101 N3
Kirkton P & K 90 E8
Kirkton Manor Border 83 P11
Kirkton of Airlie Angus 98 E13
Kirkton of Auchterhouse Angus 91 M4
Kirkton of Barevan Highld 103 M6
Kirkton of Collace P & K 90 J5
Kirkton of Glenbuchat Abers 104 D12
Kirkton of Kingoldrum Angus 98 E12
Kirkton of Lethendy P & K 90 H3
Kirkton of Logie Buchan Abers 105 R10
Kirkton of Maryculter Abers 99 R4
Kirkton of Menmuir Angus 98 J11
Kirkton of Monikie Angus 91 R4
Kirkton of Rayne Abers 104 K9
Kirkton of Skene Abers 99 Q2
Kirkton of Tealing Angus 91 P4
Kirkton of Tough Abers 104 J13
Kirktown Abers 105 R2
Kirktown Abers 105 T5
Kirktown of Alvah Abers 104 K3
Kirktown of Bourtie Abers 105 N10
Kirktown of Fetteresso Abers 99 R6
Kirktown of Mortlach Moray 104 C8
Kirktown of Slains Abers 105 S10
Kirkurd Border 83 M10
Kirkwall Ork 106 t18
Kirkwall Airport Ork 106 t19
Kirkwhelpington Nthumb 76 K9
Kirk Yetholm Border 85 L13
Kirmington N Linc 58 K4
Kirmond le Mire Lincs 59 L8
Kirn Ag & B 88 E10
Kirriemuir Angus 98 F13
Kirstead Green Norfk 41 N1
Kirtlebridge D & G 75 P11
Kirtling Cambs 39 U9
Kirtling Green Cambs 39 U9
Kirtlington Oxon 29 U4
Kirtomy Highld 111 Q4
Kirton Lincs 49 M6
Kirton Notts 57 U13
Kirton Suffk 41 N12
Kirton End Lincs 49 L5
Kirtonhill W Duns 88 J10
Kirton Holme Lincs 49 L5
Kirton in Lindsey N Linc 58 F7
Kirwaugh D & G 73 L9
Kishorn Highld 101 L4
Kislingbury Nhants 37 S9
Kitebrook Warwks 29 P1
Kite Green Warwks 36 G7
Kites Hardwick Warwks 37 N7
Kitleigh Cnwll 14 F13
Kitt Green Wigan 55 M5
Kittisford Somset 16 E12
Kittle Swans 25 U13
Kitt's Green Birm 36 G3
Kittybrewster C Aber 99 S2
Kitwood Hants 9 T2
Kivernoll Herefs 27 T1
Kiveton Park Rothm 57 Q10
Knaith Lincs 58 D10
Knaith Park Lincs 58 D9
Knap Corner Dorset 17 V12
Knaphill Surrey 20 G11
Knapp Somset 16 K11
Knapp Hill Hants 9 N4
Knapthorpe Notts 47 T2
Knapton C York 64 D9
Knapton N York 64 K4
Knapton Norfk 51 P7
Knapton Green Herefs 34 K10
Knapwell Cambs 39 M8
Knaresborough N York 63 T8
Knarsdale Nthumb 68 E2
Knaven Abers 105 P7
Knayton N York 63 U2
Knebworth Herts 31 S8
Knedlington E R Yk 64 G14
Kneesall Notts 58 B14
Kneeton Notts 47 T4
Knelston Swans 25 S13
Knenhall Staffs 46 B6
Knettishall Suffk 40 G4
Knightacott Devon 15 Q5
Knightcote Warwks 37 M10
Knightley Staffs 45 T8
Knightley Dale Staffs 45 T9
Knighton BCP 8 E9
Knighton C Leic 47 R13
Knighton Devon 5 N11
Knighton Dorset 7 R2
Knighton Powys 34 G6
Knighton Somset 16 G8
Knighton Staffs 45 R5
Knighton Staffs 45 S8
Knighton Wilts 19 L6
Knighton on Teme Worcs 35 P7
Knightsbridge Gloucs 28 G2
Knightsmill Cnwll 4 D4
Knightwick Worcs 35 R9
Knill Herefs 34 G8
Knipoch Ag & B 93 U14
Knipton Leics 48 B7
Knitsley Dur 69 P3
Kniveton Derbys 46 H3
Knock Cumb 68 E7
Knock Highld 100 f9
Knock Moray 104 G5
Knock W Isls 106 j5
Knockally Highld 112 D11
Knockan Highld 108 C2
Knockando Moray 103 U7
Knockbain Highld 102 G7
Knockbain Highld 102 H4
Knock Castle N Ayrs 88 E13
Knockdee Highld 112 E4
Knockdow Ag & B 88 D11
Knockdown Wilts 28 F10
Knockeen S Ayrs 81 L13
Knockenkelly N Ayrs 80 E7
Knockentiber E Ayrs 81 N5
Knockhall Kent 22 E13
Knockholt Kent 21 S11
Knockholt Pound Kent 21 S11
Knockin Shrops 44 H9
Knockinlaw E Ayrs 81 N5
Knockmill Kent 21 U10
Knocknain D & G 72 B7
Knockrome Ag & B 86 K11
Knocksharry IoM 60 d5
Knocksheen D & G 73 P3
Knockvennie Smithy D & G 74 E11
Knodishall Suffk 41 R8
Knodishall Common Suffk 41 R8
Knole Somset 17 N11
Knole Park S Glos 28 A11
Knolls Green Ches E 55 T11
Knolton Wrexhm 44 J6
Knook Wilts 18 D12
Knossington Leics 48 B12
Knott End-on-Sea Lancs 61 R10
Knotting Bed 38 F8
Knotting Green Bed 38 F8
Knottingley Wakefd 57 R2
Knotty Ash Lpool 54 K8
Knotty Green Bucks 20 F4
Knowbury Shrops 35 N5
Knowe D & G 72 J5
Knowehead D & G 73 Q1
Knoweside S Ayrs 80 K10
Knowle Bristl 17 R2
Knowle Devon 6 D3
Knowle Devon 6 E8
Knowle Devon 15 L5
Knowle Devon 15 S12
Knowle Shrops 35 N6
Knowle Solhll 36 G5
Knowle Somset 16 C8
Knowle Cross Devon 6 D5
Knowlefield Cumb 75 T14
Knowle Green Lancs 62 C12
Knowle Hill Surrey 20 G9
Knowle St Giles Somset 6 K2
Knowle Village Hants 9 R7
Knowle Wood Calder 56 D2
Knowl Green Essex 40 C12
Knowl Hill W & M 20 D7
Knowlton Dorset 8 E7
Knowlton Kent 13 Q5
Knowsley Knows 54 K7
Knowsley Safari Park Knows 55 L8
Knowstone Devon 15 T8
Knox N York 63 R8
Knox Bridge Kent 12 E7
Knoydart Highld 100 h9
Knucklas Powys 34 G6
Knuston Nhants 38 D7
Knutsford Ches E 55 S11
Knutsford Services Ches E 55 R11
Knutton Staffs 45 T4
Krumlin Calder 56 G3
Kuggar Cnwll 2 J13
Kyleakin Highld 100 g7
Kyle of Lochalsh Highld 100 g7
Kylerhea Highld 100 g7
Kylesku Highld 110 E10
Kylesmorar Highld 100 h10
Kyles Scalpay W Isls 106 h9
Kylestrome Highld 110 E10
Kynaston Herefs 35 P13
Kynaston Shrops 44 J9
Kynnersley Wrekin 45 Q10
Kyre Green Worcs 35 P8
Kyre Park Worcs 35 P8
Kyrewood Worcs 35 N7
Kyrle Somset 16 E12

L

La Bellieuse Guern 6 d3
Lacasaigh W Isls 106 i6
Lacasdal W Isls 106 j5
Laceby NE Lin 59 M5
Lacey Green Bucks 30 H12
Lach Dennis Ches W 55 R12
Lackenby R & Cl 70 J9
Lackford Suffk 40 C6
Lackford Green Suffk 40 C6
Lacock Wilts 18 D7
Ladbroke Warwks 37 M9
Ladderedge Staffs 46 C3
Laddingford Kent 12 C6
Lade Bank Lincs 49 N3
Ladock Cnwll 3 M6
Lady Ork 106 v15
Ladybank Fife 91 M10
Ladycross Cnwll 4 J3
Ladygill S Lans 82 H13
Lady Hall Cumb 61 M2
Ladykirk Border 85 M9
Ladyridge Herefs 28 A1
Lady's Green Suffk 40 C9
Ladywood Birm 36 E3
Ladywood Worcs 35 U8
La Fontenelle Guern 6 e1
La Fosse Guern 6 d4
Lag D & G 74 G8
Laga Highld 93 Q6
Lagavulin Ag & B 78 G6
Lagg N Ayrs 80 D8
Laggan Highld 96 B4
Laggan Highld 96 J5
Lagganlia Highld 97 P3
La Greve Guern 6 e2
La Grève de Lecq Jersey 7 b1
La Hougue Bie Jersey 7 e3
La Houguette Guern 6 b3
Laid Highld 110 J5
Laide Highld 107 R6
Laig Highld 100 d11
Laigh Clunch E Ayrs 81 P3
Laigh Fenwick E Ayrs 81 P4
Laigh Glenmuir E Ayrs 81 S8
Laighstonehall S Lans 82 D8
Laindon Essex 22 G10
Lairg Highld 108 K3
Laisterdyke C Brad 63 P13
Laithes Cumb 67 Q6
Lake Devon 5 N3
Lake Devon 15 N6
Lake IoW 9 R12
Lake Wilts 18 H13
Lake District Cumb 66 K10
Lake District National Park Cumb 66 K10
Lakenheath Suffk 40 B4
Laker's Green Surrey 10 G3
Lakes End Norfk 39 R1
Lakeside Cumb 61 R2
Laleham Surrey 20 J9
Laleston Brdgnd 26 F12
Lamanva Cnwll 2 K10
Lamarsh Essex 40 E13
Lamas Norfk 51 M9
Lambden Border 84 J10
Lamberhurst Kent 12 C8
Lamberhurst Down Kent 12 C8
Lamberton Border 85 P7
Lambeth Gt Lon 21 P7
Lambfair Green Suffk 40 B10
Lambley Notts 47 R4
Lambley Nthumb 76 D14
Lambourn W Berk 19 M5
Lambourne End Essex 21 S4
Lambourn Woodlands W Berk 19 M5
Lamb Roe Lancs 62 E12
Lambs Green W Susx 11 L3
Lambston Pembks 24 F7
Lamellion Cnwll 4 G8
Lamerton Devon 5 M5
Lamesley Gatesd 77 R14
Lamington S Lans 82 J12
Lamlash N Ayrs 80 E6
Lamonby Cumb 67 P5
Lamorick Cnwll 3 Q4
Lamorna Cnwll 2 C12
Lamorran Cnwll 3 M8
Lampen Cnwll 4 F7
Lampeter Cerdgn 33 L11
Lampeter Velfrey Pembks 25 L8
Lamphey Pembks 24 H10
Lamplugh Cumb 66 G8
Lamport Nhants 37 U6
Lamyatt Somset 17 S9
Lana Devon 14 H11
Lana Devon 14 H13
Lanark S Lans 82 G10
Lancaster Lancs 61 T7
Lancaster Services Lancs 61 U9
Lancaut Gloucs 27 U8
Lanchester Dur 69 Q3
Lancing W Susx 10 K10
L'Ancresse Guern 6 e1
Landbeach Cambs 39 Q7
Landcross Devon 15 L8
Landerberry Abers 99 N3
Landford Wilts 8 K5
Land-hallow Highld 112 E10
Landimore Swans 25 S12
Landkey Devon 15 N6
Landore Swans 26 B8
Landrake Cnwll 4 K8
Landscove Devon 5 T7
Land's End Cnwll 2 A11
Land's End Airport Cnwll 2 B11
Landshipping Pembks 24 H8
Landue Cnwll 4 K5
Landulph Cnwll 5 L8
Landwade Suffk 39 T7
Lane Cnwll 3 L4
Laneast Cnwll 4 G4
Lane Bottom Lancs 62 H12
Lane End Bucks 20 D4
Lane End Cnwll 3 Q3
Lane End Hants 9 R3
Lane End Kent 22 E13
Lane End Lancs 62 H10
Lane End Warrtn 55 Q8
Lane End Wilts 18 B11
Lane Ends Derbys 46 H7
Lane Ends Lancs 62 F13
Lane Ends N York 62 K11
Lane Green Staffs 45 U13
Laneham Notts 58 D11
Lanehead Dur 68 H4
Lane Head Dur 69 P10
Lanehead Nthumb 76 F8
Lane Head Wigan 55 P7
Lane Head Wsall 46 C13
Lane Heads Lancs 61 S12
Lanercost Cumb 76 B13
Laneshaw Bridge Lancs 62 J11
Lane Side Lancs 55 S2
Langaford Devon 14 K13
Langal Highld 93 S5
Langaller Somset 16 J11
Langar Notts 47 T7
Langbank Rens 88 J11
Langbar N York 63 M9
Langbaurgh N York 70 J10
Langcliffe N York 62 G7
Langdale End N York 65 L1
Langdon Cnwll 4 J3
Langdon Beck Dur 68 J6
Langdown Hants 9 N7
Langdyke Fife 91 M11
Langenhoe Essex 23 P4
Langford C Beds 31 Q4
Langford Devon 6 D4
Langford Essex 22 K6
Langford N Som 17 N4
Langford Notts 48 B2
Langford Oxon 29 P7
Langford Budville Somset 16 F12
Langham Dorset 17 U11
Langham Essex 23 P1
Langham Norfk 50 H5
Langham Rutlnd 48 B11
Langham Suffk 40 G7
Langho Lancs 62 E13
Langholm D & G 75 S9
Langland Swans 25 V13
Langlee Border 84 E11
Langley Ches E 56 D12
Langley Derbys 47 M4
Langley Gloucs 28 K2
Langley Hants 9 N8
Langley Herts 31 R8
Langley Kent 12 F5
Langley Nthumb 76 G13
Langley Oxon 29 Q4
Langley Rochdl 56 C5
Langley Slough 20 H7
Langley Somset 16 E11
Langley W Susx 10 C5
Langley Warwks 36 G8
Langley Burrell Wilts 18 D5
Langley Castle Nthumb 76 G13
Langley Common Derbys 46 J6
Langley Green Derbys 46 J6
Langley Green Essex 23 L3
Langley Green Warwks 36 G8
Langley Heath Kent 12 F5
Langley Lower Green Essex 39 P14
Langley Marsh Somset 16 E11
Langley Mill Derbys 47 M4
Langley Moor Dur 69 S4
Langley Park Dur 69 R3
Langley Street Norfk 51 Q13
Langley Upper Green Essex 39 P14
Langley Vale Surrey 21 M11
Langney E Susx 11 U10
Langold Notts 57 S9
Langore Cnwll 4 H3
Langport Somset 17 M11
Langrick Lincs 49 L4
Langridge BaNES 17 T3
Langridgeford Devon 15 N8
Langrigg Cumb 66 J3
Langrish Hants 9 U4
Langsett Barns 56 K6
Langside P & K 89 S3
Langstone Hants 9 U8
Langstone Newpt 27 R10
Langthorne N York 63 Q1
Langthorpe N York 63 T6
Langthwaite N York 69 M12
Langtoft E R Yk 65 N6
Langtoft Lincs 48 H11
Langton Dur 69 Q9
Langton Lincs 59 M13
Langton Lincs 59 Q12
Langton N York 64 H6
Langton by Wragby Lincs 58 K11
Langton Green Kent 11 S3
Langton Green Suffk 40 K6
Langton Herring Dorset 7 R8
Langton Long Blandford Dorset 8 C7
Langton Matravers Dorset 8 E13
Langtree Devon 15 L9
Langtree Week Devon 15 L9
Langwathby Cumb 67 S6
Langwell House Highld 112 D12
Langwith Derbys 57 R13
Langwith Junction Derbys 57 R13
Langworth Lincs 58 J11
Lanhydrock House & Gardens Cnwll 3 R4
Lanivet Cnwll 3 Q4
Lanjeth Cnwll 3 P6
Lank Cnwll 3 R1
Lanlivery Cnwll 3 R5
Lanner Cnwll 2 J9
Lanoy Cnwll 4 H5
Lanreath Cnwll 4 F9
Lansallos Cnwll 4 F10
Lanteglos Cnwll 4 D4
Lanteglos Highway Cnwll 4 E10
Lanton Border 76 C1
Lanton Nthumb 85 N12
La Passee Guern 6 d2
Lapford Devon 15 R11
Laphroaig Ag & B 78 F6
Lapley Staffs 45 U11
La Pulente Jersey 7 a3
Lapworth Warwks 36 G6
Larachbeg Highld 93 R9
Larbert Falk 82 G2
Larbreck Lancs 61 S11
Largie Abers 104 J9
Largiemore Ag & B 87 S8
Largoward Fife 91 Q10
Largs N Ayrs 88 F14
Largybeg N Ayrs 80 E8
Largymore N Ayrs 80 E8
Larkbeare Devon 6 E5
Larkfield Inver 88 F10
Larkfield Kent 12 D4
Larkhall S Lans 82 E8
Larkhill Wilts 18 H12
Larling Norfk 40 G3
La Rocque Jersey 7 f4
La Rousaillerie Guern 6 d2
Lartington Dur 69 M9
Lasborough Gloucs 28 F9
Lasham Hants 19 U12
Lashbrook Devon 14 K11
Lashbrook Devon 14 K11
Lashenden Kent 12 F7
Lask Edge Staffs 46 B2
Lasswade Mdloth 83 R5
Lastingham N York 64 G1
Latcham Somset 17 M7
Latchford Herts 31 U8
Latchford Oxon 30 E12
Latchford Warrtn 55 P9
Latchingdon Essex 23 L7
Latchley Cnwll 5 L6
Lately Common Warrtn 55 Q7
Lathbury M Keyn 30 J4
Latheron Highld 112 F10
Latheronwheel Highld 112 E10
Lathom Lancs 55 L4
Lathones Fife 91 Q10
Latimer Bucks 20 H3
Latteridge S Glos 28 C11
Lattiford Somset 17 S11
Latton Wilts 29 L8
Lauder Border 84 E9
Laugharne Carmth 25 P8
Laughterton Lincs 58 D11
Laughton E Susx 11 R8
Laughton Leics 37 S3
Laughton Lincs 48 G7
Laughton Lincs 58 D7
Laughton-en-le-Morthen Rothm 57 R9
Launcells Cnwll 14 F11
Launcells Cross Cnwll 14 G11
Launceston Cnwll 4 J4
Launton Oxon 30 D8
Laurencekirk Abers 99 N9
Laurieston D & G 73 R7
Laurieston Falk 82 H3
Lavendon M Keyn 38 D10
Lavenham Suffk 40 F11
Lavernock V Glam 16 G3
Laversdale Cumb 75 U13
Laverstock Wilts 8 H2
Laverstoke Hants 19 Q11
Laverton Gloucs 36 E13
Laverton N York 63 Q5
Laverton Somset 17 U6
La Villette Guern 6 d3
Lavister Wrexhm 44 J2
Law S Lans 82 F8
Lawers P & K 95 T11
Lawford Essex 23 Q1
Lawford Somset 16 F9
Law Hill S Lans 82 F8
Lawhitton Cnwll 4 K4
Lawkland N York 62 F6
Lawkland Green N York 62 F6
Lawley Wrekin 45 Q12
Lawnhead Staffs 45 T8
Lawrence Weston Bristl 27 U12
Lawrenny Pembks 24 H9
Lawshall Suffk 40 E10
Lawshall Green Suffk 40 E10
Lawton Herefs 34 K9
Laxay W Isls 106 i6
Laxdale W Isls 106 j5
Laxey IoM 60 g6
Laxfield Suffk 41 N6
Laxford Bridge Highld 110 E7
Laxo Shet 106 u7
Laxton E R Yk 58 C1
Laxton Nhants 38 E1
Laxton Notts 58 B13
Laycock C Brad 63 L11
Layer Breton Essex 23 M4
Layer-de-la-Haye Essex 23 N3
Layer Marney Essex 23 M4
Layham Suffk 40 H12
Layland's Green W Berk 19 N7
Laymore Dorset 7 L4
Layter's Green Bucks 20 G4
Laytham E R Yk 64 G12
Laythes Cumb 66 K1
Lazenby R & Cl 70 J9
Lazonby Cumb 67 R5
Lea Derbys 46 K2
Lea Herefs 28 C3
Lea Lincs 58 D9
Lea Shrops 34 J3
Lea Shrops 44 K12
Lea Wilts 28 J10
Leachkin Highld 102 H7
Leadburn Border 83 P7
Leadenham Lincs 48 D3
Leaden Roding Essex 22 E5
Leadgate Cumb 68 F4
Leadgate Dur 69 P2
Leadgate Nthumb 77 N14
Leadhills S Lans 74 G2
Leadingcross Green Kent 12 G5
Leadmill Derbys 56 K10
Leafield Oxon 29 R4
Leagrave Luton 31 N8
Leahead Ches W 55 Q14
Lea Heath Staffs 46 D8
Leake N York 63 U1
Leake Common Side Lincs 49 N3
Lealholm N York 71 N11
Lealholm Side N York 71 N11
Lealt Highld 100 e3
Leam Derbys 56 K11
Lea Marston Warwks 36 H2
Leamington Hastings Warwks 37 M7
Leamington Spa Warwks 36 K7
Leamside Dur 70 D3
Leap Cross E Susx 11 T8
Leasgill Cumb 61 T3
Leasingham Lincs 48 G4
Leasingthorne Dur 69 S6
Leatherhead Surrey 21 L11
Leathley N York 63 Q10
Leaton Shrops 45 L10
Leaton Wrekin 45 P11
Lea Town Lancs 61 T13
Leaveland Kent 12 K5
Leavenheath Suffk 40 G13
Leavening N York 64 H7
Leaves Green Gt Lon 21 R10
Lea Yeat Cumb 62 F2
Lebberston N York 65 P3
Le Bigard Guern 6 c4
Le Bourg Guern 6 d4
Le Bourg Jersey 7 f4
Lechlade on Thames Gloucs 29 P8
Lecht Gruinart Ag & B 86 D12
Leck Lancs 62 C4
Leckbuie P & K 95 U10
Leckford Hants 19 N13
Leckhampstead Bucks 30 F5
Leckhampstead W Berk 19 P5
Leckhampstead Thicket W Berk 19 P5
Leckhampton Gloucs 28 H4
Leckmelm Highld 108 B7
Leckwith V Glam 27 M13
Leconfield E R Yk 65 N11
Ledaig Ag & B 94 C11
Ledburn Bucks 30 K8
Ledbury Herefs 35 R13
Leddington Gloucs 35 Q14
Ledgemoor Herefs 34 K10
Ledicot Herefs 34 K8
Ledmore Highld 108 C2
Ledsham Ches W 54 J12
Ledsham Leeds 64 B14
Ledston Leeds 63 U14
Ledstone Devon 5 S11
Ledston Luck Leeds 63 U13
Ledwell Oxon 29 T2
Lee Devon 15 L3
Lee Gt Lon 21 Q7
Lee Hants 9 M5
Lee Shrops 44 K7
Leebotwood Shrops 45 L14
Lee Brockhurst Shrops 45 M8
Leece Cumb 61 N6
Lee Chapel Essex 22 G10
Lee Clump Bucks 30 K12
Lee Common Bucks 30 K12
Leeds Kent 12 F5
Leeds Leeds 63 R13
Leeds Bradford Airport Leeds 63 Q11
Leeds Castle Kent 12 F5
Leedstown Cnwll 2 G10
Lee Green Ches E 45 Q1
Leek Staffs 46 C2
Leek Wootton Warwks 36 J7
Lee Mill Devon 5 P9
Leeming C Brad 63 L13
Leeming N York 63 R2
Leeming Bar N York 63 R2
Lee Moor Devon 5 P8
Lee-on-the-Solent Hants 9 R8
Lees C Brad 63 L12
Lees Derbys 46 J6
Lees Oldham 56 E6
Lees Green Derbys 46 J6
Leesthorpe Leics 47 U11
Leeswood Flints 44 G1
Leetown P & K 90 K7
Leftwich Ches W 55 Q12
Legar Powys 27 N4
Legbourne Lincs 59 Q10
Legburthwaite Cumb 67 M9
Legerwood Border 84 F10
Legoland W & M 20 F8
Le Gron Guern 6 c3
Legsby Lincs 58 K9
Le Haguais Jersey 7 e4
Le Hocq Jersey 7 e4
Leicester C Leic 47 Q13
Leicester Forest East Leics 47 P13
Leicester Forest East Services Leics 47 P13
Leigh Devon 15 R10
Leigh Dorset 7 R3
Leigh Gloucs 28 G2
Leigh Kent 21 T13
Leigh Shrops 44 H13
Leigh Surrey 21 M13
Leigh Wigan 55 Q7
Leigh Wilts 29 L9
Leigh Worcs 35 S10
Leigh Beck Essex 22 K11
Leigh Delamere Wilts 18 C5
Leigh Delamere Services Wilts 18 C5
Leigh Green Kent 12 H9
Leigh Knoweglass S Lans 81 S2
Leighland Chapel Somset 16 D9
Leigh-on-Sea Sthend 22 K10
Leigh Park Dorset 8 E9
Leigh Park Hants 9 U7
Leigh Sinton Worcs 35 S10
Leighswood Wsall 46 E13
Leighterton Gloucs 28 F9
Leighton N York 63 P4
Leighton Powys 44 F12
Leighton Shrops 45 P12
Leighton Somset 17 T8
Leighton Bromswold Cambs 38 H5
Leighton Buzzard C Beds 30 K7
Leigh upon Mendip Somset 17 S7
Leigh Woods N Som 27 V13
Leinthall Earls Herefs 34 K7
Leinthall Starkes Herefs 34 K7
Leintwardine Herefs 34 K6
Leire Leics 37 P3
Leiston Suffk 41 R8
Leith C Edin 83 Q3
Leitholm Border 84 K10
Lelant Cnwll 2 E9
Lelley E R Yk 65 S13
Lem Hill Worcs 35 R5
Lempitlaw Border 84 K12
Lemreway W Isls 106 i7
Lemsford Herts 31 R10
Lenchwick Worcs 36 D11
Lendalfoot S Ayrs 72 E1
Lendrick Stirlg 89 N4
Lendrum Terrace Abers 105 U7
Lenham Kent 12 G5
Lenham Heath Kent 12 H6
Lenie Highld 102 F10
Lennel Border 85 M10
Lennox Plunton D & G 73 Q9
Lennoxtown E Duns 89 P10
Lent Bucks 20 F6
Lenton C Nott 47 Q6
Lenton Lincs 48 F7
Lenwade Norfk 50 J10
Lenzie E Duns 89 Q11
Leochel-Cushnie Abers 104 G13
Leomansley Staffs 46 F12
Leominster Herefs 35 L9
Leonard Stanley Gloucs 28 F7
Leoville Jersey 7 b1
Lepe Hants 9 N9
Lephin Highld 100 a5
Leppington N York 64 H7
Lepton Kirk 56 K3
Lerags Ag & B 94 B13
L'Erée Guern 6 b3
Lerryn Cnwll 4 E9
Lerwick Shet 106 u9
Les Arquêts Guern 6 b3
Lesbury Nthumb 77 Q3
Les Hubits Guern 6 e3
Leslie Abers 104 H11
Leslie Fife 91 L11
Les Lohiers Guern 6 c3
Lesmahagow S Lans 82 F11
Les Murchez Guern 6 c4
Lesnewth Cnwll 4 E2
Les Nicolles Guern 6 d4
Les Quartiers Guern 6 d2
Les Quennevais Jersey 7 b3
Les Sages Guern 6 c3
Lessingham Norfk 51 Q8
Lessonhall Cumb 66 K2
Lestowder Cnwll 2 K12
Les Villets Guern 6 c4
Leswalt D & G 72 C7
L'Etacq Jersey 7 a2
Letchmore Heath Herts 21 L3
Letchworth Garden City Herts 31 R6
Letcombe Bassett Oxon 29 S11
Letcombe Regis Oxon 29 S10
Letham Angus 91 R2
Letham Border 76 D4
Letham Falk 82 G1
Letham Fife 91 M9
Letham Grange Angus 91 T2
Lethenty Abers 104 H11
Lethenty Abers 105 N7
Letheringham Suffk 41 N9
Letheringsett Norfk 50 J6
Lettaford Devon 5 S4
Letterewe Highld 107 S10
Letterfearn Highld 101 M7
Letterfinlay Lodge Hotel Highld 96 B5
Lettermorar Highld 100 g11
Letters Highld 108 B7
Lettershaw S Lans 74 G1
Letterston Pembks 24 F5
Lettoch Highld 103 R12
Lettoch Highld 103 T9
Letton Herefs 34 H11
Letton Herefs 34 J6
Lett's Green Kent 21 S11
Letty Green Herts 31 S10
Letwell Rothm 57 S9
Leuchars Fife 91 Q7
Leumrabhagh W Isls 106 i7
Leurbost W Isls 106 i6
Levalsa Meor Cnwll 3 Q7
Levedale Staffs 45 U10
Level's Green Essex 22 C3
Leven E R Yk 65 Q10
Leven Fife 91 N11
Levens Cumb 61 T2
Levens Green Herts 31 U8
Levenshulme Manch 56 C8
Levenwick Shet 106 u11
Leverburgh W Isls 106 f10
Leverington Cambs 49 P11
Leverstock Green Herts 31 N11
Leverton Lincs 49 P4
Le Villocq Guern 6 d2
Levington Suffk 41 M13
Levisham N York 64 J1
Lew Oxon 29 R6
Lewannick Cnwll 4 H4
Lewdown Devon 5 M3
Lewes E Susx 11 Q8
Leweston Pembks 24 F6
Lewisham Gt Lon 21 Q8
Lewiston Highld 102 F10
Lewistown Brdgnd 26 G10
Lewis Wych Herefs 34 H9
Lewknor Oxon 20 B3
Leworthy Devon 14 H12
Leworthy Devon 15 Q5
Lewson Street Kent 12 J3
Lewth Lancs 61 T12
Lewtrenchard Devon 5 M3
Lexden Essex 23 N2
Lexworthy Somset 16 J9
Ley Cnwll 4 F7
Leybourne Kent 12 C4
Leyburn N York 63 N1
Leycett Staffs 45 S4
Leygreen Herts 31 Q8
Ley Hill Bucks 31 L12
Leyland Lancs 55 M2
Leyland Green St Hel 55 N6
Leylodge Abers 105 M13
Leys Abers 105 S5
Leys P & K 91 L4
Leysdown-on-Sea Kent 23 P13
Leysmill Angus 91 T2
Leys of Cossans Angus 91 N2
Leysters Herefs 35 N8
Leyton Gt Lon 21 Q5
Leytonstone Gt Lon 21 Q5
Lezant Cnwll 4 J5
Lezerea Cnwll 2 H10
Lhanbryde Moray 104 B3
Libanus Powys 26 H2
Libberton S Lans 82 J10
Libbery Worcs 36 C9
Liberton C Edin 83 Q5
Lichfield Staffs 46 F12
Lickey Worcs 36 C5
Lickey End Worcs 36 C6
Lickey Rock Worcs 36 C6
Lickfold W Susx 10 E5
Liddaton Green Devon 5 M4
Liddesdale Highld 93 T7
Liddington Swindn 18 K4
Lidgate Derbys 57 M11
Lidgate Suffk 40 B9
Lidget Donc 57 U6
Lidgett Notts 57 T13
Lidham Hill E Susx 12 F12
Lidlington C Beds 31 L5
Lidsey W Susx 10 E10
Lidsing Kent 12 E3
Liff Angus 91 M5
Lifford Birm 36 E4
Lifton Devon 4 K3
Liftondown Devon 4 K3
Lighthorne Warwks 36 K9
Lighthorne Heath Warwks 37 L9
Lightwater Surrey 20 F10
Lightwater Valley Theme Park N York 63 R4
Lightwood C Stke 46 B5
Lightwood Green Ches E 45 P5
Lightwood Green Wrexhm 44 J5
Lilbourne Nhants 37 Q5
Lilburn Tower Nthumb 85 Q14
Lilleshall Wrekin 45 R10
Lilley Herts 31 P7
Lilley W Berk 19 P5
Lilliesleaf Border 84 E13
Lillingstone Dayrell Bucks 30 F5
Lillingstone Lovell Bucks 30 F4
Lillington Dorset 7 R2
Lilliput BCP 8 E11
Lilstock Somset 16 G7
Lilyhurst Shrops 45 R11
Limbrick Lancs 55 P3
Limbury Luton 31 N8
Limebrook Herefs 34 J7
Limefield Bury 55 T4
Limekilnburn S Lans 82 D8
Limekilns Fife 83 L2
Limerigg Falk 82 G4
Limerstone IoW 9 N12
Limestone Brae Nthumb 68 G3
Lime Street Worcs 28 F1
Limington Somset 17 P12
Limmerhaugh E Ayrs 81 S7
Limpenhoe Norfk 51 Q13
Limpley Stoke Wilts 17 U4
Limpsfield Surrey 21 R12
Limpsfield Chart Surrey 21 R12
Linby Notts 47 P3
Linchmere W Susx 10 D4
Lincluden D & G 74 J10
Lincoln Lincs 58 G12
Lincomb Worcs 35 T7
Lincombe Devon 5 S12
Lincombe Devon 15 L3
Lindale Cumb 61 S3
Lindal in Furness Cumb 61 N4
Lindfield W Susx 11 N5
Lindford Hants 10 C3
Lindley Kirk 56 H3
Lindley N York 63 Q10
Lindores Fife 91 L8
Lindow End Ches E 55 T11
Lindridge Worcs 35 Q7
Lindsell Essex 22 F2
Lindsey Suffk 40 G11
Lindsey Tye Suffk 40 G11
Liney Somset 17 L9
Linford Hants 8 H7
Linford Thurr 22 G12
Lingbob C Brad 63 M12
Lingdale R & Cl 71 L9
Lingen Herefs 34 J7
Lingfield Surrey 11 P2
Lingwood Norfk 51 Q12
Liniclate W Isls 106 c14
Linicro Highld 100 c3
Linkend Worcs 28 F1
Linkenholt Hants 19 N9
Linkhill Kent 12 F10
Linkinhorne Cnwll 4 J6
Linktown Fife 91 L13
Linkwood Moray 104 A3
Linley Shrops 34 J2
Linley Green Herefs 35 Q10
Linleygreen Shrops 45 Q14
Linlithgow W Loth 82 J3
Linshiels Nthumb 76 H4
Linsidemore Highld 108 J5
Linslade C Beds 30 K7
Linstead Parva Suffk 41 P5
Linstock Cumb 75 T14
Linthurst Worcs 36 C6
Linthwaite Kirk 56 H4
Lintlaw Border 85 L7
Lintmill Moray 104 G2
Linton Border 84 K13
Linton Cambs 39 S11
Linton Derbys 46 J10
Linton Herefs 28 C2
Linton Kent 12 E5
Linton Leeds 63 T10
Linton N York 62 K7
Linton Nthumb 77 R7
Linton Heath Derbys 46 J10
Linton Hill Herefs 28 C3
Linton-on-Ouse N York 64 B7
Linwood Hants 8 H7
Linwood Lincs 58 K9
Linwood Rens 88 K13
Lionacleit W Isls 106 c14
Lìonal W Isls 106 k2
Lions Green E Susx 11 T7
Liphook Hants 10 C4
Lipley Shrops 45 R7
Liscard Wirral 54 G8
Liscombe Somset 15 U6
Liskeard Cnwll 4 H8
Lismore Ag & B 93 U10
Liss Hants 10 B5
Lissett E R Yk 65 Q8
Liss Forest Hants 10 B5
Lissington Lincs 58 K10
Liston Essex 40 E12
Lisvane Cardif 27 M11
Liswerry Newpt 27 Q10
Litcham Norfk 50 E10
Litchborough Nhants 37 R10
Litchfield Hants 19 Q10
Litherland Sefton 54 H7
Litlington Cambs 31 T4
Litlington E Susx 11 S10
Little Abington Cambs 39 R11
Little Addington Nhants 38 E6
Little Airies D & G 73 L10
Little Almshoe Herts 31 R7
Little Alne Warwks 36 F8
Little Altcar Sefton 54 H5
Little Amwell Herts 31 U10
Little Asby Cumb 68 E11
Little Aston Staffs 46 E14
Little Atherfield IoW 9 P13
Little Ayton N York 70 J10
Little Baddow Essex 22 J6
Little Badminton S Glos 28 F11
Little Bampton Cumb 67 L1
Little Bardfield Essex 22 G1
Little Barford Bed 38 J9
Little Barningham Norfk 50 K7
Little Barrington Gloucs 29 P5
Little Barrow Ches W 55 L13
Little Barugh N York 64 H4
Little Bavington Nthumb 76 K10
Little Bealings Suffk 41 M11
Littlebeck N York 71 Q12
Little Bedwyn Wilts 19 L7
Little Bentley Essex 23 R2
Little Berkhamsted Herts 31 S11
Little Billing Nhants 38 B8
Little Billington C Beds 30 K8
Little Birch Herefs 27 U1
Little Bispham Bpool 61 Q11
Little Blakenham Suffk 40 K11
Little Blencow Cumb 67 Q6
Little Bloxwich Wsall 46 D13
Little Bognor W Susx 10 G6
Little Bolehill Derbys 46 J3
Little Bollington Ches E 55 R9
Little Bookham Surrey 20 K12
Littleborough Devon 15 T10
Littleborough Notts 58 D10
Littleborough Rochdl 56 D3
Littlebourne Kent 13 P4
Little Bourton Oxon 37 N12
Little Bowden Leics 37 T3
Little Bradley Suffk 39 U10
Little Brampton Herefs 34 H8
Little Brampton Shrops 34 J4
Little Braxted Essex 22 K5
Little Brechin Angus 98 K11
Littlebredy Dorset 7 Q7
Little Brickhill M Keyn 30 K6
Little Bridgeford Staffs 45 U8
Little Brington Nhants 37 S8
Little Bromley Essex 23 Q2
Little Broughton Cumb 66 G6
Little Budworth Ches W 55 N13
Littleburn Highld 102 H5
Little Burstead Essex 22 G9
Littlebury Essex 39 R13
Littlebury Green Essex 39 Q13
Little Bytham Lincs 48 F10
Little Canfield Essex 22 E3
Little Carlton Lincs 59 Q9
Little Carlton Notts 47 U2
Little Casterton Rutlnd 48 F12
Little Catwick E R Yk 65 Q11
Little Catworth Cambs 38 H6
Little Cawthorpe Lincs 59 Q10
Little Chalfont Bucks 20 G3
Little Chart Kent 12 H6
Little Chesterford Essex 39 R12
Little Cheveney Kent 12 D7
Little Cheverell Wilts 18 E10
Little Chishill Cambs 39 P13
Little Clacton Essex 23 S4
Little Clanfield Oxon 29 Q7
Little Clifton Cumb 66 G7
Little Coates NE Lin 59 M5
Little Comberton Worcs 36 C12
Little Common E Susx 12 D14
Little Comp Kent 12 B4
Little Compton Warwks 29 Q1
Little Corby Cumb 67 Q1
Little Cornard Suffk 40 F13
Littlecott Wilts 18 H10
Little Cowarne Herefs 35 P10
Little Coxwell Oxon 29 Q9
Little Crakehall N York 63 Q1
Little Cransley Nhants 38 B5
Little Cressingham Norfk 50 E13
Little Crosby Sefton 54 H6
Little Crosthwaite Cumb 66 K7
Little Cubley Derbys 46 G6
Little Dalby Leics 47 U11
Littledean Gloucs 28 C5
Little Dewchurch Herefs 27 U1
Little Ditton Cambs 39 U9
Little Doward Herefs 27 U4
Littledown Hants 19 M9
Little Downham Cambs 39 R4
Little Driffield E R Yk 65 N8
Little Dunham Norfk 50 E11
Little Dunkeld P & K 90 F3
Little Dunmow Essex 22 G3
Little Durnford Wilts 8 G2
Little Easton Essex 22 F3
Little Eaton Derbys 47 L5
Little Ellingham Norfk 50 H14
Little Elm Somset 17 T7
Little Everdon Nhants 37 Q9
Little Eversden Cambs 39 N10
Little Faringdon Oxon 29 P7
Little Fencote N York 69 S14
Little Fenton N York 64 C12
Littleferry Highld 109 Q5
Little Fransham Norfk 50 F11
Little Gaddesden Herts 31 L10
Little Garway Herefs 27 S3
Little Gidding Cambs 38 H4
Little Glemham Suffk 41 P9
Little Gorsley Herefs 28 C3
Little Gransden Cambs 39 L9
Little Green Notts 47 T5
Little Green Somset 17 T7
Little Grimsby Lincs 59 P8
Little Gringley Notts 58 B10
Little Habton N York 64 G4
Little Hadham Herts 22 B3
Little Hale Lincs 48 H5
Little Hallam Derbys 47 N5
Little Hallingbury Essex 22 D4
Littleham Devon 6 D8
Littleham Devon 14 K8
Little Hampden Bucks 30 J12
Littlehampton W Susx 10 G10
Little Hanford Dorset 8 A6
Little Harrowden Nhants 38 C6
Little Haseley Oxon 30 D12
Little Hatfield E R Yk 65 R11
Little Hautbois Norfk 51 N9
Little Haven Pembks 24 E8
Littlehaven W Susx 10 K4
Little Hay Staffs 46 F13
Little Hayfield Derbys 56 F9
Little Haywood Staffs 46 D9
Little Heath Staffs 45 U10
Little Heath W Berk 19 U6
Littlehempston Devon 5 U8
Little Hereford Herefs 35 N7
Little Horkesley Essex 23 N1
Little Hormead Herts 22 B2
Little Horsted E Susx 11 R7
Little Horton C Brad 63 P13
Little Horton Wilts 18 F8
Little Horwood Bucks 30 G6
Little Houghton Barns 57 P5
Little Houghton Nhants 38 B9
Littlehoughton Nthumb 77 Q2
Little Hucklow Derbys 56 J11
Little Hulton Salfd 55 R6
Little Hungerford W Berk 19 R6
Little Hutton N York 64 B4
Little Irchester Nhants 38 D7
Little Kelk E R Yk 65 P8
Little Keyford Somset 17 U7
Little Kimble Bucks 30 H11
Little Kineton Warwks 36 K10
Little Kingshill Bucks 20 E3
Little Knox D & G 74 F13

Little Langdale – Mallaigvaig 135

Little Langdale Cumb 67 M12
Little Langford Wilts 18 F13
Little Laver Essex 22 D6
Little Leigh Ches W 55 P11
Little Leighs Essex 22 H4
Little Lever Bolton 55 S5
Little Linford M Keyn 30 H4
Little Load Somset 17 N12
Little London Bucks 30 D10
Little London Cambs 39 P1
Little London E Susx 11 T6
Little London Essex 22 C2
Little London Essex 39 U13
Little London Gloucs 28 D4
Little London Hants 19 N11
Little London Hants 19 T9
Little London Leeds 63 Q12
Little London Lincs 48 K9
Little London Lincs 49 P9
Little London Lincs 59 P12
Little London Norfk 49 S9
Little London Powys 34 B3
Little Longstone Derbys 56 J12
Little Madeley Staffs 45 S4
Little Malvern Worcs 35 S12
Little Mancot Flints 54 H13
Little Maplestead Essex 40 D14
Little Marcle Herefs 35 Q13
Little Marland Devon 15 M10
Little Marlow Bucks 20 E5
Little Massingham Norfk 50 C9
Little Melton Norfk 51 L12
Littlemill Abers 98 E4
Littlemill Highld 103 P5
Little Mill Mons 27 Q7
Little Milton Oxon 30 D12
Little Missenden Bucks 20 F3
Little Mongeham Kent 13 R5
Littlemoor Derbys 57 N14
Little Moor Somset 16 K10
Littlemore Oxon 30 B12
Little Musgrave Cumb 68 G10
Little Ness Shrops 44 K10
Little Neston Ches W 54 G11
Little Newcastle Pembks 24 G5
Little Newsham Dur 69 P9
Little Norton Somset 17 N13
Little Oakley Essex 23 T2
Little Oakley Nhants 38 C3
Little Odell Bed 38 E9
Little Offley Herts 31 P7
Little Ormside Cumb 68 F9
Little Orton Cumb 67 N1
Little Ouse Cambs 39 T3
Little Ouseburn N York 63 U7
Littleover C Derb 46 K7
Little Oxendon Nhants 37 T4
Little Packington Warwks 36 H4
Little Pattenden Kent 12 D6
Little Paxton Cambs 38 J8
Little Petherick Cnwll 3 N2
Little Plumpton Lancs 61 R13
Little Plumstead Norfk 51 P11
Little Ponton Lincs 48 D7
Littleport Cambs 39 S3
Littleport Bridge Cambs 39 S3
Little Posbrook Hants 9 Q8
Little Potheridge Devon 15 M10
Little Preston Leeds 63 T13
Little Preston Nhants 37 Q10
Littler Ches W 55 P13
Little Raveley Cambs 39 L5
Little Reedness E R Yk 58 D2
Little Ribston N York 63 T9
Little Rissington Gloucs 29 N4
Little Rollright Oxon 29 Q1
Little Rowsley Derbys 57 L13
Little Ryburgh Norfk 50 G8
Little Ryle Nthumb 77 L3
Little Ryton Shrops 45 L13
Little Salkeld Cumb 67 S5
Little Sampford Essex 39 U14
Little Sandhurst Br For 20 D10
Little Saredon Staffs 46 B12
Little Saughall Ches W 54 J13
Little Saxham Suffk 40 D8
Little Scatwell Highld 102 C4
Little Shelford Cambs 39 Q10
Little Shrewley Warwks 36 H7
Little Silver Devon 6 B3
Little Singleton Lancs 61 R12
Little Skipwith N York 64 F12
Little Smeaton N York 57 R3
Little Snoring Norfk 50 G7
Little Sodbury S Glos 28 E11
Little Sodbury End S Glos 28 D11
Little Somborne Hants 9 M2
Little Somerford Wilts 28 J11
Little Soudley Shrops 45 R8
Little Stainforth N York 62 G6
Little Stainton Darltn 70 D8
Little Stanion Nhants 38 C3
Little Stanney Ches W 54 K12
Little Staughton Bed 38 H8
Little Steeping Lincs 59 R14
Little Stoke Staffs 46 B7
Littlestone-on-Sea Kent 13 L11
Little Stonham Suffk 40 K8
Little Stretton Leics 47 S13
Little Stretton Shrops 34 K2
Little Strickland Cumb 67 S9
Little Stukeley Cambs 38 K5
Little Sugnall Staffs 45 T7
Little Sutton Ches W 54 J11
Little Sutton Shrops 35 M4
Little Swinburne Nthumb 76 J10
Little Sypland D & G 73 S9
Little Tew Oxon 29 S2
Little Tey Essex 23 L3
Little Thetford Cambs 39 R5
Little Thirkleby N York 64 B4
Little Thornage Norfk 50 J6
Little Thornton Lancs 61 R11
Little Thorpe Dur 70 F4
Littlethorpe Leics 37 P1
Littlethorpe N York 63 S6
Little Thurlow Suffk 39 U10
Little Thurlow Green Suffk 39 U10
Little Thurrock Thurr 22 F12
Littleton Angus 98 E13
Littleton BaNES 17 Q4
Littleton Ches W 54 K13
Littleton D & G 73 Q8
Littleton Dorset 8 B8
Littleton Hants 9 P2
Littleton Somset 17 N10
Littleton Surrey 20 G13
Littleton Surrey 20 J9
Littleton Drew Wilts 18 B4
Littleton-on-Severn S Glos 28 A10
Littleton Pannell Wilts 18 F10
Little Torrington Devon 15 L9
Little Totham Essex 23 L5
Little Town Cumb 66 K9
Littletown Dur 70 D4
Little Town Lancs 62 D12
Little Town Warrtn 55 P8
Little Twycross Leics 46 K12
Little Urswick Cumb 61 P5
Little Wakering Essex 23 M10
Little Walden Essex 39 R12
Little Waldingfield Suffk 40 F11
Little Walsingham Norfk 50 F6
Little Waltham Essex 22 H5
Little Warley Essex 22 F9
Little Washbourne Gloucs 36 C14
Little Weighton E R Yk 65 M13
Little Welnetham Suffk 40 E9
Little Welton Lincs 59 P9
Little Wenham Suffk 40 J13
Little Wenlock Wrekin 45 P12
Little Weston Somset 17 R11
Little Whitefield IoW 9 R11
Little Whittingham Green Suffk 41 N5
Little Whittington Nthumb 76 K12
Littlewick Green W & M 20 D7
Little Wilbraham Cambs 39 R9
Littlewindsor Dorset 7 M4
Little Witcombe Gloucs 28 H4
Little Witley Worcs 35 S8
Little Wittenham Oxon 19 S2
Little Wolford Warwks 36 J13
Littlewood Staffs 46 C12
Little Woodcote Gt Lon 21 N10
Littleworth Bucks 30 J8
Littleworth Oxon 29 R8
Littleworth Staffs 46 B9
Littleworth Staffs 46 D11
Littleworth W Susx 10 K6
Littleworth Worcs 35 U10
Littleworth Worcs 36 C8
Littleworth Common Bucks 20 F5
Little Wratting Suffk 39 U11
Little Wymington Bed 38 E8
Little Wymondley Herts 31 R7
Little Wyrley Staffs 46 D12
Little Wytheford Shrops 45 N10
Little Yeldham Essex 40 C13
Littley Green Essex 22 G4
Litton Derbys 56 J11
Litton N York 62 J5
Litton Somset 17 Q6
Litton Cheney Dorset 7 P6
Liurbost W Isls 106 i6
Liverpool Lpool 54 H8
Liverpool Maritime Mercantile City Lpool 54 H9
Liversedge Kirk 56 J2
Liverton Devon 5 U5
Liverton R & Cl 71 M9
Liverton Mines R & Cl 71 M9
Liverton Street Kent 12 G5
Livingston W Loth 83 L5
Livingston Village W Loth 82 K5
Lixwm Flints 54 E12
Lizard Cnwll 2 J14
Llaingoch IoA 52 B6
Llaithddu Powys 34 C4
Llan Powys 43 S13
Llanaber Gwynd 43 M10
Llanaelhaearn Gwynd 42 G5
Llanafan Cerdgn 33 N6
Llanafan-Fawr Powys 33 U9
Llanafan-fechan Powys 33 U10
Llanallgo IoA 52 H5
Llanarmon Gwynd 42 H6
Llanarmon Dyffryn Ceiriog Wrexhm 44 E7
Llanarmon-yn-Ial Denbgs 44 E2
Llanarth Cerdgn 32 H9
Llanarth Mons 27 R5
Llanarthne Carmth 25 T7
Llanasa Flints 54 D10
Llanbabo IoA 52 E5
Llanbadarn Fawr Cerdgn 33 M4
Llanbadarn Fynydd Powys 34 C5
Llanbadarn-y-garreg Powys 34 D11
Llanbadoc Mons 27 R8
Llanbadrig IoA 52 E4
Llanbeder Newpt 27 R9
Llanbedr Gwynd 43 L8
Llanbedr Powys 27 N3
Llanbedr Powys 34 D11
Llanbedr-Dyffryn-Clwyd Denbgs 44 D2
Llanbedrgoch IoA 52 H6
Llanbedrog Gwynd 42 F7
Llanbedr-y-Cennin Conwy 53 N9
Llanberis Gwynd 52 J10
Llanbethêry V Glam 16 D3
Llanbister Powys 34 D6
Llanblethian V Glam 26 H13
Llanboidy Carmth 25 M6
Llanbradach Caerph 27 L9
Llanbrynmair Powys 43 S13
Llancadle V Glam 16 D3
Llancarfan V Glam 16 D2
Llancayo Mons 27 R7
Llancloudy Herefs 27 T3
Llancynfelyn Cerdgn 33 M2
Llandaff Cardif 27 M12
Llandanwg Gwynd 43 L8
Llandarcy Neath 26 C8
Llandawke Carmth 25 N8
Llanddaniel Fab IoA 52 G8
Llanddarog Carmth 25 T7
Llanddeiniol Cerdgn 33 L6
Llanddeiniolen Gwynd 52 H9
Llandderfel Gwynd 43 U6
Llanddeusant Carmth 26 D3
Llanddeusant IoA 52 D5
Llanddew Powys 26 K1
Llanddewi Swans 25 S13
Llanddewi Brefi Cerdgn 33 N9
Llanddewi'r Cwm Powys 34 B11
Llanddewi Rhydderch Mons 27 R5
Llanddewi Velfrey Pembks 24 K7
Llanddewi Ystradenni Powys 34 D7
Llanddoged Conwy 53 P10
Llanddona IoA 52 J7
Llanddowror Carmth 25 N8
Llanddulas Conwy 53 R7
Llanddwywe Gwynd 43 L9
Llanddyfnan IoA 52 H7
Llandecwyn Gwynd 43 M6
Llandefaelog Powys 26 J1
Llandefaelog-Tre'r-Graig Powys 27 L2
Llandefalle Powys 34 D13
Llandegfan IoA 52 J8
Llandegla Denbgs 44 E3
Llandegley Powys 34 D8
Llandegveth Mons 27 Q8
Llandegwning Gwynd 42 E8
Llandeilo Carmth 26 A3
Llandeilo Graban Powys 34 C12
Llandeilo'r Fan Powys 33 S14
Llandeloy Pembks 24 E5
Llandenny Mons 27 S7
Llandevaud Newpt 27 S9
Llandevenny Mons 27 S10
Llandinabo Herefs 27 U2
Llandinam Powys 34 B3
Llandissilio Pembks 24 K6
Llandogo Mons 27 U7
Llandough V Glam 26 H13
Llandough V Glam 27 M13
Llandovery Carmth 33 Q14
Llandow V Glam 26 G13
Llandre Carmth 33 N12
Llandre Cerdgn 33 M3
Llandre Isaf Pembks 24 K5
Llandrillo Denbgs 44 B6
Llandrillo-yn-Rhos Conwy 53 P6
Llandrindod Wells Powys 34 C8
Llandrinio Powys 44 G10
Llandudno Conwy 53 N6
Llandudno Junction Conwy 53 N7
Llandulas Powys 33 S12
Llandwrog Gwynd 52 G11
Llandybie Carmth 25 V7
Llandyfaelog Carmth 25 R8
Llandyfan Carmth 26 A4
Llandyfriog Cerdgn 32 F12
Llandyfrydog IoA 52 F5
Llandygai Gwynd 52 J8
Llandygwydd Cerdgn 32 D12
Llandynan Denbgs 44 E4
Llandyrnog Denbgs 54 D13
Llandyssil Powys 34 E1
Llandysul Cerdgn 32 H12
Llanedeyrn Cardif 27 N11
Llanedi Carmth 25 U9
Llaneglwys Powys 34 C13
Llanegryn Gwynd 43 M12
Llanegwad Carmth 25 T6
Llaneilian IoA 52 G4
Llanelian-yn-Rhôs Conwy 53 Q7
Llanelidan Denbgs 44 D3
Llanelieu Powys 34 E14
Llanellen Mons 27 Q5
Llanelli Carmth 25 T10
Llanelltyd Gwynd 43 P10
Llanelly Mons 27 N5
Llanelly Hill Mons 27 N5
Llanelwedd Powys 34 B10
Llanenddwyn Gwynd 43 L9
Llanengan Gwynd 42 E8
Llanerch Gwynd 43 S10
Llanerch Powys 34 H2
Llanerchymedd IoA 52 F6
Llanerfyl Powys 44 B12
Llanfachraeth IoA 52 D6
Llanfachreth Gwynd 43 Q9
Llanfaelog IoA 52 D8
Llanfaelrhys Gwynd 42 D8
Llanfaenor Mons 27 S4
Llanfaes IoA 52 K7
Llanfaes Powys 26 J2
Llanfaethlu IoA 52 D5
Llanfair Gwynd 43 L8
Llanfair Caereinion Powys 44 D12
Llanfair Clydogau Cerdgn 33 M10
Llanfair Dyffryn Clwyd Denbgs 44 D2
Llanfairfechan Conwy 53 L8
Llanfair Kilgeddin Mons 27 R6
Llanfair-Nant-Gwyn Pembks 25 L3
Llanfairpwllgwyngyll IoA 52 H8
Llanfair Talhaiarn Conwy 53 R8
Llanfair Waterdine Shrops 34 F5
Llanfairynghornwy IoA 52 D4
Llanfair-yn-Neubwll IoA 52 D7
Llanfallteg Carmth 25 L6
Llanfallteg West Carmth 24 K7
Llanfarian Cerdgn 33 L5
Llanfechain Powys 44 E9
Llanfechell IoA 52 E4
Llanferres Denbgs 44 E1
Llanfflewyn IoA 52 E5
Llanfigael IoA 52 D6
Llanfihangel-ar-arth Carmth 25 S3
Llanfihangel Glyn Myfyr Conwy 43 U4
Llanfihangel Nant Bran Powys 33 T14
Llanfihangel-nant-Melan Powys 34 E9
Llanfihangel Rhydithon Powys 34 E7
Llanfihangel Rogiet Mons 27 T10
Llanfihangel Tal-y-llyn Powys 27 L2
Llanfihangel-uwch-Gwili Carmth 25 S6
Llanfihangel-y-Creuddyn Cerdgn 33 N5
Llanfihangel-yng-Ngwynfa Powys 44 C10
Llanfihangel yn Nhowyn IoA 52 D7
Llanfihangel-y-pennant Gwynd 42 K5
Llanfihangel-y-pennant Gwynd 43 N12
Llanfihangel-y-traethau Gwynd 43 L7
Llanfilo Powys 34 D14
Llanfoist Mons 27 P5
Llanfor Gwynd 43 T6
Llanfrechfa Torfn 27 Q9
Llanfrothen Gwynd 43 M5
Llanfrynach Powys 26 K2
Llanfwrog Denbgs 44 D2
Llanfwrog IoA 52 D6
Llanfyllin Powys 44 D10
Llanfynydd Carmth 25 U5
Llanfynydd Flints 44 G2
Llanfyrnach Pembks 25 M4
Llangadfan Powys 44 B11
Llangadog Carmth 25 R9
Llangadog Carmth 26 C2
Llangadwaladr IoA 52 E9
Llangadwaladr Powys 44 E7
Llangaffo IoA 52 F9
Llangain Carmth 25 Q7
Llangammarch Wells Powys 33 T11
Llangan V Glam 26 H12
Llangarron Herefs 27 U3
Llangasty-Talyllyn Powys 27 L2
Llangathen Carmth 25 U6
Llangattock Powys 27 N4
Llangattock Lingoed Mons 27 R3
Llangattock-Vibon-Avel Mons 27 T4
Llangedwyn Powys 44 E9
Llangefni IoA 52 G7
Llangeinor Brdgnd 26 G10
Llangeitho Cerdgn 33 M9
Llangeler Carmth 25 Q3
Llangelynin Gwynd 43 L12
Llangendeirne Carmth 25 S8
Llangennech Carmth 25 U10
Llangennith Swans 25 R12
Llangenny Powys 27 N4
Llangernyw Conwy 53 Q9
Llangian Gwynd 42 E8
Llangiwg Neath 26 C6
Llangloffan Pembks 24 F4
Llanglydwen Carmth 25 L5
Llangoed IoA 52 K7
Llangoedmor Cerdgn 32 D11
Llangollen Denbgs 44 F5
Llangolman Pembks 24 K5
Llangors Powys 27 L2
Llangorwen Cerdgn 33 M4
Llangovan Mons 27 T6
Llangower Gwynd 43 T7
Llangrannog Cerdgn 32 F10
Llangristiolus IoA 52 F8
Llangrove Herefs 27 U4
Llangua Mons 27 R2
Llangunllo Powys 34 F6
Llangunnor Carmth 25 R6
Llangurig Powys 33 T5
Llangwm Conwy 43 U5
Llangwm Mons 27 S8
Llangwm Pembks 24 G9
Llangwnnadl Gwynd 42 D7
Llangwyfan Denbgs 54 D13
Llangwyllog IoA 52 F7
Llangwyryfon Cerdgn 33 L6
Llangybi Cerdgn 33 M10
Llangybi Gwynd 42 H5
Llangybi Mons 27 R8
Llangyfelach Swans 26 A8
Llangynhafal Denbgs 54 D14
Llangynidr Powys 27 M4
Llangynin Carmth 25 N7
Llangynllo Cerdgn 32 G12
Llangynog Carmth 25 P8
Llangynog Powys 44 C8
Llangynwyd Brdgnd 26 F10
Llanhamlach Powys 26 K2
Llanharan Rhondd 26 J11
Llanharry Rhondd 26 J11
Llanhennock Mons 27 R9
Llanhilleth Blae G 27 N7
Llanidan IoA 52 G9
Llanidloes Powys 33 U4
Llaniestyn Gwynd 42 E7
Llanigon Powys 34 F13
Llanilar Cerdgn 33 M5
Llanilid Rhondd 26 H11
Llanina Cerdgn 32 H9
Llanio Cerdgn 33 M9
Llanishen Cardif 27 M11
Llanishen Mons 27 T7
Llanllechid Gwynd 52 K9
Llanlleonfel Powys 33 T10
Llanllowell Mons 27 R8
Llanllugan Powys 44 C13
Llanllwch Carmth 25 Q7
Llanllwchaiarn Powys 34 D2
Llanllwni Carmth 25 S3
Llanllyfni Gwynd 42 J3
Llanmadoc Swans 25 R12
Llanmaes V Glam 16 C3
Llanmartin Newpt 27 R10
Llanmerewig Powys 34 E2
Llanmihangel V Glam 16 C2
Llanmiloe Carmth 25 M9
Llanmorlais Swans 25 T12
Llannefydd Conwy 53 S8
Llannon Carmth 25 T9
Llannor Gwynd 42 G6
Llanon Cerdgn 32 K7
Llanover Mons 27 Q6
Llanpumsaint Carmth 25 R5
Llanrhaeadr-ym-Mochnant Powys 44 D8
Llanrhian Pembks 24 D4
Llanrhidian Swans 25 S12
Llanrhos Conwy 53 N6
Llanrhychwyn Conwy 53 N10
Llanrhyddlad IoA 52 D5
Llanrhystud Cerdgn 32 K7
Llanrothal Herefs 27 T4
Llanrug Gwynd 52 H10
Llanrumney Cardif 27 N11
Llanrwst Conwy 53 P10
Llansadurnen Carmth 25 N8
Llansadwrn Carmth 26 B1
Llansadwrn IoA 52 J7
Llansaint Carmth 25 Q9
Llansamlet Swans 26 B8
Llansanffraid Glan Conwy Conwy 53 P7
Llansannan Conwy 53 R9
Llansannor V Glam 26 H12
Llansantffraed Powys 27 L3
Llansantffraed-Cwmdeuddwr Powys 33 U7
Llansantffraed-in-Elvel Powys 34 C10
Llansantffraid Cerdgn 32 K7
Llansantffraid-ym-Mechain Powys 44 F9
Llansawel Carmth 25 V3
Llansilin Powys 44 F8
Llansoy Mons 27 S7
Llanspyddid Powys 26 J2
Llanstadwell Pembks 24 F10
Llansteffan Carmth 25 Q8
Llanstephan Powys 34 D12
Llantarnam Torfn 27 Q9
Llanteg Pembks 25 L8
Llanthewy Skirrid Mons 27 Q4
Llanthony Mons 27 P2
Llantilio-Crossenny Mons 27 R5
Llantilio Pertholey Mons 27 Q4
Llantood Pembks 32 C12
Llantrisant IoA 52 E6
Llantrisant Mons 27 R8
Llantrisant Rhondd 26 J11
Llantrithyd V Glam 26 J13
Llantwit Fardre Rhondd 26 K10
Llantwit Major V Glam 16 C3
Llantysilio Denbgs 44 E5
Llanuwchllyn Gwynd 43 S7
Llanvaches Newpt 27 S9
Llanvair Discoed Mons 27 S9
Llanvapley Mons 27 R5
Llanvetherine Mons 27 R4
Llanveynoe Herefs 27 Q1
Llanvihangel Crucorney Mons 27 Q3
Llanvihangel Gobion Mons 27 Q6
Llanvihangel-Ystern-Llewern Mons 27 S5
Llanwarne Herefs 27 U2
Llanwddyn Powys 44 B10
Llanwenarth Mons 27 P5
Llanwenog Cerdgn 32 J11
Llanwern Newpt 27 R10
Llanwinio Carmth 25 N5
Llanwnda Gwynd 52 G11
Llanwnda Pembks 24 F3
Llanwnnen Cerdgn 32 K11
Llanwnog Powys 34 B2
Llanwonno Rhondd 26 J8
Llanwrda Carmth 26 C1
Llanwrin Powys 43 Q13
Llanwrthwl Powys 33 U8
Llanwrtyd Powys 33 S11
Llanwrtyd Wells Powys 33 S11
Llanwyddelan Powys 44 C13
Llanyblodwel Shrops 44 F9
Llanybri Carmth 25 P8
Llanybydder Carmth 32 K12
Llanycefn Pembks 24 J6
Llanychaer Pembks 24 G3
Llanycil Gwynd 43 T7
Llanycrwys Carmth 33 M11
Llanymawddwy Gwynd 43 T10
Llanymynech Powys 44 G9
Llanynghenedl IoA 52 D6
Llanynys Denbgs 54 D14
Llan-y-pwll Wrexhm 44 J3
Llanyre Powys 34 B8
Llanystumdwy Gwynd 42 J6
Llanywern Powys 27 L2
Llawhaden Pembks 24 J7
Llawnt Shrops 44 F7
Llawryglyn Powys 33 T2
Llay Wrexhm 44 H2
Llechcynfarwy IoA 52 E6
Llechfaen Powys 26 K2
Llechrhyd Caerph 27 L6
Llechryd Cerdgn 32 D12
Llechylched IoA 52 D7
Lledrod Cerdgn 33 M6
Lleyn Peninsula Gwynd 42 F6
Llidiardau Gwynd 43 S6
Llidiartnenog Carmth 25 T3
Llidiart-y-parc Denbgs 44 D5
Llithfaen Gwynd 42 G5
Lloc Flints 54 D11
Llowes Powys 34 E12
Llwydcoed Rhondd 26 H7
Llwydiarth Powys 44 B10
Llwyn Denbgs 54 C14
Llwyncelyn Cerdgn 32 H9
Llwyndafydd Cerdgn 32 G9
Llwynderw Powys 44 F13
Llwyn-drain Pembks 25 N4
Llwyn-du Mons 27 P4
Llwyndyrys Gwynd 42 G5
Llwyngwril Gwynd 43 L12
Llwynhendy Carmth 25 T11
Llwynmawr Wrexhm 44 F6
Llwyn-on Myr Td 26 J5
Llwyn-y-brain Carmth 25 L8
Llwyn-y-groes Cerdgn 33 L9
Llwynypia Rhondd 26 H9
Llynclys Shrops 44 G9
Llynfaes IoA 52 F7
Llyn-y-pandy Flints 54 F13
Llysfaen Conwy 53 Q7
Llyswen Cerdgn 32 J8
Llyswen Powys 34 D13
Llysworney V Glam 26 H13
Llys-y-frân Pembks 24 H6
Llywel Powys 26 F1
Load Brook Sheff 57 L9
Loan Falk 82 J3
Loanend Nthumb 85 N8
Loanhead Mdloth 83 Q5
Loaningfoot D & G 66 E1
Loans S Ayrs 81 L6
Lobb Devon 15 L5
Lobhillcross Devon 5 M3
Lochailort Highld 93 T2
Lochaline Highld 93 R10
Lochans D & G 72 D8
Locharbriggs D & G 74 J9
Lochavich Ag & B 87 S2
Lochawe Ag & B 94 G13
Loch Baghasdail W Isls 106 c17
Lochboisdale W Isls 106 c17
Lochbuie Ag & B 93 Q13
Lochcarron Highld 101 M4
Lochdon Ag & B 93 S12
Lochdonhead Ag & B 93 S12
Lochead Ag & B 87 P10
Lochearnhead Stirlg 95 R14
Lochee C Dund 91 N5
Locheilside Station Highld 94 D3
Lochend Highld 102 G8
Locheport W Isls 106 d12
Loch Euphoirt W Isls 106 d12
Lochfoot D & G 74 G11
Lochgair Ag & B 87 S7
Lochgelly Fife 90 J13
Lochgilphead Ag & B 87 R8
Lochgoilhead Ag & B 88 F5
Lochieheads Fife 91 L9
Lochill Moray 104 B3
Lochindorb Lodge Highld 103 Q8
Lochinver Highld 110 B12
Loch Lomond and The Trossachs National Park 88 K3
Loch Loyal Lodge Highld 111 N7
Lochluichart Highld 102 B3
Lochmaben D & G 75 L9
Lochmaddy W Isls 106 e12
Loch nam Madadh W Isls 106 e12
Loch Ness Highld 102 F10
Lochore Fife 90 J12
Lochranza N Ayrs 79 S5
Loch Sgioport W Isls 106 d15
Lochside Abers 99 N11
Lochside D & G 74 J10
Lochside Highld 103 M5
Lochskipport W Isls 106 d15
Lochslin Highld 109 Q8
Lochton S Ayrs 72 H4
Lochty Angus 98 J11
Lochty Fife 91 R10
Lochuisge Highld 93 T7
Lochwinnoch Rens 88 J14
Lochwood D & G 75 L6
Lockengate Cnwll 3 Q4
Lockerbie D & G 75 M9
Lockeridge Wilts 18 H7
Lockerley Hants 9 L3
Locking N Som 17 L5
Locking Stumps Warrtn 55 P8
Lockington E R Yk 65 M10
Lockington Leics 47 N8
Lockleywood Shrops 45 Q8
Locksbottom Gt Lon 21 R9
Locksgreen IoW 9 N10
Locks Heath Hants 9 Q7
Lockton N York 64 J2
Loddington Leics 47 U13
Loddington Nhants 38 B5
Loddiswell Devon 5 S11
Loddon Norfk 51 Q14
Lode Cambs 39 R8
Lode Heath Solhll 36 G4
Loders Dorset 7 N6
Lodsworth W Susx 10 E6
Lofthouse Leeds 57 M1
Lofthouse N York 63 N5
Lofthouse Gate Wakefd 57 M2
Loftus R & Cl 71 M9
Logan E Ayrs 81 R8
Loganbeck Cumb 61 M1
Loganlea W Loth 82 J6
Loggerheads Staffs 45 R6
Logie Angus 99 M11
Logie Fife 91 P7
Logie Moray 103 R5
Logie Coldstone Abers 98 G3
Logie Newton Abers 104 K8
Logie Pert Angus 99 M11
Logierait P & K 97 R13
Logierieve Abers 105 Q10
Login Carmth 25 L6
Lolworth Cambs 39 N8
Lonbain Highld 107 L14
Londesborough E R Yk 64 K10
London Gt Lon 21 P6
London Apprentice Cnwll 3 Q7
London Beach Kent 12 G8
London Colney Herts 31 Q12
Londonderry N York 63 S2
London End Nhants 38 D7
London Gateway Services Gt Lon 21 L4
London Gatwick Airport W Susx 11 M2
London Heathrow Airport Gt Lon 20 J7
London Luton Airport Luton 31 P8
London Oxford Airport Oxon 29 U4
London Southend Airport Essex 23 L10
London Stansted Airport Essex 22 E3
Londonthorpe Lincs 48 E6
London Zoo ZSL Gt Lon 21 N6
Londubh Highld 107 Q8
Lonemore Highld 107 N9
Long Ashton N Som 17 P2
Long Bank Worcs 35 S6
Long Bennington Lincs 48 B5
Longbenton N Tyne 77 R12
Longborough Gloucs 29 N2
Long Bredy Dorset 7 Q6
Longbridge Birm 36 D5
Longbridge Warwks 36 J8
Longbridge Deverill Wilts 18 C12
Long Buckby Nhants 37 R7
Longburgh Cumb 75 R14
Longburton Dorset 7 R2
Long Cause Devon 5 T8
Long Clawson Leics 47 T8
Longcliffe Derbys 46 H2
Longcombe Devon 5 U9
Long Common Hants 9 Q6
Long Compton Staffs 45 U9
Long Compton Warwks 36 J14
Longcot Oxon 29 Q9
Long Crendon Bucks 30 E11
Long Crichel Dorset 8 D6
Longcroft Cumb 75 P14
Longcross Surrey 20 G9
Longden Shrops 44 K12
Longden Common Shrops 44 K12
Long Ditton Surrey 21 L9
Longdon Staffs 46 E11
Longdon Worcs 35 T13
Longdon Green Staffs 46 E11
Longdon Heath Worcs 35 T13
Longdon upon Tern Wrekin 45 P10
Longdown Devon 5 V2
Longdowns Cnwll 2 J10
Long Drax N York 64 F14
Long Duckmanton Derbys 57 P12
Long Eaton Derbys 47 N7
Longfield Kent 12 B2
Longford Covtry 37 L4
Longford Derbys 46 H6
Longford Gloucs 28 F3
Longford Gt Lon 20 J7
Longford Kent 21 T11
Longford Shrops 45 P7
Longford Wrekin 45 R10
Longforgan P & K 91 L6
Longformacus Border 84 H7
Longframlington Nthumb 77 N5
Long Green Ches W 55 L12
Long Green Worcs 35 T14
Longham Dorset 8 F9
Longham Norfk 50 F10
Long Hanborough Oxon 29 T5
Longhaven Abers 105 U8
Long Hedges Lincs 49 N4
Longhirst Nthumb 77 Q8
Longhope Gloucs 28 C4
Longhope Ork 106 s20
Longhorsley Nthumb 77 N7
Longhoughton Nthumb 77 Q2
Long Itchington Warwks 37 M7
Longlands Cumb 67 L5
Longlane Derbys 46 H6
Long Lawford Warwks 37 N5
Longleat Safari & Adventure Park Wilts 18 B12
Longlevens Gloucs 28 G4
Longley Calder 56 G2
Longley Kirk 56 H5
Longley Green Worcs 35 R10
Longleys P & K 91 L3
Long Load Somset 17 N12
Longmanhill Abers 105 L3
Long Marston Herts 30 J9
Long Marston N York 64 C9
Long Marston Warwks 36 G11
Long Marton Cumb 68 E8
Long Meadowend Shrops 34 K4
Long Melford Suffk 40 E11
Longmoor Camp Hants 10 B4
Longmorn Moray 104 A4
Longmoss Ches E 56 C12
Long Newnton Gloucs 28 H9
Longnewton Border 84 F13
Long Newton E Loth 84 E6
Longnewton S on T 70 E9
Longney Gloucs 28 E5
Longniddry E Loth 84 C3
Longnor Shrops 45 L13
Longnor Staffs 56 G14
Longparish Hants 19 P11
Longpark Cumb 75 T13
Long Preston N York 62 G8
Longridge Lancs 62 C12
Longridge Staffs 46 B10
Longridge W Loth 82 H6
Longriggend N Lans 82 F4
Long Riston E R Yk 65 Q11
Longrock Cnwll 2 E10
Longsdon Staffs 46 C3
Longshaw Wigan 55 M6
Longside Abers 105 S6
Long Sight Oldham 56 D5
Longslow Shrops 45 Q6
Longstanton Cambs 39 N7
Longstock Hants 19 N13
Longstone Pembks 24 K9
Longstowe Cambs 39 M10
Long Stratton Norfk 41 L2
Long Street M Keyn 37 U11
Longstreet Wilts 18 H10
Long Sutton Hants 20 B13
Long Sutton Lincs 49 P9
Long Sutton Somset 17 N11
Longthorpe C Pete 48 J14
Long Thurlow Suffk 40 H7
Longthwaite Cumb 67 P8
Longton C Stke 46 B5
Longton Lancs 55 L1
Longtown Cumb 75 S12
Longtown Herefs 27 Q2
Longueville Jersey 7 e3
Longville in the Dale Shrops 35 M2
Long Waste Wrekin 45 P10
Long Whatton Leics 47 N9
Longwick Bucks 30 G11
Long Wittenham Oxon 19 R2
Longwitton Nthumb 77 M8
Longwood D & G 73 S7
Longwood Shrops 45 P12
Longworth Oxon 29 S8
Longyester E Loth 84 E5
Lôn-las Swans 26 C8
Lonmay Abers 105 S4
Lonmore Highld 100 b5
Looe Cnwll 4 H10
Loose Kent 12 E5
Loosebeare Devon 15 R11
Loosegate Lincs 49 M8
Loosley Row Bucks 30 H12
Lootcherbrae Abers 104 J5
Lopcombe Corner Wilts 19 L13
Lopen Somset 7 M2
Loppington Shrops 45 L8
Lorbottle Nthumb 77 L4
Lordington W Susx 10 B9
Lordsbridge Norfk 49 S11
Lordshill C Sotn 9 M5
Lords Wood Medway 12 E3
Lornty P & K 90 J2
Loscoe Derbys 47 M4
Loscombe Dorset 7 N5
Losgaintir W Isls 106 f9
Lossiemouth Moray 104 A1
Lostford Shrops 45 P7
Lostock Gralam Ches W 55 Q12
Lostock Green Ches W 55 Q12
Lostock Hall Lancs 55 M1
Lostock Hall Fold Bolton 55 Q5
Lostock Junction Bolton 55 Q5
Lostwithiel Cnwll 4 E9
Lothbeg Highld 109 S2
Lothersdale N York 62 K10
Lothmore Highld 109 T2
Loudwater Bucks 20 F4
Loughborough Leics 47 P10
Loughor Swans 25 U11
Loughton Essex 21 R3
Loughton M Keyn 30 H5
Loughton Shrops 35 P4
Lound Lincs 48 G10
Lound Notts 57 U9
Lound Suffk 51 T14
Lounston Devon 5 T5
Lount Leics 47 L10
Louth Lincs 59 P9
Loveclough Lancs 55 T1
Lovedean Hants 9 T6
Lover Wilts 8 J4
Loversall Donc 57 S7
Loves Green Essex 22 F7
Lovesome Hill N York 70 E13
Loveston Pembks 24 J9
Lovington Somset 17 Q10
Low Ackworth Wakefd 57 Q3
Low Angerton Nthumb 77 M9
Lowbands Gloucs 28 E1
Low Barbeth D & G 72 C6
Low Barlings Lincs 58 J12
Low Bell End N York 71 M13
Low Bentham N York 62 C6
Low Biggins Cumb 62 C4
Low Borrowbridge Cumb 68 D12
Low Bradfield Sheff 57 L8
Low Bradley N York 63 L10
Low Braithwaite Cumb 67 P4
Low Burnham N Linc 58 C6
Low Buston Nthumb 77 Q4
Lowca Cumb 66 E8
Low Catton E R Yk 64 G9
Low Coniscliffe Darltn 69 S10
Low Crosby Cumb 75 T14
Lowdham Notts 47 S4
Low Dinsdale Darltn 70 D10
Lowe Shrops 45 L7
Lowe Hill Staffs 46 C2
Low Ellington N York 63 Q3
Lower Aisholt Somset 16 H9
Lower Ansty Dorset 7 U4
Lower Apperley Gloucs 28 G2
Lower Arboll Highld 109 R8
Lower Arncott Oxon 30 D9
Lower Ashton Devon 5 U4
Lower Assendon Oxon 20 B6
Lower Badcall Highld 110 D8
Lower Ballam Lancs 61 R13
Lower Bartle Lancs 61 T13
Lower Basildon W Berk 19 T5
Lower Bearwood Herefs 34 J9
Lower Beeding W Susx 11 L5
Lower Benefield Nhants 38 E3
Lower Bentley Worcs 36 C7
Lower Beobridge Shrops 35 S2
Lower Birchwood Derbys 47 M3
Lower Boddington Nhants 37 N10
Lower Boscaswell Cnwll 2 B10
Lower Bourne Surrey 10 C2
Lower Brailes Warwks 36 K13
Lower Breakish Highld 100 f7
Lower Bredbury Stockp 56 D8
Lower Broadheath Worcs 35 T9
Lower Broxwood Herefs 34 J10
Lower Buckenhill Herefs 35 P14
Lower Bullingham Herefs 35 M13
Lower Burgate Hants 8 H5
Lower Burrowton Devon 6 D5
Lower Burton Herefs 34 K9
Lower Caldecote C Beds 38 J11
Lower Cam Gloucs 28 D7
Lower Canada N Som 17 L5
Lower Catesby Nhants 37 P9
Lower Chapel Powys 34 B13
Lower Chicksgrove Wilts 8 D3
Lower Chute Wilts 19 M10
Lower Clapton Gt Lon 21 P5
Lower Clent Worcs 36 B5
Lower Common Hants 20 C10
Lower Creedy Devon 15 T12
Lower Crossings Derbys 56 F10
Lower Cumberworth Kirk 56 K5
Lower Darwen Bl w D 55 Q1
Lower Dean Bed 38 G7
Lower Denby Kirk 56 K5
Lower Diabaig Highld 107 N12
Lower Dicker E Susx 11 T8
Lower Dinchope Shrops 35 L4
Lower Down Shrops 34 H4
Lower Dunsforth N York 63 U7
Lower Egleton Herefs 35 P11
Lower Elkstone Staffs 46 E2
Lower Ellastone Staffs 46 F5
Lower End Bucks 30 E11
Lower End M Keyn 30 K5
Lower End Nhants 38 B9
Lower End Nhants 38 C8
Lower Everleigh Wilts 18 J10
Lower Exbury Hants 9 N9
Lower Eythorne Kent 13 Q6
Lower Failand N Som 27 U13
Lower Farringdon Hants 19 V13
Lower Feltham Gt Lon 20 J8
Lower Fittleworth W Susx 10 G7
Lower Foxdale IoM 60 d7
Lower Frankton Shrops 44 J7
Lower Freystrop Pembks 24 G8
Lower Froyle Hants 10 B2
Lower Gabwell Devon 6 B11
Lower Gledfield Highld 108 K6
Lower Godney Somset 17 N8
Lower Gornal Dudley 36 B2
Lower Gravenhurst C Beds 31 P5
Lower Green Herts 31 Q6
Lower Green Herts 39 P14
Lower Green Kent 11 T2
Lower Green Kent 12 B7
Lower Green Norfk 50 G6
Lower Green Staffs 46 B12
Lower Green Suffk 40 B7
Lower Hacheston Suffk 41 P9
Lower Halstock Leigh Dorset 7 P3
Lower Halstow Kent 12 G2
Lower Hamworthy BCP 8 D10
Lower Hardres Kent 13 N5
Lower Harpton Herefs 34 G8
Lower Hartlip Kent 12 F3
Lower Hartshay Derbys 47 L3
Lower Hartwell Bucks 30 G10
Lower Hatton Staffs 45 T6
Lower Hawthwaite Cumb 61 N2
Lower Hergest Herefs 34 G9
Lower Heyford Oxon 29 U3
Lower Heysham Lancs 61 S7
Lower Higham Kent 22 H13
Lower Holbrook Suffk 41 L13
Lower Hordley Shrops 44 J8
Lower Horncroft W Susx 10 G7
Lowerhouse Lancs 62 G13
Lower Houses Kirk 56 J3
Lower Howsell Worcs 35 S11
Lower Irlam Salfd 55 R8
Lower Kilburn Derbys 47 L5
Lower Kilcott Gloucs 28 E10
Lower Killeyan Ag & B 78 D7
Lower Kingcombe Dorset 7 Q5
Lower Kingswood Surrey 21 M12
Lower Kinnerton Ches W 44 H1
Lower Langford N Som 17 N4
Lower Largo Fife 91 P11
Lower Leigh Staffs 46 D6
Lower Lemington Gloucs 36 H14
Lower Llanfadog Powys 33 U7
Lower Lovacott Devon 15 M7
Lower Loxhore Devon 15 P5
Lower Lydbrook Gloucs 28 A4
Lower Lye Herefs 34 K7
Lower Machen Newpt 27 N10
Lower Maes-coed Herefs 27 Q1
Lower Mannington Dorset 8 F8
Lower Marston Somset 17 U8
Lower Meend Gloucs 27 V7
Lower Merridge Somset 16 H10
Lower Middleton Cheney Nhants 30 B4
Lower Milton Somset 17 P7
Lower Moor Worcs 36 C11
Lower Morton S Glos 28 B9
Lower Nazeing Essex 31 U11
Lower Norton Warwks 36 H8
Lower Nyland Dorset 17 U12
Lower Penarth V Glam 16 G3
Lower Penn Staffs 35 U1
Lower Pennington Hants 9 L10
Lower Penwortham Lancs 55 M1
Lower Peover Ches E 55 R12
Lower Place Rochdl 56 D4
Lower Pollicott Bucks 30 F10
Lower Quinton Warwks 36 G11
Lower Rainham Medway 12 F2
Lower Raydon Suffk 40 H13
Lower Roadwater Somset 16 D9
Lower Salter Lancs 62 C7
Lower Seagry Wilts 18 E4
Lower Sheering Essex 22 C5
Lower Shelton C Beds 31 L4
Lower Shiplake Oxon 20 C7
Lower Shuckburgh Warwks 37 N8
Lower Slaughter Gloucs 29 N3
Lower Soothill Kirk 57 L2
Lower Soudley Gloucs 28 C6
Lower Standen Kent 13 P7
Lower Stanton St Quintin Wilts 18 D4
Lower Stoke Medway 22 K12
Lower Stondon C Beds 31 Q5
Lower Stone Gloucs 28 C9
Lower Stonnall Staffs 46 E13
Lower Stow Bedon Norfk 40 G2
Lower Street Dorset 8 A9
Lower Street E Susx 12 D13
Lower Street Norfk 51 N6
Lower Street Suffk 40 C10
Lower Street Suffk 40 K10
Lower Stretton Warrtn 55 P10
Lower Stroud Dorset 7 N5
Lower Sundon C Beds 31 N7
Lower Swanwick Hants 9 P7
Lower Swell Gloucs 29 N2
Lower Tadmarton Oxon 37 M13
Lower Tale Devon 6 E4
Lower Tasburgh Norfk 41 L1
Lower Tean Staffs 46 D6
Lower Thurlton Norfk 51 R14
Lower Town Cnwll 2 H11
Lower Town Devon 5 S6
Lower Town Herefs 35 P12
Lower Town Pembks 24 G3
Lower Trebullett Cnwll 4 J5
Lower Treluswell Cnwll 2 K9
Lower Tysoe Warwks 36 K11
Lower Ufford Suffk 41 N10
Lower Upcott Devon 6 A8
Lower Upham Hants 9 Q5
Lower Upnor Medway 22 J13
Lower Vexford Somset 16 F9
Lower Walton Warrtn 55 P9
Lower Waterston Dorset 7 T5
Lower Weare Somset 17 M6
Lower Weedon Nhants 37 R9
Lower Welson Herefs 34 G10
Lower Westmancote Worcs 36 B13
Lower Whatcombe Dorset 8 A8
Lower Whatley Somset 17 T7
Lower Whitley Ches W 55 P11
Lower Wick Gloucs 28 D8
Lower Wick Worcs 35 T10
Lower Wield Hants 19 T12
Lower Willingdon E Susx 11 T10
Lower Withington Ches E 55 T13
Lower Woodend Bucks 20 D5
Lower Woodford Wilts 18 H13
Lower Wraxhall Dorset 7 Q4
Lower Wyche Worcs 35 S12
Lower Wyke C Brad 56 J1
Lowesby Leics 47 T12
Lowestoft Suffk 41 T2
Loweswater Cumb 66 H8
Low Fell Gatesd 77 R14
Lowfield Heath W Susx 11 M3
Low Gartachorrans Stirlg 89 L8
Low Gate Nthumb 76 J13
Low Gettbridge Cumb 75 V14
Lowgill Cumb 68 D13
Lowgill Lancs 62 D7
Low Grantley N York 63 Q5
Low Green N York 63 Q8
Low Habberley Worcs 35 T5
Low Ham Somset 17 M11
Low Harrogate N York 63 R8
Low Hawsker N York 71 R11
Low Hesket Cumb 67 Q3
Low Hutton N York 64 H6
Lowick Cumb 61 P2
Lowick Nhants 38 E4
Lowick Nthumb 85 Q11
Lowick Bridge Cumb 61 P2
Lowick Green Cumb 61 P2
Low Knipe Cumb 67 R9
Low Laithe N York 63 P7
Lowlands Dur 69 P7
Lowlands Torfn 27 P8
Low Langton Lincs 59 L11
Low Leighton Derbys 56 F9
Low Lorton Cumb 66 J7
Low Marishes N York 64 J4
Low Marnham Notts 58 D13
Low Middleton Nthumb 85 S11
Low Mill N York 71 L13
Low Moor C Brad 63 P14
Low Moorsley Sundld 70 D3
Low Moresby Cumb 66 E8
Low Newton Cumb 61 S3
Low Row Cumb 66 J4
Low Row Cumb 67 N5
Low Row Cumb 76 B13
Low Row N York 69 L13
Low Salchrie D & G 72 C6
Low Santon N Linc 58 F4
Lowsonford Warwks 36 G7
Low Street Norfk 51 P9
Low Street Thurr 22 G12
Low Tharston Norfk 41 L1
Lowther Cumb 67 R8
Lowthorpe E R Yk 65 P7
Lowton Devon 15 Q12
Lowton Somset 16 G13
Lowton Wigan 55 P7
Lowton Common Wigan 55 P7
Lowton St Mary's Wigan 55 P7
Low Torry Fife 82 K1
Low Toynton Lincs 59 N12
Low Valley Barns 57 P6
Low Wood Cumb 61 Q3
Low Worsall N York 70 E11
Low Wray Cumb 67 N12
Loxbeare Devon 16 B13
Loxhill Surrey 10 G3
Loxhore Devon 15 P5
Loxhore Cott Devon 15 P5
Loxley Warwks 36 J10
Loxley Green Staffs 46 E7
Loxter Herefs 35 R12
Loxton N Som 17 L5
Loxwood W Susx 10 G4
Lubenham Leics 37 T3
Lucasgate Lincs 49 P4
Lucas Green Surrey 20 F10
Luccombe Somset 16 B8
Luccombe Village IoW 9 R13
Lucker Nthumb 85 T12
Luckett Cnwll 4 K6
Lucking Street Essex 40 D14
Luckington Wilts 28 F11
Lucklawhill Fife 91 P7
Lucknam Wilts 18 B6
Luckwell Bridge Somset 16 B9
Lucton Herefs 34 K8
Lucy Cross N York 69 R10
Ludag W Isls 106 c17
Ludborough Lincs 59 N7
Ludbrook Devon 5 R10
Ludchurch Pembks 24 K8
Luddenden Calder 56 F1
Luddenden Foot Calder 56 F1
Luddenham Court Kent 12 J3
Luddesdown Kent 12 C2
Luddington N Linc 58 D3
Luddington Warwks 36 G10
Luddington in the Brook Nhants 38 H4
Ludford Lincs 59 L9
Ludford Shrops 35 M6
Ludgershall Bucks 30 E9
Ludgershall Wilts 19 L10
Ludgvan Cnwll 2 E10
Ludham Norfk 51 Q10
Ludlow Shrops 35 M5
Ludney Somset 7 L2
Ludwell Wilts 8 C4
Ludworth Dur 70 E4
Luffenhall Herts 31 S7
Luffincott Devon 4 J2
Luffness E Loth 84 D2
Lugar E Ayrs 81 R8
Luggate Burn E Loth 84 F4
Lugg Green Herefs 34 K8
Luggiebank N Lans 89 S11
Lugton E Ayrs 81 N2
Lugwardine Herefs 35 N12
Luib Highld 100 e7
Luing Ag & B 87 N3
Lulham Herefs 34 K12
Lullington Derbys 46 H11
Lullington E Susx 11 S10
Lullington Somset 17 U6
Lulsgate Bottom N Som 17 P3
Lulsley Worcs 35 R9
Lulworth Camp Dorset 8 A12
Lumb Calder 56 F2
Lumb Lancs 55 T2
Lumbutts Calder 56 E2
Lumby N York 64 B13
Lumphanan Abers 98 K3
Lumphinnans Fife 90 J13
Lumsden Abers 104 F11
Lunan Angus 99 M13
Lunanhead Angus 98 H13
Luncarty P & K 90 G6
Lund E R Yk 65 M10
Lund N York 64 F13
Lundie Angus 91 L4
Lundin Links Fife 91 P11
Lundin Mill Fife 91 P11
Lundy Devon 14 D3
Lundy Green Norfk 41 M2
Lunga Ag & B 87 N4
Lunna Shet 106 u7
Lunsford Kent 12 C4
Lunsford's Cross E Susx 12 D13
Lunt Sefton 54 H6
Luntley Herefs 34 J9
Luppitt Devon 6 G3
Lupridge Devon 5 S10
Lupset Wakefd 57 M3
Lupton Cumb 62 B3
Lurgashall W Susx 10 E5
Lurley Devon 16 B13
Lusby Lincs 59 P13
Luscombe Devon 5 T9
Luson Devon 5 Q10
Luss Ag & B 88 J7
Lussagiven Ag & B 87 L8
Lusta Highld 100 b4
Lustleigh Devon 5 T4
Luston Herefs 35 L8
Luthermuir Abers 99 M10
Luthrie Fife 91 M8
Lutley Dudley 36 B4
Luton Devon 6 B9
Luton Devon 6 E4
Luton Luton 31 N8
Luton Medway 12 E2
Luton Airport Luton 31 P8
Lutterworth Leics 37 P4
Lutton Devon 5 P9
Lutton Devon 5 R8
Lutton Lincs 49 P8
Lutton Nhants 38 H3
Luxborough Somset 16 C9
Luxulyan Cnwll 3 R5
Luxulyan Valley Cnwll 3 R5
Luzley Tamesd 56 E6
Lybster Highld 112 F9
Lydbury North Shrops 34 H3
Lydcott Devon 15 Q5
Lydd Kent 12 K11
Lydd Airport Kent 13 L11
Lydden Kent 13 Q6
Lydden Kent 13 S2
Lyddington RutInd 38 C1
Lydd-on-Sea Kent 13 L12
Lydeard St Lawrence Somset 16 F10
Lyde Green Hants 20 B11
Lydford Devon 5 N3
Lydford on Fosse Somset 17 Q10
Lydgate Calder 56 D1
Lydgate Rochdl 56 E3
Lydham Shrops 34 H2
Lydiard Green Wilts 29 L10
Lydiard Millicent Wilts 29 L10
Lydiard Tregoze Swindn 29 M11
Lydiate Sefton 54 J6
Lydiate Ash Worcs 36 C5
Lydlinch Dorset 7 T2
Lydney Gloucs 28 B7
Lydstep Pembks 24 J11
Lye Dudley 36 B4
Lye Cross N Som 17 N4
Lye Green Bucks 31 L12
Lye Green E Susx 11 S4
Lye Green Warwks 36 G7
Lye Head Worcs 35 S6
Lye's Green Wilts 18 B11
Lyford Oxon 29 S9
Lymbridge Green Kent 13 M7
Lyme Regis Dorset 6 K6
Lyminge Kent 13 N7
Lymington Hants 9 L9
Lyminster W Susx 10 G10
Lymm Warrtn 55 Q9
Lymm Services Warrtn 55 Q10
Lympne Kent 13 M8
Lympsham Somset 16 K6
Lympstone Devon 6 C8
Lynbridge Devon 15 R3
Lynchat Highld 97 M3
Lynch Green Norfk 51 L12
Lyndhurst Hants 9 L7
Lyndon RutInd 48 D13
Lyndon Green Birm 36 F3
Lyne Border 83 P10
Lyne Surrey 20 H9
Lyneal Shrops 44 K7
Lyne Down Herefs 28 B1
Lyneham Devon 5 V5
Lyneham Oxon 29 Q3
Lyneham Wilts 18 F5
Lyneholmford Cumb 75 V11
Lynemouth Nthumb 77 R7
Lyne of Skene Abers 105 M13
Lynesack Dur 69 N7
Lyness Ork 106 s20
Lyng Norfk 50 J10
Lyng Somset 16 K11
Lynmouth Devon 15 R3
Lynn Staffs 46 E13
Lynn Wrekin 45 S10
Lynsted Kent 12 H3
Lynstone Cnwll 14 F11
Lynton Devon 15 R3
Lynton Cross Devon 15 M4
Lyon's Gate Dorset 7 S3
Lyonshall Herefs 34 H9
Lytchett Matravers Dorset 8 C9
Lytchett Minster Dorset 8 D10
Lyth Highld 112 G4
Lytham Lancs 54 J1
Lytham St Annes Lancs 54 H1
Lythbank Shrops 45 L12
Lythe N York 71 P10
Lythmore Highld 112 C3

M

Mabe Burnthouse Cnwll 2 K10
Mablethorpe Lincs 59 T10
Macclesfield Ches E 56 D12
Macduff Abers 105 L3
Macharioch Ag & B 79 N14
Machen Caerph 27 N10
Machrie N Ayrs 79 R9
Machrihanish Ag & B 79 L11
Machrins Ag & B 86 F7
Machynlleth Powys 43 P13
Machynys Carmth 25 T11
Mackworth Derbys 46 K6
Macmerry E Loth 84 C4
Maddaford Devon 5 N2
Madderty P & K 90 E7
Maddington Wilts 18 G12
Maddiston Falk 82 H3
Madehurst W Susx 10 F8
Madeley Staffs 45 S5
Madeley Wrekin 45 Q13
Madeley Heath Staffs 45 S4
Madford Devon 6 F2
Madingley Cambs 39 N8
Madley Herefs 34 K13
Madresfield Worcs 35 T11
Madron Cnwll 2 D10
Maenaddwyn IoA 52 G6
Maenan Conwy 53 N9
Maenclochog Pembks 24 J5
Maendy V Glam 26 J12
Maenporth Cnwll 2 K11
Maentwrog Gwynd 43 N5
Maen-y-groes Cerdgn 32 G9
Maer Cnwll 14 F11
Maer Staffs 45 S6
Maerdy Carmth 26 B2
Maerdy Conwy 44 B5
Maerdy Rhondd 26 H8
Maesbrook Shrops 44 H9
Maesbury Shrops 44 H8
Maesbury Marsh Shrops 44 H8
Maes-glas Newpt 27 P10
Maesgwynne Carmth 25 M6
Maeshafn Denbgs 44 F1
Maesllyn Cerdgn 32 G12
Maesmynis Powys 34 B11
Maesmynis Powys 34 B11
Maesteg Brdgnd 26 F9
Maesybont Carmth 25 U7
Maesycwmmer Caerph 27 M9
Magdalen Laver Essex 22 D6
Maggieknockater Moray 104 C6
Maggots End Essex 22 C2
Magham Down E Susx 11 U8
Maghull Sefton 54 J6
Magna Park Leics 37 P4
Magor Mons 27 S10
Magor Services Mons 27 S10
Maidenbower W Susx 11 M3
Maiden Bradley Wilts 18 B13
Maidencombe Torbay 6 B11
Maidenhayne Devon 6 J5
Maiden Head N Som 17 Q3
Maidenhead W & M 20 E6
Maiden Law Dur 69 Q3
Maiden Newton Dorset 7 Q5
Maidens S Ayrs 80 J11
Maiden's Green Br For 20 F8
Maidenwell Lincs 59 P11
Maiden Wells Pembks 24 G11
Maidford Nhants 37 R10
Maids Moreton Bucks 30 F5
Maidstone Kent 12 E4
Maidstone Services Kent 12 F4
Maidwell Nhants 37 T5
Mail Shet 106 u9
Maindee Newpt 27 Q10
Mainland Ork 106 t19
Mainland Shet 106 u8
Mainsforth Dur 70 D6
Mains of Balhall Angus 98 J11
Mains of Balnakettle Abers 99 L9
Mains of Dalvey Highld 103 T9
Mains of Haulkerton Abers 99 N9
Mains of Lesmoir Abers 104 F10
Mains of Melgunds Angus 98 J12
Mainsriddle D & G 66 D1
Mainstone Shrops 34 G3
Maisemore Gloucs 28 F3
Major's Green Worcs 36 F5
Makeney Derbys 47 L5
Malborough Devon 5 S13
Malcoff Derbys 56 G10
Malden Rushett Gt Lon 21 L10
Maldon Essex 22 L6
Malham N York 62 J7
Maligar Highld 100 d3
Mallaig Highld 100 f10
Mallaigvaig Highld 100 f10

136 Malleny Mills – Nassington

Malleny Mills C Edin 83 N5
Mallows Green Essex 22 C2
Malltraeth IoA 52 F9
Mallwyd Gwynd 43 S11
Malmesbury Wilts 28 H10
Malmsmead Devon 15 S3
Malpas Ches W 45 L4
Malpas Cnwll 3 L8
Malpas Newpt 27 Q9
Malshanger Hants 19 S10
Malswick Gloucs 28 D3
Maltby Lincs 59 P10
Maltby Rothm 57 R8
Maltby S on T 70 G10
Maltby le Marsh Lincs 59 S10
Malting Green Essex 23 N3
Maltman's Hill Kent 12 H7
Malton N York 64 H5
Malvern Worcs 35 S11
Malvern Hills 35 S12
Malvern Link Worcs 35 S11
Malvern Wells Worcs 35 S12
Mamble Worcs 35 Q6
Mamhilad Mons 27 Q7
Manaccan Cnwll 2 K12
Manafon Powys 44 D13
Manais W Isls 106 g10
Manaton Devon 5 T4
Manby Lincs 59 Q9
Mancetter Warwks 36 K1
Manchester Manch 55 T7
Manchester Airport Manch 55 T10
Mancot Flints 54 H13
Mandally Highld 96 B3
Manea Cambs 39 Q3
Maney Birm 36 F1
Manfield N York 69 R10
Mangersta W Isls 106 f5
Mangerton Dorset 7 N5
Mangotsfield S Glos 28 C12
Mangrove Green Herts 31 P8
Mangurstadh W Isls 106 f5
Manhay Cnwll 2 H10
Manish W Isls 106 g10
Mankinholes Calder 56 E2
Manley Ches W 55 M12
Manmoel Caerph 27 M7
Mannal Ag & B 92 B10
Manningford Bohune Wilts 18 H9
Manningford Bruce Wilts 18 H9
Manningham C Brad 63 N12
Mannings Heath W Susx 11 L5
Mannington Dorset 8 F7
Manningtree Essex 23 R1
Mannofield C Aber 99 S3
Manorbier Pembks 24 J11
Manorbier Newton Pembks 24 H10
Manordeilo Carmth 26 B2
Manorhill Border 84 H12
Manorowen Pembks 24 F3
Manor Park Gt Lon 21 R5
Mansell Gamage Herefs 34 J12
Mansell Lacy Herefs 34 K11
Mansergh Cumb 62 C3
Mansfield E Ayrs 81 S10
Mansfield Notts 47 P1
Mansfield Woodhouse Notts 57 R14
Mansriggs Cumb 61 P3
Manston Dorset 17 V13
Manston Kent 13 R2
Manston Leeds 63 T13
Manswood Dorset 8 D7
Manthorpe Lincs 48 D6
Manthorpe Lincs 48 G10
Manton N Linc 58 F6
Manton Notts 57 T11
Manton Rutlnd 48 C13
Manton Wilts 18 J7
Manuden Essex 22 C2
Manwood Green Essex 22 D5
Maperton Somset 17 S11
Maplebeck Notts 47 T1
Maple Cross Herts 20 H4
Mapledurham Oxon 19 U5
Mapledurwell Hants 19 U10
Maplehurst W Susx 10 K6
Maplescombe Kent 21 U10
Mapleton Derbys 46 G4
Mapleton Kent 21 S13
Mapperley Derbys 47 M5
Mapperley Park C Nott 47 Q5
Mapperton Dorset 7 P5
Mappleborough Green Warwks 36 E7
Mappleton E R Yk 65 S11
Mapplewell Barns 57 M4
Mappowder Dorset 7 T3
Marazanvose Cnwll 2 K6
Marazion Cnwll 2 E10
Marbhig W Isls 106 j7
Marbury Ches E 45 N4
March Cambs 39 P1
March S Lans 74 J3
Marcham Oxon 29 U8
Marchamley Shrops 45 N8
Marchamley Wood Shrops 45 N7
Marchington Staffs 46 F7
Marchington Woodlands Staffs 46 F8
Marchros Gwynd 42 F8
Marchwiel Wrexhm 44 J4
Marchwood Hants 9 M6
Marcross V Glam 16 B3
Marden Herefs 35 M11
Marden Kent 12 D7
Marden Wilts 18 G9
Marden Ash Essex 22 E7
Marden Beech Kent 12 D7
Marden's Hill E Susx 11 S4
Marden Thorn Kent 12 E7
Mardlebury Herts 31 S9
Mardy Mons 27 Q4
Marefield Leics 47 T12
Mareham le Fen Lincs 49 L1
Mareham on the Hill Lincs 59 N13
Marehay Derbys 47 L4
Marehill W Susx 10 H7
Maresfield E Susx 11 R6
Marfleet C KuH 65 Q14
Marford Wrexhm 44 J2
Margam Neath 26 D10
Margaret Marsh Dorset 17 V13
Margaret Roding Essex 22 E5
Margaretting Essex 22 G7
Margaretting Tye Essex 22 G7
Margate Kent 13 S1
Margnaheglish N Ayrs 80 E6
Margrie D & G 73 P9
Margrove Park R & Cl 71 L9
Marham Norfk 50 B12
Marhamchurch Cnwll 14 F12
Marholm C Pete 48 H13
Marian-glas IoA 52 H6
Mariansleigh Devon 15 R8
Marine Town Kent 23 M13
Marionburgh Abers 99 N2
Marishader Highld 100 d3
Maristow Devon 5 M8
Marjoriebanks D & G 75 L9
Mark Somset 17 L7
Markbeech Kent 11 R2
Markby Lincs 59 S11
Mark Causeway Somset 17 L7
Mark Cross E Susx 11 T4
Markeaton C Derb 46 K6
Market Bosworth Leics 47 M13
Market Deeping Lincs 48 H11
Market Drayton Shrops 45 Q7
Market Harborough Leics 37 T3
Market Lavington Wilts 18 F10
Market Overton Rutlnd 48 C10
Market Rasen Lincs 58 K9
Market Stainton Lincs 59 M11
Market Warsop Notts 57 S13
Market Weighton E R Yk 64 K11
Market Weston Suffk 40 G5
Markfield Leics 47 N12
Markham Caerph 27 M7
Markham Moor Notts 58 B12
Markinch Fife 91 L11
Markington N York 63 R6
Markle E Loth 84 F3
Marksbury BaNES 17 S4
Mark's Corner IoW 9 P10
Marks Tey Essex 23 M3
Markwell Cnwll 4 K9
Markyate Herts 31 N9
Marlborough Wilts 18 J7
Marlbrook Herefs 35 M10
Marlbrook Worcs 36 C6
Marlcliff Warwks 36 E10
Marldon Devon 5 V8
Marle Green E Susx 11 T7
Marlesford Suffk 41 P9
Marley Kent 13 N5
Marley Kent 13 R5
Marley Green Ches E 45 N4
Marley Hill Gatesd 77 Q14
Marlingford Norfk 50 K12
Marloes Pembks 24 C9
Marlow Bucks 20 D5
Marlow Herefs 34 K5
Marlow Bottom Bucks 20 D5
Marlpit Hill Kent 21 R13
Marlpits E Susx 11 R5
Marlpits E Susx 12 D13
Marlpool Derbys 47 M4
Marnhull Dorset 17 U13
Marple Stockp 56 E9
Marple Bridge Stockp 56 E9
Marr Donc 57 R5
Marrick N York 69 N13
Marros Carmth 25 M9
Marsden Kirk 56 F4
Marsden S Tyne 77 T13
Marsden Height Lancs 62 H12
Marsett N York 62 J2
Marsh Bucks 30 H11
Marsh C Brad 63 L12
Marsh Devon 6 J2
Marshall's Heath Herts 31 Q10
Marshalswick Herts 31 Q11
Marsham Norfk 51 L9
Marsh Baldon Oxon 30 C13
Marsh Benham W Berk 19 P7
Marshborough Kent 13 R4
Marshbrook Shrops 34 K3
Marshchapel Lincs 59 Q7
Marsh Farm Luton 31 N7
Marshfield Newpt 27 P11
Marshfield S Glos 28 E13
Marshgate Cnwll 4 F2
Marsh Gibbon Bucks 30 D8
Marsh Green Devon 6 D6
Marsh Green Kent 11 Q2
Marsh Green Wrekin 45 P11
Marshland St James Norfk 49 R12
Marsh Lane Derbys 57 P11
Marsh Lane Gloucs 28 A6
Marshside Sefton 54 J3
Marsh Street Somset 16 C8
Marshwood Dorset 7 L5
Marske N York 69 P12
Marske-by-the-Sea R & Cl 70 K8
Marsland Green Wigan 55 Q7
Marston Ches W 55 Q11
Marston Herefs 34 J9
Marston Lincs 48 C5
Marston Oxon 30 B11
Marston Staffs 45 T11
Marston Staffs 46 B8
Marston Warwks 36 H2
Marston Wilts 18 E9
Marston Green Solhll 36 G3
Marston Jabbet Warwks 37 L3
Marston Magna Somset 17 Q12
Marston Meysey Wilts 29 M8
Marston Montgomery Derbys 46 F6
Marston Moretaine C Beds 31 L4
Marston on Dove Derbys 46 H8
Marston St Lawrence Nhants 30 B4
Marston Stannett Herefs 35 N9
Marston Trussell Nhants 37 S3
Marstow Herefs 27 V4
Marsworth Bucks 30 K10
Marten Wilts 19 L8
Marthall Ches E 55 S11
Martham Norfk 51 S10
Martin Hants 8 F5
Martin Kent 13 R6
Martin Lincs 48 H2
Martin Lincs 59 M13
Martindale Cumb 67 P9
Martin Dales Lincs 48 J1
Martin Drove End Hants 8 F4
Martinhoe Devon 15 Q3
Martin Hussingtree Worcs 35 U8
Martinscroft Warrtn 55 Q9
Martinstown Dorset 7 R7
Martlesham Suffk 41 M11
Martlesham Heath Suffk 41 M11
Martletwy Pembks 24 H8
Martley Worcs 35 S8
Martock Somset 17 N13
Marton Ches E 56 C13
Marton Ches W 55 P13
Marton Cumb 61 N4
Marton E R Yk 65 R12
Marton E R Yk 65 S6
Marton Lincs 58 D10
Marton Middsb 70 H9
Marton N York 63 U7
Marton N York 64 G3
Marton Shrops 44 G13
Marton Warwks 37 M7
Marton-le-Moor N York 63 T5
Martyr's Green Surrey 20 J11
Martyr Worthy Hants 9 Q2
Marvig W Isls 106 j7
Marwell Wildlife Hants 9 Q4
Marwick Ork 106 r17
Marwood Devon 15 M5
Marybank Highld 102 E5
Maryburgh Highld 102 F4
Marygold Border 85 L7
Maryhill C Glas 89 N12
Marykirk Abers 99 M10
Maryland Mons 27 U6
Marylebone Gt Lon 21 N6
Marylebone Wigan 55 N5
Marypark Moray 103 U8
Maryport Cumb 66 F5
Maryport D & G 72 E13
Marystow Devon 5 L4
Mary Tavy Devon 5 N5
Maryton Angus 99 M12
Marywell Abers 98 K4
Marywell Abers 99 S4
Marywell Angus 91 U3
Masham N York 63 Q3
Mashbury Essex 22 G5
Mason N u Ty 77 Q11
Masongill N York 62 D4
Mastin Moor Derbys 57 Q11
Matching Essex 22 D5
Matching Green Essex 22 D5
Matching Tye Essex 22 D5
Matfen Nthumb 77 L11
Matfield Kent 12 C7
Mathern Mons 27 U9
Mathon Herefs 35 R11
Mathry Pembks 24 E4
Matlask Norfk 51 L7
Matlock Derbys 46 K2
Matlock Bank Derbys 46 K1
Matlock Bath Derbys 46 J2
Matlock Dale Derbys 46 J2
Matson Gloucs 28 G4
Matterdale End Cumb 67 N8
Mattersey Notts 57 U9
Mattersey Thorpe Notts 57 U9
Mattingley Hants 20 B11
Mattishall Norfk 50 J11
Mattishall Burgh Norfk 50 J11
Mauchline E Ayrs 81 P7
Maud Abers 105 Q6
Maufant Jersey 7 e2
Maugersbury Gloucs 29 P2
Maughold IoM 60 h4
Mauld Highld 102 D8
Maulden C Beds 31 N5
Maulds Meaburn Cumb 68 D9
Maunby N York 63 T2
Maund Bryan Herefs 35 N10
Maundown Somset 16 E11
Mautby Norfk 51 S11
Mavesyn Ridware Staffs 46 E10
Mavis Enderby Lincs 59 Q13
Mawbray Cumb 66 G3
Mawdesley Lancs 55 L4
Mawdlam Brdgnd 26 E11
Mawgan Cnwll 2 J11
Mawgan Porth Cnwll 3 M3
Maw Green Ches E 45 R2
Mawla Cnwll 2 J7
Mawnan Cnwll 2 K11
Mawnan Smith Cnwll 2 K11
Mawsley Nhants 38 B5
Mawthorpe Lincs 59 S12
Maxey C Pete 48 H12
Maxstoke Warwks 36 H3
Maxted Street Kent 13 M7
Maxton Border 84 G12
Maxton Kent 13 R7
Maxwelltown D & G 74 J10
Maxworthy Cnwll 4 H2
Mayals Swans 25 V13
May Bank Staffs 45 U4
Maybole S Ayrs 80 K11
Maybury Surrey 20 H11
Mayes Green Surrey 10 J3
Mayfield E Susx 11 T5
Mayfield Mdloth 83 S5
Mayfield Staffs 46 G4
Mayford Surrey 20 G11
May Hill Gloucs 28 D3
Mayland Essex 23 M7
Maylandsea Essex 23 M7
Maynard's Green E Susx 11 T7
Maypole Birm 36 E5
Maypole Kent 13 P3
Maypole Mons 27 T4
Maypole Green Norfk 41 R1
Maypole Green Suffk 40 F9
Maypole Green Suffk 41 N7
May's Green Oxon 20 B6
May's Green Surrey 20 J11
Mead Devon 14 F9
Meadgate BaNES 17 S5
Meadle Bucks 30 H11
Meadowfield Dur 69 R5
Meadowtown Shrops 44 H13
Meadwell Devon 5 L4
Meaford Staffs 45 U6
Mealabost W Isls 106 j5
Meal Bank Cumb 67 R13
Mealrigg Cumb 66 H3
Mealsgate Cumb 66 K4
Meanwood Leeds 63 R12
Mearbeck N York 62 G7
Meare Somset 17 N8
Meare Green Somset 16 J12
Meare Green Somset 16 K11
Mearns E Rens 81 Q1
Mears Ashby Nhants 38 B7
Measham Leics 46 K11
Meath Green Surrey 11 M2
Meathop Cumb 61 S3
Meaux E R Yk 65 P12
Meavaig W Isls 106 f5
Meavy Devon 5 N7
Medbourne Leics 38 B2
Medburn Nthumb 77 N11
Meddon Devon 14 G9
Meden Vale Notts 57 S13
Medlam Lincs 49 M2
Medlar Lancs 61 S12
Medmenham Bucks 20 D6
Medomsley Dur 69 P2
Medstead Hants 19 U13
Medway Services Medway 12 F3
Meerbrook Staffs 46 C1
Meer Common Herefs 34 J10
Meesden Herts 22 B1
Meeson Wrekin 45 P9
Meeth Devon 15 M11
Meeting Green Suffk 40 B9
Meeting House Hill Norfk 51 P8
Meidrim Carmth 25 N6
Meifod Powys 44 E11
Meigle P & K 91 L3
Meikle Carco D & G 74 E3
Meikle Earnock S Lans 82 D8
Meikle Kilmory Ag & B 88 C13
Meikle Obney P & K 90 F4
Meikleour P & K 90 J4
Meikle Wartle Abers 105 L9
Meinciau Carmth 25 S8
Meir C Stke 46 B5
Meir Heath Staffs 46 B5
Melbost W Isls 106 j5
Melbourn Cambs 31 U4
Melbourne Derbys 47 L8
Melbourne E R Yk 64 H11
Melbur Cnwll 3 N6
Melbury Devon 14 J9
Melbury Abbas Dorset 8 B4
Melbury Bubb Dorset 7 Q3
Melbury Osmond Dorset 7 Q3
Melbury Sampford Dorset 7 Q3
Melchbourne Bed 38 F7
Melcombe Bingham Dorset 7 U4
Meldon Devon 5 P2
Meldon Nthumb 77 N9
Meldon Park Nthumb 77 N8
Meldreth Cambs 39 N11
Meldrum Stirlg 89 R6
Melfort Ag & B 87 Q3
Meliden Denbgs 54 C10
Melinau Pembks 25 L8
Melin-byrhedyn Powys 43 R14
Melincourt Neath 26 E7
Melin-y-coed Conwy 53 P10
Melin-y-ddol Powys 44 C12
Melin-y-wîg Denbgs 44 B4
Melkinthorpe Cumb 67 S7
Melkridge Nthumb 76 E13
Melksham Wilts 18 D8
Mellangoose Cnwll 2 H11
Mell Green W Berk 19 Q5
Mellguards Cumb 67 P3
Melling Lancs 62 B5
Melling Sefton 54 J6
Melling Mount Sefton 54 K6
Mellis Suffk 40 J6
Mellon Charles Highld 107 P6
Mellon Udrigle Highld 107 Q5
Mellor Lancs 62 D13
Mellor Stockp 56 E9
Mellor Brook Lancs 62 C13
Mells Somset 17 T7
Mells Suffk 41 R5
Melmerby Cumb 68 D5
Melmerby N York 63 M2
Melmerby N York 63 S4
Melness Highld 111 M4
Melon Green Suffk 40 D9
Melplash Dorset 7 N5
Melrose Border 84 E12
Melsetter Ork 106 r21
Melsonby N York 69 Q11
Meltham Kirk 56 H4
Meltham Mills Kirk 56 H4
Melton E R Yk 58 G1
Melton Suffk 41 N10
Meltonby E R Yk 64 H9
Melton Constable Norfk 50 H7
Melton Mowbray Leics 47 U10
Melton Ross N Linc 58 J4
Melvaig Highld 107 M7
Melverley Shrops 44 H10
Melverley Green Shrops 44 H10
Melvich Highld 111 T4
Membury Devon 6 J4
Membury Services W Berk 19 M5
Memsie Abers 105 R3
Memus Angus 98 G12
Menabilly Cnwll 3 R6
Menagissey Cnwll 2 J7
Menai Bridge IoA 52 J8
Mendham Suffk 41 N4
Mendip Hills 17 P6
Mendlesham Suffk 40 K7
Mendlesham Green Suffk 40 J8
Menheniot Cnwll 4 H8
Menithwood Worcs 35 R7
Menna Cnwll 3 N6
Mennock D & G 74 F4
Menston C Brad 63 P11
Menstrie Clacks 90 C12
Menthorpe N York 64 G13
Mentmore Bucks 30 K9
Meoble Highld 100 g11
Meole Brace Shrops 45 L11
Meonstoke Hants 9 S5
Meopham Kent 12 B2
Meopham Green Kent 12 B2
Meopham Station Kent 12 B2
Mepal Cambs 39 P4
Meppershall C Beds 31 P5
Merbach Herefs 34 H11
Mere Ches E 55 R10
Mere Wilts 17 V10
Mere Brow Lancs 54 K3
Mereclough Lancs 62 H13
Mere Green Birm 46 F14
Mere Green Worcs 36 C8
Mere Heath Ches W 55 Q12
Meresborough Medway 12 F3
Mereworth Kent 12 C5
Meriden Solhll 36 H4
Merkadale Highld 100 c6
Merley BCP 8 E9
Merlin's Bridge Pembks 24 F8
Merrington Shrops 45 L9
Merrion Pembks 24 F11
Merriott Somset 7 M2
Merrivale Devon 5 N5
Merrow Surrey 20 H12
Merry Field Hill Dorset 8 E8
Merry Hill Herts 20 K4
Merryhill Wolves 35 U1
Merry Lees Leics 47 N12
Merrymeet Cnwll 4 H7
Mersea Island Essex 23 P4
Mersey Crossing Halton 55 M10
Mersham Kent 13 L7
Merstham Surrey 21 N12
Merston W Susx 10 D10
Merstone IoW 9 Q11
Merther Cnwll 3 M8
Merthyr Carmth 25 Q6
Merthyr Cynog Powys 33 U13
Merthyr Dyfan V Glam 16 F3
Merthyr Mawr Brdgnd 26 F12
Merthyr Tydfil Myr Td 26 J6
Merthyr Vale Myr Td 26 K8
Merton Devon 15 M10
Merton Gt Lon 21 N8
Merton Norfk 50 F14
Merton Oxon 30 C9
Meshaw Devon 15 S9
Messing Essex 23 L4
Messingham N Linc 58 E6
Metfield Suffk 41 N4
Metherell Cnwll 5 L7
Metheringham Lincs 48 G1
Methil Fife 91 N12
Methilhill Fife 91 N11
Methley Leeds 57 N1
Methley Junction Leeds 57 N1
Methlick Abers 105 P8
Methven P & K 90 F6
Methwold Norfk 40 B2
Methwold Hythe Norfk 40 B2
Mettingham Suffk 41 Q3
Metton Norfk 51 M6
Mevagissey Cnwll 3 Q8
Mexborough Donc 57 Q6
Mey Highld 112 G2
Meysey Hampton Gloucs 29 M7
Miabhaig W Isls 106 f5
Michaelchurch Herefs 27 U2
Michaelchurch Escley Herefs 34 H14
Michaelchurch-on-Arrow Powys 34 F10
Michaelstone-y-Fedw Newpt 27 N11
Michaelston-le-Pit V Glam 27 M13
Michaelstow Cnwll 4 D5
Michaelwood Services Gloucs 28 D8
Michelcombe Devon 5 R7
Micheldever Hants 19 R13
Micheldever Station Hants 19 R12
Michelmersh Hants 9 L3
Mickfield Suffk 40 K8
Micklebring Donc 57 R8
Mickleby N York 71 P10
Micklefield Leeds 63 U13
Micklefield Green Herts 20 H3
Mickleham Surrey 21 L12
Mickleover C Derb 46 K7
Micklethwaite C Brad 63 N11
Micklethwaite Cumb 67 L2
Mickleton Dur 69 L8
Mickleton Gloucs 36 G12
Mickletown Leeds 57 P1
Mickle Trafford Ches W 54 K13
Mickley Derbys 57 M11
Mickley N York 63 R4
Mickley Green Suffk 40 D9
Mickley Square Nthumb 77 M13
Mid Ardlaw Abers 105 Q3
Midbea Ork 106 t15
Mid Beltie Abers 99 L3
Mid Bockhampton BCP 8 H9
Mid Calder W Loth 83 L5
Mid Clyth Highld 112 G9
Mid Culbeuchly Abers 104 K3
Middle Assendon Oxon 20 B5
Middle Aston Oxon 29 U2
Middle Barton Oxon 29 T2
Middlebie D & G 75 P10
Middlebridge P & K 97 P10
Middle Chinnock Somset 7 N2
Middle Claydon Bucks 30 F7
Middlecliffe Barns 57 P5
Middlecott Devon 5 S3
Middle Duntisbourne Gloucs 28 J6
Middleham N York 63 N2
Middle Handley Derbys 57 P11
Middle Harling Norfk 40 G3
Middlehill Cnwll 4 H7
Middlehill Wilts 18 B7
Middlehope Shrops 35 L3
Middle Kames Ag & B 87 S8
Middle Littleton Worcs 36 E11
Middle Madeley Staffs 45 S4
Middle Maes-coed Herefs 34 H14
Middlemarsh Dorset 7 S3
Middle Mayfield Staffs 46 F5
Middle Mill Pembks 24 D5
Middlemoor Devon 5 M6
Middle Quarter Kent 12 G8
Middle Rasen Lincs 58 J9
Middle Rocombe Devon 6 B11
Middle Salter Lancs 62 C7
Middlesbrough Middsb 70 G9
Middlesceugh Cumb 67 P4
Middleshaw Cumb 62 B2
Middlesmoor N York 63 M5
Middle Stoford Somset 16 G12
Middle Stoke Medway 22 K12
Middlestone Dur 69 S6
Middlestone Moor Dur 69 R6
Middle Stoughton Somset 17 M7
Middlestown Wakefd 57 L3
Middle Street Gloucs 28 E7
Middle Taphouse Cnwll 4 F8
Middlethird Border 84 H10
Middleton Ag & B 92 A10
Middleton Cumb 62 C2
Middleton Derbys 46 J2
Middleton Derbys 56 J14
Middleton Essex 40 E13
Middleton Hants 19 P12
Middleton Herefs 35 M7
Middleton Lancs 61 S8
Middleton Leeds 63 S14
Middleton N York 63 N10
Middleton N York 64 H2
Middleton Nhants 38 B3
Middleton Norfk 49 U10
Middleton Nthumb 77 M9
Middleton Nthumb 85 S11
Middleton P & K 90 H10
Middleton Rochdl 56 C5
Middleton Shrops 35 M5
Middleton Shrops 44 H8
Middleton Suffk 41 R7
Middleton Swans 25 R13
Middleton Warwks 46 G14
Middleton Cheney Nhants 37 N12
Middleton Green Staffs 46 C6
Middleton Hall Nthumb 85 P13
Middleton-in-Teesdale Dur 68 K7
Middleton Moor Suffk 41 R7
Middleton One Row Darltn 70 E10
Middleton-on-Leven N York 70 G11
Middleton-on-Sea W Susx 10 F10
Middleton on the Hill Herefs 35 M8
Middleton on the Wolds E R Yk 65 L10
Middleton Park C Aber 105 Q13
Middleton Priors Shrops 35 P2
Middleton Quernhow N York 63 S4
Middleton St George Darltn 70 D10
Middleton Scriven Shrops 35 Q3
Middleton Stoney Oxon 30 B8
Middleton Tyas N York 69 R11
Middletown Cumb 66 E11
Middle Town IoS 2 b3
Middletown N Som 17 N2
Middletown Powys 44 H11
Middle Tysoe Warwks 36 K12
Middle Wallop Hants 19 L13
Middlewich Ches E 55 R13
Middle Winterslow Wilts 8 J2
Middlewood Cnwll 4 H5
Middlewood Herefs 34 G12
Middle Woodford Wilts 18 H13
Middlewood Green Suffk 40 J8
Middle Yard Gloucs 28 F7
Middlezoy Somset 17 L10
Middridge Dur 69 R7
Midford BaNES 17 U4
Midge Hall Lancs 55 M2
Midgeholme Cumb 76 C14
Midgham W Berk 19 S7
Midgley Calder 56 F1
Midgley Wakefd 57 L4
Mid Holmwood Surrey 21 L13
Midhopestones Sheff 56 K7
Midhurst W Susx 10 D6
Mid Lavant W Susx 10 D9
Midlem Border 84 E13
Mid Mains Highld 102 D8
Midney Somset 17 N11
Midpark Ag & B 87 U14
Midsomer Norton BaNES 17 S6
Midtown Highld 111 M4
Midville Lincs 49 N2
Midway Ches E 56 D10
Mid Yell Shet 106 v4
Migdale Highld 109 L6
Migvie Abers 98 G2
Milborne Port Somset 17 S13
Milborne St Andrew Dorset 7 V5
Milborne Wick Somset 17 S12
Milbourne Nthumb 77 N10
Milbourne Wilts 28 J10
Milburn Cumb 68 E7
Milbury Heath S Glos 28 C9
Milby N York 63 U6
Milcombe Oxon 37 M14
Milden Suffk 40 G11
Mildenhall Suffk 40 B6
Mildenhall Wilts 18 K7
Milebrook Powys 34 H6
Milebush Kent 12 E6
Mile Elm Wilts 18 E7
Mile End Essex 23 N2
Mile End Gloucs 28 A5
Mile End Suffk 41 P3
Mileham Norfk 50 F10
Mile Oak Br & H 11 L9
Mile Oak Kent 12 C7
Mile Oak Staffs 46 G13
Miles Hope Herefs 35 N8
Milesmark Fife 90 G14
Miles Platting Manch 56 C7
Mile Town Kent 23 M13
Milfield Nthumb 85 N12
Milford Derbys 47 L4
Milford Devon 14 F8
Milford Powys 34 C2
Milford Staffs 46 C9
Milford Surrey 10 E2
Milford Haven Pembks 24 F9
Milford on Sea Hants 8 K10
Milkwall Gloucs 28 A6
Millais Jersey 7 a1
Milland W Susx 10 C5
Milland Marsh W Susx 10 C5
Mill Bank Calder 56 F2
Millbeck Cumb 67 L7
Millbreck Abers 105 S7
Millbridge Surrey 10 C2
Millbrook C Beds 31 M5
Millbrook C Sotn 9 M6
Millbrook Cnwll 5 L10
Millbrook Jersey 7 c3
Millbrook Tamesd 56 E7
Mill Brow Stockp 56 E9
Millbuie Abers 99 P2
Millbuie Highld 102 G5
Millcombe Devon 5 U11
Mill Common Norfk 51 P13
Mill Common Suffk 41 R4
Millcorner E Susx 12 F11
Millcraig Highld 109 M10
Mill Cross Devon 5 S8
Milldale Staffs 46 F3
Mill End Bucks 20 C5
Millend Gloucs 28 D8
Mill End Herts 31 T6
Millerhill Mdloth 83 R5
Miller's Dale Derbys 56 H12
Millers Green Derbys 46 J3
Miller's Green Essex 22 E6
Millerston C Glas 89 P12
Millgate Lancs 56 C3
Mill Green Cambs 39 T11
Mill Green Essex 22 F7
Mill Green Herts 31 R10
Mill Green Lincs 48 K9
Mill Green Norfk 40 K4
Millgreen Shrops 45 Q8
Mill Green Staffs 46 E13
Mill Green Staffs 46 E9
Mill Green Suffk 40 G12
Mill Green Suffk 40 G9
Mill Green Suffk 40 K8
Mill Green Suffk 41 P8
Millhalf Herefs 34 G11
Millhayes Devon 6 H4
Millhead Lancs 61 T5
Millheugh S Lans 82 D8
Mill Hill E Susx 11 U9
Mill Hill Gt Lon 21 M4
Millhouse Ag & B 87 T11
Millhouse Cumb 67 N5
Millhousebridge D & G 75 M8
Millhouse Green Barns 56 K6
Millhouses Barns 57 P6
Millhouses Sheff 57 M10
Milliken Park Rens 88 K13
Millin Cross Pembks 24 G8
Millington E R Yk 64 J9
Mill Lane Hants 20 C12
Millmeece Staffs 45 T7
Millness Cumb 61 U3
Mill of Drummond P & K 89 T2
Mill of Haldane W Duns 88 J9
Millom Cumb 61 M3
Millook Cnwll 14 E13
Millpool Cnwll 2 F10
Millpool Cnwll 4 E6
Millport N Ayrs 80 H2
Mill Side Cumb 61 S3
Mill Street Kent 12 C4
Mill Street Norfk 50 J10
Mill Street Suffk 40 J6
Millthorpe Derbys 57 M11
Millthrop Cumb 62 D1
Milltimber C Aber 99 R3
Milltown Abers 98 D2
Milltown Abers 104 F12
Milltown Cnwll 4 E9
Milltown D & G 75 R10
Milltown Derbys 47 L1
Milltown Devon 15 N5
Milltown Highld 100 g5
Milltown of Auchindoun Moray 104 D7
Milltown of Campfield Abers 99 M3
Milltown of Edinvillie Moray 104 B7
Milltown of Learney Abers 99 L3
Milltown of Rothiemay Moray 104 H6
Milnathort P & K 90 H11
Milngavie E Duns 89 N11
Milnrow Rochdl 56 D4
Milnthorpe Cumb 61 T3
Milnthorpe Wakefd 57 M3
Milovaig Highld 100 a5
Milson Shrops 35 P6
Milstead Kent 12 H4
Milston Wilts 18 J11
Milthorpe Lincs 48 H7
Milthorpe Nhants 37 Q11
Milton C Stke 46 B3
Milton Cambs 39 Q8
Milton Cumb 76 B13
Milton D & G 72 G9
Milton D & G 74 F11
Milton Derbys 46 K8
Milton Highld 102 E9
Milton Highld 102 G6
Milton Highld 109 P10
Milton Highld 112 H6
Milton Inver 88 J12
Milton Kent 22 G13
Milton Moray 103 U12
Milton Moray 104 G3
Milton N Som 16 K4
Milton Newpt 27 R10
Milton Notts 58 B12
Milton Oxon 29 U9
Milton Oxon 37 N13
Milton P & K 97 T11
Milton Pembks 24 H10
Milton Somset 17 N12
Milton Stirlg 89 M5
Milton W Duns 88 K11
Milton Abbas Dorset 7 V4
Milton Abbot Devon 5 L5
Milton Bridge Mdloth 83 Q6
Milton Bryan C Beds 31 L6
Milton Clevedon Somset 17 S9
Milton Combe Devon 5 M7
Milton Common Oxon 30 E12
Milton Damerel Devon 14 J10
Milton End Gloucs 28 D5
Milton End Gloucs 29 M7
Milton Ernest Bed 38 F9
Milton Green Ches W 45 L2
Milton Hill Oxon 29 U9
Milton Keynes M Keyn 30 J5
Milton Lilbourne Wilts 18 J8
Milton Malsor Nhants 37 T9
Milton Morenish P & K 95 S11
Milton of Auchinhove Abers 98 K3
Milton of Balgonie Fife 91 M11
Milton of Buchanan Stirlg 88 K7
Milton of Campsie E Duns 89 Q10
Milton of Finavon Angus 98 H12
Milton of Leys Highld 102 J7
Milton of Murtle C Aber 99 R3
Milton on Stour Dorset 17 U11
Milton Regis Kent 12 H3
Milton Street E Susx 11 S10
Milton-under-Wychwood Oxon 29 Q4
Milverton Somset 16 F11
Milverton Warwks 36 K7
Milwich Staffs 46 C7
Milwr Flints 54 E12
Minard Ag & B 87 T6
Minchington Dorset 8 D6
Minchinhampton Gloucs 28 G7
Mindrum Nthumb 85 L12
Minehead Somset 16 C7
Minera Wrexhm 44 G3
Minety Wilts 28 K9
Minffordd Gwynd 43 L6
Mingarrypark Highld 93 R5
Miningsby Lincs 59 P14
Minions Cnwll 4 H6
Minishant S Ayrs 81 L10
Minllyn Gwynd 43 S11
Minnigaff D & G 73 L6
Minnonie Abers 105 M3
Minshull Vernon Ches E 45 Q1
Minskip N York 63 T7
Minstead Hants 8 K6
Minsted W Susx 10 D6
Minster Kent 13 R3
Minsterley Shrops 44 J12
Minster Lovell Oxon 29 R5
Minster-on-Sea Kent 23 N13
Minsterworth Gloucs 28 E4
Minterne Magna Dorset 7 S4
Minterne Parva Dorset 7 S4
Minting Lincs 59 L12
Mintlaw Abers 105 R6
Minto Border 76 B1
Minton Shrops 34 K2
Minwear Pembks 24 H8
Minworth Birm 36 G2
Mirehouse Cumb 66 E9
Mireland Highld 112 H4
Mirfield Kirk 56 K3
Miserden Gloucs 28 H6
Miskin Rhondd 26 J11
Miskin Rhondd 26 J8
Misson Notts 57 U8
Misterton Leics 37 Q4
Misterton Notts 58 C8
Misterton Somset 7 N3
Mistley Essex 23 R1
Mistley Heath Essex 23 R1
Mitcham Gt Lon 21 N9
Mitcheldean Gloucs 28 C4
Mitchell Cnwll 3 M6
Mitchellslacks D & G 74 J6
Mitchel Troy Mons 27 T5
Mitford Nthumb 77 P8
Mithian Cnwll 2 J6
Mitton Staffs 45 U10
Mixbury Oxon 30 D6
Mixenden Calder 63 M14
Moats Tye Suffk 40 H9
Mobberley Ches E 55 S11
Mobberley Staffs 46 D5
Moccas Herefs 34 J12
Mochdre Conwy 53 P7
Mochdre Powys 34 C3
Mochrum D & G 72 J10
Mockbeggar Hants 8 H7
Mockbeggar Kent 12 D6
Mockerkin Cumb 66 G8
Modbury Devon 5 R10
Moddershall Staffs 46 B6
Moelfre IoA 52 H5
Moelfre Powys 44 E8
Moel Tryfan Gwynd 52 H11
Moffat D & G 75 L4
Mogador Surrey 21 M12
Moggerhanger C Beds 38 H11
Moira Leics 46 K10
Molash Kent 12 K5
Mol-chlach Highld 100 d8
Mold Flints 54 F14
Moldgreen Kirk 56 J3
Molehill Green Essex 22 E3
Molehill Green Essex 22 H3
Molescroft E R Yk 65 N11
Molesden Nthumb 77 N9
Molesworth Cambs 38 G5
Moll Highld 100 e6
Molland Devon 15 T7
Mollington Ches W 54 J12
Mollington Oxon 37 M11
Mollinsburn N Lans 82 D4
Monachty Cerdgn 32 K8
Mondynes Abers 99 P8
Monewden Suffk 41 M9
Moneydie P & K 90 G6
Moneyrow Green W & M 20 E7
Moniaive D & G 74 E7
Monifieth Angus 91 Q5
Monikie Angus 91 Q4
Monimail Fife 91 L9
Monington Pembks 32 B12
Monk Bretton Barns 57 N5
Monken Hadley Gt Lon 21 M3
Monk Fryston N York 64 C14
Monkhide Herefs 35 P12
Monkhill Cumb 75 R14
Monkhopton Shrops 35 P2
Monkland Herefs 35 L9
Monkleigh Devon 15 L8
Monknash V Glam 16 B2
Monkokehampton Devon 15 N11
Monkseaton N Tyne 77 S11
Monks Eleigh Suffk 40 G11
Monk's Gate W Susx 11 L5
Monks Heath Ches E 55 T12
Monk Sherborne Hants 19 T9
Monks Horton Kent 13 M7
Monksilver Somset 16 E9
Monks Kirby Warwks 37 N4
Monk Soham Suffk 41 M7
Monkspath Solhll 36 F5
Monks Risborough Bucks 30 H12
Monksthorpe Lincs 59 R13
Monk Street Essex 22 F2
Monkswood Mons 27 Q7
Monkton Devon 6 G4
Monkton Kent 13 Q3
Monkton S Ayrs 81 M7
Monkton S Tyne 77 S13
Monkton V Glam 16 B2
Monkton Combe BaNES 17 U4
Monkton Deverill Wilts 18 C13
Monkton Farleigh Wilts 18 B7
Monkton Heathfield Somset 16 J11
Monkton Up Wimborne Dorset 8 E6
Monkton Wyld Dorset 6 K5
Monkwearmouth Sundld 77 T14
Monkwood Hants 9 T2
Monmore Green Wolves 46 B14
Monmouth Mons 27 U5
Monnington on Wye Herefs 34 J12
Monreith D & G 72 K11
Montacute Somset 17 N13
Montcliffe Bolton 55 Q4
Montford Shrops 44 K11
Montford Bridge Shrops 44 K10
Montgarrie Abers 104 H12
Montgomery Powys 34 F1
Monton Salfd 55 S7
Montrose Angus 99 N12
Mont Saint Guern 6 c3
Monxton Hants 19 M12
Monyash Derbys 56 J13
Monymusk Abers 104 K12
Monzie P & K 90 C6
Moodiesburn N Lans 82 C4
Moonzie Fife 91 M8
Moor Allerton Leeds 63 S12
Moorbath Dorset 7 M5
Moorby Lincs 59 N14
Moorcot Herefs 34 J9
Moor Crichel Dorset 8 D7
Moordown BCP 8 F10
Moore Halton 55 N10
Moor End C Beds 31 L8
Moor End Calder 63 M14
Moor End Devon 15 Q11
Moorend Gloucs 28 D7
Moor End Lancs 61 R11
Moor End N York 64 E12
Moorends Donc 57 U3
Moorgreen Hants 9 P5
Moor Green Herts 31 T7
Moorgreen Notts 47 N4
Moorhall Derbys 57 M12
Moorhampton Herefs 34 J11
Moorhead C Brad 63 N12
Moor Head Leeds 63 Q14
Moorhouse Cumb 67 L2
Moorhouse Cumb 67 M1
Moorhouse Donc 57 Q4
Moorhouse Notts 58 C13
Moorhouse Bank Surrey 21 R12
Moorland Somset 16 K10
Moorlinch Somset 17 L9
Moor Monkton N York 64 C8
Moor Row Cumb 66 F10
Moor Row Cumb 66 K3
Moorsholm R & Cl 71 L10
Moorside Dorset 17 U13
Moorside Dur 69 N3
Moor Side Lancs 61 S13
Moor Side Lancs 61 T12
Moorside Leeds 63 Q12
Moor Side Lincs 49 L2
Moorside Oldham 56 D5
Moorstock Kent 13 M8
Moor Street Birm 36 C4
Moor Street Medway 12 F2
Moorswater Cnwll 4 G8
Moorthorpe Wakefd 57 Q4
Moortown Devon 5 N6
Moortown Hants 8 H8
Moortown IoW 9 N12
Moortown Leeds 63 R12
Moortown Lincs 58 J7
Moortown Wrekin 45 P10
Morangie Highld 109 P8
Morar Highld 100 f10
Morborne Cambs 38 H2
Morchard Bishop Devon 15 S11
Morchard Road Devon 15 S11
Morcombelake Dorset 7 M6
Morcott Rutlnd 48 D13
Morda Shrops 44 G8
Morden Dorset 8 C9
Morden Gt Lon 21 N9
Mordiford Herefs 35 N13
Mordon Dur 70 D7
More Shrops 34 H2
Morebath Devon 16 C11
Morebattle Border 84 K14
Morecambe Lancs 61 S7
Moredon Swindn 29 M10
Morefield Highld 107 V5
Morehall Kent 13 P8
Moreleigh Devon 5 T10
Morenish P & K 95 S11
Moresby Parks Cumb 66 E9
Morestead Hants 9 Q3
Moreton Dorset 7 V7
Moreton Essex 22 D6
Moreton Herefs 35 M8
Moreton Oxon 30 E12
Moreton Staffs 45 S10
Moreton Staffs 46 F8
Moreton Wirral 54 G9
Moreton Corbet Shrops 45 N9
Moretonhampstead Devon 5 T3
Moreton-in-Marsh Gloucs 29 P1
Moreton Jeffries Herefs 35 P11
Moretonmill Shrops 45 N9
Moreton Morrell Warwks 36 K9
Moreton on Lugg Herefs 35 M11
Moreton Paddox Warwks 36 K10
Moreton Pinkney Nhants 37 Q11
Moreton Say Shrops 45 P7
Moreton Valence Gloucs 28 E6
Morfa Cerdgn 32 F10
Morfa Bychan Gwynd 42 K6
Morfa Dinlle Gwynd 52 F11
Morfa Glas Neath 26 F6
Morfa Nefyn Gwynd 42 E5
Morganstown Cardif 27 L11
Morgan's Vale Wilts 8 H4
Morham E Loth 84 F4
Moriah Cerdgn 33 M5
Morland Cumb 68 D8
Morley Ches E 55 T10
Morley Derbys 47 L5
Morley Dur 69 P7
Morley Leeds 57 L1
Morley Green Ches E 55 T10
Morley St Botolph Norfk 50 J14
Mornick Cnwll 4 J6
Morningside C Edin 83 P4
Morningside N Lans 82 F7
Morningthorpe Norfk 41 M2
Morpeth Nthumb 77 P8
Morphie Abers 99 N11
Morrey Staffs 46 F10
Morridge Side Staffs 46 D3
Morriston Swans 26 B8
Morston Norfk 50 H5
Mortehoe Devon 15 L3
Morthen Rothm 57 Q9
Mortimer W Berk 19 U8
Mortimer Common W Berk 19 U7
Mortimer's Cross Herefs 34 K8
Mortimer West End Hants 19 T8
Mortlake Gt Lon 21 M7
Morton Cumb 67 N2
Morton Cumb 67 Q5
Morton Derbys 47 M1
Morton IoW 9 S11
Morton Lincs 48 G9
Morton Lincs 58 D8
Morton Lincs 58 E14
Morton Notts 47 T3
Morton Shrops 44 G9
Morton-on-Swale N York 63 S1
Morton on the Hill Norfk 50 K10
Morton Tinmouth Dur 69 Q8
Morvah Cnwll 2 C9
Morval Cnwll 4 H9
Morvich Highld 101 P7
Morville Shrops 35 Q2
Morville Heath Shrops 35 Q2
Morwenstow Cnwll 14 F9
Mosborough Sheff 57 P10
Moscow E Ayrs 81 P4
Mose Shrops 35 S2
Mosedale Cumb 67 N6
Moseley Birm 36 E4
Moseley Wolves 46 B14
Moseley Worcs 35 T9
Moses Gate Bolton 55 R5
Moss Ag & B 92 B10
Moss Donc 57 S4
Moss Wrexhm 44 H3
Mossat Abers 104 F12
Mossbank Shet 106 u6
Moss Bank St Hel 55 M7
Mossbay Cumb 66 E7
Mossblown S Ayrs 81 N8
Mossbrow Traffd 55 R9
Mossburnford Border 76 D2
Mossdale D & G 73 R5
Mossdale E Ayrs 81 P12
Moss Edge Lancs 61 S11
Moss End Ches E 55 Q11
Mossend N Lans 82 D6
Mosser Mains Cumb 66 H7
Mossley Ches E 45 U1
Mossley Tamesd 56 E6
Mosspaul Hotel Border 75 S6
Moss Side Cumb 66 J2
Moss-side Highld 103 N4
Moss Side Lancs 61 R13
Moss Side Sefton 54 J6
Mosstodloch Moray 104 C4
Mossyard D & G 73 N9
Mossy Lea Lancs 55 M4
Mosterton Dorset 7 N3
Moston Manch 56 C6
Moston Shrops 45 N8
Moston Green Ches E 45 R1
Mostyn Flints 54 E10
Motcombe Dorset 8 B3
Mothecombe Devon 5 Q11
Motherby Cumb 67 P7
Motherwell N Lans 82 D7
Motspur Park Gt Lon 21 M9
Mottingham Gt Lon 21 R8
Mottisfont Hants 9 L3
Mottisfont Hants 9 L3
Mottistone IoW 9 N12
Mottram in Longdendale Tamesd 56 E7
Mottram St Andrew Ches E 56 C11
Mouilpied Guern 6 d3
Mouldsworth Ches W 55 M12
Moulin P & K 97 Q12
Moulsecoomb Br & H 11 N9
Moulsford Oxon 19 S4
Moulsoe M Keyn 30 K4
Moultavie Highld 109 L10
Moulton Ches W 55 Q13
Moulton Lincs 49 M9
Moulton N York 69 R12
Moulton Nhants 37 U7
Moulton Suffk 39 U8
Moulton V Glam 16 E3
Moulton Chapel Lincs 49 L10
Moulton St Mary Norfk 51 Q12
Moulton Seas End Lincs 49 M8
Mount Cnwll 2 K5
Mount Cnwll 4 E7
Mount Kirk 56 G3
Mountain C Brad 63 M13
Mountain Ash Rhondd 26 J8
Mountain Cross Border 83 N9
Mountain Street Kent 13 L5
Mount Ambrose Cnwll 2 J8
Mount Bures Essex 40 F14
Mountfield E Susx 12 D11
Mountgerald Highld 102 G3
Mount Hawke Cnwll 2 J7
Mount Hermon Cnwll 2 H13
Mountjoy Cnwll 3 M4
Mount Lothian Mdloth 83 Q7
Mountnessing Essex 22 F8
Mounton Mons 27 U9
Mount Pleasant Ches E 45 T2
Mount Pleasant Derbys 46 J10
Mount Pleasant Derbys 46 K4
Mount Pleasant Dur 69 S6
Mount Pleasant E R Yk 65 T12
Mount Pleasant E Susx 11 Q7
Mount Pleasant Norfk 40 G2
Mount Pleasant Suffk 40 B11
Mount Pleasant Worcs 36 D8
Mountsorrel Leics 47 Q11
Mount Sorrel Wilts 8 E4
Mount Tabor Calder 56 G1
Mousehole Cnwll 2 D11
Mouswald D & G 75 L11
Mow Cop Ches E 45 U2
Mowhaugh Border 76 G1
Mowmacre Hill C Leic 47 Q12
Mowsley Leics 37 R3
Moy Highld 96 E7
Moy Highld 103 L9
Moyle Highld 101 M8
Moylegrove Pembks 32 B12
Muasdale Ag & B 79 M7
Muchalls Abers 99 S5
Much Birch Herefs 27 U1
Much Cowarne Herefs 35 P11
Much Dewchurch Herefs 27 T1
Muchelney Somset 17 M12
Muchelney Ham Somset 17 M12
Much Hadham Herts 22 B4
Much Hoole Lancs 55 L2
Much Hoole Town Lancs 55 L2
Muchlarnick Cnwll 4 G9
Much Marcle Herefs 35 Q14
Much Wenlock Shrops 45 P14
Muck Highld 93 L3
Mucking Thurr 22 G11
Muckleburgh Collection Norfk 50 K5
Muckleford Dorset 7 R6
Mucklestone Staffs 45 R6
Muckley Shrops 35 P1
Muckton Lincs 59 Q10
Muddiford Devon 15 N5
Muddles Green E Susx 11 S8
Mudeford BCP 8 H10
Mudford Somset 17 Q13
Mudford Sock Somset 17 Q13
Mudgley Somset 17 N7
Mud Row Kent 23 P13
Mugdock Stirlg 89 N10
Mugeary Highld 100 d6
Mugginton Derbys 46 J5
Muggintonlane End Derbys 46 J5
Muggleswick Dur 69 M3
Muirden Abers 105 L5
Muirdrum Angus 91 S4
Muiresk Abers 104 K6
Muirhead Angus 91 M5
Muirhead Fife 91 L10
Muirhead N Lans 82 C5
Muirhouses Falk 82 K2
Muirkirk E Ayrs 82 C13
Muirmill Stirlg 89 R9
Muir of Fowlis Abers 104 H13
Muir of Miltonduff Moray 103 U4
Muir of Ord Highld 102 F5
Muirshearlich Highld 94 G2
Muirtack Abers 105 R8
Muirton P & K 90 D9
Muirton Mains Highld 102 E5
Muirton of Ardblair P & K 90 J3
Muker N York 68 K13
Mulbarton Norfk 51 L13
Mulben Moray 104 D5
Mulfra Cnwll 2 D10
Mull Ag & B 93 Q12
Mullacott Cross Devon 15 M4
Mullion Cnwll 2 H13
Mullion Cove Cnwll 2 H13
Mumby Lincs 59 T12
Munderfield Row Herefs 35 P10
Munderfield Stocks Herefs 35 Q10
Mundesley Norfk 51 P6
Mundford Norfk 40 D2
Mundham Norfk 51 P14
Mundon Hill Essex 23 L7
Mundy Bois Kent 12 H6
Mungrisdale Cumb 67 N6
Munlochy Highld 102 H5
Munnoch N Ayrs 80 K3
Munsley Herefs 35 Q12
Munslow Shrops 35 M3
Murchington Devon 5 R3
Murcot Worcs 36 E12
Murcott Oxon 30 C9
Murcott Wilts 28 J9
Murkle Highld 112 E3
Murlaggan Highld 101 Q13
Murrell Green Hants 20 B11
Murroes Angus 91 Q4
Murrow Cambs 49 N12
Mursley Bucks 30 H7
Murston Kent 12 H3
Murthill Angus 98 H12
Murthly P & K 90 H4
Murton C York 64 E9
Murton Cumb 68 F8
Murton Dur 70 E3
Murton N Tyne 77 S11
Murton Nthumb 85 P9
Murton Swans 25 U13
Musbury Devon 6 J6
Muscoates N York 64 F4
Musselburgh E Loth 83 R4
Muston Leics 48 B6
Muston N York 65 P4
Mustow Green Worcs 35 U6
Muswell Hill Gt Lon 21 N5
Mutehill D & G 73 R10
Mutford Suffk 41 S3
Muthill P & K 90 C8
Mutterton Devon 6 D3
Muxton Wrekin 45 R11
Mybster Highld 112 E6
Myddfai Carmth 26 D1
Myddle Shrops 45 L9
Mydroilyn Cerdgn 32 J9
Myerscough Lancs 61 T12
Mylor Cnwll 3 L9
Mylor Bridge Cnwll 3 L9
Mynachlog ddu Pembks 24 K4
Myndd-llan Flints 54 E12
Myndtown Shrops 34 J3
Mynydd Bach Cerdgn 33 P5
Mynydd-bach Mons 27 T9
Mynydd-Bach Swans 26 B8
Mynyddgarreg Carmth 25 R9
Mynydd Isa Flints 54 G14
Mynydd Llandygai Gwynd 52 K9
Mynytho Gwynd 42 F7
Myrebird Abers 99 N4
Myredykes Border 76 B6
Mytchett Surrey 20 E11
Mytholm Calder 56 E1
Mytholmroyd Calder 56 F1
Mythop Lancs 61 R13
Myton-on-Swale N York 63 U6

N

Naast Highld 107 P8
Nab's Head Lancs 62 C14
Na Buirgh W Isls 106 f9
Naburn C York 64 D10
Naccolt Kent 13 L7
Nackington Kent 13 N5
Nacton Suffk 41 M12
Nafferton E R Yk 65 P8
Nag's Head Gloucs 28 G8
Nailbridge Gloucs 28 B4
Nailsbourne Somset 16 H11
Nailsea N Som 17 N2
Nailstone Leics 47 M12
Nailsworth Gloucs 28 F8
Nairn Highld 103 N4
Nalderswood Surrey 21 M13
Nancegollan Cnwll 2 G10
Nancledra Cnwll 2 D9
Nanhoron Gwynd 42 E7
Nannerch Flints 54 E13
Nanpantan Leics 47 P10
Nanpean Cnwll 3 P5
Nanquidno Cnwll 2 B11
Nanstallon Cnwll 3 Q3
Nant-ddu Powys 26 J5
Nanternis Cerdgn 32 G9
Nantgaredig Carmth 25 S6
Nantgarw Rhondd 27 L10
Nant-glas Powys 33 U7
Nantglyn Denbgs 53 T10
Nantgwyn Powys 33 U5
Nant Gwynant Gwynd 43 M3
Nantlle Gwynd 52 H12
Nantmawr Shrops 44 G9
Nantmel Powys 34 B7
Nantmor Gwynd 43 M4
Nant Peris Gwynd 52 K11
Nantwich Ches E 45 Q3
Nant-y-Bwch Blae G 27 L5
Nantycaws Carmth 25 S7
Nant-y-derry Mons 27 Q6
Nantyffyllon Brdgnd 26 F9
Nantyglo Blae G 27 M5
Nant-y-gollen Shrops 44 F8
Nant-y-moel Brdgnd 26 G9
Nant-y-pandy Conwy 53 L8
Naphill Bucks 20 D3
Napleton Worcs 35 U11
Nappa N York 62 H9
Napton on the Hill Warwks 37 N8
Narberth Pembks 24 K8
Narborough Leics 37 P1
Narborough Norfk 50 B11
Narkurs Cnwll 4 J9
Nasareth Gwynd 42 J4
Naseby Nhants 37 S5
Nash Bucks 30 G6
Nash Gt Lon 21 R10
Nash Herefs 34 H8
Nash Newpt 27 Q11
Nash Shrops 35 P6
Nash End Worcs 35 S4
Nashes Green Hants 19 U11
Nash Lee Bucks 30 H11
Nash Street Kent 12 B2
Nassington Nhants 38 G1

Nastend – Otterham 137

Nastend Gloucs 28 E6
Nasty Herts 31 U8
Nateby Cumb 68 G11
Nateby Lancs 61 T11
National Memorial Arboretum Staffs 46 G11
National Motor Museum (Beaulieu) Hants 9 M8
National Space Centre C Leic 47 Q12
Natland Cumb 61 U2
Naughton Suffk 40 H11
Naunton Gloucs 29 M3
Naunton Worcs 35 U13
Naunton Beauchamp Worcs 36 C10
Navenby Lincs 48 E2
Navestock Essex 22 D8
Navestock Side Essex 22 E8
Navidale Highld 112 B13
Navity Highld 103 L3
Nawton N York 64 F3
Nayland Suffk 40 G14
Nazeing Essex 22 B6
Nazeing Gate Essex 22 B6
Neacroft Hants 8 H9
Neal's Green Warwks 36 K4
Neap Shet 106 v8
Near Cotton Staffs 46 E4
Near Sawrey Cumb 67 N13
Neasden Gt Lon 21 M5
Neasham Darltn 70 D10
Neath Neath 26 D8
Neatham Hants 10 A2
Neatishead Norfk 51 P9
Nebo Cerdgn 32 K7
Nebo Conwy 53 P11
Nebo Gwynd 42 J3
Nebo IoA 52 G4
Necton Norfk 50 E12
Nedd Highld 110 C10
Nedderton Nthumb 77 Q9
Nedging Suffk 40 G11
Nedging Tye Suffk 40 H11
Needham Norfk 41 M4
Needham Market Suffk 40 J9
Needham Street Suffk 40 B7
Needingworth Cambs 39 M6
Neen Savage Shrops 35 Q5
Neen Sollars Shrops 35 Q6
Neenton Shrops 35 P3
Nefyn Gwynd 42 F5
Neilston E Rens 81 P1
Nelson Caerph 27 L8
Nelson Lancs 62 H12
Nemphlar S Lans 82 G10
Nempnett Thrubwell BaNES 17 P4
Nenthall Cumb 68 G3
Nenthead Cumb 68 G4
Nenthorn Border 84 H11
Neopardy Devon 15 S13
Nep Town W Susx 11 L7
Nerabus Ag & B 78 C4
Nercwys Flints 44 F1
Nerston S Lans 81 S1
Nesbit Nthumb 85 P12
Nesfield N York 63 M10
Ness Ches W 54 H11
Nesscliffe Shrops 44 J10
Neston Ches W 54 G11
Neston Wilts 18 C7
Netchwood Shrops 35 P2
Nether Abington S Lans 82 H14
Nether Alderley Ches E 55 T11
Netheravon Wilts 18 H11
Nether Blainslie Border 84 E10
Netherbrae Abers 105 M4
Nether Broughton Leics 47 S8
Netherburn S Lans 82 E9
Netherbury Dorset 7 N5
Netherby Cumb 75 S11
Netherby N York 63 S10
Nether Cerne Dorset 7 S5
Nethercleuch D & G 75 M8
Nether Compton Dorset 17 Q13
Nethercote Warwks 37 P8
Nethercott Devon 14 J13
Nethercott Devon 15 L5
Nether Crimond Abers 105 N11
Nether Dallachy Moray 104 D3
Netherend Gloucs 28 A7
Nether Exe Devon 6 B4
Netherfield E Susx 12 D12
Netherfield Leics 47 Q10
Netherfield Notts 47 R5
Nether Fingland S Lans 74 H3
Nethergate N Linc 58 C7
Nethergate Norfk 50 J8
Netherhampton Wilts 8 G3
Nether Handley Derbys 57 P11
Nether Handwick Angus 91 N3
Nether Haugh Rothm 57 P7
Netherhay Dorset 7 M3
Nether Headon Notts 58 B11
Nether Heage Derbys 47 L3
Nether Heyford Nhants 37 S9
Nether Kellet Lancs 61 U6
Nether Kinmundy Abers 105 T7
Netherland Green Staffs 46 F7
Nether Langwith Notts 57 R12
Netherlaw D & G 73 S11
Netherley Abers 99 R5
Nethermill D & G 74 K8
Nethermuir Abers 105 Q7
Netherne-on-the-Hill Surrey 21 N11
Netheroyd Hill Kirk 56 H3
Nether Padley Derbys 56 K11
Nether Poppleton C York 64 D9
Nether Row Cumb 67 M5
Netherseal Derbys 46 J11
Nether Silton N York 64 B1
Nether Skyborry Shrops 34 G6
Nether Stowey Somset 16 G9
Nether Street Essex 22 E5
Netherstreet Wilts 18 E8
Netherthong Kirk 56 H5
Netherthorpe Derbys 57 P12
Netherton Angus 98 J12
Netherton Devon 6 A10
Netherton Dudley 36 B3
Netherton Hants 19 N9
Netherton Herefs 27 U2
Netherton Kirk 56 H4
Netherton N Lans 82 E8
Netherton Nthumb 76 K4
Netherton Oxon 29 T8
Netherton P & K 97 U13
Netherton Sefton 54 J7
Netherton Shrops 35 R4
Netherton Stirlg 89 N10
Netherton Wakefd 57 L3
Netherton Worcs 36 C12
Nethertown Cumb 66 E11
Nethertown Highld 112 J1
Nethertown Lancs 62 E12
Nethertown Staffs 46 F10
Netherurd Border 83 M10
Nether Wallop Hants 19 M13
Nether Wasdale Cumb 66 H12
Nether Welton Cumb 67 N3
Nether Westcote Gloucs 29 P3
Nether Whitacre Warwks 36 H2
Nether Whitecleuch S Lans 74 F2
Nether Winchendon Bucks 30 F10
Netherwitton Nthumb 77 M7
Nethy Bridge Highld 103 R11
Netley Hants 9 P7
Netley Marsh Hants 9 L6
Nettlebed Oxon 19 U3
Nettlebridge Somset 17 R7
Nettlecombe Dorset 7 P5
Nettlecombe IoW 9 Q13
Nettleden Herts 31 M10
Nettleham Lincs 58 H11
Nettlestead Kent 12 C5
Nettlestead Green Kent 12 C5
Nettlestone IoW 9 S10
Nettlesworth Dur 69 S3
Nettleton Lincs 58 K6
Nettleton Wilts 18 B5
Nettleton Shrub Wilts 18 B5
Netton Devon 5 P11
Netton Wilts 18 H13
Neuadd Carmth 26 C3
Neuadd-ddu Powys 33 T5
Nevendon Essex 22 J9
Nevern Pembks 32 A12
Nevill Holt Leics 38 B2
New Abbey D & G 74 J12
New Aberdour Abers 105 P3
New Addington Gt Lon 21 Q10
Newall Leeds 63 P10
New Alresford Hants 9 R2
New Alyth P & K 90 K2
Newark C Pete 48 K13
Newark Ork 106 w15
Newark-on-Trent Notts 47 U3
New Arram E R Yk 65 N11
Newarthill N Lans 82 E7
New Ash Green Kent 12 B2
New Balderton Notts 48 B3
New Barn Kent 12 B2
Newbarn Kent 13 N7
New Barnet Gt Lon 21 N3
New Barton Nhants 38 C8
Newbattle Mdloth 83 R5
New Bewick Nthumb 77 M1
Newbie D & G 75 N12
Newbiggin Cumb 61 P6
Newbiggin Cumb 66 G14
Newbiggin Cumb 67 Q7
Newbiggin Cumb 67 S3
Newbiggin Cumb 68 D7
Newbiggin Dur 68 K7
Newbiggin Dur 69 P3
Newbiggin N York 62 K1
Newbiggin N York 63 L2
Newbiggin-by-the-Sea Nthumb 77 S8
Newbigging Angus 91 L3
Newbigging Angus 91 P4
Newbigging Angus 91 Q4
Newbigging S Lans 82 K9
Newbiggin-on-Lune Cumb 68 F12
New Bilton Warwks 37 N5
Newbold Derbys 57 N12
Newbold Leics 47 M10
Newbold on Avon Warwks 37 N5
Newbold on Stour Warwks 36 H11
Newbold Pacey Warwks 36 J9
Newbold Revel Warwks 37 N4
Newbold Verdon Leics 47 M13
New Bolingbroke Lincs 49 M2
Newborough C Pete 48 K12
Newborough IoA 52 F9
Newborough Staffs 46 F8
Newbottle Nhants 30 B5
Newbottle Sundld 70 D2
New Boultham Lincs 58 G12
Newbourne Suffk 41 N12
New Bradwell M Keyn 30 H4
New Brampton Derbys 57 N12
New Brancepeth Dur 69 R4
Newbridge C Edin 83 M4
Newbridge Caerph 27 N8
Newbridge Cerdgn 32 K9
Newbridge Cnwll 2 C10
Newbridge Cnwll 2 K8
Newbridge D & G 74 H10
Newbridge Hants 8 K5
Newbridge IoW 9 N11
New Bridge N York 64 J2
Newbridge Oxon 29 T7
Newbridge Wrexhm 44 G5
Newbridge Green Worcs 35 T13
Newbridge-on-Usk Mons 27 R9
Newbridge-on-Wye Powys 34 B9
New Brighton Flints 54 G13
New Brighton Wirral 54 H8
New Brinsley Notts 47 N3
New Brotton R & Cl 71 L8
Newbrough Nthumb 76 H12
New Broughton Wrexhm 44 H3
New Buckenham Norfk 40 J2
Newbuildings Devon 15 S12
Newburgh Abers 105 R10
Newburgh Abers 105 R4
Newburgh Fife 90 K8
Newburgh Lancs 55 L4
Newburn N u Ty 77 P12
New Bury Bolton 55 R6
Newbury Somset 17 S7
Newbury W Berk 19 Q7
Newbury Wilts 18 B12
Newbury Park Gt Lon 21 R5
Newby Cumb 67 S8
Newby Lancs 62 G10
Newby N York 62 E6
Newby N York 65 N1
Newby N York 70 H10
Newby Bridge Cumb 61 R2
Newby Cross Cumb 67 N2
Newby East Cumb 75 U14
Newby Head Cumb 67 S8
New Byth Abers 105 N5
Newby West Cumb 67 N2
Newby Wiske N York 63 T2
Newcastle Mons 27 S4
Newcastle Shrops 34 G4
Newcastle Airport Nthumb 77 P11
Newcastle Emlyn Carmth 32 F12
Newcastleton Border 75 U8
Newcastle-under-Lyme Staffs 45 T4
Newcastle upon Tyne N u Ty 77 Q13
Newchapel Pembks 25 M3
Newchapel Staffs 45 U3
Newchapel Surrey 11 P2
Newchurch Blae G 27 M5
Newchurch Herefs 34 J10
Newchurch IoW 9 R11
Newchurch Kent 13 L9
Newchurch Mons 27 T8
Newchurch Powys 34 F10
Newchurch Staffs 46 F9
Newchurch in Pendle Lancs 62 G12
New Costessey Norfk 51 L11
New Cowper Cumb 66 H3
Newcraighall C Edin 83 R4
New Crofton Wakefd 57 N3
New Cross Cerdgn 33 M5
New Cross Gt Lon 21 Q7
New Cross Somset 17 M13
New Cumnock E Ayrs 81 S10
New Cut E Susx 12 F12
New Deer Abers 105 P6
New Delaval Nthumb 77 R10
New Delph Oldham 56 E5
New Denham Bucks 20 H6
Newdigate Surrey 10 K2
New Duston Nhants 37 T8
New Earswick C York 64 E8
New Eastwood Notts 47 N4
New Edlington Donc 57 R7
New Elgin Moray 103 V3
New Ellerby E R Yk 65 R12
Newell Green Br For 20 E8
New Eltham Gt Lon 21 R8
New End Worcs 36 E8
Newenden Kent 12 F10
New England C Pete 48 J13
New England Essex 40 B12
Newent Gloucs 28 D2
New Farnley Leeds 63 R13
New Ferry Wirral 54 H9
Newfield Dur 69 R2
Newfield Dur 69 R6
Newfield Highld 109 P9
New Fletton C Pete 48 J14
New Forest National Park 8 K7
Newfound Hants 19 S10
New Fryston Wakefd 57 Q1
Newgale Pembks 24 E6
New Galloway D & G 73 Q4
Newgate Norfk 50 H5
Newgate Street Herts 31 T11
New Gilston Fife 91 P10
New Grimsby IoS 2 b1
Newhall Ches E 45 P4
Newhall Derbys 46 J9
Newham Nthumb 85 T13
New Hartley Nthumb 77 S10
Newhaven C Edin 83 Q3
Newhaven Derbys 46 G1
Newhaven E Susx 11 Q10
New Haw Surrey 20 J10
New Hedges Pembks 24 K10
New Herrington Sundld 70 D2
Newhey Rochdl 56 D4
New Holkham Norfk 50 E6
New Holland N Linc 58 J2
Newholm N York 71 Q10
New Houghton Derbys 57 Q13
New Houghton Norfk 50 C8
Newhouse N Lans 82 E6
New Houses N York 62 G5
New Houses Wigan 55 N6
New Hutton Cumb 62 B1
New Hythe Kent 12 D4
Newick E Susx 11 Q6
Newingreen Kent 13 M8
Newington Kent 12 G3
Newington Kent 13 N8
Newington Oxon 30 D13
Newington Shrops 34 K4
Newington Bagpath Gloucs 28 F9
New Inn Carmth 25 S3
New Inn Torfn 27 Q8
New Invention Shrops 34 G5
New Lakenham Norfk 51 M12
New Lanark S Lans 82 G10
New Lanark Village S Lans 82 G10
Newland C KuH 65 P13
Newland Cumb 61 Q4
Newland E R Yk 64 J14
Newland Gloucs 27 V6
Newland N York 57 U2
Newland Oxon 29 S6
Newland Somset 15 T5
Newland Worcs 35 S11
Newlandrig Mdloth 83 S6
Newlands Border 75 V7
Newlands Cumb 67 M5
Newlands Nthumb 69 N1
Newlands of Dundurcas Moray 104 B5
New Lane Lancs 54 K4
New Lane End Warrtn 55 P8
New Langholm D & G 75 S9
New Leake Lincs 49 P2
New Leeds Abers 105 R5
New Lodge Barns 57 N5
New Longton Lancs 55 M1
New Luce D & G 72 F7
Newlyn Cnwll 2 D11
Newmachar Abers 105 P12
Newmains N Lans 82 F7
New Malden Gt Lon 21 M9
Newman's End Essex 22 D5
Newman's Green Suffk 40 E12
Newmarket Suffk 39 T8
Newmarket W Isls 106 j5
New Marske R & Cl 70 K8
New Marston Oxon 30 B11
New Marton Shrops 44 H7
New Mill Abers 99 P7
Newmill Border 75 U3
New Mill Cnwll 2 D10
New Mill Herts 30 K10
New Mill Kirk 56 J5
Newmill Moray 104 E5
Newmillerdam Wakefd 57 M3
Newmill of Inshewan Angus 98 G11
Newmills C Edin 83 N5
New Mills Cnwll 3 M6
New Mills Derbys 56 F9
Newmills Fife 82 K1
Newmills Mons 27 U6
New Mills Powys 44 C13
Newmiln P & K 90 H5
Newmilns E Ayrs 81 Q5
New Milton Hants 8 J9
New Mistley Essex 23 R1
New Moat Pembks 24 J5
Newnes Shrops 44 J7
Newney Green Essex 22 G6
Newnham Hants 20 B12
Newnham Herts 31 R5
Newnham Kent 12 J4
Newnham Nhants 37 Q9
Newnham Bridge Worcs 35 P7
Newnham on Severn Gloucs 28 C5
New Ollerton Notts 57 U13
New Oscott Birm 36 E2
New Pitsligo Abers 105 P4
New Polzeath Cnwll 4 A5
Newport Cnwll 4 J3
Newport Dorset 8 B9
Newport E R Yk 64 K13
Newport Essex 39 R14
Newport Gloucs 28 D8
Newport Highld 112 D12
Newport IoW 9 Q11
Newport Newpt 27 Q10
Newport Norfk 51 T10
Newport Pembks 24 J3
Newport Wrekin 45 R10
Newport-on-Tay Fife 91 P6
Newport Pagnell M Keyn 30 J4
Newport Pagnell Services M Keyn 30 J4
Newpound Common W Susx 10 H5
New Prestwick S Ayrs 81 L8
New Quay Cerdgn 32 G9
Newquay Cnwll 3 L4
New Quay Essex 23 P3
Newquay Zoo Cnwll 3 L4
New Rackheath Norfk 51 N11
New Radnor Powys 34 F8
New Rent Cumb 67 Q5
New Ridley Nthumb 77 M14
New Road Side N York 62 K11
New Romney Kent 13 L11
New Rossington Donc 57 T7
New Row Cerdgn 33 P6
New Row Lancs 62 C12
New Sauchie Clacks 90 C13
Newsbank Ches E 55 T13
Newseat Abers 105 L9
Newsham Lancs 61 U12
Newsham N York 63 T3
Newsham N York 69 P10
Newsham Nthumb 77 S10
New Sharlston Wakefd 57 N3
Newsholme E R Yk 64 G14
Newsholme Lancs 62 G9
New Shoreston Nthumb 85 T12
New Silksworth Sundld 70 E2
New Skelton R & Cl 71 L9
Newsome Kirk 56 J4
New Somerby Lincs 48 D6
New Springs Wigan 55 N5
Newstead Border 84 F12
Newstead Notts 47 P3
Newstead Nthumb 85 T13
New Stevenston N Lans 82 E7
New Street Herefs 34 H9
New Swannington Leics 47 M10
Newthorpe N York 64 B13
Newthorpe Notts 47 N4
New Thundersley Essex 22 J10
Newtimber W Susx 11 M8
Newtoft Lincs 58 H9
Newton Ag & B 88 B6
Newton Border 76 C1
Newton Brdgnd 26 E12
Newton C Beds 31 R4
Newton Cambs 39 P11
Newton Cambs 49 P11
Newton Cardif 27 N12
Newton Ches W 45 M2
Newton Ches W 54 K13
Newton Ches W 55 M11
Newton Cumb 61 N5
Newton Derbys 47 M2
Newton Herefs 34 H14
Newton Herefs 34 J7
Newton Herefs 35 M10
Newton Highld 102 G5
Newton Highld 102 K6
Newton Highld 103 L2
Newton Highld 112 H7
Newton Lancs 61 Q12
Newton Lancs 62 B5
Newton Lincs 48 F6
Newton Mdloth 83 R5
Newton Moray 103 U3
Newton Moray 104 C3
Newton N York 64 K5
Newton Nhants 38 C4
Newton Norfk 50 D10
Newton Notts 47 S5
Newton Nthumb 76 J4
Newton Nthumb 77 L13
Newton S Lans 82 H12
Newton S Lans 89 Q13
Newton Sandw 36 D2
Newton Shrops 44 K7
Newton Somset 16 F9
Newton Staffs 46 D8
Newton Suffk 40 F12
Newton W Loth 83 L3
Newton Warwks 37 P5
Newton Wilts 8 J4
Newton Abbot Devon 5 V6
Newton Arlosh Cumb 66 K1
Newton Aycliffe Dur 69 S8
Newton Bewley Hartpl 70 G7
Newton Blossomville M Keyn 38 D10
Newton Bromswold Nhants 38 E7
Newton Burgoland Leics 47 L12
Newton-by-the-Sea Nthumb 85 U13
Newton by Toft Lincs 58 H9
Newton Ferrers Devon 5 P11
Newton Ferry W Isls 106 d11
Newton Flotman Norfk 51 M14
Newtongrange Mdloth 83 R6
Newton Green Mons 27 U9
Newton Harcourt Leics 37 R1
Newton Heath Manch 56 C6
Newtonhill Abers 99 S5
Newton Hill Wakefd 57 M2
Newton-in-Bowland Lancs 62 D9
Newton Kyme N York 64 B11
Newton-le-Willows N York 63 Q2
Newton-le-Willows St Hel 55 N7
Newtonloan Mdloth 83 R6
Newton Longville Bucks 30 H6
Newton Mearns E Rens 81 Q1
Newtonmill Angus 99 L11
Newtonmore Highld 97 L4
Newton Morrell N York 69 R11
Newton Mountain Pembks 24 G9
Newton Mulgrave N York 71 N9
Newton of Balcanquhal P & K 90 J9
Newton of Balcormo Fife 91 R11
Newton-on-Ouse N York 64 C8
Newton-on-Rawcliffe N York 64 J1
Newton on the Hill Shrops 45 L9
Newton-on-the-Moor Nthumb 77 P4
Newton on Trent Lincs 58 D12
Newton Poppleford Devon 6 E7
Newton Purcell Oxon 30 D6
Newton Regis Warwks 46 J12
Newton Reigny Cumb 67 Q6
Newton St Cyres Devon 15 U13
Newton St Faith Norfk 51 M10
Newton St Loe BaNES 17 T4
Newton St Petrock Devon 14 K10
Newton Solney Derbys 46 J8
Newton Stacey Hants 19 P12
Newton Stewart D & G 73 L6
Newton Tony Wilts 18 K12
Newton Tracey Devon 15 M7
Newton under Roseberry R & Cl 70 J10
Newton Underwood Nthumb 77 N8
Newton upon Derwent E R Yk 64 G10
Newton Valence Hants 9 U2
Newton Wamphray D & G 75 M7
Newton with Scales Lancs 61 T13
Newtown BCP 8 E10
Newtown Blae G 27 M6
Newtown Ches W 55 M11
Newtown Cnwll 2 F11
Newtown Cnwll 4 H5
Newtown Cumb 66 H3
Newtown Cumb 67 R8
Newtown Cumb 75 S13
Newtown Cumb 75 V13
Newtown D & G 74 E3
Newtown Derbys 56 E10
Newtown Devon 6 E5
Newtown Devon 15 S7
Newtown Dorset 7 N4
New Town Dorset 8 D5
New Town Dorset 8 D5
New Town Dorset 8 D7
New Town E Susx 11 R6
Newtown Gloucs 28 C7
Newtown Hants 8 K6
Newtown Hants 9 S6
Newtown Hants 19 Q8
Newtown Herefs 35 L9
Newtown Herefs 35 M14
Newtown Herefs 35 P11
Newtown Highld 96 D3
Newtown IoW 9 N10
New Town Nhants 38 E5
Newtown Nthumb 77 L5
Newtown Nthumb 85 P12
Newtown Nthumb 85 Q13
Newtown Powys 34 D2
Newtown Rhondd 26 K8
Newtown Shrops 44 K9
Newtown Shrops 45 L7
Newtown Somset 6 J2
Newtown Staffs 46 B1
Newtown Staffs 46 C13
Newtown Wigan 55 N6
Newtown Wilts 8 C3
New Town Wilts 19 L6
Newtown Wilts 19 L8
Newtown Worcs 35 U9
Newtown Worcs 36 B5
Newtown-in-St Martin Cnwll 2 J12
Newtown Linford Leics 47 P12
Newtown of Beltrees Rens 88 J14
Newtown St Boswells Border 84 F12
Newtown Unthank Leics 47 N13
New Tredegar Caerph 27 L7
New Trows S Lans 82 F11
New Tupton Derbys 57 N13
Newtyle Angus 91 L3
New Walsoken Cambs 49 Q12
New Waltham NE Lin 59 N6
New Whittington Derbys 57 N11
New Winton E Loth 84 C4
New Yatt Oxon 29 S5
Newyears Green Gt Lon 20 J5
Newyork Ag & B 87 T3
New York Lincs 48 K2
New York N Tyne 77 S11
New York N York 63 P7
Nextend Herefs 34 H9
Neyland Pembks 24 G9
Niarbyl IoM 60 c7
Nibley Gloucs 28 C6
Nibley S Glos 28 C11
Nibley Green Gloucs 28 D8
Nicholashayne Devon 16 F13
Nicholaston Swans 25 T13
Nickies Hill Cumb 76 A12
Nidd N York 63 S7
Nigg C Aber 99 S3
Nigg Highld 109 Q10
Nigg Ferry Highld 109 P11
Nimlet BaNES 17 T2
Ninebanks Nthumb 68 G2
Nine Elms Swindn 29 M10
Nine Wells Pembks 24 C6
Ninfield E Susx 12 D13
Ningwood IoW 9 M11
Nisbet Border 84 H13
Nisbet Hill Border 84 K8
Niton IoW 9 Q13
Nitshill C Glas 89 M13
Noah's Ark Kent 21 U11
Noak Bridge Essex 22 G9
Noak Hill Gt Lon 22 D9
Noblethorpe Barns 57 L5
Nobold Shrops 45 L11
Nobottle Nhants 37 S8
Nocton Lincs 58 J14
Nogdam End Norfk 51 Q13
Noke Oxon 30 B10
Nolton Pembks 24 E7
Nolton Haven Pembks 24 E7
No Man's Heath Ches W 45 M4
No Man's Heath Warwks 46 J12
No Man's Land Cnwll 4 H9
Nomansland Devon 15 T10
Nomansland Wilts 8 K5
Noneley Shrops 45 L8
Nonington Kent 13 Q5
Nook Cumb 61 U3
Nook Cumb 75 U10
Norbiton Gt Lon 21 L9
Norbreck Bpool 61 Q11
Norbridge Herefs 35 R12
Norbury Ches E 45 N4
Norbury Derbys 46 F5
Norbury Gt Lon 21 P9
Norbury Shrops 34 J2
Norbury Staffs 45 S9
Norbury Common Ches E 45 N4
Norbury Junction Staffs 45 S9
Norchard Worcs 35 T7
Norcott Brook Ches W 55 P10
Norcross Lancs 61 Q11
Nordelph Norfk 49 S13
Norden Rochdl 56 C4
Nordley Shrops 35 Q1
Norfolk Broads Norfk 51 S12
Norham Nthumb 85 N9
Norland Town Calder 56 G2
Norley Ches W 55 N12
Norleywood Hants 9 M9
Norlington E Susx 11 Q8
Normanby Lincs 58 G9
Normanby N Linc 58 E3
Normanby N York 64 G3
Normanby R & Cl 70 H9
Normanby le Wold Lincs 58 K7
Norman Cross Cambs 38 J2
Normandy Surrey 20 F12
Normans Bay E Susx 11 V9
Norman's Green Devon 6 E4
Normanton C Derb 46 K7
Normanton Leics 48 B5
Normanton Notts 47 T3
Normanton Rutlnd 48 D12
Normanton Wakefd 57 N2
Normanton Wilts 18 H12
Normanton le Heath Leics 47 L11
Normanton on Cliffe Lincs 48 D4
Normanton on Soar Notts 47 P9
Normanton on the Wolds Notts 47 R7
Normanton on Trent Notts 58 C13
Normoss Lancs 61 Q12
Norney Surrey 10 E2
Norrington Common Wilts 18 C8
Norris Green Cnwll 5 L7
Norris Green Lpool 54 J8
Norris Hill Leics 46 K10
Norristhorpe Kirk 56 K2
Northacre Norfk 50 G14
Northall Bucks 31 L8
Northallerton N York 70 E14
Northall Green Norfk 50 G11
Northam C Sotn 9 N6
Northam Devon 15 L7
Northampton Nhants 37 U8
Northampton Worcs 35 T7
Northampton Services Nhants 37 T9
North Anston Rothm 57 R10
North Ascot Br For 20 F9
North Aston Oxon 29 U2
Northaw Herts 31 S12
Northay Somset 6 J2
North Baddesley Hants 9 M4
North Ballachulish Highld 94 F6
North Barrow Somset 17 R11
North Barsham Norfk 50 F6
Northbay W Isls 106 c18
North Benfleet Essex 22 J10
North Berwick E Loth 84 E1
North Bitchburn Dur 69 Q6
North Blyth Nthumb 77 S9
North Boarhunt Hants 9 S6
North Bockhampton BCP 8 H9
Northborough C Pete 48 J12
Northbourne Kent 13 R5
North Bovey Devon 5 S4
North Bradley Wilts 18 C9
North Brentor Devon 5 M4
North Brewham Somset 17 T9
North Bridge Surrey 10 F3
Northbridge Street E Susx 12 D11
Northbrook Hants 19 R13
Northbrook Oxon 29 U3
North Brook End Cambs 31 S4
North Buckland Devon 15 L4
North Burlingham Norfk 51 Q12
North Cadbury Somset 17 R11
North Carlton Lincs 58 F11
North Carlton Notts 57 S10
North Cave E R Yk 64 K13
North Cerney Gloucs 28 K6
North Chailey E Susx 11 P6
Northchapel W Susx 10 F5
North Charford Hants 8 H5
North Charlton Nthumb 85 T14
North Cheam Gt Lon 21 M9
North Cheriton Somset 17 S11
North Chideock Dorset 7 M6
Northchurch Herts 31 L11
North Cliffe E R Yk 64 K12
North Clifton Notts 58 D12
North Close Dur 69 S6
North Cockerington Lincs 59 Q8
North Connel Ag & B 94 C12
North Cornelly Brdgnd 26 E11
North Corner Cnwll 2 K13
North Cotes Lincs 59 P6
Northcott Devon 4 J2
Northcott Devon 6 E2
Northcott Devon 6 F3
North Country Cnwll 2 H8
Northcourt Oxon 29 U8
North Cove Suffk 41 S3
North Cowton N York 69 S12
North Crawley M Keyn 30 K4
North Cray Gt Lon 21 S8
North Creake Norfk 50 E6
North Curry Somset 16 K11
North Dalton E R Yk 65 L9
North Deighton N York 63 T9
Northdown Kent 13 S1
North Downs 12 H4
North Duffield N York 64 F12
Northedge Derbys 57 N13
North Elham Kent 13 N7
North Elkington Lincs 59 N8
North Elmham Norfk 50 G9
North Elmsall Wakefd 57 Q4
Northend Bucks 20 B4
North End C Port 9 T8
North End Cumb 75 R14
North End Dorset 8 A3
North End E R Yk 65 R11
North End E R Yk 65 T13
North End Essex 22 G4
North End Hants 8 G5
North End Hants 9 R3
North End Leics 47 Q10
North End Lincs 48 K5
North End Lincs 58 H7
North End Lincs 59 P6
North End Lincs 59 R9
North End N Linc 58 K2
North End N Som 17 M3
North End Nhants 38 E7
North End Norfk 40 G2
North End Nthumb 77 N5
North End Sefton 54 H6
North End W Susx 10 F10
North End W Susx 10 J9
Northend Warwks 37 L10
Northenden Manch 55 T9
Northend Woods Bucks 20 F5
North Erradale Highld 107 M8
North Evington C Leic 47 R13
North Fambridge Essex 23 L8
North Featherstone Wakefd 57 P2
North Ferriby E R Yk 58 G1
Northfield Birm 36 D5
Northfield C Aber 99 S2
Northfield E R Yk 58 H1
Northfields Lincs 48 F12
Northfleet Kent 22 F13
North Frodingham E R Yk 65 Q9
North Gorley Hants 8 H6
North Green Norfk 41 M3
North Green Suffk 41 P8
North Green Suffk 41 Q7
North Greetwell Lincs 58 H12
North Grimston N York 64 J6
North Halling Medway 12 D2
North Haven Shet 106 r11
North Hayling Hants 9 U8
North Hazelrigg Nthumb 85 R12
North Heasley Devon 15 R6
North Heath W Susx 10 H6
North Hele Devon 16 D12
North Hill Cnwll 4 H5
North Hillingdon Gt Lon 20 J6
North Hinksey Village Oxon 29 U6
North Holmwood Surrey 21 L13
North Huish Devon 5 S9
North Hykeham Lincs 58 F13
Northiam E Susx 12 F11
Northill C Beds 38 H11
Northington Gloucs 28 D6
Northington Hants 19 S13
North Kelsey Lincs 58 H6
North Kessock Highld 102 J6
North Killingholme N Linc 58 K3
North Kilvington N York 63 U2
North Kilworth Leics 37 R4
North Kingston Hants 8 H8
North Kyme Lincs 48 J3
North Lancing W Susx 10 K9
North Landing E R Yk 65 S5
Northlands Lincs 49 M3
Northleach Gloucs 29 M5
North Lee Bucks 30 H11
North Lees N York 63 R5
Northleigh Devon 6 G5
Northleigh Devon 15 P6
North Leigh Kent 13 M6
North Leigh Oxon 29 S5
North Leverton with Habblesthorpe Notts 58 C10
Northlew Devon 15 M13
North Littleton Worcs 36 E11
Northload Bridge Somset 17 N9
North Lopham Norfk 40 H4
North Luffenham Rutlnd 48 D13
North Marden W Susx 10 C7
North Marston Bucks 30 G8
North Middleton Mdloth 83 S7
North Middleton Nthumb 85 P14
North Millbrex Abers 105 N7
North Milmain D & G 72 D9
North Molton Devon 15 R7
Northmoor Oxon 29 T7
North Moreton Oxon 19 S3
Northmuir Angus 98 F12
North Mundham W Susx 10 D10
North Muskham Notts 47 U2
North Newbald E R Yk 65 L12
North Newington Oxon 37 M12
North Newnton Wilts 18 H9
North Newton Somset 16 K10
Northney Hants 9 U8
North Nibley Gloucs 28 D8
North Oakley Hants 19 R10
North Ockendon Gt Lon 22 E10
Northolt Gt Lon 20 K6
Northolt Airport Gt Lon 20 J5
Northop Flints 54 F13
Northop Hall Flints 54 G13
North Ormesby Middsb 70 H9
North Ormsby Lincs 59 N8
Northorpe Kirk 56 K2
Northorpe Lincs 48 G10
Northorpe Lincs 48 K6
Northorpe Lincs 58 E7
North Otterington N York 63 T2
Northover Somset 17 N9
Northover Somset 17 P12
North Owersby Lincs 58 J8
Northowram Calder 56 H1
North Perrott Somset 7 N3
North Petherton Somset 16 J10
North Petherwin Cnwll 4 H3
North Pickenham Norfk 50 E12
North Piddle Worcs 36 C10
North Poorton Dorset 7 P5
Northport Dorset 8 C11
North Poulner Hants 8 H7
North Queensferry Fife 83 M2
North Radworthy Devon 15 S6
North Rauceby Lincs 48 F4
Northrepps Norfk 51 M6
North Reston Lincs 59 Q10
North Rigton N York 63 R10
North Ripley Hants 8 H9
North Rode Ches E 56 C13
North Ronaldsay Ork 106 w14
North Ronaldsay Airport Ork 106 w14
North Row Cumb 66 K6
North Runcton Norfk 49 T10
North Scale Cumb 61 M6
North Scarle Lincs 58 D13
North Seaton Nthumb 77 R8
North Seaton Colliery Nthumb 77 R8
North Shian Ag & B 94 C10
North Shields N Tyne 77 T12
North Shoebury Sthend 23 M10
North Shore Bpool 61 Q12
North Side C Pete 49 L14
North Side Cumb 66 E7
North Skelton R & Cl 71 L9
North Somercotes Lincs 59 R7
North Stainley N York 63 R4
North Stainmore Cumb 68 H9
North Stifford Thurr 22 F11
North Stoke BaNES 17 T3
North Stoke Oxon 19 T3
North Stoke W Susx 10 G8
Northstowe Cambs 39 P7
North Street Cambs 39 S7
North Street Hants 8 H5
North Street Hants 9 S2
North Street Kent 12 K4
North Street Medway 22 K13
North Street W Berk 19 T6
North Sunderland Nthumb 85 U12
North Tamerton Cnwll 14 H13
North Tawton Devon 15 Q12
North Third Stirlg 89 S8
North Thoresby Lincs 59 N7
North Togston Nthumb 77 Q5
North Tolsta W Isls 106 k4
Northton W Isls 106 e10
North Town Devon 15 M11
North Town Somset 17 Q8
North Town W & M 20 E6
North Tuddenham Norfk 50 H11
North Uist W Isls 106 c11
Northumberland National Park Nthumb 76 F9
North Walbottle N u Ty 77 P12
North Walsham Norfk 51 N7
North Waltham Hants 19 S11
North Warnborough Hants 20 B12
Northway Somset 16 F11
North Weald Bassett Essex 22 C7
North Wheatley Notts 58 C9
North Whilborough Devon 5 V7
Northwich Ches W 55 Q12
North Wick BaNES 17 Q3
Northwick S Glos 27 V10
Northwick Somset 17 L7
Northwick Worcs 35 T9
North Widcombe BaNES 17 Q5
North Willingham Lincs 59 L9
North Wingfield Derbys 57 P13
North Witham Lincs 48 D9
Northwold Norfk 40 C1
Northwood C Stke 45 U4
Northwood Derbys 57 L14
Northwood Gt Lon 20 J4
Northwood IoW 9 P10
Northwood Shrops 45 L7
Northwood Green Gloucs 28 D4
North Wootton Dorset 7 S2
North Wootton Norfk 49 T9
North Wootton Somset 17 Q8
North Wraxall Wilts 18 B5
North Wroughton Swindn 18 H4
North York Moors National Park 71 M12
Norton Donc 57 R3
Norton E Susx 11 R10
Norton Gloucs 28 G3
Norton Halton 55 N10
Norton Hants 19 Q12
Norton Herts 31 R6
Norton IoW 9 L11
Norton Mons 27 S3
Norton N Som 16 K4
Norton Nhants 37 Q8
Norton Notts 57 S12
Norton Powys 34 H7
Norton S on T 70 F8
Norton Sheff 57 N10
Norton Shrops 35 L4
Norton Shrops 35 P4
Norton Shrops 45 N12
Norton Shrops 45 R13
Norton Suffk 40 G7
Norton Swans 25 V13
Norton W Susx 10 E9
Norton Wilts 28 G11
Norton Worcs 35 U10
Norton Worcs 36 D11
Norton Bavant Wilts 18 D12
Norton Bridge Staffs 45 U7
Norton Canes Staffs 46 D12
Norton Canes Services Staffs 46 D12
Norton Canon Herefs 34 J11
Norton Corner Norfk 50 J8
Norton Disney Lincs 48 C2
Norton Ferris Wilts 17 U9
Norton Fitzwarren Somset 16 G11
Norton Green IoW 9 L11
Norton Hawkfield BaNES 17 Q4
Norton Heath Essex 22 F7
Norton in Hales Shrops 45 R6
Norton-Juxta-Twycross Leics 46 K12
Norton-le-Clay N York 63 U5
Norton-le-Moors C Stke 45 U3
Norton Lindsey Warwks 36 H8
Norton Little Green Suffk 40 G7
Norton Malreward BaNES 17 R4
Norton Mandeville Essex 22 E7
Norton-on-Derwent N York 64 H5
Norton St Philip Somset 17 U5
Norton Subcourse Norfk 51 R14
Norton sub Hamdon Somset 17 N13
Norton Wood Herefs 34 J11
Norwell Notts 47 U1
Norwell Woodhouse Notts 58 B14
Norwich Norfk 51 M12
Norwich Airport Norfk 51 M11
Norwick Shet 106 w2
Norwood Clacks 90 C13
Norwood Derbys 57 Q10
Norwood Kent 13 L9
Norwood End Essex 22 E6
Norwood Green Calder 56 H1
Norwood Green Gt Lon 20 K7
Norwood Hill Surrey 11 L2
Norwoodside Cambs 49 P14
Noseley Leics 47 T14
Noss Mayo Devon 5 P11
Nosterfield N York 63 R3
Nosterfield End Cambs 39 T12
Nostie Highld 101 M6
Notgrove Gloucs 29 M3
Nottage Brdgnd 26 E12
Notter Cnwll 4 K8
Nottingham C Nott 47 Q6
Nottington Dorset 7 S8
Notton Wakefd 57 M4
Notton Wilts 18 D7
Nounsley Essex 22 J5
Noutard's Green Worcs 35 T7
Nowton Suffk 40 E8
Nox Shrops 44 K11
Nuffield Oxon 19 U3
Nunburnholme E R Yk 64 J10
Nuncargate Notts 47 P3
Nunclose Cumb 67 Q3
Nuneaton Warwks 37 L2
Nuneham Courtenay Oxon 30 C13
Nunhead Gt Lon 21 P7
Nunkeeling E R Yk 65 Q10
Nun Monkton N York 64 C8
Nunney Somset 17 T7
Nunney Catch Somset 17 T8
Nunnington Herefs 35 N12
Nunnington N York 64 F4
Nunsthorpe NE Lin 59 N5
Nunthorpe C York 64 E9
Nunthorpe Middsb 70 H10
Nunthorpe Village Middsb 70 H10
Nunton Wilts 8 H3
Nunwick N York 63 S5
Nunwick Nthumb 76 H11
Nupdown S Glos 28 B8
Nup End Bucks 30 J9
Nupend Gloucs 28 E6
Nuptown Br For 20 E8
Nursling Hants 9 M5
Nursted Hants 10 B6
Nursteed Wilts 18 F8
Nurton Staffs 45 T14
Nutbourne W Susx 10 B9
Nutbourne W Susx 10 H7
Nutfield Surrey 21 P12
Nuthall Notts 47 P5
Nuthampstead Herts 39 P14
Nuthurst W Susx 10 K5
Nutley E Susx 11 Q5
Nutley Hants 19 T12
Nuttall Bury 55 S3
Nutwell Donc 57 T6
Nybster Highld 112 J4
Nyetimber W Susx 10 D11
Nyewood W Susx 10 C6
Nymans W Susx 11 M5
Nymet Rowland Devon 15 R11
Nymet Tracey Devon 15 R12
Nympsfield Gloucs 28 F7
Nynehead Somset 16 F12
Nythe Somset 17 M10
Nyton W Susx 10 E9

O

Oadby Leics 47 R13
Oad Street Kent 12 G3
Oakall Green Worcs 35 T8
Oakamoor Staffs 46 D5
Oakbank W Loth 83 L5
Oak Cross Devon 15 M13
Oakdale Caerph 27 M8
Oake Somset 16 G11
Oaken Staffs 45 U13
Oakenclough Lancs 61 U10
Oakengates Wrekin 45 R11
Oakenholt Flints 54 G12
Oakenshaw Dur 69 Q5
Oakenshaw Kirk 63 P14
Oakerthorpe Derbys 47 L3
Oakford Cerdgn 32 J9
Oakford Devon 16 B12
Oakfordbridge Devon 16 B12
Oakgrove Ches E 56 D13
Oakham Rutlnd 48 C12
Oakhanger Ches E 45 S3
Oakhanger Hants 10 B3
Oakhill Somset 17 R7
Oakhurst Kent 21 U12
Oakington Cambs 39 P8
Oaklands Powys 34 B10
Oakle Street Gloucs 28 E4
Oakley BCP 8 E9
Oakley Bed 38 F10
Oakley Bucks 30 D10
Oakley Fife 90 F14
Oakley Hants 19 S10
Oakley Oxon 30 G12
Oakley Suffk 41 L5
Oakley Green W & M 20 F7
Oakley Park Powys 33 U3
Oakridge Lynch Gloucs 28 H7
Oaks Lancs 62 D13
Oaks Shrops 44 K13
Oaksey Wilts 28 J9
Oaks Green Derbys 46 G7
Oakshaw Ford Cumb 75 V10
Oakshott Hants 9 U3
Oakthorpe Leics 46 K11
Oak Tree Darltn 70 E10
Oakwood C Derb 47 L6
Oakwood Nthumb 76 J12
Oakworth C Brad 63 L12
Oare Kent 12 K3
Oare Somset 15 S3
Oare Wilts 18 J8
Oasby Lincs 48 F6
Oath Somset 17 L11
Oathlaw Angus 98 H12
Oatlands Park Surrey 20 J9
Oban Ag & B 94 B13
Oban Airport Ag & B 94 C11
Obley Shrops 34 H5
Obney P & K 90 F4
Oborne Dorset 17 S13
Obthorpe Lincs 48 G11
Occold Suffk 41 L6
Occumster Highld 112 G9
Ochiltree E Ayrs 81 Q8
Ockbrook Derbys 47 M6
Ocker Hill Sandw 36 C2
Ockeridge Worcs 35 S8
Ockham Surrey 20 J11
Ockle Highld 93 P4
Ockley Surrey 10 J2
Ocle Pychard Herefs 35 N11
Octon E R Yk 65 N6
Odcombe Somset 17 P13
Odd Down BaNES 17 T4
Oddendale Cumb 67 S10
Oddingley Worcs 36 B9
Oddington Gloucs 29 P2
Oddington Oxon 30 C9
Odell Bed 38 E9
Odham Devon 15 L12
Odiham Hants 20 B12
Odsal C Brad 63 P14
Odsey Cambs 31 S5
Odstock Wilts 8 G3
Odstone Leics 47 L12
Offchurch Warwks 37 L7
Offenham Worcs 36 E11
Offerton Stockp 56 D9
Offerton Sundld 70 D1
Offham E Susx 11 Q8
Offham Kent 12 C4
Offham W Susx 10 G9
Offleymarsh Staffs 45 S8
Offord Cluny Cambs 38 K7
Offord D'Arcy Cambs 38 K7
Offton Suffk 40 J11
Offwell Devon 6 G5
Ogbourne Maizey Wilts 18 J6
Ogbourne St Andrew Wilts 18 J6
Ogbourne St George Wilts 18 K6
Ogden Calder 63 M13
Ogle Nthumb 77 N10
Oglet Lpool 54 K10
Ogmore V Glam 26 F12
Ogmore-by-Sea V Glam 26 F12
Ogmore Vale Brdgnd 26 G9
Ogwen Bank Gwynd 52 K9
Okeford Fitzpaine Dorset 7 V2
Okehampton Devon 15 N13
Oker Side Derbys 46 J1
Okewood Hill Surrey 10 J3
Olchard Devon 6 A9
Old Nhants 37 U6
Old Aberdeen C Aber 99 S2
Old Alresford Hants 9 R2
Oldany Highld 110 B10
Old Auchenbrack D & G 74 E6
Old Basford C Nott 47 Q5
Old Basing Hants 19 U10
Old Beetley Norfk 50 G10
Oldberrow Warwks 36 F7
Old Bewick Nthumb 77 M1
Old Bolingbroke Lincs 59 Q13
Old Bramhope Leeds 63 Q11
Old Brampton Derbys 57 M12
Old Bridge of Urr D & G 74 E12
Old Buckenham Norfk 40 J2
Old Burghclere Hants 19 Q9
Oldbury Kent 21 U11
Oldbury Sandw 36 C3
Oldbury Shrops 35 R2
Oldbury Warwks 36 K2
Oldbury Naite S Glos 28 B9
Oldbury-on-Severn S Glos 28 B9
Oldbury on the Hill Gloucs 28 F10
Old Byland N York 64 D2
Old Cantley Donc 57 T6
Old Cassop Dur 70 D5
Oldcastle Mons 27 Q3
Oldcastle Heath Ches W 45 L4
Old Catton Norfk 51 M11
Old Churchstoke Powys 34 G2
Old Clee NE Lin 59 N5
Old Cleeve Somset 16 D8
Old Colwyn Conwy 53 Q7
Oldcotes Notts 57 S9
Old Coulsdon Gt Lon 21 P11
Old Dailly S Ayrs 80 J13
Old Dalby Leics 47 S9
Old Dam Derbys 56 H11
Old Deer Abers 105 R6
Old Ditch Somset 17 P7
Old Edlington Donc 57 R7
Old Eldon Dur 69 R7
Old Ellerby E R Yk 65 R12
Old Felixstowe Suffk 41 P13
Oldfield C Brad 63 L12
Oldfield Worcs 35 T8
Old Fletton C Pete 38 J1
Oldford Somset 17 U6
Old Forge Herefs 27 V4
Old Furnace Herefs 27 T3
Old Glossop Derbys 56 F8
Old Goole E R Yk 58 B2
Old Grimsby IoS 2 b1
Old Hall Green Herts 31 U8
Oldhall Green Suffk 40 E9
Old Hall Street Norfk 51 P7
Oldham Oldham 56 D6
Oldhamstocks E Loth 84 J4
Old Harlow Essex 22 C5
Old Heath Essex 23 P3
Old Hunstanton Norfk 49 U5
Old Hurst Cambs 39 M5
Old Hutton Cumb 62 B2
Old Inns Services N Lans 89 S10
Old Kea Cnwll 3 L8
Old Kilpatrick W Duns 89 L11
Old Knebworth Herts 31 R8
Old Lakenham Norfk 51 M12
Oldland S Glos 17 S2
Old Langho Lancs 62 E12
Old Laxey IoM 60 g6
Old Leake Lincs 49 P3
Old Malton N York 64 H5
Oldmeldrum Abers 105 N10
Oldmill Cnwll 4 K6
Old Milverton Warwks 36 J7
Oldmixon N Som 16 K5
Old Newton Suffk 40 J8
Old Oxted Surrey 21 Q12
Old Portlethen Abers 99 S4
Old Quarrington Dur 70 D5
Old Radford C Nott 47 Q5
Old Radnor Powys 34 G9
Old Rayne Abers 104 K10
Old Romney Kent 12 K11
Old Shoreham W Susx 11 L9
Oldshoremore Highld 110 E5
Old Soar Kent 12 B5
Old Sodbury S Glos 28 E11
Old Somerby Lincs 48 E7
Oldstead N York 64 C4
Old Stratford Nhants 30 G4
Old Struan P & K 97 N10
Old Swarland Nthumb 77 P5
Old Swinford Dudley 36 B4
Old Tebay Cumb 68 D11
Old Thirsk N York 63 U3
Old Town Calder 63 L14
Old Town Cumb 62 B3
Old Town Cumb 67 Q4
Old Town E Susx 11 T11
Old Town IoS 2 c2
Old Trafford Traffd 55 T7
Old Tupton Derbys 57 N13
Oldwall Cumb 75 U13
Oldwalls Swans 25 S12
Old Warden C Beds 31 P4
Oldways End Somset 15 U8
Old Weston Cambs 38 G5
Old Wick Highld 112 J7
Old Windsor W & M 20 G8
Old Wives Lees Kent 13 L5
Old Woking Surrey 20 H11
Old Wolverton M Keyn 30 H4
Old Woodhall Lincs 59 M13
Old Woods Shrops 45 L9
Olgrinmore Highld 112 C6
Olive Green Staffs 46 F10
Oliver's Battery Hants 9 P3
Ollaberry Shet 106 t5
Ollach Highld 100 e6
Ollerton Ches E 55 S11
Ollerton Notts 57 U13
Ollerton Shrops 45 P8
Olmarch Cerdgn 33 M9
Olmstead Green Cambs 39 T12
Olney M Keyn 38 C10
Olrig House Highld 112 E3
Olton Solhll 36 F4
Olveston S Glos 28 B10
Ombersley Worcs 35 T8
Ompton Notts 57 U13
Once Brewed Nthumb 76 E12
Onchan IoM 60 f7
Onecote Staffs 46 D2
Onehouse Suffk 40 H9
Onen Mons 27 S5
Ongar Street Herefs 34 J7
Onibury Shrops 35 L5
Onich Highld 94 E6
Onllwyn Neath 26 E5
Onneley Staffs 45 S5
Onslow Green Essex 22 G4
Onslow Village Surrey 20 G13
Onston Ches W 55 N12
Openwoodgate Derbys 47 L4
Opinan Highld 107 M10
Orbliston Moray 104 C4
Orbost Highld 100 b5
Orby Lincs 59 S13
Orchard Portman Somset 16 H12
Orcheston Wilts 18 G11
Orcop Herefs 27 T2
Orcop Hill Herefs 27 T2
Ord Abers 104 J4
Ordhead Abers 104 K13
Ordie Abers 98 H3
Ordiequish Moray 104 C4
Ordley Nthumb 76 J14
Ordsall Notts 58 B11
Ore E Susx 12 F13
Oreleton Common Herefs 35 L7
Oreton Shrops 35 Q4
Orford Suffk 41 R10
Orford Warrtn 55 P8
Organford Dorset 8 C10
Orgreave Staffs 46 F10
Orkney Islands Ork 106 t19
Orkney Neolithic Ork 106 s18
Orlestone Kent 12 K9
Orleton Herefs 35 L7
Orleton Worcs 35 R7
Orlingbury Nhants 38 C6
Ormathwaite Cumb 67 L7
Ormesby R & Cl 70 H9
Ormesby St Margaret Norfk 51 S11
Ormesby St Michael Norfk 51 S11
Ormiscaig Highld 107 Q6
Ormiston E Loth 83 T5
Ormsaigmore Highld 93 M6
Ormsary Ag & B 87 N11
Ormskirk Lancs 54 K5
Ornsby Hill Dur 69 Q3
Oronsay Ag & B 86 F8
Orphir Ork 106 s19
Orpington Gt Lon 21 S9
Orrell Sefton 54 H7
Orrell Wigan 55 M6
Orrell Post Wigan 55 M5
Orrisdale IoM 60 e4
Orroland D & G 73 T10
Orsett Thurr 22 F11
Orsett Heath Thurr 22 F11
Orslow Staffs 45 T10
Orston Notts 47 U5
Orthwaite Cumb 67 L6
Ortner Lancs 61 U9
Orton Cumb 68 D11
Orton Nhants 38 B5
Orton Staffs 35 U1
Orton Longueville C Pete 38 J1
Orton-on-the-Hill Leics 46 K13
Orton Rigg Cumb 67 M2
Orton Waterville C Pete 38 J1
Orwell Cambs 39 N10
Osbaldeston Lancs 62 C13
Osbaldeston Green Lancs 62 C13
Osbaldwick C York 64 E9
Osbaston Leics 47 M13
Osbaston Shrops 44 H9
Osborne IoW 9 Q10
Osborne House IoW 9 Q10
Osbournby Lincs 48 G6
Oscroft Ches W 55 M13
Ose Highld 100 c5
Osgathorpe Leics 47 M10
Osgodby Lincs 58 J8
Osgodby N York 64 E13
Osgodby N York 65 P3
Oskaig Highld 100 e6
Oskamull Ag & B 93 M10
Osmaston Derbys 46 G5
Osmington Dorset 7 T8
Osmington Mills Dorset 7 T8
Osmondthorpe Leeds 63 S13
Osmotherley N York 70 G13
Osney Oxon 29 U6
Ospringe Kent 12 K3
Ossett Wakefd 57 L2
Ossington Notts 58 C14
Ostend Essex 23 M8
Osterley Gt Lon 21 L7
Oswaldkirk N York 64 E4
Oswaldtwistle Lancs 55 R1
Oswestry Shrops 44 G8
Otford Kent 21 T11
Otham Kent 12 E5
Otham Hole Kent 12 F5
Othery Somset 17 L10
Otley Leeds 63 Q10
Otley Suffk 41 M9
Otley Green Suffk 41 M9
Otterbourne Hants 9 P4
Otterburn N York 62 H8
Otterburn Nthumb 76 H7
Otter Ferry Ag & B 87 S9
Otterham Cnwll 4 F2

Otterhampton Somset 16 H8
Otterham Quay Kent 12 F2
Otterham Station Cnwll 4 F3
Otternish W Isls 106 e11
Ottershaw Surrey 20 H10
Otterswick Shet 106 v5
Otterton Devon 6 E7
Otterwood Hants 9 N8
Ottery St Mary Devon 6 F5
Ottinge Kent 13 N7
Ottringham E R Yk 59 N2
Oughterby Cumb 67 L1
Oughtershaw N York 62 H3
Oughterside Cumb 66 H4
Oughtibridge Sheff 57 M8
Oughtrington Warrtn 55 Q9
Oulston N York 64 C5
Oulton Cumb 66 K2
Oulton Leeds 63 T14
Oulton Norfk 50 K8
Oulton Staffs 45 S9
Oulton Staffs 46 B6
Oulton Suffk 41 T2
Oulton Broad Suffk 41 T2
Oulton Street Norfk 51 L8
Oundle Nhants 38 F3
Ounsdale Staffs 35 U2
Our Dynamic Earth C Edin 83 Q4
Ousby Cumb 68 D6
Ousden Suffk 40 B9
Ousefleet E R Yk 58 D2
Ouston Dur 69 S2
Outchester Nthumb 85 S12
Out Elmstead Kent 13 P5
Outgate Cumb 67 N13
Outhgill Cumb 68 G12
Outhill Warwks 36 F7
Outlands Staffs 45 S7
Outlane Kirk 56 G3
Out Newton E R Yk 59 Q2
Out Rawcliffe Lancs 61 S11
Out Skerries Shet 106 w6
Outwell Norfk 49 R13
Outwick Hants 8 G5
Outwood Surrey 21 P13
Outwood Wakefd 57 M2
Outwood Gate Bury 55 S5
Outwoods Leics 47 M10
Outwoods Staffs 45 S10
Ouzlewell Green Leeds 57 M1
Ovenden Calder 56 G1
Over Cambs 39 N6
Over Ches W 55 P13
Over Gloucs 28 F4
Over S Glos 28 A11
Over Burrows Derbys 46 J6
Overbury Worcs 36 C13
Overcombe Dorset 7 S8
Over Compton Dorset 17 Q13
Over End Cambs 38 G2
Overgreen Derbys 57 M12
Over Green Warwks 36 G2
Over Haddon Derbys 56 K13
Over Kellet Lancs 61 U6
Over Kiddington Oxon 29 T3
Overleigh Somset 17 N9
Overley Staffs 46 G10
Over Monnow Mons 27 U5
Over Norton Oxon 29 R2
Over Peover Ches E 55 S12
Overpool Ches W 54 J11
Overscaig Highld 110 J12
Overseal Derbys 46 J10
Over Silton N York 70 F14
Oversland Kent 13 L4
Oversley Green Warwks 36 E9
Overstone Nhants 37 U7
Over Stowey Somset 16 G9
Overstrand Norfk 51 M5
Over Stratton Somset 17 M13
Overstreet Wilts 18 G13
Over Tabley Ches E 55 R11
Overthorpe Nhants 37 N12
Overton C Aber 105 P13
Overton Ches W 55 M11
Overton Hants 19 R11
Overton Lancs 61 S8
Overton N York 64 D8
Overton Shrops 35 M6
Overton Swans 25 S13
Overton Wakefd 57 L3
Overton Wrexhm 44 J5
Overton Bridge Wrexhm 44 J5
Overton Green Ches E 45 T1
Overtown Lancs 62 C4
Overtown Lancs 62 H14
Overtown N Lans 82 F8
Overtown Swindn 18 J5
Overtown Wakefd 57 N3
Over Wallop Hants 19 L13
Over Whitacre Warwks 36 J2
Over Woodhouse Derbys 57 Q12
Over Worton Oxon 29 T2
Overy Oxon 19 S2
Oving Bucks 30 G8
Oving W Susx 10 E10
Ovingdean Br & H 11 P10
Ovingham Nthumb 77 M13
Ovington Dur 69 P10
Ovington Essex 40 C12
Ovington Hants 9 R2
Ovington Norfk 50 F13
Ovington Nthumb 77 M13
Ower Hants 9 L5
Ower Hants 9 P8
Owermoigne Dorset 7 U7
Owlbury Shrops 34 H2
Owlerton Sheff 57 M9
Owlpen Gloucs 28 E8
Owl's Green Suffk 41 N7
Owlsmoor Br For 20 D10
Owlswick Bucks 30 G11
Owmby Lincs 58 H9
Owmby Lincs 58 J6
Owslebury Hants 9 Q4
Owston Donc 57 S4
Owston Leics 47 U12
Owston Ferry N Linc 58 D6
Owstwick E R Yk 65 T13
Owthorne E R Yk 65 U14
Owthorpe Notts 47 S7
Owton Manor Hartpl 70 G7
Oxborough Norfk 50 B13
Oxbridge Dorset 7 N5
Oxcombe Lincs 59 P11
Oxcroft Derbys 57 Q12
Oxen End Essex 22 G2
Oxenholme Cumb 61 U2
Oxenhope C Brad 63 L13
Oxen Park Cumb 61 Q2
Oxenpill Somset 17 M8
Oxenton Gloucs 28 J1
Oxenwood Wilts 19 M9
Oxford Oxon 30 B11
Oxford Airport Oxon 29 U4
Oxford Services Oxon 30 D12
Oxhey Herts 20 K3
Oxhill Dur 69 Q2
Oxhill Warwks 36 K11
Oxley Wolves 46 B13
Oxley Green Essex 23 M5
Oxley's Green E Susx 12 C11
Oxlode Cambs 39 Q3
Oxnam Border 76 D2
Oxnead Norfk 51 M9
Oxshott Surrey 20 K10
Oxshott Heath Surrey 20 K10
Oxspring Barns 57 L6
Oxted Surrey 21 Q12
Oxton Border 84 D8
Oxton N York 64 C11
Oxton Notts 47 R3
Oxton Wirral 54 H9
Oxwich Swans 25 S13
Oxwich Green Swans 25 S13
Oxwick Norfk 50 F8
Oykel Bridge Highld 108 F4
Oyne Abers 104 K10
Oystermouth Swans 25 V13
Ozleworth Gloucs 28 E9

P

Pabail W Isls 106 k5
Packers Hill Dorset 7 T2
Packington Leics 47 L11
Packmoor C Stke 45 U3
Packmores Warwks 36 J7
Padanaram Angus 98 G13
Padbury Bucks 30 F6
Paddington Gt Lon 21 N6
Paddington Warrtn 55 P9
Paddlesworth Kent 12 C3
Paddlesworth Kent 13 N8
Paddock Wood Kent 12 C7
Paddolgreen Shrops 45 M7
Padfield Derbys 56 F7
Padgate Warrtn 55 P9
Padhams Green Essex 22 F8
Padiham Lancs 62 F13
Padside N York 63 P8
Padstow Cnwll 3 N1
Padworth W Berk 19 T7
Page Bank Dur 69 R5
Pagham W Susx 10 D11
Paglesham Essex 23 M9
Paignton Torbay 6 A12
Pailton Warwks 37 N4
Paine's Cross E Susx 11 U6
Painleyhill Staffs 46 D7
Painscastle Powys 34 E11
Painshawfield Nthumb 77 M13
Painsthorpe E R Yk 64 J8
Painswick Gloucs 28 G6
Painter's Forstal Kent 12 J4
Paisley Rens 89 L13
Pakefield Suffk 41 T2
Pakenham Suffk 40 F7
Pale Gwynd 43 U6
Pale Green Essex 39 U12
Palestine Hants 19 L12
Paley Street W & M 20 E7
Palfrey Wsall 36 D1
Palgrave Suffk 40 K5
Pallington Dorset 7 U6
Palmersbridge Cnwll 4 F5
Palmers Green Gt Lon 21 P4
Palmerston E Ayrs 81 Q9
Palmerstown V Glam 16 F3
Palnackie D & G 73 U8
Palnure D & G 73 M7
Palterton Derbys 57 Q13
Pamber End Hants 19 T9
Pamber Green Hants 19 T9
Pamber Heath Hants 19 T8
Pamington Gloucs 36 B14
Pamphill Dorset 8 D8
Pampisford Cambs 39 Q11
Panborough Somset 17 N7
Panbride Angus 91 S4
Pancrasweek Devon 14 G11
Pancross V Glam 16 D3
Pandy Caerph 27 M10
Pandy Gwynd 43 M13
Pandy Gwynd 43 S8
Pandy Mons 27 Q3
Pandy Powys 43 T13
Pandy Wrexhm 44 E6
Pandy'r Capel Denbgs 44 C3
Pandy Tudur Conwy 53 Q10
Panfield Essex 22 H2
Pangbourne W Berk 19 T5
Pangdean W Susx 11 M8
Panks Bridge Herefs 35 P11
Pannal N York 63 S9
Pannal Ash N York 63 R9
Pant Shrops 44 G9
Pantasaph Flints 54 E11
Panteg Pembks 24 F4
Pantersbridge Cnwll 4 F7
Pant-ffrwyth Brdgnd 26 G11
Pant Glas Gwynd 42 J4
Pantglas Powys 43 Q14
Pant-Gwyn Carmth 25 U5
Pant-lasau Swans 26 B7
Pant Mawr Powys 33 R4
Panton Lincs 59 L11
Pant-pastynog Denbgs 53 T10
Pantperthog Gwynd 43 P13
Pant-y-dwr Powys 33 U6
Pant-y-ffridd Powys 44 E13
Pantyffynnon Carmth 25 V8
Pantygaseg Torfn 27 P8
Pantygelli Mons 27 Q4
Pant-y-gog Brdgnd 26 G9
Pantymenyn Carmth 24 K5
Pant-y-mwyn Flints 54 E14
Panxworth Norfk 51 Q11
Papa Stour Shet 106 r7
Papa Stour Airport Shet 106 r8
Papa Westray Ork 106 t14
Papa Westray Airport Ork 106 t14
Papcastle Cumb 66 H6
Papigoe Highld 112 J6
Papple E Loth 84 F4
Papplewick Notts 47 P3
Papworth Everard Cambs 39 L8
Papworth St Agnes Cambs 39 L8
Par Cnwll 3 R6
Paramour Street Kent 13 Q3
Parbold Lancs 55 L4
Parbrook Somset 17 Q9
Parbrook W Susx 10 H5
Parc Gwynd 43 S7
Parcllyn Cerdgn 32 D10
Parc Seymour Newpt 27 S9
Pardshaw Cumb 66 G8
Parham Suffk 41 P8
Park D & G 74 H7
Park Nthumb 76 D13
Park Bottom Cnwll 2 H8
Park Bridge Tamesd 56 D6
Park Corner E Susx 11 S3
Park Corner Oxon 19 U3
Park Corner W & M 20 E6
Park End Bed 38 E10
Parkend Gloucs 28 B6
Park End Nthumb 76 H10
Parker's Green Kent 12 B6
Parkeston Essex 23 T1
Parkeston Quay Essex 41 M14
Park Farm Kent 12 K8
Parkgate Ches W 54 G11
Parkgate Cumb 66 K3
Parkgate D & G 74 K8
Parkgate E Susx 12 D13
Parkgate Essex 22 G2
Park Gate Hants 9 Q7
Parkgate Kent 12 G9
Parkgate Kent 21 T10
Park Gate Leeds 63 P11
Parkgate Surrey 11 L2
Park Gate Worcs 36 B6
Park Green Essex 22 C2
Park Green Suffk 40 K8
Parkhall W Duns 89 L11
Parkham Devon 14 J8
Parkham Ash Devon 14 J8
Park Head Derbys 47 L3
Park Hill Gloucs 27 V8
Parkhouse Mons 27 U7
Parkmill Swans 25 T13
Park Royal Gt Lon 21 L6
Parkside Dur 70 F3
Parkside N Lans 82 F7
Parkside Wrexhm 44 J2
Parkstone BCP 8 E10
Park Street Herts 31 P12
Park Street W Susx 10 J4
Parkway Herefs 35 R13
Parley Green BCP 8 G9
Parmoor Bucks 20 C5
Parracombe Devon 15 Q3
Parrog Pembks 24 J3
Parsonby Cumb 66 H5
Parson Cross Sheff 57 M8
Parson Drove Cambs 49 N12
Parson's Heath Essex 23 P2
Parson's Hill Derbys 46 J8
Partick C Glas 89 M12
Partington Traffd 55 R8
Partney Lincs 59 R13
Parton Cumb 66 E8
Partridge Green W Susx 10 K7
Partrishow Powys 27 P3
Parwich Derbys 46 G3
Paslow Wood Common Essex 22 E7
Passenham Nhants 30 G5
Passfield Hants 10 C4
Passingford Bridge Essex 22 D8
Paston C Pete 48 J13
Paston Norfk 51 P7
Pasturefields Staffs 46 C9
Patchacott Devon 15 L13
Patcham Br & H 11 N9
Patchetts Green Herts 20 K3
Patching W Susx 10 H9
Patchole Devon 15 P4
Patchway S Glos 28 B11
Pateley Bridge N York 63 P6
Paternoster Heath Essex 23 M4
Pathe Somset 17 L10
Pathhead Fife 91 L13
Pathhead Mdloth 83 S6
Pathlow Warwks 36 G9
Path of Condie P & K 90 G9
Patmore Heath Herts 22 B2
Patna E Ayrs 81 N10
Patney Wilts 18 G9
Patrick IoM 60 c6
Patrick Brompton N York 63 Q1
Patricroft Salfd 55 S7
Patrington E R Yk 59 P2
Patrington Haven E R Yk 59 P2
Patrixbourne Kent 13 N4
Patterdale Cumb 67 N9
Pattingham Staffs 45 T14
Pattishall Nhants 37 S10
Pattiswick Green Essex 22 K3
Patton Shrops 35 N1
Patton Bridge Cumb 67 S13
Paul Cnwll 2 D11
Paulerspury Nhants 37 T11
Paull E R Yk 59 L1
Paulton BaNES 17 S5
Paultons Park Hants 9 L5
Paunton Herefs 35 Q10
Pauperhaugh Nthumb 77 N6
Pave Lane Wrekin 45 S10
Pavenham Bed 38 E9
Pawlett Somset 16 J8
Pawston Nthumb 85 M12
Paxford Gloucs 36 G13
Paxton Border 85 N8
Payden Street Kent 12 H5
Payhembury Devon 6 E4
Paynter's Lane End Cnwll 2 H8
Paythorne Lancs 62 G9
Paytoe Herefs 34 K6
Peacehaven E Susx 11 Q10
Peak Dale Derbys 56 G11
Peak District National Park 56 J8
Peak Forest Derbys 56 H11
Peak Hill Lincs 49 L10
Peakirk C Pete 48 J12
Pearson's Green Kent 12 C7
Peartree Green Herefs 35 N14
Peasedown St John BaNES 17 T5
Peasehill Derbys 47 M4
Peaseland Green Norfk 50 J10
Peasemore W Berk 19 Q5
Peasenhall Suffk 41 Q7
Pease Pottage W Susx 11 M4
Pease Pottage Services W Susx 11 M4
Peaslake Surrey 10 H2
Peasley Cross St Hel 55 M8
Peasmarsh E Susx 12 G11
Peasmarsh Somset 6 K2
Peasmarsh Surrey 20 G13
Peathill Abers 105 Q2
Peat Inn Fife 91 Q10
Peatling Magna Leics 37 Q2
Peatling Parva Leics 37 Q3
Peaton Shrops 35 M3
Pebmarsh Essex 40 E14
Pebsham E Susx 12 E14
Pebworth Worcs 36 F11
Pecket Well Calder 62 K14
Peckforton Ches E 45 M2
Peckham Gt Lon 21 P7
Peckleton Leics 47 N13
Pedairffordd Powys 44 D9
Pedlinge Kent 13 M8
Pedmore Dudley 36 B4
Pedwell Somset 17 M9
Peebles Border 83 Q10
Peel IoM 60 c6
Peel Lancs 61 R13
Peel Common Hants 9 R8
Peene Kent 13 N8
Peening Quarter Kent 12 G10
Peggs Green Leics 47 M10
Pegsdon C Beds 31 P6
Pegswood Nthumb 77 Q8
Pegwell Kent 13 S3
Peinchorran Highld 100 e6
Peinlich Highld 100 d4
Pelcomb Pembks 24 F7
Pelcomb Bridge Pembks 24 F7
Pelcomb Cross Pembks 24 F7
Peldon Essex 23 N4
Pell Green E Susx 12 B9
Pelsall Wsall 46 D13
Pelsall Wood Wsall 46 D13
Pelton Dur 69 S2
Pelton Fell Dur 69 S2
Pelutho Cumb 66 H3
Pelynt Cnwll 4 G9
Pemberton Carmth 25 T10
Pemberton Wigan 55 N6
Pembles Cross Kent 12 G6
Pembrey Carmth 25 R10
Pembridge Herefs 34 J9
Pembroke Pembks 24 G10
Pembroke Dock Pembks 24 G10
Pembrokeshire Coast National Park Pembks 24 D6
Pembury Kent 12 B7
Pen-allt Herefs 27 V2
Penallt Mons 27 U5
Penally Pembks 24 K11
Penare Cnwll 3 P8
Penarth V Glam 16 G2
Penblewin Pembks 24 K7
Pen-bont Rhydybeddau Cerdgn 33 N4
Penbryn Cerdgn 32 E10
Pencader Carmth 25 R3
Pencaenewydd Gwynd 42 H5
Pencaitland E Loth 84 C5
Pencarnisiog IoA 52 E8
Pencarreg Carmth 32 K11
Pencarrow Cnwll 4 E4
Pencelli Powys 26 K2
Penclawdd Swans 25 T11
Pencoed Brdgnd 26 H11
Pencombe Herefs 35 N10
Pencoyd Herefs 27 U2
Pencraig Herefs 27 V3
Pencraig Powys 44 B8
Pendeen Cnwll 2 B10
Penderyn Rhondd 26 G6
Pendine Carmth 25 M9
Pendlebury Salfd 55 S6
Pendleton Lancs 62 F12
Pendock Worcs 35 S14
Pendoggett Cnwll 4 C5
Pendomer Somset 7 P2
Pendoylan V Glam 26 K12
Penegoes Powys 43 Q13
Penelewey Cnwll 3 L8
Pen-ffordd Pembks 24 J6
Pengam Caerph 27 M8
Pengam Cardif 27 N12
Penge Gt Lon 21 Q8
Pengelly Cnwll 4 D4
Pengenffordd Powys 27 M2
Pengorffwysfa IoA 52 G4
Pengover Green Cnwll 4 H7
Pen-groes-oped Mons 27 Q6
Pengwern Denbgs 53 T7
Penhale Cnwll 2 H13
Penhale Cnwll 3 N5
Penhale Cnwll 3 R4
Penhale Cnwll 5 L10
Penhallow Cnwll 2 K6
Penhalurick Cnwll 2 J9
Penhalvean Cnwll 2 J9
Penhill Swindn 29 N10
Penhow Newpt 27 S9
Penhurst E Susx 12 C12
Peniarth Gwynd 43 M12
Penicuik Mdloth 83 P7
Peniel Carmth 25 R6
Peniel Denbgs 53 T10
Penifiler Highld 100 d5
Peninver Ag & B 79 P11
Penisarwaun Gwynd 52 J10
Penistone Barns 56 K6
Penjerrick Cnwll 2 K10
Penketh Warrtn 55 N9
Penkill S Ayrs 80 J13
Penkridge Staffs 46 B11
Penlean Cnwll 14 F13
Penleigh Wilts 18 C10
Penley Wrexhm 44 K5
Penllergaer Swans 25 V11
Pen-llyn IoA 52 E6
Penllyn V Glam 26 H12
Pen-lôn IoA 52 F9
Penmachno Conwy 43 Q3
Penmaen Caerph 27 M8
Penmaen Swans 25 T13
Penmaenan Conwy 53 M7
Penmaenmawr Conwy 53 M7
Penmaenpool Gwynd 43 N10
Penmark V Glam 16 E3
Penmon IoA 52 K6
Penmorfa Gwynd 42 K5
Penmynydd IoA 52 H8
Penn Bucks 20 F4
Penn Wolves 35 U1
Pennal Gwynd 43 N13
Pennan Abers 105 N2
Pennant Cerdgn 32 K8
Pennant Denbgs 44 B7
Pennant Powys 43 S14
Pennant-Melangell Powys 44 B8
Pennar Pembks 24 G10
Pennard Swans 25 U13
Pennerley Shrops 44 J14
Pennicott Devon 15 U12
Pennines 62 K12
Pennington Cumb 61 P4
Pennington Hants 9 L9
Pennington Green Wigan 55 P5
Pennorth Powys 27 L2
Penn Street Bucks 20 F3
Pennsylvania S Glos 28 D13
Penny Bridge Cumb 61 Q3
Pennycross Ag & B 93 N13
Pennygate Norfk 51 P9
Pennyghael Ag & B 93 N13
Pennyglen S Ayrs 80 K10
Penny Green Derbys 57 R11
Penny Hill Lincs 49 N8
Pennymoor Devon 15 U10
Pennywell Sundld 70 E1
Penparc Cerdgn 32 D11
Penparcau Cerdgn 33 L4
Penpedairheol Caerph 27 L8
Penpedairheol Mons 27 Q7
Penpergwm Mons 27 Q5
Penperlleni Mons 27 Q7
Penpethy Cnwll 4 D3
Penpillick Cnwll 3 R5
Penpol Cnwll 3 L9
Penpoll Cnwll 4 E10
Penponds Cnwll 2 G9
Penpont Cnwll 3 R2
Penpont D & G 74 F7
Penpont Powys 26 H2
Penquit Devon 5 Q10
Penrest Cnwll 4 J5
Penrherber Carmth 25 N3
Pen-rhiw Pembks 32 D12
Penrhiwceiber Rhondd 26 K8
Pen Rhiwfawr Neath 26 C5
Penrhiwllan Cerdgn 32 G12
Penrhiw-pal Cerdgn 32 F11
Penrhos Gwynd 42 F7
Penrhos IoA 52 C6
Penrhos Mons 27 S5
Penrhos Powys 26 E5
Penrhos garnedd Gwynd 52 J8
Penrhyn Bay Conwy 53 P6
Penrhyn-coch Cerdgn 33 M4
Penrhyndeudraeth Gwynd 43 M6
Penrhyn-side Conwy 53 P6
Penrhys Rhondd 26 J9
Penrice Swans 25 S13
Penrioch N Ayrs 79 R7
Penrith Cumb 67 R6
Penrose Cnwll 3 M2
Penruddock Cumb 67 P7
Penryn Cnwll 2 K10
Pensarn Conwy 53 S7
Pensax Worcs 35 R7
Pensby Wirral 54 G10
Penselwood Somset 17 U10
Pensford BaNES 17 R4
Pensham Worcs 36 B12
Penshaw Sundld 70 D2
Penshurst Kent 11 S2
Penshurst Station Kent 21 T13
Pensilva Cnwll 4 H6
Pensnett Dudley 36 B3
Penstone Devon 15 S12
Penstrowed Powys 34 C2
Pentewan Cnwll 3 Q7
Pentir Gwynd 52 J9
Pentire Cnwll 2 K4
Pentlepoir Pembks 24 K9
Pentlow Essex 40 D11
Pentlow Street Essex 40 D11
Pentney Norfk 50 B11
Pentonbridge Cumb 75 T10
Penton Grafton Hants 19 M11
Penton Mewsey Hants 19 M11
Pentraeth IoA 52 H7
Pentre Denbgs 54 C14
Pentre Flints 54 H13
Pentre Mons 27 Q6
Pentre Mons 27 S7
Pentre Powys 34 C3
Pentre Powys 34 E3
Pentre Powys 34 G2
Pentre Rhondd 26 H8
Pentre Shrops 44 J10
Pentre Wrexhm 44 G5
Pentre-bâch Cerdgn 33 L11
Pentre Bach Flints 54 F11
Pentrebach Myr Td 26 K7
Pentre-bach Powys 33 T14
Pentrebeirdd Powys 44 E11
Pentre Berw IoA 52 G8
Pentre-bont Conwy 43 P3
Pentre-cagel Carmth 32 F12
Pentrecelyn Denbgs 44 D3
Pentre-celyn Powys 43 S12
Pentre-chwyth Swans 26 B9
Pentre-clawdd Shrops 44 G7
Pentre-cwrt Carmth 25 Q3
Pentredwr Denbgs 44 E4
Pentrefelin Gwynd 42 K6
Pentrefelin IoA 52 F4
Pentre Ffwrndan Flints 54 G12
Pentrefoelas Conwy 43 S3
Pentregalar Pembks 25 L4
Pentregat Cerdgn 32 G10
Pentre-Gwenlais Carmth 25 V7
Pentre Gwynfryn Gwynd 43 L8
Pentre Halkyn Flints 54 F12
Pentre Hodrey Shrops 34 H5
Pentre Isaf Conwy 53 S8
Pentre Llanrhaeadr Denbgs 54 C14
Pentre Llifior Powys 44 E14
Pentre-llwyn-llwyd Powys 33 U10
Pentre-llyn Cerdgn 33 M5
Pentre-llyn-cymmer Conwy 43 U3
Pentre-Maw Powys 43 S13
Pentre Meyrick V Glam 26 H12
Pentre-piod Torfn 27 P7
Pentre-poeth Newpt 27 P10
Pentre'rbryn Cerdgn 32 G10
Pentre'r-felin Cerdgn 33 M11
Pentre'r Felin Conwy 53 P9
Pentre'r-felin Powys 26 G1
Pentre Saron Denbgs 53 T10
Pentre-tafarn-y-fedw Conwy 53 P10
Pentre ty gwyn Carmth 33 R13
Pentrich Derbys 47 L3
Pentridge Dorset 8 E5
Pen-twyn Caerph 27 N7
Pen-twyn Mons 27 U6
Pen-twyn Torfn 27 P7
Pentwynmaur Caerph 27 M8
Pentyrch Cardif 27 L11
Penwithick Cnwll 3 Q5
Penwood Hants 19 P8
Penwyllt Powys 26 F4
Penybanc Carmth 25 V6
Penybont Powys 34 D8
Pen-y-bont Powys 44 F9
Penybontfawr Powys 44 C9
Pen-y-bryn Pembks 32 C12
Pen-y-cae Powys 26 E5
Penycae Wrexhm 44 G4
Pen-y-cae-mawr Mons 27 S8
Penycaerau Gwynd 42 C8
Pen-y-cefn Flints 54 D11
Pen-y-clawdd Mons 27 T6
Pen-y-coedcae Rhondd 26 K10
Penycwn Pembks 24 E6
Pen-y-fai Brdgnd 26 F11
Pen-y-felin Flints 54 E13
Penyffordd Flints 44 H1
Pen-y-ffordd Flints 54 D10
Penyffridd Gwynd 52 H11
Pen-y-garn Cerdgn 33 M3
Pen-y-Garnedd Powys 44 D9
Pen-y-graig Gwynd 42 D7
Penygraig Rhondd 26 J9
Penygroes Carmth 25 U8
Penygroes Gwynd 52 G12
Penygroeslon Gwynd 42 D7
Pen-y-Gwryd Gwynd 53 L11
Pen-y-lan V Glam 26 H12
Pen-y-Mynydd Carmth 25 S10
Penymynydd Flints 44 H1
Pen-y-pass Gwynd 52 K11
Pen-yr-Heol Mons 27 S5
Penysarn IoA 52 G4
Pen-y-stryt Denbgs 44 F3
Penywaun Rhondd 26 H7
Penzance Cnwll 2 D10
Peopleton Worcs 36 B10
Peover Heath Ches E 55 S12
Peper Harow Surrey 10 E2
Peplow Shrops 45 P9
Pepper's Green Essex 22 F5
Pepperstock C Beds 31 N9
Perceton N Ayrs 81 M4
Percyhorner Abers 105 R2
Perelle Guern 6 c3
Perham Down Wilts 19 L11
Periton Somset 16 C7
Perivale Gt Lon 21 L6
Perkins Village Devon 6 D6
Perkinsville Dur 69 S2
Perlethorpe Notts 57 T12
Perranarworthal Cnwll 2 K9
Perranporth Cnwll 2 K6
Perranuthnoe Cnwll 2 E11
Perranwell Cnwll 2 K6
Perranwell Cnwll 2 K9
Perran Wharf Cnwll 2 K9
Perranzabuloe Cnwll 2 K6
Perrott's Brook Gloucs 28 K6
Perry Birm 36 E2
Perry Barr Birm 36 E2
Perry Green Essex 22 K3
Perry Green Herts 22 B4
Perry Green Wilts 28 J10
Perrystone Hill Herefs 28 B2
Perry Street Somset 6 K3
Pershall Staffs 45 T8
Pershore Worcs 36 B11
Pertenhall Bed 38 G7
Perth P & K 90 H7
Perthy Shrops 44 J7
Perton Herefs 35 N12
Perton Staffs 45 U14
Pertwood Wilts 18 C13
Peterborough C Pete 48 J14
Peterborough Services Cambs 38 H2
Peterchurch Herefs 34 H13
Peterculter C Aber 99 Q3
Peterhead Abers 105 U6
Peterlee Dur 70 F4
Petersfield Hants 9 U4
Peter's Green Herts 31 P9
Petersham Gt Lon 21 L8
Peters Marland Devon 15 L10
Peterstone Wentlooge Newpt 27 P12
Peterston-super-Ely V Glam 26 K12
Peterstow Herefs 27 V3
Peters Village Kent 12 D3
Peter Tavy Devon 5 N5
Petham Kent 13 M5
Petherwin Gate Cnwll 4 H3
Petrockstow Devon 15 M11
Petsoe End M Keyn 38 C11
Pet Street Kent 13 L6
Pett E Susx 12 G13
Pettaugh Suffk 41 L9
Pett Bottom Kent 13 N5
Petterden Angus 91 P4
Pettinain S Lans 82 J10
Pettistree Suffk 41 P9
Petton Devon 16 D12
Petton Shrops 44 K8
Petts Wood Gt Lon 21 S9
Pettycur Fife 83 Q1
Petty France S Glos 28 E10
Pettymuk Abers 105 Q11
Petworth W Susx 10 F6
Pevensey E Susx 11 U9
Pevensey Bay E Susx 11 V10
Pewsey Wilts 18 J8
Pewsham Wilts 18 D6
Pheasant's Hill Bucks 20 C5
Phepson Worcs 36 B9
Philadelphia Sundld 70 D2
Philham Devon 14 G8
Philiphaugh Border 84 C13
Phillack Cnwll 2 F9
Philleigh Cnwll 3 M9
Philpot End Essex 22 F4
Philpstoun W Loth 83 L3
Phocle Green Herefs 28 B2
Phoenix Green Hants 20 C11
Pibsbury Somset 17 M11
Pica Cumb 66 F8
Piccadilly Warwks 46 H14
Piccotts End Herts 31 M11
Pickburn Donc 57 R5
Pickering N York 64 H3
Picket Piece Hants 19 N11
Picket Post Hants 8 H7
Picket Twenty Hants 19 N11
Pickford Covtry 36 J4
Pickford Green Covtry 36 J4
Pickhill N York 63 S3
Picklescott Shrops 44 K14
Pickmere Ches E 55 Q11
Pickney Somset 16 G11
Pickstock Wrekin 45 R9
Pickup Bank Bl w D 55 R2
Pickwell Devon 15 L4
Pickwell Leics 47 U11
Pickwick Wilts 18 C6
Pickworth Lincs 48 F7
Pickworth Rutlnd 48 E11
Picton Ches W 54 K12
Picton Flints 54 D10
Picton N York 70 F11
Piddinghoe E Susx 11 Q10
Piddington Bucks 20 D4
Piddington Nhants 38 B10
Piddington Oxon 30 D9
Piddlehinton Dorset 7 T5
Piddletrenthide Dorset 7 T5
Pidley Cambs 39 M5
Piercebridge Darltn 69 R9
Pierowall Ork 106 t15
Piff's Elm Gloucs 28 H2
Pigdon Nthumb 77 P8
Pigeon Green Warwks 36 H8
Pig Oak Dorset 8 E8
Pig Street Herefs 34 J11
Pikehall Derbys 46 G2
Pilford Dorset 8 E8
Pilgrims Hatch Essex 22 E8
Pilham Lincs 58 E8
Pill N Som 27 U12
Pillaton Cnwll 4 K8
Pillatonmill Cnwll 4 K8
Pillerton Hersey Warwks 36 J11
Pillerton Priors Warwks 36 J11
Pilleth Powys 34 G7
Pilley Barns 57 M6
Pilley Hants 9 L9
Pilley Bailey Hants 9 L9
Pillgwenlly Newpt 27 Q10
Pillhead Devon 15 L7
Pilling Lancs 61 S10
Pilling Lane Lancs 61 R10
Pilning S Glos 27 V10
Pilot Inn Kent 13 L12
Pilsbury Derbys 56 H14
Pilsdon Dorset 7 M5
Pilsgate C Pete 48 G12
Pilsley Derbys 47 M1
Pilsley Derbys 56 K12
Pilson Green Norfk 51 Q11
Piltdown E Susx 11 Q6
Pilton Devon 15 N6
Pilton Nhants 38 F4
Pilton Rutlnd 48 D13
Pilton Somset 17 Q8
Pilton Green Swans 25 R13
Pimbo Lancs 55 L6
Pimlico Herts 31 N11
Pimlico Lancs 62 E11
Pimlico Nhants 30 D4
Pimperne Dorset 8 C7
Pinchbeck Lincs 48 K8
Pinchbeck Bars Lincs 48 J8
Pincheon Green Donc 57 U3
Pinchinthorpe R & Cl 70 J10
Pincock Lancs 55 M3
Pinfold Lancs 54 J4
Pinford End Suffk 40 D9
Pinged Carmth 25 R10
Pingewood W Berk 19 U7
Pin Green Herts 31 S7
Pinhoe Devon 6 C6
Pinkett's Booth Covtry 36 J4
Pinkney Wilts 28 G10
Pinkneys Green W & M 20 E6
Pinley Covtry 37 L5
Pinley Green Warwks 36 H7
Pin Mill Suffk 41 M13
Pinminnoch S Ayrs 80 H14
Pinmore S Ayrs 72 G1
Pinn Devon 6 F7
Pinner Gt Lon 20 K5
Pinner Green Gt Lon 20 K4
Pinsley Green Ches E 45 N4
Pinvin Worcs 36 C11
Pinwherry S Ayrs 72 G2
Pinxton Derbys 47 N3
Pipe and Lyde Herefs 35 M12
Pipe Aston Herefs 35 L6
Pipe Gate Shrops 45 R5
Pipehill Staffs 46 E12
Piperdam Angus 91 M5
Piperhill Highld 103 N5
Pipers Pool Cnwll 4 H4
Pipewell Nhants 38 B3
Pippacott Devon 15 M5
Pippin Street Lancs 55 N2
Pipton Powys 34 E13
Pirbright Surrey 20 F11
Pirbright Camp Surrey 20 F11
Pirnie Border 84 H13
Pirnmill N Ayrs 79 R7
Pirton Herts 31 P6
Pirton Worcs 35 U11
Pisgah Cerdgn 33 N5
Pishill Oxon 20 B5
Pistyll Gwynd 42 F5
Pitblae Abers 105 R3
Pitcairngreen P & K 90 G6
Pitcalnie Highld 109 Q10
Pitcaple Abers 105 L10
Pitcarity Angus 98 E10
Pitchcombe Gloucs 28 G6
Pitchcott Bucks 30 G8
Pitcher Row Lincs 49 L7
Pitchford Shrops 45 M13
Pitch Green Bucks 30 G12
Pitch Place Surrey 10 D3
Pitch Place Surrey 20 G12
Pitchroy Moray 103 U8
Pitcombe Somset 17 S10
Pitcot V Glam 26 F13
Pitcox E Loth 84 G3
Pitfichie Abers 104 K12
Pitglassie Abers 104 K7
Pitgrudy Highld 109 P6
Pitlessie Fife 91 M10
Pitlochry P & K 97 Q12
Pitmachie Abers 104 K10
Pitmain Highld 97 L3
Pitmedden Abers 105 P10
Pitmedden Garden Abers 105 P10
Pitminster Somset 16 H13
Pitmuies Angus 91 S2
Pitmunie Abers 104 K13
Pitney Somset 17 N11
Pitroddie P & K 90 K6
Pitscottie Fife 91 P9
Pitsea Essex 22 H10
Pitses Oldham 56 D6
Pitsford Nhants 37 U7
Pitstone Bucks 30 K9
Pitt Devon 16 D13
Pitt Hants 9 P3
Pittarrow Abers 99 N9
Pitt Court Gloucs 28 D8
Pittenweem Fife 91 S11
Pitteuchar Fife 91 L12
Pittington Dur 70 D4
Pittodrie House Hotel Abers 104 K11
Pitton Wilts 8 J2
Pitt's Wood Kent 12 B6
Pittulie Abers 105 R2
Pityme Cnwll 3 P1
Pity Me Dur 69 S3
Pivington Kent 12 H6
Pixey Green Suffk 41 M5
Pixham Surrey 21 L12
Plains N Lans 82 E5
Plain Street Cnwll 4 B5
Plaish Shrops 35 M1
Plaistow Gt Lon 21 R6
Plaistow W Susx 10 G4
Plaitford Hants 8 K5
Plank Lane Wigan 55 P7
Plas Cymyran IoA 52 C7
Plastow Green Hants 19 R8
Platt Bridge Wigan 55 P6
Platt Lane Shrops 45 M6
Platts Heath Kent 12 G5
Plawsworth Dur 69 S3
Plaxtol Kent 12 B5
Playden E Susx 12 H11
Playford Suffk 41 M11
Play Hatch Oxon 20 B7
Playing Place Cnwll 3 L8
Playley Green Gloucs 28 E1
Plealey Shrops 44 K12
Plean Stirlg 89 T8
Pleasance Fife 90 K9
Pleasington Bl w D 55 P1
Pleasley Derbys 57 R14
Pleasleyhill Notts 57 R14
Pleasurewood Hills Suffk 41 T1
Pleck Dorset 7 T2
Pledgdon Green Essex 22 E2
Pledwick Wakefd 57 M3
Pleinheaume Guern 6 d2
Plemont Jersey 7 a1
Plemstall Ches W 55 L12
Plenmeller Nthumb 76 E13
Pleshey Essex 22 G5
Plockton Highld 100 h6
Plowden Shrops 34 J3
Plox Green Shrops 44 J13
Pluckley Kent 12 H6
Pluckley Station Kent 12 H7
Pluckley Thorne Kent 12 H7
Plucks Gutter Kent 13 Q3
Plumbland Cumb 66 J5
Plumgarths Cumb 67 Q14
Plumley Ches E 55 R12
Plump Hill Gloucs 28 C4
Plumpton Cumb 61 Q4
Plumpton Cumb 67 Q5
Plumpton E Susx 11 P8
Plumpton Nhants 37 Q11
Plumpton End Nhants 30 F4
Plumpton Green E Susx 11 P7
Plumpton Head Cumb 67 R5
Plumstead Gt Lon 21 R7
Plumstead Norfk 50 K7
Plumstead Green Norfk 50 K6
Plumtree Notts 47 R7
Plumtree Green Kent 12 F6
Plungar Leics 47 U7
Plurenden Kent 12 H8
Plush Dorset 7 T4
Plusha Cnwll 4 H4
Plushabridge Cnwll 4 J6
Plwmp Cerdgn 32 G10
Plymouth C Plym 5 M10
Plympton C Plym 5 N9
Plymstock C Plym 5 N10
Plymtree Devon 6 E4
Pockley N York 64 E2
Pocklington E R Yk 64 J10
Pode Hole Lincs 48 K9
Podimore Somset 17 P12
Podington Bed 38 D8
Podmore Staffs 45 S6
Point Clear Essex 23 R5
Pointon Lincs 48 H7
Pokesdown BCP 8 G10
Polbain Highld 107 S2
Polbathic Cnwll 4 J9
Polbeth W Loth 82 K6
Polbrock Cnwll 3 Q3
Poldark Mine Cnwll 2 H10
Polebrook Nhants 38 G3
Pole Elm Worcs 35 T10
Polegate E Susx 11 T10
Pole Moor Kirk 56 G3
Polesden Lacey Surrey 20 K12
Polesworth Warwks 46 J13
Polgigga Cnwll 2 B12
Polglass Highld 107 T3
Polgooth Cnwll 3 P6
Polgown D & G 74 D5
Poling W Susx 10 G10
Poling Corner W Susx 10 G9
Polkerris Cnwll 3 R6
Pollard Street Norfk 51 P7
Pollington E R Yk 57 T3
Polloch Highld 93 T5
Pollokshaws C Glas 89 N13
Pollokshields C Glas 89 N13
Polmassick Cnwll 3 P7
Polmear Cnwll 3 R6
Polmont Falk 82 H3
Polnish Highld 93 T2
Polperro Cnwll 4 G10
Polruan Cnwll 4 E10
Polsham Somset 17 P8
Polstead Suffk 40 G13
Polstead Heath Suffk 40 G12
Poltalloch Ag & B 87 Q6
Poltescoe Cnwll 2 J13
Poltimore Devon 6 C5
Polton Mdloth 83 Q6
Polwarth Border 84 J8
Polyphant Cnwll 4 H4
Polzeath Cnwll 4 A5
Pomathorn Mdloth 83 P7
Pomeroy Derbys 56 H13
Ponde Powys 34 D13
Pondersbridge Cambs 39 L2
Ponders End Gt Lon 21 Q3
Ponsanooth Cnwll 2 K9
Ponsonby Cumb 66 G11
Ponsongath Cnwll 2 K13
Ponsworthy Devon 5 S6
Pont Abraham Services Carmth 25 U9
Pontac Jersey 7 e4
Pontamman Carmth 26 A5
Pontantwn Carmth 25 R8
Pontardawe Neath 26 C7
Pontarddulais Swans 25 U10
Pont-ar-gothi Carmth 25 T6
Pont-ar-Hydfer Powys 26 F2
Pont-ar-llechau Carmth 26 C3
Pontarsais Carmth 25 R5
Pontblyddyn Flints 44 G1
Pont Cyfyng Conwy 53 M11
Pontcysyllte Aqueduct Wrexhm 44 G5
Pont Dolgarrog Conwy 53 N9
Pontdolgoch Powys 34 B2
Pont-Ebbw Newpt 27 P10
Pontefract Wakefd 57 Q2
Ponteland Nthumb 77 P11
Ponterwyd Cerdgn 33 P4
Pontesbury Shrops 44 J12
Pontesbury Hill Shrops 44 J12
Pontesford Shrops 44 K12
Pontfadog Wrexhm 44 F6
Pontfaen Pembks 24 H4
Pont-faen Powys 33 U14
Pontgarreg Cerdgn 32 F10
Pontgarreg Pembks 32 B12
Ponthenri Carmth 25 S9
Ponthir Torfn 27 Q9
Ponthirwaun Cerdgn 32 E11
Pontllanfraith Caerph 27 M8
Pontlliw Swans 25 V10
Pontllyfni Gwynd 42 H3
Pontlottyn Caerph 27 L6
Pont Morlais Carmth 25 T9
Pontnêddféchan Neath 26 G6
Pontnewydd Torfn 27 P8
Pontnewynydd Torfn 27 P7
Pont Pen-y-benglog Gwynd 53 L10
Pontrhydfendigaid Cerdgn 33 P7
Pont Rhyd-sarn Gwynd 43 S8
Pont Rhyd-y-cyff Brdgnd 26 F10
Pont-rhyd-y-fen Neath 26 D9
Pontrhydygroes Cerdgn 33 P6
Pontrhydyrun Torfn 27 P8
Pontrilas Herefs 27 R2
Pont Robert Powys 44 D11
Pont-rug Gwynd 52 H10
Ponts Green E Susx 12 C12
Pontshaen Cerdgn 32 H11
Pontshill Herefs 28 B3
Pontsticill Myr Td 26 K5
Pont Walby Neath 26 F6
Pontwelly Carmth 32 H12
Pontyates Carmth 25 S9
Pontyberem Carmth 25 T8
Pont-y-blew Wrexhm 44 H6
Pontybodkin Flints 44 G2
Pontyclun Rhondd 26 J11
Pontycymer Brdgnd 26 G9
Pontyglasier Pembks 24 K3
Pontygwaith Rhondd 26 J9
Pontygynon Pembks 24 K3
Pontymister Caerph 27 N9
Pont-y-pant Conwy 53 N12
Pontypool Torfn 27 P7
Pontypridd Rhondd 26 K10
Pont-yr-hafod Pembks 24 F5
Pont-yr-Rhyl Brdgnd 26 G10
Pontywaun Caerph 27 N9
Pool Cnwll 2 H8
Pool IoS 2 b2
Poole BCP 8 E10
Poole Keynes Gloucs 28 J8
Poolewe Highld 107 Q8
Pooley Bridge Cumb 67 Q8
Pooley Street Norfk 40 J4
Poolfold Staffs 45 U2
Pool Head Herefs 35 N10
Poolhill Gloucs 28 D2
Pool in Wharfedale Leeds 63 Q10
Pool of Muckhart Clacks 90 F11
Pool Quay Powys 44 G11
Pool Street Essex 40 C13
Pooting's Kent 21 S13
Popham Hants 19 S12
Poplar Gt Lon 21 Q6
Poplar Street Suffk 41 R7
Porchfield IoW 9 N10
Poringland Norfk 51 N13
Porkellis Cnwll 2 H10
Porlock Somset 15 U3
Porlock Weir Somset 15 U3
Portachoillan Ag & B 79 P4
Port-an-Eorna Highld 100 g6
Port Appin Ag & B 94 C9
Port Askaig Ag & B 86 G12
Portavadie Ag & B 87 S12
Port Bannatyne Ag & B 88 C12
Portbury N Som 27 U12
Port Carlisle Cumb 75 P13
Port Charlotte Ag & B 78 D4
Portchester Hants 9 S7
Port Clarence S on T 70 G8
Port Driseach Ag & B 87 T11
Port Ellen Ag & B 78 F6
Port Elphinstone Abers 105 M11
Portencalzie D & G 72 C5
Portencross N Ayrs 80 H3
Port Erin IoM 60 b9
Portesham Dorset 7 R7
Portessie Moray 104 E2
Port e Vullen IoM 60 h4
Port Eynon Swans 25 S13
Portfield Gate Pembks 24 F7
Portgate Devon 5 L3
Port Gaverne Cnwll 4 C4
Port Glasgow Inver 88 H11
Portgordon Moray 104 D3
Portgower Highld 109 U2
Porth Cnwll 3 L4
Porth Rhondd 26 J9
Porthallow Cnwll 2 K12
Porthallow Cnwll 4 G10
Porthcawl Brdgnd 26 E12
Porthcothan Cnwll 3 M2
Porthcurno Cnwll 2 B12
Porthdinllaen Gwynd 42 E5
Port Henderson Highld 107 N10
Porthgain Pembks 24 D4
Porthgwarra Cnwll 2 B12
Porthill Staffs 45 T4
Porthkea Cnwll 3 L8
Porthkerry V Glam 16 E3
Porthleven Cnwll 2 G11
Porthmadog Gwynd 43 L6
Porthmeor Cnwll 2 C9
Porth Navas Cnwll 2 K11
Portholland Cnwll 3 P8
Porthoustock Cnwll 3 L12
Porthpean Cnwll 3 Q6
Porthtowan Cnwll 2 H7
Porthwgan Wrexhm 44 J4
Porthyrhyd Carmth 25 T7
Porth-y-Waen Shrops 44 G9
Portincaple Ag & B 88 F7
Portinfer Jersey 7 a1
Portington E R Yk 64 H13
Portinnisherrich Ag & B 87 T3
Portinscale Cumb 67 L8
Port Isaac Cnwll 4 B4
Portishead N Som 27 T12
Portknockie Moray 104 F2
Portland Dorset 7 S10
Portlethen Abers 99 S4
Portling D & G 66 C2
Portloe Cnwll 3 N9
Port Logan D & G 72 D11
Portlooe Cnwll 4 G10
Portmahomack Highld 109 S8
Portmeirion Gwynd 43 L6
Portmellon Cnwll 3 Q8
Port Mòr Highld 93 L3
Portmore Hants 9 L9
Port Mulgrave N York 71 N9
Portnacroish Ag & B 94 C9
Portnaguran W Isls 106 k5
Portnahaven Ag & B 78 B5
Portnalong Highld 100 c6
Port nan Giuran W Isls 106 k5
Port nan Long W Isls 106 d11
Port Nis W Isls 106 k2
Portobello C Edin 83 R4
Portobello Gatesd 69 S1
Portobello Wolves 46 C14
Port of Menteith Stirlg 89 N5
Port of Ness W Isls 106 k2
Porton Wilts 18 J13
Portontown Devon 5 L5
Portpatrick D & G 72 B9
Port Quin Cnwll 4 B4
Port Ramsay Ag & B 94 B9
Portreath Cnwll 2 H7
Portreath Harbour Cnwll 2 H7
Portree Highld 100 d5
Port Righ Ag & B 79 Q8
Port St Mary IoM 60 c9
Portscatho Cnwll 3 M9
Portsea C Port 9 S8
Portskerra Highld 111 T3
Portskewett Mons 27 T10
Portslade Br & H 11 M9
Portslade-by-Sea Br & H 11 M9
Portslogan D & G 72 B8
Portsmouth C Port 9 S9
Portsmouth Calder 56 D1
Portsmouth Arms Devon 15 P9
Portsmouth Dockyard C Port 9 S8
Port Soderick IoM 60 e8
Port Solent C Port 9 S7
Portsonachan Hotel Ag & B 88 B1
Portsoy Abers 104 H2
Port Sunlight Wirral 54 H10
Portswood C Sotn 9 N6
Port Talbot Neath 26 D10
Port Tennant Swans 26 B9
Portuairk Highld 93 L5
Portway Herefs 35 L12
Portway Herefs 35 L13
Portway Sandw 36 C3
Portway Worcs 36 E6
Port Wemyss Ag & B 78 B5
Port William D & G 72 J11
Portwrinkle Cnwll 4 K10
Portyerrock D & G 73 M12
Posbury Devon 15 T13
Posenhall Shrops 45 Q13
Poslingford Suffk 40 C11
Posso Border 83 P12
Postbridge Devon 5 R5
Postcombe Oxon 30 F12
Post Green Dorset 8 D10
Postling Kent 13 M8
Postwick Norfk 51 N12
Potarch Abers 99 L4
Potsgrove C Beds 31 L6
Potten End Herts 31 M11
Potten Street Kent 13 Q2
Potter Brompton N York 65 M4
Pottergate Street Norfk 41 L2
Potterhanworth Lincs 58 J13
Potterhanworth Booths Lincs 58 J13
Potter Heigham Norfk 51 R10
Potterne Wilts 18 E9
Potterne Wick Wilts 18 E9
Potter Row Bucks 30 K12
Potters Bar Herts 31 R12
Potters Brook Lancs 61 T9
Potter's Cross Staffs 35 T4
Potters Crouch Herts 31 P11
Potter's Forstal Kent 12 G6
Potters Green Covtry 37 L4
Potter's Green E Susx 11 S6
Potter's Green Herts 31 U8
Pottersheath Herts 31 R9
Potters Marston Leics 37 N1
Potter Somersal Derbys 46 F6
Potterspury Nhants 30 G4
Potter Street Essex 22 C6
Potterton Abers 105 Q12
Potterton Leeds 63 U12
Potthorpe Norfk 50 F9
Pottle Street Wilts 18 B12
Potto N York 70 G12
Potton C Beds 38 K11
Pott Row Norfk 50 B9
Pott's Green Essex 23 M3
Pott Shrigley Ches E 56 D11
Poughill Cnwll 14 F11
Poughill Devon 15 U11
Poulner Hants 8 H7
Poulshot Wilts 18 E9
Poulton Gloucs 29 L7
Poulton Wirral 54 H8
Poulton-le-Fylde Lancs 61 Q12
Poulton Priory Gloucs 29 L8
Pound Bank Worcs 35 R6
Poundbury Dorset 7 S6
Poundffald Swans 25 U12
Poundgate E Susx 11 R5
Pound Green E Susx 11 S6
Pound Green Suffk 40 B10
Pound Green Worcs 35 S5
Pound Hill W Susx 11 M3
Poundon Bucks 30 D7
Poundsbridge Kent 11 S2
Poundsgate Devon 5 S6
Poundstock Cnwll 14 F13
Pound Street Hants 19 Q8
Pounsley E Susx 11 S6
Pouton D & G 73 M10
Pouy Street Suffk 41 Q6
Povey Cross Surrey 11 M2
Powburn Nthumb 77 M2
Powderham Devon 6 C8
Powerstock Dorset 7 P5
Powfoot D & G 75 M12
Pow Green Herefs 35 R12
Powhill Cumb 66 K1
Powick Worcs 35 T10
Powmill P & K 90 F12
Poxwell Dorset 7 T8
Poyle Slough 20 H7
Poynings W Susx 11 M8
Poyntington Dorset 17 S12
Poynton Ches E 56 D10
Poynton Wrekin 45 N10
Poynton Green Wrekin 45 N10
Poyston Cross Pembks 24 G7
Poystreet Green Suffk 40 G9
Praa Sands Cnwll 2 F11
Pratt's Bottom Gt Lon 21 S10
Praze-an-Beeble Cnwll 2 G9
Predannack Wollas Cnwll 2 H13
Prees Shrops 45 N7
Preesall Lancs 61 R10
Prees Green Shrops 45 N7
Preesgweene Shrops 44 G6
Prees Heath Shrops 45 N6
Prees Higher Heath Shrops 45 N6
Prees Lower Heath Shrops 45 N7
Prendwick Nthumb 77 L3
Pren-gwyn Cerdgn 32 H12
Prenteg Gwynd 43 L5
Prenton Wirral 54 H9
Prescot Knows 55 L8
Prescott Devon 6 E2
Prescott Shrops 35 Q4
Prescott Shrops 44 K9
Presnerb Angus 98 B10
Pressen Nthumb 85 L11
Prestatyn Denbgs 54 C10
Prestbury Ches E 56 C11
Prestbury Gloucs 28 J3
Presteigne Powys 34 H8
Prestleigh Somset 17 R8
Prestolee Bolton 55 S5
Preston Border 84 K7
Preston Br & H 11 N9
Preston Devon 5 V6
Preston Dorset 7 T8
Preston E R Yk 65 R13
Preston Gloucs 28 K7
Preston Herts 31 Q8
Preston Kent 12 K3
Preston Kent 13 P3
Preston Lancs 61 U14
Preston Nthumb 85 T13
Preston Rutlnd 48 C13
Preston Shrops 45 M11
Preston Somset 16 E9
Preston Torbay 6 A12
Preston Wilts 18 F5
Preston Wilts 19 L6
Preston Bagot Warwks 36 G7
Preston Bissett Bucks 30 E7
Preston Bowyer Somset 16 F11
Preston Brockhurst Shrops 45 M9
Preston Brook Halton 55 N10
Preston Candover Hants 19 T12
Preston Capes Nhants 37 Q10
Preston Crowmarsh Oxon 19 T2
Preston Deanery Nhants 37 U9
Preston Green Warwks 36 G7
Preston Gubbals Shrops 45 L10
Preston Montford Shrops 44 K11
Preston on Stour Warwks 36 H11
Preston on Tees S on T 70 F9
Preston on the Hill Halton 55 N10
Preston on Wye Herefs 34 J12
Prestonpans E Loth 83 S4
Preston Patrick Cumb 61 U3
Preston Plucknett Somset 17 P13
Preston St Mary Suffk 40 F10
Preston Street Kent 13 Q3
Preston-under-Scar N York 63 M1
Preston upon the Weald Moors Wrekin 45 Q10
Preston Wynne Herefs 35 N11
Prestwich Bury 55 T6
Prestwick Nthumb 77 P11
Prestwick S Ayrs 81 M7
Prestwick Airport S Ayrs 81 M7
Prestwood Bucks 30 J12
Prestwood Staffs 35 U3
Price Town Brdgnd 26 G9
Prickwillow Cambs 39 S4
Priddy Somset 17 P6
Priestacott Devon 14 K11
Priestcliffe Derbys 56 H12
Priestcliffe Ditch Derbys 56 H12
Priest Hutton Lancs 61 U5
Priestland E Ayrs 81 R5
Priestley Green Calder 56 H1
Priest Weston Shrops 34 G1
Priestwood Green Kent 12 C3
Primethorpe Leics 37 P2
Primrose Green Norfk 50 J10
Primrosehill Border 84 K7
Primrose Hill Cambs 39 N3
Primrose Hill Derbys 47 M2
Primrose Hill Dudley 36 B3
Primrose Hill Lancs 54 J5
Primsidemill Border 85 L13
Prince of Wales Bridge Mons 27 U10
Princes Gate Pembks 24 K8
Princes Risborough Bucks 30 H12
Princethorpe Warwks 37 M6
Princetown Devon 5 P6
Prinsted W Susx 10 B9
Prion Denbgs 44 C1
Prior Rigg Cumb 75 U12
Priors Halton Shrops 35 L5
Priors Hardwick Warwks 37 N9
Priorslee Wrekin 45 R11
Priors Marston Warwks 37 N9
Priors Norton Gloucs 28 G3
Priory Wood Herefs 34 G11
Prisk V Glam 26 J12
Priston BaNES 17 S4
Pristow Green Norfk 40 K3
Prittlewell Sthend 23 L10
Privett Hants 9 T3
Prixford Devon 15 N5
Probus Cnwll 3 M7
Prora E Loth 84 E3
Prospect Cumb 66 H4
Prospidnick Cnwll 2 G10
Protstonhill Abers 105 N3

Prudhoe – Salterforth 139

Prudhoe Nthumb 77 M13
Prussia Cove Cnwll 2 F11
Pubil P & K 95 P10
Publow BaNES 17 R4
Puckeridge Herts 31 U8
Puckington Somset 17 L13
Pucklechurch S Glos 28 C12
Puckrup Gloucs 35 U13
Puddinglake Ches W 55 R13
Puddington Ches W 54 H12
Puddington Devon 15 T10
Puddledock Norfk 40 J2
Puddletown Dorset 7 U6
Pudleston Herefs 35 N9
Pudsey Leeds 63 Q13
Pulborough W Susx 10 G7
Puleston Wrekin 45 R9
Pulford Ches W 44 J2
Pulham Dorset 7 T3
Pulham Market Norfk 41 L3
Pulham St Mary Norfk 41 M3
Pullens Green S Glos 28 B9
Pulloxhill C Beds 31 N6
Pulverbatch Shrops 44 K13
Pumpherston W Loth 83 L5
Pumsaint Carmth 33 N12
Puncheston Pembks 24 H5
Puncknowle Dorset 7 P7
Punnett's Town E Susx 11 U6
Purbrook Hants 9 T7
Purfleet Thurr 22 E12
Puriton Somset 16 K8
Purleigh Essex 22 K7
Purley Gt Lon 21 P10
Purley on Thames W Berk 19 U5
Purlogue Shrops 34 G5
Purlpit Wilts 18 C7
Purls Bridge Cambs 39 Q3
Purse Caundle Dorset 17 S13
Purshull Green Worcs 35 U6
Purslow Shrops 34 J4
Purston Jaglin Wakefd 57 P3
Purtington Somset 7 L3
Purton Gloucs 28 C6
Purton Gloucs 28 C7
Purton Wilts 29 L10
Purton Stoke Wilts 29 L9
Pury End Nhants 37 T11
Pusey Oxon 29 S8
Putley Herefs 35 P13
Putley Green Herefs 35 P13
Putloe Gloucs 28 E6
Putney Gt Lon 21 M8
Putsborough Devon 14 K4
Puttenham Herts 30 J10
Puttenham Surrey 20 F13
Puttock End Essex 40 D12
Putton Dorset 7 R8
Putts Corner Devon 6 F5
Puxley Nhants 30 G4
Puxton N Som 17 M4
Pwll Carmth 25 S10
Pwllcrochan Pembks 24 F10
Pwll-du Mons 27 N5
Pwll-glâs Denbgs 44 D3
Pwllgloyw Powys 34 B14
Pwllheli Gwynd 42 G6
Pwllmeyric Mons 27 U9
Pwll-trap Carmth 25 N7
Pwll-y-glaw Neath 26 D9
Pydew Conwy 53 P7
Pye Bridge Derbys 47 M3
Pyecombe W Susx 11 M8
Pye Corner Newpt 27 Q10
Pye Green Staffs 46 C11
Pyle Brdgnd 26 E11
Pyleigh Somset 16 F10
Pylle Somset 17 R9
Pymoor Cambs 39 Q3
Pymore Dorset 7 N6
Pyrford Surrey 20 H11
Pyrton Oxon 30 E13
Pytchley Nhants 38 C6
Pyworthy Devon 14 H12

Q

Quabbs Shrops 34 F4
Quadring Lincs 48 K7
Quadring Eaudike Lincs 48 K7
Quainton Bucks 30 F8
Quaker's Yard Myr Td 26 K8
Quaking Houses Dur 69 Q2
Quantock Hills Somset 16 G9
Quarff Shet 106 u10
Quarley Hants 19 L12
Quarndon Derbys 46 K5
Quarr Hill IoW 9 R10
Quarrier's Village Inver 88 J12
Quarrington Lincs 48 G5
Quarrington Hill Dur 70 D5
Quarrybank Ches W 55 N13
Quarry Bank Dudley 36 B3
Quarrywood Moray 103 U3
Quarter N Ayrs 88 E13
Quarter S Lans 82 D8
Quatford Shrops 35 R2
Quatt Shrops 35 S3
Quebec Dur 69 Q4
Quedgeley Gloucs 28 F5
Queen Adelaide Cambs 39 S4
Queenborough Kent 23 M13
Queen Camel Somset 17 Q12
Queen Charlton BaNES 17 R3
Queen Dart Devon 15 T9
Queen Elizabeth Forest Park Stirlg 89 M5
Queenhill Worcs 35 U13
Queen Oak Dorset 17 U10
Queen's Bower IoW 9 R12
Queensbury C Brad 63 N13
Queensferry Flints 54 H13
Queensferry Crossing Fife 83 M2
Queen's Head Shrops 44 H8
Queen's Hills Norfk 51 L11
Queenslie C Glas 89 Q12
Queen's Park Bed 38 F11
Queen's Park Nhants 37 U8
Queen Street Kent 12 C6
Queen Street Wilts 28 K10
Queenzieburn N Lans 89 Q10
Quendon Essex 22 D1
Queniborough Leics 47 R11
Quenington Gloucs 29 M7
Quernmore Lancs 61 U8
Queslett Birm 36 E2
Quethiock Cnwll 4 J8
Quick's Green W Berk 19 S5
Quidenham Norfk 40 H3
Quidhampton Hants 19 R10
Quidhampton Wilts 8 G2
Quina Brook Shrops 45 M7
Quinbury End Nhants 37 R10
Quinton Dudley 36 C4
Quinton Nhants 37 U10
Quinton Green Nhants 37 U10
Quintrell Downs Cnwll 3 L4
Quixhall Staffs 46 F5
Quixwood Border 84 K6
Quoditch Devon 14 K13
Quoig P & K 90 B7
Quorn Leics 47 Q10
Quothquan S Lans 82 J11
Quoyburray Ork 106 u19
Quoyloo Ork 106 r17

R

Raasay Highld 100 e5
Rabbit's Cross Kent 12 E6
Rableyheath Herts 31 R9
Raby Cumb 66 J2
Raby Wirral 54 H11
Rachan Mill Border 83 M12
Rachub Gwynd 52 K9
Rackenford Devon 15 U9
Rackham W Susx 10 G8
Rackheath Norfk 51 N11
Racks D & G 74 K11
Rackwick Ork 106 r20
Radbourne Derbys 46 J6
Radcliffe Bury 55 S5
Radcliffe Nthumb 77 R5
Radcliffe on Trent Notts 47 R6
Radclive Bucks 30 E6
Radcot Oxon 29 Q8
Raddery Highld 102 K4
Raddington Somset 16 D11
Radernie Fife 91 Q10
Radford Covtry 36 K4
Radford Semele Warwks 36 K8
Radlet Somset 16 H9
Radlett Herts 31 Q12
Radley Devon 15 R8
Radley Oxon 30 B13
Radley W Berk 19 N7
Radley Green Essex 22 F6
Radmore Green Ches E 45 N2
Radnage Bucks 20 C3
Radstock BaNES 17 S6
Radstone Nhants 30 C4
Radway Warwks 37 L11
Radwell Bed 38 F9
Radwell Herts 31 R5
Radwinter Essex 39 T13
Radwinter End Essex 39 T13
Radyr Cardif 27 L11
RAF College (Cranwell) Lincs 48 F4
Rafford Moray 103 S4
RAF Museum Cosford Shrops 45 S12
RAF Museum Hendon Gt Lon 21 M4
Ragdale Leics 47 S10
Ragdon Shrops 35 L2
Raginnis Cnwll 2 D11
Raglan Mons 27 S6
Ragnall Notts 58 D12
Raigbeg Highld 103 M10
Rainbow Hill Worcs 35 U9
Rainford St Hel 55 L6
Rainham Gt Lon 22 D11
Rainham Medway 12 F2
Rainhill St Hel 55 L8
Rainhill Stoops St Hel 55 M8
Rainow Ches E 56 D11
Rainsough Bury 55 T6
Rainton N York 63 T4
Rainworth Notts 47 Q2
Raisbeck Cumb 68 D11
Raise Cumb 68 F3
Raisthorpe N York 64 K7
Rait P & K 90 K6
Raithby Lincs 59 P10
Raithby Lincs 59 Q13
Raithwaite N York 71 Q10
Rake Hants 10 C5
Rakewood Rochdl 56 D4
Ralia Highld 97 L4
Ram Carmth 33 L11
Ramasaig Highld 100 a5
Rame Cnwll 2 J10
Rame Cnwll 5 L11
Ram Hill S Glos 28 C12
Ram Lane Kent 12 J6
Rampisham Dorset 7 Q4
Rampside Cumb 61 N6
Rampton Cambs 39 P7
Rampton Notts 58 D11
Ramsbottom Bury 55 S3
Ramsbury Wilts 19 L6
Ramscraigs Highld 112 D11
Ramsdean Hants 9 U4
Ramsdell Hants 19 S9
Ramsden Oxon 29 S4
Ramsden Worcs 36 B11
Ramsden Bellhouse Essex 22 H9
Ramsden Heath Essex 22 H8
Ramsey Cambs 39 L3
Ramsey Essex 23 T1
Ramsey IoM 60 h4
Ramsey Forty Foot Cambs 39 M3
Ramsey Heights Cambs 38 K4
Ramsey Island Essex 23 M6
Ramsey Island Pembks 24 B6
Ramsey Mereside Cambs 39 L3
Ramsey St Mary's Cambs 39 L3
Ramsgate Kent 13 S2
Ramsgill N York 63 N5
Ramshaw Dur 69 L3
Ramshaw Dur 69 P7
Ramsholt Suffk 41 P12
Ramshope Nthumb 76 E5
Ramshorn Staffs 46 E4
Ramsley Devon 5 R2
Ramsnest Common Surrey 10 E4
Ranby Lincs 59 M11
Ranby Notts 57 U10
Rand Lincs 58 K11
Randwick Gloucs 28 F6
Ranfurly Rens 88 J12
Rangemore Staffs 46 G9
Rangeworthy S Glos 28 C10
Rankinston E Ayrs 81 P10
Ranksborough Rutlnd 48 B11
Rank's Green Essex 22 H4
Rannoch Station P & K 95 N7
Ranscombe Somset 16 B8
Ranskill Notts 57 U9
Ranton Staffs 45 U9
Ranton Green Staffs 45 T9
Ranworth Norfk 51 Q11
Raploch Stirlg 89 S7
Rapness Ork 106 u15
Rapps Somset 16 K13
Rascarrel D & G 73 T10
Rashfield Ag & B 88 D9
Rashwood Worcs 36 B7
Raskelf N York 64 B5
Rassau Blae G 27 M5
Rastrick Calder 56 H2
Ratagan Highld 101 N8
Ratby Leics 47 P12
Ratcliffe Culey Leics 46 K14
Ratcliffe on Soar Notts 47 N8
Ratcliffe on the Wreake Leics 47 R11
Rathen Abers 105 R3
Rathillet Fife 91 N7
Rathmell N York 62 G8
Ratho C Edin 83 M4
Ratho Station C Edin 83 M4
Rathven Moray 104 E2
Ratlake Hants 9 N4
Ratley Warwks 37 L11
Ratling Kent 13 P5
Ratlinghope Shrops 34 K1
Rattar Highld 112 G2
Ratten Row Cumb 67 M4
Ratten Row Cumb 67 N3
Ratten Row Lancs 61 S11
Rattery Devon 5 S8
Rattlesden Suffk 40 G9
Ratton Village E Susx 11 T10
Rattray P & K 90 J2
Raughton Cumb 67 N3
Raughton Head Cumb 67 N3
Raunds Nhants 38 E6
Ravenfield Rothm 57 Q7
Ravenglass Cumb 66 G13
Ravenhills Green Worcs 35 R10
Raveningham Norfk 41 Q1
Ravenscar N York 71 S12
Ravenscraig N Lans 82 E7
Ravensdale IoM 60 f4
Ravensden Bed 38 G10
Ravenseat N York 68 J12
Ravenshead Notts 47 Q3
Ravensmoor Ches E 45 P3
Ravensthorpe Kirk 56 K2
Ravensthorpe Nhants 37 S6
Ravenstone Leics 47 M11
Ravenstone M Keyn 38 B10
Ravenstonedale Cumb 68 F12
Ravenstruther S Lans 82 H9
Ravensworth N York 69 P11
Raw N York 71 R11
Rawcliffe C York 64 D9
Rawcliffe E R Yk 57 U2
Rawcliffe Bridge E R Yk 57 U2
Rawdon Leeds 63 Q12
Rawling Street Kent 12 H4
Rawmarsh Rothm 57 P7
Rawnsley Staffs 46 D11
Rawreth Essex 22 J9
Rawridge Devon 6 H3
Rawtenstall Lancs 55 T2
Raydon Suffk 40 H13
Raylees Nthumb 76 J7
Rayleigh Essex 22 K9
Raymond's Hill Devon 6 K5
Rayne Essex 22 H3
Raynes Park Gt Lon 21 M9
Reach Cambs 39 S7
Read Lancs 62 F13
Reading Readg 20 B8
Reading Services W Berk 19 U7
Reading Street Kent 12 H9
Reading Street Kent 13 S2
Reagill Cumb 68 D9
Realwa Cnwll 2 G9
Rearquhar Highld 109 N6
Rearsby Leics 47 S11
Rease Heath Ches E 45 P3
Reay Highld 111 V4
Reculver Kent 13 P2
Red Ball Devon 16 E13
Redberth Pembks 24 J10
Redbourn Herts 31 P10
Redbourne N Linc 58 G7
Redbrook Gloucs 27 U6
Redbrook Wrexhm 45 M5
Redbrook Street Kent 12 H8
Redburn Highld 103 P6
Redburn Nthumb 76 F13
Redcar R & Cl 70 K8
Redcastle D & G 74 F12
Redcastle Highld 102 G6
Red Dial Cumb 67 L3
Redding Falk 82 H3
Reddingmuirhead Falk 82 H3
Reddish Stockp 56 C8
Redditch Worcs 36 D7
Rede Suffk 40 D9
Redenhall Norfk 41 N4
Redenham Hants 19 M11
Redesmouth Nthumb 76 H9
Redford Abers 99 P9
Redford Angus 91 S3
Redford W Susx 10 D5
Redfordgreen Border 75 S2
Redgate Rhondd 26 J10
Redgorton P & K 90 G6
Redgrave Suffk 40 H5
Redhill Abers 99 P3
Red Hill BCP 8 F9
Redhill Herts 31 T6
Redhill N Som 17 N4
Redhill Surrey 21 N12
Red Hill Warwks 36 F9
Redisham Suffk 41 R4
Redland Bristl 28 A12
Redland Ork 106 s17
Redlingfield Suffk 41 L6
Redlingfield Green Suffk 41 L6
Red Lodge Suffk 39 U6
Red Lumb Rochdl 55 T3
Redlynch Somset 17 T10
Redlynch Wilts 8 J4
Redmain Cumb 66 H6
Redmarley Worcs 35 S7
Redmarley D'Abitot Gloucs 28 E1
Redmarshall S on T 70 E8
Redmile Leics 47 U6
Redmire N York 63 L1
Redmyre Abers 99 P8
Rednal Birm 36 D5
Rednal Shrops 44 J8
Redpath Border 84 F11
Redpoint Highld 107 M11
Red Post Cnwll 14 G11
Red Rock Wigan 55 N5
Red Roses Carmth 25 M8
Red Row Nthumb 77 R6
Redruth Cnwll 2 H8
Redstocks Wilts 18 D8
Redstone P & K 90 J5
Redstone Cross Pembks 24 K7
Red Street Staffs 45 T3
Redvales Bury 55 T5
Red Wharf Bay IoA 52 H6
Redwick Newpt 27 S11
Redwick S Glos 27 U10
Redworth Darltn 69 R8
Reed Herts 31 U5
Reedham Norfk 51 R13
Reedness E R Yk 58 C2
Reeds Beck Lincs 59 M13
Reeds Holme Lancs 55 T2
Reepham Lincs 58 H12
Reepham Norfk 50 K9
Reeth N York 69 M13
Reeves Green Solhll 36 J5
Regaby IoM 60 g3
Regil N Som 17 P4
Reiff Highld 107 S2
Reigate Surrey 21 N12
Reighton N York 65 Q4
Reinigeadal W Isls 106 h8
Reisque Abers 105 P12
Reiss Highld 112 H6
Rejerrah Cnwll 2 K5
Releath Cnwll 2 H10
Relubbus Cnwll 2 F10
Relugas Moray 103 Q6
Remenham Wokham 20 C6
Remenham Hill Wokham 20 C6
Rempstone Notts 47 Q9
Rendcomb Gloucs 28 K6
Rendham Suffk 41 P8
Rendlesham Suffk 41 P10
Renfrew Rens 89 M12
Renhold Bed 38 G10
Renishaw Derbys 57 Q11
Rennington Nthumb 77 Q2
Renton W Duns 88 J10
Renwick Cumb 67 S4
Repps Norfk 51 R10
Repton Derbys 46 K8
Reraig Highld 100 h7
Resaurie Highld 102 K6
Rescassa Cnwll 3 P8
Rescorla Cnwll 3 P7
Resipole Burn Highld 93 S6
Reskadinnick Cnwll 2 G8
Resolis Highld 102 J2
Resolven Neath 26 E7
Rest and be thankful Ag & B 88 F4
Reston Border 85 M6
Restronguet Cnwll 3 L9
Reswallie Angus 98 J13
Reterth Cnwll 3 N4
Retford Notts 58 B10
Retire Cnwll 3 Q4
Rettendon Essex 22 J8
Retyn Cnwll 3 M5
Revesby Lincs 49 L1
Rew Devon 5 S13
Rew Devon 5 T6
Rewe Devon 6 B5
Rew Street IoW 9 P10
Rexon Devon 5 L3
Reydon Suffk 41 S5
Reymerston Norfk 50 H12
Reynalton Pembks 24 J9
Reynoldston Swans 25 S13
Rezare Cnwll 4 K5
Rhadyr Mons 27 R7
Rhandirmwyn Carmth 33 Q12
Rhayader Powys 33 U7
Rheindown Highld 102 F6
Rhenigidale W Isls 106 h8
Rhes-y-cae Flints 54 E12
Rhewl Denbgs 44 D1
Rhewl Denbgs 44 E5
Rhewl Mostyn Flints 54 E10
Rhicarn Highld 110 B11
Rhiconich Highld 110 F6
Rhicullen Highld 109 M10
Rhigos Rhondd 26 G6
Rhives Highld 109 Q4
Rhiwbina Cardif 27 M11
Rhiwbryfdir Gwynd 43 N4
Rhiwderyn Newpt 27 P10
Rhiwen Gwynd 52 J10
Rhiwinder Rhondd 26 J10
Rhiwlas Gwynd 43 T6
Rhiwlas Gwynd 52 J9
Rhiwlas Powys 44 E7
Rhiwsaeson Rhondd 26 K11
Rhode Somset 16 J10
Rhoden Green Kent 12 C6
Rhodesia Notts 57 S11
Rhodes Minnis Kent 13 N7
Rhodiad-y-brenin Pembks 24 C5
Rhonehouse D & G 74 D14
Rhoose V Glam 16 E3
Rhos Carmth 25 Q3
Rhos Denbgs 44 D1
Rhos Neath 26 C7
Rhosaman Carmth 26 C5
Rhosbeirio IoA 52 E4
Rhoscefnhir IoA 52 H7
Rhoscolyn IoA 52 C7
Rhoscrowther Pembks 24 F10
Rhosesmor Flints 54 F13
Rhos-fawr Gwynd 42 G6
Rhosgadfan Gwynd 52 H11
Rhosgoch IoA 52 F5
Rhosgoch Powys 34 E11
Rhos Haminiog Cerdgn 32 K8
Rhoshill Pembks 32 C12
Rhoshirwaun Gwynd 42 D8
Rhoslan Gwynd 42 J5
Rhoslefain Gwynd 43 L12
Rhosllanerchrugog Wrexhm 44 G4
Rhôs Lligwy IoA 52 G5
Rhosmaen Carmth 26 A3
Rhosmeirch IoA 52 G7
Rhosneigr IoA 52 D8
Rhosnesni Wrexhm 44 J3
Rhôs-on-Sea Conwy 53 P6
Rhosrobin Wrexhm 44 H3
Rhossili Swans 25 R13
Rhostrehwfa IoA 52 F8
Rhostryfan Gwynd 52 G11
Rhostyllen Wrexhm 44 H4
Rhosybol IoA 52 F5
Rhos-y-brithdir Powys 44 D9
Rhosygadfa Shrops 44 H7
Rhos-y-garth Cerdgn 33 M6
Rhos-y-gwaliau Gwynd 43 T7
Rhos-y-llan Gwynd 42 D6
Rhosymedre Wrexhm 44 G5
Rhos-y-meirch Powys 34 G7
Rhu Ag & B 88 G9
Rhuallt Denbgs 54 C11
Rhubodach Ag & B 88 B11
Rhuddall Heath Ches W 45 N1
Rhuddlan Cerdgn 32 J12
Rhuddlan Denbgs 53 T7
Rhulen Powys 34 D11
Rhunahaorine Ag & B 79 N6
Rhyd Gwynd 43 M5
Rhydargaeau Carmth 25 R5
Rhydcymerau Carmth 25 U3
Rhydd Worcs 35 T11
Rhyd-Ddu Gwynd 52 J12
Rhydding Neath 26 C8
Rhydgaled Conwy 53 S10
Rhydlanfair Conwy 53 P12
Rhydlewis Cerdgn 32 F11
Rhydlios Gwynd 42 C8
Rhydlydan Conwy 43 S3
Rhydowen Cerdgn 32 H11
Rhydroser Cerdgn 33 L7
Rhydspence Herefs 34 F11
Rhydtalog Flints 44 F3
Rhyd-uchaf Gwynd 43 T6
Rhyd-y-clafdy Gwynd 42 F7
Rhydycroesau Shrops 44 F7
Rhydyfelin Cerdgn 33 L5
Rhydyfelin Rhondd 26 K10
Rhyd-y-foel Conwy 53 R7
Rhydyfro Neath 26 C6
Rhyd-y-groes Gwynd 52 J9
Rhydymain Gwynd 43 R9
Rhyd-y-meirch Mons 27 Q6
Rhydymwyn Flints 54 F13
Rhyd-y-pennau Cerdgn 33 M3
Rhyd-yr-onnen Gwynd 43 M13
Rhyd-y-sarn Gwynd 43 N5
Rhyl Denbgs 53 T6
Rhymney Caerph 27 L6
Rhynd P & K 90 J7
Rhynie Abers 104 F10
Rhynie Highld 109 Q9
Ribbesford Worcs 35 S6
Ribbleton Lancs 62 B13
Ribby Lancs 61 S13
Ribchester Lancs 62 D12
Riber Derbys 46 K2
Riby Lincs 59 L5
Riccall N York 64 E12
Riccarton Border 76 A7
Riccarton E Ayrs 81 N5
Richards Castle Herefs 35 L7
Richings Park Bucks 20 H7
Richmond Gt Lon 21 L8
Richmond N York 69 Q12
Richmond Sheff 57 P9
Rich's Holford Somset 16 F10
Rickerscote Staffs 46 B9
Rickford N Som 17 N5
Rickham Devon 5 T13
Rickinghall Suffk 40 H5
Rickling Essex 22 C1
Rickling Green Essex 22 D2
Rickmansworth Herts 20 J4
Riddell Border 84 E14
Riddings Derbys 47 M3
Riddlecombe Devon 15 P10
Riddlesden C Brad 63 M11
Ridge BaNES 17 Q5
Ridge Dorset 8 C11
Ridge Herts 31 R12
Ridge Wilts 8 D2
Ridgebourne Powys 34 C8
Ridge Green Surrey 21 P13
Ridge Lane Warwks 36 J2
Ridge Row Kent 13 P7
Ridgeway Derbys 57 P10
Ridgeway Worcs 36 D8
Ridgeway Cross Herefs 35 R11
Ridgewell Essex 40 B12
Ridgewood E Susx 11 R7
Ridgmont C Beds 31 L5
Riding Mill Nthumb 77 L13
Ridley Kent 12 B3
Ridley Nthumb 76 F13
Ridley Green Ches E 45 N3
Ridlington Norfk 51 P7
Ridlington Rutlnd 48 B13
Ridlington Street Norfk 51 P7
Ridsdale Nthumb 76 J9
Rievaulx N York 64 D2
Rigg D & G 75 Q12
Riggend N Lans 82 E4
Righoul Highld 103 N5
Rigmadon Park Cumb 62 C3
Rigsby Lincs 59 R11
Rigside S Lans 82 G11
Riley Green Lancs 55 P1
Rileyhill Staffs 46 F11
Rilla Mill Cnwll 4 H6
Rillaton Cnwll 4 H6
Rillington N York 64 K5
Rimington Lancs 62 G10
Rimpton Somset 17 R12
Rimswell E R Yk 65 U14
Rinaston Pembks 24 G5
Rindleford Shrops 35 R1
Ringford D & G 73 R8
Ringinglow Sheff 57 L10
Ringland Norfk 50 K11
Ringles Cross E Susx 11 R6
Ringlestone Kent 12 G4
Ringley Bolton 55 S5
Ringmer E Susx 11 Q8
Ringmore Devon 5 R11
Ringmore Devon 6 B10
Ringorm Moray 104 B7
Ring's End Cambs 49 N13
Ringsfield Suffk 41 R3
Ringsfield Corner Suffk 41 R3
Ringshall Herts 31 L10
Ringshall Suffk 40 H10
Ringshall Stocks Suffk 40 J10
Ringstead Nhants 38 E5
Ringstead Norfk 50 B5
Ringwood Hants 8 H7
Ringwould Kent 13 S6
Rinmore Abers 104 E12
Rinsey Cnwll 2 F11
Rinsey Croft Cnwll 2 G11
Ripe E Susx 11 S8
Ripley Derbys 47 L3
Ripley Hants 8 H9
Ripley N York 63 R7
Ripley Surrey 20 J11
Riplingham E R Yk 65 M13
Riplington Hants 9 T4
Ripon N York 63 S5
Rippingale Lincs 48 G8
Ripple Kent 13 S5
Ripple Worcs 35 U13
Ripponden Calder 56 F3
Risabus Ag & B 78 E7
Risbury Herefs 35 M10
Risby N Linc 58 F4
Risby Suffk 40 D7
Risca Caerph 27 N9
Rise E R Yk 65 R11
Riseden E Susx 11 U4
Riseden Kent 12 D8
Risegate Lincs 48 K8
Riseholme Lincs 58 G11
Risehow Cumb 66 F6
Riseley Bed 38 F8
Riseley Wokham 20 B10
Rishangles Suffk 41 L7
Rishton Lancs 62 E13
Rishworth Calder 56 F3
Rising Bridge Lancs 55 S1
Risley Derbys 47 N6
Risley Warrtn 55 Q8
Risplith N York 63 Q6
Rivar Wilts 19 M8
Rivenhall End Essex 22 K4
River Kent 13 Q7
River W Susx 10 E6
River Bank Cambs 39 R7
Riverford Highld 102 F5
Riverhead Kent 21 T11
Rivers Corner Dorset 7 U2
Rivington Lancs 55 P4
Rivington Services Lancs 55 P4
Roachill Devon 15 U8
Roade Nhants 37 U10
Road Green Norfk 41 N2
Roadhead Cumb 75 V11
Roadmeetings S Lans 82 G9
Roadside E Ayrs 81 R9
Roadside Highld 112 E4
Roadwater Somset 16 D9
Roag Highld 100 b5
Roa Island Cumb 61 N6
Roan of Craigoch S Ayrs 80 K12
Roast Green Essex 39 Q14
Roath Cardif 27 M12
Roberton Border 75 T3
Roberton S Lans 82 H13
Robertsbridge E Susx 12 D11
Roberttown Kirk 56 J2
Robeston Wathen Pembks 24 J7
Robgill Tower D & G 75 P11
Robin Hill Staffs 46 B2
Robin Hood Lancs 55 M4
Robin Hood Leeds 57 M1
Robinhood End Essex 40 B13
Robin Hood's Bay N York 71 S11
Roborough Devon 5 N8
Roborough Devon 15 N9
Robroyston C Glas 89 P12
Roby Knows 54 K8
Roby Mill Lancs 55 M5
Rocester Staffs 46 F6
Roch Pembks 24 E6
Rochdale Rochdl 56 C4
Roche Cnwll 3 P4
Rochester Medway 12 D2
Rochester Nthumb 76 G6
Rochford Essex 23 L9
Rochford Worcs 35 P7
Roch Gate Pembks 24 E6
Rock Cnwll 3 N1
Rock Neath 26 D9
Rock Nthumb 77 Q1
Rock W Susx 10 J8
Rock Worcs 35 R6
Rockbeare Devon 6 D6
Rockbourne Hants 8 G5
Rockcliffe Cumb 75 S13
Rockcliffe D & G 66 B2
Rockcliffe Cross Cumb 75 R13
Rock End Staffs 45 U2
Rockend Torbay 6 B12
Rock Ferry Wirral 54 H9
Rockfield Highld 109 S8
Rockfield Mons 27 T5
Rockford Devon 15 S3
Rockford Hants 8 H7
Rockgreen Shrops 35 M5
Rockhampton S Glos 28 C9
Rockhead Cnwll 4 D4
Rockhill Shrops 34 G5
Rock Hill Worcs 36 C7
Rockingham Nhants 38 C2
Rockland All Saints Norfk 40 G1
Rockland St Mary Norfk 51 P13
Rockland St Peter Norfk 40 G1
Rockley Notts 58 B12
Rockley Wilts 18 J6
Rockliffe Lancs 56 C2
Rockville Ag & B 88 F7
Rockwell End Bucks 20 C5
Rockwell Green Somset 16 F12
Rodborough Gloucs 28 F7
Rodbourne Swindn 29 M10
Rodbourne Wilts 28 H11
Rodd Herefs 34 H8
Roddam Nthumb 77 L1
Rodden Dorset 7 R8
Roddymoor Dur 69 Q5
Rode Somset 18 B10
Rode Heath Ches E 45 T2
Rode Heath Ches E 56 C13
Rodel W Isls 106 f10
Roden Wrekin 45 N10
Rodhuish Somset 16 D9
Rodington Wrekin 45 N11
Rodington Heath Wrekin 45 N11
Rodley Gloucs 28 D5
Rodley Leeds 63 Q12
Rodmarton Gloucs 28 H8
Rodmell E Susx 11 Q9
Rodmersham Kent 12 H3
Rodmersham Green Kent 12 H3
Rodney Stoke Somset 17 N7
Rodsley Derbys 46 H5
Rodway Somset 16 J8
Roecliffe N York 63 T6
Roe Cross Tamesd 56 E7
Roe Green Herts 31 R11
Roe Green Herts 31 T6
Roe Green Salfd 55 R6
Roehampton Gt Lon 21 M8
Roffey W Susx 10 K4
Rogart Highld 109 N4
Rogate W Susx 10 C6
Roger Ground Cumb 67 N13
Rogerstone Newpt 27 P10
Roghadal W Isls 106 f10
Rogiet Mons 27 T10
Roke Oxon 19 T2
Roker Sundld 77 U14
Rollesby Norfk 51 R10
Rolleston Leics 47 T13
Rolleston Notts 47 T3
Rollestone Wilts 18 G11
Rolleston on Dove Staffs 46 H8
Rolston E R Yk 65 S11
Rolstone N Som 17 L4
Rolvenden Kent 12 F9
Rolvenden Layne Kent 12 G9
Romaldkirk Dur 69 L8
Romanby N York 70 E14
Romanno Bridge Border 83 N9
Romansleigh Devon 15 R8
Romden Castle Kent 12 G7
Romesdal Highld 100 d4
Romford Dorset 8 F7
Romford Gt Lon 22 D10
Romiley Stockp 56 D8
Romney Street Kent 21 U10
Romsey Cambs 39 Q9
Romsey Hants 9 M4
Romsley Shrops 35 S4
Romsley Worcs 36 C4
Rona Highld 100 f4
Ronachan Ag & B 79 N5
Rood Ashton Wilts 18 C9
Rookhope Dur 68 K4
Rookley IoW 9 Q12
Rookley Green IoW 9 Q12
Rooks Bridge Somset 17 L6
Rooks Nest Somset 16 E10
Rookwith N York 63 Q2
Roos E R Yk 65 T13
Roose Cumb 61 N6
Roosebeck Cumb 61 P6
Roothams Green Bed 38 G9
Ropley Hants 9 S2
Ropley Dean Hants 9 S2
Ropley Soke Hants 9 T2
Ropsley Lincs 48 E7
Rora Abers 105 T5
Rorrington Shrops 44 H13
Rosarie Moray 104 D5
Rose Cnwll 2 K6
Roseacre Lancs 61 S12
Rose Ash Devon 15 S8
Rosebank S Lans 82 F9
Rosebush Pembks 24 J5
Rosecare Cnwll 14 E13
Rosecliston Cnwll 3 L5
Rosedale Abbey N York 71 M13
Rose Green Essex 23 M2
Rose Green Suffk 40 F13
Rose Green Suffk 40 G12
Rose Green W Susx 10 E11
Rosehall Highld 108 H4
Rosehearty Abers 105 Q2
Rose Hill E Susx 11 R7
Rose Hill Lancs 62 G13
Rosehill Shrops 45 L10
Roseisle Moray 103 T2
Roselands E Susx 11 U10
Rosemarket Pembks 24 G9
Rosemarkie Highld 102 K4
Rosemary Lane Devon 6 G2
Rosemount P & K 90 J3
Rosenannon Cnwll 3 P3
Rosenithon Cnwll 3 L12
Roser's Cross E Susx 11 S6
Rosevean Cnwll 3 Q5
Rosevine Cnwll 3 M9
Rosewarne Cnwll 2 G9
Rosewell Mdloth 83 Q6
Roseworth S on T 70 F8
Roseworthy Cnwll 2 G9
Rosgill Cumb 67 R9
Roskestal Cnwll 2 B12
Roskhill Highld 100 b5
Roskorwell Cnwll 2 K12
Rosley Cumb 67 M3
Roslin Mdloth 83 Q6
Rosliston Derbys 46 H10
Rosneath Ag & B 88 G9
Ross D & G 73 Q11
Ross Nthumb 85 S11
Rossett Wrexhm 44 J2
Rossett Green N York 63 R9
Rossington Donc 57 T7
Ross-on-Wye Herefs 28 A3
Roster Highld 112 G9
Rostherne Ches E 55 R10
Rosthwaite Cumb 67 L10
Roston Derbys 46 F5
Rosudgeon Cnwll 2 F11
Rosyth Fife 83 M2
Rothbury Nthumb 77 M5
Rotherby Leics 47 S10
Rotherfield E Susx 11 T5
Rotherfield Greys Oxon 20 B6
Rotherfield Peppard Oxon 20 B6
Rotherham Rothm 57 P8
Rothersthorpe Nhants 37 T9
Rotherwick Hants 20 B11
Rothes Moray 104 B6
Rothesay Ag & B 88 C13
Rothiebrisbane Abers 105 L8
Rothiemurchus Lodge Highld 97 R2
Rothienorman Abers 105 L8
Rothley Leics 47 Q11
Rothley Nthumb 77 L8
Rothmaise Abers 104 K9
Rothwell Leeds 63 S14
Rothwell Lincs 58 K7
Rothwell Nhants 38 B4
Rotsea E R Yk 65 P9
Rottal Lodge Angus 98 F10
Rottingdean Br & H 11 P10
Rottington Cumb 66 E10
Roucan D & G 74 K10
Roud IoW 9 Q12
Rougham Norfk 50 D9
Rougham Suffk 40 F8
Rough Close Staffs 46 B6
Rough Common Kent 13 M4
Roughlee Lancs 62 G11
Roughpark Abers 104 C13
Roughton Lincs 59 M14
Roughton Norfk 51 M6
Roughton Shrops 35 S2
Roughway Kent 12 B5
Roundbush Essex 23 L7
Round Bush Herts 20 K3
Roundbush Green Essex 22 E5
Round Green Luton 31 P8
Roundham Somset 7 M3
Roundhay Leeds 63 S12
Rounds Green Sandw 36 C3
Round Street Kent 12 C2
Roundstreet Common W Susx 10 H5
Roundswell Devon 15 M6
Roundway Wilts 18 F8
Roundyhill Angus 98 F13
Rousay Ork 106 s16
Rousdon Devon 6 J6
Rousham Oxon 29 U3
Rous Lench Worcs 36 D10
Routenburn N Ayrs 88 E13
Routh E R Yk 65 P11
Rout's Green Bucks 20 C3
Row Cnwll 3 R1
Row Cumb 61 T2
Row Cumb 68 D6
Rowanburn D & G 75 T10
Rowardennan Stirlg 88 J6
Rowarth Derbys 56 F9
Row Ash Hants 9 Q6
Rowberrow Somset 17 N5
Rowborough IoW 9 P12
Rowde Wilts 18 E8
Rowden Devon 15 P13
Rowen Conwy 53 N8
Rowfield Derbys 46 G4
Rowfoot Nthumb 76 D13
Rowford Somset 16 H11
Row Green Essex 22 H3
Rowhedge Essex 23 P3
Rowhook W Susx 10 J4
Rowington Warwks 36 H7
Rowland Derbys 56 K12
Rowland's Castle Hants 9 U6
Rowlands Gill Gatesd 77 P14
Rowledge Surrey 10 C2
Rowley Dur 69 N3
Rowley E R Yk 65 M13
Rowley Shrops 44 H12
Rowley Hill Kirk 56 J4
Rowley Regis Sandw 36 C3
Rowlstone Herefs 27 R2
Rowly Surrey 10 G2
Rowner Hants 9 R8
Rowney Green Worcs 36 D6
Rownhams Hants 9 M5
Rownhams Services Hants 9 M5
Rowrah Cumb 66 G9
Rowsham Bucks 30 H9
Rowsley Derbys 57 L13
Rowstock Oxon 29 U10
Rowston Lincs 48 G2
Rowthorne Derbys 57 Q14
Rowton Ches W 54 K14
Rowton Shrops 34 K4
Rowton Shrops 44 J11
Rowton Wrekin 45 P10
Row Town Surrey 20 H10
Roxburgh Border 84 H12
Roxby N Linc 58 F3
Roxby N York 71 N9
Roxton Bed 38 J10
Roxwell Essex 22 F6
Royal Leamington Spa Warwks 36 K7
Royal Oak Darltn 69 R8
Royal Oak Lancs 54 K6
Royal's Green Ches E 45 P5
Royal Sutton Coldfield Birm 36 F1
Royal Tunbridge Wells Kent 11 T3
Royal Wootton Bassett Wilts 29 L11
Royal Yacht Britannia C Edin 83 Q3
Roy Bridge Highld 96 B7
Roydhouse Kirk 56 K4
Roydon Essex 22 B5
Roydon Norfk 40 K4
Roydon Norfk 50 B9
Roydon Hamlet Essex 22 B6
Royston Barns 57 N4
Royston Herts 31 U4
Royton Oldham 56 D5
Rozel Jersey 7 e2
Ruabon Wrexhm 44 H5
Ruaig Ag & B 92 D9
Ruan High Lanes Cnwll 3 N9
Ruan Lanihorne Cnwll 3 M8
Ruan Major Cnwll 2 J13
Ruan Minor Cnwll 2 J13
Ruardean Gloucs 28 B4
Ruardean Hill Gloucs 28 B4
Ruardean Woodside Gloucs 28 B4
Rubery Birm 36 C5
Rubha Ban W Isls 106 c17
Ruckcroft Cumb 67 R4
Ruckhall Herefs 35 L13
Ruckinge Kent 12 K9
Ruckland Lincs 59 P11
Ruckley Shrops 45 M13
Rudbaxton Pembks 24 G6
Rudby N York 70 G11
Rudchester Nthumb 77 N12
Ruddington Notts 47 Q7
Ruddle Gloucs 28 C5
Ruddlemoor Cnwll 3 Q6
Rudford Gloucs 28 E3
Rudge Somset 18 B10
Rudgeway S Glos 28 B10
Rudgwick W Susx 10 H4
Rudhall Herefs 28 B2
Rudheath Ches W 55 Q12
Rudheath Woods Ches E 55 R12
Rudley Green Essex 22 K7
Rudloe Wilts 18 B6
Rudry Caerph 27 N10
Rudston E R Yk 65 P6
Rudyard Staffs 46 C2
Ruecastle Border 76 C1
Rufford Lancs 55 L3
Rufford Abbey Notts 57 T14
Rufforth C York 64 C9
Rug Denbgs 44 C5
Rugby Warwks 37 P5
Rugeley Staffs 46 D10
Ruigh'riabhach Highld 107 T5
Ruisgarry W Isls 106 e10
Ruishton Somset 16 J11
Ruisigearraidh W Isls 106 e10
Ruislip Gt Lon 20 J5
Rùm Highld 100 c10
Rumbach Moray 104 D5
Rumbling Bridge P & K 90 F12
Rumburgh Suffk 41 P4
Rumby Hill Dur 69 Q6
Rumford Cnwll 3 M2
Rumford Falk 82 H3
Rumney Cardif 27 N12
Rumwell Somset 16 G12
Runcorn Halton 55 M10
Runcton W Susx 10 D10
Runcton Holme Norfk 49 T12
Runfold Surrey 20 E13
Runhall Norfk 50 J12
Runham Norfk 51 S11
Runham Norfk 51 T12
Runnington Somset 16 F12
Runsell Green Essex 22 J6
Runshaw Moor Lancs 55 M3
Runswick N York 71 P9
Runtaleave Angus 98 D10
Runwell Essex 22 J9
Ruscombe Wokham 20 C7
Rushall Herefs 35 P13
Rushall Norfk 41 L4
Rushall Wilts 18 H9
Rushall Wsall 46 D13
Rushbrooke Suffk 40 E8
Rushbury Shrops 35 M2
Rushden Herts 31 T6
Rushden Nhants 38 E7
Rushenden Kent 23 M13
Rusher's Cross E Susx 11 U5
Rushford Devon 5 M5
Rushford Norfk 40 F4
Rush Green Essex 23 S4
Rush Green Gt Lon 22 D10
Rush Green Herts 31 R8
Rush Green Warrtn 55 Q9
Rushlake Green E Susx 11 U7
Rushmere Suffk 41 S3
Rushmere St Andrew Suffk 41 L11
Rushmoor Surrey 10 D2
Rushock Herefs 34 H9
Rushock Worcs 35 U6
Rusholme Manch 56 C8
Rushton Ches W 55 N14
Rushton Nhants 38 B4
Rushton Shrops 45 P12
Rushton Spencer Staffs 46 B1
Rushwick Worcs 35 T10
Rushyford Dur 69 S7
Ruskie Stirlg 89 P5
Ruskington Lincs 48 G3
Rusland Cross Cumb 61 Q2
Rusper W Susx 11 L3
Ruspidge Gloucs 28 C5
Russell Green Essex 22 H5
Russell's Water Oxon 20 B5
Russel's Green Suffk 41 N6
Russ Hill Surrey 11 L2
Rusthall Kent 11 T3
Rustington W Susx 10 G10
Ruston N York 65 M3
Ruston Parva E R Yk 65 P7
Ruswarp N York 71 Q11
Ruthall Shrops 35 N2
Rutherford Border 84 G12
Rutherglen S Lans 89 P13
Ruthernbridge Cnwll 3 Q3
Ruthin Denbgs 44 D2
Ruthrieston C Aber 99 S3
Ruthven Abers 104 G6
Ruthven Angus 91 L2
Ruthven Highld 97 M4
Ruthven Highld 103 M9
Ruthvoes Cnwll 3 N4
Ruthwaite Cumb 66 K5
Ruthwell D & G 75 L12
Ruxley Corner Gt Lon 21 S8
Ruxton Green Herefs 27 U4
Ruyton-XI-Towns Shrops 44 J9
Ryal Nthumb 77 L11
Ryall Dorset 7 M5
Ryall Worcs 35 U12
Ryarsh Kent 12 C3
Rycote Oxon 30 E11
Rydal Cumb 67 N11
Ryde IoW 9 R10
Rye E Susx 12 H11
Ryebank Shrops 45 M7
Ryeford Herefs 28 B3
Rye Foreign E Susx 12 G11
Rye Harbour E Susx 12 H12
Ryehill E R Yk 59 M1
Ryeish Green Wokham 20 B9
Rye Street Worcs 35 S13
Ryhall Rutlnd 48 F11
Ryhill Wakefd 57 N4
Ryhope Sundld 70 F2
Rylah Derbys 57 Q13
Ryland Lincs 58 H11
Rylands Notts 47 P6
Rylstone N York 62 K8
Ryme Intrinseca Dorset 7 Q2
Ryther N York 64 D12
Ryton Gatesd 77 P13
Ryton N York 64 H4
Ryton Shrops 45 S13
Ryton Warwks 37 M3
Ryton-on-Dunsmore Warwks 37 L6
Ryton Woodside Gatesd 77 N13
RZSS Edinburgh Zoo C Edin 83 P4

S

Sabden Lancs 62 F12
Sabine's Green Essex 22 D8
Sacombe Herts 31 T9
Sacombe Green Herts 31 T9
Sacriston Dur 69 R3
Sadberge Darltn 70 D9
Saddell Ag & B 79 P9
Saddington Leics 37 S2
Saddlebow Norfk 49 T10
Saddlescombe W Susx 11 M8
Sadgill Cumb 67 Q11
Saffron Walden Essex 39 R13
Sageston Pembks 24 J10
Saham Hills Norfk 50 F13
Saham Toney Norfk 50 E13
Saighton Ches W 44 K1
St Abbs Border 85 N5
St Agnes Border 84 H6
St Agnes Cnwll 2 J6
St Agnes IoS 2 b3
St Agnes Mining District Cnwll 2 J7
St Albans Herts 31 P11
St Allen Cnwll 3 L6
St Andrew Guern 6 d3
St Andrews Fife 91 R8
St Andrews Botanic Garden Fife 91 R8
St Andrews Major V Glam 16 F2
St Andrews Well Dorset 7 N6
St Anne's Lancs 61 Q14
St Ann's D & G 75 L7
St Ann's Chapel Cnwll 5 L6
St Ann's Chapel Devon 5 R11
St Anthony-in-Meneage Cnwll 2 K11
St Anthony's Hill E Susx 11 U10
St Arvans Mons 27 U8
St Asaph Denbgs 53 T8
St Athan V Glam 16 D3
St Aubin Jersey 7 c3
St Austell Cnwll 3 Q6
St Bees Cumb 66 E10
St Blazey Cnwll 3 R6
St Blazey Gate Cnwll 3 R6
St Boswells Border 84 F12
St Brelade Jersey 7 b3
St Brelade's Bay Jersey 7 b3
St Breock Cnwll 3 P2
St Breward Cnwll 3 R1
St Briavels Gloucs 27 V7
St Brides Pembks 24 D8
St Bride's Major V Glam 26 F13
St Brides Netherwent Mons 27 S10
St Brides-super-Ely V Glam 26 K12
St Brides Wentlooge Newpt 27 P11
St Budeaux C Plym 5 M9
Saintbury Gloucs 36 F13
St Buryan Cnwll 2 C11
St Catherine BaNES 17 U3
St Catherines Ag & B 88 D4
St Chloe Gloucs 28 F7
St Clears Carmth 25 N7
St Cleer Cnwll 4 G7
St Clement Cnwll 3 M8
St Clement Jersey 7 e4
St Clether Cnwll 4 G4
St Colmac Ag & B 88 B12
St Columb Major Cnwll 3 N4
St Columb Minor Cnwll 3 L4
St Columb Road Cnwll 3 N5
St Combs Abers 105 T3
St Cross South Elmham Suffk 41 N4
St Cyrus Abers 99 N11
St David's P & K 90 D7
St Davids Pembks 24 C5
St Davids Cathedral Pembks 24 C5
St Day Cnwll 2 J8
St Decumans Somset 16 E8
St Dennis Cnwll 3 P5
St Devereux Herefs 27 S1
St Dogmaels Pembks 32 C11
St Dogwells Pembks 24 G5
St Dominick Cnwll 5 L7
St Donats V Glam 16 B3
St Edith's Marsh Wilts 18 E8
St Endellion Cnwll 4 B5
St Enoder Cnwll 3 M5
St Erme Cnwll 3 L7
St Erney Cnwll 4 K9
St Erth Cnwll 2 F9
St Erth Praze Cnwll 2 F9
St Ervan Cnwll 3 M2
St Eval Cnwll 3 M3
St Ewe Cnwll 3 P7
St Fagans Cardif 27 L12
St Fagans: National History Museum Cardif 27 L12
St Fergus Abers 105 T5
St Fillans P & K 95 T14
St Florence Pembks 24 J10
St Gennys Cnwll 14 D13
St George Conwy 53 S7
St Georges N Som 17 L4
St George's V Glam 27 L12
St George's Hill Surrey 20 J10
St Germans Cnwll 4 K9
St Giles in the Wood Devon 15 M9
St Giles-on-the-Heath Devon 4 K2
St Gluvia's Cnwll 2 K10
St Harmon Powys 33 U6
St Helen Auckland Dur 69 Q7
St Helens Cumb 66 F6
St Helens E Susx 12 F13
St Helens IoW 9 S11
St Helens St Hel 55 M7
St Helier Gt Lon 21 N9
St Helier Jersey 7 d3
St Hilary Cnwll 2 E10
St Hilary V Glam 26 J13
Saint Hill Devon 6 E3
Saint Hill W Susx 11 P3
St Illtyd Blae G 27 N7
St Ippolyts Herts 31 Q7
St Ishmael's Pembks 24 D9
St Issey Cnwll 3 N2
St Ive Cnwll 4 J7
St Ive Cross Cnwll 4 J7
St Ives Cambs 39 M6
St Ives Cnwll 2 E8
St Ives Dorset 8 G8
St James Norfk 51 N9
St James's End Nhants 37 T8
St James South Elmham Suffk 41 P4
St Jidgey Cnwll 3 N3
St John Cnwll 5 L10
St John Jersey 7 c1
St Johns Dur 69 N6
St John's E Susx 11 S4
St John's IoM 60 d6
St John's Kent 21 T11
St Johns Surrey 20 G11
St Johns Worcs 35 T10
St John's Chapel Devon 15 M7
St John's Chapel Dur 68 J5
St John's Fen End Norfk 49 R11
St John's Highway Norfk 49 R11
St John's Kirk S Lans 82 J11
St John's Town of Dalry D & G 73 Q3
St John's Wood Gt Lon 21 N6
St Judes IoM 60 f3
St Just Cnwll 2 B10
St Just-in-Roseland Cnwll 3 L9
St Just Mining District Cnwll 2 B10
St Katherines Abers 105 M9
St Keverne Cnwll 2 K12
St Kew Cnwll 3 Q1
St Kew Highway Cnwll 3 Q1
St Keyne Cnwll 4 G8
St Lawrence Cnwll 3 Q3
St Lawrence Essex 23 N7
St Lawrence IoW 9 Q13
St Lawrence Jersey 7 c2
St Lawrence Kent 13 S2
St Leonards Bucks 30 K11
St Leonards Dorset 8 G8
St Leonards E Susx 12 F14
St Leonard's Street Kent 12 C4
St Levan Cnwll 2 B12
St Lythans V Glam 27 L13
St Mabyn Cnwll 3 Q2
St Madoes P & K 90 J7
St Margarets Herefs 34 J14
St Margarets Herts 31 U10
St Margaret's at Cliffe Kent 13 S7
St Margaret's Hope Ork 106 t20
St Margaret South Elmham Suffk 41 P4
St Marks IoM 60 d8
St Martin Cnwll 2 J12
St Martin Cnwll 4 H9
St Martin Guern 6 d3
St Martin Jersey 7 e2
St Martin's IoS 2 c1
St Martin's P & K 90 J5
St Martin's Shrops 44 H6
St Martin's Moor Shrops 44 H6
St Mary Jersey 7 c2
St Mary Bourne Hants 19 P10
St Marychurch Torbay 6 B11
St Mary Church V Glam 16 D2
St Mary Cray Gt Lon 21 S9
St Mary Hill V Glam 26 H12
St Mary in the Marsh Kent 13 L10
St Mary's IoS 2 c2
St Mary's Ork 106 t19
St Mary's Bay Kent 13 L10
St Mary's Hoo Medway 22 K12
St Mary's Platt Kent 12 B4
St Maughans Mons 27 T4
St Maughans Green Mons 27 T4
St Mawes Cnwll 3 L10
St Mawgan Cnwll 3 M3
St Mellion Cnwll 4 K7
St Mellons Cardif 27 N11
St Merryn Cnwll 3 M2
St Mewan Cnwll 3 P6
St Michael Caerhays Cnwll 3 P8
St Michael Church Somset 16 K10
St Michael Penkevil Cnwll 3 M8
St Michaels Kent 12 G8
St Michaels Worcs 35 N7
St Michael's Mount Cnwll 2 E11
St Michael's on Wyre Lancs 61 T11
St Michael South Elmham Suffk 41 P4
St Minver Cnwll 4 B5
St Monans Fife 91 R11
St Neot Cnwll 4 F7
St Neots Cambs 38 J8
St Newlyn East Cnwll 3 L5
St Nicholas Pembks 24 F3
St Nicholas V Glam 26 K13
St Nicholas-at-Wade Kent 13 Q2
St Ninians Stirlg 89 S7
St Olaves Norfk 51 S14
St Osyth Essex 23 R4
St Ouen Jersey 7 b2
St Owen's Cross Herefs 27 U3
St Paul's Cray Gt Lon 21 S9
St Paul's Walden Herts 31 Q8
St Peter Jersey 7 b2
St Peter Port Guern 6 e3
St Peter's Guern 6 c3
St Peter's Kent 13 S2
St Peter's Hill Cambs 38 K6
St Petrox Pembks 24 G11
St Pinnock Cnwll 4 G8
St Quivox S Ayrs 81 M8
St Ruan Cnwll 2 J13
St Sampson Guern 6 e2
St Saviour Guern 6 c3
St Saviour Jersey 7 d3
St Stephen Cnwll 3 N6
St Stephens Cnwll 4 J3
St Stephens Cnwll 5 L9
St Teath Cnwll 4 D4
St Thomas Devon 6 B6
St Margaret's Bay Kent 13 S7
St Tudy Cnwll 3 R1
St Twynnells Pembks 24 G11
St Veep Cnwll 4 E9
St Vigeans Angus 91 T3
St Wenn Cnwll 3 P4
St Weonards Herefs 27 T3
St Winnow Cnwll 4 E9
St y-Nyll V Glam 26 K12
Salcombe Devon 5 S13
Salcombe Regis Devon 6 G7
Salcott-cum-Virley Essex 23 M5
Sale Traffd 55 S8
Saleby Lincs 59 S11
Sale Green Worcs 36 B9
Salehurst E Susx 12 E11
Salem Carmth 25 V5
Salem Cerdgn 33 N4
Salen Ag & B 93 P10
Salen Highld 93 R6
Salesbury Lancs 62 D13
Salford C Beds 30 K5
Salford Oxon 29 Q2
Salford Salfd 55 T7
Salford Priors Warwks 36 E10
Salfords Surrey 21 N13
Salhouse Norfk 51 P11
Saline Fife 90 F13
Salisbury Wilts 8 G2
Salisbury Plain Wilts 18 G12
Salkeld Dykes Cumb 67 R5
Salle Norfk 50 K9
Salmonby Lincs 59 P12
Salperton Gloucs 29 L3
Salph End Bed 38 G10
Salsburgh N Lans 82 F6
Salt Staffs 46 C8
Salta Cumb 66 G3
Saltaire C Brad 63 N12
Saltaire C Brad 63 N12
Saltash Cnwll 5 L9
Saltburn Highld 109 N10
Saltburn-by-the-Sea R & Cl 71 L8
Saltby Leics 48 C8
Salt Coates Cumb 66 J2
Saltcoats Cumb 66 G13
Saltcoats N Ayrs 80 J4
Saltcotes Lancs 61 R14
Saltdean Br & H 11 P10
Salterbeck Cumb 66 E7
Salterforth Lancs 62 H10